Dictionary of Literary Biography

1 *The American Renaissance in New England*, edited by Joel Myerson (1978)

2 *American Novelists Since World War II*, edited by Jeffrey Helterman and Richard Layman (1978)

3 *Antebellum Writers in New York and the South*, edited by Joel Myerson (1979)

4 *American Writers in Paris, 1920–1939*, edited by Karen Lane Rood (1980)

5 *American Poets Since World War II*, 2 parts, edited by Donald J. Greiner (1980)

6 *American Novelists Since World War II, Second Series*, edited by James E. Kibler Jr. (1980)

7 *Twentieth-Century American Dramatists*, 2 parts, edited by John MacNicholas (1981)

8 *Twentieth-Century American Science-Fiction Writers*, 2 parts, edited by David Cowart and Thomas L. Wymer (1981)

9 *American Novelists, 1910–1945*, 3 parts, edited by James J. Martine (1981)

10 *Modern British Dramatists, 1900–1945*, 2 parts, edited by Stanley Weintraub (1982)

11 *American Humorists, 1800–1950*, 2 parts, edited by Stanley Trachtenberg (1982)

12 *American Realists and Naturalists*, edited by Donald Pizer and Earl N. Harbert (1982)

13 *British Dramatists Since World War II*, 2 parts, edited by Stanley Weintraub (1982)

14 *British Novelists Since 1960*, 2 parts, edited by Jay L. Halio (1983)

15 *British Novelists, 1930–1959*, 2 parts, edited by Bernard Oldsey (1983)

16 *The Beats: Literary Bohemians in Postwar America*, 2 parts, edited by Ann Charters (1983)

17 *Twentieth-Century American Historians*, edited by Clyde N. Wilson (1983)

18 *Victorian Novelists After 1885*, edited by Ira B. Nadel and William E. Fredeman (1983)

19 *British Poets, 1880–1914*, edited by Donald E. Stanford (1983)

20 *British Poets, 1914–1945*, edited by Donald E. Stanford (1983)

21 *Victorian Novelists Before 1885*, edited by Ira B. Nadel and William E. Fredeman (1983)

22 *American Writers for Children, 1900–1960*, edited by John Cech (1983)

23 *American Newspaper Journalists, 1873–1900*, edited by Perry J. Ashley (1983)

24 *American Colonial Writers, 1606–1734*, edited by Emory Elliott (1984)

25 *American Newspaper Journalists, 1901–1925*, edited by Perry J. Ashley (1984)

26 *American Screenwriters*, edited by Robert E. Morsberger, Stephen O. Lesser, and Randall Clark (1984)

27 *Poets of Great Britain and Ireland, 1945–1960*, edited by Vincent B. Sherry Jr. (1984)

28 *Twentieth-Century American-Jewish Fiction Writers*, edited by Daniel Walden (1984)

29 *American Newspaper Journalists, 1926–1950*, edited by Perry J. Ashley (1984)

30 *American Historians, 1607–1865*, edited by Clyde N. Wilson (1984)

31 *American Colonial Writers, 1735–1781*, edited by Emory Elliott (1984)

32 *Victorian Poets Before 1850*, edited by William E. Fredeman and Ira B. Nadel (1984)

33 *Afro-American Fiction Writers After 1955*, edited by Thadious M. Davis and Trudier Harris (1984)

34 *British Novelists, 1890–1929: Traditionalists*, edited by Thomas F. Staley (1985)

35 *Victorian Poets After 1850*, edited by William E. Fredeman and Ira B. Nadel (1985)

36 *British Novelists, 1890–1929: Modernists*, edited by Thomas F. Staley (1985)

37 *American Writers of the Early Republic*, edited by Emory Elliott (1985)

38 *Afro-American Writers After 1955: Dramatists and Prose Writers*, edited by Thadious M. Davis and Trudier Harris (1985)

39 *British Novelists, 1660–1800*, 2 parts, edited by Martin C. Battestin (1985)

40 *Poets of Great Britain and Ireland Since 1960*, 2 parts, edited by Vincent B. Sherry Jr. (1985)

41 *Afro-American Poets Since 1955*, edited by Trudier Harris and Thadious M. Davis (1985)

42 *American Writers for Children Before 1900*, edited by Glenn E. Estes (1985)

43 *American Newspaper Journalists, 1690–1872*, edited by Perry J. Ashley (1986)

44 *American Screenwriters, Second Series*, edited by Randall Clark, Robert E. Morsberger, and Stephen O. Lesser (1986)

45 *American Poets, 1880–1945, First Series*, edited by Peter Quartermain (1986)

46 *American Literary Publishing Houses, 1900–1980: Trade and Paperback*, edited by Peter Dzwonkoski (1986)

47 *American Historians, 1866–1912*, edited by Clyde N. Wilson (1986)

48 *American Poets, 1880–1945, Second Series*, edited by Peter Quartermain (1986)

49 *American Literary Publishing Houses, 1638–1899*, 2 parts, edited by Peter Dzwonkoski (1986)

50 *Afro-American Writers Before the Harlem Renaissance*, edited by Trudier Harris (1986)

51 *Afro-American Writers from the Harlem Renaissance to 1940*, edited by Trudier Harris (1987)

52 *American Writers for Children Since 1960: Fiction*, edited by Glenn E. Estes (1986)

53 *Canadian Writers Since 1960, First Series*, edited by W. H. New (1986)

54 *American Poets, 1880–1945, Third Series*, 2 parts, edited by Peter Quartermain (1987)

55 *Victorian Prose Writers Before 1867*, edited by William B. Thesing (1987)

56 *German Fiction Writers, 1914–1945*, edited by James Hardin (1987)

57 *Victorian Prose Writers After 1867*, edited by William B. Thesing (1987)

58 *Jacobean and Caroline Dramatists*, edited by Fredson Bowers (1987)

59 *American Literary Critics and Scholars, 1800–1850*, edited by John W. Rathbun and Monica M. Grecu (1987)

60 *Canadian Writers Since 1960, Second Series*, edited by W. H. New (1987)

61 *American Writers for Children Since 1960: Poets, Illustrators, and Nonfiction Authors*, edited by Glenn E. Estes (1987)

62 *Elizabethan Dramatists*, edited by Fredson Bowers (1987)

63 *Modern American Critics, 1920–1955*, edited by Gregory S. Jay (1988)

64 *American Literary Critics and Scholars, 1850–1880*, edited by John W. Rathbun and Monica M. Grecu (1988)

65 *French Novelists, 1900–1930*, edited by Catharine Savage Brosman (1988)

66 *German Fiction Writers, 1885–1913*, 2 parts, edited by James Hardin (1988)

67 *Modern American Critics Since 1955*, edited by Gregory S. Jay (1988)

68 *Canadian Writers, 1920–1959, First Series*, edited by W. H. New (1988)

69 *Contemporary German Fiction Writers, First Series*, edited by Wolfgang D. Elfe and James Hardin (1988)

70 *British Mystery Writers, 1860–1919*, edited by Bernard Benstock and Thomas F. Staley (1988)

71 *American Literary Critics and Scholars, 1880–1900*, edited by John W. Rathbun and Monica M. Grecu (1988)

72 *French Novelists, 1930–1960*, edited by Catharine Savage Brosman (1988)

73 *American Magazine Journalists, 1741–1850*, edited by Sam G. Riley (1988)

74 *American Short-Story Writers Before 1880*, edited by Bobby Ellen Kimbel, with the assistance of William E. Grant (1988)

75 *Contemporary German Fiction Writers, Second Series*, edited by Wolfgang D. Elfe and James Hardin (1988)

76 *Afro-American Writers, 1940–1955*, edited by Trudier Harris (1988)

77 *British Mystery Writers, 1920–1939*, edited by Bernard Benstock and Thomas F. Staley (1988)

78 *American Short-Story Writers, 1880–1910,* edited by Bobby Ellen Kimbel, with the assistance of William E. Grant (1988)

79 *American Magazine Journalists, 1850–1900,* edited by Sam G. Riley (1988)

80 *Restoration and Eighteenth-Century Dramatists, First Series,* edited by Paula R. Backscheider (1989)

81 *Austrian Fiction Writers, 1875–1913,* edited by James Hardin and Donald G. Daviau (1989)

82 *Chicano Writers, First Series,* edited by Francisco A. Lomelí and Carl R. Shirley (1989)

83 *French Novelists Since 1960,* edited by Catharine Savage Brosman (1989)

84 *Restoration and Eighteenth-Century Dramatists, Second Series,* edited by Paula R. Backscheider (1989)

85 *Austrian Fiction Writers After 1914,* edited by James Hardin and Donald G. Daviau (1989)

86 *American Short-Story Writers, 1910–1945, First Series,* edited by Bobby Ellen Kimbel (1989)

87 *British Mystery and Thriller Writers Since 1940, First Series,* edited by Bernard Benstock and Thomas F. Staley (1989)

88 *Canadian Writers, 1920–1959, Second Series,* edited by W. H. New (1989)

89 *Restoration and Eighteenth-Century Dramatists, Third Series,* edited by Paula R. Backscheider (1989)

90 *German Writers in the Age of Goethe, 1789–1832,* edited by James Hardin and Christoph E. Schweitzer (1989)

91 *American Magazine Journalists, 1900–1960, First Series,* edited by Sam G. Riley (1990)

92 *Canadian Writers, 1890–1920,* edited by W. H. New (1990)

93 *British Romantic Poets, 1789–1832, First Series,* edited by John R. Greenfield (1990)

94 *German Writers in the Age of Goethe: Sturm und Drang to Classicism,* edited by James Hardin and Christoph E. Schweitzer (1990)

95 *Eighteenth-Century British Poets, First Series,* edited by John Sitter (1990)

96 *British Romantic Poets, 1789–1832, Second Series,* edited by John R. Greenfield (1990)

97 *German Writers from the Enlightenment to Sturm und Drang, 1720–1764,* edited by James Hardin and Christoph E. Schweitzer (1990)

98 *Modern British Essayists, First Series,* edited by Robert Beum (1990)

99 *Canadian Writers Before 1890,* edited by W. H. New (1990)

100 *Modern British Essayists, Second Series,* edited by Robert Beum (1990)

101 *British Prose Writers, 1660–1800, First Series,* edited by Donald T. Siebert (1991)

102 *American Short-Story Writers, 1910–1945, Second Series,* edited by Bobby Ellen Kimbel (1991)

103 *American Literary Biographers, First Series,* edited by Steven Serafin (1991)

104 *British Prose Writers, 1660–1800, Second Series,* edited by Donald T. Siebert (1991)

105 *American Poets Since World War II, Second Series,* edited by R. S. Gwynn (1991)

106 *British Literary Publishing Houses, 1820–1880,* edited by Patricia J. Anderson and Jonathan Rose (1991)

107 *British Romantic Prose Writers, 1789–1832, First Series,* edited by John R. Greenfield (1991)

108 *Twentieth-Century Spanish Poets, First Series,* edited by Michael L. Perna (1991)

109 *Eighteenth-Century British Poets, Second Series,* edited by John Sitter (1991)

110 *British Romantic Prose Writers, 1789–1832, Second Series,* edited by John R. Greenfield (1991)

111 *American Literary Biographers, Second Series,* edited by Steven Serafin (1991)

112 *British Literary Publishing Houses, 1881–1965,* edited by Jonathan Rose and Patricia J. Anderson (1991)

113 *Modern Latin-American Fiction Writers, First Series,* edited by William Luis (1992)

114 *Twentieth-Century Italian Poets, First Series,* edited by Giovanna Wedel De Stasio, Glauco Cambon, and Antonio Illiano (1992)

115 *Medieval Philosophers,* edited by Jeremiah Hackett (1992)

116 *British Romantic Novelists, 1789–1832,* edited by Bradford K. Mudge (1992)

117 *Twentieth-Century Caribbean and Black African Writers, First Series,* edited by Bernth Lindfors and Reinhard Sander (1992)

118 *Twentieth-Century German Dramatists, 1889–1918,* edited by Wolfgang D. Elfe and James Hardin (1992)

119 *Nineteenth-Century French Fiction Writers: Romanticism and Realism, 1800–1860,* edited by Catharine Savage Brosman (1992)

120 *American Poets Since World War II, Third Series,* edited by R. S. Gwynn (1992)

121 *Seventeenth-Century British Nondramatic Poets, First Series,* edited by M. Thomas Hester (1992)

122 *Chicano Writers, Second Series,* edited by Francisco A. Lomelí and Carl R. Shirley (1992)

123 *Nineteenth-Century French Fiction Writers: Naturalism and Beyond, 1860–1900,* edited by Catharine Savage Brosman (1992)

124 *Twentieth-Century German Dramatists, 1919–1992,* edited by Wolfgang D. Elfe and James Hardin (1992)

125 *Twentieth-Century Caribbean and Black African Writers, Second Series,* edited by Bernth Lindfors and Reinhard Sander (1993)

126 *Seventeenth-Century British Nondramatic Poets, Second Series,* edited by M. Thomas Hester (1993)

127 *American Newspaper Publishers, 1950–1990,* edited by Perry J. Ashley (1993)

128 *Twentieth-Century Italian Poets, Second Series,* edited by Giovanna Wedel De Stasio, Glauco Cambon, and Antonio Illiano (1993)

129 *Nineteenth-Century German Writers, 1841–1900,* edited by James Hardin and Siegfried Mews (1993)

130 *American Short-Story Writers Since World War II,* edited by Patrick Meanor (1993)

131 *Seventeenth-Century British Nondramatic Poets, Third Series,* edited by M. Thomas Hester (1993)

132 *Sixteenth-Century British Nondramatic Writers, First Series,* edited by David A. Richardson (1993)

133 *Nineteenth-Century German Writers to 1840,* edited by James Hardin and Siegfried Mews (1993)

134 *Twentieth-Century Spanish Poets, Second Series,* edited by Jerry Phillips Winfield (1994)

135 *British Short-Fiction Writers, 1880–1914: The Realist Tradition,* edited by William B. Thesing (1994)

136 *Sixteenth-Century British Nondramatic Writers, Second Series,* edited by David A. Richardson (1994)

137 *American Magazine Journalists, 1900–1960, Second Series,* edited by Sam G. Riley (1994)

138 *German Writers and Works of the High Middle Ages: 1170–1280,* edited by James Hardin and Will Hasty (1994)

139 *British Short-Fiction Writers, 1945–1980,* edited by Dean Baldwin (1994)

140 *American Book-Collectors and Bibliographers, First Series,* edited by Joseph Rosenblum (1994)

141 *British Children's Writers, 1880–1914,* edited by Laura M. Zaidman (1994)

142 *Eighteenth-Century British Literary Biographers,* edited by Steven Serafin (1994)

143 *American Novelists Since World War II, Third Series,* edited by James R. Giles and Wanda H. Giles (1994)

144 *Nineteenth-Century British Literary Biographers,* edited by Steven Serafin (1994)

145 *Modern Latin-American Fiction Writers, Second Series,* edited by William Luis and Ann González (1994)

146 *Old and Middle English Literature,* edited by Jeffrey Helterman and Jerome Mitchell (1994)

147 *South Slavic Writers Before World War II,* edited by Vasa D. Mihailovich (1994)

148 *German Writers and Works of the Early Middle Ages: 800–1170,* edited by Will Hasty and James Hardin (1994)

149 *Late Nineteenth- and Early Twentieth-Century British Literary Biographers,* edited by Steven Serafin (1995)

150 *Early Modern Russian Writers, Late Seventeenth and Eighteenth Centuries,* edited by Marcus C. Levitt (1995)

151 *British Prose Writers of the Early Seventeenth Century,* edited by Clayton D. Lein (1995)

152 *American Novelists Since World War II, Fourth Series,* edited by James R. Giles and Wanda H. Giles (1995)

153 *Late-Victorian and Edwardian British Novelists, First Series,* edited by George M. Johnson (1995)

154 *The British Literary Book Trade, 1700–1820,* edited by James K. Bracken and Joel Silver (1995)

155 *Twentieth-Century British Literary Biographers*, edited by Steven Serafin (1995)
156 *British Short-Fiction Writers, 1880–1914: The Romantic Tradition*, edited by William F. Naufftus (1995)
157 *Twentieth-Century Caribbean and Black African Writers, Third Series*, edited by Bernth Lindfors and Reinhard Sander (1995)
158 *British Reform Writers, 1789–1832*, edited by Gary Kelly and Edd Applegate (1995)
159 *British Short-Fiction Writers, 1800–1880*, edited by John R. Greenfield (1996)
160 *British Children's Writers, 1914–1960*, edited by Donald R. Hettinga and Gary D. Schmidt (1996)
161 *British Children's Writers Since 1960, First Series*, edited by Caroline Hunt (1996)
162 *British Short-Fiction Writers, 1915–1945*, edited by John H. Rogers (1996)
163 *British Children's Writers, 1800–1880*, edited by Meena Khorana (1996)
164 *German Baroque Writers, 1580–1660*, edited by James Hardin (1996)
165 *American Poets Since World War II, Fourth Series*, edited by Joseph Conte (1996)
166 *British Travel Writers, 1837–1875*, edited by Barbara Brothers and Julia Gergits (1996)
167 *Sixteenth-Century British Nondramatic Writers, Third Series*, edited by David A. Richardson (1996)
168 *German Baroque Writers, 1661–1730*, edited by James Hardin (1996)
169 *American Poets Since World War II, Fifth Series*, edited by Joseph Conte (1996)
170 *The British Literary Book Trade, 1475–1700*, edited by James K. Bracken and Joel Silver (1996)
171 *Twentieth-Century American Sportswriters*, edited by Richard Orodenker (1996)
172 *Sixteenth-Century British Nondramatic Writers, Fourth Series*, edited by David A. Richardson (1996)
173 *American Novelists Since World War II, Fifth Series*, edited by James R. Giles and Wanda H. Giles (1996)
174 *British Travel Writers, 1876–1909*, edited by Barbara Brothers and Julia Gergits (1997)
175 *Native American Writers of the United States*, edited by Kenneth M. Roemer (1997)
176 *Ancient Greek Authors*, edited by Ward W. Briggs (1997)
177 *Italian Novelists Since World War II, 1945–1965*, edited by Augustus Pallotta (1997)
178 *British Fantasy and Science-Fiction Writers Before World War I*, edited by Darren Harris-Fain (1997)
179 *German Writers of the Renaissance and Reformation, 1280–1580*, edited by James Hardin and Max Reinhart (1997)
180 *Japanese Fiction Writers, 1868–1945*, edited by Van C. Gessel (1997)
181 *South Slavic Writers Since World War II*, edited by Vasa D. Mihailovich (1997)
182 *Japanese Fiction Writers Since World War II*, edited by Van C. Gessel (1997)

183 *American Travel Writers, 1776–1864*, edited by James J. Schramer and Donald Ross (1997)
184 *Nineteenth-Century British Book-Collectors and Bibliographers*, edited by William Baker and Kenneth Womack (1997)
185 *American Literary Journalists, 1945–1995, First Series*, edited by Arthur J. Kaul (1998)
186 *Nineteenth-Century American Western Writers*, edited by Robert L. Gale (1998)
187 *American Book Collectors and Bibliographers, Second Series*, edited by Joseph Rosenblum (1998)
188 *American Book and Magazine Illustrators to 1920*, edited by Steven E. Smith, Catherine A. Hastedt, and Donald H. Dyal (1998)
189 *American Travel Writers, 1850–1915*, edited by Donald Ross and James J. Schramer (1998)
190 *British Reform Writers, 1832–1914*, edited by Gary Kelly and Edd Applegate (1998)
191 *British Novelists Between the Wars*, edited by George M. Johnson (1998)
192 *French Dramatists, 1789–1914*, edited by Barbara T. Cooper (1998)
193 *American Poets Since World War II, Sixth Series*, edited by Joseph Conte (1998)
194 *British Novelists Since 1960, Second Series*, edited by Merritt Moseley (1998)
195 *British Travel Writers, 1910–1939*, edited by Barbara Brothers and Julia Gergits (1998)
196 *Italian Novelists Since World War II, 1965–1995*, edited by Augustus Pallotta (1999)
197 *Late-Victorian and Edwardian British Novelists, Second Series*, edited by George M. Johnson (1999)
198 *Russian Literature in the Age of Pushkin and Gogol: Prose*, edited by Christine A. Rydel (1999)
199 *Victorian Women Poets*, edited by William B. Thesing (1999)
200 *American Women Prose Writers to 1820*, edited by Carla J. Mulford, with Angela Vietto and Amy E. Winans (1999)
201 *Twentieth-Century British Book Collectors and Bibliographers*, edited by William Baker and Kenneth Womack (1999)
202 *Nineteenth-Century American Fiction Writers*, edited by Kent P. Ljungquist (1999)
203 *Medieval Japanese Writers*, edited by Steven D. Carter (1999)
204 *British Travel Writers, 1940–1997*, edited by Barbara Brothers and Julia M. Gergits (1999)
205 *Russian Literature in the Age of Pushkin and Gogol: Poetry and Drama*, edited by Christine A. Rydel (1999)
206 *Twentieth-Century American Western Writers, First Series*, edited by Richard H. Cracroft (1999)
207 *British Novelists Since 1960, Third Series*, edited by Merritt Moseley (1999)
208 *Literature of the French and Occitan Middle Ages: Eleventh to Fifteenth Centuries*, edited by Deborah Sinnreich-Levi and Ian S. Laurie (1999)

209 *Chicano Writers, Third Series*, edited by Francisco A. Lomelí and Carl R. Shirley (1999)
210 *Ernest Hemingway: A Documentary Volume*, edited by Robert W. Trogdon (1999)
211 *Ancient Roman Writers*, edited by Ward W. Briggs (1999)
212 *Twentieth-Century American Western Writers, Second Series*, edited by Richard H. Cracroft (1999)
213 *Pre-Nineteenth-Century British Book Collectors and Bibliographers*, edited by William Baker and Kenneth Womack (1999)
214 *Twentieth-Century Danish Writers*, edited by Marianne Stecher-Hansen (1999)
215 *Twentieth-Century Eastern European Writers, First Series*, edited by Steven Serafin (1999)
216 *British Poets of the Great War: Brooke, Rosenberg, Thomas. A Documentary Volume*, edited by Patrick Quinn (2000)
217 *Nineteenth-Century French Poets*, edited by Robert Beum (2000)
218 *American Short-Story Writers Since World War II, Second Series*, edited by Patrick Meanor and Gwen Crane (2000)
219 *F. Scott Fitzgerald's The Great Gatsby: A Documentary Volume*, edited by Matthew J. Bruccoli (2000)
220 *Twentieth-Century Eastern European Writers, Second Series*, edited by Steven Serafin (2000)
221 *American Women Prose Writers, 1870–1920*, edited by Sharon M. Harris, with the assistance of Heidi L. M. Jacobs and Jennifer Putzi (2000)
222 *H. L. Mencken: A Documentary Volume*, edited by Richard J. Schrader (2000)
223 *The American Renaissance in New England, Second Series*, edited by Wesley T. Mott (2000)
224 *Walt Whitman: A Documentary Volume*, edited by Joel Myerson (2000)
225 *South African Writers*, edited by Paul A. Scanlon (2000)
226 *American Hard-Boiled Crime Writers*, edited by George Parker Anderson and Julie B. Anderson (2000)
227 *American Novelists Since World War II, Sixth Series*, edited by James R. Giles and Wanda H. Giles (2000)
228 *Twentieth-Century American Dramatists, Second Series*, edited by Christopher J. Wheatley (2000)
229 *Thomas Wolfe: A Documentary Volume*, edited by Ted Mitchell (2001)
230 *Australian Literature, 1788–1914*, edited by Selina Samuels (2001)
231 *British Novelists Since 1960, Fourth Series*, edited by Merritt Moseley (2001)
232 *Twentieth-Century Eastern European Writers, Third Series*, edited by Steven Serafin (2001)
233 *British and Irish Dramatists Since World War II, Second Series*, edited by John Bull (2001)
234 *American Short-Story Writers Since World War II, Third Series*, edited by Patrick Meanor and Richard E. Lee (2001)
235 *The American Renaissance in New England, Third Series*, edited by Wesley T. Mott (2001)

236 *British Rhetoricians and Logicians, 1500–1660*, edited by Edward A. Malone (2001)

237 *The Beats: A Documentary Volume*, edited by Matt Theado (2001)

238 *Russian Novelists in the Age of Tolstoy and Dostoevsky*, edited by J. Alexander Ogden and Judith E. Kalb (2001)

239 *American Women Prose Writers: 1820–1870*, edited by Amy E. Hudock and Katharine Rodier (2001)

240 *Late Nineteenth- and Early Twentieth-Century British Women Poets*, edited by William B. Thesing (2001)

241 *American Sportswriters and Writers on Sport*, edited by Richard Orodenker (2001)

242 *Twentieth-Century European Cultural Theorists, First Series*, edited by Paul Hansom (2001)

243 *The American Renaissance in New England, Fourth Series*, edited by Wesley T. Mott (2001)

244 *American Short-Story Writers Since World War II, Fourth Series*, edited by Patrick Meanor and Joseph McNicholas (2001)

245 *British and Irish Dramatists Since World War II, Third Series*, edited by John Bull (2001)

246 *Twentieth-Century American Cultural Theorists*, edited by Paul Hansom (2001)

247 *James Joyce: A Documentary Volume*, edited by A. Nicholas Fargnoli (2001)

248 *Antebellum Writers in the South, Second Series*, edited by Kent Ljungquist (2001)

249 *Twentieth-Century American Dramatists, Third Series*, edited by Christopher Wheatley (2002)

250 *Antebellum Writers in New York, Second Series*, edited by Kent Ljungquist (2002)

251 *Canadian Fantasy and Science-Fiction Writers*, edited by Douglas Ivison (2002)

252 *British Philosophers, 1500–1799*, edited by Philip B. Dematteis and Peter S. Fosl (2002)

253 *Raymond Chandler: A Documentary Volume*, edited by Robert Moss (2002)

254 *The House of Putnam, 1837–1872: A Documentary Volume*, edited by Ezra Greenspan (2002)

255 *British Fantasy and Science-Fiction Writers, 1918–1960*, edited by Darren Harris-Fain (2002)

256 *Twentieth-Century American Western Writers, Third Series*, edited by Richard H. Cracroft (2002)

257 *Twentieth-Century Swedish Writers After World War II*, edited by Ann-Charlotte Gavel Adams (2002)

258 *Modern French Poets*, edited by Jean-François Leroux (2002)

259 *Twentieth-Century Swedish Writers Before World War II*, edited by Ann-Charlotte Gavel Adams (2002)

260 *Australian Writers, 1915–1950*, edited by Selina Samuels (2002)

261 *British Fantasy and Science-Fiction Writers Since 1960*, edited by Darren Harris-Fain (2002)

262 *British Philosophers, 1800–2000*, edited by Peter S. Fosl and Leemon B. McHenry (2002)

263 *William Shakespeare: A Documentary Volume*, edited by Catherine Loomis (2002)

264 *Italian Prose Writers, 1900–1945*, edited by Luca Somigli and Rocco Capozzi (2002)

265 *American Song Lyricists, 1920–1960*, edited by Philip Furia (2002)

266 *Twentieth-Century American Dramatists, Fourth Series*, edited by Christopher J. Wheatley (2002)

267 *Twenty-First-Century British and Irish Novelists*, edited by Michael R. Molino (2002)

268 *Seventeenth-Century French Writers*, edited by Françoise Jaouën (2002)

269 *Nathaniel Hawthorne: A Documentary Volume*, edited by Benjamin Franklin V (2002)

270 *American Philosophers Before 1950*, edited by Philip B. Dematteis and Leemon B. McHenry (2002)

271 *British and Irish Novelists Since 1960*, edited by Merritt Moseley (2002)

272 *Russian Prose Writers Between the World Wars*, edited by Christine Rydel (2003)

273 *F. Scott Fitzgerald's* Tender Is the Night: *A Documentary Volume*, edited by Matthew J. Bruccoli and George Parker Anderson (2003)

274 *John Dos Passos's* U.S.A.: *A Documentary Volume*, edited by Donald Pizer (2003)

275 *Twentieth-Century American Nature Writers: Prose*, edited by Roger Thompson and J. Scott Bryson (2003)

276 *British Mystery and Thriller Writers Since 1960*, edited by Gina Macdonald (2003)

277 *Russian Literature in the Age of Realism*, edited by Alyssa Dinega Gillespie (2003)

278 *American Novelists Since World War II, Seventh Series*, edited by James R. Giles and Wanda H. Giles (2003)

279 *American Philosophers, 1950–2000*, edited by Philip B. Dematteis and Leemon B. McHenry (2003)

280 *Dashiell Hammett's* The Maltese Falcon: *A Documentary Volume*, edited by Richard Layman (2003)

281 *British Rhetoricians and Logicians, 1500–1660, Second Series*, edited by Edward A. Malone (2003)

282 *New Formalist Poets*, edited by Jonathan N. Barron and Bruce Meyer (2003)

283 *Modern Spanish American Poets, First Series*, edited by María A. Salgado (2003)

284 *The House of Holt, 1866–1946: A Documentary Volume*, edited by Ellen D. Gilbert (2003)

285 *Russian Writers Since 1980*, edited by Marina Balina and Mark Lipoyvetsky (2004)

286 *Castilian Writers, 1400–1500*, edited by Frank A. Domínguez and George D. Greenia (2004)

287 *Portuguese Writers*, edited by Monica Rector and Fred M. Clark (2004)

288 *The House of Boni & Liveright, 1917–1933: A Documentary Volume*, edited by Charles Egleston (2004)

289 *Australian Writers, 1950–1975*, edited by Selina Samuels (2004)

290 *Modern Spanish American Poets, Second Series*, edited by María A. Salgado (2004)

291 *The Hoosier House: Bobbs-Merrill and Its Predecessors, 1850–1985: A Documentary Volume*, edited by Richard J. Schrader (2004)

292 *Twenty-First-Century American Novelists*, edited by Lisa Abney and Suzanne Disheroon-Green (2004)

293 *Icelandic Writers*, edited by Patrick J. Stevens (2004)

294 *James Gould Cozzens: A Documentary Volume*, edited by Matthew J. Bruccoli (2004)

295 *Russian Writers of the Silver Age, 1890–1925*, edited by Judith E. Kalb and J. Alexander Ogden with the collaboration of I. G. Vishnevetsky (2004)

296 *Twentieth-Century European Cultural Theorists, Second Series*, edited by Paul Hansom (2004)

297 *Twentieth-Century Norwegian Writers*, edited by Tanya Thresher (2004)

298 *Henry David Thoreau: A Documentary Volume*, edited by Richard J. Schneider (2004)

299 *Holocaust Novelists*, edited by Efraim Sicher (2004)

300 *Danish Writers from the Reformation to Decadence, 1550–1900*, edited by Marianne Stecher-Hansen (2004)

301 *Gustave Flaubert: A Documentary Volume*, edited by Éric Le Calvez (2004)

302 *Russian Prose Writers After World War II*, edited by Christine Rydel (2004)

303 *American Radical and Reform Writers, First Series*, edited by Steven Rosendale (2005)

304 *Bram Stoker's* Dracula: *A Documentary Volume*, edited by Elizabeth Miller (2005)

305 *Latin American Dramatists, First Series*, edited by Adam Versényi (2005)

306 *American Mystery and Detective Writers*, edited by George Parker Anderson (2005)

307 *Brazilian Writers*, edited by Monica Rector and Fred M. Clark (2005)

308 *Ernest Hemingway's* A Farewell to Arms: *A Documentary Volume*, edited by Charles Oliver (2005)

309 *John Steinbeck: A Documentary Volume*, edited by Luchen Li (2005)

310 *British and Irish Dramatists Since World War II, Fourth Series*, edited by John Bull (2005)

Dictionary of Literary Biography Documentary Series

1 *Sherwood Anderson, Willa Cather, John Dos Passos, Theodore Dreiser, F. Scott Fitzgerald, Ernest Hemingway, Sinclair Lewis*, edited by Margaret A. Van Antwerp (1982)

2 *James Gould Cozzens, James T. Farrell, William Faulkner, John O'Hara, John Steinbeck, Thomas Wolfe, Richard Wright*, edited by Margaret A. Van Antwerp (1982)

3 *Saul Bellow, Jack Kerouac, Norman Mailer, Vladimir Nabokov, John Updike, Kurt Vonnegut*, edited by Mary Bruccoli (1983)

4 *Tennessee Williams*, edited by Margaret A. Van Antwerp and Sally Johns (1984)

5 *American Transcendentalists*, edited by Joel Myerson (1988)

6 *Hardboiled Mystery Writers: Raymond Chandler, Dashiell Hammett, Ross Macdonald*, edited by Matthew J. Bruccoli and Richard Layman (1989)

7 *Modern American Poets: James Dickey, Robert Frost, Marianne Moore*, edited by Karen L. Rood (1989)

8 *The Black Aesthetic Movement*, edited by Jeffrey Louis Decker (1991)

9 *American Writers of the Vietnam War: W. D. Ehrhart, Larry Heinemann, Tim O'Brien, Walter McDonald, John M. Del Vecchio*, edited by Ronald Baughman (1991)

10 *The Bloomsbury Group*, edited by Edward L. Bishop (1992)

11 *American Proletarian Culture: The Twenties and The Thirties*, edited by Jon Christian Suggs (1993)

12 *Southern Women Writers: Flannery O'Connor, Katherine Anne Porter, Eudora Welty*, edited by Mary Ann Wimsatt and Karen L. Rood (1994)

13 *The House of Scribner, 1846–1904*, edited by John Delaney (1996)

14 *Four Women Writers for Children, 1868–1918*, edited by Caroline C. Hunt (1996)

15 *American Expatriate Writers: Paris in the Twenties*, edited by Matthew J. Bruccoli and Robert W. Trogdon (1997)

16 *The House of Scribner, 1905–1930*, edited by John Delaney (1997)

17 *The House of Scribner, 1931–1984*, edited by John Delaney (1998)

18 *British Poets of The Great War: Sassoon, Graves, Owen*, edited by Patrick Quinn (1999)

19 *James Dickey*, edited by Judith S. Baughman (1999)

See also DLB 210, 216, 219, 222, 224, 229, 237, 247, 253, 254, 263, 269, 273, 274, 280, 284, 288, 291, 294, 298, 301, 304, 308, 309

Dictionary of Literary Biography Yearbooks

1980 edited by Karen L. Rood, Jean W. Ross, and Richard Ziegfeld (1981)

1981 edited by Karen L. Rood, Jean W. Ross, and Richard Ziegfeld (1982)

1982 edited by Richard Ziegfeld; associate editors: Jean W. Ross and Lynne C. Zeigler (1983)

1983 edited by Mary Bruccoli and Jean W. Ross; associate editor Richard Ziegfeld (1984)

1984 edited by Jean W. Ross (1985)

1985 edited by Jean W. Ross (1986)

1986 edited by J. M. Brook (1987)

1987 edited by J. M. Brook (1988)

1988 edited by J. M. Brook (1989)

1989 edited by J. M. Brook (1990)

1990 edited by James W. Hipp (1991)

1991 edited by James W. Hipp (1992)

1992 edited by James W. Hipp (1993)

1993 edited by James W. Hipp, contributing editor George Garrett (1994)

1994 edited by James W. Hipp, contributing editor George Garrett (1995)

1995 edited by James W. Hipp, contributing editor George Garrett (1996)

1996 edited by Samuel W. Bruce and L. Kay Webster, contributing editor George Garrett (1997)

1997 edited by Matthew J. Bruccoli and George Garrett, with the assistance of L. Kay Webster (1998)

1998 edited by Matthew J. Bruccoli, contributing editor George Garrett, with the assistance of D. W. Thomas (1999)

1999 edited by Matthew J. Bruccoli, contributing editor George Garrett, with the assistance of D. W. Thomas (2000)

2000 edited by Matthew J. Bruccoli, contributing editor George Garrett, with the assistance of George Parker Anderson (2001)

2001 edited by Matthew J. Bruccoli, contributing editor George Garrett, with the assistance of George Parker Anderson (2002)

2002 edited by Matthew J. Bruccoli and George Garrett; George Parker Anderson, Assistant Editor (2003)

Concise Series

Concise Dictionary of American Literary Biography, 7 volumes (1988–1999): *The New Consciousness, 1941–1968; Colonization to the American Renaissance, 1640–1865; Realism, Naturalism, and Local Color, 1865–1917; The Twenties, 1917–1929; The Age of Maturity, 1929–1941; Broadening Views, 1968–1988; Supplement: Modern Writers, 1900–1998.*

Concise Dictionary of British Literary Biography, 8 volumes (1991–1992): *Writers of the Middle Ages and Renaissance Before 1660; Writers of the Restoration and Eighteenth Century, 1660–1789; Writers of the Romantic Period, 1789–1832; Victorian Writers, 1832–1890; Late-Victorian and Edwardian Writers, 1890–1914; Modern Writers, 1914–1945; Writers After World War II, 1945–1960; Contemporary Writers, 1960 to Present.*

Concise Dictionary of World Literary Biography, 4 volumes (1999–2000): *Ancient Greek and Roman Writers; German Writers; African, Caribbean, and Latin American Writers; South Slavic and Eastern European Writers.*

Dictionary of Literary Biography® • Volume Three Hundred Ten

British and Irish Dramatists Since World War II
Fourth Series

Dictionary of Literary Biography® • Volume Three Hundred Ten

British and Irish Dramatists Since World War II
Fourth Series

Edited by
John Bull
University of Reading

Detroit • New York • San Francisco • San Diego • New Haven, Conn. • Waterville, Maine • London • Munich

ST. PHILIP'S COLLEGE LIBRARY

Dictionary of Literary Biography
Volume 310: British and Irish Dramatists Since World War II
Fourth Series
John Bull

Editorial Directors
Matthew J. Bruccoli and Richard Layman

© 2005 Thomson Gale, a part of The Thomson Corporation.

Thomson and Star Logo are trademarks and Gale is a registered trademark used herein under license.

For more information, contact
Thomson Gale
27500 Drake Rd.
Farmington Hills, MI 48331-3535
Or you can visit our Internet site at
http://www.gale.com

ALL RIGHTS RESERVED
No part of this work covered by the copyright hereon may be reproduced or used in any form or by any means—graphic, electronic, or mechanical, including photocopying, recording, taping, Web distribution, or information storage retrieval systems—without the written permission of the publisher.

For permission to use material from this product, submit your request via Web at http://www.gale-edit.com/permissions, or you may download our Permissions Request form and submit your request by fax or mail to:

Permissions Department
Thomson Gale
27500 Drake Rd.
Farmington Hills, MI 48331-3535
Permissions Hotline:
248-699-8006 or 800-877-4253, ext. 8006
Fax: 248-699-8074 or 800-762-4058

While every effort has been made to ensure the reliability of the information presented in this publication, Thomson Gale does not guarantee the accuracy of the data contained herein. Thomson Gale accepts no payment for listing; and inclusion in the publication of any organization, agency, institution, publication, service, or individual does not imply endorsement of the editors or publisher. Errors brought to the attention of the publisher and verified to the satisfaction of the publisher will be corrected in future editions.

LIBRARY OF CONGRESS CATALOGING-IN-PUBLICATION DATA

British and Irish dramatists since World War II. Fourth series / edited by John Bull.
  p. cm. — (Dictionary of literary biography ; v. 310)
"A Bruccoli Clark Layman book."
Includes bibliographical references and index.
ISBN 0-7876-8128-8 (alk. paper)
 1. English drama—20th century—Bio-bibliography—Dictionaries. 2. English drama—Irish authors—Bio-bibliography—Dictionaries. 3. Dramatists, English—20th century—Biography—Dictionaries. 4. Dramatists, Irish—20th century—Biography—Dictionaries. 5. English drama—Irish authors—Dictionaries. 6. English drama—20th century—Dictionaries. I. Bull, John (John Stanley) II. Title. III. Series.

PR736.B683 2005
822'.91409'03—dc22   2005000217

Printed in the United States of America
10 9 8 7 6 5 4 3 2 1

Contents

Plan of the Series xiii
Introduction xv

Alan Bennett (1934-) 3
Kara McKechnie

Edward Bond (1934-) .19
Peter Billingham

John Boyd (1912-2002) .34
Roy Connolly

Ian Brown (1945-) 42
Susanne Kries

Caryl Churchill (1938-) 51
Frances Gray

Maureen Duffy (1933-) 66
Lucy Kay

Robin Glendinning (1938-) 73
David Grant

Sue Glover (1943-) 79
Ksenija Horvat

David Hare (1947-) 87
Catherine MacGregor

Sarah Kane (1971-1999) 105
Aleks Sierz

Tom Kempinski (1938-) 115
Peter Billingham

Deborah Levy (1959-) 120
Margaret Llewellyn-Jones

Saunders Lewis (1893-1985) 126
Ioan Williams

Liz Lochhead (1947-) 134
Lucy Kay

Martin Lynch (1950-) 143
Roy Connolly

Owen McCafferty (1961-) 151
David Grant

David Mercer (1928-1980) 158
Jeremy Ridgman

Tom Murphy (1935-) 170
Ben Francombe

G. F. Newman (1946-) 179
Jeremy Ridgman

Joe Orton (1933-1967) 187
Francesca Coppa

Harold Pinter (1930-) 203
Ronald Knowles

Meic Povey (1950-) .219
Nic Ros

Mark Ravenhill (1966-) 230
Aleks Sierz

Ian Rowlands (1964-) 239
Andy W. Smith

W. Gordon Smith (1928-1996) 249
Ian Brown

Ed Thomas (1961-) .257
Andy W. Smith

Michelene Wandor (1940-) 268
Margaret Llewellyn-Jones

Arnold Wesker (1932-) 278
Anne Etienne

E. A. Whitehead (Ted Whitehead) (1933-) 299
Tony Dunn

Christopher Wilkinson (1941-) 307
Derek Paget

Ted Willis (1918-1992) 313
Derek Paget

Appendix 1: Playwriting for the Seventies 323

Appendix 2: Michael Billington Reviews the
    Past in British Theatre and Celebrates
    the New Breed 361

Books for Further Reading 365
Contributors 371
Cumulative Index 375

Plan of the Series

. . . Almost the most prodigious asset of a country, and perhaps its most precious possession, is its native literary product—when that product is fine and noble and enduring.

Mark Twain*

The advisory board, the editors, and the publisher of the *Dictionary of Literary Biography* are joined in endorsing Mark Twain's declaration. The literature of a nation provides an inexhaustible resource of permanent worth. Our purpose is to make literature and its creators better understood and more accessible to students and the reading public, while satisfying the needs of teachers and researchers.

To meet these requirements, *literary biography* has been construed in terms of the author's achievement. The most important thing about a writer is his writing. Accordingly, the entries in *DLB* are career biographies, tracing the development of the author's canon and the evolution of his reputation.

The purpose of *DLB* is not only to provide reliable information in a usable format but also to place the figures in the larger perspective of literary history and to offer appraisals of their accomplishments by qualified scholars.

The publication plan for *DLB* resulted from two years of preparation. The project was proposed to Bruccoli Clark by Frederick G. Ruffner, president of the Gale Research Company, in November 1975. After specimen entries were prepared and typeset, an advisory board was formed to refine the entry format and develop the series rationale. In meetings held during 1976, the publisher, series editors, and advisory board approved the scheme for a comprehensive biographical dictionary of persons who contributed to literature. Editorial work on the first volume began in January 1977, and it was published in 1978. In order to make *DLB* more than a dictionary and to compile volumes that individually have claim to status as literary history, it was decided to organize volumes by topic, period, or genre. Each of these freestanding volumes provides a biographical-bibliographical guide and overview for a particular area of literature. We are convinced that this organization—as opposed to a single alphabet method—constitutes a valuable innovation in the presentation of reference material. The volume plan necessarily requires many decisions for the placement and treatment of authors. Certain figures will be included in separate volumes, but with different entries emphasizing the aspect of his career appropriate to each volume. Ernest Hemingway, for example, is represented in *American Writers in Paris, 1920–1939* by an entry focusing on his expatriate apprenticeship; he is also in *American Novelists, 1910–1945* with an entry surveying his entire career, as well as in *American Short-Story Writers, 1910–1945, Second Series* with an entry concentrating on his short fiction. Each volume includes a cumulative index of the subject authors and articles.

Between 1981 and 2002 the series was augmented and updated by the *DLB Yearbooks*. There have also been nineteen *DLB Documentary Series* volumes, which provide illustrations, facsimiles, and biographical and critical source materials for figures, works, or groups judged to have particular interest for students. In 1999 the *Documentary Series* was incorporated into the *DLB* volume numbering system beginning with *DLB 210: Ernest Hemingway*.

We define literature as the *intellectual commerce of a nation*: not merely as belles lettres but as that ample and complex process by which ideas are generated, shaped, and transmitted. *DLB* entries are not limited to "creative writers" but extend to other figures who in their time and in their way influenced the minds of a people. Thus the series encompasses historians, journalists, publishers, book collectors, and screenwriters. By this means readers of *DLB* may be aided to perceive literature not as cult scripture in the keeping of intellectual high priests but firmly positioned at the center of a nation's life.

DLB includes the major writers appropriate to each volume and those standing in the ranks behind them. Scholarly and critical counsel has been sought in deciding which minor figures to include and how full their entries should be. Wherever possible, useful refer-

From an unpublished section of Mark Twain's autobiography, copyright by the Mark Twain Company ences are made to figures who do not warrant separate entries.

Each *DLB* volume has an expert volume editor responsible for planning the volume, selecting the figures for inclusion, and assigning the entries. Volume editors are also responsible for preparing, where appropriate, appendices surveying the major periodicals and literary and intellectual movements for their volumes, as well as lists of further readings. Work on the series as a whole is coordinated at the Bruccoli Clark Layman editorial center in Columbia, South Carolina, where the editorial staff is responsible for accuracy and utility of the published volumes.

One feature that distinguishes *DLB* is the illustration policy–its concern with the iconography of literature. Just as an author is influenced by his surroundings, so is the reader's understanding of the author enhanced by a knowledge of his environment. Therefore, *DLB* volumes include not only drawings, paintings, and photographs of authors, often depicting them at various stages in their careers, but also illustrations of their families and places where they lived. Title pages are regularly reproduced in facsimile along with dust jackets for modern authors. The dust jackets are a special feature of *DLB* because they often document better than anything else the way in which an author's work was perceived in its own time. Specimens of the writers' manuscripts and letters are included when feasible.

Samuel Johnson rightly decreed that "The chief glory of every people arises from its authors." The purpose of the *Dictionary of Literary Biography* is to compile literary history in the surest way available to us–by accurate and comprehensive treatment of the lives and work of those who contributed to it.

The *DLB* Advisory Board

Introduction

This volume of the *British and Irish Dramatists Since World War II* series is a continuation of the work in *DLB 233* (2001) and *DLB 245* (2001). The series updates entries on major figures from *DLB 13: British Dramatists Since World War II* (1982) and includes many writers who have come to prominence since then. This volume includes a mix of playwrights from England, Scotland, Wales, and Ireland, from those whose careers were established shortly after World War II to others who are just beginning to find a voice and an audience. Together, they give a good idea of the quality and range of theater in the period.

The senior figure in this volume is Saunders Lewis, arguably the single most important figure in twentieth-century Welsh drama. He was born into a Victorian world and lived to see Margaret Thatcher installed as the first female prime minister of Britain in 1979. A passionate supporter of Welsh culture and a founder of the Welsh National Party in 1925, he must also be considered as part of a larger European tradition—as is demonstrated, for instance, by the fact that in 1970 he translated into his own language the seminal play of the modern period, Samuel Beckett's *Waiting for Godot* (1952).

W. Gordon Smith was a product of an earlier Scottish theatrical tradition; yet, before he began to write for the stage in the 1970s, he first embraced the new medium of television, having previously worked as a radio producer. Like Lewis in his eclecticism—although different in the form it took—Smith was a published photographer, a television presenter and producer working in both highbrow and popular cultural areas, a writer of revues, a journalist, and, of course, a playwright. To look at the details of his career is to become aware of his dedication to Scottish culture in its many manifestations.

Ted Willis's work also links the worlds of stage and television. A committed left-wing writer in his youth, Willis wrote his earliest theatrical pieces for the activist group Unity Theatre. After a brief period of army service in World War II (brief because he was dismissed for political activity), he returned to work with Unity. However, disillusioned with the Communist Party, of which he had been a longtime member, he returned to the Labour Party and increasingly found employment in radio and the new medium of television. His output included scripts for the first radio soap opera in Britain, *Mrs. Dale's Diary* (beginning in 1948). His work for all mediums gradually became more populist, and he is perhaps best known for creating and writing for the long-running BBC television series *Dixon of Dock Green* (beginning in 1955), a rather cozy police show broadcast early on Saturday evenings. The facts that this series evolved from his own stage play about the shooting of a policeman, *The Blue Lamp* (performed in 1951), and that this play had also been transposed by him into a highly successful 1950 motion picture, are in themselves an indication of his versatility and of his popular appeal as a writer. Now inevitably seen as a part of a theater world that was supposedly destroyed by the "New Wave" dating from the mid 1950s, Willis was in his time one of the most important and prolific writers for television.

One of the new figures encouraged by the Royal Court Theatre in London was Arnold Wesker, whose first forays into the new naturalism caused a considerable sensation. His most successful play has been *Chips with Everything* (performed in 1962), a bitter attack on the Establishment, for which he drew from his experiences as a national serviceman; but from the outset he declared himself as a left-wing dramatist and champion of kitchen-sink theater. His other claim to fame is as founder and director of Centre 42, a project that eventually and briefly was located at London's Roundhouse and aimed at bringing culture to a popular audience. Once the project collapsed in the face of an impossible financial burden, Wesker retreated from the public and political arena. He has continued to write plays, but they get little exposure in Britain. However, his place in British theater history is secure, and he continues to enjoy considerable success abroad.

Under George Devine, the English Stage Company at the Royal Court Theatre had actively sought to encourage new writing through the creation of a Writers' Workshop. One of the earliest successes was Edward Bond, whose first three staged plays were all produced there. His initial submission was not produced, but he was invited to join the group, and in

1962 *The Pope's Wedding* was staged. However, the furor that greeted his 1965 play, *Saved,* with a scene in which a baby is stoned to death in a pram, brought him the most public attention. Similar controversy surrounded his surrealistic take on the Victorian age in *Early Morning* (performed in 1968), with scenes of cannibalism and a lesbian relationship between Florence Nightingale and Queen Victoria. Bond went on to produce a series of epic plays, rivaling the output of Bertolt Brecht and establishing himself as a playwright of worldwide importance. Latterly, he lost faith in the British theater and has turned increasingly to writing for young people. However, even more than Wesker, his work continues to be treated with veneration in continental Europe and elsewhere.

The Royal Court Theatre also provided the launchpad for E. A. Whitehead, whose first three plays were all performed there in the 1970s. Having attended the Old Vic Drama School, Maureen Duffy was asked to join the Royal Court Theatre Writers' Group under Devine and director William Gaskill after she turned to writing because she was increasingly unhappy about being limited to female roles as an actor. In 1972, ten years after Bond had made his public entrance at the Royal Court Theatre, Caryl Churchill's *Owners* premiered there, followed three years later by *Objections to Sex and Violence.* Churchill had also received encouragement and gained experience through the activities of the Writers' Workshop, and both these plays were performed in the Theatre Upstairs, a new and smaller space created specifically to allow new writers to be showcased. Most of her long and impressive career has involved frequent returns to the Royal Court Theatre as well as commissions from Joint Stock, a touring theater company formed by Gaskill (after he had left the Royal Court Theatre) and Max Stafford-Clark shortly before he went on to become the longest-serving artistic director at the theater. She has also produced work for Out of Joint, the theater company later formed by Stafford-Clark. Churchill continues to produce work, and her reputation as one of the major playwrights since the 1970s remains undiminished.

The success of the Royal Court Theatre's policy of producing new work was initially linked to the naturalistic theater associated with, in particular, Wesker, and most epitomized by the phenomenal success of John Osborne's *Look Back in Anger* in 1956. Joan Littlewood's Theatre Workshop at the Theatre Royal Stratford East was the other London venue most responsible for encouraging new writing, and in 1958 it introduced the young Shelagh Delaney with her *A Taste of Honey,* a play that soon transferred to the West End. However, the mid 1950s also marked the beginning of a Continental invasion of absurdist drama, and most important was a 1955 production of Beckett's *Waiting for Godot* that influenced young Harold Pinter, who was an actor at the time. Pinter's early plays owe a considerable debt to the emerging absurdist tradition and also to the emphasis on the new naturalism, and he explored social territory that was virtually uncharted in the British theater. His was not an overnight success, however, and his first London production, *The Birthday Party,* met largely with baffled incomprehension at the Lyric Theatre Hammersmith in May 1958 and closed after less than a week. By 1960 *The Caretaker* had established him as a major writer, and this reputation was consolidated by *The Homecoming* (performed in 1965), which opened in Cardiff before transferring to London's Aldwych Theatre. As well as becoming a writer of notable screenplays, Pinter continued to write for the stage with popular success and the accumulation of increasing critical esteem. Highlights have included *Old Times* (performed in 1971), *No Man's Land* (performed in 1975), and *Betrayal,* which was staged at the new National Theatre on London's South Bank in 1978. He continues to hold his reputation as one of the major playwrights of his generation.

Joe Orton clearly owed something of a debt to Pinter in his earliest work, borrowing from the techniques of the "comedy of menace" so memorably conjured in plays such as *The Birthday Party.* However, Orton's savage and frequently farcical examinations of the complicated mores of sexual behavior were intended to outrage audiences in a way never aimed at by Pinter. Paradoxically, even as Orton set out to shock audiences, he was desirous of all the trappings of fame and success, and he resolutely refused to be produced other than in the commercial theater. Since his promising career was cut short by his murder at the hands of his longtime lover, Kenneth Halliwell, one can only conjecture about what he might have gone on to achieve had he lived beyond the 1960s, whose quasi-mythical aura of permissiveness he, more than any writer of the decade, seemed to embody.

Although Orton had three of his plays televised, *The Erpingham Camp* (broadcast in 1966) was the only one written specifically for that medium. However, there have been many playwrights in the modern period who have seen the stage as secondary to television in their desire to reach a wider audience. This approach became true of Willis, but G. F. Newman and David Mercer are thought of almost exclusively as writers for television; and between them they produced some of the most important and exciting dramas to appear in that medium. Other writers besides Pinter have written for radio, television, and the movies as well as for the stage; another of the most media-dexterous writers in the postwar years has been David Hare. His extraordinary career had its roots in the alternative-theater movement of the late 1960s, and he was co-founder (in 1968) of Portable Theatre, a company that launched several playwrights, including Howard Brenton and Christopher Wilkinson, whose Portable production of *Plays for Rubber Go-Go Girls* was the most controversial piece offered at the 1971 Edinburgh Festival. But even as Hare was working in the alternative-theater field, his *Slag* was being produced at the Hampstead Theatre Club in London in 1970. His first real breakthrough into the mainstream came with his collaboration with Brenton on *Brassneck* (performed in 1973), an epic piece tracing the decline of Britain through the progress of the Bagley family into local politics and corruption. It was produced at the Nottingham Playhouse, which was, under the artistic direction of Richard Eyre, the most important regional theater in England at the time. *Brassneck* was followed by *Knuckle* (performed in 1974), the first of Hare's plays to be performed in the United States when it opened in New York the following year. Then came one of many changes of theatrical strategy as Hare worked with the Joint Stock Company on a stage adaptation of William Hinton's 1967 book *Fanshen*, which traces the progress of the Chinese Revolution through events in a single village. *Teeth 'n' Smiles* (performed in 1975) retreated from this epic model to look at the chaotic events of a single Cambridge May Ball. By 1978 Hare was at the National Theatre for the first time with *Plenty*, the second of his plays to open in the United States (in 1980) and the first to be made into a movie (in 1985). He has since gone on to produce a steady stream of highly successful plays, many of them staged at the National Theatre, with which he has enjoyed a long and fruitful relationship. Between 1990 and 1993 he created a trilogy of "state of the nation" plays (*Racing Demon* [performed in 1990], *Murmuring Judges* [performed in 1991], and *The Absence of War* [performed in 1993]) that reemphasized his career-long interest in the presentation and analysis of history. Hare's theatrical output has also included adaptations of plays by writers as divergent in their aims as Brecht and Luigi Pirandello. If there is a consistent theme in his work, it is his interest in what happens when history and psychology collide. His commitment to continuing to write for the stage is accompanied by an ever more impressive list of screen credits.

Shortly after the start of Hare's writing career, Tom Kempinski began an eleven-year career as a professional actor, appearing at the Royal Court Theatre among other venues. However, his subsequent career as a playwright, which dates from 1971, has never been associated with that theater. His early work can be seen as a part of that radical agitprop tradition associated with groups such as General Will, which David Edgar produced work for in his early writing career. Much of Kempinski's work through the 1970s was produced at alternative venues such as the Bush Theatre in London, where his best-known play, *Duet for One*, was first staged in 1980. That play emphasized the way in which the writer's work had been increasingly moving from the political to the psychological in its approach.

Alan Bennett first came to prominence in 1960, as a member of the *Beyond the Fringe* company, along with Peter Cook, Dudley Moore, and Jonathan Miller. That revue had started life at the Edinburgh Festival Fringe, and more than anything else, it can lay claim to having been the catalyst for the satire movement of the 1960s. Bennett's first stage play, *Forty Years On*, did not come for a further eight years, exactly at the point when the alternative-theater movement was really beginning to take off with the work of writers such as Hare. *Forty Years On*, a somewhat ambivalent comedy set in a boys' public school and testing the state of the nation, seemed somewhat out of line with contemporary theatrical developments; and, in many ways, this ambivalence has characterized Bennett's work throughout his career. Immensely popular, especially after his first series of *Talking Heads* television plays in 1988, he has continued to quietly go his own way, becoming enshrined as something of an English institution as he does so. From quite modest theatrical beginnings he has slowly developed into a major figure whose work has been produced at the National Theatre, an occurrence that would probably have seemed unlikely to him at the outset.

Deborah Levy also started her stage career at the Edinburgh Festival, with *On New Land* in 1981, a piece that later toured London fringe venues; unlike Bennett, however, she has continued to work in the alternative theater, with commissions from companies such as Common Stock, the Women's Theatre Group, and Loose Change, and using venues such as London's Oval House and the Institute of Contemporary Arts (ICA) and Cardiff's Chapter Arts. Many critics came to conceive of the 1980s in British theater as a decade dominated by women writers. Apart from obvious precursors such as Delaney and, most important, Churchill, the writer who can be considered the most influential in this development is Michelene Wandor. Her work was regularly performed at alternative venues throughout the 1970s, but she was also responsible for bringing women's theater to prominence through the volumes of *Plays for Women* that she edited (1982–1985). Her critical books *Understudies: Theatre & Sexual Politics* (1981) and *Look Back in Gender: Sexuality and the*

Family in Post-War British Drama (1987) also proved to be influential. Sue Glover, whose first play, *The Seal Wife,* opened in Edinburgh in 1980, has premiered virtually all of her work in Scotland, as is the case with Liz Lochhead. The latter's first staged play, *Mary and the Monster,* actually opened at the Coventry Belgrade in 1981 but only came to critical attention when it was revised as *Blood and Ice* and produced at the most important Scottish venue for new writing, Edinburgh's Traverse Theatre, the following year. The fact that Lochhead's best-known play is *Mary Queen of Scots Got Her Head Chopped Off* (performed in 1987) is indicative of the problem faced by writers working self-consciously out of the English mainstream: the tension between the wish to remain true to one's roots and the desire to reach a wider audience and thus perhaps to risk writing on less "local" subjects.

Ian Brown is a classic example of this tension: his first and third staged productions (*Antigone* in 1969 and *The Bacchae* in 1972) drew from classical sources and were produced in Glasgow and Brighton, on England's south coast, respectively. However, most of his work has been specifically placed in Scotland, geographically or thematically. Furthermore, he has written plays both in English and in Scots.

As the separation of inherited and lived cultures in England, Ireland, Scotland, and Wales has become more acute in the latter half of the twentieth century, this sense of distinct theatrical traditions has increased. But it can be seen with the work of an earlier writer such as Lewis: because he chose to write not only about Welsh concerns but also in Welsh, he is somewhat inaccessible beyond the borders of Wales (and even to a considerable extent within them). Thus, he is not placed alongside Bond and Brecht, for example, as one of the great European playwrights of the twentieth century.

In the modern renaissance of Welsh drama, the dilemma facing a playwright who wishes to find an audience remains unchanged. Unlike the dramas of his contemporary Dic Edwards, which are marked by the absence of Welsh locales, characters, and concerns, Ian Rowlands's plays are concerned with specifically Welsh themes. As a result, only two of his plays have ever had professional productions outside his own country. Meic Povey's work, with the exception of *Indian Country* (performed in 2003), is entirely in Welsh and clearly indicates a sense of security in the audience he wishes to reach. However, Ed Thomas, whose first play was *House of America* (performed in 1988), has shown that it is possible to enjoy both a Welsh and an international acclaim, even though his work is rooted in the problems besetting modern Wales. This balance is something that writers such as Sean O'Casey and, in contemporary terms, Brian Friel have been able to do with their plays about Ireland.

Although the Belfast writer John Boyd did not have his first stage play produced until 1967, his work as a BBC Radio producer in Northern Ireland already had led to a prolific output of drama for that medium. Since that first theatrical production he became an active contributor to the Belfast theater scene and was the first Irish playwright to write about the Troubles. Boyd's first work for the stage coincided not only with his retirement, at the age of fifty-five, from the BBC, but also with the beginnings of a real renaissance in the Irish theater both north and south of the border. Boyd's concern was always with the ways in which the lives of ordinary people are unwittingly caught up in the implications of the political struggle. In this respect his work may be compared to that of another Northern Irish writer, Martin Lynch, whose impressive list of stage productions began in 1976. Owen McCafferty is a more recent arrival on the Northern Irish stage (his first play having been staged in 1992); and, although he writes about the contemporary situation, he talks of the political/sectarian strife as more of a backdrop to his work. Robin Glendinning (whose first staged play was in 1982) writes more about the actual political processes of the struggle. Tom Murphy, born in the Republic of Ireland in 1935, had his first play produced at London's Royal Court Theatre in 1961; yet, unlike his contemporary and friend Friel, Murphy is little known to audiences outside of the republic, despite his enormous reputation and the continuing success of his work in Ireland. However, what the work of all these, and many more, writers points to is that the theater in Ireland, as in Scotland and Wales, is in a healthy state, and that the different nations of the two islands really are finding their own voices in the context of the changing nature of the relationships between them.

In England, the theater has also undergone enormous change since the 1990s, at least if one looks away from the plethora of frequently anodyne musicals that constitute the bulk of the mainstream tradition. A new post-Quentin Tarantino, post-Irvine Welsh's *Trainspotting* (1993) generation of writers have brought an innovative toughness and vigor to the stage. Among them, and perhaps most important, the work of Sarah Kane and Mark Ravenhill has figured prominently in what can loosely be defined as a new brutalism, with its insistence on the harshest facts of living in a postmodern age. Kane's *Blasted* (performed in 1995) caused a wave of controversy reminiscent of that which greeted Bond's *Saved* forty years earlier (and Bond was quick to defend her work, as were Pinter and Churchill), and the furor confirmed the ability of live theater to provoke debate. One year later, Ravenhill's *Shopping and Fucking* caused a different kind of stir in its first stage production, an uproar that went beyond the fact that theater box-office personnel found themselves unable to tell telephone customers the full title of the play. The fact that both of these major theatrical breakthroughs started in the space created for trying out new work in London, the Royal Court Theatre Upstairs, is evidence that although successive generations of writers come seemingly afresh to the theater, they do so with the legacy of the past offering them support and, more than occasionally, ideas and inspiration.

A Note on the Structure of the Volumes

A decision was made early in the planning of the *British and Irish Dramatists Since World War II* series not to follow a straight alphabetical ordering from volume to volume. Thus, each volume has its own alphabetical order. The intention was to make each volume a mixture in which the old and the new sit alongside each other. This arrangement has the further advantage of allowing some "breathing space" for playwrights who, as the first volumes are published, may not yet have produced a body of work sufficient to justify inclusion but who, in the interim, may well do so. The entries in these volumes have been commissioned from a wide variety of theater scholars, all of them experts in their field. Many of the pieces have been written in collaboration with their subjects, and we are extremely grateful to all the playwrights who have responded to detailed questions about the exact dates of production and the like, as well as to their agents, and, in some cases, to members of their families who have done likewise. Although the present volume is designated *Fourth Series* in acknowledgment of *DLB 13,* it is really the third volume in a new series that began with *DLB 233.*

—*John Bull*

Acknowledgments

This book was produced by Bruccoli Clark Layman, Inc. Tracy Simmons Bitonti was the in-house editor.

Production manager is Philip B. Dematteis.

Administrative support was provided by Carol A. Cheschi.

Accountant is Ann-Marie Holland.

Copyediting supervisor is Sally R. Evans. The copyediting staff includes Phyllis A. Avant, Caryl Brown, Melissa D. Hinton, Philip I. Jones, Rebecca Mayo, Nadirah Rahimah Shabazz, and Nancy E. Smith.

Pipeline manager is James F. Tidd Jr.

Editorial associates are Jessica R. Goudeau, Joshua Shaw, and Timothy C. Simmons.

In-house vetter is Catherine M. Polit.

Permissions editor is Amber L. Coker.

Layout and graphics supervisor is Janet E. Hill. The graphics staff includes Zoe R. Cook and Sydney E. Hammock.

Office manager is Kathy Lawler Merlette.

Photography editors are Anthony J. Scotti Jr., Mark J. McEwan, and Walter W. Ross.

Digital photographic copy work was performed by Joseph M. Bruccoli.

Systems manager is Donald Kevin Starling.

Typesetting supervisor is Kathleen M. Flanagan. The typesetting staff includes Patricia Marie Flanagan and Pamela D. Norton.

Walter W. Ross is library researcher. He was assisted by the following librarians at the Thomas Cooper Library of the University of South Carolina: Elizabeth Suddeth and the rare-book department; Jo Cottingham, interlibrary loan department; circulation department head Tucker Taylor; reference department head Virginia W. Weathers; reference department staff Laurel Baker, Marilee Birchfield, Kate Boyd, Paul Cammarata, Joshua Garris, Gary Geer, Tom Marcil, Rose Marshall, and Sharon Verba; interlibrary loan department head Marna Hostetler; and interlibrary loan staff Bill Fetty, Nelson Rivera, and Cedric Rose.

Dictionary of Literary Biography® • Volume Three Hundred Ten

British and Irish Dramatists Since World War II
Fourth Series

Dictionary of Literary Biography

Alan Bennett
(9 May 1934 -)

Kara McKechnie
University of Leeds

PLAY PRODUCTIONS: *Beyond the Fringe,* by Bennett, Peter Cook, Jonathan Miller, and Dudley Moore, Edinburgh, Royal Lyceum, 22 August 1960; London, Fortune Theatre, May 1961; New York, John Golden Theatre, 27 October 1962;
Forty Years On, London, Apollo Theatre, 31 October 1968;
Getting On, London, Queen's Theatre, 14 October 1971;
Habeas Corpus, London, Lyric Theatre, 10 May 1973; New York, Martin Beck Theatre, 25 November 1975;
The Old Country, London, Queen's Theatre, 7 September 1977;
Enjoy, London, Vaudeville Theatre, 15 October 1980;
Kafka's Dick, London, Royal Court Theatre, 23 September 1986;
An Englishman Abroad and *A Question of Attribution,* London, National Theatre, 1 December 1988;
The Wind in the Willows, adapted from Kenneth Grahame's book, London, National Theatre, 14 December 1990;
The Madness of George III, London, National Theatre, 28 November 1991;
Talking Heads, London, Comedy Theatre, 6 February 1992;
The Lady in the Van, London, Queen's Theatre, 19 November 1999;
Hymn, book by Bennett, music by George Fenton and the Medici String Quartet, Harrogate International Festival, July 2001;
The History Boys, London, National Theatre, 18 May 2004.

BOOKS: *Beyond the Fringe,* by Bennett, Peter Cook, Jonathan Miller, and Dudley Moore (London:

Alan Bennett (photograph by John Timbers; from the dust jacket for the 2002 U.S. edition of The Laying On of Hands, *2001; Richland County Public Library)*

Souvenir Press, 1963; New York: Random House, 1963);
Forty Years On (London: Faber & Faber, 1969);
Getting On (London: Faber & Faber, 1972);
Habeas Corpus: A Play in Two Acts (London: Faber & Faber, 1973);
The Old Country (London: Faber & Faber, 1978);

Enjoy (London: Faber & Faber, 1980);
Office Suite: Two One-Act Plays (London: Faber & Faber, 1981)—comprises *Green Forms* and *A Visit from Miss Prothero;*
Objects of Affection and Other Plays for Television (London: BBC, 1982; revised, 1984)—comprises *Our Winnie, A Woman of No Importance, Rolling Home, Marks, Say Something Happened, A Day Out, Intensive Care,* and *An Englishman Abroad;*
A Private Function: A Screenplay (London: Faber & Faber, 1984);
Forty Years On and Other Plays (London: Faber & Faber, 1985; expanded, 1991); republished as *Plays One* (London: Faber & Faber, 1996)—comprises *Forty Years On, Getting On, Habeas Corpus,* and *Enjoy;*
The Writer in Disguise (London: Faber & Faber, 1985)—includes *Me! I'm Afraid of Virginia Woolf, All Day on the Sands, One Fine Day, The Old Crowd,* and *Afternoon Off;*
Kafka's Dick (London: Faber & Faber, 1986);
Two Kafka Plays (London: Faber & Faber, 1987)—comprises *Kafka's Dick* and *The Insurance Man;*
Prick Up Your Ears: The Screenplay (London: Faber & Faber, 1987);
Talking Heads (London: BBC Books, 1988)—comprises *A Chip in the Sugar, Bed Among the Lentils, A Lady of Letters, Her Big Chance, Soldiering On,* and *A Cream Cracker Under the Settee;*
Single Spies: A Double Bill (London: Faber & Faber, 1989)—comprises *An Englishman Abroad* and *A Question of Attribution;*
The Lady in the Van (London: London Review of Books, 1990; revised edition, London: Profile Books, 1999);
Poetry in Motion (London: Channel 4 Television, 1990);
The Wind in the Willows, adapted from Kenneth Grahame's book (London: Faber & Faber, 1991);
The Madness of George III (London: Faber & Faber, 1992);
Poetry in Motion 2 (London: Channel 4 Television, 1992);
Mr Bennett's Pictures (Leeds: Leeds City Art Gallery, 1994);
Writing Home (London: Faber & Faber, 1994; New York: Random House, 1995; revised edition, London: Faber & Faber, 1997);
The Madness of King George [screenplay] (London: Faber & Faber, 1995);
Talking Heads 2 (London: BBC Worldwide, 1998);
The Complete Talking Heads (London: BBC Books, 1998);
The Clothes They Stood Up In (London: Profile Books in association with London Review of Books, 1998; New York: Random House, 2001);

Plays Two (London: Faber & Faber, 1998)—comprises *Kafka's Dick, The Insurance Man, The Old Country, An Englishman Abroad,* and *A Question of Attribution;*
Father! Father! Burning Bright (London: Profile Books in association with London Review of Books, 2000);
Telling Tales (London: BBC Worldwide, 2000);
The Laying On of Hands (London: Profile Books in association with London Review of Books, 2001; New York: Picador USA, 2002);
Three Stories (London: Profile Books, 2003)—comprises *The Laying On of Hands, The Clothes They Stood Up In,* and *Father! Father! Burning Bright;*
Rolling Home (London: Faber & Faber, 2003)—comprises *Our Winnie, All Day on the Sands, One Fine Day, Marks, Say Something Happened, Rolling Home,* and *Intensive Care;*
Me! I'm Afraid of Virginia Woolf (London: Faber & Faber, 2003)—comprises *A Day Out, Sunset Across the Bay, A Visit from Miss Prothero, Me! I'm Afraid of Virginia Woolf, Green Forms, The Old Crowd,* and *Afternoon Off;*
The History Boys (London: Faber & Faber, 2004);
Loose Canon: A Portrait of Brian Brindley, by Bennett and Ned Sherrin, edited by Damian Thompson (London: Continuum, 2004);
A Private Function (London: Faber & Faber, 2004)—comprises *The Old Crowd, A Private Function, Prick Up Your Ears, 102 Boulevard Haussmann,* and *The Madness of King George.*

PRODUCED SCRIPTS: *On the Margin,* television, BBC, 9 November 1966;
A Day Out, television, London Weekend Television, 24 December 1972;
Sunset Across the Bay, television, London Weekend Television, 20 February 1975;
A Little Outing, television, BBC, 1977;
A Visit from Miss Prothero, television, BBC, 11 January 1978;
Me! I'm Afraid of Virginia Woolf, television, London Weekend Television, 2 December 1978;
Doris and Doreen, television, London Weekend Television, 16 December 1978;
The Old Crowd, television, London Weekend Television, 27 January 1979;
Afternoon Off, television, London Weekend Television, 3 February 1979;
One Fine Day, television, London Weekend Television, 17 February 1979;
All Day on the Sands, television, London Weekend Television, 24 February 1979;
Intensive Care, television, BBC, 9 November 1982;
Our Winnie, television, BBC, 12 November 1982;

A Woman of No Importance, television, BBC, 19 November 1982;
Rolling Home, television, BBC, 3 December 1982;
Marks, television, BBC, 10 December 1982;
Say Something Happened, television, BBC, 17 December 1982;
An Englishman Abroad, television, BBC, 29 November 1983;
A Private Function, by Bennett and Malcolm Mowbray, motion picture, Handmade Films, 1984;
The Insurance Man, television, BBC2, 23 February 1986;
Prick Up Your Ears, adapted from John Lahr's book, motion picture, Civilland/Zenith, 1987;
Talking Heads, television, BBC, 19 April – 24 May 1988–comprised *A Chip in the Sugar, Bed Among the Lentils, A Lady of Letters, Her Big Chance, Soldiering On,* and *A Cream Cracker Under the Settee;*
Dinner at Noon, television, BBC, 8 August 1988;
Poetry in Motion, 6 parts, television, Channel 4, June 1990;
A Question of Attribution, television, BBC, 20 January 1991;
102 Boulevard Haussmann, television, BBC, 17 February 1991;
Poetry in Motion 2, television, Channel 4, 1992;
Portrait or Bust, television, BBC, March 1993;
The Madness of King George, motion picture, Samuel Goldwyn/Channel 4 Films, 1994;
The Abbey, television, BBC, 25–27 December 1995;
Talking Heads 2, television, Slow Motion Ltd./BBC, 13 October – 11 November 1998–comprised *Miss Fozzard Finds Her Feet, The Hand of God, Playing Sandwiches, Nights in the Gardens of Spain, The Outside Dog,* and *Waiting for the Telegram;*
Telling Tales, television, Slow Motion Ltd./BBC, November–December 2000.

SELECTED PERIODICAL PUBLICATIONS– UNCOLLECTED: "What I Did in 1996," *London Review of Books,* 19, no. 1 (January 1997): 3;
"Notes on 1997," *London Review of Books,* 20, no. 1 (January 1998): 3;
"What I Did in 1998," *London Review of Books,* 21, no. 2 (January 1999): 3;
"Untold Stories," *London Review of Books,* 21, no. 19 (September 1999): 11;
"What I Did in 1999," *London Review of Books,* 22, no. 2 (January 2000): 3;
"Memories of Lindsay Anderson," *London Review of Books,* 22, no. 14 (July 2000): 17;
"A Cure for Arthritis and Other Tales," *London Review of Books,* 22, no. 21 (November 2000): 21;
"Alan Bennet's 2000 Diary," *London Review of Books,* 23, no. 2 (January 2001): 3;
"Seeing Stars," *London Review of Books,* 24, no. 1 (January 2002): 12;
"Alan Bennett Gives a Personal View of 25 Years of the National on the South Bank," *National Theatre Website* (19 July 2002) <http://website-archive.nt-online.org/platforms/Alan_Bennett_NT25_article.html>;
"Secrets Are Best Kept by Those Who Do Not Have a Sense of Humour," *London Review of Books,* 25, no. 1 (January 2003): 3;
"Two in Torquay," *London Review of Books,* 25, no. 13 (July 2003): 13;
"A Shameful Year," *London Review of Books,* 26, no. 1 (January 2004): 26;
"Postscript," *London Review of Books,* 26, no. 4 (February 2004): 7;
"A Common Assault," *London Review of Books,* 26, no. 21 (June 2004): 25.

Alan Bennett defies categorization, not least because of the ease with which he contributes to a wide range of media: he writes for stage, television, movies, and printed media, and he also acts and directs. Bennett's works transfer easily across media boundaries. Equally, his plays for the stage have a variety of themes, settings, and forms: history play, farce, monologue, and autobiographical play, to name but a few. Successful with West End and regional audiences, Bennett's plays result in sold-out runs before they even open. The general critical reaction to Bennett's work suggests that his accessibility and popularity (especially with an audience of a certain age) can be seen as bland and middlebrow. Bennett has been undervalued for supposedly promoting a safe concern with the past and writing to reinforce the political status quo. However, the perception of Bennett as a safe and "cozy" writer does not hold true when one actually examines his work, which could be described as often subversive but not agitational, often political but not always topical. Bennett applies his first profession as an historian to his analyses of past politics in comparison with contemporary political occurrences. For Bennett, politics is to be understood primarily through its effects on the individual. He examines what he loves and hates about Englishness with a sharp sense of observation.

Bennett was born in Leeds, West Yorkshire, on 9 May 1934. The more famous he has become, the more his origins and his childhood have featured in his works. Bennett has jokingly claimed that he lacks the necessary prerequisites to be a writer, specifically a northern writer, whose life should ideally be grim and bleak, conforming to clichés brought about by social realist conventions. Bennett claims he was thus deprived of deprivation, as he and his family were sim-

Bennett at Oxford in 1955 (from Writing Home, *1994; Richland County Public Library)*

ply normal. His father, Walter Bennett, was a butcher, and his mother, Lillian (née Peel), was the kind of Yorkshire woman who has often inhabited Bennett's plays: class-conscious, preoccupied with hygiene, and funny without realizing it. Bennett's grandmother, and especially his mother's sisters, Aunty Myra and Aunty Kathleen, further added to Bennett's later repertoire of characters. Bennett also has one older brother, Gordon, who was born on 9 May 1931.

His family moved to Guildford just before World War II, but his father's business failed, and the Bennetts had to admit defeat and return to Leeds. Bennett's way of escaping his humdrum surroundings at first seemed to be through education: he went to Leeds Modern Boys School (the school song was called "Forty Years On," which later became the title of Bennett's first play). Thinking of himself as a "frightful little creep" in childhood, Bennett has also often talked about himself dismissively as an adult; but his unauthorized biographer, Alexander Games, describes the young Bennett as "opinionated, articulate, naturally intelligent and communicative."

After passing his A-level exams, Bennett was chosen for Russian language training during his compulsory national military service, which he recalls as a thoroughly enjoyable time. Because he was already familiar with Cambridge and because he had what he called in his diary *Writing Home* (1994) a "hopeless crush" on a fellow cadet bound for Oxford, Bennett then went to read history at Exeter College, Oxford. In the 1997 edition of *Writing Home,* he described the entrance of the dons into the college dining hall as a favorite theatrical experience. After gaining a first-class degree in modern history in 1957, Bennett embarked on research on Richard II at Magdalen College, Oxford, as a junior don. History, however, was not to be his career: in 1960 Bennett, with three other aspiring student writers and performers, conceived, wrote, and performed the revue *Beyond the Fringe.* His collaborators were Peter Cook, Jonathan Miller, and Dudley Moore. The show was commissioned by the official Edinburgh Festival in an attempt to capitalize on the growing success of satirical revues being produced for the Fringe, one of the many festivals held in Edinburgh; it opened on 22 August 1960 at the Edinburgh Royal Lyceum. Kenneth Tynan, writing for *The Observer,* called the revue a watershed for English satire.

Although always expressing feelings of inferiority opposite his more extroverted collaborators, Bennett is remembered as bringing his particular brand of comedy to the show, based on acute linguistic and behavioral observation. The mock-Anglican sermon he created ("And my brother Esau is an hairy man, but I am a smooth man") is still quoted several decades later. Bennett was already torn between his original, northern Yorkshire voice and the metropolitan southern language of literary London. When a northern monologue about death was not understood by American audiences after *Beyond the Fringe* transferred to Broadway in 1962, it seemed to confirm that "speaking properly" was the only option for a playwright. *Beyond the Fringe* won a London *Evening Standard* award in 1961 and an Antoinette Perry (Tony) Award and a New York Drama Critics Circle Award in 1963. Bennett still taught and researched at Oxford, but his history career was gradually abandoned.

Walter Bennett had retired in 1966, and Bennett's parents had moved to Clapham, a village on the edge of the Yorkshire Dales. Walter and Lillian Bennett's marriage was a happy one; Bennett remembers his parents, although inhibited in company, "laughing, still silly and full of fun" in their old age. He realized that his own social embarrassment and feelings of inferiority were a question of temperament rather than class background. His parents' move was meant to give them a new lease on life from "mucky Leeds" but instead brought on a serious bout of depression and delusion in his mother. As Bennett wrote in a short memoir, "Untold Stories" (1999), she was unsettled by the lack of anonymity in a small village "where folks know all your business." During the course of his mother's illness and recuperation in a psychiatric hospital, Bennett learned that there was more to his humdrum family history than he had known: his mother's father had committed suicide. As he recalled in "Untold Stories," "In 1966 I have just begun to write but have already given up on my own background because the material seems so thin. This perks things up a bit." Despite being intrigued, Bennett felt guilty for seeing a family tragedy as potential "material," something detected by his father, who refused to disclose more than the bare facts.

Bennett's first project after *Beyond the Fringe* was to write and star in an acclaimed television comedy series, *On the Margin* (1966), for which he won the Guild of Television Producers Award in 1967. Bennett portrayed characters such as a camp antique-shop owner and the male half of the Stringalongs, a couple who personified the upmarket, house-converting, vaguely left-wing couple typical of his own surroundings in affluent but left-wing Camden Town in northwest London. Tapes were erased by the BBC in those days, so the programs have been lost, as much contemporary work was. Some of Bennett's sketches caused angry complaints to the BBC. Games remarks that it is illuminating, given Bennett's near-sacrosanct status since the 1980s, to see that he was capable of provoking hostility.

Critics agree that there is a clear divide in Bennett's work: his stage work is set in predominantly southern environments, and the ideas expressed are not directly connected to Bennett's Yorkshire roots but set more in those surroundings he inhabited after he moved south. Richard Eyre states that in the theater Bennett has "moved from form to form, never quite settling." His first play, *Forty Years On* (performed in 1968, published in 1969), demonstrates the voice that Bennett acquired through education: the play is a hybrid between a revue and an animated history lesson. In the introduction to *Writing Home* Bennett describes *Forty Years On* as an elaborate life-support system for the preservation of bad jokes. A play within a play, it abounds with cross-references and quotations, genre parodies, and pastiche. Albion House, the boys' school in which the work is set, also carries the weight of being a loose metaphor for England. In this frame, Bennett explores the ambiguity of nostalgia he feels at events such as Remembrance Day, being repelled politically and profoundly moved emotionally. While the play is not a biting political satire and shows fondness for the traditions and historical characters it explores, it is not the harmless history revue it is sometimes portrayed to be. It was a widely noticed West End debut, with John Gielgud playing the part of the Headmaster and Bennett himself playing a junior master. It won Bennett his second London *Evening Standard* award in 1968.

In 1969 Bennett bought a house in Camden Town, which remains his London base. Bennett's next play, *Getting On* (performed in 1971, published in 1972), started out as a critique of the change of government in 1970 from Harold Wilson (Labour) to Edward Heath (Conservative) and ended up winning the London *Evening Standard* award for best comic play in 1971. Bennett remarks in *Writing Home* that this outcome was similar to entering a marrow in an agricultural show and being given the cucumber prize. The main reason for this change in perception seemed to be the casting of Kenneth More in the main part, M.P. George Oliver. More was not comfortable playing a ruthless and unsympathetic character, as it did not suit his image. According to Bennett, he thus made the play fit around his wish to give the audience what they wanted: a simple, straightforward, good-natured guy in a comic play. Comments by More himself and other contemporaries suggest that Bennett was banned from the theater for being dogmatic about how the play should come to life and for putting undue pressure on the actors.

Habeas Corpus (performed and published in 1973), Bennett's next play for the stage, had little in common

Frontispiece and title page from the first U.S. edition (1963) of the 1960 revue that was Bennett's first theatrical success (Thomas Cooper Library, University of South Carolina)

with the previous two. Exploring the impact of sexual liberation and a permissive society, it is a pastiche of farce, music-hall, and seaside-postcard styles. Eyre attributes this stylistic overcompensation to the critical misunderstanding of *Getting On*. Alec Guinness took the main part of Wicksteed, a doctor trying to compensate for his own physical decline by groping his female patients. Bennett himself took over the part of the cleaning woman, Mrs. Swabb, when the play was re-cast.

While the plays continued to show considerable formal and thematic diversity, in the early 1970s Bennett started to discover the medium most suited to his original voice: television drama. Bennett's television work is not distinctive because of its richness in narrative and plot; it can be quite limited in both these areas and is often set in similar environments, involving similar characters, frequently with a personal connection to Bennett's life. The fact that critics took less notice of his television work than of his stage work provided a sanctuary for Bennett, in which, as he said in a 1984 interview with Martin Auty, he could write in the "internal voice I hear most clearly." He added that, when he was writing for television, it did not feel "as though I'm going to be marked on it in the same way as I am with theatre." Consequently, Bennett's writing for television has always seemed more confident than his work for the stage. In television, what started as "jottings" of unlinked memorized or overheard dialogue went on to form Bennett's largest number of works.

In the 1960s and early 1970s the BBC was an extraordinary environment for drama. Young writers were given relative freedom to develop their talent, carefully guided and nurtured by experienced senior staff. Producer Irene Shubik referred to this environment as "the nursery school," stressing that most of the aspiring young writers were Cambridge graduates. Bennett, like his friend and collaborator Stephen Frears, who was debuting as a television director, was on the margins of this nursery school. Frears describes Bennett as developing ideas for plays in ways different from the other clever young men. Bennett did not conform politically; his plays were against the trend, nonagitational, and he was not afraid to break out from the generally Left-leaning culture when the idea demanded it. This opposition meant provocatively parochial stories instead of agitprop-inspired drama about homelessness in the fashion of Bennett's contemporaries. One could term Bennett as a nonconformist by content. His formal evolution within television, however, seems to conform to general trends, which can be summarized as the development from the dominance of the single play in the 1970s to the series from the mid 1980s onward.

Bennett states in *Me! I'm Afraid of Virginia Woolf* (broadcast in 1978, published in 1985) that in many of his television plays he is documenting a world about to be lost, with an "ecological regret for loss of habitat." *Sunset Across the Bay* (1975), for example, follows Mam and Dad, an old couple from Leeds whose house is being demolished and who are retiring to Morecambe, a slightly run-down seaside resort on the west coast. Losing his function (work) and place (Leeds) simultaneously, Dad feels redundant and out of place. He dies of a heart attack, leaving Mam to face an uncertain future. In 1974, when *Sunset Across the Bay* was already written but not yet shot, Bennett's father died suddenly of a heart attack. Bennett felt guilty both about seemingly helping to bring about his father's death by writing such a similar story and in general about exploiting real people in his writing. This conflict has since surfaced often in his work. Biographer Games notes that, while Bennett found it hard to come to terms with his father's death and his mother's ongoing mental and physical decline, his father's death also meant liberation. Bennett did not produce work of a personal nature (diaries, memoirs, autobiographical material) until after his father died.

Themes such as pretense and disguise became constants in Bennett's works for television, and they also cross over into his stage plays. *The Old Country* (performed in 1977, published in 1978) establishes its protagonist, Hilary, and his wife, Bron, as a traditional aging English couple. Only late in the play does the audience discover that the location is Moscow, not the home counties. Hilary is a former spy and has built his own little England in exile. The play naturally evoked resonances of the Cambridge Spies (four British intelligence agents who had met at Cambridge University in the 1930s and who became infamous spies for the KGB), particularly Harold "Kim" Philby, but Bennett focuses less on the political dimension and claims to be more interested in the personal aspect. Hilary's love-hate relationship with the England he knew (which, of course, has since changed, but is frozen in time in his mind) evokes Bennett's own deeply ambiguous feelings on what England means to him. This theme led to other explorations on the notion of treachery, notably in the two one-act plays *An Englishman Abroad* (published in 1982, broadcast in 1983, performed in 1988) and *A Question of Attribution* (performed in 1988, published in 1989), based on Guy Burgess and Anthony Blunt, two more Cambridge Spies. *The Old Country* won the Plays and Players Award for best new play in 1977.

In the mid 1970s Bennett produced his first season of television plays. He had approached the BBC with six plays but had been told that only one could be produced per year. Michael Grade, then director of programs at London Weekend Television, provided an alternative working environment for Bennett and his trusted collaborators, Frears and Innes Lloyd. These first plays were later published under the title *The Writer in Disguise* (1985). Bennett aligns some of the male protagonists in the plays with his own public persona, not going as far as saying that they are autobiographical sketches but that they represent a certain aspect of his own personality. These Bennettian protagonists present a curious void within the plays, as they are passive, not moving events but merely being moved by them. In the tales of small failures (and occasionally, small victories, often sexual), audiences get a notion of silent frustration and the inability to break free and live, because of the most powerful of English restraints: embarrassment.

Obsolescence is another theme that surfaces in many of these works: the play *Doris and Doreen* (broadcast in 1978; published as *Green Forms,* 1981) shows the cozy and predictable world of two secretaries being threatened by possible redundancy. Another, *A Visit from Miss Prothero* (broadcast in 1978, published in 1981), shows how the world of a happily retired office manager is destroyed through a short visit by a bitter colleague. Miss Prothero tells her former boss, Mr. Dodsworth, how his lifetime achievement, an office docketing system, is being declared obsolete and replaced, making its inventor feel just as outdated. Critics praised Bennett's ability to turn seemingly boring, parochial subjects into funny and touching accounts of real life. *All Day on the Sands* (1979) documents a day in the vacation of a family destabilized by the father's being laid off, as seen from the perspective of the two children. Bennett mentions in *Writing Home* that they are based on families he used to see during seaside vacations who were "cross that they were not happy."

Me! I'm Afraid of Virginia Woolf is an intriguing play: it responds to the question asked by Edward Albee in *Who's Afraid of Virginia Woolf?* (1962) and is both a portrait of an inhibited polytechnic lecturer and a deconstruction of the worth of art. Hopkins, the lecturer, undergoes a development that might suggest he is ready to embark on a fulfilling homosexual relationship, through recognizing that "literature was not much help" and that he needs to embrace life instead. The theme of feeling overlooked is prominent in Bennett's works of this period, and it also surfaces in diaries and other nondramatic writing of the time.

unpredictable territory. Most critics blamed Anderson for his damaging influence on Bennett, who, they felt, would otherwise have delivered another gentle comedy to enjoy. As the other plays in the season are not exactly gentle, one gets an early impression of the Bennett persona being the most influential factor in the reception of his works.

Enjoy (performed and published in 1980) is a crossover: it is Bennett's only work for the stage that is set in the north of England among "ordinary" people. It builds on realist conventions, only to turn them into a play that has touches of Ortonesque comedy and of the Theatre of the Absurd. *Enjoy* is different from Bennett's northern plays for television. It bewildered audiences and critics in 1980 because the combination of absurdist plot and Bennett's acerbic criticism of his Yorkshire roots were seen as out of character. Set in the "last back-to-back England" (modest, terraced houses, associated with the working class) in Leeds, shortly before the local council turns it into a museum, *Enjoy* satirizes northern realism. It exposes the familiar Bennett templates of ordinary folk, trying to be as typical as possible, as mere performers. Daphne Turner argues that Bennett's presentation of the north as "fake" in *Enjoy* is a symptom of his own disillusionment with it and a realization of the staying power of destructive northern clichés. Most critics hated *Enjoy,* and Bennett publicly expressed disappointment about their vindictiveness. As was the case with *The Old Crowd,* he found his writing being rejected when he produced "problem plays" laced with feelings of anger and bitterness.

The BBC had turned down Bennett's proposal for a television season in the late 1970s, but his name was now a guarantee for ratings and critical success. Relations with the BBC were thus restored in 1982 when they accepted six plays to be shown in sequence. All were published in the collection *Objects of Affection* (1982). His characters are predominantly middle-aged or elderly, and they are disillusioned and disappointed by their inability to "live!" Some plays deal with alienation and the breakdown of communication within a family. Meaning is normally not placed within the characters' speech, which is proof of their difficulty expressing themselves, but within the joint subtext of reactions, silences, and visual signifiers.

The first of these plays, *Intensive Care* (broadcast in 1982), evolves around the universal themes of sex and death in the slightly less universal surroundings of Keighley Hospital. It tells the story of Midgley, a typical Bennett protagonist—shy, neurotic, and on the margins of life—who wants to support his dying father. In his quest to catch up with the life that has eluded him, Midgley seduces a night nurse, and while the two are having sex, Midgley's father dies. To his profound

Alan Bates and Coral Browne in the 1983 BBC television premiere of Bennett's play An Englishman Abroad, *in which Bates played exiled British spy Guy Burgess (photograph by John Jeffords; from the revised 1984 edition of* Objects of Affection and Other Plays for Television, *1982; Thomas Cooper Library, University of South Carolina)*

Formally part of the *Writer in Disguise* season, *The Old Crowd* (broadcast in 1979) is unlike anything else Bennett has written. This difference is attributed largely to his collaboration with Lindsay Anderson, who inserted surrealist elements into the plot. The play shows a party in an almost empty house that has cracks appearing in the ceiling and black holes appearing outside. As the guests arrive, one engages in furtive toe-sucking under the table, and another one dies, but that seems no great surprise. The dialogue, often consisting of non sequiturs, is spoken in an oddly heightened way, and the audience catches glimpses of the production team on the set, reminding them of the artificiality of the play. Bennett remarked that the greatest virtue of the play was "that it didn't seem like mine." The critical reaction, however, was so savage that *The Old Crowd* remained one of Bennett's few ventures into radical and

shock, Midgley also finds out that his father had a secret affair with a glamorous woman. Bennett played the role of Midgley, and two actresses who appear frequently in Bennett's works were also involved: Thora Hird as Aunty Kitty and Julie Walters as the Night Nurse.

A Woman of No Importance (broadcast in 1982) features Patricia Routledge and is the story of Peggy Schofield, a middle-aged office clerk who goes to the hospital with an unspecified stomach complaint and eventually dies of the illness. Peggy is related to Doris and Doreen and to Miss Prothero as another of Bennett's portraits of small lives. Peggy's story of borrowing the salt from a colleague in the canteen illustrates the merciless detail with which the tellers of such stories try to make their lives more important in an indifferent world. This monologue was the formal blueprint that later led to two innovative series of television monologues: *Talking Heads* (1988) and *Talking Heads 2* (1998).

The plays from *Objects of Affection* look at characters who are on the margins of society for a variety of reasons: Winnie, in *Our Winnie* (broadcast in 1982), is disabled; old Mr. Wyman in *Rolling Home* (broadcast in 1982) is losing not only his physical functions but also contact with his family as he languishes in a nursing home; teenage truant Les and his mother in *Marks* (broadcast in 1982) cannot communicate, and the boy faces a bleak future without work. *Say Something Happened* (broadcast in 1982) is similar to *Enjoy* in its depiction of the marginalization of old people and their ways of life. Bennett points out his preoccupations in the introduction to the collection: "If I have a favourite, imaginary landscape it seems to be an empty corridor." He adds a comment about the characters that seem to be recurring frequently: "The number of ladies in little costumes in these plays must be well above the national average (though vicars in civvies come hard on their heels)." Like the plays of *The Writer in Disguise,* these six works show Bennett's determination to portray the unspectacular, parochial, and provincial and to raise the audience's interest in them.

An Englishman Abroad and *A Question of Attribution,* normally performed as a double bill under the name *Single Spies,* seem to form a stylistic unity, but the two originated in different media: *An Englishman Abroad* was first conceived as television drama in 1983. It was then adapted for the National Theatre and presented with *A Question of Attribution* in 1988 with Bennett taking the role of Blunt. Finally, *A Question of Attribution* was also adapted as a television drama. *Single Spies* received the Olivier Award for best comedy in 1989.

An Englishman Abroad is based on a true story: in 1958, on tour in Moscow with the Royal Shakespeare Company, the actress Coral Browne met the exiled (and completely drunk) spy Burgess. She was invited to his apartment to take measurements for some new Saville Row suits: "Nobody will believe me when I go home. 'What did you do in Moscow, darling?' 'Not much. I measured Guy Burgess's inside leg.'" Bennett's play won the Broadcasters Press Guild TV Award and a British Academy of Film and Television Arts Writers Award in 1983, as well as a Royal Television Society Award in 1984. Browne played herself in the television production.

A Question of Attribution parallels the similarities between a man with a hidden identity and forgery in art. Anthony Blunt, Keeper of the Queen's Pictures and director of the Courtauld Institute, was publicly unmasked as one of the Cambridge Spies in 1979. The play takes place just before his downfall. Bennett juxtaposes the discovery of a concealed fourth and fifth man, revealed through X ray, in a *Triple Portrait* misattributed to Titian, and Blunt's imminent unmasking as "the fourth man," after Philby, Burgess, and Donald MacLean. A scene between Queen Elizabeth II (HMQ) and Blunt is the centerpiece of the play, full of double entendres:

HMQ: Portraits are supposed to be frightfully self-revealing, aren't they? Have you had your portrait painted?

Blunt: No, Ma'am.

HMQ: So we don't know whether you have a secret self.

A Private Function (1984) was Bennett's first movie script. The topic was an illegally obtained pig during the period when meat was still being rationed in postwar Britain, on the eve of the royal wedding in 1947. Gilbert Chilvers, a chiropodist trying to establish his business in a small town, comes up against the provincial powers and, through his wife's hunger for social status, is driven to crime and subversion. *A Private Function* displays accurate period detail, depicting the context of postwar food deprivation and the battle for social status (as Mrs. Chilvers puts it: "It's not about steak, Gilbert, it's about status!"). The script always stays on the comic or satirical side, and the dialogue is written in a slightly mannered style.

More seriously, Turner comments that *A Private Function,* with its focus on the black market, shows both sides of the English north-south divide as morally corrupt. This theme would have been a familiar one from Bennett's childhood–Bennett's father refused lucrative black-market deals but knew colleagues who went along with the practice. Bennett had started to interweave private and public histories in *A Private Function*

verse, and consequently has an unreal, nightmarish quality. Bennett also uses a plot similar to that of Kafka's *The Trial* (1925) to show the case of a young dye worker, Franz, who becomes ill as a consequence of working with toxic materials. It is his quest to find out what is wrong with him, but answers evade him as he tries to fathom the administrative procedures. Bennett's preoccupation with ethical questions a writer faces surfaces in *The Insurance Man*: Kafka, through trying to do a good deed in getting young Franz a job in the asbestos factory, is indirectly responsible for his death decades later.

Whereas *The Insurance Man* depicts Kafka's daytime job, the comedy *Kafka's Dick* (performed and published in 1986) focuses on the literary monument Franz Kafka. Parallels between Kafka and Bennett include the two writers' meticulous attention to detail, their sense of absurdity, and their isolation in a world they are unable to be included in, condemned to the role of the observer. The absurdist influence in *Enjoy* is also detectable in *Kafka's Dick*. It has characteristics of farce but combines them with biographically oriented drama, although Bennett is not pursuing factual authenticity in his exploration of Kafka. Factuality would be hard to justify in a play that starts with Kafka's friend and disobedient literary executor, Max Brod, urinating on a tortoise that metamorphoses into Kafka—all in a respectable middle-class couple's front room in Leeds. The play could be described as a farcical, stylized biography of a writer that also carries a skeptical message about the dangers of biography, summarized economically in the play: Kafka says, "This is persecution!" Brod replies, "No, it's not. It's biography." *Kafka's Dick* is also influenced by *The Trial*, as Kafka is tried for being famous and for not behaving in the way he is seen by readers and critics. *Kafka's Dick* won the Plays and Players Award for best new play in 1986.

In 1986 Bennett's second motion picture, *Prick Up Your Ears* (1987), reached production after many rewrites and a lengthy struggle by Bennett and director Frears to secure funding. The movie is an adaptation of John Lahr's biography of playwright Joe Orton, which was largely based on Orton's diaries, also edited by Lahr. It shows Orton's development from ignorant boy from the provinces to one of the most exciting playwrights of his time. In 1967, at the age of thirty-four, Orton was murdered by his longtime partner, Kenneth Halliwell, who then killed himself.

The script went through several rewrites because Bennett found he was telling the story, supposedly Orton's, too much from the perspective of Halliwell. Orton's story was framed by scenes of agent Peggy Ramsay supplying Orton's diaries to Lahr. There were certain parallels between Lahr's marriage—his wife, Anthea, was expected to blend into the background—and the "mar-

Prunella Scales and Bennett in the 1988 National Theatre premiere of his play A Question of Attribution, *about Anthony Blunt, who was Keeper of the Queen's Pictures and director of the Courtauld Institute before it was revealed that he had been a spy for the KGB (photograph by John Haynes; from* Writing Home, *1994; Richland County Public Library)*

and in *An Englishman Abroad*. Throughout the 1980s he focused specifically on the lives of writers.

The play *The Insurance Man* was produced for BBC2 in 1986, directed by one of Bennett's regular collaborators, Eyre, with Daniel Day-Lewis in the title role. Bennett had discovered that Franz Kafka, an author preoccupied with disease and dying, had involvements with his brother-in-law's asbestos factory. *The Insurance Man* is about Kafka's daytime job for Royal Assekuranz Insurance in Prague. It is among Bennett's best work for television, filmed in a style that evokes Kafkaesque mazes and the surrealist and frightening world of a powerless individual struggling against the merciless machinery of inflexible bureaucracy. Bennett comments in the introduction to *Two Kafka Plays* (1987) that Kafka's fearful universe is constructed out of burrows and garrets and cubbyholes on back staircases. The movie visually and atmospherically evokes this uni-

riage" of Orton and Halliwell. Bennett and Frears produced a movie that paid meticulous attention to period detail and language. Bennett, without losing the character of Lahr's biography, had told the well-known story of an outsider, of his sexual flowering, and of his provincial origins and transformation in the literary London of the 1960s. He has since stated that he was also attracted by Orton's confidence in his own abilities and the lack of concern over how he was perceived.

The first series of Bennett's *Talking Heads* monologues was broadcast in 1988 to great public and critical acclaim, earning Bennett the Hawthornden Prize in 1989. They suited developments in television drama in the 1980s, a decade Jonathan Bignell calls "oppressively reactionary" in its approach to innovative television drama. Although formally innovative, *Talking Heads* fit into an age that was concerned with the creation of brands and the re-creation of familiar formats, and the series has lent itself to marketing outside the broadcast medium, based on Bennett's familiar appeal. The monologues are cheap to produce and keep the risk of failure to a minimum. The supposed simplicity of these works and the familiarity of the voices Bennett creates betray a formally innovative miniature: they can be seen as a new kind of monologue that takes inspiration from all the known kinds but does not conform completely to the formal rules of any. Soliloquy, music-hall act, dramatic monologue, stream of consciousness, and radio play can all be seen as influences on the *Talking Heads* format, but in the amalgamation of all these influences, a new form emerges.

The principle is simple: a character talks about his or her life directly to the camera (although the presence of a viewer or listener is not acknowledged by the character). The characters are the types "taken from life" who have populated Bennett's television work for a long time. *Talking Heads* is "pure" Bennett, without the "frills" of location or relationships between different characters. Audiences are drawn into the world of a character and get a clear sense of the unspoken subtext in the monologues, which always presents an alternative history to what the character is telling: for example, Graham in *A Chip in the Sugar* would like to be seen as an educated man who looks after his aging mother; but he is revealed as mentally unstable and totally dependent on his mother. Lesley in *Her Big Chance* tells of acting skills and location filming with Roman Polanski; the reality is that she gets work as an extra in cheap German porn movies.

In a foreword, Bennett describes the American photographer Chauncey Hare's portraits as conveying what he tries to do in *Talking Heads*: he allows people to pose as they wish to be seen, which in itself is revelatory. The monologues first transferred to the stage in 1992 and have been popular programming choices with both professionals and amateurs.

Bennett found dealing with the media increasingly problematic. In his 1988 funeral address for Russell Harty, a popular television presenter, Bennett accused reporters of "hounding" his longtime friend. Harty had been suffering from hepatitis, and throughout his illness there had been a constant pursuit from the press, hoping to catch an exclusive photo of a terminally ill man and trying to fuel rumors that he was dying, as Bennett pointed out with bitter sarcasm, of "the wrong kind of disease."

Bennett himself soon felt the impact of heightened media interest: questions about his sexual orientation had always been met with "there's been something of both in my life, but not enough of either." As Games records, when Bennett was encouraged to out himself at a charity event, he replied to the openly homosexual actor Ian McKellen that the question of whether one prefers men or women was like asking a man crawling across the desert whether he preferred Malvern or Perrier water.

Bennett and director Jonathan Stedall produced three television documentaries for the BBC: *Dinner at Noon* (1988), *Portrait or Bust* (1993), and *The Abbey* (1995). All three documentaries are hybrids: although well researched and informative about their subjects—behavior in public places, the Leeds City Art Gallery in Yorkshire, and Westminster Abbey in London—they are about Bennett's life in relation to these topics.

As in his documentaries, Bennett makes it his mission to facilitate understanding of aspects of British culture in the Channel 4 series *Poetry in Motion* (1990). He discusses British poets such as Thomas Hardy, Philip Larkin, and W. H. Auden, offering accessible interpretations but also addressing the question of the relationship between art and life.

Critics have commented on similarities between Marcel Proust's cork-lined room and Bennett's wood-paneled one in Camden Town, and between both authors mining their lives to explore the working of mind and memory. Bennett's television play *102 Boulevard Haussmann* (1991) is the story of Proust's infatuation with a young viola player but also shows Proust's rapport with his housekeeper, Celeste, who is not the slightest bit interested in his writing. He found this indifference liberating. Bennett shared a similar relationship with Anne Davies, his partner at the time. This play was Bennett's last collaboration with his friend and ally, producer Lloyd, who died in 1991.

During the late 1980s Eyre, then artistic director of the National Theatre in London, asked Bennett to adapt Kenneth Grahame's classic children's book, *The Wind in the Willows* (1908), for the stage. The adaptation was initially intended to incorporate Grahame's biogra-

Nigel Hawthorne in the 1991 National Theatre premiere of Bennett's The Madness of George III, *which Bennett adapted into the 1994 motion picture* The Madness of King George, *earning an Oscar nomination for best adapted screenplay (photograph by Donald Cooper; from* Writing Home, *1994; Richland County Public Library)*

phy, but Bennett found this integration impossible because of the tragic and unfulfilled nature of Grahame's life. *The Wind in the Willows* was thus adapted as a Christmas show for the National Theatre in 1990, directed by Nicholas Hytner. Bennett produced an adaptation relevant both to Grahame's times and to the late 1980s: rabbits argue about political correctness; weasels are property speculators; and Albert the cart horse is encouraged by his doctor to seek "a less stressful position." The play still retains elements of Grahame's pastoral idyll. Whereas A. A. Milne's adaptation, *Toad of Toad Hall* (1929), centers on the adventures and character of Toad, Bennett's version is the story of four friends: Mole, Ratty, Badger, and Toad. He comments, though, that it is essentially Mole's bildungsroman. It is Mole who is allowed to express doubt over the "re-education" of Toad, stating that Toad's behavior might have improved but that he is much duller as an effect. But, reassuringly, Bennett does not end the play on this note; he shows that Toad has simply learned to "keep it under" and delights in the effects of his new modesty, because "everybody loves me."

The Madness of George III (performed in 1991, published in 1992) was Bennett's next collaboration with the National Theatre and was also directed by Hytner (who in 2002 was appointed artistic director). With the revival of *The Wind in the Willows,* Bennett became the first contemporary playwright who had two productions in repertory at the same time. He describes the work on these two plays as a happy period in his career, as he was fully involved in the production process, and the plays were developed and rewritten during rehearsals.

The Madness of George III is a large-scale history play that focuses on events during the Regency Crisis of 1788–1789. King George's mind and behavior were unstable, puzzling doctors and family alike. He eventually recovered in time to prevent a Regency bill being passed, which would have given reigning power to the Prince of Wales, later George IV. Bennett incorporated modern research that shows the king was suffering from a hereditary neurological disease, porphyria. This knowledge made the audience even more sympathetic toward the monarch, who was losing control over his body and his reigning power at the same time, while tortured by babbling, incompetent physicians. Just as *The Wind in the Willows* shows that Toad has to learn to control his behavior, the play *The Madness of George III* makes important points about behavior as performance. When, after his recovery, the king is congratulated on seeming more like himself, he responds, "I have always been myself, even when I was ill. Only now I seem myself."

From a psychologically poignant history drama on stage, with Nigel Hawthorne giving the performance of a lifetime in the title role, *The Madness of George III* underwent a transformation to large-scale motion picture. *The Madness of King George* (1994) is Bennett's "textual recycling" of his own work. Turner calls it a tragicomedy, and it can also be seen as a costume or period movie with certain heritage conventions, as a biopic, or as an historical movie based on factual sources, as well as a case study of mental illness. It visually complies with the period, drawing from eighteenth-century portraits, landscape paintings, and caricatures. *The Madness of King George* makes links with contemporary politics and royalty, presented to the "knowing" audience.

Bennett and Hytner were accused of thinking mainly of an American audience in their screen adaptation of the stage play, which they had also developed together. But what is deemed an "Americanization" (mainly by British critics) can also be seen as an acknowledgment of the different needs of different media. In an interview with Duncan Wu for *Making Plays: Interviews with Contemporary British Dramatists and Directors* (2000) Hytner commented that with the stage play, "it immediately became apparent that you could either do everything, and make it the biggest pile of scenery ever seen on the London stage, or do nothing–so we did nothing." The movie version, by contrast, "was everything. Yes. Because that's what films are."

When Bennett mentioned his relationship with Davies, his former housekeeper, in an interview in *The New Yorker* in 1994, he found himself under siege from the British press, who came up with headlines about his "charlady sweeping him off his feet." Bennett sarcastically referred to himself during this period as "London's most prominent heterosexual," according to Games, since everyone had previously assumed he was homosexual, without that ever being explicitly confirmed. Bennett had been gradually withdrawing from public life before this incident, but it put an end to interviews and television appearances. His standard written response to students and academics inquiring about his works is "treat me as a dead author, and make quotations up. Nobody will know." Bennett was claiming ownership of his life; since it was fast becoming the most important source in his works, he thus became increasingly unwilling to share its contents with journalists. Bennett resented being portrayed as the eternal flaxen-haired northern English lad and harmless national treasure, and being misrepresented: in an article in the *Guardian* (25 May 1992) he complained about being misunderstood in his objections to Margaret Thatcher and stated that the only solution was not to be interviewed. He broke this rule on occasion, but on the whole, journalists who call Bennett have been told that he was "putting the phone down now, very nicely."

Writing Home, first published in 1994, is an unconventional autobiography, a retrospective of Bennett's works. It is a loose chronology of texts that were obviously all written at different times but that are meaningfully grouped together to illustrate a life and a career. It could be called a "reader" or "collected nondramatic works." Its core is formed by Bennett's diaries between 1980 and 1990 (with material from three more years added in a later edition). The collection also includes essays, prefaces to plays, reviews, and obituaries, most of them originally published in the *London Review of Books,* a fortnightly literary magazine edited by Bennett's friend Mary Kay Wilmers. Typically, the diaries attracted the most attention. Games explains that the diaries "made the reader feel as if Bennett's inner thoughts had become public property." Bennett was compared with classical chroniclers such as Samuel Pepys in his ability to juxtapose public and private history as well as giving a strong sense of his own moral standings and convictions.

Writing Home became an instant best-seller in 1994 and was still selling well ten years later. Bennett has mentioned on occasion that there will be a second volume of miscellanea, scheduled for 2005.

Bennett's mother features regularly in the diaries. In addition to her lifelong affliction with depression, she developed Alzheimer's disease and gradually lost her memory and speech. She lived in a nursing home in Weston-super-Mare, close to Bennett's brother, who lived in Bristol. Bennett's entries on her utterances make the relevant point that creativity can still originate in the absence of words. He even juxtaposes his mother's expressions with Ludwig Wittgenstein's theory that things only exist through nomenclature when he quotes her as saying about sheep that she knows what they are but does not know what they are called. Looking at a grand view, she exclaimed, "Oh, what a lot of about!" Lillian Bennett died in 1995.

Bennett wrote three short novellas that originally appeared in the *London Review of Books*. The first, *The Clothes They Stood Up In* (1997), begins with an unusual occurrence: the mysterious removal of the complete contents of a couple's flat. The story then concentrates on the effects of this event. The solution to the crime, when it comes at the end of the story, has lost its importance. The liberation of the wife through the emptying of her life, first through the removal of her possessions and then through the death of her husband, has become the focus. *Father! Father! Burning Bright* (1999) is an adaptation of the television play *Intensive Care*. In *The Laying On of Hands* (2001) Bennett returns to the theme of exposure, already explored in works such as *The Insurance Man* or *Kafka's Dick*. It is the story of a masseur's funeral, at which a panic suddenly erupts as people speculate on the cause of his death. Nobody explicitly refers to AIDS, but everyone is worried: quite a few high-profile public figures are attending, and everyone is pretending that they did not have sexual contact with the deceased.

Kevin McNally, Nicholas Farrell, and Maggie Smith in the 1999 Queen's Theatre premiere of Bennett's autobiographical play
The Lady in the Van, *in which two actors portray different aspects of Bennett's response to a homeless woman who lived in his driveway for twenty years (photograph © Robbie Jack/CORBIS)*

During the 1990s Bennett became more reclusive while at the same time concentrating on his life in his works. He suffered two bouts of serious illness in the early and late 1990s. He remained close to Davies, his partner for more than ten years, and helped to finance a café that she ran in the Yorkshire Dales village of Clapham, next door to the house Bennett bought for his parents and now uses as a weekend and holiday home. During the 1990s he started a relationship with Rupert Thomas, art historian and editor of *World of Interiors* design magazine. Although he was a trustee of the National Gallery from 1993 to 1998, Bennett continued to avoid public occasions such as the first performances of his plays, interviews, or television contributions, and he turned down an honorary degree from Oxford University in 1998 as a protest against the installation of the Rupert Murdoch Chair in Language and Communication. (He had previously been named an honorary fellow of Exeter College, Oxford, in 1987 and received a D.Litt. from the University of Leeds in 1990.) His voice is seldom heard in the media, but his life, as he himself tells it, is public property.

Bennett states that the success of the first series of *Talking Heads* made the second more difficult to write. In *Talking Heads 2* he reproduced the format introduced ten years earlier, but the characters' stories were arguably darker and more connected to contemporary issues than in 1988. Consequently, *The Sunday Times* (10 May 1998) ran the headline "Bennett Pens TV Child Sex Drama" in reaction to one of the monologues, *Playing Sandwiches*. It is the story of a repeat-offender pedophile, and it caused consternation because it shows the case from the perspective of the offender, neutrally. Bennett certainly does not plead for understanding but demands that the viewer listen to the characters' stories. The other 1998 *Talking Heads* monologues are also full of unexpected, dark turns: Miss Fozzard, in *Miss Fozzard Finds Her Feet*, sells soft furnishing in a department store and also comes to sell sexual services to her chiropodist, a foot fetishist, without actually quite admitting it to herself. Marjory, in *The Outside Dog*, discovers that she holds the crucial clue by which her husband could be convicted as a murderer. Her overpowering cleaning obsession can be linked to her wish to keep the "dirt" he is bringing into the house at bay. Thora Hird, in one of her best performances for television, starred in *Waiting for the Telegram* as Violet, a nonagenarian inmate of a nursing home. She tells of her lifelong regret of not having sex with her fiancé before he went to the front in World War I and was killed.

In *Telling Tales* (2000) Bennett presents yet another hybrid form for television, one he seems to have invented to match his thematic and narrative concerns. It is a mixture of monologue, documentary, and storytelling. *Telling Tales* is delivered in ten installments. The visual conventions are close to those of *Talking Heads*: a single person–in this case, Bennett himself– addressing the camera. The narrative, however, is not based on gradual revelation of the duality of a character's story. *Telling Tales* consists of Bennett's densely detailed confessions and reminiscences, grouped thematically rather than chronologically. The form is less plot-based, less theatrically driven, but just as protagonist-centered as the *Talking Heads* monologues. The technique of taking a "snapshot" and developing it into a narrative, associated with the medium of short story, can also be found in *Telling Tales;* the blurb on the front cover of the published scripts calls them "Ten childhood snapshots from the master of the monologue."

The Lady in the Van (published in 1990, performed in 1999) was Bennett's first new stage play since *The Madness of George III* in 1991. It tells the story of Bennett's life over a period of twenty years during which he allowed Miss Shepherd, a cantankerous and ill-smelling eccentric, to live in her van in his driveway until her death in 1989. The play opened in the Queen's Theatre in London's West End in November 1999, directed by one of Bennett's favorite collaborators, Hytner, with Maggie Smith in the title role. There were two actors to play Alan Bennett and Alan Bennett 2, and this fact makes the play, although based on a well-known source, innovative and distinctive. After the diary of Bennett's and Miss Shepherd's coexistence had been published initially in *Writing Home,* Bennett states in the preface to the play he unsuccessfully tried to adapt it for the stage: "Miss Shepherd's story was not difficult to tell; it was my own story over the same period that defeated me. Not that there was a good deal to be said, but somehow the two stories had to interconnect. It was only when I had the notion of splitting myself into two that the problem seemed to solve itself."

The two Bennetts personify the ongoing conflict between the "ruthless and exploitative" writer and the "caring, considerate human being." Alan Bennett 2 is charitable toward Miss Shepherd, who does not respond with gratitude and leaves him frustrated. The other Alan Bennett, however, sees the literary potential of his deranged lodger. Bennett commented: "The device of having two actors playing me isn't just a bit of theatrical showing off and does, however crudely, correspond to the reality." Games remarks that having made the point himself that the play was exploitative, it was as if Bennett had eluded further criticism, as reviews and audience reaction were hugely enthusiastic, and the ethical considerations of laughing at a deluded, increasingly disabled old woman were brushed aside.

Previously, Bennett has not been preoccupied with autobiography in his stage works; it was something associated with his television work or diaries, his life often coded and in disguise. *The Lady in the Van,* by comparison, is an extraordinarily confessional text, but it also playfully presents its author's story as only one possible version of "the truth." This difference could be seen as a postmodern breakthrough in Bennett's work, as it allows him to retreat to the claim of fictionality.

Again inventing a format of his own, in 2001 Bennett wrote a loose narrative about music and its place in his childhood, *Hymn;* though not published, the play was first performed at the Harrogate International Festival in July 2001. The title can be seen as a pun, also meaning "him," as it focuses on himself as a child and adolescent, and on his father. The piece took the form of Bennett narrating, accompanied by the Medici String Quartet. At times, the musicians played school hymns, took the parts of father and son Bennett in a violin lesson gone wrong, or simply provided a "soundscape" for Bennett's impressionistic narrative.

Although fragmented, the central narrative is a scene in the attic of the Bennett family home in Leeds. A talented violinist, Walter Bennett gives his son his first violin lesson. Tempers flare as Bennett does not copy his father's skill with enough aptitude. The encounter is an epiphany for Bennett, forming the nucleus of a lifelong feeling of inability to be the right kind of son to his father. His father wants a son who does not "show off" or behave pretentiously. When Bennett received his first-class degree from Oxford through the mail and was not at home to receive it, his father decided not to tell anyone else in the family, certain that his son would not want any "fuss."

In 2004 Bennett wrote a stage play for the National Theatre, *The History Boys,* and an autobiographical essay for the *London Review of Books,* "A Common Assault," in which he discusses a homosexual attack on him and his partner Thomas. *The History Boys* premiered in March 2004 and is set to run until the summer of 2005. Tours of the United Kingdom and the United States are planned. It is a play about the nature of the teaching of history, reflecting on matters of factuality, the editing of truth, and the British educational system.

Throughout Alan Bennett's life and works there are both linear developments and ongoing contradictions. Among the developments, there is a clear sense of Bennett's life as an increasingly dominant source. First, he hid behind his characters in works such as *The Writer in Disguise* season. During the 1990s he became popular as a diarist and social commentator, mining his life as the main source of his works. This direction culminated in *The Lady in the Van,* where he appears onstage, not only out of disguise but also twofold. He supposedly reveals his "real" self onstage but makes sure that the play remains ambiguous.

In Bennett's work, close observation often results in ambivalence. He has effectively presented himself as politically left-wing, socially right-wing, and a strong sense of being in two minds runs through his whole body of work. Bennett rejected his own Englishness at the height of the Falklands War in 1982 (in *Writing Home* he states, "This is just where I happen to have been put down. No country. No party. No church. No voice"). He has refused to condemn the Cambridge Spies as traitors and turned down an honorary doctorate from Oxford. Despite these refusals to join the establishment, Bennett is the chairman of the Settle Conservation Society, launched a passionate protest in *Writing Home* against the replacement of the Book of Common Prayer, and is seen as the very personification of traditional Englishness. This sense of ambivalence provides the crucial tension within Bennett's work.

Interviews:

Martin Auty, "A Yorkshireman Abroad," *Time Out* (13 September 1984): 13;

Duncan Wu, "Alan Bennett, The Madness of George III" and "Nicholas Hytner," in his *Making Plays: Interviews with Contemporary British Dramatists and Directors* (London: Macmillan, 2000), pp. 74–110;

Amelia Hill, "A Bad Case of Writer's Block Deepens the Dark Mood of Alan Bennett," *Observer* (9 December 2001) <http://books.guardian.co.uk/print/0,3858,4316231-102285,00.html>.

Biographies:

Ronald Bergan, *Beyond the Fringe . . . and Beyond: A Critical Biography of Alan Bennett, Peter Cook, Jonathan Miller and Dudley Moore* (London: Virgin, 1989);

Alexander Games, *Backing into the Limelight: The Biography of Alan Bennett* (London: Headline, 2001).

References:

Jonathan Bignell, Stephen Lacey, and Madeleine Macmurraugh-Kavanagh, eds., *British Television Drama: Past, Present and Future* (Basingstoke: Palgrave, 2000), p. 1;

John Bull, "Whither Britain" and "Alan Bennett: The Leftovers," in his *Stage Right: Crisis and Recovery in British Contemporary Mainstream Theatre* (London: Macmillan, 1994), pp. 3–13, 178–191;

Richard Allen Cave, *New British Drama in Performance on the London Stage* (Gerrards Cross: Colin Smythe, 1987);

Richard Eyre, *Changing Stages* (London: Bloomsbury, 2000);

Ian Goode, "A Pattern of Inheritances: Alan Bennett, Heritage and British Film and Television," *SCREEN,* 44, no. 3 (Autumn 2003): 295–313;

Albert Hunt, "*Talking Heads:* Bed Among the Lentils," in *British Television Drama in the 1980s,* edited by G. Brandt (Cambridge: Cambridge University Press, 1993), p. 19;

Kara McKechnie, "Homely Northern Women in Sensible Shoes: Alan Bennett and the Pleasures of the Provincialism," in *Global Challenges and Regional Responses,* edited by Martin Middecke, Birgit Daewes, and Ina Bergmann (Trier: Wissenschaftlicher Verlag, 2003), pp. 189–201;

McKechnie, "Mrs Brown's Mourning and Mr King's Madness," in *Retrovisions,* edited by Deborah Cartmell, I. Q. Hunter, and Imelda Whelehan (London: Pluto Press, 2001), pp. 102–119;

McKechnie, "Taking Liberties with the Monarch: The Royal Biopic in the 1990s," in *British Historical Cinema,* edited by Claire Monk and Amy Sargeant (London: Routledge, 2002), pp. 217–234;

Joseph O'Mealey, *Alan Bennett: A Critical Introduction* (London: Routledge, 2001);

Margaret Rose, "The Repression of the Melodramatic in Alan Bennett's *Talking Heads* Monologue Plays," in *I linguaggi della passione,* edited by Romana Rutelli and Anthony Johnson (Udine: Campanotto Editore, 1993), p. 9;

Richard Scarr, "Alan Bennett–Political Playwright," *New Theatre Quarterly,* 12, no. 48 (November 1996): 309–322;

David Sexton, "National Treasure," *Sunday Telegraph,* 23 December 2001, p. 20;

Irene Shubik, *Play for Today* (London: Davis-Poynter, 1975);

Daphne Turner, *In a Manner of Speaking* (London: Faber & Faber, 1997);

Roger Wilmut, *From Fringe to Flying Circus* (London: Eyre Methuen, 2000), p. 17;

Peter Wolfe, *Understanding Alan Bennett* (Columbia: University of South Carolina Press, 1999);

Duncan Wu, "Alan Bennett: Anarchists of the Spirit," in his *Six Contemporary Dramatists* (London: Macmillan, 1995), pp. 17–33.

Edward Bond
(18 July 1934 -)

Peter Billingham
Bath Spa University College

See also the Bond entry in *DLB 13: British Dramatists Since World War II*.

PLAY PRODUCTIONS: *The Pope's Wedding,* London, Royal Court Theatre, 9 December 1962;
Saved, London, Royal Court Theatre, 3 November 1965;
A Chaste Maid in Cheapside, adapted from Thomas Middleton's play, London, Royal Court Theatre, 13 January 1966;
The Three Sisters, translated by Bond and Richard Cottrell from Anton Chekhov's play, London, Royal Court Theatre, 18 April 1967;
Early Morning, London, Royal Court Theatre, 31 March 1968;
Narrow Road to the Deep North, Coventry, Belgrade Theatre, 24 June 1968; London, Royal Court Theatre, 19 February 1969; New York: Vivian Beaumont Theatre, 6 January 1972;
Black Mass, London, Lyceum Theatre, 22 March 1970;
Passion, London, Alexandra Park Racecourse, 11 April 1971;
Lear, London, Royal Court Theatre, 29 September 1971;
The Sea, London, Royal Court Theatre, 22 May 1973;
Bingo: Scenes of Money and Death, Exeter, Northcott Theatre, 14 November 1973;
Spring Awakening, translated from Frank Wedekind's play, London, National Theatre, 28 May 1974;
The Fool: Scenes of Bread and Love, London, Royal Court Theatre, 18 November 1975;
Stone, London, Institute of Contemporary Arts Theatre, 8 June 1976;
The White Devil, adapted from John Webster's play, London, Old Vic Theatre, 12 June 1976;
We Come to the River, libretto by Bond, music by Hans Werner Henze, London, Royal Opera House, 12 July 1976;
Grandma Faust: A Burlesque (part one of *A-A-America!*), London, Almost Free Theatre, 25 October 1976; San Francisco, EXIT on Taylor, 20 March 2003;

Edward Bond (from the cover for Plays: 1, *1977; Thomas Cooper Library, University of South Carolina)*

The Swing: A Documentary (part two of *A-A-America!*), London, Almost Free Theatre, 22 November 1976; San Francisco, EXIT on Taylor, 20 March 2003;
The Bundle, or, New Narrow Road to the Deep North, London, Warehouse Theatre, 13 January 1978;
The Woman: Scenes of War and Freedom, London, Olivier Theatre (National Theatre), 10 August 1978;

The Worlds, Newcastle upon Tyne, Newcastle Playhouse, 8 March 1979; London, New Half Moon Theatre, 16 June 1981;

Restoration, London, Royal Court Theatre, 22 July 1981;

Summer, London, Cottesloe Theatre (National Theatre), 27 January 1982;

Derek, Stratford-upon-Avon, The Other Place, 18 October 1982;

After the Assassinations, Colchester, University of Essex, 1 March 1983;

The Cat (performed as *The English Cat*), libretto by Bond, music by Henze, Stuttgart, Stuttgart Opera House, 2 June 1983;

Red Black and Ignorant, London, Barbican Theatre, 19 January 1984;

The Tin Can People, Birmingham, Cannon Hill Arts Centre, 4 May 1984;

Great Peace, London, Barbican Theatre, The Pit, 17 July 1985; performed with *Red Black and Ignorant* and *The Tin Can People* as *The War Plays,* London, Barbican Theatre, The Pit, 25 July 1985;

Human Cannon, Manchester, Quantum Theatre, 2 February 1986;

Jackets, Lancaster, University of Lancaster, Nuffield Studio, 24 January 1989;

September, Canterbury, Canterbury Cathedral, 16 September 1989;

In the Company of Men, Paris, Théâtre de la Ville, 29 September 1992;

At the Inland Sea, Birmingham, Big Brum Theatre, Broadway School, Aston, 16 October 1995;

Coffee, Cardiff, Chapter Arts Centre, 27 November 1996; Paris, Le Théâtre National de la Colline, 12 May 2000;

Eleven Vests, Birmingham, Big Brum Theatre, Broadway School, Aston, 7 October 1997;

The Crime of the Twenty-First Century, Bochum, Germany, Schauspielhaus, 28 May 1999; Paris, Le Théâtre National de la Colline, 9 January 2001;

The Children, Cambridge, Manor Community College, Classwork Theatre, 11 February 2000;

Have I None, Birmingham, Big Brum Theatre, Castle Vale Artsite, 2 November 2000;

Existence, Altfortville, Studio Théâtre, 28 October 2002; Paris, Le Théâtre National de la Colline, 2002;

The Balancing Act, Birmingham, Big Brum Theatre, Broadway School, Aston, October 2003.

BOOKS: *Saved* (London: Methuen, 1966; New York: Hill & Wang, 1966);

Early Morning (London: Calder & Boyars, 1968; New York: Hill & Wang, 1969; revised edition, London: Eyre Methuen, 1977);

Narrow Road to the Deep North (London: Methuen, 1968; New York: Hill & Wang, 1969);

The Pope's Wedding (London: Methuen, 1971; revised, 1977)–comprises *The Pope's Wedding* and *Black Mass;*

Lear (London: Eyre Methuen, 1972; New York: Hill & Wang, 1972; revised, London: Eyre Methuen, 1978);

The Sea (London: Eyre Methuen, 1973; revised, 1978); published as *The Sea: A Full-Length Play* (Chicago: Dramatic Publishing, 1974);

Bingo: Scenes of Money and Death (London: Eyre Methuen, 1974)–comprises *Bingo: Scenes of Money and Death* and *Passion;*

Bingo & The Sea: Two Plays (New York: Hill & Wang, 1975);

The Fool and We Come to the River (London: Eyre Methuen, 1976);

We Come to the River: Actions for Music, libretto by Bond, music by Hans Werner Henze (Mainz & New York: B. Schott's Söhne/Schott Music, 1976);

A-A-America! & Stone (London: Eyre Methuen, 1976; revised, 1981);

Plays: 1 (London: Eyre Methuen, 1977)–comprises *Saved, Early Morning,* and *The Pope's Wedding;*

The Bundle, or, New Narrow Road to the Deep North (London: Eyre Methuen, 1978);

Plays: 2 (London: Eyre Methuen, 1978)–comprises *Lear, The Sea, Narrow Road to the Deep North, Black Mass,* and *Passion;*

Theatre Poems and Songs, edited by Malcolm Hay and Philip Roberts (London: Eyre Methuen, 1978);

The Woman: Scenes of War and Freedom (London: Eyre Methuen, 1979; New York: Hill & Wang, 1979);

Spring Awakening, translated from Frank Wedekind's play (London: Eyre Methuen, 1980);

The Worlds, with The Activist Papers (London: Eyre Methuen, 1980);

Restoration (London: Eyre Methuen, 1981; Woodstock, Ill.: Dramatic Publishing, 1982); revised version in *Restoration & The Cat* (London: Methuen, 1982);

Summer, and Fables; with Service, a Story (London: Methuen, 1982);

Summer: A Full-Length Play (Chicago: Dramatic Publishing, 1982);

Derek; and, Choruses from After the Assassinations (London: Methuen, 1983);

The English Cat: A Story for Singers and Instrumentalists, libretto by Bond, music by Henze (Mainz & New York: Schott Music, 1983);

The War Plays: A Trilogy, 2 volumes (London & New York: Methuen, 1985)–comprises *Red Black and Ignorant, The Tin Can People,* and *Great Peace;*

Human Cannon (London: Methuen, 1985; Woodstock, Ill.: Dramatic Publishing, 1989);

Poems, 1978-1985 (London & New York: Methuen, 1987);

Plays: 3 (London: Methuen, 1987)—comprises *Bingo, The Fool, The Woman,* and *Stone;*

Two Post-Modern Plays (London: Methuen, 1990)—comprises *Jackets, In the Company of Men,* and *September;*

Plays: 4 (London: Methuen, 1992)—comprises *The Worlds, The Activist's Papers, Restoration,* and *Summer;*

Tuesday (London: Methuen, 1993);

Olly's Prison (London: Methuen, 1993);

Coffee: A Tragedy (London: Methuen, 1995);

Plays: 5 (London: Methuen, 1996)—comprises *Human Cannon, The Bundle,* and *In the Company of Men;*

At the Inland Sea: A Play for Young People (London: Methuen, 1997);

Eleven Vests & Tuesday (London: Methuen, 1997);

Plays: 6 (London: Methuen, 1998)—comprises *The War Plays* and *Choruses from After the Assassinations;*

The Crime of the Twenty-First Century (London: Methuen, 1999);

The Children & Have I None (London: Methuen, 2000);

The Hidden Plot: Notes on Theatre and the State (London: Methuen, 2000);

Selections from the Notebooks of Edward Bond, volume 1, 1959-1980, edited by Ian Stuart (London: Methuen, 2000);

Selections from the Notebooks of Edward Bond, volume 2, 1980-1995, edited by Stuart (London: Methuen, 2001);

Plays: 7 (London: Methuen, 2003)—comprises *Olly's Prison, Coffee, The Crime of the Twenty-First Century, The Swing, Derek,* and *Fables and Stories.*

PRODUCED SCRIPTS: *Blow-Up,* adapted from Julio Cortázar's story by Michelangelo Antonioni and Tonino Guerra, with English dialogue by Bond, motion picture, Bridge Films, 1966;

Laughter in the Dark, adapted by Bond and others from Vladimir Nabokov's novel, motion picture, United Artists, 1969;

La Monaca di Monza, by Bond, Giampiero Bona, and Eriprando Visconti, motion picture, Clesi Cinematografica/San Marco, 1969;

Walkabout, adapted by Bond from James Vance Marshall's novel, motion picture, 20th Century-Fox, 1971;

Nicholas and Alexandra, adapted by James Goldman from Robert K. Massie's book, additional dialogue by Bond, motion picture, Horizon Pictures, 1971;

Derek, television, BBC Schools, 1983;

Tuesday, television, BBC Schools, 1993;

Olly's Prison, television, BBC2, 1993;

Bingo, television, BBC2, 1995;

Chair, radio, BBC Radio 4, 8 April 2000;

Existence, radio, BBC Radio 4, May 2002.

TRANSLATIONS: Frank Wedekind, *Spring Awakening* (London: Methuen, 1984);

Wedekind, *Plays: One,* translated and introduced by Bond and Elisabeth Bond-Pablé (London: Methuen Drama, 1993).

Edward Bond is one of the major British dramatists of the postwar period and arguably one of the most provocative voices in British theater, principally as dramatist but also as essayist and poet. Throughout his career as a professional playwright, dating back to *The Pope's Wedding* (performed in 1962, published in 1971), his work has been characterized by a rigorously rational, materialist view of human nature, society, and culture. He is an advocate of the imperative necessity of a theater whose central function is, as he said in a 2000 *Guardian Unlimited* interview, "to recreate what it means to be human, to redefine our relationship with the world." The dramatist's problem, he added, is "how do you speak sanity to the insane?" His work has often provoked controversy among critics and audiences, especially with early seminal plays such as *Saved* (performed in 1965, published in 1966), in which a baby is stoned to death in its pram.

Bond's output as a dramatist demonstrates an ongoing evolution of ideological discourse and stylistic innovation over a period of some forty years. The defining characteristics of Bond's theater emerge out of a compelling interplay of heightened, textured dramatic language and the impact of what he calls "theater events" such as the stoning of the baby in *Saved.* This interplay is always toward a political end—not in a narrow, sectarian sense but rather in a deeper concern for what it means to be human and how a more just and equal human society can be built.

Bond's early opportunities as a playwright and his subsequent reputation are inescapably bound up with a crucial period in postwar British theater, during which the English Stage Company (ESC) emerged at the Royal Court Theatre, London, under the initial leadership of the director and actor George Devine. This period, the first "New Wave" of which might be marked between that company's production of John Osborne's *Look Back in Anger* in 1956 and William Gaskill's seminal ESC production of Bond's *Saved* in 1965, brought a profound renewal in British writing for the stage. This work, the product of a new generation

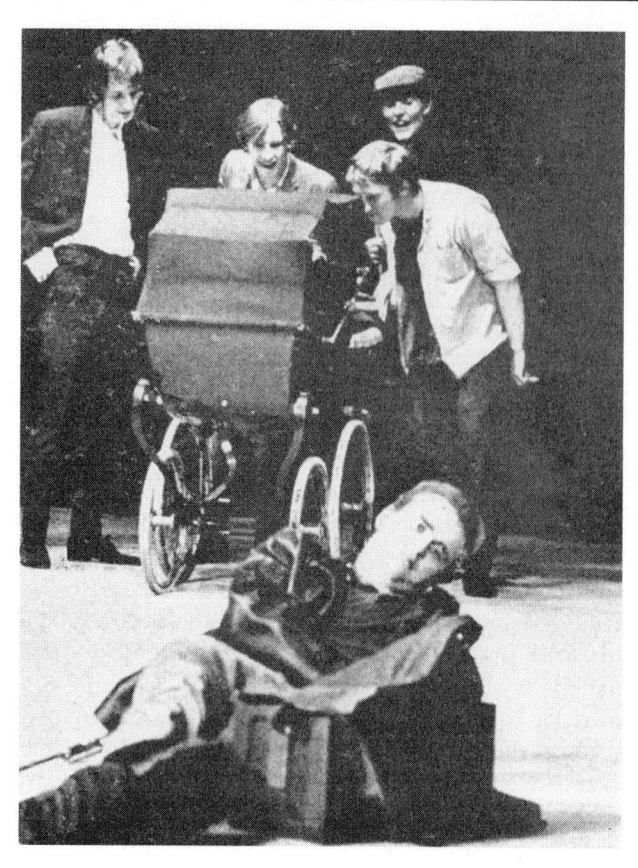

Scene from the 1969 Royal Court Theatre production (the first unrestricted public production) of Bond's controversial 1965 play, Saved, *in which a baby is stoned to death by a group of frustrated working-class youths (photograph by Zoë Dominic; from Richard Scharine,* The Plays of Edward Bond, *1976; Thomas Cooper Library, University of South Carolina)*

of writers (some of them, like Bond and Arnold Wesker, from working-class backgrounds), emerged out of the relative economic optimism of the period—which facilitated the building of new theaters. While the election of Harold Wilson's Labour government in 1964 hardly heralded in a radical alternative to the previous thirteen years of Conservative rule, this period nevertheless was one in which writers who defined themselves as Marxist (Bond), democratic socialist (Wesker of that period), and liberal humanist (Osborne of that period) found stages and audiences for their work. In an unpublished 6 July 2003 letter Bond remarked that "I was lucky enough to enter professional theatre during what diplomats called a 'window of opportunity.'"

Bond was born on 18 July 1934 in Holloway, North London, one of four children. His father, Gaston Cyril Bond, was a farm laborer and later an auto painter in a garage; his mother, Florence Kate (née Baker), remained at home bringing up the family. In *Bond on File* (1985), edited by Philip Roberts, Bond describes his upbringing as "Lower working class. But not London working class—my parents had come up to London during the depression because they couldn't get work on the land. My father had been a labourer in Suffolk and he did various kinds of labouring jobs when he was in London." As a direct consequence of the German bombing of the capital, in 1940 the six-year-old Bond was evacuated to Cornwall and subsequently to Ely in Cambridgeshire, East Anglia, where he lived with his grandparents. In 1944 he returned to London and attended Crouch End Secondary Modern School. However, he was not considered academically able enough to take the selection examination (commonly known as the "Eleven-Plus"). He later observed in *Bond on File:* "That was the making of me, of course. You see, after that nobody takes you seriously. The conditioning process stops. Once you let them send you to grammar school and university, you're ruined."

In 1948, at the age of fourteen and in his penultimate year at school, he attended a production of *Macbeth* produced by the last of the great touring British actor-managers, Donald Wolfit, who was known for the epic scale, grandeur, and intense emotional range of his acting. The young Bond was indelibly impressed, as he recalls in *Bond on File,* calling the event "The first thing that made sense of my life for me. . . . Naturally, when I wrote, I wrote for the theatre." His profound sense of engagement with theater and performance was also enhanced by regular visits to the music hall where his sister worked; he remembered years later that "It's the most incredible way to develop an understanding of timing and control on the stage. . . . A wonderful way to learn about theatre."

After leaving school at fifteen without formal qualifications, Bond worked as an office junior before being called up in 1953, at the age of nineteen, to fulfill his compulsory two years of national military service. He served in the army as an infantryman and wrote his first serious work (the first part of a novel, left unfinished) while stationed in Vienna. Bond's traumatic experience of military culture and practice was a key event in his life; he recalls in *Bond on File,* "I was in the infantry, cut off from the outside world for six weeks—degrading, hair cut, strange clothes, shouted at, screamed at. We were turned into automata." This dehumanizing and alienating conditioning of the human being into a robotic "automaton" programmed to obey orders, hate, and kill for the monarch and the state is a recurring theme in Bond's work. In his introduction to *Plays: 1* (1977) he says, "I write about violence as naturally as Jane Austen wrote about manners"—and violence always has for Bond a specific material and ideological site: frequently and predictably sanctioned by the monarchy or the state as a means and expressions of power, control, and the crushing of resistance to the political hierarchy.

On completing his national service, Bond began to write plays; he had written about fifteen and had unsuccessfully submitted some of them to the BBC before being invited, in 1958, to join one of the writers' groups established at the Royal Court Theatre by Gaskill, at that time an assistant director to Devine. Bond also became a regular play reader for the theater. He remembered later how useful the experience was: "In this group we practised improvisation and a few elementary acting exercises. The group was always run by directors and not writers. This was good because it made the members aware of the plastic, visual nature of theatre." In the context of a jaded postwar British theater that, with rare exceptions, was controlled and defined by a commercial, West End mentality, Devine's values and aims—while not revolutionary—offered a more thoughtful and challenging form of theater, reflecting a time of significant change.

On 9 December 1962 Bond's first produced play for the Royal Court Theatre, *The Pope's Wedding,* was staged as a single performance as part of a season that the company instituted called "Sunday Night Productions without Décor." It was directed by Keith Johnstone. What might now more commonly be described as platform performances or rehearsed readings, these Sunday evening productions provided new, untested writers such as Bond with an opportunity to have their dramatic voices heard and nurtured through the fundamentals of performance.

Bond's play is set in East Anglia, where he had spent some of his formative years during the wartime evacuation. The characters are the rural working class, living precariously on subsistence wages, constantly needing to subsidize their social lives and routines through borrowing cigarettes or the price of the next pint of beer from each other. The characters speak with an acutely observed East Anglian dialect. However, unlike Wesker's play from the same period, *Roots* (1959), Bond's play, for all of its equivalent geographical location and class setting, is not a piece of left-wing social realism. Indeed, and critically, Bond's work is simply not engaged in a realist political discourse in any sense. What is a common factor in both of these East Anglian plays is that those rural farming communities in the east of England are characteristically isolated, creating a powerful sense of entrapped and marginalized lives.

The Pope's Wedding is the dramatic narrative of Scopey, a young farm laborer who initially embodies his class contemporaries' prejudice and violence toward an old hermit, Alen, who lives on the edge—literally and metaphorically—of the village. Scopey's wife, Pat, has been visiting the old man and cleaning and cooking for him, her actions contingent upon a promise made by her late mother to Alen. While at first Scopey is frustrated with the unpaid time and attention that Pat devotes to Alen, almost irresistibly he begins to assume her role of caregiver to this estranged, uncommunicative, older man. This evolutionary process of a social relationship located in even the most basic sense of identification and empathy is ultimately, bleakly realized when Scopey, having murdered Alen, assumes his clothes and persona—having sought to "become him."

This play and its distinctive treatment of its themes of an alienated, rural working class, along with Bond's recognition of the violence latent within that class context, helped to establish him as a major young writer. However, for Bond, the construct of individual subjectivity and interior motivation is both problematic and, at best, only a symptom of the wider social, cultural, and political influences that define human beings.

Throughout his career, Bond has continually pondered on the nature, causes, and function of violence in society. With its unflinching demonstration of a violent act—the stoning to death of a baby in a pram in a public park by a group of young men—his next play, *Saved,* shocked contemporary reviewers and audiences. There were angry disturbances—including actual fights—on its opening night. For Bond, violence is always a product and issue of corrupt and exploitative social organization. Therefore, within the dramatic site of the park in *Saved* the violence may be viewed and analyzed from multiple but complicit standpoints. On one level it is a savagely premeditated demonstration of socially gendered codes of masculinity-as-violence. Simultaneously, this public exhibition of violence is also reflective and expressive of the wider metanarratives of state-sanctioned violence, as Bond observes in his *Plays: 1* introduction: "Clearly the stoning to death of a baby in a London park is a typical English understatement. Compared to the 'strategic' bombing of German towns it is a negligible atrocity, compared to the cultural and emotional deprivation of most of our children its consequences are insignificant."

Another significant issue that the depiction of violence in the play raised for some contemporary reviewers was what one might term the "politics of representation." The prevailing style of many of the other writers of the "New Wave" was dramatic naturalism complemented with the relative social realism of Wesker in plays such as *Roots* and *The Kitchen* (1961). A play like Bond's *Saved,* with its urban location and its heightened, "realist" working-class idiom, was therefore presumed to be located within that broader generic territory. However, Bond's approach was exploring stylistic and narrative

Shirley Ann Field as Florence Nightingale and Moira Redmond as Queen Victoria in a 1969 Royal Court Theatre production of Bond's 1968 play Early Morning, *the original production of which was initially banned by the Lord Chamberlain and then raided by police (photograph by Zoë Dominic; from David L. Hirst,* Edward Bond, *1985; Thomas Cooper Library, University of South Carolina)*

territory that—while initially influenced by the alienation effects of Brechtian methodology—developed into a performance language and political analysis that became distinctive.

In the same year that *Saved* was first produced, Bond was a short-listed finalist for the prestigious award of Most Promising Playwright of 1965. *Saved* opened at the Royal Court Theatre on 3 November 1965. Bond had submitted *Saved* to the theater on 18 September 1964, but the Lord Chamberlain (the official state censor) would not grant a license for the play to be produced without severe and unacceptable cuts to Bond's script. Gaskill had therefore made a decision to present the play in an implicitly private production for an audience from those ten thousand affiliated members of the English Stage Society. The production was thus a club production, which could be presented outside of the jurisdiction of the censor, whose authority existed only over public performances. On 13 December 1965 police officers acting under the authority of the Lord Chamberlain's Office visited the theater to see a performance of *Saved*. They were not asked to show their membership cards and so, on a technicality (they were in fact members), effectively undermined the "private" status of the performance. In January 1966 the Royal Court Theatre was charged (under the 1843 Theatres Act) with presenting an unlicensed play. On 14 February 1966 court proceedings opened, while on 17 February, theater censorship was debated in the House of Lords. On 1 April the Royal Court Theatre was found guilty, although the defendants were given a conditional discharge. *Saved* was the last play prosecuted under the censorship laws.

Meanwhile, Bond's next play, *Early Morning* (1968), commissioned by Gaskill, was banned in its entirety by the Lord Chamberlain. The Royal Court Theatre decided to launch a sustained fight over the wider, ongoing issues of artistic integrity and freedom of speech that the censorship laws symbolized. This conflict was further provoked by Bond's play-in-waiting; Gaskill must have anticipated that *Early Morning* would not secure the censor's approval, since it portrays Queen Victoria ("Call me Victor") in a lesbian relationship with Florence Nightingale. Following the same strategy that had ultimately failed with *Saved*, Gaskill decided once more to stage a "private" performance for members of the English Stage Society. This planned production only served to heighten the controversy, and the situation reached a public crisis point when the Arts Council threatened to withdraw its funding to the Royal Court Theatre for that specific play if the presentation went ahead. The Royal Court Theatre withdrew the production, although Gaskill did endeavor to produce a Sunday evening private performance of the play; the production was raided by the police on 31 March 1968, though no charges were filed. *Early Morning* proved to be the last play ever to be actually prevented from production by the Lord Chamberlain, although Bond's next play, *Narrow Road to the Deep North* (performed and published in 1968), premiered at the Belgrade Theatre, Coventry, in defiance of cuts demanded by the censor. However, the battle was finally won as legislation was passed in Parliament on 28 September 1968 to abolish censorship.

In this same year, 1968, Bond continued to receive further recognition, even as the critics remained virulently divided over his work. In May he received the George Devine Award for both *Saved* and *Early Morning* and won the John Whiting Award for *Narrow Road to the Deep North*. Meanwhile, in April 1968 the Tory (Conservative) politician Enoch Powell had delivered an inflammatory, racist speech concerning the "tide of immigrants" from the Commonwealth and former British Empire, predicting that without compulsory "repatriation," British cities would flow with "rivers of blood." The Royal Court Theatre organized an agitprop event against Powell's speech and the racial unrest and violent prejudice that it unleashed. To this event, Bond contributed *The Enoch Show* (1969), which on its first performance was disrupted by members of the English neo-Nazi party, the National Front.

In 1969, following the abolition of censorship in the previous spring, Gaskill brought together a short season of Bond plays (*Saved* and *Early Morning*), each to be given its first unrestricted public performance, along with the Royal Court Theatre premiere of *Narrow Road to the Deep North*. The first public production of *Saved* opened on 19 February 1969 with a new cast featuring Kenneth Cranham as protagonist Len. It was tellingly reviewed by Martin Esslin for *Plays and Players* (April 1969):

> Nothing could have shown up the idiocy of British stage censorship in its declining phase than the reaction of the public—and even critics!—to the revival of *Saved* at the Royal Court.... What a brilliant play *Saved* is, and how well it has stood the test of time! ... *Saved* is a deeply moral play: the scene of the stoning of the baby, which led to the first outcry about it, is one of the key points of its moral structure.

Early Morning represents a change in location and, in that sense, scale and focus from Bond's first two plays, while remaining a play that, as Bond asserted, "is essentially about working-class life." It is a savage comedy in which some of the principal historical characters from the late-Victorian political era are relocated in an effectively postmodern domain: a microcosm of the violence and power dynamics within British imperialism. This dramatic landscape features not only a lesbian relationship between Victoria and Nightingale but also cannibalistic murders erupting out of the queues waiting to enter the cinema, as well as a plot between Benjamin Disraeli and the prince regent, Albert, to violently overthrow the monarchy and assassinate Victoria. Bond's savage criticism of the brutal self-interest and callous pragmatism of the ruling classes in some senses anticipates both the murdering British missionary regime of his *Narrow Road to the Deep North* and, more completely, the nightmarish fusion of Stalinism and Auschwitz in the geo-ideological landscape of *Lear* (performed in 1971, published in 1972).

Some of Bond's most exciting work came in the 1970s, a decade of political unrest and activism leading up to the election of Margaret Thatcher's Conservative government in 1979. It was a decade of mass oppositional left-wing political activity, particularly in industrialized northern England and especially focused upon the major miners' strikes. In 1971 there was a strike of 280,000 British miners, and in 1973 the second strike provoked Edward Heath's Conservative government into declaring a state of emergency and initiating a three-day working week in order to conserve energy resources. Bond's engagement with some of the major political events of that era may be seen in shorter plays such as *Black Mass* (performed in 1970, published in 1971) and *Passion* (performed in 1971, published in 1974). Significantly, both plays were written for specific politically motivated organizations, respectively the antiapartheid movement and the Campaign for Nuclear Disarmament. Of further interest is that Bond himself played the part of Christ in the opening performance of *Black Mass*. Also in 1971, Bond married Elisabeth Pablé.

With *Lear*, Bond produced one of his landmark achievements as a dramatist. In this work the playwright's dramatic vision and political analysis challenges, with clear implications, some of the central tenets of dramatic tragedy. Simultaneously, Bond questions the concept of a passive, fatalistic catharsis—human suffering must and will happen—with a savage exposure of the strategic imperative of violence used not only by the ruling class (Lear himself and then his daughters after they have ousted him from power) but also by Cordelia's revolutionary forces. In Bond's deconstruction of William Shakespeare's classic Elizabethan tragedy, Cordelia is portrayed, not as Lear's youngest and compassionate daughter, but as "a rural female Castro," as Bond describes her in *Bond on File*, who leads a revolutionary army against the regime of

Scene from the 1971 Royal Court Theatre premiere of Bond's play Lear, *a reworking of William Shakespeare's tragedy, with Harry Andrews in the title role (photograph by John Haynes; from David L. Hirst,* Edward Bond, *1985; Thomas Cooper Library, University of South Carolina)*

Bodice and Fontanelle, Lear's elder daughters. In a program note for a production of *Lear* at the Liverpool Everyman Theatre in October 1975 Bond wrote:

> Shakespeare's *Lear* is usually seen as an image of high, academic culture. The play is seen as a sublime action and the audience are expected to show the depth of their culture by the extent to which they penetrate its mysteries. . . . But the social moral of Shakespeare's *Lear* is this: endure till in time the world will be made right. That's a dangerous moral for us. We have to have a culture that isn't an escape from the sordidness of society, the "natural" sinfulness or violence of human nature, that isn't a way of learning how to endure our problems—but a way of solving them.

When Bond's Lear, in the final scene of the play, starts to try to dig away the wall that he had previously ordered to be built for "protection" and "defense," he enacts an iconic moment from postwar British theater. However, Lear's death is neither poetic nor tragic. From Bond's view, Lear's death is a rational action in which the character accepts responsibility for his life and action, as he wrote in the 1975 program note: "My Lear's gesture mustn't be seen as final. . . . Lear is very old and has to die anyway. He makes his gesture only to those who are learning how to live."

Bond's next play, *The Sea,* was first produced at the Royal Court Theatre on 22 May 1973, directed by Gaskill. There is a strong biographical resonance, as Bond was inspired by profound images from his childhood experiences as an evacuee in East Anglia. Bond recalled these memories in an interview in the *Radio Times* (4–10 March 1978, referenced in *Bond on File*):

> The images I had when I wrote *The Sea* go back to my childhood, the war. I was evacuated. Like now, the war was a time of great horror and fear. As if all the horrors in the movies were really coming to life, happening. One afternoon, I remember so clearly being taken to a photographer's shop. By the coast. . . . The studio was upstairs. . . . Suddenly I was up there at a giant's height, looking out. And I realised how vast the sea was. . . . And suddenly all the dreadful things about war became very small. The same afternoon I was told the story of somebody walking along the beach, finding the body of someone who had been torpedoed. Washed up. . . . It was one of those things when suddenly the world starts asking you questions.

Set in an Edwardian east coast town, the play presents a microcosm of a world in which the pathologically sustained insanity of the character Hatch, a small-town shopkeeper, is exposed in all of its petit bourgeois, xenophobic paranoia. Hatch leads a group of local men in a continuous and furtive search for aliens who are intent on taking over the planet by inhabiting human bodies. Thus, when a drowned young man is washed up on the beach, he becomes for Hatch another chilling example of the endless lengths to which the aliens will go in order to infiltrate decent, conventional human society.

Hatch's rampant paranoia exists alongside of and in diametrical opposition to the small-town social hierarchy presided over by Mrs. Rafi, a marvelous comic creation. Mrs. Rafi is directing her female socially conformist acolytes in a classical drama, the sanctimonious rationale being to raise funds for the local coast guard. The production is being rehearsed in the grande dame's drawing room. Bond wittily uses this play-within-the-play as a means of exposing the underlying tensions, jealousies, and neuroses underlying the social status of these female characters, ably supported by a classic comic vicar. To the same extent that this scene foregrounds the essentially enacted roles and power strategies of provincial bourgeois life, Hatch's pathological worldview is, in fact, a perfectly logical extension and consequence of the manipulated social charade that passes as polite, decent society. The soundings of the military batteries throughout the play—invisible but present and gradually intruding—remind the audience of pre-1914 Britain and Europe beyond the narrow confines of the coastal community.

Within this metaphor of the insanity and ideological chaos of late-empire Britain, Bond employs characters who offer some sense of relative calm, sanity, and provisional hope for escape and change. Evens, an older man who lives in self-chosen isolation on the beach at the farthest edge of this society, is able to offer a rational perspective upon the underlying causes of the social pathology of the community. It is an act of conscious irony that the playwright's Cambridgeshire home in the village of Great Wilbraham is, in Bond's own words in *Bond on File*, "on the edge of Wilbraham, and I'm known here as 'the last man in the village.'"

Bingo: Scenes of Money and Death was written in the same year as its first production at the Northcott Theatre, Exeter, on 14 November 1973, featuring Bob Peck as the protagonist, Shakespeare himself. It transferred to the Royal Court Theatre on 14 August 1974, with John Gielgud taking on the role of Shakespeare. The subtitle points to the context of the play: the dawn of mercantile capitalism and of a contemporary Elizabethan society ruled with brutal authoritarianism. It was also a period of imperialist expansionism (in both Ireland and the New World) and of a monarchist feudal society and economy facing massive and potentially destabilizing social and economic change. Not only "foreigners" were perceived and manufactured as a "threat" but also those increasingly large numbers of the rootless and wandering poor—their suffering and plight a direct and (within the rationale of capitalism) acceptable consequence of "reform" and productive efficiency (the enclosure of common land and increase of privatized cash profit).

Bond uses an episodic scene structure to expose the potentially devastating contradictions inherent within the rationale and structures of embryonic capitalism. His Shakespeare is seen as a writer and individual who is complicit with and within those structures as a result of the commercial success of his plays. Having made a financially shrewd investment in the popular theaters that produced those plays, he has become a wealthy bourgeois who, effectively at the end of his working life, has bought a country property near Stratford-upon-Avon to live out his retirement. There are plans for enclosure of the common land and active and organized resistance to it by armed groups of peasants, personified particularly by the character of the Son—a young man whose mother is Shakespeare's housekeeper. Out of this ongoing violent resistance, the Son's father is eventually killed on the snow-driven heath above and beyond Shakespeare's home. In reflecting upon the moral contradictions confronting his constructed Shakespeare, Bond was revisiting and revaluating his own relationship to the enduring political inequalities, injustices, and violent oppressions of not only the 1970s but also the twentieth century as a whole:

> SHAKESPEARE: What does it cost to stay alive? I'm stupefied at the suffering I've seen. The shapes huddled in misery that twitch away when you step over them. Women with shopping bags stepping over puddles of blood. What it costs to starve people. The chatter of those who hand over prisoners. The smile of the men who see no further than the end of a knife. Stupefied. How can I go back to that? What can I do there? I talk to myself now. I know no one will ever listen.

In November 1974 Bond contributed to "Poets for the People" at the Mermaid Theatre in London, an event that raised funds for the Defense Aid Fund of Southern Africa. In 1975 Bond's play *The Fool: Scenes of Bread and Love* opened, another play that takes a writer from a specific historical context and uses him as a means of exploring wider issues. In the case of *The Fool* the writer is the poet John Clare, who lived and worked in rural Northamptonshire in the English Midlands. In a letter to a theater director in 1977, Bond observed:

John Gielgud as William Shakespeare and Arthur Lowe as Ben Jonson in the 1974 Royal Court Theatre production of Bond's 1973 play Bingo: Scenes of Money and Death, *which depicts Shakespeare as a bourgeois landowner near the end of his life (photograph by Douglas H. Jeffrey; from David L. Hirst,* Edward Bond, *1985; Thomas Cooper Library, University of South Carolina)*

We mustn't only write problem plays, we must write answer plays—at least plays which make answers clearer and more practical. . . . The answers aren't always light, easy, or even straightforward, but the purpose—a socialist society—is clear.

These sentiments throw interesting light upon the plays of what Bond has called his Second Series: *The Fool; The Bundle, or, New Narrow Road to the Deep North* (performed and published in 1978); *The Woman: Scenes of War and Freedom* (performed in 1978, published in 1979); *The Worlds* (performed in 1979, published in 1980); and *Restoration* (performed and published in 1981). In their different ways, these plays all seek to propose answers—no matter how provisional and perhaps problematic—to the crucial ideological and ethical issues of human beings and their society in the late twentieth century. *The Bundle* is a reworking of *Narrow Road to the Deep North*, offering an extension of its allegorical structure; as Bond explained in *The Guardian* (13 January 1978; included in *Bond on File*): "The people in *The Bundle* all live by a river. Directly or indirectly they all live from it. From time to time it floods and destroys them. If, as the play invites, you substitute factories and offices—all industrialism—for the river, then my purpose is plain."

Bond directed *The Woman* himself in the Olivier Theatre of the National Theatre in London. This play is set at the time of the Trojan War, and its use of Greek mythology allowed the playwright to further universalize his expression of the horrors of war and superstition. Bond states it was the first full modern play presented on the main stage of the National Theatre.

The Worlds was given its first production at Newcastle Playhouse on 8 March 1979 and subsequently performed by the Activists' Youth Theatre Club on 21 November 1979 at the Royal Court Theatre Upstairs. Both productions were directed by Bond. Its professional premiere was at the New Half Moon Theatre, London, on 16 June 1981. It broke into newly developed territory, as Bond made clear in *Bond on File:* "I'm trying to move towards a theatre in which very often the character is not relating the voice to himself but is relating his voice, his words, to the 'pictoriality,' the picture of the whole stage." This shift and development in dramatic strategy and focus enables Bond's central characters to speak with an even more vigorous and direct manner and style. However, they are not reduced to being mouthpieces but rather change the assumptions and the prejudices of the ruling classes.

In the play, Trench is a managing director of an unnamed company whose motivating force is money and its acquisition with a veneer of high-cultural sensibility. Following the usurpation of his power in a boardroom coup, armed revolutionary political activists aim to kidnap Hubbard, Trench's successor, in order to force the company to meet the wage demands of the workers, whose livelihood is diminishing while the directors continue to increase profits. However, instead of kidnapping Hubbard, they succeed only in abducting his chauffeur. This scenario provides an opportunity for a rigorous examination of the ways in which human life may be reduced to a commodity within capitalism. Far from being willing to pay the ransom for the chauffeur, Hubbard and his capitalist, bourgeois-gangster associates cynically calculate that the victim has cost them more than the ransom fee and, accordingly, is in debt to them.

The character who is most articulately resistant to Trench and his self-serving cronies is the trade-union activist Terry. This choice was particularly significant at the time the play premiered, as Thatcher's government had set about passing new legislation that seriously weakened the function of trade unions as representatives and protectors of workers' interests. Terry has several powerful speeches marked by a strong sense of passionate opposition. The revolutionary activist Anna also articulates the significance of the title of the play while embodying a political perspective that is central to Bond's own worldview:

> ANNA. Listen. There are two worlds. Most people think they live in one but they live in two. First there's the daily world in which we live. The world of appearance. There's law and order, right and wrong, good manners. How else could we live and work together? But there's also the *real* world. The world of power, machines, buying, selling, working. That world depends on capital: money! Money can do anything. It gives you the power of giants. The real world obeys the law of money. And there's a paradox about this law: whoever owns money is owned by it.... Our lives, our minds, what we are, the way we see the world, are not shaped by human law but by the law of money.

The major plays from this decade thus deal with perennial issues in Bond's work.

Restoration opened in a production at the Royal Court Theatre on 21 July 1981, directed by Bond. In a letter to *The Guardian* on 31 July 1981, Bond wrote: "I was deeply depressed over the last [1979] election and, indeed, I wrote *Restoration* as a consequence. I saw [protagonist] Bob as being the typical, working-class Tory voter, and the play is about his betrayal." The election result of 1979 restored the dominant party and political doctrine of twentieth-century British politics to power. Meanwhile in some of the most deprived areas of England's major cities, such as Toxteth in Liverpool and St Paul's in Bristol (areas of dense long-term unemployment, slum housing, and established British ethnic communities), riots raged in the streets.

Although Bond describes the setting for the play as "England, eighteenth century–or another place at another time," *Restoration* depicts contemporary Britain in 1981, using the setting of eighteenth-century England as a critical mirror. In doing so, Bond exposes contemporary British society while distancing those events into an historical frame. The action of the play is interspersed with nonnaturalistic songs to comment upon the principal themes and concerns.

Bob, a young man from the East Anglian peasant class, arrives at the stately home of the socially aristocratic but financially bankrupt Lord Are. Bob's mother works as a housekeeper in Are's service and perfectly embodies the unthinking deference of the reactionary English working class to their ruling class. The compliant Bob has been framed by Are as the murderer of the aristocrat's wife, whom Are himself has callously and carelessly killed over breakfast. Their marriage had been predicated upon mutual economic advantage to her industrialist father, Hardache, and Are, whose sole concern now is to avoid the hangman's noose. Bob's mother sees her son's situation as a remarkable opportunity for social advancement:

> MOTHER. . . . This is his big chance. Doo his lordship a favour like this an' he's set up for life. Poor people can't afford to waste a chance like this, god know it don't come often. Time our luck change . . . Ont expect his lordship to goo in the dock for the like of her. Jist drag his family name through the mire. Whatever next! Ont know where to look next time I went to the village, they knew I work for someone like that.

Prior to his arrest, Bob and his mother sought to detain for punishment one of their own servant class, Frank, for daring to steal some of the Are family silver to subsidize his own paltry wage and poor living conditions. Within the play, only Frank and Rose–Bob's young, black, Afro-Caribbean wife–offer any critique and resistance to the corrupt status quo and to Bob's and his mother's internalized acceptance of the submission and oppression that it inflicts upon them. On realizing that Bob is not the murderer–Are's wife, by Bob's admission, had blood on her before his arrival at the scene–Rose desperately seeks to raise the awareness of the other working-class characters. She commits herself to working for justice for Bob, who otherwise will face the death penalty. Exasperated and exhausted by her failure to make him understand his actual class position and fate, she asserts:

basis for the English eighteenth century. His dementia in Scene 10 is the basis for modern fascism—which is a corruption of his alliance with Hardache. In other words, the play points at us from the eighteenth century and into the modern world.

By the final scene of the play, Bob has been executed, and the power and status of the English ruling class has been even more rooted and cemented by the "new politics" of self-interest and expediency forged through Hardache's capital and the myth—constructed and sustained by Are and his class—of themselves as keepers of the sacred flames of nationhood, tradition, and law-abiding godliness. In the final scene, Rose acknowledges: "What have I learned? If nothing, then *I* was hanged." Determined not to be disempowered in an equivalent way to her dead husband, she exits with lines filled with the poignancy of loss but the commitment to return to the city and her part in the struggle for political change.

Other plays by Bond in the 1980s were *Summer* (performed and published in 1982), which Bond directed and in which he returned, as in *The Sea,* to Shakespeare's *The Tempest* as a source; *Derek* (performed in 1982, published in 1983), an ideological fable about the political manipulation of a young man's identity and genius; and *The Cat* (published in 1982, performed as *The English Cat* in 1983, with music by Hans Werner Henze), an example of music theater used for the exploration of political concerns, with all of the characters having animal personae. *Red Black and Ignorant* is a short play that was originally written between December 1983 and January 1984. Its first London production was at the Barbican Theatre, London, in January 1984, directed and designed by Nick Hamm. The following May, a play with the working title "The Birmingham Play" became *The Tin Can People*. With the addition of *Great Peace* (performed in 1985), these plays were published in 1985 as a new trilogy, *The War Plays*. The war in question is the terrifying possibility, even likelihood, of nuclear holocaust.

In an interview with *The Guardian* on 16 January 1984 (included in *Bond on File*), Bond spoke of the circumstances surrounding his writing of *Red Black and Ignorant* and of his key concerns expressed in that play:

> When I was asked to write for "Thoughtcrimes" at the Barbican, I decided to write about nuclear war. A society which does not "know itself" does not act rationally. If the processes by which the state organises society's various strata and activities are corruptions of the truth, then these corruptions will affect all its decisions. . . . I created a character who in fact never lives: he is burned in the womb in a nuclear war. His "ghost" comments on the people who, to preserve freedom, condemn him and millions of others to the perpetual imprisonment of death. He argues that a society that

Simon Callow as Lord Are in the 1981 Royal Court Theatre premiere of Bond's play Restoration, *in which an eighteenth-century peasant is framed and executed for the murder of an aristocrat's wife (photograph by John Haynes; from David L. Hirst,* Edward Bond, *1985; Thomas Cooper Library, University of South Carolina)*

ROSE. You're a slave but you don't know it. My mother *saw* her chains, she's had marks on her wrists all her life. There are no signs on *you* till you're dead. How can yer fight for freedom when yer think you've got it? What happens to people like you? It's a circus! The clown kicks the mongrel and it licks his boots. He kicks it harder and it rolls on its back an' wags its tail—an' all the dogs laugh. Yer won't go. If there was a chance he'd put yer a mile underground an' chain yer to the wall. Then yer'd be free: yer'd know what you are.

The alliance between the aristocratic Are and the industrialist Hardache is an intrinsic and essential part of the treatment of the themes of the play and its historical counterreferencing. As Bond observed in 1981 (as quoted in *Bond on File*):

> The second half [of the play] concerns the creation of a new Lord Are—his alliance with Hardache was the

invests and labours to make that possible, and gambles on having to do it, ought not to be called civilization.

With this play, Bond enters into a darkly poetic, epic piece of theater; in nine relatively short scenes with such titles as "Work," "The Army," and "No one can willingly give up the name of human," his characters emerge and engage as a means by which Bond can express his concerns. The unborn child, named and viewed as "the Monster," serves as both a viewing and distancing frame through which the audience may respond to the central themes and concerns of the play.

In the opening sequence of the play, the Monster and his Mother speak directly to the audience in a dramatic language rich and painful with the overwhelming sense of loss and the destruction of what Bond writes about in his commentary on the plays as "radical innocence." The nine scenes expose the unjust, oppressive power relations and the inequalities that arise from, and are endemic to, the conditions in which nuclear war might happen. The global violence and destruction unleashed upon the world is seen as the complex but direct consequence of the rationale of capitalism as an economic system and social organization centered on exploitation: a world in which social morality is psychological oppression, sanity is insanity, and justice is barely disguised, brutal, ruling-class self-interest.

The whole of *The War Plays* lasts seven hours. Bond was originally going to codirect the trilogy with Hamm for the Royal Shakespeare Company at the Barbican in 1985. He left the project in frustration at the standard of the work, however, and described the ensuing Royal Shakespeare Company production as disastrous. He has frequently said that it is one reason why he turned his back on British theater. *The War Plays* was later produced in Paris at the Odéon (Théâtre de l'Europe) in 1995, and there have been many productions in Europe of the whole or parts of the trilogy.

Continuing through the mid and late 1980s, Bond wrote other significant plays, such as *Jackets* (performed in 1989, published in 1990), in which a woman has two sons, one a soldier and the other a political revolutionary (terrorist). This short play examines the interweaving of public and personal narratives within a dramatic site of urban violence and political unrest. The decade came to a close with the production of *September* (performed in 1989, published in 1990) at Canterbury Cathedral, a seemingly unlikely setting for a Bond play. Most of his subsequent work has been written specifically for performance by community and children's groups or for Le Théâtre National de Colline in Paris, because, in Britain at least, Bond has become disillusioned with the general theatrical climate. In an unpublished 6 May 2003 letter he commented:

usually, except at a few places in France, my plays are misdirected and misacted. It's as if I write for piano and the plays were performed on a triangle. But this isn't anyone's "fault"–it's simply that the site of theatre (which is also the–historically shifting–place "where theatre comes from") has to be rediscovered. In this strict sense, there is no theatre in this country and none is possible. It is really "substitute theatre"–at best the theatre of symptoms.

However, he has continued to be produced in mainland Europe, with premieres of *In the Company of Men* (published in 1990, performed in 1992) and *Coffee* (performed in 2000) at Le Théâtre National de la Colline. In France he is the second most-produced writer, after Molière.

Bond's desire to communicate to young audiences has been synonymous with his working relationship with the Birmingham-based Theatre in Education company, Big Brum ("Brum" is a well-known English colloquialism for Birmingham, Britain's second-largest city after London). Bond's plays for young audiences include *Eleven Vests,* first presented by Big Brum Theatre on 7 October 1997 prior to a regional tour of the play. The two parts of this work explore the events surrounding a character known only as the Student. The Student is a teenager who, in the opening part of the play, has been marginalized and subsequently expelled for the seemingly random destruction of other pupils' property. He remains quiet throughout a long interrogation from his Head Teacher, who tries various strategies of inducement and judgmental criticism to try to understand the teenager's actions. Ultimately, the events lead to the Student murdering the Head Teacher with a knife. This dramatic enactment was a powerfully disturbing and controversial echo of an incident that shocked British society in 1995, the knifing to death of a well-respected head teacher, Philip Lawrence, by one of his former pupils outside the school gates. In the 1997 Methuen edition of the play, Bond comments: "I'm sure Philip Lawrence was as innocent as his killer. But in one shape or another, violence always returns to unleash its wrath on the ignorance that creates it. And we are an ignorant society."

In the second half of the play, based again on an actual incident (this time from World War II), the audience sees the Student on active service in the army at war, as he murders two defenseless prisoners of war. The juxtaposing of the violence enacted outside the school gates with the state-sanctioned violence of war conveys several challenging issues to young audiences: principally the nature of violence within human life and the social and ideological site in which that violence is enacted. In an interview published in the supporting educational materials of the text, Bond recalled once again the impact that national military service had on him and its relevance to *Eleven Vests* and an accompanying short play for teenagers, *Tuesday* (first published in 1993):

> I didn't like what I saw and I wanted to write about it. There was an atmosphere of violence and coercion. It was a very brutal society. Various ranks were given very unjust powers over other people and if you were an offender you could be publicly humiliated, degraded and brutalised. I saw in it an image of the society outside the army.

Tuesday, which was a BBC Schools television drama (and marked Bond's debut as a television director), and other plays such as *At the Inland Sea* (performed in 1995) were written against the background of a major centralization of the English educational system by the Thatcher government, with the introduction of a national curriculum for all schools. This national curriculum was based on a "core subjects" structure in which creative subjects such as drama, music, and art were viewed as being of secondary and minor importance.

Through the late 1990s and into the early years of the twenty-first century, Bond's plays continued to attract interest and sometimes scandal with productions in France and Germany. After a May 1999 German premiere, *The Crime of the Twenty-First Century* was produced on 9 January 2001 at Le Théâtre National de la Colline, Paris, and was directed by Alain Françon. On the title page of the 2003 Methuen version of this play, Bond has placed the infamous quotation from Thatcher, "There is no such thing as society." This statement both epitomizes the core ideological values of the Thatcher period (1979–1990) and provides a parallel for a dramatic site in which Bond envisions the implications of a brutally autocratic, postmodern State. The setting of the piece is, to quote from Bond's stage directions, "an open space that was once a yard or two or three ground-floor rooms. It is in the 'clearance,' a vast desert of ruins that stretch for hundreds of miles and have been flattened to discourage resettlement." This landscape of material devastation and decay might be analogous to post-atomic Hiroshima, Belsen, or the war-ravaged, occupied territory of Palestine or Iraq. However, this dramatic site is more powerfully and significantly a scenic political metaphor rather than literal. Four characters inhabit this bleak landscape: two men, Grig and Sweden, and two women, Hoxton and Grace, mother and daughter. These characters speak in a savagely clipped, idiomatic, postholocaust dialect:

> GRIG. Let the effect a' the water wear off. Why's the road so straight? Army made it when they flat all this. White makes yer eyes run. Left me place—no permit. Wife was dyin. Scream—yer could count the interval, regular as a siren. . . . Death takes its time to tell its tale:
> 'ers was cancer. When it reached 'er mouth she scream as if it's arguing with 'er in 'er throat.

Reduced to the most elemental scavenging for water, food, and shelter, these characters engage in fearful bartering and sharing of the most basic ingredients for survival. Beyond these brutally marginalized "clearances" (redolent of ethnic cleansing) the characters speak of a wider world of prisons, punishment camps, suburbs, and ghettos where an undefined privileged class continues to enjoy the residual benefits of consumer capitalism—particularly cars. It is a world in which—bereft of any social organization other than an army that continually patrols the clearances, dismembering and blinding those from the marginalized underclass such as Sweden—only the desperately fundamental instinct for survival holds sway. Yet, even under such conditions, Bond creates characters who, though stripped of all socially and culturally conditioned attitudes, still seek some fundamental form of social interaction. Hoxton gives water, and subsequently shelter, to Grig when he arrives at her minimal lodging; and at the conclusion of the play, when Sweden has murdered both Hoxton and Grace, Grig offers him the possibility of human company, care, and protection. As in all of his work, Bond is not arguing that beneath the surface of human civilization lies a primitive, savage human nature; rather, *The Crime of the Twenty-First Century* advocates once again the rational imperative of justice and shows that, without the sanity of art and imagination to inform the struggle for justice, only the "rationale" of the insane atrocities of Auschwitz and Dubrovnik will continue to prevail. The crime of the twenty-first century is the formal, systematic denial (enforced by the use and threatened use of nuclear weapons) of the possibility or need for human society.

Bond's remorseless questioning of human existence and human society has been pursued through a new language of political theater that centers upon the human and humanity. Bond believes that political theater needs to reoccupy—or discover—a new ontological site of human existence. For Bond, this quest necessitates a continuous critiquing of postmodern capitalism and the discovery and implementation of a new site for theater and a new methodology of performance within that site. Yet, Bond has remained largely unperformed on the main theater stages of his native country since the early 1990s; in fact, he has refused to permit his plays to be staged by the Royal Shakespeare Company, the Royal Court Theatre, and the National Theatre, in spite of their requests to do so. This omission reflects the profound changes in the political and cultural climate in Britain within Bond's working life and also Bond's concern that his plays should be properly understood in the process of their rehearsal and production. Bond says that the most important thing about his career is the necessity he has found of concentrating his work on the European mainland. He frequently comments that he finds it ironic that a British dramatist must go abroad to save British theater from what he sees as its present tragedy.

Bond continues to produce new work and was involved on a movie project based on *In the Company of Men,* adapted by director Arnaud Desplechin, Emmanuel Bourdieu, and Nicolas Saada, titled *En jouant "Dans la compagnie des hommes."* It premiered at the Cannes Film Festival in May 2003.

Have I None, a play originally produced at the Big Brum Theatre in 2000, was staged by Le Théâtre National de la Colline in 2003–2004 and revised in 2005. In 2004 Bond wrote *Born,* the third play of the "Colline Triptych," which is dedicated to Françon. *Born* is scheduled to premiere at the Avignon Drama Festival in 2006, which will also feature the first stage production of the 2000 radio play *Chair* and a revival of the Colline production of *Have I None.* There will also be a production of Bond's farce *The Balancing Act,* first staged by Big Brum Theatre in 2003.

In 2000 Bond published a major book on drama and social theory, *The Hidden Plot: Notes on Theatre and the State.* L'Arche, Bond's French publisher, published the French translation in 2003. Among his controversial critical assessments in this volume is his judgment of Bertolt Brecht's work as "the theatre of Auschwitz."

Bond frequently holds actors' workshops in Belgium and France under the title "Acting the Invisible Object." From actors' exercises developed in such a workshop in Vincennes in 2003, Bond created the play "The Short Electra," which is among the plays to be published by Methuen in 2005. These workshops are part of a radical new form of theater, the fullest description of which can be found in David Davis and David Allen's 2005 study, *Edward Bond and the Dramatic Child: Edward Bond's Plays for Young People.* This volume also examines Bond's radical ideas on the nature of reason and imagination, which he considers as hitherto misunderstood. He is in the process of creating "a rational tragedy."

Two volumes of selections from Bond's notebooks were published in 2000 and 2001. In one entry dated 16 April 1980 he wrote:

> I find that my work is more than I had thought. I began writing simply as a criticism of certain things I saw around me and in praise of certain other things. I wanted to understand and so I had to analyse. I didn't at that time understand the implications this would have on my theatrical technique. I find it increasingly useless when an actor tries to find out how to play one of my roles by trying to understand his character. He must understand the whole play. What he has to act are the situations. . . . He shows us not a character acting but a character being formed . . . in interaction with the world.

Letters:

Edward Bond Letters, 5 volumes, edited by Ian Stuart (Chur, Switzerland & Philadelphia: Harwood Academic, 1994–2000).

Interview:

Brian Logan, "Still Bolshie After All These Years," *Guardian Unlimited,* 5 April 2000 <http://www.guardian.co.uk/arts/story/0,,177739,00.html>.

References:

Tony Coult, *The Plays of Edward Bond* (London: Eyre Methuen, 1977);

David Davis and David Allen, eds., *Edward Bond and the Dramatic Child: Edward Bond's Plays for Young People* (Stoke on Trent: Trentham Books, 2005);

Macolm Hay and Philip Roberts, *Bond: A Study of His Plays* (London: Theatre Quarterly Publications, 1980);

David L. Hirst, *Edward Bond* (London: Macmillan, 1985);

Stephen Lacey, *British Realist Theatre* (London: Routledge, 1995);

Michael Mangan, *Edward Bond* (Plymouth, U.K.: Northcote House, 1998);

Philip Roberts, *The Royal Court Theatre and the Modern Stage* (Cambridge: Cambridge University Press, 1999);

Roberts, ed., *Bond on File* (London: Methuen, 1985);

Richard Scharine, *The Plays of Edward Bond* (London: Associated University Presses, 1976);

Jenny S. Spencer, *Dramatic Strategies in the Plays of Edward Bond* (Cambridge: Cambridge University Press, 1992);

Ian Stuart, *Politics in Performance–The Production Work of Edward Bond, 1978-1990* (London: Peter Lang, 1996);

John Russell Taylor, "British Dramatists: The New Arrivals, no. 5: Edward Bond," *Plays and Players,* 17 (August 1970): 16–18;

Simon Trussler, *Edward Bond* (Harlow: Longman, 1976).

John Boyd
(19 July 1912 – 2 July 2002)

Roy Connolly
Edge Hill College

PLAY PRODUCTIONS: *The Blood of Colonel Lamb,* Belfast, Circle Theatre, 1967; revised as *The Assassin,* Dublin Theatre Festival, Gaiety Theatre, 29 September 1969;

The Flats, Belfast, Lyric Theatre Belfast, 15 March 1971;

The Farm, Belfast, Lyric Theatre Belfast, 10 May 1972;

Guests, Belfast, Lyric Theatre Belfast, 25 September 1974;

The Street, Belfast, Lyric Theatre Belfast, 8 March 1977;

Facing North, Belfast, Lyric Theatre Belfast, 6 March 1979;

Speranza's Boy, Belfast, Lyric Theatre Belfast, 21 April 1982;

Summer Class, Belfast, Lyric Theatre Belfast, 19 November 1986;

Wuthering Heights, adapted from Emily Brontë's novel, Belfast, Lyric Theatre Belfast, 17 February 1988;

A Christmas Carol, adapted from Charles Dickens's novella, Belfast, Lyric Theatre Belfast, 7 December 1988;

Ghosts, translation by Boyd and Louis Muinzer of Henrik Ibsen's play, Lyric Theatre Belfast, 1 March 1990;

Round the Big Clock, Belfast, Lyric Theatre Belfast, 5 November 1992.

John Boyd (courtesy of the Linen Hall Library, Belfast)

BOOKS: *The Assassin* (Belfast: Linen Hall Library, 1969);

The Flats (Belfast: Blackstaff, 1973);

Collected Plays, 2 volumes (Belfast: Blackstaff, 1981, 1982)—comprises volume 1, *The Flats* [revised], *The Farm,* and *Guests;* and volume 2, *The Street* and *Facing North;*

Mrs Martin's Man, adapted from St. John Ervine's novel (Belfast: Linen Hall Library, 1983);

Out of My Class (Belfast: Blackstaff, 1985);

The Middle of My Journey (Belfast: Blackstaff, 1990).

PRODUCED SCRIPTS: *Out of Exile,* radio, BBC Northern Ireland, 22 October 1947;

Letters from Abroad, radio, BBC Northern Ireland, 8 December 1948;

The Mother, adapted from Michael McLaverty's short story, radio, BBC Northern Ireland, 22 January 1953;

Mrs Martin's Man, adapted from St. John Irvine's novel, radio, BBC Northern Ireland, 13 July 1954;

The Younger Son, adapted from Ronald Mason's novel, radio, BBC Northern Ireland, 4 December 1957;

Last Voyage, radio, BBC Northern Ireland, 17 July 1959;

The Rise of the City, radio, BBC Northern Ireland, 24 November 1961;

Evening with a Gunman, radio, BBC Northern Ireland, 17 September 1963;

Strictly Private, radio, BBC, 7 April 1964;
All Fall Down, radio, BBC Northern Ireland, 13 September 1965;
The Assassin, radio, BBC, 8 October 1969;
The Flats, radio, BBC, 26 January 1971;
The Flats, television, RTE, 26 September 1975;
Noble Doctor, radio, BBC, 27 March 1979;
Alchemy, radio, BBC, 9 January 1981.

OTHER: *Lagan,* edited by Boyd, 1943–1946;
Lagan: A Miscellany of Ulster Writing, edited by Boyd (Belfast: Lagan, 1945);
"Ulster Prose," in *The Arts in Ulster: A Symposium,* edited by Sam Hanna Bell, Nesca Robb, and John Hewitt (London: Harrap, 1951), pp. 99–130;
Threshold, edited by Boyd, 1972–1993;
A Needle's Eye: The Lyric Players Theatre, Belfast 1979, edited by Boyd and Mary O'Malley (Dublin: ELO Press, 1979);
The Selected Roy McFadden, edited by Boyd (Belfast: Blackstaff, 1983).

SELECTED PERIODICAL PUBLICATIONS–UNCOLLECTED: "Poems Reprinted," *Community Forum,* 4, no. 1 (1969);
"John Boyd," *Campus Carrier* (Berry College, Georgia), (20 April 1995): 10–14.

John Boyd is widely held to be the originator of the modern Irish "Troubles" play. He was the first dramatist to attempt documenting day-to-day life in Belfast after the outbreak of violence in the late 1960s, and over the next twenty years he produced a body of work that offers a panoramic yet detailed vision of a city in conflict. Furthermore, this vision quickly entered both the local and national consciousness, as Boyd–alone among Northern Irish writers–had his plays consistently produced at Belfast's premier theatrical venue, the Lyric Theatre Belfast (also called the Lyric Players Theatre), and also found an audience for his work in the Republic and beyond Ireland. Boyd's career as playwright runs almost exactly parallel with the period of the Troubles (1968–1994), and his contribution to, and impact on, local theater history is unrivaled. His work documents a period of civil and social disintegration and offers an intimate insight into the way of life of the people living amid these conditions. Moreover, in retrospect, as the critic Louis Muinzer has suggested, Boyd's achievement in bringing Northern Ireland to the stage is all the more significant, as his plays pull into focus a way of life–the Troubles, the "poor neighborhoods," the "people of the countryside," and "the milieu of the local artist"–that is now fast fading from view.

Boyd's plays confront contemporary issues in a direct and impartial manner and thus often display the method of a documentary or feature writer. They are, nevertheless, infused with a sense of passion and social concern, with a compulsion to tell people about the society in which they live and to communicate a social vision. Rather than succumb to received historical readings of Ireland, Boyd seeks to expose what he sees as the false consciousness of unionism and nationalism. Thus, rather than engage with and be diverted by the national debate, he directs his sympathies toward the struggle of the working class. His message is given with striking simplicity in his most famous play, *The Flats* (performed in 1971, published in 1973): "What's the difference, tell me, between a working-class Catholic family an' a working-class Protestant family? Well there's none, is there? What's the difference between the Falls Road and the Shankhill Road?"

Boyd was born at 9 Templemore Avenue, a small redbrick house in Ballymacarrett, east Belfast, on 19 July 1912. He was the eldest of three children–one brother and one sister–from a working-class Protestant family. His grandfather was staunchly Loyalist and a member of the Orange Order; his father, Robert, was a locomotive engine driver; and his mother, Jane (née Leeman), was a housewife. Boyd remembers his childhood fondly in his two autobiographies, *Out of My Class* (1985) and *The Middle of My Journey* (1990), but his youth was not without discord. Belfast experienced successive economic depressions in the early part of the century, and his parents' home was far from happy. His mother was an alcoholic who would regularly pawn the family's belongings in order to buy wine, and his father would punish her with severe beatings.

Boyd was educated at Mountpottinger National School, the Royal Belfast Academical Institution, and the Queen's University Belfast, where he earned an M.A. in 1938. He was married on 11 November 1939 to Elizabeth, two months after Prime Minister Neville Chamberlain's declaration of war on Germany. The Boyds had three children: a daughter, Deirdre–who was born in 1941 at the Royal Victoria Hospital in Belfast during an air raid by the Luftwaffe–and two sons, Brian and Gavin. Boyd worked as a teacher before joining BBC Northern Ireland as "talks" director in 1946. In this position, he produced radio broadcasts featuring virtually all of Northern Ireland's leading authors and also worked closely with well-established literary and theatrical figures from the Republic and England. Thus, he developed relationships, and in some cases close friendships, with artists including Philip Larkin, John Hewitt, Frank O'Connor, Louis MacNeice, Denis Johnston, Brian Friel,

Sam Thompson, Sam Hanna Bell, Joseph Tomelty, Tyrone Guthrie, and Seamus Heaney. At the BBC he acquired a reputation for quiet determination and efficiency and became one of the most influential regional producers in the corporation. He also took his first steps toward establishing a literary reputation in his own right with adaptations of short stories and novels—such as Michael McLaverty's *The Mother* (1953), St John Irvine's *Mrs Martin's Man* (1954), and Ronald Mason's *The Younger Son* (1957)—for radio broadcast. At the same time, he was working on his own early forays into playwriting with the radio scripts *An Evening with a Gunman* (1963) and *All Fall Down* (1965). These examinations of local political tensions offered some intimation of the concerns that dominated his later, more renowned works.

During the 1950s and 1960s Boyd also had extensive contact with live theater, in a professional capacity as reviewer for the BBC and, as a pastime, as a devotee of local cultural activity. Belfast had many professional and amateur theater companies, and Boyd was an active patron of popular and avant-garde venues alike. This patronage extended across well-established producing houses such as the Empire Theatre, the Group Theatre, and the Grand Opera House, as well as what were then up-and-coming venues such as the Arts Theatre and the Circle Theatre, which catered to special-interest groups. As a theatergoer, Boyd reserved his most enthusiastic support for the Lyric Theatre Belfast, which was committed to poetic drama and in particular the works of William Butler Yeats. Boyd's own work was in marked contrast to "the poetic," but the influence such material exerted over his imagination and sense of what theater might be was, nevertheless, considerable. Later he joined the Lyric Theatre Belfast as literary adviser (1971), honorary director (1972), and editor of its associate journal, *Threshold* (1972–1993); in these positions he acted as custodian of the artistic standards of the theater for more than two decades.

Boyd's career writing for the stage began as he approached retirement from the BBC at the end of the 1960s. In *The Middle of My Journey* he notes: "I was 55 years old, and beginning when most playwrights have already written a body of work and are maybe thinking of retiring." His first play, *The Blood of Colonel Lamb*, was produced by the Circle Theatre in 1967. Two years later, a revised version of the same play, retitled *The Assassin*, was presented at the Dublin Theatre Festival. Boyd's concern with confronting events in contemporary Northern Ireland, however, proved an obstacle to a professional production in Belfast; in future work he exercised a careful self-censorship in order to ensure production of his work in his native city. In making that desire a priority, Boyd is in marked contrast to his southern counterparts and to fellow Ulster writers such as Friel, whose preference during the 1970s lay with giving their work its first airing in Dublin or London.

Boyd's reputation as a dramatist was secured on a Sunday night in January 1971, when his play *The Flats* was given a rehearsed reading at the Lyric Theatre Belfast. It was sufficiently well received to prompt a full production. Two months later, the play was staged before packed houses and immediately hailed as a "minor Irish classic" (*Belfast Telegraph*, 16 March 1971). *The Flats* addressed the issue of sectarianism in a direct fashion and in the local idiom. It came to define the genre of the modern Troubles play, was translated into several languages, and has been produced throughout the world.

The Flats is above all a play of its time. It depicts events that had been taking place in a variety of working-class areas throughout Belfast in the early 1970s. In the months before its presentation, Protestant youths had mounted a sustained attack on Unity Flats (the building that provided the inspiration for the play), and there had been rioting on the Shankhill Road, on the Catholic Ballymurphy estate, and in the Ardoyne. The opening of the play is, consequently, infused with the zeitgeist of the era. The stage directions call for the songs and slogans of the civil-rights marchers, familiar throughout the province, to be sung before the curtain rises: "One man, one vote . . . An end to Special Powers . . . We want more jobs and houses . . . Ireland for the Irish." The use of local sound is complemented by the use of other local detail. The stage directions pick out the defining features of the Belfast landscape and condense them into the scenography. A cyclorama is called for at the back of the stage with images of "Catholic and Protestant church steeples," "barrack like factories," "backstreets," "the hills of Antrim," and, looming over all, "the yellow shipyard cranes." The combined effect of these sights and sounds would have been to tap the sense consciousness of a Belfast audience.

At the start of the play, a radio announcer tells the audience that the residents of the flats are under siege by a mob from the Shankhill Road. However, rather than develop this strand of plot, Boyd undercuts the political with the domestic and the dynamics of family life. The Donellans, the occupants of the ground-floor unit of the flats, are the focus of attention. They first appear in their kitchen—the setting traditionally depicted by playwrights of the Ulster Literary Theatre (1902–1939) as the hub of the Irish household. The narrative does not dwell on a single character's case history or a theme; instead, it explores a range of story lines, simultaneously presenting the drama of the returning relative from England, the disaffected youth, and the fledgling love of the native and the foreigner.

Boyd places a cross-section of characters around the family to create a microcosm of the community. The army is represented by Phil, a soldier on duty outside the flats. The Protestant perspective is supplied by a neighbor, Monica Moore. The rationalist position is presented by Brid Donnellan's fiancé, Sean. And the opportunist is also on hand, as Adam, a local street vagrant who has developed survival instincts enough to know that it is advisable to carry both Union Jacks and Irish tricolors. The characters provide a range of political perspectives and communicate some of the attitudes present in the community. Each of them expresses and defends a position. Amid these exchanges, it emerges that the principal tension is between the mother, Kath, and the son, Gerard Donnellan. Gerard offers a broad justification for the actions of a gunman: "We're fighting for the right to live—to live as human beings . . . The fact we're Catholics is irrelevant . . . the Protestants should be alongside us fighting for the same ideals." Kath provides moral perspective against this point by arguing that political inequity is no defense for shootings and murder. Gradually, though, her position is overrun. The events overtake her appeals for restraint, as guns are smuggled into her home, and the flat is commandeered first by the local political activist, Malachi, and then by the army. The frustration of being caught up in the crossfire of the militarists is explicit. Kath, and the ordinary people like her, are revealed as the victims of the Troubles.

Boyd is, however, circumspect about attributing blame. The characters are shown to be victims of circumstance, less accountable for their actions than the external forces that act upon them. His analysis of the political situation continually emphasizes this point:

> The objective facts are that Catholics are discriminated against—in housing, in jobs, in culture, in everything. But the Protestant workers are discriminated against too—they both have the same enemies . . . They have—they've the same enemies as workers all over the world—the ruling capitalist class who fester their minds with mythologies that keep them apart and blind them to the truth. Mythologies falsely called religion. . . .

Boyd emphasizes common, unifying elements. Phil, the soldier, is marked by his worthiness and good nature. Monica, the Protestant presence in the play, is "beautiful" and "somehow unawakened." Furthermore, Boyd is at pains to make clear that intimidation cuts both ways, with Monica announcing to Kath: "We're going to leave the Flats, Mrs Donnellan? Sure we're the only Protestants left here. We'd have left a long time ago if it hadn't been for you an' Mr Donellan helpin' us."

Boyd's description of the genesis of *The Flats* (included in the first volume of his *Collected Plays*, 1981) gives a clear indication of his distance from the material:

> I was walking along the streets near the centre of town one afternoon when I stopped and stood for a long time studying Unity Flats. It isn't an attractive building, but that day it looked forbidding with British soldiers on guard. I began to wonder about the lives of the people inside. And that was the germ: one family, one day, one death.

Similarly, in the play, the audience encounters the characters from a distance. They see the large view, a depiction of social tragedy. The climax of the play typifies this approach. When Monica rushes into the street and is shot dead, the audience is not told who is responsible. Instead, they are invited to recognize her death on a human level and be suitably disaffected with the political prevarications of all. A Protestant girl and her would-be lover, a British soldier, become the martyrs of the play. Phil is the final focus of attention as he delivers an elegy over Monica's body. Boyd invites audiences to recognize the vacuity of the situation. His point is a simple one: in the factional dispute resulting in the intimidation of the residents of the flats, it is not the militarists but the innocent who suffer.

At the time the play premiered, the *Irish News* (a paper that aligns itself with the nationalist community) found fault with this approach (as has more recent criticism that operates from a similar perspective), noting that in being fair to everyone, Boyd "destroyed the play's vitality" (*Irish News*, 22 March 1971). But such attacks, mounted from a safe spatial and temporal distance, can be disingenuous. They fail to bring to attention the hazardous political context in which the play appeared. Certainly, *The Flats* marked a considerable advance on previous works on the sectarian theme, such as Sam Thompson's *Over the Bridge* (1959), which had offered an even more oblique account of the political tensions in the North. *The Flats* thus represented an important and transitional achievement in the history of theater in the province. It also drew the attention of the Arts Council of Northern Ireland to the potential of theater as a platform for social exchange.

With *The Flats*, Boyd established a precedent for documentary drama and brought local themes and preoccupations to the forefront of Northern Irish theater. Furthermore, the play met with an enthusiastic

Cover for Boyd's second autobiography (1990), in which he chronicles the beginning of his playwriting career when he was fifty-five years old (Jean and Alexander Heard Library, Vanderbilt University)

public response, which demonstrated that audiences wanted to see plays that addressed, in a recognizable idiom, a situation with which they were familiar. Boyd's next play, *The Farm* (performed in 1972, published in 1981), built upon this foundation. The play, which Boyd described in a program note for the premiere production as a "realistic study of family relationships," again has a documentary tone. It explores the life of the Protestant middle classes and borrows another familiar Irish setting–the family farm. The play evokes issues with ready appeal for local audiences, with its principal conflict concerning whether the farm of the title should be inherited by the venerable and rugged MacCann or by MacCann's effete son and daughter-in-law, Ed and Dolly. Several other story lines–chiefly a ménage à trois and a subplot about Irish American emigration–run alongside the main plot, while the local vagrant, Ben, provides persistent comic interjections. In his introduction to the first volume of Boyd's *Collected Plays* Daniel Casey identifies the method at work:

> *The Farm* is of course a dramatic allegory that could, in the hands of a lesser talent, degenerate to a type of child's play, but Boyd is too clever to let that happen. He introduces psychological conflicts–divided loyalties, marital rifts, and broken dreams–that balance the dramatic action.

The principal appeal of the work lay in its depiction of MacCann ("Mac"), a working-class hero and indeed Boyd's personification of the working masses: masculine, intelligent, and principled. He was a character ideally suited for one of Belfast's best-known and most venerated actors, Louis Rolston, a former shipyard worker idolized by many among the local theater community. On several occasions, therefore, Mac is given opportunity to flaunt his physical prowess or parade his political commitment, a commitment so avid that during the course of his career in the shipyard, Mac turned down the opportunity for promotion many times.

The vitality of the play was increased by its immediacy. It retains the context of the modern Troubles depicted in *The Flats* and offers several swipes at the rigid political context, with Ben expressing traditional sectarian values: "Yer right there! Not an inch!" and "What we have we hold!" Mac offers angry resistance to such thinking:

> Ye're like one o' them ventiloquist's dummies. (Makes a gesture with his mouth and his hands, of a fish opening and closing–the dummy) What we have we hold! What have you? What have ye to hold? Nothin' but a lot o' oul' slogans ye picked up when you were a nipper. An' now ye're near dotin' yer cacklin' them out like an oul' rooster! Have a titter o' wit, man, an' don't go scavengin' in the gutter.

Again, Boyd projects his political philosophy, using Mac to articulate his worldview: "The land belongs to the people. . . . The land to the farmers, the sea to the fisherman, the factories to the workers . . . That's the way of it."

The play, a fusion of soap opera and political tract, proved a successful mix. It provided audiences with both topical commentary and local issues with which they could readily identify. *The Farm* received an enthusiastic reception. The response iterated the point, to local writers and producers alike, that there was a desire for plays about contemporary Ulster.

Guests (performed in 1974, published in 1981), Boyd's next play, is difficult not to interpret as a direct critique of the middle-class, theatergoing public. A reviewer for *The Irish Press* (30 September 1974) went as far as to suggest that many of the characters were drawn from people locally known. *Guests* imaginatively reconstructs the ambience of a middle-class theater coterie made up of teachers, artists, and writers from the University area of Belfast. The central character is Maria Carey, and her home is the meeting place of the group. The play is set on a summer evening during a party held to commemorate Maria's late husband. In an article published in *Campus Carrier* in 1995, Boyd cited his intention as documentary: "All that takes place in the two hours of the play took place in reality. The people who were there, were real people. They were friends of mine." It soon emerges that this social clique is riddled with discontent. The characters have few redeeming features; their conversation is vacuous, and their arguments are petty and opinionated. They are all in decline. Charley, the journalist, has become an alcoholic. Tegwen, the professor's wife, is an adulteress. Matt, the would-be artist, is an embittered failure. The consequence of this decline is a pervasive sense of world-weariness, which psychically reflects the mood elsewhere in the city, and this sense is heightened by explicit references to the state of Belfast:

> Don't stay it's like livin' in a graveyard—only not as quiet nor as safe . . . Everbody's gettin' out. What is there for anybody? Nothin'. Nothin'. No life, no joy, no art . . . nothin' . . . it's all a pretence. They don't want to live! And they don't want anybody else to live . . . they've never lived . . . they're afraid.

The first part of the play is taken up with exploring the interpersonal relationships of the characters. At the end of the first act, a bomb explodes outside a nearby pub. When the second act opens, the audience learns that the local barman has been killed. Even this event, however, does not jar the other characters from their self-absorption. The people carry on as before—the same animosities and relationships in evidence. There is even the suggestion that the party should continue. Commentary at the time reminded people involved in the theater that a degree of self-examination was not out of place (*The Irish Press*, 30 September 1974). And in terms of the indifference "real people" show for the Troubles, the play is a telling indictment of middle-class introspection.

Boyd's next two plays, *The Street* (performed in 1977, published in 1982) and *Facing North* (performed in 1979, published in 1982), were directed at the working-class Ulster public rather than more privileged audiences. *The Street,* set in 1930s Ballymacarett, was Boyd's most overtly political play since *The Flats*. It is the story of two brothers, Bob and Willie Downie, living amid the economic depression of the 1930s. Bob contends with an alcoholic wife and a hostile father-in-law, while Willie and his wife, Elsie, campaign for social reform, acting as the voice of socialism, as did Gerard in *The Flats* and Mac in *The Farm*. Boyd's message is reinforced by juxtaposing a story of alcoholism alongside the campaign for better social welfare, thus providing the implication that social problems will be eradicated when the workers unite.

However, according to some commentators, Boyd's work had begun to lose its impetus. His concern with social issues was still evident, but critics argued that his "politicising" was now working to the detriment of his plays. The *Sunday News* response (13 March 1977) to *The Street* circumscribed the growing criticism of his "one note opera": "*The Street* at the Lyric has little to recommend it. A poor show from start to finish, where tags like 'boring' 'trivial' 'provincial' 'unenlightened' 'pedestrian' and 'badly constructed' are none of them out of place." In this unfocused criticism lay a deep malaise and disaffection with Boyd's output.

With *Facing North,* Boyd returned to the preoccupation of his earliest play and promised to confront the sectarian issue head-on. He introduces the Grant family, prosperous Northern Irish Protestants and the owners of a local factory. The Grants are at the center of a dispute at the factory over a worker displaying a Union flag, in spite of the risk of provocation to Catholic workers. This play appeared to be a more frank portrait of the tensions in the North. In this case it is not an anonymous authority but the proletariat who is the instigator of dispute. An allegory is established, with the factory as a microcosm of Northern Ireland. The dispute threatens to escalate into a walkout or even riot. Principle is at stake, as one of the protagonists articulates: "Hasn't a worker every right to put up a Union Jack in front of her machine. What's the harm in that eh. . . . This is still a free country." The Protestant and Catholic workers present opposite and intractable positions: to Protestant workers, the Union Jack is a symbol of loyalty, while to Catholics, its presence is a mark of imperialism that fosters a mood of intimidation, or, at the least, one of sectarian inequity. This dispute encapsulates the wider social problem.

After setting up the scenario, Boyd finds a solution. A ballot is held in which the workers vote against displaying emblems in the workplace. The potentially irresolvable is resolved. Again he presents the thesis that conflict can be resolved when the workers unite. Having presented its parable, *Facing North* loses focus altogether. In the latter part of the play a kidnapping subplot comes to the fore, and the play culminates in melodrama rather than debate over the implications of what has taken place.

The public response to *Facing North* was mixed. Audiences turned out in droves, but reviews suggested the critical community was developing Troubles-play fatigue. Signs of disaffection with the genre had been evident as early as 1973, when the *Racine Journal* had published audience criticism of Belfast's "heavy" and "morbid" theater programming (15 April 1973). And by January 1987 a critic for the *Belfast Telegraph* was suggesting this perspective had come to dominate: "Oh no not another play about the Troubles . . . What other dramatic variation could there possibly be on this theme?" Trudy Kelly, one of Belfast's best-known actors, summed up the mood among her fraternity by exclaiming in the press in 1988 that she hoped "never to do another 'troubles' play" (*The Irish Press*, 22 April 1988).

In confronting matters of topical and local interest, Boyd moved Northern Irish theater a considerable distance forward. Most notably, he encouraged discussion on the question of the relevance of theater to the community it serves. Boyd's work initiated a much delayed self-examination among Belfast theater of its own complacencies and affectations. These traits are thoroughly set out in the declarations of Belfast's principal theater personalities of the 1950s, 1960s, and 1970s, such as the founder of the Lyric Players, Mary O'Malley, who spent her entire career preoccupied with the Yeatsian desire to impart the style of the aristocracy to the Irish public, and thus rather than building on indigenous artistic strengths, ultimately confounded herself, and public alike, in pursuit of a theater that would Hellenize the local middle classes.

Boyd died in July 2002, two weeks short of his ninetieth birthday. In the last two decades of his life, he completed three additional original plays, though with less vivid social intentions than his previous work. After reflecting in the second volume of his *Collected Plays* (1982) that the genre he had established had "been well and truly turned over," he spoke of turning to "open up a new field." Taking up this theme, his following plays—*Speranza's Boy* (performed in 1982), a biography of Oscar Wilde; *Summer Class* (performed in 1986); and *Round the Big Clock* (performed in 1992)—displayed a newfound interest in dramatizing relationships between culture, art, and personality. This change of direction offered some insight into his long-held sympathy with the cause of individuals such as O'Malley and his concomitant frustration with the audience to whom he had so long directed his attention. He summed up this feeling in a 1973 article for *Threshold*:

> So we in Ireland—the country of Yeats and Shaw, O'Casey and Synge, the Abbey Theatre in Dublin and the Lyric Theatre in Belfast—have little to congratulate ourselves on. Few theatres; a dearth of first class directors; unemployed actors in Dublin; a scarcity of actors in Belfast; middle class audiences (in the main) that relish the ready laugh, the unthinking, "unfeeling" immediate response; managements unwilling to experiment, being too timid (a timidity born perhaps from poverty and the fear it engenders): these are some of our handicaps.

There was, then, some unresolved tension in Boyd's aspiration for the public theater relative to his actual output. However, in giving some indication of the potential for theater to deal with contemporary issues (and raising public expectation that it would do so), he had a significant impact on the local theatrical landscape, and, in particular, on the activities of the successive generation of Ulster writers.

In his latter career, the encouragement and incentives Boyd gave to new writers were as significant as his own literary output. He was instrumental in ensuring the appointment of two writers in residence at the Lyric Theatre—the community activist Martin Lynch, and the Lyric's first female writer in residence, Christina Reid. These writers took their place in a dramatic tradition stretching back to the Ulster Literary Theatre. Following Boyd's lead, these writers were able to think more freely and creatively about their locale—traditionally the strength of Ulster drama, but until Boyd began writing, largely set aside in the cause of more esoteric aims. With increasing confidence, the new generation of writers—exemplified by Lynch, Reid, and Lynch's collaborator Marie Jones—were able creatively to move Northern Irish theater forward to deal with issues pertinent to local theater audiences. Embodied in this activity was a clear concern with what a theater might contribute to community education. In encouraging this endeavor, John Boyd may well have exceeded his own modest and self-effacing aims, as expressed in volume two of his *Collected Plays*: "My hope is that when these dark days pass I may have left some record, in dramatic form, of how things seemed to me, here, during my time."

Interviews:

Irish News, 15 March 1971;

"Fine Words with a Message for All," *Belfast Telegraph*, 16 March 1971;

Sunday Independent, 21 March 1971;

Belfast Telegraph, 2 September 1972;

Ian Kirk-Smith, "John Boyd: The Thoughtful Man Who Cannot Retire From Thinking," *Belfast Telegraph*, 21 April 1982.

References:

Roy Connolly, *The Evolution of the Lyric Players Theatre* (Lampeter: Edwin Mellen, 2000), pp. 167–199;

Lynda Henderson, "The Green Shoot: Transcendence and the Imagination in Contemporary Ulster Drama," in *Across the Roaring Hill: The Protestant Imagination in Modern Ireland,* edited by Gerald Dawe and Edna Longley (Belfast: Blackstaff, 1985), pp. 205–207;

E. Lehmann, "England's Ireland: An Analysis of Some Contemporary Plays," in *Studies in Anglo-Irish Literature,* edited by Heinz Kosok (Bonn: Bouvier, 1982), pp. 88–96;

Christopher Morash, *A History of Irish Theatre 1601–2000* (Cambridge: Cambridge University Press, 2002), pp. 245–246;

Louis Muinzer, "Between the World & the Stage: A Tribute to John Boyd," *Fortnight* (April 2003): 19;

Christopher Murray, *Twentieth-Century Irish Drama: Mirror Up to Nation* (Manchester: Manchester University Press, 1997), pp. 189–190;

Frank Ormsby, ed., *Northern Windows: An Anthology of Ulster Autobiography* (Belfast: Blackstaff, 1987), pp. 138–145;

Lionel Pilkington, "Theatre and Cultural Politics in Northern Ireland: The *Over the Bridge* Controversy, 1959," *Éire-Ireland,* 30 (Winter 1996): 76–93;

Pilkington, *Theatre and the State in Twentieth Century Ireland* (London: Routledge, 2001), pp. 203–209.

Papers:

A collection of John Boyd's papers is part of the Lyric Theatre Archive at the Lyric Theatre Belfast.

Ian Brown
(28 February 1945 –)

Susanne Kries
Universität Potsdam

PLAY PRODUCTIONS: *Antigone,* adapted from Sophocles' play, Glasgow, Lecture Theatre of John Street Union, 25 November 1969;

Mother Earth, by Brown and others, Edinburgh, Traverse Workshop Company, 30 July 1970;

The Bacchae, adapted from Euripides' play, Brighton, Gardner Arts Centre, January 1972;

Positively the Last Final Farewell Performance, ballet scenario, Glasgow, Close Theatre Club, 29 June 1972;

Carnegie, Edinburgh, Royal Lyceum Theatre, 19 April 1973; Pittsburgh, Pa., Old Post Office, 7 May 1976;

Rune, choral text, Stirling, MacRobert Centre, 27 April 1973;

Rabelais, readings, Edinburgh, Lodge Canongate Kilwinning, 23 August 1973;

The Knife, Edinburgh, Royal Lyceum Theatre, 27 August 1973;

The Fork, London, Contemporary Arts Theatre, 6 April 1976;

New Reekie, Edinburgh, Traverse Theatre, 21 April 1977;

Mary, Edinburgh, Royal Lyceum Theatre, 18 August 1977;

Runners, London, Bush Theatre, 14 June 1978;

Mary Queen and the Loch Tower, Cairnhill Primary School, 23 April 1979;

Pottersville, documentary reading, Stoke-on-Trent, Victoria Theatre, 19 May 1982;

Joker in the Pack, Alsager, Alsager Arts Centre, 17 October 1983;

Beatrice, Edinburgh, Traverse Theatre, 11 April 1989;

First Strike, by Brown and others, London, Soho Theatre, 1990;

The Scotch Play, Perth, Perth Theatre, 23 February 1991;

Bacchai, translated from Euripides, Cardiff, Memory Lane Cake Works, 16 October 1991;

Wasting Reality, Perth, Perth Theatre, 23 October 1992;

Margaret, Edinburgh, Gateway Theatre, 15 February 2000;

Ian Brown (courtesy of Ian Brown)

A Great Reckonin, Perth, Perth Theatre, 10 November 2000.

BOOK: *Poems for Joan* (Perth: Perth Theatre, 2001).

OTHER: *Poems,* in Visual Arts/Poetry Exhibition, Alsager, Alsager Gallery, September 1981;

"Plugged into History: The Sense of the Past in Scottish Theatre," in *Scottish Theatre Since the Seventies,* edited by Randall Stevenson and Gavin Wallace (Edinburgh: Edinburgh University Press, 1996), pp. 84–99;

"Antigone–A Scots/Welsh Experience of Mythical and Theatrical Translation," by Brown and Ceri Sherlock, in *Unity in Diversity? Current Trends in Translation Studies,* edited by Lynne Bowker and others (Manchester: St. Jerome, 1998), pp. 25–37;

Antologija Suvremene Škotske Drame, edited by Brown, translated by Ksenija Horvat (Zagreb: Hryatski centar ITI-UNESCO, 1999);

Kulturniy turizm: Konvergentsiya kultury i turizma na poroge XXI veka, edited by Brown, Vivien Andersen, and Valery Gordin (St. Petersburg: St. Petersburg State University of Economics and Finance, 2001);

Journey's Beginning: The Gateway Theatre Building and Company, 1884–1965, edited by Brown (Bristol, U.K. & Portland, Ore.: Intellect Press, 2004).

SELECTED PERIODICAL PUBLICATIONS–UNCOLLECTED: "Cultural Centrality and Dominance: The Creative Writer's View–Conversations Between Scottish Poet/Playwrights and Ian Brown," *Interface,* 3 (Summer 1984): 17–67;

"'Scots Wha Ha'e' – The Politics of Literary Language," *Interface,* 3 (Summer 1984): 68–77;

"Problems of Defining 'Standard' Scots: Some Linguistic and Theatrical Aspects," *Zeitschrift für Anglistik und Amerikanistik,* 43 (1995): 291–302;

"When Theatre Was For All: The Cork Report, After Ten Years," by Brown and Rob Brannen, *New Theatre Quarterly,* 12 (1996): 367–383;

"A New Spirit Abroad in the North: MacDiarmid and Cultural Identity in Contemporary Scottish Theatre," *Etudes Ecossaises,* 5 (1998): 111–125;

"Scots and Welsh: Theatrical Translation and Theatrical Languages," by Brown, Ceri Sherlock, and John Ramage, *International Journal of Scottish Theatre,* 1 (December 2000) <http://arts.qmuc.ac.uk/ijost/Volume1_no2/I_Brown.htm>;

"Renaissance Re-examined: The Diversification of Scottish Playwriting, 1970–2000," by Brown, Ramage, and Ksenija Horvat, *Revista Canaria de Estudios Ingleses,* 41 (2000): 13–27;

"Referendum to Referendum and Beyond: Political Vitality and Scottish Theatre," by Brown and Ramage, *Irish Review,* 28 (2001): 46–57;

"Thrawn Themes and Dramatic Experiment: W. Gordon Smith and the Paradoxes of Creative Iconoclasm," *Scottish Studies Review,* 4 (2003): 98–120.

Ian Brown's plays are marked by a surprising lightness of touch in treating serious topics such as human relationships, liberation and social oppression, moral obligations toward self and society, and the subtle mechanisms of social control and manipulation. During more than thirty years of playwriting, he has also explored the presentation of history and historical figures onstage, especially figures representing his native country, Scotland. Deeply influenced by the late extravaganzas of George Bernard Shaw and by post-Brechtian Epic Theater, with its alienating effects, Brown has sought to deconstruct and subvert long-established myths, though without being narrowly political or tied to easy moral responses. To achieve this aim, he has explored several dramaturgical techniques–such as his use of comic effects, often verbal in nature–to modify the perceptions and preconceptions of the audience. Several of his plays blend different theatrical traditions (such as pantomime, music-hall, or burlesque). Besides examining the interaction of history, ideology, myth, and dramaturgy, and the greater questions of reenacting and rearranging history, Brown has also dealt with issues of contemporary society, such as the abuse of drugs in sports (in *Runners,* performed in 1978). Brown uses English as well as Scots, and some of his plays exist in both languages.

Ian James Morris Brown was born in Barnet, an outer borough of London, on 28 February 1945, the son of Bruce Beveridge Brown and Eileen Frances Scott Carnegie, who were then on war service in London. His father was a department store manager and his mother a nurse. Ian Brown is the oldest of three children and has one sister, Sheena, and one brother, Gavin. After living in Dunfermline in Scotland from 1945 to 1951, the family settled in Alloa, Clackmannanshire, which is the place Brown considers his hometown. He was educated at Dollar Academy and Edinburgh University, where he graduated in 1967 with an honors M.A. in English literature and language. Brown has followed three professions: not only has he been a practicing playwright since 1969, but he has also worked as a teacher in both secondary and higher education and as a cultural manager. In 1968 he married Judith Ellen Sidaway, with whom he has two children: Emily, born in 1972, and Joshua, born in 1977. (The couple later divorced.)

Besides its strong focus on Scottish history and various contemporary issues, Brown's work also shows his interest in classical traditions. His first produced play, written during the time he worked as a schoolteacher, was a version in Scots of Sophocles' *Antigone* (performed in 1969). It is, however, a free rendering of the story. The political aspects of Sophocles' play gain less prominence in Brown's version. In Sophocles' play, Creon stresses that the interests of the state have to secure priority over personal wishes, such as Antigone's desire to bury her brother Polynices, who is declared a traitor. However, this attitude gradually gives way to a selfish pride (hubris) that challenges the gods. Brown's *Antigone,* unlike the Greek tragedy, starts with a lament that sets the mood for the entire play. It recounts Oedipus's incestuous relationship with his mother and his subsequent self-mutilation, followed by a scene showing his two sons, Eteocles and Polynices, quarrelling over the rule of Thebes. The struggle for peace and love in a world overshadowed by the tragic family background of the kin of Oedipus is the actual subject of the play.

From the beginning, Creon's role is that of a patronizing despot, especially since in Brown's play Polynices' rights to the throne of Thebes are stated as an argument against his assumed treason. In the Greek tragedy, the collision of religious and political principles, forcefully performed by Antigone and Creon, also appears as a collision of the sexes, since performing the funeral rites was the duty and privilege of the women in ancient Greece. Less concerned with the aspects of power, Brown's *Antigone* includes, however, an important addition: the hope for change in the future, embodied by the pregnancy of Antigone's sister, Ismene, whose lover was one of Polynices' officers. What Antigone has given up by defending her integrity and ideals to the death—namely marriage with Creon's son Haemon and the children that might have arisen from the bond—finds continuation in Ismene. Brown's *Antigone* emphasizes the family realm, even replacing the figure of the leader of the citizens of Thebes with a nurse. Creon does not achieve wisdom in the end and does not publicly admit his transgression of divine rule by burying Polynices in all honor. All that remains is an old man who still thinks he has done the right thing for the people, the right thing to achieve political but not personal peace—as Teiresias says, "the peace o haein rule an order, and bein empty."

The Bacchae (performed in 1972), like Brown's adaptation of *Antigone,* is based on ancient mythology, this time centering on the Olympian deity Bacchus (or Dionysus), the god of wine and ecstasy. As in Euripides' tragedy (and in an earlier treatment of the myth in Aeschylus's *Pentheus*), Dionysus returns to Thebes to take revenge on the city and its rulers, who have denied his existence and his origin. Dionysus appears as the embodiment of change—born twice, to a mortal and a god, and a leader of an all-female cult associated with sexual licentiousness. Although most of the time Brown closely follows Euripides' play, he changes Euripides' general message by shifting the emphasis from revenge to the liberating influence of the deity and release from oppressive moralities. The focus is not so much on the individual, since humans do not appear as the gods' playthings (as in Euripides), but on society in general and on Dionysus's achievements in bringing down philistine narrow-mindedness. Dionysus's last words in the play are "I am inevitable," stressing once again the necessity of change within societies.

Carnegie (performed in 1973) embodies many of the characteristics of Brown's art as a playwright. It is a biographical play, the story of the successful multimillionaire and philanthropist Andrew Carnegie, who made his immense fortune in steel and related industries. Brown himself is related to Carnegie through his mother's family. Carnegie's Scottish roots are represented by his mother, a speaker of broad Scots, and his memories of holidays in Scotland. The narrator of the play is Uncle Sam, who invites the audience to his "school of business," teaching them sardonic lessons on how to be a successful businessperson. The examples are all taken from Carnegie's life and reveal a businessman who enjoys presenting himself as an idealistic self-made man but who appears at the same time as a ruthless exploiter not only of his working-class employees but also of his business associates. Carnegie's idealized and romantic view of industrial capitalism is presented in several speeches throughout the play, many in the historic Carnegie's own words, beginning with "I believe absolutely in the dignity of Labour. I pity the son of the idle rich for he has money but has not earned it." However, his pompous statements are immediately contrasted by songs and choral sequences of Carnegie's exploited workmen, who reshape Carnegie's assertions and mold the audience's understanding of the historical figure, who is probably best-known for his benefactions for cultural purposes and educational institutions. Carnegie appears as the embodiment of the American dream—the Scottish "lad o'pairts" who managed to climb to the top of the social ladder. He is presented as a man of principle, a figure full of pathos but without emotion, a man whose moral values seem to be staged rather than lived. His grand speeches and his generous donations are countered by his obviously small-minded private life.

From 1973 to 1975 Brown served as the founding chairman of the Scottish Society of Playwrights; he later chaired it twice more, from 1984 to 1987 and from 1997 to 1999. In 1975 he also received an M.Litt. from Edinburgh University. His two next plays, *The Knife* (performed in 1973) and *The Fork* (performed in 1976), were written as companion pieces and are inextricably linked, although they have never been presented as a double bill despite plans by the Traverse Theatre in Edinburgh to do so. Had this plan come to fruition, it would have involved a coupling of roles for each actor. *The Knife* is set in a Scottish high school, where the stern atmosphere throws ominous light on Scotland's educational system. "Poor wee bugger probably doesn't know which is left and which is right," the liberal teacher Grant comments when a pupil is criticized for drawing the margins on the wrong side of the page. Brown depicts an educational system calculated to subject rather than to inspire young people. Of the four teachers presented in *The Knife,* Grant is the only one to leave his job in the end, unable to bear the oppressive and unjust atmosphere anymore. The pupils do not

Jeff Chiswick and Anthony Sher in the 1976 Contemporary Arts Theatre premiere of Brown's The Fork, *in which two gay men, one of whom hides his sexuality and one of whom is open about it, meet over tea at their landlady's flat (courtesy of Ian Brown)*

gain a voice during the entire play—their stories are told by the staff alone, who at different times turn the audience into their classes by addressing them directly. But aggression is not restricted to the staff, as one boy stabs his classmate with a knife, an act of violence that nevertheless seems to take even the teachers by surprise.

Stabbing also features in *The Fork*. The protagonists are two gay men (Tom and Jack), who have just met; Jack's landlady (Maggy), who earns her living as a prostitute; and a young man (Sandy), who is ignorant of Maggy's profession and tries to get involved with her. The four characters meet accidentally at Maggy's flat, where they share tea, chips, and conversation. Tom, whose reminiscences of Greece the others initially take as an innocuous report of a prolonged holiday, reveals to the others that he once planted a bomb in Athens to oppose the totalitarian Greek regime. Though the bomb did not explode, both he and his Greek lover were imprisoned and tortured, and his friend was finally beaten to death. Tom's open attitude toward his own sexuality provokes Sandy and embarrasses Jack, until Sandy pierces Tom's hand with a fork.

In both plays, aggressors and victims merge. This merging is exemplified by the figure of the disillusioned teacher Pringle in *The Knife,* whose energy is being drained by his fruitless efforts to become a good teacher while simultaneously conforming to a flawed system, and Jack in *The Fork,* who refrains from publicly acknowledging his homosexuality and accepts the offensive jokes his colleagues make at his expense.

Grant in *The Knife* and Tom in *The Fork* are the two characters who refuse to accept the current system. They are willing to stand up to make a difference. The most striking coupling, however, appears in the form of the stern teacher Masterton in *The Knife* and the student Sandy in *The Fork*. Despite their differences in age and experience, they evidently share a belief in traditional, stern moral values: Sandy calls Greece the very cradle of civilization, thus revealing his romantic lack of interest in the problem of the dictatorship as compared to past achievements, while Masterton obviously enjoys using the belt (the "popular educator") to keep up discipline in a Scottish educational system that he claims is the best in the world. Apart from their generally conservative attitudes toward life, they share a belief in traditional gender roles and the appropriateness or otherwise of male and female behavior. They are both insecure, socially and emotionally. Brown's two plays are also tales about male aggression; but since Tom, who calls himself a terrorist, is gay, the author avoids easy stereotyping. The final complexity of the two plays lies in the fact that the ages of the male characters make it clear that the actor who plays the authoritarian Masterton would play the closeted Jack; the defeated Pringle would play the activist Tom; and the radical Grant would play the repressive Sandy.

In 1976 Brown left Dunfermline College, Edinburgh, where he had taught as a lecturer in drama since 1971, and turned toward cultural management, working with the British Council as assistant representative for Scotland (1976–1977) and then as assistant regional director in Istanbul (1977–1978). The setting of Brown's next play, *New Reekie,* produced in 1977, is a flat in the south side of Edinburgh. The story revolves around Douglas Allan, a university lecturer about thirty years of age; his wife, Jenny; her brother, Andrew Innes; and three of their friends. The action takes place on two consecutive weekends when Douglas brings home a friend, Rob, from whom he had not heard in a long time. The play explores male-female relationships, the ups and downs of coupledom, and the occasional extramarital affair. The main focus is on the shy Jenny, who has on more than one occasion been betrayed by her self-obsessed husband and finally manages, with the help of Rob, to liberate herself from Douglas and her own ideas about an ideal marriage. Douglas's efforts at the end of the play to restore his grip on their relationship show that he has not understood at all why Jenny left him in the first place, and still less why she came back.

With his next play, *Mary* (performed in 1977), Brown returned to writing in Scots, though he continued to write plays in English as well. The version of *Mary* produced in 1977 in Edinburgh was in fact the author's second rendering of the theme. The first version, written in 1967, presented Mary, Queen of Scots, in a traditionally romantic way and was rejected by Brown himself, despite the offer of Bill Bryden, who was then associate director of the Royal Lyceum Theatre in Edinburgh, to produce it in 1974. Brown had by then turned to more Shavian and post-Brechtian styles of presenting history and felt the need to rework the original script. Like his other plays presenting Scottish characters, *Mary* was written to address a wider audience, not distinctly a Scottish one. The play features a Mary who is both aware of her role in history and yet unable to step out of the circumstances leading to her own death. Brown achieves this exploration of historical role-playing by repeatedly exchanging the characters' roles within the play. For example, Lord Darnley, Mary's second husband, appears as Mary in the first scene, introducing the queen immediately after John Knox's mocking call to prayer, "For whit you are aboot te see, may the Lord mak you truly gratefu," with the words:

> I'm going to be Mary, Queen of Scots. Really. Well, for the time being. Now, some people have said I'm a gay queen. And some people have said I'm a romantic queen. And some people have even said I'm the great Catholic martyr.

The only person who plays just one role is the actress playing Mary, who thus appears as what Brown called a "dramaturgic anchor." This image of constancy is, however, illusory, since Mary does not appear in a fixed position but is constantly redefined by the people interacting with her.

Not only are the characters' roles exchanged, but the scenes switch between naturalism and highly theatrical modes: Shakespearean, music-hall, and melodrama are three of the forms parodied to meaningful effect. Mary appears as a victim both of circumstances and historical mythmaking, forsaken by her fellow countrymen and unable to see through the intentions of the political and religious interest groups that surround her. By deconstructing her role in history, Brown manages to make her appear as an ordinary, all-too-human, and naive person. Some absurdly humorous scenes—for example, the mock trial of the deceased rebel Lord Huntly, whose corpse is presented to the court in a coffin (as it in fact was, under an obscure Scots law)—are used to alienate the audience from the scenes presented. The female victim in a male-dominated, repressively puritan society is put at the center of a play that reveals itself, however, as being more a play about manipulation by men than one about a woman. The audience cannot empathize with Mary, since she appears as too naive and empty of real personality, but can sympathize with her as a victim of power politics. Her identity is shaped by the men surrounding her. "Who cares about me?" Mary asks at the end of the play; "I could be neither public nor private." Indeed, even the representation of the Mary/Darnley courtship, usually presented in terms of romance, is embodied in a pastiche scene in the style of Noel Coward.

In the 1980s Brown headed the performing arts division and then the drama studies degree program at Crewe and Alsager College. He also ran the Alsager Arts Centre before being seconded to act as secretary to the influential Cork Enquiry into Professional Theatre in England (1985–1986). He was then one of the more successful drama directors of the Arts Council of Great Britain (1986–1994) and increased both the number of properly funded touring companies and the public funding of regional and national building-based theater companies. Even more significantly, not a single theater building was closed during his tenure at the Arts Council.

Beatrice (performed in 1989), Brown's last play of the 1980s, differs in many ways from his previous work. First and foremost, it consists of a long monologue uttered by the protagonist, Beatrice de Planissoles, who has just been released from captivity by the Inquisition. Beatrice is an historical figure but different from Brown's other historical portrayals. The story of her life clearly strikes a more personal note than that of Carnegie or Mary, Queen of Scots. Though her experience is personal, she stands for the multitude of women who had to (and have to) face the forces of the male-dominated church and state. The still-disoriented Beatrice identifies the stage as her "home," inviting the audience to listen to her thoughts and feelings outside the public sphere. Brown establishes Beatrice's individuality on the basis of the material recorded by the Inquisition as presented in Emmanuel Le Roy Ladurie's book *Montaillou* (1975). The account of her experience in a mountain community in the south of France during the thirteenth and early fourteenth centuries reveals her as an individual who somehow survived ecclesiastical and state oppression and as a woman who had to grapple with male hegemony and violence in a society where the only security women had came through marriage: "the men have sought the tidiness of dogma and authority and control." The fact that she repeats and comments on her confessions in front of the audience, reenacting them, draws the listeners directly into the story.

In 1991 Brown completed his Ph.D. through Crewe and Alsager College of Higher Education (now part of Manchester Metropolitan University) with a dissertation titled "History as Theatrical Metaphor."

Moreover, he was made a Fellow of the Royal Society of Arts. The same year, the Perth Theatre company performed *The Scotch Play,* in which Brown blends the historical past with the present by combining two elements that are uniformly associated with Scotland: William Shakespeare's tragedy *Macbeth* (1606) and soccer. Not only does he present Harry Lauder (alias Macbeth, Thane of Glamis) as trainer of a small Scottish soccer team, Auchenwhinnie Star, and Duncan Yuill (alias Duncan, King of Scotland) as the manager of the club, but he also imitates the form of Shakespeare's play by writing blank verse. With the help of his wife, Grace, Harry succeeds in getting Duncan's job as manager of the team and is about to lead them to the cup final when Duncan, with the help of Stewart Duff (alias Banquo/Macduff), returns to regain his position. Brown's verbal humor is at its best when Harry, plotting against Duncan, starts a famous Shakespearean monologue rather mockingly with the words: "This is the shirt I see before me, / Fresh laundered and te hand. Come let me hold." Harry's increasing alienation (from his wife, the team, and Stewart) and his self-centeredness become evident linguistically, as he increasingly uses Standard English rather than Scots or Scottish English expressions. The name Harry Lauder is itself significant, since Scottish audiences will associate him with the famous music-hall entertainer by that name, who has been repeatedly seen as the ambiguous personification of Scottish life.

Wasting Reality (performed in 1992) addresses the problems of members of a family who are confronted with the death of a son or sibling. The setting is the flat of the deceased Michael on the south side of Edinburgh. His parents, Jock and Meg, and his sister Shona have begun clearing his flat, sorting out what to keep, what to give away, and what to dump. It slowly becomes apparent that Michael was gay and that he died of AIDS. The family members employ different strategies in publicly and privately dealing with Michael's death that also involve thinking about the public status of gay relationships and their acceptance. Later, Morag, the older of Michael's sisters, turns up to help but also to come to terms with her own feelings over Michael's life and death. To judge from her Christian background, she strongly disapproves of homosexuality. Moreover, Morag neither visited her brother when he became ill nor came to his funeral. The play evokes questions of guilt and responsibility, of public shame and personal sorrow. The discussion of Michael's death finally makes way for larger questions of family bonds, and the audience learns that Meg and Jock have separated some time ago, a reality with which their children have thus far been unable to deal.

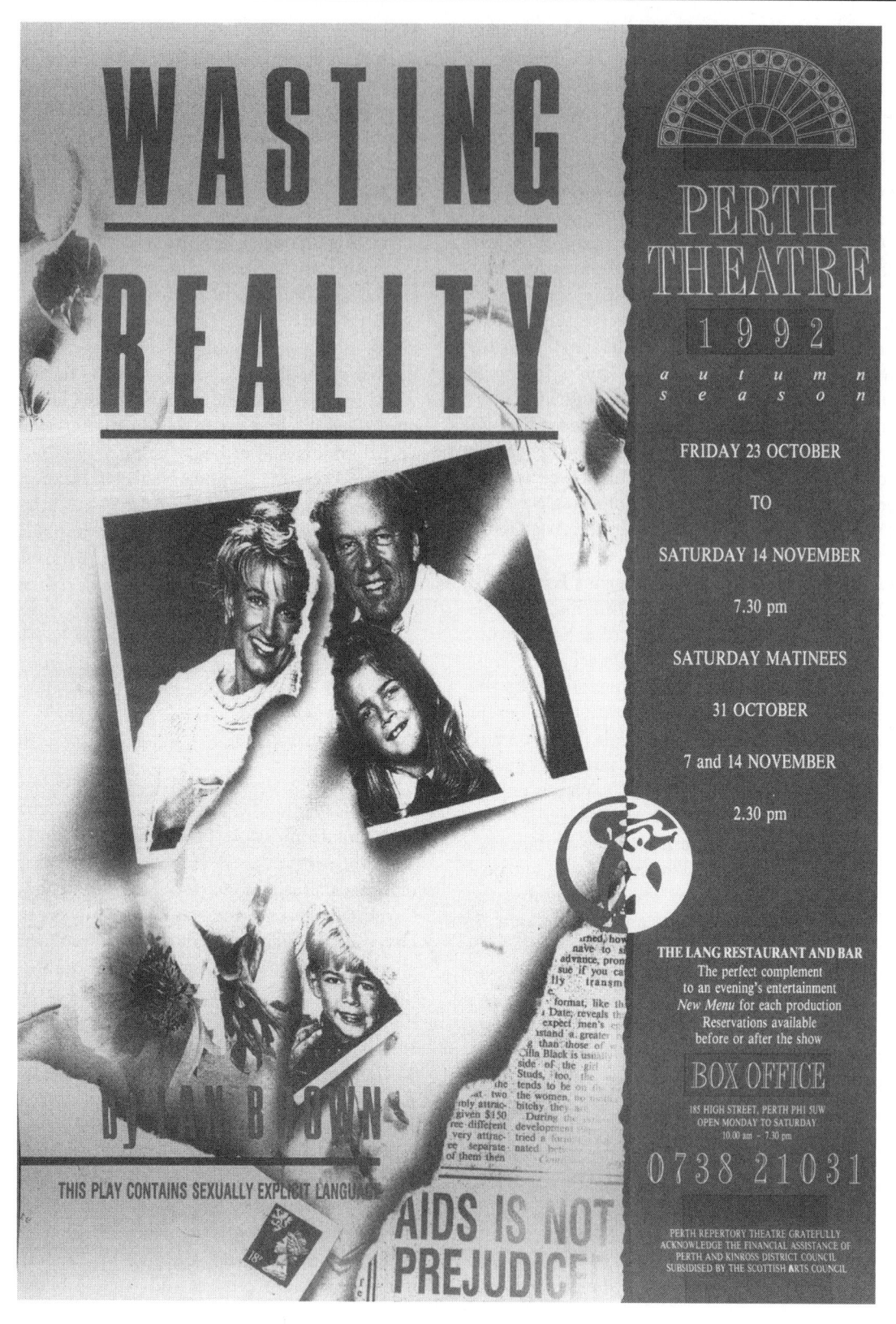

Poster for the premiere of Brown's play about a family's efforts to cope with the death of a gay son from AIDS (courtesy of Ian Brown)

Though Brown's play "Livingstone and Rowland" has never been produced, it shares similarities with the earlier *Mary* and *Carnegie*. The play was first written in 1982 on commission for Manchester Contact Theatre, but before it could be produced, the director left, and the new director wanted to move in a different direction. The protagonists, all famous Scots, also all spent most of their lives outside Scotland. The central issue of "Livingstone and Rowland" is, however, to show the processes of the manipulation of one's public image—a theme that already occurred in *Carnegie* and *Mary*—and mythmaking. John Rowland, who is better known as Henry Morton Stanley, is financed by James Gordon Bennett, publisher of the *New York Herald,* to find David Livingstone on his exploration and missionary activities in southern Africa and to sell his life story to the readers of the *Herald*. The so-called achievements of the "Livingstones" in history have for some time been criticized from a postcolonial point of view—and Brown assumes a similar position. Stanley's search for Livingstone becomes a quest for his own identity, one that he feels able to approve. In fact, in many instances, Stanley's ideas about how Livingstone's life should be staged immediately lead to some appropriate action by the latter. Again Brown uses different dramaturgical techniques to detach the audience from the protagonists' actions (songs, comic relief, mise-en-scène). The famous historical utterance by Stanley, "Doctor Livingstone, I presume," runs through the entire play. It is emptied of its mythical character since it is repeatedly used with different addressees; it is no longer unique to the situation of the actual meeting but appears as a well-rehearsed phrase. At the end of the play Stanley sings: "I used to be John Rowland / Now I'm Henry Morton Stanley / He used to be David Livingstone / Now he belongs to me."

Until 2002, Brown was based at Queen Margaret University College, Edinburgh—first as reader in drama (1994–1995), then as professor and head of the Department of Drama (1995–1999), director of the Scottish Centre for Cultural Management and Policy (1996–2002), and dean of the Faculty of Arts (1999–2002). In 1997 he married Nicola Dawn Axford.

After a gap of some eight years in Brown's playwriting, two new plays were performed in 2000: *Margaret* and *A Great Reckonin*. Despite the fact that Brown turns in both plays to the familiar matter of Scotland's history, his approach in dealing with the past is quite different compared to the earlier *Mary* or *The Scotch Play*. Both *Margaret* and *A Great Reckonin* are much less pessimistic with regard to the question of what chance there is of recovering the past. After all the years of deconstructing the ideological intent behind the very endeavor of writing history and of revealing the ways by which mythologies are forged, Brown chooses in these plays another approach to the presentation of his protagonists, one that centers more on the person than on his or her public portrayal. This change might have something to do with the contexts in which the plays were performed, since both *Margaret* and *A Great Reckonin* reflect in some ways Scotland's new political identity after the inauguration of the new Scottish parliament in July 1999.

Margaret is a play about politics at home and abroad, about the relationship between man and woman, and about the question of when passion turns into possession. Margaret, second wife to the Scottish king Malcolm Canmore (1031–1093), was later canonized for her life of devotion and piety—or perhaps because of her suppression of the Scottish Celtic church structures and forms. Both Margaret and Malcolm are known for their achievements as reformers, one in the area of state diplomacy and military strategy, the other for her success in uniting the Scottish church again with the practices of Roman Catholicism. The personal and public spheres emerge as one in Brown's play, and Margaret reflects more than once on her own role as woman and as stranger in the sphere of man's worldly ambitions. Since Malcolm and Margaret do not directly compete with each other, their relationship is portrayed as unusually understanding and mutually respectful. Underlying the play is a recognition that these powerful people form a close and lovingly cooperative relationship, although Margaret by the end begins to feel alienated from Malcolm's commitment to his diplomatic aims. In the end, both protagonists perish in pursuit of their main goals: Malcolm is killed in Northumberland, an area he tried to annex by different means more than once during his life, and Margaret dies worn out from devotion to her religious duty.

A Great Reckonin, produced later in 2000, is set in Perth in February 1437. A group of actors, the Royal Company of Guisers, arrives at the Royal Palace at Blackfriars Abbey only to find that two circumstances have rendered their prospect of performing before the king futile. First, Lent has just started, preventing them from delivering public entertainment; and second, their royal patron, King James I, has just been assassinated. Since the prospect of zero income will displease the rest of the troupe, which is already on its way to Perth with most of the company's accessories, the actors decide to seize the historic moment and make a play about the death of their former monarch. To obtain some information on King James, the actors turn to Andra, the king's butler, who takes them on a guided tour of the palace, reiterating the major events of the dead king's life. Andra becomes the director of the play but also acts as the historian. In effect Andra and the actors make explicit the dramatic rewriting of history that was implicit in the theatrical varieties adopted in *Mary,* a case made in a key article by Steve Cramer.

Andra tries to capture a version of the king by drawing attention to the circumstances of James's times and his contemporaries, a method that the artists find difficult to understand. "But whit has it got tae dae wi the life o James?" is the question repeatedly asked by the members of the troupe. They, at least initially, do not see a connection between the events in James's youth, his captivity at the court of the English kings Henry IV and V, or the recollection of the Battle of the North Inch—a clan trial-by-combat organized by James's father, Robert III—and the actual death of the king, although it becomes clear that those earlier events affected the politics of James's kingship. Andra's efforts are especially opposed by the troupe's leader, Shug Welsh. Shug, a bully who claims his inconsiderate behavior is a reflection of his artistic temperament, insists on playing James himself, despite his obvious lack of the musical talent for which James was famous. "I can match the script tae suit ma talents" is his answer to the troupe's open criticism. The audience thus becomes aware of the swift move from historic moment to historical interpretation and artistic reception. In the end, the actors are satisfied with the results, being now in a position to offer a play, however qualified its version of reality, to the rest of the company, whose arrival is expected the next morning.

Since 2002 Brown has worked as a consultant on cultural, theatrical, and educational matters, offering expert advice, for example, on behalf of the Council of Europe to the govenments of Armenia, Azerbaijan, and Georgia and conducting a wide range of studies for U.K. bodies. He is a member of the International Advisory Committee of the Eugene O'Neill Theatre Center in Waterford, Connecticut, and was one of the founders and sometime chairman of the Dionysia World Festival of Contemporary Playwriting in Veroli, Italy. Moreover, he has been a member of various advisory boards and panels both for arts funding bodies and for academic organizations. Brown has been an important influence in the development of modern Scottish theater. His critical writing and research have contributed to modern perceptions of Scottish language, culture, and theater. Finally, during his time at Queen Margaret University College he was a prime mover in raising the funds to refurbish the historic Gateway Theatre and then led the team who reopened the venue in 1999.

History and identity are the two recurring subjects of Ian Brown's writing, whether in his adaptations or his original work. His plays have received less academic critical comment than those of some of his contemporaries, in part because none of his plays has been formally published, a fact that also reflects the general difficulties of playwrights to find a publisher in the adverse climate for drama publishing that prevailed in Scotland at that time. The general newspaper response has been positive, noting Brown's theatrical inventiveness and willingness to address large or controversial issues. He is an innovative playwright, one who puts historical figures into a new context and creates contemporary characters who face painful and incisive questioning of received wisdom, inviting his audience to revisit long-cherished national stereotypes, secondhand values, and identity myths. Brown's principal historical protagonists derive from identifiable historical individuals, but they assume a representative status as exemplars of the human condition. He is the only heterosexual playwright besides Edward Bond to have a play presented by Gay Sweatshop *(The Fork)* and the only man, apart from David Edgar, to have one presented by the feminist troupe Monstrous Regiment *(Beatrice).* Moreover, his main strengths lie in his verbal and theatrical expressiveness, his puns and wordplays, his dramatic allusions, and the power and intimacy achieved through the use of Scots and English.

References:

Steve Cramer, "History, Ideology and Performance in Ian Brown's *Mary* and *A Great Reckonin',*" *International Journal of Scottish Theatre,* 3 (June 2002) <http://arts.qmuc.ac.uk/ijost/Volume3_no1/3_cramer_s.htm>;

Randall Stevenson and Gavin Wallace, eds., *Scottish Theatre Since the Seventies* (Edinburgh: Edinburgh University Press, 1996), pp. 84–99.

Caryl Churchill
(3 September 1938 –)

Frances Gray
University of Sheffield

See also the Churchill entry in *DLB 13: British Dramatists Since World War II*.

PLAY PRODUCTIONS: *Downstairs*, Oxford, Oriel College, 4 November 1958;
You've No Need to Be Frightened (Student Production), 1959;
Having a Wonderful Time, Oxford, Oxford University, 1960; London, Questors Theatre, 1960;
Easy Death, Oxford, Oxford Playhouse, 9 March 1961;
Owners, London, Royal Court Theatre Upstairs, 22 November 1972; New York, Mercer Shaw Theatre, 14 May 1972;
Schreber's Nervous Illness, London, King's Head Lunchtime Theatre, 6 December 1972;
Perfect Happiness, London, Soho Poly Lunchtime Theatre, 10 March 1974;
Objections to Sex and Violence, London, Royal Court Theatre Upstairs, 2 January 1975;
Moving Clocks Go Slow, London, Royal Court Theatre Upstairs, 2 June 1975;
Light Shining in Buckinghamshire, Edinburgh, Traverse Theatre, July 1976; London, Royal Court Theatre Upstairs, 27 September 1976;
Vinegar Tom, Hull, Hull Arts Centre, 7 September 1976;
Traps, London, Royal Court Theatre Upstairs, 27 January 1977; New York, Remains Theatre, March 1983;
Floorshow, by Churchill, David Bradford, Bryony Lavery, and Michelene Wandor, London, North London Polytechnic Theatre, October 1977; London, Theatre Royal, Stratford East, 18 January 1978;
Cloud Nine, Devon, Dartington College of Arts, 14 February 1979; London, Royal Court Theatre, 27 March 1979; revised, London, Royal Court Theatre, 30 August 1980; New York, Lucille Lortel Theatre, 18 May 1981;
Three More Sleepless Nights, London, Soho Poly Theatre, 9 June 1980; transferred to the Royal Court Theatre Upstairs, 5 August 1980;

Caryl Churchill (photograph © Guardian/David Sillitoe; from Richard Eyre and Nicholas Wright, Changing Stages: A View of British and American Theatre in the Twentieth Century, *2001; Richland County Public Library)*

Top Girls, London, Royal Court Theatre, 28 August 1982; New York, Public Theater, 28 December 1982; New York, Newman Theater, 24 February 1983;
Fen, Colchester, University of Essex, 20 January 1983; London, Almeida Theatre, 16 February 1983; New York, LuEsther Hall, 24 May 1983;
Softcops, London, Barbican Theatre, The Pit, 2 January 1984;
Midday Sun, London, Institute of Contemporary Arts, 8 May 1984;
A Mouthful of Birds, by Churchill and David Lan, Birmingham, Birmingham Repertory Theatre, 29

August 1986; London, Royal Court Theatre, 26 November 1986;

Serious Money, London, Royal Court Theatre, 21 March 1987; New York, Royale Theatre, 20 January 1988;

Ice Cream, London, Royal Court Theatre, 6 April 1989; performed with *Hot Fudge,* New York, Newman Theater, July 1990;

Hot Fudge, London, Royal Court Theatre Upstairs, 11 May 1989; performed with *Ice Cream,* New York, Newman Theater, July 1990;

Mad Forest, London, Central School of Speech and Drama, 25 June 1990; Bucharest, National Theatre, June 1990; London, Royal Court Theatre, 10 October 1990;

Lives of the Great Poisoners, Bristol, Arnolfini, 13 February 1991;

The Skriker, London, Cottesloe Theatre (Royal National Theatre), 20 January 1994; New York, Joseph Papp Public Theater, 1996;

Thyestes, adapted from Seneca's play, London, Royal Court Theatre Upstairs, 7 June 1994;

Hotel, Hanover, Schauspielhauss, 15 April 1997; London, The Place, 22 April 1997–comprises *Eight Rooms* and *Two Nights;*

Blue Heart, Bury St. Edmunds, Theatre Royal, 14 August 1997; London, Duke of York's Theatre, 17 September 1997–comprises *Heart's Desire* and *Blue Kettle;*

This Is a Chair, London, Royal Court Theatre Downstairs, 1997;

Far Away, London, Royal Court Jerwood Theatre Upstairs, 23 November 2000; transferred to Albery Theatre, 18 January 2001;

A Number, London, Royal Court Jerwood Theatre Downstairs, 23 September 2002.

BOOKS: *Owners* (London: Eyre Methuen, 1973);

Vinegar Tom (London: Theatre Quarterly Publications, 1978; New York: S. French, 1982);

Light Shining in Buckinghamshire (London: Pluto Press, 1978; New York: Theatre Communications Group, 1996);

Traps (London: Pluto Press, 1978);

Cloud Nine (London: Pluto Press, 1979; New York: S. French, 1979);

Top Girls (London: Methuen in association with the Royal Court Theatre, 1982; New York: S. French, 1982);

Fen (London: Methuen in association with Joint Stock Theatre Group, 1983; New York: S. French, 1984);

Softcops (London & New York: Methuen, 1984);

Plays One (London & New York: Methuen, 1985)–comprises *Owners, Traps, Vinegar Tom, Light Shining in Buckinghamshire,* and *Cloud Nine;*

A Mouthful of Birds, by Churchill and David Lan (London: Methuen in association with Joint Stock Theatre Group, 1986);

Softcops & Fen (London & New York: Methuen, 1986);

Serious Money (London & New York: Methuen in association with the Royal Court Theatre, 1987);

Icecream (London: Nick Hern, 1989);

Mad Forest: A Play from Romania (London: Nick Hern, 1990; New York: Theatre Communications Group, 1996);

Icecream with Hot Fudge (New York: S. French, 1990);

Plays Two (London: Methuen, 1990; New York: Routledge, 1990)–comprises *Softcops, Top Girls, Fen,* and *Serious Money;*

Churchill Shorts: Short Plays (London: Nick Hern, 1990; New York: Theatre Communications Group, 1990)–comprises *Three More Sleepless Nights, Lovesick, The After-Dinner Joke, Abortive, Schreber's Nervous Illness, The Judge's Wife, The Hospital at the Time of the Revolution, Hot Fudge, Not Not Not Not Not Enough Oxygen,* and *Seagulls;*

Lives of the Great Poisoners: A Production Dossier, by Churchill, Orlando Gough, and Ian Spink (London: Methuen, 1993);

Mad Forest: A Play from Romania and The Skriker: Two Plays (London & New York: Nick Hern/Fireside Theatre, 1993);

Not Not Not Not Not Enough Oxygen and Other Plays, edited by Terry Gifford and Gill Round (Harlow: Longman, 1993)–comprises *Seagulls, Not Not Not Not Not Enough Oxygen,* and *The Judge's Wife;*

The Skriker (London: Nick Hern, 1994; New York: Theatre Communications Group, 1994);

The After-Dinner Joke and Three More Sleepless Nights, edited by Lib Taylor (Cambridge: Cambridge University Press, 1995);

Thyestes, adapted from Seneca (London: Nick Hern, 1995);

Blue Heart (London: Nick Hern, 1997; New York, Theatre Communications Group, 1998)–comprises *Heart's Desire* and *Blue Kettle;*

Hotel: In a Room Anything Can Happen, by Churchill, Gough, and Spink (London: Nick Hern in association with Second Stride, 1997; New York, Theatre Communications Group, 1997)–comprises *Eight Rooms* and *Two Nights;*

Plays Three (London: Nick Hern, 1998; New York: Theatre Communications Group, 1998)–comprises *Icecream, Mad Forest, Thyestes, The Skriker, Lives of the Great Poisoners,* and *A Mouthful of Birds;*

This Is a Chair (London: Nick Hern, 1999; New York: Theatre Communications Group, 2000);

Far Away (London: Nick Hern, 2000; New York: Theatre Communications Group, 2001);

A Number (London: Nick Hern, 2002; New York: Theatre Communications Group, 2003).

PRODUCED SCRIPTS: *The Ants,* radio, BBC Third Programme, 27 November 1962;

Lovesick, radio, BBC Third Programme, 8 April 1967;

Identical Twins, radio, BBC Radio 3, 21 November 1968;

Abortive, radio, BBC Radio 3, 4 February 1971;

Not Not Not Not Not Enough Oxygen, radio, BBC Radio 3, 31 March 1971;

Schreber's Nervous Illness, radio, BBC Radio 3, 25 July 1972;

The Judge's Wife, television, BBC2, 2 October 1972;

Henry's Past, radio, BBC Radio 3, 5 December 1972;

Perfect Happiness, radio, BBC Radio 3, 30 September 1973;

Turkish Delight, television, BBC2, 22 April 1974;

Save It for the Minister, television, BBC2, 26 July 1976;

The After-Dinner Joke, television, BBC1, 14 February 1978;

The Legion Hall Bombing, television, BBC1, 22 August 1978 (Churchill removed her name from the credits after some passages were censored);

Crimes, television, BBC1, 13 April 1982;

Fugue, television, Channel 4, 26 June 1988.

OTHER: *The Ants,* in *New English Dramatists 12,* edited by Irving Wardle (Harmondsworth, U.K.: Penguin, 1969), pp. 89–103;

Objections to Sex and Violence, in *Plays by Women 4,* edited by Michelene Wandor (London: Methuen, 1985), pp. 13–53.

Now established as one of the most important contemporary British playwrights, Caryl Churchill is often grouped with the dramatists of the late 1960s who revitalized and reshaped British theater, not only in terms of their political subject matter but also in terms of their chosen venues and company structures. While this connection is an accurate reflection of both her importance and her socialist perspective, the trajectory of her career is remarkably different from that of contemporaries such as Howard Brenton or David Hare. While the male dramatists of the period generally proceeded from university to the founding of a fringe theater company and thence to the major subsidized playhouses, Churchill's path was fragmented and complex, marked by several major shifts in direction.

Churchill was born in London on 3 September 1938. She was an only child; her mother was a model and actress, and her father, Robert Churchill, was a cartoonist. When she was ten the family moved to Montreal, Canada, where she was educated at the Trafalgar School. She returned to England to study at Lady Margaret Hall, Oxford, in 1957, and finished her degree in English in 1960, just as the first wave of British postwar playwrights was beginning to make its presence felt. While this development may have prompted her to write several pieces for the stage, which received student productions, her own dramaturgy was shaped more by radio than the theater, and her first professional radio production, *The Ants* (1962), originally envisaged for television, was submitted to the BBC Third Programme on the advice of her agent, Margaret "Peggy" Ramsay. *The Ants* was also included in the Penguin *New English Dramatists* volume covering radio drama in 1969. What made *The Ants* outstanding was not so much the youth of the author—Churchill was twenty-four—as a remarkable clarity of design that gives it an unusual authority. The story of a child who cannot articulate his feelings about either the war that occupies the headlines or the corrosive breakup of his parents, and who joins his grandfather in the destruction of an ants' nest he had formerly loved to watch, reflects preoccupations that recur throughout Churchill's work: the interrelation of the personal and the political; the ways in which the silenced struggle to find expression; and the idea of alternative worlds, both utopia and dystopia.

Churchill married the barrister David Harter in 1961, and between 1963 and 1969 they had three sons. She claimed in Catherine Itzin's *Stages in the Revolution* (1980) that the years she spent at home with the children "politicized" her. They were also instrumental in her early choice of medium. Radio has, from the outset, offered women opportunities to experiment and work. Its large output and relatively low profile mean that an author's gender is not emphasized. As plays are rehearsed and recorded at speed, the writer can work almost entirely from home; and, in a life filled with differing responsibilities, a play that is structured in small, often vividly contrasting, scenic units can be easier to build.

Because a radio play has no embodied form, it is also a medium in which the line between the abstract and the concrete can be blurred; ideas are colored by the voice that speaks them; and scenes of vigorous action derive their strength from the movement they create within characters rather than from spectacle. In Churchill's *Abortive* (1971), for example, a husband and wife reflect on her recent abortion; their thoughts seem to be drawn out of them by the carefully orchestrated sound effects of wind and rain. Gradually, the audience

David Swift, Jill Bennett, and Richard O'Callaghan in the 1972 Royal Court Theatre Upstairs premiere of Churchill's Owners, *in which a landlord and her husband pressure an impoverished tenant into giving them her baby (photograph by John Haynes; from Geraldine Cousin,* Churchill the Playwright, *1989; Thomas Cooper Library, University of South Carolina)*

becomes aware that the couple read past events differently. The wife seems to have been raped by Billy, the father of her aborted child. Both she and her husband, however, hold Billy in affection, though their accounts of him do not tally. The husband, for instance, remembers a day on the river, "an English scene so remarkable for its pale green that it seemed even at the time like a memory," a moment made beautiful by Billy's vulnerability as he told their small daughter that he had never been in a boat and was tenderly encouraged by her to step in. The wife comments, "He was certainly lying because he told me he'd worked his passage to South America." There is no "true" version of the story, and the audience never hears Billy himself; what is important is the concrete effect his actions have had upon the relationship, on the ways the couple define themselves, their sexuality, their child, the possible lives that have now been closed to them, and those that remain.

Schreber's Nervous Illness (1972) enters the mind of the protagonist, a judge at the turn of the century and a patient of Sigmund Freud, to render concrete the images that afflict him. Schreber sees himself as assailed by "nerve rays" that speak to him in a variety of voices; in an arresting first speech he claims that "the Order of the World has been broken and God and I find ourselves in a situation that has never arisen before." As his illness progresses he sees himself as participating in "miracles" and as undergoing a transformation into a female state, his body becoming quick with new life. His monologues and the interruptions of the "rays" are intercut with statements from the Director of the Asylum, who never addresses the protagonist directly. As Elaine Aston has pointed out, this image parallels other plays in the 1970s, such as David Edgar's *Mary Barnes* (performed in 1978, published in 1979), that explore the "anti-psychiatry" of R. D. Laing. Churchill's use of radio puts the listener in the position of a Laingian psychiatrist: the audience hears, as Schreber does, the voices of the "rays" and of God himself—and with no visual dimension to suggest otherwise, their presence is not measurably different from that of the doctor. The audience has no choice, therefore, but to accept the validity of Schreber's experience—not to believe in the existence of the rays, but to acknowledge the significance of the psychological journey that he undergoes and the newly strengthened self with which he emerges. Churchill's interest in the ways the human subject can make and remake, articulate, and express itself is an abiding preoccupation.

What she has described as the second stage of her career, the period that marked a return to the theater, this time as a professional playwright, was inaugurated in 1972 with *Owners* at the Royal Court Theatre Upstairs. The darkly funny *Owners* tells with elegant symmetry the story of two couples: property owner Marion and her pushy capitalist husband, Clegg, and tenants Alec and Lisa. Written in three days as Churchill recovered from a miscarriage, *Owners* explores sexual and familial, as well as financial, ownership. Clegg likes to think of himself as owning Marion: "It's very like having a talking dog." His stereotypical chauvinism is so outrageous that the audience is set up to expect an uncomplicated enjoyment of Marion's refusal to conform; they are instantly challenged by her shameless adoption of the "dog" image. She converts it from Samuel Johnson's dismissive type of ineptitude ("A woman preaching is like a dog walking on its hind legs: it is not well done, but you are surprised to find it done at all") to that of the "capitalist running dog" of Mao Tse-tung: "I work like a dog. Most women are fleas but I'm the dog." Marion and Clegg both assume that they have the right to own Lisa's child: Marion because she desires her former lover Alec, Clegg because he has slept with Lisa, and both because they can afford to exploit Lisa's poverty. In contrast, when Marion gets her go-between Worsely to set the house on fire, Alec not only saves his family but sacrifices his life to save a neighbor's baby. While he sees life as something that can be spent in a good cause, he is equally willing to assume the responsibility of taking life: when his elderly mother goes into a permanent coma, he releases her. In contrast, Worsely, who subscribes to the capitalist assumption that life is what one makes it, is always trying to commit suicide; his failures are a running gag, as is his ongoing debate with a Samaritan: "I told him I wanted to kill myself and could he help. He said in a very feeling voice he would certainly try. But does he hell. The bastard's always trying to stop me."

Like many of Churchill's plays, *Owners* became more topical with time: the right-wing government elected in 1979 increasingly preached individual responsibility for life. Margaret Thatcher characteristically invoked the story of the Good Samaritan who could afford to do good. The extent of this responsibility was explored in real-life events such as the "Baby Cotton" case in 1984, which raised questions about payment for surrogate parenthood, and the Hillsborough Stadium disaster in 1989 (when ninety-six football fans were crushed to death in the press of a badly managed crowd), which left one young victim in a permanent coma from which his parents struggled for the right to release him.

Churchill saw the mid 1970s as marking the beginning of a third phase in her work. As she became active in the women's movement she also moved from solitary to collaborative work, a process she described in Rob Ritchie's *The Joint Stock Book* (1987) as leaving her "as thrilled as a child at a pantomime." For many dramatists, collaborative writing, or "workshopping" material with a company, was a useful apprenticeship to be discarded as competence developed. Churchill had been a playwright for eighteen years when she encountered the feminist company Monstrous Regiment on an abortion march; the result was *Vinegar Tom* (performed in 1976, published in 1978), about the seventeenth-century witch trials. At the same time, she worked with the socialist company Joint Stock on a play about the same period, *Light Shining in Buckinghamshire* (performed in 1976, published in 1978). Working with companies from the outset gave her the support she needed to work on a broader canvas with larger casts and to make use of their personal experiences and stage skills.

Churchill's plays differ from those of most of her male contemporaries, even those of broadly leftist/feminist sympathy, whose works frequently track the career of a female hero, a romantic conscience for a corrupt world, leaving old assumptions about gender and personality unshaken. Churchill's dramaturgy reflects the collective process that engendered the play. To watch *Light Shining in Buckinghamshire,* for example, is to experience a disorienting shift of focus. The play presents the experiences of the ordinary people who made the English revolution in the seventeenth century. There are no heroes with whom to identify; characters are played by several different actors, so they may be seen to grow in terms of understanding their situation, but not in terms of "personality." This undercutting of audience identification made *Light Shining in Buckinghamshire*—along with *Vinegar Tom,* which broke up the seventeenth-century story with modern songs—Churchill's most Brechtian work to date.

Like much of Bertolt Brecht's work, the play is charged with an excitement that stems from its ability to catch a political process and make it human and concrete. In one key scene, two women are looking in a mirror. The conversation concentrates on the material aspects of their situation. One explains to the other that they can take what they need, blankets and cattle, from the manor house, and she claims their right to do so as Saxons dispossessed by Norman aristocrats, as workers on the land betrayed by those whose title lies only in paper: "We're burning his papers . . . that's like him burnt." Feminist critiques of Churchill identify this scene as a liminal moment embodying the idea that the act of becoming a subject, a political being, is open to all. Throughout the play characters take hold of the language that has constructed them and shape new selves: a woman claims the right to preach; a butcher refuses meat to the rich; a vagrant ceases to identify herself as "evil" and can allow herself to be touched, in a meeting charged with a sense that "you're God, you're God, no one's more God than you if you could know it yourself, you're lovely, you're perfect." Yet, even in this scene it is clear that the revolution has been betrayed. Oliver Cromwell refuses the chance to set up a democracy and invests the government of the country in the propertied classes; the preacher who recruited for the New Model Army evicts his tenants while assuring himself he is doing it to provide corn for all. "Jesus Christ did come," one of the empowered women tells us, "and nobody noticed." The last lines of the play are spoken by men while the women keep silent.

Churchill's subsequent plays with Joint Stock and the Royal Court Theatre, especially *Cloud Nine* (performed and published in 1979), *Top Girls* (performed and published in 1982), and *Fen* (performed and published in 1983), brought her to much greater prominence. All three transferred to New York, where *Cloud Nine* and *Top Girls* won Obie Awards. *Fen* won the Susan Smith Blackburn Award in 1984, and Churchill's first collection of plays was published by Methuen in 1985. Since then all three works have been revived frequently by both amateur and professional companies. It was an extraordinary achievement, given the combination of political complexity and theatrical innovation in the plays. Their reception was prompted by the uprush of feminist consciousness in all aspects of life: novels, consciousness-raising groups, rape crisis centers, shelters for battered women, and an increasing body of feminist theory began to transform life at many levels, and Churchill's works took on the status of classics.

She continued to be active in the women's movement and in 1977 contributed to the Monstrous Regiment cabaret, *Floorshow*. The heady sense of new possibilities and the swift and stylized cabaret medium generated ideas that emerged in the bold imagery and cartoon-like tableaux of *Cloud Nine,* developed with Joint Stock in 1979 out of a series of workshops exploring sexuality and sexual politics. The title was taken from the term for orgasm used by the caretaker of the rehearsal room, who had been drawn into the discussions. In the middle of the second act the whole company unite to celebrate the varieties of love and sing "It'll be fine when you reach Cloud Nine." This scene is, however, a utopian moment that can only exist outside the narrative; within it, characters have to struggle and engage with the legacy of Victorian patriarchy. Churchill reveals the complexity of this legacy only gradually. The first act, which takes place circa 1879, is a wildly comic parody of the television series of the 1970s such as *Upstairs Downstairs*, which cast a nostalgic glow over the days of the British Empire; Churchill mocks the enforced sexual and social passivity of women and the insensitivity and colonizing greed of men:

BETTY Do you think of me sometimes then?
HARRY You have been thought of where no white woman has been thought of before.
BETTY It's one way of having adventures. I suppose I will never go in person.

In this act Churchill continually subverts the idea that the bodies of women (or of any oppressed group) are to be looked at as powerless and unchanging objects by the white male hierarchy. Because Betty is solely defined by male desire, she is played by a man; her son, Edward, who likes dolls, has yet to be made a man, and is played by a woman; her daughter, Victoria, the most passive of all, is a doll; and the black servant Joshua, who sings English Christmas carols and flogs native rebels but eventually shoots Betty's husband, Clive, is played by a white actor in unconvincing makeup that reveals him as a construct of white culture. The pattern the actors weave onstage also echoes the trap in which women are caught. The sexually articulate Mrs. Saunders speaks of desire, but as Clive vanishes underneath her skirts, emerging moments later to disguise the damp patch on his trousers with champagne, she can only ponder her dislike of him; the lesbian governess Ellen is played by the actress playing Mrs. Saunders, thus simultaneously embodying the attraction and the impossibility of a union between them. Ellen is married off to Harry Bagley, neatly crushing her hopeless desire for Betty and his for Clive in a single miserable union.

While the cross-dressing and farce-like speed are outrageously comic, reflecting the enthusiasm Churchill found in the workshops, they have an underlying savagery that emerges fully in the second act. The action moves to 1979, but Betty, Edward, and Victoria have aged only twenty-five years, and they are played by actors of the appropriate gender. They may thus be understood to have "matured" or "grown up" and absorbed the experience of earlier generations, but their engagement with the sexual politics of the 1970s is still warped and distorted despite the distance they have traveled. Betty has left her painful marriage; so has Victoria, now a mother and tentatively exploring a relationship with another woman. Edward is gay and struggling to come to terms with his lover Gerry's promiscuity. While the action—apart from the wild energy of Victoria's daughter, Cathy, played by a man with no attempt to disguise the incongruity—is primarily naturalistic, it borders on surrealism. If the Victorian Age can now be viewed as comic caricature, Churchill implies, humans are still far from utopia; a better world can be glimpsed in the moments when characters are at their least ratio-

Anthony Sher, Carole Hayman, and Julie Covington in the 1979 Royal Court Theatre production of Churchill's Cloud Nine, *which explores sexual politics and role conditioning by casting actors in roles for the opposite gender (photograph by John Haynes; from Geraldine Cousin,* Churchill the Playwright, *1989; Thomas Cooper Library, University of South Carolina)*

nal—as when Edward, Victoria, and her lover Lin make a drunken and giggly attempt to evoke the Goddess. Their language suggests an ideal past, the "history we haven't had," and, through Victoria's socialist-feminist analysis, explains how this past is so rooted in a long-dead economic system that it can never be recovered. They raise not a goddess but evidence of patriarchal corruption: first, Victoria's husband, Martin, who is nostalgic for the 1960s, "when liberation just meant fucking"; and second, the ghost of Lin's brother Bill, a soldier in Northern Ireland, who sees brutal sex as an antidote to his rage as a victim of a still-operative colonialism.

The closing moments of the play measure the distance between what 1970s feminism has achieved and what still has to be overcome. Visited by the ghosts of her mother and Ellen, Betty narrates her attainment of selfhood through self-induced orgasm:

> I thought well there is somebody there. It felt very sweet.... Afterwards I thought I'd betrayed Clive. My mother would kill me. But I felt triumphant because I was a separate person from them. And I cried because I didn't want to be. But I don't cry about it any more. Sometimes I do it three times in one night and it really is great fun.

Betty can now begin to renegotiate her relationship with her children, acknowledging their sexuality and articulating, through an awkward attempt to pick up Gerry, the hope that she may have a sexual relationship herself. At this point, the last image in the play, it is possible for her to embrace the Betty of the previous act; it is an image of great tenderness and optimism, and also one that only exists in imagined as opposed to real space, implying that the reconciliation of past and present has still to occur. Its echo of the mirror scene in *Light Shining in Buckinghamshire*, however, implies that it is not impossible.

Top Girls and *Fen* mark a new phase in feminist political drama; as the 1970s gave way to the Thatcher era, images of women united in a struggle against a patriarchal legacy gave way to a more fragmented picture. In both plays Churchill turns to an examination of the position of women in contemporary capitalism. In the opening scene of *Top Girls,* the protagonist, Marlene, places herself in a continuum of "successful" women in history who gather to celebrate her promotion at a dinner: Isabella Bird, the Victorian explorer and traveler; Pope Joan, an apocryphal figure who allegedly served as the pontiff from 855 to 858; Lady Nijo, a thirteenth-century Japanese imperial court concubine and Buddhist nun;

Patient Griselda, the "obedient wife" character from medieval and Renaissance sources such as Giovanni Boccaccio's *Decameron* and Geoffrey Chaucer's *Canterbury Tales;* and Dull Gret, the key figure in a painting by Pieter Brueghel the Elder. The scene itself is theatrically and politically uplifting, with an energy arising both from obstacles transcended and heroic failure, sometimes sharply juxtaposed: Joan, for instance, reduces the company to ribald and delighted laughter with an account of giving birth unexpectedly during a papal procession, a laughter she suddenly ruptures with the comment, "They took me by the feet and dragged me out of town and stoned me to death." Much of the vigor of the first scene derives from the way lines overlap, so that the rhythms of nineteenth-century reminiscence or Japanese haiku collide with those of the Latin Mass or the twitterings of Griselda. As virtually every critique of the play has since pointed out, this overlap dramatizes the point that these historical heroines could function only on the individual level; they lack the power to support one another or to offer help to their contemporaries—except, perhaps, for Gret, monosyllabic apart from one speech in which she describes organizing her neighbors to go and beat the devils in hell: "We'd had worse, you see, we'd had the Spanish. We'd all had family killed. Men on wheels. Babies on swords. I'd had enough, I was mad, I hate the bastards."

In the next act, the actress who plays Gret, powerful but unheard, becomes the equally marginalized figure of Angie, Marlene's slow-witted daughter. Churchill tracks their relationship backward; the audience first meets Angie in the country, announcing that she is going to run away to London to visit her aunt, Marlene, whom she believes to be her mother. When she arrives at Marlene's office, she sits ignored, sometimes asleep, through a series of interactions between Marlene and various colleagues that are notable not simply for their infectious ruthlessness (Angie gapes in admiration as Marlene tells a wife interceding for her failed husband to "piss off" and a would-be saleswoman intones like a mantra, "I'm not very nice") but also for their linguistic poverty. Marlene's role in sustaining the capitalist culture is more overtly argued out in the following section, which takes place one year earlier. She visits her sister Joyce and confirms that she is Angie's true mother. The sisters bicker, at first with affection, then corrosively as the row becomes political; Joyce hurls the epithet "Hitlerina," while Marlene, who has won over Angie with presents, is confronted with the personal implications of her beliefs:

> MARLENE . . . Anyone can do anything if they've got what it takes.
>
> JOYCE And if they haven't?
>
> MARLENE If they're stupid or lazy or frightened, I'm not going to help them get a job, why should I?
> JOYCE What about Angie?
> MARLENE What about her?
> JOYCE She's stupid, lazy and frightened, so what about her?

Angie closes the play with a single word born out of the nightmare she has been having offstage: "Frightening," a word that sums up both her own future and that of a country in which feminism can contemplate an alliance with capitalism.

Fen is also a state-of-the-nation play, but in this play the gulf between those who control the land and those who work it is so wide that not even the acrid dialogue of Joyce and Marlene is possible. Rather, the opening, in which a Japanese businessman gazes at the Fens and looks for someone to tell him "old tales" of the Fen Tigers' resistance to the draining of their land, serves to stress that the figures of power in the play, such as the landowner Tewson, are themselves at the mercy of the multinational corporations. The lives of the sixteen women in the play are shaped by these forces, whose impact on the most intimate parts of their lives was indicated by the set designed by Annie Smart. Domestic paraphernalia was surrealistically planted in the soil on which they worked, so that they were never wholly free of the land. Economic conditions were seen to dictate vicious and frustrated relationships like that between Angela and her stepdaughter Becky, and the doomed love affair of Val, shuttling between her lover Frank, who cannot afford to support her, and her husband and children, until she finally asks Frank to kill her.

The women speak the same debased language of the *Top Girls* clientele: when Val bids her daughter a last good-bye it is subtextual, beneath an exchange of elephant jokes; as she seeks for God, a woman testifies to finding Jesus in the words "More jam, mum." Men do not tell stories, as Churchill's doubling plot stresses; they are all played by a single actor, indicating a failure to negotiate, or unite, or provide any kind of community. (At one point, Frank considers the futility of asking for a raise, taking the part of his boss as well as himself, and finally hits himself in the face.) The women, however, speak together. Nell tells stories of the past and refutes the chants of "witch" by telling the village children that she is a princess; and the ghost of a woman whose child died starving continues to challenge the landowners, warning them that she watches television alongside them and sees both their greed and the suffering they cause. As Val herself becomes a ghost, she liberates the dream-lives of the women: Nell is a Fen Tiger on stilts; Shirley, the worker, is ironing the field, but recalls the days when workers fought back and killed the owners' cattle; her mother, who would never sing, now does so in a burst of glory that brings the play to its end. The dream-lives create a context for the documentary material of which Churchill makes extensive use, much of it derived from interviews in Mary Chamberlain's book *Fenwomen* (1975), which narrates the lives of women in an English village. They show that the most tightly circumscribed daily lives have still a capacity for energy and vision; they alert both characters and audience to utopian possibilities not yet dead.

Serious Money (performed and published in 1987), Churchill's second play to win a Susan Smith Blackburn Award and the third in what might be called her state-of-the-nation plays at the Royal Court Theatre, is far less optimistic. Set at the time of the "Big Bang" that transformed the stock exchange in the 1980s, it narrates the takeover of a company, significantly called Albion. It is also a murder story—except that no one actually cares about justice, and with the murder unsolved, the cast ends the play with an exuberant song welcoming in five more years of the Thatcher administration. The play was, disconcertingly, a huge success with the very community it satirized, and during the West End transfer, the Wyndham was filled with city speculators. The action presents a self-contained world, a capitalist dystopia with its own language and logic. The theatrical pleasure is rooted in the energy of the presentation: the play bounds along in verse, deriving comedy from the sort of outrageous rhymes associated with Cole Porter's witty love lyrics rather than the language of finance.

The verse, however, offers more than just pantomime energy. Studies of Churchill's language point out how she habitually defamiliarizes words; in this play she concentrates on those once used to denote tangible commodities, such as copper and cocoa (and cocaine), on which the lives of Third World communities depend. In the face of the Big Bang they have assumed the status of paper money, with a fluctuating face value. This volatile status is as true for those in a position to save those communities as it is for the young Thatcherites who now dominate the city. Jacinta Condor, for example, does not see herself as in any way responsible for the workers in her copper mine or for the political destiny of her country; the pat rhythms betray her lack of real concern while the drop into prose indicates the area in which she is prepared to engage with complex ideas:

> I lose every quarter
> The cash goes like water
> Is better to close the mine.
> I choose very well
> The moment to sell,

I benefit from the closures in Surinam because of guerrilla activity, and also I leak the news I am closing my mines, which puts the price up a little, so it is fine.

Everything, in this world, can be reduced to commodities, and there is no longer a vocabulary outside that of trading. In the last moments, the ghost of the murder victim appears, perfunctorily; unlike the long-dead woman in *Fen,* he cannot speak of what has happened to him. While in *Fen* the women have the power to see spirits and imagine other worlds, in *Serious Money* there is no apparent possibility of a considered and vigorous dissent—no words, no societies or actions that are not ultimately controlled and corroded by city values. *Serious Money* won a London *Evening Standard* award for best comedy and the Laurence Olivier/BBC Award for best new play, both in 1987.

Mad Forest (performed and published in 1990) is a work on an equally ambitious scale about the revolution in Romania. The project was suggested to Churchill by Mark Wing-Davey, the artistic director of the Central School of Speech and Drama, who knew Churchill from Monstrous Regiment, just weeks after the execution of overthrown Romanian president Nicolae Ceausescu and his wife on Christmas Day 1989. By April 1990, Churchill, Wing-Davey, ten students, and a team of designers were working with students from the Caragiale Institute of Theatre and Cinema in Bucharest. The techniques Churchill had developed in her Joint Stock work were used to explore the experience of the Romanian students and other Romanian people whom they interviewed. The result was a play that combined a sense of being still under construction, like a series of dispatches from a war zone, with great formal coherence. The play has three acts. Acts 1 and 3 center on two weddings involving the working-class Vladu family and the Antonescu family, members of the intelligentsia. The weddings take place before and after the revolution. The revolution is presented in Act 2 through a series of testimonies by ordinary Romanians—including students, doctors, and artists. The documentary quality of this act is reinforced by the use of the Romanian accent; elsewhere characters speak unaccented English or Romanian. The division is not between the personal and the political—politics permeates the lives of the fictional families, while the testimonies are as concerned with the feelings of parents and children as they are with the actions of the army—rather, it is between the fact of the revolution and its implications for a complex society. Churchill's structure refutes any suggestion that her exploration of these implications can be comprehensive: the action proceeds in a series of vignettes, each introduced with a short sentence in Romanian; the effect is of a phrase book,

Lindsay Duncan, Carole Hayman, Gwen Taylor, and Selina Cadell in the 1982 Royal Court Theatre premiere of Churchill's Top Girls, *which features a dinner for the businesswoman-protagonist attended by female historical figures (photograph by Catherine Ashmore; from Geraldine Cousin,* Churchill the Playwright, *1989; Thomas Cooper Library, University of South Carolina)*

eclectic and sometimes surreal, each "lesson" defamiliarizing the one before.

The pressures of the Ceausescu regime are presented in a series of scenes linking material and linguistic deprivation. In Act 1 the Vladus have a row about Lucia's forthcoming marriage to an American. It is conducted in shouts masked by a loud radio, a strategy employed to avoid bugging. Meanwhile, a subtext about poverty plays itself out as Lucia offers eggs and cigarettes. When her father smashes one of the eggs, her mother and sister carefully gather it up. As the play progresses it is clear that sexual life is similarly circumscribed: Lucia conducts a (bugged) conversation with a doctor who tells her "There is no abortion in Romania. I am shocked that you even think of it," while they exchange notes and a large wad of money. Even the spiritual is touched: a priest talks to his angel, hoping that his flock can still retreat into a "blue" of peace but realizing that while no words can be safely spoken there is no meaning in silence. "I try to keep clear of the political side," explains the angel blandly.

Churchill explains in her notes to the play that "the play goes from the difficulty of saying anything to everyone talking." The play rejects obvious theatrical opportunities—flags, shooting, heroics—to present the attempts of Romanian citizens to use their apparent newfound freedom of speech to analyze what has happened to them. For many, this freedom means speaking about confusion. This confusion is borne out by the final act, which centers on the wedding of Florina Vladu, who is marrying Radu Antonescu. It opens, not with one of the central characters, but with a scene between a vampire and a dog. The connotations the figure of the vampire bears in the West are complex: potent religion; forbidden sexuality; luxury and decadence; a specifically Eastern European culture; a near-feudal social structure; superstition; and, as a staple of the movies, capitalism itself. In vampire movies arcane knowledge has to be resurrected to make sense of the world, and everyone is under the threat of death. The image sets an agenda for the final part of the play.

Occasionally, briefly, there is a glimpse of utopia: Florina's old aunt seems to embody a new national awareness as she chants peasant wedding verses. But the overall picture is dark. In the hospital, Lucia's brother Gabriel is feted as a hero, but an unnamed patient asks again and again, "Who was shooting on the 22nd? . . . Did we have a revolution or a putsch?" Radu and Florina welcome Gabriel home with a bit of impromptu theater, acting out the execution of the Ceausescus; the scene is wildly funny but displays a disturbing level of mimic violence, which becomes real as Lucia (who married and dumped her American) is embraced by her lover Ianos and Gabriel lashes out with "Get your filthy Hungarian hands off her." No one is clear what they have been liberated to: their choices, their identity, their purchasing power, their rights. The play ends with everyone speaking at once, nobody listening, no new identity articulated except that of the vampire, whose speech cuts through the rest: "You begin to want blood, your limbs ache, your head burns, you have to keep moving faster and faster."

The confidence with which Churchill was able to engage with the two different student companies and with audiences in London and Bucharest is reflected in the experimentalism of much of her work since 1985, the year Joint Stock fell victim to Arts Council cuts. Her final work with them, *A Mouthful of Birds* (performed and published in 1986), on which she collaborated with David Lan and the choreographer Ian Spink, indicated the direction much of her later work took in making the stage a place of magical transformation. Churchill dates her interest in working with dance and song from seeing a production of Brecht's *Seven Deadly Sins* (1933) in 1979 and the politically resonant dance work of Pina Bausch in the 1980s at Sadlers Wells. However, while the images in *Fen* made the dreams of the characters concrete, and *Mad Forest* dredged up the vampire from the Romanian subconscious to articulate new political nightmares, *A Mouthful of Birds* was her first real attempt to use dance and speech in equal measure to explore extreme states of feeling.

Its starting point is Euripides' *Bacchae*, but while characters act out the story of Dionysus and Pentheus, the focus is different. *The Bacchae* tells the story of one man's opposition to the cult, which destroys him, and of the possession of a group of women who tear him to pieces in their ecstasy and then, horrified, resume their lives. Much of its fascination lies in its subversive images of authority brought down by its own rigidity, of women consumed by a violence that not only runs counter to all accepted forms of female behavior but that is in some degree holy. Churchill echoes the subversion of sexual stereotypes, exploring both female violence and male tenderness, but lays new emphasis on the variety of possibilities inherent in the idea of possession and the variety of characters who experience it. In workshops she explored different kinds of "being beside ourselves," as she explained in the published version of the play, including spiritualism, hypnotic regression, and living in the open, and developed the idea of the "undefended day," in which seven characters would step out of their normal lives and explore extremes. Lena, for example, hears the voice of her husband droning on about everyday defeats in counterpoint to the insistence of a spirit that she kill her baby in order to exist. The act of killing is symbolized by the washing of a shawl; Churchill is concerned to explore the feeling of power generated by violence rather than to evoke horror. Paul, working in an office and dealing in statistics and reports, falls in love with a pig, and they dance with great tenderness. Derek is unemployed, and works out to avoid the sense of emasculation experienced by his father when out of work. His journey through the play is the most extraordinary, as he takes on the identity of Herculine Barbin, the hermaphrodite, and then becomes Pentheus as the other men become Dionysus and the women Bacchantes. He is torn to pieces, but in the final section, as the characters all decide how to lead their lives after the "undefended day," he is born into a female body in which he finds peace and happiness.

Churchill continued to develop her work with Spink and his company Second Stride, and with *Lives of the Great Poisoners* (performed in 1991, published in 1993), they also explored the use of song with the composer Orlando Gough. The company consisted of four dancers, four singers (one of whom acted), and an actor, and explored the idea of "poison"–mythological, with the story of Medea; historical, with the cases of Cora Crippen (a music-hall singer murdered by her husband in 1910) and Madame de Brinvilliers (beheaded in 1676 for poisoning her father and two brothers); and environmental, with the story of Thomas Midgley Jr., the American engineer and chemist who put lead into gasoline with benevolent intentions. Modes of expression and historical periods flow into one another: Cora Crippen does her lamentable music-hall turn, is sung to death by a Chorus of Poisons, and returns as Medea to take her revenge; Jason discusses his forthcoming marriage to Creusa with Midgley as she dances her death with the Poisons.

What is perhaps most important about both these plays with Spink is their attempt to explore political questions by using resources no longer normally associated with political theater; they turn back to the spectacle and excess of melodrama, a medium whose political dynamic is gradually being rediscovered. The play on which Churchill worked steadily throughout the whole period of her association with Gough, *The Skriker,* completed and staged at the National in 1994, made this political aspect more explicit through its choice of central characters. Josie and Lily are everything the Tory values of the 1990s reviled–unemployed single mothers. Josie is in a psychiatric hospital after killing her baby. Alongside their gray and deprived world is another, inhabited by spirits, grotesque folkloric figures who dance, silently, their own stories and interactions with humanity. The only one to engage in dialogue, however, is the Skriker, described by Churchill as "a shapeshifter and death portent, ancient and damaged." Dazzlingly portrayed by Katherine Hunter in the original production, the Skriker continually transforms herself into social victims such as mental patients and lost children, into pieces of furniture, into psychotic men, and–most signficantly, perhaps, in a play employing the persecuted young mothers of melodrama–into a pantomime fairy in pink tulle and glitter. She offers what otherworld spirits have always offered in folktales: wishes interpreted with dangerous literalmindedness, gifts that cause only pain–Josie and Lily find their

The second cast of the 1987 Royal Court Theatre premiere of Serious Money, *Churchill's satire of the London stock exchange and the insider trading of the 1980s (photograph by John Haynes; from Geraldine Cousin,* Churchill the Playwright, *1989; Thomas Cooper Library, University of South Carolina)*

mouths dropping toads and pound coins like Rose Red and Snow White—and visits to her own world that savagely skew the time frame in this one.

While folk stories tend to construct spirits as troublesome but nonetheless in overall harmony with the natural world, the Skriker's "damage" is a product of an environment wrecked by twentieth-century capitalism:

> Sunbeam sunburn in your eye socket to him. All good many come to the aids party. When I go uppety, follow a fellow on a dark road dank ride and jump thrump out and eat him how does he taste? toxic waste paper basket case, salmonelephantiasis, blue blood bad blood blad blodd blah blah blah. I remember dismember the sweet flesh in the panic, tearing limb from lamb chop you up and suck the tomorrowbones. Lovely lively lads and maiden England. . . .

Her language is breaking down, corrupted by a Nature abused by men. Toxic waste and the poisoning of the food chain break up the balance between the real and the supernatural. Lily, marginalized and despised, behaves as the heroine of a fairy-tale should and tries to save the world; but the twentieth century has destroyed the possibility of a fairy tale ending, and she finds herself on a blasted Earth whose inhabitants bellow at her in blind hatred. *The Skriker* never shows a figure who might be held responsible for what happens. At one point the Skriker tries to understand how the earth has been poisoned, but Lily cannot explain it. The paradox of the play lies in the theatrical complexity and richness that is used to depict the deprivation imposed by capitalism—a deprivation not only material but also spiritual and linguistic.

Churchill's preoccupation with the relationships between politics, language, and excess continued with her translation of Seneca's *Thyestes* in 1994. After seeing Ariane Mnouchkine's landmark production of the Greek tragic cycle *The House of Atreus* two years previously, Churchill researched the beginnings of the story in Latin and became attracted to the possibilities of the language. While earlier translators had tended to equate Latin itself with the Latinate borrowings in English that make for grandiloquence, producing an overblown rhetoric to match the extremes of violence in the plays, Churchill was attracted to the speed and compression possible in an inflected language. Her verse translation was fast, rough, and plain. Seneca's focus upon drought and a damaged Earth, the hellish landscapes in which he sets the narratives of murder, revenge, and cannibalism, echo the imagery of *The Skriker,* and much of the text reads like a more rhythmic and immediate version of the descriptions of a polluted world in that play:

> Have we been chosen
> out of everyone

somehow deserving
to have the world smash up and fall on us? or have the last days come
in our lifetime? It's
a hard fate, whether we've lost the sun
or driven it away.

Churchill's work of the late 1990s continued to experiment with language; her plays also took on a new intimacy, an intense preoccupation with the personal. This intimacy springs from the way Churchill deploys subtext. The double bill *Hotel* (performed and published in 1997) was once again worked out in collaboration with Second Stride, directed and choreographed by Spink with music by Gough. The first piece, *Eight Rooms,* is an opera rather than a play with song and dance; both Churchill and Gough were interested in the way language works at the high points in an opera when a whole ensemble is singing different words. In *Hotel,* Churchill developed a text of fragments, incomplete sentences that the audience might grasp at different points as repeats were sung. The scraps form a mosaic that offer glimpses into the lives of fourteen hotel guests, couples and singles, who occupy the same room oblivious of one another. Their stories hint at pain and loss: one couple is silent; a woman having an affair cannot sleep because she is worried about her children; a gay couple fail to communicate; a drunken couple quarrel and wake everyone up. While the audience works to extrapolate stories from these fragments of private unhappiness, the onstage action is full of wit: Spink coordinated the everyday actions of the guests—brushing teeth, watching TV, making phone calls—into a complex choreography that culminate in a point at which fourteen people lie on the bed, moving in a weird synchronicity that still reflects their own characters. The effect of the whole is a Bergsonian comedy—in which the human figures become cogs in a machine—which nevertheless implies the existence of tragedy.

The companion piece, *Two Nights,* was a dance to what Gough called "a kind of song cycle" built out of scraps from a diary. The theme of these scraps is disappearance; phrases come from an account of a magician making a building vanish, a Greek spell, and a manifesto that posits disappearance, not confrontation, as the ultimate way of taking power. The subtext is dark and disturbing; one can infer the possibility of suicide in lines such as: "will I still have a shadow? / will I still have a mind?" Dancers appear and disappear through cracks in the walls of the room. It is for the audience, finally, to decode the room and its inhabitants, as with the projects of Sophie Calle in the 1990s. Calle worked as a chambermaid in a Venice hotel and photographed the rooms she cleaned, exposing the lives of the occupants through their intimate debris: underwear slung across a chair, scribbled notes, and casual purchases. Both Calle and Churchill push the audience to reflect on the fragility of identity in an urban society lacking the old certainties of community.

The same theme is echoed in *Blue Heart,* the paired plays *Heart's Desire* and *Blue Kettle* (performed and published in 1997), which marked a reunion for Churchill and Joint Stock, resurrected by Max Stafford-Clark as Out of Joint. The use of actors' games and exercises creates a surface playfulness, but the precision of the subtext has the darkness of *Hotel*. *Heart's Desire* uses a technique Churchill developed in her 1977 play *Traps,* in which the actors play out different versions of the same event, so that as the story advances the audience become aware of multiple possibilities. *Heart's Desire* shows a couple in their sixties, Brian and Alice, who with Brian's sister Maisie are waiting for their daughter Susy to arrive from Australia. The wait, and later the arrival, are played out many times in different ways: sometimes the action is replayed at double speed with the smallest of variations; sometimes there are radical differences in what occurs—a horde of small children stampedes onstage, or two gunmen burst in and kill everybody. Each time the scene is reset to the beginning. When the play reaches the ring at the door, Susy does arrive, but so, as the scene resets again and again, do an anonymous "official," a friend of Susy from Australia, and an enormous bird. The speed and surrealism give the play a wild comic edge; but what remains consistent is the undertone of bitterness between the couple ("I've thought for forty years that you were a stupid woman, now I know you're simply nasty," says Brian time and again as the scene continually resets), and what the narrative seems to aspire to—the articulation of Brian's love for his daughter—takes place only once, in the penultimate run. "You are my heart's desire," he tells her—and at once the whole scene begins again, this time cutting itself off as he begins to speak the line for the second time. The narrative structure dramatizes the fact that the expression of love is far rarer than the corrosive rows engendered by a family politics shaped by a society growing less free, as rare as Churchill's carnival bird, which appears only once.

Blue Kettle is also about family politics in a capitalist world—this time, specifically about the marketing of family values. Derek operates a scam: he tracks down women who gave up babies for adoption in their youth and pretends to be their long-lost son. He denies that he is interested in anything but their money; but his motives, and those of the "mothers" he meets, become more complex and opaque as the play progresses. This complexity is partly because language itself is undergoing a metamorphosis, with the words "blue" and "ket-

Cover with photograph by Man Ray for Churchill's 1994 play about a shape-shifting crone pursuing two unemployed young single mothers (Thomas Cooper Library, University of South Carolina)

tle" replacing words the audience comes to expect by their context. At first this substitution occurs only a few times in a scene, and it is always simple to guess the replaced word; it is as if Churchill is combining a naturalistic text with a party game. Later, however, more words are substituted, until the final scene is almost entirely languageless:

MRS PLANT Tle hate k later k, k bl bl bl shocked.
DEREK K, t see bl.
MRS PLANT T b k k k k l?
DEREK B.K.

This tactic makes for a radical shift in the relationship between actors and audience. The audience is neither passively accepting a naturalistic illusion, or judging a Brechtian *gestus;* rather, the process of decoding forces them to confront the values they normally bring to scenes dealing with mother-child relationships, to select for themselves a vocabulary that is adequate to both the emotional and economic aspects. "Mother," "son," "love," "money," all become fluid signs whose meaning is constantly being negotiated between the actors and the audience. It remains, though, a comic process, a party game in which the possibility of a wrong inflection can lead to a collapse like the fall of a house of cards.

Since the early 1990s Churchill has not been prolific, but the plays she has written continue to challenge actor, director, and audience alike. The short play *Far Away* (performed and published in 2000) shows a world at war. Its opening scenes between a girl, Joan, and her Aunt Harper set out the theme of complicity. Joan wakes in the night to see her uncle loading prisoners on a lorry; she is told that he is "part of a big movement now to make things better." Her willingness to accept the lie is pushed into a deeper complicity: the second section shows her in a workshop making elaborate, fantastic hats—their purpose to enliven processions of the condemned on their way to execution. The image of this parade—Churchill writes, "five is too few and twenty better than ten. A hundred?"—is horrifying. It tempts an audience to respond with delight in its own refined sensibility. It proves, however, to be only a preparation for a more searching analysis. A dialogue between Joan and her coworker Todd deconstructs that very response. They debate the nature of art and beauty—"It seems so sad to burn them [the hats] with the bodies. . . . No, that's the joy of it"—and determine to expose not the realities that horrified the younger Joan but the "corrupt financial basis of how the whole hat industry is run."

The debate pushes the audience further from the assurance that the events of the last century cannot repeat themselves. In fact, it is only logical that the evasions and betrayal implicit in the narrow liberalism of Todd and Joan lead to world war in the literal sense—not simply involving nations, but dragging all existence into destruction. Todd says, matter-of-factly, "I've shot cattle and children in Ethiopia. I've gassed mixed troops of Spanish, computer programmers and dogs. I've torn starlings apart with my bare hands." As the play ends, the audience is confronted with scores of these verbal images, as unstageable as they are disturbing. Joan's last question is "Who's going to mobilize darkness and silence?" The trajectory Churchill traces from a single act of unthinking and almost innocent collaboration to the destruction of a planet is accomplished with such apparent simplicity that its frightening implications only dawn on the audience after the power of the text has already done its work.

In *A Number* (performed and published in 2002), the setting is one of extreme simplicity: two men, "father" and "son," in a room. What makes it troubling is that although the same actors play every scene, each "son" proves to be different—an "original" and two clones, Bernard 1, Bernard 2, and Michael. All three—aware that "a number" of them exist, created by scientists without reference to their future needs or desires—are engaged in a struggle to discover and articulate an identity for themselves. It becomes increasingly apparent, however, that no language exists for their situation. Stories about origins shift. Salter, the "father," tells Bernard 2 that the "original" died in a car crash and that he wanted to replicate his perfection—immediately exposed as a lie as he confesses to Bernard 1 he abandoned him as delinquent in order to start afresh with "the same basic the same raw materials because they were perfect." Bernard 1 destroys Bernard 2 and then himself. Salter searches out the unauthorized clones, and the play closes as he struggles to connect with Michael, who is happy with his life for reasons that undermine all Salter's investment in the notions of individuality and parenthood: "We've got ninety-nine per cent the same genes as any other person. We've got ninety per cent the same as a chimpanzee. We've got thirty per cent the same as a lettuce. Does that cheer you up at all? I love about the lettuce. It makes me feel I belong."

Every mythology of Western selfhood that seems to bear on the story—Cain and Abel, Oedipus, nature and nurture, scientific progress, capitalism—proves inadequate. Salter, Bernard 1, and Bernard 2 all find themselves deprived of a language in which to describe their relationship, and their syntax flounders, as when Bernard 2 says:

> Maybe he shouldn't blame you, maybe it was a genetic, could you help drinking we don't know or drugs at the time philosophically as I understand it it wasn't viewed as not like now when our understanding's different and would a different person not have been so vulnerable because there could always be some genetic additive and then again someone with the same genetic exactly the same but at a different time a different cultural and of course all the personal. . . .

Michael, centered on other people and the world around him, speaking of concrete things such as lettuce and his wife's ears, is the only one at ease with language and himself. *A Number* won the 2002 London *Evening Standard* award for best play.

Caryl Churchill's name may be less well known than those of, say, Harold Pinter or Tom Stoppard, but this relative lack of visibility is a reflection of her continuing engagement with theater rather than with movies, her loyalty to the Royal Court Theatre rather than the larger subsidized theaters (the National Theatre has produced only two of her plays, the Royal Shakespeare Company only one), and her love of personal privacy. However, there is a considerable body of critical material about her, and the critical consensus places her as a major force in shaping the contemporary theatrical landscape. She not only has raised feminist concerns within the theater but also has provided a new theatrical vocabulary with which to investigate sexual politics. Her influence has been acknowledged by playwrights as diverse as Mark Ravenhill and Tony Kushner; it also reaches out to impact coming generations.

References:

Elaine Aston, *Caryl Churchill* (London: British Council, 1998; revised edition, Plymouth, U.K.: Northcote House, 2004);

Sue Ellen Case, ed., *Performing Feminisms* (Baltimore: Johns Hopkins University Press, 1990);

Geraldine Cousin, *Churchill the Playwright* (London: Methuen, 1989);

Elin Diamond, "Invisible Bodies in Churchill's Theater," in *Making a Spectacle*, edited by Lynda Hart (Ann Arbor: University of Michigan Press, 1989), pp. 259–281;

Gisela Ecker, *Feminist Aesthetics* (London: Women's Press, 1985);

Richard Eyre and Nicholas Wright, *Changing Stages: A View of British and American Theatre in the Twentieth Century* (New York: Knopf, 2001);

Linda Fitzsimmons, *File on Churchill* (London: Methuen, 1989);

Christopher Innes, "Caryl Churchill: Theatre as a Model for Change," in his *Modern British Drama, 1890–1990* (Cambridge: Cambridge University Press, 1992), pp. 460–472;

Catherine Itzin, *Stages in the Revolution* (London: Eyre Methuen, 1980), p. 278;

Amelia Howe Kritzer, *The Plays of Caryl Churchill: Theatre of Empowerment* (London: Macmillan, 1991);

Phyllis Randall, ed., *Caryl Churchill: A Casebook* (London: Garland, 1988);

Janelle Reinelt, *After Brecht: British Epic Theater* (Ann Arbor: University of Michigan Press, 1994), pp. 81–107;

Rob Ritchie, *The Joint Stock Book* (London: Methuen, 1987);

Jane Thomas, "The Plays of Caryl Churchill: Essays in Refusal," in *The Death of the Playwright?* edited by Adrian Page (London: Macmillan, 1992), pp. 160–185.

Maureen Duffy
(21 October 1933 -)

Lucy Kay
Liverpool Hope University College

See also the Duffy entry in *DLB 14: British Novelists Since 1960.*

PLAY PRODUCTIONS: *The Lay-Off,* London, Guildhall School of Drama, 1962;

The Silk Room, Watford, Hertfordshire, Watford Civic Theatre, 1966;

Rites, London, Jeannetta Cochrane Theatre (National Theatre), 1969;

Solo and *Olde Tyme,* London, Cambridge Theatre, 1970;

A Nightingale in Bloomsbury Square, London, Hampstead Theatre, 1973;

Afterword, Manchester, Manchester University Drama Society, 1983;

Megrim, Winchester, King Alfred's School of Speech and Drama, 1984;

The Masque of Henry Purcell, London, Southwark Playhouse, 1995.

BOOKS: *That's How It Was* (London: Hutchinson, 1962; Garden City, N.Y.: Dial, 1984);

The Single Eye (London: Hutchinson, 1964);

The Microcosm (London: Hutchinson, 1966; New York: Simon & Schuster, 1966);

The Paradox Players (London: Hutchinson, 1967; New York: Simon & Schuster, 1968);

Lyrics for the Dog Hour (London: Hutchinson, 1968);

Rites, published together with Carey Harrison's *Lovers* and Rochelle Owens's *Futz* as *New Short Plays 2* (London: Methuen, 1969);

Wounds (London: Hutchinson, 1969; New York: Knopf, 1969);

Love Child (London: Weidenfeld & Nicolson, 1971; New York: Knopf, 1971);

The Venus Touch (London: Weidenfeld & Nicolson, 1971);

The Erotic World of Faery (London: Hodder & Stoughton, 1972; New York: Avon, 1980);

I Want to Go to Moscow: A Lay (London: Hodder & Stoughton, 1973); republished as *All Heaven In a Rage* (New York: Knopf, 1973);

Maureen Duffy (photograph by Nick Cook; from the cover for Illuminations: A Fable, *1991; Thomas Cooper Library, University of South Carolina)*

Capital (London: Cape, 1975; New York: Braziller, 1976);

Evesong (London: Sappho Publications, 1975);

The Passionate Shepherdess: Aphra Behn, 1640-89 (London: Cape, 1977; New York: Avon, 1979);

Housespy (London: Hamilton, 1978);

Memorials of the Quick and the Dead (London: Hamilton, 1979);

Inherit the Earth: A Social History (London: Hamilton, 1980);

Gor Saga (London: Eyre Methuen, 1981; New York: Viking, 1982);

Scarborough Fear, as D. M. Cayer (London: Macdonald, 1982);

Londoners: An Elegy (London: Methuen, 1983);

Men and Beasts: An Animal Rights Handbook (London: Paladin, 1984);

Collected Poems (London: Hamilton, 1985);

Change (London: Methuen, 1987);

A Thousand Capricious Chances: A History of the Methuen List, 1889–1989 (London: Methuen, 1989);

Illuminations: A Fable (London: Sinclair-Stevenson, 1991);

Occam's Razor (London: Sinclair-Stevenson, 1993);

Henry Purcell (London: Fourth Estate, 1994);

Restitution (London: Fourth Estate, 1998);

England: The Making of the Myth (London: Fourth Estate, 2001);

Alchemy (London: Fourth Estate, 2004).

PRODUCED SCRIPTS: *Josie,* television, BBC, 1961;

Sanctuary, television, Granada, 1967;

Upstairs, Downstairs, television, London Weekend Television, 1971;

The Passionate Shepherdess, radio, BBC, 1979;

Only Goodnight, radio, BBC, 1981.

OTHER: *A Nightingale in Bloomsbury Square,* in *Factions,* edited by Giles Gordon and Alex Hamilton (London: Joseph, 1974);

Aphra Behn, *Oroonoko and Other Stories,* edited by Duffy (London: Methuen, 1986);

Behn, *Five Plays,* edited by Duffy (London: Methuen, 1990).

Maureen Duffy is a lesbian playwright, poet, novelist, critic, and editor. Her work is complex and anarchic, often experimental in form and dealing with taboo subjects. She is concerned with inequality of all kinds, including class, race, gender, and age, and her own experience as a lesbian informs her investigations into the performative nature of gender and the construction of sexuality. She enjoys writing through a male persona and sees the writer as an androgynous figure. Duffy often uses cross-dressing and role reversal to destabilize meaning and unfix identity. She is an intensely political person with a keen interest in animal welfare and authorial rights. She dismantles androcentric assumptions through her work and challenges her audience, often through savage humor, to rethink the world.

Maureen Patricia Duffy was born on 21 October 1933 in Worthing, Sussex, to Cahia Patrick Duffy and Grace Rose Wright. Her mother suffered from tuberculosis, and Duffy has acknowledged the political and psychological effects of her mother's prolonged absences in sanatoriums. Duffy was educated at Trowbridge High School for Girls in Wiltshire and the Sarah Bonnell High School for Girls. She studied English at King's College, London, and after earning her B.A. with honors in 1956, she taught for two years in Italy. She wrote from an early age and acted in school plays. At the age of seventeen she was offered a place at the Old Vic Drama School, and during her university years she performed in plays by William Shakespeare and Sean O'Casey.

Unwilling to be confined to female roles as an actor, she concentrated on writing, and in her final year at King's College she wrote "Pearson," a modern adaptation of William Langland's fourteenth-century poem *Piers Plowman,* set in a contemporary factory during a strike. "Pearson" was submitted to Kenneth Tynam, the drama critic for *The Observer,* who was running a competition to find new playwrights. Though "Pearson" did not win the competition, Duffy was invited to join one of the writers' groups at the Royal Court Theatre under the direction of George Devine and William Gaskill. "Pearson" was performed in 1962 as *The Lay-Off* (the title was changed by the producer), but it remains unpublished. She won the City of London Festival Playwright's Award in 1962 for this work. After the publication of her first novel, *That's How It Was* (1962), her writing career was established. This period was an exciting time in her life when she was introduced to experimental theater forms, improvisation, mask work, and discussion/evaluation groups. In 1969 her play *Rites* was produced at the Jeannetta Cochrane Theatre (a branch of the National Theatre) under the direction of Joan Plowright, who recognized the lack of parts for women in the theater. It was then produced at the Old Vic and, subsequently, internationally. It remains Duffy's most performed play to date.

Rites is the first in a trilogy of plays that rework Greek myths in a contemporary context. The piece is a fusion of comedy and tragedy, and the voyeurism in Euripides' *The Bacchae* informs the gruesome treatment of a lesbian cross-dresser who is slaughtered and cremated in the incinerator of a ladies' public restroom, the setting for the play. Duffy deliberately manipulates and distorts style, form, and genre to produce a funny yet disturbing piece of theater that addresses issues of class and sexuality and explores gender as a performative act.

The play opens with a group of workmen literally constructing the set with tongue-in-cheek solemnity as all the niceties of the "ceremony" are observed. Duffy points to ways in which men define and construct female experience. The ritual is conducted in silence, apart from the noises of banging, hammering, and the clanking of chains. The first entrance of Meg and Ada, the toilet attendants, sustains the ritualistic flavor in their enactment of their well-rehearsed routines, including not only their official duties but also the process of applying make-up. The adoring Meg quickly establishes Ada as a figure of power. Ada occupies her nights with a variety of men and, by day, rules her lavatorial empire with authority and pride, taking a keen—and unlikely—interest in the stock market, investing her gains as a madam.

The figure of an old woman eating her breakfast (noisily) in the first cubicle is both funny and sinister in a Pinteresque style. Duffy's enjoyment of language, its sounds and rhythms and potential for playful subversion and ambiguity, is clear: "Have you done number Five? There's bound to be writing. Brings them all out in a hot flush of words, number Five." Three office girls, who are in the restroom on their way to work, are initially presented as stereotypes who eventually reveal more complex personalities and varied experiences. In the security of this all-female space they draw on their memories and fantasies, moving toward a rejection of men: "*All:* Don't need them. Don't need them."

The introduction of a mother with a boy doll evokes hilarity and fear in the women and makes oblique reference to the original myth. The boy doll is placed on a chair, stripped, and scrutinized by the women. "There's no harm in looking," states the First Office Girl, parodying the voyeurism of the myth. The humor of this scene is undercut by the attempted suicide of another girl. The scene is, however, given farcical treatment as the Third Office Girl falls down the toilet pan in the course of her rescue attempt, and Ada instructs Meg to "clean up that mess." Duffy deals with themes common to her work—rejection, self-hatred, and violence—with a comic and satirical touch. Finally, as the old woman "cowers down making little noises of fear," a figure, whom they believe to be a man, emerges from number Seven. In a coup de théâtre of violence, with "frenzied activity" and menacing whispers, the figure is destroyed and shoved into the incinerator in an undignified and practical fashion, again disrupting expectations of the genre.

Wash House is a one-act play written as a sequel to *Rites* and set in a laundromat. It received a platform reading by the Oxford University Dramatic Society but remains unpublished. Duffy again demonstrates her skill as both a poet and dramatist. Her uses of wordplay, rhyme, patterns, repetitions, echoes, and a chorus serve as a reminder of the construction of meaning and its shifting contexts. Audience expectation is frequently disrupted, sometimes by the persistent alarm that interrupts the narrative, lending the washing machines a powerful, almost Gothic presence, and at other times by Brechtian techniques of alienation. The play is essentially optimistic but offers fierce criticism of patriarchal society and the difficulties women face in finding ways to create themselves. By juxtaposing the mundane with the quasi-religious and mythical, Duffy parodies aspects of cleansing and catharsis: "Remember it'll all come out in the wash."

The piece is a mixture of styles, with music-hall and absurdist elements juxtaposed with naturalistic settings and near-naturalistic dialogue. The cast is all female, apart from the attendant, Georgie, who is in the process of having a sex change and draws attention throughout to gender as performance. Again, the often farcical plot explores the role of the "outsider" and considers issues of race and culture. The love story, which is central to the piece, is between Venus and Diana, mythical figures given contemporary resonance, and their masks of identity are constructed by society. This theme is developed by the introduction of three generations of Arab women, the eldest of whom wears a facemask. When Diana removes the Arab mother's mask, she discovers another one lying underneath, pointing to the multiple layers of identity and the internalization of cultural codes and assumptions: "But the mask has grown into my flesh like another skin." The Arab mother is unable to imagine different lives for future generations of Arab women, and the youngest child is both symbolically and literally dumb. Language is seen as a means of both freedom and imprisonment for women. Despite differences of class, culture, and sexuality, the women are united as "sisters" and use the laundromat, like the restroom in *Rites,* as a woman's space: "Here in London we come to the washeteria where we can meet away from the eyes of men and laugh together."

Although Georgie occupies a central role—he controls the space and services the machines—he can never succeed in his desire to become a woman; thus, his singing and dancing disguise a strong sense of sadness and isolation. His obsession with female saints in his search for a name is at once funny and tragic. His research leads him to identify the systematic violence with which women have been treated throughout history, and he draws parallels with the experience of contemporary women. Georgie acts as mediator between the audience and the events onstage and uses direct audience address: "And then there's you lot looking in as if we couldn't see you and us looking out as if you couldn't see us." The play draws attention to the act of looking, through the use of an onstage mirror and references to voyeurism and the power of the gaze.

Georgie wants to be a Hollywood queen, "with my broken heart on the sleeve of my filmy negligee," but "They don't make women like that anymore so I've got to make myself." Duffy, whose interest in ambiguity is apparent in the character, treats his sexuality in a playful manner. In his final speech he warns himself against envy in an amusing inversion of the Freudian concept of "penis envy."

The lesbian relationship in the play is dealt with honestly and sensitively. Free from the stereotyping suffered and internalized by the other women in the piece, the relationship is simple, equal, erotic, and optimistic. Although the play explores various positions of resistance to stereotyping, this relationship is perhaps the most powerful and the one most likely to give pleasure. The play treats other areas of female life and history comically, parodying witchcraft, folklore, cliché, and "old wives' tales." Two older women act as a chorus and parody the notion of old wives' tales; in an entertaining double act with the repeated refrain "Happy times," they offer a critique of heterosexual relationships and the domestic role of women.

Duffy's concern with suicide is evident in her next play, *Solo* (1970), a reworking of the Narcissus myth that was performed together with *Old Tyme* as part of an evening of plays. The two are linked by their Greek themes. Nigel, the central character, uses a mirror to highlight his lack of identity and negative image of himself. The play is set in the bathroom, where Nigel revisits his childhood. The set is dazzlingly white, with a "gilt and ornate bathroom stool" that parodies the pretensions of this otherwise mundane character. Nigel adopts a variety of roles, replaying earlier experiences and indicating forces and attitudes that have shaped his life. Duffy's imaginative use of props in the creation of roles provides humor and suggests disturbing parallels between religion and state violence. His mother, played by Nigel in a falsetto voice, draws attention to the working-class background from which he is never fully able to escape: "Now we've moved darling there's no need to tell anyone at your new school that we once had an outside pennyhouse." The audience is made aware of Nigel's ambitious nature by the Yorkshire accent of, presumably, his father: "Yer like a bloody lift always on the up. One day yer'll go clean through t'roof." However, Nigel's final exit into the bottomless bath points to death and failure. The piece is highly amusing in Nigel's acting out of fantasies and attempts to make himself important. The repeated sentiments of "Change and decay in all around I see" undercut the lighthearted tone of childish innocence in Nigel's performances and suggest a desperation in his actions and despair at his inability to escape the realities of aging: "You're like a whored out drab," he tells the critical alter ego reflected in his mirror.

Duffy's use of language and range of discourses add theatrical interest and keen insights into this pathetic figure who is obsessed with perfection. Much of the language is nonsensical, yet familiar—Nigel's cries of "Quark, quark; quark, quark" as he plays with his ducks in the bathtub suggest a blend of innocence and madness, revealing the chaos masked by the exterior calm of his rituals of ablution. His wife appears on several occasions in the shadows, vainly calling for him. This offstage presence reinforces his isolation and coldness as he moves toward his final descent in the paradoxical cold of the bath. Having stripped off his silk boxer shorts with yellow monogram, Nigel stands naked, facing himself in the mirror, and tells himself, "It's time; it's really time. You're crying. It's alright. I'm here. Come on." Duffy creates a moving picture of a solitary figure of despair who, like many of her characters, is unable to find a satisfactory identity and is alienated from himself.

Writing about *Olde Tyme* in *Contemporary Literature: Women Dramatists* Frank Marcus commented that it "is in many ways her most interesting and original play. . . . studded with brilliant Pirandellian ideas." The play concerns a television tycoon who is metaphorically castrated when his workers rebel and overcome his tyranny. He has fond memories of his mother, a music-hall queen, and plans to re-create an old music-hall evening, starring his mother. However, here arrival undermines his sense of self as a prosperous tycoon and shatters his sexual fantasies about her. Class and identity issues are again given theatrical treatment, and there is a clash of styles and a mixture of humor and social criticism.

"Sarah Loves Caroline" is an undated three-act play that was never performed or published that explores the complexities of lesbian romance. Reunited after twenty-five years, two former pupils of St. Friday's School fall in love and revisit their childhood experiences from a new perspective. The play is unusual and ahead of its time in staging the physical, emotional, and psychological states of two women in their forties reflecting on their choices and coming to terms with their sexuality. In the opening act, Caroline rewrites *Twelfth Night* (circa 1601) so that Olivia and Viola confess their love for each other; Shakespeare's play becomes a metaphor for Sarah and Caroline's relationship. The kiss at the end of the act is both a parody of the notion of "the happy ending" and a brave acknowledgement of the physical and sexual needs of older women. Sarah and Caroline sing, both together and to each other, throughout the play, conveying their warmth, tenderness, and sense of fun. They tell bawdy jokes and stories, talking openly about their previous sexual experiences and crushes.

Glimpses into their developing relationship are offered in a series of telephone conversations, for which Duffy uses lighting economically to indicate their responses to each other. Their conversations are a blend of the poetic and the mundane, with a range of intertextual references that subtly challenge patriarchal assumptions and raise questions of class, age, parenthood, and politics. Duffy's interest in animal rights is also apparent in this play, in a critique of foxhunting and in Sarah's story of a blackbird injured by a cat, presaging future events.

Act 3 takes place in Sarah's flat after her death in a car crash in New York. Sarah appears as a ghost, and the scene has a gentle lyricism that avoids sentiment. The two women kiss and dance in a tender moment that combines elements of myth and fairy tale with images of death and absence. As Sarah departs, she writes "Sarah loves Caroline" on the mirror, inscribing herself in her relationship; Duffy frequently uses mirrors, pictures, photographs, and verbal references to draw attention to the constructed nature of identity. The piece has a rather ambiguous conclusion, leaving the audience to wonder if Caroline's early pessimism really has succeeded in "disarming whatever powers there are." In the final scene, Sarah's son, Robin, outlines his struggle in accepting his mother's sexual choice and demonstrates the complexity of parent-child relationships.

Similar in theme, the undated "Unfinished Business" is a television play that has not been produced, set in the school hall of the Harriet Busby Comprehensive School, formerly the High School for Girls. The play explores the relationship between Jo and Marion at the Old Girls' reunion, and Duffy uses flashbacks to offer an insight into their early experiences and pleasures. The complex nature of lesbian desire is emphasized, and Marion finally admits to Jo, "I want you. I always have." Although Jo reciprocates the love, it is never consummated, and the business remains unfinished at the end of the play.

Many aspects of female experience are considered in the piece, in particular those of aging and change. Marion highlights the contradiction between the inner and outer self when she states, "You feel just the same inside and then you look in the mirror and know that old woman is you." Issues of class are addressed with specific reference to women—Jo is a successful artist in London and has high status, whereas Marion leads a domestic life in Southampton, married with two children and running a personnel department because "Women are supposed to be good with people." Although separated by class, their gender experiences are similar, and Duffy re-creates childhood experiences to illustrate this point, using frank language and period detail: "The senior washroom was the only place you could talk, in the privacy of the bogs and the Dr White's machine that was always empty when you needed it most," reminisces Jo. Duffy also raises the question of child abuse in Marion's reference to her stepfather, and the ambiguous nature of its presentation adds tension to the piece. Marion's desire for power and revenge on her stepfather draws on mythology as she declares, "I want to be one of those tough old goddesses with blood on their hands."

Dancing is used intermittently throughout the play to establish the romantic and physical nature of Jo and Marion's relationship. The sword dance that the girls reenact from a childhood experience is highly erotic, yet charged with images of violence and death. The appropriation of traditionally male roles is theatrically exciting, and the phallic swords suggest a playful reversal of prescribed roles. Sex and death are juxtaposed in the context of childhood rituals and fantasy play. Although the play ends on a sad and wistful note, the final image—the grin between the protagonists—conveys a sense of optimism and secret pleasures available only to the girls/women.

Duffy's reputation as a writer and critic developed significantly during the 1970s and 1980s as she continued to write poems and novels as well as plays. She was a founder of the Writers Action Group in 1972 and served as joint chairman of the Writers' Guild of Great Britain from 1977 to 1978 and president from 1985 to 1989. She was chairman of the Greater London Arts Literature Panel from 1979 to 1981 and of the British Copyright Council, Authors Lending and Copyright Society in 1982. She received Arts Council bursaries in 1963, 1966, and 1975, as well as a Society of Authors traveling scholarship in 1985. She also became a fellow of the Royal Society of Literature (1985). Her keen interest in literary figures, especially female ones, influenced much of her writing in the 1970s and beyond.

A Nightingale in Bloomsbury Square (performed in 1973, published in 1974), one of several biographical pieces, is set in Monk's Lodge, Rodmell, on 28 March 1941 as Virginia Woolf contemplates her suicide in the presence of two ghosts, Sigmund Freud and Vita Sackville-West. Images of death are evident in the "long funeral drapes" of the opening set, and the play also addresses issues of childlessness, war, and the role of the woman writer. Duffy makes intertextual reference to Woolf's writing in order to make sense of her decision to kill herself: Woolf says, "I killed my mother. I murdered the angel in the house," a decision necessary for her as a female writer but fraught with feelings of guilt. She tells Freud that "No one is ever truthful. Everyone shifts, makes shift, is shifty and shiftless together, is a chameleon and a shape-changer," indicating her distrust of people and the fragility and instability of human behavior. Freud is presented as a shrunken old man who employs psychoanalytical thought for comic effect: "You are suffering from post-natal depression after the birth of your book: that is all." Woolf replies, "All books by women are stillbirths, born out of their mother's madness."

Duffy uses cross-dressing in the play in order to establish Sackville-West as a homoerotic figure; the stage directions indicate her likeness to Marlene Dietrich as she enters in male evening dress. Her slow dance with Woolf offers an insight into the deeply sensual nature of their relationship, enriched by a kiss toward the end of the play. Woolf is able to name her oppression but is unable to find a way of escaping it: "How will they place us in order of merit, the patriarchy that judges these things?"

Sackville-West's epilogue is in rhyming couplets and offers a cynical view of the exploitation of the woman writer:

> A classic, hidebound or in Penguin dress,
> Her academic rape ensures success;
> Witness a throng of dusty PhDs
> Who gut her books to further their degrees.
> (Dead writers please them most who can't spit back,
> Point out perceptions that most critics lack).

Marcus commented in *The Sunday Telegraph* (23 September 1973), "Miss Duffy recreates her [Woolf] with sympathy in a work of immense distinction." Duffy uses a range of theatrical styles in the piece to highlight feminist concerns and raise questions about sexuality and its performance and the complex position of the woman writer.

Between the years of 1973 and 1995 Duffy's artistic efforts were more fully concentrated on the writing of her poems and novels. She was also politically active and involved in environmental and feminist movements. During this time period, she published eighteeen books, including novels, essays, and play collections.

Duffy's next play, *The Masque of Henry Purcell* (performed in 1995, though never published) was written to coincide with the three hundredth anniversary of Purcell's death. It is a highly theatrical piece that utilizes music, dancing, ghosts, trap doors, special effects, and mime to recall the life of the seventeenth-century composer as he lies dying. The piece employs flashback and caricature to evoke the political and social positions influencing his life and work; but, by contrast, the naturalistic portrayal of his wife, Frances, offers perceptive commentary on the role of women in both an historical and contemporary setting. Paul Taylor, writing in *The Independent* (9 October 1995), stated: "this new play–with music–sticks up for the wife." Purcell is a thoroughly human character, drinking to excess so frequently that Frances is obliged to lock him out and is subsequently blamed for his death. Frances has a strong narrative presence in the piece and makes incisive commentary on the hypocrisy and moral ambiguities of her time. Duffy plays with a range of theatrical conventions, using the masque form as a framework and drawing on the grotesque medieval representations of heaven and hell and the courtly rituals of formal dance, which give delightfully sinister undertones to the piece as a whole. In the program for the Southwark Playhouse premiere, Duffy states that she is setting Purcell "not only against the background of his times but also of his family and to explore the tensions in what I believe was a complex personality."

"The Passionate Shepherdess" is an unpublished, unproduced radio play that tells the story of seventeenth-century writer Aphra Behn's life through use of letters and a range of narrative voices. (Duffy's 1977 book by the same title is a biography.) Yet again, the role of the female writer is called into question, and the androgynous nature of the writer is considered: "All I ask is the privilege for my masculine part the poet in me." The contemporary language gives the play immediacy, and the political context is linked directly to events in Behn's life. Duffy has demonstrated a consistent interest in Behn's work and plans to write an opera or musical based on Behn's novel *Oroonoko* (1688).

François Villon, major French poet of the Middle Ages, is the subject of Duffy's unpublished play "Villon." The piece is funny, violent, anarchic, slapstick, and antiestablishment, as the protagonist turns to crime and finally goes into exile. Duffy's introduction to this work is interesting not only for her comments on the character but also for her views on theater and its function. She explains, "Every period creates and needs its own myths and heroes. . . . By using a historical period or character to parallel a contemporary situation we are able to distance ourselves from the myth, to see it in a mirror and therefore more wholly." She describes Villon as "a petty criminal because of his own wanton drive for self destruction egged on by a society which educated him to a high standard and then gave him no acceptable outlet for his abilities." Duffy is interested in paradoxes and contradictions: "I want them [the audience] to identify in Villon the conflicts in their own natures: the urge to violence and non-conformity; the loneliness of non-communication; the self-pity and frenetic self aggrandisement."

Maureen Duffy is both a respected professional and a committed political figure whose lifelong involvement in local and global politics informs her artistic agendas. Duffy's work for the stage is often disturbing and radical, experimental, and employing contradictory discourses. In many ways, it could be said that her work is "total theater," reminiscent of the ideas of Antonin Artaud and Jean Genet, employing Brechtian techniques and often grotesque styles. Her work is complex and exciting, and her unperformed scripts offer opportunities for future national and international performances.

References:

Dulan Barber, *Transatlantic Review,* 45 (Spring 1973);

Beate Neumeier, ed., *Engendering Realism and Postmodernism: Contemporary Women Writers in Britain* (Amsterdam: Rodopi, 2001);

Jane Rule, *Lesbian Images* (London: Peter Davies, 1976);

Lorna Sage, *Maureen Duffy* (London: Book Trust in conjunction with the British Council, 1989);

Christine Sizemore, *A Female Vision of the City* (Knoxville: University of Tennessee Press, 1989).

Papers:

King's College, London, has a collection of Maureen Duffy's papers.

Robin Glendinning
(1 September 1938 –)

David Grant
Queen's University, Belfast

PLAY PRODUCTIONS: *Jennifer's Vacation,* Dublin, Gate Theatre (Dublin Theatre Festival), 14 October 1981; produced as *Stuffing It,* London, Tricycle Theatre, 1982;

Mumbo Jumbo, Manchester, Royal Exchange Theatre, 8 May 1986; Belfast, Lyric Theatre Belfast, 28 Jaunary 1987; London, Lyric Theatre Hammersmith, 15 May 1987;

Culture Vultures, Belfast, Lyric Theatre Belfast, 12 October 1988;

Donny Boy, Manchester, Royal Exchange Theatre, 1 November 1990; Dublin, Tinderbox Theatre Company (Dublin Theatre Festival), 7 October 1991;

Summerhouse, Galway, Druid Lane Theatre, 20 April 1994.

BOOKS: *Mumbo Jumbo* (London: Chappell Plays, 1987);

Donny Boy (London: Warner Chappell Plays, 1990);

Three Plays: Mumbo Jumbo; Donny Boy; Summerhouse (Belfast: Lagan Press, 2004).

PRODUCED SCRIPTS: *The Artist,* radio, BBC, 4 August 1977;

Conversations with a Child, radio, BBC, 7 September 1979;

Stuffing It, radio, BBC Radio 3, 4 June 1981;

A Night of the Campaign, by Glendinning and Leonard Kingston, television, BBC1, 4 August 1985;

Culture Vultures, radio, BBC, 18 July 1986;

Condemning Violence, radio, BBC, 16 March 1987;

Mumbo Jumbo, radio, BBC, 25 July 1988;

The Words Are Strange, radio, BBC, 6 May 1991;

Shooting the Moon, radio, BBC, 25 June 1994;

Stopping the Rising, radio, BBC, 8 December 1997;

Emergency, radio, BBC, 5 February 1999.

OTHER: *The Words Are Strange,* in *Best Radio Plays of 1991: The BBC Giles Cooper Award Winners* (London: Methuen, 1992), pp. 1–63.

Amid the flurry of playwriting that arose from the Troubles that began in Ireland in 1968, Robin Glendin-

Robin Glendinning (from the cover for Mumbo Jumbo, *1987; Bruccoli Clark Layman Collection)*

ning has been distinctive in having offered a middle-class establishment response to what has been widely regarded as a working-class problem. Where other writers such as Martin Lynch, Graham Reid, Christina Reid, and Marie Jones have all helped reveal the social roots of Northern Ireland's violent past, only Glendinning has directly engaged in the political process. He is the first Irish dramatist since Richard Brinsley Sheridan to stand for Parliament, and his work is founded on a depth of understanding that merits lasting attention.

Robert James "Robin" Glendinning was born in Belfast on 1 September 1938. His father, Acheson Harden Glendinning, who had served with distinction in the Royal Engineers during World War II, moved to County Armagh at the end of the war and took up farming but never settled back into civilian life. He and Robin's mother, Christina, had three other children: Will, Rosemary, and Johnny. The family was closely associated with the linen industry, the principle economic engine of nineteenth-century Belfast, but his background was also a highly political one. His great-grandfather had been a Home Rule M.P. for North Antrim in the Westminster Parliament, aligning himself to the 1906 Liberal government. His mother's father was a Unionist M.P. As he recalled in an unpublished interview with David Grant on 4 June 2003, "politics was always discussed at home."

Glendinning attended Rockport School in Holywood, just outside Belfast. It was a preparatory school for those destined for the English public (that is, private) school sector, and Glendinning proceeded to Belfast's nearest equivalent, Campbell College, which later became the model for the school in his play *Mumbo Jumbo* (performed in 1986, published in 1987). He went on to study history at Trinity College, Dublin, with the intention of becoming a clergyman in the Church of Ireland. After graduating, however, and taking several temporary teaching jobs around Northern Ireland, he completed the teacher-training course at Stranmillis College in Belfast, which led in 1964 to a job at Omagh Academy, where he taught for the next eleven years.

Glendinning's lifelong interest in politics had up to this point been focused principally on events in London. Although Northern Ireland had maintained its own parliament at Stormont since the partition of Ireland in 1921, local politics tended to be a stagnant and parochial affair. But with the election in 1963 of Terence O'Neill as prime minister of Northern Ireland, there seemed to be some possibility of reform. The Unionist audience in whose company Glendinning heard O'Neill speak in Omagh shortly after his arrival there, however, only served to awaken Glendinning to the full absurdity of the local political scene, in which complicity between Unionists and Nationalists maintained the status quo.

As the Civil Rights movement gathered momentum, he found himself one of few Protestants attending meetings in Omagh, but he resisted attempts by the organizers to make him the "token Protestant" on the committee. But he continued to have an active interest in politics, in 1969 setting up Omagh's first meeting of the New Ulster Movement, an organization that campaigned for political, economic, and social reforms in Northern Ireland. This activity soon led to the foundation of the Alliance Party, in which Glendinning and his brother Will were both key players.

He worked full-time for two and a half years as party organizer of the nonsectarian Alliance Party during one of the most turbulent periods in the political history of Northern Ireland, standing twice for Parliament without success. In 1976 he returned to Belfast with his wife, Lorna Kyle, whom he married on 4 July 1968, and three children to take up a teaching post in the English department of the Royal Belfast Academical Institution ("Inst"); he worked there until 1992, when he left to become a full-time writer.

He continued, however, as campaign manager for his brother Will in local elections. Will Glendinning's constituency was in West Belfast, the crucible of sectarian division, and canvassing in the area familiarized Glendinning with every shade of Northern Ireland's complex political spectrum. He remembers the period of the Hunger Strikes in 1981 as especially tense. Such experiences encouraged Glendinning to devote more of his energies to writing plays.

He had started writing short stories in the mid 1970s and had gotten some published in Dublin's *Irish Press* newspaper, winning a Hennessey Award. A radio play, *The Artist,* based on his time at Trinity College, Dublin, was produced by the BBC in 1977. But he was drawn above all to live performance. He had become heavily involved in amateur drama while at Omagh Academy, directing several school plays and even appearing as Henry VIII in a pageant for the Omagh Inter-Schools History Society. On his return to Belfast, he began in earnest to expand his understanding of acting and performance. "The Linen Hall Library," he told Grant, "was on my way home and I really started to get educated in Irish drama. History began to take second place."

Another radio play followed, and in 1979 he was awarded a Schoolmaster Fellowship to Trinity College, Dublin, which allowed him to spend a term in Dublin away from teaching. This period resulted in a new play, *Stuffing It,* about a middle-class Belfast Christmas. The head of the BBC's radio drama department, Robert Cooper, produced it for BBC Radio 3 in 1981, leading to a production at Dublin's Gate Theatre in October of the same year for the Dublin Theatre Festival. The Gate management insisted on a change of title to the less provocative *Jennifer's Vacation,* but the original title was restored when Cooper directed the London premiere at the Tricycle Theatre in 1982. Throughout his career, producers (and by implication, audiences) in England have proved more receptive to his plays than his fellow countrymen in Northern Ireland.

Glendinning eschews the comfortable vernacular preoccupations that characterize the work of many of his Northern Ireland contemporaries. Despite the fact that Belfast audiences are still predominantly middle class, the preference for new plays in the early 1980s was almost exclusively for representations of working-class life. While such plays have undoubtedly helped to extend understanding of the social and political roots of Northern Ireland's tragic history, Glendinning's work has fulfilled an important complementary role in its analysis of Northern Ireland's Protestant middle class. Though much has been made of the attractiveness to audiences of hearing drama in their "own voice," it may well be that middle-class audiences in Belfast have been more receptive to drama that explains the Troubles as a working-class problem and have been resistant to seeing their own kind exposed onstage.

The reception of *Stuffing It* in London revealed other ironies, however. The location of the Tricycle Theatre in Kilburn, an area of London long associated with the Irish, may have seemed appropriate for an Irish play, but this play offered an unaccustomed brand of Irishness. "If it wasn't for the politics," wrote Irving Wardle in *The Times,* "this could be set in Hampstead." In fact, it was set in Belfast's equivalent of that prosperous London suburb, the Malone Road. The teenage daughter of a well-to-do Belfast family returns home for Christmas at the end of her first term at university, bringing with her a radically left-wing young Englishman, whose part, says Glendinning, came straight out of a political pamphlet. Glendinning is scathing about the ignorance of both political extremes in England about the nuances of the Northern Ireland situation. That this ignorance extends across the full spectrum of English life is a point reinforced by Wardle's mystification that Hampstead attitudes could exist in Belfast. Nevertheless, the play was well received.

The success of *Stuffing It* secured Glendinning an agent, who recommended he send his next play, *Mumbo Jumbo,* to the Mobil Playwriting Competition, and in 1985 it was declared the joint winner of this prestigious award. This honor led to a full production at Manchester's Royal Exchange Theatre, directed by Nicholas Hytner (who later became artistic director of the National Theatre of Great Britain). Glendinning was unequivocal about this opportunity in his interview with Grant: "The whole experience of the Royal Exchange was fantastic."

Mumbo Jumbo is set in a leading Belfast school and owes much of its detail to the author's experiences as a pupil at Campbell College and a teacher at Inst. As he explained in a program note for the Lyric Theatre Belfast's 1987 production, "it was inspired by a suggestion from Robert Cooper that I should write something about the crisis of identity faced by Ulster Protestants and in particular their relationship with the English." One of the things that struck audiences in England was the familiarity of the educational system illustrated by this play, in which young men play cricket amid all the traditions of a typical English "public" school. This irony is absolutely at the heart of the drama, as

Cover for the 1987 publication of Glendinning's 1986 play, about the conflicts of Irish boys in a Belfast school that is modeled on British public schools and has an Englishman as dean (Bruccoli Clark Layman Collection)

Glendinning is showing the unconscious colonialism of the world in which he grew up.

For most of the twentieth century, the headmasters and many of the teachers in Northern Ireland's most influential schools tended to be appointed from England. Outsiders are often bewildered at the dogmatic assertion of Ulster Protestants that they are British rather than Irish, but that is essentially what Unionism means. And it is a position fostered not least by the Protestant part of the segregated educational system, of which those schools modeled on the English public-school system are the most highly regarded. Since the 1990s, the development of an integrated sector has begun to challenge this dominance, but in 1986, when *Mumbo Jumbo* was first produced, this movement was in its infancy.

The use in the play of American writer Vachel Lindsay's poem "The Congo" (1914), from which its title is drawn, points to the tribal nature of Northern

Ireland life and triggers an indignant response from Creaney, a proud young Orangeman (a member of the loyalist institution dedicated to the memory of the victory in Ireland of the Protestant king William III over the Catholic king James II at the Battle of the Boyne in 1690) who resents what he perceives as the sneering disdain of his teacher, the school dean. The dean is an Englishman who has no time for the outlandish trappings of the Orange Order. But *Mumbo Jumbo,* written in the early 1980s, the most intractable period of the Troubles in the aftermath of the Hunger Strikes, is above all about the need to move on. Another pupil, Barry Dunham, the son of a judge, wrestles with the inconsistencies between his education and the changing world around him, and unlike Creaney, is less secure in an alternative Protestant value system. But following the dramatic climax of the play, in which he learns of his father's assassination by the IRA, he seeks out the Black Pig's Dyke, an ancient archaeological feature that he believes provides evidence of an Ulster identity, distinct from concepts of Britishness or Irishness. He does so in an effort to escape both the dead hand of a colonial tradition and also cultural disenfranchisement in an Ireland where to succeed as a poet "you have to be called Seamus."

Glendinning's express aim in writing *Mumbo Jumbo* was to present onstage an Ulster Protestant who was not a caricature. In his interview with Grant, he cherished the memory of hearing the reviewer for BBC Radio 4's *Kaleidoscope* arts magazine confess to the appalling realization that he would have to rethink totally his attitude to Northern Ireland.

The acclaim accorded Hytner's excellent production of *Mumbo Jumbo* resulted in Glendinning's belated acknowledgment by the Lyric Theatre Belfast, who produced the play in 1987. While it attracted reasonable audiences, the response was less enthusiastic than in England. This reaction may have been caused in part by the economic necessity of casting real schoolboys to fill out the classroom, whereas in Manchester every role had been played by an experienced professional. But there was also a sense of resistance to the play itself. Audience members walked out on the first night during a sexually explicit scene between two schoolboys, and the reviewer for the *Belfast News Letter,* Charles Fitzgerald, dismissed the play as "two and a half hours of bludgeoning junk" (30 January 1987). Although this critique generated protests in the Letters Page a few days later from a theatergoer rallying to defend the play, the underlying message seemed clear. Belfast did not welcome this kind of scrutiny of its mores being aired on an English stage.

Nevertheless, the Lyric Theatre Belfast went on to produce Glendinning's next play, *Culture Vultures,* in 1988. This work was an extended version of his 1986 radio play by the same name, which had centered on the amateur production of an "Ulsterised" version of Anton Chekhov's *The Cherry Orchard* (1904), titled *The Brambly Orchard.* The stage play included a fuller evocation of small-town life in Northern Ireland. Roly Miller, a would-be playwright and director of the amateur group, struggles to get his performers to see the relevance of Chekhov's play to their own lives. Roly's own hotel (significantly called The Imperial), his old family business and symbol of Unionist power in the divided town, is up for sale. Roly is ready, even anxious, to see it sold to a Catholic friend from "across the bridge." But at the auction, the weight of his heritage and the sad look in the eyes of his father, Colonel Miller, cause him to renege. Glendinning substitutes for Chekhov's felling of the cherry trees the more topical image of the hotel being blown up by an IRA bomb. The fact that Roly's father, the standard-bearer of the old order, is portrayed in his dotage, symbolizes the decline of traditional Unionism and foreshadows the character of Eva Ross in *Summerhouse* (performed in 1994, published in 2004).

The difficulty experienced by Roly's actors in understanding the metaphorical import of Chekhov's play resonates with Glendinning's own frustration at the response of his home audience. As he put it in his interview with Grant: "I'd like to think it is too hard for them to take and what they really like here is what they consider to be raunchy working class work that they can patronise."

By contrast, Casper Wrede, cofounder of the Manchester Royal Exchange, eagerly committed to a production of Glendinning's next play, *Donny Boy* (performed and published in 1990), within a few days of reading it. A riposte perhaps to the Belfast appetite for working-class drama, *Donny Boy* is a world apart from *Mumbo Jumbo.* Instead of targeting outmoded establishment values, it sets out to investigate the impact of nationalist mythology in working-class Catholic communities. Like *Stuffing It,* this play draws on the polemical rhetoric of political pamphlets (of which Glendinning has an encyclopedic knowledge) to inform the dialogue. As he explained to Grant: "I thought I knew the voice.... I wasn't removed from it because I was in there talking to people and my brother. The mother is an examination of traditional Republicanism as seen in Belfast."

Donny is the apple of his mother's eye, with the body of a man but the mind of a child. Regardless of his arrested mental development, when he returns home with a revolver that has been foisted on him by Cahill, an escaping terrorist, Donny assumes in his mother's mind the heroic proportions of the iconic figures of Irish history such as eighteenth-century rebel Wolfe Tone and nationalist leader Robert Emmet. When Cahill arrives in the house to check that Donny has disposed of the weapon, he is horrified to discover it still on the premises. As a British Army patrol approaches, he flees, leaving Ma to face the full impact of their search. The second act opens on a highly theatrical vision of the ensuing devastation, with Donny hanging Christ-like from the shattered beams of the house. When Cahill returns to face Ma's wrath, the ambivalence of his own situation becomes clear. He is a police informer turned reluctant assassin. When he again makes his escape, Ma is left nursing not only her battered son but also the inconsistencies inherent in the Republican ideology that has been at the center of her system of values.

For a Northern Ireland audience, the play proved highly provocative. Responses ranged from accusations of the play being "anti-working class" to a letter from a retired army officer in Enniskillen's *Impartial Reporter* newspaper that it was Republican propaganda. *The Irish Times* (9 October 1991), on the other hand, welcomed "this black comedy turned loose on the patriot game. Republican myths, as remoulded in Northern Ireland, fall prey to a knife that twists its way through the heart and soul of IRA iconography and its four green fields." Coming half a tempestuous decade after *Mumbo Jumbo*, it shares with the earlier play a rejection of entrenched opinions, and it anticipates the imminent historic changes within Republicanism itself. *Donny Boy* was named best new play in the Martini-Rossi Regional Theatre Awards and received a Manchester Evening News Theatre Award in 1991.

Stylistically, Glendinning's next play, *Summerhouse*, falls somewhere between the relative naturalism of *Mumbo Jumbo* and the expressionism of *Donny Boy*. The protagonist, Eva Ross, is the last descendant of the "Big House" (home of the ruling family) in an Ulster village, who knows that she is soon to die from cancer. Socially and politically she is the polar opposite of Donny's Ma, but she too is having to cope with a relentless tide of change.

Summerhouse received its first production not in Manchester, but at Galway's Druid Lane Theatre in the Republic of Ireland in 1994. For a Galway audience, unfamiliar with the subtleties of Northern Ireland society, the bold (almost hysterical) portrayal of Eva was highly entertaining and succeeded on the level of farce. And there are many aspects of the play that lend themselves to such an approach, not least the clever parodies of traditional hymn lyrics. But what the production failed to capture was the passionate truthfulness and real pathos of Eva's predicament. Like the establishment figures in *Mumbo Jumbo*, she is challenged by a

Cover for Glendinning's 1990 play, in which a fleeing terrorist leaves his gun with a mentally handicapped man and thereby exposes the man and his mother to the wrath of the British army (Bruccoli Clark Layman Collection)

younger generation to come to terms with rapid changes to the accepted order. Her son, Gerald, a television producer, clearly sees the world to which she belongs as quaint and outdated. Her daughter is more nostalgic, regretting the decay around her, as symbolized by the summerhouse itself, quietly "jungled" by nettles. The image recalls the dean's charge of Ulster tribalism in *Mumbo Jumbo*. But while her solicitor husband resorts to drink, Eva retains throughout a quiet dignity.

Glendinning was influenced in the early stages of writing the play by the ideas of Elisabeth Kübler-Ross, who in her classic treatise *On Death and Dying* (1969) analyzed the process of coming to terms with fatal illness as a progression from denial to anger to bargaining to depression to acceptance. The playwright told Grant, "It occurred to me that here was a paradigm for the Unionist position in Northern Ireland. The first draft had scenes corresponding to these stages, but then the characters upset that—which was just as well!" However schematic the initial vision, the play evolved into a passionate and compassionate exploration of the intricacies of Unionism, as necessary as it is unfashionable.

Disease and disability are frequent metaphors in Glendinning's work: Eva's cancer, Donny's mental incapacity, the dean's war wound, Colonel Miller's senility. "Disease provides a catalyst for the drama," he explained to Grant. "It sets up all sorts of strange things happening which might not otherwise happen."

When not engaged in new projects, Glendinning is invariably revisiting established works in a restless process of refinement and revision. Each of his plays inhabits a distinct world, but there are preoccupations that draw them together. In each play, the protagonist is at odds with the almost overwhelming pressure of heritage and expectation.

What characterizes Robin Glendinning's work is a profound intelligence, a capacity to speak his mind, and an observational humor that can find a comic twist in even the most difficult of ideas. He draws on a lifetime of real experience for some of the most telling moments in his plays, be it the inherent absurdity of cross-dressing in a public-school play or the gentle pomposity of a village rector. Unlike some so-called Troubles dramas (a genre to which they do not belong), his plays are built around characters and ideas that have enduring relevance. As he told Grant: "Those voices are in my head so it's natural that they should speak."

Sue Glover
(1 March 1943 –   )

Ksenija Horvat
Queen Margaret University College, Edinburgh

PLAY PRODUCTIONS: *The Seal Wife,* Edinburgh, Lyceum Little Theatre, 21 April 1980; London, Attic Theatre, 29 January 1997;

The Bubble Boy, Pitlochry, Pitlochry Festival Theatre, 1981; Glasgow, Tron Theatre, 27 May 1981;

An Island in Largo, St. Andrews, Byre Theatre, 3 October 1981;

The Straw Chair, Edinburgh, Traverse Theatre, 24 March 1988;

Bondagers, Edinburgh, Traverse Theatre, 3 May 1991; London, Donmar Warehouse, 27 March 1996;

Sacred Hearts, Dundee, Dundee Repertory Theatre, 11 February 1994; London, Drill Hall, 1994;

Artist Unknown, Glasgow, Turnbull High School, 29 January 1996; Scottish tour, 1996;

Shetland Saga, Edinburgh, Traverse Theatre, 28 July 2000.

BOOKS: *Bondagers & The Straw Chair* (London: Methuen, 1997);

Bondagers (Woodstock, Ill.: Dramatic Publishing Company, 1998);

Shetland Saga (London: Nick Hern, 2000; New York: Theatre Communications Group, 2001).

PRODUCED SCRIPTS: *The Watchie,* radio, BBC Scotland, 1976;

Shift Work, radio, BBC Scotland, 1979;

Home Front, television, STV, 1980;

The Spaver Connection, television, STV, 1982;

The Benjamin, radio, BBC Scotland, 1983;

The Wish House, radio, BBC Scotland, 1984;

Take the High Road, television, fifty episodes, STV, 1984–1988;

Mme Perle, radio, BBC1, 1986;

Mme Montand and Mrs Miller, television, BBC, 1992;

Strathblair, television, two episodes, BBC, 1992;

Dear Life, television, BBC, 1993;

The Child and the Journey, radio, BBC, 1994.

Sue Glover (from <http://www.virtualtraverse.com/productions/productions.htm>)

OTHER: *The Bubble Boy,* in *You Don't Know You're Born,* edited by Rony Robinson (London: Hodder & Stoughton, 1991);

Bondagers, in *Made in Scotland: An Anthology of New Scottish Plays,* edited by Ian Brown and Mark Fisher (London: Methuen, 1995), pp. 123–179.

Sue Glover is a leading Scottish playwright whose career includes works for the stage, radio, and television. She considers herself an outsider in theater circles, however, partly because she falls between two groups of women playwrights in Scotland: the authors who had written their major works long before the 1970s (such as Ena Lamont Stewart, Ada Stewart, and Netta Blair), and those authors who appeared on the Scottish playwriting scene during the mid and late 1980s (such as Liz Lochhead, Marcella Evaristi, Rona Munro, and Ann Marie di Mambro). Another reason may be that, following her initial success, Glover found her use of structure and language ardently criticized. As she told Jackie McGlone in 2000, Glover has always thought herself to be unfashionable, since much of her work is set outside the urban Scottish environment: "I don't think I am an urban writer and urban plays are very much the thing in Scottish theatre now. I don't write about factories and high-rise flats."

In her writing, Glover is chiefly concerned with the issues of power and autonomy, authority and freedom, (quasi)historicity and contemporary comment. Her plays largely belong to a strand in Scottish playwriting that has been influenced by the storytelling tradition, and, to an extent, they have remained within the naturalistic canon. However, she often introduces chimerical and mythic elements into the realistic structure. Another common feature of her writing is the linguistic and emotional fragmentation of the protagonists, individuals who communicate in broken, dislocated ways. Glover's protagonists, especially the female ones, are always outsiders in relation to society. Susan Triesman suggests that in her writing Glover concentrates on "difference, transgression and the outcast as images central to women's experience."

Glover was born Susan Claire Hall on 1 March 1943 to Ronald Hall, an Edinburgh veterinary surgeon, and his wife, Lucy Hall. She graduated from the University of Edinburgh in 1965 with a degree in English and French languages and literature. Apart from two years spent in London, where she worked as a teacher and a secretary, and a year in France, during which she attended Montpelier University for six months and worked the other six as an au pair before enrolling at Edinburgh University, she has lived most of her life in Scotland. Since 1968 she has lived in Fife, and the desolate seascape and rich oral tradition of the region have been powerful sources of inspiration in her writing. Glover is separated from her husband and has two sons, Garry Hardie Glover (born in 1967) and Donald Pattulio Glover (born in 1969).

Glover began writing for radio in the 1970s, but little information is available about those works. Her professional playwriting career began in 1980, when, through her membership in the Scottish Society of Playwrights, she came to the attention of Tom Gallagher, who was then a writer-in-residence at the Royal Lyceum Theatre in Edinburgh. Gallagher commissioned her to write her first full-length play, *The Seal Wife* (performed in 1980), for the Lyceum Little Theatre. Glover used elements of the Scottish folk tradition: the play is based on the legend of the Selkies, the Seal People who live in an underwater world or on lonely skerries. According to legends from the Western Isles, the Selkies' natural form is human, but they put on seal skins and the appearance of seals to enable them to pass through the waters from one realm to another. Against the background of these legends, Glover weaves a tale about the complex relationship between man and nature.

The play is set on the beaches around Wemyss, Dysart, and Kircaldy, "an eerie blend of beauty and industrial clutter," as it says in the program note, and it depicts the people who live on the margin of Scottish society—the impoverished, the disillusioned, the forgotten. Agnes Grey and her son, Alec, live on a secluded beach, out on the limb of a small Fife fishing community. Branded as outsiders, they have made the beach their private universe. Agnes is looked upon with suspicion by the community because of her single-parent status, while Alec is shunned because he is a seal hunter, an illegal profession associated by others with violence. The intrusion into this world of a mysterious young woman, Rona, whose apparent connection with the sea and seals kindles Alec's imagination, presses the events to a tragic conclusion. During the play the characters undergo a process of self-discovery that leaves them changed and alone.

In her plays Glover uses two recurrent metaphors that represent aspects of human nature—sea and island. Triesman notes that the sea and wildness epitomize sexuality as the chaos "that is implicit in the boundary-crossing capacity of the seal people." According to the legends, the Selkies are thought to have magical seductive powers over mortals, and on occasion, young men trick Selkie girls into marrying them by stealing the seal skins that the Selkies shed upon transforming into their human form. In *The Seal Wife,* Alec wounds the seal, while the skin is found by two beachcombers and eventually returned to Rona. Glover strays a bit from the legend: while the Selkie must always return to the sea once a human finds the skin, Rona keeps hers in the cottage that she shares with Alec. In this sense the seal skin becomes both the remainder of Rona's "transgressive" nature and a symbol of her freedom to choose. Only when Alec's controlling nature threatens to stifle her, at the end of the play, does she take the skin and return to the sea, leaving behind her husband and baby daughter.

Following the successful Scottish premiere, the Attic Theatre Company and the Warehouse opened their production of *The Seal Wife* in London on 29 January 1997 as the English premiere and a part of the

Attic's tenth-anniversary celebration. On that occasion, Douglas McPherson wrote in *What's On in London* that "such [is] the skill with which Glover [evokes] the atmosphere of the place that the odd cliché [is] easily forgiven." McPherson praised the play for its restraint, dialogue, and cast, as well as Jenny Lee's energetic directing. Similarly, Adrian Turpin commented in *The Independent* (5 February 1997) that "both play and production [boasted] a low-key naturalism which [rubbed] up neatly against the more opaque, symbolic aspects of the tale."

Glover's second play, *The Bubble Boy*, was originally written for television, but after its initial acceptance for a Saturday morning workshop at Pitlochry Festival Theatre in early 1981, it was produced by Tron Theatre, Glasgow, on 27 May 1981. The play was subsequently re-adapted for television and shown as *Dear Life* for the BBC Education series *Scene* on 19 March 1993.

The Bubble Boy deals with eighteen-year-old Tuscan, who suffers from a rare immunity disorder. Because his body is incapable of fighting viruses, he is condemned to live inside a self-contained, bubble-shaped laboratory, continually monitored by a small team of scientists. It is a story of a rite of passage, under circumstances of extreme deprivation of privacy. In an interview included with the play in the collection *You Don't Know You're Born* (1991), Glover said that she read an article years ago about a "bubble boy" in Houston: "He was about four years old, and he couldn't come out of the bubble. I thought: 'It's bad enough when you're four—but how would you feel at fourteen? Sixteen?' It was the photograph of the doctor and the child looking at each other through this perspex wall that got to me." Another incentive to write about this subject was an incident much closer to her heart. Her second son had spent some time in an incubator after he was born and, in her own words, "would have either died, or been brain-damaged, if it hadn't been for medical research." Furthermore, on several occasions, she herself suffered a severe kind of allergy that left her with extensive swellings, and in complete isolation, for long periods of time.

In the same interview Glover described the evolution of the play. She was asked to make changes to the text that was used in the Tron production. In retrospect she believed that the alterations improved the piece:

> The Glasgow theatre didn't want five characters because of the expense, so there are now only four. An improvement, I think. It had been a double-set play (the bubble and an outer office), but the theatre space was small, so it became a single-set play. Another improvement, actually.

Cover for the 1997 publication of two of Glover's plays. *Bondagers* (1991) depicts a group of female agricultural workers, and *The Straw Chair* (1988) is an historical play about an eighteenth-century abduction (Arizona State University Libraries).

The 1993 television version of the play was directed by Jane Howell. Its cast included Jamie Hinde, Tom Georgeson, Gemma Jones, Indra Ové, and John Darling. Set in the year 2018, *Dear Life* does not differ radically from the original stage play and is infused with Orwellian elements and subtle science-fiction references.

Glover's following play, *An Island in Largo*, was first performed at the Byre Theatre, St. Andrews, in October 1981 as part of a showcase of two plays by Scottish women writers, alongside Evaristi's *Wedding Belles and Green Grasses*. Although Glover's main concerns remain the topics of female identity and sexuality, in this play she chooses to explore the correlation between myth and reality and the ways in which people, regardless of gender, are seen, as opposed to who they are. The play tells the life story of Scottish mariner and buccaneer Alexander Selkirk, who inspired Daniel Defoe's novel *Robinson Crusoe* (1719). Glover explores the Selkirk myth in this analysis of an individual's alienation from society. Like Tuscan in *The Bubble Boy*, whose immune system has confined him to life in laboratory conditions away from any physical contact, Selkirk has been emotionally and physically removed from his social environment. While in Tuscan's case the oppressive agent is medical science, in *An Island in Largo* Glover attacks the Church as another agent of social containment. The oppression of an individual by the Church is shown in act 2, scene 1, when, upon his return to Largo after many years of buccaneering, Selkirk is ignored by the local minister during a sermon about the return of a prodigal son. In this scene an ironic discrepancy is established between the Christian dogma, founded on the concepts of love and forgiveness, which is represented in an allegory about a prodigal son, and the theological practice steeped in prudery and dogmatism, as depicted in the minister's renunciation of Largo's prodigal son.

The play shows Selkirk's alienation as twofold. First, it shows his physical alienation on a deserted island in the Juan Fernández cluster, where he asked to be put ashore after a quarrel with Captain Stradling and his crew. Second, it reflects his emotional and spiritual alienation, symbolized in the misunderstanding and ridicule of his family and community at large. Glover introduces Defoe as a character in the story to comment on different ways in which a writer adapts and reinterprets history. Defoe distorts the truth in order to make it acceptable: "A Moral Tale cannot be founded on a quarrel, Mr Selkirk. But it can very well be founded on a shipwreck.... It must have a moral ending. And the people will prefer it to be a happy one also." Any fact about people's lives and identities that might be seen as subversive in the eyes of a social order must be silenced. The writer shrugs off Selkirk's identity to fulfill creative and political agendas, and his experience becomes a literary construct in the same way that his Scottishness is suppressed as undesirable to an English audience. Defoe turns Selkirk, a Scottish buccaneer from Largo, into Robinson Crusoe, an imaginary York mariner, shipwrecked on an uninhabited island on an American coast and strangely delivered by pirates.

Some critics felt that the introduction of Defoe into the story was not an effective device. For example, Allen Wright suggested, in his review of the play in *The Scotsman* (5 October 1981), that "a flippantly contrived encounter with Defoe" creates an "anti-climax to the stimulating scenes on the island." Though Wright felt that actor Alec Heggie gave "a fine performance as the proudly defiant adventurer" and that the play began "splendidly" and was "graced with some excellent lines and imaginative touches," he also suggested that it "ran out of steam long before the end." He thought it a great shame that the author and the director, Adrian Reynolds, did not tighten up the second act.

In subsequent plays Glover explores the gender and economic exploitation of the feminine through its removal from a public sphere. *The Straw Chair* (performed in 1988, published in 1997) is based on the life of a real person, Rachel Chiesley, Lady Grange. Her abduction in 1732 was arranged by her husband, James Erskine of Grange, to prevent her revealing his links with the Jacobites in the highest circles of Edinburgh society. She was subsequently taken to the island of St. Kilda (Hirta), where she was held prisoner until her death. The play begins with the arrival of a middle-aged minister, Aneas, and his young bride, Isabel, on the island, where they encounter not only mistrust from the locals but also the drunken antics of a half-crazed Rachel.

The Straw Chair was first produced on 24 March 1988 by the Traverse Theatre Company, in association with Focus Theatre Company Scotland and with financial support from the Scottish Post Office Board, as part of Traverse's twenty-fifth-anniversary season. This production is also significant because it opened a new era of Traverse Theatre, their first public season upon obtaining a public theater license after a quarter century of club status. Wright noted this historical moment in his review in *The Scotsman* (28 March 1988): "The first production in the 'open' Traverse is exceedingly well acted, and very sensitively written." He further described a scene in which the three female protagonists—Rachel, Isabel, and Oona, Rachel's keeper—fall under the influence of alcohol and throw off all of the restraints imposed upon them by the patriarchy. "It is this episode which seems to encapsulate the spirit of the play," Wright suggested, "but there is much to admire in the way the dramatist establishes the feeling of being on the edge of the world and yet being part of a more civilized society than that of supposedly sophisticated Edinburgh." Wright praised the performances of the actresses—Anne Lacey, Sharon Muircroff, and Alyxis Daly—as well as Derek Anders as Aneas. After a three-week run in Traverse, this "subdued" production by Jeremy Raison toured Scotland from Islay and Inverness to Glasgow (Mayfest).

In *The Straw Chair*, Glover sets out to disclose the hypocrisy of eighteenth-century Scottish society, which removed women from the public sphere at their husbands' volition. She attacks the double standard by which a woman's role is defined through virtues of chastity and duty. While viewing Isabel as a virginal figure, a Madonna, Aneas rejects Rachel as "a godless,

Cover for Glover's 2000 play, about the crew of a Bulgarian ship as they try to gain acceptance from the Shetland Islands community while their ship is docked during a strike (James Cabell Library, Virginia Commonwealth University)

mischievous, evil creature," a "strumpet," whereas her sins are only a passion for life and a belief in romantic love. He sees her as a constant menace to his established worldview, and not until late in the play does he realize that, like her, he has been yet another pawn in the game of social forces.

In her next play, *Bondagers,* Glover returned to issues of the exploitation of women. The play was first produced in 1991 by the Traverse Theatre Company, under the direction of Ian Brown, and has since toured in the United States, Canada, and Sweden. *Bondagers* explores the themes of female labor, sexuality, and madness by means of the elements of traditional storytelling, folk songs, and modern soap opera. The hypnotic musical quality of the rural Lallans language and the dynamic choruses and dance sequences give the play a communal, ritualistic mood. Peter Zenzinger refers to this frequent use of song as a "major distinctive characteristic of recent Scottish drama" and an extension of the Scottish *ceilidh* (informal gathering for music and dancing) tradition.

Glover's interest in theater comes from her love of language, its audible and visual qualities. She believes that only through words can a playwright convey the spirit of a play to her audience, a director, actors, and a designer. In an unpublished 15 October 1996 interview with Ksenija Horvat, Glover commented about her work on *The Straw Chair:*

> the language has to tell you that it is happening in the eighteenth century, that this is Isabella, and she is very young and quite timid but that she actually has got guts. And it has to tell you that this is St. Kilda. And it has to tell you it is raining. . . . That's why the beginning is so difficult. Because you cannot do anything until you find out how they talk.

There has always been controversy about Glover's use of language. Several critics challenged the authenticity of the Lallans that Glover uses in *Bondagers*. Glover's response was that a textbook Lallans was an academic invention that had little to do with the way people had spoken through the ages. Although Glover admitted to Horvat that there have been plays written in "very good" Scots, it is, nevertheless, her belief that one cannot be accurate "because there is no such thing as being accurate. Scots is not a rigid language." Her additional concern with *Bondagers* was that if it had been written in broad Borders dialect, it might have been well received in the Borders but utterly incomprehensible anywhere else. For this reason, she argues against "putting a Scottish cork on something to make it acceptable" and favors a freer language use–English, Scots, Gaelic, or otherwise–in Scottish playwriting in general, and in her playwriting in particular.

The opening scene in *Bondagers* is set at a February hiring fair, and it focuses on a group of four women hired by farmhands to work on a Borders farm during an agricultural year. In the course of the play it transpires that, though they do the same work as men, these women are subject to various facets of discrimination: their salaries are much lower, and they are sexually abused by the men who hire them. Glover shows the conventional objectives of womanhood, such as marriage and motherhood, as the stabilizers of the fundamentally male-dominated system of economic, political, and sexual exploitation. The birth-giving power of woman is compared to the creative power of nature. From the sense of this link between woman and land develops the concept of economic exploitation of both by the man-dominated community.

In an article posted on a website devoted to "Scottish Events in New Scotland (Nova Scotia)" <http://www.chebucto.ns.ca/Heritage/FSCNS/Scots_NS/Events/Events_Scots.html> Ken Schwartz, artistic codirector of Two Planks and a Passion Theatre Company, commented on the Canadian premiere of *Bondagers* by his company at the Wolfville Festival Theatre on 14 October 1998. He thought the play interesting because "it raises questions about how women define and value women's work." Schwartz's wife and associate Chris O'Neill added in the same article that she felt the play dealt with "incredibly strong women laboring as indentured workers and struggling with their roles as workers, mothers, mentors, lovers."

In a 15 April 1996 article in the *Toronto Sun*, John Coulbourn reviewed another production of *Bondagers,* that of the Traverse Theatre Company at Harbourfront's du Maurier Theatre Centre, Toronto, on 11 April 1996. He described the characters with "feet planted firmly in the soil," adding that "playwright Glover paints their lives in monochromatic shades of bleak Calvinism." He commented that each of the "six magnificent performances" by the actresses "is stripped bare of sentimentality and easy artifice, enlivened only by truthful characterization and the simple but exquisite power of the playwright's dialogue." Coulbourn praised the vitality with which these characters transformed a minimal, evocative set by Stewart Laing into "a powerful testament to community and the female spirit."

Glover further examined the theme of women's exploitation in her next play, *Sacred Hearts*. The play was commissioned by Communicado Theatre Company and premiered at Dundee Repertory Theatre on 11 February 1994. It is concerned with the French prostitutes' protest in Lyons in 1975 against the lack of police protection from the so-called Lyons Ripper. Glover cited Ned Polsky's "The Sociology of Pornography," the last chapter of his *Hustlers, Beats and Others* (1985), and Claude Jaget's book *Prostitutes, Our Life* (1980) as the main sources for her play. Jaget's book was particularly haunting because it included reports on the Yorkshire Ripper, who coincidentally went on his murder rampage at the time of the Lyons protest. However, Glover insisted that murders were a motif, not the focus of the play. *Sacred Hearts* is not a story about the Lyons Ripper, or any other man. It is about a group of women who seek sanctuary in a Catholic cathedral; about impotence and the unwillingness of the Church and the State to offer any protection; and about men's violent attitudes toward women's sexuality. The main theme is starkly illustrated by Jack Vettriano's painting, specially commissioned in 1993, which accompanied the Communicado's production of the play.

In the program note, Glover points out that the male-dominated monetary economies have brought about prostitution and pornography, and she condemns the hypocritical Madonna-strumpet dichotomy constructed by Christian theologies. This dichotomy is perhaps best illustrated in the words of Raymond, one of the few male characters, who offers a monologue about the women in his family:

> RAYMOND. A disgrace to their sex. An insult to my mother. Don't tell me they can't get work. My mother worked. She worked in the mill. There were five of us at home. We never tasted meat. She cooked, she cleaned, she sewed. She never had a new coat. The priest called her a saint. An example, he said, a good woman, above rubies. (*Pause. Thoughtfully.*) Asking for it. . . . The old man ruled her with a rod of iron. When he was at home. Ruled us all, even the girls. Especially the girls. The big stick. The rod of iron.

Though Glover does not moralize, she is clear about the choices that any woman is given in a modern society. Unheedingly, Raymond describes his mother as a slave to her family, devoid of any independence and abused by her husband. The iron rod becomes a symbol of power; it is also a symbol of male sexuality that suppresses female sexuality. When the prostitutes leave the streets and barricade themselves in the cathedral in protest, they gain control through denying sexual services to the same individuals who persecute them in court. Their control is short-lived, however, and their former allies—journalists, women's organizations, men and women in the street—soon turn against them or stand silent as the police break down the front door of the cathedral and undertake an unspeakable act of violence against them.

Sacred Hearts is not a play against men. They are not seen as menace; on the contrary, they are as powerless as women are. Glover seeks responsibility elsewhere, in the authority of the State and the Church who fail to act against the invisible Ripper and who jointly wear these women down.

Reviewer Mark Fisher acknowledged that he had found the production "smart" and "stylish" but, nevertheless, slightly disappointing. In his opinion, director Myra McFadyen made good use of familiar Communicado tools such as chimes, chants, candles, and drums, and the best sequences in the play were those "when Glover's script takes a back seat to form a mantra of repeated sound, while the actors create impressionistic images of street scenes, confessionals and confrontations." However, once the production returned to the script, the result was far more conventional.

In her next play, *Artist Unknown* (performed in 1996), Glover explores the theme of the marginalization of women from the creative process, which coincides with their invisibility in a social hierarchy. When Glover was originally commissioned by Tag Theatre Company in 1996, the idea was to write a play about celebrated Scottish architect and artist Charles Rennie Mackintosh to introduce his life and art to schoolchildren. Instead, *Artist Unknown* focuses on his fellow artist and wife, Margaret Macdonald Mackintosh, and mid-twentieth-century painter Joan Eardley. Glover introduces a third character, a young aspiring artist, Cassie, who belongs to a new generation of women striving toward independence and recognition. Through an elaborate fusion of past and present, the author explores the position of female artists whose work and very existence have often been rendered anonymous by society. Margaret comments on the views in the 1900s:

MARGARET. Women are equal—but different. Ladies may draw and paint and sculpt—but in classes on their own, segregated from the men. Ladies may not study architecture at all. And it is absolutely unheard of for a lady to "draw from life." No nude must ever be seen by the lady pupils. . . . So: the lady pupils will have to study the male, and female, form—elsewhere.

Glover seeks to make connections between past and present attitudes: in some areas, female creativity is still met with suspicion and derision, as some believe "women can't paint," they "always compromise," and they "haven't got the balls for Art." While observing Joan's and Margaret's struggles to be recognized as artists, Cassie goes through her personal purgatory, trying to come to terms with self-doubt in both her art and her sexuality. Only after she has ceased to perceive the world as a series of abstracts and has accepted the interchangeability of reality and creativity, does she begin to grow as an artist and as a woman.

Glover's next play, *Shetland Saga* (originally titled "Klondykers"), was first performed by the Traverse Theatre Company in Edinburgh on 28 July 2000 under the direction of Philip Howard. In this play, Glover returns to the topics of identity, individuality, and transgression of boundaries in the modern world, by, as the program note states, "depicting a community which defies stereotypes and constantly surprises."

Shetland Saga, based on a true incident, tells the story of a Bulgarian ship, *Ludmilla,* which is stranded near the Shetland Islands as the unpaid crew goes on strike, holding their valuable cargo. As they wait, the crew members are gradually integrated into the local community. Glover shows how the sailors are turned into pawns in an international deal, on the one hand, and how they struggle to be accepted among the locals, on the other. Amid the political and personal games, a love affair develops between Svetan, a married Bulgarian engineer, and Mena, the niece of a local hotel owner, despite cultural and linguistic barriers. The feelings of claustrophobia and intrusion of one world into the other are emphasized by the set, which the stage directions specify is never absolute and "should, at any necessary point, be able to invade and utilize what space there is." The only reminder of the spaciousness of the world outside is the image of the *Ludmilla* in the distance, which brings with it "a sense of sea and sky."

The Traverse premiere of *Shetland Saga* received mixed reviews. Though most critics praised the topic of the play, they felt that the author failed to explore it in innovative ways. Joyce McMillan wrote in *The Scotsman* (9 August 2000) that the play started well, "with a fine, feisty range of characters and some strong dialogue," but that "as soon as the focus shifts to the complex dilemmas facing the Bulgarian crew, the structure begins to waver, the quality of the writing fades." She added that the result was "something more akin to a particularly strong episode of a long-running television soap than a single play strong enough to stand alone." Similarly, Michael Billington suggested in *The Guardian* (8 August 2000) that Glover's play was "clearly authentic but, as the title implies . . . more saga than drama: a discursive, folkloristic narrative rather than something tightly focused." These arguments, though, can be seen both as a fault and as a virtue. This elegiac work displays Glover's poetic and passionate writing, which is powerfully embedded in the rhythmic and verbal plenitude of Scottish language.

The play reflects Glover's own political involvement with human-rights organizations. For example, she was one of the cosignatories of a letter from well-known Scottish women calling on the British government to act in support of the women of Srebrenica, Bosnia. The letter was published on 7 March 2000 in *The Scotsman* as part of the celebrations of International Women's Days, 5–11 March 2000.

Although not all of Sue Glover's plays deal with a Scottish milieu, one can always find in them an echo of the author's fascination with the ways in which Scotland has changed through time and how these changes, resulting from different political and economic developments, have affected her people. Her plays deal with an individual's claim on singular physical and emotional space, especially with regard to women and their position as social, sexual, and creative participants in the Scottish community. They also deal with the sense of belonging to a community and the effects that economic and political relationships have on the minds of individuals and entire nations. Glover has enriched Scottish contemporary theater and has proven that she belongs among the most talented Scottish playwrights today.

Interview:

Jackie McGlone, "Glued to Her Seat," *Scotsman*, 24 July 2000, pp. 14–15.

References:

Susan Triesman, "Transformations and Transgressions: Women's Discourse on the Scottish Stage," in *British and Irish Women Dramatists Since 1958: A Critical Handbook,* edited by Trevor R. Griffiths and Margaret Llewellyn-Jones (Buckingham, U.K. & Philadelphia: Open University Press, 1993), pp. 124–134;

Peter Zenzinger, "The New Wave," in *Scottish Theatre Since the Seventies,* edited by Randall Stevenson and Gavin Wallace (Edinburgh: Edinburgh University Press, 1996), pp. 125–137.

David Hare

(5 June 1947 -)

Catherine MacGregor

See also the Hare entry in *DLB 13: British Dramatists Since World War II.*

PLAY PRODUCTIONS: *Inside Out,* adapted by Hare and Tony Bicât from Franz Kafka's *Diaries,* London, Arts Lab, September 1968;

How Brophy Made Good, Brighton, Brighton Combination Theatre, March 1969; Edinburgh, Traverse Theatre, 1 April 1969;

Slag, London, Hampstead Theatre Club, 2 April 1970; New York, Public Theatre, 21 February 1971; London, Royal Court Theatre, 24 May 1971;

What Happened to Blake? London, Royal Court Theatre Upstairs, 28 September 1970;

The Rules of the Game, adapted by Hare and Robert Rietty from Luigi Pirandello's play, London, New Theatre, 15 June 1971; London, Almeida Theatre, 12 May 1992;

Lay-By, by Hare, Howard Brenton, Brian Clark, Trevor Griffiths, Steven Poliakoff, Hugh Stoddart, and Snoo Wilson, Edinburgh, Traverse Theatre, 24 August 1971; London, Royal Court Theatre, 26 September 1971;

Deathsheads, Edinburgh, Traverse Theatre, December 1971;

The Great Exhibition, London, Hampstead Theatre Club, 28 February 1972;

England's Ireland, by Hare, Tony Bicât, Brenton, Clark, David Edgar, Francis Fuchs, and Wilson, Amsterdam, Mickery Theatre, September 1972; London, Round House Theatre, 2 October 1972;

Brassneck, by Hare and Brenton, Nottingham, Nottingham Playhouse, 10 September 1973;

Knuckle, Oxford, Oxford Playhouse, 29 January 1974; London, Comedy Theatre, 4 March 1974; New York, Playhouse II, 23 January 1975;

Fanshen, based on William Hinton's book, Sheffield, Crucible Theatre, 10 March 1975; London, Institute of Contemporary Arts, 22 April 1975;

Teeth 'n' Smiles, book by Hare, music by Nick Bicât, lyrics by Tony Bicât, London, Royal Court Theatre,

David Hare (photograph courtesy of Greenpoint Films, Ltd.; from Judy Lee Oliva, David Hare: Theatricalizing Politics, *1990; Thomas Cooper Library, University of South Carolina)*

2 September 1975 (transferred to Wyndham's Theatre, 24 May 1976); Washington, D.C., Folger Theatre, 4 April 1980;

Deeds, by Hare, Brenton, Ken Campbell, and Griffiths, Nottingham, Nottingham Playhouse, 8 March 1978;

Plenty, London, Lyttelton Theatre (National Theatre), 7 April 1978; Washington D.C., Arena Stage, 4 April 1980; New York, Public Theatre, 21 October 1982; New York, Plymouth Theatre, 28 December 1982;

A Map of the World, Adelaide, Opera Theatre, March 1982; Sydney, Sydney Opera House, March 1982; London, Lyttelton Theatre (National Theatre), 20 January 1983; New York, Public/Mortinson Hall, 28 October 1985;

Pravda: A Fleet Street Comedy, by Hare and Brenton, London, National Theatre, 2 May 1985;

The Bay at Nice and *Wrecked Eggs,* London, Cottesloe Theatre (National Theatre), 4 September 1986;

The Knife, libretto by Hare, lyrics by Tim Rose-Price, music by Nick Bîcat, New York, Shakespeare Festival, 1987;

The Secret Rapture, London, Lyttelton Theatre (National Theatre), 4 October 1988; New York, Ethel Barrymore Theatre, 10 October 1989;

Racing Demon, London, Cottesloe Theatre (National Theatre), 1 February 1990; New York, Vivian Beaumont Theatre, 1 November 1995;

Murmuring Judges, London, Olivier Theatre (National Theatre), 10 October 1991;

The Absence of War, London, Olivier Theatre (National Theatre), 2 October 1993;

The Life of Galileo, adapted from Bertolt Brecht's play, London, Almeida Theatre, 11 February 1994;

Skylight, London, Cottesloe Theatre (National Theatre), 4 May 1995; New York, Royale Theatre, 9 September 1996;

Mother Courage and Her Children, adapted from Brecht's play, London, National Theatre, 14 November 1995;

Ivanov, adapted from Anton Chekhov's play, London, Almeida Theatre, 2 June 1997; New York, Vivian Beaumont Theatre, 23 October 1997;

Amy's View, London, Lyttelton Theatre (National Theatre), 13 June 1997; New York, Ethel Barrymore Theatre, 3 April 1999;

The Judas Kiss, London, Playhouse Theatre, 19 March 1998; New York, Broadhurst Theatre, 23 April 1998;

Via Dolorosa, London, Royal Court Theatre, 8 September 1998; New York, Booth Theatre, 5 March 1999;

The Blue Room, adapted from Arthur Schnitzler's *La Ronde,* London, Donmar Warehouse, 10 September 1998; New York, Cort Theatre, 27 November 1998;

My Zinc Bed, London, Royal Court Theatre, 14 September 2000;

Platonov, adapted from Chekhov's play, London, Almeida Theatre, 11 September 2001;

The Breath of Life, London, Theatre Royal Haymarket, 15 October 2002;

The Permanent Way, York, York Theatre Royal, 13 November 2003; London, National Theatre, January 2004;

Stuff Happens, London, Olivier Theatre (National Theatre), 3 September 2004; New York, New York Theatre Workshop, 18 October 2004; Hartford, Conn., Hartford Stage, 24 October 2004; Los Angeles, Mark Taper Forum, 25 May 2005.

BOOKS: *Slag* (London: Faber & Faber, 1971);

Lay-By, by Hare, Howard Brenton, Brian Clark, Trevor Griffiths, Steven Poliakoff, Hugh Stoddart, and Snoo Wilson (London: Calder & Boyars, 1972);

The Great Exhibition (London: Faber & Faber, 1972);

Brassneck, by Hare and Brenton (London: Eyre Methuen, 1974);

Knuckle (London: Faber & Faber, 1974);

Teeth 'n' Smiles, book by Hare, music by Nick Bicât, lyrics by Tony Bicât (London: Faber & Faber, 1976);

Fanshen, based on William Hinton's book (London: Faber & Faber, 1976);

Licking Hitler (London & Boston: Faber & Faber, 1978);

Plenty (London & Boston: Faber & Faber, 1978);

Dreams of Leaving (London & Boston: Faber & Faber, 1980);

A Map of the World (London: Faber & Faber, 1982; revised, 1983);

Saigon: Year of the Cat (London & Boston: Faber & Faber, 1983);

The History Plays: Knuckle; Licking Hitler; Plenty (London & Boston: Faber & Faber, 1984);

Pravda: A Fleet Street Comedy, by Hare and Brenton (London & New York: Methuen, 1985);

Wetherby (London & Boston: Faber & Faber, 1985);

The Asian Plays: Fanshen; Saigon; A Map of the World (London & Boston: Faber & Faber, 1986);

The Bay at Nice; Wrecked Eggs (London & Boston: Faber & Faber, 1986);

Paris by Night (London: Faber & Faber, 1988);

The Secret Rapture (London: Faber & Faber, 1988; New York: Grove Weidenfeld, 1989);

Strapless (London & Boston: Faber & Faber, 1989);

Racing Demon (London: Faber & Faber, 1990);

Heading Home; Wetherby; and, Dreams of Leaving (London: Faber & Faber, 1991);

Murmuring Judges (London: Faber & Faber, 1991; revised, 1993);

The Early Plays (London: Faber & Faber, 1991)—comprises *Slag, The Great Exhibition,* and *Teeth 'n' Smiles;*

Writing Left-Handed (London & Boston: Faber & Faber, 1991);

Asking Around: Background to the David Hare Trilogy, edited by Lyn Haill (London: Faber & Faber in association with Royal National Theatre, 1993);

The Absence of War (London: Faber & Faber, 1993);

The Rules of the Game, translated and adapted from Luigi Pirandello's play (Bath: Absolute Classics, 1993);

Skylight (London & Boston: Faber & Faber, 1995);

Mother Courage and Her Children, adapted from Bertolt Brecht's play (London: Methuen, 1995; New York: Arcade, 1996);

Plays One (London & Boston: Faber & Faber, 1996)—comprises *Slag; Teeth 'n' Smiles; Knuckle; Licking Hitler;* and *Plenty;*

Plays Two (London & Boston: Faber & Faber, 1997); published as *The Secret Rapture and Other Plays* (New York: Grove, 1997)—comprises *Fanshen; A Map of the World; Saigon: Year of the Cat; The Bay at Nice;* and *The Secret Rapture;*

Amy's View (London: Faber & Faber, 1997);

Ivanov, adapted from Anton Chekhov's play (London: Methuen, 1997);

The Judas Kiss (London: Faber & Faber, 1998; New York: Grove, 1998);

The Blue Room, adapted from Arthur Schnitzler's *La Ronde* (London: Faber & Faber, 1998; New York: Grove, 1998);

Via Dolorosa; & When Shall We Live? (London: Faber & Faber, 1998);

Acting Up: A Diary (London & New York: Faber & Faber, 1999);

My Zinc Bed (London: Faber & Faber, 2000);

Platonov, adapted from Chekhov's play (London & New York: Faber & Faber, 2001);

The Breath of Life (London: Faber & Faber, 2002);

Collected Screenplays (London: Faber & Faber, 2002)—comprises *Wetherby; Paris by Night; Strapless; Heading Home;* and *Dreams of Leaving;*

The Hours: A Screenplay, adapted from Michael Cunningham's novel (New York: Miramax, 2002; London: Faber & Faber, 2003);

The Permanent Way or La Voie Anglaise (London: Faber & Faber, 2003).

PRODUCED SCRIPTS: *Man Above Men,* television, BBC "Play for Today," 19 March 1973;

Brassneck, by Hare and Howard Brenton, television, BBC "Play for Today," 22 May 1975;

Fanshen, television, BBC Television, 18 October 1975;

Licking Hitler, television, BBC 1, 10 January 1978;

Dreams of Leaving, television, BBC 1, 17 January 1980;

Knuckle, radio, BBC, 1981;

Saigon: Year of the Cat, television, Thames TV, 30 November 1983;

Wetherby, motion picture, Greenpoint Films/Zenith, 1985;

Plenty, motion picture, RKO/Pressman, 1985;

Paris by Night, motion picture, British Screen Productions/Zenith/Film Four International, 1988;

Strapless, motion picture, Channel Four Films/Granada Film Productions, 1989;

Knuckle, television, BBC Television "Theatre Night," 7 May 1989;

Pravda, with Howard Brenton, radio, BBC, 28 September 1990;

Heading Home, television, BBC, 13 January 1991;

The Secret Rapture, radio, BBC World Service, 1991;

Damage, adapted from Josephine Hart's novel, motion picture, Channel Four Films/Le Studio Canal/Skreba Films/TFI, 1992;

The Secret Rapture, motion picture, Channel Four Films/Greenpoint Films, 1993;

The Absence of War, television, BBC, 1995;

Via Dolorosa, television, BBC, 2000;

The Hours, adapted from Michael Cunningham's novel, motion picture, Miramax, 2002.

OTHER: "Time of Unease," in *At the Royal Court: 25 Years of the English Stage Company,* edited by Richard Findlater (New York: Grove, 1981), pp. 139–142.

SELECTED PERIODICAL PUBLICATIONS–UNCOLLECTED: *Deeds,* by Hare, Howard Brenton, Ken Campbell, and Trevor Griffiths, *Plays and Players* (May 1978);

"Theatre's Great Malcontent," *Guardian,* 8 June 2002 <http://books.guardian.co.uk/guardianhayfestival2002/story/0,11873,729201,00.html>.

David Hare is one of the most successful playwrights of his generation, and his concern with the politics of contemporary life have taken him from the oppositional fringe, with Portable Theatre, to the bastion of the theater establishment with, in particular, a long-standing relationship with the National Theatre. Hare's work focuses on the interlinking of the personal and the political in English life. The stance that Hare takes as a writer reflects his experience as one simultaneously within and outside of the culture of the British establishment.

Hare was born in St. Leonard's in Sussex on 5 June 1947. His parents were Clifford Hare, a ship's purser on the P & O line, and Agnes Gilmour. They also had an older daughter. When he was five years old the family moved a short distance, to Bexhill-on-Sea, also in Sussex, and Hare attended the local preparatory school. In 1960 he obtained a scholarship to attend the

Jeremy Piven and Steve Trovillion in a 1989 Next Theater Company (Evanston, Illinois) production of Hare's 1974 play Knuckle, *about a gun dealer investigating the disappearance of his sister and expressing distaste for the shady business ethics of his stockbroker father (photograph by J. B. Spector; from Judy Lee Oliva,* David Hare: Theatricalizing Politics, *1990; Thomas Cooper Library, University of South Carolina)*

Anglo-Catholic Lancing College as a boarder. One of his contemporaries there was playwright Christopher Hampton. Hare was an avid cinemagoer, but from early on had an interest in the theater. Richard Eyre, who was artistic director of the National Theatre from 1988 to 1997 and who has directed several of Hare's plays, comments in Richard Boon's *About Hare: The Playwright and the Work* (2003):

> There's this wonderful paradox, of the excoriating voice of British political theatre emerging from the petty bourgeois world of Bexhill-on-Sea. He went to the theatre a lot with his mother, so he'd seen a lot more theatre than I had when I first met him, and he knew a lot more. He was also an usher at the National Theatre during Olivier's time, so he had a rather, I suppose, unfashionable curiosity about the theatre. Where most of his generation would be gravitating towards the movies or television, the allure for him was the theatre.

Eyre also believes that Hare's ability to tap into "the world of petty bourgeois gentility, and the quiet desperation of people's lives" that surrounded him in Bexhill is crucial to his theatrical work. After leaving Lancing College, Hare spent some time in California and then, in 1965, went to Jesus College, Cambridge, to study English, specifically to be taught by postwar cultural historian and theorist Raymond Williams. However, he found his years at university to be a time of disillusionment, particularly with the activities of the organised Left in Britain at that time. He did, however, direct some undergraduate plays. After graduating from Cambridge in 1968 he worked briefly for movie production company A. B. Pathe, screening Pathe Pictorials in pursuit of material for sex-education movies, but he soon found himself drawn to theatrical activity.

That same year Hare formed Portable Theatre with Tony Bicât, who had been at Cambridge with him. Portable Theatre was formed with the express purpose of working outside the theatrical establishment. The company's credo, as described in a 1978 article by Peter Ansorge, was straightforward: it was a small "mobile group equipped to carry a handful of harsh, explosive shows to England's campuses, post-68 Arts Labs, and even theatres, in a calculated series of three monthly cycles." The company's first production was *Inside Out,* a one-act adaptation of Franz Kafka's *Diaries* by Hare and Bicât, which was performed at the Arts Lab in Drury Lane in September 1968.

Hare's first play, *How Brophy Made Good,* was directed by its author and Bicât and performed by Portable Theatre at Brighton Combination in March 1969. In the late summer of that year playwright Howard Brenton came to see a Portable Theatre production, an adaptation of Kafka's *Amerika,* at the Arts Lab. Since he was the only person to show up, the company adjourned with him to a neighboring pub. From this meeting came the beginning of a lifelong friendship between Hare and Brenton and a commission for the latter to write a play for Portable Theatre. The play, *Christie in Love* (1969), was directed by Hare and proved to be one of the most memorable of all the Portable Theatre offerings. In September 1970 Portable Theatre presented a double-bill at the Royal Court Theatre Upstairs: it consisted of Hare's *What Happened to Blake?* and Brenton's *Fruit,* directed by Hare. Thereafter, the two collaborated on many ventures.

In April 1970 Michael Codron, the theater impresario who had been responsible for introducing Harold Pinter to a London public with *The Birthday Party* in 1958, produced Hare's play *Slag* at the Hampstead Theatre Club. *Slag,* which was reprised at the Royal Court Theatre in 1971, is set in a girls' boarding school called Brackenhurst. The play opens with three teachers at the school swearing to abstain from all contact with men. This vow is the beginning of a new order, with Brackenhurst seen as the vanguard in feminist revolution. Joanne is the most revolutionary of the three women, in contrast to Ann, the headmistress, who wants to leave politics out of the perfect new society. Elise, who is obsessed with love and sex, makes up the trio. The pupils are never seen, although the audience is informed that their number is slowly dwindling, leaving just one who is nicknamed Lucrecia Bourgeois. Hare began the play in 1969, in the wake of the French student riots of 1968, which British counterculture could only palely imitate. In the introduction to his *Plays One* (1996) Hare wrote of his inspiration for *Slag:* "By one of those coincidences of timing that have been a feature of my life as a writer, I had started reading some of the wilder feminist writings of the period, and in between the time when I began writing the play and its subsequent production the whole subject of women's liberation had become hotly topical."

The comedy or tragicomedy of the piece lies in the fact that the revolution is pointless and contained within the class boundaries of the English public school. The fact that audiences only see the three teachers also highlights the stagnation of this particular revolutionary impulse. Rather than having a strong narrative thrust, building to a climatic moment where revolutionary potential is either seized or abandoned, the protagonists of *Slag* merely endlessly replay their ideological conflicts. Within the setting of the deserted boarding school, their clashes become parodies of the revolutionary angst of the 1960s. After all else has failed, the pupils have left; the feminist community is a series of conflicts; and the workers are silent. In *Slag,* Hare pinpoints the problems and disappointments in revolution: the stasis and rigidity of "Englishness" he parodies in *Slag* is a continuing theme explored more forcefully in later works.

As a result of the success of *Slag,* Hare won the 1970 *Evening Standard* award for the most promising playwright. He became resident dramatist at the Royal Court Theatre, a post he held for a year, and married Margaret Matheson, a television and motion-picture producer, with whom he had three children, Joe (who played Richard Forbes in Hare's 1988 movie *Strapless*) and twins Lewis and Darcy. The couple were divorced in 1980.

In February 1971 *Slag* was produced by Joe Papp at the New York Shakespeare Festival's Public Theatre, his first play to open in America, and in June his adaptation of Luigi Pirandello's *The Rules of the Game,* written with Robert Rietty, was staged by the National Theatre at the New Theatre. He was, however, still involved with Portable Theatre. Hare's two most significant pieces for Portable Theatre were the collaborative *Lay-By* (performed in 1971, published in 1972) and *England's Ireland* (performed in 1972), the latter an early attempt, using the shock tactics of Portable Theatre, to consider the Troubles in Ireland; and a play that, because of its nature, caused theaters to refuse it, thus bringing about the end of Portable Theatre.

The theme of disillusionment was taken up in Hare's next play, *The Great Exhibition* (performed and published in 1972), which is concerned with the crumbling world of a Labour M.P. who "decided to be a politician about three days before the rest of the world became revolutionaries," as he announces dramatically. In September 1972 *England's Ireland,* directed by Hare, finally found a stage, at the Mickery Theatre, Amsterdam, and the following year Hare resumed a working relationship with both Brenton and Eyre, who had directed *The Great Exhibition* and was by then running the Nottingham Playhouse, which for much of the 1970s was the most important venue for new theatrical work in England. Hare was appointed resident dramatist at the Playhouse and with Brenton produced *Brassneck* (performed in 1973, published in 1974). This play

Pleasure Principle at the Royal Court Theatre Upstairs as well as a production of Sir John Vanbrugh's *The Provoked Wife* (1697) at the Palace Theatre, Watford. Freed from his association with Portable Theatre, he founded Joint Stock Theatre with Max Stafford-Clark and David Aukin (shortly to be joined by William Gaskill, fresh from his role as artistic director of the Royal Court Theatre). Joint Stock Theatre was a touring company that became a significant agent in the production and encouragement of new theater work, committed to the company working with the playwrights.

In 1974, after previewing at the Oxford Playhouse, Hare's next stage play, *Knuckle,* opened at the Comedy Theatre in London's West End. It was produced by Codron, and the fact that it did not play at, for instance, the Royal Court Theatre, gives further evidence of the versatility of approach that characterizes Hare's work. In *Knuckle* the values of the new aristocracy in Britain–the stockbrokers, the moneymakers–are put under scrutiny. The action at first unfurls as a thriller or murder mystery. International gun dealer Curly Delafield has returned to England after twelve years to investigate the disappearance of his sister, Sarah. The initial setting of the Moonlight Club gives the piece a *film noir* ambience, but the action then shifts and alternates with suburban Guildford. Sarah, in common with many of Hare's female figures, acts as the moral axis of the play, not through irreproachable behavior but by a distaste for hypocrisy and the facades of morality that prop up English society. Sarah, though absent throughout the play, is nevertheless the point around which all the other characters revolve, and they are defined by their relationships with and attitudes toward her.

Sarah's excoriating desire for truth is mirrored by her brother Curly's disgust with the sort of attitude toward life represented by their father, the stockbroker, Patrick: "He made his money with silent indolence. Part of a club. In theory a speculator. But whoever heard of a speculator who actually speculated and lost? Once you were in, you had it sewn up from paddock to post." Both Sarah and Curly are outsiders to this world of establishment respectability that their father represents; yet, both of them are also too close to it through their connection to Patrick and their upbringing. The play stages the tension between the need to know uncomfortable truths about the way society really works, represented by Sarah and Curly, and the desire to live a quiet life, despite the half-truths and evasions that doing so may require. Patrick Delafield represents this desire, which Hare identifies with a quintessential type of Englishness that, in the modern world, has become increasingly debased. Patrick's housekeeper mourns the loss of values, while Curly situates the

Cover for the 1976 publication of Hare's 1975 play Teeth 'n' Smiles, *which starred Hugh Fraser and Helen Mirren as members of a second-rate rock band performing at the Cambridge May Ball (Thomas Cooper Library, University of South Carolina)*

moved the action directly into the political arena, tracing the wheeler-dealer history of the Bagley family from the formation of the postwar Labour government under Clement Atlee in 1945 through disillusionment and the property speculation of the 1960s. It ends with an ironic toast to "the death of capitalism," as the family prepares to market the ultimate consumer product, Chinese heroin: "a product for our times, the perfect market, totally artificial, man-made, creating its own market, if there's a glut the demand goes up, if there's a famine the market goes up, an endless spiral of need and profit."

In 1973 *Man Above Men,* Hare's first work for television, aired in the prestigious BBC "Play for Today" slot, and he directed the premiere of Snoo Wilson's *The*

blame with men like his father, representatives of a class that has used the ideology of Englishness to disguise its own machinations.

The play won its author the John Llewellyn Rhys Prize. In the same year Hare directed Trevor Griffiths's *The Party,* a reexamination of the political events of 1968, at the National Theatre. In 1974 Hare was asked by Stafford-Clark and Gaskill to adapt William Hinton's book *Fanshen* (1967) for Joint Stock Theatre; it was performed in 1975. Hinton's book is a study of a single Chinese village, Long Bow, in light of the land reforms of the communist revolution. Joint Stock Theatre was set up as a radical left-wing collective, whose aim was to find a working method that was inclusive and nonhierarchical; the attractions of Hinton's book for such a group are obvious. The company's working method involved workshops with the writer and cast before the play was written, therefore the text was intended to be a collective effort. In his introduction to his *Plays Two* (1997) Hare explained that he did not use much of this material directly but was "crucially affected by the spirit of it." This influence comes across most clearly in the structure of the play, which adopts a dialectical method that was a reinvention of Bertolt Brecht's didactic theater for the 1970s. Yet, as Hare was at pains to make clear, *Fanshen* was not a Brechtian play, which made the familiar seem remarkable through alienation, but "a classical play about revolution." Hare uses the events in Long Bow to give a European audience a glimpse of the struggles and contradictions of successful revolution. Hare does not present a utopian vision of the process of land reform in China but, rather like the methods of the Chinese peasants, the play is self-critical and dramatizes a process of revision. The play is divided into sections, and the narrative focuses around "asking basic questions" about how humans live together and formulate "society." The villagers' attempts to answer these questions form the basis of their education into revolution.

The representational style of performance calls for nine actors to play the thirty-two parts regardless of age or gender. The opening section of the play gives the audience information about the setting and allows some of the villagers to introduce themselves. Their identity is formed by the experience of living in a land-based feudal economy: the villagers define themselves in terms of how much, if any, land that they own. The notion of theater as a forum for debate is heightened by the use of slogans to summarize the action in the different sections of the play. However, Hare is not utopian in his vision of China and its revolutionary promise, as so many other intellectuals were at this time; Hare shows the pitfalls and problems of redefinition that come with the notion of building a new world. Yet, *Fanshen* does not suggest that revolution is wrong; rather that it is such a leap in the dark that mistakes and confusion are necessarily part of the process. In later plays Hare showed the impossibility of revolution in England; with *Fanshen,* Hare examines the consequences of a "successful" revolution and the problems it brings. Hare subtitled *Fanshen* "a play for Europe," thereby negating Brecht's antiuniversalism; it is a play about China but one that has ramifications for the West in its salutary version of the compromises and contradictions involved in "wiping the slate clean."

Teeth 'n' Smiles was first performed in 1975, directed by Hare. Like *Slag,* it is informed by the inability to achieve real change in the British class system. The play shows the events of the Cambridge May Ball, a gig for a second-rate rock band fronted by the enigmatic, destructive Maggie. *Teeth 'n' Smiles* transforms the theater into a rock venue, and the audience is identified with the Cambridge revellers to whom the band are playing. This simple structuring of the action automatically sets up the aggressiveness of the piece, with the audience being placed as the "them" in contrast to the band's working-class "us." The clash between the rock band as icon of youth and modernity and the weight of tradition carried by the Cambridge college opens an unbridgeable gap where the revolution of rock 'n' roll becomes merely empty rhetoric.

The ambivalent nature of class in post-1960s Britain is shown by the absurdity of the confrontation the play stages, as in the entrance of Snead, the college porter, carrying the drunken Maggie over his shoulder. The potential for change opened up by the events of the 1960s is illustrated by the band's privileged position, rock stars as the new aristocracy: "Don't look at us pal, we're too famous, we're like the Queen, we don't carry actual money." Yet, this comment is undercut with irony, reflecting the fact that the band will never quite make it to the top. The old class structures as represented by Snead and Anson, the medical student organizing the ball, are still firmly in place but now fixed by the demands of a postwar, consumer-driven economy: Maggie comments to Saraffian, the band's manager, that the band is "Just merchandise to you. . . . We could be anything. Soapflakes we could be."

Arthur, the Svengali-like figure who found Maggie and gave her the songs on which she based her career, personifies the anomalies of social positioning felt by scholarship boys like Hare. Arthur is onstage at the beginning of the play, set up as an uneasy outsider, mediating between the worlds of the band and the college. Maggie performs the pain she feels, but Arthur is characterized by an overwhelming sense of displacement and self-loathing. Arthur's desire to make things matter, to impose meaning on the world, is contrasted with Maggie. Whereas Arthur seeks to change the rules

Bill Paterson as Archie MacLean in Licking Hitler, *Hare's 1978 television play about a British counterpropaganda unit during World War II (photograph by the BBC; from Judy Lee Oliva,* David Hare: Theatricalizing Politics, *1990; Thomas Cooper Library, University of South Carolina)*

of the games and make new meanings, Maggie is caught up in a spiral of free-falling nihilism.

Hare makes Maggie the center of the action, even when she is not onstage. She seems to fit the stereotype of Dionysian, doomed rock star, yet her capacity for survival denies that easy pigeonholing: "there's something in me that won't lie down." Maggie, like Hare's other central female figures, is a catalyst employed to call attention to the invisible systems and ideologies that control the characters around them.

In 1976 Hare directed Brenton's *Weapons of Happiness* at the Lyttelton auditorium of London's National Theatre, and in 1977 he was awarded a US/UK Bicentennial Fellowship, which allowed him to write and travel in England and the United States. He returned to direct Tony Bicât's *Devil's Island* for Joint Stock Theatre. During this period he also was working on his next two plays, one for television and one for the stage, which premiered the following year.

Licking Hitler (1978), which won a British Academy of Film and Television Arts (BAFTA) award for best play of the year, was written for television as a companion piece to *Plenty,* which was performed at the National Theatre in the same year. Both plays use World War II to explore debates around the personal and the political that still have resonance in contemporary life. The war is shown as a time of potential for change and revision in British life, which was ultimately not realized. Hare wrote of the impact of the war on his imagination as a time when the British were radicalized; citing Angus Calder's *The People's War: Britain 1939–1945* (1969) as his stimulus for this fascination, Hare began to explore the impact of what Carol Homden has termed "a war on two fronts–the class war and the Second World War."

Licking Hitler focuses on the activities of a British counterpropaganda unit based in an appropriated country house. Yet, the wartime activities are merely the window dressing for an exploration of the interlinking effects of class and sexuality on the characters. The play features two characters who typify that ambiguous status found in many of Hare's plays: the outsider who is also an insider. Archie MacLean, in his late twenties, is a working-class Glaswegian who has risen through the ranks of British intelligence to devise and write the counterpropaganda broadcasts. Anna Seaton, nineteen, comes from an upper-class family and is characterized by a naiveté about life that is quickly rubbed off by the vagaries of war. Anna and Archie's relationship provides the impetus for Hare's narrative. As in *Plenty*, the activities of the counterintelligence or Special Operations Executive (SOE) provide a matrix within which to situate the characters' interactions, but this wartime matrix is one that produces a period of almost carnivalesque liberation from prevailing attitudes, especially those relating to class and sex. This notion of the revolutionary aspect of the war is reinforced in the first few minutes of the screenplay as Lord Minton, the owner of the house, is turned into a refugee in his own home:

> Also waiting outside is an old Rolls-Royce. At the very centre of the hall Lord Minton is sitting on his suitcase. He has a stick, a big black coat and is very old and ill. Around him, and taking no notice, soldiers carry filing cabinets and wireless equipment through the hall and off down the corridor.

The sense of class revolution is reinforced by Archie's farewell to Minton:

> ARCHIE: Very kind. Of you. To lend us. Your place. Tell him we appreciate his sacrifice. Having to spend the rest of the war in that squalid wee single end in Eaton Square.
> *[The Chauffeur smiles thinly as he closes the door, and goes round to drive away. Anna arrives in time to hear Archie as he waves from the steps.]* That's right Minton, you bugger off.

Archie is the first occupant of the house whom Anna meets when she arrives to work as a translator, and he is consistently antagonistic to her. Yet, underlying this antagonism, both characters are united by a sense of otherness—Archie by virtue of his class and attitude, Anna through her gender and overwhelming naiveté. One of the most problematic aspects of the plot is Anna and Archie's sexual relationship, which begins with his raping her. Prior to this event it is made clear that Archie is unsettled by Anna. On her second night he bursts into her room clutching a bottle of scotch and shouting: "I'll smash a bloody bottle in yer if yer bloody come near me." This defensive/aggressive attitude to Anna could be explained by the ambivalent feelings Anna raises in Archie: hostility to her class, coupled with attraction and an underlying shared sense of not belonging. Hare cites Anna as the conscience of the piece, and Archie's refusal of her desire to share a sense of intimacy with him can be seen as symptomatic of his own self-loathing and sense of disjuncture resulting in the betrayal of his own class origins. Anna's rape may be problematic in terms of sexual politics, but metaphorically it represents an awakening that she chooses to repeat and that spills over into other areas of her life:

> ANNA: I literally didn't know there was such a thing as an electricity bill. I was sheltered, I suppose. . . . and I said you mean, you have to pay? For what you use? You have to pay? Gas, electricity, water. It had never occurred to me. *(Silence. She shivers.)* Archie, I am trying to learn.

She even comes to implicitly defend Archie in what can be seen as the awakening of a class-consciousness that after the war she will not lose. More so than even Archie, Anna is reinvented by her experience of war.

In *Licking Hitler,* Hare makes the macronarrative of the political peripheral to the micronarrative of the personal and uses one to comment on the other. This technique was taken further in *Plenty,* Hare's first full-length play for the National Theatre.

Plenty represents the culmination of the first period of Hare's work. Unlike the other "history plays," it achieves a broad sweep chronologically without losing its tight focus on individual characters. Hare merges the personal and the political more successfully than in *Licking Hitler,* and in Susan Traherne he creates his most fully realized female character, one who is the center of the narrative in every way. Women in Hare's plays are often used as mirrors to reflect the disruption of society back on itself; in Susan the catalytic potential of Maggie from *Teeth 'n' Smiles* is placed firmly center stage, and the audience sees the action from the woman's point of view rather than hearing about her as an object of speculation. In his introduction to the published text, Hare described *Plenty* as "a play about the cost of spending your whole life in dissent." The price of dissent for the individual reflects the concerns displayed in earlier plays such as *Knuckle* and *Fanshen* about the inability of society to cope with individuality that questions its mores.

The structure of *Plenty* juxtaposes youthful hope and its destruction. The opening of the play starts at the end of the narrative proper, showing the dystopian realism of life—literally and metaphorically—the morning after World War II. This scene is followed by the beginning of the narrative proper, which shows Susan's life in France as an agent of the SOE. The excitement and hope for change present in the young Susan in this scene is echoed in the final scene of the play with Susan's drug-induced utopian vision of a new postwar order; however, this promise has already been negated by the reality shown at the beginning of the play. Any dreams of change through the era of plenty and post-

Kate Nelligan and Kelsey Grammer in the 1982 New York Public Theater production of Hare's 1978 play Plenty, *about a woman whose postwar life cannot match the excitement and idealism of her work as a counterintelligence agent during World War II (photograph by Martha Swope; from* Plenty, *1978; Richland County Public Library)*

war prosperity engendered by the radicalism of the war are dismissed from the outset of the play.

Susan places herself outside of notions of class, sexuality, and femininity, but what were strengths in the SOE are failings in the postwar world of the diplomatic service. Hare was inspired to write *Plenty* through a footnote he found in a history of the SOE, stating that the majority of female operatives went on to have broken marriages. Susan's inability to conform to the role of postwar femininity and her sexual freedom result in her finding herself ill-adapted to everyday life. Sexuality is used not only to point up the strictures of British society but also to represent most clearly the melancholy of a lost dream, the potential of war to produce a cataclysmic change upon society and the individuals who experience it. Society did not change substantially, but individuals like Susan did. The postwar society that ushered in the consumer age is also shown as a time of lost opportunity, as abundance stifled the radicalism born in the war and channelled the desire of the people into plans for buying fridges through hire-purchase. Susan's life is one lived in dissent because she chooses to place herself at the heart of bourgeois 1950s society while living as an outsider.

In 1982 Hare directed a production of *Plenty* for Joe Papp at the Public Theatre in New York, the first time that he had directed in America. In late December it transferred to the Plymouth Theatre, a first Broadway production for Hare and one that led to him winning the New York Drama Critics Circle Award for best foreign play as well as an Antoinette Perry Tony Award nomination for best play in 1983.

The compromises of wealth and power, in the sense of both political power and moral responsibility, are explored through the colonial experience in Hare's television screenplay *Saigon: Year of the Cat* (1983) and play *A Map of the World* (performed and published in 1982); along with *Fanshen*, they were published under the title *The Asian Plays* in 1986. These two plays, unlike *Fanshen*, which is set in China but has a more universal scope, deal explicitly with the colonial experience and the imbalance of power between West and East, the developed and the developing world.

In *Saigon,* written in 1979, the juxtaposition between love story and action war movie provides a structuring contrast between the personal and the political and the ramifications of both. The protagonist is Barbara Dean, an Englishwoman working for an international bank in Saigon. If, unlike Susan in *Plenty,* Barbara does not thrive on crisis, she at least seems unruffled by it; one of the first shots follows Barbara walking imperviously through a bustling Saigon street. The first part of the teleplay is seen through Barbara's eyes, with her voice-over replacing the generic American male voice of popular Vietnam war movies such as *Apocalypse Now* (1979). Barbara falls into a pattern replicated by many of Hare's female protagonists of appearing enigmatic, yet also functioning as the conscience of the piece. She makes her younger lover, Bob Chesneau, uneasy:

> CHESNEAU: We weren't any better at losing the war than we were at winning it. And Barbara . . . you made it worse for me. Every time I saw you, you made me feel guilty. I couldn't take that after a while. That's why I stopped coming to see you.

Chesneau's betrayal of the Vietnamese mirrors his neglect of Barbara, and her reply is inspired by grief both for her personal situation and for the moral tragedy that is unfolding. The inadequacy of the responses of the colonizers to the colonized is reflected in the lack of communication between Barbara and Chesneau. As in *A Map of the World,* the problems of individual and collective responsibility in relation to power and privilege are addressed but are not prescribed. Hare wrote of the mood evoked by *Saigon* as indicative of the prevalent mood in Britain in the early 1980s:

> This feeling of living somewhere which you know is doomed is one which a lot of us who lived in England during the sixties and seventies felt, that it can't go on like this and yet seeing no way of being able to change it or to protest against the end. But I wouldn't stretch the analogy too far, it's a mood that the film is trying to catch and it's a mood in which people will not face reality.

This experience of living in a doomed era ended not in left-wing revolution but in the commercial boom of the 1980s that was explored with savage wit in *Pravda: A Fleet Street Comedy* (performed and published in 1985), a blistering attack on the world of tabloid journalism that was the second collaborative effort between Hare and Brenton.

In *A Map of the World,* Hare extends the analysis of Eurocentrism begun in *Saigon* to encompass the whole notion of the contingency of truth. The play is set during a UNESCO conference on world poverty in Bombay, but as in *Saigon,* the political and moral dialectic is refracted through personal conflict. The play centers around a debate between the influential novelist Victor Mehta and a young journalist, Stephen Andrews. Mehta, an Anglicized Indian, despises the socialist project of many developing countries and refuses to admit the ideological bias inherent in fiction; Stephen, an intense left-wing journalist, is all too aware of his own Western burden of guilt.

Alongside the political impulse of the debate, however, lies a more elemental rivalry for sexual possession of the young American Peggy Whitton. The debate of the play is further refracted by the surprise revelation in the middle of act 1 that the audience is actually watching the filming of Mehta's novel of these events. What has appeared to be actual is a movie set peopled by actors; this framing device serves to further underline the debate between fact and fiction expounded in the main plot. Mehta's refusal to admit that as a writer of fiction he "is already half-way towards admitting that a great deal of what he makes up and invents is as much with an eye to entertainment as it is to presenting literal historical truth," becomes part of a bigger debate about whose truth is "fact" anyway, as M'Bengue, the Senegalese envoy, declares:

> All your terms are political, and your politics is the crude fight between your two great blocs. Is Angola pro-Russian? Is it pro-American? These are the only questions you ever ask yourselves. As if the whole world could be seen in those terms. In your terms. In the white man's terms and through the white man's media.

The whole nature of the dialectic between fact and fiction, whose "truth" is being shown, is made more ironic by the fact that these words are spoken by an actor within the narrative.

The dissolution into the "reality" of the movie set is accompanied by the arrival of the real Peggy Whitton with her declaration: "My God, it's terrible. That wasn't the point of the original scene." Changing fact into fiction becomes the starting point for what, at the end of the play, is an even more universal moral debate, that of the possibility of change. The real Victor Mehta says at the end of the play: "This feeling, finally, that we may change things–this is at the centre of everything that we are. Lose that . . . lose that, lose everything." While he admits the contingency of interpretation, Mehta goes on to assert his feeling of admiration for Stephen's conviction; thus, Stephen, initially decried as a cultural tourist and bleeding-heart liberal, is ultimately seen as the moral center of the play. Yet, despite the debates raised over Western imperialism, fact and fiction, and the notion of moral decision making, the utopian dream is seen to have a bitter reality. At the end of the play, another scene from the movie leaves the audience with the message that the whole notion of moral debate with which they have been entertained is merely another Western luxury. The UNESCO official Martinson outlines the conditions of the proposed aid package to the Senegalese M'Bengue. Even altruism is contextual and provisional, with Martinson effectively demanding the abandonment of socialism within the country; as M'Bengue remarks, "You throw us a lifeline. The lifeline is in the shape of a noose."

In 1984 Hare was appointed associate director of the National Theatre, and he directed his motion picture *Wetherby*, which won the Golden Bear Best Film Award at the Berlin Film Festival when it was released the following year. In 1985 he directed his and Brenton's *Pravda* at the National Theatre. It won the *Plays and Players*, *City Limits*, and *Evening Standard* Best Play awards. The movie version of *Plenty* was also released, starring Meryl Streep, and Hare was made a Fellow of the Royal Society of Literature. The following year he was almost entirely involved in work at the National Theatre, directing his own double bill of *The Bay at Nice* and *Wrecked Eggs* and directing Anthony Hopkins in *King Lear*. In 1987 his opera *The Knife* played at the Public Theatre in New York, and then the following year he returned to the National Theatre.

The Secret Rapture (performed and published in 1988) is conditioned by Hare's experience of the Thatcherite 1980s, and, like *A Map of the World*, the play is occupied with the value decisions people make. Isobel Glass fulfils the role of many of Hare's female protagonists in being the moral center of the play, and in *The Secret Rapture*, Hare has made the contrast between Isobel and the other characters more pronounced. Isobel's sense of herself, her self-containment and spirituality, make her an anachronism in the materialism of the 1980s, and her death at the end of the play almost has the air of the ritual sacrifice of a scapegoat. There is a similarity between Isobel and Jean Travers in *Wetherby* in their sense of alienation from the values of 1980s Britain and their self-imposed isolation, which makes others uneasy. Isobel is contrasted most strikingly with the other main female characters: her sister, Marion, a conservative cabinet minister, and her father's widow, Katherine, an emotionally unstable alcoholic.

The play opens just after the death of Robert Glass; in the first scene Isobel is sitting with her father's body when Marion enters. The conflict between the sisters' values is seen initially over Marion's reclaiming a ring that was a gift to Robert. Marion justifies her search for the ring pragmatically, to prevent Katherine selling it for alcohol, and sentimentally, as a memento mori, yet she still feels uneasy in Isobel's presence. Their exchange typifies the tension between the two sisters and, by extension, the unease that Isobel inspires in other characters in the play, such as Irwin, her business partner and lover. There is a sense in that, with the character of Isobel, Hare is showing the problems of goodness as well as its virtues. Isobel's inability to express what she feels leads to Marion's projecting her own anxieties onto her sister and to Marion's explosion of frustration. Isobel's self-containment continually leads to her being a screen for the projection of others' insecurities, as Isobel acknowledges when she snaps: "Why is everyone so eager to tell me what I think?"

Isobel's desire to be fair and good makes her both a target to be taken advantage of and an irritant to those who do not see the world in her terms. Marion is irritated by Isobel's hesitance to take Katherine on in her design firm or at least to lie to Katherine and pretend that this employment will be the case. Throughout the play Isobel is implicitly linked with her dead father in the sense that they both share the same values. These values are not religious or overtly political but more to do with having a sense of decency. However, with Isobel, Hare seems to be much more interested in debating the nature of goodness, a debate that was heightened by the increasing materialism of the 1980s. As Hare wrote: "I was interested to show what choices good people might have to make in order to survive or prosper among some of the other typical characters of the age." However, Isobel is too good to prosper or survive; Marion screams at her, "You are truly insufferable. Hide behind your father for the rest of your life. Die there!" Isobel simply answers, "Yes, well no doubt I shall."

The catalyst for the eruption of the conflict between the sisters and between Isobel and Irwin is the fate of Katherine. By allowing Katherine into her business and, metaphorically, into her and Irwin's bed, Isobel is living the consequences of choosing to help Katherine, as her father had done, and this choice is one that has ramifications for all aspects of her life. To keep Katherine in the business and give her something to do, Marion and her Christian businessman husband, Tom, decide to bankroll an expansion. Isobel's lack of enthusiasm for this idea is defeated by Irwin's acceptance of a doubling of his salary; Isobel, weakened by this betrayal, accepts the expansion, but her relationship with Irwin is in its death throes. The expansion fails, leading Isobel to remark, "I was out of my depth, no, I was weak, but putting that aside I have been–

what is the word for it?—I think I have just been asset-stripped." Isobel has been asset-stripped emotionally by both Irwin and Katherine, as well as financially by the imprudent expansion of the business. The final denouement comes when Isobel is confronted by the distraught Irwin, whose inability to cope with the end of their relationship leads to his shooting her to death. Although the title of the play, *The Secret Rapture,* refers to the moment of a nun's unification with Christ, Isobel does not emerge as a saint or a martyr, except in the imaginations of others. This quality is both Isobel's tragedy and that of those around her, as Hare remarked of the play: "I wanted to show how goodness can bring out the worst in all of us."

Isobel's death does shake Marion and Tom into a new awareness of the values of emotion, family, and love, but Hare's overwhelming point in the play seems to be that the values of humanity and decency are being strangled by the modern world. The personal and social repercussions of this debate are displayed in Hare's plays of the 1990s, which expand and refine the personal debate of *The Secret Rapture.*

In the 1990s Hare created a trilogy that focuses on British institutions: the Church of England in *Racing Demon* (performed and published in 1990), the judiciary in *Murmuring Judges* (performed and published in 1991), and modern politics in *The Absence of War* (performed and published in 1993). In their themes and breadth these three plays seem to act as addenda to the earlier "history plays." The thesis that World War II offered the last real possibility of revolution through the radicalization of the working class and the democratization of traditional hierarchies surfaces again.

The problem of trying to "do good" in the modern world provides an elemental basis for each of the three plays. In *Racing Demon,* the contrasting styles of two ministers, Lionel Espy and Tony Ferris, form the dialectic of the play situated around the question, what is the Church for in a secular world? Lionel's feeling is that the Church's only valid role is in social work rooted in the needs of the community:

> Lionel: I wouldn't even say the Church was a joke. In our areas it's an irrelevance. It has no connection with most people's lives. A lot of people are struggling to make a life at all. Now I feel we should be humble about this. Our job is mainly to listen and to learn. From ordinary working people. We should try to understand and serve them. *(Shrugs slightly)* Perhaps with time, I do find that more important than ritual.

Lionel's view of the Church as a dispenser of natural justice is contrasted with Tony's view of the Church as a scourging force that must be fundamentalist in its approach:

Cover for Hare's 1993 play about modern politics, the third in a trilogy examining British institutions, featuring John Thaw as party leader George Jones (photograph by Mark Douet; Thomas Cooper Library, University of South Carolina)

> Tony: People must be converted. There is only one religion. Yes, one. Whatever your background. And the only way to God is through Jesus Christ. . . . Because the alternative, going round smiling, sitting people down, have a little chat, very nice, nice to see you, arrivederci . . . that doesn't work. I've seen it. *(Smiles.)* Christ came not to bring peace but the sword.

This conflict of humanity and professionalism also features in the other two plays. In *Racing Demon,* the conflict comes to a head when the Bishop of Southwark decides that Lionel is to be made a scapegoat, a test case, and will be fired for running his parish ineffectually. The definition of "ineffectual" is political, however. The initial complaints come from a group of middle-class parishioners who feel that Lionel does not display enough belief. This charge is further compounded by other political dissatisfaction with Lionel's expression of faith, as one character points out that Lionel's sermons "tend to harp a bit on certain themes. The divided nation. The failings of materialism. The importance of devoting our lives to the poor."

The dialectic in *Racing Demon* is mediated once again by a female figure. Frances Parnell is the scion of a churchgoing family who works in advertising; the family business has just taken on the Church of England as a client. At the beginning of the play Frances is in a relationship with Tony, but she tips Lionel off as to what Southwark is planning. Hare obviously wants the audience to feel that Lionel and Frances are more naturally compatible, and although there is the hint of sexual interest, the relationship seems ultimately to be based more on shared values than on physical attraction.

Frances and an abused parishioner, Stella, both serve to illuminate the different approaches of Tony and Lionel and, through these approaches, the problem of the Church's position in modern Britain. Hare seems to be arguing that the Church has essentially lost sight of its values. At the end of the play, Lionel and his wife, Heather, are searching for somewhere to go; Stella feels that Tony's charity has deprived her of the life she has made for herself, by changing it so irrevocably that it is not hers anymore; another cleric, Harry Henderson, has left England with his lover when a newspaper threatens to unmask the scandal of his homosexuality; and Frances is also about to leave. The Church thus fails to include the community, whether that is the poor and uneducated or gay clergy. Hare demonstrates, through Lionel's loss of faith, the wider cultural loss of faith in the the role of the Church. At the end of the play, the audience is left with three different responses: despair from Lionel; reforming, professional zeal from Tony; and escape from Frances.

The debate between humanity and professionalism is continued and extended in *Murmuring Judges*. The action focuses on all aspects of the judiciary: police, courts, and prison. The catalyst for the action is a young black barrister, Irina Platt. Irina's dissatisfaction with a defense she has worked on leads her to dig deeper into the case, and, while doing so, she discovers the disjunction between "justice" and the criminal justice system. The case that concerns her is that of Gerard MacKinnon, a first-time offender who is an unwilling accomplice in an armed robbery. Gerard is sentenced to five years, an unusually harsh sentence, which Irina suspects has more to do with his Irishness than his actual crime. It emerges that Semtex, an explosive preferred by terrorists, was found at the scene of the men's arrest, but Gerard insists that it was planted by the police, which Irina comes to believe is true. In the play, Hare juxtaposes the worlds of the law, the police, and the prison, demonstrating the systematic inertia and lack of interest in individuals that is built into these institutions of justice. The micro level of coping and/or caring undertaken by individuals is contrasted with the rigidity of the systems within which these individuals work or are incarcerated. The prison warder, Beckett, warns Irina of the hopelessness of her type of intervention:

Beckett: We call them Something-Must-Be-Dones. Oh look we say, there's another bunch of Something-Must-Be-Dones. This place is their monument.

Irina: And is nothing done?

(He looks at her a moment, a sudden quiet flash of real feeling.)

Beckett: Only by us, Miss Platt. It's left to us.

Irina is mirrored by the character of Sandra, an ambitious young police officer who still believes in the notion of right and wrong. Sandra is contrasted with her colleague and lover, Barry, who believes in getting results, even if the methods used are not always aboveboard.

By putting characters in different settings on the stage at the same time, Hare underlines the gaps between those within the different parts of the judicial system. These gaps are institutionalized in the same way as the distance felt by Lionel from the reality of most of his parishioners' lives. Irina's boss tries to persuade her to drop her idea of an appeal for MacKinnon by underlining this sense of distance and noncommunication: "There is a glass screen. And our clients, I'm afraid, live on the other side of it. We on the other. And much as you wish it we cannot break through." Hare interrogates the notion of professionalism, and in a theme that recurs in the trilogy, professionalism and compassion seem to be incompatible. This point is made clear during Irina's meeting with Sandra at Crystal Palace, when she tries to persuade the policewoman to testify against her colleagues. By the end of the play, though, Sandra has decided it is time to take a stand.

The subject for the third part of Hare's trilogy was not, at first, obviously apparent. As he wrote in *Asking Around: Background to the David Hare Trilogy* (1993), he toyed for a while with writing about the army, but with the anticipation of a general election in the early 1990s, Hare decided "to capture that strange moment at which a small part of the State is compelled, for a few weeks at least, to offer itself up to the public's inspection." *The Absence of War* centers around the figure of George Jones, a political leader presiding over a demoralized and divided opposition. George is a grassroots man who has risen from the ranks. His main rival is Malcolm Pryce, the shadow chancellor, a university-educated career politician. The problems of what the Labour Party is and what it is trying to be are emphasized throughout the play by this conflict between the values of socialism and the need to succeed. George sums up the problem when he states: "But our master is different. And causes more argument. Our master is justice. *(He spreads his hands ironically.)* And no two people agree what that is."

George's dilemma is both personal and political. Hare does not seem to suggest a way by which George could have been elected. He is constrained by what politics has become in the 1990s. While the public-relations consultant, Lindsay Fontaine, identifies the party's stifling of George's natural vitality as the cause of his lack of public support, when George does speak without his script he finds that his years in the party machine have robbed him of his natural oratory skills:

> George: All those hours in hotel rooms working at speeches, drafting, redrafting, polishing, changing every word and all you're doing is covering up for what really's gone wrong. What you know in your heart. What really happened. What really happened . . .
>
> *(He pauses a moment. The others are suddenly still in the middle of his stream of consciousness.)*
>
> You once had the words. Now you don't.

As in the other two plays in the trilogy, Hare shows the detrimental effects of professionalism on these key institutions, as they have now lost sight of the abstract values that are fundamental to their conception.

The Labour Party's lack of debate and their overwhelming concern with both the Tories' and the media's representation of them is shown to be strangling George's natural passion as a leader and a politician. Hare takes this theme and reveals it to be more than George's personal tragedy but also that of a country that cannot deal with truth and passion in its political life. The stultifying effect of "ancestor worship" and national heritage is highlighted again. At the close of the play, when George addresses the audience after his defeat, he asks a question that is central to Hare's philosophy throughout his work, both personally and politically: "Is this history? Is everything history? Could we have done more? Was it possible? And how shall we know?"

Racing Demon won four Best Play of the Year awards when it was first performed in 1990, and in 1993 the entire trilogy played in repertory for two months. In 1992 Hare married fashion designer Nicole Farhi.

Cover for Hare's 1999 diary, in which he chronicles writing and acting in Via Dolorosa *(performed and published in 1998)*, his one-man show about visiting Israel and Palestine *(photograph by Alistair Muir; Thomas Cooper Library, University of South Carolina)*

The broad social sweep of the trilogy was replaced by more intimate concerns in Hare's 1995 play *Skylight*. The protagonists, Kyra Hollis and Tom Sergeant, had a long affair that ended when Tom's wife, Alice, found out. Kyra used to work for Tom, a successful restaurateur, but has given that up to teach in an inner-city comprehensive. The play gives a more personal view of the debate between competing value systems seen in the trilogy but also focuses on the importance of choice, rather than the absence of choice.

The meeting between Kyra and Tom that provides the main action is prefigured by a visit from Tom's son, Edward, who is concerned about his father's loss of direction after Alice's death: "He's sitting there alone in this bloody great house. Like some stupid animal. Licking his pain." Edward's attitude toward

Hare performing his monologue Via Dolorosa *on* The MacNeil/Lehrer Report, *25 October 2000 (photograph by PBS; MacNeil/Lehrer Productions, 2000)*

life is closer to Kyra's than that of his father, whose love of opportunity and enterprise are now out of date, or at least, Hare seems to say, they should be. Edward sees Kyra's life, for all its difficulties, as embodying a kind of purity that is lacking from his father's. Kyra's depiction mirrors that of Isobel Glass in *The Secret Rapture* or Stephen Andrews in *A Map of the World* in that she has chosen a certain set of rules to live by, even if these are out of joint with the values of the majority of society. Kyra has the freedom of making a choice, but Hare does not celebrate her position as necessarily wholly virtuous. One of the strengths of the play is that the debate Hare sets up is not constructed through polarized abstractions but through complex human emotions.

The dialectic between Kyra and Tom is further complicated by the conflicting emotions that each of them feel in the light of their previous love affair. Yet, the personal connection between Kyra and Tom is colored by their individual ways of looking at the world. Tom's visit is inspired by a desire to go back to the comfort that Kyra represents, as he tells her at the end of act 1, "Kyra, Kyra, I'm back." Kyra, on the other hand, cannot go back, feeling that the choice she made in giving up that part of her life was too much of a change to be undone.

Kyra's reasons behind her decisions are expounded in a long speech that expresses Hare's feelings of dissatisfaction with the dearth of humanity and responsibility in modern life. Those who try to deal with society's problems, the social workers and the probation officers, are sneered at, as Kyra angrily points out:

> They try and clear out society's drains. They clear out the rubbish. They do what no one else is doing, what no one else is willing to do. And for that, oh Christ, do we thank them? No, we take our own rotten consciences, wipe them all over the social worker's face, and say, "If . . ." FUCK! "if I did the job, then of course if I did it . . . oh no, excuse me, I wouldn't do it like that . . ." *(She turns, suddenly aggressive.)* Well I say: "O.K, then, fucking do it, journalist. Politician, talk to the addicts. Hold families together. Stop the kids from stealing in the streets. Deal with couples who beat each other up. You fucking try it, why not? Since you're so full of advice. Sure come and join us."

Kyra's impassioned outpouring crystallizes the fury with the impossibility of social responsibility in a modern world that is characterized by greed and individualism. But Tom sees Kyra's zeal as indicative of something deeper, a refusal, expressing a fear of commitment and love. *Skylight* dramatizes both sides of the dialectic, juxtaposing the need for personal salvation through love with the need to make a difference. In terms of performance conventions, the piece is daring in its simplicity; no more than two people on stage at any one time, talking, in a world where, as Tom puts it in the play, "Language belongs to the past. This is the world of Super-Mario. Bang! Splat! Spit out your venom and go."

The same importance of language is evident in *Amy's View* (performed and published in 1997). Like *Skylight,* the title of which refers not only to the window built for Alice to look out at the birds as she is dying but also, metaphorically, to a different way of looking at things, *Amy's View* also juxtaposes a variety of different ways of looking at life and love. The play depicts the relationship between Amy and her actress mother, Esme, and the effect of Amy's relationship with a young man, Dominic Tyghe. The play blends the concerns of *Skylight*–life, love, and responsibility–with a debate on the value of theater. "Amy's view" refers both to the newspaper she produced as a child and, more importantly, to the philosophy by which she lives her life: "you have to love people. You just have to love them. You have to give love without any conditions at all. Just give it. And one day you will be rewarded. One day you will get it back."

The play opens in 1979, as Amy has just brought Dominic home for the first time. They wait along with Amy's grandmother, Evelyn, for Esme's return from the theater in the West End where she is playing. Problems in Amy's relationship with Dominic are revealed when Esme guesses that Amy is pregnant. Amy has asked her mother for £5,000 so that she can be independent and not force Dominic into a situation that he cannot handle. Despite promising to keep quiet, Esme drops the bombshell of Amy's pregnancy just before she goes to bed.

Act 2 takes place six years later; Amy and Dominic are now a couple with two children. Dominic chairs a successful arts program and is trying to find ten minutes to interview Esme. The interview becomes a debate on the place of theater in modern society. Dominic's view is that image, exemplified by movies and television, is now tantamount to the word: "But who does theatre reach? Who is it talking to? Obvious to me, it's just wank time." Esme counters with an attack on the media and Dominic: "Have you noticed? It's always the death of the theatre. The death of the novel. The death of poetry. The death of whatever they fancy this week. Except there's one thing it's never the death of. Somehow it's never the death of themselves."

Esme is able to offer advice to Amy as to how to live her life but remains unable to face up to her own problems. This attitude becomes apparent when her investment fund collapses and her income is wiped out. Esme refuses to take responsibility or to take account of the part played by Frank, her fund manager, who advised her and now wants to marry her. She refuses to conflate Frank the man with his actions, which angers Amy: "We are what we do, for Christ's sake. Have you never grasped that? We are nothing else. There's no 'us' apart from the things that we do."

Amy's view takes in the notion of social responsibility that characterized Kyra in *Skylight* and, like Isobel in *The Secret Rapture*, Amy is the moral center of the play whose death produces profound effects that are displayed through a continuation of the debate on the value of theater. In act 3 Esme has given up a lucrative television series and is appearing in a play by a new writer; she is surprised by a visit from Dominic. Hare conflates Dominic's need to take responsibility and to make amends with Esme with his admittance of enjoying the matinee he had seen earlier. When he asks what Esme thinks is the reason for the appeal of theater, she replies, "People like it because they feel it's sincere."

Hare has continued to develop the relationship between the public and private worlds. In *The Judas Kiss* (performed and published in 1998), first performed the year that he received a knighthood for his services to theater, he revisited the relationship between Oscar Wilde and Lord Alfred ("Bosie") Douglas. *Via Dolorosa* (performed and published in 1998) is a one-man piece, written and performed by Hare, that provides an account of his visit to Israel and Palestine. He wrote about the experience of composing and acting the piece in *Acting Up: A Diary* (1999). It is characteristic of his stamina as a writer that *The Blue Room*, his adaptation of Arthur Schnitzler's *La Ronde* (1903), was playing simultaneously to packed and enthusiastic audiences at London's Donmar Warehouse. *My Zinc Bed* (2000), at the Royal Court Theatre, took him back to the territory of personal relationships that he had been developing in his plays after the trilogy; and then, in 2002, *The Breath of Life* opened at the Theatre Royal Haymarket, about which Michael Billington wrote in *The Guardian* (16 October 2002), "Hare's strength has always been his ability to interweave private and public concerns."

The Permanent Way (performed and published in 2003) was Hare's response to the privatization of the railways and the ensuing disasters as a result of the destruction of the railway infrastructure. The play was created collectively with Stafford-Clark's Out of Joint Company. Their collaborative, improvisational way of working harked back to the days of Joint Stock, their forerunner, whose working methods and research resulted in Hare's 1974 piece *Fanshen*. The group started their research for *The Permanent Way* with a list of people involved in the railways and victims of railway disasters; the nine company actors were sent out in groups of two or three to interview these people and report back via improvisations based on these interviews. Thus Hare often had to create a character from two conflicting reports or opinions.

Although the play may seem at first to be a specific piece of documentary theater, it raises issues such as the fate of individuals at the mercy of government and management restructuring. As Hare commented in a 2004 interview with Richard Boon:

> There are a lot of people who don't see this as a play about the railways at all, and I love that. There are people who see it as being about what it's now like at their own place of work—in other words it's run by managers who don't know what they're doing, and where management culture has replaced expertise culture.

Hare commented further in the same interview: "The play to me is about honor and dishonor; a group of people who are behaving honorably and another group who are behaving dishonorably." This comment could also ring true about *Plenty* or *The Secret Rapture*, as well as more overtly political plays such as *Pravda*, *Murmuring Judges*, or Hare's controversial 2004 play, *Stuff Happens*.

Stuff Happens is based on the events leading up to the invasion of Iraq by U.S. and British Coalition forces in 2003. The title was lifted from U.S. Defense Secretary Donald Rumsfeld's response (at an 11 April 2003 press conference) to the looting of Baghdad: "Stuff happens . . . and it's untidy, and freedom's untidy, and free people are free to make mistakes and commit crimes and do bad things." The play depicts the real-life figures from the U.S. and British governments–including George W. Bush, Colin Powell, and Tony Blair–trying to decide the pros and cons for a full invasion of Iraq. The characterization of current political figures led to mixed reviews from critics, who made accusations of political caricature and agitprop. Many, however, praised Hare's courage in so fulsomely attacking and engaging with current political events.

The action takes place with the characters sitting around tables onstage as if in an interminable political meeting. Most of the dialogue is based on real-life quotes and documentary material. For this reason, the play has more of a docudrama feel than some of Hare's other political plays such as *The Permanent Way* or *The Absence of War*.

The strengths of the play, for most commentators, lie in the way in which Hare lets the material speak for itself and the way in which he allows the prowar rhetoric to become convincing. This position is juxtaposed with the experience of the "nameless" victims of the war. At the end of the play, one of Hare's characters comes downstage to stand in an imaginary Iraq. He asks why nobody has bothered to calculate figures for the Iraqi dead. Then he says, "Until this country takes charge of itself, it will continue to suffer. If you don't do it yourself, this is what you get!" This sentiment echoes the sense of social and moral responsibility that is key in many of Hare's plays: the need for the individual, and therefore the playwright, to take notice of one's place in the world.

Esme's comments in *Amy's View* echo David Hare's own views about the revival of theater: that there is still an appetite for what plays have to say, even if theatergoing as a social ritual is dead. Hare ends the play by depicting the first moments of stepping out onto the stage. This play within a play is a bold stylistic device in a work otherwise characterized by the conventionality of its staging. By his use of this convention Hare seems to be asserting the special power of theater; as he told Billington in a 1998 interview, "my claim has always been that people think more deeply when they think together. That's what theatre does."

Interviews:

Catherine Itzin and Simon Trussler, "From Portable Theatre to Joint Stock . . . via Shaftesbury Avenue," *Theatre Quarterly,* 5 (September–November 1975): 108–115;

Michael Billington, "A Knight at the Theatre," *Guardian,* 4 September 1998;

Richard Boon, "David Hare on *The Permanent Way,*" *National Theatre Backstage: Platform Papers* (27 January 2004) <http://www.nationaltheatre.org.uk/?lid=8304>.

References:

Peter Ansorge, "David Hare: A War on Two Fronts," *Plays and Players,* 25 (April 1978);

Richard Boon, *About Hare: The Playwright and the Work* (London: Faber & Faber, 2003);

John Bull, *New British Political Dramatists* (Basingstoke: Macmillan, 1984);

Angela Carter, *The Sadeian Woman* (London: Virago, 1979);

John FitzPatrick Dean, *David Hare* (New York: Twayne, 1990);

Carol Homden, *The Plays of David Hare* (Cambridge: Cambridge University Press, 1995);

Catherine Itzin, *Stages in the Revolution: Political Theatre in Britain Since 1968* (London: Eyre Methuen, 1980);

Judy Lee Oliva, *David Hare: Theatricalizing Politics* (Ann Arbor & London: UMI Research Press, 1990).

Papers:

The Harry Ransom Humanities Research Center at the University of Texas at Austin houses David Hare's papers.

Sarah Kane
(3 February 1971 – 20 February 1999)

Aleks Sierz

PLAY PRODUCTIONS: *Comic Monologue,* Edinburgh Festival Fringe, 12 August 1991;

Starved and *What She Said,* Theatre Zoo, Roman Eagle Lodge, Edinburgh Festival Fringe, 17 August 1992;

Blasted, London, Royal Court Theatre Upstairs, 12 January 1995;

Phaedra's Love, London, Gate Theatre, 15 May 1996;

Cleansed, London, Royal Court Theatre Downstairs, 30 April 1998;

Crave, Edinburgh, Traverse Theatre, 13 August 1998; London, Royal Court Theatre Upstairs, September 1998;

4.48 Psychosis, London, Royal Court Theatre Upstairs, 23 June 2000.

BOOKS: *Blasted; &, Phaedra's Love* (London: Methuen, 1996);

Cleansed (London: Methuen, 1998);

Crave (London: Methuen, 1998);

4.48 Psychosis (London: Methuen, 2000);

Complete Plays (London: Methuen, 2001)—comprises *Blasted, Phaedra's Love, Cleansed, Crave, 4.48 Psychosis,* and *Skin.*

PRODUCED SCRIPT: *Skin,* motion picture, Tapson Steel Films, 1995.

OTHER: *Blasted* and afterword, in *Frontline Intelligence 2: New Plays for the Nineties,* edited by Pamela Edwardes (London: Methuen, 1994), pp. 1–50;

"Sarah Kane: from *Blasted,*" in *Live 3: Critical Mass,* edited by David Tushingham (London: Methuen, 1996), pp. 5–17.

SELECTED PERIODICAL PUBLICATIONS–UNCOLLECTED: "The Only Thing I Remember Is," *Guardian,* 13 August 1998;

"Drama with Balls," *Guardian,* 20 August 1998.

Sarah Kane (photograph by Pau Ros; from Graham Saunders, "Love Me or Kill Me": Sarah Kane and the Theatre of Extremes, 2002; Howard-Tilton Memorial Library, Tulane University)

Sarah Kane was arguably one of the most talented and controversial British writers to emerge during the 1990s, and, since her death by suicide at the age of twenty-eight, she has become an icon, symbolizing the writer who is uncompromising in her vision and openly provocative. In a short career, she completed five plays, of which four were performed during her lifetime, plus one screenplay. Each of the plays is different in structure from the previous work, and her output represents a constant experiment with theater form.

Although her writing is contemporary in its 1990s sensibility, there are few specific local references in her work, and it is clear that she was writing with an eye on future productions of her plays. As examples of what she called "experiential theatre" (which seeks to make audiences feel as if they have actually experienced the acts shown on stage), her plays were originally most successful when put on in studio theaters, especially the Royal Court Theatre Upstairs, where three of them were performed. Since their premieres, her plays have been translated and performed in several European languages, and productions have been mounted all over the world.

Public perception of Kane has been affected by two circumstances: the reception of her first full-length play and the manner of her death. In 1995 her debut, *Blasted* (published in 1994), caused the biggest controversy in British theater since Howard Brenton's *The Romans in Britain* in 1980. The sheer extremism and overwhelming rawness of the work gave her a notoriety that made it difficult for both critics and audiences to view her subsequent plays dispassionately. The fact of her suicide has also made it hard to view her work with detachment. Since her death, her work and her life have become entangled. Some critics have seen her suicide as a validation of the genuineness of the extreme emotions that run through her plays, while others have read her work as a literal reflection of her life. However, drawing too many parallels between her life and her writing tends to narrow the meaning of a body of work that has the potential for a range of interpretations.

Kane has also attracted radical disagreement as to her significance. To her supporters, she "enriched British playwriting more powerfully and enduringly than any other writer of her generation," in the words of theater academic Dan Rebellato in *New Theatre Quarterly* (1999), and her work was characterized by "unforgiving internal landscapes: landscapes of violation, of loneliness, of power, of mental collapse and, most consistently, the landscape of love," according to playwright David Greig in his introduction to Kane's *Complete Plays* (2001). To her critics, such as theater academic Mary Luckhurst, she is not a great writer, nor did her plays represent "a defining moment." Even Dominic Dromgoole, director of the Bush Theatre in the 1990s, argues that "I'm not sure she's a natural writer," meaning that dialogue did not come easily to her.

Born on 3 February 1971, Sarah Marie Kane was the only daughter and second child of Peter Kane, a journalist working for Mirror Group newspapers, and his wife, Jeannine, née Potter. Kane grew up in Kelvedon Hatch, near Brentwood, Essex, and in 1989 began studying drama at Bristol University. In 1991 she wrote and performed the twenty-minute *Comic Monologue* at the Edinburgh Festival Fringe, and the following year she created two more Fringe monologues, *Starved* and *What She Said*. These works were never published, because Kane later considered them juvenilia. After graduating with a First Class Honours degree in 1992, she took an M.A. course in playwriting at Birmingham University, during which she wrote the first drafts of *Blasted;* the first forty-five minutes of the play were presented as a workshop production on Saturday, 3 July 1993, during the end-of-term performance weekend. After completing her studies, Kane became a literary associate at the Bush fringe theater in west London in early 1994, leaving about six months later. She successfully submitted *Blasted* to the Royal Court Theatre, which staged a reading of the play in January 1994, directed by James Macdonald—an associate director at the theater—and the play had a full production a year later, with Macdonald again as director.

In *Blasted*, Ian, a racist, middle-aged journalist with terminal lung cancer, takes twenty-something Cate, a good-natured family friend, to a Leeds hotel room. She is nervous and prone to epileptic fits; he wears a gun and claims he once worked for the secret services. Apparently, Cate was once his girlfriend. He tries to seduce her, then rapes her during the night. In the morning, when she tries to leave, he obstructs her. She goes to the bathroom, and a nameless Soldier suddenly bursts in, demanding food. Then the room is hit by a mortar shell. As they recover, the Soldier tells Ian about the agonies of fighting a civil war and about the death of his girlfriend. Then he rapes Ian, sucks out his eyes, and finally commits suicide. Cate, who escaped through the bathroom window, returns with a baby that has been handed to her by one victim of the war raging outside. It dies, and the blind and hungry Ian tries to eat it. He finally dies. Rain pours in on his head, which is poking out of the floorboards. Having left again in order to sell herself for something to eat, Cate returns to this hellhole with some food, and the dead Ian thanks her.

Blasted is an example of experiential theater: it conveys the unexpected shock of war by means of a sudden change in form (the bomb blast) and reproduces the disruption of war by means of a dislocation of plot. The Leeds hotel room suddenly explodes into a war zone reminiscent in the mid 1990s of the conflict in the former Yugoslavia, although Kane eliminated any explicit references to Bosnia between her first drafts and the published play text. While the first half of the play is recognizably naturalistic, the second half is symbolic or metaphorical and clearly nonnaturalis-

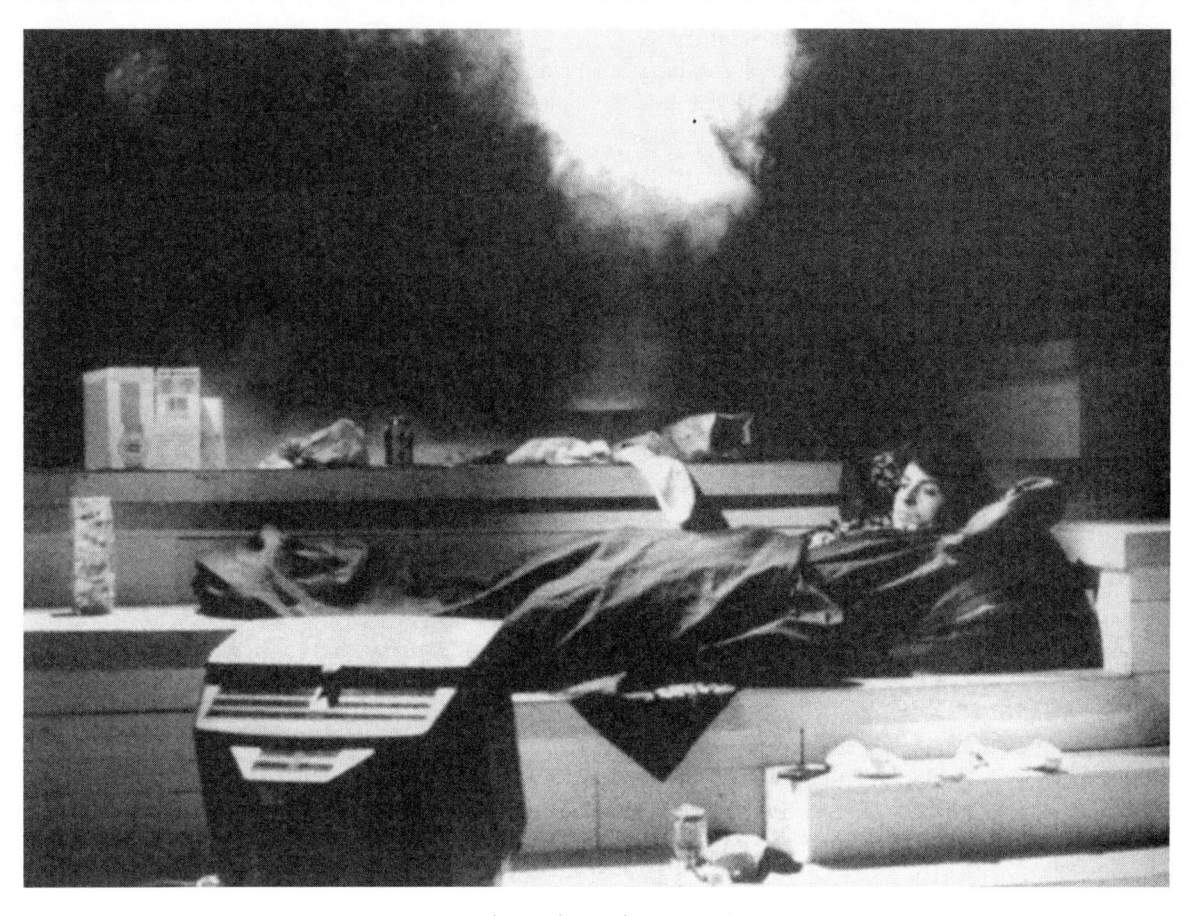

Cas Harkins as Hippolytus in the 1996 Gate Theatre (London) premiere of Phaedra's Love, *Kane's modern reworking of Seneca's* Phaedra *that focuses on Phaedra's depressed and narcissistic stepson (photograph by Pau Ros; from Graham Saunders,* "Love Me or Kill Me": Sarah Kane and the Theatre of Extremes, *2002; Howard-Tilton Memorial Library, Tulane University)*

tic. For example, the stage directions specify that Ian speaks even after "*He dies with relief.*" Raw in sensibility, horrifying in content, and experimental in form, *Blasted* received some of the most hostile reviews of the decade.

First put on in the sixty-seat Royal Court Theatre Upstairs on 12 January 1995, *Blasted* had its press night on 18 January. During that performance, one critic walked out, and two others–Jack Tinker of the *Daily Mail* and Charles Spencer of the *Telegraph*–decided that the play was so shockingly explicit in its portrayal of sex and violence that it was itself a news story. During the following days, many newspapers carried articles about it–headlined, for example, "Walk-Outs at Royal Court 'Atrocity' Play" (London *Evening Standard,* 19 January 1995)–as well as regular reviews. These reviews usually acknowledged Kane's youth and writing abilities but also expressed shock at her subject matter: "scenes of masturbation, fellatio, frottage, micturition, defecation–ah, those old familiar faeces–homosexual rape, eye gouging and cannibalism," wrote Michael Billington in the *Guardian* (20 January 1995). Tinker's review appeared under the headline "This Disgusting Feast of Filth" (*Daily Mail,* 18 January 1995). Some critics called for the Royal Court Theatre's government grant to be cut; Sheridan Morley, in the *Spectator* on 28 January 1995, argued that it would have been better for the theater to "close for the winter" than to stage "this sordid travesty of a play." But others, such as John Peter of *The Sunday Times* and Louise Doughty of the *Mail on Sunday,* praised *Blasted* for its unflinching view of war and its moral integrity.

As the controversy grew, Stephen Daldry, the Royal Court Theatre's artistic director, returned early from a fund-raising trip to New York to appear on television and defend Kane's play. Macdonald wrote an article explaining its importance in the *Observer* newspaper (22 January 1995). While cartoons mocking Kane appeared in some newspapers, playwrights Harold Pinter, Edward Bond, Caryl Churchill, Martin Crimp, and Greig publicly defended her. In a 1996 issue of

Theater, academic Tom Sellar sums up the significance of the play: "Just as [John] Osborne tapped an angry national psyche of class resentment in the 1950s—and as Edward Bond made fierce characters and language speak for poverty and cruelty in the 1960s and 70s—Kane ventures into extremity, terror, and social decay in the late 1990s." The lingering notoriety of her play is reflected by the fact that most reviews of her later work continued to refer to her debut.

In summer 1995 Kane completed the final drafts of *Skin,* a screenplay for a ten-minute motion picture directed by Vincent O'Connell, her mentor at the time (he staged her early monologues, and her first two plays are dedicated to him). She had written the first drafts of *Skin* in autumn 1994, and the movie was short-listed for production during its *Short & Curlies* series by Channel Four/British Screen at the beginning of 1995, just as *Blasted* was being produced. The movie is about Billy, a young skinhead who participates in a brutal racist attack on a black wedding party in Brixton and then finds himself drawn to Marcia, a black woman whose flat is visible from Billy's window. He visits Marcia, and they have sex. She then carves her name on his back but finally rejects him, finding solace with Kath, her flatmate, while Billy unsuccessfully takes an overdose. *Skin* was filmed in September 1995 and previewed at the London Film Festival the following month. It was eventually broadcast by Channel Four television on 17 June 1997, causing controversy when its original screening time of 9:40 P.M. was changed to 11:35 P.M. because, according to the *Daily Mail* of 16 June 1997, television executives were worried by what they considered to be "one of the most violent and racially offensive programmes ever to be made for television in this country."

After the furor over *Blasted,* and on the suggestion of Mel Kenyon, her agent, Kane accepted a commission from the Gate Theatre in London to adapt a European classic. Her original choice was Georg Büchner's *Woyzeck* (1879), but the theater was already planning a Büchner season and had assigned *Woyzeck* to another writer. Her second choice was Bertolt Brecht's *Baal* (1922), although this idea was dropped after the theater anticipated problems with his literary estate. Finally, the Gate suggested a Greek tragedy, and Kane chose Seneca's *Phaedra* because she had seen Churchill's version of another of his plays, *Thyestes,* directed in 1994 by Macdonald at the Royal Court Theatre. Kane's version of Seneca's *Phaedra,* titled *Phaedra's Love,* eventually included one scene—between Hippolytus and the priest—which she had originally written for *Baal,* and the play, directed by the author herself, was first performed at the Gate Theatre in May 1996.

Kane's version of the Phaedra story is not a translation of Seneca's original but a completely new play. Its title refers both to Phaedra's feelings and to the object of her love, her stepson, Hippolytus. Set in modern times, the play focuses on Hippolytus, seeing him as a depressed and narcissistic member of a satirically dysfunctional royal family. In Phaedra's words, he is "Moody, cynical, bitter, fat, decadent, spoilt." Despite these flaws, she feels an intense and irrational desire for him. On his birthday, she performs fellatio on him. He rejects her, telling her that he has had sex with her daughter, Strophe, and that he suffers from gonorrhea. In the next scene, Strophe informs Hippolytus that Phaedra has hung herself, leaving a note accusing Hippolytus of rape, and that a vengeful mob is rioting in the streets. Hippolytus surrenders to the police, but in prison he refuses the priest's offer of forgiveness, asserting his pride in sinning and demanding to be punished. The scene ends with the priest performing fellatio on him. Theseus (Phaedra's husband and Hippolytus's father) returns, mingles with the populace, and watches as Hippolytus throws off his guards and leaps into the crowd, which tries to kill him. When Strophe, in disguise, tries to help her half brother, Theseus rapes her and cuts her throat. When he realizes who she is, he kills himself. The mob cuts off Hippolytus's genitals and throws them on a fire. His last words, as vultures circle, are: "If there could have been more moments like this."

Kane's version of this Greek tragedy concentrates more on Hippolytus than on Phaedra and radically rethinks his character. Instead of having the puritanical attitude of the classical original, Kane's Hippolytus is sexually experienced, even if he gets no pleasure from sex. His motivation is the pursuit of honesty, even to the point of self-destruction. Paul Taylor, in *The Independent* (26 February 1997), wrote that the inversion of Hippolytus's character "cleverly accentuated Phaedra's plight: it was no problem getting into her stepson's knickers but impossible to get through to his heart." As fanatical as the original, he languishes in depression until Phaedra's suicide inspires him to seek feeling through confrontation. His dialogues with his stepmother and his rejection of her advances are cruel, but his "rape" of her is not literal; it is an emotional violation, and her suicide is a desperate response to the impossibility of finding love. Finally, Kane inverts classical conventions by showing rather than just describing violence. Her staging, in which the whole of the small Gate Theatre was turned into a set, with the audience seated on benches around the edges and in the center, enhanced the feeling of participating in the action, as actors sat next to audience members or spoke over their heads.

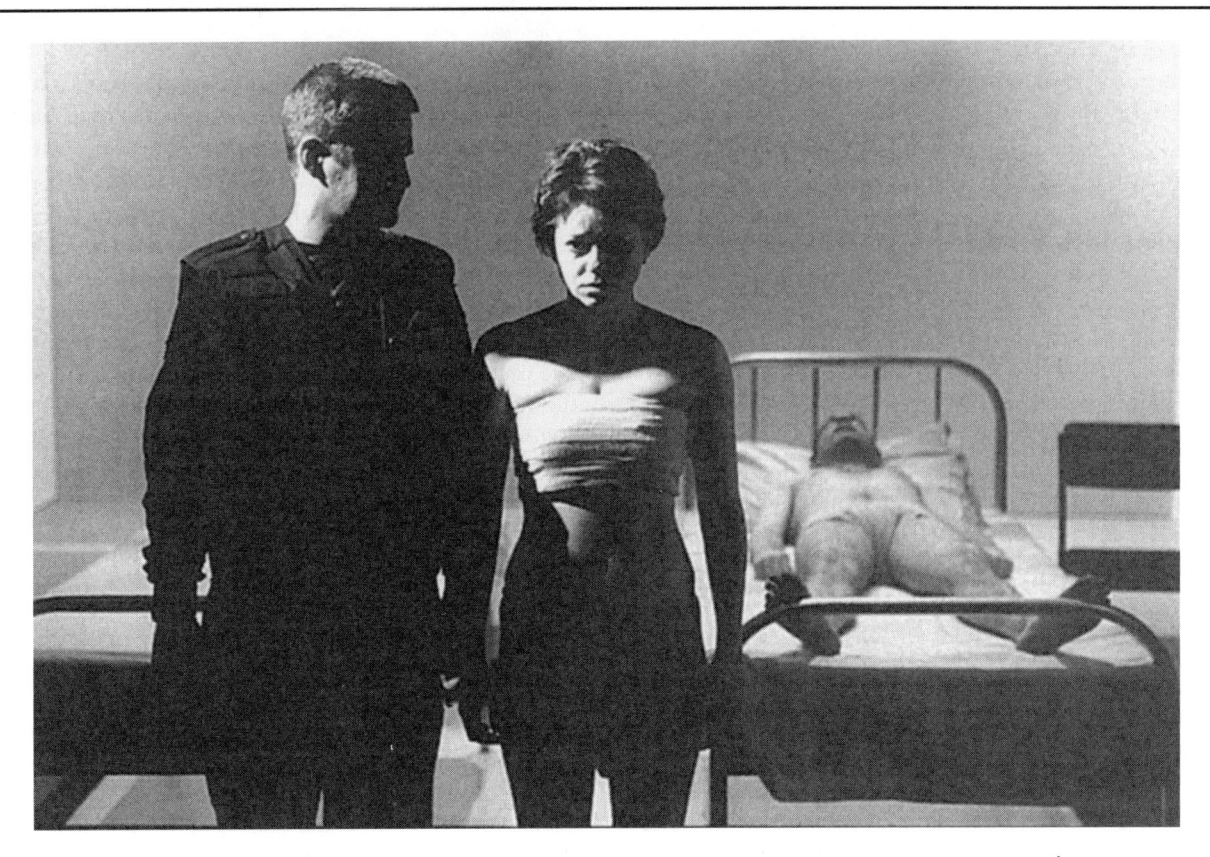

Stuart McQuarrie as Tinker, Suzan Sylvester as Grace, and Daniel Evans as Robin in the 1998 Royal Court Theatre Downstairs premiere of Kane's play Cleansed, *in which an institutionalized woman desires a union with her murdered addict brother (photograph by Ivan Kynel; from Elaine Aston and Janelle Reinelt, eds.,* The Cambridge Companion to Modern British Women Playwrights, *2000; Richland County Public Library)*

After *Blasted,* Kane was widely seen by the media as an "angry young woman," and reviews of *Phaedra's Love* were mixed. For example, in the *Guardian* (21 May 1996), Billington wrote, "Viscerally, her play has undeniable power: intellectually, it's hard to see what point it is making." In the *Telegraph* (21 May 1996), Spencer claimed to be "seriously concerned about Sarah Kane's mental health" and ended his review by saying: "It's not a theatre critic that's required here, it's a psychiatrist." By contrast, Michael Coveney, in the *Observer* (26 May 1996), saw the play as "an entirely serious, utterly absorbing attempt to re-imagine themes of revulsion, audacity and vile lust." In the *Times* (22 May 1996), Kate Bassett wrote: "Speech is terse, truncated. Violence does not reach us by word of mouth. It is in our faces, almost literally as the cast thwack between clumps of seats. The trouble is that lashings of stage violence are not really shocking, just hard to believe."

In August 1996 Kane was appointed writer-in-residence at Paines Plough, a theater company that develops new writing, and ran the Wild Lunch series of writers' workshops. In February 1997 *Phaedra's Love* was performed at the Deutsche Theater Baracke in Berlin as part of the Royal Court Theatre's annual International Exchange Programme (New English Drama). In October 1997, Kane returned to the Gate Theatre to direct Büchner's *Woyzeck,* on an open set, for the theater's season of his work. She then spent much of the following year running workshops for writers in Britain, Europe, and the United States, and was awarded the 1998 Arts Foundation Fellowship in Playwriting. Under the aegis of the British Council, she worked with Dutch writers in Amsterdam (May 1998). As part of the Royal Court Theatre's International Play Development Programme, she participated in writers' groups in the Varna Festival Bulgaria in June, helping set up a writers' group in Sofia. Kane led playwriting workshops (with participants from seventeen countries) at the Royal Court Theatre's International Residency in London (July and August) and worked with the Centro Andaluz de Teatro in Seville, Spain, part of the International Play Development Programme (November). In August 1998 she also wrote a couple of articles for *The Guardian,* reporting from the Edinburgh Festival. In the last year of her life she also premiered two of her most ambitious plays.

On 30 April 1998 *Cleansed* was first performed at the Royal Court Theatre Downstairs at the Duke of York's, St. Martin's Lane (its temporary location while its historic base in Sloane Square was being refurbished). Set in "an institution designed to rid society of its undesirables," according to the cover of the first edition of the play text, *Cleansed* is about "a group of inmates [who] try to save themselves through love." Using four interview-style story lines, Kane explores the theme of love, testing her characters by putting them in a concentration camp where they are subjected to horrendous atrocities. The main story is about Grace's search for Graham, her brother, an addict who has been murdered by Tinker, a sadistic guard or doctor. Grace wears Graham's clothes, dances with and makes love to his spirit, and finally—after receiving a penis transplant—becomes him. Juxtaposed with this story of sibling bonding is the romance of two men, Carl and Rod. Carl, after promising eternal love, betrays his lover; Rod, who lives for the moment, dies for love. In a subplot, Robin, a disturbed nineteen-year-old, falls for Grace when she tries to teach him to read. After learning to use an abacus, he realizes the length of his sentence and hangs himself in despair. The last story is Tinker's: he visits a peep show and imposes Grace's identity onto that of the erotic dancer. He seduces her, then rejects her. By the end of the play, the intensity of desire has made gender identity fluid. In a final speech reminiscent of Hippolytus's last words, Grace declares, "And when I don't feel it, it's pointless," and the play ends in a blaze of sunlight.

Critics were divided over *Cleansed.* While David Benedict of *The Independent* (9 May 1998) wrote that Kane's "handling of image and metaphor sets her apart from almost every other playwright of her generation," Spencer of *The Telegraph* (7 May 1998) called the play "a deadly, entirely predictable bore" by a "writer arrested in a permanent state of doomy adolescence." Sympathetic critics picked up on the echoes in the play of Franz Kafka's *In the Penal Colony* (1919), George Orwell's *Nineteen Eighty-Four* (1949), and Harold Pinter's *The Hothouse* (1980), as well as its central theme of the redemptive power of love. Peter, in *The Sunday Times* of 10 May 1998, summed up: "Love survives, if that is the word, as an incestuous dream, a form of blissful death wish, or a visceral loyalty between mutilated men whose wounds are being gnawed at by rats." The symbolic aspects of the title, which suggests purification through pain as well as ethnic cleansing, and the name of the main character, Grace, were acknowledged, and director Macdonald's production, which used expressionistic devices such as slanted staging and tilting furniture, matched the symbolism with a well-received nonnaturalistic aesthetic.

In August 1998 Kane's next play, *Crave,* marked a further innovation in dramatic structure. While she was developing the play, Kane gave it a rehearsed reading on 21 March 1998, during one of the Wild Lunch workshops she was running for Paines Plough. To avoid the expectations aroused by her reputation, she presented it under the pseudonym of Marie Kelvedon. The first edition of the published play text (1998) states: "Anonymity liberated Sarah to write for—and see her work played in front of—an audience unswayed by the influence of the *Blasted* phenomenon." With characteristic humor, she included a short fictional biography of Kelvedon. But Kane was a perfectionist, and another reason for using a pseudonym was that, at the time of the reading, the play was not completely finished.

Crave is more like a tone poem than a naturalistic drama. The published play text says: "*Crave* marks a departure in Sarah's work. Having pioneered a new theatre where brutality and action express an emotional narrative, here she deploys language like music. Rhythm and orchestration are as vital here as content to understanding and responding to the play." *Crave* has four characters—A, B, C, and M—but no stage directions. While the characters speak in turn, and occasionally seem to answer each other, there is no conventional dialogue. Each character could be addressing one or more of the other characters, and many lines can have more than one meaning, depending on which character one imagines is being addressed. Although their relationships with each other are unstable, each character has a coherent personality: A is an older pedophile; C is a young woman haunted by abuse; M is older and wants to have a baby; and B is a youthful opportunist. The play makes sense as a series of fragmented exchanges between A and C, and between M and B. But *Crave* can be read in several different ways: as an account of two couples, as one mind's mental collapse, or even as the overlapping feelings of four people who may or may not have met. The cover of the first edition states that *Crave* "charts the disintegration of a [single] human mind under the pressures of love, loss and desire." The ending is also ambiguous, and can be understood as a final exhalation of happiness before death, a moment of rage against the fading of the light, or the quiet drifting of a mind into unconsciousness.

In the first full production by Paines Plough, the four actors were seated in a row on swivel chairs. They spoke, sometimes to each other, sometimes to themselves, sometimes to the audience, and sometimes as parts of a poetic whole. At one point, the actors swapped chairs so that the two women were seated next to each other. Directed by Vicky Featherstone, *Crave* lasted about forty-five minutes and was performed in August 1998 at the Traverse Theatre, Edinburgh, transferring to the Royal Court Theatre Upstairs the following month. The critical response was relatively enthusiastic. Some critics, such as Billington of *The Guardian* (15 August 1998), tried to create a coherent story from the text: "An anguished young woman (C) is trying to free herself from an older man (A). Meanwhile, a mature woman (M) terrified of passing time is both drawn to and repelled by a younger man (B)." In this case, A stands for abuser, B for boy, C for child, and M for mother; but this approach tends to limit interpretations of a deliberately open-ended text. Peter pointed out that as the title implies, the message of the play is that "You crave what could destroy you" (*The Sunday Times,* 23 August 1998). The writing, said Peter, "has the dark, edgy poetry and shocking precision of nightmares." Certainly, Kane's use of language is richer, more allusive, and more sensuous than before. Several critics pointed out the echoes of the King James Bible, William Shakespeare, T. S. Eliot, and Samuel Beckett. However, Alastair Macaulay in *The Financial Times* (22 August 1998) interpreted the play as "a flashy feminist maze," pointing out that while the two men located their needs in the women, the women wanted "to be free of these men and their demands." Such differing interpretations suggest the richness of the work, which embodies Kane's characteristic themes: the search for love, and how love can be expressed in adversity. Violence is present but has been internalized.

Kane's final play, *4.48 Psychosis* (performed and published in 2000), was also her most experimental and exemplifies her desire to represent abstract ideas, as well as being the culmination of her quest to align form and content. As with *Crave,* the play text has no character descriptions, and moreover there is no indication of how many actors are required. The text resembles a modernist poem, both visually and verbally suggesting the experience of psychological collapse, and in particular what happens to a person's mind when he or she suffers a psychotic breakdown, when the barriers between reality and different forms of imagination come down. Yet, the play is also clear in its content: it includes dialogues between patients and therapists, jokes about grief, diary entries, caustic accounts of the therapeutic use of drugs to treat depression, and religious passages. One speech gives various reasons for cutting one's wrists; another expresses a yearning for love; and a third voices disbelief that the intensity of one's feelings for another person are not reciprocated. Each line could be spoken by a man or a woman. The effect, once again, is of a mind full of competing voices. But the style is both controlled and refined, and there is a mix of poetic images, idiomatic conversation, satires on psychobabble, and repetitive, quasi-liturgical rhythms. The title refers to 4:48 A.M., a time when the human will to live, according to Kane, is at low ebb: "At 4.48 / when desperation visits." Despite its humor, the play represents the terminal stage in a writing career that had moved from the apparently objective to the completely subjective.

Kane suffered from clinical depression and was a voluntary patient at the Royal Maudsley (Psychiatric) Hospital in London more than once. On 20 February 1999, while recovering in King's College Hospital from an earlier suicide attempt, she hanged herself. An inquest held on 22 September 1999 recorded a verdict of "suicide while the balance of her mind was disturbed." Obituaries by drama critics and theater colleagues paid tribute to her. In *The Independent* (23 February 1999) her friend and fellow playwright Mark Ravenhill wrote: "Sarah Kane was a contemporary writer with a classical sensibility who created a theatre of great moments of beauty and cruelty." In *The Observer* (28 February 1999) Macdonald praised the "brave, angry, poetic body of work quite unlike anything else" and pointed out that "she chose to talk about the political through the personal, and found new forms for doing so."

4.48 Psychosis was first performed in June 2000 at the newly refurbished Royal Court Theatre Upstairs, in Sloane Square. It was directed by Macdonald, who chose to use three actors. Just as the fragmented thought of mental disturbance is echoed by the fractured form of Kane's text, so Macdonald's imaginative production used a huge mirror and projections of street scenes and electronic static to emphasize the disjunction of the inner life of the troubled psyche. At the end, the windows of the Theatre Upstairs attic studio were thrown open, and the inrush of natural air acted as a refreshing contrast to the claustrophobia of the play.

The posthumous staging of Kane's last play inevitably created a controversy; some commentators viewed the work as an "extended suicide note" (Coveney in *The Daily Mail,* 30 June 2000), while others defended the intensity of her vision. In the *Observer* (2 July 2000), Susannah Clapp called the play "Kane's most nakedly autobiographical work," while Sarah Hemming in *The Financial Times* (30 June 2000) said it was "disjointed, dense, bitter and desolate," pointing out that "words such as 'shame,' 'betrayal' and 'anger' echo through the writing, and it is driven by merciless

Ingrid Craigie, Lan Williams, Sharon Duncan-Brewster, and Paul Thomas Hickey in a 1998 Paines Plough production in Copenhagen of Kane's 1998 play Crave, *in which four characters known only as A, B, C, and M take turns speaking in overlapping, interwoven dialogue (photograph by Manuel Harlan; from Graham Saunders, "Love Me or Kill Me": Sarah Kane and the Theatre of Extremes, 2002; Howard-Tilton Memorial Library, Tulane University)*

self-scrutiny." In *The Guardian* (30 June 2000) Billington compared Kane to Sylvia Plath and called *4.48 Psychosis* "a rare example of the writer recording the act she is about to perform," and Paul Taylor in *The Independent* (3 July 2000) argued that the play "testifies to a harrowing, almost skinned personal vision of the world—a vision which, in the end, she refuses to blur with anti-depressants."

Although the initial responses to Kane's work were divided between uncomprehending hostility and unstinting praise, subsequent criticism is producing a more balanced view of her achievement. Much more work has been done on the sources of her inspiration, for example by Graham Saunders (2004), who compares *Blasted* with *King Lear,* and Christopher Innes, who sees Kane's work as "fulfilling all the requirements of Artaud's 'Theatre of Cruelty.'" Other academics, such as Elaine Aston, have seen Kane's informal trilogy—*Blasted, Cleansed,* and *Crave*—as "a cycle of plays that variously treats and critiques the damaging and brutalising force of the masculine." Apart from the shocking "in-yer-face" sensibility of her work, Kane also has a firm political standpoint that is critical of the norms of contemporary society, and especially of its sexual mores. While some of her work can be seen as a critique of traditional notions of masculinity *(Blasted)* or gender identity *(Cleansed),* Kane fiercely rejected being categorized as either a feminist or a woman writer, seeing such labels as inherently limiting.

It should also be remembered that although Kane's vision was powerful, it was also narrow. Each of her plays has a character who commits or attempts to commit suicide, and—like many other 1990s playwrights—she virtually ignores family life, concentrating instead on individuals. Certainly, a mature engagement with her work has to recognize those moments of awkwardness in her writing: some clumsy contrasts between dirty realism and Beckettian poetry in *Blasted,* some trite writing in *Phaedra's Love,* and some moments of juvenile petulance in *4.48 Psychosis.* Still, her distinctive voice, with its mixture of passionate intensity and raw feeling, remains instantly recognizable, and her style—utterly bleak yet wryly comic, always direct and well crafted—does create beauty out of despair and affirms a sense of hope. If her confrontational style and sheer aggression suggest an antagonistic personality, they are balanced by those moments of gentleness when a romantic faith in the power of love and the human capacity for goodness are powerful evidence of an idealistic nature. Kane wrote her contradictions into her work. While its rawness suggests that she wrote from the gut, it should also be remembered that her plays are the product of constant rewriting and a full-time immersion in a community of writers in Britain and abroad. Her work as a theater-maker—reading plays, running workshops, and encouraging others—was exceptional. As fellow playwright Greig said at her memorial event, organized by the Royal Court Theatre, on 18 April 1999: "Sarah Kane was not some petulant *enfant terrible* who simply gloried in shocking audiences; she was a committed, sophisticated, challenging playwright who had a fine sense of the traditions she came from, and had a generous respect and love for and from the community of writers she moved in."

Interviews:

David Benedict, "Disgusting Violence? Actually It's Quite a Peaceful Play," *Independent*, 22 January 1995;

Clare Bayley, "A Very Angry Young Woman," *Independent*, 23 January 1995;

Benedict, "What Sarah Did Next," *Independent*, 15 May 1996;

James Christopher, "Her First Play Was about Defecation, Cannibalism, and Fellatio. The New One's about Love," *Observer*, 2 November 1997;

Heidi Stephenson and Natasha Langridge, "Sarah Kane," in *Rage and Reason: Women Playwrights on Playwriting*, edited by Stephenson and Langridge (London: Methuen, 1997), pp. 129–135;

Kate Stratton, "Extreme Measures," *Time Out* (25 March – 1 April 1998);

Simon Fanshawe, "Given to Extremes," *Sunday Times*, 26 April 1998;

Claire Armitstead, "No Pain, No Kane," *Guardian*, 29 April 1998;

Caroline Egan, "The Playwright's Playwright," *Guardian*, 21 September 1998;

Nils Tabert, "Gespräch mit Sarah Kane," in *Playspotting: Die Londoner Theaterszene der 90er*, edited by Tabert (Reinbeck: Rowohlt, 1998), pp. 8–21;

Anon, "The Late Sarah Kane: In Her Own Words," *Independent*, 24 February 1999;

Johan Thielemans, "Sarah Kane and Vicky Featherstone," in *Rehearsing the Future: 4th European Directors Forum–Strategies for the Emerging Director in Europe*, edited by Andrew McKinnon (London: Directors Guild of Great Britain et al, 1999), pp. 9–15;

Aleks Sierz, "The Short Life of Sarah Kane," *Daily Telegraph*, 27 May 2000;

Simon Hattenstone, "A Sad Hurrah," *Guardian Weekend*, 1 July 2000.

Bibliography:

Aleks Sierz, "Sarah Kane Checklist," *New Theatre Quarterly*, 67 (August 2001): 285–290.

References:

Elaine Aston, "Sarah Kane: The 'Bad Girl of Our Stage,'" in her *Feminist Views on the English Stage: Women Playwrights 1990–2000* (Cambridge: Cambridge University Press, 2002), pp. 77–97;

Aston and Janelle Reinelt, eds., *The Cambridge Companion to Modern Women British Playwrights* (Cambridge & New York: Cambridge University Press, 2000), pp. 1–2, 17, 71, 154, 214, 237;

Stefani Brusberg-Kiermeier, "Re-writing Seneca: Sarah Kane's *Phaedra's Love*," in *Crossing Borders: Intercultural Drama and Theatre at the Turn of the Millennium*, edited by Bernhard Reitz and Alyce von Rothkirch, Contemporary Drama in English 8 (Trier: Wissenschaftlicher Verlag Trier, 2001), pp. 165–172;

Dominic Dromgoole, "Sarah Kane," in his *The Full Room: An A–Z of Contemporary Playwriting* (London: Methuen, 2000), pp. 161–165;

Christopher Innes, "Sarah Kane," in his *Modern British Drama: The Twentieth Century* (Cambridge: Cambridge University Press, 2002), pp. 528–537;

Mary Luckhurst, "An Embarrassment of Riches: Women Dramatists in 1990s Britain," in *British Drama of the 1990s*, edited by Bernhard Reitz and Mark Berninger (Heidelberg: Universitätsverlag C Winter, 2002), pp. 65–78;

Peter Morris, "The Brand of Kane," *Areté*, no. 4 (Winter 2000): 142–155;

Dan Rebellato, "Sarah Kane: An Appreciation," *New Theatre Quarterly*, 59 (August 1999): 280–281;

Graham Saunders, "'Just a Word on a Page and There Is the Drama': Sarah Kane's Theatrical Legacy," *Contemporary Theatre Review*, 13, no. 1 (February 2003): 97–110;

Saunders, *"Love Me or Kill Me": Sarah Kane and the Theatre of Extremes* (Manchester: Manchester University Press, 2002);

Saunders, "'Out Vile Jelly': Sarah Kane's *Blasted* and Shakespeare's *King Lear*," *New Theatre Quarterly*, 77 (February 2004): 69–78;

Tom Sellar, "Truth and Dare: Sarah Kane's *Blasted*," *Theater*, 27, no. 1 (1996): 29–34;

Aleks Sierz, "Cool Britannia? 'In-yer-face' Writing in the British Theatre Today," *New Theatre Quarterly*, 56 (November 1998): 324–333;

Sierz, "'The Element That Most Outrages': Morality, Censorship and Sarah Kane's *Blasted*," in *Morality and Justice: The Challenge of European Theatre,* edited by Edward Batley and David Bradby, special issue of *European Studies: A Journal of European Culture, History and Politics,* no. 17 (2001): 225–239;

Sierz, "Sarah Kane," in his *In-Yer-Face Theatre: British Theatre Today* (London: Faber & Faber, 2001), pp. 90–121;

Mal Smith, "Sarah Kane: A Nineties 'Take' on Cruelty," in *Antonin Artaud and His Legacy,* edited by Smith (London: Theatre Museum Education Pack, 1999);

Eckart Voigts-Virchow, "Sarah Kane, a Late Modernist: Intertextuality and Montage in the Broken Images of *Crave* (1998)," in *What Revels Are in Hand: Assessments of Contemporary Drama in English in Honour of Wolfgang Lippke,* edited by Bernhard Reitz and Heiko Stahl (Trier: Wissenschaftlicher Verlag Trier, 2001), pp. 205–220;

Clare Wallace, "Dramas of Radical Alterity: Sarah Kane and Codes of Trauma for a Postmodern Age," in *Extending the Code: New Forms of Dramatic and Theatrical Expression,* edited by Hans-Ulrich Mohr and Kerstin Mächler, Contemporary Drama in English 11 (Trier: Wissenschaftlicher Verlag Trier, 2004), pp. 117–130;

Heiner Zimmermann, "Theatrical Transgression in Totalitarian and Democratic Societies: Shakespeare as a Trojan Horse and the Scandal of Sarah Kane," in *Crossing Borders: Intercultural Drama and Theatre at the Turn of the Millennium,* edited by Bernhard Reitz and Alyce von Rothkirch, Contemporary Drama in English 8 (Trier: Wissenschaftlicher Verlag Trier, 2001), pp. 173–182.

Papers:

Sarah Kane's papers are in the possession of her estate, which is privately administered by her brother, Simon Kane.

Tom Kempinski

(24 March 1938 –   )

Peter Billingham
Bath Spa University College

PLAY PRODUCTIONS: *The English Revolution,* Northampton, Town Hall, 1971;

Chartism, The First International, Wembley, Empire Pool, 1972;

The English Civil War, London, 1972;

The Peasants Revolt, Colchester, 1972;

The Ballad of Robin Hood, by Kempinski and Roger Smith, London, 1973;

The General Strike, London, 1973;

October, by Kempinski and Smith, London, 1973;

Ramsay MacDonald, London, Hammersmith Palais, 1974;

1917, London, Alexander Palace, 1975;

Moscow Trials, London, 1975;

1871, The Paris Commune, London, 1976;

Sell-Out, by Kempinski and Smith, London, Cottesloe (National Theatre), 1978;

The Brothers, London, 1979;

The Life of Trotsky, London, Alexander Palace, 1979;

Flashpoint, London, New End Theatre, 1979;

Japanese Noh Plays, Leicester, Haymarket Theatre, 1979;

Mayakovsky, translated from Stefan Schultz, London, Half Moon, 1980;

Duet for One, London, Bush Theatre, 13 February 1980; New York, Royale Theatre, 17 December 1981;

Dreyfuss, translated from Jean-Claude Grumberg's play, London, Half Moon, 1982;

The Beautiful Part of Myself, Watford, Palace Theatre, 1983;

Life of Karl Marx, by Kempinski and Smith, London, 1984;

Self-Inflicted Wounds, Mold, Northeast Wales, Theatr Clwyd, 1985;

Separation, London, Hampstead Theatre, 14 October 1987;

What About Borneo? London, King's Head, Islington, 1988;

The Workshop, translated from Grumberg's play, Oxford, Oxford Playhouse, 1989;

Sex Please, We're Italian, London, Young Vic Theatre, 4 July 1991;

Tom Kempinski (photograph by John Haynes; from Plays and Players, *July 1991; Thomas Cooper Library, University of South Carolina)*

A Free Country, translated from Grumberg's play, London, 1991;

When the Past is Still To Come, London, Finborough Arms, 2 September 1992;

What a Bleedin' Liberty! London, Theatre Royal, Stratford East, April 1996;

Addicted to Love, Bristol, Bristol Old Vic, September 1996;

Salus Populi, Glasgow, Citizens Theatre, 1996;

Heinrich Heine vs Nikolai Gogol, London, New End Theatre, 1997;

Don Quixote and the Jewish Question, London, New End Theatre, 1997;

Penthesilea, adapted from Heinrich von Kleist's play, London, Mountview Theatre, 1998;

Chatterton, London, New End Theatre, 2001;

Family, London, New End Theatre, 2001;

High Jumpers, adapted from Xenophon's *Anabasis,* London, New End Theatre, 2001.

BOOKS: *Duet for One* (London & New York: S. French, 1981);

Separation (London & New York: S. French, 1989).

PRODUCED SCRIPTS: *Duet for One,* television, BBC, 1981;

Duet for One, by Kempinski, Andrei Konchalovsky, and Jeremy Lipp, motion picture, Golan-Globus, 1986;

Separation, television, BBC, 1987;

Lovejoy, television, BBC, 1992.

A writer of formidable productivity, Tom Kempinski has written an eclectic range of work, from powerful political satires such as *Sell-Out* (performed in 1978) through the award-winning *Duet for One* (performed in 1980, published in 1981) to later comedies such as *What a Bleedin' Liberty!* (performed in 1996). His writing, particularly in plays such as *Duet for One*—with which he has enjoyed major international success—needs to be placed in the context of British theater since 1960. His early output of explicitly political dramas (usually for performance at left-wing political rallies), while bearing interesting comparison with the earlier political work of contemporaries such as David Edgar, has remained effectively unknown and unacknowledged. Kempinski has a particular capacity for exploring the deeply painful life experiences of characters enmeshed within the grip of profound psychological conflicts. His plays also reflect crucial and fundamental aspects of Kempinski's own life experience.

Kempinski was born on 24 March 1938 in London to German Jewish parents who had fled Germany to England during Adolf Hitler's rise to power. His father was a successful actor, while his mother was a restaurateur. Fearing the continued rise of Nazism on the Continent, his parents sent Kempinski to America with his grandparents in 1940. His early years, by his own acknowledgment, imprinted a traumatic mark that characterized and defined Kempinski's later, adult life; as he told Peter Billingham in an unpublished 1998 interview:

> I had very bad early experiences in terms of developing a personality. Basically. . . . because of the Second World War, I was sent away to America. . . . with my grandparents. After three months in America, my grandfather died—so that was the second loss—my grandmother couldn't handle a child on her own, and so I was sent to a foster family—so that was the third loss within a very short time—after four years with this foster family, I was sent back at the end of the war, which of course was another break. I didn't know about the war, I didn't know these original, real parents.

Kempinski's father died in 1947, and his mother, concerned for her son's emotional state after this sudden bereavement, sent him to a neurologist. Also at about this time, he was sent consecutively to two different preparatory schools. He then went as a boarding pupil to Abingdon Grammar School. After initially faring unevenly, he underwent a steep curve of academic development, resulting in his winning a major open scholarship to Cambridge University. Kempinski went to Cambridge in 1957, managing to avoid the final year of national conscription on medical grounds. Suffering from symptoms of persistent, acute anxiety, Kempinski went to a general practitioner who, realizing the seriousness of his patient's condition, referred him to a psychologist at Maudsley Hospital. Out of this encounter with the psychologist, Kempinski told Billingham, he discovered and articulated his desire to be an actor:

> He said to me, "What do you want to be?" And I heard this voice—I don't mean in a mystical sense—but a voice said, "I want to be an actor," and that's when I allowed myself to say that I wanted to be an actor.

After a ten-week stay at Maudsley Hospital, Kempinski successfully auditioned for the Royal Academy of Dramatic Arts (RADA) in 1957. He graduated from RADA in 1960, and in eleven years as a professional actor, he was unemployed for only ten months. His roles included lead parts in productions of Lionel Bart's *Blitz* (1962) and Charles Wood's *Dingo* (1967) at the Royal Court Theatre. He was also a member of the National Theatre, where his performances included a production of William Congreve's *Love for Love* (1695) that starred Laurence Olivier, Maggie Smith, Albert Finney, and Lynn Redgrave.

During this period Kempinski's political awareness and ideological views began to develop. Although he had been effectively apolitical until this point in his life, in his interview with Billingham he reflected upon his exposure to political discussions as a child:

> Whereas other young people sit with grown-ups and they're talking about insurance, jobs. . . . I sat in the middle of people with German accents discussing politics. . . . people going past with wheelbarrows of money in 1926. . . . that was what was being talked about. The Nazis. . . . it was just "normal." In a sense, politics was going in. . . . it was very one sided, despairing, they didn't know why it had happened. . . . they were all Conservatives.

Kempinski's exposure to those repeated discussions on the economic collapse of 1926 and the rise of the Nazis undoubtedly played its part in the later development of his political activism. In 1964, following the election of

Harold Wilson's Labour government after "thirteen years of Tory misrule," Kempinski joined the Labour Party. Within a short time of his making this decision, he was shocked at Wilson's failure to send in troops to Rhodesia following Ian Smith's Unilateral Declaration of Independence. In an effort to define his own position and beliefs, Kempinski bought and read several books on communism and thus began the gradual development of his political understanding. This study culminated in a chance meeting with other like-minded actors and theater people in 1969 that led him into revolutionary Marxist politics.

Kempinski continued to commit himself to his life as an actor, combining his serious work on the stage with relatively lucrative movie or television work. However, simultaneously, he felt the urge to try to express his growing political awareness in stage terms. His lead in Wood's antiwar drama *Dingo* was a clear sign of that impetus. Kempinski found himself in Paris amid the revolutionary events of 1968, albeit as an actor in Peter Brook's experimental company. He had also started to meet several left-wing directors and writers and became increasingly involved in political activities. By 1969 Kempinski had aligned himself with the International Committee of the Fourth International, a Bolshevik group. Toward the end of the 1960s and the early years of the 1970s, Kempinski began to write overtly political plays for that movement. His output over the next decade was phenomenal, and he often collaborated with his friend and fellow activist Roger Smith.

A particularly good example of their agitprop plays was *Sell-Out*, a musical that views, with savage irony and satire, the fatal compromises and ultimate capitulation of Ramsay MacDonald's Labour administration in the early 1930s. The play is characteristically Brechtian in tone and effect and opens, for example, with the American Eagle suspended above the stage while assorted Stock Brokers watch as a Chorus of Flapper Girls enters to sing "Boom Time":

> Everybody knows it's boom time
> Everybody knows its spoon time
> Buy stock Be bold
> They're better than gold.

Nonnaturalistic and episodic in structure, the piece employs similar strategies from Bertolt Brecht's alienation effect (dramatic devices designed to challenge the audience into critical reflection rather than emotional empathy with the stage events) to communicate its indictment of the seemingly imminent collapse of capitalism at the time of the Wall Street crash. MacDonald's Labour government was elected in 1929

Cover for the VHS release of the 1986 movie version of Kempinski's 1980 play about the psychiatric sessions of a musician with multiple sclerosis (Hollywood Video)

against a background of massive unemployment and poverty, reflected in the "Song of the Unemployed":

> Let's get it straight now
> We're not a bunch of bums or jerks
> We're in this state now
> But we're the guys who did the work
> We built your railways
> We worked your mines and made your cars
> We met the deadlines
> Now we're on breadlines
> Where are the red lines?

Kempinski and Smith cleverly used the process of historicization to comment not only upon the compromise and impotency of MacDonald's government but also upon the centrist-right paralysis of the contemporary administration of James Callaghan, brought down by a series of labor strikes in 1978 and 1979. *Sell-Out* is an interesting example of Kempinski's political writing and displays both the characteristic qualities and limitations of that genre. Characters are inevitably simplified to represent stereotypes, while the nature of the episodic narrative contrives to present complex ideological issues in a clear–if simplistic–manner.

Kempinski's next major play was the one that established his wider reputation both at the time and in the intervening years. *Duet for One* was originally produced at the Bush Theatre on 13 February 1980 with Frances de la Tour in the lead role of violinist Stephanie Abrahams. Kempinski had met the actress through their shared political beliefs and activities, and they were married and had two children.

An assumption grew around the subject matter of the play–the traumatic emotional and psychological descent of a violinist afflicted by multiple sclerosis–that Kempinski had written it as a direct result of the similar circumstances surrounding famed cellist Jacqueline du Pre. Nevertheless, the play is not in any sense about her, although Kempinski was clearly aware of her situation. More significantly, the play is a profound and complex metaphor of Kempinski's own lifelong psychiatric illness. At the time of this play, that illness and its symptoms had reached a critical point. Beginning in 1980 Kempinski was effectively a prisoner of his pathological agoraphobia for seventeen years. He told Billingham, "*Duet for One* is about struggle. . . . the play is about that person's battle to survive. . . . The play is a symbol of my emotional paralysis. . . . To me, it was a metaphor for my emotional struggles."

The play was an immediate success and was awarded the London Theatre Critic's Award for best play of the year in 1980. The play has a core of authentic emotional truth, wrested from the author's own experience. The action of the play takes place across two acts and six separate scenes, delineated as "Sessions." This structuring of the play emphasizes the central context of Stephanie's interaction with her psychiatrist, Dr. Feldmann. The "duet" these two characters play is one of life against death, liberty against imprisonment within the soul, light against darkness. Kempinski cleverly delineates the characters and reveals Stephanie as a woman of intelligence, tenacity, and an artist's pride in her own achievements, which makes the irreversible diminishing and ultimate destruction of that personality and genius even more painful. Feldmann is an astute and experienced physician of the soul, who carefully seeks to help Stephanie recognize the life-threatening psychological vortex into which she is being inexorably pulled.

At first Stephanie tries to dismiss the seriousness of her psychological condition and attempts to fend Feldmann off with her acerbic social style and manner. However, Feldmann recognizes her defensive strategies of denial and, toward the end of session 1, quietly but firmly confronts her: "I really think that it is very important for you to understand these feelings you have. Very important. Indispensable, I should say." As the play progresses, the relationship between the two characters unfolds like some complex game of chess, with Stephanie especially employing bluffs and double bluffs to try to keep Feldmann at bay.

As her journey into the dark night of her soul is steadily revealed, Kempinski provides her with some longer, evocative speeches that are almost arias of inner torment and confusion:

> STEPHANIE: JESUS CHRIST! What is this? What the hell is going on here, what are you bloody after anyway? I come here in good faith, I come because there may be a problem, I come willingly, openly, . . . Do you have many patients at all, Dr Feldmann, eh? Do you? Have you? I mean, do you, because as far as I can see, you must be sending people out of here to see other doctors as fast as their legs, or their wheelchairs can carry them? I think you must send them to other doctors with a whole new set of illnesses and problems which you have specially and skilfully created by sheer determined hard work and bloody bloody-mindedness and insensitivity and rudeness. . . . though I am, of course not the great white-coated expert on the sub-conscious that you obviously, mistakenly think you are. . . .

The audience witnesses the awful degeneration of Stephanie both physically and emotionally, so that by the penultimate scene or session, she is a darkly harrowing shadow of herself at the start of the play. When Feldmann seeks to present Stephanie with a vision of life that is positive and inspirational, she callously undermines his plea. She recalls, in cruel, self-destructive, matter-of-fact terms, her account of an alleged sexual encounter with a totter (someone who makes a living collecting scrap metal or sellable waste of any kind to sell for a modest profit; seen as a poor and demeaning occupation). Just when it seems that her tidal wave of self-destruction has, perhaps, unnerved and overwhelmed him, Feldmann responds with his first–and only–expression of anger. He castigates her dark and manipulative self-destructive games:

> . . . . it is I who am bored by your displays of depression and cynicism and pretended unconcernedness, because they are just stupid games. . . . the game here is a real one, a deadly earnest one, a life and death game, as a matter of fact. Let me give it to you straight, Madame, you are close to killing yourself. . . . We must

give battle to these dark forces, and I do, and I am asking you, or rather I am telling you, Miss Abrahams, to add your weight to mine in this fight.

In the final scene of the play, Stephanie, shaken for the first time into an acknowledgment of her condition, admits to Feldmann, "The violin isn't my work; it isn't a way of life. It's where I live. It's when I play that I actually live in the real world; mine, of course. . . . It's not your fault. . . . It's just that I'm over here—and I can't sing." Kempinski allows for the dialectical interplay of their relationship and its potential for her inner healing to remain tantalizingly alive with Feldmann's final line: "Is the same time next week still convenient?"

The dynamics at the heart of *Duet for One* are resumed, redefined, and reworked in Kempinski's later play *Separation* (performed in 1987, published in 1989). Nominated for the Olivier Award for best comedy in 1987, the play is a bittersweet, poignant, but unsentimental exploration of the relationship between a playwright, Joe Green, and a disabled young American actress, Sarah. Premiered at the Hampstead Theatre on 14 October 1987 with David Suchet and Saskia Reeves in its two roles, *Separation* presents Joe, like Stephanie, as someone who is enmeshed in a complex web of fear and insecurity. Clearly autobiographical, Joe is agoraphobic and effectively consigned to a solitary life. When he is contacted by Sarah, who asks for permission to produce an adapted version of one of his best-selling plays, an unlikely friendship and intimate relationship develop. Kempinski had in fact been approached by a young actress to do an Off-Off-Broadway production of *Duet for One*, a request to which he had agreed.

In the play, through a relationship that for most of the first half of the play is mediated via transatlantic telephone calls, Joe gradually and painfully finds a way of loving and trusting someone in a nonaddictive, nondependent sense. Sarah represents, in Freudian terms, the mother figure whose love Joe wants while he simultaneously despises her for the threat that she constitutes to the life-denying security of his neurosis. The play is written with emotional courage and honesty, interwoven with a sharp-edged humor born out of adversity. After an ill-fated attempt to try living together in London is aborted by Joe's self-destructive rejection of Sarah, she returns to America. Joe, belatedly and sorrowfully realizing his culpability, telephones her to negotiate a reconciliation. Slowly, Joe and Sarah realize that they can start again, but this time with a relationship based on mutual trust and Joe's ability to live with the precarious nature of life itself.

In the years since *Separation*, Kempinski's personal and professional life found a renewed focus and serenity. Through the help of continuing therapy and the loving support of his partner and their daughter, he has over-

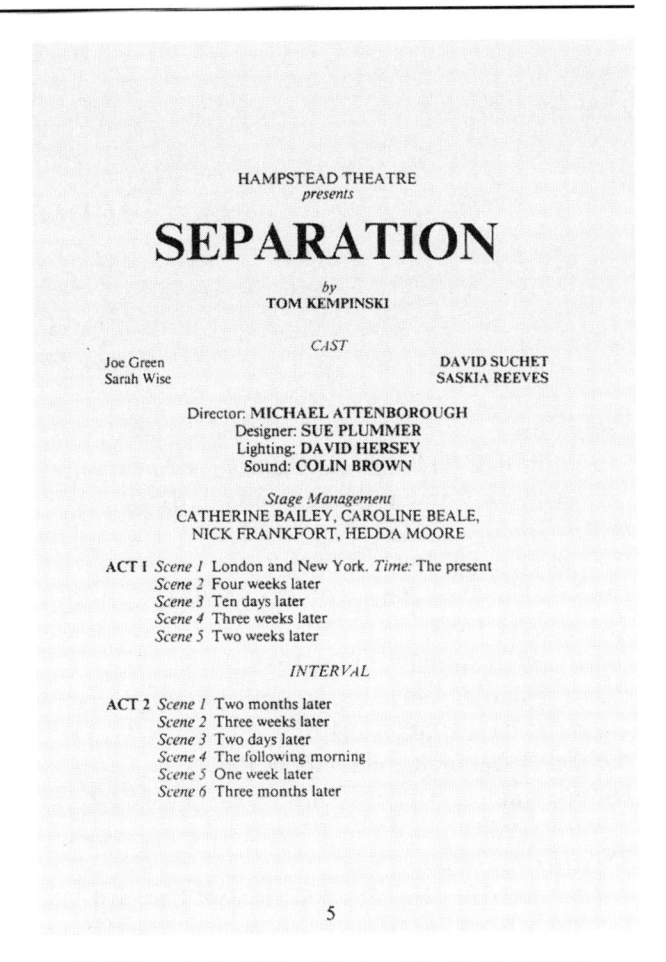

Playbill page in the 1989 publication of Kempinski's 1987 play, in which an agoraphobic playwright conducts a long-distance relationship with a disabled American actress (University of Tennessee Libraries)

come the crippling agoraphobia and anxiety that had previously beset him. He has continued to write prolifically, with plays ranging from the more overtly political *Salus Populi* (performed in 1996) to *What a Bleedin' Liberty!* his humorous response to the bleak nihilism of Samuel Beckett's play.

Tom Kempinski remains an idiosyncratic author who writes with unflinching honesty, passion, and some humor about both his political and private preoccupations. Through the creativity of his writing—especially in plays such as *Duet for One*—he has found a therapeutic means of identifying and transcending the traumatic insecurity of his early life. *Duet for One* will remain one of the landmark plays of British theater in the 1980s. In its passionate appeal for life, truth, and liberty over repressive conformity and denial, it offers a vibrant, theatrical antidote to the political and cultural philistinism of the Margaret Thatcher years. It will remain an essential reference point for any future attempts to plot the personal and political journeys and developments of the decade whose beginning it marked.

Deborah Levy

(13 January 1959 -)

Margaret Llewellyn-Jones
London Metropolitan University

PLAY PRODUCTIONS: *On New Land,* Edinburgh Festival and London Fringe venues, 1981;

Eva and Moses, staged reading, London, Women's Theatre Group, 1983;

Pax, London, Oval House, 20 August 1984;

Dream Mama, 1985;

Ophelia and the Great Idea, Aire, 1985;

Clam, London, Oval House, 25 April 1985;

The Naked Cake, 1986;

Our Lady, Edinburgh and London, 1986;

Heresies, London, Barbican Theatre, The Pit, 10 December 1986;

Silver Herrings, 1989;

Judith & Holofernes, by Levy and Howard Barker, 1990;

Pushing the Prince into Denmark, Stratford, Memorial Theatre, 1991; London, Riverside Studio, 1991;

Nights at the Circus, adapted from Angela Carter's novel, 1991;

The B File: An Erotic Interrogation of Five Female Personas, Cardiff, Chapter Arts Theatre, October 1991; European tour, November 1992;

Call Blue Jane, Cardiff, Chapter Arts Theatre, 1992; London, ICA and Royal Court Theatre, 1992;

Blood Wedding, adapted from Federico García Lorca's play, libretto by Levy, music by Nicola Le Fanu, London, Jacob Street Studios, 26 October 1992;

Shiny Nylon, London, Warehouse, Royal Docks, 1994;

Honey Baby: 13 Studies in Exile, Melbourne, Australia, LaMama Theatre, 1995;

Wife of Sade: The Misfortunes of Virtue, Women's Playhouse Trust, 1997;

Macbeth–False Memories, London, Waterman's Arts Centre, 9 March 2000.

BOOKS: *Ophelia and the Great Idea* (London: Cape, 1985; New York: Viking, 1989);

Beautiful Mutants (London: Cape, 1987; New York: Viking, 1989);

Heresies & Eva and Moses (London & New York: Methuen, 1987);

An Amorous Discourse in the Suburbs of Hell (London: Cape, 1990);

Swallowing Geography (London: Cape, 1993; New York: Vintage, 1993);

The Unloved (London: Cape, 1994; New York: Vintage, 1994);

Billy and Girl (London: Bloomsbury, 1996; Normal, Ill.: Dalkey Archive Press, 1999);

Blood Wedding (London: Novello, 1997);

Diary of a Steak, edited by Michael Bracewell and Jane Rolo (London: Book Works, 1997);

Deborah Levy: Plays 1 (London: Methuen, 2000)—comprises *Pax, Clam, The B File, Pushing the Prince into Denmark, Macbeth–False Memories,* and *Honey Baby;*

Pillow Talk in Europe and Other Places (Normal, Ill.: Dalkey Archive Press, 2004).

PRODUCED SCRIPTS: *Celebrating Quietly,* television, 1988;

Lickin' Bones, television, 1990;

The Open Mouth, television, 1991;

Pushing the Prince into Denmark, radio, Radio Copenhagen, 1991;

"Suburban Psycho," television, *The Talent,* BBC 2, 23 January 1999;

Unless, adapted from Carol Shields's novel, radio, BBC Radio 4, 28 June 2004.

OTHER: *Clam,* in *Peace Plays,* edited by Stephen Lowe (London: Methuen, 1985);

Pax, in *Plays by Women,* volume 6, edited by Mary Remnant (London: Methuen, 1987), pp. 85–113;

The B File, in *Walks on Water: Five Performance Texts,* edited by Levy (London: Methuen, 1993), pp. 139–157;

"Games," in *Grand Street,* edited by Jean Stein (New York: Grand Street Press, 1994);

"The Eros of Rose: The Work of Rose English," in *A Split Second of Paradise: Live Art, Installation and Performance,* edited by Nicky Childs and Jeni Walwin (London: Rivers Oram Press, 1998).

SELECTED PERIODICAL PUBLICATION–
UNCOLLECTED: "My Frozen Father," *Granta*, 63 (September 1998).

As she wrote in her introduction to *Walks on Water: Five Performance Texts* (1993), Deborah Levy is intent on exploring "a theatre language that uses poetics, physical and visual metaphors and the abstraction of domestic situations, but is nevertheless rooted in the political and personal conflicts of our culture now." Certain themes run through her plays, including the contrast between the destructive quality of the scientific rational in contrast to the positive qualities of the emotional or irrational; the importance of female values; and the culture and history of Eastern Europe. As is often the case with work created with or for small fringe groups and venues, much of Levy's early work remains unpublished. Among such unpublished works is Levy's first play, *On New Land*, performed at the Edinburgh Festival and Fringe venues in London in 1981. Levy was involved in the evolution of different kinds of feminist theater practice in Britain during the 1980s.

Levy was born in South Africa on 13 January 1959 and undertook higher education in Britain from 1978 to 1981. In 1981 she obtained an honors B.A. in theater language, specializing in writing for performance, at Dartington College of Arts, Devonshire. From 1989 to 1991 she was awarded a fellowship in creative arts at Trinity College Cambridge. Her interest in bridging creative and academic activities is evident both in involvement with conferences on performance issues and appointments such as her post as creative writer in residence at the University of North London from 1996 to 1999. Levy is also a journalist whose work includes features and theater reviews for the major British newspapers, and she has written a considerable amount of fiction as well.

A stress on visual articulacy underlies the development of Levy's work for the theater, which seems to have moved further toward performance art and includes collaborations with visual artists. The predominantly postmodern form of her work is in tune with her preference for working with ensemble companies. Nevertheless, an intellectual depth, a concern with certain ideological issues, and vivid experiments with language mark Levy's work as original and distinctive from other avant-garde or feminist movements whose perspectives she to some extent shares. She believes that the economic crisis in theater is also a spiritual and aesthetic crisis, and in her introduction to *Walks on Water* she criticizes both "doddery naturalism" and "flattened postmodern pastiche."

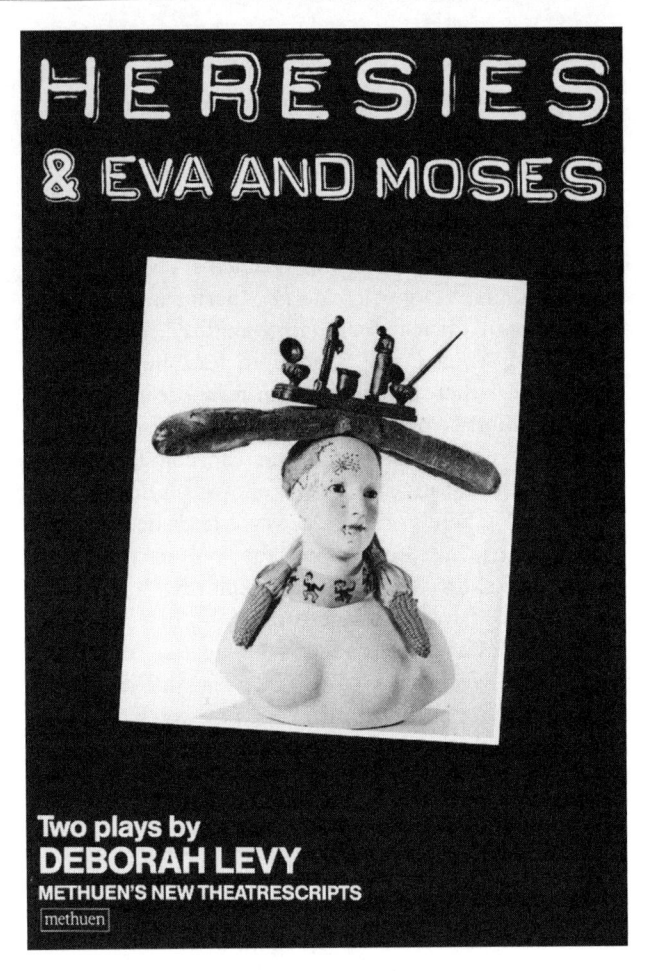

Cover for the 1987 publication of two of Deborah Levy's plays. Heresies *(1987) contrasts the rational world of an architect with the creative world of a composer, while* Eva and Moses *(1983) is a duologue in which a long-married couple recall their life together (Thomas Cooper Library, University of South Carolina).*

In April 1983 the Women's Theatre Group staged a reading of Levy's second play, *Eva and Moses*. In some ways this duologue seems atypical of Levy's work; the characters sit facing the audience while crickets chirp offstage throughout, and the phases of conversation occur in bright light interspersed with silent blackouts. Yet, despite the simplicity of the visual image, the conversation about the nature of relationships touches on complex themes, including love and gender differences, that she explores elsewhere more adventurously. Moses claims that "After so many years of marriage we can predict each other's conversation," while Eva attempts to retain her private persona. She points out, "You fill your belly to fill the silence, Moses." Disappointments throughout their life together include Moses' becoming a pharmacist instead of a doctor and Eva's wish for new shoes. Ultimately, there is some suggestion of communication when Moses acknowledges, "I've thought for the first time in twenty-five years—I have no right to expect love (pause). Great love, as if it were a debt the world owed me." The piece ends as he repeats the opening lines about taking their dog for a walk. Thus, the play explores the nature of love as it may underlie the banal routines of every day.

After *Eva and Moses,* the Women's Theatre Group commissioned Levy to create *Pax* (performed in 1984), a play about nuclear war. *Pax* was directed by Susan Todd and Anna Furse, who both had close involvement with other fringe and feminist theater groups, namely Blood Group and Monstrous Regiment. Furse, a trained dancer, enhanced the choreographical elements of the creative process. Following a fortnight in April 1984 when Todd and Levy established a framework scenario, the entire company took part in a two-week workshop period. After exploring a common vocabulary of word and gesture in the first week, the members devised ways of developing the scenario in the second week, as well as selecting and discarding from the material produced in the first week. A seven-week research and writing period followed, until the company could resume rehearsals, joined by a musician.

Levy wrote in the program note that she wanted to examine how nuclear war "has been absorbed into our culture." As her afterword notes, the play involves four archetypal roles: the Keeper, who embodies the past, burdened with history; HD, the Hidden Daughter, symbolic of the future while trying to make sense of the present; the Mourner, representing the present, in mourning for her "stuck" life; and the Domesticated Woman, indicative of the past and the present as well as the contradictions of capitalism and patriarchy. Levy suggests that the power of images may cure society's sicknesses such as the threat of nuclear power, although this threat is not mentioned during the play until an oblique one-word reference in the last lines.

During the play, the Mourner—a paleontologist—comments that she is good at "Taking the fragments of history left to us . . . and putting them back together again." This remark encapsulates the postmodern dramatic techniques Levy uses, which make it possible for her to convey a multiplicity of discourses and intertextual references within a relatively short piece. The play has passages of ritual and a dream-like collage structure that is poetic rather than linear. Within a "desolate house in the wilderness, which could be called 'The Retreat,'" properties and set are symbolic of both past and present, East and West, Buddhism and Christianity. During the play, bread, fruit, and eggs are used to suggest the basic elements of living. Sound effects include bells and offstage music, as well as the sinister sound of helicopters. The naming of HD, the Keeper's daughter, presumably after the American writer Hilda Doolittle, evokes the modernist movement and hence is appropriate for the intertextual echoes within the play. Events seem limited but signify a wide range of concerns, from identity to political and personal ideologies: The Keeper receives a visit from the Mourner for the funeral of her mother; the Domesticated Woman, perhaps The Keeper's aunt, arrives; HD asks questions about her father, whose funeral also occurs. The other women finally leave the Keeper, who seems to represent a mythic "wise woman" associated with matriarchies.

Although some of the exchanges between the women ring true with the tensions that may exist between women with different attitudes—especially across generations—sometimes the weight of historical and philosophical reference is rather heavily allegorical, at least on the page rather than in performance. Science is critiqued through the Mourner's arid study of dinosaur eggs, the genetic engineering apparently practiced by HD's father, and a general proecological (and vegetarian) tone. The Keeper's longing for a return to Eastern Europe, where her family died in the Holocaust, and her allusion to the Mourner's mother as a musician are echoed in Levy's later play *Heresies* (performed in 1986, published in 1987).

Clam, later published with a selection of *Peace Plays,* was first presented by Blood Group at the Oval House in London on 25 April 1985. It was directed by Furse, and she and Levy were jointly responsible for the design. Levy commented in *British & Irish Women Dramatists Since 1958* (1993) that "*Clam* was turned down by the Arts Council when Blood Group applied for funds to put it on. They didn't know what it was." One male and one female actor each play three roles. In the original production, Mine Kaylan played Alice, Nadia Krupskaya, and a Patient, while Andrzey Borkowski played Harry, Vladimir Lenin, and a Doctor. The simple yet symbolic design for the set included a large fish tank, one large and one small chair, one large and one small cup. Harry's costume included a top hat with dollar label and white gloves, while Alice wore a scarlet puffed-sleeve dress and black patent-leather shoes. Their conversation during tea has overtones of the "too close for comfort" tensions between Eva and Moses in Levy's earlier play. In a surreal moment Alice fishes a clam for Harry's tea out of the fish tank to the sound of Friedrich von Schiller's hymn "Ode to Joy" (1787), and the scene finishes with some child-like jokes.

In postmodern mode, the next scene flashes back in time and across Europe to a conversation between Lenin and Krupskaya—who enters wearing a feathered headdress and doing a Russian dance. Lenin gargles and spits into the fish tank, turning the water red. Typical of Levy's themes elsewhere, Lenin epitomizes science and revolution, while Krupskaya embodies emotion and imagination: "Imagination, Vladimir, like revolution, is the last resort of the underprivileged." At the culmination of their verbal struggle, Krupskaya holds Lenin's head underwater–having put goldfish in the samovar. For the next scene, Lenin's concern that Krupskaya must be cured of her "sickness" shifts into an encounter between the Doctor and the Patient, but at the end both erupt into inconsolable sobbing, followed by hollow laughter. In the fourth scene, Harry and Alice fish a variety of objects, from sweets and a dinosaur bone to William Shakespeare's complete works and a Union Jack, out of the tank–a mixture of items symbolic of the random nature of cultural values. Alice speaks of walking across a radioactive beach and discovering a range of extinct and exotic creatures from across the whole world. Harry's refusal to kiss a possibly radioactive Alice flows into another Doctor/Patient exchange–until the Patient speaks of the next war as "the war men fought against women."

The next scene satirically explores the limitations of aesthetics through Harry's reduction of their relationship to abstract and logical formulas, observed by Alice in the terms of abstract paintings. She offers him a clam without tea. A metatheatrically framed TV interview given by Harry shows his reaction to the death of Alice–shot by a soldier–which he has transmuted into a book, which he uses the opportunity to advertise: "Poor Alice and her unhatched egg." True to Levy's tendency to see Eastern Europe as a site of possibilities, Lenin and Krupskaya, in spite of his anger at her reported dalliance with a poet, come to a compromise symbolized through a dance to the faint music of the "Internationale," as embodying a marriage of science and intuition. The oppositions between male and female, science and art, West and East sound rather contrived in summary, but reviewers generally agreed that the surreal dimension, humorous actions, and flowing movement, combined with lighting and musical effects, made this postmodern piece visually effective and elliptically rather than heavily didactic in performance.

An indicator of Levy's growing reputation is the fact that *Heresies* was performed in The Pit at the Barbican by the Women's Group of the Royal Shakespeare Company (RSC) in 1986. This particular group was relatively short-lived. However, this production was directed by Todd and designed by Iona McLeish with movement by Furse. Again, collaborative workshopping was an important part of the process, as indicated in the program for the production. Levy and Todd put some ideas into four weeks of workshop activities with a changing group of actors–mostly women, but some men. Key words included in some improvisational contexts included "faith," "ambition," "bargain," "allegiance," and "belief"–and these words applied to sexual and personal situations, public declarations, and physical images. Work happened in and around real buildings in the city as the actors explored key moments for particular characters in specific places. Levy then wrote the play, drawing upon these experiences as well as her original ideas. In a 1986 interview with Angela Neustatter, Levy talked about the increasing displacement of modern life and the denial of space for the subversive imagination, which she hopes her images will prompt within the audience. She suggested that, with the easy money and technology of the 1980s, "we became fickle and shifting. Old allegiances grow rusty." She further claimed that human needs and demands underlie her archetypes and that the connected relationships of the play show how "fragments of experience link us in a grand chain reaction."

McLeish worked closely with both the writer and director, and as the project had been allotted only £8,000, she brought her experience of designing traveling fringe shows usefully into play. She contrasted the rational approach of Pimm, the architect, and the creative, imaginative world of the composer, Leah, within the same space. Alcoves with religious icons and the presence of a piano helped create Leah's home, while a metal fish tank was a key fixture in the architect's office. The flexible use of light and screens helped to suggest change of location. The set was also intended to show a mixture of the future and the past.

Besides Pimm and Leah, the cast of characters includes Cholla, a displaced person; Mayonnaise, a courtesan and Pimm's lover; Mary, a housekeeper; Violet, an educator; Edward, a lonely businessman; Betty, a mother; and Bridie, a student. The production included three additional characters who were cut from the published version. Cholla has had a child, Lydia, by Pimm, but she does not want him to find her; she tells him in act 2 that he is not part of the family she has made with Lydia and also with Leah and Violet, who help educate the child. Leah is first seen with candles on her head as she plays her piano. She had once taught Pimm and now rebukes him for putting his energies into aesthetics when once he had worked for people. Throughout the play a variety of experimental music underpins the themes. A sense of alienation and displacement at both personal and political levels infects the characters. Cholla longs to return to Hungary, remembering her mother. Although Mayonnaise claims she "wouldn't know how to be a mother," she arranges to steal Cholla's child because Pimm wants her. Mary

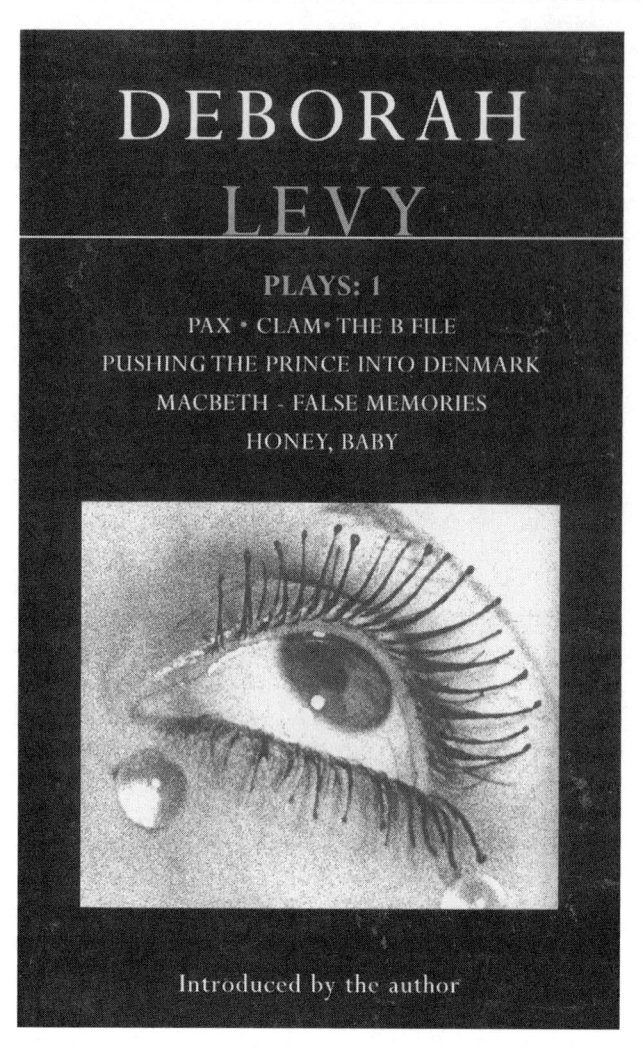

Cover for Levy's 2000 collection of plays, all of which premiered between 1984 and 2000 (Bruccoli Clark Layman Collection)

longs to see her sister, Bridie, who had been a political prisoner, and they both want to go home to Ireland. Mayonnaise ultimately insists that Cholla take the child back to Hungary, because Mary has—for money—told Pimm where they are. The last scene shows the women dancing, following a moment when the others touch Mayonnaise's head in a healing gesture. Leah and the music seem to have fostered some kind of resolution.

Lizbeth Goodman reports that reviewers of *Heresies,* while praising the play as a challenge to the low profile of women in the RSC, tended to disapprove of it as "A sludgy concoction" composed by "committee-style collaboration." Critical consensus was divided between those who welcome collaborative processes and the often complex, open, postmodern structures that result, and those who prefer single authorship and more straightforward narrative drive.

Levy's Trinity College fellowship and her University of North London appointment facilitated her involvement in the academy as well as in the world of performance. While she pursued her theatrical endeavors, she also participated in conferences and continued journalistic activities. A typical example of her activity is *The B File,* published in *Walks on Water,* an anthology Levy edited. The play was originally written as a workshop session that she had been asked to direct in Cardiff during October 1991 for the Magdalena Project, which is dedicated to exploring women's performance languages; the reworked piece, as commissioned by Chapter Arts, toured with five professional performers in November 1992. In the preface Levy indicates that this play explores issues prompted by her fiction *Swallowing Geography* (published later in 1993): feeling homesick at home, missing someone never met, wanting to be someone else. This sense of searching and marginality she links with wishing for things to be different but not knowing quite how to meet the fragmented, half-formed imagined possibilities. *The B File* manifests qualities that some theater practitioners have suggested are in tune with French feminist theoreticians such as Hélène Cixous. The play is subtitled *An Erotic Interrogation of Five Female Personas* because the protagonist, Beatrice, is split into five roles. Each of these is introduced and questioned by an Interpreter in a way that lays bare the processes through which the female persona is constructed. For example: "Is Beatrice a character? If she is a character is she dressed for the part? Is Beatrice a persona? If she is a persona what are her voices?"

The deconstructive Interpreter role is played by Beatrice 5, until it is her turn to be interrogated by Beatrice 1. In the original, one performer spoke in Welsh, another in Italian, and another in Greek; one Beatrice is pregnant, another is lesbian. Each is questioned on identity, whether she loves her lovers, what words are spoken, what effect they have, and who sleeps first after lovemaking. In this sense the play makes manifest female desire. Each Beatrice expresses her different ideas and feelings, in some instances enhancing the notion of the split between the unspoken and speaking self by speaking of Beatrice in the third person. The concerns of the Beatrices echo the questions and desires expressed in Levy's preface. Properties used are symbolic, for instance of different kinds of entrapment, and include a microwave, a picture of the Pope, a compact-disc player, and a computer. Slides are shown, sometimes projected onto the Beatrices' suitcases or bodies. The piece was choreographed in great detail, so that on some occasions the Beatrices move ritually almost as one—sometimes dancing, sometimes coughing, sometimes moving their suitcases. Finally, Beatrice 5 says, "I think Beatrice is just an actress playing out what has been staged for her." Music follows; all Beatrices snap their fingers; Beatrice 1 stands naked with her back to the audience; and then after music and a blackout, a red poppy and its stem is projected on her back as Beatrice 1 and Beatrice 2 sing "Take Me Higher." Thus the piece expresses feminist concerns while using theatrical forms and stylistic strategies that could be considered as an overlapping of the postmodern and feminine writing. In contrast, *Call Blue Jane* (1992), which also originated at Chapter Arts with MANACT, was a highly choreographed piece performed by two men, with little verbal content, strong music, and blue light.

The volume of Levy's plays published by Methuen in 2000 should make Levy's creative development more accessible. This collection includes *Pushing the Prince into Denmark* (performed in 1991) and *Macbeth–False Memories* (performed in 2000), two plays that rework elements taken from Shakespeare's *Hamlet* and *Macbeth* in ways that show their powerful resonance in modern times. Her plays continue to be wide-ranging in scope. For example, she spent time in Australia, where *Honey Baby: 13 Studies in Exile* premiered at the LaMama Theatre in 1995, and then created *Wife of Sade: The Misfortunes of Virtue* for the Women's Playhouse Trust in London during 1997. Levy has also been writing fiction and working on other kinds of visual collaborations, including installation—for instance, *Shiny Nylon* at the Royal Docks in 1994. She has been researching and writing narrative nonfiction, a book of ideas titled "The Snowman: Exile and Belonging." Its concerns include questions of the nature of home and of the relationship between nonfiction, fiction, and autobiography. Her collection of short stories *Pillow Talk in Europe and Other Places* appeared in 2004. She is also collating her unpublished theater texts and writing a critical commentary about them.

Whereas the early development of women's theater writing in the late 1970s and early 1980s began to challenge realist forms through theatrical devices similar to Bertolt Brecht's Epic Theater practice, often in the now outmoded agitprop style, Deborah Levy's work is more adventurous and expressionistic. Her involvement with the use of untraditional performance spaces is a factor significant for current postmodern experimental dramatic practice.

Interview:

Angela Neustatter, "The Power and the Glory," *Guardian,* 12 October 1986.

References:

Lizbeth Goodman, *Contemporary Feminist Theatres: To Each Her Own* (London & New York: Routledge, 1993), pp. 25, 42–43, 54, 64, 96, 224;

Trevor R. Griffiths and C. Woddis, *Bloomsbury Theatre Guide* (London: Bloomsbury, 1988), pp. 177–178;

Griffiths and Margaret Llewellyn-Jones, eds., *British & Irish Women Dramatists Since 1958* (Buckingham: Open University Press, 1993), pp. 28, 146–147;

Claire Macdonald, *The Artistry of Deborah Levy* (Cambridge: Cambridge University Press, 1999).

Saunders Lewis

(15 October 1893 – 1 September 1985)

Ioan Williams
University of Wales Aberystwyth

PLAY PRODUCTIONS: *The Eve of St. John*, Glasgow, April 1921;

Gwaed yr Uchelwyr, Cardiff, Town Hall, 13 May 1922;

Amlyn ac Amig, amateur production, Llangefni, December 1946; professional production, Garthewin, 31 January 1947;

Blodeuwedd, Garthewin, 15 October 1948;

Eisteddfod Bodran, Garthewin, 24 August 1950;

Gan Bwyll, Garthewin, 3 June 1952;

Siwan, Garthewin, 23 August 1954;

Gymerwch Chi Sigaret? Llangefni, 23 May 1955;

Brad, Ebbw Vale National Eisteddfod, 7 August 1958;

Esther, Theatr Fach Llangefni, 22 September 1959;

Serch Yw'r Doctor, libretto by Lewis, music by Arwel Hughes, Cardiff, Cory Hall, 23 February 1960;

Cymru Fydd, Bala National Eisteddfod, Neuadd Ysgol y Berwyn, 7 August 1967;

Problemau Prifysgol, Barry National Eisteddfod, Ysgol Gyfun Ganol, 7 August 1968;

Excelsior, Bangor, Theatr Gwynedd, 18 March 1992.

BOOKS: *The Eve of St. John: A Comedy of Welsh Life (in Two Scenes)* (Newtown: Welsh Outlook Press, 1921);

Gwaed yr Uchelwyr: Drama Mewn Tair Act (Cardiff: Educational, 1922);

A School of Welsh Augustans: Being a Study in English Influences on Welsh Literature During Part of the 18th Century (Wrexham: Hughes, 1924);

Egwyddorion Cenedlaetholdeb, Plaid Genedlaethol Cymru, 1 (Machynlleth: Evan Jones, Argraffydd, 1926);

An Introduction to Contemporary Welsh Literature (Wrexham: Hughes & Son, 1926);

Williams Pantycelyn (London: Foyle's Welsh Depôt, 1927);

Ceiriog, Yr Artist yn Philistia, 1 (Aberystwyth: Gwasg Aberystwyth, 1929);

Monica (Aberystwyth: Gwasg Aberystwyth, 1930);

Ieuan Glan Geirionydd, Cyfres y Clasuron, 1 (Cardiff: University of Wales Press, 1931);

Saunders Lewis (from Alun R. Jones and Gwyn Thomas, eds., Presenting Saunders Lewis, *1973; Thomas Cooper Library, University of South Carolina)*

The Banned Wireless Talk on Welsh Nationalism (Carnarvon: Swyddfa'r Blaid Genedlaethol, 1931);

Braslun o Hanes Llenyddiaeth Gymraeg: Y Gyfrol Gyntaf: Hyd 1535 (Cardiff: Gwasg Prifysgol Cymru, 1932);

The Local Authorities and Welsh Industries (Carnarvon: Welsh National Party, 1932);

The Case for a Welsh National Development Council (Carnarvon: Swyddfa'r Blaid Genedlaethol, 1933);

Cywydd gan Thomas Jones, Dinbych (Wrexham: Y Llenor, 1933);

Y Frwydr Dros Ryddid (Carnarvon: Swyddfa'r Blaid Genedlaethol, 1935);

Paham y Gwrthwynebwn yr Ysgol Fomio (Carnarvon: Plaid Genedlaethol Cymru, 1936);

Daniel Owen, Yr Artist yn Philistia, 2 (Aberystwyth: Gwasg Aberystwyth, 1936);

Buchedd Garmon; Mair Fadlen (Aberystwyth: Gwasg Aberystwyth, 1937);

Paham y Llosgasom yr Ysgol Fomio, by Lewis and Lewis Valentine (Carnarvon: Plaid Genedlaethol Cymru, 1937);

Canlyn Arthur: Ysgrifau Gwleidyddol (Aberystwyth: Gwasg Aberystwyth, 1938);

Is There an Anglo-Welsh Literature? (Cardiff: Cardiff Branch of the Guild of Graduates, University of Wales, 1939);

Amlyn ac Amig: Comedi (Aberystwyth: Gwasg Aberystwyth, 1940);

Byd a Betws: Cerddi (Aberystwyth: Gwasg Aberystwyth, 1941);

Cymru Wedi'r Rhyfel (Aberystwyth: Gwasg Aberystwyth, 1942);

Plaid Cymru Gyfan, by Lewis and J. E. Daniel (Carnarvon: Swyddfa'r Blaid, 1942); published as *The Party for Wales: Replies . . . to Mr. Gwilym Davies* (Carnarvon: Nationalist Offices, 1942);

Straeon Glasynys, by Lewis and Owen Wynne Jones (Llandysul: Y Clwb Llyfrau Cymreig, Gwasg Gee, 1943);

Y Newyn yn Ewrop (Dinbych: Gwasg Gee, 1943);

Ysgrifau Dydd Mercher (Llandysul: Y Clwb Llyfrau Cymreig, 1945);

Blodeuwedd: Drama Mewn Pedair Act (Dinbych: Gwasg Gee, 1948);

Dwy Gomedi (Dinbych: Gwasg Gee, 1952)—comprises *Eisteddfod Bodran* and *Gan Bwyll;*

Siwan a Cherddi Eraill (Llandybie: Llyfrau'r Dryw, 1955);

Gymerwch Chi Sigaret? (Llandybie: Llyfrau'r Dryw, 1956);

Brad (Llandybie: Llyfrau'r Dryw, 1958);

Esther; a, Serch Yw'r Doctor (Abertawe: Christopher Davies, 1960);

Tynged yr Iaith (London: BBC, 1962);

Merch Gwern Hywel: Rhamant Hanesiol (Llandybie: Llyfrau'r Dryw, 1964);

Cymru Fydd (Llandybie: Llyfrau'r Dryw, 1967);

Gramadegau'r Penceirddiaid (Cardiff: Gwasg Prifysgol Cymru, 1967);

Problemau Prifysgol (Llandybie: Llyfrau'r Dryw, 1968);

Dwy Briodas Ann (Abertawe: John Perry, 1973);

Meistri'r Canrifoedd: Ysgrifau ar Hanes Llenyddiaeth Gymraeg, selected by R. Geraint Gruffydd (Cardiff: Gwasg Prifysol Cymru, 1973);

Dramâu'r Parlwr (Llandybie: Christopher Davies, 1975)—comprises *Branwen* and *Dwy Briodas Ann;*

Excelsior (Abertawe: Christopher Davies, 1980);

Meistri a'u Crefft: Ysgrifau Llenyddol, edited by Gwynn ap Gwilym (Cardiff: Gwasg Prifysol Cymru, 1981);

Ati, Wŷr Ifainc, edited by Marged Dafydd (Cardiff: Gwasg Prifysol Cymru, 1986);

Cerddi Saunders Lewis, edited by Gruffydd (Newtown: Gwasg Gregynog, 1986);

Y Cyrnol Chabert; a, 1938: Dwy Ddrama (Pen-y-groes, Carnarvon: Gwasg Dwyfor, 1989);

Dramâu Saunders Lewis: Y Casgliad Cyflawn, 2 volumes, edited by Ioan Williams (Cardiff: Gwasg Prifysol Cymru, 1996, 2000).

Editions in English: *The Plays of Saunders Lewis Translated from the Welsh,* 4 volumes, edited and translated by Joseph P. Clancy (Llandybie: Christopher Davies, 1985–1986)—comprises volume 1, *The Vow, The Woman Made of Flowers,* and *The King of England's Daughter;* volume 2, *Have a Cigarette, Treason,* and *Esther;* volume 3, *Excelsior, Academic Affairs, Tomorrow's Wales,* and *On the Train;* and volume 4, *The Daughter of Gwern Hywel, The Condemned Cell,* and *The Two Marriages of Ann Thomas;*

Selected Poems, translated by Clancy (Cardiff: University of Wales Press, 1993);

Monica, translated by Meic Stephens (Bridgend: Seren / Chester Springs, Pa.: Dufour, 1997).

PRODUCED SCRIPTS: *Buchedd Garmon,* radio, BBC Radio Wales, 1 March 1937;

Siwan, radio, BBC, 1 March 1954;

Excelsior, television, BBC, 1 March 1962;

Tynged yr Iaith, radio, BBC Wales, 1 March 1962;

Wrth Aros Godot, translation of Samuel Beckett's play, radio, BBC, 20 November 1962;

Yn y Trên, radio, BBC Welsh Home Service, 8 May 1965; television, BBC, 4 December 1969;

Merch Gwern Hywel, radio, BBC Radio Wales, 11 May 1968; expanded, television, BBC, 1 March 1976;

Cyrnol Chabert, adapted from Honoré Balzac's short story, radio, BBC Radio 4, 19 October 1968;

Branwen, television, BBC, 1 March 1971;

Dwy Briodas Ann, television, BBC, 16 October 1973;

Cell y Grog, radio, BBC Wales Radio 4, 2 March 1974;

1938, television, BBC, 27 February 1978.

TRANSLATIONS: Molière, *Doctor er ei Waethaf* (Wrexham: Hughes a'i Fab, 1924);

Samuel Beckett, *Wrth Aros Godot* (Cardiff: University of Wales Press, 1970).

OTHER: *Crefft y Stori Fer,* edited by Lewis (Aberystwyth: Y Clwb Llyfrau Cymreig, 1949).

SELECTED PERIODICAL PUBLICATIONS–
UNCOLLECTED:
DRAMA
Blodeuwedd, Act 1, *Y Llenor* (Winter 1923): 231–244;
Blodeuwedd, Act II, *Y Llenor* (Winter 1925): 196–210;
Mair Fadlen, Llenor, Haf (1935);
Mair Fadlen II, Yr Efrydydd, Hydref (1944);
Serch yw'r Doctor, Llafar, 6, no. 2 (1957): 9–28;
Yn y Trên, Barn (August 1965): 274–276;
Cell y Grog, Taliesin, 27 (December 1973): 8–20.
NONFICTION
"Profiad Cymro yn y Fyddin," two parts, *Y Cymro* (23 July 1917): 4; (30 July 1917): 4;
"Rhufain,–yr ymweliad cyntaf," *Y Cymro* (12 February 1919);
"Celfyddyd y Ddrama," three parts, *Y Darian* (20 May 1920): 2; (27 May 1920): 7; (10 June 1920): 7;
"Nodyn ar Ibsen," *Y Darian* (23 December 1920): 8;
"Y Ddrama yn Ffrainc," *Y Darian* (7 July 1921): 3;
"Maurice Barrès," *Y Faner* (24 January 1924): 5;
"Pasiant neu Sagrafan," *Y Faner* (8 July 1926): 5;
"Trasiedi," *Y Ddraig Goch* (July 1926): 5;
"Llythyr Ynghylch Catholigiaeth," *Y Llenor* (Summer 1927): 73–77;
"The Banned Talk," *Western Mail*, 9 December 1930, p. 9;
"Cwrs y Byd" [weekly articles on cultural and political affairs], *Y Faner,* January 1939 – July 1951;
"Pierre Corneille," *Y Faner* (28 December 1949): 8;
"Efrydwyr a'r Offeren," *Efrydiau Catholig,* 7 (1955): 3;
"Tynged Darlith," *Barn* (1 March 1963): 143;
"Am Weddi'r Terfyn," *Y Tyst,* 75 (3 June 1974): 1.

It would be difficult to overstate the importance of Saunders Lewis in terms of his influence on the life of Welsh-speaking Wales in the period following World War I. Considered separately, his achievements as a scholar, poet, literary and cultural historian, politician, journalist, and dramatist would place him among the most outstanding figures of the twentieth century. Taken as a whole, however, his work in all these modes embodies a complex network of interrelated insights and values that has transformed Welsh culture and political life. Though he spoke of himself as a failure, because he had aimed at nothing less than to reverse the main cultural drive of the century, his achievement was astounding. His drama was based on the fundamental assumption that the moral integrity of the human subject was the foundation of all culture and civilization. His plays were therefore constructed from units of dialogue and debate, which reflected the predominance he accorded to the conscious, reflective mind.

John Saunders Lewis was born on 15 October 1893 in Wallasey (in the English county of Cheshire), the second of three sons, to the Reverend Lodwig Lewis and Mary Lewis. His maternal grandfather was Owen Thomas, famous as a preacher in his own right. Beyond that, again through his mother, Lewis was descended from William Roberts, Amlwch, one of the major figures in the great age of Welsh Calvinist Methodism. Mary Lewis died not long after giving birth to her third son, and Saunders was brought up among the Welsh-speaking community in Wallasey by one of her sisters, Ellen; but by virtue of the many boyhood holidays he spent with family in Anglesey, he claimed to belong there much more than to Cheshire. After attending the private Liscard High School for Boys, he went in 1911 to study English under Oliver Elton at the University of Liverpool. In World War I he served as an infantry officer in France until May 1917, when he was wounded. After convalescence he was posted to Athens, where he remained until December 1918.

In 1919 Lewis returned to Liverpool, where he graduated with First Class Honours in English and completed an M.A. thesis on the Augustan element in eighteenth-century Welsh literature. In 1921 he took up a position as county librarian in Glamorganshire; the following year, he was appointed as a lecturer in the Department of Welsh at Swansea University College, where he remained until his dismissal in 1936. In July 1924 he married Margaret Gilcriest, an Irish girl he had met in Liverpool and a convert to Roman Catholicism from her family's Methodism. Lewis himself waited until after his father's death in 1933 before converting, in the knowledge that he was thereby isolating himself from the sympathies of the majority of his countrymen. Lewis and his wife had one daughter, Mair.

A self-confessed disciple of Walter Pater when he went off to France, Lewis came into contact there with the work of Maurice Barrès, whose novels revealed to him how aestheticism could be reconciled with an awareness of the social and cultural determinants of personality, implicit in Welsh culture and in the work of the Irish writers William Butler Yeats and John Millington Synge in particular, whose influence he had already felt. Later, in his final year at the University of Liverpool, he was uncertain as to the direction of his own career, although he was fairly sure even then he would have something to do with drama. Articles he wrote on stagecraft and design at this time show him close to the group of contemporary French practitioners gathered around Gaston Baty and known as the Cartel, and his early theatrical experiments betray the same tendencies. However, the influence of French neoclassical drama was also strong at this time and later became dominant.

To the extent that Lewis's work can be subdivided, it could be said that in the earliest period, roughly from 1921 to 1932, the basic structure of his thought was put together. The first two substantial works of this period were plays—one in English, and the other in Welsh, after he made an irreversible decision to write in that language from then on. *The Eve of St. John* (performed and published in 1921) was a two-act playlet in the manner of Synge, in which Lewis experimented with an Anglo-Welsh literary dialogue. *Gwaed yr Uchelwyr* (performed and published in 1922; Blood of Noblemen), though technically more clumsy, was a more substantial step toward maturity. Set in the 1820s, it presents the story of Luned Griffiths, whom he described as "a Welsh Antigone," who takes on herself the responsibility of maintaining a proud tradition of cultural idealism at the cost of sacrificing her love and leaving Wales for exile in Wisconsin. There is a good deal in that play that remained typical of Lewis, but it embodies idealist tendencies that were burned out of him during the study that led to his 1927 book on William Williams, Pantycelyn (one of the leaders of the eighteenth-century Methodist movement in Wales and the country's greatest hymn writer), and his first novel, *Monica* (1930).

By 1932, when he published his influential *Braslun o Hanes Llenyddiaeth Gymraeg: Y Gyfrol Gyntaf: Hyd 1535* (A Sketch for a History of Welsh Literature up to 1535), the complex framework of his mature thought had been put together. The first step in this process was to extend the cultural model he had borrowed from Barrès so as to be able to reconcile the hierarchical, Platonist aesthetic of the European Middle Ages with a critical analysis of human personality derived from eighteenth-century materialism. The next step was to elaborate a conception of tradition not unlike that which T. S. Eliot proposed a little later. Having done that, Lewis was able to develop his early aestheticism into a critical vision of what he identified as the "Welsh aesthetic," which inspired the great achievement of the fourteenth- and fifteenth-century poets who employed the strict meter known as the *cywydd*. The study of Pantycelyn he undertook at this time was the catalyst for a further development. Grafting the ideas of Sigmund Freud onto the combination of Calvinism and Enlightenment realism that he found in Pantycelyn's work, he elaborated a complex model of human personality as a site within which spiritual experience could be developed, which proved to be closely compatible with contemporary existentialism. Developing traditional European Christian civilization, he believed, was the best guarantee that the personality could continue to exist at all, particularly as individuals became more isolated and more vulnerable to the effects of the late-capitalist market economy. In the world immediately around him, Welsh culture, and particularly the Welsh language, represented a precious form of that continuing European tradition; and he came to believe that it had to be preserved at all costs. That conviction shaped his life and underlay all his work from the moment it took shape.

From 1925 to 1936 Lewis wrote no drama, largely because he was heavily involved in political life. Early in the 1920s he had come to see that the continuing existence of the Welsh language and culture would depend on direct political intervention; and in that conviction he helped to set up Plaid Cymru (the Welsh National Party) in 1925 and served as its president for the next eleven years. However, that activity eventually brought him back to drama. In 1936, after a long national campaign to prevent the destruction of an important cultural site in Anglesey for the construction of a bombing range, Lewis, together with the Independent minister Lewis Valentine and schoolteacher D. J. Williams (fellow members of Plaid Cymru), set fire to materials gathered there and presented themselves subsequently to the police. A preliminary trial at Carnarvon having failed to find them guilty, the trial was removed to London, where a result more satisfactory to the authorities was easily obtained. A nine-month term at Wormwood Scrubs followed, but even before the verdict, Swansea University College dismissed Lewis from his lectureship. The arson incident and the speech Lewis made in the dock at Carnarvon are probably the most important single events in twentieth-century Welsh political history; but their immediate importance for his work as a dramatist were that they freed him from the pressure of his political engagements and his work as a lecturer and put him in a position where he was more than glad to accept commissions, such as the one given to him by BBC Wales Radio while he was waiting for his second trial and that led to the composition of *Buchedd Garmon* (broadcast and published in 1937; Life of Garmon). After his release from prison, Lewis supported himself for several years by working in a private Catholic school in Aberystwyth, by farming and journalism, and as an inspector of education. He was never reinstated in Swansea but did return to lecture at the University of Wales, this time at Cardiff, where he remained from 1952 to 1957.

The first plays he wrote after his return to drama invite comparison with Eliot's plays in terms of subject matter and manner. *Buchedd Garmon* is a four-part presentation of the life of the fifth-century saint Germanus, to whom is attributed the defeat of Pelagianism and of a combined attack by heathen Picts and Saxons in what remained of Roman Britain. Its importance in Lewis's dramatic canon relates to the fact that it is a powerful embodiment of his central concept of the spiritual and material community inherited from Rome and developed in Catholic Christendom, through the medium of a form of free verse more pliant than anything achieved before in Welsh. *Amlyn ac Amig* (published in 1940, performed in 1946) resulted from another BBC commission, although wartime restrictions prevented its being broadcast. It also developed a medieval subject, presenting the trial of faith of a father required by God to slaughter his sons to cure his friend of leprosy.

Neither of these two radio plays shows Lewis's full power as a dramatist, which was revealed for the first time with the stage play *Blodeuwedd* (performed and published in 1948; Flowerface). Early versions of the first two acts of this play had been written in 1923 and 1925 and published in the periodical *Y Llenor,* but the impulse to complete the whole play was provided by the establishment of Garthewin Theatre on the estate of the dramatist's Catholic friend Robert Wynne. *Blodeuwedd* develops a story taken from the *Mabinogion* but shows nothing of the relative crudity of the two previous radio plays. Here for the first time and in powerful dramatic verse, Lewis succeeded in presenting an action that conveyed the full complexity of his view of human character. Inspired originally by actress Sybil Thorndike's presentation of Medea, which Lewis saw in Liverpool in 1921, *Blodeuwedd* is a sophisticated adaptation of the medieval writer's tale of a girl made from flowers to satisfy the yearning of a prince cursed by his mother never to know a woman's love. Each one of the three central characters experiences the tension presented in the imagery of the play between the yearning for self-fulfilment, more or less absolute, and the awareness that human happiness is ultimately dependent on accepting the limitations of the self. Lewis acknowledged that contemporary existentialism was an important element in the process that led to *Blodeuwedd,* which reminds one how central it is to the discourse of contemporary European theater. That it is also central to the predominant discourse taking shape in Welsh culture at the time underlines the particular importance of Lewis in reminding audiences of the extent to which Welsh culture remains an integral part of the extended, international debate.

Lewis's activity as a dramatist after *Blodeuwedd* was governed partly by the fact that at Garthewin and later at the dramatic festival at Llangefni he had access to stages and to theatrical companies sufficiently sophisticated to perform his work. The next six plays he wrote, in verse and prose, represent a major dramatic achievement in themselves. Two comedies followed *Blodeuwedd,* both derived to greater or lesser extent from the *Mabinogion* and both further developing ideas about the relationship between the sexes that first appeared in that play. Neither *Eisteddfod Bodran* (performed in 1950, published in 1952) nor *Gan Bwyll* (performed and published in 1952; Take Care) are of substantial importance in themselves, though they gave Lewis opportunities to develop his psychological analysis and his dramatic technique in a heavily literary comic mode. The historical play *Siwan* (Joan), which followed next, however, was a major achievement. Though written for the stage, *Siwan* was broadcast on the radio in 1954 before it was staged at Garthewin that year. In three acts, it presents the situation of the Princess Siwan—daughter of King John and wife of Llywelyn ap Iorwerth, Prince of Gwynedd—and her lover, William Breos, Earl of Brecon, hanged by Llywelyn for his adultery with her. As with *Blodeuwedd,* much of the power of *Siwan* derives from the fact that beneath the surface of the sharply dramatic situation, all three characters experience essentially the same existential crisis. Breos, incorrigibly adventurous, leaps to his death at the end of a rope, in defiance of everything that wears out the human spirit. Llywelyn, carrying his guilt for the savage jealousy that made him hang Siwan's lover, learns to accept himself and his love for his wife. Siwan herself, less resilient than her husband, returns to his bed at the end of a year, scarred by the inescapable sadness of her knowledge that not even love can overcome loneliness.

Lewis chose to publish *Siwan* in a volume with the title *Siwan a Cherddi Eraill* (1955; Siwan and Other Poems), emphasizing the poetic quality which in itself sets the play apart in the history of drama in Welsh; and yet, at that same time, he abandoned verse drama. His next two plays relate directly to contemporary historical events. The origins of *Gymerwch Chi Sigaret?* (performed in 1955, published in 1956; Have a Cigarette?) were in newspaper reports of a notorious spy case, set in Cold War Europe, but the play culminates in a leap of faith explicitly related to Blaise Pascal's *Pensées* (1669). *Gymerwch Chi Sigaret?* has been misinterpreted in several ways—as anti-Communist propaganda and Roman Catholic apology, for example, but Lewis denied that he was writing anything other than drama. The center of the play is the hero's encounter with the instinctive fear that only love can combat.

In different ways the two plays that followed *Gymerwch Chi Sigaret?* were also controversial. The first, *Brad* (Betrayal), was criticized by left-wing commentators because it was a sympathetic treatment of the situation of the German officers involved in the July 1944 bomb plot against Adolf Hitler. It was presented first on the stage of the National Eisteddfod (Festival) held in Nye Bevan's Ebbw Vale in 1958. The central character of this historical drama is Lieutenant Colonel Caesar von Hofacker, hanged by the Gestapo in Berlin after prolonged torture, who had voluntarily accepted the consequence of what he believed was the only responsible action open to him. Anything else, Lewis's Hofacker argues, would be *brad,* betrayal of the fundamental principles of the civilization in terms of which his character and his role in life had been formed. To Lewis, the failure of the plot in France, where it might have succeeded even after Hitler had escaped death, was itself a betrayal of that same civilization, marking out the tragic difficulty of heroic action in a fundamentally compromised world.

Almost as if by reaction, *Esther* (performed in 1959, published in 1960) presented a story that turned on precisely the kind of heroic action the characters of *Brad* had failed to achieve: the biblical story of Esther's willingness to sacrifice herself to preserve the people of God from the destruction threatened by their enemies in Persia. However, the dramatist's fundamental preoccupation in this play remains with the existential crisis of the character, who experiences fear and escapes from it by virtue of her capacity to abandon the very self whose existence is the source of that fear. Lewis's Esther faces death in order to assert her belief in her husband's love for her, and by that means, she becomes an instrument in the hands of God. She is, however, an uncompassionate heroine, merciless in revenge against the enemy of her people; and her lack of sentiment continues to disturb some commentators.

Shortly before writing *Esther,* Lewis had completed the libretto for an operetta composed by Arwel Hughes, *Serch Yw'r Doctor* (performed and published in 1960; Love's the Doctor). This lighthearted piece of work, modeled on Molière, could be said to herald the beginning of a new phase in Lewis's career, although it is quite different in tone from his major works of this period. The latter, without dispute, are the radio lecture *Tynged yr Iaith* (broadcast and published in 1962; The Fate of the Language) and the stage play *Cymru Fydd* (performed and published in 1967; Future Wales). In *Tynged yr Iaith,* Lewis presented the situation of the Welsh language in terms more bleakly realistic than had been done before. One result of that lecture was the setting up of the Welsh Language Society and a campaign of civil disobedience, which led gradually to a change of attitude toward the language in Wales and beyond and eventually to the setting up of the Welsh Television Channel S4C. That same uncompromising bleakness was found in the play *Cymru Fydd,* which presented a vision of Wales that left many of the young people who had been stimulated to positive action by *Tynged yr Iaith* nonplussed. Lewis's vision of modern Wales was by this time highly satirical, which is the factor that links the sometimes wickedly irresponsible humor of *Serch yw'r Doctor* with *Cymru Fydd* and other plays of the period.

These other plays included *Excelsior,* a penetratingly satirical portrait of a young politician who turns from nationalism to success in the Labour Party in the interests of romantic love. It had only one showing on BBC Television in 1962 before succumbing to a writ for libel served by the Labour M.P. who considered himself the model for the central character. (The play was, however, later published in 1980 and performed in 1992.) Frightened by their experience on that occasion, the BBC also refused to broadcast the next drama it commissioned from Lewis, even though that play was later staged at the National Eisteddfod of 1968 without attracting legal action. This play was the comedy *Problemau Prifysgol* (University Problems), which grew out of contemporary debates concerning the future of the University of Wales.

Cymru Fydd, perhaps Lewis's most unpopular play and the hardest-hitting criticism of contemporary life, presents the situation of two lovers: Dewi Rhys, son of a Nonconformist minister, and Bet Thomas. The play begins with Dewi's return home after escaping from an open prison, where he was serving a sentence for a series of robberies he undertook while a graduate student of philosophy, in protest against what he felt was the impossibility of taking any coherent stance in contemporary Wales. Bet, on the other hand, remains faithful to what Dewi calls the "shibboleths" of love, family, and nationality. Dewi's return is not undertaken in the hope of any real escape, but as a bitter attempt to force his parents and Bet to adopt and to approve his own nihilism. In the process he is drawn by Bet herself into a desperate game, in which she pledges her love, her religious faith, and her hope in an attempt to save him from the suicide that she clearly sees is the logical consequence of his position. In that, however, she fails. Dewi betrays her and turns on her in a savage attempt to destroy those qualities in her that attract his love. That he fails does not reduce the tragic quality of *Cymru Fydd,* because it is implicit throughout the play that Dewi's childish refusal to accept reality as he finds it is another version of that same crisis depicted in *Gymerwch chi Sigaret?, Brad,* and in other plays. *Cymru Fydd* reflects a world in which corruption is the almost inevitable consequence of sensitivity and sophistication.

Critics have often suggested that the work of this period betrays a gradual slackening of the religious faith that had sustained all of Lewis's drama until then. This observation has been made partly on the basis of readings of his poetry, but also because of the tone and manner of radio plays such as *Yn y Trên* (broadcast and published in 1965; In the Train) and *Cell y Grog* (published in 1973, broadcast in 1974; The Condemned Cell), both of which are experiments in the manner of absurdist drama. A reading of the preface Lewis wrote for his translation of Samuel Beckett's 1952 play *Waiting for Godot* (broadcast in 1962, published in 1970), however, shows how firmly he placed the absurdist vision within his own religious perspective. His appreciative criticism of the writings of the philosopher J. R. Jones is another indication of the complexity and resilience of his own version of the mainstream Catholic tradition.

During Lewis's last years as a dramatist and particularly after the departure of the director Wilbert Roberts from Cwmni Theatr Cymru (The Welsh Theatre Company), who had been responsible for several major Eisteddfod productions of his plays, Lewis wrote exclusively on commission for BBC radio and television, although his adjustment to the latter medium was never more than partial. His last play, commissioned by the BBC producer George Owen, was broadcast on 28 February 1978. Seven years later, at the age of ninety-two, Lewis died and was buried in the Catholic cemetery in Penarth, near Cardiff. In that last play, *1938* (published in 1989), Lewis returned to recent German history, with a study of the failure of the early plot against Hitler in September 1938, which he attributed to Neville Chamberlain's determined appeasement of Hitler at all costs. It is notable that this play was written in defiance of the many attacks made since the 1960s by revisionist historians interested in demolishing claims that real resistance had been offered to Hitler by members of the Officer Corps. Lewis refused to be drawn into this debate, perhaps partly because for his purposes as a dramatist, its ultimate historical validity was irrelevant. In the dilemma of these men, faced with the frightening reality of barbarism in their immediate world and its correlative in the weakmindedness of Western politicians, Lewis saw an extreme and dramatic version of the position of all honest men and women.

Other plays of these last years present different versions of that same dramatic crisis, such as *Cyrnol Chabert* (broadcast in 1968, published in 1989; Colonel Chabert), adapted for the radio from a story by Honoré Balzac, and *Branwen* (broadcast in 1971, published in 1975), another adaptation of a story from the second branch of the *Mabinogion*. But two other plays produced toward the end of his long career embody a different mood. The first is a 1968 radio version of his own 1964 historical romance, *Merch Gwern Hywel* (The Daughter of Gwern Hywel), which told the love story of his great-grandfather and great-grandmother, Williams Roberts and Sarah Jones; the second, *Dwy Briodas Ann* (broadcast and published in 1973; Ann's Two Marriages), is a dramatization of the history of the serving girl Ann Williams's two astonishing marriages, one to Sir John Bulkeley of Presaddfed, the other to the greatest of all Calvinist preachers, John Elias. Both of these plays can be placed in relation to everything else Lewis wrote. Their characters reflect the same psychological and moral conformation as Siwan and Dewi Rhys, and they embody the same critical attitude toward the realities of Welsh culture. However, they are also positive, showing another aspect of the penetrating criticism that pervaded all of Lewis's work. William Roberts in the earlier play and John Elias in the later embody the same complexity of nature seen in all the characters who inhabit this dramatic world, and they experience the same internal crisis; but they are at the same time more fortunate, by virtue of the honesty and consistency they acquire from their education in the world and share with the women they love.

Neither Roberts nor Elias, however, for all their heroic stature in the real world, is actually the most important character in *Merch Gwern Hywel* or *Dwy Briodas Ann*—they are important as the lovers of two of the many women who dominate the theatrical world of Lewis from the beginning to the end. Megan Morris of *The Eve of St. John* was the first of these, Luned Griffiths of *Gwaed yr Uchelwyr* the second; later heroines share the same essential nature and the same fundamental dramatic role, offering a spiritual and moral test to the men who love them or who refuse their love.

The nature of his heroines helps to place Saunders Lewis's work firmly in the tradition of what Peter Szondi calls the "classic" European drama, arising from interpersonal relationships. Lewis's work is certainly interpersonal rather than intrapersonal, which in itself accounts for his return to the structural pattern of neoclassical French drama after his brief experiments in the 1920s with the theories of the Cartel and with Anglo-Irish symbolism. Of his European contemporaries he was perhaps closer to Jean-Paul Sartre than to Eliot insofar as he created his drama around moments of self-definition that were stimulated by external circumstances. Modernist and postmodernist aesthetics and resulting experiments in dramatic form failed to interest him greatly. By choice, he upheld a tradition that honored the highly conscious human mind and that was deeply engaged with the torments and the victories experienced therein.

Letters:

Annwyl Kate, Annwyl Saunders, Gohebiaeth 1923–1983, edited by Dafydd Ifans (Aberystwyth: National Library of Wales, 1992);

Letters to Margaret Gilcriest, edited by Mair Saunders Jones, Ned Thomas, and Harri Pritchard Jones (Cardiff: Univerity of Wales Press, 1993).

Interviews:

"By Way of Apology," *Dock Leaves* (Winter 1955): 10–13;

Aneurin Talfan Davies, "Dylanwadau: Saunders Lewis," *Taliesin,* 2 (Christmas 1961): 5–18;

Ann Clwyd, "Dim Gwers i neb yn Brad," *Y Gwrandawr* (November 1964): 2–3;

Meirion Edwards, "Treiswyr sy'n ei chipio hi," *Y Gwrandawr* (December 1968): 1–3;

"Holi Saunders Lewis," *Mabon,* 1 (Winter 1974–1975): 7–10.

Biography:

D. Tecwyn Lloyd, *John Saunders Lewis Y Gyfrol Gyntaf* (Dinbych: Gwasg Gee, 1988).

References:

Hazel Ann Davies, *Saunders Lewis a Theatr Garthewin* (Llandysul: Gwasg Gomer, 1995);

Pennar Davies, ed., *Saunders Lewis: Ei feddwl a'i waith* (Dinbych: Gwasg Gee, 1950);

Bruce Griffiths, *Saunders Lewis* (Cardiff: University of Wales Press, 1979);

Emyr Humphreys, *Theatr Saunders Lewis* (Bangor: Cymdeithas Theatr Cymru, 1979);

Alun R. Jones and Gwyn Thomas, *Presenting Saunders Lewis* (Cardiff: University of Wales Press, 1973);

Dafydd Glyn Jones, "Saunders Lewis a Thraddodiad y Ddrama Gymraeg," *Llwyfan,* 9 (Winter 1973): 1–12;

Robert M. Jones, *Llên Cymru a Chrefydd* (Abertawe: Christopher Davies, 1977), pp. 10–12;

D. Tecwyn Lloyd and Gareth Rees, *Saunders Lewis* (Abertawe: Christopher Davies, 1975);

John Rowlands, *Saunders Lewis y Beirniad, Llên y Llenor* (Carnarvon: Gwasg Pantycelyn, 1990);

Mair Saunders, *Saunders Lewis 1893–1985* (Cardiff: Welsh Arts Council, 1987);

Peter Szondi, *Theory of the Modern Drama: A Critical Edition* (Cambridge: Polity, 1987);

Ioan Williams, *A Straitened Stage: A Study of the Theatre of J. Saunders Lewis* (Bridgend: Seren, 1991).

Papers:

There are no major archives of Saunders Lewis's papers, most of which he took great care to destroy.

Liz Lochhead

(26 December 1947 –)

Lucy Kay
Liverpool Hope University College

PLAY PRODUCTIONS: *Sugar and Spite,* by Lochhead and Marcella Evaristi, 1978;

Mary and the Monster, Coventry, Belgrade Theatre, 1981; revised and performed as *Blood and Ice,* Edinburgh, Traverse Theatre, 19 August 1982; revised again, London, New Merlin's Cave, 27 February 1984; revised again, Edinburgh, Royal Lyceum Theatre, 24 October 2003;

True Confessions, by Lochhead and others, Glasgow, Tron Theatre, August 1981;

Tickly Mince, by Lochhead, Tom Leonard, Alisdair Gray, and Jim Kelman, Glasgow, Tron Theatre, July 1982; Edinburgh Fringe Festival, August 1982;

Disgusting Objects, toured by Scottish Youth Theatre, Autumn 1982;

A Bunch of Fives, by Lochhead, Leonard, Dave Anderson, Dave McLennan, and Sean Hardie, Glasgow, 1983;

The Pie of Damocles, by Lochhead, Leonard, Gray, and Kelman, Edinburgh Fringe Festival, August 1983;

Same Difference, toured by Wildcat Theatre Company, 1983;

Shanghaied, toured by Borderline Theatre Company, 1983; revised as *Britannia Rules,* Edinburgh, Royal Lyceum Theatre, September 1998;

Red Hot Shoes, Glasgow, Tron Theatre, December 1983;

Rosaleen's Baby, Scottish Youth Theatre, 1984;

Silver Service, 1984;

Dracula, adapted from Bram Stoker's novel, Edinburgh, Royal Lyceum Theatre, 13 March 1985;

Tartuffe, adapted from Molière's play, Edinburgh, Royal Lyceum Theatre, 24 January 1986;

Consuming Passions, May 1987;

Mary Queen of Scots Got Her Head Chopped Off, Edinburgh, Lyceum Studio Theatre, 10 August 1987; London, Donmar Warehouse, 16 September 1987;

The Big Picture, Dundee, Dundee Repertory Theatre, 1988;

Liz Lochhead (photograph by Sean Hudson; from Robert Crawford and Anne Varty, eds., Liz Lochhead's Voices, *1993; Thomas Cooper Library, University of South Carolina)*

Patter Merchants, adapted from Molière's play *Les Precieuses ridicules,* Edinburgh Fringe Festival, August 1989;

Them Through the Wall, adapted from Bertolt Brecht's play by Lochhead and Kyra Dietz, music by Wagner Regeny, Cumbernauld, Cumbernauld Theatre, 1989;

Jock Tamson's Bairns, by Lochhead and Gerry Mulgrew, Glasgow, Tramway Theatre, February 1990;

Mozart and Salieri, Glasgow, Royal Scottish Academy of Music and Drama, 1990;

Quelques Fleurs, Edinburgh Fringe Festival, August 1991;

The York Cycle of Mystery Plays, York, Theatre Royal, 12 June 1992 and May/June 1996;

The Magic Island, adapted from William Shakespeare's *The Tempest,* London, Unicorn Children's Theatre, February 1993;

Carmen, Wildcat Theatre, 1997;

Cuba, London, Cumbernauld Youth Theatre, 27 March 1997;

In Flagrant Delicht, by Lochhead and Michael Marra, Glasgow, Tron Theatre, 1997;

Perfect Days, Edinburgh, Traverse Theatre, 7 August 1998; London, Hampstead Theatre, January 1999; London, Vaudeville Theatre, 11 June 1999;

Medea, Glasgow, The Old Fruitmarket, 17 March 2000; Edinburgh Fringe Festival, August 2000; toured 2000–2001;

Three Sisters, adapted from Anton Chekhov's play, Edinburgh, Royal Lyceum Theatre, 2000;

Beauty and the Beast, book by Lochhead, music by Marra, Glasgow, Tron Theatre, 3 December 2001;

Miseryguts, adapted from Molière's play *The Misanthrope,* Edinburgh, Royal Lyceum Theatre, 22 March 2002;

Little Girl Lost, adapted from Sandra Brown's book *Where There Is Evil,* staged reading, Glasgow, Tron Theatre, 20 October 2002;

Thebans, Edinburgh Fringe Festival, 2 August 2003;

Good Things, by Lochhead and Joe Ahearne, Glasgow, Tron Theatre, 10 September 2004.

BOOKS: *Riddle-me-ree* (London: Compton Poetry Fund/University of London, 1970);

Memo for Spring (Edinburgh: Reprographia, 1972);

Islands (Glasgow: Print Studio Press, 1978);

The Grimm Sisters (London: Next Editions, 1981);

Blood and Ice (Edinburgh: Salamander Press, 1982);

Dreaming Frankenstein & Collected Poems (Edinburgh: Polygon, 1984);

Silver Service (Edinburgh: Salamander Press, 1984);

True Confessions & New Clichés (Edinburgh: Polygon, 1985);

Tartuffe: A Translation into Scots from the Original by Molière (Glasgow: Third Eye Centre / Edinburgh: Polygon, 1985 [i.e., 1986]);

Mary Queen of Scots Got Her Head Chopped Off; & Dracula (Harmondsworth, U.K.: Penguin, 1989);

Bagpipe Muzak (London: Penguin, 1991);

The York Cycle (York: Theatre Royal, 1992);

Perfect Days (London: Nick Hern, 1998);

Medea (London: Nick Hern, 2000);

Cuba, published with *Dog House* by Gina Moxley (London: Faber & Faber, 2001);

Miseryguts & Tartuffe: Two Plays by Molière (London: Nick Hern, 2002);

Britannia Rules: A Playscript for Higher Drama and English (Dundee: Learning + Teaching Scotland, 2003);

The Colour of Black & White (Edinburgh: Polygon, 2003);

Thebans (London: Nick Hern, 2003).

PRODUCED SCRIPTS: "Sweet Nothings," television, *End of the Line,* BBC, 1984;

Fancy You Minding That, radio, BBC Radio 4, 1986;

Blood and Ice, radio, BBC Radio 4, 1990;

Latin for a Dark Room, motion picture, Gold Star Films, 1994;

Mary Queen of Scots Got Her Head Chopped Off, radio, BBC Radio 3, 11 February 2001.

RECORDING: *Competent at Peever,* selections read by Lochhead, Glasgow, Book Trust Scotland GAL BT1, 1991.

OTHER: *Blood and Ice,* in *Plays By Women,* volume 4, edited by Michelene Wandor (London: Methuen, 1985), pp. 82–117;

Cuba, in *New Connections: New Plays for Young People* (London: Faber & Faber, 1997), pp. 116–162;

Quelques Fleurs, in *Scotland Plays: New Scottish Drama,* edited by Philip Howard (London: Nick Hern in association with Traverse Theatre, 1999);

"The Man in the Comic Shop," in *The Year's Best Fantasy and Horror: Fifteenth Annual Collection,* edited by Ellen Datlow and Terri Windling (New York: St. Martin's Press, 2002).

Liz Lochhead has explored Scottish identity through her work as poet, playwright, director, and performer, and her keen awareness of theatrical styles, forms, and genres has established her as an authoritative practitioner and popular voice of the people. Applauded by feminists for her rich and diverse female characters and generally admired for her ironic wit and subversive strategies, Lochhead focuses on themes of cultural identity, female identity, and childhood identity in a world fraught with violence, contradictions, and confusions. Her penetrating sense of humor offers challenges to institutionalized prejudices, and her sense of imagery makes her work at once memorable and disturbing. She has worked collaboratively on many of her projects and has long associations with Communicado Theatre Company and the Edinburgh Fringe Festival. Susan C. Triesman locates Lochhead in the context of Scottish women writers: "Women dramatists in Scotland work from the twin sites of gender and national cross-culture to cross discursive patriarchal modes, inflecting, and sometimes transforming, the meanings of both." In an unpublished interview with Lucy Kay on 9 July 1997, Lochhead commented that she sees drama as being about "choices being made and not made."

Born in Motherwell, Lanarkshire, on 26 December 1947, Elizabeth Anne Lochhead was brought up with her sister, Janice, in a traditional Scottish Presbyterian context. Her father, John Lochhead, was a clerk in local government, and the family lived in a council house near Motherwell. Her mother was Margaret Forrest Lochhead. After graduating from Dalziel High School in Motherwell, Lochhead attended Glasgow School of Art between 1965 and 1970, attaining a diploma in art. She then taught art for eight years before receiving the Scottish-Canadian Writers Exchange Fellowship in 1978. By this time she had taken part in many writing workshops, and her interest in poetry was well established. Lochhead's early performance work was as a poet while she was still in art school. Her professional career as a writer and performer can be dated from 1971, when she won the BBC Radio Scotland Poetry Competition, and in 1973 she received a Scottish Arts Council Award for her first collection of poetry, *Memo for Spring* (1972).

Lochhead had published three volumes of poetry by the time her first play was produced. Many of the themes of her early work appear in more sophisticated form in the later plays. Her particular fondness for rewriting myths was evident in her first full-length play, *Blood and Ice* (originally titled *Mary and the Monster*, performed in 1981), a retelling of the Frankenstein tale. Although the play was not initially well received, its revised version a year later at the Traverse Theatre in Edinburgh—a venue already associated with new work and bold experimentation—received more favorable critical attention.

Blood and Ice retells the story of Frankenstein from a new perspective, that of Mary Shelley, who is presented throughout as a complex character evoking a range of audience responses. As in many of her plays, Lochhead utilizes the material of the original text to make incisive comments on identity and its construction. Through Mary Shelley, the contradictions presented to the female writer are explored, and the images of blood and ice vividly represent the binary oppositions of emotion versus intellect, male versus female. *Blood and Ice* draws parallels with contemporary issues, and the skillful manipulation of history reveals close links between past and present. The epic structure of the play serves the additional Brechtian purpose of alienation, encouraging the audience to engage with a complex mesh of conflicting ideologies and positions. Lochhead experiments throughout the piece with language, drawing attention to the multiplicity of meanings available: "Sometimes I wake up. Cold. Bathed in a moon sweat. And I rub myself slowly to life again," says Mary in scene 1 of the play. Issues of sexuality and gender, such as motherhood, menstruation, and the construction of a gendered identity, are linked to class and "otherness," a recurring feature of Lochhead's work.

The constant presence of Frankenstein's Creature on the stage problematizes the act of creation and its particular complexities for women. The death of Mary Shelley's mother, Mary Wollstonecraft, in childbirth adds further poignancy to the birth of Percy Florence Shelley, as Mary Shelley herself is only saved from death by being packed in a bath of ice, her "natural" element. Her husband, Percy Bysshe Shelley, states, "Yes I am a man. I shall never die of childbirth. Oh no. We are a different species!" This sense of otherness and difference is central to Lochhead's concern with identity.

Blood and Ice interrogates the act of creativity. Attention is also drawn to wider issues of representation, such as women's role in art history, through intertextual references and the emphasis on the creation of the female body. This early play demonstrates many of the issues and concerns of Lochhead's subsequent work.

In 1982 and 1983 Lochhead worked extensively in revues and was a performer and writer at the Edinburgh Fringe Festival. Working with Tom Leonard and Alisdair Gray in a new, experimental fashion, she developed a strong relationship with Communicado Theatre Company (which, in its new identity as Archipelago Theatre, closed in January 2000 after losing its annual £200,000 grant from the Scottish Arts Council). Formed by Gerry Mulgrew and a group of fellow actors, Communicado was an Edinburgh-based touring company that, as Mark Fisher wrote in *The Observer* (7 August 1994), flouted convention and "epitomises the energy, innovation and eclecticism of Scottish Theatre." During this period Lochhead contributed to and appeared in *Tickly Mince* (1982), *Disgusting Objects* (1982), *Red Hot Shoes* (1983), and *A Bunch of Fives* (1983). Her interest in young people was already extending to the stage in her tour with the Scottish Youth Theatre. Her love of comic reappropriations was developed through her work at the Tron Theatre, which gave her wide exposure to a range of audiences. Her work with the Wildcat and Borderline Theatre companies provided further opportunities to play with conventions of theater and adopt political strategies through subversive techniques. Founded in 1974, Borderline's aim was to produce new, popular, accessible, quality Scottish touring theater. Borderline encouraged new writing for the theater and held workshops with many local groups and organizations, which proved especially useful to Lochhead. Role reversals, multiple perspectives, linguistic experiments, and playful approaches to world issues characterized her dramatic techniques and processes.

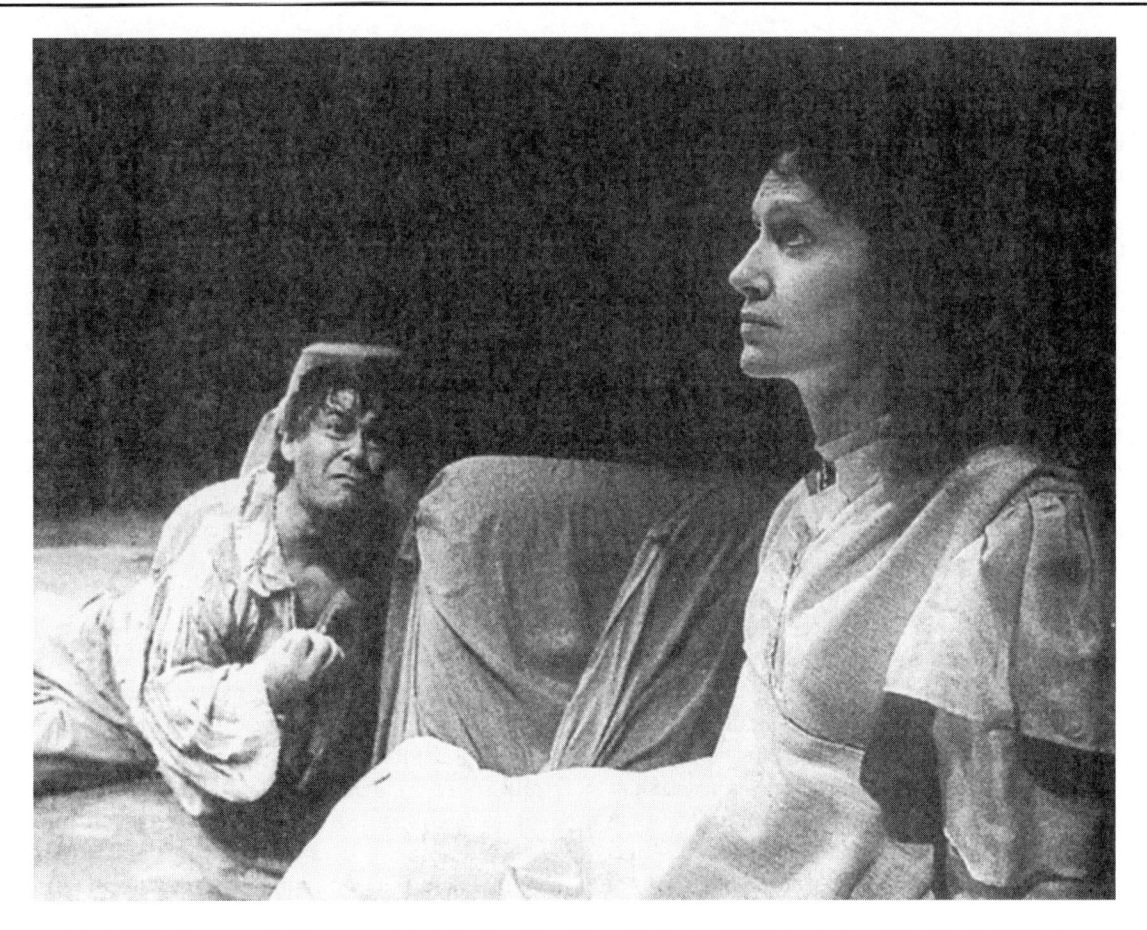

Michael Mackenzie as the Creature and Isabella Jarrett as Mary Shelley in a 1986 production of Lochhead's 1982 play
Blood and Ice, *which depicts the creation of Shelley's 1818 novel,* Frankenstein, *from the author's perspective (photograph by Douglas Robertson; from Robert Crawford and Anne Varty, eds.,* Liz Lochhead's Voices, *1993; Thomas Cooper Library, University of South Carolina)*

Shanghaied and *Same Difference,* both performed in 1983, evolved from actor workshops, and in both works, adults play children's roles. *Shanghaied* (later expanded as *Britannia Rules,* performed in 1998, published in 2003) involves three poor evacuees from Clydebank living in Ayrshire. The play raises issues of class, privilege, and alienation. Lochhead's interest in children's games is used to explore prejudices. In *Same Difference,* Lochhead employs the Shakespearean device of swapping and mixing identities. As a peripheral issue, the difficulties of "coming out" are hinted at—an issue addressed again in her later writings.

Lochhead's interest in the gory and the Gothic, evident in *Blood and Ice,* surfaced again in *Dracula* (performed in 1985, published in 1989). In adapting Bram Stoker's novel for a contemporary stage, Lochhead again addresses the concept of the monster—and the monstrous—with particular reference to female desire. In identifying with the monstrous, she, like other feminist thinkers of the time, acknowledges the pleasures of excess in both theatrical and personal frameworks. Melanie Reid of *The Scotsman* (16 March 1985) described Lochhead's achievement: "she has managed to sweep aside the celluloid and get close to universal fears about blood, life, love and death which give Dracula the potential for true tragedy."

The play opens with an exaggerated scene of innocence and natural beauty. Lucy, the aristocratic young woman whom Dracula will seduce, sings to herself as she looks in the mirror and kisses her own image, alerting the spectator from the onset to forbidden pleasures. Lochhead employs witty, anarchic, and subversive strategies to rewrite the myth, telling new stories and challenging the Christian values underpinning the original. Lucy draws attention to the constructed nature of women by her initial enjoyment of her liberation from her stays followed by her masochistic demand: "I want it tighter. I want to feel it nip me in. . . . I wasn't going to suffer for nothing and not be noticed." In direct contrast to Stoker's novel, Lucy is presented in scene 1 as a thoroughly bad girl, teasing her friend Mina with sexual innuendo and expressing her desire for a man.

Scene 2 opens in Bedlam and establishes the pattern of alternating locations. The exaggerated characterizations lend an air of superrealism to the scene and give a comic touch to an otherwise depressing environment. The flavor is of myth or fairy tale, nightmare figures with sadomasochistic tendencies and practices playing out their Brueghelesque roles. Throughout the play Lochhead utilizes the character of Dr. Seward's mental patient Renfield to draw attention to language and its slippery and unstable qualities. Through Renfield, the audience is led to question the oppositions of madness and sanity as Lochhead blurs the distinctions between them. The stage directions suggest that Renfield "*knows everything,*" and he is a constant onstage presence.

The character of Jonathan Harker, Mina's fiancé, first appears in Seward's private study, and his upper-class status and snobbery are soon evident. Their conversation reveals Jonathan to be an unscrupulous man of business; he has duped Dracula into buying Carfax, unaware of the madhouse next door. Lochhead denies Jonathan, the "hero," audience sympathy and offers, instead, Count Dracula as an outsider, a victim, and perhaps an object of pity.

Not until scene 7 does Dracula finally emerge—from "*out of us,*" according to the stage directions. Dracula appears to be a welcoming and warm character, sharing and libertarian, who draws attention to his own foreignness—"I have the manners of a barbarian"—thus highlighting racial and national difference. This fusion of discourses and references demonstrates the links between class, race, religion, consumerism, colonialism, and identity.

The irreverent treatment of Christianity in Lochhead's work is often amusing and incisive. Many of the references to blood are reminders of the body and blood of Christ. Lochhead's understanding of structure and ability to disrupt audience expectation and continuity of narrative with humorous effect are again apparent.

Attention is frequently drawn to the act of dressing as a means of constructing identity; for example, Mina puts on her wedding dress at the same time as Renfield is put into a straitjacket. Meaning is constantly destabilized through these devices, and the short scenes add pace and tension to the play. Toward the end of act 1 the weather becomes increasingly tempestuous as the climax approaches. The imagery is vivid and animalistic; as Lucy sleepwalks, she chants, "Coming, coming, coming, coming, coming." Mina and Lucy entertain each other with tales of folklore, and women's inequality is clearly identified through jokes about menstruation and her servant Florrie's comment, "Well, us Eve's daughters got to laugh, I reckon, else we'd sit down and cry." Although divided by class, the three women are unified by gender.

When *Dracula* opened at the Edinburgh Royal Lyceum Theatre, Joyce McMillan wrote in *The Guardian* (16 March 1985): "It delves deep beneath the psychosexual surface of Stoker's story in an attempt to marry his imagery with modern ideas about women's sexuality; its language is a daring and often highly successful mixture of domestic naturalism and high melodrama, pun, alliteration, and pure poetry."

In 1986 Lochhead married Tom Logan, an architect; the couple lives in Glasgow. Lochhead's adaptation of Molière's 1664 play, *Tartuffe,* premiered in January 1986. This play is in rhyme throughout, though not in the alexandrines of Molière's original, and utilizes an invented Scottish language that, according to Ilona Koren-Deutsch, "draws on the different accents of various regions of Scotland to create one unified stage language that nonetheless echoes the sound of old Scots." The play is set in 1920s Scotland, a significant time in the renaissance of Scottish literary tradition, and a 1995 revival at the Tron Theatre in Glasgow was described by John Peter in *The Sunday Times* (21 May 1995) as "fruity, bawdy, wickedly funny," with an ending "full of sharp Caledonian sarcasm."

In another of her best-known plays, *Mary Queen of Scots Got Her Head Chopped Off* (performed in 1987, published in 1989), Lochhead utilizes a mixture of genres and styles, influenced strongly by carnival and circus, to explore a range of national identities and the theme of women's uneasy relationship with power. The piece is episodic and fast-moving, cutting across perspectives, and the similarities and differences between Mary and Elizabeth I are highlighted. The ghoul-like character La Corbie (The Crow) acts as a narrator and constant onstage presence, offering visual and linguistic reminders of the themes of the play, in particular the death drive.

La Corbie opens the play with the question, "Country: Scotland. Whit like is it?" and answers, "It depends. It depends." Lochhead uses elements of the grotesque, dance, movement, and image to subvert the ambience of the child-like narrative, and her "strange circus" distorts the audience's expectations of the history play. The fairy-tale narrative is deconstructed, alerting the audience to the more subtle narratives of power and abuse. Lochhead rewrites history from a female perspective, drawing on her own experiences of growing up as a woman in Scotland, a land steeped in tradition and contradictions.

The two queens, although separated by distance and material concerns, are ultimately unified in their inability to operate as both woman and queen in a patriarchal society. The responses of the commoners to the various suitors for each queen demonstrate the extent of religious bigotry in both countries and the impossibility of a compromise for either. Both Mary and Elizabeth forgo their personal and sexual freedoms in order to retain the status of queen and, while Mary is determined to marry "wha I can love," Elizabeth understands the price that must be paid for such freedom. In scene 2 attention is drawn to the artificiality of the play by Lochhead's unrealistic setting, use of dance (a mad tango), and the mirrored positions of Mary and Elizabeth on the stage. This parodied treatment of the characters, characteristic of Lochhead's work, creates a sense of unreality, and their puppet-like natures are reinforced by comic use of repetition. La Corbie says, "I ask you, when's a queen a queen / And when's a queen juist a wummin?" Her question proves to be central to the play and a question to which neither queen can find an answer.

In her 2001 adaptation of *Mary Queen of Scots Got Her Head Chopped Off* for BBC Radio 3, Lochhead uses music and sound to re-create the play in, as she said in a preface, "a brand new imaginative sound-scape kind of way . . . keeping the anachronisms, the cheek, the nerve that was there in the theatre show." In this preface Lochhead identifies this play as her favorite and concludes, "It's a play that doesn't seem to be going to lie down and die."

Jock Tamson's Bairns, written with Mulgrew, was first performed at the Tramway Theatre in Glasgow in 1990. As Helen Roberts pointed out in her review in *The Tribune* (9 February 1990), this play "re-enacts some of the least desirable aspects of Scottish history and culture," including drunkenness and womanizing. It takes place on Burns Night (25 January, the birthday of Scottish poet Robert Burns) and uses multilayered images to explore the Bairns, whom Lochhead in the 1997 interview with Kay called "a community of the dispossessed." The Reverend John Thomson (Jock Tamson) was a minister in Duddingston Kirk, Edinburgh, from 1805 to 1840. He called the members of his congregation "ma bairns" (my children), which resulted in the folk saying "We're all Jock Tamson's bairns." This sentiment gave a sense of belonging to a small but special group. Images of Scottishness abound, and the cult of tartanry (the excessive use of tartan and other Scottish imagery to produce a distorted, sentimental view of Scotland) is given comic treatment. The 1990 production utilized surreal cartoons, clowning, dance, documentary, physical comedy, image, and music to create a grotesque fusion of theatrical styles and "total theater," in what Triesman calls "a ritual of deconstruction and renovation." James Mavor, in his 29 January 1990 review in *The Independent*, commented: "*Jock Tamson's Bairns* takes a look at the state of the nation and comes to the conclusion . . . that the nation is in a right old state, struggling to be reborn from the debris of kitsch and false pride."

Quelques Fleurs (performed in 1991, published in 1999) is a two-person play in the form of monologues that deal emotionally and physically with isolation and separation. The structure of the play is interesting: the man's monologue goes backward in time, from being extremely drunk on Christmas Eve to being sober at the start of the journey. The woman's monologue goes forward in time, from events of the previous year until their current meeting; thus there are two different versions of the same events working in counterpoint. The characters are skillfully constructed through the use of trivia and casual remarks that offer keen insights into their lives, and Lochhead gradually reveals the tragedy of the couple's relationship. In a 10 August 1995 review in *The Guardian*, Joy Hendry stated, "Lochhead treads that tightrope of intermingling humour and tragedy, touching with sympathy and understanding the soft underbelly of her characters and their alienating predicament."

Lochhead produced another adaptation in 1992 with her version of the York Mystery Plays, a fourteenth-century cycle depicting the biblical story of man's Fall and Redemption. In the 1997 interview with Kay, Lochhead commented, "quite a lot of the actual original . . . is very similar indeed to the language of the Scottish ballads." Reviewer Robin Thornber commented in *The Guardian* (15 May 1992) that "poet Liz Lochhead has produced a new version which respects the vigorous, vivid and often passionate language of the original 56 pageants but toughens and tightens it." The performance broke with tradition in that it was staged indoors, set in a building site with contemporary casting. In a 1996 Theatre Royal production, cut to less than four hours, God was played by a local woman. This version was described by Lyn Gardner in *The Guardian* (13 June 1996) as "cunning and bristly as a ratcatcher's glove." As Lochhead herself stated, "I have kept it archaic, even knowing that God might be wearing a cardigan."

The Magic Island (performed in 1993) is a version of William Shakespeare's *The Tempest* that opened at the Unicorn Children's Theatre in London. It involves the transferral of power from adults to children and has an environmental theme. Heather Neill, in an article in *The Sunday Times* (2 February 1993), suggested that "*The Magic Island* is an original play which stands in relation to Shakespeare rather like a child acting out its parents' role. It is respectful but cheeky, and sometimes innocently direct." As in many of Lochhead's plays, the search for freedom and the different ways of approaching it is an underlying theme. The play acts as a vehicle for her belief that "living in harmony is worth more than material success."

In the 1997 interview with Kay, Lochhead described her play *Cuba* (performed and published in 1997): "it is about the Cuba crisis, it's *set* around the Cuba crisis but it's *about* two girls and their betrayal so it is a play about friendship and a play about life and death. So it is about rewriting history in the light of what stories ought to have been heard and asking the question, 'what if?'" *Cuba* was commissioned by the Royal National Theatre as one of twelve new plays for the BT National Connections scheme for young people. In his introduction to the accompanying published collection, *New Connections* (1997), Nick Drake called *Cuba* "a beautifully detailed and very funny large-scale theatrical extravaganza." The play demonstrates many of Lochhead's concerns: the relationship of the personal to the political, the wisdom of children, friendships between women, and class identities. Lochhead juxtaposes the present with the past, recreating history and telling the stories of two children who, influenced by world events, internalize the betrayals that characterize the wider conflicts.

Throughout the piece a chorus of girls comments on the action onstage and gives specific references to the period by snatches of song, slogans, and chants. The ageless narrator is referred to as B, so that only at the end of the play does the audience know which of the two girls she was. As in *Mary Queen of Scots Got Her Head Chopped Off*, the play explores issues of sameness and difference. While Barbara's parents spend the evening at a dinner dance at the golf club in aid of the Rotary, Bernadette's go "round the pub . . . for a little drink." However, Barbara is able to identify similarities: "OK, different class, different attitudes, different standard of living, granted. Different sides of the track maybe, but I'd say they were far more alike than—well, certainly *much* more alike than they thought they were."

The play is a sequence of flashbacks crafted into short scenes. Articles from advertisements and magazines demonstrate the construction of "women" in comic form. The girls' innocent dreams acquire a more sinister flavor in the context of the potential violence in the current crisis. The attitudes—and platitudes—of the parents are caricatured in their clichéd responses and simultaneous presence on stage. Their identical dress and actions mock their class differences, and their nonnaturalistic characterizations draw attention to the constructed nature of their stereotypes.

As Jim Mulligan suggested in "The Time When Next Week Might Be Cancelled," an interview with Lochhead included in *New Connections*, "In *Cuba* Liz Lochhead is exploring conformity, the effects of stepping out of line and what makes a rebel." The two girls plan to write "Cuba Libre" in spray paint on headmaster Miss Arthur's door; this foray is an exciting adventure into an "other" world forbidden to them, and their titillation is apparent. In the same way as Cuba is the pawn in the game of world politics, so Bernadette's friendship is enjoyed, then abandoned, by Barbara. Miss Arthur resigns, in an amusingly futile gesture of early feminist resistance; and Barbara, years later, is left to make sense of her own history and her failure to support her friend. The cyclical nature of the piece, the blend of humor and sadness, naiveté and understanding, and the fusion of history with the present, act as a poignant reminder of the internalization of oppression and its effects on the actions of individual people.

Britannia Rules opened at the Royal Lyceum Theatre in September 1998. The young evacuees of *Shanghaied* are relocated in the countryside a decade later on Coronation Day. In a program note, Catherine Lockerbie, literary editor of *The Scotsman,* commented: "Lochhead is in her blissful element in this nostalgia (the national pastime . . .) and conjures with uncanny accuracy a complete, bygone world of spam and piccalilli sandwiches, of nylons and National service, of empire biscuits and adoration of royalty." Lochhead's sharp sense of linguistic cadence and love of stories old and new are again evident.

Also in 1998 Lochhead was again working with the Traverse Theatre, where she developed a short script into the highly acclaimed piece *Perfect Days,* a single-set stage play. Lochhead worked closely with directors Philip Howard and John Tiffany, playwright Iaian Heggie, and literary manager Colin Chambers on this piece about a modern Glasgow woman who desperately wants to have a baby. The audience follows Barbs Marshall, a celebrity hairdresser, through nine different days of her life as she grapples with being forty and childless. The play is a sort of romantic comedy with dark undertones and bitingly funny situations, often verging on farce. The reviewer for *The Times* (August 1998) commented that the dialogue is "arrestingly crisp and idiomatic," and many themes are explored: the middle-aged woman, mother/daughter relationships, artificial insemination, and the desire to reproduce with the assistance of a gay donor. *Perfect Days* concludes on a triumphant note by describing Barbs and her best friend Brendan: *"They laugh together in sheer joy. It comes streaming out from them, expanding, lifting."* Matt Wolf's review of a production at the Vaudeville Theatre in London (*Variety,* 28 June 1999) offered a less favorable view than the Edinburgh Fringe Festival reviews, suggesting the play "at heart is so TV sitcom retrograde." However, he was also identifying one of the strengths of the play—its sense of kitsch, camp, and playful excess, which is the source of much of its humor. *Perfect Days* was nominated for an Olivier Award for best new play in 2000.

While she was still developing *Perfect Days,* Lochhead was invited by Graham McLaren of Theatre Babel—a company founded in 1994 with the principal aim of reinvestigating classical drama and bringing it to life for a contemporary audience—to take part in a "Greeks" program. The result was her version of *Medea* (performed and published in 2000). As she comments in a foreword to *Medea,* "there was a frisson of slight perverse attraction in the notion of next working on a play that would be—in every way—exactly the opposite [of *Per-*

Alison Peebles as Elizabeth I in the 1987 Edinburgh premiere of Mary Queen of Scots Got Her Head Chopped Off, *one of Lochhead's best-known plays, in which she uses carnival-inspired elements to highlight the comparison of the two queens (photograph by Ginny Atkinson; from Robert Crawford and Anne Varty, eds.,* Liz Lochhead's Voices, *1993; Thomas Cooper Library, University of South Carolina)*

fect Days]: a tragedy, absolutely timeless and ancient, about a woman driven by female desperation of a quite different sort, to killing her children." She explained the difference in her approach:

> It was only after seeing the play in performance here in Glasgow this Spring, that it struck me the conventional way of doing *Medea* in Scotland until very recently would have been to have Medea's own language Scots and the, to her, alien Corinthians she lived under speaking, as powerful "civilised" Greeks, patrician English. That it did not occur to me to do other than give the dominant mainstream society a Scots tongue and Medea a foreign-speaking-English refugee voice must speak of a genuine in-the-bone cultural confidence here.

Medea previewed at The Old Fruitmarket in Glasgow on 17 March 2000 before opening at the Edinburgh Assembly Rooms in August prior to touring. The play received much acclaim; a reviewer for *The Scotsman* (27 August 2000) wrote:

> Liz Lochhead's stunning new version of *Medea* is the kind of interpretation–brave, visionary, risky–that blows a well-known text apart and reassembles it in a completely new light. . . . What Lochhead does is to recast *Medea* as an episode–ancient but new, cosmic yet agonisingly familiar–in a sex war which is recognisable to every woman, and most of the men, in the theatre.

The published version of the play won the prestigious Saltire Society Literary Award for Scottish book of the year in 2001.

In March 2002 *Miseryguts,* Lochhead's Scots adaptation of Molière's *Le Misanthrope* (1666), opened at the Royal Lyceum Theatre in Edinburgh. The play is updated to take place in a contemporary Scottish parliament. Elisabeth Mahoney, writing in *The Guardian* (26 March 2002), said of the piece:

> The name change says it all. In her new translation of *Le Misanthrope,* Liz Lochhead brings a spiky, colloquial and often delicious immediacy to Molière's comedy of morals and manners. Moving the seventeenth-century play into the world of media and politics in devolved Scotland, Lochhead satirises with deadly precision. . . . Here are a pretty blonde newsreader, an Old Etonian posh Scot, a feminist cultural commentator who is fairer to men than to other women, and even a prolific

poet/playwright with some success at translating Molière. Doubtless, MSPs, TV people and hacks will be booking seats just to see if they are included.

Mahoney concluded that "the play's moral question—whether it is better to tell the truth and be damned, or flatter fools and flourish—is convincingly and hilariously translated into the present day."

Lochhead's keen interest in reworking classical dramas is further demonstrated in *Thebans*, which premiered at the Edinburgh Fringe Festival in August 2003. In this play, Lochhead intermingles Sophocles' *Oedipus Rex* with a variety of other sources to produce a tragic tale of epic proportions. Phillip Fisher, an Edinburgh *Fringe* reviewer, called *Thebans* "a very satisfying and entertaining trip through Greek tragedy, with a Scottish twang, in a really gripping two hours." Mark Brown, writing in *Scotland on Sunday* (10 August 2003), summarized the power of Lochhead's writing: "An innocent, wretched population stand before us, medical masks strapped across their faces. The objects of pestilence and war, they are suffering for the misdeeds of another. It is as if the Iraq War and the magnified SARS pandemic had become combined into one. The stories of Sophocles and Euripides have hit the contemporary mark in this way in every age. We, in Scotland, are fortunate that we have a dramatist of the abilities of Liz Lochhead to mould them to our times and our culture."

Lochhead returned to her first play, *Blood and Ice*, with an extensively rewritten script produced in October 2003 at the Royal Lyceum Theatre in Edinburgh. It is characteristic of her approach to theater that she constantly rewrites and revisits old material in order to keep her work vibrant and contemporary.

Good Things, a romantic farce, premiered on 10 September 2004 at the Tron Theatre in Glasgow. The play, which was written with Joe Ahearne, was short-listed under the Fast Forward Feature Film Initiative sponsored by Scottish Screen, BBC Scotland Drama, BBC Films, and Content Films to be produced by Arabella Croft for Black Camel Pictures.

Liz Lochhead's achievements in theater continue to be recognized in Scotland and abroad. Lochhead has received honorary degrees from the Universities of Aberdeen, Glasgow, Strathclyde, Stirling, Edinburgh, St. Andrews, and Dundee. She is also a Fellow of the Royal Scottish Academy of Music and Drama. Her love of performance and performing, her bold theatrical sense, and her vision for a better future make her work stunningly contemporary. Her experiments with language and performance modes and her interest in identities past and present enrich Scottish theater.

Interviews:

Joyce McMillan, "Liz Lochhead: An Interview," *Scottish Theatre News*, no. 18 (August 1982): 3–7;

Rebecca E. Wilson, "Liz Lochhead," in *Sleeping with Monsters: Conversations with Scottish and Irish Women Poets*, edited by Wilson and Gillean Somerville-Arjat (Edinburgh: Polygon, 1990), pp. 8–17;

Gillian Glover, "A Thing About Poetic Justice," *Scotsman*, 6 June 2003 <http://thescotsman.scotsman.com/s2.cfm?id=626422003>;

Lesley McDowell, "Liz Lochhead: Hooked on Classics," *Independent*, 5 July 2003 <http://enjoyment.independent.co.uk/books/interviews/story.jsp?story=421731>.

Bibliography:

Alison Walker and Craig W. McLuckie, "Liz Lochhead: An Annotated Bibliography" <http://www.kalwriters.com/archive/lochhead.html>.

References:

Robert Crawford and Anne Varty, eds., *Liz Lochhead's Voices* (Edinburgh: Edinburgh University Press, 1993);

Jennifer B. Harvie, "Desire and Difference in Liz Lochhead's *Dracula*," *Essays in Theatre*, 11 (May 1993): 133–143;

Harvie, "Liz Lochhead's Drama," dissertation, University of Glasgow, 1996;

Ilona Koren-Deutsch, "Feminist Nationalism in Scotland: *Mary Queen of Scots Got Her Head Chopped Off*," *Modern Drama*, 35 (September 1992): 424–432;

J. McDonald, "*Dracula*: Freudian Novel and Feminist Drama," in *Novel Images: Literature in Perspective*, edited by P. Reynolds (London: Routledge, 1993), pp. 80–104;

B. Nuemeier, "Past Lives in Present Drama: Feminist Theatre and Intertextuality," in *Frauen und Frauemdastellung in der Englischen und Amerikanischen Literatur*, edited by T. Fischer-Seidel (Tübingen, 1991), pp. 181–191;

Susan C. Triesman, "Transformations and Transgressions: Women's Discourse on the Scottish Stage," in *British and Irish Women Dramatists Since 1958*, edited by Trevor Griffiths and Margaret Llewellyn-Jones (Buckingham: Open University Press, 1993), pp. 124–134.

Papers:

The Scottish Theatre Archive at the University of Glasgow includes typescripts of Liz Lochhead's plays *Blood and Ice* and *Shanghaied*. The National Library of Scotland, Edinburgh, houses additional papers related to her poetry.

Martin Lynch
(22 November 1950 -)

Roy Connolly
Edge Hill College

PLAY PRODUCTIONS: *We Want Work, We Want Bread*, Group Theatre, 1976;

Is There Life Before Death, Belfast, Group Theatre, 1978;

They're Taking Down the Barricades, Belfast, Group Theatre, 1979;

A Roof Under Our Heads, Belfast, Group Theatre, 29 March 1980; revised as *Castles in the Air*, Belfast, Lyric Theatre Belfast, 8 June 1983;

Dockers, Belfast, Lyric Theatre Belfast, 12 January 1981;

What About Your Ma, Is Your Da Still Workin'? Belfast, Group Theatre, 16 November 1981;

The Interrogation of Ambrose Fogarty, Belfast, Lyric Theatre Belfast, 27 January 1982;

Ricochets, Belfast, Ulster Youth Theatre, August 1982;

Lay Up Your Ends, by Lynch, Marie Jones, and the Charabanc Theatre Company, Belfast, Arts Theatre, 15 May 1983;

Crack Up, Belfast, Stage '80, Group Theatre, 10 November 1983;

Oul' Delf and False Teeth, by Lynch, Jones, and the Charabanc Theatre Company, Dublin, Project Theatre, 15 April 1984;

Can't Pay Won't Pay, adapted from Dario Fo, Belfast, Arts Theatre, 21 September 1984;

Minstrel Boys, Belfast, Lyric Theatre Belfast, 6 November 1985;

Welcome to Bladonmore Road, Belfast, Arts Theatre, 14 November 1988;

The Stone Chair, Belfast, Grand Opera House, 16 June 1989;

Rinty, Belfast, Group Theatre, 27 August 1990;

Moths, Belfast, Arts Theatre, May 1992;

Bonjour Mucker, Belfast, Old Museum Arts Centre, February 1993;

Pictures of Tomorrow, Belfast, Lyric Theatre Belfast, 14 April 1994;

The Wedding Community Play, by Lynch, Jones, Jo Egan, and the company, Belfast, Belfast Festival at Queen's, November 1999;

Martin Lynch (Grand Opera House, Belfast; courtesy of the Linen Hall Library, Belfast)

Main Hall: What Did I Know When I Was Nineteen? part of *Convictions* by Lynch and others, Belfast, Crumlin Road Courthouse, 30 October 2000;

The History of the Troubles (Accordin' to My Da), Belfast, Northern Bank, 2 May 2002;

The Belfast Carmen, by Lynch and Mark Dougherty, Belfast, Grand Opera House, 6 November 2002;

Titanic, Belfast, Ulster Hall, 24 April 2003.

BOOKS: *Dockers* (Belfast: Farset, 1982);

The Interrogation of Ambrose Fogarty (Dundonald: Blackstaff, 1982);

Three Plays, edited by Damian Smyth (Belfast: Lagan, 1996)—comprises *Dockers, The Interrogation of Ambrose Fogarty,* and *Pictures of Tomorrow;*

Dockers & Welcome to Bladonmore Road (Belfast: Lagan, 2003);

The Interrogation Of Ambrose Fogarty & Castles in the Air (Belfast: Lagan, 2003);

Pictures of Tomorrow & Rinty (Belfast: Lagan, 2003).

PRODUCED SCRIPTS: *Dockers,* radio, BBC Radio, 21 November 1980;

A Prayer for the Dying, by Lynch and Edmund Ward, adapted from Jack Higgins's novel, motion picture, M-G-M, 1987;

Jamesy Baker and the 22 Walls, radio, BBC Radio, 27 April 1990;

Sailortown, by Lynch and Mark Bussell, television, Carlton Television, 20 April 1993;

Pictures of Tomorrow, radio, BBC Radio, 9 April 1995;

The Clearance of Audleystown, radio, BBC Radio, 29 June 1995;

Personal Visions, television, BBC Northern Ireland, 7 March 1996;

Needles and Pins, radio, BBC Radio, 19 July 1997.

Martin Lynch is one of Northern Ireland's most politically and socially conscientious playwrights. Since the late 1970s he has produced a body of work resolutely committed to celebrating the voice of the people of Belfast and highlighting issues pertinent to that city's working-class communities. In an interview for *The Gown* (June 1981) he stated that his early inspiration came not from other playwrights but from political thinkers such as Vladimir Lenin, Fidel Castro, and James Connolly, and that he perceives theater to be at its most valuable when providing a platform for political self-expression and protest. He noted in the *Sunday Tribune* (12 June 1983) that in playwriting, he believes he had found a means to a pragmatic end: "a better way of getting to people than going around the doors selling newspapers." His plays concern themselves not with voguish narratives and concepts but with the minutiae of daily life in Belfast.

Throughout his career, Lynch has been less concerned with servicing orthodox cultural values than with writing about, and for, the community of which he is a part. His solidarity with his community and dedication to place has not, however, come without a price. He has often fallen foul of local criticism, coming under fire for excessive reliance on dramatic cliché, for engaging in propaganda, and for his apparent lack of development as a playwright. Most critics would acknowledge that such censure has been warranted, but alongside these evaluations it is also important to note that Lynch's plays provide a series of valuable social documents. They stage a constructive dialogue between "place" and the meaning of that place in human terms and offer significant insights into life in Northern Ireland during the Troubles. Furthermore, as literary works, they are sustained by the strength of their storytelling and the force and freshness of their observations. They conjure up vivid, domestic worlds and, in sharing local knowledge, "in-jokes," and urban myths with an audience, they deflate the pomposity and mannerisms of middle-class theater.

Lynch was born in Gilnahurk on 22 November 1950 and moved to Turf Lodge in West Belfast in 1963. His father, James Lynch (known as Jimmy), was a dockworker, extremely fond of quoting William Butler Yeats and other Irish poets when he had a few drinks, an activity that introduced Lynch to literature. His mother, Veronica (known as Bina), was a casual mill worker, and the family estimated that she had spent approximately nine and a half years of her life pregnant: Martin Lynch is the middle child of thirteen, one of whom died. He attended St. Malachy's Primary and St. Patrick's Secondary School, both on the New Lodge Road in Belfast, but he left school at fifteen and went to work as a clothes cutter. He married Moira in 1974, and together they had two daughters, Graine and Briege, although the couple later separated.

His political awakening came at the age of nineteen and was provoked, he says, by the arrival of British troops in Belfast in 1969. Shortly after soldiers appeared on the streets, he became an active member of the Republican Clubs Organization (now the Workers' Party) and subsequently served as their administrator. In his 1996 television documentary, *Personal Visions,* Lynch stated that in this post he spent "most of the 1970s working for a thirty-two-county-socialist-workers-and-small-farmers' republic," although he acknowledged that he was "never actually to meet a small farmer, let alone free one."

His introduction to theater was forestalled "by growing up amid a community where there was no grounding for engaging in the Arts," as he said in *Personal Visions.* Consequently, he did not see a theater production until he was twenty-five years of age. When this introduction finally came, it was courtesy of the Republican Clubs Organization: as the administrator, Lynch was given the task of hunting out venues for a community production of John Arden's *The Nonstop Connolly Show* (1975). The Marxist politics and celebration of working-class resistance in this play held an immediate fascination and provided Lynch with the impetus to write. Within a year he had written his own play, *We Want Work, We Want Bread* (performed in 1976), and he quickly followed it with three more: *Is There Life Before Death* in 1978, *They're Taking Down the Barricades* in 1979, and *A Roof Under Our Heads* in 1980.

These plays, performed at the Group Theatre by the Turf Lodge Fellowship Community Theatre group, established Lynch's formula for dramatic writing: good characters, a good story, plenty of humor, a concern to highlight social injustice, and, most of all, "the attempt to depict the lives of the audience members themselves." *A Roof Under Our Heads* (later revised and retitled *Castles in the Air*) depicts the real-life tragedy of a resident of Turf Lodge, Rosie Nolan, who committed suicide after repeatedly having her requests to be rehoused turned down by Belfast City Council. Lynch noted in *Personal Visions,* "That happened. I was there at the time. I knew the woman. It greatly affected me and I wanted to do something about it, and so I wrote a play about it." The stinging critique of economic deprivation in the play, its documentary origins, and its sincere intentions provided a new kind of insight into life in urban Belfast for theatergoers, and the critical response demonstrated that as much as Lynch had detractors, he had equally enthusiastic supporters.

Chief among these supporters was John Boyd, the literary advisor of the Lyric Theatre Belfast (also known as the Lyric Players Theatre) and author of the first modern Troubles plays. Boyd was quick to espouse the merits of Lynch's drama, and upon his recommendation, Lynch was offered a post at the Lyric Players Theatre in 1980. Four years after he began writing, his career thus underwent a paradigm shift: as he said in *Personal Visions,* he "moved from being on the dole to being a Resident Playwright."

Lynch's initial rise to prominence was bound up with the growth of, and increasing subventions for, community drama in Belfast in the late 1970s. It also coincided with a shift in the artistic establishment from a concern for traditional aesthetics to a concern with reflecting the fault lines in the politics of Northern Ireland through community participation and education. As a proactive representative of the minority Catholic culture, yet well regarded across the political spectrum, Lynch was well placed to benefit from this cultural sea change.

Lynch's first play for the professional theater and his breakthrough work, *Dockers* (performed in 1981, published in 1982)—which is set in the shipyards and takes as its hero a trade unionist—evokes the most famous Ulster play of the 1960s: Sam Thompson's *Over the Bridge* (1960). Lynch identifies *Dockers* as his history, his family, the very color of his existence, and to emphasize the point, he made use of the names of real people for many of its characters and real locations for

Cover for the 1982 publication of Lynch's first professionally produced work, a 1981 play about the shipyard community, in which the hero defies a corrupt union (Lavinger Memorial Library, Georgetown University)

many of its settings. The play is thus aimed squarely at the shipyard community and only secondarily at the general public. To guarantee it found its target audience, dockworkers were bussed in to see the play. In *Personal Visions,* Lynch fondly recollects the impact the material had on this audience:

> When you put a play like *Dockers* on, dock workers are almost watching their lives go by in two hours—their entire lives. If it's a biography of anybody it's a biography of a community, and so these people can collectively watch their lives go by in two hours and it's a pretty powerful emotion.... They don't see their lives on TV or in the newspapers or anywhere else; and suddenly they see it.

The play has clear didactic intentions, with the character of John Graham acting as the vehicle for most of them. At times the play seems to sacrifice the character's voice in favor of direct appeals from playwright to audience. Most notably, in pursuing its message, the play understates the sectarian issue. The climax, set on the route of a Workers Day March, sweeps aside sectarian difference as Catholics and Protestants exchange songs in a Catholic pub with minimal discord, and instead talk of the communities "living together," of showing "toleration" and respecting "the other man's point of view." With sectarianism in silhouette, Lynch is able to direct sympathy toward the social idealist Graham and allow his theme to emerge: that the workers hold the key to resolving the North's problems.

Dockers was a big hit. Its success is owed in part to its close relative, director Elia Kazan's 1954 motion picture *On the Waterfront*, written by Budd Schulberg, and Lynch played explicitly on a knowledge of the movie. Thus, Lynch's hero, Graham, takes a stand against the corrupt union, is ostracized by his coworkers, faces a campaign of intimidation, and finally is beaten up by the union heavies (for singing "The Red Flag")—though, in Marlon Brando fashion, he gets up for more. The public appeal was further assured by comic characters such as Buckets McGuinness, the local wag in constant search of a free lunch.

Lynch claimed that with this play he "revolutionised" the nature of the theater audience and spoke of the theatrical establishment being "devastated" by the public response, which drew a new working-class audience to the theater. Despite the hyperbole, by dint of naive enthusiasm and commitment to the issues, *Dockers* shifted local theater onto a new plateau of community interaction.

Lynch's follow-up play for the professional theater, *The Interrogation of Ambrose Fogarty* (performed and published in 1982), sustained the public interest in his work. It is a Troubles play that tells of the arrest of a suspect in a bank robbery and of his subsequent abuse and torture while in police custody. Unlike most Troubles plays—which are conciliatory, condemn violence, and attempt to promote understanding—*The Interrogation of Ambrose Fogarty* is an indictment of internment and, as such, it was one of the most controversial plays ever produced in Northern Ireland. It appeared in 1982 before the events surrounding the release of the Guildford Four and Birmingham Six—two groups of people who were wrongfully convicted for bombings on the British mainland in the 1970s and were eventually released from prison and exonerated, but not before serving substantial jail sentences.

In an attempt to preempt criticism, the play came with a conciliatory program note from Ciaran McKeown, leader of the Peace People, the local organization that had won the Nobel Peace Prize in 1976:

> If violence begetting violence is to be replaced by an understanding begetting understanding, whether on the streets of Belfast or across the nuclear threatened divide of the Northern hemisphere, human beings must have the courage to look at the unpleasantness, the crude viciousness, the mind-freezing bitterness, the heart-hardening cruelty, then look beyond to find the humanity on the other side of the rubble-strewn wasteland. . . . Martin Lynch, a child of one tradition, and long-time resident of Turf Lodge which knows so much of barricades, of terrorism, of official and unofficial regression, has taken a courageous step for all of us with *The Interrogation of Ambrose Fogarty*.

Nevertheless, the play provoked acute controversy. There were accusations that it engaged with bigotry and "tribal propaganda," that it would repel and embitter and "drive yet another wedge between the two [Catholic and Protestant] communities" (*Belfast Telegraph*, 2 February 1982). In the same article Lynch's contemporary, the playwright Graham Reid, also added his voice in condemnation, accusing Lynch of being arrogant and politically irresponsible and of attempting "to unite the working class behind their discontent."

The controversy surrounding the play was tied up with Lynch's approach to his subject. In his concern to focus on the rights of the individual, he directs all his sympathies to the internee and overlooks the wider political picture. Furthermore, in the figure of Ambrose Fogarty, he presents not just a working-class hero but (like John Graham in *Dockers*, who keeps singing despite being beaten up) a working-class martyr. Where Fogarty practices noncooperation, he does so in defense of the rights of the individual rather than to obstruct police procedure. And eventually, when he emerges from the police station, having been tortured for three days, he does so unbowed and with his ideals intact. The police force, meanwhile, are presented as unprincipled, cynical, and brutish. They assume the guilt of those they arrest, and they employ "no holds barred" tactics including bribery, blackmail, and violence to obtain convictions. After Fogarty has been beaten, he asks: "Why do they do it?" and later makes the statement: "Christ, it's a sick society that can throw up police stations where people are beaten up systematically. And a sick police force that carries it out."

In a 1982 interview with Ian Kirk-Smith, Lynch acknowledged his prejudices, admitting he was brought up "despising policemen" and thinking of them as "*Black* bastards" (in Northern Ireland, *Black* is a derogatory term for Protestants). However, he also vouched that the play is not a misrepresentation of the experience of being interned—he was arrested twenty-two times during the Troubles but never charged with any criminal offenses—and that everything depicted onstage had happened to him. In this respect, Lynch identifies the play not only as a protest but also as part of a campaign designed to bring the methods of the Royal Ulster Constabulary (RUC) to public attention and to advance the case for an independent police complaints tribunal. Amid the controversy, the play achieved full houses, successfully promoting both debate on the issue of police brutality and Lynch as Northern Ireland's most angry young playwright.

Having attracted working-class audiences to the theater with these two plays, Lynch next sought to bring the theater to working-class Belfast. In 1983 Marie Jones, a local actress (and later writer of plays such as *A Night in November* [1995] and the Broadway-produced *Stones in His Pocket* [1997]), approached him with a request to write a play for the newly formed Charabanc Theatre Company. This group was made up of five actresses frustrated by the scarcity of good theatrical roles available to them. Lynch agreed to help out, but as a collaborator rather than author. The plays that followed—*Lay Up Your Ends* (performed in 1983), which deals with the 1911 linen industry strike in Belfast, and *Oul' Delf and False Teeth* (performed in 1984), which deals with the election of 1949—were dedicated simultaneously to documenting forgotten social histories and celebrating local cultural identity.

This initiative had several far-reaching effects. The first of these concerned the working process that the company instigated. Based on the method of composition developed by Ann Jellicoe in the south of England in the late 1970s, this process entailed researching and conducting interviews in the community and creating improvisations from the results. This approach, though well established elsewhere, was revolutionary in the context of Northern Irish theater and consequently provided a new impetus and a new model for other local theater groups. In addition, the initiative had a significant impact on the complexion of Northern Irish theater. It provided the first step toward establishing Charabanc as a theatrical force that went on to become—along with Field Day—among the most important, and most exported, British/Irish theater companies of the 1980s. Moreover, it launched Jones as a dramatist in her own right. Following her collaborations with Lynch, she continued as writer in residence for Charabanc for the next seven years and subsequently founded her own company, Dubbel Joint.

For its own part, Lynch's career continued to consolidate. Having been adopted by the theatrical establishment, he was appointed in 1985 as writer in residence at the University of Ulster, a position he held for three years. However, the anticipated synergy between an active and contemporary writer and the local literary establishment was underrealized. There

Cover for the published version of Lynch's controversial 1982 play about a bank-robbery suspect who is beaten and abused while in police custody (Howard-Tilton Memorial Library, Tulane University)

was an unresolved tension in the idea of how his skills might best be put to use in this new setting. Lynch's brand of populism was predicated on operating not from within, but from outside the establishment. His aesthetic fundamentally opposed ruling-class, academic values. Some indication of this tension is evident in the works he produced during this period, which were a significant departure from his early explorations.

The first of these works concerned a brief flirtation with Hollywood when Lynch became co-author of the screenplay for *A Prayer for the Dying* (1987), a potboiler based on the best-selling novel by Jack Higgins about an IRA terrorist who, while attempting to blow up a British military target, accidentally bombs a bus full of schoolchildren. Wracked with guilt, the terrorist escapes to London and strikes up a deal with a British gangster to get papers and cash to go to America. In return, however, he must carry out one last hit—which gets complicated when it is witnessed by a priest. The cast included Bob Hoskins as the priest, Alan Bates as the gangster, Mickey Rourke as the terrorist, and Liam Neeson in a supporting role. But the project was, nevertheless, awash with problems both pre- and postproduction. The original director, Franc Roddam, left the shoot midway through, while Rourke attempted to disassociate himself from the movie after its release, and critics panned it as politically crass.

Lynch followed this celluloid venture with a return home and the play *Welcome to Bladonmore Road* (performed in 1988, published in 2003), which premiered at the Arts Theatre in Belfast. This comic examination of the clash of working-class and middle-class manners seemed to offer some indication of the anxiety attendant with his own recently altered social and economic status. The critical responses to the work were, however, among the most negative of his career (*Irish Times*, 29 November 1988). Lynch's time at the University of Ulster thus brought the early and most prolific phase of his career to a close.

He emerged from the experience with a desire to return to his roots. Claiming to be "fed up" with the rigors of professional theater and to yearn once again to "make theatre with ordinary people," he involved himself with the Short Strand Community Group. His play for the Short Strand, *The Stone Chair* (performed in 1989), was another sociohistorical documentary based on the recollections of the people of East Belfast during the Blitz of 1941. *The Stone Chair*, Belfast's first large-scale community play, ran at the premier local theatrical venue, the Grand Opera House, for ten nights and proved Lynch's biggest critical success for nearly a decade.

This high point could not, however, mask the erratic relationship that he had had with local critics. In his most generous reviews, he had been designated a "folk hero," a writer of "social drama at its best" (*Irish News*, 8 June 1983), and, in one particularly unrestrained piece of criticism, "a modern day Sean O'Casey" (*Coleraine Chronicle*, 12 February 1982). But in general the perception was that his work was technically deficient and hampered by political affectation. As if acknowledging the validity of these assessments, as the 1980s progressed, Lynch began to express a new attitude toward his work. He rejected his early "starry-eyed" desire to change the world and instead spoke of the intention to "simply write good theatre and drama" (*Belfast Newsletter*, 6 November 1985, and *Irish Times*, 13 June 1989).

Pictures of Tomorrow (performed in 1994, published in 1996) is set in London in the 1990s and tells the story of a reunion of Len, Ray, and Hugo, three old comrades from the Spanish Civil War. At first glance the play appears typical of Lynch's work. The reunion serves as a frame for a recollection of another of Belfast's forgotten histories: Irish and British involvement—and cooperation with each other—in the war against General Francisco Franco's Fascist Party. Initially, the memory of this event appears to be underpinned by romance. There is an idealistic yearning for the comradeship of wartime and that special period of social history when men and women from all over the world joined "the most unusual army assembled in the history of the world," the International Brigade.

However, there is an increasing degree of unreality to this depiction of the past. The utopian moment has passed, and in light of the political events of the late 1980s and early 1990s, it is now forever unattainable:

> The Berlin Wall coming down was like one of those slow motion dreams you have, where you're falling from a high building and you're powerless to do anything about it. When the Soviet Union collapsed I hit the ground . . . I stuck it out, right through Hungary, 1956. I remember feeling uneasy about Czechoslovakia in 1968, but I believed it had to be done. The doubts were shoved all the way to the back of my head. But now even the Russian people have rejected it. It's all come to a very, very sad and confusing end.

These words, spoken by Ray, indicate that a new realism seems to be setting in. With an awareness that "the Spanish civil war ended years ago," idealism is displaced by a questioning of youthful convictions, by late-life anxiety, and by a dissection of socialist mythology. Consequently, the play is pervaded by a sense of regret and disappointment, a sense of "all those wasted years." Past commitment has led not to fulfillment but to mistakes and unhappiness. The choices made in the name of political duty have haunted the characters throughout their lives, and all three experience disquiet over those choices: Ray for breaking off an engagement; Hugo for estranging himself from his father; and Len for "driving his mother to an early grave." And of course above these past hurts, most of all, is the regret for the lost lives of the young men who did not come home. As if to emphasize the inability to transcend the past, the phrase "manos arriba" (hands up) is the refrain throughout the play. This sense is intensified as the play culminates in a roll call of the dead—a dramatic device widely employed in Irish literature. Here, however, the incantation of the "heroes" of the past is not romantic indulgence, it is rather a means of providing closure. Thus, the play ends not in reverie but in a return to the present as Ray goes off to a retirement home—and a fresh start, of a kind.

In light of this period of reevaluation, Lynch's later plays have increasingly been the site of heterogeneous cultural influences. Adopting the methodologies of companies such as Welfare State, his community work has demonstrated a new sophistication and readiness to experiment in its use of space, time, scale, and spectacle.

Similarly, his plays for mainstream theater have evidenced a new willingness to engage with established cultural traditions. This shift has made explicit what has been present throughout his career: a desire less to reject orthodox cultural values than to somehow accommodate them within the frame of community work. Finally, his political work has also taken on a new complexion in making use of methodologies that blur the line between fact and fiction further than ever before and stretch the formal constraints of theater with the techniques of street theater, the political rally, and stand-up comedy.

This phase of Lynch's career began with *The Wedding Community Play* (performed in 1999), a return to collaboration with Jones as part of the Belfast Festival at Queen's University. It took fifteen months to develop and involved more than ninety performers from six community theater groups from across East and West Belfast. The piece began in the center of Belfast and involved the audience moving from site to site. The spectators were first taken by bus to a house in the Catholic Short Strand to witness the preparations of the groom, followed by a trip to the Protestant Templemore Avenue to observe the bride and her family. At these sites, the sense of ceremony was ensured by splitting the audience into groups and taking them from room to room and house to house. The performers, meanwhile, remained stationary and repeated their scenes for each new audience. The characters established, the audience was then taken back to the city center and a church, where a mock wedding ceremony was held. Finally, the day was capped with celebration and a trip to a nightclub for the reception, where the event ended in music, dancing, and refreshments. In terms of its theme and content, the play offered little more than a reworking of what Christopher Murray has referred to as the "Romeo and Juliet typos," the much-explored topic of a love affair between protagonists from the Catholic and Protestant communities. However, the separation of the audience into different constituencies, the use of multiple performance spaces, the simultaneous and repeated action, and the promenade technique that involved actors and audience journeying through real time and space marked a merging of theatrical and paratheatrical elements unprecedented in Northern Irish theater. The production was thus hailed by many critics as one of "the most affecting" pieces of theater in their experience (*The Guardian*, 16 November 1999).

A similarly innovative approach was evident in Lynch's next collaboration, *Convictions* (performed in 2000). This work was a site-specific piece produced by the local group Tinderbox Theatre Company at the Crumlin Road Courthouse (site of many of Northern Ireland's most notorious paramilitary trials), and it involved seven separate scenes provided by some of Belfast's best-known playwrights. Again, the show was con-

Cover for the 2003 collection that includes Lynch's 1994 play about three Spanish Civil War comrades who reunite and reevaluate their commitment to political idealism and what it cost (O'Neill Library, Boston College)

ceived for a mobile, touring audience, with spectators being conducted in groups around various parts of the courthouse—the holding cells, the courtrooms, the toilets, the jury room, and the judges' chambers—to witness a series of dramatic scenes. The physical characteristics of the space conditioned the content of the piece, with the scenes tailored to their various environments. Giving an indication of the regard with which he is held locally, Lynch provided the centerpiece of the show, *Main Hall: What Did I Know When I Was Nineteen?* a return to the theme that whatever their religious or political differences, the "victims" of the Crumlin Road Court were consistently united by their working-class origin.

This project was, like so many of Lynch's works, a theatrical experience that derived its power from elements beyond the text, but here it drew not on a community aesthetic but rather on place consciousness, on social legacy, on the evocative atmosphere of the building, and on physical impression. The fictional inhabiting of a real setting produced an altered relationship between theater and reality. For many, the performance acted as a reclaiming of the space and as such marked not only a theatrical experience but also an important social and historical event in its own right.

Lynch's subsequent works, *The History of the Troubles (Accordin' to My Da)* and *The Belfast Carmen* (both performed in 2002), have been lighter in tone but continue to offer evidence of an expanding theatrical imagination along with a concern to accommodate diverse cultural influences. As an antidote to the earlier "forgotten history" plays, *The History of the Troubles (Accordin' to My Da)* offers a conventional reading of the Ulster past. It employs the device of personal odyssey as the local innocent, Gerry Courtney, negotiates the landmarks of the Troubles over the previous thirty-five years. Using the method of radical textual and historical compression developed by the Reduced Shakespeare Company, the actors take the audience through rapprochement, civil-rights marches, the arrival of British troops, internment, power sharing, the peace movement, the hunger strikes, and the Anglo-Irish Treaty. The mix of social history, personal tragedy, and stand-up comedy in the play ensured that it had significant marketability. In 2003 it toured Ireland and Irish communities in England. With this play, too, the sense of social conscience persisted, albeit postproduction, with the play returning to Northern Ireland from a run at its most high-profile venue, the Tricycle Theatre in London, to play Maghaberry, Hyde Bank, and Magill Prisons, after which question-and-answer sessions were held with the cast and playwright.

Throughout Lynch's career there has been a clear and particular emphasis in his work. His plays have acted at a level of cultural intervention that has sought to assist individual and community advancement rather than a reconfiguration of society. *The Belfast Carmen,* which was specially written as the centerpiece of the 40th Belfast Festival at Queen's University, and which integrated professional and community aesthetics, brought together opera singers, actors, and the musicians of the Ulster Orchestra with a one-hundred-strong community cast and chorus. This project is the most telling indication to date of an aesthetic imagination less motivated by a desire for radical change, as is the case with many British community drama groups, than for a democratization of the arts.

More than thirty years since the start of the Troubles, Martin Lynch continues to display his origins as a civil-rights and Republican Clubs activist with a concern for egalitarianism above all else. His statements also reinforce this sense by continuing to echo the call for equal opportunities. He speaks of his aim to "raise awareness," to "widen access," to "build structures for ordinary people to participate in the arts," to "empower those who have traditionally been excluded," and to "change the mindset of an arts establishment that looks down on community arts as a kind of social work." This consistent ambition is perhaps, though, most lucidly and neatly summed up in *Personal Visions* as a modest reflection on the overriding aim of his career as a theater-maker: "My hope is that, unlike my father's generation, the next generation will be able to enjoy the arts unhindered by accidents of class, gender or socio-economic background."

Interviews:
"Interview," *Sunday Press,* 1 February 1981;
Cassidy, "Interview with Martin Lynch," *Gown* (June 1981): 23;
Ian Kirk-Smith, "Martin Lynch, The Political Activist, Who Has Turned to Fighting the Vicious Circle of Violence with a Powerful Pen," *Belfast Telegraph,* 26 January 1982;
Fintan O'Toole, "Fun and Laughter and Story Telling," *Sunday Tribune,* 12 June 1983;
Gerald Rafferty, "The Voice of the Dispossessed," *Belfast Telegraph,* 26 March 1984;
"Interview with Martin Lynch," *Irish Press,* 27 April 1984;
In Dublin, 3 May 1984;
Sunday News, 20 October 1985;
Belfast Newsletter, 6 November 1985;
Irish Times, 13 June 1989.

References:
Fintan Brady, "The Politics of Community Theatre," *Causeway* (Spring 1994);
Ophelia Byrne, ed., *The State of Play* (Belfast: Linen Hall Library, 2001);
Roy Connolly, *The Evolution of the Lyric Players Theatre* (Lampeter: Edwin Mellen Press, 2000), pp. 201–226;
Baz Kershaw, *The Politics of Performance: Radical Theatre as Cultural Intervention* (London: Routledge, 1992);
Margaret Llewellyn-Jones, *Contemporary Irish Drama and Cultural Identity* (Bristol: Intellect Books, 2002), pp. 101–106, 146–160;
D. E. S. Maxwell, *Modern Irish Drama* (Cambridge: Cambridge University Press, 1984);
Christopher Murray, *Twentieth Century Irish Drama: Mirror Up to Nation* (Manchester: Manchester University Press, 1997), pp. 188–194;
Our Wedding Video, documentary about the making of *The Wedding Community Play,* Northern Visions, 1999.

Papers:
Papers relating to Martin Lynch may be found in the Lyric Players Theatre Archive in Belfast, and in the Theatre Archive at Linen Hall Library in Belfast.

Owen McCafferty

(13 March 1961 -   )

David Grant
Queen's University, Belfast

PLAY PRODUCTIONS: *Winners, Losers and Non-Runners,* staged reading, Belfast, Lyric Theatre Belfast; full production, Belfast, Old Museum Arts Centre, 13 April 1992;

I Won't Dance, Don't Ask Me, Belfast, Ulster Arts Club, 15 November 1993;

The Waiting List, part of *Angels with Split Voices* by McCafferty and others, Belfast, Old Museum Arts Centre, 18 April 1994;

The Private Picture Show, Belfast, Lyric Theatre Belfast, 22 November 1994;

Freefalling, Enniskillen, Ardhowen Theatre, 2 February 1996;

Shoot the Crow, Galway, Druid Lane Theatre, 26 February 1997; Manchester, Royal Exchange, February 2003;

Mojo-Mickybo, Dublin, Andrews Lane Theatre, 15 October 1998;

Court Room No. 1, part of *Convictions* by McCafferty and others, Belfast, Crumlin Road Courthouse, 30 October 2000;

A Scene from the Bridge, by McCafferty and Damian Gorman, Armagh, The Market Place, 20 August 2001;

No Place Like Home, Belfast, Northern Bank Building, Bridge Street, 27 October 2001;

Closing Time, London, National Theatre, 9 September 2002; Dublin, Tivoli Theatre, 8 October 2002;

The Chairs, adapted from Eugène Ionesco's *Les Chaises,* Armagh, The Market Place, 5 March 2003;

Scenes from the Big Picture, London, Cottesloe Theatre (National Theatre), 10 April 2003; Pasadena, Pasadena Playhouse Balcony Theatre, 19 October 2004;

Days of Wine and Roses, adapted from J. P. Miller's script, London, Donmar Warehouse, 17 February 2005.

BOOKS: *Mojo-Mickybo* (Belfast: Lagan, 1998);

Plays & Monologues (Belfast: Lagan, 1998)—comprises *Shoot the Crow; Damage Done; The Waiting List; Free-*

Owen McCafferty (National Theatre, Belfast; courtesy of the Linen Hall Library, Belfast)

falling; I Won't Dance, Don't Ask Me; and *The Private Picture Show;*

Convictions (Belfast: Tinderbox Theatre Company, 2000);

No Place Like Home (Belfast: Tinderbox Theatre Company, 2001);

Closing Time (London: Nick Hern, 2002);

Mojo-Mickybo: Three Plays (London: Nick Hern, 2002)—comprises *Mojo-Mickybo; The Waiting List;* and *I Won't Dance, Don't Ask Me;*

The Chairs, adapted from Eugène Ionesco (Belfast: Tinderbox Theatre Company, 2003);

Shoot the Crow (London: Nick Hern, 2003);

Scenes from the Big Picture (London: Nick Hern, 2003).

PRODUCED SCRIPTS: *The Elasticity of Supply and Demand,* radio, BBC Radio 3, 30 December 2000; *The Law of Diminishing Returns,* radio, BBC Radio 3, 25 October 2002.

The recognition of Owen McCafferty's work outside Ireland through productions of his plays at the Royal Exchange in Manchester and London's National Theatre in 2002 and 2003 vindicates his long-held position that Irish playwrights should not be circumscribed by external expectations of what constitutes an "Irish play." Throughout his work he has resisted the pressure to conform to categorization, a risk to which writers from the north of Ireland are especially prone. To this extent, his work sits outside the well-established genre of "Troubles Drama" into which many of the plays from and about Northern Ireland between 1970 and 1994 can usefully be grouped. Although his work is inevitably influenced by the environment in which he has grown up, the headline-catching events in Northern Ireland since 1970 provide the backdrop rather than the themes for his drama.

McCafferty was born in Belfast on 13 March 1961. With his father, Gerry McCafferty, the manager of a bookmaker's office, and his mother, Rosemary (née Crosby), a civil servant, he moved to London shortly after he was born. Despite the absence of an overt theatrical heritage, he acknowledges the influence of both his parents. His mother took him to the movies and big musicals in London, and his father took him to see Sammy Davis Jr. perform live. Later, he saw productions of plays by writers such as Sean O'Casey and the northern Irish writer George Shiels, each of whom wrote in a distinctive vernacular style. He recalls that his mother was a beautiful singer and that his father, who was involved in amateur drama as a young man, had a way with language—an inventiveness that allowed him to create his own words.

The family returned to Belfast in 1971, when McCafferty was ten years old. The demographic tide in Belfast as the Troubles took hold in the early 1970s was emphatically in the opposite direction, and young McCafferty, with his alien Cockney accent, was thrown into the shifting world of Belfast's Lower Ormeau Road—an area known for the increasing polarization of its Protestant and Catholic communities.

Born into the Roman Catholic tradition, McCafferty attended the local St. Augustine's Secondary School until 1979. Having worked for a year in the government civil service, he went to the United States for four months, after which he returned to Belfast and found work in an abattoir. He then took his A-level examinations at Belfast's College of Business Studies, which qualified him in 1984 at the age of twenty-three for admission to a degree course in philosophy and linguistics at the Ulster Polytechnic in Jordanstown. In that same year, he married Peggy Carlin, an office worker. Finding the linguistics course not to his taste, he switched to pure philosophy, graduating three years later.

He toyed with the idea of enrolling for a Ph.D. in existentialism, with a view to becoming a university lecturer, but on being advised that employment prospects in Northern Ireland in that field were poor, he chose instead to train as an accountant. After two years he realized that this career path was not a life option and left to run an office, which he did for two years. He then stopped working to look after his children, Matthew and Paula. A subsequent government job proved short-lived, and eventually he went to work with his wife's brother as a tiler.

McCafferty's father died in 1985, and shortly afterward McCafferty began to write short stories. He joined the Belfast Writers Group at the Linen Hall Library (an important Belfast cultural landmark dating from the radical days of the United Irishmen's failed rebellion in 1798 and retaining much of that movement's thwarted spirit), but he did not really feel he had the drive to live the life of a writer. After he made a few unsuccessful attempts to get published, his wife observed that his stories were full of dialogue and that perhaps he should try writing a play. During his university studies, he had written a dissertation as a duologue between two living philosophers, and his tutor, who had been taught by one of them, commented that he had captured exactly the man's pattern of speech. Encouraged by this experience, McCafferty turned his hand to playwriting.

When his wife's father became involved in *The Stone Chair,* a large-scale community play at Belfast's Grand Opera House in 1989, McCafferty took the opportunity to make contact with its author, the well-established Belfast playwright Martin Lynch. He sent Lynch a copy of his first play, *Winners, Losers and Non-Runners;* Lynch recommended the script to the Lyric Theatre Belfast, where it was included in a season of rehearsed readings. Although it was well received, in an uncertain time for the Lyric, the hope that it would receive a full production came to nothing. In the meantime, disenchanted with the Lyric, Lynch and McCafferty revived the Point Fields Theatre Company banner under which Lynch had staged his boxing play, *Rinty* (1990), and in 1992 he directed *Winners, Losers and Non-Runners* as part of a double bill with *Justice* by Hugh Murphy. Although he received mixed reviews and the play remains unpublished, McCafferty was encouraged by frequent references to his good ear for dialogue.

McCafferty's dissatisfaction with his first play centered on the need he perceived for its protagonist to have more time on the stage on his own. "His voice wasn't big enough," McCafferty recalled in an unpublished interview with David Grant on 24 May 2003, "The drama that was surrounding him seemed to me to be tacked on." The Belfast-based actor-manager Sean Caffrey had been in the cast of the reading of the play at the Lyric, and one night at Belfast's Arts Club he and McCafferty discussed the possibility of a play for one actor based on the central character of *Winners, Losers and Non-Runners.* Caffrey performed the resulting play, *I Won't Dance, Don't Ask Me,* to great acclaim in 1993, convincing McCafferty that his analysis of the shortcomings of his earlier play had been right.

In *I Won't Dance, Don't Ask Me,* fifty-four-year-old Gus McMahon is awake in his living room at four o'clock in the morning with only Sparky the cat for company. Now unemployed and with prostate trouble, he recalls the key choices in his life, his career as a bookie's clerk, and the missed opportunities that might have prevented him from ending up disregarded by his wife and son, who are asleep upstairs. The play is McCafferty's first attempt to put a whole life onstage.

McCafferty stayed with the monologue form for his next play, *The Waiting List* (performed in 1994, published in 1998), but whereas *I Won't Dance, Don't Ask Me* told the story of a man nearing the end of a long life full of frustration and disappointment, *The Waiting List* drew more directly on McCafferty's personal life. The play presents the night thoughts of a man locking up his house at bedtime in a so-called interface area of Belfast (that is, where Catholic and Protestant districts met) at a period (in early 1994, just months before the first IRA cease-fire) when there had been enough frequent, random sectarian killings to make him reflect on his own mortality. His life meanders rather than flashes before him, and the text touches fleetingly on an idea that McCafferty returns to more extensively in his later success *Mojo-Mickybo* (performed and published in 1998): the loss of childhood innocence that was a reality for so many Belfast children of his generation. The questions "Where you from?" "What school do you go to?" "What football team do you support?" and the request "Say the alphabet" all mean the same thing–"Are you a Catholic or a Protestant?" The alphabet question is an insidious reflection of the segregated education system in Northern Ireland that results in young Catholics and Protestants pronouncing the letter *H* in different ways.

One incident during McCafferty's teenage years, which he alludes to in several plays, made an indelible impression on him. The murder of one of his teachers in his local youth club is described vividly in *The Waiting List:*

Cover for the 2003 edition of McCafferty's 1997 play about four tile workers who plot to steal construction materials while they ponder their roles as workers and providers (University of Tennessee–Knoxville Libraries)

I'm standing in the gym this night, not half-a-brick's throw away from the table tennis room, watching fellas with low cheek bones beat the shit out of each other. Bang, bang, bang, bang. You see there was a pane of glass missing from one of the windows in the table tennis room, and if you had a mind to, if you put yourself out a bit, you could have climbed over the wall, crawled through the long grass on your elbows and knees like a commando, aimed a gun through the missing pane and [Pause] if you had a mind to. A hole in the head, thick purple blood on a cord jacket. A smart man with brains hanging out of him.

Running through the narrator's history in *The Waiting List* is a sense of the unpredictability of the course life takes, a feeling reflected in the course of McCafferty's own emergence as a playwright.

Point Fields Theatre Company presented *The Waiting List* as part of a program called *Angels with Split*

Voices, which offered opportunities for emerging writers (including Gary Mitchell) to present short monologues. In the same year, the Lyric Theatre expressed interest in McCafferty's new short play, *The Private Picture Show,* which its new artistic director, Robin Midgley, directed for the 1994 Belfast Festival. Midgley also invited Caffrey to revive *I Won't Dance, Don't Ask Me.*

Although produced later, *The Private Picture Show* was actually written before *The Waiting List* and was an attempt to follow up the success of *I Won't Dance, Don't Ask Me* by reverting to a multiple-character format. *The Private Picture Show* rapidly introduces six inhabitants of an old Victorian terrace house that has been converted into flats. It is, as one of these characters describes it, "a dangerous place . . . everyone thinks they're just passing through, there's something better round the corner and then without knowing it they're stuck here, forever." The action of the play shifts in and out of focus, sometimes seeming real but more often conjuring up the dope-driven imagination of Iggy, the thirty-eight-year-old writer who is its central character. The play ends poised on the moment in which Iggy takes up his pencil to write, suggesting that everything the audience has seen has been a snapshot in his mind's eye.

McCafferty has both good and bad memories of the play. As he explained to Grant: "I was trying to be too smart by half–trying to experiment with the notion of form–and forgot to tell a story." But, he added, "it was *The Private Picture Show* that allowed me to be inventive, because once you've written something like that and you realise that you've got away with it . . . you're not frightened any more of something not being naturalistic."

McCafferty analyzes the development of his own craftsmanship in dialectical terms: *I Won't Dance, Don't Ask Me* placed the emphasis on narrative; *The Private Picture Show* emphasized form; and *The Waiting List* represented a synthesis of the two. He sees *The Waiting List* as a pivotal point in his development as a dramatist. As he told Grant: "Once *The Waiting List* had gone on, that completely freed me up. I realised then you can use the stage in a much freer way." He stated that the play "also showed me how important the contribution of the director and the actor was. All three elements are needed to create the entire world. That has stood me in good stead over the years."

After *The Waiting List* came *Freefalling* (performed in 1996, published in 1998) and *Shoot the Crow* (performed in 1997, published in 1998), which he wrote back-to-back. *Freefalling* was commissioned by a newly formed young people's theater company called Virtual Reality. The play built on what he had learned in *The Waiting List* but was different from anything he had been asked for before: it was to be for a young audience and a cast of two.

Virtual Reality teamed up with a new Belfast theater company called Kabosh, whose director, Karl Wallace, directed the production. In many ways *Freefalling,* in which the two actors shift seamlessly between multiple roles in a kind of staged "road movie," became the prototype for the later *Mojo-Mickybo.* The main characters in *Freefalling* are named simply Him and Her. Each is facing the routine frustrations of teenage life, their exotic ambitions contrasting markedly with the humdrum existence of college and dead-end jobs. Her lures Him into a stolen car, and they briefly enjoy an unfamiliar freedom, until the discovery of a revolver results in a murderous escalation of their reckless adventure.

Where *Freefalling* adopted the fluid physicality of *The Waiting List,* McCafferty's next play, *Shoot the Crow,* was more naturalistic in style. McCafferty has described *Shoot the Crow* as his "work-play" in that it sets out to capture the whole of a working life in one day. He achieves this aim by providing a range of tile workers' perspectives, from that of the nineteen-year-old Randolph to that of the sixty-five-year-old Ding Ding, who is on his last day of work before retirement. The other two characters, Petesy and Socrates, are both in their thirties. The plot revolves around rival schemes to pilfer tiles, but the real substance of the drama concerns the role of men in a changing world. Ding Ding is terrified of the implied meaninglessness of a life in retirement, while Petesy and Socrates are both preoccupied with their paternal responsibilities. Socrates' situation is heightened by the fact that he is separated from his wife and child. The dialogue displays an idiomatic energy and an authenticity grounded in McCafferty's own work as a tiler.

Point Fields, the company that had commissioned *Shoot the Crow,* folded before the play could be produced, but one of its directors, Joe Devlin, sent the play to Garry Hynes, the artistic director of the Druid Theatre Company in Galway. Hynes recognized the originality of the writing and immediately offered to put the play into production. It had a successful six-week run in Galway, and although critics drew comparisons with the similar structure of Jimmy Murphy's *Brothers of the Brush* (1993), *Shoot the Crow* clearly sits apart from such traditional socialist drama, just as McCafferty's other work cannot be confined within the boundaries of "Troubles plays." *Shoot the Crow* is, if anything, more concerned with sexual politics than socialism.

McCafferty is sanguine about the connections critics choose to make between himself and other writers. As he told Grant: "You get used to comparisons. At the moment I'm Belfast's answer to David Mamet, Eugene O'Neill, Gorky, Sean O'Casey and Edward Bond!" A more obvious running theme in McCafferty's work is the classic preoccupation of good drama with "the human condition." *The Waiting List* was a continuation of McCafferty's conscious ambition to put a complete life onstage. To that extent it can be seen as the precursor of *Closing*

Time (performed and published in 2002) and *Scenes from the Big Picture* (performed and published in 2003), both of which evoke what McCafferty described to Grant as a "normal but generic day." The fact that the ordinary and the extraordinary enjoy such a close coexistence in these plays is at the heart of McCafferty's philosophy.

"I begin with the structure of the play," he said in his interview with Grant. "Then I write three drafts, and by the time I do that the play is near enough complete. I write the first draft and there will always be something in the first draft, which at the start I thought wasn't that significant. I'll discover it in the second draft, and then consequently the play will be about that in the third draft."

The success of *Shoot the Crow* led to an invitation from Kabosh to write a stage version of director Alan Parker's 1984 motion picture *Birdy* (based on William Wharton's 1979 novel), in keeping with the company's then-current "film and theatre" policy. When rights turned out not to be available, McCafferty offered to write an original play to the same specifications—a two-person play with a cinematic connection. An initial idea about two boys united by a bonding game based around the movie *Butch Cassidy and the Sundance Kid* (1969) developed into a telling evocation of a child's growing awareness of sectarianism in McCafferty's phenomenally successful *Mojo-Mickybo*. Two boys in Belfast in the summer of 1970 meet and become firm friends. They play at being cowboys, team up against the bullying of rival kids, meet each other's families and neighbors, and go on a spontaneous outing to the seaside. On returning home they find that Mickybo's father has been shot dead and are confronted by the cruel reality that their Protestant and Catholic backgrounds are ultimately what define them. Given McCafferty's English accent as a child, his portrayal of the Catholic youngster who narrates the story of the play cannot be entirely autobiographical, but the writing carries an undeniable hallmark of authenticity.

The stark memory of the killing of McCafferty's youth-club leader, described in *The Waiting List,* also informed the unexpectedness of the moment of brutality that is the catalyst for Mojo's and Mickybo's loss of innocence. The fast-moving text, in which two actors play seventeen characters, inspired award-winning performances from original actors Niall Shanahan and Fergal McElherron, and the production toured widely, changing casts several times.

When McCafferty was approached in 1999 by Tinderbox Theatre Company to contribute to *Convictions* (performed in 2000), an imaginative site-specific project in Belfast's disused Crumlin Road Courthouse, the youth-club incident found yet another manifestation. Lalor Roddy, who had performed in *The Waiting List*, became in this play, as Ian Hill described him in the *Belfast News Letter* (1 November 2000), "the ghost of victims past, caught

Cover for the 2002 collection that includes McCafferty's 1998 play about two boys in 1970 Belfast who realize that their friendship cannot transcend the fact that one is Catholic and the other Protestant (University of Tennessee–Knoxville Libraries)

in Owen McCafferty's Kafkaesque *Huis Clos* from which he will be released only when the murderer is made amenable." The haunting quality of McCafferty's language established *Courtroom No. 1* (each of the seven plays by different writers were named after the rooms in which they were performed), in which the dead victim of a terrorist murder accuses his attacker before an unseen interrogator, as one of the most memorable components of this extraordinary theatrical event.

Seeking to build on the success of *Convictions,* and in particular the way in which it had drawn on the creativity of an amalgam of different kinds of artists, Tinderbox then invited McCafferty to work alongside a visual artist, a composer, actors, and a choreographer to create *No Place Like Home* (performed in 2001), a new kind of theatrical event for Belfast. Video and installation art were combined with drama and movement. This ambition was one for which he had great sympathy. "I was very enthu-

Cover for the published text of McCafferty's 2003 play, a collection of vignettes about Irish life that emphasizes universal concerns (University of Tennessee–Knoxville Libraries)

siastic about *No Place Like Home,*" he said in his interview with Grant; "This was an opportunity for a group of artists to see if there was a theatrical way of telling a uniquely Belfast story. I didn't feel that had ever happened. We hadn't created a form of theatre that suited our own environment. I felt this was a genuine attempt to do that. There was something very interesting about going into a situation where all the elements had equal power."

The significance of this experiment was not lost on Fintan O'Toole, the influential critic of *The Irish Times,* who began his 2 November 2000 review by observing that the reason the Troubles had inspired relatively little lasting drama was because naturalism has been its dominant form:

> Owen McCafferty's text is superbly effective when it gives a wry Belfast inflection to broad metaphors. The notion of Archimedes (who first grasped the principle of displacement) as a Belfast plumber . . . is inspired.

The reduction of victims to banal clichés rings more bells than a royal wedding.

The text is poetically impressionistic rather than narrative. It evokes images of exile and dispossession, which, while rooted in the Belfast experience of the 1970s when hundreds of families were driven from their homes, have clear associations with the plight of refugees everywhere.

At the same time that he was working on *No Place Like Home,* McCafferty also collaborated with his close contemporary Damian Gorman on a new commission for the Ulster Youth Theatre. Delays in confirming funding prevented this project from being the integrated process both had hoped for, but McCafferty contributed the overall structure as well as the second half of the text, with Gorman providing the characters and the first half. Influenced by Luigi Pirandello's *Six Characters in Search of an Author* (1921), the eventual text, *A Scene from the Bridge* (performed in 2001), deconstructed established youth theater practice, depicting the well-meaning author of a documentary play confronted with the acid response of her young subjects. Invited to see a dress rehearsal, the youths persuade the actors to reenact their own version of the truth, but this scenario in turn gives way to a flashback to the real events. In the first version a boy who has fallen to his death is represented as having heroically tried to remove a Nazi flag from a symbolic Peace Bridge. In his friends' version, he is shown to have been putting the flag up in protest at the facile symbolism of the bridge. In the real version, there is no such clear intent, and he is revealed to have been just clowning around. The subjectivity of each of the earlier theatrical versions is thus laid bare. The sparse truthfulness of McCafferty's final representation of the real events foreshadowed the authenticity of his portrayal of the younger characters in *Scenes from the Big Picture,* just as the more mature characters in that play have their prototypes in McCafferty's next work, *Closing Time.*

Closing Time, McCafferty told Grant, "is about closure. In order to move on you need closure. Even though it was seen as quite a bleak play, all the characters do move on, if only in a tiny way. There's a chink of light." Aptly described by Paul Taylor in his subsequent review of *Scenes from the Big Picture* (London *Independent,* 22 April 2003) as a "Long Night's Boozing into Day," the play is set in a run-down hotel, probably in the same section of Belfast as *The Waiting List* and *Mojo-Mickybo.*

Robbie is the publican, who begins each day nurturing hope for the future development of his business, only to lose faith as night and the drink set in. His wife, Vera, seems perpetually on the verge of leaving him but somehow never does. And his customers also dwell in an expectant torpor. The critic Michael Billington (*The Guardian,* 11 September 2002) considered it "impossible not to see the play as a metaphor for Northern Ireland's own political stasis." The older characters have lived their entire adult lives through the Troubles, but as so often in McCafferty's portrayal of the city, history is a shadow hanging over the action, not its driving force. As in *Mojo-Mickybo,* it makes its explicit presence felt only once, toward the end of the play.

As if to underline the fact that lost illusions are not unique to Northern Ireland, McCafferty's next production was *The Chairs* (performed in 2003), a new version of Eugène Ionesco's *Les Chaises* (1952). As Karen Fricker observed in *The Guardian* (2 April 2003), "McCafferty has a wonderfully poetic ear for language . . . exploiting the musicality of local speech to ironically point up the emptiness that the couple are trying to fill through their compulsive storytelling." Despite an occasional local reference, however, topical resonances were light. Paul Devlin commented in the *Irish Theatre Magazine* (Summer 2003): "McCafferty's version of *The Chairs* succeeds so well precisely because it doesn't insist on the analogy (with Northern Ireland). It's a bigger play than that." *The Chairs* has connections with McCafferty's own unperformed short play, *Damage Done* (published in 1998), which, like the Ionesco play, hovers between reality and the absurd with telling poignancy.

Director Peter Gill's fast-moving production of McCafferty's next play opened at the National Theatre just weeks after *The Chairs* premiered. *Scenes from the Big Picture* has a cast of twenty-one, although each is only in the spotlight for moments at a time. "Whereas *Mojo-Mickybo* evokes a whole community," McCafferty explained to Grant, "in *Scenes from the Big Picture* you actually see them on stage. Scale in a small space has an impact in its own right. The play is linked in a way to *Mojo-Mickybo* and *The Waiting List* where you see lives criss-crossing, but in style it's different. I wanted to tell as many stories on stage as I could in one go."

As Peter Hepple observed in *The Stage* (17 April 2003), "McCafferty takes pains not to differentiate his characters, never letting us know whether they are Catholics or Protestants." McCafferty is quick to confirm that this ambiguity is a conscious policy, motivated by the desire not to instantly alienate a proportion of his local audience once they work out which side they should be on. But outside Northern Ireland this approach has had the additional benefit of lifting his work out of the Troubles groove, allowing Taylor (*London Independent,* 22 April 2003) to conclude that although the Troubles "are an issue in these people's lives . . . *Scenes*—where the sectarian divide is scarcely mentioned—is not an issue-play."

Stylistically, the play represents a synthesis of the strengths of his most successful earlier works, fusing the fluidity of *Mojo-Mickybo* with the depth of characterization of *Closing Time* and *Shoot the Crow*. Gill's decision to place all twenty-one actors like an extra row of the audience at the front of the stage, from where they glided in and out of the action, was much more than a Brechtian conceit. It replicated for each actor the psychology of the multirole performances of *Mojo-Mickybo* by ensuring that despite the fragmented structure of the play, they were kept constantly in touch with the way in which their roles intersect with the "big picture." There is no dominant plot or narrative, rather a kaleidoscope of vignettes.

The success of *Scenes from the Big Picture* depended largely on the deftness with which McCafferty allowed the different story lines to interlink without seeking to tie up loose ends. It is a kind of "chaos theory" onstage, where one character's actions can be seen reflected in another's without the audience's being aware of any explicit causal link. This approach is best exemplified by the closing moment of the play, when a young courting couple crosses the path of the oldest character shortly before he looks heavenward in gentle communion with his dead wife. McCafferty received the Charles Wintour Award for New Playwriting for *Scenes from the Big Picture* in December 2004.

Perhaps Owen McCafferty's greatest achievement to date has been to represent his home environment in a way that convinces his fellow citizens of the truthfulness of what he writes without arousing their innate sense of allegiance, while at the same time providing an insight for outsiders that challenges the stereotypes that the works of many of his Northern Ireland contemporaries often reinforce. His training as a philosopher, combined with his strong sense of identity with the place in which he lives, have produced a growing sense of confidence as he has demonstrated his increasing command of his chosen craft.

On the BBC's website, in one of his few published comments on his work, McCafferty observes,

> being in Belfast, being brought up and living there . . . hasn't influenced my writing a great deal from the point of view of what the outside world sees Belfast as. I'm not a political writer in the sense that my contemporaries probably are . . . I concentrate on the notion of telling human stories as opposed to sticking to political themes.

But the world he portrays, and especially the way in which he uses the English language, clearly displays the importance of his Belfast heritage.

David Mercer

(27 June 1928 - 8 August 1980)

Jeremy Ridgman
Roehampton University

See also the Mercer entry in *DLB 13: British Dramatists Since World War II.*

PLAY PRODUCTIONS: *The Buried Man,* Manchester, Library Theatre, 1 October 1962;

The Governor's Lady, London, Aldwych Theatre, 4 February 1965;

Ride a Cock Horse, London, Piccadilly Theatre, 24 June 1965;

Belcher's Luck, London, Aldwych Theatre, 17 November 1966;

After Haggerty, London, Aldwych Theatre, 26 February 1970;

Flint, London, Criterion Theatre, 5 May 1970;

White Poem, London, Institute of Contemporary Arts, 20 August 1970;

Blood on the Table, London, 1971;

Let's Murder Vivaldi, London, King's Head Evening Theatre, 24 October 1972;

In Two Minds, London, Bush Theatre, May 1973;

Duck Song, London, Aldwych Theatre, 5 February 1974;

Cousin Vladimir, London, Aldwych Theatre, 20 September 1978;

Then and Now, London, Hampstead Theatre, 21 May 1979;

No Limits to Love, London, Warehouse Theatre, 2 October 1980.

BOOKS: *The Generations: A Trilogy of Plays* (London: Calder, 1964); republished as *Collected T.V. Plays: Volume One* (London: Calder, 1981)—comprises *Where the Difference Begins, A Climate of Fear,* and *The Birth of a Private Man;*

Three T.V. Comedies (London: Calder & Boyars, 1966)—comprises *A Suitable Case for Treatment, For Tea on Sunday,* and *And Did Those Feet;*

Ride a Cock Horse (London: Calder & Boyars, 1966; New York: Hill & Wang, 1966);

Belcher's Luck (London: Calder & Boyars, 1967; New York: Hill & Wang, 1967);

David Mercer (photograph by Irving Teitelbaum; from the cover for Cousin Vladimir & Shooting the Chandelier, *1978; Thomas Cooper Library, University of South Carolina)*

The Parachute with Two More T.V. Plays (London: Calder & Boyars, 1967)—comprises *The Parachute, Let's Murder Vivaldi,* and *In Two Minds;*

The Governor's Lady (London: Methuen, 1968);

After Haggerty (London: Methuen, 1970);

On the Eve of Publication, and Other Plays (London: Methuen, 1970)—comprises *On the Eve of Publication, The Cellar and the Almond Tree,* and *Emma's Time;*

Flint (London: Methuen, 1970);

The Bankrupt, and Other Plays (London: Eyre Methuen, 1974)—comprises *The Bankrupt, You and Me and Him, An Afternoon at the Festival,* and *Find Me;*

Duck Song (London: Eyre Methuen, 1974);

Huggy Bear and Other Plays (London: Eyre Methuen, 1977)—comprises *Huggy Bear, The Arcata Promise,* and *A Superstition;*

Providence: Un film pour Alain Resnais, translated into French by Claude Roy (Paris: Gallimard, 1977);

Cousin Vladimir & Shooting the Chandelier (London: Eyre Methuen, 1978);

The Monster of Karlovy Vary & Then and Now (London: Eyre Methuen, 1979);

No Limits to Love (London: Eyre Methuen, 1980).

Collections: *Collected T.V. Plays: Volume Two* (London: Calder, 1981)—comprises *A Suitable Case for Treatment, For Tea on Sunday, And Did Those Feet, Let's Murder Vivaldi, In Two Minds,* and *The Parachute;*

Plays: One (London: Methuen, 1990)—comprises *Where the Difference Begins, A Suitable Case for Treatment, The Governor's Lady, On the Eve of Publication, The Cellar and the Almond Tree, Emma's Time,* and *After Haggerty;*

Plays: Two (London: Methuen, 1994)—comprises *Flint, The Bankrupt, An Afternoon at the Festival, Duck Song, The Arcata Promise, Find Me,* and *Huggy Bear.*

PRODUCED SCRIPTS: *Where the Difference Begins,* television, BBC, 15 December 1961;

A Climate of Fear, television, BBC, 22 June 1962;

A Suitable Case for Treatment, television, BBC, 21 October 1962;

The Birth of a Private Man, television, BBC, 1 February 1963;

The Buried Man, television, Associated Television, 12 February 1963;

For Tea on Sunday, television, BBC, 17 March 1963; another production, 29 March 1978;

A Way of Living, television, ABC, 29 December 1963;

Ninety Degrees in the Shade, English dialogue by Mercer, story by Jiri Mucha and Jiri Weiss, motion picture, Ceskoslovensky Film/Raymond Stross Productions/Filmové Studio Barrandov, 1965;

And Did Those Feet, television, BBC, 2 June 1965;

Morgan: A Suitable Case for Treatment, motion picture, Quintra Films, 1966;

In Two Minds, television, BBC, 1 March 1967;

The Parachute, television, BBC, 21 January 1968;

Let's Murder Vivaldi, television, BBC, 10 April 1968;

On the Eve of Publication, television, BBC, 27 November 1968;

The Governor's Lady, radio, BBC, 31 August 1969;

The Cellar and the Almond Tree, television, BBC, 4 March 1970;

Emma's Time, television, BBC, 13 May 1970;

Family Life, adapted from *In Two Minds,* motion picture, Kestrel Films, 1971;

The Bankrupt, television, BBC, 27 November 1972;

You and Me and Him, television, BBC, 22 February 1973;

An Afternoon at the Festival, television, Yorkshire Television, 6 May 1973;

Barbara of the House of Grebe, adapted from Thomas Hardy's story, television, BBC, 12 December 1973;

A Doll's House, adapted from Henrik Ibsen's play, motion picture, World Film Services, 1973;

Folie á Deux, radio, BBC, 29 January 1974;

The Arcata Promise, television, Yorkshire Television, 22 September 1974;

Find Me, television, BBC, 8 December 1974;

Huggy Bear, television, Yorkshire Television, 11 April 1976;

A Superstition, television, Yorkshire Television, 14 August 1977;

Shooting the Chandelier, television, BBC, 25 October 1977;

Providence, motion picture, Action Films, 1977;

Flint, television, BBC, 15 January 1978;

The Ragazza, television, Yorkshire Television, 23 May 1978;

A Rod of Iron, television, Yorkshire Television, 29 April 1980;

A Dinner of Herbs, television, BBC, 4 August 1988.

By the time of his death at the age of fifty-two, David Mercer had written ten stage plays, five produced movie scripts, and twenty-six plays for television. This "precisely Shakespearean output," as it was described in the (London) *Times* (11 October 1980) by Christopher Hampton, the young dramatist for whom Mercer had acted as a mentor, is all the more remarkable given how much of it was produced for the often derided medium of television. Although first motivated by a belief in theater as "the abiding dramatic expression," he quickly turned to television and can be regarded as the first *auteur* of the medium, responsible for a series of plays that, in Hampton's words, "were to alter, fundamentally, the weight and scope of British television drama."

Mercer was born on 27 June 1928 in Wakefield, in the West Riding section of Yorkshire, the son of an engine driver. His parents, he later recalled in a 1973 interview for *Theatre Quarterly,* were highly respectable and ambitious for their two sons; his father, Edward Mercer, was a staunch union man, and his mother, Helen Steadman Mercer, who had worked as a housemaid, was conservatively puritanical. His early life almost follows the archetypal trajectory of the postwar scholarship boy—the working-class (usually northern) socialist intellectual, uprooted from his class and struggling with his social identity—who populates the work of writers such as David Storey, Dennis Potter, and Trevor Griffiths. However, Mercer failed the "eleven

Leslie Sands as Wilf, Pauline Letts as Margaret, and Nigel Stock as Edgar in Mercer's 1961 BBC television drama Where the Difference Begins, *about the conflicts between a working-class socialist and his educated sons, who come home when their mother is dying (photograph by the BBC; from Don Taylor,* Days of Vision–Working with David Mercer: Television Drama Then and Now, *1990; University of Tennessee–Knoxville Libraries)*

plus" examination that provided the passport to grammar school and university, though his elder brother, Reuben, passed and went on to professional eminence as a scientist. Leaving elementary school at fourteen, Mercer began work as a pathology laboratory technician, a trade he continued to practice during a spell in the Royal Navy from 1945 to 1948. At the age of twenty he went back to education, enrolling at Wakefield Technical College and then winning a place at Durham University to study chemistry. Within a year he had made up his mind to leave the sciences and went to study fine art at King's College, Newcastle upon Tyne, graduating in 1953. There he discovered politics, psychiatry, history, and philosophy, which helped him begin to make ideological sense of his background and upbringing. Urged on by his friend Stanley Eveling, he also started writing short stories.

In Newcastle he met his first wife, Jitka, a Czech exile from the 1948 coup d'état, with whom he moved to Paris, determined to set up as a painter. This personal identification with Czechoslovakia, intensified by life in Paris among Czech, Polish, and Russian émigrés, fed his already developing concern with Central and Eastern European history and the repercussions of the Bolshevik revolution, Nazi occupation, and Stalinism. Much of his work explores the classic dilemma of the "communist without a party," the left-wing Western intellectual alienated from revolutionary politics by the effects of Stalinism in Eastern Europe. Visits to Cuba and the Soviet Union in 1967 and 1968 also fueled this debate, leading Mercer to emerge as one of the most internationalist writers of his generation.

Abandoning his career as a painter within only a few months, Mercer turned to writing; then, with the collapse of his marriage in 1955, he returned to London and a brief, unhappy spell as a teacher. His novel writing also proved fruitless, and in 1957 he suffered a nervous breakdown and was admitted to the Tavistock Clinic in London, where he came into contact with the work of the radical psychoanalyst R. D. Laing. This experience was a crystallizing moment in Mercer's decision to start writing drama. Psychoanalysis not only enabled him to confront the formative forces of family, class, the present, and the past; it also allowed his ideas to take form as dialogue and image. Marxism and madness began to emerge as the principle axes along which

Mercer attempted to synthesize what he later referred to in a 1973 interview with Francis Jarman as the problems of "the individual and society" and "the society that produces the individuals."

In 1958, inspired by having seen Shelagh Delaney's working-class drama *A Taste of Honey* (which premiered that year) and deciding that he could do better, Mercer wrote his first play, the classically autobiographical "A Death in the Family." Originally intended for the stage, the script was optioned by several producers before it found its way, almost by accident, into the hands of the charismatic agent Margaret "Peggy" Ramsay, who took Mercer under her wing. Their relationship developed into one of the most intense of both careers. Failure, Ramsay recalled in an interview with John Ezard in 1988, had made Mercer so nervous he could hardly speak when she first met him, but underneath he was "like a young bull, with a tremendous latent rather dangerous energy." Ramsay helped instill in Mercer the confidence he needed to persevere as a dramatist, quickly getting commissions for him in radio and television and sending him other scripts and classic work–most notably by Georg Büchner and August Strindberg–as models in stagecraft, even obtaining a visa for him to visit Eastern Europe. She also persuaded him to rewrite "A Death in the Family," which she thought was overliterary and needed more of his own personality in it, and showed it to Don Taylor, then a writer and recently BBC-trained drama director. Taylor was keen to work with Mercer in adapting the play for television and persuaded the head of BBC drama to let him direct it. The play was broadcast in 1961 under the new title *Where the Difference Begins*.

This success marked the beginning of a highly fruitful collaboration with Taylor, a relationship that helped to establish Mercer's preeminence within television at a time when, under the patronage of the BBC, a new generation of working-class writers was being attracted to and courted by the medium. East End born and Oxford educated, Taylor was passionate about television drama and compelled by the politics and poetry of Mercer's work. He was also greatly influential in shaping the creative development of the scripts themselves. The collaboration ended in 1965, after six plays together, partly at the behest of Ramsay, who believed that Taylor was now hindering Mercer's development. The two worked together again in 1974 on *Find Me*, a play commissioned by the BBC on the theme of the artist and society, and in 1978 on a remake of their early success *For Tea on Sunday* (broadcast in 1963, published in 1966). Mercer went on to develop similar partnerships with the television director Alan Bridges, the movie director Joseph Losey, and David Jones, who directed much of his stage work at the Royal Shakespeare Company.

During rehearsals for *Where the Difference Begins*, Taylor pressed Mercer to produce a synopsis for a sequel and persuaded the BBC to give him a second commission. This play, *A Climate of Fear* (broadcast in 1962, published in 1964), was followed within another year by *The Birth of a Private Man* (broadcast in 1963, published in 1964), completing what has come to be known as the "Generations" trilogy. With its historical and political scope, as well as its increasingly ambitious experimentation with dramatic form, the trilogy established Mercer's reputation as a television dramatist committed to extending the frontiers of the medium. A seminal drama of class displacement and deracination, *Where the Difference Begins* explores the tensions between Wilf, a working-class socialist in his sixties (like Mercer's father, an engine driver), and his educated sons: one an embittered and directionless idealist, clinging to his socialist beliefs, and the other an aspirational, conservative-minded scientist. From its classic naturalism–the domestic setting, the family gathering as a mother lies dying–springs dialogue marked by an intense sense of poetry, not least in Wilf's final aria, "a savage and dignified testament," as Taylor has described it in an appendix to the first volume of Mercer's *Collected T.V. Plays* (1981), "on a breed of rank and file socialist now vanished or vanishing, and the way of life that was lived by them." Across the rest of the trilogy, however, form and ideological perspective open up as the inherited social tensions are lived out by new generations in the ever more complex political theaters of the Campaign for Nuclear Disarmament and Cold War Europe. The final nightmarish scene of the trilogy, as Colin (Wilf's grandson) is mowed down by a hail of bullets in a deliberately suicidal attempt to climb the Berlin Wall, provides a potent symbol of Mercer's symbiosis of psychological and political dislocation in a world where the grand narratives of ideological certainty already appear to be fracturing.

So-called madness, Mercer maintained in a distinctive echo of Laing, was a function of modern social existence, "a painful and violent attempt by human beings," as he told Sonia Copeland in 1969, "to assert something of themselves which is authentic and valid and individual." The relationship between politics and mental breakdown is further explored in Mercer's most comic work, *A Suitable Case for Treatment* (broadcast in 1962, published in 1966), written at the same time as the trilogy; in the far bleaker *In Two Minds* (broadcast and published in 1967, performed in 1973); and the apocalyptic *For Tea on Sunday*. At the same time, these plays stretch in different directions the formal boundaries of television drama, demonstrating Mercer's

Sarah Badel and Douglas Wilmer in Mercer's 1962 BBC television drama A Climate of Fear, *which followed* Where the Difference Begins *as the second play in Mercer's "Generations" trilogy (photograph by the BBC; from Don Taylor,* Days of Vision–Working with David Mercer: Television Drama Then and Now, *1990; University of Tennessee–Knoxville Libraries)*

growing affinity with the expressionist possibilities of the medium. *A Suitable Case for Treatment* was written in the space of three weeks and, as Mercer later claimed, "broke every rule in the television drama book." It is a quasi-absurdist blend of comic action and surreal fantasy, in which Morgan, a disillusioned communist and failed artist, wreaks havoc in his personal relations in a series of anarchic practical jokes and confrontations, punctuated by movie sequences depicting his obsession with gorillas and dreams of his own Eastern European show trial and execution mixed with footage from movies such as *Battleship Potemkin* (1925).

Motion pictures increasingly became a point of reference in Mercer's work for television. He not only incorporated movie clips into several plays but also wrote about people working in and around the movie industry. In 1965 he provided the English dialogue for a Czech-British coproduction, *Ninety Degrees in the Shade,* the tale of a shop assistant who commits suicide after realizing that her boss has been exploiting her infatuation with him to protect himself from arrest for theft. He adapted *A Suitable Case for Treatment* and later *In Two Minds* for the cinema—the former as *Morgan: A Suitable Case for Treatment* for director Karel Reisz in 1966, and the latter as *Family Life* in 1971, for Ken Loach and producer Tony Garnett. *Morgan* lost much of its surprise in the transfer from the small screen but became a key work in the British "new wave" cinema.

The television version of *A Suitable Case for Treatment* won Mercer a Screenwriters' Guild Award and a carte blanche commission from the BBC. Within a few months, he had sent Taylor the script of *For Tea on Sunday,* a piece of work the producer recognized immediately as "utterly original." What starts off as a light satire on the mores of a group of complacently wealthy young friends is violently disrupted by the arrival of Nicholas, an acquaintance of one of the women, who without warning sets about destroying their flat with an ax. This act is an apocalyptic assault not only on the complacent materialism of Western civilization represented by the friends' world but also on the comfortable, lightweight naturalism of a certain strand of British boulevard comedy that has often embodied that worldview. Of the three hundred phone calls and four hundred letters received by the BBC denouncing the play, the main complaint, Mercer later told Copeland, was about the sight of beautiful furniture being chopped up.

In contrast with these experiments in comic style, *In Two Minds* falls into the category of documentary realism that was beginning to emerge in British television drama during the 1960s. Modeled as a case study in schizophrenia, it charts the descent into eventual catatonia of Kate, a vibrant girl unable to handle the competing expectations of her social world, particularly those exerted by repressive (and in their turn repressed) lower-middle-class parents. In its provocative stance against the medical establishment and institutionalized methods of treatment, particularly electroconvulsive therapy, the play bears the clear imprint of Mercer's affiliation with Laingian antipsychiatry. "The diagnosis schizophrenia," he told the *Times* (London) in 1966, quoting Laing, "is a political act." An opening scene, cut during production, in which Kate watches a television interview about a military crisis and weeps, would have situated the trauma in an even wider ideological context; but the politics throughout is underscored in production by Loach's distinctively forensic, neorealist methods of shooting and editing.

Mercer continued his experimentation with comic artifice, however, in the insidiously unsettling *Let's Murder Vivaldi* (published in 1967, broadcast in 1968, performed in 1972), an account of distrust and infidelity in the relationships of two couples: a well-heeled, middle-aged husband and wife, and a young draftsman and his girlfriend. With its tight, symmetrical structure, its conventional settings (a sleekly modern kitchen and dining room, a shabby, one-room flat, and a country hotel bedroom), and, above all, its brittle, witty dialogue, this play consciously evoked the feel of an elegantly wrought piece of theatrical high comedy: "[Noel] Coward updated and gift-wrapped in razor wire" was how the critic of the *Guardian* (24 June 1988) described it on a rescreening in 1988. The neurotic tension underlying the tightly organized interplay of discreet, middle-class sexual infidelity erupts in moments of unpredictable violence as first the young man slashes his girlfriend's face with a knife and, toward the end, the husband neatly stabs his wife in the stomach.

Fantasy and psychological breakdown as functions of ideological and social crisis are also at the heart of Mercer's early works for the theater. His first stage play, *The Buried Man*, was produced, after a series of rejections and redrafts, by the Library Theatre Manchester in 1962 and dealt with a Yorkshire factory worker who decides to return to the hospital after a mental breakdown rather than live with his family. Although thriving on a certain level of ambiguity, the play was a predominantly naturalistic attempt at capturing with emotional directness the realities of working-class life, and its 1963 adaptation for television remains one of Mercer's most conventional works for the medium. *The Governor's Lady* (performed in 1965, published in 1968), on the other hand, shows the influence of the Theater of the Absurd, as the widow of a British governor in a colonialist territory imagines her husband to be still alive and, in an image reminiscent of Eugène Ionesco's work, he gradually begins to change into a gorilla. Originally written for radio, the play was left unproduced by the BBC until 1969. In the meantime, it was staged in 1965 by the Royal Shakespeare Company as part of an evening of experimental new plays, the first in a series of collaborations with the company that made Mercer, alongside Harold Pinter, the closest they had to a contemporary house dramatist during the 1960s and 1970s.

Mercer's concern with the British upper class and the trauma of historical change is further developed in the television drama *And Did Those Feet* (broadcast in 1965, published in 1966), a bizarre portrayal of the impotence of the British aristocracy, based on the relationship between a Lord Fountain and his illegitimate twin sons. With its interplay of studio action, location movie shooting, voiceover narration, stock footage and animation, and especially in its final setting of a candle-lit indoor swimming pool adorned with inflatable rubber animals and a circus trapeze—the womb-like world to which the brothers have retreated—this work is perhaps Mercer's most fantastical and (for its time) technically demanding television play.

If television presented itself to Mercer as the medium of experiment and imagination, his first full-length plays for the theater seem to follow the more conventional, John Osborne–like contours of bourgeois realism and stylishly trenchant invective. *Ride a Cock Horse* (performed in 1965, published in 1966) develops the narrative of the deracinated working class. It follows Peter, a successful working-class novelist, through a series of bitterly sardonic scenes as he plays out the guilt of his empty celebrity and Hampstead wealth through tempestuous relationships with the three women in his life: wife, mistress, and mother of his eventually aborted child. Behind Peter stands the paradoxical social legacy of his parents, a father who is a mixture of staunch socialism and working-class racism and a mother who cannot decide whether her son has "transcended her ambitions or betrayed them." In the closing scene, after a speech to the absent parents on the dilemma of feeling "nothing but gratitude for having been spared, indeed absolved, from conviction long ago," Peter finally retreats into complete infantilism. As the curtain falls, the mother and father appear on stage, finally to give succor to the impotent and rootless son.

The absent child and the infantile withdrawal of the adult are key metaphors in Mercer's dramatization of the isolation of man from the wider humanity and political complexities of history and his circumscription by the social institutions of class and family. In *Belcher's Luck* (proclaimed by the critic of the *Daily Telegraph* the best play of the year when it was staged by the Royal Shakespeare Company in 1966) the position of the handyman and factotum Belcher and his inheritance from the impotent lord he has served since World War I are threatened by the reappearance of Belcher's bastard son, who has been adopted by the master and cared for as his own. Belcher's anarchic vitality is eventually forced into an accommodation with the class system he has manipulated for so long. In the Joe Ortonesque comedy *Flint* (performed and published in 1970), Mercer sets up a septuagenarian vicar whose agnosticism, benign humanity, and outrageous lust for life are compromised by the machinations of his wife and sister-in-law and the demands of the institution he is supposed to represent. A relationship with Dixie, a pregnant young Irish Liverpudlian, and a fire in the church, started by his wife as an act of revenge for his infidelities, eventually motivate him to escape for the ancient cultures and "wine dark seas" of the Mediterranean. He meets his death in a motorbike crash with an army truck in an unspecified Middle Eastern state, a self-liberation doomed by this final brush with the realities of international politics and military struggle. There is perhaps even an underlying irony in the fact that this deluded journey of romantic escape has been rendered by means of a series of movie clips projected onto the stage set.

In *After Haggerty* (performed and published in 1970), his most critically successful play for the stage, Mercer nails down this self-reflexive metaphor of the enclosed and isolating world of the bourgeois stage. The protagonist, Bernard Link, is a former Marxist theater critic whose political seclusion in the comfort and privacy of his London flat is broken only by regular lecture appearances in Iron Curtain cities in which he meditates uneasily on the significance of British theater since Osborne's *Look Back in Anger* (1956) as a home-grown cultural revolution. The disruptive effect of these direct-address scenes is given added piquancy by the inclusion of a brief parody of a Living Theatre performance: Mercer had little time for the countercultural fringe theater movement of the late 1960s and its strident demands for self-liberation. Domestic concerns intrude on Bernard's privatized world in the form of Claire, a feisty American who arrives at the flat looking for the eponymous previous tenant and father of her baby, and then his father, who has been flooded out of his Yorkshire home. Pitched between the patriarchal figures of *Where the Difference Begins* and *Ride a Cock Horse*, old Link is a personification of working-class conservatism, a force Bernard finally resists as he moves toward an affinity with Claire and her own disillusioned past. These personal accommodations are set against the offstage figure of Haggerty himself, first through the telegrams that periodically arrive from him and finally through the coffin that is delivered with the news of his death fighting as an antigovernment guerrilla in an unnamed African state. The new centers of revolutionary struggle, as New Left thinkers recognized in the early 1970s, were no longer in the West, and certainly not in the drawing rooms of the metropolitan elite, but in the postcolonial liberation movements of the Third World. Mercer's commitment to this issue is embodied in *White Poem,* a short monologue written for the antiapartheid movement in 1970. In this rare foray into fringe theater, a Rhodesian farmer stands on guard, waiting to shoot his first black target and pondering his situation. As he speaks, he gradually reveals his muddled racial bigotry, before a black figure finally bursts into the theater and guns him down.

Mercer's other great figure of disillusioned withdrawal is Robert Kelvin, the dying Marxist novelist at the center of the television play *On the Eve of Publication*. The dramatic premise for this play, produced in 1968 and published in 1970, is deceptively simple. A dinner party has been convened by his agent to celebrate the publication of Kelvin's latest novel, and it becomes an occasion for drunkenly acerbic wit as the writer lambastes his guests; taunts his young mistress, Emma, for her selfless dedication to his various bodily and emotional needs; and recounts stories from his working-class boyhood. Out of this theatrically closed mise-en-scène, however, springs a dynamic televisual narrative. Voiceover, flashbacks, and cinematic inserts map a journey into the dreams, memories, and reflections of the ailing Kelvin, at the center of which lies the bitter awareness of being "a Marxist without the unbearable problem of having to live in a so-called socialist society." This "ironic fate" is epitomized by the torture of his Czech friend and fellow writer Sladek at the hands of the communist authorities and by a recurring scene in which Kelvin projects his own narratives into the white-tiled chamber of his alter ego's incarceration. In the final scene, Kelvin lies dead, and the dinner itself turns out to have been planned but never to have taken place—another layer in the projection of his self-analytical interior fiction.

Two further plays, broadcast and published in 1970, broaden the perspective and ideological implications of the Kelvin story as well as resolving its narrative enigmas. In *The Cellar and the Almond Tree,* Sladek is himself the protagonist, a torture victim of successive

Ian Hendry as Morgan in Mercer's 1962 BBC television play A Suitable Case for Treatment, *a comic fantasy in which a disillusioned artist obsessed with gorillas sabotages his personal relationships (photograph by the BBC; from Don Taylor,* Days of Vision–Working with David Mercer: Television Drama Then and Now, *1990; University of Tennessee–Knoxville Libraries)*

Nazi and Stalinist regimes and now, under the name of Volubin, a party functionary whose path crosses with that of a countess, Isabel von Reger, who is still living on the top floor of her requisitioned palace. Their interweaving pasts are windows onto the convoluted logic of mid-century, middle-European history, a vision widened even further by scenes from Sladek's friendship with Kelvin at an earlier stage in his career. *Emma's Time* reconstructs Emma's relationship with Kelvin as she sifts through the remnants of his life and makes contact with his various acquaintances. In the final scenes she is found by Sladek in a large white room–an image that unites the interrogation chamber of Kelvin's dreams with the harsh reality of Sladek's cellar–and agrees to assist in writing his memoirs of the Czech communist party. This recovery of the socialist ideal from the failures of Stalinism sounds a final note of optimism, an honest confrontation with historical realities out of which a new, perhaps feminine, future might be born.

Mercer dedicated the Kelvin trilogy to the memory of the Polish actor Zbigniew Cybulski. Clips of the movie *Ashes and Diamonds* (1958), in which Cybulski starred, appear in *Emma's Time,* and Kelvin confusedly recalls his meeting with the legendary figure, "a grieving romantic" and "obdurate communist," who comes to embody the distance between the position of the artist under the repressive tolerance of the liberal West and in the active resistance movements of the East. In the later play *Find Me,* commissioned for the BBC arts series *Omnibus,* Mercer extended the homage to Cybulski with a portrait of a Polish novelist living in drunken misery in the West and haunted by memories of his life in the Resistance and by his anger at Stalinism.

The countess's brief references in *The Cellar and the Almond Tree* to her relationship with the von Reger family forge a subtle narrative link between this play and *The Parachute,* broadcast in the same year as *On the Eve of Publication.* The result is a tetralogy of intricately textured and interrelated dramas that replaces the linear narrative form of the Generations trilogy with a more complex synchronic analysis of key oppositions–past and present, personal and political, and East and West. *The Parachute* is Mercer's most cinematic television play, a study of doomed aristocratic hauteur and the impotence of noncommitment, lived out once again in the crucible of European politics. It is 1940, and

Werner von Reger, the son of a Prussian baron, eschews the commission that would be his by right and joins the ranks of the Luftwaffe, volunteering to risk his life in a series of trials for a new parachute. Dreams and flashbacks reveal Werner's authoritarian upbringing and his father's belief in the glorious destiny of his class. His rejection of this patriarchal legacy and his ineffectual loathing for Germany's blind surrender to the Nazi cause are set against his cousin Anna's militant involvement in the communist-led resistance. The probably deliberate bungling of his final jump, in which he breaks his back (recalling Colin's suicidal attempt on the Berlin Wall), leads to the final image of impotence as he watches, wheelchair bound, on the terrace of the family home while conquering Russian paratroopers float from the sky.

At the beginning of the 1970s, in an interview for the theater journal *Gambit,* Mercer provocatively declared that the Kelvin trilogy was to be his swan song to overt politics. Later, in the *Theatre Quarterly* interview, he explained that what he meant was the end of ten years of developing explicitly political and autobiographical themes and the beginning of concerns that he predicted would be more "subjective." He also appeared to be acknowledging the ideological cul de sac of his commercial success. The aptly titled *Duck Song,* written for the Royal Shakespeare Company in 1974, embodies much of this crisis of belief. In many ways it is an ambitiously imaginative stage metaphor for a feckless and destabilized postimperialist West struggling for some sense of identity and faith in the future. A cluster of related but oddly disparate characters, each bemoaning his or her own loss of direction and self-belief—material, political, artistic, and psychoanalytical—gather in the "leathery comfort" of a composite interior, part study and library, part drawing room, only to find the environment evaporate before their eyes at the end of the first act. Act 2 is played out on a white set denuded of props and furniture, either a postapocalyptic setting or a parallel universe, where the characters are, as one of them observes, "all in extremis": actions appear to be reversible, and dialogue becomes ever more allusive. This work is Mercer's most experimental stage play but at the same time perhaps his most obscure—an attempt, as he described it in the Jarman interview, "to create an invented world, in which the preoccupations of my middle age will begin to express themselves."

This shift into more abstract territory and the poor critical reception that greeted Jones's production marked a low point in Mercer's critical popularity and self-confidence as a writer. He found no one ready to produce *The Monster of Karlovy Vary* (published in 1979), a satire on the politics of movie coproduction and East-West relationships partly based on his experience of the Czech motion-picture industry; and the theater pieces that were staged generally suffered at the hand of the critics. In *Cousin Vladimir* (performed and published in 1978), a far from heroic fugitive from the Soviet system arrives in London to find himself in the even more morally bankrupt company of a group of hard-drinking, middle-class intellectuals. "My intention," Mercer explained to Ronald Hayman in a 1978 interview, "is for the notion of alcohol to represent the general fog of insulation and isolation from general world reality in which most people live." This theme of English insularity and ideological complacency was developed in *Then and Now* (performed and published in 1979), a two-act juxtaposition of England in 1945, alive with the possibility of change, and the disillusion and moral bankruptcy of "now," seen through the life of a once-idealistic Yorkshire doctor now living in metropolitan affluence. That the "now" was 1979, the year that the new Conservative Right triumphed under Margaret Thatcher, gives the play a strangely prophetic air. In *No Limits to Love,* produced by the Royal Shakespeare Company in tribute shortly after his death in 1980, Mercer returned to the formalized style of *Let's Murder Vivaldi* with a chamber piece for four players based around sexual manners, music, and middle-class affluence.

Much of Mercer's television work during the mid 1970s is rooted in a sense of spiritual absence and political isolation. *The Bankrupt* (broadcast in 1972, published in 1974) is the story of a catatonic mental patient returning to his father's house—a journey that takes him through sequences of dream, memory, and ritual into an ideological vacuum similar to that of *Duck Song. You and Me and Him* (broadcast in 1973, published in 1974) is a thirty-minute psychodrama in which three characters—essentially the protagonist's warring id, ego, and superego—are all played by the same actor in what was, for 1973, a technical feat of videotape editing. Other plays from this period, particularly those commissioned by Yorkshire Television for the Independent Television network, are more conventional in form, relying on dialogue to capture the sense of spiritual wreckage, both through verbal dexterity and the evocation of past events and relationships. *An Afternoon at the Festival* (broadcast in 1973, published in 1974), set in an unnamed East European capital, focuses on the brief relationship between a jaded, second-rate movie director and a local female music student to explore what is summarized in a final monologue as "the moral squalor of human emptiness." In a bold move, however, Mercer refers back to the *On the Eve of Publication* cycle by having the director working on a movie version of Kelvin's final novel, *The Last Days of Buster Crook,* a self-reflexive trope reinforced by the casting of the actor Leo McKern (who played Kelvin in *On the Eve of Publica-*

tion) in the central role. *The Arcata Promise* (broadcast in 1974, published in 1977) is a portrait of an alcoholic, misogynistic actor, "more frightened by death than I am incompetent at life." *A Superstition* (broadcast and published in 1977) deals with the sexual relationships among three men; but drawn into their highly charged and eventually violent drama, played out on the terrace of an elegant Italian villa, is a back story of international intrigue and political cynicism. *Huggy Bear* (broadcast in 1976, published in 1977) is a farcical incursion into the erotic game-playing of male menopause, with images of infantile regression reminiscent of *Ride a Cock Horse* and *And Did Those Feet*.

Against this trend toward the more introspective chamber play, two later works for television stand out as manifestations of Mercer's resolute commitment to a more internationalist perspective. With *Shooting the Chandelier* (broadcast in 1977, published in 1978), his most favorably received television play of the late 1970s, Mercer returns to the historical and political territory of the Kelvin trilogy with a confrontation between two Russian soldiers as a unit of the Red Army moves into a Czechoslovakian country house following the defeat of Adolf Hitler. Nikolai, the officer, embodies the cool detachment of political orthodoxy, while Simon—his former professor and now a shambling, alcoholic infantry cook—embodies the confused impotence of the intellectual dissident. In an even bolder departure, Mercer's last and posthumously produced television play, *A Dinner of Herbs* (broadcast in 1988), struggled with the highly charged political contradictions of Israel, where he had settled with his third wife, Daphna, herself an Israeli. (Mercer had been married a second time, to an Englishwoman, Dilys.) Significantly, the familiar, semi-autobiographical protagonist—cynical, hard-drinking, and sexually predatory—is rendered as a female character, a journalist whose pro-Palestinian stance is challenged by falling in love with an Israeli man. Colin Chambers has argued that Mercer's almost primitive misogyny had been continually challenged by his intellectual struggle with feminism, and it is tempting to speculate as to what further shifts might have taken place in the sexual politics of his work had he continued to write into the 1980s.

If Mercer's output during the 1970s lacked the consistency of his earlier work, it may be partly because of his increasing devotion to the time-consuming process of writing movie scripts. In 1973, with his screen adaptation of Henrik Ibsen's *A Doll's House* (1879), Mercer began a working relationship with the movie director Joseph Losey that was one of the most energetic and tumultuous of his career, although their collaborations, as Losey's biographer has noted, were "constantly bedevilled." Mercer's script for *A Doll's House* was

Cover for the published versions of two of Mercer's plays. Cousin Vladimir *was performed in London in 1978;* Shooting the Chandelier *was televised by the BBC in 1977 and starred Denholm Elliott and Edward Fox, who are pictured (photograph by the BBC; Thomas Cooper Library, University of South Carolina).*

attacked by the star, Jane Fonda, for its apparent betrayal of Ibsen's feminism. The resulting feud was a bitter one, but Losey stuck by Mercer. Despite his lack of sympathy with the overt politics of Mercer's stage work, Losey admired his skill in adapting works for the screen, and together they developed several such projects, none of them completed.

Mercer's single greatest achievement in the cinema was his screenplay for Alain Resnais's *Providence* (1977), a work that earned him the coveted César Award from the French Film Academy. Resnais had approached Mercer after seeing *Duck Song* in London (also regarded by Losey as Mercer's best play), and the project grew out of a shared desire to make what Mercer called a "slightly theatrical film." In its portrait of a dying writer weaving fictions of his relationships with his wife and grown children into a series of retributive narratives, it owes much to *On the Eve of Publication;* but the meeting with Resnais's nonlinear experiment in time and memory, presaged in the interweaving of psychological and historical subjectivities in *The Parachute,* creates a far more unsettling experience. Mercer's writing here provides the formalized and unequivocally literary texture for a journey through the complexity of a writer's imagination as it struggles to reconcile itself with the painful realities of the past and present. The images of mortality bring to a head one of the underlying preoccupations of Mercer's work and, with hindsight, serve as ominous premonitions of his own untimely death. (Like many of his protagonists, Mercer was a heavy drinker; despite a late period of abstinence, he died of a heart attack on 8 August 1980.)

In his 1973 play *The Party,* Mercer's near contemporary Griffiths created the character of Sloman, a successful working-class television playwright whose political cynicism and passion are displayed through a mixture of lyrical articulacy and shambling alcoholic vituperation. Few have missed the reference to Mercer in what is at one level a *pièce à clef*. Mercer's hard drinking was one aspect of a highly emotional temperament that often veered toward violence and contained the seeds of self-destruction. Griffiths's depiction, however, is less biographical than philosophical, one in a range of positions in the discourse of cultural politics in the play, which captures in particular Mercer's awareness of the tragic crisis of socialist commitment in the face of Stalinist reaction and Western inertia. Griffiths is just one of several dramatists who have acknowledged the debt they owe to Mercer's pioneering drama of ideas and his belief in television as the stage on which it could be most passionately and penetratingly delivered. In *A Rod of Iron* (1980), the last television play to be broadcast before his death and, for Hampton, one of his "most powerful and haunting works," Mercer returns to the narrative material of *Where the Difference Begins*. Two seemingly successful brothers return home to confront their aged father, a former miner, who has been waiting for his wife to die. In a reprise of Wilf's final aria, the father speaks of a life spent in "numb bitterness" and of the transcendental enlightenment he now seeks in life as a *sanyasin* (holy man who has renounced all possessions), destined to wander the roads with his begging bowl. If this uncanny and self-referential late play can be seen as Mercer's version of William Shakespeare's *The Tempest,* it is perhaps appropriate that, in a testimony to his particular artistic vocation, he has the old man deliver a eulogy to television itself as "a window on the magnificence and pathos of man."

David Mercer's output for the stage is considerable, but he has been most highly regarded as a pioneering and inspirational television dramatist. As early as 1963, his collaborator Taylor could claim that Mercer had "killed forever the idea that . . . deep thought and complex language have no place on the small screen," and in a tribute shortly after Mercer's death, Taylor reiterated that he was "the first major English dramatist to have emerged from television." Not only did Mercer establish the idea of television drama as a space for the passionate exploration of serious and often difficult ideas; he also stretched the boundaries of the medium, forging a new aesthetic out of the tension between naturalistic social observation, richly poetic dramatic dialogue, and the allusive potentialities of cinematic narrative. As John Caughie has observed, both in his historical and ideological vision and in his readiness to combine the European avant-garde aesthetics of the absurd, the epic, and the *nouveau roman* (new novel) with the inherent realism of television, Mercer can now be recognized as the major modernist of British television drama and perhaps its only truly internationalist writer.

Interviews:

Bert Baker, "David Mercer and the Man Among the Ruins," *Morning Star,* 17 November 1966, p. 2;

Lionel Birch, "Mercer: In Two Minds About Success," *Daily Telegraph,* 19 April 1968, pp. 24–25;

Penelope Mortimer, "David Mercer Talking to Penelope Mortimer," *Evening Standard,* 17 November 1968, p. 7;

Sonia Copeland, "Drama of Conflict," *Sunday Times,* 20 April 1969, p. 58;

Joan Bakewell, Interview with David Mercer, in *The New Priesthood,* by Bakewell and Nicholas Garnham (London: Penguin, 1970), pp. 84–86;

Ronald Hayman, "Cases for Treatment," *Times,* 14 February 1970, pp. I, III;

Helena Matheopoulos, "Women Are People Too, in a Way . . . ," *Vanity Fair* (March 1971): 68;

Irving Wardle, "Political Theatre in Britain: An Interview with David Mercer and Geoffrey Reeves," *Gambit,* 5, no. 20 (1971): 75–86;

Joseph F. McCrindle, *Behind the Scenes: Theatre and Film Interviews from the Transatlantic Review* (London: Pitman, 1971), pp. 88–98;

Francis Jarman, "Birth of a Playwriting Man," *Theatre Quarterly,* 3 (January–March 1973): 43–57, 90;

Hayman, Interview with David Mercer, in his *Playback 2* (London: Davis-Poynter, 1973), pp. 122–144;

Hayman, "Mercer's Cousin Vladimir," *Plays and Players,* 26 (November 1978): 10–11;

John Orr, "Portrait of a Turncoat," *AIP and Co,* 29 (October–November 1980): 13–20.

Bibliography:

Francis Jarman, John Noyce, and Malcolm Page, *The Quality of Mercer: A Bibliography of Writings By and About David Mercer* (Brighton: Smoothie Publications, 1974).

References:

John Caughie, *Television Drama: Realism, Modernism and British Culture* (Oxford: Oxford University Press, 2000);

David Caute, *Joseph Losey: A Revenge on Life* (London: Faber & Faber, 1994), pp. 351–359;

Colin Chambers, *Peggy: The Life of Margaret Ramsay, Play Agent* (London: Nick Hern, 1997), pp. 124–131;

John Ezard, "Spotting the Talent in a Shy Young Bull," *Guardian*, 30 June 1988, p. 2;

Christopher Hampton, "The Climate of David Mercer," *Times*, 11 October 1980, p. 8;

Ronald Hayman, "The Quality of Mercer," *Listener*, 9 July 1981, p. 40;

Derek Hill, "Intellectual Attitudes," *Contrast*, 2, no. 2 (Winter 1962): 116–123;

Albert Hunt, "The Quack Theatre," *New Society*, 14 February 1974, pp. 393–394;

Catherine Itzin, *Stages in the Revolution: Political Theatre in Britain Since 1968* (London: Eyre Methuen, 1980), pp. 91–101;

D. A. N. Jones, "Mercer Unmarxed," *Listener*, 14 May 1970, p. 652;

Alan Lovell, "Television Playwright: David Mercer," *Contrast*, 2, no. 4 (Summer 1963): 251–258;

Paul Madden, ed., *David Mercer: Where the Difference Began* (London: British Film Institute, 1981);

Khalil El Mubarak Mustafa, "David Mercer," in *British Television Drama*, edited by George W. Brandt (Cambridge: Cambridge University Press, 1981), pp. 82–109;

Don Taylor, "David Mercer," *New Statesman*, 15 August 1980, p. 23;

Taylor, *Days of Vision–Working with David Mercer: Television Drama Then and Now* (London: Methuen, 1990);

Taylor, "The Legacy of David Mercer," *Broadcast*, 24 November 1980, pp. 14–15;

John Russell Taylor, "British Dramatists; The New Arrivals, No 2: David Mercer," *Plays and Players*, 17 (May 1970): 48–50;

Taylor, *The Second Wave: British Drama for the Seventies* (London: Methuen, 1971), pp. 36–58;

Katharine J. Worth, *Revolutions in Modern English Drama* (London: G. Bell, 1972), pp. 40–44.

Tom Murphy

(23 February 1935 –)

Ben Francombe
University College Chichester

PLAY PRODUCTIONS: *A Whistle in the Dark,* London, Theatre Royal, Stratford East, 1961;

Famine, Dublin, Peacock Stage (Abbey Theatre), 21 March 1968;

The Orphans, Dublin, Gate Theatre, 1968;

A Crucial Week in the Life of a Grocer's Assistant, Dublin, Abbey Theatre, 1969;

The Morning After Optimism, Dublin, Abbey Theatre, 15 March 1971;

The White House, Dublin, Abbey Theatre, 1972; revised and performed as *Conversations on a Homecoming,* Galway, Druid Lane Theatre, 16 April 1985;

On the Outside, by Murphy and Noel O'Donoghue, Dublin, Project Arts Centre, 30 September 1974;

On the Inside, Dublin, Peacock Stage (Abbey Theatre), 18 November 1974;

The Vicar of Wakefield, adapted from Oliver Goldsmith's novel, Dublin, Abbey Theatre, 1975; revised as *She Stoops to Folly,* Costa Mesa, California, South Coast Repertory Theater, 1995; Dublin, Abbey Theatre, 9 October 1996;

The Sanctuary Lamp, Dublin, Abbey Theatre, 7 October 1975; revised edition, Dublin, Abbey Theatre, 31 October 1985;

The J. Arthur Maginnis Story, Dublin, Pavilion Theatre Dun Laoghaire, 1976;

Epitaph Under Ether, adapted from J. M. Synge's works, Dublin, Abbey Theatre, 30 August 1979;

The Blue Macushla, Dublin, Abbey Theatre, 6 March 1980;

The Informer, adapted from Liam O'Flaherty's novel, Dublin, Olympia Theatre, 13 October 1981;

She Stoops to Conquer, adapted from Goldsmith's play, Dublin, Abbey Theatre, 11 February 1982;

The Gigli Concert, Dublin, Abbey Theatre, 29 September 1983;

A Thief of a Christmas, Dublin, Abbey Theatre, 1985;

Bailegangaire, Galway, Druid Lane Theatre, 5 December 1986;

Too Late for Logic, Dublin, Abbey Theatre, 3 October 1989;

Tom Murphy (photograph by Michael Slevin; from Nicholas Grene, ed., Talking About Tom Murphy, *2002; Thomas Cooper Library, University of South Carolina)*

The Patriot Game, Dublin, Peacock Stage (Abbey Theatre), 15 May 1991;

The Wake, Dublin, Abbey Theatre, 28 January 1998;

The House, Dublin, Abbey Theatre, 12 April 2000;

The Drunkard, adapted from W. H. Smith's play, Galway, Town Hall Theatre, 18 July 2003;

The Cherry Orchard, adapted from Anton Chekhov's play, Dublin, Abbey Theatre, 17 February 2004.

BOOKS: *The Fooleen* (Dixon, Cal.: Proscenium Press, 1968); republished as *A Crucial Week in the Life of a Grocer's Assistant* (Dublin: Gallery Press, 1978);
A Whistle in the Dark (New York: S. French, 1971; Dublin: Gallery Press, 1984);
The Morning After Optimism (Dublin & Cork: Mercier Press, 1973);
The Orphans (Newark, Del.: Proscenium Press, 1974);
On the Outside; On the Inside, by Murphy and Noel O'Donoghue (Dublin: Gallery Press, 1976);
The Sanctuary Lamp (Dublin: Poolbeg Press, 1976; revised edition, Dublin: Gallery Press, 1984);
Famine (Dublin: Gallery Press, 1977);
The Gigli Concert (Dublin: Gallery Press, 1984);
Conversations on a Homecoming (Dublin: Gallery Press, 1986);
Bailegangaire (Dublin: Gallery Press, 1986);
After Tragedy: Three Irish Plays (London: Methuen, 1988)—comprises *The Gigli Concert, Conversations on a Homecoming,* and *Bailegangaire;*
A Whistle in the Dark & Other Plays (London: Methuen, 1989); republished as *Plays: Four* (London: Methuen, 1997)—comprises *A Whistle in the Dark, A Crucial Week in the Life of a Grocer's Assistant, On the Outside,* and *On the Inside;*
Too Late for Logic (London: Methuen, 1990; revised, 2001);
Plays: One (London: Methuen, 1992)—comprises *Famine, The Patriot Game,* and *The Blue Macushla;*
Plays: Two (London: Methuen, 1993)—comprises *Conversations on a Homecoming, Bailegangaire,* and *A Thief of a Christmas;*
Plays: Three (London: Methuen, 1994)—comprises *The Morning After Optimism, The Sanctuary Lamp,* and *The Gigli Concert;*
The Seduction of Morality (London: Little, Brown, 1994);
She Stoops to Folly (London: Methuen, 1996);
The Wake (London: Methuen, 1998);
The House (London: Methuen, 2000);
The Cherry Orchard, adapted from Anton Chekhov's play (London: Methuen, 2004);
The Drunkard, adapted from W. H. Smith's play (Dublin: Carysfort Press, 2004).

PRODUCED SCRIPT: *On the Outside,* by Murphy and Noel O'Donoghue, radio, Radio Eireann, 1962.

Tom Murphy is one of the leading Irish dramatists of his generation. Since the 1960s he has written more than twenty plays and has become closely associated with the Abbey, Ireland's National Theatre, both as a member of the board from 1972 to 1983 and as writer-in-association from 1986 to 1989. He has also worked closely with other leading Irish theater companies, in particular Druid Theatre Company of Galway, for whom he was writer-in-association from 1983 to 1985. He is a member of Aosdana—the national affiliation of leading creative artists—and the Irish Academy of Letters. Several major critical studies of Murphy's work have been published, including Fintan O'Toole's seminal book *The Politics of Magic: The Work and Times of Tom Murphy* (1987), and in the spring of 1987, *Irish University Review,* the journal of Irish studies, devoted a whole issue to Murphy. In October 2001, a six-play Murphy celebration took place at the Abbey, accompanied by an international symposium on his work at Trinity College Dublin. In a program note for the 2001 Abbey production of *The Blue Macushla* (first performed in 1980, published in 1992), fellow playwright Brian Friel described Murphy as "the most distinctive, the most restless, the most obsessive imagination at work in Irish theatre today."

In spite of his gradual rise within Ireland's literary and theatrical establishment, Murphy has not won much recognition outside his native country. Consideration of Murphy's work and his reputation, however, can be made alongside that of Friel. The two writers share much in common beyond close friendship, having been brought up in similar communities at the same time and both conforming to the agenda of the defined "Generation of Playwrights" who wrote with a degree of critical detachment on Ireland since the beginning of Eamon de Valera's presidency (1959-1973). But there are also differences, with Murphy, on occasions, choosing a demanding, psychologically complex, and allegorical approach to the examination of "Irishness" that has, perhaps, prevented appreciation from the international audience that has venerated the work of Friel. There is also bluntness in Murphy's writing, offering a vision that is brutal, restless, and uncompromising. Murphy refuses, at times, to show any of the warmth or compassion that is central to Friel's more Chekhovian vision of Ireland. In short, Murphy makes extreme demands upon his audience, both theatrically and emotionally.

Thomas Bernard Murphy was born in Tuam, County Galway, on 23 February 1935, the youngest of ten children of John Murphy, a carpenter, and Winifred Shaughnessy Murphy. His early life was in many ways paradigmatic of rural Ireland in the early years of the Irish Free State. His was an uncompromising, often violent, Catholic education provided by the local Christian Brothers within a small-town community that was not yet prepared to admit the economic reality of industrialization. Murphy spent a large part of his childhood waiting for occasional visits from his father and other members of his family who, like so many, were forced to find work in England. Murphy took an apprenticeship in welding before training as a teacher in Dublin

Máire ní Dhomhnaill and Dan O'Herlihy in the 1972 Abbey Theatre premiere of The White House, *in which an actor returns from New York to a run-down Galway pub and discovers how his friends have changed (photograph by Fergus Bourke; from Christopher Fitz-Simon,* The Abbey Theatre: Ireland's National Theatre: The First 100 Years, *2003; Thomas Cooper Library, University of South Carolina)*

and returning to County Galway to take a post as engineering teacher in 1957. He married Mary Hamilton-Hippisley in 1966, and the couple has three children: Bennan, Nell, and Johnny.

Some of these biographical facts filter into his plays, particularly those written during the early part of his career. Economic frustration and envy; the tedium of employment and the triviality of social life; the suffocation and paternalistic assumption of Catholic establishment; the precarious tension found in extended families; and brutal tribalism and inward-looking pride are all themes that confront Murphy's characters.

Murphy's interest in writing was encouraged and assisted by his longtime friend Noel O'Donoghue, with whom he wrote his first play, the one-act *On the Outside*, in 1959. This play, broadcast on Radio Eireann in 1962 but not receiving a stage production until 1974, captures the sense of boredom and frustration in Tuam during the late 1950s. The two central characters, Frank and Joe, are excluded from a small-town dance hall—first, in tangible terms, by not having the money for the admission fee, and second, by their own feelings of worthlessness as they watch others who have money enough for entry taking an unfair advantage in the pursuit of love and perceived happiness. The play would be a straightforward morality tale if it were not for the dark and underlying sense of violent frustration felt by the excluded. Frank has no comeback at the end and responds to events only through a hopelessly irrelevant attack on the dance-hall poster. Somberly, Joe encourages him away with the words "come on out of here to hell," suggesting that there is little liberation anywhere from their purgatory. In this play Murphy demonstrates an uncompromising approach to character and conflict and an ability to take a cold, detached, and allegorical look at the changing, yet frustratingly constant, face of modern Ireland.

The delayed production history of *On the Outside* is reflective of the slow start to Murphy's career. Throughout the early 1960s Murphy had to battle against the limiting cultural preconceptions of the Irish theatrical establishment. The Abbey Theatre, an institution that, at the time, served with enthusiasm the dogma of an outdated Catholic and rural Ireland, could find no place for a new generation of playwrights—Murphy, Friel, Thomas Kilroy, Eugene McCabe—who

Scene from the 1975 Abbey Theatre premiere of Murphy's play The Sanctuary Lamp, *in which two former circus performers and an orphan who has lost her baby seek shelter and understanding in a church (from D. E. S. Maxwell,* A Critical History of Modern Irish Drama 1891–1980, *1984; Thomas Cooper Library, University of South Carolina)*

chose to challenge old assumptions of Irishness. Ernest Blythe, the Abbey's long-standing managing director, stood firm (and increasingly alone) as guardian of the Abbey tradition of romantic peasant drama. The Abbey management also rejected outright Murphy's second play, one of the great Irish plays of the 1960s, *A Whistle in the Dark* (performed in 1961, published in 1971).

A Whistle in the Dark tells the story of the Carney family, displaced from their native Mayo and ensconced in the Coventry home of the oldest brother, Michael, and his English wife, Betty. Michael is a reluctant host, drawn into accommodating his brothers—Harry, Hugo, and Iggy—through the last vestiges of family loyalty. But his heart is now in England, believing that respect and respectability have come with his modest house, job, and wife. Michael has followed textbook emigration: he has an ingrained sense of what self-betterment means, a belief in integration, and a rigorous work ethic. It is not clear why the three brothers have come to Coventry; they have fallen easily into a violent and unseemly world of the criminal economy, choosing to fight and threaten their way to a sense of position in this new community. They have no care for betterment or integration: they find their money where they can and spend it on beer as soon as they can; they show no interest in the home that Michael has made, and their contempt for Betty is constant and vicious. These two opposites meet with bloody consequences upon the arrival of Dada and the youngest brother, Des, when Michael is finally goaded into a violent response to his family's challenging behavior. This encounter leaves him isolated from any identifiable purpose as well as hopelessly entwined in the tribalism of his family.

Murphy's ambivalence toward Michael—his sympathy for the character's confusion, isolation, and provocation, tempered by the harsh observation of his character's stifling sense of propriety and subservience—shows a clear link with *On the Outside* and the cool exposé of Frank's emotional impotence. At the heart of

A Whistle in the Dark is the fact that nothing has changed for the Carney family, not even for Michael with his smug reliance on emigration, and his frustration with this reality leads to the tragic climax.

Premiered to great acclaim in London at the Theatre Royal, Stratford East (previously the home of Joan Littlewood's Theatre Workshop), in 1961, *A Whistle in the Dark* moved Murphy into the center of London's vibrant theater scene. Murphy was an overnight success, fitting neatly into a theater world that had recently embraced the idea of the Angry Young Man. But the regard of the London critics did not lead to a breakthrough in terms of sustained career; their praise was fulsome but superficial. An English audience at this time probably could not have realized the cultural sensitivity behind the violence in *A Whistle in the Dark,* and the generalized nature of one infamous review may have reinforced the prejudice of Blythe and others at the Abbey. Kenneth Tynan's review in *The Observer,* in particular, seemed to class Murphy as an English stage Irishman, a second Brendan Behan: loud, uncompromising, aggressive, and ill-disciplined, even though in fact Murphy was a shy, well-mannered young schoolteacher. Such a review allowed Blythe to continue believing that *A Whistle in the Dark* painted an inaccurate, untruthful image of Ireland.

In 1962 the Abbey swiftly vetoed Murphy's second full-length play, *The Fooleen* (published in 1968). After this third rejection from Ireland's national theater, Murphy moved to London, where he made a living writing for television for the remainder of the 1960s. *The Fooleen* was finally staged in 1969 at the Abbey, under the more revealing title of *A Crucial Week in the Life of a Grocer's Assistant.*

The irrelevance of emigration as a solution to Ireland's social and emotional crisis is at the heart of *A Crucial Week in the Life of a Grocer's Assistant.* It tells the story of one week in the life of John Joe, a surprisingly old (age thirty-three) grocer's assistant in a small Irish town. At first, John Joe seems to be another frustrated and impotent character, an aging teenager, a desperately reluctant yet hopelessly compliant participant in his mother's demands for small-time respectability in this deeply entrenched society. The emotional turmoil expressed by John Joe appears to be nothing more than some trivial rebellion: he stresses that he is determined to leave, to find escape through emigration from the sense of repression; but through his boss's simple dismissal ("you're only a dreamer"), John Joe's timidity is easily exposed. Never is there any doubt that John Joe will remain at home, and it seems likely that he will sink back into his mother's world of tragic hypocrisy and exploitation hidden under a facade of community. But at the ultimate moment of crisis, the moment when he seems prepared to admit his cowardice, John Joe takes a bold step away from the tragedy of defeated ambition as he discovers the essential truth: that escape cannot be found through emigration. The real escape comes from confronting the stifling repression of the community within. Angrily, John Joe attacks his mother: "a person can hardly breathe in that street. I don't know what started it. Whether it's just badness or whether it came from a hundred years ago." The slow realization of centuries-old repression leads him to confront the ghosts of respectability, dramatically shouting the secrets of the town from his door step. "We're disgraced!" his mother gasps, but John Joe has found a way to declare his independence.

A Crucial Week in the Life of a Grocer's Assistant follows on from Murphy's previous two plays in the way that it chooses a specific and isolated incident as a metaphor for wider conflicts in 1960s Irish society. Characters created in a form of brutal realism, whose acts of emotional and physical violence are seen in the context of the time, forge the allegorical nature of all three plays. But *A Crucial Week in the Life of a Grocer's Assistant* departs from its predecessors in two ways that signal a gradual change in approach, developed in Murphy's later plays. First is the departure from tragedy. John Joe finds an answer to confront the repression of past ideals, choosing to avoid the hopeless acts of climactic violence that leave the characters in the previous plays no further ahead. In the process John Joe finds a calm that is beyond tragedy. Second is a reticent move away from naturalism. While Murphy in *A Crucial Week in the Life of a Grocer's Assistant* attempts an accurate reflection of modern Irish life, using well-drawn and emotionally demanding characters, he also attempts a more episodic and distinctly theatrical structure that allows for the representation of fantasy as well as realism.

This movement toward greater philosophical and theatrical experimentation continued upon Murphy's return to Dublin and informed a sustained period of activity at the Abbey Theatre. This belated collaboration between theater and playwright had little to do with the changing nature of the playwright's approach and more to do with the changing nature of the Abbey management. After 1966, when the Abbey moved into a new building, the directorate started to develop a far more modern understanding of the role of a national theater. Blythe retired as director, allowing for a series of artistic directors, Tomás Mac Anna in particular, who set about meeting the challenge of the demanding and flexible stages of the new building with an artistic policy to match.

Murphy's first new play to be accepted unequivocally by the Abbey came a year before the production of *A Crucial Week in the Life of a Grocer's Assistant* and dem-

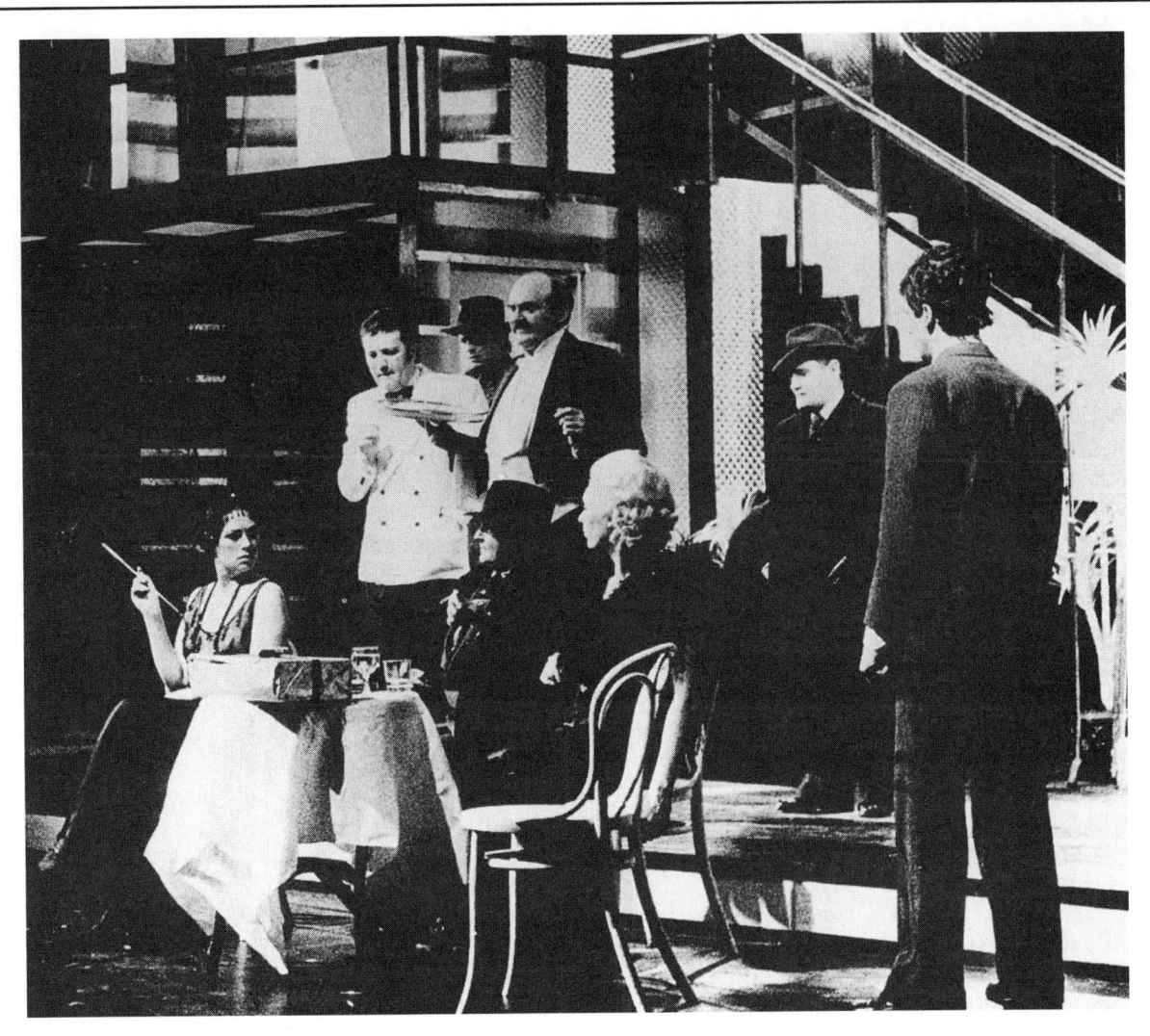

Fedelma Cullen, Donal McCann, Emmet Bergin, Peadar Lamb, Pat Leavy, Deirdre Donnelly, Paddy Long, and Stephen Rea in the 1980 Abbey Theatre premiere of Murphy's gangster play, The Blue Macushla *(photograph by Fergus Bourke; from Christopher Fitz-Simon,* The Abbey Theatre: Ireland's National Theatre: The First 100 Years, *2003; Thomas Cooper Library, University of South Carolina)*

onstrates clearly greater international influence upon mainstream Irish theater. *Famine* (performed in 1968, published in 1977), staged by Mac Anna in the Abbey's studio, the Peacock, is a large, episodic, history play with a cast of more than twenty. It tells the story of John Conner, a village elder—seen by his community as their "King"—who is powerless, emotionally and physically, to lead a coherent response to the economic crime enacted upon the Irish people by the British Empire at the time of the Great Hunger of the 1840s. *Famine* subscribes, in part, to the Brechtian tradition of showing how a definitive moment in history can inform later cultures: in this case, the culture of doubt and nervous impotency found in contemporary Irish life. Murphy is being overtly political, but he avoids the simple explanation of intent found in many epic plays. According to Christopher Murray, *Famine* subscribes more closely to the Theatre of Cruelty by the way the play "becomes a process to be experienced traumatically." The emotional drive of the play draws Murphy away from the easy identification of social realism and social conflict toward an underlying tension, a conflict determined as much by his understanding of theater as his understanding of Ireland.

The 1970s and early 1980s are punctuated by three interesting plays produced at the Abbey: *The Morning After Optimism* (performed in 1971, published in 1973); *The Sanctuary Lamp* (performed in 1975, published in 1976); and *The Gigli Concert* (performed in 1983, published in 1984). All three plays show considerable evidence of experimentation with form and language. *The Morning After Optimism* is the first, and perhaps only, play by Murphy that deliberately steps outside a realistic context into a fantastic and universal world. Staged by Hugh Hunt, another of the pioneering artistic directors of the Abbey, and revived by the same theater in 1977, the play exploits a totality of theater form—abstract design, absurd props, expressive movement, heightened use of song—to create a dream-like "Forest of Arden": a world that is beyond a clear Irish context. While the context is deliberately vague and unusual in Murphy's drama, there are aspects consistent with the playwright's tendency toward potentially challenging and critical definitions of human nature. The play presents the oppositional and ultimately violent interaction between the uncompromisingly drawn characters of a pimp and a whore on the one hand and "star-crossed lovers" on the other. According to Murray, *The Morning After Optimism* remains "occupied with the spiritual deprivation and a social humiliation that are endemically Irish."

The first production of *The Morning After Optimism*, while generally well received, left certain critics bemused by the lack of clear contextual foundation. For his next major play, Murphy retained the undisputed strength of *The Morning After Optimism*—the uncompromising portrayal of character beyond simple narrative intentions—but ensured that his Dublin audience would have a proactive response to the characters' contextual situation.

By setting *The Sanctuary Lamp* in "A Church in a City," ostensibly a Catholic church in the city of Dublin, Murphy is prompting a reaction from his audience that comes from a distinctly Irish identity. To the bemusement of some international critics, the 1975 production caused disturbances by audience members convinced that the play was blasphemous. While there is an iconoclastic tone to *The Sanctuary Lamp*, the play reaches beyond the specifics of Catholic identity to consider the wider issues of spirituality within a community and its value for the individual who remains outside of the community. Three outcasts from society find shelter in the church: Harry and Francisco, who used to have a circus act together, and Maudie, an orphan who has lost her baby and, consequently, feels considerable guilt. Harry has also lost a child but has a greater sense of anger and is determined to exact revenge against God. Francisco, who arrives demanding an explanation for Harry's sudden departure, instigates passionate debate and argument about the way that the Church restricts them. This debate climaxes with a drunken sermon given from the pulpit by Francisco that is one of the bitterest attacks against Catholicism ever heard on the Irish stage. But again, Murphy moves beyond crisis and conflict toward a kind of acceptance and understanding in which all three become the custodians of the Sanctuary Lamp (the visual indicator of the presence of the sacrament) in a determination to preserve themselves and the ultimate "human" presence they find in the church.

The Morning After Optimism and *The Sanctuary Lamp* indicate a transition in Murphy's work, away from narrative and toward a kind of realistic expressionism. In an article from the 1987 Murphy issue of *Irish University Review,* Harry White observes in Murphy's work from the mid 1970s onward a preference for "the poetic and dramatic impact of . . . a pattern or mosaic, with its inherent attractions of ambiguity (and risk of incomprehensibility)." Perhaps the most illustrative example of this approach comes from *The Gigli Concert*.

At the heart of *The Gigli Concert* is the theatrical exploration and representation of miracle brought on by the profound interaction of two complex and contrasting elements: the enactment of high drama within the mundane surroundings of a dingy, modern Dublin office. A gruff, taciturn, self-made Irishman (his name is never stated) chooses to visit J. P. W. King, a practitioner of a failed American quasi science: "Dynamatology." Murphy does not explain exactly what Dynamatology is or, crucially, how King can make a living from practicing it; certainly, the appearance of the Irishman as a customer is a rare event for King, and it quickly transpires that the Irishman's needs are way beyond the therapeutic offerings of Dynamatology. The Irishman has a deeply felt need to sing like the famed operatic tenor Beniamino Gigli. King becomes intensely fascinated and, ultimately, emotionally involved in this need. The contrasting ways in which each deals with this impossible demand become the central focus of the play. The Irishman, in spite of coming near to a form of full emotional catharsis, draws back from the brink and responds to emotional crisis in conventional terms by readjusting to, and reentering, the world outside. King, on the other hand, is compelled to carry on—there is no outside world for him. In a theatrical climax, King presents to the audience the "impossible" image of actually singing like Gigli: he has broken through the barriers of a confining logic and finds liberation beyond the restraints of social convention.

The Gigli Concert was given a standing ovation when first seen at the Abbey in spite of its running time of more than three hours. It brings together many of the familiar theatrical attributes from earlier Murphy plays—harsh, uncompromising, and oppositional characterization; oblique dialogue; fantasy merged with mundanity; and scenic expressionism merged with scenic naturalism. O'Toole articulates the strength of the play: "when JPW [King] opens his windows at the end of the play and lets in the morning light, we know that we have been with one of the few playwrights now writing who is able to let the full, unfiltered light of European culture in on his plays and not be dazzled by the glare." Revived in 1991 at the Abbey, *The Gigli Concert* played to full houses.

The Gigli Concert was the climax of a sustained relationship between Murphy and the Abbey Theatre. By the 1980s, the Abbey had become a creative ally of Murphy, protecting "their man" even at moments of failure, as in 1980 when his gangster play, *The Blue Macushla,* did not capture the imagination of critics and audiences. Murphy, in return, served on the theater board and, with others, assisted the Abbey through a remarkable period of artistic transformation: from complacent repertory theater to experimental producing house.

In 1983 Murphy took an extended sabbatical from the Abbey and moved west, returning to Galway to work with Garry Hynes and the emerging Druid Theatre Company. Hynes directed two of Murphy's plays. First was *Conversations on a Homecoming* (performed in 1985, published in 1986), which was a reworking of his stage play *The White House* (performed in 1972). The second was an original play, *Bailegangaire* (performed and published in 1986). In *Bailegangaire,* Murphy takes the linguistic juggling, realistic expressionism, and oppositional characterization found in his later Abbey plays and returns with them to small-town Ireland. The setting for *Bailegangaire* is a kitchen in a cottage: the one setting he vowed, when discussing the possibilities of dramatic writing with O'Donoghue back in 1959, that he would never use. The ironic self-consciousness in the setting seems to be consolidated by the way the play also returns to narrative. *Bailegangaire* draws on the notion of storytelling; the title of the play—Irish for "The Town Without Laughter"—is also the title of the story retold, but never finished, by Mommo, the old, almost senile central character, whose bed dominates the kitchen. But her narrative appears, at first, to be almost incidental: a background noise in the lives of her granddaughters, Mary and Dolly, who are charged to act as nurses for her. The conversations between Mary and Dolly are fueled by the tension of sibling rivalry, of years of waste and conflict. The image created is of repressed lives in a repressed community, until Mary realizes that her shapeless and formless life is reflected in Mommo's inability to finish her story. Mary and Dolly encourage Mommo to finish her tale, discovering in the process information within the story that helps them to understand the great emotional turmoil that has scarred their grandmother. This knowledge and understanding, discovered at the end of the story, draws the play to a peaceful and moving close. With the first

Pauline Flanagan as Mommo in the 2001 Abbey Theatre production of Murphy's 1986 play Bailegangaire, *in which an old woman keeps trying to retell a story to her two granddaughters but cannot finish it (photograph by Paul McCarthy; from Christopher Fitz-Simon,* The Abbey Theatre: Ireland's National Theatre: The First 100 Years, *2003; Thomas Cooper Library, University of South Carolina)*

production of *Bailegangaire,* Murphy reached the pinnacle of critical reception within his career.

Since 1985, Murphy's dramatic output has decreased. He returned to Dublin and to the Abbey, where he became writer-in-association in 1986. This period of formal contact produced one full-length play, *Too Late for Logic* (performed in 1989, published in 1990). The play depicts Christopher, a university lecturer who, wrapped up in the pessimistic philosophies of Arthur Schopenhauer and divorced from the logic of his family, decides to take his own life. The play exploits the theatrical convention of duality of time to allow Christopher the opportunity to observe the gradual buildup to his own failure. The self-observation at the heart of the play, together with the subject of that observation—the self-obsession of middle-aged crisis—allows for a good deal of dry humor, but some critics felt that *Too Late for Logic* is almost too reflective in its tone, lacking the dramatic passions of *The Gigli Concert* and *Bailegangaire*.

With his plays *The Wake* (performed and published in 1998) and *The House* (performed and published in 2000), Murphy returned to the small-mindedness of small-town Ireland, now entrenched in the class-ridden morality of the postindustrial 1990s and the hypocrisy of high-minded family politics. Of the two, *The Wake* best represents the maturity and calm clarity in his subject matter. *The Wake* was staged by the Abbey in 1998, under the direction of Patrick Mason. The play is an adaptation of Murphy's 1994 novel, *The Seduction of Morality,* and tells the story of Vera, an aging New York prostitute returning to her native Irish town for the funeral of her mother. The rejection felt by Vera as the family prepares to cheat her out of her inheritance prompts her to declare war. Desperate yet defiant, she fights back with her sexuality. The highlight comes in a joyful three-in-a-bed romp in the family hotel between Vera, her old boyfriend Finbar, and her ironically bombastic brother-in-law Henry. Drunk, loud, yet sadly self-conscious, the three defy the family and the community that remain locked outside the hotel. The inevitable armistice in the family war prompts a beautifully observed Irish family gathering, complete with liberal amounts of drink, sing-alongs, and the overloud laughter of enforced bonhomie. Understanding and acceptance is sought but never fully found; Vera is befriended but remains isolated. In the microcosm of this small-town family, Murphy observes a divided Ireland, similar to that of the early 1960s, but an Ireland now prepared to accept difference. The effect is sad but compassionate, negative yet mature.

By returning to the setting of his early plays, albeit with the assured and reflective touches of a mature and established playwright, Tom Murphy has drawn a full circle in his career. He is still concerned with exposing the myth of the Irish homogenous society, still the individual on the outside, still confrontational and uncompromising. What has changed is Murphy's audience. No longer shocked or disbelieving, the Abbey audience's response to *The Wake* was one of celebration, laughter, and above all, recognition. Murphy's portrait hangs in the foyer of the Abbey alongside those of William Butler Yeats, John Millington Synge, Sean O'Casey, and Friel.

References:

Michael Etherton, "The Plays of Thomas Murphy," in his *Contemporary Irish Dramatists* (London: Macmillan, 1989), pp. 107–146;

Christopher Fitz-Simon, *The Abbey Theatre: Ireland's National Theatre: The First 100 Years* (London: Thames & Hudson, 2003);

Nicholas Grene, ed., *Talking About Tom Murphy* (Dublin: Carysfort Press, 2002);

Irish University Review, special Murphy issue, edited by Christopher Murray, 17 (Spring 1987);

D. E. S. Maxwell, "Explorations 1956–1982," in his *A Critical History of Modern Irish Drama 1891–1980* (Cambridge: Cambridge University Press, 1984), pp. 158–187;

Maxwell, "New Lamps for Old: The Theatre of Tom Murphy," *Theatre Research International,* 15 (Spring 1990): 57–66;

Christopher Murray, "Revolutionary Times: 'A Generation of Playwrights,'" in his *Twentieth-Century Irish Drama, Mirror up to Nation* (Manchester: University Press, 1997), pp. 162–186;

Fintan O'Toole, *The Politics of Magic: The Work and Times of Tom Murphy* (Dublin: Raven Arts Press, 1987; revised, Dublin: New Island Books, 1994; London: Nick Hern, 1994);

Anthony Roche, "Murphy's Drama: Tragedy and After," in his *Contemporary Irish Drama, from Beckett to McGuinness* (Dublin: Gill & Macmillan, 1994), pp. 129–188.

G. F. Newman

(22 May 1946 -)

Jeremy Ridgman
Roehampton University

PLAY PRODUCTIONS: *Operation Bad Apple,* London, Royal Court Theatre, 4 February 1982;

An Honourable Trade, London, Royal Court Theatre, 11 October 1984.

BOOKS: *Sir, You Bastard* (London: W. H. Allen, 1970; New York: Simon & Schuster, 1970);

Billy: A Family Tragedy (London: New English Library, 1971);

The Abduction (London: New English Library, 1972);

The Player & the Guest (London: New English Library, 1972);

You Nice Bastard (London: New English Library, 1972);

The Split (London: New English Library, 1972);

3 Professional Ladies (London: New English Library, 1973);

The Price (London: New English Library, 1974); republished as *You Flash Bastard* (London: Sphere, 1978);

The Guvnor (London: Hart-Davis MacGibbon, 1977);

A Prisoner's Tale (London: Sphere, 1977);

A Villain's Tale (London: Sphere, 1977);

A Detective's Tale (London: Sphere, 1977);

The List (London: Secker & Warburg, 1979);

The Obsession (London & New York: Granada, 1980);

Charlie and Joanna (London: Granada, 1981);

The Men with the Guns (London: Secker & Warburg, 1982);

Operation Bad Apple (London: Methuen in association with The Royal Court Theatre, 1982);

Law and Order (London: Granada, 1983; revised edition, New York & London: Pocket Books, 1993);

The Nation's Health (London: Granada, 1983);

An Honourable Trade (London: Methuen in association with The Royal Court Theatre, 1984);

Set a Thief (London: Joseph, 1986);

The Testing Ground (London: Joseph, 1987);

Trading the Future (London: Macdonald, 1991);

Circle of Poison (London: Pocket Books, 1995).

G. F. Newman (from the dust jacket for the American edition of Sir, You Bastard, *1970; Boynton Beach City Library)*

PRODUCED SCRIPTS: *Law and Order,* television, BBC, 6, 13, 20, and 27 April 1978;

Billy, television, *Play for Today,* BBC, 13 November 1979;

The Nation's Health, television, Channel 4 (Euston Films), 6, 13, 20, and 27 October 1983;

Here Is the News, television, BBC, 5 March 1989;

Nineteen 96, television, BBC, 17 September 1989;

For the Greater Good, television, BBC, 20 and 27 March and 3 April 1991;

Black and Blue, television, BBC, 27 September 1992;

The Healer, television, BBC, 19 and 20 September 1994;

Woe to the Hunter, motion picture, 1995;

Judge John Deed, television, BBC, 9 January, 26 November, and 3, 10, and 17 December 2001; 21 and 28 November and 12 and 19 December 2002.

SELECTED PERIODICAL PUBLICATIONS–UNCOLLECTED: "If the Face Fits," *Radio Times*, 1 April 1978, pp. 4–5, 10;

"The Friction Over Faction," *Guardian*, 15 May 1989, p. 21;

"Truth Ache," *Time Out* (30 May 1990): 21;

"A Likely Story," *Guardian (G2)*, 15 July 2002, pp. 16–17.

Since the broadcast of his four-part television series *Law and Order* in 1978, G. F. Newman has earned a formidable reputation as one of Britain's most uncompromising television dramatists. His forensic concern with corruption and professional self-interest in the police, the legal system, the health service, and government, conveyed through a highly charged and sometimes sensational realism, has split critical opinion and sometimes sparked anger and debate, particularly within the professions and institutions whose conduct he has laid bare. Tirelessly researched and bolstered by a remarkable degree of insider knowledge, yet frequently prey to charges of dramatic hyperbole, his work has been at the heart of the drama documentary movement in British television, with all the controversy that has dogged that form. While frequently defending his work on the grounds of accuracy, Newman has acknowledged its hyperbolic tendency: "Exaggeration," he wrote in "A Likely Story" in 2002, "is sometimes essential. . . . Drama and fiction is not–and must never be–about consensus; it must remain about position."

Newman remained a relatively anonymous figure for much of his early career but, as his broadly anarchist politics became increasingly shaped by his commitment to spiritualism and radical veganism in the 1980s, his "new age" image was seized upon in the press, both to cast him as a messianic extremist and to throw doubt onto the veracity of his work. Producers, directors, and actors who have worked with him, however, have frequently testified to his integrity, passion, and sensitivity.

Much about Newman's biography remains obscure, the result largely of his own deliberately enigmatic reaction to expressions of interest in his life. Not only has he maintained a certain reticence in press interviews, but there have been moments when he has seemed prepared to weave a mythology around his background and personal experiences, to the point of inventing a fictional identity with the authority to write the work on which he was currently engaged. During a public discussion of *Law and Order*, for example, he casually informed the audience that he had worked as a policeman and had served time in prison, neither of which is true. What is certain is that Gordon Frank Newman was born in Kent on 22 May 1946, the son of an engineer. He failed the "11-plus" examination and left regular education at the age of sixteen to attend a local acting school. Over the next few years he took a variety of jobs, eventually investing his earnings in a flat in Mayfair. In the meantime he began to write fiction and, at the age of twenty-four, published the crime novel *Sir, You Bastard* (1970), partly based on information he had gleaned from a friend in the police force. The book sold two hundred thousand copies and introduced the character of Terry Sneed, the unscrupulous police officer whose unstoppable rise is charted through the subsequent "Bastard" novels and whom Newman later placed at the center of his stage play *Operation Bad Apple* (performed and published in 1982).

The success of *Sir, You Bastard* led to a meeting with Troy Kennedy Martin, scriptwriter on the popular police series *Z-Cars*, noted for its new brand of social realism. Martin in turn introduced Newman to the radical producer Tony Garnett, whose work had included the pioneering documentary drama *Cathy Come Home* (1966) and the four-part drama series on the 1926 General Strike, *Days of Hope* (1975). Garnett commissioned a single script from Newman, then helped him to develop it into the four-part *Law and Order*. In a 1993 BBC television documentary about the changing representation of the police in British television drama, *Barlow, Regan, Pyall and Fancy: Cops on the Box*, Newman summed up his premise thus:

> The person who becomes a policeman has almost the same pathology as the criminal, to express that susceptibility towards crime, if you like. . . . As I've looked at television over the years and particularly television dealing with the police, I've seen nothing other than the contribution to the propaganda battle that the police have been waging to promote this heroic image. And in fact they're anything but heroes.

Using the quartet form that Garnett had developed for *Days of Hope*, Newman wrote four interconnected, eighty-minute episodes–"A Detective's Tale," "A Villain's Tale," "A Brief's Tale," and "A Prisoner's Tale"– each offering a different protagonist's perspective of the same scenario, the frame-up and conviction of a known criminal by the Sneed-like Detective Inspector Fred Pyall. The format was crucial in exposing the processes of detection and conviction to reveal systematic bribery, intimidation, perjury, and above all, a symbiotic relationship between the police and the criminal fraternity based on the reliance on paid informants. The texture of the drama, however–created by dialogue convincingly peppered with the casual use of police and underworld argot, by observational camera work, and by low-key, semi-improvised performances by a cast of unknown actors–emphasized the sense of these actions as typical and simply part of a system that was taken for granted. The impact of the series was enormous. It prompted debate in Parliament, and the BBC came under fire from the Prison Officers' Association and from the Metropolitan Police, who began to push for an agreement that would allow them to approve programs for their representation of the police. At a time when BBC officials were increasingly nervous of government interference, there was a considerable delay before they agreed to repeat the series, and the director general placed a ban on its overseas sale, despite interest from several countries.

In the *Barlow, Regan, Pyall and Fancy* documentary, *Law and Order* was described by one senior police officer as "outrageous . . . a sickening travesty of police work . . . [that] picked up on the small minority of bad behaviour and pretended that that was the normal behaviour for all police officers." Other officers, however, were disturbed by the attention to authentic detail and admitted that "most of the scenes [had] happened in the job without a doubt." It fell to one former chief constable to endorse Newman's underlying proposition by confirming that, because of the constant contact with criminals, "There is a sense in which the policeman and the crook have more in common than the policeman has with other people. He's always doing deals, which are not moral deals. He's undermining his own morality all the time."

At one level, as John Caughie has observed, *Law and Order* stands as "an event within the history of the relations between the police and one of the major media." Despite its status as a four-part one-off rather than a long-running popular series, the production represents a watershed in the development of police drama as a television genre. Newman's Pyall was an officer operating out of control but, in his understated ordinariness, he emerged as representative of an entire institution rather than at odds with it. Furthermore, as the four-part narrative unfolded, he could be seen as a cog in a wider structure that went beyond the police community to include not only the criminal underworld but also a corrupt judicial system and a dysfunctional prison service.

Both in its keen observation of process and in the journey taken through intersecting social institutions to reveal conspiracy and corruption, *Law and Order* became the model for much of Newman's later work. His next work, *Billy,* a single drama transmitted in the BBC *Play for Today* strand in 1979, is perhaps untypical

Dust jacket for the American edition of Newman's first novel (1970), which introduced the character of corrupt police officer Terry Sneed, who reappears in Newman's plays (Boynton Beach City Library)

in this respect, focusing as it does on institutional inadequacy rather than duplicity. The play starts with the situation faced by a boy, the child of teenage parents living in poverty in a high-rise flat, who is physically abused by his father. The canvas broadens to examine the failure of the welfare agencies to tackle the case, as social workers give up and foster parents collapse under the weight of the responsibility placed on them.

With *Operation Bad Apple,* performed at the Royal Court Theatre in 1982, Newman took up where *Law and Order* had left off. The action follows the course of an investigation into corruption in the Metropolitan Police Force (the Met) by a rural constabulary, a scenario clearly based on the real-life Operation Countryman inquiry in 1978 into allegations of corruption against officers in the Metropolitan Police and the City of London Police, conducted by investigating officers from the Dorset Constabulary. Newman strategically emphasizes the fictional nature of his account by placing at its center his larger-than-life antihero, Detective Chief Inspector Terry Sneed. A highly effective thief-taker, with several commendations to his name, Sneed is, in the words of one colleague, "the bentest Old Bill around," massively involved in what is euphemistically referred to as "private enterprise," framing some criminals and taking bribes to protect others. He is also well connected with more senior officers, and especially with the assistant commissioner, who launches the investigation in the opening scene. Once apprehended, Sneed threatens to reveal the extent of the corruption, thereby implicating those above him. In a conspiratorial meeting, the assistant commissioner, the attorney general, and the director of public prosecutions decide to cut short the operation, handing the final inquiries back to the Met itself and focusing attention on a few junior officers, with Sneed himself appointed to guard against further incriminating revelations.

Operation Bad Apple goes even further than *Law and Order* in tracing the pervasiveness of police malpractice. Working in the less regulated environment of the stage, in particular the Royal Court Theatre with its anti-establishment tradition, Newman was also able to be both bolder in the blatancy of his character's behavior and more abrasive in his verbal style. The play moves rapidly from one intense meeting to another, its narrative drive and pungent dialogue reinforcing the sense of Machiavellian intrigue. Nevertheless, the close parallels with an actual ongoing trial of Metropolitan Police led to a legal injunction to prevent the play from opening and threats of action from the attorney general, both of which were ineffective but which succeeded in turning the play into a cause célèbre and ensured a sell-out run. The attacks also prompted a riposte from Newman in the shape of *An Honourable Trade* (performed and published in 1984), again performed at the Royal Court Theatre, in which Sir Walter Pursar, the attorney general from *Operation Bad Apple,* is placed at the center of a network of Parliamentary corruption and sexual exploitation. Called in for an opinion on the strength of the legal cases emanating from the earlier police investigations, Sir Walter advises against prosecution in order to save the government embarrassment. At the same time, he advises against prosecuting in a case of marital rape, only to find himself embroiled in a scandal involving his own sexual mistreatment of his wife and a prostitute. The play ends with an epilogue similar to that of *Operation Bad Apple,* as, following a pact designed simultaneously to head off scandal and to forestall rumors of a cover-up in the police corruption cases, Sir Walter is elevated to the supreme judicial position of lord chancellor.

An Honourable Trade leans further than its companion play in the direction of satirical caricature and, with its direct references to the prime minister of the day, Margaret Thatcher, seems intended much more as a comic broadside against the morality of the new conservatism. In a display of the prescience that characterizes much of Newman's work, it also manages to foreshadow the discourse of "sleaze," the public revelation of sexual scandal and financial self-interest, that dogged the Conservative Party in government some ten years later.

Newman returned to the format of the four-part television drama with *The Nation's Health* in 1983. Given the storm of controversy raised by *Law and Order,* it is unsurprising that the new series was produced not by the BBC but for the newly established Channel 4, whose very remit gave it license to "encourage innovation and experiment in the form and content of programmes." The series follows the progress of a young doctor, Jessie Marvill, as she joins the surgical staff of a large teaching hospital, each episode homing in on a particular area of care or treatment: cancer, obstetrics, geriatrics, and psychiatry. The four episode titles—"Acute," "Decline," "Chronic," and "Collapse"—give an indication of the growing sense of crisis both in the system and in Jessie's sense of vocation. However, although the action unfolds against a backdrop of underresourcing, Newman's concern lies less with the issue of depleted National Health Service (NHS) funding, which was providing the terrain on which the Labour opposition was fighting the Conservative government of the mid 1980s, than with the philosophical foundations of modern medicine itself.

The series certainly depended on Newman's assiduous research into the day-to-day workings of an NHS hospital—bolstered once again by Les Blair's verité-style direction—and was typically critical of the medical establishment and the condescending power wielded by its senior figures; but its politics was also informed by Newman's increasing commitment to the idea of alternative medicine. A key character is Laurence James, a radical doctor who confronts Jessie with the argument for holistic medicine and the concentration on prevention through care rather than intervention through expensive drugs and surgery. Thus, at ground level viewers see a young doctor being rebuked by a consultant for assessing his patient's condition in terms of environmental and social pressures while, higher up, increasing evidence is uncovered of pharmaceutical and equipment manufacturers' economic stake in the running of the hospital. Unsurprisingly, the series met with strong opposition, in particular from the British Medical Association. Notwithstanding its commitment to innovation, Channel Four felt obliged to run a four-part follow-up discussion series in the interests of public-service balance. Newman himself appeared on the viewer feedback program *Right to Reply* in October 1983, where he locked horns with representatives of the medical profession and where his unrepentant defense of the series earned him a scathing reception in the press.

There followed a break of five years in Newman's work for television. He returned in 1989 with two dramas, the single play *Here Is the News* and a three-part adaptation of his 1987 novel, *The Testing Ground*, titled *Nineteen 96*. Both ran into legal difficulties over their closeness to actual events. *Here Is the News* sets out as a conspiracy drama about a journalist working on a story about germ warfare and government cover-up. The real focus of the play, however, is a satirical attack on the faux heroism, hypocrisy, and treachery of press and television journalism. At its center is an investigative journalist, David Dunhill, who leads a secret double life as a kleptomaniac with a penchant for dressing in women's underwear. Newman and the BBC found themselves sued for libel by the real-life investigative journalist Duncan Campbell, who recognized enough details in the protagonist's background to believe that he had been the model for Dunhill. Despite Newman's insistence that he had never based the character on any specific person, Campbell won the suit.

The problems the dramatization of *The Testing Ground* encountered were of a different order. The work concerned the "shoot to kill" policy that the Royal Ulster Constabulary were alleged to have used in policing the unrest in Northern Ireland during the 1980s, a subject also tackled by Peter Kosminsky's docu-drama *Shoot to Kill* (1990) and Ken Loach's movie *Hidden Agenda* (1990). Newman's narrative was based on the case of John Stalker, a senior Manchester police officer who had been sent to Belfast to lead an inquiry into the policy, only to be removed following an apparent conspiracy to discredit him. There were also references to the scandal of the Kincora Boys' Home, where accusations had emerged over several years that members of the security service, civil servants, and many Loyalists had been involved in the sexual abuse of young boys, as well as references to the role played by the former chief of British counterintelligence, Sir Maurice Oldfield—Sir Michael Newfield in Newman's script—in coordinating the work of the various security forces in Northern Ireland. The BBC were not only concerned about the possibility of libel action but also keen to protect their own delicate journalistic relationship with the security forces in Northern Ireland, and Newman was forced to make several revisions. The original three-part serialization was compressed into a single play; names were amended; the setting was transferred to Wales; and, to ensure that there would be no doubt that the action took place in the future and had

Cover for Newman's first play, performed and published in 1982, in which Detective Chief Inspector Sneed is at the enter of a conspiracy to thwart the investigation by a rural constabulary into corruption in the Metropolitan Police Force (University of Alabama Libraries)

no connection to the ongoing police investigation, the title was changed to *Nineteen 96*.

Both in the complexity of its narrative and in the dark mood that prevails in the mise-en-scène, *Nineteen 96* marked a shift in Newman's work toward a dystopian vision of state secrecy that puts it firmly alongside other conspiracy thrillers of the 1980s such as *Edge of Darkness* (1985) by Martin and *A Very British Coup* (1989) by Alan Plater. The same bleak pall hangs over Newman's three-part series *For the Greater Good* (1991) and his single drama *Black and Blue* (1992). *For the Greater Good*, set again in the near future, concerns a government investigation into the critical state of the country's prisons, where the effects of massive overcrowding have been compounded by drug abuse and the spread of AIDS. The crisis is instigated by the revolt of a black prisoner who has been deliberately infected with AIDS by drug-pushing prison officers. Against this background, each episode focuses on the dilemma of a figure within the government, as policy-making is steadily undermined by the quest for personal gain and by darker political motives. In the first episode, "Member," a progressive backbench Conservative member of Parliament is concerned about increasing police power but distracted by the breakdown of his marriage and by his own unrealized political ambitions. "Mandarin" homes in on a senior civil servant and the temptation that she faces to leak confidential information; and in the final play, "Minister," the home secretary, a liberal member of the government, is threatened by a conspiracy among his more hard-line colleagues on the one hand and by the sexual attraction of the young woman who is feeding him information on the other.

In *Black and Blue,* Newman returned to the issue of police corruption, placing it now in the context of racial tension and drug dealing on a run-down inner-city estate—the iconic dystopian landscape of socially aware television drama in the 1990s. An idealistic, inexperienced young black police constable from Devon, Maurice Knight, is brought up to the city to conduct an undercover investigation of the murder of a black councillor. Behind the death lies not only routine police harassment of the black community but a drug-pushing racket conducted by a group of detectives on the street and controlled by the officer who has been deputed to watch over Knight's operation. In an uncanny premonition of what by the end of the 1990s would become officially recognized as institutional racism in the police force, the treatment of the black community is legitimated by attitudes further up the hierarchy. "If you're going to kick a black," advises the chief superintendent, "do it right." The situation is rendered all the more pernicious by Newman's depiction of how members of the black community are recruited by the white officers to do their dirty work for them and, more subtly, how the few black police officers in the force are pressured to subscribe to the racist discourse that surrounds them.

Against this gloomy background and in counterpoint to the apocalyptic imagery of crooks being disposed of in the local crematorium and cars ablaze in the final street riot, the crusading optimism of Knight shines through at every stage of the narrative. Not only does *Black and Blue,* constructed as it is along the lines of a full-blown police thriller rather than the fly-on-the-wall naturalism of *Law and Order,* mark a shift in Newman's acceptance of the genre requirements of television drama; it also introduces the figure of the good man among villains, a protagonist who may not prevail but whose uncluttered commitment to human well-being cuts through the perfidy that surrounds him.

Such a vision lies behind Newman's return to the topic of medicine and health in *The Healer* (1994), a two-part drama about a young doctor, John Lassiter, who starts work in an NHS teaching hospital and discovers that he has the power of healing through touch. The play shows even more clearly than *The Nation's Health* the influence of Newman's spiritualist belief and his advocacy of alternative and holistic medicine. While one of the key themes is Lassiter's inability to perform miracles on demand, there is little ambiguity about the central scene, in which he brings a boy out of a life-threatening coma, or the final moment, in which a man with cerebral palsy is "cured" by his passing touch. At the BBC, however, Newman had to negotiate with more skeptical forces. The project was delayed for several months by the controller of BBC1, Alan Yentob, who was concerned that Lassiter should not come across as an untarnished hero, while the director, Mike Hodges, sought to create an ironic distance from the scenario by overlaying it with a tone of whimsical comedy.

The appeal of the play hinges on a tension between fantasy and realism, rendered all the more intriguing by the verisimilitude of the hospital-drama conventions within which the drama is embedded. Lassiter, for all his doubts and imperfections, is a utopian figure whose unsettling presence serves to challenge not just the hospital's institutionalized practices—especially those governed by power politics, personal ambition, and cost-effectiveness—but the wider culture of contemporary medicine. At the center of the narrative is a conflict with the hospital management, who seek at first to discredit Lassiter but are then persuaded to accede to a public manifestation of his powers by the promise of an endowment for a new scanner by the young coma patient's grateful mother. At the other end of the spectrum, the Christ-like following generated by Lassiter's gift among the hospital patients, gently comic at first but increasingly manic as the desire for miracles snowballs, can be read as a critique of society's dependency on the power of doctors. The problem with the NHS, Newman argues in "A Likely Story," was not its failure but the "burgeoning expectations it fosters in the people who use it. None of us are encouraged to take care of our own health."

Honored by the British Academy of Film and Television Arts (BAFTA) in 1992 with the Writer's Award for the achievement of his work up to that date and then in 1996 for *The Healer,* Newman nevertheless found it increasingly difficult during the 1990s to interest broadcasting executives in his particular brand of polemical and investigative drama. He began to act as producer, promoting his own work and later that of other writers, and forming his own company, One-Eyed Dog Ltd.

With his partner Rebecca Hall, a writer on animal rights, Newman became increasingly committed during the 1990s to the politics of radical veganism. This passionate, campaigning concern is expressed in *Woe to the Hunter,* the short motion picture he wrote, directed, and produced in 1995. Ten minutes long, it shows a farmer rising early in the morning to meet a shooting party coming up from the city. As he shaves and dresses and while his wife sleeps, he is visited by images of earlier kills, images that haunt him through the rest of the day. The movie was broadcast by the BBC in 1996 in a series of shorts titled *10 x 10* but later submitted by Newman as an independent short in experimental-film festivals.

In sharp contrast with this project, and after more than half a decade working outside the mainstream, Newman returned to the heart of television drama in 2001 with the highly popular *Judge John Deed.* First broadcast in January as a one-off pilot, it was immediately commissioned by the BBC as a series, running for three four-episode seasons over the next two years. Produced by One-Eyed Dog Ltd., it was developed under the BBC's aegis by Ruth Caleb (who had also produced *Nineteen 96* and *Black and Blue*) and Mal Young, the corporation's controller of continuing drama series. Young has been credited as the executive largely responsible for leading a populist revival in drama commissioning and scheduling at the BBC, and it is thus no coincidence that, more than any previous work by Newman, *Judge John Deed* locks onto recognizable conventions of the formula-led, ongoing television series.

At its center is the classic maverick protagonist, juggling the demands of his profession with his personal and domestic commitments. John Deed is an unconventional high-court judge, a lawyer from a working-class background, who is prepared to take a stand against rules and bureaucracy, risking his professional standing in defense of his liberal principles and, above all, allowing his emotions and instincts to guide his decisions. He is witty, charming, and attractive; but, like all such mavericks, he is also a flawed character, sometimes arrogant, occasionally misguided, and something of a womanizer, still balancing unresolved relationships with his former wife and a former mistress (also a barrister). The series was built around the potential for high-profile casting, not only through the choice of the television star Martin Shaw—a longtime friend and collaborator of Newman's—for the central role, but also with a group of regular parts played by such charismatic actors as Jenny Seagrove, Caroline Langrishe, Christopher Cazenove, and Donald Sinden, and individual slots for guest actors along the way. With its

Cover for Newman's 1984 play, a satire of Parliamentary scandal and sexual exploitation, in which an abusive attorney general is ultimately promoted to lord chancellor (University of Mississippi Libraries)

own website (<http://www.bbc.co.uk/drama/crime/judge/>) and with a plethora of interviews and previews prior to the launch of the successive seasons, *Judge John Deed,* in a dramatic contrast with most of Newman's earlier work, functioned as a marketable commodity, with all the allure of post-1990s "quality" television.

Within this populist genre framework, however, Newman strategically pursues story lines that continue to express his concerns with institutional corruption, political conspiracy, and medical ethics. Some threads, such as Deed's perennially hostile relationship with his former father-in-law, a traditionalist senior appeal-court judge, or the campaign by the Lord Chancellor's Department to discredit him, are extended over several episodes; others, such as the case of a corrupt senior judge, are buried, only to resurface later in the series. The backbone of the series, however, is formed by the individual cases upon which Deed must adjudicate and which involve him in complex political and ethical decisions and, in accordance with the expectations of the genre, his own behind-the-scene investigations. At one end of the scale there is the case of an Arab sheik who is implicated in a murder but whose role in an arms deal with a British aircraft manufacturer leads first to government pressure on Deed and then to the mysterious death of the prosecuting counsel. At the other lies the decision Deed must take in the case of a boy with heart disease who has brought an injunction, against the wishes of his parents, to prevent surgeons attempting a possibly life-saving transplant. Deed's parental instincts govern his decision, and he lifts the injunction; but the boy dies on the operating table, having spent his final weeks not at peace but still pleading for surgery not to take place.

If *Judge John Deed* can be seen as the product of the inevitable negotiation between a highly individual author and the new commercialist scheduling practices of public-service television, it also represents a change in G. F. Newman's approach to the injustices he sees around him and an attempt to tell what he has referred to as more "aspirational" stories. "One has to change," he declared in "Natural Lawman" in 2000; "First you go behind the closed doors into the secret rooms of the police and hospitals, you open them up and shine some light in. Then the next stage is taking the people on the journey from wanting to be in the dark, to the light; from bad to good." There is, nevertheless, no doubting the unremitting belief in the potential of drama and fiction to promote social reform that has continued to sustain Newman's commitment to writing for television. It is not surprising, then, that in "A Likely Story" he should have cited as his antecedents such writers as Charles Dickens, Upton Sinclair, John Steinbeck, and Jeremy Sandford (the author of *Cathy Come Home*). Above all, he has testified to the continued value of television drama as a form of polemic that sits at the heart of the national consciousness and that has the power not only to shock and disturb but also to challenge society's most cherished, and at times most casually held, assumptions and beliefs.

Interviews:

Eithne Power, "Doctors on the Critical List," *TV Times* (1 October 1983): 67;

Martyn Auty, "The Body Politic," *Time Out* (6 October 1983): 5–6;

Simon Hattenstone, "The Guardian Profile: Natural Lawman," *Guardian B Saturday Review,* 30 December 2000, pp. 6–7.

References:

Barlow, Regan, Pyall and Fancy: Cops on the Box, BBC, 31 May 1993;

Richard Brooks, "BBC Cuts Play on 'Shoot to Kill,'" *Observer,* 9 July 1989, p. 4;

Brooks, "In Politics, Cynicism Rules OK," *Observer,* 17 March 1991, p. 27;

John Caughie, "Progressive Television and Documentary Drama," in *Popular Television and Film,* edited by Tony Bennett, Sue Boyd-Bowman, Colin Mercer, and Janet Woollacott (London: BFI/Open University, 1981), pp. 333–349;

Bernard Davies, "One Man's Television," *Broadcast* (17 April 1978): 14, 38; (8 May 1978): 8–9;

Sean Day-Lewis, "A Tradition of Self-Censorship," *Broadcast* (12 April 1991): 56;

David Downes and Rod Morgan, "Dumping the 'Hostages to Fortune'? The Politics of Law and Order in Post-War Britain," in *The Oxford Handbook of Criminology,* edited by Mike Maguire and others (Oxford: Oxford University Press, 1997), pp. 87–134;

Paul Nathanson, "Why Judges Need More Emotion," *Times Law Supplement* (9 January 2001): 11;

"Nursing Hope for Society," *Television Today,* no. 5918 (15 September 1994): 19;

C. H. Rolph, "Nothing But the Worst," *Radio Times,* 219, no. 2844 (13 May 1978): 70;

James Saynor, "Astral Tweaks," *Guardian,* 12 September 1994, G2, pp. 14–15;

John Stalker, "The Wrong Arm of the Law," *Sunday Times,* 20 September 1992, p. 25;

Patrick Stoddart, "Off Air," *Broadcast* (21 October 1983): 15; (4 November 1983): 24;

John Tulloch, *Television Drama: Agency, Audience and Myth* (London: Routledge, 1990), p. 73;

John Wyver, "Dirty Coppers," *Time Out* (31 March 1978): 8–9.

Joe Orton
(1 January 1933 – 9 August 1967)

Francesca Coppa
Muhlenberg College

See also the Orton entry in *DLB 13: British Dramatists Since World War II.*

PLAY PRODUCTIONS: *Entertaining Mr. Sloane,* London, New Arts Theatre, 6 May 1964 (transferred to Wyndham Theatre, 29 June 1964; transferred to Queen's Theatre, 5 October 1964); New York, Lyceum Theatre, 12 October 1965;

Loot, Cambridge, Arts Theatre, 1 February 1965; revised, Manchester, University Theatre, 11 April 1966; revised again, London, Jeanetta Cochrane Theatre, 27 September 1966; New York, Biltmore Theatre, 18 March 1968;

The Ruffian on the Stair, London, Royal Court Theatre, 21 August 1966; produced with *The Erpingham Camp* as *Crimes of Passion,* London, Royal Court Theatre, 6 June 1967; New York, Astor Place Theatre, 26 October 1969;

The Erpingham Camp, produced with *The Ruffian on the Stair* as *Crimes of Passion,* London, Royal Court Theatre, 6 June 1967; New York, Astor Place Theatre, 26 October 1969;

What the Butler Saw, London, Queen's Theatre, 5 March 1969; New York, McAlpin Rooftop Theatre, 4 May 1970;

The Good and Faithful Servant, London, King's Head Theatre, 17 March 1971;

Fred and Madge, Oxford, Oxford Playhouse, 1 March 2000.

BOOKS: *Entertaining Mr. Sloane* (London: Hamish Hamilton, 1964; New York: Grove, 1965);

Loot (London: Methuen, 1967; New York: Grove, 1967);

Crimes of Passion (London: Methuen, 1967)—comprises *The Ruffian on the Stair* [revised] and *The Erpingham Camp;*

What the Butler Saw (London: Methuen, 1969; New York: S. French, 1969);

Funeral Games; and, The Good and Faithful Servant (London: Methuen, 1970);

Joe Orton (photograph by Lewis Morley, National Portrait Gallery, NPG P512 [16])

Head to Toe (London: Anthony Blond, 1971; New York: St. Martin's Press, 1986);

Up Against It: A Screenplay for the Beatles (London: Eyre Methuen, 1979; New York: Grove, 1979);

The Orton Diaries: Including the Correspondence of Edna Welthorpe and Others, edited by John Lahr (London: Methuen, 1986; New York: Harper & Row, 1986; republished, New York: Da Capo Press, 1996);

Between Us Girls: A Novel (London: Nick Hern, 1998; New York: Grove, 1998);

Fred and Madge; The Visitors: Two Plays (London: Nick Hern, 1998; New York: Grove, 1998);

The Boy Hairdresser; and, Lord Cucumber: Two Novels, by Orton and Kenneth Halliwell (London: Nick Hern, 1999).

Collection: *The Complete Plays* (London: Eyre Methuen, 1976; New York: Grove, 1976)—comprises *Entertaining Mr. Sloane, Loot, What the Butler Saw, The Ruffian on the Stair, The Erpingham Camp, Funeral Games,* and *The Good and Faithful Servant.*

PRODUCED SCRIPTS: *The Ruffian on the Stair,* radio, BBC Third Programme, 31 August 1964;

The Erpingham Camp, television, Rediffusion Television, 27 June 1966;

The Good and Faithful Servant, television, Rediffusion Television, 6 April 1967;

Funeral Games, television, Yorkshire Television, 25 August 1968.

SELECTED PERIODICAL PUBLICATION– UNCOLLECTED: "Until She Screams," *Evergreen Review,* no. 78 (May 1970).

Joe Orton wrote high comedy about working-class characters and changed the face of gay theater while he was at it. Orton's work brought two distinct theatrical traditions together, combining the epigrammatic comedy of manners (as practiced by such writers as William Congreve, Oscar Wilde, and Noel Coward) and the 1950s drama of social anger and circumstantial menace (as pioneered by John Osborne, Arnold Wesker, and Harold Pinter). The result was a hilarious, terrifying hybrid: plays about characters whose high language belies their low circumstances.

Orton's fusion of society comedy and social anger had important ramifications for the history of gay drama and performance. High comedy had, by Orton's time, become associated with homosexuality because of its link to Wilde, and its cast of aristocrats, dandies, and grandes dames personified mid-twentieth-century gay stereotypes. Such characters were effeminate, aesthetic, leisured, amoral, witty, and charming; and while those qualities did not necessarily read as queer in Wilde's time, in the years after the Wilde trials they came to have strong homosexual associations. In contrast, the "angry" drama of 1956 and after was hailed not only for bringing working-class authors to the forefront and working-class characters to the stage, but for being an implicitly heterosexual theater. The new theater was described by its champions as "vigorous," "vital," and even "virile," in explicit contrast to the supposed artificiality, feyness, and sterility of the previous tradition. It is difficult not to see these two stage traditions as divided both in terms of class (upper vs. lower) and of sexuality (effeminate vs. manly; queer vs. straight), which makes Orton's ability to combine them both significant and provocative.

Because of his youth, his class, and his Leicester upbringing, Orton was originally grouped with the working-class dramatists, though his work was both liked and supported by the old guard as well. (Sir Terence Rattigan admired Orton's first play, *Entertaining Mr. Sloane* [performed and published in 1964], well enough to invest in it; Laurence Olivier and Vivien Leigh were also fans.) Orton's characters are, like Wilde's, insouciant and charming, but they are from the opposite end of the class spectrum; if they appear leisured, for instance, it is because they are on the dole or involved in something criminal. While Wilde's aristocrats threatened middlebrow sensibilities from above, Orton's hooligans threaten from below, challenging the pieties and values of conventional society by being amoral, streetwise, and carelessly, almost defiantly, bisexual. Orton's affection for such characters extended even to the remaking of his own image; the asthmatic Royal Academy of Dramatic Arts (RADA)-trained actor "John Orton" reinvented himself as the leather-clad, former-convict playwright "Joe Orton," a process that took the better part of thirty years.

John Kingsley Orton was born in Leicester on 1 January 1933, the first child of William Orton, a gardener, and his wife, Elsie, a machinist. Leicester was at the time a key center for garment manufacturing, which meant that there were plenty of jobs for women, who were therefore able to maintain a certain kind of economic and social strength. Elsie Orton had ambitions for her eldest son, who was quiet and a reader and consequently thought to be more gifted than his three siblings. But Orton was also sickly, suffering particularly from asthma attacks that kept him out of school for long periods of time. When Orton flunked his "eleven plus" exam, which prevented him from continuing his education at an academically oriented grammar school, Elsie Orton pawned her wedding ring to send him to a private, fee-paying school in defiance of all local convention. However, the school she chose, Clark's College, was a secretarial college rather than an academic one; Orton was taught typing and shorthand instead of Latin and Greek.

In later years, Orton made satire out of this disjunction between his mother's pretensions and his actual circumstances, but at the time, it only made him more desperate. Biographer John Lahr reveals that despite Elsie Orton's belief in her son's intellectual gifts, Orton was, according to his teachers, "semi-literate. He couldn't spell. He couldn't string a sentence together. He couldn't express himself. He used to start a sentence and then get

Beryl Reid as Kath and Malcolm McDowell as Sloane in the 1975 Royal Court Theatre revival of Orton's 1964 play,
Entertaining Mr. Sloane, *in which a tough young lodger is blackmailed into becoming the lover of a woman and her brother (photograph by John Haynes; from his* Taking the Stage: Twenty-one Years of the London Theatre. Photographs, *1986; Richland County Public Library)*

all het up. He had no vocabulary." Orton's adolescent diaries confirm his teachers' assessments of him, at least as far as spelling and grammar goes: "27 January 1949 Not a very good day. Finished all my work so asked Horace he gave me some work. I didn't like cleaning ink wells." But these early diaries also show Orton's determination to improve himself. He took notes on the books he read and the movies he attended. He vowed to practice his tennis and work on his physique.

Orton had already focused his ambitions on the theater, which required him to save money for cast albums, playscripts, and, perhaps most important, elocution lessons, which he began in 1950 in an attempt to improve his Midlands-inflected speaking voice. He joined the Leicester Dramatic Society, where he was soon cast as a messenger in a production of William Shakespeare's *Richard III*. Orton had only three lines, but he found the experience exhilarating and immediately joined two other dramatic societies, the Bats Players and the Vaughn Players, so that all his evenings were taken up with rehearsals. The lowly and frail office clerk dreamed of his glorious future as an actor.

By 1950 Orton had identified a goal that, by all contemporary accounts, was beyond the reach of both his talent and his finances: he wanted to be accepted at England's premiere drama school, RADA. Inspired partly by a newspaper article in which Olivier mentioned the possibility of scholarships for talented youngsters, Orton began to save his money and work up audition pieces. He got good marks on an early technical exam, placed third at the Nottingham Festival of Music and Drama, and then, to his elocution teacher's surprise, won a place at RADA with what Orton himself called an "alarming" audition piece, a dialogue "from Peter Pan between Captain Hook and Smee, both at the same time, a kind of schizophrenic act" (quoted in Lahr, *Prick Up Your Ears: The Biography of Joe Orton*, 1978).

Orton left Leicester for London in 1951. A month after the term started, he stopped writing his juvenile diary, though not before he recorded having met Kenneth Halliwell, who was also enrolled in the acting classes. As is often the way with diaries, as events get more exciting, the descriptions of those events become more elliptical, though the future playwright is already demonstrating a knack for dramatic construction:

12 June 1951 Ken offers to share flat again.

13 June 1951 I say no.

14 June 1951 Ken offers again.

15 June 1951 We accept because we must.

16 June 1951 Move into Ken's flat

17 June 1951 Well!

18 June 1951 Well!!

19 June 1951 Well!!!

20 June 1951 The rest is silence.

Halliwell, Orton's literary partner and lover for sixteen years, radically changed Orton's life, although it is often difficult to evaluate that constructive impact on Orton's development in light of the fact that Halliwell murdered Orton in August 1967.

Halliwell was seven years older than Orton, a sophisticated twenty-five to Orton's eighteen when they met. Halliwell was middle-class, the only child of a senior chartered accountant at a large company, and grew up in Bebington, a suburb of Liverpool. Unlike Orton, Halliwell had been a promising student and was sent to grammar school, where he excelled in classics and was expected to go on to Oxford or Cambridge. But like Orton, Halliwell fell in love with the theater. Halliwell had been a successful local actor in Bebington, and consequently he approached RADA with a confidence that bordered on arrogance. Both of his parents were dead (his mother by an accident, his father by suicide), which left Halliwell independent and with inherited money to spend. And, perhaps most important for Orton's future, Halliwell considered himself both an actor and a writer, whereas Orton's "literary" work before meeting Halliwell was confined exclusively to his diaries.

However, despite being the younger and less experienced actor of the two, Orton was more successful at RADA. Halliwell was better educated, more analytical, more intellectual, but perhaps consequentially, too cerebral in his approach to acting. Orton, not Halliwell, was chosen to be in RADA's public show the year they graduated, and Orton landed the better job after graduation, as an assistant stage manager at Ipswich Rep. But neither Orton nor Halliwell succeeded in the world of repertory theater, and soon they were back in London and living together while Halliwell attempted to become a novelist. They lived in that same studio apartment for the rest of their lives.

Initially, Orton served as Halliwell's assistant. But Halliwell served as a mentor to Orton, directing his education and encouraging Orton to collaborate with him. They formed a writing partnership, though in the early days there was no question as to who was the senior partner. In *Prick Up Your Ears*, Charles Monteith, an editor at the publishers Faber and Faber, describes the pair in the early 1950s:

> I had a very clear impression at the first meeting that Kenneth was the one that did the writing. Kenneth was the talker. He liked to turn words around and savour them. Kenneth's talk, his appearance, his age vis-a-vis Orton certainly gave the impression that Kenneth was the literary figure. I thought that John was quite simply his young, pretty, and rather vivacious boyfriend.

But Orton was applying the same quiet diligence to writing that he had previously applied to acting. He was reading the writers that Halliwell was telling him to read: the ancient Greeks, Christopher Marlowe, Wilde, Ronald Firbank, and Jean Genet; he was developing his vocabulary, compiling pages of unusual adjectives (*affably, athletically, allergically, apocalyptically*); and he was testing the way words fit together, composing page after page of impressionistic Firbankian sentences.

In the earliest part of his literary career, 1953 to 1956, Orton wrote as a junior partner in collaboration with Halliwell. Together they produced *Lord Cucumber* (written in 1954, first published in 1999), as well as at least four other novels, now lost, including "The Silver Bucket" (1953), "The Mechanical Womb" (1955), "The Last Days of Sodom" (1955), and the first of three works to be titled "The Boy Hairdresser" (1956).

Lord Cucumber details the life of the orphaned Helen Hagg, Lord Cucumber's young secretary, and her love for and eventual marriage to Richard Cucumber, Lord Cucumber's heir and son. Helen is armed against a cruel, class-stratified world with only her typing and shorthand skills and must face a considerable number of difficulties before getting her man and literally walking off with him into the sunset.

The novel satirizes the literary obsession with the aristocracy and specifically engages with the reader's desire for a worthy but poor heroine to claim her rightful (moral) place among the (idealized) upper classes. As with much of Halliwell and Orton's work, Jane Austen is a starting point. Halliwell and Orton also mock genres where a naive class-lust reoccurs, such as Hollywood movies, the British murder mystery (Agatha Christie's *Death on the Nile* [1937] seems to be referenced particularly), and Mills and Boon novels (the British equivalent of Harlequin Romances). More important, each of the characters seems to be covertly pursuing a member of the same sex even as they overtly pursue more-suitable mates. But while *Lord Cucumber* and Orton and Halliwell's other collaborative works attracted the attention of various publishers, none were ever published in Halliwell and Orton's lifetime.

Sheila Ballantine as Fay, Gerry Duggan as McLeavy, Kenneth Cranham as Hal, and Michael Bates as Truscott in a 1966 production of Orton's 1965 play, Loot, *in which a bank-robbing son, a murderous nurse, and a corrupt detective triumph over a law-abiding man's faith in the system (photograph by Romano Cagnoni–Report London; from the 1996 edition of* The Orton Diaries: Including the Correspondence of Edna Welthorpe and Others, *1986; Thomas Cooper Library, University of South Carolina)*

In the latter part of 1956, Orton and Halliwell decided to write separately. Between 1956 and 1962, Orton produced a diary novel (*Between Us Girls,* written in 1957 but not published until 1998), a Swiftian satiric fable ("The Vision of Gombold Proval," written in 1961 and published in 1971 as *Head to Toe*), and two startlingly different plays: *Fred and Madge* (published in 1998, performed in 2000) and *The Visitors* (published in 1998). Orton's second-phase work reveals a writer who was interested in experimentation and paying attention to trends in contemporary writing. While Halliwell continued to write in the style of Firbank, producing the now-lost novel "Priapus in the Shrubbery" in 1959, Orton experimented with new styles and forms.

In *Between Us Girls,* Orton's first solo literary work, his preoccupation with the disjunction between his characters' lives and their language can already be seen. The novel chronicles the adventures of Susan Hope, aspiring starlet. The humor of the story lies in the fact that Susan lives in a fantasy world created by romantic fiction and the movies, and she refuses to recognize the corruptness of the real world in which she lives. Susan chooses to focus on the correctness of her grammar rather than the fact that she is auditioning for sex shows, though not even her excellent syntax can save her from being sold into white slavery in the second half of the novel. Orton ultimately allows Susan to escape to Hollywood, where she becomes a singing and dancing sensation. With her concern for good manners and her ability to ignore unpleasant realities, Susan prefigures the character of Kath in Orton's *Entertaining Mr. Sloane* six years later.

Orton's first play, *Fred and Madge,* written in 1959, shows that he was paying attention to trends in contemporary writing; the play fused the "angry" drama of the mid 1950s and the absurdism of Samuel Beckett. Fred and Madge are a working-class couple who are trying to break out of the dehumanizing routines of everyday life. However, those routines are partially represented by the rituals of theater itself; the characters are aware that they are in a play, and one of Fred's menial jobs is to move the props and scenery (a

Orton in London, 1966 (photograph by John Haynes; from his Taking the Stage: Twenty-one Years of the London Theatre. Photographs, *1986; Richland County Public Library)*

job Orton, a former assistant stage manager, knew well). As the play progresses, the action becomes increasingly absurd, the language more fantastic.

Like many of the characters who populated the social drama of the 1950s, Fred and Madge have spent their lives working at brutal and pointless jobs, but Orton plays the familiar "angry" tune in an absurd key: Fred rolls boulders up a ramp, and Madge transports water in a sieve. Fred demonstrates his pride in this good, honest work; bourgeois clichés such as "work is recognized as a virtue," the need for "security," and being a "useful member of society" both entrap and sustain him in his Sisyphean task. Similarly, Madge and her coworkers at the water-sieving plant break into virtual choruses of proverbs: "Look on the bright side," "Take the rough with the smooth," and "Into each life some rain must fall."

Orton argues that the exploitation of the working class is greatly aided by this kind of thinking in proverbs and clichés—the limitations of these characters' lives are reflected in the limitations of their speech and their ideas. Throughout his career, Orton created humor from the disjunction between what people say and what they do. In *Fred and Madge* the characters who have been most oppressed by the class system are those most deeply immersed in its rules and values and most brainwashed by its language. However, as in *Between Us Girls,* Orton again allows his characters to escape their circumstances. This time, the Fantasyland is not Hollywood, but India—not the real, postcolonial India, but a fantasy India:

> Fred. We shall be the favourites of princes; ride in howdahs and palanquins; live in purple-hued throne rooms; dine off golden platters; listen to the music of flutes; watch the dancing of exotic slaves—
>
> Petrie.—of either gender.
>
> Madge. How marvellous!

The characters of *Fred and Madge* reject the English for the exotic, while Orton explodes his characters' clichéd speech patterns and substitutes baroque, Firbankian lavishness: "The swaying palms and the camels and the seductive dances of the Murri-murri, oh I can see it all," exclaims Fred, glorying in his new vocabulary. The characters bid farewell to the audience and leave the play for the promise of an unlikely Indian utopia, but as the play spells out for its audience, "We shall not despise the unlikely."

Orton followed *Fred and Madge* with a different kind of play: *The Visitors,* written in 1961. Originally intended for television, *The Visitors* is quiet where *Fred and Madge* is exuberant, realist where *Fred and Madge* is fantastic; but although it got the attention of both the Royal Court Theatre and the BBC, both ultimately rejected it. The play tells the story of Mrs. Platt's visit to her dying father in the hospital and shows Orton attempting a more straightforward illustration of his mastery of working-class syntax: both the Royal Court Theatre and the BBC thought the dialogue "excellent" but rejected the play on structural grounds. Kemp, the dying father, is forced to listen to the relentless and false cheeriness of his daughter, who, like Madge and her friends, speaks in platitudes, generalities, and clichés. Mrs. Platt, in fact, appears to be Madge's sister, and in her flow of gossip she mentions many of the characters of *Fred and Madge,* while referring to different events: in *The Visitors,* Orton apparently decided to flesh out the same characters in a more naturalistic way. Orton repeatedly and obsessively rewrote his own work: in fact, Mrs. Platt and Kemp are themselves the first drafts of daughter and father duo Kath and Kemp in *Entertaining Mr. Sloane.*

Like Kath, Mrs. Platt is both infantile and infantalizing ("Have a grape? Grapie? A little one?" she coaxes her father), and through a stultifying combination of childish optimism and fatuous propriety, she prevents discussion of almost everything that Orton thinks important. Like Kath, and like Susan from *Between Us Girls,* Mrs. Platt censors unpleasant language in herself and others, and the thoughts and ideas that such language expresses. In Orton's work, women are generally made to represent the false social niceties that prevent realities—work, sex, death—from being articulated and understood. The keynote of Mrs. Platt's personality is represented by such censorious lines as: "You're not to talk like that!" "I won't have that kind of talk!" and "You can stop *dwelling* on that subject." The fact that Kemp is actually about to die cannot be acknowledged in public, either by Mrs. Platt or by the nurses who attend Kemp, although they admit as much in the safety of the nurses' room.

Orton and Halliwell reunited as collaborators once, briefly, in 1960, to write the second work titled *The Boy Hairdresser* (the one published in 1999), a novel in which Orton and Halliwell fictionalize themselves as hip London antiheroes. Donelly, the character clearly inspired by Halliwell, is a writer (albeit one "too good to be published"), a social rebel ("how could even God love the wives of stockbrokers and the pigs who run and are run by materialism?"), and a defiant homosexual. By contrast, Peterson, Orton's represenative in the novel, is portrayed as a charming ideological waffler, a "crypto-beat, a fraudulent rebel, a man whose anger was not strictly on the level." Peterson is torn between conventional values ("I know it sounds stupid," said Peterson, "but I don't want to drift . . . I'd like to put down roots before its too late. I can't go on in this way forever.") and a more rebellious life with Donelly. But Peterson's murder by a hit man at the end of the novel brings their relationship to a tragic end. The grief-stricken Donelly races out into the streets with a gun, but his attempt at revenge is a failure.

Orton's final attempt at novel writing was "The Vision of Gombold Proval," a satiric fantasy in which Gombold travels over the body of a giant, considering questions of sex and language and meeting various "disreputable" working-class men along the way. However, the centerpiece of the book is his encounter in prison with Doktor von Pregnant—another thinly disguised portrait of Halliwell. A great scholar, the Doktor takes on the task of educating Gombold and helps him dig his way to freedom. But Doktor von Pregnant himself never escapes the prison: he is shot by the guards before he reaches the end of the tunnel.

While Gombold manages to escape his prison with the help of the Doktor, prison was about to become a reality for Orton. He and Halliwell were arrested on 28 April 1962 for stealing 72 library books from the Islington Public Library, "unlawfully and maliciously causing damage" to an additional 62, and "wilfully" damaging others by removing from them a total of 1,653 art plates. Orton and Halliwell pleaded guilty and were sentenced to six months in jail as well as a substantial fine.

Lahr records in *Prick Up Your Ears* that Orton was privately convinced that their sentences were so harsh "because we were queers." Lahr notes that Orton and Halliwell attracted the suspicion of a branch librarian because they always visited the library together and shared the same address. The crime was described as "childish . . . prompted by feelings that are unusual," and in *Because We're Queers: The Life and Crimes of Kenneth Halliwell and Joe Orton* (1989) Simon Shepherd observes that these phrases are easily recognizable code words for homosexuality. Additionally, the severe sentence that Orton and Halliwell received for defacing library books was in line with the punishment other homosexuals then received for the sexual crime of "gross indecency."

Although technically the pair were charged with stealing and defacing books, their real crime was refacing those books. Orton and Halliwell altered the dust jackets and texts of many of the books they stole, and replaced those doctored books on the library shelves. The most famous of their visual alterations was "Gorilla in the Roses," which was also the title of the *Daily Mirror* headline announcing their arrest: Orton and Halliwell redesigned the *Collins Guide to Roses,* sticking a monkey's head into the large yellow rose on the cover. Orton and Halliwell also altered the texts themselves, adding obscene subtitles (such as "Up the Back," "Knickers Must Fall," and "Fucked by Monty"), photographic captions, or back-cover summaries. These works got the attention of library personnel and caused them to investigate; only later did the librarians realize that Orton and Halliwell had perpetrated a large-scale theft. However, in court the crime was repeatedly emphasized as the alteration of books, not their absence, and it was noted by the senior probation officer that "in a sense both defendants were frustrated authors."

When Orton and Halliwell came out of prison, they were broke, unemployed, and socially disgraced. But oddly enough, prison was just the break that Orton needed. "I tried writing before I went into the nick . . . but it was no good," Orton told the *Leicester Mercury* in

Avril Elgar as Joyce and Michael Standing as Wilson in a 1967 production of Orton's 1966 play The Ruffian on the Stair, *in which a man tries unsuccessfully to expose his brother's murderer (photograph by Douglas Jeffery; from the 1996 edition of* The Orton Diaries: Including the Correspondence of Edna Welthorpe and Others, *1986; Thomas Cooper Library, University of South Carolina)*

1964. "Being in the nick brought detachment to my writing. I wasn't involved any more" (quoted in *Prick Up Your Ears*). It did not hurt his career, either; in the early 1960s, working-class artists were dominating London, and a prison term was the ultimate sign of credibility.

Orton's work had come to the attention of the BBC Third Programme with a radio script titled "The Boy Hairdresser," the third Orton work to bear the title. The play was accepted in August 1963, subject to revision—and during the time between its acceptance and its broadcast, Orton not only revised his play but re-created himself. This version of "The Boy Hairdresser" became *The Ruffian on the Stair* (broadcast in 1964, performed in 1966, published in 1967), and John Kingsley Orton became Joe Orton.

The name change from "John Kingsley" to "Joe" was not purely superficial. Having finally attracted the attention of the theatrical establishment and the greater public, "Joe" crafted a personality and a history to go with his new name. Asked for an autobiographical sketch for the program of *Entertaining Mr. Sloane,* Orton delivered a calculated mix of fact and fiction:

> I was born in Leicester. I didn't get the 11 plus. I went to what, I suppose, is now called a secondary modern school. I've been married. And divorced. I've worked at various jobs, including unloading chocolates at Cadbury's railway sidings, helping in the making of sex hormones at the British Drug Houses and cleaning the lenses on spectacles. I was in prison for six months in 1962 for larceny (not really as grand as it seems.) This is my first full-length play, though I wrote one before this which the BBC have bought. Nobody knows when it's to be put on . . . Oh, I'm thirty-one. Since I came out of prison in September 1962 I've been living on the National Assistance.
>
> Is that enough?

The version of himself that Orton promoted was calculated to emphasize the authenticity of his working-class background and the rawness of his talent; it also suggested heterosexuality. To further support this image of Joe Orton, novice writer, Orton lowered his age from thirty-one to twenty-five in the final version of his program biography.

The press fell in love with the idea of the young, working-class, novice playwright and thrust him into the national spotlight. They turned the attractive and photogenic Orton into a poster boy for the new British theater, and his image—the playwright in T-shirt and leather jacket, arms crossed, pouting into the camera against the background of a seedy North London street—accompanied articles with headlines such as "Theatre's New Star Signs on the Dole," "What Prison Did for This Playwright," and "It's Still Fish and Chips for Joe Orton." At the center of these articles were what one newspaper wit quickly catalogued as the five clichés of the Orton story—his prison record, working-class background, failure to pass the eleven plus, time on the National Assistance, and tough public image, complete with chic leather jacket. While all of these clichés were in fact true, they were also elements of a role that Orton, the former actor, played to the hilt. They also served to distract attention from the fact that Orton was far from a novice writer; by 1963 he had been working hard at his craft for more than ten years.

In *The Ruffian on the Stair* Orton moves elements of his and Halliwell's novel *The Boy Hairdresser* from the streets of Northern London to the inside of a room; in fact, he works the story into the schema of Pinter's play *The Room* (1960). In Pinter's play, Rose fears that her room is about to be invaded by a mysterious stranger. When the intruder—Riley, a blind black man—finally appears, he is beaten savagely (perhaps killed) by

Rose's silent but menacing partner, Burt. At the end of the play, Rose is herself mysteriously struck blind. In *The Ruffian on The Stair,* a young man, Wilson, arrives at the apartment of Joyce and Mike, wanting to rent a room that does not exist. Joyce is unnerved by the young man's repeated, and often vaguely violent, appearances. It turns out that Mike, a hit man, has murdered Wilson's brother, with whom Wilson was having an incestuous, homosexual love affair. Wilson is grief-stricken and angry and intends, by worming his way into the apartment, to provoke Mike into murdering him both as a way of committing suicide and a means of exposing Mike as a murderer. Mike shoots Wilson in cold blood, but Joyce decides to lie and claim that Wilson tried to rape her. As the play ends, it is made clear that Mike will never be brought to justice for his crimes.

While Pinter's play was famously cryptic—for instance, the audience never learns who Riley is, why Rose fears him, why Burt kills him, or why Rose goes blind—Orton's play, while following the same basic plot arc, supplies concrete motivations for the action. Orton tells the audience why Wilson is there, why Joyce fears him, and why Mike shoots him. If Pinter deliberately refuses to give information, Orton deliberately gives too much. In fact, Wilson's suicidal gesture is also a coming out:

WILSON. We had separate beds—he was a stickler for convention—but that's as far as it went. We spent every night in each other's company. It was the reason we never got any work done.

MIKE. There's no word in the Irish language for what you were doing.

WILSON. In Lapland they have no word for snow.

Wilson straddles important categories and transcends clichés—he is both working-class and homosexual, a threatening tough and a "sensitive" lad, a hooligan and a victim, and while he should, by some of these criteria, be the villain of the play, he is easily done in by Mike and Joyce, the heterosexual couple whose union Orton figures as an alliance between hit man and whore. Joyce, in fact, sheds more tears for her goldfish—which have been inadvertently killed by a stray bullet—than for the dead man on her floor. The blackly funny ending lines, "I'll fetch the police. This has been a crime of passion. They'll understand. They have wives and goldfish of their own," show that Orton believed that while his young queer hooligan appeared to be threatening, all the power was really on the side of the establishment.

The script of *The Ruffian on the Stair* brought Orton's work to the attention of theatrical insiders such as BBC producer John Tydeman and agent Margaret (Peggy) Ramsay, and Orton wasted no time in producing more material. By the time *The Ruffian on the Stair* was broadcast on BBC radio in August of 1964, Orton had a full-length stage play, *Entertaining Mr. Sloane,* in production at the New Arts Theatre. This play, too, has a young hooligan at its center—the titular Mr. Sloane, who is taken into Kath's house as a lodger. Sloane kicks Kath's father, Kemp, to death at the end of the second act (because Kemp witnessed Sloane's offstage murder of Kemp's former employer), thus proving what a tough character he can be when threatened. But again, the power dynamics are not quite what they seem. Rather than report their father's murderer to the police, Kath and her brother, Ed, instead use their knowledge of his crime to blackmail Sloane into sexual servitude: he will spend six months of the year with Kath, and six months living with Ed. As in *The Ruffian on the Stair,* the character who should be the villain of the play ultimately ends up as one of its victims.

The play also ends up being a contest between Kath and Ed for the sexual attention of Sloane. Orton provocatively presents Sloane as an almost universal object of desire, an amoral youth who is willing to have sex with men or women. "I'm an all rounder," Sloane explains as he flirts with Ed; "A great all rounder. In anything you care to mention. Even in life." Ed is immediately and ardently attracted; however, while Ed has a clear preference for boys, he does not seem to regard himself as homosexual—rather, he claims that his behavior is typical in the powerful circles within which he travels. While he is clearly attempting to seduce Sloane, he tightens up whenever Sloane seems on the verge of making the real intent of his actions explicit. For example, Ed balks at Sloane's sympathetic characterization of him as "sensitive"—a popular euphemism for homosexual. In fact, Ed, in his dealings with the beautiful, young Sloane, hides behind the rhetoric of a hearty, moral, masculinity:

ED: Why am I interested in your welfare? Why did I give you a job? Why do thinking men everywhere show young boys the strait and narrow? Flash chequebooks when delinquency is mentioned? Support the Scout movement? Principles, boy, bleeding principles. And don't you dare say otherwise or you'll land in serious trouble.

To "say otherwise" would be to imply that these "thinking men everywhere" are interested in young boys for less altruistic reasons. Orton thereby casts suspicion upon the two most powerful forms of masculinity at the time: the established older man and the tough

Donald Pleasence and Hermione Baddeley in Orton's 1967 television play The Good and Faithful Servant, *about a man whose retirement after fifty years of service is rewarded with a broken toaster. The stage version of the play premiered in 1971 (photograph by Rediffusion Television; from the 1996 edition of* The Orton Diaries: Including the Correspondence of Edna Welthorpe and Others, *1986; Thomas Cooper Library, University of South Carolina).*

working-class youth. This move was a radical gesture that challenged the stereotype of the effeminate homosexual.

Orton's next work was the teleplay *The Good and Faithful Servant*, written in 1964 (although not broadcast until 1967). *The Good and Faithful Servant* tells the story of George Buchanan, a man who has given fifty years of his life (and lost one of his arms) to his job at "the firm." He retires, old and broken, his faithful service rewarded by the firm with gifts of a broken toaster and a clock that runs backward. Buchanan dies shortly thereafter, but not before he and his wife, Edith, have coerced their rebellious young grandson, Ray, into taking a conventional job and a wife, dooming him to repeat his grandfather's life. While *The Good and Faithful Servant* is funny (particularly the character of Mrs. Vealfoy, the relentlessly cheerful personnel manager who wants to micromanage not only the characters' work lives but also their inner lives and emotions: "We're going to sing in a minute. That will cure your depression, won't it?"), it is black comedy, steeped in pathos, bitterness, and regret. As Maurice Charney notes, "Orton would never again speak so directly and so poignantly about the evils of contemporary industrial life."

Orton's second stage play, *Loot* (performed in 1965, published in 1967), went through two productions and several significant rewrites before going on to be a major London success, ultimately winning both the *Evening Standard* and *Plays and Players* Awards for best play of 1966. *Loot* is, in a way, an elaborate revenge against the character of Mr. McLeavy–a good man whose only crime is his blind faith in a corrupt establishment. Orton attacks McLeavy by satirizing his language, which consists almost entirely of cringing and deferential statements toward authority: "We can rely on public officials to behave themselves. We must give this man every opportunity to do his duty. As a good citizen I ignore the stories which bring officialdom into disrepute." Such remarks are the secular commandments of twentieth-century society; they codify the beliefs that underlie common participation in the Western democratic system of government. McLeavy is punished for believing in them; at the end of the play he becomes a victim of the very system in which he placed his trust.

McLeavy's son, Hal, and his boyfriend Dennis have robbed a bank of £104,000. They are planning to leave the country but are detained by the need to attend Hal's mother's funeral. Detective-Inspector Truscott, suspecting the boys, gains entrance to the McLeavy house by disguising himself as an official of the water board (because the water board, or so he claims, does not need a search warrant), to search for the stolen money. Truscott is a stupid, corrupt, and brutal policeman. Panicked, the boys hide the money in Mrs. McLeavy's coffin and attempt to hide the corpse in the house until it can be dumped in the woods. Assisted by Mrs. McLeavy's unscrupulous nurse, Fay, who has murdered the old woman for her money, the boys juggle the corpse, the coffin, and the police inspector until the situation inevitably unravels. Ultimately, however, Truscott agrees to split the money with Hal, Dennis, and Fay and arrests the outraged McLeavy for refusing to keep quiet. Once McLeavy is dragged away, the others plan for his "accidental" death while in prison.

The play deeply divided its audiences, scandalizing those audience members who identified with McLeavy and his investments in British authority. There were walkouts (Orton named this group "the Bump and Trot Brigade" from the noise their seats made as they rose up), and Orton requested that the box office provide refunds to elderly couples who requested them. Orton felt that *Loot* was a play for young people, and in a 1990 article Alan Sinfield notes that young people were energized by the play, particularly its critique of the police. In interviews about *Loot*, Orton expounded on his views of the police:

> Obviously you've got to have police; they're a necessary evil. I've no objection to them tracking down murderers and bank robbers, clearly you can't have people behaving in a completely anarchic way. I believe, though, that they interfere far too much with private morals—whether people are having it off in the backs of cars or smoking marijuana, or doing the interesting little things that one does.... (quoted in *Prick Up Your Ears*)

This issue is not simply an intellectual one for Orton, who was not only a former convict but also involved in criminal activity for most of his adult life. Homosexuality was illegal in Britain until two weeks before Orton was murdered, and the police entrapment of homosexuals was at its height in the late 1940s and early 1950s, during the formative stages of Orton's development. *Loot* makes the point that the question of innocence or guilt is irrelevant in a corrupt society—so all things being equal, one might as well be guilty. In *Loot*, all the heroic characters are guilty. In Orton's imagination, the bank robbers are subversive working-class lads who are criminals because of both their burglary and their sexuality: in addition to being thieves, these "perfectly ordinary boys" also "happen to be fucking each other." As in *Entertaining Mr. Sloane,* in which the audience's sympathy goes out to Sloane despite his having killed two

Kenneth Halliwell, Orton's longtime lover, who murdered Orton and committed suicide in August 1967 (from the 1996 edition of The Orton Diaries: Including the Correspondence of Edna Welthorpe and Others, *1986; Thomas Cooper Library, University of South Carolina)*

people, *Loot* is constructed so that one roots for the boys to get away with their crimes.

Lahr reports that during the highly stressful time before *Loot* was a hit, Orton wrote an angry letter to his agent threatening to quit writing for the stage: "I shall earn my living on TV." Perhaps as a form of insurance, Orton wrote two more television plays during this period: *The Erpingham Camp* (broadcast in 1966, performed and published in 1967) and *Funeral Games* (broadcast in 1968, published in 1970). *The Erpingham Camp* is a rewrite of Euripedes' *The Bacchae* set in a working-class holiday camp or vacation resort. In Orton's hands the camp becomes a metaphor for England itself, and the portrait is not a flattering one. Erpingham, the camp leader, is the stuffiest type of British bureaucrat, the kind of petty official without whom the Empire could not have been maintained. The holidaymakers are working class and run riot when a pregnant woman believes herself to have been insulted. When Erpingham tries to quell the revolt by locking down the camp and denying the campers food, the campers decide to "take by force those common human rights which should be denied no man." Erpingham's petty dictatorship is overthrown, and Erpingham is killed; but neither masters nor servants, colonizers or colonized, come off looking well.

In *Funeral Games,* Orton turns his satirical attention to organized religion. Pringle, the head of a religious sect called "the Brotherhood," hires a young tough named Caulfield to investigate his wife, Tessa, whom he suspects of adultery. He finds out that Tessa is innocently spending her afternoons as a home companion to an elderly defrocked priest named McCorquodale. But, as so often in Orton, innocence does not matter: "It's too late now to say she's chaste." Pringle has publicly given a sermon, "Thou shalt not suffer an adulteress to live," and now he must live up to his own image and murder his wife. However, when push comes to shove, he is incapable of doing the deadly deed. A solution is easily reached, however: Tessa agrees to "vanish" so that Pringle can publicly take credit for murdering her. But this solution is jeopardized by Tessa's discovery that old McCorquodale actually has murdered his wife and buried her body in the coal cellar. Caulfield then attempts to kill Tessa to keep her from exposing both McCorquodale (for killing his wife) and Pringle (for not killing his wife). After finding out that Mrs. McCorquodale was herself an adulteress, Tessa is willing to conceal her murder, but the play nonetheless ends with the arrival of the police and the arrest of all involved.

With two television plays in production and *Loot* a hit on the West End, Orton was riding high at the end of 1966. At his agent's suggestion, he began to keep a journal–a "Diary Of A Somebody" (a title reversing that of George Grossmith and Weedon Grossmith's 1892 comic novel, *Diary Of A Nobody*). The protagonist of the resulting *Orton Diaries* (published in 1986) is "Joe Orton," successful playwright and urbane wit, a man who could detail his theatrical and sexual exploits with equal aplomb. *The Orton Diaries* exudes good humor and confidence as Orton swaggers and struts his way through London in the Summer of Love. He tells funny stories and jots down his wry observations of people– the actors in his shows, celebrities such as Olivier and Paul McCartney, his friends and neighbors, old people on buses, the men he picks up for sex in restrooms– treating all equally, giving each his or her narrative due.

The only sour note in *The Orton Diaries* is the subtle, slow emotional breakdown of Halliwell, which occurs in the background of the more colorful events. Orton records that Halliwell complains of various (potentially psychosomatic) symptoms–palpitations, rashes, allergies, loss of appetite, constipation, stomach pains, and tightness in the chest. He sees various doctors for various medications, and his mood frequently veers between a numb sort of depression and a desperate rage: "Exhausting wrangles over trivia. Kenneth, lying in bed, suddenly shouted, 'I hope I die of heart disease! I'd like to see you manage then.'" Orton chronicles their fights and Halliwell's moods and ailments, but he does not seem to understand what is happening to his partner. Sometimes he reacts to Halliwell's complaints with tender concern; other times, he merely placates; still other times, his frustration with Halliwell is evident.

Despite the strain in his relationship with Halliwell, the last nine months of Orton's life were extremely productive. In addition to his comic diaries, Orton wrote his final stage play, *What the Butler Saw* (performed and published in 1969); rewrote his 1961 novel "The Vision of Gombold Proval" as a movie script for the Beatles (retitled *Up Against It,* published in 1979); and revised the teleplay of *The Erpingham Camp* for the stage. While the Beatles' management eventually rejected *Up Against It* (which was not all that surprising, considering that, as Orton noted in his diaries: "the boys, in my script, have been caught in flagrante, become involved in dubious political activity, dressed as women, committed murder, been put in prison and committed adultery. And the script isn't finished yet"), Orton managed to sell the screenplay to the producer Oscar Lewenstein, who also coproduced *What the Butler Saw* with Binkie Beaumont in 1969, after Orton's death. *Up Against It* was first adapted as a musical by Edward Ball (with songs by Ball) for the Royal Court Theatre in 1986; it was later adapted as an entirely different musical by Joseph Papp (with songs by Todd Rundgren) for the Public Theatre in New York in 1989.

Orton's last play targets the psychiatric establishment. *What the Butler Saw* is set in the consulting room of Dr. Prentice's private psychiatric clinic. The set calls for doors leading to the wards, the dispensary, and the hall. Additionally, French windows open onto the gardens. As Robert Brustein noted in a review of a 1989 production of the play, "multiple exits are the design required by the lunatic logic of farce, but it is Orton's inspiration to set this farce in a madhouse" (*New Republic,* 17 April 1989). Orton also draws attention to the strange construction of this room in the dialogue: "Why are there so many doors?" asks Dr. Rance, a supervisory doctor whose unexpected visit to the clinic sets much of the farce in motion. "Was this house designed by a lunatic?" Dr. Prentice notes that he has the architect of his clinic "here as a patient from time to time."

The plot of *What the Butler Saw* concerns Dr. Prentice's botched attempt to seduce his new secretary, Geraldine Barclay. He has gotten Geraldine undressed when his wife returns home in her underwear; her dress has been confiscated by Nick, the bellboy at the

Station Hotel, and so she takes Geraldine's discarded dress as her own. When Dr. Rance suddenly appears to inspect the clinic, Prentice explains away the naked Geraldine as a mental patient, and Dr. Rance has her taken into custody and certified. However, now Prentice has to account for the missing Geraldine. He persuades Nick, who has come to the clinic to blackmail Mrs. Prentice, to impersonate Geraldine; however, now he has the sudden disappearance of the bellboy to explain. Geraldine, who has escaped, takes Nick's clothes to cover herself and pretends to be Nick so that she will be removed from the premises. However, Mrs. Prentice, who knows what Nick looks like, asserts that s/he is not the missing bellboy. Dr. Prentice then lies and identifies Geraldine as Gerald Barclay.

Through these machinations, Orton succeeds in splitting the secretary Geraldine into two: she becomes both Geraldine and Gerald Barclay. The original object of lust has been divided into two genders, and this split is further complicated by the fact that neither of the two is recognizable by sex: the boy is impersonating a girl, and vice versa. These gender games provide the opportunity for some of Orton's best lines, such as: "This is a boy, sir. Not a girl. If you're baffled by the difference it might be as well to approach both with caution."

In *What the Butler Saw*, Orton's creation of the nonexistent Gerald Barclay serves, as in Wilde's *The Importance of Being Earnest* (1895), as a precursor to the revelation of an actual brother: Geraldine and Nick are discovered to be twins, and the female ingenue of traditional farce is revealed to have a male counterpart—a twin, a double, a doppelgänger—in the form of Nick. Geraldine is an innocent, naive, and sexually inexperienced young woman of middle-class pretensions; Nick is a sexually experienced, vaguely criminal, amoral young man of the working classes. But they are two sides of the same coin; two sex objects, in fact: one traditional, and one subversive.

Geraldine and Nick are sexually desired by the older characters in the play, Dr. and Mrs. Prentice: Dr. Prentice has attempted to seduce Geraldine, and Mrs. Prentice and Nick have had a sexual encounter at the Station Hotel. But it turns out that not only are Nick and Geraldine related, but also the Prentices are their parents: each of the two has therefore been the victim of an incestuous assault. Orton stacks the deck against heterosexuality by making the "natural" male-female sexual affairs incestuous; all the Prentices' sexual inclinations are revealed to be socially taboo. As in Orton's play *The Ruffian on the Stair*, incest is made to parallel homosexuality (as another socially unacceptable form of desire); here, it simultaneously complicates heterosexuality by showing that not all heterosexual relationships are free of social stigma. As in *Loot*, where Orton constructs the play so as to make the

Bill Fraser as McCorquodale, a defrocked priest who has murdered his adulterous wife, in Orton's television drama Funeral Games, *broadcast posthumously in 1968 (photograph by Yorkshire Television; from John Lahr,* Prick Up Your Ears: The Biography of Joe Orton, *1978; Thomas Cooper Library, University of South Carolina)*

audience root for the criminals, in *What the Butler Saw* audiences are made to recoil from the heterosexual relationships in the play.

Orton refused to treat homosexuality as a problem, as even liberals were doing in the mid 1960s. Rather, he turned the tables on mainstream society, and even on liberal society, by setting his play in a psychiatrist's office and showing that it was the psychiatric establishment and the institutions it supported and that supported it—such as heterosexual marriage, the nuclear family, and patriotism—that were in need of "help." In *What the Butler Saw*, Orton subjects the "normal" lusts of conventional farce to the hysterical language used to discuss perceived abnormality. As a result of his desire to seduce his secretary, Dr. Prentice is mistakenly labeled "one of the most remarkable lunatics of all time," a "transvestite, fetishist, bi-sexual murderer" who displays "considerable deviation overlap." Dr. Rance, the head psychiatrist, always frames his analyses of the characters in terms that are directed toward a sensationalist media discussion of their problems:

Everything is now clear. The final chapters of my book are knitting together: incest, buggery, outrageous women and strange love-cults catering for depraved appetites. All the fashionable bric-à-brac. A beautiful but neurotic girl has influenced the doctor to sacrifice a white virgin to propitiate the dark guns of unreason. "When they broke into the evil-smelling den they found her poor body bleeding beneath the obscene and half-erect phallus." My "unbiased account" of the case of the infamous sex-killer Prentice will undoubtedly add a great deal to our understanding of such creatures. Society must be made aware of the growing menace of pornography.

Orton is doing something strikingly modern: he is attacking the hypocrisy of a media that revels in the presentation of sensationalistic detail in its discussion of social "problems" while shaking its collective head in moral disapproval. ("What a dreadful story," declares Mrs. Prentice. "I'd condemn it in the strongest terms if it were fiction.") And Dr. Rance blames the fiction-makers— "the whole treacherous avant-garde movement"—for "inciting decent citizens to commit bizarre crimes against humanity and the state!" From this perspective, plays such as Orton's are part of "the growing menace of pornography," while Rance's work is permitted as an unbiased nonfictional "discussion." Just as *The Importance of Being Earnest* sends up the "revolting sentimentality" of the three-volume novel, *What the Butler Saw* targets the revolting sensationalism and exploitation of tabloid journalism and media "expertise."

Orton himself was soon at the center of this kind of sensational story. On 9 August 1967 a chauffeur coming to pick up Orton for a meeting with the movie director Dick Lester found Orton and Halliwell dead in their apartment. Halliwell had killed Orton with nine hammer blows to the head before committing suicide via overdose. The murder-suicide made the front page of the *Evening Standard* with language as lurid as any Orton satirized in *What the Butler Saw:* "In this flat with the cross on the wall, West End playwright found dead with friend. 'LOOT' MAN IN DOUBLE DEATH." Furthermore, Halliwell left a suicide note that has intrigued academics, amateur psychologists, and mystery readers for more than three decades:

If you read his diaries, all will be explained.

K.H.

P.S. Especially the latter part.

But Orton's published *Diaries* do not explain everything, and it is unclear to which "latter" part Halliwell was referring. Adding to the mystery is the fact that Orton normally kept his diary faithfully, writing every day or every other day; yet, the last extant entry is for 1 August, a full eight days before the murder. Have pages gone missing or been stolen? Halliwell's note points toward an obvious explanation, but no explanation is to be had.

Critics, caught up in the mystery of it, have felt compelled to create narratives that fill in the blanks. Lahr's 1978 biography implicitly blames Orton for his own murder: "Orton died from his short-sighted and indecisive loyalty to a friend." Lahr argues that Orton betrayed Halliwell both literally, by refusing to acknowledge his contributions as mentor, editor, and partner, and sexually, by being promiscuous. In *Because We're Queers,* Shepherd claims that Orton was killed because he reentered (and was apparently contaminated by) mainstream homophobic society. In Shepherd's reading, Orton made the fatal choice of aligning himself with a masculine mainstream culture, and that culture destroyed him and Halliwell by teaching them to hate each other: Orton was taught to hate Halliwell's effeminacy, and Halliwell was taught to hate Orton's promiscuity. The result: the murder-suicide.

There is also a more prosaic explanation. Halliwell's father committed suicide; Halliwell himself discovered his father with his head in the oven. Halliwell's own eventual suicide cannot be coincidental, entirely dependent on the particular circumstances of his life with Orton; to argue such would be to ignore the extent to which mental illness runs in families. Lahr also notes that "Halliwell had already attempted suicide once, in 1962." If true, Halliwell's emotional problems clearly predate their supposed "cause": Orton's success. Halliwell also took a great number of prescription drugs, mostly antidepressants and tranquilizers. At the time of the murder-suicide, Halliwell was in the process of arranging his admission to a hospital for psychiatric treatment, and as Lahr rightly notes, "there was always a high incidence of suicide between arranging hospitalization and the patient's actual admission, because of the depressive's feelings of unworthiness and sense of being a burden."

In light of these facts, Orton can hardly be held responsible for provoking his own murder. It seems reasonable to place some blame at the door of the psychiatric establishment, as Orton himself did in *What the Butler Saw*. Homosexuality itself was considered a mental illness at the time, so Halliwell had little hope of unbiased psychiatric treatment. In fact, Dr. Ismay, the general practitioner who was treating Halliwell before the murder-suicide, said in a taped interview with Lahr that he thought Orton was "psychopathic or very disturbed" (on the basis of seeing *Entertaining Mr. Sloane*) and that homosexuality was a demonstration of infantile behavior. It would have been difficult for Halliwell to have gotten help without having his identity as a homosexual attacked; Orton even wrote a play making the point.

Critics and audiences generally use words such as "outrageous," "fantastic," and "macabre" to describe Joe Orton's work, but Orton always insisted on the truth of

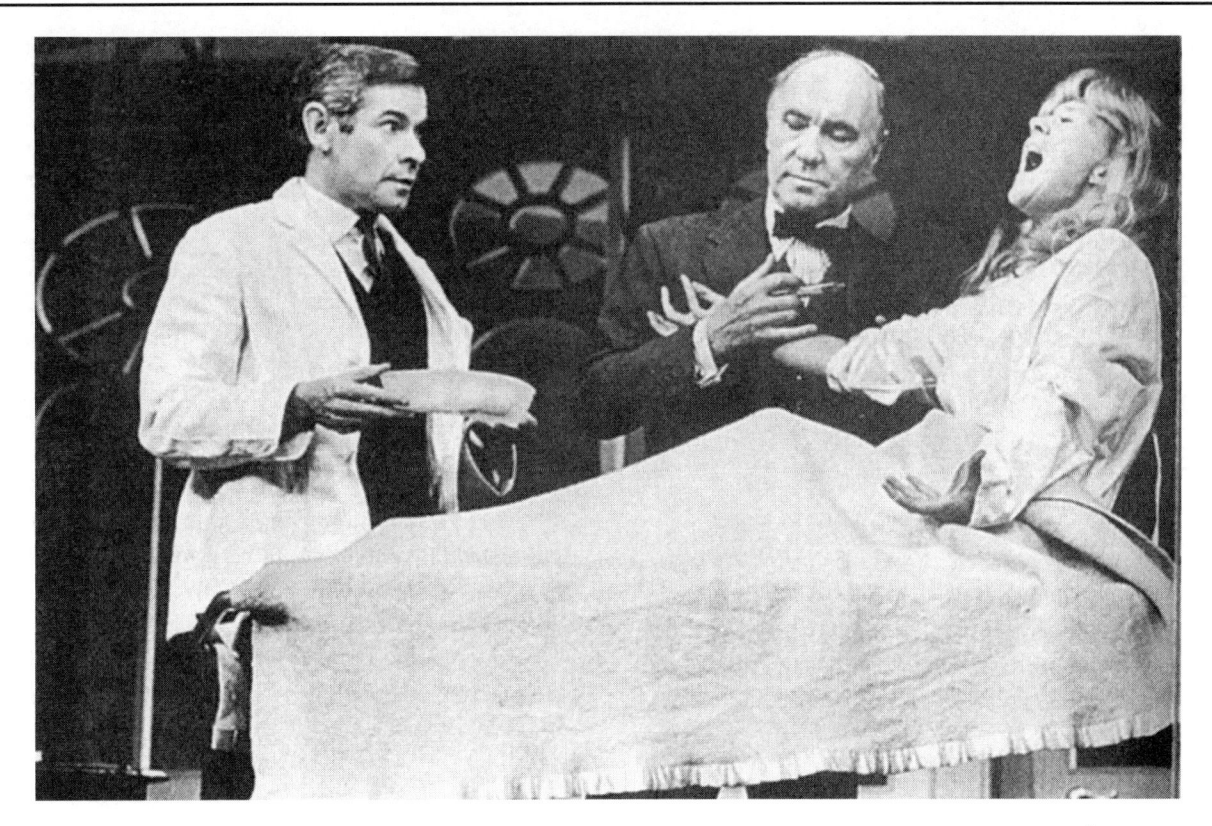

Stanley Baxter as Dr. Prentice, Ralph Richardson as Dr. Rance, and Julia Foster as Geraldine, in the 1969 Queen's Theatre (London) premiere of Orton's play What the Butler Saw, *a farce set in the clinic of a psychiatrist who is trying to hide his botched attempt at seducing his secretary (photograph by Douglas Jeffery; from the 1996 edition of* The Orton Diaries: Including the Correspondence of Edna Welthorpe and Others, *1986; Thomas Cooper Library, University of South Carolina)*

his vision. In a production note to the Royal Court Theatre describing *The Ruffian on the Stair,* Orton noted that "Everything the characters say is *true.* Mike has murdered the boy's brother. Joyce is an ex-call girl. Wilson has an incestuous relationship with his brother." If the world was "shocked" by his stories, refusing to believe in bisexual punks, corrupt policemen, and insane psychiatrists, then the world, like McLeavy in *Loot,* was brutally naive. As Orton noted when he won the *Evening Standard* Award for *Loot* in 1967:

> In the early days we used to give complimentary tickets to various organizations. We sent a few to Scotland Yard. And the police loved the play so much that they rang up asking for more tickets. Everyone else thinks the play is a fantasy. Of course the police know it's true.

Interview:

Glenn Loney, "Entertaining Mr. Loney: An Early Interview with Joe Orton," *New Theatre Quarterly,* 4 (November 1988): 300–305.

Bibliography:

Kimball King, *Twenty Modern British Playwrights: A Bibliography, 1956 to 1976* (New York: Garland, 1977), pp. 77–83.

Biography:

John Lahr, *Prick Up Your Ears: The Biography of Joe Orton* (London: Allen Lane, 1978; New York: Knopf, 1978).

References:

Michael Beehler, "Joe Orton and the Heterogeneity of the Book," *Sub-stance,* 33–34 (1982): 84–98;

C. W. E. Bigsby, *Joe Orton* (London: Methuen, 1982);

Joseph A. Boone, "Vacation Cruises: or, The Homoerotics of Orientalism," *PMLA,* 110 (January 1995): 89;

John Bull and Frances Gray, "Joe Orton," in *Essays on Contemporary British Drama,* edited by Hedwig Bock and Albert Wertheim (Munich: Hueber, 1981), pp. 71–96;

Mary I. Casmus, "Farce and Verbal Style in the Plays of Joe Orton," *Journal of Popular Culture*, 13 (1980): 461–468;

Maurice Charney, *Joe Orton*, Grove Press Modern Dramatists (New York: Grove, 1984);

John M. Clum, *Acting Gay: Male Homosexuality in Modern Drama* (New York: Columbia University Press, 1992);

Francesca Coppa, "Coming Out In The Room: Joe Orton's Epigrammatic Re/Vision of Harold Pinter's Menace," *Modern Drama*, 40 (Spring 1997): 11–22;

Coppa, "A Perfectly Developed Playwright: Joe Orton and Homosexual Reform," in *The Queer Sixties*, edited by Patricia Juliana Smith (New York: Routledge, 1999), pp. 87–104;

Coppa, ed., *Joe Orton: A Casebook* (New York: Routledge, 2003);

Joan F. Dean, "Joe Orton and the Redefinition of Farce," *Theatre Journal*, 34 (December 1982): 481–492;

Jonathan Dollimore, "Post/Modern: On The Gay Sensibility, or the Pervert's Revenge on Authenticity—Wilde, Genet, Orton and Others," in his *Sexual Dissidence: Augustine to Wilde, Freud to Foucault* (Oxford: Clarendon Press, 1991), pp. 307–325;

Manfred Draudt, "Comic, Tragic, or Absurd? On Some Parallels between the Farces of Joe Orton and Seventeenth Century Tragedy," *English Studies: A Journal of English Language and Literature*, 59 (1978): 202–217;

Martin Esslin, "Joe Orton: The Comedy of (Ill) Manners," in *Contemporary English Drama*, edited by C. W. E. Bigsby (New York: Holmes & Meier, 1981), pp. 95–107;

Esslin, "The Sacred Force," *Plays and Players* (1966): 19;

John Haynes, *Taking the Stage: Twenty-one Years of the London Theatre. Photographs* (New York: Thames & Hudson, 1986);

Christopher Innes, *Modern British Drama 1890–1990, Parts I and II* (Cambridge: Cambridge University Press, 1992);

Nicholas de Jongh, *Not In Front of the Audience: Homosexuality On Stage* (New York: Routledge, 1992);

James R. Keller, "Tennessee Williams' *Orpheus Descending* and Joe Orton's *Entertaining Mr. Sloane*," *Notes on Contemporary Literature*, 22 (March 1992): 8–10;

John Lahr, *Automatic Vaudeville* (London: Methuen, 1984);

Lahr, *Light Fantastic: Adventures in Theatre* (London: Bloomsbury, 1996);

Mark Lilly, "The Plays of Joe Orton," in his *Gay Men's Literature in the Twentieth Century* (New York: New York University Press, 1993), pp. 168–179;

Randall S. Nakayama, "Domesticating Mr. Orton," *Theatre Journal*, 45 (May 1993): 185–195;

Goran Nieragden, "Neglected Yet Respectable: Joe Orton's *Head to Toe* as Political Satire," *English Studies*, 75 (July 1994): 350–356;

Mark Ravenhill, "Looking Back Warily at a Heterosexual Classic," *New York Times*, 17 October 1999, Arts and Leisure, p. 1;

Susan Rusinko, *Joe Orton* (New York: Twayne, 1995);

Simon Shepherd, *Because We're Queers: The Life and Crimes of Kenneth Halliwell and Joe Orton* (London: Gay Men's Press, 1989);

Shepherd, "Edna's Last Stand, or Joe Orton's Dialectic of Entertainment," *Renaissance & Modern Studies*, 22 (1978): 87–110;

Shepherd and Mick Wallis, eds., *Coming On Strong: Gay Politics and Culture* (London: Unwin Hyman, 1989);

Alan Sinfield, "Who Was Afraid Of Joe Orton?" *Textual Practice*, 4 (Summer 1990): 259–277;

Leslie Smith, "Democratic Lunacy: The Comedies of Joe Orton," *Adam: International Review* (1976): 394–396;

Smith, *Modern British Farce* (Houndsmills: Macmillan, 1989);

Grant Stirling, "Ortonesque/Carnivalesque: The Grotesque Realism of Joe Orton," *Journal of Dramatic Theory and Criticism*, 11 (Spring 1997): 41–63;

John Russell Taylor, *The Second Wave: British Drama of the Sixties* (London: Eyre Methuen, 1978);

David Van Leer, *The Queening of America: Gay Culture in Straight Society* (New York: Routledge, 1995);

Peter Walcot, "An Acquired Taste: Joe Orton and The Greeks," in *Legacy of Thespis: Drama Past and Present*, edited by Karelisa V. Hartigan (Lanham, Md.: University Press of America, 1984), pp. 99–123;

Michelene Wandor, *Look Back In Gender: Sexuality and the Family in Postwar British Drama* (London & New York: Methuen, 1987);

Katherine J. Worth, "Form and Style in the Plays of Joe Orton," in *Modern British Dramatists*, edited by John Russell Brown (Englewood Cliffs, N.J.: Prentice-Hall, 1984), pp. 75–84;

Worth, *Revolutions in Modern English Drama* (London: G. Bell & Sons, 1973).

Papers:

The Orton Collection of Joe Orton's personal and literary papers, photographs, and memorabilia can be found at the University of Leicester Library. John Lahr's notes for the Orton biography *Prick Up Your Ears*, including additional biographical testimony and Orton's prison letters, can be found in the John Lahr Collection at Mugar Memorial Library, Boston University. Orton's defaced and refaced book jackets can be found in the Islington Public Library's Local History Collection.

Harold Pinter

(10 October 1930 -   )

Ronald Knowles
University of Reading

See also the Pinter entry in *DLB 13: British Dramatists Since World War II*.

PLAY PRODUCTIONS: *The Room,* Bristol, Bristol University Drama Studio, 15 May 1957; produced with *The Dumb Waiter,* London, Hampstead Theatre Club, 21 January 1960 (transferred to Royal Court Theatre, 8 March 1960); produced with *A Slight Ache,* New York, Writers Stage Theatre, 9 December 1964;

The Birthday Party, Cambridge, Arts Theatre, 28 April 1958; London, Lyric Theatre Hammersmith, 19 May 1958; New York, Booth Theatre, 3 October 1967;

The Dumb Waiter, translated into German by Willy H. Thiem, Frankfurt am Main, Kleines Haus, 28 February 1959; produced with *The Room,* London, Hampstead Theatre Club, 21 January 1960 (transferred to Royal Court Theatre, 8 March 1960); produced with *The Collection,* New York, Cherry Lane Theatre, 26 November 1962;

Trouble in the Works and *The Black and White,* in *One to Another* (revue), London, Lyric Theatre Hammersmith, 15 July 1959;

Request Stop, Last to Go, and *Special Offer,* in *Pieces of Eight* (revue), London, Apollo Theatre, 23 September 1959;

The Caretaker, London, Arts Theatre, 27 April 1960 (transferred 30 May 1960 to Duchess Theatre); New York, Lyceum Theatre, 4 October 1961;

A Slight Ache, London, Arts Theatre, 18 January 1961; produced with *The Room,* New York, Writers Stage Theatre, 9 December 1964;

A Night Out, London, Comedy Theatre, 2 October 1961;

The Collection, London, Aldwych Theatre, 18 June 1962; produced with *The Dumb Waiter,* New York, Cherry Lane Theatre, 26 November 1962;

The Dwarfs, produced with *The Lover,* London, New Arts Theatre, 18 September 1963; produced with *The Dumb Waiter,* New York, Abbey Theatre, 3 May 1974;

The Lover, produced with *The Dwarfs,* London, New Arts Theatre, 18 September 1963; New York, Cherry Lane Theatre, 4 January 1964;

The Homecoming, Cardiff, New Theatre, 22 March 1965; London, Aldwych Theatre, 3 June 1965; New York, Music Box Theatre, 5 January 1967;

Tea Party and *The Basement,* New York, Eastside Playhouse, 15 October 1968; London, Duchess Theatre, 17 September 1970;

Night, in *We Who Are About To . . . ,* London, Hampstead Theatre Club, 6 February 1969; produced again in *Mixed Doubles: An Entertainment on Marriage* (revised version of *We Who Are About To . . .*), London, Comedy Theatre, 9 April 1969;

Landscape and *Silence,* London, Aldwych Theatre, 2 July 1969; New York, Forum Theatre, 2 April 1970;

Old Times, London, Aldwych Theatre, 1 June 1971; New York, Billy Rose Theatre, 16 November 1971;

Monologue, Hampstead, King's Head Theatre, 29 August 1973;

No Man's Land, London, Old Vic (National Theatre), 23 April 1975; New York, Longacre Theatre, 9 November 1976;

Betrayal, London, Lyttelton Theatre (National Theatre), 15 November 1978; New York, Trafalgar Theatre, 5 January 1980;

The Hothouse, London, Hampstead Theatre, 24 April 1980 (transferred to Ambassador Theatre, 25 June 1980); New York, Playhouse Theatre, 6 May 1982;

Family Voices, London, National Theatre, 13 February 1981;

A Kind of Alaska and *Victoria Station,* London, Cottesloe Theatre (National Theatre), 14 October 1982;

Precisely, London, Apollo Theatre, 19 December 1983;

One for the Road, London, Lyric Theatre Studio, 13 March 1984;

Harold Pinter (photograph by John Haynes; from his Taking the Stage: Twenty-One Years of the London Theatre. Photographs, *1986; Richland County Public Library)*

Mountain Language, London, Lyttelton Theatre (National Theatre), 20 October 1988;

The New World Order, London, Royal Court Theatre Upstairs, 19 July 1991;

Party Time, London, Almeida Theatre, 31 October 1991;

Moonlight, London, Almeida Theatre, 7 September 1993;

Ashes to Ashes, London, Ambassadors Theatre, 12 September 1996;

God's Own District, London, Lyric Theatre Hammersmith, 27 March 1997;

Celebration, London, Almeida Theatre, 16 March 2000;

Remembrance of Things Past, adapted by Pinter and Di Trevis from Pinter's *The Proust Screenplay,* London, Cottesloe Theatre (National Theatre), 23 November 2000;

Sketches, London, National Theatre, 8 and 11 February 2002–comprised *That's Your Trouble, The Black and White, Tess, Trouble in the Works, Last to Go, Special Offer, That's All, Night,* and *Press Conference.*

SELECTED BOOKS: *The Birthday Party* (London: Encore, 1959);

The Birthday Party and Other Plays (London: Methuen, 1960); republished as *The Birthday Party and The Room* (New York: Grove, 1960)–includes *The Birthday Party, The Room,* and *The Dumb Waiter;*

The Caretaker (London: Methuen, 1960);

The Caretaker and The Birthday Party (Garden City, N.J.: Doubleday, 1960);

A Night Out (London: S. French, 1961);

A Slight Ache and Other Plays (London: Methuen, 1961)–comprises *A Slight Ache, A Night Out, The Dwarfs, Trouble in the Works, The Black and White, Request Stop, Last to Go,* and *Applicant;*

Three Plays: A Slight Ache, The Collection, The Dwarfs (New York: Grove, 1962);

The Collection and The Lover (London: Methuen, 1963)–includes "The Examination";

The Dwarfs and Eight Revue Sketches (New York: Dramatists Play Service, 1965)–comprises *The Dwarfs, Trouble in the Works, The Black and White, Request Stop, Last to Go, Applicant, Interview, That's All,* and *That's Your Trouble;* augmented with *The New World Order* as *The Dwarfs and Nine Revue Sketches* (New York: Dramatists Play Service, 1999);

The Homecoming (London: Methuen, 1965; New York: Grove, 1967);

Tea Party (London: Methuen, 1965; New York: Grove, 1966);

Tea Party and Other Plays (London: Methuen, 1967)–comprises *Tea Party, The Basement,* and *Night School;*

The Lover, Tea Party, The Basement (New York: Grove, 1967);

Landscape (London: Pendragon, 1968);

Poems (London: Enitharmon, 1968);

A Night Out, Night School, Revue Sketches (New York: Grove, 1968);

Mac (London: Pendragon, 1968);

Landscape and Silence (London: Methuen, 1969; New York: Grove, 1970)–includes *Night;*

Five Screenplays (London: Methuen, 1971); republished as *The Servant and Other Screenplays* (London & Boston: Faber & Faber, 1991)–comprises *The Servant, The Pumpkin Eater, The Quiller Memorandum, Accident,* and *The Go-Between;*

Old Times (London: Methuen, 1971; New York: Grove, 1973);

Monologue (London: Covent Garden, 1973);

No Man's Land (London: Eyre Methuen, 1975; New York: Grove, 1975);

The Proust Screenplay, adapted from Marcel Proust's *A la recherche de temps perdu* (London: Eyre Methuen/Chatto & Windus, 1978; New York: Grove, 1978);

Poems and Prose 1949–1977 (London: Eyre Methuen, 1978; New York: Grove, 1978); revised and republished as *Collected Poems and Prose* (London: Methuen, 1986; expanded edition, London: Faber & Faber, 1990; New York: Grove, 1996);

Betrayal (London: Eyre Methuen, 1978; New York: Grove, 1979);

I Know the Place: Poems (Warwick: Greville Press, 1979);

The Hothouse (London: Eyre Methuen, 1980; New York, Grove, 1980);

Family Voices (London: Next Editions/Faber & Faber, 1981; New York: Grove, 1981);

The Screenplay of The French Lieutenant's Woman (London: Cape, 1981); republished as *The French Lieutenant's Woman: A Screenplay* (New York: Little, Brown, 1981);

The French Lieutenant's Woman and Other Screenplays (London: Methuen, 1982)–comprises *The French Lieutenant's Woman, The Last Tycoon,* and *Langrishe, Go Down;*

Other Places: Three Plays (London: Methuen, 1982; New York: Grove, 1983)–comprises *Family Voices, Victoria Station,* and *A Kind of Alaska;* augmented with *One for the Road* as *Other Places: Four Plays* (New York: Dramatists Play Services, 1984);

One for the Road (London: Methuen, 1984; augmented, 1985; New York: Grove, 1986);

Mountain Language (London & Boston: Faber & Faber, 1988);

The Heat of the Day (London & Boston: Faber & Faber, 1989);

The Comfort of Strangers and Other Screenplays (London & Boston: Faber & Faber, 1990)–comprises *The Comfort of Strangers, Reunion, Turtle Diary,* and *Victory;*

The Dwarfs: A Novel (London & Boston: Faber & Faber, 1990);

Party Time: A Screenplay (London & Boston: Faber & Faber, 1991);

Plays One (London: Faber & Faber, 1991; New York: Grove, 1991)–comprises "Writing for the Theatre," *The Birthday Party, The Room, The Dumb Waiter, A Slight Ache, The Hothouse, A Night Out, The Black and White,* and *The Examination;*

Plays Two (London: Faber & Faber, 1991; New York: Grove, 1991)–comprises "Writing for Myself," *The Caretaker, The Dwarfs, The Collection, The Lover, Night School, Trouble in the Works, The Black and White, Request Stop, The Last to Go,* and *Special Offer;*

Ten Early Poems (Warwick: Greville Press, 1992);

Party Time and The New World Order (New York: Grove, 1993);

The Trial: Adapted from the Novel by Franz Kafka (London & Boston: Faber & Faber, 1993);

Moonlight (London: Faber & Faber, 1993; New York: Grove, 1994);

Ashes to Ashes (London: Faber & Faber, 1996; New York: Grove, 1997);

Plays Three (London: Faber & Faber, 1997; New York: Grove, 1997)–comprises *The Homecoming, Tea Party, The Basement, Landscape, Silence, Old Times, No Man's Land, Night, That's Your Trouble, That's All, Applicant, Interview, Dialogue for Three,* and "Tea Party" [story];

Plays Four (London: Faber & Faber, 1998; New York: Grove, 1998)–comprises *Betrayal, Monologue, Family Voices, A Kind of Alaska, Victoria Station, One for the Road, Mountain Language, Party Time, Ashes to Ashes, Precisely,* and *The New World Order;*

Various Voices: Poetry, Prose, Politics, 1948–1988 (London: Faber & Faber, 1998; New York: Grove, 1998);

Celebration and The Room (New York: Grove, 1999; London: Faber & Faber, 2000);

Remembrance of Things Past, adapted by Pinter and Di Trevis from Pinter's *The Proust Screenplay* (London: Faber & Faber, 2000);

The Disappeared and Other Poems (London: Enitharmon, 2002);

Press Conference (London: Faber & Faber, 2002);

War (London: Faber & Faber, 2003).

PRODUCED SCRIPTS: *A Slight Ache,* radio, BBC Third Programme, 29 July 1959;

A Night Out, radio, BBC Third Programme, 1 March 1960; television, ABC Weekend Television, 24 April 1960;

The Birthday Party, television, ITV, 22 March 1960;

The Dwarfs, radio, BBC Third Programme, 2 December 1960;

The Collection, television, Associated Rediffusion Television, 11 May 1961;

Night School, television, Associated Rediffusion Television, 21 July 1961;

The Lover, television, Associated Rediffusion Television, 28 March 1963;

The Servant, adapted from Robin Maugham's novel, motion picture, Springbok/Elstree, 1963;

The Guest (UK title, *The Caretaker*), motion picture, Janus, 1964;

The Pumpkin Eater, adapted from Penelope Mortimer's novel, motion picture, Rank, 1964;

Tea Party, television, BBC, 25 March 1965;

The Quiller Memorandum, adapted from Elleston Trevor's novel, motion picture, 20th Century-Fox, 1966;

The Basement, television, BBC, 20 February 1967;

Accident, adapted from Nicholas Mosley's novel, motion picture, Cinema V, 1967;

Landscape, radio, BBC Third Programme, 25 April 1968;

The Birthday Party, motion picture, Continental, 1968;

The Go-Between, adapted from L. P. Hartley's novel, motion picture, EMI, 1970;

Monologue, television, BBC, 13 April 1973;

The Homecoming, motion picture, American Film Theatre, 1973;

The Collection, television, Granada, 1976;

The Last Tycoon, adapted from F. Scott Fitzgerald's novel, motion picture, Paramount, 1976;

Langrishe, Go Down, adapted from Aidan Higgins's novel, television, BBC, 20 September 1978;

No Man's Land, television, BBC Four, 1978;

Family Voices, radio, BBC Radio Three, 22 January 1981;

The French Lieutenant's Woman, adapted from John Fowles's novel, motion picture, United Artists, 1981;

Betrayal, motion picture, 20th Century-Fox/Horizon, 1983;

Turtle Diary, adapted from Russell Hoban's novel, motion picture, United British Artists/Britannic, 1985;

The Heat of the Day, adapted from Elizabeth Bowen's novel, television, Granada, 1989;

Reunion, adapted from Fred Uhlman's novel, motion picture, C.L.G. Films/France 3 Cinema/Les Films Ariane/NEF Diffusion, 1989;

The Comfort of Strangers, adapted from Ian McEwan's novel, motion picture, Rank/Sovereign, 1990 [i.e., 1991];

The Handmaid's Tale, adapted from Margaret Atwood's novel, motion picture, Cinecom, 1990;

The Trial, adapted from Franz Kafka's story, motion picture, BBC/Europanda, 1993;

The Proust Screenplay, radio, BBC Radio Three, 31 December 1995.

Harold Pinter is now firmly established as a major playwright with an international reputation. He is, indeed, generally recognized as being the preeminent living British dramatist. The importance of his life's work was attested in letters nominating the writer for the Nobel Prize in literature (see *The Pinter Review,* 1999). Like the greatest dramatists of the past and present, such as Euripides, George Bernard Shaw, Luigi Pirandello, and Samuel Beckett, Pinter has found a new language and a new form for the theater. These elements give expression to Pinter's fundamentally political vision of the individual inescapably vulnerable to different kinds of power, whether private or public, recognized or inscrutable. As a consequence, existence becomes a power struggle against the abuse of authority. Pinter adds the revelation that the seemingly most insignificant speech, laughter, or gesture within the domestic sphere could reflect the immanent outside world. The significance of his original contribution is summed up, paradoxically, in one familiar word, the "Pinteresque." As with the "Ibsenesque" and "Chekhovian," the distinctly personal that earns the epithet also embodies a general truth of experience, language, and society.

Harold Pinter, the only child of Jewish parents, Hyman (Jack) Pinter and Frances Mann Pinter, was born on 10 October 1930 in Hackney, in London's East End. He was brought up in a modest house on Thistlewaite Road, near Clapton Pond. His predecessors were Sephardic Jews from Portugal who had come to England from Hungary around the turn of the century. His surname is probably an anglicized version of the Portuguese original, and his first published works, two poems in *Poetry London* (1950), were credited to Harold Pinta. His father was originally a ladies' tailor, but he subsequently lost his business and worked for someone else.

Following wartime evacuation to Cornwall, Pinter returned to Hackney. In a 25 February 1967 article for *The New Yorker,* he vividly recalls the Little Blitz of 1944: "there were times when I would open our back door and find our garden in flames. . . . Our house never burned, but we had to evacuate several times. Every time we evacuated, I took my cricket bat with me." He has retained his love of cricket, and in an introduction to Pinter's *Plays One* (1991) fellow playwright Simon Gray remembers that when Pinter was directing Gray's *Quartermaine's Terms* in 1981, the pair of them frequently dropped in to watch cricket at the Kennington Oval, which was near the rehearsal rooms. Since 1989 Pinter has been a member of the editorial board of *Cricket World*.

From the age of six, Pinter attended an elementary school close to Clapton Pond and then won a scholarship to Hackney Downs Grammar School, which he attended from 1941 to 1947. There he became a champion athlete and fledgling actor, thriving among intellectually challenging friends. He was encouraged greatly by the senior English master, Joseph Brearley. He played the lead role in school productions of *Macbeth* and *Romeo and Juliet,* and on leaving Hackney Downs he successfully applied for a grant to study acting at the Royal Academy of Dramatic Art. However, he felt alienated by the middle-class assurance of his contemporaries, faked a nervous breakdown, and left to wander around London, always attentive to the rhythms of speech that surrounded him. Having declared himself a conscientious objector in 1948, Pinter was tried twice and fined for refusing national military service, in protest against the Cold War.

In 1949 he wrote the first fragment of his dramatic dialogue "Kullus," which was eventually published in his *Poems* in 1968; and the following year he found work as an actor with BBC Radio. Sufficiently encouraged, in 1951 he restarted his actor training, this time at the Central School of Speech and Drama. That summer he was engaged to perform in Anew McMaster's company and toured Ireland, beginning a repertory actor's career that continued through the 1950s. The tour over, he returned to London and acted in Donald Wolfit's 1953 season at the King's Theatre, Hammersmith, where he first met the actress Vivien Merchant. In 1954 Pinter took the stage name David Baron and toured the English repertory theaters, again meeting up with Merchant when they played the leads in a 1956 Bournemouth production. They married the same year and continued to tour together until she became pregnant, and they went back to London to settle. Their first home was a basement room in a building where Pinter worked as a caretaker to offset the rent. Their son, Daniel, was born on 29 January 1958, and after moving to better accommodations, both Pinter and Merchant returned to acting full-time. He continued to write, however; in 1955 he had completed a novel, *The Dwarfs,* which was finally published in 1990.

In 1957 an old friend at Bristol University persuaded Pinter to write a one-act play, *The Room,* for a student production. He wrote it quickly while appearing in a production of Terence Rattigan's *Separate Tables* (1955) in Torquay.

From the outset Pinter displayed a fascination for the "living moment" of the "engendering" image of two people in a room. Ordinary domestic familiarity is made strange, or defamiliarized, by what takes place and what

Beatrix Lehmann as Meg and Richard Pearson as Stanley in the 1958 Lyric Theatre Hammersmith staging of The Birthday Party, *Pinter's first major production and a box-office failure at the time (from Michael Billington,* The Life and Work of Harold Pinter, *1996; Thomas Cooper Library, University of South Carolina)*

is said or unsaid. Pinter's early working-class milieu was permeated by the influence of the radio and movies. His basic dramatic technique was to take the visual primacy of motion-picture close-up and transfer it to sound with the exposure of onstage dialogue—an aural close-up—by means of the now notorious pause/silence method. Beneath both a torrent of language that evades any real communication, and silence itself, a Chekhovian subtext resonates.

Pinter's brand of naturalism turned away from the repertory theater norm of educated middle-class articulacy. The difficulty of verifying either what had taken place or what was actually intended behind the ambiguity of utterance and feeling, combined with frequent resorts to the comic techniques of radio, revue sketch, and music hall, destabilized the audience. Pinter rejected the traditional genre distinctions of tragedy and comedy as stale and empty and instead seemed to wildly juxtapose uproarious laughter with moments of great seriousness while rigorously resisting any compensatory sentimentalism. Moreover, Pinter disassociated himself from his "kitchen-sink" contemporaries by insisting that his plays were realistic but not the domestic realism of

John Osborne or Arnold Wesker. Though conventional in some respects—the use of "curtain lines" and writing for the proscenium arch theater—Pinter turned from the cut-and-dried formula of "the well-made play" (cause and effect of intrigue speedily alternated over exposition, development, complication, catastrophe, and denouement).

Pinter's early plays were celebrated initially for their verisimilitude, but eventually the careful structuring was recognized, both in plot and language. Patterns of duplication, reversal, and circularity are signaled in the almost musical variation of verbal repetition and permutation. Pinter thereby transcends the limitations of domestic realism, projecting the character's inner being by superimposing the psychological on the social plane of reality. Within this aesthetic emerged Pinter's master themes that evolved throughout his writing career—insecurity and betrayal in varying psychological, sexual, and social permutations.

The Room takes place in the humdrum lower-class apartment of a middle-aged woman, Rose. She is uncertain about who lives in the rest of the house. Mr. Kidd, who enters nervously, seems almost deaf to her questions; he is reluctant to confirm whether he is the landlord or not; whether he is or is not Jewish; or how many floors the house has. A young couple then appear, claiming they have been told that Rose's room is vacant. Rose's position is questioned further by the appearance from the basement of a blind black man, Riley. Far from her professed comfort and security, the subtext of Rose's edgy monologue beside the morose and silent Bert, her husband, reveals her deep insecurity, which is finally acknowledged as she adopts Riley's symbolic blindness—whereupon the returning Bert erupts into violence.

Though heavily symbolic, the figure of Riley is partly used to draw on the atavistic racism in London that erupted with the Notting Hill race riots of 1958. The play begins as a sketch-like comedy of lower-class manners, which is then compromised by the nightmarish accretion of contemporary absurdism, and culminates in the reality of racism past and present as Bert kicks Riley's head against a gas oven. Franz Kafka and Beckett are always raised in discussion of early Pinter, and rightly so since they have always been acknowledged influences (though perhaps Eugène Ionesco's *The New Tenant* [1956] is a greater influence here). But the distinctive amalgam of modes in *The Room* signaled something entirely new in English drama.

Although *The Room* attracted some local interest in Bristol, it certainly did not provide Pinter with an immediate breakthrough. Extremely short of money, he and Merchant continued to tour as actors. BBC Radio expressed some interest in producing the play, but this avenue came to nothing. Then in December 1957 *The Room* was presented in a new production at the National Student Drama Festival at Bristol University. Harold Hobson, the influential theater critic of the newspaper that sponsored the event, the *Sunday Times,* saw the production, and in January 1958 he praised it extravagantly in his column. This review brought Pinter to the notice of the budding theater impresario Michael Codron, who had booked the Lyric Theatre in Hammersmith for a season of new plays. Codron was presented with the script of a play called "The Party," later renamed *The Birthday Party* (performed in 1958, published in 1959). Pinter had also written another play in 1957, *The Dumb Waiter* (performed in 1959, published in 1960), and he was beginning to see his future in terms of writing rather than the acting that still gave him a slender income.

The Dumb Waiter draws on contemporary gangster motifs that Pinter found in Ernest Hemingway's short story "The Killers" (1927). But of greater general significance is the clear introduction of power and subservience as a key to individual relationships and to society itself. At first Gus and Ben are like a cross-talk vaudeville act of dominant partner and querulous sidekick, with their comic exchanges on topical trivia. With the appearance of a gun, however, the tone changes, as it becomes apparent that this comic duo are professional killers in a situation that grows more bizarre as they are forced to respond to requests sent through the dumbwaiter—set in the wall of what appears to be an abandoned kitchen beneath a restaurant—for increasingly exotic dishes.

Ben is metaphorically a dumb waiter, embodying unquestioning acceptance of authority, while Gus queries everything. Consequently, the puzzling but insignificant becomes momentous—why do matches appear under the door when the gas supply to the oven has run out? For Gus, the "organisation" is called into question; for Ben, there is all the more need for authority to be asserted in the due execution of his partner, who turns out to be the awaited victim. The criminality of Ben reflects the bureaucratic unquestioning conformism to state-sanctioned orders that must extinguish the questioning of the individual.

The genesis of *The Birthday Party* came from Pinter's experience of meeting a man in a pub when he was looking for somewhere to stay while performing in Eastbourne in 1954. The man took him to a seedy guesthouse, where they shared an attic room; biographer Michael Billington records that the man later told Pinter, "I'm a pianist, I used to play in the concert-party here and I gave that up." When asked why he stayed, he said "There's nowhere else to go." The remark stayed with Pinter "and, three years later, the image was still there and . . . this idea came to me about two men coming down to get him."

In *The Birthday Party* the sole, scruffy lodger in Meg and Petey's seaside boardinghouse, Stanley, who is already unstably immured in their world of stolid routine, grows increasingly alarmed when he hears of the impending arrival of two more guests. Goldberg and McCann arrive, confirming Stanley's fears, and eventually subject him to a grotesque interrogation. In the course of the following birthday party Stanley undergoes a nervous breakdown. The next day the traumatized lodger is driven off by his abductors to an unstated destination, while Meg and Petey resume their routine.

The play proved to be one of the most famous modern box-office flops. It was met with blank incomprehension that might have announced the end of Pinter's writing career, and yet, after a highly successful television production on 22 March 1960, the play soon became established as a modern classic; it was produced by the Royal Shakespeare Company in 1964. Throughout the work Pinter strikes a balance between theatricality and realism to destabilize genre and audience. He deliberately mixes "low" and "high" art forms, shifting from a realism of set and character to revue-sketch format and comic timing; juxtaposing aspects of gangster thriller with music-hall comedy; and undermining Hitchcockian domestic suspense with farce. Consequently, the audience is made to laugh at what is also recognized as frightening. As Jewish straight man and lugubrious Irish stooge, Goldberg and McCann echo the cross-talk act of stage and radio comedy while, as critics point out, Stanley's situation seems almost a burlesque of that of Kafka's hero "K" in *The Trial* (1925): K is arrested on his birthday, is interrogated by his two tormentors, and is finally executed, all for an assumed offense that is never identified. To complicate responses in *The Birthday Party* there are allusions to Stanley possibly being caught up in contemporary IRA activity.

While seeking to adjust to the commercial failure of *The Birthday Party* and finding it hard to support his wife and child, Pinter worked (over the summer of 1958) on a play commissioned by the BBC. *A Slight Ache* (broadcast, performed, and published in 1961) once again features an intruder, a tramp match seller who brings menace and breakdown, both social and psychological, into the upper-class country home of Edward, a private gentleman-scholar, and his wife, Flora. The initial slight ache in Edward's eyes prefigures the entry of the match seller, whose silent presence releases Flora's social fantasies and deflates Edward's intellectual pretensions. Parody characterizes the play, with its adaptation of Noel Cowardish elements of social comedy, while anthropological allusions to Flora as fertility goddess and Edward as the dying god suggest a partial burlesque of T. S. Eliot's allusive method in *The Cocktail Party* (1949). From a social point of view the parody parallels the anachronism of the parvenu couple and the class they emulate, while the match seller acts as a symbolic reminder of the lower orders.

Even in apparent excesses, the language is controlled in *A Slight Ache*; but with the 1961 television drama *Night School* (published in 1967) Pinter became aware of the dangers of self-parody, particularly where it was closely related to the parodic element in the repetitious habits of everyday speech. When this element is used artistically for comic purposes it runs the risk of caricature. "Night school" and night clubs are the ambivalent venues of Sally, a lodger whom petty forger Wally discovers in his old room when he returns home from a prison sentence to his aunt's house. Intrusion and dispossession of a kind is once again the theme, but the play has smaller comic touches such as the bravura protestations of Mr. Solto, the landlord, against the tax collector: "What are you trying to do, bring me to an early death? Buy me a cheap spade I'll get up first thing in the morning before breakfast and dig my own grave."

Another play Pinter had doubts about was *The Hothouse*, written in 1958 but put aside until the first successful production in 1980. In this play the blustering bully Roote presides over what appears to be a mental institution. Having possibly murdered one patient and impregnated another, Roote withdraws on Christmas Day into the seclusion of his office, where he undergoes something of a mental breakdown. The power, subservience, and vicious emptiness of authority was later viewed by Pinter in political terms as part of the preoccupation in his earlier plays with authoritarian systems, though at the time he thought the characters "purely cardboard" and the whole play "heavily satirical" (quoted in Arthur Ganz, ed., *Pinter: A Collection of Critical Essays*, 1972). Pinter acted the part of Roote in August and September of 1995 in a production that relished and emphasized the farcical elements—such as an exploding cigar—in spite of the conclusion, in which it is revealed that the inmates have been allowed by one of Roote's rival subordinates to slaughter the staff.

Pinter came to criticize sensationalistic aspects of his early work as "cabaret turns." In writing his most popular early work, *The Caretaker* (performed and published in 1960), he moved away from that tendency. In a manner similar to *The Birthday Party,* this new play started from an experience in Pinter's own life, when he and Merchant were living in a first-floor flat in Chiswick. As he told Billington, the house was owned by a builder and his brother, who lived in the house as a handyman and who had had "some kind of electric shock treatment. . . . Anyway, he did bring a tramp back one night . . . a homeless old man who stayed three or four weeks." The man was eventually thrown out: "I met him one day on Chiswick roundabout. We had a

Warren Mitchell as Davies in a 1980 National Theatre production of Pinter's 1960 play The Caretaker, *in which two brothers argue over one's efforts to rehabilitate an untrustworthy tramp (photograph by John Haynes; from his* Taking the Stage: Twenty-One Years of the London Theatre. Photographs, *1986; Richland County Public Library)*

chat and I asked him how he was getting on. I didn't mention the play, which I'd by then written."

In *The Caretaker* an old Welsh tramp, Mac Davies, is rescued from a fight, after losing his café job, by Aston, a former mental patient, who takes him back to his squalid attic home. The owner of the house, Mick, Aston's brother, who self-consciously aspires to be an interior decorator to the upper classes, is less accommodating. Davies opportunistically sides with each, depending on whom he considers holds power and the offer of a job as caretaker. But the work-shy Davies eventually turns on Aston, who finally joins his brother in rejecting the tramp.

The plot is made even simpler by Pinter's abandoning the symbolic, mystifying aspects of his earlier plays. Character, action, and language remain within the conventions of social realism; verisimilitude and naturalism prevail. Nevertheless, critical response included the wildest symbolism and allegory. The characters were variously interpreted in Freudian, Marxist, and theological terms as representing, respectively, the struggle between ego, superego, and id; the class war arising from dialectical materialism; and the Old and New Covenants of the Bible. Such blunt extremes entirely overlooked the real subtlety of the work. By renegotiating the distinction between comedy and tragedy, and by orchestrating utterance and object with a musical sense of form, Pinter signaled his affiliation with and development from predecessors such as Beckett, August Strindberg, and Anton Chekhov, providing something distinctly his own. *The Caretaker* engages the audience in a structure of feeling that begins by exploring the predisposition to respond to Davies as a comic type—a whining old hypocrite and liar whose pretensions are comically at odds with what he manifestly is. But subsequently the tramp is revealed as a victim of circumstance that has shaped his character, and seriousness supervenes as the audience is forced to recognize him as a vulnerable human being.

To work almost subliminally on the audience, Pinter uses a contrapuntal technique of repetition that functions like musical augmentation. Pinter uses the objects obsessively referred to by Davies and Aston (such as shoes and the shed) to alternate in the middle of acts 1 and 2. The alternation is carefully placed in relation to fade or blackout and to the visibly dominant objects of the Buddha on the stove and the bucket suspended from the ceiling. Pinter thereby finds an expressive means, in spite of the seeming limitation of his characters' evasiveness and prevarication, which culminates in the overwhelming power of Davies's closing lines.

The Caretaker brought Pinter fame and financial security. But this success was anticipated by the national impact of his work in other media: on 1 March 1960 *A Night Out* was produced on BBC radio's Third Programme; on 22 March 1960 a production of *The Birthday Party* for Independent Television (ITV) caused a national sensation; on 24 April 1960 *A Night Out* reappeared in Sydney Newman's Armchair Theatre series for ABC Television; and a few days later, on 27 April, *The Caretaker* opened at the Arts Theatre to immediate acclaim and then transferred to the Duchess Theatre for a year's run. Pinter was now a household name, and the word "Pinteresque" entered the English language in *The Times* of 28 September 1960. The success that *The Caretaker* enjoyed meant that for the first time Pinter's family could do more than simply survive economically. They moved to Kew and then, in 1964, to Hanover Terrace in Regent's Park, at the heart of fashionable London. Five years elapsed before the next stage play, *The Homecoming* (performed and published in 1965), but Pinter was busy at work in other mediums in the interim.

Broadly speaking, Pinter's writing for television in the 1960s showed increasing sophistication and experiment in the visual medium. This development is unsurprising, since during this period he was collaborating as screenwriter with distinguished directors: Jack Clayton for *The Pumpkin Eater* (1964); Michael Anderson for *The Quiller Memorandum* (1966); and Joseph Losey for *The Servant* (1963) and *Accident* (1967).

A Night Out fitted television producer Newman's agenda for contemporary social realism. Pinter evokes the world of 1950s psychological entrapment in Albert, the preternaturally middle-aged image of his dead father, emotionally coerced by his mother as he attempts to leave for an office party. At the party, the wider social entrapment of the office hierarchy becomes apparent as Albert is blamed for his superior's sexual misdemeanor. Albert, in turn, intimidates and ridicules a shabby-genteel prostitute before final capitulation to maternal wheedling: "You're a good boy . . . I know you are." The clarity of motive and action in *A Night Out* is unusual in Pinter, since he saw ambiguity as the core of his work.

The Collection (broadcast in 1961, performed and published in 1962) shares part of the theme of marital betrayal but with the added twist of the problem of verification. In this latter-day comedy of manners James, the proprietor of a Chelsea dress shop, is presented with stories of the infidelity of his wife and partner, Stella. She says she was seduced by Bill at a Leeds exhibition of dress collections; Bill admits to relatively innocent kissing and flirtation; Harry, Bill's wealthy Belgravia boyfriend, claims to Stella that Bill made up the story, and then claims to Bill and James that Stella made up the story; finally Bill revises his story and insists that nothing but talk took place. Fluidity of camera work and the subtextual possibilities of the close-up are disciplined by parallelism and complementarity of plot. In the course of the play it becomes apparent that James's pursuit of the "truth" is really just an evasion of the ulterior truth of the breakdown of his marriage, which may derive from latent homosexuality. Thus the central irony of Bill's observation: "Surely the wound heals when you know the truth, doesn't it? I mean, when the truth is verified?"

The Lover (broadcast, performed, and published in 1963) shifts from verification to role-playing in an erotic game of shifting power/subservience relationships. Richard and Sarah live in upper-middle-class, stockbroker-belt Windsor. During the day Sarah is visited by her lover "Max," the very opposite of her conventional husband—but they are the same person. The sexual games played by Sarah as "Dolores/Mary" are on her terms as they both alternately play seducer/innocent. This fantasy is undermined by Richard enquiring after Max, and vice versa. Max further claims that he can no longer deceive his wife, whereas Richard criticizes his wife's "debauchery." Camera close-ups in the first production were important in revealing the increasing disorientation of Sarah, who finally has to accept the reversal of the initiative for fantasy role-playing as Richard installs her as his "lovely whore."

The European Broadcasting Union commissioned *Tea Party* (broadcast and published in 1965, performed in 1968), which was shown to all sixteen member countries. Visual techniques create the meaning as Disson, a self-made managerial bureaucrat who has married into the upper class, finds that his sight is failing, like that of Edward in *A Slight Ache*. Disson's dictatorial bluster, comparable to Roote's in *The Hothouse*, is undermined by what he dreads most—"I don't like self-doubt"—as his new secretary and his new wife and her brother appear to be taking over his life and business. But clever use of the camera creates another kind of doubt: does Disson actually see what really takes place, or is what appears from his point of view no more than paranoid delusion? At the closing office party, when Disson's bandage is removed, revealing his open eyes, the audience is forced to reconsider that the betrayal, conspiracy, and incest they have witnessed are both within and without him.

The most experimental visual techniques are found in *The Basement* (broadcast and published in 1967, performed in 1968), in places subordinating the function of dialogue. Pinter utilizes fluid camera work in depicting the social and psychological rivalry in male friend-

Ian Holm as Lenny and Vivien Merchant, Pinter's first wife, as Ruth in the 1965 Aldwych Theatre premiere of The Homecoming, *in which a philosopher introduces his hostile brothers, father, and uncle to his new wife (photograph © Friedman-Abeles; from Michael Billington,* The Life and Work of Harold Pinter, *1996; Thomas Cooper Library, University of South Carolina)*

ship, love, and possession. The lonely Law is surprised one night when an old friend, Stott, with his girlfriend Jane, turns up on his doorstep. A struggle for territory and mate ensues. "Action," however, is largely replaced by alternating shots: between exterior and interior, between winter and summer, between day and night, and between the alternating decor of the basement flat. Intercut shots eliminate narrative cause and effect to emphasize the primal condition of savagery beneath the cultural veneer. Correspondingly, in the closing shots the circular form is completed with the reversal of roles and dialogue as Law, with Jane, enters Stott's flat—suggesting the truer identity of common masculine instinct and impulse, rather than that of individual character.

Merchant played the lead female roles in all of Pinter's works from 1960 and *The Room* on and took the part of the newly introduced wife, Ruth, in *The Homecoming*. However, the relationship was steadily disintegrating during this period, and in 1962 Pinter embarked on a seven-year affair with the television presenter Joan Bakewell, a relationship and its aftermath that provided the starting point for *Betrayal* (performed and published in 1978).

Probably the most contentious of Pinter's plays, *The Homecoming* is also considered by many to be his greatest accomplishment. It was inspired when one of Pinter's oldest friends returned from North America to visit his family in London with a wife he had never even mentioned to them. Pinter used the incident to create a scenario far from the warm sentimental connotations of "homecoming." Indeed, almost all of Pinter's early work may be considered as written in reaction to the sentimental mode of popular culture of the postwar years.

In *The Homecoming,* Teddy, a lecturer in philosophy, returns with Ruth from America to the all-male household of his brothers Lenny, a pimp, and Joey, a demolition worker-cum-boxer; uncle Sam, a chauffeur; and Max, the father, a retired butcher. The couple's reception is antagonistic, denigratory, and savage, yet with touches of sentimental cliché that offer a travesty of family values: throughout the play familial names are mocked. Jessie, the mother of the family, died many years ago, and her absence is overtly symbolized by obtrusive reference to a demolished wall, as Teddy explains: "We knocked it down . . . years ago . . . to make an open living area. The structure wasn't affected, you see. My mother was dead." The play explores how, bereft of love, men revert to animality and degradation but cannot quite expunge the need for all that motherhood implies. Consequently, Ruth, like Jessie, is finally enthroned as mother, lover, and whore in response to the men's offer to stay on as concubine and prostitute. Some critics have interpreted the atrocious treatment of Ruth as blatant misogyny, but others argue that this reading is far from the case.

Once again Pinter offers a mixed mode that derives from the necessity of finding an expressive means beyond that of available realism. In the course of the play Pinter exposes the subjective reality of a buried need and superimposes it on the surface reality—social and psychological realities are intercut and juxtaposed. The conflict between these realities is formally heightened by the binary oppositions of civility and animality, domesticity and violence, and sentimentality and sexuality. The men enact the collective compulsion to degrade womanhood as whoredom—a clear deflection of their individual need for love. In the closing tableau Ruth acts out the fantasies of male obsessions, fears, and privation, but as a redemptive figure, replacing that demolished wall and symbolizing the emotional mainstay that can save them from degradation.

If *The Caretaker* established Pinter as a major dramatist, the reaction to *The Homecoming* represented more than simply a confirmation of this fact, as it played in theaters all over the world; it also can be seen as the end of the first stage of his writing career. His stage plays to this point had drawn heavily from his East London roots and from incidents in his life as an impecunious actor. From this point the work increasingly reflected the newer, more affluent world in which he found himself; and though he never lost contact with his earlier life, there was an increasing sense of isolation.

Landscape (broadcast and published in 1968, performed in 1969), *Silence* (performed and published in 1969), *Old Times* (performed and published in 1971), *No Man's Land* (performed and published in 1975), and *A Kind of Alaska* (performed and published in 1982), along with the screenplays *The Go-Between* (1970), *The Proust Screenplay* (written in 1972 but unproduced as a movie, published in 1978) and *Langrishe, Go Down* (1978), together represent a major shift in Pinter's development. All the established concerns continue, apart from that early sensationalist menace, but with the added dimension of memory: drama derives from the conflict of past and present, within and between individual memories. *Landscape* and *Silence* were immediately considered Beckettian in their minimalist use of theater resources. *Landscape* dramatizes separation, symbolized by the long kitchen table centrally placed between married protagonists Duff and Beth, and by speech, since they appear never to hear each other (though Duff looks at Beth, she never looks at him). Furthermore, separation characterizes the content of the frustrated dialogue. Duff speaks of his betrayal, while Beth recalls, or re-creates, romantic fulfillment; Duff crudely recalls "dogshit, duckshit," while Beth's artistic sensibility ponders on "the principles of shadow and light." Will the parallel lines never meet, or suddenly coincide, as the dialogue hints? Absolute separation closes the play with the impotence of Duff's verbal rape and Beth's retreat into the landscape of memory.

In *Silence* each of the three characters (who sit in chairs in separate areas on the bare stage) speaks with a young and a considerably older voice, alternating around silences. Ellen's younger voice speaks of an unfulfilled relationship with the older Rumsey, whose stoically fortified loneliness resists love and anticipates age. Bates, his rival, mouths antiromantic crudities. The older voice of each speaks of isolation: Bates in anger, Rumsey with resignation, Ellen with anguish as identity implodes on the fallibility of memory. As this brief play unfolds, patterns of repetition recur in increasing fragments of the young and old voices, thus making the silences encroach more.

Old Times continued the preoccupation with memory, but Beckettian minimalism was put aside as Pinter returned to his characteristic mixed mode, involving dramatized planes of reality and the withholding of a clear distinction between past and present. At the opening of act 1, in a remote country farmhouse, Deeley and Kate await the visit of Anna, Kate's London friend of twenty years ago. This scene is perfectly naturalistic except for the fact that another figure stands in silence looking out of the window with her back to the audience, in a Dior dress of the postwar period (in Peter Hall's original production). Eventually the figure, Anna of course, turns and joins in the conversation as if she had been chatting all evening. A power struggle follows between Deeley and Anna, with Kate as prize.

Anna provides a key statement: "There are some things one remembers even though they may never have happened. There are things I remember which may never have happened but as I recall them so they take place." Memory may be accurate or fallible, and seeming verification or doubt may not be impartially truthful but for ulterior motives. When Anna seems to be winning the struggle for Kate, the past prevails over the present and is re-enacted onstage. Conversely, upon final rejection of both by Kate, Deeley's sobbing is a re-enactment of a past incident of twenty years ago, as related by Anna in act 1. Yet, throughout the play the evident crisis in Deeley's life is offset by constant humor. Of this combination Pinter remarked, "I agree that more often than not the speech only *seems* to be funny—the man in question is actually fighting for his life" (quoted in Ganz, ed.) Many critics agree that Deeley's rejection in *Old Times* is one of the most profound moments in all of Pinter's drama.

Pinter spent almost all of 1972 on *The Proust Screenplay*: it proved, as Billington argues, "something of a watershed in both his public and private life." In 1973, at Hall's prompting, Pinter became an associate director at the National Theatre just as it was about to take up permanent residence on the South Bank of the Thames in London; this association lasted for a decade. In that same year Pinter also began to play a more public role in political debate, condemning the U.S. government's role in the overthrow of President Salvador Allende of Chile and, building on his self-declaration as a conscientious objector, taking a strong interest in the bloody machinations of regimes as far apart as Chile (under General Augusto Pinochet) and Russia. His marriage was also increasingly turbulent; in 1975 he fell in love with the writer Antonia Fraser, the wife of a conservative politician with a family of six children. His next stage play, *No Man's Land,* speaks of personal unhappiness: as Fraser later said of it (in Billington's biography), "*No Man's Land* is a very bleak play—not the work of someone who was

Michael Gambon as Jerry and Penelope Wilton as Emma in the 1978 Lyttelton Theatre premiere of Betrayal, *an adultery play inspired by Pinter's direction of James Joyce's* Exiles *(1918) in 1970 and by other events in his own life (photograph © Sally Fear; from Michael Billington,* The Life and Work of Harold Pinter, *1996; Thomas Cooper Library, University of South Carolina)*

going to take a banner and protest about the state of the world."

Pinter's screenplays for *The Go-Between* and *Langrishe, Go Down*, as well as *The Proust Screenplay*, are each reflected in different ways in *No Man's Land*. In *The Go-Between*, flash-forwards reveal that the aging Leo Colston was emotionally destroyed by the enforced witnessing of illicit copulation while on a boyhood visit to an aristocratic estate in 1900. Yet, the equally aged Marian still idealizes in recollection what for Leo had been poisonous: like the central symbol of the deadly nightshade, experience is beautiful and corrupting. In *No Man's Land*, similarly, bucolic recollections of an idealized past vie with memories of sexual corruption. Imogen in *Langrishe, Go Down*, doting on her love letters, may be compared with protagonist Hirst in the alcoholic stasis of *No Man's Land*, as he is obsessed with the fixity of the past

enclosed within his photograph album. The writer-hero of Marcel Proust's *A la recherche du temps perdu* (1913–1927, Remembrance of Things Past) resorts to an inner world of memory transformed into artistic epiphany to triumph over the refined crassness and sexual corruption around him. A pattern of mock or failed epiphanies also partly structures *No Man's Land*, in which Hirst, a distinguished writer, struggles to retain an epiphanic sense of the past.

No Man's Land is like an upper-class version of *The Caretaker*. Hirst brings to his wealthy Hampstead household a down-at-heel poet, Spooner, after a pub encounter. Spooner immediately senses opportunities of a secretarial rather than a caretaking kind, but this plan is thwarted by the appearance of two picaresque servants, Foster and Briggs, whose sarcasm barely conceals real threat. The brilliance of the play derives from the way Pinter is able to suggest wildly contrasted social worlds by idiolect and allusion: Briggs's barrack-room pornography ("a mingejuice bottler, a fucking shitcake baker"); Hirst's socially exclusive prewar world of scholarly society ("I knew him at Oxford"); Spooner's sexual, social, and literary ambivalence ("Let me live with you and be your secretary"); and Foster's opportunistic acculturation ("Nothing duff, nothing ersatz"). In action and dialogue the whole play is structured around refinement and vulgarity, degradation and dignity, loneliness and friendship, as it moves from night to day and back to the artificial, alcoholically induced, perpetual "night" of Hirst's no-man's-land, "Which never moves, which never changes, which never grows older, but which remains forever, icy and silent."

In the short play *Monologue* (broadcast, performed, and published in 1973), the sole, unnamed speaker, seated on one chair and addressing an empty one, asks: "Who was your best mate, who was your truest mate?" Pinter is particularly drawn to rivalry as a form of power struggle within friendship, and this subject takes two forms: rivalry in love, predictably, and rivalry in competitive sport and games. This struggle may be considered as a single rivalry in love, but of a hetero- and homosexual kind, the latter socially sublimated into sport. Guido Almansi and Simon Henderson's 1983 study is devoted to the concept of "games" in Pinter's writing, and literal references to sport are found throughout his work. The speaker's opening lines in *Monologue* invite his missing friend to "a game of ping pong" and "a categorical thrashing." Both are lovers of the same beautiful black girl, and as in *The Basement*, individual identity coalesces in sex: "My spasms could be your spasms," the speaker declares. *Betrayal*, in title and content, fully realized the theme.

On the surface, *Betrayal* appears to be a 1970s comedy of manners concerned with intrigue, betrayal, and hypocrisy among the London literati. Immediately unusual in the play is its backward-moving time sequence, from a 1977 meeting between Jerry and Emma, whose adulterous liaison ended two years earlier, to 1968, when Jerry first makes a pass at her at a party hosted by Emma and her husband, Robert. But there is considerably more to the play than technical innovation.

Pinter dramatizes the homosocial conflict between bonds of male friendship and the oaths of marital fidelity. Jerry betrayed Robert for years, yet maintained their friendship. When he learns that Robert has known of the affair for some time, he feels that his friend has betrayed him by not letting him know. To Jerry the exclusive primacy of maleness in friendship should be inviolable; the bonds of marriage are something lesser. Jerry's whole life—from sport (squash) to intellectual interests (William Butler Yeats)—has been in complementary adulation of his friend. Robert mockingly reciprocates this feeling when he says to Emma: "I've always liked Jerry. To be honest, I've always liked him rather more than I've liked you. Maybe I should have had an affair with him myself."

Inevitably, the homoerotic view arises of the central psychological paradox that in loving Emma, Jerry has taken the closest step possible to loving Robert, short of actual homosexuality. In doing so he betrayed the greatest thing in his life, the homosocial bond with Robert. Such moral distortion yet psychological insight goes beyond a simple comedy of manners. Revelations in Billington's biography indicate that Pinter drew on personal experience of an affair in the late 1960s, but an equal if not greater source was the experience of directing a 1970 production of James Joyce's *Exiles* (1918), from which much of *Betrayal* is derived. After a divorce from Merchant in 1980, Pinter married Fraser.

Pinter's later plays take on a more explicitly political tone, as the playwright was becoming involved in the activities of organizations such as Amnesty International. In the 1970s he became a member of the Campaign for Nuclear Disarmament; for many years he has been a member of PEN International. But the coup against Allende's democratically elected government in Chile in 1973 was what galvanized his political sympathies. The political plays can be directly related to the world of public affairs in the 1980s: torture in Turkey and elsewhere relates to *One for the Road* (performed and published in 1984); Turkey's suppression of the Kurds is related to *Mountain Language* (performed and published in 1988); and in Britain, Prime Minister Margaret Thatcher's political authoritarianism is related to *Party Time* (performed and published in 1991).

The screenplay for *The Quiller Memorandum* had been concerned with resurgent fascism in postwar Germany. Several screenplays of the 1980s took up this theme again: *The Heat of the Day* (1989) explored a love triangle that included political betrayal and fascism; *The Comfort of Strangers* (1990) linked authoritarian right-wing politics with fascistic homosexuality; *The Handmaid's Tale* (1990; Pinter's name remained in the credits, but work by others on the final shooting script dissuaded him from publication) evokes a futuristic fascist dystopia; finally, Pinter acknowledged a lifetime's debt in his 1993 screenplay for Kafka's *The Trial,* the archetypal story of bureaucratic nightmare and political abduction. For Pinter the stark reality of an individual's and whole people's suffering and death through torture or bombing displaced any aesthetic or absurdist niceties about existence, and this atrocity is confronted in *One for the Road.*

Indeterminacy of place, person, and country in *One for the Road* is sedulously contrasted with the hard facts of torture (offstage) as Victor faces his tormentor, Nicolas. His offense, like K's in *The Trial,* is never named. Fascistic allusions suggest some police state, but the commonplace office setting implies that these events could be happening at any time, in any place—even England. Invoking civilization and civility, friendship and respect, Nicolas's sadistic strategy becomes apparent: to reduce life to a condition worse than death but to refrain from actual killing. Nicolas is pathologically corrupted by the power he wields much more than by his evident alcoholism. Intoxicated by both, he toasts, "One for the road." But such bonhomie has meant multiple rape for Gila, Victor's wife, and death for their son Nicky.

In *The New World Order* (performed in 1991, published in 1993), two interrogators gloat over their blindfolded victim, congratulating each other on their mutual sadism. As in *One for the Road* and *Mountain Language,* the condition of speechlessness is a symbol of totalitarian oppression (anticipated as far back as *The Birthday Party*). The forbidden "mountain language" in the play of that title is that of prisoners and their visitors, who are compelled to speak the language of the capital. Audiences immediately assumed that the play derived from Pinter's horror at Turkey's suppression of the Kurds. However, the playwright indicated that the significance of the work was more far-reaching than that and even applied to the United Kingdom. This relevance is signaled powerfully in the play when a visitor reveals that her name is the completely English "Sara Johnson." In this brief work a woman visitor cannot speak the language of the capital; but when the language prohibition is lifted, the sight of her son's blood renders the woman speechless, and the son is consequently traumatized. In *One for the Road* Victor's tongue is mutilated, and at the end of *Party Time* a spectral, presumably tortured victim is finally left with nothing but "The dark . . . in my mouth."

Pinter and his second wife, writer and historian Lady Antonia Fraser, on their wedding day in 1980 (photograph © Daily Telegraph; from Michael Billington, The Life and Work of Harold Pinter, *1996; Thomas Cooper Library, University of South Carolina)*

The title *Party Time* puns on the contexts of social entertainment and political organization. The slight action of the play consists entirely of banal chitchat of an upper-class, snobbish kind, which tends to focus on the virtues of an exclusive sports club. Talk of "elegance, style, grace, taste" jars somewhat with remarks such as one made by Terry, friend of the great and arbiter of "real class," on his wife, Dusty: "The only thing she doesn't like on boats is being fucked on boats." Behind this social satire, however, is something more sinister. In the streets around the party a political "round up" involving troops and roadblocks is taking place. Given several offhand hints, the audience becomes aware that an authoritarian fascist party, represented by Gavin at the social gathering, is seizing power and suppressing dissidents. In Britain of the 1980s many people believed that the government was steadily encroaching on a whole range of democratic institutions. *Party Time* is Pinter's oblique critique.

Pinter's next two stage plays offer a dramatic recapitulation of virtually a lifetime of writing. There are three stage areas in *Moonlight* (performed and published in 1993). Andy lies in bed awaiting death, with his wife, Bel, in attendance. Jake and Fred, his estranged sons, play anguished word games of paternal rejection and affection around another bed. Intermittently, in the third area, appears the ghostly figure of their sister, Bridget, who died at sixteen. Old family friends, Maria and Ralph, reappear with stories of the past. For the premiere, veteran actor Ian Holm returned to the stage after many years, and his performance as Andy—compounding grief and anger with a vibrant, foul-mouthed hilarity—won awards and drew acclaim from the critics, who, in spite of quickly recognizing echoes of Pinter's earlier works, such as the radio play *Family Voices* (broadcast, performed, and published in 1981), nevertheless were a little uncertain about how to take *Moonlight*.

Pinter wrote *Moonlight* while acting the part of Hirst in *No Man's Land*. In a central speech the audience learns that "moonlight" represents Andy's no-man's-land between life and death, a place of guilt-ridden consciousness of which Bridget is the ghost-like projection.

The whole set was designed to emphasize silver and blackness, guilt and nothingness. Though her death is never discussed, Bridget is the emotional heart of the play. Andy has to insist that the "past is a mist," otherwise he would have to acknowledge the precise nature of his failings. Instead he fantasizes that Bridget has given him grandchildren. In retrospect the audience sees that the intruding menace is death itself; that "evasion of communication" concerning Bridget is the subtext of the play; that in spite of estrangement, the sons are manifestly still caught up in power relationships with their father; that delusive memory reacts on the past and present; and that again the theatrical vies with realism, seriousness with laughter.

Critics immediately recognized that *Ashes to Ashes* (performed and published in 1996) could be compared to the memory plays, particularly *Landscape* and *Old Times*. In a simple room setting, Devlin questions his lover Rebecca about a former boyfriend who sadistically made her kiss his clenched fist (an image in *Party Time*) as he half throttled her. Even more alarmingly, Rebecca's memory seems to conflate her personal history with earlier historical memory of images of the Holocaust—babies snatched from mothers, lemming-like crowds herded to their deaths, and submissive slave-laborers. From one point of view the play presents a subjective ahistorical transference of guilt, as if simply being human makes everyone retroactively guilty for what one group of humans did to another, since one can never know whether one would have acted otherwise. From another, perhaps more frightening point of view, a psychosexual need for retributive punishment seems to create the very fascism that is evoked. As a kind of compliance Devlin finally reenacts the role of sadistic lover just as Rebecca recalls a baby being snatched from her, long before she was born.

Pinter's play *Celebration* (published in 1999) opened at the Almeida Theatre in London in March 2000 in a double bill with a revival of his first play, *The Room*. Set in a smart restaurant, the play is concerned with the interaction between two tables of diners and the waiters. Susannah Clapp said of it that it is "a direct descendant of *The Room;* both are stories about power and intruders" (*The Observer*, 26 March 2000).

In addition to his significant contribution as a writer of major screenplays, Pinter has continued to work sporadically as an actor, mostly in revivals of his own work, as well as a theatrical director. As early as 1964 he directed his own *The Birthday Party*, and he has continued to direct both his own and others' works, starting with Robert Shaw's *The Man in the Glass Booth* in 1967. He has been particularly associated with the work of his close friend Gray. Pinter has received a host of awards, including the Berlin Film Festival Silver Bear in 1963, BAFTA awards in 1965 and 1971, the Cannes Film Festival Palme D'Or in 1971, and the Commonwealth Award in 1981. He was made a Companion of the British Empire in 1966, and in 1996 he was awarded the Laurence Olivier Award for lifetime achievement in theater. He has continued to speak out against political abuse, taking the opportunity of his acceptance speech for an honorary doctorate at the University of Turin on 27 November 2002 to talk about the larger context of violence in the wake of the 11 September 2001 terrorist attacks in America and to condemn the invasion of Iraq. This talk was reprinted in a small collection of poems titled *War* (2003), written in response to the conflict in the Middle East. Pinter received the Wilfrid Owen Award for poetry for this collection in 2004.

In February of 2002 he revealed that he was undergoing treatment for cancer of the esophagus. A complete recovery was announced, and in the same year Harold Pinter was appointed Companion of Honour, the highest award for any British citizen. In October and November of 2002, "Pinter at the BBC," the most extensive festival accorded any living writer by the BBC, was presented over the national media to crown one of the most influential careers in British drama—one that continues into the twenty-first century.

Interviews:

Lawrence Bensky, "Harold Pinter: An Interview," *Paris Review*, 10 (Fall 1966): 13–37; republished in *Writers at Work: The Paris Review Interviews*, third series (New York: Viking, 1967), pp. 347–368;

Mel Gussow, *Conversations with Pinter* (London: Nick Hern / New York: Limelight Editions, 1994).

Bibliographies:

David S. Palmer, "A Harold Pinter Checklist," *Twentieth Century Literature*, 16 (1970): 287–296;

Herman T. Schroll, *Harold Pinter: A Study of His Reputation (1958–1969) and a Checklist* (Metuchen, N.J.: Scarecrow Press, 1971);

Rudiger Imhof, *Pinter: A Bibliography* (London & Los Angeles: TQ Publications, 1975);

Steven H. Gale, *Harold Pinter: An Annotated Bibliography* (Boston: G. K. Hall, 1978);

Francis Gillen and Gale, eds., *Pinter Review: Collected Essays* (Tampa: University of Tampa Press, 1987–   );

Susan Hollis Merritt, "The Harold Pinter Archive in the British Library," in *Pinter Review: Collected Essays 1994* (Tampa: University of Tampa Press, 1994), pp. 14–53;

William Baker and John C. Ross, *Harold Pinter: A Bibliographical History* (New Castle, Del.: Oak Knoll press, forthcoming 2005).

Biography:

Michael Billington, *The Life and Work of Harold Pinter* (London: Faber & Faber, 1996).

References:

Guido Almansi and Simon Henderson, *Harold Pinter* (London: Methuen, 1983);

Raymond Armstrong, *Kafka and Pinter: Shadow-Boxing* (New York: St. Martin's Press, 1999);

Mark Batty, *Harold Pinter* (Tavistock, U.K.: Northcote House, 2001);

Katherine H. Burkman and John L. Kundert-Gibbs, eds., *Pinter at Sixty* (Bloomington & Indianapolis: Indiana University Press, 1993);

Martin Esslin, *Pinter, the Playwright*, sixth edition (London: Methuen, 2000);

Steven H. Gale, ed., *Critical Essays on Harold Pinter* (Boston: G. K. Hall, 1990);

Arthur Ganz, ed., *Pinter: A Collection of Critical Essays* (Englewood Cliffs, N.J.: Prentice-Hall, 1972);

Lois Gordon, ed., *Harold Pinter: A Casebook* (New York & London: Garland, 1990); revised as *Pinter at 70: A Casebook* (New York: Routledge, 2001);

Harold Pinter: A Celebration (London: Faber & Faber, 2000);

HaroldPinter.Org <http://www.haroldpinter.org>;

John Haynes, *Taking the Stage: Twenty-One Years of London Theatre. Photographs* (New York: Thames & Hudson, 1986);

Leslie Kane, ed., *The Art of Crime: The Plays and Films of Harold Pinter and David Mamet* (New York: Routledge, 2004);

Ronald Knowles, *Understanding Harold Pinter* (Columbia: University of South Carolina Press, 1995);

Susan Hollis Merritt, *Pinter in Play: Critical Strategies and the Plays of Harold Pinter* (Durham & London: Duke University Press, 1990);

Bill Naismith, *Harold Pinter: The Caretaker, The Birthday Party, The Homecoming* (London: Faber & Faber, 2000);

Peter Raby, ed., *The Cambridge Companion to Harold Pinter* (Cambridge: Cambridge University Press, 2001);

Linda Renton, *Pinter and the Object of Desire: An Approach Through the Screenplays* (Oxford: Legenda, 2002);

Elizabeth Sakellaridou, *Pinter's Female Portraits* (London & Totowa, N.J.: Macmillan, 1988);

Michael Scott, ed., *Harold Pinter: The Birthday Party, The Caretaker, The Homecoming* (Basingstoke, U.K.: Macmillan, 1986);

Marc Silverstein, *Harold Pinter and the Language of Cultural Power* (Lewisburg, Pa.: Bucknell University Press, 1993).

Papers:

The Harold Pinter Archive at the British Library is the most extensive collection of Pinter material, including manuscript and typescript drafts of plays, screenplays, poetry, and prose, donated by Pinter in September 1993. The Lilly Library, Indiana University, also has three drafts of *The Caretaker*.

Meic Povey

(28 November 1950 –   )

Nic Ros
University of Wales Bangor

PLAY PRODUCTIONS: *Y Pry,* Theatr Ddieithr, Spring 1971;

Aderyn, Theatr yr Ymylon, Autumn 1972;

Y Cadfridog, Theatr yr Ymylon, Autumn 1975;

Terfyn, Theatr yr Ymylon, February 1978;

Chwarae Plant, Rhosybol, Neuadd y Ganolfan, Theatr Bara Caws, 6 December 1983;

Perthyn, Harlech, Theatr Ardudwy, Whare Teg, August 1987;

Gwaed Oer, Felinfach, Theatr Felinfach, Whare Teg, 25 September 1992;

Wyneb yn Wyneb, Cardiff, Chapter, Dalier Sylw, 11 March 1993;

Diwedd y Byd, Neuadd Goffa Chwilog, Theatr Bara Caws, 28 September 1993;

Yn Debyg Iawn i Ti a Fi, Carnarvon, Theatr Seilo, Theatr Bara Caws, 11 April 1995; revised, Theatr Genedlaethol Cymru tour, 23 April 2004;

Fel Anifail, Cardiff, Chapter, Dalier Sylw, 3 August 1995;

Bonansa! Cardiff, Chapter, Dalier Sylw, 20 February 1997;

Tair, Pencoed, Ysgol Pencoed, Dalier Sylw, 3 August 1998; translated by Simon Harris as *Three Women,* Edinburgh, Traverse Theatre, 12 May 2001;

Yr Hen Blant, Pontyberem, Neuadd Pontyberem, Sgript Cymru, 8 August 2000;

Sylw, Cardiff, Theatr Bute, Coleg Cerdd a Drama Cymru, 5 February 2002;

Indian Country, Cardiff, Chapter, Sgript Cymru, 31 April 2003; Edinburgh, Traverse Theatre, 11 June 2003;

Owain Mindwr, Theatr Bara Caws tour, 25 November 2004.

BOOKS: *Mae'r Sgwar yn Wag* (Swansea: Christopher Davies, 1975);

Perthyn (Llanrwst: Gwasg Carreg Gwalch, 1995);

Wyneb yn Wyneb (Cardiff: Canolfan Astudiaethau Addysg, 1995);

Meic Povey (from <http://www.sgriptcymru.com/english/playwright/description.php?author_id=19>)

Fel Anifail (Cardiff: Canolfan Astudiaethau Addysg, 1995);

Bonansa! (Cardiff: Canolfan Astudiaethau Addysg, 1997);

Tair (Cardiff: Canolfan Astudiaethau Addysg, 1998);

Diwedd y Byd / Yr Hen Blant (Cardiff: Sgript Cymru, 2000);

Yn Debyg Iawn i Ti a Fi (Llanrwst: Gwasg Carreg Gwalch, 2000);

Sylw (Cardiff: Coleg Cerdd a Drama Cymru, 2002);

Indian Country (Cardiff: Canolfan Astudiaethau Addysg, 2003).

PRODUCED SCRIPTS: *Deryn,* by Povey and Mei Jones, television, Ffilmiau'r Nant, 11 February 1986;

Sul y Blodau, television, BBC, 23 March 1986;
Nel, television, Opus 30, 1 March 1990;
Yr Ynys, television, Opus 30, 25 February 1992;
Y Weithred, television, Opus 30, 17 September 1995;
Cerddwn Ymlaen, television, Ffilmiau'r Eryri, 27 September 1998;
Talcen Caled, television, Ffilmiau'r Nant, 10 January 1999;
Bob A'i Fam, television, Tonfedd Eryri, 19 September 2002.

Meic Povey is Wales's foremost late-twentieth-century playwright, praised by Bob Roberts in the *Western Mail* (1 October 1993) as "one of the most gifted and prolific dramatists working in Wales today." Povey refers to his television work as his day job, as theater is particularly poverty-stricken in Wales, but his stature as a writer in both media has grown exponentially. He is in a rare position of certitude in Wales: whatever he writes in whatever medium will be produced. Working in movies as well as television and theater, he almost always knows instinctively to what format a story is best suited. With a thoroughly conventional style of writing, his virtues are classical ones; he freely confesses his dependence on plot as a dynamic device. He has often admitted that he writes the same play, that of the conflicts within a family, and the focus remains the same, even in his movie work that can be considered more political and engaged. His own personal creative project is the assertion of the common humanity of the underdog and the outcast, even a character such as an incestuous pedophile, and the most shocking element of his work is his understanding and even alliance with this type of vilified figure.

Michael Povey was born on 28 November 1950 to Gruffydd John Povey, a farm laborer, and his wife, Margaret Emma. He was raised on a farm in the Welsh highlands of Nant Gwynant, Snowdonia, North Wales, where he lived for eleven years before the family moved to the village of Garndolbenmaen. The movement to a village some fifteen miles hence seems a small hike, but it was a turning point in his young life; given the extreme isolation of Nant Gwynant, Garndolbenmaen must have appeared as a metropolis in comparison. The move seems to have set in stone for him the idyllic glories of his former home, to which Povey's work returns often.

His childhood was certainly not lonely, given that he was the fifth of ten children, with his five brothers and four sisters a ready-made community with whom he could play. Home was similar to school, where he shared space with just sixteen other children. Not all his memories are celebratory, however: his mother told him when he was seven years old that she would not be with him forever. The significance of this early indication of the fragility of life was multiplied when he was sixteen: his fifteen-year-old brother, with whom Povey had shared a bedroom, was killed in a car accident. Povey remembers not being able to mourn at the time, but the effect on his parents, and his mother in particular, was tangible. One consolation of being in Garndolbenmaen was that escape was nearby in the form of the cinema in Penrhyndeudraeth, which was where Povey dreamed of becoming a movie star.

Having left school early at fifteen, he worked for a firm of solicitors. More importantly, he began his acting career with Wil Sam (W. S. Jones) and Cwmni'r Gegin of Criccieth, one of the great Welsh amateur companies. Sam's writing was an influence on Povey, particularly in the realm of dialogue. Povey's knowledge of stagecraft was undoubtedly increased by his engagement as a stage manager for Cwmni Theatr Cymru—a national Welsh-language theater company—for whom he worked between 1968 and 1970. This apprenticeship in the practical aspects of staging gave him a utilitarian knowledge of theatrical possibilities, and when writing plays he can "see" them onstage.

Moving to Cardiff in 1971, which he subsequently referred to as an "emigration," he had a brief sojourn with the children's programming department of HTV (an independent television company) before joining the drama department of the BBC in 1974, falling under his most obvious Welsh-language influence, writer Gwenlyn Parry. With Parry he worked on the first three seasons of the long-running Welsh-language soap opera *Pobl y Cwm* (People of the Valley). Parry made his greatest contribution to Welsh culture as a stage writer, in a series of semi-absurdist plays given a rigidly realist treatment, and his influence on Povey's theatrical work is most obvious in the areas of characterization and dialogue as well as in a shared sense of inevitable decline in the Welsh heartlands. Povey also learned a great deal about the craft of writing for television and the crucial discipline of writing to a deadline.

The 1970s were characterized by Povey's attempt to discover his own writing style. In early works such as *Y Cadfridog* (produced in 1975; The General), the desire to shock was evident. In 1975 this play was entered in the drama-writing competition at the annual Welsh-language culture festival, the National Eisteddfod. The fact that the play featured two homosexual characters was seen by some as a positive in the conservative Welsh heartland, with the esteemed playwright John Gwilym Jones praising its "daring novelty" in the adjudications of the festival. Jones also noted the uncannily good ear for dialogue and speech rhythm evident in this future-set play. Also in 1975 Povey published an ambitious novel, *Mae'r Sgwar Yn Wag* (The Square Is

Empty), in which there is the first inkling of his uncanny appropriation of the feminine and female psyche. His experimentation with form is evident in his collaboration on the satirical revue *Cofiant y Cymro Olaf* (Memoirs of the Last Welshman), produced by Cwmni Theatr Cymru in the late 1970s. Many years later Povey practically disowned these early works and condemned such attempts at shock tactics as "unforgivable," taking the opposite route in his mature work. His concern for the linguistic and cultural heritage of Wales and in particular the North became more oblique: he approached the same material but focused on character and story.

Povey's confession and probable exaggeration that he spent the years between ages seventeen and twenty-seven drinking in public houses might mislead the reader into a vision of a Dylan Thomas model, but Povey in fact puts great store by craft and discipline. He writes something every day and has a strict regimen admired by fellow writers, with whom he often creates comedies for television. The period of Thomasesque drinking came to an end when he met his future wife, Gwenda Hughes-Jones, a teacher, and settled down. The couple married in 1985, and Povey has a stepdaughter, Catrin Awgharad, and a stepson, Llion Maldwyn. Around the same time he met Hughes-Jones, in 1977, he left the BBC. Povey considers himself a budding writer from that date forward, but it was some years before he reached the nation's consciousness in the mid 1980s. Looking back at his writing in his mid thirties, he agrees with a comment made by his friend the television writer Wilfred Greatorex, who said that Povey would not write anything of quality until he was forty. He sees the 1986 television movie *Sul y Blodau* (Palm Sunday) as a turning point.

Sul y Blodau is a direct and angry response to an historical situation. The problem of the erosion of the Welsh culture and language in the western and northern heartland by second-home owners primarily from England, who could better afford house prices than economically deprived natives, was an increasing social problem throughout the latter half of the twentieth century. The problem has been exacerbated by economic migrants who settle permanently in the heartlands without any integrational intention. In the face of the refusal of the politicians to become involved, in the late 1980s there was a spate of arson attacks on second homes that were partially or completely burned down; since none of the homes were at the time occupied, no one was hurt. This campaign by Meibion Glyndwr (The Sons of Glyndwr, named after the fourteenth-century Welsh prince who defeated the English) was fantastically successful in two senses: potential second-home owners were put off moving to Wales, and the police and MI5 (the British Secret Service) had little or no idea of who was responsible. The Palm Sunday arrest of several dozen "suspects," using strong-arm tactics, was interpreted as an attempt to frighten the arsonists, and while it was not particularly successful, the date is seen as a pivotal one in recent Welsh history and as a great injustice.

One of the elements that emerges from Povey's screenplay is an obvious guilt complex, since he had left the North for Cardiff. His emphasis is primarily but not wholly on a typical family with two brothers of almost the same age. One has moved away to England and is returning with his English girlfriend for the first time. The other has stayed at home to work the farm and has done the right thing in the eyes of the community, but his brother's financial success riles him. One can understand Povey's desire to show the effect of the Palm Sunday raids on the whole community, but looking back he feels he should have restricted the action to this one family. He himself is obviously in part the returning exile, although in the movie he played the role of the more heroic brother, the good son.

Like *Sul y Blodau,* the stage play *Perthyn* (performed in 1987, published in 1995; Belonging) is based on real events, this time a child-abuse case in South Wales. This play was commissioned for the 1987 National Eisteddfod at Porthmadog, the town where Povey went to high school, and it was staged in the local theater at Harlech. Certainly a great deal of the audience was shocked by both the subject matter and the location, which is obviously southern Snowdonia; but most shocking is the matter-of-fact tone, and one of the greatest virtues of *Perthyn* is to make the story not just believable but unexceptional, with the obvious inference that the mother has suffered the same horrible fate as her daughter.

Since the total number of Welsh speakers of all ages is just half a million, few Welsh plays of the last twenty years have been revived. When *Perthyn* was given a second professional production (in 2002) it was owing as much to the status of the play and author as the fact that it was a school set text. The first production served as both manifesto and calling card. In the fifteen years after its premiere Povey only occasionally strayed from the form and style of this piece, which is almost Ibsenesque in its gradual unveiling of dark family secrets. In many ways Povey is reminiscent of Henrik Ibsen, but his use of theatrical space is completely different. Povey's episodic structure means that he uses several locations and times, suggesting minimal staging. In *Perthyn* he recommends the splitting of the action into five spaces, and the debut production accomplished that mainly through the use of light. This utilitarian approach particularly suits the outdoor scenes that frame the play.

Owain Garmon and Christine Pritchard in the 1995 Dalier Sylw premiere of Povey's Fel Anifail *(Like an Animal), in which an old married couple quarrel over history and faith as they wait to die (from <http://www.users.globalnet.co.uk/~dalsylw/archif/anifail.htm>)*

Povey's plotting and characterization are particularly strong, giving actors and directors huge possibilities in terms of emotional engagement from the audience. The most striking element of *Perthyn* is that Povey makes the sexually abusive father, Tom, a sympathetic figure, while Gwen, the mother, is an almost equally culpable presence, and the daughter, Mari, is an infuriatingly willful teenager who seldom tells a consistent truth. The actions of the father of course garner no sympathy, but the context makes them wholly believable. The fragility of the father, the coldness of the mother, and the responsiveness of the daughter all make the traumatic events almost inevitable. The understatement of the whole is contrasted with a single use of expletive to state bald fact when the mother asks the daughter why she does not date as her older brother, Edward, does:

Mari: Mae gen i gariad.
Gwen: Cariad go iawn, rhywun o'r un oed, ma' Edward efo rhes o gariadon, be sy'n dy rwystro di?
Mari: Ddaru Dad rioed ffwcio Edward.

(Mari: I have a boyfriend.
Gwen: A proper boyfriend, the same age as you, Edward has a string of girlfriends, what's stopping you?
Mari: Dad never fucked Edward.)

Povey places these lines late in the play, by which time the audience has no doubt as to the father's guilt, so the declaration serves not as melodramatic revelation but as the opposite. What surprises is the previous lack of clear statement of what viewers know to be fact. The play leaves no doubt that nothing good can come from the revelation—such are the hypocritical forces of repression weighing against the girl. To tell seems to be the equal of the act itself. Yet, the most horrific line is reserved for the mother in a flashback scene as she and the nine-year-old Mari watch a program on child abuse. Povey creates tension by gradually increasing the audience's doubts as to how much the mother knows and by subtly making it clear that Mari is about to talk, before she is cut off with the mother's brutally banal "Gwna baned imi, gwael" (Make us a cuppa, love). Povey has a precise ear for the rhythms of everyday North Walian speech, and here (in contrast to later work) he offers a homogenous style of speech for everyone in the family without falling into the trap of insufficient differentiation between them.

While Povey later developed a predilection for a single-act, seventy- to eighty-minute play, *Perthyn* is much longer. The main action is played out between the three family figures, but Povey has added an unnamed Psychiatrist who questions the others, adding another third to the length of the work. Under the possible influence of Peter Shaffer's *Equus* (1973), the trendy psychobabble offers only one significant revelation, that of the equally abusive childhood of the mother. Particularly unconvincing are the confessions of desire by the father in an attempt to elicit a similar response from the Psychiatrist. As with *Sul y Blodau,* Povey believes in retrospect that he could have and maybe should have restricted the action to the family home.

Despite these imperfections, the play was unanimously well received, with one review for *Y Faner* (August 1987) commenting on the generality of the relevance: "Certainly it is a valuable contribution to the continual discussion of our values and a great step towards the eradication of the overriding hypocrisy that is such an integral part of the fabric of the Welsh way of life." In the majority of his plays Povey exposes a particularly Welsh incarnation of hypocrisy and prejudice.

In a September 2000 article, Gwenno Hughes claims that *Gwaed Oer* (performed in 1992; Cold Blood) is a more effective play than *Perthyn,* with better characterization. This lurid little melodrama with too much action, however, remains unpublished, though years later Povey successfully converted it into a television series titled *Talcen Caled* (1999; Hard Times). The play revisits some of the themes of *Perthyn,* with a teenage daughter in whom the rather twisted father and grandfather show too much interest; significantly, these unwholesome elements have been banished from the small-screen version. Povey's love of theater is multiplied by the opportunity it gives for "the individual voice of the author," and he can push boundaries onstage, while his television audience needs to be treated more carefully to avoid displeasing what he calls "our little middle of the road nation."

Wyneb yn Wyneb (performed in 1993, published in 1995; Face to Face) is a deliberately disingenuous title, for little is stated openly as the audience once again sees a domestic situation with family secrets being suppressed. The play deals with a young man's coming to terms with his homosexuality and the subsequent arc of his relationship with his mother. The author has on several occasions stated that "it is the mother's play," and certainly the son's lover, Steff, is almost peripheral. Much of the action unfolds in flashback, but the monologues give the audience the clearest perception of the mother's burgeoning acceptance. There is little in the way of revelation, and one of the greatest subtleties of the work is the way it implies that the mother, Laura, has always known the truth of her son Tom's persuasion. Instead of a hackneyed coming-out scene between son and mother, Povey presents a scene where the battle is between appearance and reality, with Laura craving for Tom to at least appear to behave in a "normal" fashion.

The shame accruing from the public knowledge of homosexual behavior is deemed to be worse than the behavior itself, and as in *Perthyn,* the domestic pressure is to cover up the truth at all costs. This rather antiquated hypocrisy is another tie to Ibsen, and *Wyneb yn Wyneb* echoes Ibsen's *Ghosts* (1881) in many ways: the focus on the mother/son relationship, with the emphasis on the mother's experience; the father's absence from the stage; and the terminal illness of the son, which is necessary for her to accept the reality of the situation beyond the social stigma. The relationship between son and lover is secondary but crucial in its addition of another level, as Steff refuses to accept Tom's reticence to tell his mother of their relationship, questioning Tom's seriousness of purpose and ultimately feeling that he is treated as a second-class citizen by the individual who purports to love him. That Tom cannot completely avoid in himself the peculiarly Welsh hypocrisy of his mother, even in London, is a crucial point of the play. Steff is from South Wales, but in his ease with his own sexuality he might as well be from Mars.

The deliberate understatement of the play generally works in its favor, but the narrow focus mostly on two characters means that at times it can play rather flatly. Certainly of all Povey's works it is the one that would work best as a radio play. The isolation of the milieu is in contrast to the all-pervasive influence of social niceties but serves to emphasize the nonpolitical bent of Povey's writing. Whereas *Perthyn* keeps one eye on the world, as it accelerates toward the day of the father's trial and his possible incarceration, *Wyneb yn Wyneb* focuses on the mother/son relationship and Laura's eventual acceptance of her son's lover. Ultimately, she realizes that she gains a second son rather than losing her one and only.

Formally, the play has the same episodic structure as *Perthyn,* but Laura's monologues, which frame the piece, bring the play into the present, while the flashback sequences are chronological. The play happens in the two domestic spaces of the family home and Tom's London lodging, and the stage should serve to emphasize the split between Tom's real and pretend lives. Once again dependent on note-perfect performances and subtlety, this drama has since gained the seal of approval of the Welsh Joint Education Committee, which placed *Wyneb yn Wyneb* on its syllabus.

Diwedd y Byd (performed in 1993, published in 2000; The End of the World) is the most obviously autobiographical of Povey's early works, as its time and place are clearly established. Set in 1962, this play concentrates on the twilight zone of childhood as two sets of brothers and sisters play on the Snowdonian mountainside for the last time before they ascend to the "big school." Extremes of experience and maturity are designated by the girls, who offer a contrast between Rhi's quiet self-assurance and sexual curiosity on the one hand, and Mags's crybaby innocence on the other. Between these extremes the boys begin with a similar hierarchy, as Deio always calls the shots in his cowboy game with Em. Deio has even "borrowed" his father's Luger in an attempt to impose himself on the group, and only Rhi is not impressed. Deio's actions follow the downward spiral of the vanquished: he ends the play having soiled himself following the accidental firing of the gun by Mags. One of the more interesting implications of the play is that he, the junior top dog, is the one who will struggle most in high school. The battle for control between Rhi and Deio is centered on Em, who ultimately chooses to ascend the mountain further with the apparently sexually forthcoming Rhi. His journey through the play is toward maturity and in direct contrast to that of Deio, who ends the play desperately pleading with Em to continue their boyhood games. Em, however, has already moved beyond such immaturity and will obviously be fine in high school.

Despite its obvious debt to the television play *Blue Remembered Hills* (1979) by Dennis Potter, a writer for whom Povey has confessed his appreciation, *Diwedd y Byd* is a mature and considered portrayal of youth. The setting gives the play its sense of nostalgia, and the interplay of comedy and gravity is balanced. Once again the characters are sharply drawn, although they speak with a homogeneity that reveals much of the close-knit community that spawned them. Povey's continual insistence in interviews that he is not from Garndolbenmaen (where he went to school) but Nant Gwynant says as much about that community as it does about the man and his perception of his world. Even at his most urban, Povey's rural background remains pertinent, and he later revisited not only the period and place but also the characters.

The warm, nostalgic glow of the play and its comparative lack of issues meant that some of the generally positive reception was qualified; a few critics commented that the lack of greatness in the play should not affect its popularity. After some of Povey's earlier stage work, the personal nature of this play surprised other reviewers: "Here is emotion rather than a sermon," said Meleri Wyn James in *Golwg* (14 October 1993). The play was inevitably popular with children, and the proximity of audience and performers enhanced the ambience in a production that toured community venues and schools in autumn 1993. While in some of these venues the emphasis seems to have been on the lighter side of events, the delicate interplay of seriousness and levity was praised by the more perceptive critics.

The first production of *Diwedd y Byd* was also directed by Povey, with simplicity and unfussiness. His work as a director is bolstered by the strictness of his own editing, with his writing in the 1990s characterized by a compactness of vision and a clear move toward a seventy-five-minute model of drama. *Diwedd y Byd* telescopes time, and although the play is presented as happening continuously, it in fact takes place over several hours as the day gets gradually darker. In his next work, which he also directed, his use of time is far more daring.

Yn Debyg Iawn i Ti a Fi (performed in 1995, published in 2000; Just Like You and I) is the work above all others by Povey that is read as an issue play. Community care for the mentally ill was certainly an issue at the time the play was conceived, but the phrase is not used, and neither are there direct references to schizophrenia, in the same way that *Wyneb yn Wyneb* does not mention AIDS. The suffering Derec's illness is not specified, but Povey at times drowns out the actual conversation of the characters with the dissonant sounds and voices in Derec's head. Theatrically, this technique is not as irritating as it reads, because it also indicates that one does not need to hear the dialogue to know what is being said: as the future care of Derec is discussed, everyone adopts platitudes. There is a far more important element with which Povey is experimenting here: his use of real time. The play believably takes place in the seventy minutes after the family returns home following the funeral of the mother.

The semidysfunctional family unit is once again under the microscope, but this time there are four characters all of the same generation and no parental figure. Glyn sees his own chronic lack of ambition and drive reflected in the eyes of his doormat wife, Elin, who allows him to bully her with withering put-downs. His sister, Olwen, has escaped and seldom returns home from her safe place in England, half a step up the social ladder. Her greatest fear, however, is the same as that of Glyn: sharing the same genes as her brother Derec. Both have more in common with their problematic brother than they would wish, and she distances herself geographically while Glyn does so intellectually: he hates the idea that his brother writes poetry too. His relationship with Derec is presented in an evenhanded manner. From the opening raised thumb and "Iawn, boi?" (A'right, lad?), his approach is patronizing but understandable: he is the one who has remained on hand to help with Derec and who can discipline him at times, which is painful but necessary. Elin brings a rare note of tenderness and proper Christian values to Povey's work, as she is the virtuous matriarch of the piece. Her faith and attendant selflessness are wholly admirable but affect the perception of her as possibly the most simpleminded of all four characters.

The play was seen as a major development in the writer's craft, and the unanimously positive reception was influenced by the actors' performances, in particular that of Myrfyn Jones as the troubled Derec: Sian Gwynedd wrote in *Y Cymro* (20 October 1993), "Every physical movement and facial gesture combined with a monotone speech thoroughly discomfort the viewer."

The cast of the 1997 Dalier Sylw premiere of Povey's Bonansa! *(Bonanza!), in which an animal-rights activist eats her morally corrupt family's winning lottery ticket (photograph © ffotofictions; from <http://www.users.globalnet.co.uk/~dalsylw/archif/bonansa.htm>)*

While some journalists focused on the difficult subject of schizophrenia, other reviewers were more perceptive of the real theme of the piece; as Aled Islwyn wrote in *Barn* (May 1995), "the theme and the subject of drama are not the same. If the subjects of Meic Povey's plays sometimes appear to be taken from the bold headlines of the daily papers, the themes more often than not dwarf them, displaying a greater maturity than the marketing machine will imply." This statement is a summation of one of Povey's greatest attributes, that of finding the human under the headline.

First staged by Theatr Bara Caws in 1995, the play offered Povey his second chance to direct a professional production of his own play. He freely confesses his own limitations as a director, saying that knowing where and when actors should move is not something he does. His clear inference is that the script is almost enough on its own, and should be. His production of *Yn Debyg Iawn i Ti a Fi* had a simplicity of direction and decor that placed the emphasis on the script and the performances.

Povey's next project, as he described it in an unpublished October 2001 interview with Nic Ros, was "Nid drama am nhad a'n fam, ond dyna lle y dechreuodd hi" (Not a play about my mother and father, but that was the starting point). In the eighty-minute two-hander *Fel Anifail* (performed and published in 1995; Like an Animal), an old married couple, Defi and Mair, argue over the details of the past while they wait to join whatever spirit kingdom there is. Nothing happens in the play, and little is resolved; yet, it is gripping despite its grim theme of coming to terms with the past before leaving this world. Despite their fierce renunciation of the other's version of history and faith, the two display a curious dependence on each other, which gives them a Beckettian tenderness. Christian as well as pagan mythology is ransacked for its comforts, but it is the dead figures of their past and not a divinity who will pass judgment, with the implication that one version of history will finally be sanctioned.

The land is the third character in this play, and the possible journey from farmhouse to retirement bungalow is symbolic of the movement to death and beyond. In Povey's television movie *Nel* (1990), the female title character wishes to stay at the farm, despite the selling of the land, while her brother wants to move to town for the sake of convenience; but in *Fel Anifail* the roles are reversed. Mair is the practical woman, seeing great benefit in the acquisition of a bungalow, the horizontal opposite to Defi's beloved mountain that he now struggles to climb.

As with Harold Pinter's play *Old Times* (1971), the audience has to decide for itself where the truth of the past lies, and whether either of the couple is absolutely reliable. But *Fel Anifail* is in fact more reminiscent of Pinter's *Landscape* (broadcast and published in 1968, performed in 1969), which features two overlapping monologues by a husband and wife. Although Mair and Defi do maintain a dialogue, they are in fact as entrenched in their own singular views of the past as are the farmhouse inhabitants of *Landscape*. Equally if not more likely an influence is Brian Friel's *Faith Healer* (performed in 1979, published in 1980), and all three plays have a similar view of patriarchal inefficacy and a greater sympathy for the female character.

Fel Anifail was staged in 1995 by Dalier Sylw, the company that almost exclusively produced the author's work in the second half of the 1990s, and it had a female director, Bethan Jones, with whom Povey enjoyed a formidable partnership. Jones has talked of Povey's affinity with female roles, and this ability to write so well for both sexes ensures that the best actors and actresses want to perform in his work. *Fel Anifail* is another example of a successful production based ostensibly only on the script and performances. With the emphasis on the writing and so little happening, Povey's skill was recognized; as Meg Elis wrote in *Barn* (September 1995), "Here is the difference between those who record everyday speech without polishing the dust, and the artist who hears speech rhythms and turns our ordinary words into shining weapons."

Disappointment, however, followed with *Bonansa!* (produced and published in 1997; Bonanza!), a problematic play that combines elements of satire and sitcom, of absurdity and farce, in an uneasy mélange. Its biggest drawback is the lack of sympathy for any of the characters, who have little depth to ameliorate their somewhat obvious faults, and even the single virtuous character, the politically correct but naive Anwen, is irritatingly one-dimensional. She is the only member of this extended family untouched by greed, and she seems an almost incredible creation given the context of her uncultured working-class background. This milieu itself provides difficulty, as the characters are without ambitions. The title refers to the winning of the National Lottery, which offers only material escape from mundane realities, and while the element of satire is strongest, the chronic lack of any kind of a future vision in the family's schemes means again a lack of sympathy for them; indeed, the play can even be read as a satire of a certain patronizing view of the working classes.

The wimpish Iori is married to the unfaithful Rosina, who is flagrantly having an affair with their neighbor Bob. Their daughter, Anwen, is a believer in animal rights and minority rights and is patently ill at ease with the modern world. There is also a South Walian lodger, Rhydian, who embarks on an affair with Rosina later in the play. Anwen is responsible for the collection of the money for the group's lottery tickets, but neither Rhydian nor Bob has paid. The group wins and all go out to celebrate, the aftermath of which includes Rosina's failed attempt to keep Bob to his promise of leaving his wife for her, the point being that money makes these changes possible. The following day the nonpaying members of the circle are excluded as Anwen is in control. The play takes a surreal turn as Anwen is suddenly struck blind in a reverse symbolism, for she alone sees the sudden fortune for what it is. This blindness is explained in the play by an offstage doctor who says it is the shock of the sudden fortune. However, Anwen has a vision that the winning ticket brings only destructive change, and she eats the ticket. This action is accompanied by a heavenly flash and Anwen's quoting of Jesus while on the cross: "Forgive them Father for they know not what they do." The initial shock of the family is short-lived, and the play ends with a depiction of them waiting again for the magic numbers. The message, as in other Povey plays, is that dreams should remain in their own realm.

Bonansa! earned tentative reviews and reactions that hinted at the obviousness of the author's targets of scorn, but critics ultimately decided that the play was humorous enough to justify its place. The most interesting view came from Islwyn, who suggested in *Barn* (October 1998) that the implied inclusion of the audience in the action resulted in an example of "metatheatre."

Tair (performed and published in 1998; Three) benefits from its classical simplicity: three generations of the same family realize they have much more in common than they would like to admit. The characters are named only the Gran, the Mother, and the Daughter to emphasize the universality of their predicament. The plot is extremely simple, dealing with the pregnancy of the Daughter by her college tutor, with whom she is having an affair, and while this situation may seem to be a particularly contemporary issue, the play slyly undermines such presumptions. While humor has almost always been a factor in Povey's work, in this play it is crucial to the mix as a comedy of misunderstandings is played out between the generations. This leavening effect is justified by the happy ending as the Daughter realizes that she was merely late with her period.

Language in the play is simultaneously naturalistic and symbolic, as there is a clear line of degradation through the three generations. The difference between the Gran and the Daughter is most evident in the younger's use of English and blasphemy. The Daughter's statement "God, saethwch fi pan dwi'n thirty" (God, shoot me when I'm thirty) is extremely funny in the context of the Gran's confusion, but the precise linguistic mix of colloquial Welsh with the preceding oath and emphasis on the English "thirty" highlights the absurdity of her worldview. In contrast, the Gran's Welsh is classical and reverend; but the underlying experience is ostensibly the same, as all three women have been abandoned by their menfolk in various ways.

The use of space and time are deliberately vague, as the set for almost all of the action is a living room, but the play remains episodic because of its elliptical time scheme, which seems to imply a continual time frame but in fact takes place over a week or so. The one scene that has to be staged or lit differently is a brief chapel scene. Under much pressure from the Mother, the Daughter acquiesces in accompanying the others to the chapel but chooses this location to reveal her worry to her Mother, who replies comically with an expletive. The Mother's use of swearing takes her idiomatically closer to her Daughter, and the language reveals most clearly where the mother's sympathies lie: her values are closer to that of her own mother, but common circumstances mean that a direct expression of abjectivity has a purging effect–she enjoys the release of saying the pointedly English words of "Fucked, basically." The linguistic change between the generations is mirrored in the shift from country to town: the older generation is indicative of a rural, almost traditional Wales, while the younger's experience is different. Povey said in a 1993 interview, "Faswn i byth yn sgwennu dim byd am Gaerdydd achos . . . dydw i ddim yn perthyn yno" (I would never write anything about Cardiff because . . . I don't belong there), but in *Tair* he certainly approaches the urban. While the characters do not represent his family, the play was inspired by being surrounded by women–mother-in-law, wife, and stepdaughter–and in the initial production, his stepdaughter was cast as the rebellious Daughter.

Tair was a commissioned play at the National Eisteddfod and was again staged simply and efficiently by Dalier Sylw. It was praised for its comic touch; some, but not all, of the reviewers also perceived the darker edge of the play and its continuation of an old Povey theme: as Islwyn wrote in *Barn* (October 1998) "This was a play from an age of decay."

The difficult *Yr Hen Blant* (performed and published in 2000; The Old Children) returns to the characters and community of *Diwedd y Byd* thirty years later, and fifteen years after a tragedy that made Em leave. His return from London, in an attempt to save the junior school that was the glue of these four, is the catalyst for the action. The tone is much darker, and the contrast was emphasized in the production of the new play in tandem with a new version of the earlier work as a double bill. The intervening years have not been kind to anyone, and the person least changed, Mags, is the most pathetic and childish of the four. Deio is a drunk and virtually destitute, selling bacon from the back of a Land Rover, but he is unchastened and at heart as much of a bully as previously. Rhi, his sister, has lost none of her superiority despite its now apparent lack of foundation, and her latent sexual sophistry has become a kind of sadism.

The role of the English settler Mel, who lives in the same village as the four, is bifurcate, as Povey makes her arty worthiness and political correctness rather contemptible, and even her attempt to learn Welsh seems emblematic of a kind of tokenness. However, Povey reverses her role completely, and when she becomes the oppressed minority, the audience is both sympathetic and guilty, as they have colluded in her attack. The central theme of the play is that those who say nothing are as culpable as those who encourage violence and injustice, who are in turn almost as guilty as those who take the violent actions. The reader or viewer might find it difficult to accept this point of rather Grand Guignol reversal as a device of realism, as Em and subsequently Deio ride Mel as they would a horse, with active encouragement from Mags and sly collusion from Rhi. The group is attempting to exorcise the memory of the earlier tragedy, when a combination of strong drink and a mob mentality was responsible for the killing of Gareth Ty Isa, a special-needs boy mentioned several times in the original play. Stylistically the play needs careful staging, as the gradually emerging contextual history combined with the latent hatred of Mel and her ilk should render the bullying scene credible, but there is a definite stylistic shift, with Em ordering Mags to turn off the light.

The audience viewing this play immediately after its predecessor will be shocked by its difference in tone, which is of course deliberate, with the author stating that the halcyon days of *Diwedd y Byd* are but a prelude to the process of disillusionment in the real world. It would be too easy for Deio the erstwhile bully to be the perpetrator of the assault on Mel, and Em's behavior needs to be viewed in the context of the others, as his bestiality is in everyone. The fact that his homosexuality is the main reason for his social as well as geographical exile should not be overemphasized. Deio in fact appears to be in the only genuinely selfless relationship in this play, in which there is mention of a plethora of warped temporary and permanent partnerships.

The double bill offered audiences and reviewers alike the opportunity to compare two different vintages, with most seeing a two-act play that homogenized perfectly. The addled people that the characters have become are the direct descendants of their childhood actions and choices. Others noted the difference in craft, claiming that the first play displays a writer whose strength is dialogue, while the latter shows greater playwriting craft.

Povey was familiar with the restraints of writing for a small-scale theater company, as all of his works since *Perthyn* featured no more than five actors, and usually fewer. A different challenge was offered in 2002 with a commission from the Welsh College of Music and Drama, which requested a play for six actors (two female, four male) of ostensibly the same age. For Povey, making college the common ground between the six characters was logical. He also needed to make the parts roughly of the same size, and in addition he

Lisabeth Miles, Betsan Llywd, and Catrin Powell in the 1998 Dalier Sylw premiere of Povey's Tair *(Three), about three generations of women who recognize the common elements in their experiences when the youngest woman confesses that she might be pregnant (from <http://www.users.globalnet.co.uk/~dalsylw/archif/tair.htm>)*

took on the natural accents of the six actors with whom he was working, representing a broader range of vernacular Welsh than he had previously attempted.

At the heart of the resulting play, *Sylw* (performed and published in 2002; Attention), is a discussion of youthful mores, as six students prepare for the wedding and subsequently the funeral of John and Jane, who do not appear in the play. Gradually, the truth of the relations among these eight is uncovered, with the unwholesome mess including bisexuality, infidelity, anal sex, a pregnancy of indeterminate fatherhood, and attempted murder. There is a great deal of revelation in the play, but the humor, not the plot, is what sustains the work. Whereas in previous works Povey's use of explicit language and detail is subtle, here the drama explodes in a barrage of bad language and a thorough quest for the details of any sordid liaison.

Sylw presents a somewhat jaundiced view of Welsh youth, with none of the six characters being particularly likable and none of them able to control their raging desires; Kylie and Proff, the two professed Christians, are as loose as the laddish Baz and Lewis. Sei is only saved from active indiscretion by his predilection for voyeuristic entertainment, while Ruth is too busy analytically studying who is doing what to whom to take part. The video that launches the second half of the revelations is placed in the bedroom by Ruth; similarly, the climax of the wedding is relayed with a recording of John's speech. Dramatically, this technique presented the young cast with a huge task, to react appropriately to two sets of external stimuli; but the greatest challenge was to engage the theater audience for scenes that required reacting more than acting.

Povey's next stage work was both a departure and a return. *Indian Country* (performed and published in 2003) is arguably his most personal play, yet in an unfamiliar language—though the characters occasionally speak Welsh, the majority of the text is in English. It is, like *Tair,* a work that plays far funnier than it reads, without compromising the integrity of the characters or the seriousness of the conceit, which is an imagined triangle of relationships with an historically correct setting: the filming of the movie *The Inn of the Sixth Happiness,* starring Ingrid Bergman, in Gwynedd in 1958. The central figure is Mos, seen as both a naive boy of fourteen and an older commentator on the action. Mos's fixation on the movies recalls that of Povey himself, and he dreams of meeting Bergman and becoming a movie star. His brief meeting with her offstage toward the end of the play is one of the more subtle examples of the disillusionment that is at the core of the play:

> Young Mos: Two minutes. We talked for two minutes. Not much to say. Talked funny. Had a pimple on her chin. And she was smoking! Never seen a woman smoking before. Seen a woman pissing in a field, but never smoking.

Mos and his mother, Gwyneth, are both in need of financial and emotional support following the twin blows of the death of his father, Alun, and a tough winter. But while Gwyneth is in denial about her own needs, Mos is wide-eyed with optimism and belief when the charismatic American drifter Gregg staggers into their lives, having been kicked out of his menial post on the movie set for drunken behavior. His eventual seduction of Gwyneth, which is to her at least partly a business exchange, is the most obvious support for critic David Adams's political reading of the play as "an allegory of imperialist domination" (*The Guardian*, May 2003).

Such a reading surely implies a greater sympathy with the invaded, and a necessary breaking up of the rural idyll. But in *Indian Country*, the "invader" Gregg is probably the one who gains least from the exchanges between Hollywood and hillbilly. Mos is unharmed but wiser for the incursion, while Gwyneth's giving birth to a daughter is not seen in negative terms, although the "half breed" daughter, Elin, would obviously have added to the financial burden. The actress playing Gwyneth also appears as Elin at her mother's funeral in the present day, emphasizing that the tough, indomitable line of Welsh women has been continued. The political allegory that connects the Welsh with the American Indians (referenced first in the boy's gunslinger fantasies) does not extend to equating the English-language circus of the movie filming with the suppression of the natives of the Wild West. The dramatist's point is that the more subtle force of American culture, of which cinema is the most potent weapon, is at the heart of any imperialism, dangerous in its appeal to young and old alike. Even Gwyneth at the beginning is susceptible to memories of *Casablanca* (1942), which is the first common ground between her and Gregg.

Two of the three main characters speak English as their second language, and in the hands of a less practiced craftsman could emerge as either country buffoons or sentimental ciphers. In fact, the role of the American drifter Gregg is the one closest to cliché. The greatest challenge for the writer is to ensure that the situation remains realistic despite being predominantly in English, and so Povey gives mother and son little time alone together onstage, meaning that their relationship is most enlightened by their contrasting reactions to Gregg. The action is framed by the meditations of Mos as an old man, played by another actor onstage, and while the language is a challenging departure for Povey's stage writing, some reviewers felt that it added to the burden of words; one critic commented that it was "untheatrical" (*The Scotsman*, 12 June 2003). Nevertheless, the majority of reviews praised both the writing and the performances, despite the comparative slowness of the action.

There is a rare consensus in Welsh Wales that Meic Povey's craft is thoroughly admirable, and as he moves further away from the experimentation with form and style that characterized his youth, he is more at home stylistically. Even in the English language his strengths are the same: "writing that's lyrical, funny, sharp as tacks, and then as bleak as the high, dark crags," as a reviewer for *The Scotsman* (12 June 2003) put it. Povey's work shows him to be as defined by the "high, dark crags" of his Snowdonian spiritual home as he is by his language.

Interviews:

Gareth William Jones, *Cyntedd* (Summer 1987);

Dylan Iorwerth, "Chwarae Plant?" *Golwg* (23 September 1993);

Dafydd Llywelyn, "Speaking Two Spokes," *New Welsh Review*, 60 (Summer 2003).

References:

Gwenno Hughes, "Perthyn," *Astudiaethau Theatr Cymru*, no. 9 (September 2000): 6–21;

Nic Ros, "Leaving the Twentieth Century," in *Staging Wales: Welsh Theatre 1979–1997*, edited by Anna-Marie Taylor (Cardiff: University of Wales Press, 1997);

Rhiannon Tomos, "Roeddwn Innau Yno," *Barn* (May 1995);

Robin Tomos and Robin Gwyn, "Gofal yn y Gymuned," *Golwg* (May 1995).

Mark Ravenhill

(7 June 1966 -)

Aleks Sierz

PLAY PRODUCTIONS: *Blood Brood,* Edinburgh, Calton Centre, Edinburgh Festival Fringe, 10 August 1987;

Close to You, London, Old Red Lion Theatre, May 1993;

Fist, part of *I'll Show You Mine,* by Ravenhill and others, London, Finborough Theatre, 12 December 1994;

Shopping and Fucking, London, Royal Court Theatre Upstairs, 26 September 1996; London, Gielgud Theatre, 24 June 1997;

Faust, Hemel Hempstead, Old Town Hall Arts Centre, 13 February 1997; London, Lyric Hammersmith Studio, March 1997; performed as *Faust Is Dead,* Los Angeles, Zephyr Theatre, 23 May 1998;

Sleeping Around, by Ravenhill, Hilary Fannin, Stephen Greenhorn, and Abi Morgan, Salisbury, Salisbury Playhouse, 11 March 1998;

Handbag, London, Lyric Hammersmith Studio, 14 September 1998;

Some Explicit Polaroids, Bury St. Edmunds, Theatre Royal, 30 September 1999; London, New Ambassadors Theatre, November 1999;

Mother Clap's Molly House, book by Ravenhill, music by Matthew Scott, London, Lyttelton Theatre (National Theatre), 24 August 2001; transferred to Aldwych Theatre, 8 February 2002;

Die Fledermaus, adapted from Johann Strauss's work, Cardiff, Welsh National Opera, 14 September 2002;

Totally Over You, London, Cottesloe Theatre (National Theatre), 15 July 2003;

Education, London, Olivier Theatre (National Theatre), 12 October 2004.

BOOKS: *Shopping and Fucking* (London: Methuen in association with the Royal Court Theatre, 1996);

Faust (Faust Is Dead) (London: Methuen, 1997);

Handbag (London: Methuen, 1998);

Sleeping Around, by Ravenhill, Hilary Fannin, Stephen Greenhorn, and Abi Morgan (London: Methuen, 1998);

Some Explicit Polaroids (London: Methuen, 1999);

Mother Clap's Molly House (London: Methuen, 2001);

Plays 1 (London: Methuen, 2001)—comprises *Shopping and Fucking, Faust Is Dead, Handbag,* and *Some Explicit Polaroids;*

Totally Over You (London: S. French, 2003).

PRODUCED SCRIPTS: *Lulu,* adapted from Frank Wedekind's "Lulu" plays, radio, BBC World Service, 2 and 9 October 1994—comprised *Earth Spirit* and *Pandora's Box;*

"Lost and Found," television, *Black Cab,* BBC2, 10 May 2000;

"Feed Me," radio, *The Wire,* BBC Radio 3, 18 November 2000.

OTHER: "Plays about Men: Mark Ravenhill," in *State of Play: Playwrights on Playwriting,* edited by David Edgar (London: Faber & Faber, 1999), pp. 48–51;

Totally Over You, in *Shell Connections 2003: New Plays for Young People,* edited by Suzy Graham-Adriani (London: Faber & Faber, 2003), pp. 571–621.

SELECTED PERIODICAL PUBLICATIONS–
UNCOLLECTED: "Dramatic Moments," *Guardian,* 9 April 1997;

"The Difference a Day Made," *Guardian,* 19 January 1998;

"The Bland National," *Observer,* 30 May 1999;

"Help! I'm Having an Art Attack," *Guardian,* 18 November 2000;

"The Bottom Line," *Guardian,* 20 June 2001;

"Good Golly Mr Molly," *Time Out* (29 August–5 September 2001);

"Almost Famous," *Guardian,* 2 February 2002;

"A Touch of Evil," *Guardian,* 22 March 2003;

Mark Ravenhill (photograph © David Tolley; from <http://www.davidtolley.com/Theatre%20Large/mark_ravenhill.htm>)

"A Tear in the Fabric: The James Bulger Murder and New Theatre Writing in the Nineties," *New Theatre Quarterly,* 80 (November 2004): 305–314.

With his notorious debut, *Shopping and Fucking,* in 1996, Mark Ravenhill emerged as one of the most controversial of the new generation of 1990s playwrights. In the space of a decade, he rose from putting on small productions at tiny fringe venues to becoming an associate at the National Theatre in 2003 under artistic director Nicholas Hytner, who had staged Ravenhill's large-cast play, *Mother Clap's Molly House,* on the Lyttelton stage in 2001 before transferring it to the West End. While Ravenhill's later work commands main stages, his first plays were put on in studio theaters and are examples of experiential theater (which seeks to make audiences feel as if they have experienced the acts shown on stage). Ravenhill's first full-length play, *Shopping and Fucking,* catapulted him into notoriety, with a title that was censored in newspapers and on public billboards, but succeeded in entering the public mind in a way few other plays have done since John Osborne's *Look Back in Anger* in 1956. Ravenhill's achievement is summarized by theater academic Dan Rebellato in his introduction to Ravenhill's *Plays 1* (2001): "He has a reputation among some critics as a theatrical *enfant terrible* purveying sexually explicit, sensationalist, shock-loaded drama, and there's stuff in the plays one could point to, but Ravenhill is profoundly moral in his portraiture of contemporary society. His vision is elliptically but recognisably social, even socialist." Since their premieres, all of his plays have been translated and performed in several European languages, and productions have been put on all over the world. Ravenhill's work has been admired for its ability to sum up the zeitgeist, its entertainingly witty and ironic tone, and its ability to mix disturbing stage pictures of social discontent with an intelligent attitude to left-wing politics.

Born on 7 June 1966, Ravenhill was the elder of two sons of draftsman Ted Ravenhill and his wife, Rita, a shorthand typist. Ravenhill has described growing up in Haywards Heath, West Sussex, as "pleasant and untroubled," and in Michael Kustow's book *Theatre@Risk* (2000) he recalled his early interest in theater: "We didn't have any money to go to the theatre, so my brother and I started making theatre before we knew what it was. . . . From when we were about four to eight we put on plays." Using cardboard boxes and makeshift props, they entertained family and friends. Then Ravenhill attended after-school drama classes at his comprehensive secondary school. When he was about thirteen, he read a biography of Louis Braille and wrote a play about it; at school, he appeared in a version of *Anne of Green Gables* (1937). After school, Ravenhill took A-levels at a sixth-form college in Chichester and became the first in his family to go to a university, studying drama and English at Bristol University from 1984 to 1987. He originally wanted to act but soon realized that his talent was for directing and writing. In 1987 he wrote a short play, *Blood Brood,* for the Edinburgh Festival.

Ravenhill's first job was as an administrative assistant at the Soho Poly, a new writing theater in London, where he was a workshop director from 1989 to 1991. After leaving the company, he became a freelance director, taught drama, worked at the Finborough fringe theater, and directed productions of Giacomo Puccini's *La Bohéme* (1896) and Giuseppe Verdi's *Rigoletto* (1851) for Opera East. In 1993, Carl Miller directed Ravenhill's controversial *Close to You,* a short comedy about "outing" a gay M.P., for the London New Play Festival. In 1994 Ravenhill wrote a radio adaptation of Frank Wedekind's "Lulu" plays. Then, for Christmas, he directed *Hansel and Gretel,* a show written by Sheila Goff for the Midlands Arts Centre in Birmingham, before returning to London to help stage *I'll Show You Mine,* a weeklong festival of short erotic plays at the Finborough Theatre, as a fund-raiser for Red Admiral, an AIDS counseling project. For this event he wrote *Fist,* a ten-minute short. Director Max Stafford-Clark attended the festival and asked if Ravenhill had a full-length play; although he did not, Ravenhill said yes, and then had to write one.

Ravenhill finished the first draft, titled "Fucking Diana," in the spring of 1995. At the time, he was living in a cheap flat in Brixton, south London, which he shared with actress Emily Watson. After a conversation with Goff, he changed the title to *Shopping and Fucking,* which seemed to sum up perfectly its main themes of sex and consumerism. In May 1996 Ravenhill returned to the Finborough to direct David Eldridge's second play, *A Week with Tony.* A month later, Stafford-Clark directed *Shopping and Fucking* in a two-week workshop at the National Studio, and rehearsals followed in August. The play went through several drafts and revisions. By this time, Ravenhill was living in Camden, north London. His theatrical influences were varied, including not only playwrights Caryl Churchill, Anthony Neilson, David Mamet, and Brad Fraser but also the "blank fictions" of North American novelists such as Dennis Cooper, Bret Easton Ellis, and Douglas Coupland, as well as cult movies such as those of Greg Araki. In a 2004 article for *New Theatre Quarterly* Ravenhill also emphasized the importance of the notorious 1993 abduction and murder of Liverpool toddler James Bulger by two ten-year-old boys as a subconscious influence on images of child abuse in his work.

When *Shopping and Fucking* was accepted for production by Stafford-Clark's Out of Joint theater company, Sonia Friedman, the producer, was warned that the title legally could not appear on posters or in advertisements. Under a Victorian law—the Indecent Advertisements Act of 1889, amended by the Indecent Displays (Control) Act of 1981—words such as "fuck" are banned from public display. To solve the problem, the first posters for *Shopping and Fucking* used the image of a splintered fork to obscure the offending word. The next solution involved asterisks, so the title (in advertising, reviews, and on the covers of published editions of the play) became *Shopping and F***ing.*

The play is about twentysomethings Lulu and Robbie, who share a flat with Mark, a young man as addicted to sex as he is to drugs. All three keep trying to improve themselves and failing. Mark checks into a clinic to cure his drug addiction, has sex with another patient, and is expelled. On the streets, he finds Gary, a teenage hustler who falls for him. Meanwhile, Lulu's attempt to get a job involves stripping for middle-aged Brian, who gives her three hundred Ecstasy tablets to sell; but an idealistic—and stoned—Robbie gives the drugs away. To raise the money they now owe Brian, they sell telephone sex. The climax of the story comes when Mark brings Gary to meet Lulu and Robbie. They play a truth-or-dare game, which includes a gross story about having sex with royals Diana and Fergie in a men's lavatory, and which culminates in Gary's offer to pay off their debts if they penetrate him with a knife and give him "a good hurt." Later, Brian settles his accounts with Robbie and Lulu, and the play ends with harmony restored.

The critical reaction to the play, which premiered at the Royal Court Theatre Upstairs while it was located temporarily in the specially adapted Ambassadors Theatre in London's West End, was generally favorable. In the *Daily Mail* on 4 October 1996, critic Jack Tinker reminded readers that "whereas I led the chorus of disapproval" against Sarah Kane's violent and explicit play *Blasted* in 1995, "I can only applaud" the Royal Court Theatre's "courage in staging this dangerous and, no doubt to some, offensive work." Although several critics mentioned the scenes of rape and oral sex—in what Michael Billington in *The Guardian* (3 October 1996) called a "deeply uneven, in-your-face play"—most praised its achievement in putting on stage a world where sex is a commercial transaction and consumption is sexually arousing. Many critics noted the balance in the play between raw dialogue and bigger themes. James Christopher, in a *Sunday Express* review (6 October 1996) that was reprinted in the program when the play transferred to the West End, said that scandal was what made the Royal Court Theatre "chic." Only John Gross in *The Sunday Telegraph* (6 October 1996) made a sustained case against the play, arguing that it encourages "complacent self-pity (it is always somebody else's fault) and glib pessimism (taking the worst for the most representative)" and adding that it "wallows in the conditions it describes." *Shopping and Fucking* was put on twice at the Ambassadors Theatre, toured Britain, and then, with help from the British Council, toured internationally. In June 1997 it transferred to the Gielgud Theatre in London's West End and was revived there again six months later.

Subsequent assessments of the play stress its contemporary references–Ravenhill's typically playful attitude to his characters involved naming them after members of the pop group Take That–and its characteristic mix of anarchic energy, social realism, and fantasy. Director Dominic Dromgoole, in his book *The Full Room: An A–Z of Contemporary Playwriting* (2000), compares Ravenhill to George Bernard Shaw: "There's a gamut of parallels between the writers—verbal wit, a resistance to the morality of the preceding generation, and a keen sense of sociology." He stresses Ravenhill's "huge debt" to his mentor Stafford-Clark and summarizes his weaknesses: "a taste for journalism rather than drama, and a prurient fascination with a netherworld that exists more garishly in the imagination of the middle class, than it does in life." By contrast, Rebellato emphasizes the thematic coherence of *Shopping and Fucking*—"globalisation is Ravenhill's theme"—and his humanistic concerns: "Like the individual microwave meals that Lulu, Mark and Robbie eat, there is no sharing in these characters' lives." In her study *Post-War British Drama: Looking Back in Gender* (2001) playwright Michelene Wandor (2001) criticizes the gender politics in the play: "The overall vision is profoundly nihilistic. . . . Women do not exist here—except as implicitly absent mothers." More sympathetically, Rebellato has pointed out that "Ravenhill's work has a complex and difficult relationship with fathers, who are variously abusing, absent, sugar daddies, roles adopted for daddy/son sexual role play, and even appear in absurdly mythpoeic form in references to [1994 Disney movie] *The Lion King*."

Shopping and Fucking was one of the first plays of the 1990s in which the sexual orientation of the characters was rarely mentioned in reviews. Although Ravenhill openly referred to his sexuality, neither he nor his work were attacked for being gay. Indeed, he has described himself as "queer" rather than "gay," meaning that he sees himself as a confrontational sexual outlaw rather than an assimilated, trendy homosexual. In a frank interview published in the *Evening Standard* on 14

Cover for a 1997 edition of Ravenhill's 1996 play, in which the misadventures of a trio of flatmates express the themes of consumerism and sex announced in the title (Howard-Tilton Memorial Library, Tulane University)

August 2001, when asked "How long have you been HIV positive?" he replied, "For ever!" and gave details of his medical regimen.

Ravenhill's next three plays are often seen as minor, experimental works. *Faust* (performed and published in 1997) was commissioned by Nick Philippou of the Actors Touring Company (ATC), which at the time specialized in radically updating classic drama. Ravenhill knew the Christopher Marlowe and Johann Wolfgang von Goethe versions of the story, and Philippou introduced him to the work of Nikolaus Lenau, a German Romantic poet who wrote his version of *Faust* in 1836. After a weeklong workshop in October 1996, followed by a further rehearsal period, Ravenhill's eighty-minute *Faust* began a tour of Britain in Hemel Hempstead in February 1997, although most reviewers saw it in March at the Lyric Hammersmith Studio in London.

The two-hander, a free adaptation of the Faust story, features Alain, a French postmodernist philosopher reminiscent of Michel Foucault, Jean Baudrillard, and Francis Fukayama, who is making the rounds of American talk shows to publicize his book on the subject of the Death of Man and the End of History. After upsetting the sponsors of his university, he quits his academic job and takes up with Pete, the wayward son of a computer-software magnate. They travel through the Californian desert indulging in drugs and sex. On the Internet, they meet Donny, a disturbed boy who cuts himself, and when they challenge him to prove that he is really doing that, Donny commits suicide. Alain is then beaten up by Pete, who returns to his father.

After reading John Peter's review in *The Sunday Times* (2 March 1997), which pointed out that in a Godless world "the Faust legend is dead," Ravenhill changed the title of his play to *Faust Is Dead*. The published play text was titled *Faust (Faust Is Dead)*, and subsequent productions used the new name. The second production, in May 1998 by the Tuesday Laboratory company at the Zephyr Theatre in Los Angeles, gave Ravenhill the chance to make other changes. For example, Donny—who in the first version only appeared on a video monitor because the company could not afford more than two actors—became the third character. Scene 14 was rewritten and put Donny onstage, so that audiences could see him cutting himself, which effectively made him more human.

In 1997 Ravenhill became literary director of Paines Plough, a new writing company, and he developed his flair for attracting media attention: for example, in April he appeared in an orange "Girl Power" T-shirt at the Eighth Birmingham Theatre Conference. In a later article, he explored his childhood obsession with the BBC television science-fiction series *Dr Who*. He also attracted controversy in 1997 when he worked on the third season of the BBC's cult soap opera *This Life*. After the story line he devised was dropped, there was media speculation that he had killed off the main characters and introduced several new gay ones. Although these rumors were untrue, the collapse of the project marked a temporary end of his involvement with television. In the same year, his health got worse: he developed a treatable illness, AIDS-related toxoplasmosis, which at first was misdiagnosed as brain cancer.

After he recovered, his next play was *Sleeping Around* (1998), a collaborative project conceived at Paines Plough. The idea was to use several writers to create a contemporary version of Arthur Schnitzler's *Reigen* (Round Dance/La Ronde, 1903; translated as *Hands Around*, 1920). Paines Plough chose writers from Scotland, Wales, and Ireland; and Ravenhill developed the play with Stephen Greenhorn, Abi Morgan, and Hilary Fannin at the National Studio, each writer contributing a couple of scenes. First put on at the Salisbury Playhouse in March 1998, *Sleeping Around* was performed by John Lloyd Fillingham and Sophie Stanton, who played all the roles.

In March 1998 Ravenhill also attracted more controversy when Education Secretary David Blunkett belatedly denounced *Shopping and Fucking* as full of foul language and a waste of public money. In May, at the London New Play Festival, when Ravenhill appeared on a public platform with David Hare to discuss new writing, some journalists wanted to turn the amicable occasion into a battle between the old generation and the new. On another occasion, Ravenhill was criticized for refusing an invitation to meet the queen at a Buckingham Palace reception; he argued that while he was happy to promote Britain as "a young creative country" through work abroad with the British Council, he was a republican at heart.

Ravenhill's next play, *Handbag* (1998), was an ambitious project developed by ATC and directed by Philippou, touring in 1998. The play tells two stories simultaneously—one about contemporary parenting and one about Oscar Wilde's *The Importance of Being Earnest* (performed in 1895, published in 1899). In the 1990s story line, a pair of middle-class lesbian and gay couples—Mauretta and Suzanne; David and Tom—decide to create a baby by artificial insemination and bring it up together. By the time the baby boy is born, however, their relationships are unraveling: David has taken up with Phil, a homeless drug addict, and Suzanne is trying to seduce Lorraine, a vulnerable girl the women have hired as a nanny. When Lorraine falls for Phil, her subsequent neglect of the baby leads to her firing; she then steals the baby and runs off with Phil. When the baby develops breathing problems, Phil tries to revive it by burning it with a cigarette; as a result, the baby dies. The Victorian story line is a prequel to *The Importance of Being Earnest*, set twenty-eight years before Wilde's play begins. Augusta, the future Lady Bracknell, is staying with her sister, Constance, whose new baby boy has been entrusted to a nanny, Miss Prism. Meanwhile, Cardew, a philanthropist with a penchant for boys, is forced to flee to the seaside town of Worthing when a hostile crowd burns down his house. Prism encounters him at the railway station, and, after he tells her about his charitable deeds, she gives him the baby because she wants peace to write her novel. The boy grows up to become the Jack Worthing of Wilde's play.

Ravenhill's title refers to Jack's statement in Wilde's play that he was found as an infant in a handbag; but in Ravenhill's version, baby Jack is given to Cardew deliberately and not lost accidentally. Equally deliberate is the subtitle of the first production: "The Importance of Being Someone." In this play, identity is a quest and a construct. As usual, Ravenhill managed to sum up the zeitgeist, voicing contemporary anxieties about parenting in an age of sexual diversity: *Guardian* critic Michael Billington pointed out in a 16 September 1998 article that *Handbag* was part of a "theatrical baby-boom," a rash of plays about babies. But while some critics, notably Alastair Macaulay of the *Financial Times* (16 September 1998), saw *Handbag* as one of a "post-mod genre of clever plays" that refer to playwrights such as Alan Bennett and Tom Stoppard, other references eluded older spectators. Only Samantha Marlowe in *What's On* (23 September 1998) noted that "handbag" is a form of dance-club music. In such ways, *Handbag* appealed to both young and old.

In 1999, work on Ravenhill's next play was delayed when he collapsed because of a severe epileptic seizure and had to receive hospital treatment. After recovering, he finished *Some Explicit Polaroids,* which was widely seen as the follow-up to *Shopping and Fucking,* with some commentators unaware that Ravenhill had written three plays in the interim. But while *Some Explicit Polaroids* has much in common thematically with the earlier play, casting another ironic look at contemporary consumer society, it is based on Ernst Toller's 1927 play, *Hoppla, wir leben!* (Hurrah, This Is Life!), which tells of a revolutionary who returns home after eight years in an asylum to find that his old comrades have become corrupt conformists. Ravenhill's version blends a 1970s state-of-the-nation play with a critique of both traditional leftist militancy and 1990s youth culture.

Nick, a left-wing radical, calls on Helen, his former partner, after his release from prison on finishing a sentence of fifteen years for a savage attack in 1984 on Jonathan, a capitalist entrepreneur. He finds that Helen, once a militant, has turned into a New Labour councillor and wants to become an M.P. She rejects him, so he wanders across the city, meeting Nadia, a lap dancer, and eventually living with Tim, an HIV-positive man whose boyfriend is Victor, a "Russian doll" addicted to cheap "trash" aesthetics. Nick struggles to adjust to a world whose values he does not understand, surrounded by the phrases and gadgets of contemporary life: Nadia talks in self-help clichés; Victor wears a spiky, sadomasochist-chic collar; Tim says he discovered Victor after downloading photos of his "fucking crazy body" from the Internet. With its scenes set in a hospital as Tim dies of AIDS, and its final confrontation between Nick and Jonathan, the play combines irony with emotional power. As its title suggests, the Polaroid photograph, instantly gratifying but also short-lived, is the metaphor for 1990s pop culture.

Cover for the publication of Ravenhill's 1998 play, which combines the history of Jack Worthing from Oscar Wilde's The Importance of Being Earnest *(1895) with a modern story line about the artificial-insemination baby of two homosexual couples (Z. Smith Reynolds Library, Wake Forest University)*

Produced by Out of Joint in September 1999, *Some Explicit Polaroids* was directed by Stafford-Clark on the main stage at the New Ambassadors, by then restored to its former role as a West End proscenium theater. The critical responses no longer focused on the outrageous stage images or explicit sex. But while the play was praised as an account of contemporary social rootlessness—with a reviewer for *The Daily Express* (15 October 1999) calling Ravenhill "the poet for the off-message, off-your-face Britain"—its politics were less well received. One critic for *The Times* (16 October 1999) said it was "a nostalgic lament for the end of class struggle," while another for *The Independent* (18 October 1999) saw Nick as "a hollow Rip Van Winkle-figure." Just as one reviewer in *The Sunday Telegraph* (24 October 1999) mocked the "nonsense" of having a "Hard

Left tough" representing a "vanished idealistic past, and the best hope for the future," another critic for *The Guardian* (16 October 1999) felt that the play "sometimes falls prey to the soundbite values it condemns."

While *Some Explicit Polaroids* was on tour, Ravenhill provoked further controversy when he was quoted in a *Guardian* article (8 November 1999) as saying that the original Angry Young Men—such as Osborne, Arnold Wesker, and John Arden—were "straight boys" whose historic mission was to clear theater of the "feyness and falseness" of gay writers such as Noel Coward and Terence Rattigan. Although the year 1956, when *Look Back in Anger* opened, was usually viewed in terms of class, with gritty kitchen-sink realists driving out "snobbish, dilettante and pampered" effeminates, most commentators missed the question of sexual orientation. This reinterpretation of the 1950s was apt, because *Some Explicit Polaroids* is a good illustration of David Edgar's idea, also quoted in the article, that "without Osborne we certainly wouldn't have had Ravenhill."

In 2000 Ravenhill finally broke into television with "Lost and Found," an episode in the BBC2 series *Black Cab*, for which ten writers each wrote a short movie set in the back of a London cab. It was broadcast in May, and, in November, his radio play "Feed Me" was broadcast as part of *The Wire* series on BBC Radio 3. Ravenhill's next theater project, *Mother Clap's Molly House*, was his most large-scale to date. Subtitled "A Play with Songs," it was a collaboration with Matthew Scott, who wrote the music, and was developed with a group of students at the London Academy of Music and Dramatic Arts (LAMDA). Premiered on the large Lyttelton stage at the National Theatre, the play signaled Ravenhill's arrival at the summit of the British theater system.

Similar in structure to *Handbag*, *Mother Clap's Molly House* has two parallel stories, in this case taking place three centuries apart. In 1726 London, Mrs. Tull helps her husband run a secondhand clothing shop that hires out dresses to local prostitutes. Following his sudden death, she has to run the establishment by herself and discovers new skills such as bookkeeping. When business falls, she turns the building into a "molly house," a private gay club where men can dress in women's clothing, drink, sing, and dance. Some of them even "give birth" to wooden dolls. The point of this picture of merriment and bawdiness is that the men's desires are viewed as relatively innocent, unaffected by categories such as the distinction between being gay and straight. The scenes set in 2001, however, focus on a gay orgy at a London flat and are much more critical of social conventions: although all behavior, however gross, is permitted, everything seems to be predictable and clichéd. Today's gay identity is presented as being as stifling to human needs as any repressive morality.

One of the most often quoted song lyrics from the play was "You call it sodomy. We call it fabulous," and along with the play came "The Bottom Line" and "Good Golly Mr Molly," 2001 articles in which Ravenhill pointed out that "anyone who has been to the theatre regularly in the last 10 years cannot have helped noticing that there's been an awful lot of anal sex on the British stage." He argued that most of these encounters feature "violence and humiliation" and said that in *Mother Clap's Molly House* his intention was to show "men on the British stage having anal sex much as they do in life—frequently and for fun." Commentators remarked, however, that audiences were becoming shockproof to explicit sex: Mark Simpson, in *The Independent on Sunday* (26 August 2001), defended the use of sodomy as a symbol of "non-reproductive, sex-for-its-own-sake," while Stephen Pollard in *The Independent* (3 September 2001) thought that audiences would be "more shocked if a man had smoked a cigarette live on stage." Indeed, Jonathan Croall (2001) records that a middle-aged woman at one preview said: "I was expecting to be shocked, but it was really very touching, and rather moving."

Critical reaction was divided. In *The Guardian* (5 September 2001) Billington praised "an evening rich in rudery and ambivalence," and John Peter in *The Sunday Times* (9 September 2001) hailed Hytner's "spectacular, vigorous, uninhibited and civilised" direction. However, Nicholas de Jongh in the *Evening Standard* (5 September 2001) wrote: "*Mother Clap's Molly House* is a daring, impassioned lament for decadent gay lives, but becomes too captivated by the gay high-jinks it presents and condemns," while Gross in *The Sunday Telegraph* (9 September 2001) found it "muddled, narrow in perspective and not very funny," and Macaulay in *The Financial Times* (6 September 2001) said that "Ravenhill is less a serious playwright than a clever sensationalist."

In February 2002, *Mother Clap's Molly House* transferred to the Aldwych Theatre in the West End. Despite more favorable reviews and good publicity, this expensive show, with its large cast and musicians, was not a commercial success. In *The Stage* newspaper on 21 March 2002, the coproducer, Phil Cameron, acknowledged that the play "has sustained considerable losses since transferring to the West End." Meanwhile, the playwright had moved on, writing a contemporary version of the libretto of Johann Strauss's *Die Fledermaus* (1874) that was directed in September 2002 by Spanish director Calixto Bieito for the Welsh National Opera in Cardiff to mixed reviews.

Ravenhill is a generous advocate of British theater and not only attends many events and workshops

Deborah Findlay and Danielle Tilley in the 2001 National Theatre premiere of Ravenhill's play Mother Clap's Molly House, *in which an eighteenth-century homosexual club is contrasted with the gay scene in present-day London (photograph by Mark Douet; from <http://web.axelero.hu/sudabala/kanko/kanko.htm>)*

all over Europe but is also a supporter of annual festivals such as the National Student Drama Festival, held every Easter in Scarborough. His own sixty-minute play for young people, *Totally Over You,* was put on during the 2003 Shell Connections youth theater festival at the National Theatre. In this play, Kitty is a teenager obsessed with dreams of celebrity. She persuades her "sistas" (girlfriends) that in order to date some A-list celebrities, they have to dump their "zitty boyfriends." But while she eggs on her reluctant girlfriends with visions of fame, the boyfriends get together and decide to teach the girls a lesson by posing as the latest boy band that is heading straight for stardom. This morality tale–based on Moliere's *Les Précieuses ridicules* (1659)– mixes contemporary ideas about the glamor of stardom with witty barbs about the reality of teenage life. In addition to this contribution, Ravenhill was characteristically outspoken during the summer. In *The Stage* newspaper (21 August 2003) his controversial speech at the launch of the British Council's fourth annual Edinburgh Festival showcase was quoted as arguing that, because of a worldwide "general suspicion" of the government's foreign policy, "Britain's theatre companies have been isolated from the rest of the world by the recent [coalition] invasion of Iraq." In 2004 Ravenhill returned to the National Theatre with *Education,* an uncharacteristic "verbatim theatre" monologue about the problems of Britain's schoolteachers.

At his best, Ravenhill has made a career from successfully blending the bleakness of "apocalypse culture"–inspired by the "blank fictions" of contemporary North American culture, which emphasize the extreme, the marginal, and the violent–with more traditional socialist concerns. His characteristic tone is irony, but there is also a pervasive feeling of anger in his work. His violent stage images are never gratuitous but are designed to impress powerful metaphors of social alienation on the minds of his audience. Most of all, he is well-read and deeply critical about the state of the capitalist economy and trends such as globalization and increasing social conformity. Caridad Svich has concluded from a 2003 study of Ravenhill's work that "From *Shopping and Fucking* to *Mother Clap's Molly House*, sex is the constant field where all transactions are played out in Ravenhill's theatrical world. It is the source of enquiry and the act that defines who we are at any given moment, how we give ourselves to someone else, and what price we pay for doing so."

As a writer, Ravenhill relies on collaboration and workshopping: he is more a collective theater-maker than a solitary author. He is also much more than just a playwright: acting as a publicist and advocate of new writing for theater, he has had an important role in championing younger writers such as Linda McLeon and Glyn Cannon. More than most of his contemporaries, he has been seen as an exemplar of 1990s "in-yer-face theatre" and has worked hard to publicize a new range of contemporary sensibilities, including a provocative sense of queerness. But while his plays show clearly the problematic social conditions that he believes must be changed, they are also affirmations of the human spirit. In a witty and self-aware manner, his work offers a panorama of contemporary Britain, warts and all.

Interviews:

Mark Ravenhill, Max Stafford-Clark, and Stephen Daldry, "Do New Writers Have Hearts?" *New Sceptics,* public platform, session 1, Theatre Museum, 15 October 1996;

Michael Coveney, "His Last Play Was Full of Sodomy and Vomiting. This Time the Mood Is a Bit Darker," *Observer,* 9 February 1997;

Paul Taylor, "Damned If He Does, Damned If He Don't," *Independent,* 26 February 1997;

Interview on *Theatreland,* London Weekend Television, 9 March 1997;

David Benedict, "At Last! Exclusive! What Really Killed Off *This Life.* By the Writer Many Blame," *Independent,* 6 November 1997;

Andrew Marshall, "My Life Was a Voyage with Dr. Who. Then the Tardis Turned to Cardboard," *Independent,* 27 January 1998;

John Whitley, "The Importance of Being Shocking," *Telegraph,* 4 September 1998;

Veronica Lee, "Clicking into Place," *Guardian,* 6 October 1999;

Andrew Smith, "Play for Today," *Observer Magazine,* 31 October 1999;

Aleks Sierz, "Planned Offensive," *Stage,* 4 January 2001;

Nick Curtis, "How Long Have You Been HIV Positive? 'For Ever!'" *Evening Standard,* 14 August 2001;

Sierz, "Immorality Plays," *Stage,* 16 August 2001;

"Dr. Who Started Him on Some Weird Stuff," *Sunday Times,* 26 August 2001;

Sierz, "Mollygamous," *What's On,* 29 August 2001;

Siobhan Murphy, "Sixty Second Interview: Mark Ravenhill," *Metro,* 6 February 2002;

Kate Mikhail, "Significant Others," *Observer,* 16 February 2003;

Heather Neill, "We're Doing It for the Kids," *Independent on Sunday,* 23 March 2003;

Rachel Halliburton, "It's Play Time," *Evening Standard Metro Life,* 11–17 July 2003.

References:

Michael Billington, "Would You Like Your Children To Be Brought Up by a Rich, Kindly Old Pervert?" *Guardian,* 16 September 1998;

Jonathan Croall, *Inside the Molly House: The National Theatre at Work* (London: National Theatre, 2001);

Dominic Dromgoole, *The Full Room: An A–Z of Contemporary Playwriting* (London: Methuen, 2000), pp. 235–238;

Fiachra Gibbons, "Angry Young Men Under Fire from Gay Writer," *Guardian,* 8 November 1999;

Michael Kustow, *Theatre@Risk* (London: Methuen, 2000);

Aleks Sierz, "Chapter 5: Mark Ravenhill," in his *In-Yer-Face Theatre: British Theatre Today* (London: Faber & Faber, 2001), pp 122–152;

Sierz, "Cool Britannia? 'In-Yer-Face' Writing in the British Theatre Today," *New Theatre Quarterly,* 56 (November 1998): 324–333;

Sierz, "In-Yer-Face Theatre: Mark Ravenhill and 1990s Drama," in *British Drama of the 1990s,* edited by Bernhard Reitz and Mark Berninger (Heidelberg: Winter, 2002), pp. 107–121;

Sierz, "Still In-Yer-Face? Towards a Critique and a Summation," *New Theatre Quarterly,* 69 (February 2002): 17–24;

Caridad Svich, "Commerce and Morality in the Theatre of Mark Ravenhill," *Contemporary Theatre Review,* 13 (February 2003): 81–95;

Michael Thornton, "A Shop Window for Outrage," *Punch,* 21–27 September 1996;

Michelene Wandor, *Post-War British Drama: Looking Back in Gender* (London & New York: Routledge, 2001).

Ian Rowlands

(28 June 1964 -)

Andy W. Smith
University of Wales, Newport

PLAY PRODUCTIONS: *In Search of Tregaron Man,* Llanfyllin, Old New Inn, 1 May 1989;

The Adventures of Rhys and Hywel Parts 1-4, Cardiff, Four Bars Inn, 17 November 1991—comprised *In Search of Tregaron Man, Jeran & M19, Something Comes of Nothing,* and *Consumatum Est;*

The Sin Eaters, Llanelli, Theatr Elli, 9 April 1992;

Solomon's Glory, Dublin, City Arts Centre, 26 January 1993;

Glissando on an Empty Harp, Swansea, Taliesin Arts Centre, 3 March 1994;

Love in Plastic, Swansea, Glynn Vivian Art Gallery, 25 May 1995;

Marriage of Convenience, Dolgellau, Coleg Meirion Dwyfor, 19 November 1996; Edinburgh, Edinburgh Festival, 8 August 1997;

New South Wales, Bristol, Young Vic Studio, 18 September 1997; revised, Edinburgh, Venue 13, 8 August 1999;

Blue Heron in the Womb, Glasgow, Tron Theatre, 21 May 1998;

Môr Tawel, Llanelli Eisteddfod, Theatr Elli, 7 August 2000; revised and translated as *Pacific,* Cardiff, Sherman Theatre, 1 March 2001; London, Attic Theatre, 2001.

BOOKS: *The Ogpu Men* (Cardiff: Drama Association of Wales, 1994);

Glissando on an Empty Harp (Cardiff: Theatr y Byd, 1994);

Love in Plastic and Glissando on an Empty Harp: Companions in Words (Cardiff: Bydbooks, 1995);

Marriage of Convenience (Moments on Mountains) (Cardiff: Bydbooks, 1996);

A Trilogy of Appropriation: Three Plays (Cardiff: Parthian / Chester Springs, Pa.: Dufour, 1999)—comprises *Blue Heron in the Womb, Love in Plastic,* and *Glissando on an Empty Harp;*

New South Wales (Cardiff: Bydbooks, 1999);

Môr Tawel / Pacific (Cardiff: Bydbooks, 2000).

Ian Rowlands (courtesy of Ian Rowlands)

PRODUCED SCRIPTS: *3 0'Clock at Ponty,* radio, BBC Radio Wales, 30 March 1996;

The Dough Boys, radio, BBC Radio Wales, 22 March 1997;

The Ogpu Men, television, HTV Wales, 1997;

A Light in the Valley, by Rowlands and Michael Bogdanov, television, BBC Wales, 8 December 1998.

OTHER: *The Ogpu Men,* in *Act One Wales,* edited by Phil Clark (Bridgend: Seren, 1996), pp. 253-270;

Marriage of Convenience, in *One Man, One Voice: Plays,* edited by David Adams (Cardiff: Parthian, 2001);

Môr Tawel, in *Llais Un yn Llefain: Monologau cyfoes Cymraeg,* edited by Rowlands (Llanrwst: Gwasg Carreg Gwalch, 2002);

"A View from the Operating Table," *Theatre in Wales,* 17 December 2002 <http://www.theatre-wales.co.uk/critical/index.asp>.

Since the 1980s there has been a marked resurgence in Wales of theater that has at its center a debate concerning cultural identity. This debate has coincided with key political and social changes in the fabric of Welsh public life, culminating in the 1997 referendum on devolution that led to the formation of the Welsh Assembly, a political body set up in Cardiff that was awarded a vestige of self-government distinct from Westminster. At the same time in the 1990s there was a sense of a new beginning that permeated aspects of Welsh cultural life, typified by the phrase "Cool Cymru," a catchall designation that was intended to appeal to a post-Thatcherite generation aware of the stereotypes of Welshness that were prevalent in the United Kingdom. This reawakening of nationhood, language, and culture was articulated by several Welsh dramatists and theater companies throughout the 1990s, consistently challenging assumptions and stereotypes projected onto external definitions of Welsh identity.

The dramatist, actor, administrator, and director Ian Rowlands has been at the forefront of this new wave of writing in Wales. Rowlands's drama explores issues surrounding the derivation and direction of Welsh identity in contradictory ways, encompassing a wide range of dramatic techniques that reveal his ability to switch between different theatrical styles, registers, and voices. In particular, the relationship between biography and writing establishes his work within a distinct Welsh tradition. The Welsh archetype for chronicling history in epic verse dramas such as the *Mabignon* means that the idea of "Welshness" operates through oral traditions of storytelling. For Rowlands the Welsh are frequent witnesses to historical events, a concern that runs through much of his drama, as he said in an unpublished May 2003 interview with Andy W. Smith: "The Welsh never push history forward but we are always witness to it."

For Rowlands, the chronicling of contemporary Welsh experience is partly drawn from the need to write up what he describes as "hybrid histories," an attempt to draw upon personal situations in order to construct compelling statements about the state of the Welsh nation. This intention is most evident in his one-man play *Marriage of Convenience* (performed and published in 1996), a play that is semi-autobiographical in its depiction of growing up bilingual in the rapidly changing landscape of the South Wales valleys. The interplay of language, belonging, and eventual escape, of writing oneself into and out of the drama, makes Rowlands stand out among his Welsh contemporaries, composing a theater that is as nakedly autobiographical as the intense family dramas of Eugene O'Neill.

Rowlands was born on 28 June 1964 in Porth, a small town in the postindustrial Rhondda Valley. His immediate antecedents were located in the now-defunct mining industry of South Wales: his grandfather on his father's side was a collier who was invalided out of Wattstown mine, while his grandfather on his mother's side was a superintendent ambulance worker in Tylorstown mine. His father, David Chard Rowlands of Porth, served in the merchant marine and by the time of his retirement had risen to the rank of commodore chief engineer. His mother, Shirley Margaret Rowlands (née Davies), was from Tylorstown and had the responsibility of maintaining the household while her husband was away at sea. Ian Rowlands has one brother, Matthew. Growing up in the South Wales valleys during the 1960s offered two different education pathways—one through the medium of Welsh and the other through English schools. Though his parents spoke English, Rowlands attended Ysgol Gymraeg Pontygwaith in Porth, one of the first Welsh-language primary schools in South East Wales. After this school he attended the Ysgol Gyfun Rhydfelen in Pontypridd, again one of the first secondary Welsh-language schools in the area. This experience placed Rowlands in the position of speaking Welsh at school and English at home, a bilingual rift dramatized in *Marriage of Convenience*.

After high school, Rowlands enrolled in an acting course at the Welsh College of Music and Drama in Cardiff. His first professional job as an actor was in the movie *Boy Soldier* (1985), directed by Karl Francis. He is married to the poet Elinor Wyn Reynolds and has two daughters, Hannah and Saran, and one son, Caspar. Rowlands worked as an actor in different theater companies across Wales between 1984 and 1990, touring with Welsh-language productions. In 1989 and 1990 he began his career as a writer by writing for BBC Radio Education, and with the actor Dafyd Wyn Roberts he started touring a two-man show that he had written, called *In Search of Tregaron Man* (performed in 1989), a darkly surreal comic routine exploring the contradictions of life in rural Wales. This tour led to the formation of Rowlands's first theater company, Theatr y Byd, followed by the company's first Arts Council–funded production: Rowlands's *The Sin Eaters,* premiering on 9 April 1992, a combination of the themes and ideas explored in *The Adventures of Rhys and Hywel Parts 1–4* (performed in 1991).

What linked all of these pieces was an irreverent and satirical response toward prevalent Welsh cultural mores, drawing upon Rowlands's gift for creating bold, comedic characters strongly influenced by the structural patterns of commedia dell'arte. In association with the Wales Actors' Company, *The Sin Eaters* toured Wales, Ireland, and Britain and was nominated for best regional theater play of 1992 by the Writers Guild of Great Britain. This show also instituted what became a concurrent practice with Theatr y Byd: the collaboration of artists in creating exhibitions based on and inspired by the texts, which toured with the productions.

After *The Sin Eaters* Theatr y Byd undertook an extensive ten-week tour of Rowlands's first major full-length production that, unlike *The Sin Eaters,* was not based on previous material. This production, *Solomon's Glory,* toured Ireland, Wales, Scotland, England, and France during January and February 1993. In a story reminiscent of Henrik Ibsen's *The Master Builder* (1892), *Solomon's Glory* dramatizes the attempt of a believer to build a cathedral to worship God, until he realizes that such an entity does not exist. As Rowlands related in a 1999 interview with Hazel Walford Davies, this play "presents debate rather than emotions and characters," and much of his early work is concerned with offering archetypal figures who operate theatrically as ciphers in order to explore issues surrounding the complex nexus of identity, communication, and language. In this respect his early theatrical style rejects psychological naturalism in favor of an expressionist technique, where time, space, and action are not causal but frequently discontinuous and fragmented. This approach is most evident in his next play, *Glissando on an Empty Harp,* which toured "the familiar Celtic circuit," as Rowlands said in "A Decade of Debt" (published in *A Trilogy of Appropriation: Three Plays,* 1999), after premiering at the Taliesin Arts Centre, Swansea, on 3 March 1994.

Glissando on an Empty Harp is an important play in Rowlands's career because it forms the first part of what subsequently became published as *A Trilogy of Appropriation,* along with *Love in Plastic* (performed and published in 1995) and *Blue Heron in the Womb* (performed in 1998, published in 1999). *Glissando on an Empty Harp* articulates much of what Rowlands returned to in subsequent dramas–the sterility of consumerist culture, the irony of nationhood in a nation divorced from self-government, and the purpose of art in defining "Self" and "Other." *Glissando on an Empty Harp* is an adaptation of the Greek myth of Pandora's Box within the context of a multimedia performance piece, utilizing a video installation of a "talking head" that becomes an integral part of the theatrical experience. The play begins with a monologue as the head talks directly to the audience, noting that "all around me is chaos waiting to happen whilst no one hopes it will." The head's references are deliberately postmodern, a kaleidoscope of intertextual commentary combining modern art, poetry, physics, biblical myth, and pop culture:

> They've crucified Euclid, Pythagoras, and there Newton defies gravity, suspended in mid theory, whilst Einstein plays dice and washes his hands of it, completely. Things dart around like words flailing for sentences in the napalm of "isms," like extras in Sci Fi movies bewailing the end with high conviction, like Thomas before the nails.

This introduction sets the tone for a play in which language becomes the process through which the theatrical event is defined, a style of performance that rejects identifiable realist scenarios. The main characters are two hungover bardic tramps waiting for dawn to come. There is no indication of where they are besides "onstage." The affinities with Samuel Beckett's *Waiting for Godot* (1952) are obvious and deliberate, including the insertion of a mute character who doubles as the talking video head; unlike Beckett's play, however, *Glissando on an Empty Harp* is the antithesis of a minimalist aesthetic. The two tramps, Eric and Emrys, bear witness to the birth of a box by a woman called Dora, while the mute Fergus rings a bell three times. The polyphonic tonal qualities of the text are designed by Rowlands to surround the spectator with a multitude of sensory experiences, in defiance of his own character's preferences:

> Eric: I am a realist. I hate the surreal. I hate the perversion of sanity in the satanic mills of night; the skewering of my soul on the points of Dali's moustache. I like daylight and the ethics of predictability; the smell of soldiers sweating on parade, the twitching of the hanged, the gaggling of the near dead at funerals, the repulsion of it all.

The use of drunken Welsh bards is significant for several reasons; partly an excuse for Rowlands to immerse himself in wordplay and language games, a common factor in his work, it is also an ironic commentary on the historical role of bardic poets in the Welsh consciousness. Comparing the possible "myriad of infections and afflictions" contained in Pandora's Box, of which the video head is a interior voice, with the way Wales is viewed by outsiders, Rowlands is able to be both funny and disturbing at the same time: "Listed in a nineteenth century guide book, this box would share honours with industrial Llanelli; 'Not worth the detour, avoid it completely.'"

The bards believe the perfect poem exists inside the box, and they hatch a plan to appropriate it from its "mother." This attempt at appropriation–of language and art–is a key practice of Rowlands's theater, and as the two bards violently penetrate the box with a knife, the play ends in a synthesis of silence and sound, as the video head "trapped" in the box is revealed to be the mute fool Fergus. The final stage direction reads, "Hope is released into the world," in a vision of possibilities amid the deafening white noise of consumerist culture. This play can be read as an allegory of several political concerns, as the collapse of Eastern Europe and the rise of Thatcherism (both referred to in the text) seem to indicate the contemporaneous victory of late capitalism.

The surreal and anti-illusionist style of the play– which Declan Gorman described (in "Thoughts on a Play," included in *A Trilogy of Appropriation*) as "Meta-

Gareth Potter in the 1996 Dolgellau premiere of Rowlands's Marriage of Convenience, *a semi-autobiographical one-man play in which the speaker recalls the difficulties of growing up speaking Welsh at school and English at home (photograph by Beth MacDonald; Collection of Andy W. Smith)*

physics meets the Marx brothers"–is followed up by the next part of the loose trilogy, *Love in Plastic,* which continues along the same thematic concerns of identity, loss, and desire within a more fixed and "realistic" setting. The play was first performed as part of Swansea Year of Literature 1995 at the Glynn Vivian Art Gallery, Swansea, on 25 May 1995. This original performance context was rather unusual. As Rowlands said in "A Decade of Debt," *Love in Plastic* was "unique as it combined several elements . . . a retrospective of Theatr y Byd's 'Experiments in Multi Media' was mounted at the Glynn Vivian Gallery which comprised all art work commissioned by the company to date plus an installation inspired by the text created by conceptual artist, Tim Davies." The performance of *Love in Plastic* took place inside the art installation, merging an artist's conception of the play with the text itself. As Rowlands noted, while "the artist had reacted with the text in order to create an installation, in performance the actors interacted with the art."

This original performance space defamiliarizes the setting of the text, which, when the play opens, is described in the stage directions as "an empty restaurant." The proprietor of the restaurant is looking through a magnifying glass, searching for "economic recovery." Throughout Rowlands's work there is a trenchant understanding of underlying political tensions. The restaurateur's playing of "pre-recorded crowd atmosphere to give the impression that the restaurant is full" shows his desperation at the lack of customers. This stage direction is indicative of the main theme of the play, namely, the relationship between the real and the imagined. The play focuses on a clandestine meeting in this empty restaurant between Harold, a middle-aged man protected in a plastic bubble space suit, and Isabel, a bourgeois actress reduced to appearing in detergent ads. In a fit of jealous rage the actress's agent follows them to the restaurant, where, intent on protecting his "property," he convinces the owner to poison his space-suited rival.

Love in Plastic is a contemporary farce, using the stylistic conventions of asides, irony, and absurd narrative developments to expose social attitudes about death, ambition, and the manipulation of emotions. Its black humor has a distinct Welsh context, with several jokes—about places, roads, and celebrities—that will make sense only to audience members who have spent any time in Wales. Some critics have seized upon this technique to criticize Rowlands as a writer whose drama only functions within a national specificity. This criticism does not take account of the success of the play outside of Wales, nor does it acknowledge Rowlands's concern with creating scenarios about human behavior that are universal yet happen to be placed in a Welsh context. This critique of Rowlands ignores a central facet about his writing—that he is coming from a distinct tradition that sees Wales as a colonized space, but unlike other countries that experienced an English hegemony, the only thing that geographically separates England from Wales is "a little sign 5mm thick: Croeso Cymru/Welcome to Wales." This close geographical relationship compels Rowlands to make the concerns of contemporary Welsh theater as visible as possible to a wider British and European audience.

Love in Plastic articulates with wit and style the various comic characters ranged against each other: the actress is prefaced by a stage direction that reads, "Enter woman pursued by Ego"; Harry, having covered his house in plastic after the deaths of his parents in a car crash, becomes obsessed with Isabel after seeing her in a cleaning ad; and the agent is a suitably mendacious, conniving figure, obsessed with the ramifications of losing his 15 percent: "Why does she cripple me whilst crutching him—the Woolworth's Yuri Gagarin?" But the choice comedic role is reserved for the restaurant owner, a creation of pastiche who highlights Rowlands's penchant for experimenting with dialect and verbosity. The use of a South Walian vernacular makes this character both pitiful and disturbing in equal measure, relating his willingness to collude with the agent in a game of murder as a sign of his economic desperation. *Love in Plastic* is a commentary on modern alienation, about stripping away forms of communication until what is left is lies, untruth, deception, and eventually murder. Harry's plastic suit protects him from the trauma of his parents' immolation, closing him off in a plastic environment of sterility, his only point of connection with the outside world an advertising jingle. Rowlands has concocted a modern fable that, quoting Jean Baudrillard in the epigraph to the published text of *Love in Plastic,* suggests "to each his own bubble, that is the law today."

Rowlands followed *Love in Plastic* with a play that is different in tone and style. The Arts Council of Wales commissioned *Marriage of Convenience* as part of "A Season of Work" by Theatr y Byd, along with a Welsh translation of a Quebec play by Daniel Danis. It opened on 19 November 1996 at Coleg Meirion Dwyfor in Dolgellau, North Wales. After a two-week tour of Wales, it reopened the following year at the Edinburgh Festival on 8 August 1997, where it won a Herald Angel award, followed by the award for best play at the Dublin Festival, and it was later performed at the British Festival of Visual Theatre in 1997.

Having toured Wales, Scotland, and Ireland, with more than a hundred performances, *Marriage of Convenience* is Rowlands's most performed text. It is ostensibly a childhood "coming of age" memoir tinged with political and cultural awakenings. Rowlands's most personal and transparently political work takes as its starting point the royal wedding of Charles, the Prince of Wales, and Diana Spencer in July 1981. This most public of events forms the backdrop to an interrogation of cultural identity, a meditation on language and how it constructs private and (more importantly) public personas. It is a one-man play, so the connection with the audience is immediate, starting with a voice-over that introduces the importance of place and space: "There were nights spent on the Whiterock reading omens in the disappearing clouds. Sardis Road, as dead as The Beatles beneath me, and the neon G of the Graig corkscrewing out of the cwm towards Beddau, The Lamb and Flag and beyond."

The geography of the South Wales valleys is rendered in the imagination of the speaker through a poetic use of language that frequently employs different registers of emotional and tonal qualities. Hemmed in by the mountains, the narrator articulates what the Welsh call *Hiraeth*—a word that defies translation but is often taken to connote an archaic and atavistic pull for home. The speaker fashions for the audience several conflicting situations: a dead father, a tyrannical stepfather, a mother unable to deal with her teenage son's fermenting sexuality; and into this Oedipal scenario is placed the clash of language and culture—between the "Welshies," those children going to Welsh school, and the predominantly English-speaking valley towns that resent and fear the ancient tongue. The speaker comments:

> When I was a kid, Welsh was a shift language, nine to four Monday to Friday with overtime on Thursdays for club; it was a Cinderella language, it didn't live beyond the school gates. . . . We were given a language all right, but not the social context to place it in.

This dialectic of language and identity, of belonging and not belonging, is synthesized through the political event of the royal wedding; instead of joining his

Scott Bailey and Tony Longhurst in the 1997 Bristol Young Vic Studio premiere of Rowlands's New South Wales, *which mostly consists of a conversation between a London cab driver and his Welsh passenger on the day of the referendum that approved creation of the Welsh Assembly (photograph by Richard Bosworth; Collection of Andy W. Smith)*

English-speaking family for the Royalist street party, the narrator joins his school friends' family for a Welsh-language republican picnic on top of a mountain, a choice that eventually leads to a violent confrontation with his reactionary stepfather. The play concludes, like *Glissando on an Empty Harp,* with the prospect of hope amid desolation:

> Born in the valley, we can never truly escape it, though we may rise to the brim and glimpse freedom promised in a beam of light, we are allowed only instants of hope before sliding back under the weight of our legacy, back into the pit where all our pits have been and gone. But still we climb on, because in our moments of light lie our reason for living.

That *Marriage of Convenience* is Rowlands's most performed play to date is not surprising; it has an aesthetic simplicity of language and style resulting from the first-person narration. As Rowlands points out, the play arrived at a precipitous moment in British public life: it is contemporaneous with several plays that came out in 1996 and 1997 that seemed to offer new ways of reading the "State of the Nation" through an isolated, disaffected, and marginalized youth culture. This culture was envisaged most famously through the 1996 movie and play of Irvine Welsh's novel *Trainspotting* (1993); but Edna Walsh's *Disco Pigs* (1996), Mark Ravenhill's *Shopping and Fucking* (1996), and *Caledonia Dreaming* by 7:84 Theatre Company (1997) also each offered radical new perspectives on Irish, English, and Scottish subcultures, a generation of the Margaret Thatcher era growing up under the complex negotiations of a globalized economy. *Marriage of Convenience* extended this debate to a Welsh context, prefiguring the end of eighteen years of Conservative government and the rise of New Labour in May 1997 as well as the consequences of that new political class for Wales and Scotland—the promise of devolution.

The play marked a new direction for Rowlands in his drama, an attempt to connect with issues of national identity and how that is inscribed through family conflict. *Marriage of Convenience* is more subdued in tone than the anarchic, surreal comedies that preceded it. This new register is most obvious in Rowlands's next major stage play, the intense family drama *Blue Heron in the Womb.*

Blue Heron in the Womb premiered at the Tron Theatre in Glasgow on 21 May 1998. This production cemented the previous working relationship between the Tron Theatre and Theatr y Byd with *Marriage of Convenience*. *Blue Heron in the Womb* takes its title from the bird that recurs in the poetry of Dylan Thomas—a writer who, Rowlands noted in the 1999 interview with Walford Davies, is the "most powerful voice that Wales has produced this century." *Blue Heron in the Womb* is an evocative text of burial, sacrifice, death, and rebirth that highlights several concerns that have run through Rowlands's drama. It is the most sexually explicit of all of Rowlands's plays, centering around the conflicts between men and women, fathers and daughters, and fathers and mothers. Situated around twin sisters who share the same lover, it is the most problematic of Rowlands's plays in terms of how it appropriates the feminine language of sexual desire and in the provocative way it presents female sexuality, a deliberate strategy by Rowlands of "using methods of appropriation to deal with a play about appropriation."

Blue Heron in the Womb uses the classical motifs of Greek tragedy to depict the unraveling of a family as past secrets are exposed, watched over by "A MAN HOVERING SIX FEET ABOVE WALES." This narrator figure is a malevolent chorus, outside of the action yet implicated within it. The play begins with the family preparing to scatter the ashes of a dead baby; the two Daughters iron their Father's clothes as the Mother prepares a picnic. The stage directions reveal no names, just roles, as if to emphasize the generic function of the "Family." The characters switch between dialogue and extended monologues, creating a montage of interior voices that imparts upon the text a fractured, dreamlike quality, a technique that both uses and rejects naturalistic modes of expression. The present—the ritual laying to rest of the dead—merges with the past, the stories of desire and rejection between men and women, fathers and daughters, that shatter the family unit. The Father embodies the monolithic instruments of tradition, a Welshman defined by church and language, trapped inside archaic rituals:

> FATHER: Let us pray.... They say babies gurgle in dialect, rehearsing the language they will eventually speak. If this is true, then Welsh babies are doubly blessed, for their gurglings are not only the formative sounds of the divine tongue, but their linguistic passports to life everlasting.

As the Family makes their pilgrimage to the cliff top to scatter the ashes, Rowlands exposes the fault lines that run between them—the twins' reciprocation of envy, loving the same abusive man; the loathing that the Mother feels for the Father, a direct rebellion against his phallocentric and reactionary Law. These fissures are enacted as the "spirit of the Man" hovers above them, the architect of the tragedy, father of the dead child, and source of the sisters' desire.

As the narrative unfolds and the past merges with the present, the characters exorcise their personal demons in a flurry of confessions. The play traces the causes of the tragedy and enacts the consequences of the loss of the infant son: a repetition of deaths as the Father is killed in a road accident that mirrors the death of the baby, and the Mother and one twin drown themselves in the sea. The play carries its narrative arc through a series of visual images: the Family getting dressed at the beginning of the play, ritually preparing for the journey; the picnic on top of a Welsh mountain, eating sandwiches as they wait to scatter the baby's ashes; the Man hovering in the air, clutching onto the wrists of the Daughter and Mother as they commit suicide.

Like *Marriage of Convenience*, *Blue Heron in the Womb* conveys what Rowlands described in the 1999 interview as putting the "English language through a process of syntactic shock," where the rhythms and cadences of the Welsh language are re-presented through an English syntax to create a distinctive way of describing the world. Rowlands's heritage as a bilingual writer is most apparent in this work, as *Blue Heron in the Womb* concludes with the birth of the baby conducted entirely in Welsh, as the ghosts of the dead mother and sister become the midwives to this uncanny event. This distortion of temporal space and time is part of the stylistic effect of the play on viewers as they are taken back in time to the birth of the baby, yet still contained in the present tense with the dead mother and sister speaking Welsh while delivering the child: "Gwerth y byd o boen?" (Worth a world full of pain?).

Birth, and what it represents symbolically, is a metaphor that Rowlands has returned to several times. *Blue Heron in the Womb* forms the last part of the Trilogy of Appropriation, and birth is a recurrent theme in all three plays. In *Glissando on an Empty Harp*, the woman gives birth to a box that becomes a source of artistic contestation. Harry in *Love in Plastic* undergoes a self-induced gestation as he covers his home and body in plastic, waiting for the moment to be reborn following the deaths of his parents. This imagery indicates a desire for transformation on the part of Rowlands, a political urge to begin anew—"the beginning is now." Alongside this birth motif runs the figure of the tyrannical father figure, a critique that equates fatherhood with damaging and oppressive patriarchal systems. This reading is fraught with problems for Rowlands; as he acknowledged in the interview with Smith, "some women found it difficult to stomach" the way the female characters articulated their sexuality, partly because of the frankness but more crucially because the author is male. In a retrospective of Rowlands's work published with *A Trilogy of Appropriation,* the theater critic David Adams writes, "While criticizing male appropriation of women, Rowlands exercises his power as author to appropriate his female characters." While it is facile to suggest that male writers are excluded from writing about female sexuality, Rowlands's willingness to explore these issues make his work challenging, provocative, and political.

Significantly, *Blue Heron in the Womb* was written postdevolution, and it appears to offer the possibility of closing out the past and looking forward to, in Rowlands's words, "the new political landscape in Wales." This new political landscape forms the basis for Rowlands's next stage play, *New South Wales,* an earlier version of which was first read in its one-act form at the Bristol Young Vic Studio on 18 September 1997. This date also happened to be the day of the Welsh Referendum (in which voters approved, by only a small margin, the creation of a Welsh Assembly), an irony not lost on Rowlands, who subsequently rewrote the play to take into account this synchronous event.

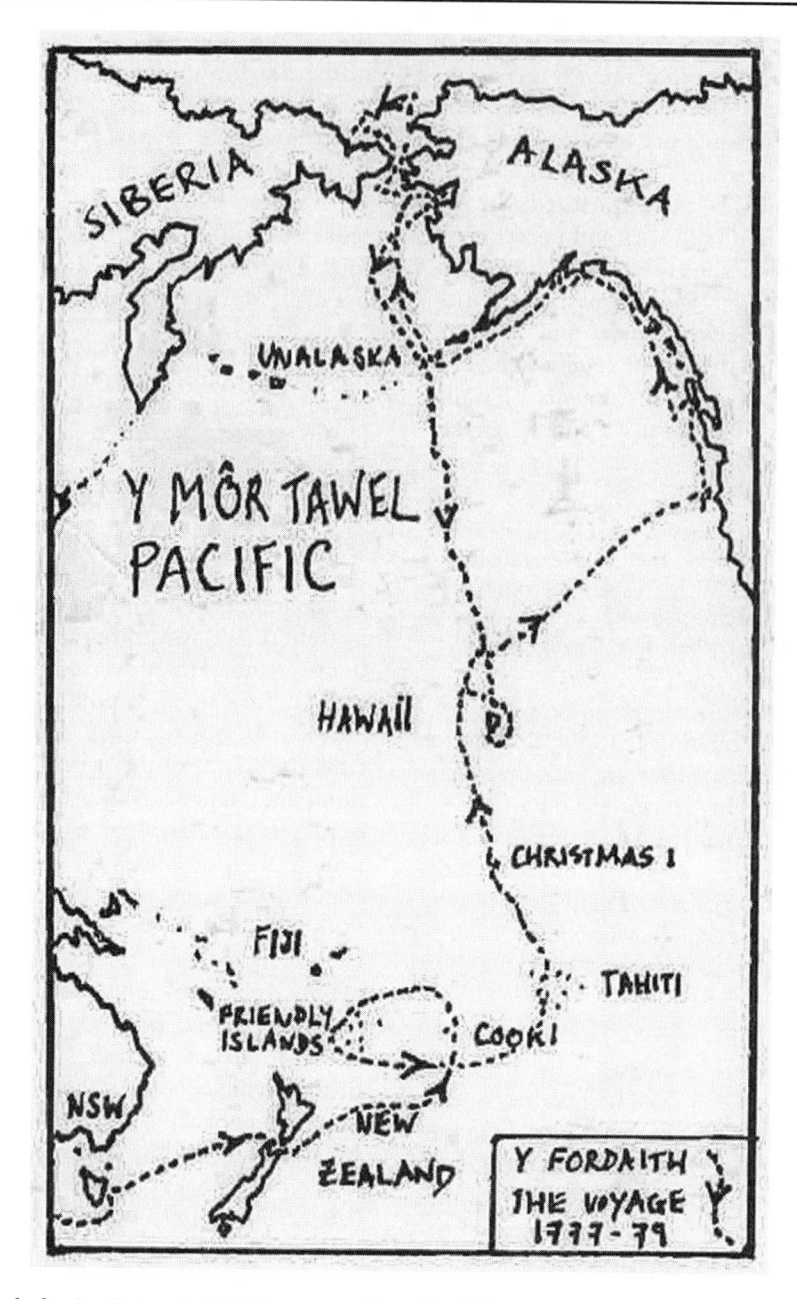

Map by Rowlands showing the travels of Welsh surgeon and poet David Samwell, whose chronicling of Captain James Cook's 1779 voyage is the subject of Rowlands's 2000 play Môr Tawel *(Calm Sea), translated in 2001 as* Pacific
(from Môr Tawel / Pacific, *2000; courtesy of Ian Rowlands)*

The redrafted *New South Wales* opened at the Edinburgh Fringe Festival on 8 August 1999. The play is a two-hander that takes place on the day of the Welsh Referendum and is set mainly in a taxicab traveling from London to Cardiff in the early hours of the morning down the M4, the motorway that joins the two capital cities. The play is reminiscent of Rowlands's television script *The Ogpu Men* (published in 1994, broadcast in 1997), which is set in a Department of Social Security (DSS) office in the Rhondda Valley, and his radio play *The Dough Boys* (1997), a tale of thwarted love in a bakery. These three plays share recognizable naturalistic settings and realistic language, an anarchic sense of humor, and an obsession with the mutations of an Anglo-Welsh dialect. *New South Wales* depicts with insouciance the various ways Wales is seen by an outsider, in this case the London cabdriver, as he is taking his fare to Cardiff:

CABBY: 'Welcome to Cardiff'. Crowsow eye Gar . . . How do you say that?

MAN: Croeso I Gaerdydd.

CABBY: Speak the lingo then, do you?

MAN: A bit . . .

CABBY: I knew this girl once who spoke Welsh.

MAN: Oh yeah?

CABBY: Yeah, we had a bit of a thing going for a while, you know. Clinos, her name was, Clinos Evans.

MAN: Llinos.

CABBY: Oh, you know her?

MAN: No.

CABBY: From up North somewhere, weird voice, sounded as if she had adenoids or something. Do they all sound like that up there?

MAN: Not all.

CABBY: It was strange to think she was from Britain because she couldn't speak English proper, you know what I mean?

The "New South Wales" of the title refers to both the dawning of a new political era in Wales and the fantasy of the promised land of Australia, a place where Alex, the man in the cab, dreams of going. He concocts a story for the cabdriver about lost love and traveling through Bangkok on his way to Sydney: "Memories I wish I had; other people's stories; stolen moments regurgitated." At Gatwick Airport, about to leave for Sydney, New South Wales, Alex gives up his dream of the "Promised Land" to return and vote for a new Wales in the referendum. Incandescent with rage at having fallen for Alex's lies, the cabdriver threatens violence until he is placated by the realization that his life is also a series of concoctions: "I live a life of lies; a cage of self deceit, it's my only defense against the pain." This exploration of where "truth" resides returns to the central concern of *Love in Plastic*: the impossibility of living a life free from mendacity and the roles that are adopted in order to become someone other than oneself. For Rowlands, the need for Wales to become a nation-state in a wider European context requires the dissolution of fantasies; prime among these are the myths of a Celtic past and the obsession by certain contemporary Welsh writers and moviemakers with empty signifiers of what constitutes "Welshness." Claire Powell's review of the play (*Theatre in Wales*, 1 November 1999) expounds upon the way Rowlands perceives this new political world, calling *New South Wales* "a forward-looking, hopeful and witty play, which intelligently examines issues pertinent to Welsh life but is not obsessed with self-identity like a recurrent nervous cultural twitch."

In 2000 Rowlands wrote *Môr Tawel* (Calm Sea), his first commissioned play in the Welsh language. Written for the Welsh Eisteddfod and first performed on 7 August 2000, *Môr Tawel* marks another new direction for Rowlands's drama, toward the use of historicization to comment upon contemporary issues. The English-language version of the text, *Pacific,* opened in London in 2001. This one-man play takes as its subject Captain James Cook's mission to locate a northwest passage between the Pacific and Atlantic Oceans on his last voyage in 1779 and his eventual death in Hawaii. The play is narrated by David Samwell—opium addict, Welsh surgeon, poet, and official documenter of Cook's voyage. The play locates Cook's journey within the context of the nascent empire building of the eighteenth century and the irony of colonial exploitation as told from the perspective of a Welshman: "Oh Iolo, we are the first and last colony, our conquest is complete."

Samwell is writing his last will and testament in Deptford, recounting his travels for Iolo Morganwg, who was one of the prime shapers of the Romantic Celtic movement of the eighteenth century and was subsequently found out by twentieth-century scholars to have forged documents he claimed were historical proof of ancient bardic ceremonies. Rowlands is able to conflate these historical characters—Cook, Samwell, and Morganwg—in order to explore issues surrounding the complex relationship of colonial discourse with cultural appropriation: "What's the point of going to the trouble of naming the world if you're not going to abuse it?"

The Welsh bardic tradition of forging the idea of nationhood through verse and song—historically, Samwell was the second bard after Morganwg to speak at Primrose Hill in 1792, the origins of the modern Eisteddfod—is juxtaposed against the brutal racist and genocidal impulse of empire building. The concept of the colonized becoming colonizers imbues *Môr Tawel* with its ironic displacement of shame and regret, as Samwell writes: "Oh, my dear Iolo, my imperial sins are embossed upon the pages of my reckoning." Although *Môr Tawel* and *Pacific* are not literal translations of each other, because of the differences in constructing sentences in Welsh and English and because they were performed by different actors, the experiment of creating two distinct texts in different languages from the same source material is an indication of the possibilities for Welsh theater in the twenty-first century.

While Rowlands wrote all of his work prior to *Môr Tawel* in English, his work as a theater director was predominantly for Welsh-language theater companies. Part of the problem that Welsh-language theater currently faces is the dominance of the Welsh-language media in radio and especially television, which Rowlands views as wholly detrimental for the forging of new young writers and actors in theater. As he noted in the interview with Smith, Wales "is the only country that I know of that had a professional television culture before professional theatre." This comment points up the absence of any Welsh-language dramatists regularly working in theater, drawn instead to the generously funded provisions of Welsh-language television. As a theater administrator and artistic director Rowlands has become one of the major figures in Welsh theater attempting to right this imbalance.

In 1998 he became artistic director of Bara Caws, the Welsh-language national community touring company. In 2000 he became the artistic director of Theatr Gwynedd, possibly the most important Welsh-language touring company. Since 2002 he has been the artistic director of Cwmni Theatr Gogledd Cymru, a theater company based in North Wales. Rowlands is thus in a position of taking forward the development of Welsh-language theater. At a conference in November 2002, debating the future of Welsh theater, Rowlands delivered a paper titled "A View from the Operating Table," mapping out his plans for the future, embarking on a new phase where Welsh-language theater can be "not a sick art form on its death bed, but a vital force, pumping with creativity, in rude health, a living theatre."

His next, as yet unperformed play, "Blink" (2003), returns Rowlands to the territory that he had previously mapped out in *Marriage of Convenience*. Set in a deindustrialized South Wales valley community, the play explores the lives of a working-class family through the double narratives of an immobile, dying father who can only blink and the uncovering of the trauma of child abuse visited upon a group of friends by their drama teacher. Like *Marriage of Convenience*, it conveys the sense of struggle that impoverished, post-Thatcherite communities deal with and the possibilities of breaking out of the cycle of violence and poverty. The young man, Si, acknowledges the abuse he suffered at the hands of his father and teacher: "He was my teacher, my fucking teacher; a surrogate father. I hate them both; both bastards abused me in their fashion."

This melding of personal lives with the social world imbues Rowlands's drama with a sense of urgency and passion about political systems and how people are used and oppressed by them. The abusive fathers of Rowlands's work signify much that is wrong with the normative values of late capitalism, and they are just as much victims of the system as they are perpetrators. His vision as a playwright is concerned with contradictory experiences, between hope and despair, love and violence, but in these contradictions his stated aim of fashioning an "epic vocabulary to create a common existence" resonates with wit, passion, and empathy for alienated and traumatized individuals.

Ian Rowlands believes that "theatre can carry the consciousness of a nation," and he views himself primarily as a postcolonial writer using language and imagery to make political statements about the current state of the Welsh nation. Rowlands's work as a dramatist plots the social tribulations of contemporary Welsh culture; but ultimately his overarching social humanism defines him as a writer who happens to set his plays in Wales, using themes, ideas, and theatrical styles that are not reducible to a set of cultural tick boxes. As he told Walford Davies:

> As a nation we should stop bemoaning the fact that Welshness is our greatest problem and concentrate, as Welsh people, on becoming citizens of the world. I am looking forward to an unselfconscious cultural future.

This position is a curious one for a self-confessed postcolonial writer, but Rowlands's theater thrives on these contradictions, like the opium-wrecked, guilt-bearing Samwell, who demands that his role in history be "fabricated." Rowlands is, then, not solely a Welsh dramatist, but a British and, indeed, European theater practitioner.

Interview:

Hazel Walford Davies, "Theatre as Exorcism," *New Welsh Review*, no. 44 (Spring 1999): 70–75.

W. Gordon Smith

(13 December 1928 – 13 August 1996)

Ian Brown

PLAY PRODUCTIONS: *Vincent,* Leicester, Phoenix Theatre, 18 November 1970;

Jock, Glasgow, Clyde Fair International at the King's Theatre, June 1972;

Knox, Edinburgh, Edinburgh Festival Fringe, 19 August 1974;

Sweeter Than All the Roses, Ochtertyre (Perthshire), Ochtertyre Festival Theatre, 26 September 1974;

Who Me? London, Royal Court Theatre (Student Drama Festival), 1975;

The North British Working Man's Guide to Arts [revue], Edinburgh, Moray House Theatre, 1975;

Cinderella and the Marvellous Mice, Inverness, Eden Court Theatre, 1976;

Wizard, Perth (Scotland), Perth Theatre, 23 May 1977;

On the Road to Avizandum, Perth (Scotland), Perth Theatre, 24 May 1977;

The Marvellous Mice and the Moon, Inverness, Eden Court Theatre, 1977;

Marie of Scotland, Perth (Scotland), Perth Theatre, 18 May 1978;

Xanadu, Dundee, College of Education Theatre, 1978; Edinburgh, Broughton High School Theatre, 16 August 1978;

The Northern Echo [revue], Edinburgh, Royal Lyceum Theatre, February 1979;

Cock Up Your Lugs [revue], Edinburgh, Stockbridge House, 1980;

Coq au Leekie [revue], Edinburgh, L'Alliance Club des Vins, 1981;

Half Past High Noon [revue], Edinburgh, Bermuda Triangle, 1982;

Smithereens [revue], Edinburgh, Dragonara Hotel, 1982;

What a Way to Go, Wick, Wick Assembly Rooms, 13 August 1983;

Scots Wha Who? [revue], Edinburgh, Bermuda Triangle, 1983;

Mister Carnegie's Lantern Lecture, Dunfermline, Carnegie Hall, 1 August 1985;

Gardyloo [revue], Edinburgh, Stockbridge House, 1985;

W. Gordon Smith (portrait by Alexander Moffat; Collection of Belinda Dewar)

Vincent By Himself, Edinburgh, St. Bernard's Church, 1986;

Mister Jock, Edinburgh, Royal Museum of Scotland, 17 August 1987;

Haggis Yoghourt [revue], Edinburgh, Royal Museum of Scotland, 1987;

This Is My Country [revue], Edinburgh, Netherbow Arts Centre, 1987;

Jock—On the Skite [revue], Edinburgh, Royal Museum of Scotland, 1988;

Going For a Love Song, Edinburgh, Stockbridge House, 24 August 1991;

Bowff [revue], Edinburgh, Stockbridge House, 1991.

BOOKS: *Edinburgh,* Portraits of Cities (London: Lutterworth, 1967);

Jock (Edinburgh: Cacciatore Fabbro, 1977);

Mister Carnegie's Lantern Lecture (Dunfermline: Carnegie Dunfermline Trust, 1985);

Mister Jock (Edinburgh: Inverleith Music, 1988);

W. G. Gillies: A Very Still Life (Edinburgh: Atelier, 1991);

Philipson: A Biography of Sir Robin Philipson (Edinburgh: Atelier, 1995);

David Donaldson: Painter and Limner to Her Majesty the Queen in Scotland (Edinburgh: Mainstream, 1996).

OTHER: *AA/Readers Illustrated Guide To Britain,* Scottish text and photographs by Smith (London: Drive Publications Ltd for the AA, 1971);

This Is My Country: A Personal Blend of the Purest Scotch, compiled by Smith (London: Souvenir Press, 1976);

Edinburgh, photographs by Douglas Corrance, captions by Smith (Glasgow: Collins, 1979);

Sir Robin Philipson, PPRSA, RA [exhibition catalogue], text by Smith (Edinburgh: Scottish Gallery, 1983);

Fallen Angels: Paintings by Jack Vettriano, edited by Smith (London: Pavilion, 1994).

W. Gordon Smith was a leading Scottish broadcaster, television producer, art and theater critic, and journalist as well as a dramatist. His distinction is marked perhaps most particularly by the inclusion of his portrait in the Scottish National Portrait Gallery, a mark of honor accorded to few. While he was certainly polymathic, he is best remembered as a playwright. This reputation is based on a series of remarkable plays written between 1970 and 1991, in which he experimented with and developed small-cast forms and above all the potential and actuality of the one-person play. He stood somewhat aside from the theatrical establishment: his own production companies most often presented his work during the Edinburgh Fringe Festival. Yet, his work remained highly popular as he explored both complex morality and Scottish history and society with wit and irony.

Despite the popularity of his plays, only a handful have been published. Scottish theater in general has had this long-standing problem: relatively few plays, even ones that are professionally produced and highly regarded, are published. The reasons include the size of the perceived market, the absence of Scottish publishers interested in dramatic texts, and the absence of significant teaching of Scottish drama in schools and universities, which might provide a stronger market. The situation began to improve in the 1990s but is still problematic.

William Gordon Smith was born in Edinburgh on 13 December 1928, the son of William Smith, a shoemaker, and his wife, Robina Ewart, a former domestic servant. He had one brother, Michael, and a sister, Constance. He was educated at Boroughmuir High School in Edinburgh, from which he was expelled in 1942 for burning down the school garden shed. From 1945 to 1948 he served in the Royal Air Force. He married Joan Elizabeth Harrower on 14 February 1952, and the marriage produced two sons and two daughters. His first wife died in August 1987, and he married Jay Flett on 8 November 1991. He died of liver cancer on 13 August 1996.

Smith was a communicator in various forms besides the theater. While in 1948 he joined an amateur dramatic company, something in which he participated throughout his twenties, he also began a career in journalism, starting with the *Dalkeith Advertiser* and moving in 1952 to the *Leith Gazette* and in 1953 to the *Edinburgh Evening News.* In 1956 he joined the BBC in Scotland as a radio producer, moving in 1964 to work as television director and producer, becoming producer/presenter of BBC Scotland's folk-music program *Hootenanny* (1963–1966) and its leading arts programs *Scope* (1969–1976) and its successor, *Spectrum* (1977–1980). His engaging presence conveyed energetic, but critically sensitive, enthusiasm for all the arts. He was known as having an excellent ear and eye for developing talent: in the 1960s he discovered and produced Paddie Bell and the Corrie Folk Trio and was the supporter of several rising visual artists, including John Bellany and Sandy Moffat. He used his position as a television arts producer to promote the best emerging talent, a role he considered proper to a discerning critic. He himself was an able photographer, having produced in 1967 a photographic and verbal portrait of his home city, Edinburgh.

The bare facts demonstrate how much Smith was an artistic polymath, but his central creative processes were connected with the theater. Surprisingly, however, his first major play was not professionally presented until 1970, when he was forty-two. This work was *Vincent,* a portrait of Vincent Van Gogh. Written for actor Tom Fleming and performed by him with gusto, the play explores the nature of the artist and Van Gogh's struggle to establish himself. Smith draws on his own knowledge of the ways of dealers and critics to present an artist in search of recognition, both of his art by others and of his own creative nature by himself. The form of the play is remarkable. When others might have followed existing models, choosing a moment at the end of the artist's life from which to reflect backward rather statically, Smith journeys dynamically from city to city through Van Gogh's career as Vincent seeks to develop his art and find some security. Smith shows Vincent's language breaking down, with the longer speeches of the earlier part giving way to fractured language and discourse that spills images, often from the paintings. In act 2 Vincent observes, "I've painted my fears as faithfully as I painted the sunflowers for my friend." *Vincent* embodies Van Gogh's inner conflict and developing breakdown of sensibility.

Smith's next play marked his talent as one that would achieve particular rapport with a broad-based audience. Smith explored Scottish history and mythology with wit and, often, acerbity in *Jock,* first presented in 1972 as part of Clyde Fair International at the King's Theatre, Glasgow, and performed by Russell Hunter, whose association with Smith thereafter was one of the great creative partnerships of late-twentieth-century theater. Smith frequently wrote plays for Hunter, whose respect for and creative sympathy with the playwright produced a series of popular and critically respected dramaturgical experiments. *Jock* is set in a Scottish military museum, whose keeper, the eponymous Jock, is a retired soldier. The audience become in effect visitors to the museum, which is Jock's mind and memory of the history of Scotland and the experience of soldiers in war.

The play opens with Jock addressing the audience, reciting his battle honors—including, with a typical Smith jeu d'esprit, the first Edinburgh Tattoo (military entertainment involving bands and dance) in 1950—when, on a lighting change, he enacts a patrol under fire in Northern Ireland. The play shifts through time and place, exploring the mythology of militarism, questioning the nature of power, and vividly narrating key moments of Scottish experience. Smith relished the potential of the Scots language, though writing more often himself in Scots-accented English. He was fascinated by the mythology of authority and the deflation of pretensions of power; his evocative representation of the execution of Mary, Queen of Scots, is followed immediately by an anecdote illustrating the stupidity of Dundee policemen. Smith examines authority figures and their effects on the common man through a variety of lenses and recognizes self-delusion as prevalent, perhaps necessary.

At the conclusion, Jock recalls the Suez crisis as the end of the British, or, as modern writers would say, Anglo-Scottish, imperialist dream. Jock asserts, with typical iconoclasm, that, if there had been a "real call-up," then "every able-bodied man in the country would have taken to the hills." Immediately after he makes this claim, the final paradoxical image of the play is of Jock, the disaffected common soldier who has seen through the ironies of history, marching on the spot in thrall to the sounds of a regimental band playing "Scotland the Brave." This ambiguous image suggests that reason and atavism lie in Everyman and may be roused despite one's own rational skepticism. *The Scotsman* critic Allen Wright's review of the first production talked of Smith's having "devised a brilliant way of combining boastfulness with disrespect," moving gloriously "from the elegiac to the bawdy." *Jock* embodies the postcolonial ambivalence of Scots, and indeed the British in general, toward the symbols and myths of their imperialist past. Smith contributed theatrically to the contemporary debate about the problematic deconstruction of the myths of "Britain" and Scotland's "hidden history." This debate formed part of the Scottish cultural renaissance that has played a role in the larger process of constitutional change.

Jock was produced by Smith's own company, Cacciatore Fabbro (from his name and Hunter's in Italian), setting a pattern that he maintained through his life of seeking whenever possible to present his own work. His experience as a producer in radio and television, of course, perhaps fed this ambition, but he also enjoyed the artistic control and freedom available as his own producer. At times, Hunter was a partner in these companies. Nevertheless, Smith's work was in demand by other companies. Not until the later 1970s and 1980s did Smith insist on producing all his new work himself. His next two plays demonstrate this point, the first being presented by Smith's company, the second by a regional theater.

The former, *Knox* (performed in 1974), revisits historical themes, and the title suggests another one-person play. Smith, however, always engaged in paradox. He has sixteenth-century clergyman and Scottish Reformation leader John Knox addressing the audience as if it were a church congregation, but his rhetorical flow is interrupted by a young man and woman who challenge both his philosophy and "truths." The play manages, thus, to achieve the interior quality of the one-person form while breaking its theatrical rules. Again, Smith seeks dramatically to humanize Scottish historical figures and simultaneously explore their legacy of conflict.

Smith's challenge to established, or establishment, values continued in *Sweeter Than All the Roses* (performed in 1974). In this play, two lavatory attendants, a man and a woman, are engaged in an act of resistance, fighting to keep their place of work and public service open against an official decision to demolish it. The play is concerned with day-to-day human aspirations, finding joy in the humblest occupations against "management's" autocracy. The final image of the play,

Smith during the period he participated in an amateur dramatic company, circa 1950 (courtesy of Belinda Dewar)

a bulldozer breaking down walls as the attendants flee for their lives, is a powerful image of the crushing of aspirations by those in authority. The premiere, at Ochtertyre Theatre in rural Perthshire, added another layer of subversion. Ochtertyre was a brief attempt to create experimental theater in a conservative part of the country. The subject and setting of Smith's play challenged an audience that might see theater as conventional. Hunter, who played the man, has observed in an unpublished interview with Ian Brown that the earliest walkout was of a front-row couple who left as soon as the lights rose and he emerged carrying toilet rolls and sanitary towels.

The variety of Smith's dramatic output is marked by his next play. A revision of a play he had earlier written for his own children in 1960, *Cinderella and the Marvellous Mice* was rewritten for production over the Christmas period of 1976–1977. As the title suggests, the work took traditional fare and subverted it in a way typical of Smith. It begins with a traditional fairy addressing the audience; but she is forty, and "No-one loves a fairy when she's forty." The surreal quality of the play is reinforced by the key roles of the mice Tomintoul and Tomingarry, with their Highland place names. The play is concerned with the healing and regenerative effect of imagination and forgiveness: "Just because a thing isn't in a book doesn't mean it isn't in somebody's head," says Tomingarry. The major denouement is not the marriage of Cinderella, almost incidentally treated, but the rejuvenation of the forty-year-old fairy.

In 1977 Smith's *On the Road to Avizandum,* whose central characters, Madame Doubtfire and Mr. Virtue, derived their names from two famous junk-shop proprietors in Edinburgh, was produced at the Perth (Scotland) Festival. The characters exist in the limbo of secondhand goods shops, thriving on the receipt of stolen property and tax fraud. As the play opens, they are revealed tied up by thieves who have robbed Madame Doubtfire; and, as it unfolds, Madame Doubtfire emerges as a concentration-camp survivor whose experience of inhumanity is unrelenting as she sees theft and betrayal around her. The ironically named Mr. Virtue seeks to steal or blackmail £2,000 from Madame Doubtfire to relieve himself of debt to criminals. Virtue obtains his £2,000 from Madame Doubtfire, but she has palmed him off with a bag mainly of Monopoly money. The double-crossing Virtue, double-crossed, must flee because when those to whom he has given the false money find out, they will return for revenge. In a preface to his typescript of the play, Smith noted:

> Avizandum is not, so far as I know, a place. It is the peculiar Scottish judicial limbo to which tough cases are taken for mature consideration. The road is one we all travel in the certain knowledge that the great majority have [sic] already arrived.

Smith's capacity to handle the zany, sweet humor of his children's play at the same time as exploring darker issues of human cruelty in *On the Road to Avizandum* typifies his range.

Smith sustained key themes with *Wizard,* a 1977 play for children; *The Marvellous Mice and the Moon,* originally written in 1961 for his own children and rewritten for production over the Christmas period of 1977–1978; and *Marie of Scotland,* a one-person play written for actress Edith McArthur, produced in 1978. Yet, throughout the period of these plays, he was continuing to produce the weekly BBC television arts programs *Scope* and *Spectrum* as well as writing prose texts. As presenter of *Spectrum,* he affected the consciousness of the public, shaping understanding and debate on the variety and nature of the arts.

His next play, *Xanadu,* also produced in 1978, marked another development in his tightly focused small-cast form, opening new dimensions of expression. As the title suggests, the play draws on Samuel Taylor Coleridge's poem about altered states of mind. Its concern is with consciousness and imagination. An apparent survivor of a car crash is under observation. In this clinical context–"blindingly white if possible," notes the opening stage direction–it seems he is being both examined and treated. In this presumed hospital (which may be a research laboratory) he desperately seeks the significance of his own life. Repeatedly, memories that he seeks in order to help re-form his damaged consciousness arise; yet, he seems to be suppressing others, perhaps fearing their potential for pain. One memory about his childhood friends reflects this sense of human frailty, the failures and joys of imagination and understanding:

> Valentino Fassone, café proprietor, Clackmannan, Fascist, June 1940, repatriated at his own request, sails home, intercepted by U-boat . . . arrivaderci . . . The trouble was, he'd taken his two sons with him–Bruno, aged 8, and Mario, aged 10. We had planned to swim the Channel and conquer Everest the following year.

The character's name, William McAdam (McAdam meaning "son of Adam"), suggests that his quandary is not simply that of an individual accident victim but something existential–the search, against the scientific and clinical, for the individual soul's nature, truth, and pain. McAdam is constantly questioned by a faceless Voice, presumably of a scientist, whether doctor or therapist. At the core of the patient, for whose identity a scientific search is undertaken, lies a seeker after the spiritual poetry of life, an artist-venturer, almost like Smith himself. The quotation from Coleridge, the poet of the "fancy" or imagination, with which Smith closes his play focuses this point: "For he on honey-dew has fed, / And drunk the milk of Paradise."

The complexity of *Xanadu* lies in the elusiveness of truth and the evasion, both by doctor and patient, of different truths. It also lies in the vision presented of the possibility of altered consciousness, that even brain damage may be a potential healing of societal suppression and control. The play is more disturbing and philosophically complex than anything Smith had written previously. His interest in myth, history, and personal identity finds in *Xanadu* a metaphor allowing him to challenge the most basic assumptions about what is good and healthy. Finally, the son of Adam and the apparently all-powerful Voice of science must work together to seek some truth from fractured, incoherent experience.

This play was followed by a five-year gap in playwriting, although Smith's creative work did not cease for this time. In 1979, following a tryout in 1975, he began a series of satirical revues presented at the Edinburgh Fringe Festival. A new revue appeared in nine of the subsequent twelve years. During this period Smith also retired from the BBC after the last *Spectrum* was broadcast in 1980 and returned to his original career as a print journalist. Published widely as a freelance journalist and broadcaster, he also worked as television critic for the *Sunday Standard* from 1981 to 1983.

Smith returned to playwriting proper in 1983 with *What a Way to Go,* in which his speculative existential challenge continued. The play is launched with a typically bold coup. As audiences enter, they face a covered coffin ceremoniously laid out. When the lights go down, the coffin bursts open, and the hero (played in the premiere by Hunter), hidden for more than half an hour, emerges. The shock to the cozy assumptions of the settling audience brings theatrical and thematic reward: as the play ruminates on the nature of death and humanity's fearing and welcoming it, the audience has observed with sentimental reverence one of its symbols, and had that reverence undermined, even shocked. Throughout, audience expectations continue to be overturned: after, for example, achieving a powerful emotional impact with the "Poor Yorick" speech from *Hamlet,* the actor mimes kicking the skull away, as if playing rugby. Presumption and false emotion are deflated. Smith's exploration of mortality itself achieves lightness of humor, eschewing cloying sentimentality.

Smith's next play, *Mister Carnegie's Lantern Lecture,* was commissioned by the Carnegie Dunfermline Trust to mark the 150th anniversary of Andrew Carnegie's birth. The play first appeared in the Carnegie Hall, Dunfermline, on 1 August 1985, before proceeding to the Edinburgh Festival. Smith faced the challenge in such a commission of avoiding seduction into hagiography of the iconic Scottish philanthropist. Founder of the public-library service in the English-speaking world, Carnegie is, of course, seen as a clear embodiment of the Scottish educational myth, the "lad o pairts." Yet, he was a "robber baron" of the nineteenth-century United States. Smith embraces the conflict in the opening of his play:

> There's two sides to most things and–as my uncle Dod Lauder used to say, God rest his soul–there's many a man who's a saint in the street but who's the deil himsel' incarnate behind his own front door . . . I was never as bad as that . . . Heh-heh, I was never as good as that either.

The form of the play, appropriately for such an autodidact and promoter of the virtues of education as Carnegie, is a lantern lecture of the kind popular at the turn of the twentieth century. Carnegie, the self-publicist in life, becomes the self-publicist and apologist onstage. Smith's vision of Carnegie reflects the "three-faced bugger" of Ian Brown's *Carnegie* (1973) as he achieves millions, drives his partners hard, and yet constantly aspires to self and social improvement. Smith, in working with a format usually focused on informational communication, faces an uphill struggle in achieving theatrical impact rather than didactic effect. He does so by flashes of insight into Carnegie's character and context and facing fully such crises in Carnegie's career as the excoriated breaking of the Homestead strike. His Carnegie says:

> Public reaction was predictable. The "St. Louis Post Dispatch" spoke for an angry America: "Count no man happy until he is dead. Three months ago Andrew Carnegie was a man to be envied. Today he is an object of mingled pity and contempt . . . Ten thousand Carnegie public libraries would not compensate the country for the direct and indirect evils resulting from the Homestead lock-out. Say what you will of Frick [Carnegie's partner who stayed in America to manage the lock-out when Carnegie absented himself in Scotland], he is a brave man. Say what you will of Carnegie, he is a coward. And gods and men hate cowards."

Smith's direct quotation of the American press exemplifies one way he achieves a sense of dramatic conflict in this play, presenting a variety of viewpoints, however dominated by Carnegie's self-image. This text, quoting Greek tragedy and half-quoting Aristotle's *Poetics*, "pity and contempt" substituting for "pity and terror," marks Smith's theatrical sensitivity. This device achieves a self-reference that is not merely indulgent but sets his Carnegie as a tragic figure, a man who aspires, fails, and aspires again. The final image is of an energetic man striving, against the sterility of industrial achievement, to do good. The play finishes:

> there, in the special vault which the new consortium, United States Steel, had to build for them, lay three hundred million dollars worth of newly printed bonds in my name, earning 15 million dollars a year just lying there. I never set eyes on them . . . I didn't riffle them greedily though my fingers. . . . I spent the rest of my life—and untold time beyond that—giving all these millions away.

With those words, Carnegie "*strides off as the lights fade to black.*"

Smith's next two plays expanded on earlier works: *Vincent By Himself* (performed in 1986) revisited Van Gogh, and *Mister Jock* (performed in 1987) returned to Smith's character of fifteen years before. Jock now works in a civilian museum, a setting allowing further examination of the historic myths of Scottishness, now from the problematic perspective of Scotland's recovering from the disappointing 1979 devolution referendum and rediscovering the identity that, in the year after Smith's death, brought about the successful 1997 referendum. Smith's typical quixotic humor is evident in this play:

> It's queer about the Bruce. He should be more famous for Bannockburn than anything else, but think how Scottish history and the impressionable Scottish character might have changed if yon stupid spider had never managed to swing to the other side of the cave. "If, at the sixteenth attempt, you don't succeed—bugger it, try something else."

A new dimension for Jock, though not for Smith's work, is a sense of Scotland as European. Jock, demonstrating Smith's love of the play of language, remembers a NATO exercise:

> Somebody says there's a town called Siena along the road. Off we go and demolish a few fiascos of vino in the square and chat up the mammary mias. I get bored with the banter and wander up the hill in the sun. And right in front of me's the biggest church I've ever seen—and it's green. Well, green and white stripes—marble I think. A Jock Stein cathedral.

The juxtaposition of Siena Cathedral and the Celtic football strip (team uniform) is startling and somehow apt as Smith's popular—even populist—imagination achieves the conjunction of religion and the secular saint of soccer, Stein. Later, Jock meets a Catholic priest. Speaking halting Scottish-Italian and satirizing futile West-of-Scotland sectarianism, he recognizes a cathedral painting representing the 1435 presentation at James I's Scottish court of Aeneas Sylvius, later Pope. His own history and culture are at once more surprising, international, and internationally recognized than he had imagined. While *Mister Jock* reprises the cultural, historic, and class themes of the earlier *Jock*, it achieves its own take on them.

In the four years before Smith's last play, he continued as a freelance journalist and broadcaster until, in 1990, he formed a long-term association with one of his freelance employers, *Scotland on Sunday*. For this newspaper, he was, until his death, both columnist and critic—first for theater, then visual arts—while continuing on occasion to broadcast.

His last play was produced in 1991. *Going For a Love Song* again explored a new variation of the one-person theme. The central character, Ariadne Christy, owner of a junk shop, has a son, Josh, a talented musician who does not speak. Throughout, he communicates by "speaking" musical sounds on his synthesizer. Sharing her first name with the Cretan princess who married Dionysus, god of holy ecstasy, Ariadne emerges as passionately and promiscuously sensual. Josh was the result of one of three liaisons in one month—with a downstart noble, a Lascar seaman, and a Jewish lawyer. When Josh first attended school, he sat facing the back of the class, bored facing front; the system tried to force him to face front again, and he has not spoken since. Music is his language, and pagan Ariadne, with the nearly Christian surname, sings to his accompaniment a series of love songs, including those of Robert Burns and Edith Piaf, exploring the range from the vulgar to the profound. Her hedonistic life has brought fulfillment, though she still feels longing, and her trade as a junk dealer has offered insight into human frailty. She talks tragicomically and with pathos of house-clearances after a death:

> Of course there are embarrassments. . . . I mean, what do you do when the widow knows nothing about the girlie magazines in the shoe boxes? . . . The women, in my experience are just as bad—or sad, as the case may be. Brand new peep-hole bras and very impractical knickers, whorishly scarlet and black, bought mail order in some moment of frustrated daring, never worn, and still in plain brown envelopes.

She lives in an overflowing basement below her junk shop. The strange glamour of her sensual, aspirational life is expressed by her changing, song after song, into frock after vividly different frock from her stock. She reflects on the sad humiliations experience brings, on how hard it is for a prostitute to escape even when she has become a "cuddly wee dumpling" like "Jenny across the road":

> The police picked her up last month for soliciting a young man in the street. She was seen taking money from him. They arrested her in front of him. Turned out he was her son. . . . She'd just scrounged a tenner off him for booze.

Ariadne is an archetypal Smith hero, achieving an ironic and distanced calm, which never becomes complacency or a refusal to care. She becomes the wise woman, with the stigmatized son, because of life's *thrawnness* (a Scots word meaning roughly *cross-grainedness*). Smith is always interested in matters of perception: at one point Ariadne says, "Lust isn't classified as a deadly sin because it's wicked, it's because it's enjoyable. Love, on the other hand, is painful, and as perishable as fish."

Smith with his dog Zeebo in the early 1990s (courtesy of Belinda Dewar)

In "the junk business" she has become "the janitor of this charnel-house of vanities," the charnel house being both human society and human body. Nonetheless, hope continues: having lusted after a young window cleaner, she has written a personal advertisement by the end of the play in an act of bravado. After some comic or desperate responses, she comes to the last, from her Adonis window cleaner. The play concludes as Ariadne Christy, the humane pagan, and her son "jive to some very loud and happy rock."

Smith continued, despite the need for a serious operation in his final years, to work as a critic and to broadcast, arguing his enthusiasms, taking iconoclastic and often controversial positions, and advocating and celebrating the irony of life. He produced three important monographs on the Scottish painters W. G. Gillies, Sir Robin Philipson, and David Donaldson, while being an early advocate of the paintings of Jack Vettriano. When he died, the announcement of his death in *The*

Scotsman invited those who would attend his funeral at Warriston Crematorium to wear "bright colours"; a broad cross-section of colleagues, artists, and critics did just that. In a cheerfully pagan and overflowing service, Hunter and the painters Bellany and Moffat paid tributes to Smith. When Ronnie Browne, the surviving member of the Corries, sang one of Smith's songs and insisted the entire congregation join in, it did. An attendant afterward said that he had never heard so much laughter in a funeral service.

W. Gordon Smith was a playwright particularly interested in the dramaturgical problems of work small in scale and large in scope. He wrote sometimes for larger casts but preferred to work with one, two, or three actors, exploring consciousness and varying perceptions of the nature of society and history. He developed the one-person form beyond its rather arid, often anthology-based 1960s form. He discovered new ways to explore major issues through the focus the one-person form allows on the individual mind and its refraction of the world it lives in, its myths, values, and hypocrisies. His work came sometimes to be identified with its original performers, who often in turn had worked closely with him in its creation. His work, nevertheless, has wider and deeper significance and was a key element in the development of Scottish theater throughout the 1970s and 1980s and into the 1990s.

References:

Ian Brown, "Thrawn Themes and Dramatic Experiments: W. Gordon Smith and the Paradoxes of Creative Iconoclasm," *Scottish Studies Review*, 4 (Autumn 2003): 98–120;

Randall Stevenson and Gavin Wallace, *Scottish Theatre Since the Seventies* (Edinburgh: Edinburgh University Press, 1996).

Ed Thomas
(17 July 1961 -   )

Andy W. Smith
University of Wales, Newport

PLAY PRODUCTIONS: *When the River Runs Dry,* Cardiff, Sherman Theatre, 1984;

Last Orders in Hope, Cardiff, Sherman Theatre, 1985;

House of America, Cardiff, St. Stephen's Theatre, 1 May 1988; revised, London, Battersea Arts Centre, January 1989;

Adar Heb Adenydd, Ystradgynlais, Miners Welfare Hall, 29 May 1989; performed with *House of America* as *Raiders of the Western Shore,* Edinburgh Festival, August 1989;

The Myth of Michael Roderick, adapted from *Adar Hen Adenydd,* Cardiff, St. Stephens's Theatre, November 1990; performed with *Flowers of the Dead Red Sea,* Brentford, Watermans Art Centre, November 1991;

Flowers of the Dead Red Sea, Glasgow, Tramway, 9 September 1991; revised, performed with *The Myth of Michael Roderick,* Brentford, Watermans Art Centre, November 1991;

East from the Gantry, Glasgow, Tramway, 10 October 1992; revised, Cardiff, Chapter Arts Centre, 2 February 1994;

Hiraeth/Strangers in Conversation, Cardiff, Oriel Art Gallery, 2 October 1993;

Envy, Cardiff, Chapter Arts Centre, 1993;

Song from a Forgotten City, Cardiff, Chapter Arts Centre, 14 February 1995; London, Royal Court Theatre, June 1995;

Gas Station Angel, Newcastle, Newcastle Playhouse, 8 May 1998; Cardiff, Sherman Theatre, 27 May 1998; London, New Ambassadors Theatre (Royal Court Theatre Upstairs), 3 June 1998;

Rain Dogs, by Thomas, Mike Brookes, and Mike Pearson, Cardiff, Chapter Arts Centre, 8 November 2002;

Stone City Blue, Mold, Theatr Clywd, 21 October 2004; Cardiff, Chapter Arts Centre, 16 November 2004.

BOOKS: *Hiraeth,* bilingual edition, text by Thomas, paintings by Iwan Bala (Cardiff: Oriel, 1993);

Ed Thomas (photograph by Jo Mazelis; from '95–'98 Selected Work, 2002; University of Kentucky Libraries)

Three Plays, edited by Brian Mitchell (Bridgend: Seren, 1994)—comprises *House of America, Flowers of the Dead Red Sea,* and *East from the Gantry;*

Gas Station Angel (London: Methuen in association with the Royal Court and Fiction Factory, 1998);

'95–'98 Selected Work (Cardiff: Parthian, 2002)—comprises *Song from a Forgotten City, House of America* [screenplay], and *Gas Station Angel.*

PRODUCED SCRIPTS: *Flowers of the Dead Red Sea,* radio, BBC Radio Three, 30 June 1992;

East from the Gantry, radio, BBC Radio Wales, 1992;
Silent Village/Pentre Mud, television, BBC, 1993;
Fallen Sons, television, BBC, 1993;
House of America, motion picture, September Films/British Screen, 1997.

OTHER: *East from the Gantry,* in *Frontline Intelligence 1: New Plays for the Nineties,* edited by Pamela Edwardes (London: Methuen, 1993);

Hiraeth/Strangers in Conversation, in *Act One Wales,* edited by Phil Clark (Bridgend: Seren, 1997), pp. 161–181;

Envy, in *One Man, One Voice,* edited by David Adams (Cardiff: Parthian, 2001), pp. 61–82.

Ed Thomas has been at the vanguard of innovative practice in Welsh theater since 1988. In conjunction with his production company Fiction Factory (formerly Y Cwmni), Thomas has written plays and has adapted his stage writing for radio and movies. He has become a successful television writer and producer, directed his first full-length feature motion picture, and is overseeing Fiction Factory producing major movie and television projects. His plays have toured in countries as diverse as Ukraine, Germany, Australia, and Romania, coinciding with translations into French, German, Catalan, Spanish, Galacian, and Croatian. This burgeoning international recognition has bestowed upon Thomas the burdensome accolade of the theatrical "voice of his generation." As Thomas stated in a 1998 interview with Hazel Walford Davies: "I find that our culture is sometimes very servile to stereotypes, and my argument is that we have to have the confidence to construct our own sense of who we are."

Thomas's call for a "theatre of imagination" that corresponds to a reimagining of what it means to be Welsh at the end of the twentieth century is an attempt to recognize both the symbolic necessity and political futility of devolution and the new political map of Wales since 1997, the year of the Welsh Referendum (in which voters approved the creation of an independent Welsh Assembly, but only by a scant margin). In an unpublished May 2001 interview with Andy W. Smith, Thomas talked of a postdevolution Wales as a place where "people are loathe to criticise too easily because it's a Mickey Mouse parliament, and anything called 'national' would be impossible because a large majority of Welsh people said no. So 'Wales' would just be forever an idea." Rather than assert a collective sense of national identity, Thomas's drama exposes the suffocating symbolism of defunct and empty national archetypes.

Edward Jenkins Thomas was born in Abercraf, a staunch Presbyterian community in the Swansea valleys, West Wales, on 17 July 1961, to Thomas Edward Jenkins Thomas and his wife, Mair. Although Thomas grew up in what was predominantly a mining community, his father owned the local butcher shop and slaughterhouse. Thomas's childhood spent around the slaughtering of animals influences the setting of his play *Flowers of the Dead Red Sea* (performed in 1991, published in 1994). His childhood was further marked by three major traumatic familial events that have subsequently found their way into his fiction and stories. His grandfather, Thomas Jenkins Thomas, committed suicide in a hotel room in Aberystwyth, a small remote Welsh seaside town, four days after Thomas was born. The reasons for this suicide still remain a family mystery. Even more strange was the death of his great-grandmother, who was accidentally shot in the head by his grandfather's brother in the family butcher shop. This incident has found its way into two Thomas plays, *East from the Gantry* (performed in 1992, published in 1994) and *Envy* (performed in 1993, published in 2001), in scenarios so fanciful that they comes across in the retelling as bleakly comic.

When he was six years old, Thomas nearly drowned in the local river while swimming, a powerful childhood memory that is poignantly dramatized in his play *Gas Station Angel* (performed and published in 1998). As Thomas noted in an unpublished September 2003 interview with Smith, in his memory of the event, the experience of near death is not borne out by the facts: Thomas remembers it as a light green river, when in truth it was dirty brown. This reliance upon the shifting allegiances of memory and place mark Thomas's plays as expressionistic evocations of frozen time, his characters returning to the unreliability of memory as their negotiation with a world defined by language.

As the first language spoken in the family was Welsh, Thomas attended the Welsh-speaking primary school Ysgol Cymraeg Ynyscedwyr in the nearby town of Ystradgynlais. Thomas then went to the English school Maesydderwen Secondary Comprehensive School in Ystradgynlais, mainly because his sister, Cynthia, older than he by four years, was already a student there. After high school Thomas went to University College Cardiff (now called Cardiff University) to read English in 1979, although he admitted in the September 2003 interview that the sole reason for him to go to college was to play rugby.

During this time in the late 1970s University College Cardiff was at the forefront of the rising dominance of critical theory in English literature, placing an emphasis on structuralism. Thomas found this new intellectual environment deeply alienating and spent most of his time socializing and playing rugby, until a serious arm injury forced him to give up the sport.

Steven Mackintosh as Sid and Lisa Palfrey as Gwenny in Thomas's 1997 movie version of his 1988 play, House of America, *in which a brother and sister create an incestuous, escapist fantasy by pretending to be Jack Kerouac and Joyce Johnson (from '95–'98* Selected Work, *2002; University of Kentucky Libraries)*

Encouraged by a creative-writing tutor, and influenced by reading the Beat writings of Jack Kerouac and Allen Ginsberg, Thomas took up writing poetry, his first foray into experimenting with language and words. Thomas graduated in 1982 with a "sociable" lower second-class degree and went to work in France for six months. On his return, through the influence of a friend, Wyndham Price, Thomas started work as a stagehand at the Prince of Wales fringe theater in Fulham, West London, though he had never previously been involved with or interested in theater.

Thomas became fascinated with the relationship of language and image through doing a whole range of jobs at the theater, from stage management to operating lights and sound. While working in London, he was given the opportunity to direct his first play for the fringe company Reality Sandwich, a 1983 production of Lanford Wilson's *Home Free* (1964). From 1984 to 1986 Thomas was an Arts Outreach worker at Battersea Arts Centre. During this period Thomas wrote his first two plays for Made in Wales Theatre Company, *When the River Runs Dry* in 1984 and *Last Orders in Hope* in 1985, both directed by Jamie Garven but unpublished. This last play was an early version of his later play *The Myth of Michael Roderick* (performed in 1990), his first attempt at writing a satirical absurdist drama influenced by Samuel Beckett.

From 1986 to 1989 Thomas played the regular role of Dr. Gareth Protheroe on the Welsh-language television soap opera *Pobol y Cwm* (People of the Valley), a remarkable feat considering that he had received no formal training as an actor. He wrote his first major play, *House of America,* during 1987 and 1988, and it was staged by Geoff Moore as part of a festival of new writing at the St. Stephen's Theatre in Cardiff in May 1988. In *House of America,* siblings Sid and Gwenny play out an incestuous fantasy based on the romanticized visions of Thomas's postcollege obsession with Kerouac's *On the Road* (1957); Sid takes on the persona of Kerouac while Gwenny "becomes" Kerouac's lover Joyce Johnson. Their brother, Boyo (the name itself an inversion of a clichéd masculine "Welshness"), rejects their role-playing–"pretending to be somebody else for a living, lies, all lies." The spark for these escapist fantasies lies in the mysterious disappearance of their father, whom they presume has left for America but who has in fact been murdered by their mother, Mam. His body has been deposited in an abandoned mine shaft, and the threat of its discovery in renewed open-cast mining leads to the unraveling of this South Walian family's patricidal and incestuous secrets. The first production of *House of America* used a narrative device of flashbacks, as told by Boyo to a psychiatrist, which framed the action in a similar way to Peter Shaffer's *Equus* (1973). Thomas subsequently rewrote the play and cut this device, bringing in the monologue of Mam at the start of the play, and she becomes the unreliable narrator of the story:

> Thing is with a story is that you've got to be sure of the facts, or people will only get the wrong end of the stick, and you end up upsetting people without meaning to. I didn't mean any harm you say, but its too late, the damage has already been done.

At the conclusion of *House of America* Mam is left catatonic by the eruption of this Freudian nightmare, as the South Wales valleys become redolent of the incest, murder, and eventual destruction of the House of Atreus in Greek tragedy. As Sid and Gwenny delve deeper into Kerouac's *On the Road*, the distinction between fantasy and reality becomes blurred, and the play ends, like Sam Shepard's *True West* (1980), in fratricide: "To the music of Lou Reed's *Perfect Day*, Boyo strangles his brother. Sid dies." Gwenny is left insane, carrying her brother's child, randomly quoting from *On the Road*.

Families, and the fault lines that run through them, are placed at the center of Thomas's drama, as Katie Gramich writes: "The dramas are littered with dead, buried, or lost fathers, with questing sons, rival brothers, mad mothers, and sexually-troubled, father-fixated daughters." In the September 2003 interview Thomas acknowledged the importance of this observation, noting that all his plays "involve the search for fathers."

The rewritten *House of America* opened at the Battersea Arts Centre in January 1989 and then toured around Wales, quickly becoming the Welsh theatrical sensation of that year. It was sold out in Cardiff for weeks and won the *Time Out* Award for best new play of 1989. This attention had partly to do with its cultural context: a young writer and cast, performing a play of power and energy that seemed to tap into the cynicism, anger, and sense of frustration felt by that 1980s Thatcherite generation, looking toward American cultural forms for inspiration. As Thomas explained to Walford Davies:

> American dramatists are lucky in having an exportable mythology. Take Sam Shepard for instance. . . . A dramatist writing in Wales has no global myths although we do have myths and stories that sustain us at home. But, unlike Sam Shepard, we have no *exportable* myths. And so a dramatist who works from a country without global myths has to work with primary colours.

Thomas realizes this obsession with American pop culture is ultimately self-defeating; like Sid in *House of America*, who awakes from his sub-Kerouac fantasy to confront his annihilation at the hands of his brother, Thomas admits to his own "love/hate" relationship with America, recognizing, like Shepard, the falsity and vacuousness of the American Dream. Thomas instead turns to those "primary colours," the signifiers of Welsh identity that are both celebrated and made strange in his dramatic works.

Along with his longtime collaborators Richard Lynch and Russell Gomer, Thomas created Y Cwmni (The Company), mostly to produce his own plays. Funded by the Welsh Arts Council, Y Cwmni became one of the most important Welsh theater companies of the 1990s, along with Brith Gof, Moving Being, Volcano, and Theatr Y Byd. This period marked a high point in Welsh cultural arts, with a thriving arts scene developing in Cardiff along with the regeneration of the city docklands. The next major work that Thomas wrote is the only Welsh-language play he has written to date, for the theater company Dalier Sylw. Called *Adar Heb Adenydd* (Birds Without Wings), this play opened in the Miners Welfare Hall, Ystradgynlais, on 29 May 1989. Y Cwmni and Dalier Sylw took *Adar Heb Adenydd* and *House of America* to the Edinburgh Festival that year under the double-bill heading *Raiders of the Western Shore*. Opening in August 1989, both plays had the same cast, with *House of America* performed in the evening and *Adar Heb Adenydd* in the afternoon, becoming the first Welsh-language production to play at the festival.

Thomas's next stage work, *The Myth of Michael Roderick*, was performed under the aegis of the *Mam Iath* (Mother Tongue) season at St. Stephens's Theatre, Cardiff, in November 1990. This play was an extension of the themes and ideas explored in *Adar Heb Adenydd*, although it cannot be viewed as a straight translation. David Adams writes that Thomas had become a de facto spokesperson for a "Welsh attachment to romantic ideas, the addiction of the return-of-Arthur dream, the resort to mythology, all expressed in a form that was a parody of Welsh anti-naturalism."

Thomas's next major play for Y Cwmni was *Flowers of the Dead Red Sea*, which was first performed at the Tramway, Glasgow, in September 1991 as part of the Theatre and Nations series, a program of plays exploring national identity within the United Kingdom. In *Flowers of the Dead Red Sea* two butchers in a "world of chains, knives, steel, blood and falling objects" dispute the validity of memory, art, and the singer Tom Jones's "dicky bow" (bow tie). The original stage version had a cast of seven, but Thomas subsequently rewrote the play to focus on the two butchers, Mock and Joe, whose verbal sparring takes in a range of subjects and stories, principally the refusal of Mock to accede to Joe's request to slaughter more than forty sheep a day:

> This steel was given to me by my father to put an edge on a blade to kill forty a day. FORTY AND NO MORE. If forty come in here, meet with my knife, leave their better parts on hooks and head, feet and skins on the floor, I will know that I have killed them with dignity, with a sharp blade; if I kill any more my blade will be blunt and they will die in shame. I am a craftsman, Joe, and I will not work in a bloodbath of shame.

Mock dreams of an oppressive silence, "a whole language, a way of life, a people drowning," ending in a vision of an artist dancing and "sprinkling yellow flowers on a dead red sea." This powerful image is an evocation of a language and culture slowly dying, the yellow flowers representing the daffodil, an icon of Welsh identity, drained of its symbolic value. This metaphor of "drowning" is an important motif in Welsh politics, as the flooding of the Cwm Celyn valley in the 1960s, obliterating the village of Capel Celyn to build the Tryweryn reservoir supplying Liverpool with water, resulted in an upsurge in Welsh nationalism in the next three decades.

With elements such as the detritus of modern life (including microwaves and prams) falling from the sky, disputes over the ownership of a dicky bow that may once have belonged to Jones, and the ritual slaughtering of sheep, *Flowers of the Dead Red Sea* highlights the ambiguous relationship of a cultural identity in crisis. That one of the objects falling from the sky is a kitchen sink reinforces the self-reflexivity of Thomas's writing, as his drama is antithetical to the conventions of a "kitchen-sink" theater—he rejects mimetic realism through his use of language and powerful stage images. David Ian Rabey describes this play as "a desperate vision of a shrinking island, increasingly submerged by shame, where memory is suffocated, forcing the characters into a relentless plunge inwards, hurtling to find something or someone to hold on to, amidst the grim sense of time running out." At the conclusion of the play, Mock, having lost his word duel with Joe, is hung on a hook "like a carcass," although his defiance is still articulated with the force of a nation refusing to submit to subjugation: "I am still here, Joe. I AM STILL HERE."

The reviews of *Flowers of the Dead Red Sea* at the Tramway exposed the critical obsession with social realism as the only legitimate source for exploring issues of national identity; Simon Berry's review from *The Scotsman* (11 September 1991) described the play as a "spluttering, incoherent, self-indulgent tirade with sporadic bursts of violence," while John Linklater for the *Glasgow Herald* (10 September 1991) wrote, "It is an extremely unpleasant experience, cacophonous, frenetic, brutal, and virtually unintelligible." In response to these negative reviews, an article in *The Scotsman* (14 September 1991) by the artistic director of the Tramway justified the play and its place in the Theatres and Nations series: "Such polarised reactions do remind me that hope is one of the essential commodities for a producing organisation like Tramway, or any other, when they choose to present artists who work in new contexts, who may be wilfully controversial or unpredictable, but whose work one believes in before just about any other consideration."

Flowers of the Dead Red Sea offers theatrical scenarios that point the way forward for Thomas's theatrical sensibility, leading to dialogue that is resolutely antinaturalistic, often employing a rhythmic cadence to the language that draws upon a heightened lyricism. In the September 2003 interview Thomas described this way of working as writing words and language independent of characterization, starting with rhythm and only later creating characters for the words.

House of America and *Flowers of the Dead Red Sea* introduce the major themes and concerns that subsequently dominated Thomas's drama: characters epitomized by the shifting of names and identity, and role-playing informed by the residue of pop music, cinema, and television. Music references as varied as The Velvet Underground, Nancy Sinatra, Dionne Warwick, and Iggy Pop litter his plays, with constant mentions of figures from popular culture. His reinvention of "Welshness" is dependent on knowingly deconstructing images of national identity. The characters that populate his dramas are dispossessed, suffering from a crisis of the self and lacking something. As Thomas said in the May 2001 interview, "one's identity is always in flux."

Thomas's next major play was *East from the Gantry,* which opened at the Tramway in October 1992 and then subsequently went on a major tour along with *House of America* and *Flowers of the Dead Red Sea* as the New Wales Trilogy. These works were published by Seren Press under the title *Three Plays* in 1994. The setting of *East from the Gantry* is "a derelict house," visually realized by the gradual revelation of several household objects hidden underneath white sheets. The play is one of Thomas's most subdued and evocative dramas, rich with metaphors and comic dialogue. The text combines

Cover for the 1994 collection of the plays that have become known as Thomas's "New Wales Trilogy" and that gained wider audiences for Welsh theater (Tulane University Library)

extended monologues with songs, creating a wistful meditation on the unpredictability of love and desire. The character Trampas takes his name and persona from the 1960s American television series *The Virginian*, speaking in an imitation of a classic Westerner: "Could be a good place in the right hands." He only reverts to his real name when faced with the consequences of his solitude—a life disconnected from "a house of love." Trampas's monologue from *East from the Gantry* becomes a powerful expression of longing for a sense of belonging:

> I thought I could be somebody, that's all, that I'd make it . . . get re-born, start again. *(pause)* I thought the stars would shine down on me and it would be there, in front of me, within grasp, reachable, to be had, felt, taken in hand and held, squeezed, there in front of me, a light flickering, a good thing, not far away, mine. . . .

Bella and Ronnie, husband and wife, are trapped inside a disintegrating marriage as Bella mourns her lost love Martin Bratton, who flew "east from the gantry"—a romantic metaphor for a prosaic death. But the play ends in an image of hope for the future, among the ruins of a burned-out house, as a "feast of friends" gathers to celebrate a new beginning: "Ronnie leads Trampas to the table. Bella pours some wine and lights some candles. The table looks beautifully laid, ready for something good to happen. They toast."

This New Wales Trilogy quickly established Thomas's reputation as the most important young dramatist to have emerged from Wales in the previous thirty years, and the plays made the concerns of Welsh theater visible to a wider audience in many productions outside of Wales and Britain. After the trilogy Thomas began filming *Silent Village/Pentre Mud* (1993), a documentary in Welsh and English that he had written in 1992. It was Thomas's first collaboration with the director Marc Evans, who subsequently went on to direct the 1997 movie version of *House of America*. It was also Y Cwmni's first nontheater project and was the first step toward the creation of Fiction Factory. In June 1992 *Flowers of the Dead Red Sea* was broadcast on BBC Radio 3, and in the same year a radio version of *East from the Gantry* was also broadcast. *East from the Gantry* toured Kiev and Ukraine in November 1992, becoming the first play from Wales to be performed in the former Soviet republics.

Thomas's next two theater projects were relatively different from his previous output. In 1993 Thomas collaborated with the artist Iwan Bala to create a bilingual theater installation, *Hiraeth/Strangers in Conversation*, performed at the Oriel Art Gallery in Cardiff. In it, two heads "appear in a landscape as if being born. They have no bodies. Both are blind." What is most notable about this piece is its specificity—it is the only play of Thomas's that exists inside its original performance context, rare for a writer most noted for reworking and restaging his plays. The two heads, Gwenny and Tyrone, are in "limbo," discussing apparently random subjects ranging from *Star Trek* to *The Magic Roundabout*, a British children's show from the 1960s. Many of the topics discussed are fragments from Thomas's plays and events from his life, drawing upon his obsession with rugby, pop culture, and myth; one speech by the head called Gwenny conflates Sid's murder in *House of America* with Thomas's own rugby injury:

> My brother went bananas see, killed my other brother with his own hands. Nobody thought he'd ever do such a thing, but it happened. They gave him fifteen years for that. He's served five. He reads a lot now. I

wrote him a letter a couple of years ago. I told him I forgave him. . . . He could have played international rugby if he hadn't got injured playing an away game in Merthyr. Ligaments, they said.

The heads compare their plight to the myth of Orpheus, still singing after his head is ripped from his body by the Bacchae; this allusion to classical myth is interesting in its attempt to make visible the situation of the heads, who can exist as long as they can speak, like Mock at the end of *Flowers of the Dead Red Sea*.

Hiraeth, a Welsh word evoking "home," spells out the longing for an existence defined by family, friends, and common factors connecting strangers. Tyrone berates Gwenny for her lack of pop-culture knowledge—"Fancy you not knowing who Spock is"—as the piece builds to Gwenny's speech detailing a horrific and violent assault played out to the sound of Frank and Nancy Sinatra singing "I Love You." This nightmare scenario ends, like the myth of Orpheus, with Gwenny's body desecrated on a beach. The speech concludes with her dead mother cradling her on this deserted beach: "She said that she was happy and she loved me. . . ." In Thomas's work the domestic arena frequently becomes symbolic as it roots down into mythic archetypes; the maternal body is the locus for a corporeal intimacy that disrupts patriarchal authority, an authority capable only of committing terrible, violent acts.

Hence the proliferations of absent fathers and mutilated (psychically and physically) mothers in Thomas's theater. Mam in *House of America* eats an imaginary bowl of cawl (a type of Welsh stew) in traditional Welsh costume. In *East from the Gantry* Trampas tells stories about his grandmother being accidentally shot and his mother dying "looking up at the ceiling with a Turkish Delight on her chest." Thomas's next play, *Envy*, also revolves around a dead mother and absent father. A one-man show written specifically for Y Cwmni regular Gomer, *Envy* is a bleakly comic routine about Ted John, caretaker of Cwmgiedd Miners Hall, whose obsession is to appear on *Mastermind*, a famous British television quiz show, to win the glass bowl his dead mother once liked to have on her mantelpiece. First performed in 1993 at the Chapter Arts Centre in Cardiff, *Envy* started life as a commission from Channel 4 television that was never broadcast. Thomas also started directing *A Mind to Kill*, a television police drama, between 1994 and 1997, and began his career as a broadcast producer with *Satellite City*, a radio serial on BBC Wales that transferred to television in 1996. In 1993 Thomas also wrote a television movie called *Fallen Sons*, which won him a Welsh British Academy of Film and Television Arts (BAFTA) award for best screenplay in 1994; his documentary *Silent Village/Pentre Mud* also won best documentary at the Celtic Film Festival in 1993. In 1994 the composer John Hardy wrote an opera based on *Flowers of the Dead Red Sea* called *Flowers*, which toured Germany with Music Theatre Wales to great acclaim until 1996.

In February 1995 *Song from a Forgotten City* opened at the Chapter Arts Centre in Cardiff before embarking on a long European tour. It played at the Royal Court Theatre in London in June 1995 as a Barclays New Stages Award winner before going on to tour in Bucharest, Bonn, and Melbourne. *Song from a Forgotten City* is a complex and disturbing drama. Ostensibly set in Cardiff on International Day when Wales has just lost to England at rugby, an event regarded as a catastrophe in Wales, the play is a lament for a moribund culture of defeat.

The reinvention of cultural identity is crucial to Carlyle, the protagonist of *Song from a Forgotten City*, a writer who constructs his own narrative surrounding his suicide. The first scene of the play is set in the Angel Hotel in Cardiff, a famous landmark in the city, where the generic characters of the Night-Porter and the Bellboy perform their roles according to Carlyle's script. The action of the play begins with a dead Carlyle in his hotel room, a tape recorder repeating: "'Binoculars' said my father. 'Whatever you do don't let him have the binoculars.'" The narrative then unfolds as if it were a flashback in a movie.

This cinematic technique is further enhanced by the flashing up of the title of the play accompanied by Iggy Pop's song "Passenger," creating the illusion of a movie title sequence. The specified lighting is a full moon and a neon sign, making it clear that the play is encased within the cinematic mise-en-scène of film noir. This playing with genre and theatricality is both strangely evocative and compelling for the audience, as the surreal and dislocated atmosphere governs the spectator's responses to this milieu. As a play on cinematic intertextuality there are intimations of Ethan and Joel Coen's movie *Barton Fink* (1991), a story of a writer trapped in a hotel that becomes the embodiment of hell.

Carlyle informs the Night-Porter and the Bellboy that they are minor characters in a fiction that he is creating, as the "phone" for the hotel becomes a gun, and then a carrot, much to the Night-Porter's disgust: "DOESN'T THE MANAGEMENT IN THIS PLACE KNOW THAT A BANANA MAKES A BETTER IMAGINARY PHONE THAN A CARROT?" This constant distortion of imaginative space impinges on the reliability of what is being presented. The competing narratives surrounding each character's response to the rugby defeat illustrate these conflicting versions of "reality." The Bellboy, the Night-Porter, and Carlyle

Dorien Thomas as Carlyle, Richard Lynch as the Bellboy, and Russ Gomer as the Night-Porter in the 1995 Royal Court Theatre production of Thomas's Song from a Forgotten City, *in which a writer creates a narrative of fictions and memories around his suicide (photograph by Brian Tarr; from '95–'98* Selected Work, *2002; University of Kentucky Libraries)*

situate themselves in a specific scenario and place where they watch or hear of the catastrophe. The Night-Porter is in "A bog. Hayes Island cubicle three, frosted glass looking up at the street" with "A four-pack, a spliff and some liquorice allsorts." He knows of the defeat by the sound of the heavy tread of the defeated Welshmen making their way home above him: "ten thousand. . . . In defeat." The Bell Boy listens to the defeat on the radio by the river opposite the stadium, watching a plastic Sindy doll being masturbated over by a fellow Welshman who states his identity with no sense of irony: "I'm Welsh and I'm fucked in the head. We're losing." Carlyle's account is a longing for a collective experience—his simple desire to sing after the match. In search of company to sing with, Carlyle goes to the Albert pub in St. Mary's Street, another famous Cardiff landmark, to be greeted by "a silent Welsh crowd." In despair at the crowd's inability to sing, the barman slits his wrists and bleeds to death in silence; meanwhile,

> somebody switched on the TV. To watch the highlights. In the Welsh language. A bloke with a moustache. "Anelu at y pissed" said the commentator. Don't know what the fuck it meant. We all watched the highlights in a language we don't understand. But the score was the same.

Each story locates the action within the specific geography of the city. Each story imagines responses to defeat that are resigned (drugged), narcissistic (masturbatory), and catastrophic (suicidal). Carlyle—the "writer" of the story—articulates the loss of collective expression, juxtaposed against the absurdity of the Welsh-language TV highlights that the rugby supporters in the pub are unable to comprehend (since Welsh is a minority language spoken by only a small percentage of the population, even in Wales).

The absence at the center of a reinvented Welsh identity is dramatized in *Song from a Forgotten City* as the lack of a thriving metropolis, as Carlyle dreams of a utopian capital:

> This ain't the city for dreamers man. Sometimes I'm not sure it's a city at all, more like a place waiting for something good to happen. Like it hasn't been invented yet. Like it doesn't really believe it exists.

And a country without a metropolis is not a country: "I came to the city in search of a metropolis and found only Cardiff." Instead, what is presented is a squalid, nihilistic existence of prostitution, drug abuse, and murder, as act 2 opens in a docklands squat, where Carlyle and two "smack heads," Jojo and Benny, play out drug-induced scenarios of conflicting anecdotes, centering around the figure of Carlyle's dead "woman" Yvonne. Act 2 unravels this alienation of the dispossessed, as Carlyle acknowledges that his unfolding narratives are caused by his addiction to heroin, and memory itself becomes an illusion: "Wouldn't it be good to have a pure memory . . . a pure recollection of good things that have happened." Carlyle articulates a longing that is both personal and social; his desire for a "giant family" full of laughter betrays his alienation, as he rejects the squalid realism of Jojo and Benny's flat for the safety of his imagination.

The final image of the play is Carlyle pointing a gun at his head, locked into the fictional world of the Angel Hotel. The narrative does not end with the final stage direction, although of course the play does: *"CARLYLE brings the gun to his head and laughs. He pulls the trigger. He stands there smiling."* This action begins the cycle of fictions and memory that the play circles around.

Song from a Forgotten City attempts to "give a voice to the voiceless," as Carlyle explains to the Night-Porter:

> Our voices must be heard Night-Porter, we must play our part on the world stage. We've got to show that the way we live, love and die means something, that we are part of the world, not unique but similar, universal, like small countries all over the world! You're a minor character Night-Porter.

Song from a Forgotten City is arguably Thomas's darkest and most elaborately constructed play to date. The review from *Scotland on Sunday* described it as "a post-modern theatrical car crash, a mind blowing evening, a fierce elaborate brilliant stream of consciousness." It was hugely popular in Germany, where Thomas played the part of Carlyle in Bonn in June 1996, and it played the Four Nations festival at the Donmar Warehouse in London in October 1996. It has been translated into German and Catalan and marks the high point of Y Cwmni/Fiction Factory's theater work.

While touring *Song from a Forgotten City* Fiction Factory collaborated on a motion picture version of *House of America*, which opened in London in October 1996 and became the first Welsh movie to be shown at the Sundance Film Festival in Utah in January 1997 (it was released generally in the United Kingdom in October 1997). The movie won Welsh BAFTA awards for best picture and best director for Evans and won the same awards at the Göteborg International Film Festival. At the same time Fiction Factory also embarked on a major tour of the play version of *House of America,* starting in Cardiff in October 1997 and ending up in Perth, Australia, on 25 February 1998.

Thomas's next new stage play opened in Newcastle on 8 May 1998 before transferring to the Royal Court Theatre Upstairs, London, on 3 June 1998. *Gas Station Angel* again marked out Thomas's concerns with family conflict; but rather than focus on a single family, *Gas Station Angel* relates the story of two families whose lives become inextricably and tragically entwined. The Aces of Gaerlishe live in a house that is crumbling into the sea. Bron and Marshall James are mourning the disappearance of their brother, Bri, who, unable to accept his place in the family schematic after Marshall was rescued from drowning, departed into nowhere. Hywel Ace, the narrator of the story, becomes the focus for audience identification, guiding the spectator through the past events that bring the two families in contact with one another. If *Song from a Forgotten City* is Thomas's most nihilistic, despairing play, then *Gas Station Angel* is optimistic, looking forward to the future rather than being trapped in a cycle of negation. At the center of this optimism is the relationship between Ace and Bron, a romantic and nostalgic vision of teenage love: "Some people are born lucky; others are born to lose. I want me and Bron to be the lucky ones. In sixteen hours forty eight minutes she's turned my world upside down and I know in my bones things are never going to be the same again."

At the core of this play is a delight in playing with realist convention, as Thomas creates an "underworld of faeries, angels and demons" that invade the "real" space and create the closest thing to "magic" on the stage. As the Aces' house falls into the sea, the mother, Mary Annie, mourns her lost babies, taken by "the fairies from the otherworld," while the father, Manny, rages against the storm that swallows his house: "So rip down our house, sea . . . do your worst. Because you'll never beat me. We'll still be here. I'll still be here. I WILL STILL BE HERE!!!" This speech has echoes of Mock's defiance at the end of *Flowers of the Dead Red Sea*, a willful refusal to back down in the face of overwhelming odds. Thomas has achieved his stated intention of making Wales visible in a wider European context, and *Gas Station Angel,* more than any other play, looks forward to the role that postdevolution Wales will play in the new Europe of the twenty-first century:

> ACE: As I sat in the car that night looking out from the back of beyond to the shores of North Africa, I felt in my bones the times are a-changing. Maybe I can soon call myself a European. A Welsh European, with my

Russ Gomer as Gruff and Roger Evans as Marshall in the 1998 Newcastle Playhouse premiere of Thomas's Gas Station Angel, *in which a romance and secrets connect two families (from '95–'98 Selected Work, 2002; University of Kentucky Libraries)*

own language and the rudiments of another on the tip of my tongue, German, French, Spanish, Portuguese, Russian, Czech, even English.

Like most of Thomas's plays, *Gas Station Angel* ends in death, the mystery of Bri's vanishing revealed as his accidental killing by Ace's mother, a story told by Ace in segments that slowly fit together. This manipulation of narrative time is one way in which Thomas is able to disrupt the linear progression of continuity in his plays. In a review from June 1998, Heike Roms described the effect of *Gas Station Angel* in performance:

> Formally, the play combines the strong characterisation of Thomas's early work, most notably *House of America*, with the conceptual sharpness and lyricism of the later plays, which makes it as emotionally moving as it is intellectually satisfying. The poeticism of the writing, however, produces a strangely non-dramatic effect, for the plot seems of less importance than the way in which the characters interpret and retell it. This creates a narrative complexity which, though maybe undramatic, is nonetheless very theatrical: one is never quite sure whether what is told in the present is a memory of things past or an imagining of the future–an effect which Thomas, as his own director, manages to underline by his fluid staging.

After *Gas Station Angel*, Thomas directed his first major motion picture, a 2000 adaptation of James Hawes's novel *Rancid Aluminium* (1997). It was not a productive experience for Thomas, who admitted in *'95–'98 Selected Work* (2002) that the project "was the worst thing I ever got involved with." This period was also an unhappy one in Thomas's personal life, as he separated from and divorced his wife, Helen, whom he had married in 1991. His theater work was still being produced overseas, with productions of *Gas Station Angel* in Berlin and Rome and productions of *House of America* in Zagreb and Montreal. But for all intents and purposes Thomas had given up working in the theater, "burnt out" by a constant workload of a play a year since 1988 and running his own production company. As he cheerfully admitted in the September 2003 interview, between 1998 and 2002 he was "a retired playwright," continuing to produce and direct *A Mind to Kill* in 1999 and directing a Welsh-language television series called *Fondue, Rhyw A Deinosors* (2001–2004; Fondue, Sex and Dinosaurs), a fantastical delve into altered states of being, not unlike the magic realism of Dennis Potter. He won a Welsh BAFTA award in 2002 for directing this series, becoming the only person to have won Welsh BAFTA awards for writing, producing, and directing.

Thomas returned to the theater in November 2002 in collaboration with Mike Pearson and Mike Brookes on *Rain Dogs*, a fluid multimedia piece that mixed movies and storytelling. Thomas found this collaborative work intriguing and challenging as the three played around with form and structure to create a performance context that changed every evening. He wrote and read text that was mixed and intercut with live and recorded video footage of the city at night, moving his approach to theater in radical new directions. In the September 2003 interview Thomas expressed his desire to work with areas not limited to a stage, actors, and set, but to branch out into installation work, to experiment with mixed media and sonic art, to create something new. As a writer Thomas was always mixing up threads of narrative, writing free-form dialogue that was only grafted onto characterization at a later date. This new collaborative work is an extension of his previous mode of working, building arbitrary constructions of narrative threads in order to create a continuity of meaning. Thomas describes this working technique as "free association," and it is a return to what started him writing in the first place, the complex language weaving of Kerouac.

Thomas's next play, *Stone City Blue,* opened on 21 October 2004 in Mold, North Wales, directed by the author. It represents a new departure in his work, moving toward the poetic evocation of place and time in a dramatic form that is both challenging and, in places, strangely comforting. The play depicts the unreliability of memory by presenting the distorted mind of a character known as Ray, played by four different actors, two male and two female. The refracted voices belong to several different, competing selves, all struggling for dominance within the same psyche. Whatever is or is not true is up for grabs in the play; instability lies at the heart of this drama that plays around with genre, sexual identity, and the debilitating accumulation of memories that cannot be exorcised. Reviewer Cathryn Scott commented, "*Stone City Blue* is by no means perfect, but it's an innovative work that pushes boundaries. If this comeback piece is the sign of things to come from Thomas, then the future looks very promising indeed."

Interview:

Hazel Walford Davies, "Not Much of a Dream, Then Is It?" in *State of Play: Four Playwrights of Wales,* edited by Walford Davies (Llandysul: Gomer, 1998).

References:

Katie Gramich, "Edward Thomas: Geography, Intertextuality and the Lost Mother," in *State of Play: Four Playwrights of Wales,* edited by Hazel Walford Davies (Llandysul: Gomer, 1998);

David Ian Rabey, "Why Can't This Crazy Love Be Mine," in *Frontline Intelligence 1: New Plays for the Nineties,* edited by Pamela Edwardes (London: Methuen, 1993).

Michelene Wandor
(20 April 1940 –   )

Margaret Llewellyn-Jones
London Metropolitan University

PLAY PRODUCTIONS: *You Two Can Be Ticklish,* London, Lamb and Flag Theatre, 1970;

Brag-a-Fruit, London, 1971;

The Day After Yesterday, London, Act Inn Theatre Club, 1972;

Spilt Milk and *Mal de Mere,* London, Portable Theatre, 1972;

To Die Among Friends, London, Paradise Foundry, 1973;

Friends & Strangers, tour, 1974;

The Old Wives' Tale, London, Soho Poly, 21 March 1977;

Penthesilia, adapted from Heinrich von Kleist's play, London, Salt Theatre, 1977;

Care and Control, London, Drill Hall, May 1977;

Floorshow, by Wandor, Caryl Churchill, Bryony Lavery, and David Bradford, London, North London Polytechnic, October 1977;

Whores D'Oeuvres, Nottingham, Midland Theatre, 8 February 1978;

Scissors, London, Almost Free Theatre, 2 April 1978;

AID Thy Neighbour, London, Theatre at New End, 10 October 1978;

Aurora Leigh, adapted from Elizabeth Barrett Browning's verse-novel, London, 1979; London, Olivier Theatre (National Theatre), 14 April 1981;

Correspondence, London, Institute of Contemporary Arts, 1979;

Rutherford & Son, adapted from Githa Sowerby's play, London, Royal Court Theatre, 1980;

The Blind Goddess, adapted from Ernst Toller's play, London, Red Ladder Theatre Company, 1981;

Future Perfect, by Wandor, Steve Gooch, and Paul Thompson, Wakefield, Wakefield Tricycle, 1981;

Whose Greenham and *Mal de Mere,* London, Barbican, 1986;

The Wandering Jew, adapted by Wandor and Mike Alfreds from Eugène Sue's novel, London, Lyttleton Theatre (National Theatre), August 1987;

Wanted, London, Drill Hall, 16 March 1988;

York, text by Wandor, music by Malcolm Singer, York, St. Michael le Belfrey, 1990;

Spain, adapted from John Cornford's poem, text by Wandor, music by Matthew Linley, Oxford, Oriel College, 1993;

Samson Agonistes, adapted from John Milton's poem, text by Wandor, music by Matthew Power, London, Hillingdon Church, 1994;

The Indian Queen, adapted from John Dryden and Sir Robert Howard's play, text by Wandor, music by Henry Purcell, London, Queen Elizabeth Hall, 1995;

Brecht & Weill: A Diversion, London, Greenwich Festival, 1995.

BOOKS: *Sink Songs: Plays,* by Wandor and Dinah Brooke (London: Playbooks, 1975)—includes *To Die Among Friends, Mal de Mere, Joey, Christmas, Pearls,* and *Swallows;*

The Great Divide: The Sexual Division of Labour, or, Is It Art? by Wandor and others (London: Open University Press, 1976);

Understudies: Theatre & Sexual Politics (London: Methuen, 1981); revised as *Carry On, Understudies: Theatre & Sexual Politics* (London & New York: Routledge & Kegan Paul, 1986);

Touch Papers, by Wandor, Judith Kazantzis, and Michèle Roberts (London & New York: Allison & Busby, 1982);

Upbeat: Poems and Stories (London & West Nyack, N.Y.: Journeyman Press, 1982; New York: Riverrun, 1985);

Five Plays (London & West Nyack, N.Y.: Journeyman Press, 1984; New York: Riverrun, 1985)—comprises *To Die Among Friends, The Old Wives' Tale, Whores D'Oeuvres, Scissors,* and *AID Thy Neighbour;*

Gardens of Eden: Poems for Eve & Lilith (London: Journeyman, 1984; New York: Riverrun, 1985);

Guests in the Body (London: Virago, 1986);

Look Back in Gender: Sexuality and the Family in Post-War British Drama (London & New York: Methuen,

1987); revised and expanded as *Post-War British Drama: Looking Back in Gender* (London & New York: Routledge, 2001);

Arky Types, by Wandor and Sara Maitland (London: Methuen, 1987);

The Wandering Jew, adapted by Wandor and Mike Alfreds from Eugène Sue's novel (London & New York: Methuen, 1987);

Wanted (London: Playbooks, 1988);

Once A Feminist: Stories of a Generation (London: Virago, 1990);

Gardens of Eden: Selected Poems (London: Hutchinson, 1990); revised and expanded as *Gardens of Eden Revisited* (Nottingham: Five Leaves, 1999);

Drama Today: A Critical Guide to British Drama, 1970–1990 (London & New York: Longman in association with the British Council, 1993);

False Relations (Nottingham: Five Leaves, 2004).

PRODUCED SCRIPTS: *Correspondence,* radio, BBC Radio 4, 1978;

Dust in the Sugar House, radio, BBC Radio 3, 1979;

Aurora Leigh, adapted from Elizabeth Barrett Browning's verse-novel, radio, BBC Radio 3, 1981;

The Ultimate Astonisher, radio, BBC Radio 3, 1982;

An Uncommon Love, radio, BBC Radio 4, 1984;

Kipps, adapted from H. G. Wells's novel, radio, BBC Radio 4, 1984;

Friend to Friend, radio, BBC Radio 4, 1984;

Venus Smiles, adapted from J. G. Ballard's story, radio, BBC Radio 4, 1985;

A Consoling Blue, radio, BBC Radio 4, 1985;

The Nine Tailors, adapted from Dorothy L. Sayers's novel, radio, BBC Radio 4, 1986;

The Brothers Karamazov, adapted from Fyodor Dostoevsky's novel, radio, BBC Radio 4, 1986;

Persuasion, adapted from Jane Austen's novel, radio, BBC Radio 4, 1986;

The Belle of Amherst, adapted from William Luce's play, television, Thames TV, 1986;

Gardens of Eden, text by Wandor, music by Michael Nyman, radio, BBC Radio 4, 1987;

The Story of an Hour, adapted from Kate Chopin's short story, television, Thames TV, 1988;

Separation, adapted from Tom Kempinski's play, radio, BBC World Service, 1989;

Frenchman's Creek, adapted from Daphne du Maurier's novel, radio, BBC Radio 4, 1989;

Ben Venga Maggio, radio, BBC Radio 3, 1990;

The Courtier, the Prince and the Lady, text by Wandor, music by Josquin and others, radio, BBC Radio 3, 1990;

The Mill on the Floss, adapted from George Eliot's novel, radio, BBC Radio 4, 1991;

A Summer Wedding, radio, BBC Radio 3, 1991;

Love & Friendship, radio, BBC Radio 3, 1992;

Bitter Medicine, adapted from Sara Paretsky's novel, radio, BBC Radio 4, 1993;

Jane Eyre, adapted from Charlotte Brontë's novel, radio, BBC Radio 4, 1994;

The Jungle Book, adapted from Rudyard Kipling's stories, radio, BBC Radio 5, 1994;

Power Cut, radio, BBC Radio 4, 1994;

Body of Glass, adapted from Marge Piercy's novel, radio, BBC Radio 4, 1995;

The Piano, adapted from Jane Campion and Kate Pullinger's novel, radio, BBC Radio 4, 1995;

Arms & the Man, adapted from George Bernard Shaw's play, radio, BBC World Service, 1995;

Orlando & Friends, adapted from Ludovico Ariosto's poem, text by Wandor, music by Wandor and The Siena Ensemble, radio, BBC Radio 3, 1995;

New For Old: Myths Retold, radio, BBC Radio 3, 1996;

Gone to Earth, adapted from Mary Webb's novel, radio, BBC Radio 4, 1996;

Crumbs, radio, BBC Radio 4, 1996;

Ethan Frome, adapted from Edith Wharton's novel, radio, BBC Radio 4, 1997;

The Queen of Spades, adapted from Aleksandr Pushkin's story, radio, BBC Radio 4, 1997;

Greensleeves, radio, BBC Radio 4, 1997;

The Moonstone, adapted from Wilkie Collins's novel, radio, BBC World Service, 1998;

Corridors of Light and Shadow, radio, BBC Radio 3, 1999;

A Lifelong Passion, radio, BBC Radio 4, 1999;

A Mist of Fine Rain, radio, BBC Radio 4, 1999;

The Cage, adapted from Henry James's story, radio, BBC Radio 4, 1999;

The Clock of Heaven, radio, BBC Radio 4, 1999;

Via Angelica, radio, BBC Radio 4, 2002;

Out of Sweetness, radio, BBC Radio 3, 2002;

Enchantment, radio, BBC Radio 4, 2002.

OTHER: *The Body Politic: Writings from the Women's Liberation Movement in Britain, 1969–1972,* edited, with contributions, by Wandor (London: Stage One, 1972);

Cutlasses & Earrings, edited, with contributions, by Wandor and Michèle Roberts (London: Playbooks, 1977);

"Feminist Fiction and Language," "Keep It Clean," "Radio Times," and "Time, Gentlemen," in *Tales I Tell My Mother: A Collection of Feminist Short Stories,* edited by Zoe Fairbairns (London & West Nyack, N.Y.: Journeyman Press, 1978; Boston: South End Press, 1980);

Mary Webb, *Precious Bane,* introduction by Wandor (London: Virago, 1978);

"The Personal is Political: Feminism & Theatre," in *Dreams and Deconstructions: Alternative Theatre in Britain,* edited by Sandy Craig (Ambergate, U.K.: Amber Lane Press, 1980);

Care and Control, in *Strike While the Iron is Hot: Three Plays on Sexual Politics,* edited, with an introduction, by Wandor (London & West Nyack, N.Y.: Journeyman Press, 1980);

"Motherhood," in *Why Children?* edited by Stephanie Dowrick and Sibyl Grundberg (London: Women's Press, 1980; New York: Harcourt Brace Jovanovich, 1980);

Spilt Milk and *Mal de Mere,* in *Play Nine: Nine Short Plays,* edited by Robin Rook (London: Edward Arnold, 1981);

British Alternative Theatre Directory, foreword by Wandor (Eastbourne, U.K.: John Offord, 1982);

Plays by Women, volumes 1–4, edited by Wandor (London & New York: Methuen, 1982–1985);

On Gender and Writing, edited, with contributions, by Wandor (London & Boston: Pandora, 1983);

Essay, in *Walking on the Water: Women Talk about Spirituality,* edited by Sara Maitland and Jo Garcia (London: Virago, 1983);

Short story, in *Passion Fruit: Romantic Fiction with a Twist,* edited by Jeanette Winterson (London: Pandora, 1986);

"Judy's Kiss," in *Stepping Out: Short Stories on Friendships Between Women,* edited by Ann Oosthuizen (London & New York: Pandora, 1986);

Short story, in *Close Company: Stories of Mothers and Daughters,* edited by Christine Park and Caroline Heaton (London: Virago, 1987);

Contributions, in *More Tales I Tell My Mother: Feminist Short Stories,* edited by Fairbairns (London: Journeyman Press, 1987);

Essay-poem, in *Very Heaven: Looking Back at the 1960's,* edited by Sara Maitland (London: Virago, 1988).

Michelene Wandor has played an extraordinary role within the development of contemporary British theater as both a critical commentator upon its evolution and as a dramatist. Her range of work includes stage plays, poetry, short stories, a co-authored novel, television and radio drama—especially dramatizations of novels—and influential books, articles, and reviews on issues including gender, theater, and sexual politics. Her interest in music is also reflected in her librettos. Wandor inaugurated and edited the first four volumes of the Methuen *Plays by Women* series beginning in 1982, providing a groundbreaking opportunity for publication of new, especially fringe work: many of these playwrights have since become well-known.

Born in London on 20 April 1940, Wandor attended Chingford Secondary School in northeast London, moving in 1956 to the County High School and then to Newnham College Cambridge from 1959 to 1962, where she obtained a B.A. (honors) degree in English. In 1963 Wandor married Ed Victor, a literary agent; they divorced in 1975. She has two sons. Wandor further earned an M.A. in the sociology of literature from the University of Essex (1976); an L.T.C.L., and a Dip.T.C.L. from the Trinity College of Music in London; and an M.Mus. from the University of London and Trinity College of Music. As a performer of Renaissance and baroque music, Wandor is the director of two early-music groups: The Siena Ensemble and Pizza Baroque. She has been poetry editor of *Time Out* magazine (1971–1982), contributed to *Spare Rib* magazine (1972–1977), and reviewed for *Plays & Players, The Listener, New Statesman,* and the BBC Radio 4 programs *Kaleidoscope* and *Saturday Review.* She has been playwright-in-residence at the University of Kent, Canterbury (1982–1983), and has throughout her career taught a variety of fiction, poetry, and drama courses and workshops, including a regular playwriting course at the Guildhall School of Drama; a weekly playwriting class at the City Lit; and short courses at the Actors' Centre, all in London. She is also a part-time lecturer in creative writing at the University of North London. This wide range of experience has contributed to Wandor's evolution as a writer and her perspectives on theater and society, which are integral to her plays.

Although Wandor has been closely involved with groups prominent in the post-1968 flowering of radical theater, including Portable Theatre, Gay Sweatshop, Mrs. Worthington's Daughters, Red Ladder, and Monstrous Regiment, her theater work is not narrowly political or mechanistically didactic in form. As she explains in her introduction to the collection *Strike While the Iron is Hot: Three Plays on Sexual Politics* (1980):

> Theatre does not by itself produce theory or claim to head political organisation. It reflects and transforms theoretical and political knowledge and practice into Works of art—even the crudest piece of instrumental agitprop touches an emotional and personal response in a way that a political pamphlet cannot—cooperation and immediacy enhance both art and politics.

From the first, her plays have been driven by a concern for and awareness of the details of human experience, through which the ideological concerns are effectively explored without the overemphasis of an overtly post-Brechtian approach. Paradoxically, although her characters often evoke strong emotional responses, Wandor generally eschews the limitations of realism as a form, while her strongest work draws upon powerful theatrical metaphor and is sometimes surreal. In an unpublished 22 March 1999 interview with Margaret Llewellyn-Jones, Wandor stated: "I don't think form is politically an issue. I think content determines form.... I don't have an attitude on form. It is just what works."

Further, although the plays are concerned with feminist issues, such as questions of sexual identity, motherhood, surrogacy, and prostitution, Wandor does not consider that there is a particular feminist aesthetic or "écriture feminine"—theatrical forms, styles, and languages peculiar to women—as claimed by some practitioners and critics on the basis of French feminist theories. Wandor examines the social context within which her characters live, combining critical, creative, and political elements that in her introduction to her contributions in *Play Nine: Nine Short Plays* (1981) she claims were seen as separate until the early 1970s. She writes, "I would describe my plays as political rather than polemical." The settings within which the plays take place are simple, with a mixture of functional and symbolic elements—typical of the inexpensive, easily reassembled effects needed for traveling fringe performance.

Wandor's earliest piece, *You Two Can Be Ticklish*, about a couple who tickle a stranger to death, was seen at the Lamb and Flag Theatre in 1970, while *The Day After Yesterday*, at the Act Inn Theatre Club in 1972, was about "Miss World and the rest of us." Events such as the feminist attack on the Miss World contest in 1970, and the celebratory International Women's Day parade of 1971 led by the newly formed Women's Theatre Group, suggest the close relationship between Wandor's work and radical activities.

Spilt Milk and *Mal de Mere* were both originally performed by Portable Theatre in 1972. Both are about the traps associated with motherhood and daughterhood. The former, flowing quickly from one brief scene to another, features a Voice expressing authoritarian views; a Toddler and a Judge, played by the same person; a couple, Helen and Graham; and a Woman and a Man. The disembodied Voice opens the play with a dispassionate description of the birth process, followed by a cacophony of domestic sounds, then the Toddler crying "I want a drink." Next, in a bedroom scene, Helen and Graham discuss a prospective baby; then a Judge demands of a Mrs. A whether she is guilty or not guilty, saying later "I charge you with being a mother." Constant intercutting between episodes with contrasting levels of domestic and institutional discourse highlights different gender attitudes to child care. A Woman at a party says "Such beautiful children," while the Man replies, "Children should be seen and not heard." The doubling of Judge and Toddler suggests the way that society, like a child, demands from mothers what is sometimes the impossible. The tension between the public or institutional perspective and the personal runs through Wandor's work.

Mal de Mere had further performances in the Almost Free Lunch Hour Theatre during 1973. Two women, A and V, are in a circle with invisible edges, with a central chair as the only prop as they act out relationships fraught with emotional struggle. A remains within the circle until the end, when she speaks her last line—"My name is Jenny"—from outside it. V, who initially seems dominant and capable of moving in and out of the circle, finally remains trapped and silent. Throughout the five sections of the play, a constant slippage of roles generally gives V more aggressive positions, including those of the overly possessive

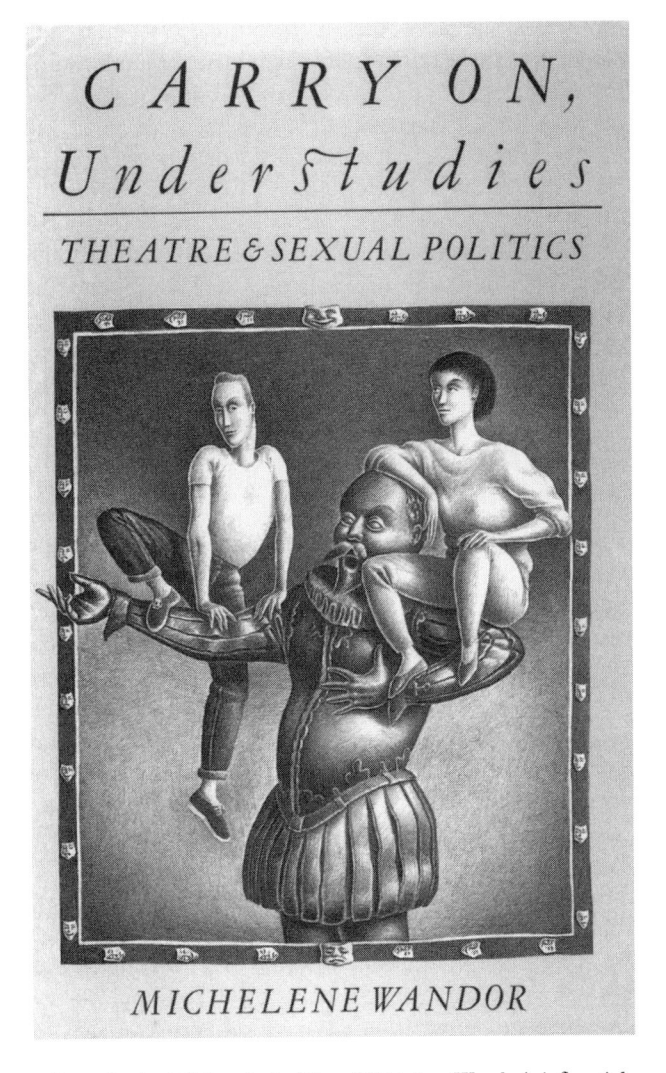

Cover for the 1986 revised edition of Michelene Wandor's influential 1981 study, which includes her own experiences in her examination of the "Second Wave" of postwar women playwrights (Thomas Cooper Library, University of South Carolina)

mother, while A is the overprotected daughter and sometimes speaks of herself in the third person, echoing her mother's attitudes: "I can't come out, she's not feeling very well, I can't get out." This splitting of the self indicates the internalized self-censorship that arises from being compelled to live up to the expectations of others. V also adopts the roles of censorious neighbors ("That Mrs. Roberts really spoils her kid"); the Father, who is starved for time to know the child; and the Headmistress, who criticizes Jenny as "Very talented and self-centred, she finds it hard to make friends." Events flow quickly to Jenny's marriage and motherhood, in which V constantly interferes. Jenny suffers from postnatal depression, with nightmares about the baby and motherhood: "the smell is suffocating me," she says, "I want to get out." Again, the doubling, abstract form and fluid performance style enable the audience to perceive the pressure behind the traditional, socially constructed mother/daughter roles while also recognizing the emotional accuracy of a claustrophobic relationship.

To Die Among Friends, first performed by the Paradise Foundry in London in 1973, included *Mal de Mere* in a series of five similarly minimalist duologues about identity and sexual politics. The other four are *Joey, Christmas, Pearls,* and *Swallows.* The first, between Joey and a female called M, starts with Joey's being prevented from going out to play. From child-like interchanges with stereotypical references to muddy rough boys and frilly girls, the piece develops through time, showing the pressures to conform to traditional masculine behavior in terms of competition and sexuality. M plays a girl who sets one boy against another, then wheedles Joey to like her best. From this scenario, suggestive of confused adolescent sexuality, evolves a triangular situation between wife, husband, and Joey, in which it is not certain who loves and who hates whom. The situation, like Joey's gender preference, is unresolved, with a potential for endless repetition.

Christmas is a duologue between two males, A and B, that at one level is about presents but at another reveals class and economic differences, acting as a critique of masculinity and competition. A obtains a "trophy wife," while B finds a partner and develops a more egalitarian attitude to gender and marriage, quoting a socialist maxim, "From each according to his ability, to each according to his needs." He seems to persuade A that compromise is needed both at work and home.

Pearls starts with "Happy Birthday" sung as He gives She a pinafore and a box of chocolates. These uninspired gifts and the husband's repeated requests for cups of tea prompt the revelation of the couple's subtextual resentments. After various exchanges, stage directions state "the couple become rather younger" and behave like a "modern liberated couple." This section now reads rather ironically, despite She's heartfelt offstage cry "And no self," prompted by He's complaints about the damaging influence of feminism. A positive ending suggests that although, as the proverb states, "one swallow does not make a summer," small personal choices do matter.

In the *Swallows* duologue, O is an older woman and Y a younger one. Y is reluctant to hear O's views; they argue about roles, freedom, fulfillment, and whether children hold women back, as Y fears. Y exhorts O to step outside what she sees as her already defined role, and to come away with Y and her friends. O says, "You cannot be free of yourself," and learns that Y's aim is "To die among friends," presumably rather than in a conventional family. Despite the accuracy of some attitudes shown, some critics feel these duologues now seem dated, since progress has been made in challenging traditional gender roles.

Following these early plays, Wandor acknowledges in *Carry On, Understudies: Theatre & Sexual Politics* (1986) that the tension between collective work and the individual voice, as well as the demands of caring for two small children, prompted her to explore her own motivation and aims in writing. The consequent slight gap in Wandor's theater output can also be partly attributed to her work on her M.A. through part-time study that took her out of the creative community within which she had been working. She returned to theater with *The Old Wives' Tale,* directed by Caroline Eves at Soho Poly in London in 1977. In this play about three women in retirement—Gertie, Ellie, and Katie—the performance space is divided among three tables: one in a North London Evening Institute canteen, one in Gertie's home, and one in Ellie's home. Within a realist narrative are woven intertextual references to William Shakespeare's *Macbeth* (circa 1606), in which the women are to perform as witches with one of the Evening Institute classes. Meg, a young and pregnant canteen worker who may return to college, provides a frame/contrast with the older women. Gertie has retained her radical, uninhibited spirit, joking about a condom found in the canteen; Ellie, more circumspect and childless, apparently happily married to Fred, becomes a "lollipop lady" (a children's crossing guard); Katie, about to retire, doubts that her daughter is sincere in suggesting she move to the seaside to be near the grandchildren. Reminiscences at rehearsal reveal that Gertie's illegitimate wartime son hopes to meet her, and that Fred unknowingly was the father. Though she never loved a man, Gertie cautions Meg against having her baby adopted. A last rehearsal in an empty space shows Katie has cleared out furniture, emphasizing the entrapping walls. The last scene reveals that the *Macbeth* production has been postponed after Katie's suicide attempt. As the others leave to visit her in the hospital, Gertie tells Meg an old wives' tale about finding out the gender of an unborn baby. This use of the witches and their spells enhances a deconstructive approach to societal attitudes toward aging women, while exploration of their different characters, class, lifestyles, political attitudes, and economic backgrounds creates a full picture of them as individuals. This play about older women shows not only potential loneliness and isolation but also mutual friendship and support.

Care and Control (performed in 1977, published in 1980), created collaboratively with Gay Sweatshop, is considered a landmark play in its approach to the custody rights of lesbian mothers. Lizbeth Goodman cites it as the group's most influential work, the "first play produced by the Sweatshop Women's Company as an autonomous group" after the split with the Men's Company. Wandor wrote the script "after extensive periods of research, workshops and devising by the company." Actor and director Nancy Diuguid was responsible for the research, and the play was first performed in the Drill Hall during May 1977, then recast for the Edinburgh Festival that August. Jill Posener, photographer and author of *Any Woman Can* (1976), one of the first coming-out plays about lesbians, was in the cast. *Care and Control* was also performed at Rose Bruford Drama School in London in 1978. The simple set, as indicated in the text, consisted of straw mats, a blank wall upstage for showing slides, cushions indicative of living spaces, and boxes downstage. The first act follows the evolution of three parallel domestic relationships, heterosexual and lesbian, in relatively realist contexts. The second act follows intercut formal court cases about access to the care and control of their children by one heterosexual and two lesbian mothers.

During the first act, nine swift-flowing scenes introduce the audience to four mothers. Unmarried Sarah seems happy to be a mother; she and the father, Stephen, are students. Elizabeth (Liz) is pregnant but not yet keen to have a baby, although Gerald, her husband, is. Sue and Peter are married with children, and Carol was encouraged to marry Nick by her mother when she became pregnant. Sounds of breathing and slides of delivery show the actuality of birth, while the following scenes trace the progress of the parental relationships. Sarah and Stephen feel the pressures of studying and child care are eroding the quality of their life. Carol, Sue, and their (offstage) children are shown getting to know each other, playing football in the park. Gerald reveals a patriarchal attitude to women's liberation meetings, and his overpossessiveness of Liz drives him to rape her. Stephen and Sarah disagree about postgraduate study opportunities, and she rejects his suggestion of joining a commune. Violent at realizing Carol's lesbianism, Nick calls her "a filthy lesbian and a pervert," but Sue decides to leave Lennie, her son, with Peter and to live with Carol and her children, Julie and Alex. Gerald accuses Liz's female friend Chris of stealing Liz from him when he finds out that they have enjoyed time out together with Dan, his child.

For act 2, stage directions indicate the cast should all wear red, and the actors playing Authority Figures also carry black folders. There are boxes downstage left and right, with two chairs placed centrally. The more stylized performance, including doubling (the actors play not only characters introduced in the first act but also a range of Authority Figures), enhances the critique of society, since it demonstrates in a somewhat Brechtian way that social conditioning molds the human being in terms of gender, class, and thus access to power. Thus *Care and Control*, although not conventionally written, is typical of Wandor's concern with the clash between institution and individual, while the dramatic technique develops further the form used in *Spilt Milk*. The opening Authority comments, "The family is still the backbone of society," while the parallel cases are intercut with some personal discussion interspersed with formal aspects of court procedure and other Authority statements. The second scene reveals that although Stephen had not seen his daughter, Lisa, for one and a half years, he has been granted custody on the grounds that his respectable job (as polytechnic lecturer) and a new wife offer the child better prospects than can Sarah. This unfair situation, like Peter's reluctance to bring Lennie to see Sue, sets up an anxious climate for the main cases: Nick, a rare visitor to Carol's two children, is also trying to obtain custody, while Gerald is determined to wrest Dan from Liz. Gerald's ridiculous attitude toward the "corrupting power" of women's liberation might now seem exaggerated despite the research basis of the play; yet, in spite of improvements since 1977, lived experience still suggests that many concerns in the play—such as male domestic laziness and the problem of sharing power within heterosexual relationships—are still relevant. The question of one Authority Voice, "Are you suggesting you can be married and independent?" is balanced against Chris's defense: "I was trying to find a warm, loving relationship. You see, in the marriage ceremony my husband said he would love and cherish me and he didn't."

The play airs a range of risible prejudices against lesbianism—such as fear that sons will be emasculated—as well as counterarguments that sexual orientation is not relevant to being a good mother. The doubling of Sarah with the Authority Figure who delivers the speech awarding care and control to Gerald emphasizes the force of community hostility toward the unconventional yet supportive relationship between Liz and Chris. In contrast, Carol is allowed to keep her children, providing that her relationship with Sue remains as "private as possible"—a decision based by the authorities solely on "bricks and mortar," because unlike Nick, she is able to provide a home. This apparent victory for a lesbian mother is thus shown as atypical and questionable. The final slides show Carol alone with her children, and each of the other women alone, implying that their relationships have faltered under the pressure of the court cases.

According to Goodman, not only was *Care and Control* the first play created in response to a Gay Sweatshop audience survey about potential topics, but it was "both theatrically successful (critically well received) and politically effective." In detailed discussion of the cultural context of the play and especially its deconstruction of institutional language, Goodman considers the mix of social realism and agitprop was probably less significant for the potential longevity of the play than the popularity of the content. However, the formal tension between public and personal values created by the mixed styles makes the play effective within and beyond the context of lesbian parenting.

In October 1977 Wandor collaborated with Caryl Churchill, Bryony Lavery, and David Bradford on *Floorshow,* a cabaret about women and work, for the company Monstrous Regiment. Wandor's next piece, *Whores D'Oeuvres,* was first performed by the Omoro Theatre Group at the Midland Theatre, Nottingham, on 8 February 1978; it was then seen at the Institute of Contemporary Arts in London. It is a surreal piece about two prostitutes, Pat and Tina, marooned on a makeshift raft after a freak hurricane has swept them along the Thames and out to sea. There are seven short scenes, alternating between Day and Night: some are subdivided. Whereas Day scenes explore the relative reality of the women's experience on the raft, Night scenes titled "Dream" seem to echo the unconscious other selves of the women—past, present, and perhaps future—providing a range of opportunities for deconstructive role-playing about gender relations. As in all of Wandor's plays, the socio-economic elements that underpin sexism are made critically clear.

Pat, the older woman, wears a policewoman's oufit—though eventually she reveals that she has adopted this disguise not as a working girl's turn-on strategy but for leafleting about prostitutes' rights and possible unionization. Pat had apparently taken Tina under her wing, introducing her to prostitution. After fishing out debris including a Hollywood-style phone from the water, the women settle down to sleep, despite Tina's worries about her daughter. The first Night section includes three of Tina's streetwalking episodes: arriving in the city, waiting for a male customer (played by Pat), and being harassed by a corrupt policeman (also played by Pat). Again, this cross-gender doubling plays a typically deconstructive role. Other Night sections include comic pornographic poses as well as a menacing seduction during which Pat as coy feminine flirt gradually changes into an aggressive male client who rapes Tina, reversing the power roles from the first episode. The fifth Day emphasizes the role of class and economics in creating different types of prostitutes. The women contrast the sexual appetites of Members of Parliament with the potential politics of unionizing the profession and compare the economics of marriage and prostitution. An interrogative ending shows that Tina has decided to give up the profession, but Pat sees no other economically viable future for herself. Most critics agree that the surreal style and the energetic, often highly physical roleplay are thought-provoking, with both the strong sense of a supportive friendship between the women and comedy preventing heavy didacticism.

Scissors, produced at the Almost Free Theatre in 1978, relies more heavily on apparent social realism, although it is overtaken by a sense of satirical and melodramatic excess. Events occur in the northeast London home of Max, a Jewish pattern cutter who had lost a job years ago through Gerry, who then left tailoring for success in America. Stage directions suggest a room set with a few bits of furniture, a menorah, and a tailor's dummy wearing a half-finished suit. Max has thoroughly patriarchal attitudes toward his wife, Martha, and daughter, Norma. Gerry is expected to arrive bringing news of Martha's sister Leah, lost during the Holocaust. Family bickering is interrupted by the arrival of Josh, a young Orthodox Jew from Israel, who has been beaten up because he intervened at a racist meeting. Thus the play deploys a range of attitudes to Jewish identity, from the reported atheism of Martin, son of socialist feminist Norma, with her ability to consider the Palestinians; to Martha, who has not kept a kosher kitchen since her in-laws died; to Max, who is keen to keep some traditions; to Josh, whose extreme views make him hostile toward "lax" Western European attitudes. Tension is increased when it seems that Gerry's plane has been hijacked by Palestinians. In an attempt to cover the repercussions of the Holocaust and link it to contemporary problems of immigration, cultural misconceptions, and violence, the (offstage) hijackers turn out to be Indians who were protesting against the British government sending their pregnant sister back to India. In the penultimate moment Josh cuts off his Orthodox hair locks with a tailor's scissors: "Now, you tell me. Who is a Jew?" The audience is left to ask questions about cultural identity and tolerance across issues of race, class, and history.

AID Thy Neighbour, a comedy about two couples and their desires for parenthood, was one of the first feminist plays to deal with Artificial Insemination by Donor (AID). It was directed by Kate Crutchley at the Theatre at New End, 1978. Stage directions suggest a split stage space, so on either side of the missing "dividing wall," the living rooms of both couples can be seen at once. Areas at the back of the set indicate the two kitchens, while two separate bedroom areas should be seen on the upper level. As the play starts, both sides of the set are lighted so the audience can see simultaneous action in both homes, although at later points action may be visible in only one. One childless couple, ironically named Mary and Joseph, are heterosexual; the other, Sandy and Georgina, are lesbians, relatively new to the district. At a dinner party instigated by Mary for the newcomers, domestic tensions in both households echo recognizable behavior and language. The second scene, when Georgina and Mary make excuses for their cross, late, reluctant partners, is made uncomfortably comic by Sandy's outrageous behavior, which is a response both to Georgina's nervousness about coming out and her supposedly "champagne socialist" background. The next two scenes depict Georgina's bloody miscarriage and the unromantic scientific precision of the sexual maneuvers undertaken by Joseph and Mary in attempting conception. Later, Mary is shocked but not hostile on realizing her new friends are lesbians and that the miscarried pregnancy had been negotiated through a cooperative male. Both Georgina, a photographer, and Mary, who has given up work for the purpose of getting pregnant, are shown as similarly desperate in their need for motherhood. At first Mary and Joseph try Artificial Insemination by Husband, while Sandy and Georgina try Artficial Insemination by Donor. Despite their different sexual partnerships, the similarity of their attitudes to AI becomes evident: Joseph's comment, "I'd never thought you'd commit adultery with a test-tube," echoes Sandy's remark, "In all my struggles against the nuclear couple, I never thought I would aid and abet you to be unfaithful to me with a plastic syringe."

Georgina's subsequent pregnancy begins to make Mary feel slightly resentful, though she is becoming more politically aware. Sandy is denied promotion, implicitly because of her sexual orientation. Daphne, a reporter who knew both Joseph and Sandy in the past, arrives with the intention of outwitting journalist Geraldine Kramer's plans to write hostile investigative articles on the availability of AID for lesbians. As act 2 starts, Sandy and Georgina deliberately overplay their relationship in comic sterotypical terms for the benefit of Geraldine, whom Daphne has brought to visit them, and who has a concealed tape recorder. Geraldine and Sandy attempt to get each other drunk in order to get incriminating evidence. Geraldine's drunken self-revelations include a pretended lesbianism and the implication that her journalist former husband, Harry, had abandoned her when pregnant, before a miscarriage. Georgina takes incriminating photographs, stealing the tape, while Sandy manages to keep Geraldine's contact notebook. At the end of the scene, Geraldine addresses Joseph as "Harry," but this potential plot complication is made ambiguous because she then addresses Mary as "Mum."

In the following scenes, Mary admits to Joseph that she does not really want a baby, and Geraldine fails to retrieve her evidence. Shocked to have been outwitted, still unable to see any similarity between the rights and needs for women—whether gay or straight—to have access to AI, she later leaves the newspaper and

Cover for the revised edition (2001) of Wandor's 1987 critical study of key British plays since 1950 (Thomas Cooper Library, University of South Carolina)

returns to Australia. Since Mary intends to resume the contraceptive pill, Joseph—at least for now—will satisfy his wish for fatherhood through babysitting. The play ends with Daphne suggesting that the two households could merge, allowing space for herself and her daughter to join them all in communal living. Some twenty years after the play premiered, this suggestion may seem old-fashioned, but the major theme is still as important for the millenium, since surrogacy and cloning make the issues of parenthood even more complex.

Aurora Leigh, Wandor's dramatization of Elizabeth Barrett Browning's 1857 verse-novel, explores the themes of love, writing, and female independence. Originally performed by the company Mrs. Worthington's Daughters, touring in 1979, it was also performed as a rehearsed reading directed by Nicholas Wright at the Olivier stage of the National Theatre in 1981, and then broadcast by BBC Radio 3 that same year. In her afterword to the published text, Wandor comments that although there was some unevenness in the original production, Mary Moore's design of a "white abstract set . . . which swept up at one corner and had chairs placed at the other corners" enhanced the simplicity and fluidity of time and space that with "naturalistic paraphernalia at an absolute minumum" facilitates exciting theater. The modern-dress National Theatre reading, with the elegantly poised cast on two rows of chairs, emphasized most effectively the rich language. Wandor writes that Aurora, as pivot of the play, "controls it—narrating, re-enacting, commenting. She is a woman in charge of her life and of a work of art."

Aurora has been liberally educated by her father and then, orphaned, is put in the care of an elderly, traditional aunt. Her wish that Aurora be more conventionally womanly and occupy herself with crocheting does not appeal to the imaginative, bookish Aurora, who intends to write and spends time with her cousin Romney and other painters. Romney, however, despite his socialism, has sexist attitudes typical of the period, considering women to be less able than men: "this same world / Uncomprehended by you, must remain / Uninfluenced by you." Aurora therefore rejects his proposal. Although Lady Waldemar, a rich widow, is vexed that Romney, whom she loves, is now likely to marry Marian, who is of lowly birth, Aurora supports his marriage plans. When she later discovers the pregnant Marian has left Romney waiting at the altar because of Lady Waldemar's trickery, she supports Marian. Eventually, sisterly generosity rather than selfish competition for a mate wins the day. Aurora will accept Romney's offer only after Marian rejects him, and she insists on her right to work with him and to write, while all three will live together and care for the child: "Two mothers and a father now, / He's rich as no child has been before him."

Mrs. Worthington's Daughters went on to perform Wandor's adaptation of Githa Sowerby's play *Rutherford & Son* (1912) at the Royal Court in 1980. Apart from Red Ladder's production of Wandor's adaptation of *The Blind Goddess,* a 1932 play by Ernst Toller, and *Future Perfect,* written with Steve Gooch and Paul Thompson for the Wakefield Tricycle in 1981, production of Wandor's plays in the theater began to dwindle in the 1980s, although her radio work escalated. Two commissioned plays—"Wild Diamonds," which contrasted the views of South Africa held by Cecil Rhodes and Olive Schreiner, and "Silk Thistle," about the Pankhursts, written for Hampstead Theatre Club and the Contact Theatre Manchester respectively—remain unproduced. *Mal de Mere* was revived with *Whose Greenham* for the Royal Shakespeare Company at the Barbican in 1986. The last major stage productions to date are *The Wandering Jew,* a dramatization of Eugène Sue's ten-volume novel (1844–1845) about Paris and the Jesuits, directed by Mike Alfreds at the National Theatre in 1987, and *Wanted,* an experimental piece performed by the Arc Theatre Company at the Drill Hall in London on 16 March 1988.

The Wandering Jew took four and a half hours to perform and involved seventeen actors in more than fifty roles. According to Peter Kemp's review in the *Independent* (10 August 1987), the novel was "splendidly caught" in this version, and well performed: "Amidst this preposterous farrago of happenings, rudimentary feminist and socialist sentiments are voiced." The reception otherwise was less favorable; for example, Irving Wardle castigated the National for wasting its resources on an "Ill Told Melodrama" (*Times,* 10 August 1987), suggesting that Wandor's prolonged verbal descriptions—filling out what was a staging with basic furniture and curtains—could be replaced by a time-saving designer. On the other hand, while wishing that the "show could have been richer visually," Stephen Romer (*TLS: The Times Literary Supplement,* 21 August 1987) suggested that the "stylized gesture of the time has been meticulously researched, and is a joy to watch." Although critics disagreed about this theater production, Wandor's skills in novel dramatization have since been clearly effective on radio.

The epigraphs to *Wanted* refer to the biblical story of Sarah and Hagar, found in Genesis; the idea that a child knows the Torah in the womb but is silenced by an angel at birth; the Warnock Report (a government study about surrogacy, fertility, and abortion); a statement by Kim Cotton, the first surrogate mother; and an American surrogate mother who refused to relinquish the baby after birth. Although this theme of problematic pregnancy echoes some of Wandor's earlier works, the adventurous surreal form is indicative of the variety and skill in her writing. The text fuses the mythic past of the infertile Sarah with the present of a modern woman in dialogues between the Angel, Sarah, and Someone, interspersed with childhood rhymes and poems. The printed text uses lines and asterisks to indicate pauses and changes in mood. The name "Someone" is not printed near certain anonymous lines, but presumably these lines are his or hers as the voice of the baby who is eventually, if reluctantly, born. The voice of the Angel also seems at times to be the voice of the unborn child, while this slippage of identity is at points echoed by fragmentation of language. Thus the piece uses those postmodern techniques that some critics read as ecriture feminine. Sarah keeps up a certain wry resistance to the Angel's blandishments; as it coaxes "You've got to have a baby, everyone wants a baby," Sarah points out that she has not menstruated for forty-nine years. Although it draws upon information about AID and surrogacy, the role-playing retains a warmth typical of Wandor's ability to strike emotional chords in the audience. The final speech affectionately conveys an image of a roomy armchair and that of a baby with "a warm little mouth . . . I hope she washes the shawl carefully. It's very delicate."

Despite her record of early and effective experiment in theater, Wandor in the late 1980s and 1990s chose to further develop a successful career in radio dramas. Goodman quotes Wandor's statement that:

> If theatre had not become so conservative so quickly, and if theatre had retained its 1970's openness, more of my work would have been done in theatre. Basically to be successful in theatre as a woman playwright you need to have patrons who will bandwagon you. To work well in radio some similar things apply, but I genuinely believe that there are more radio producers whose commitment is to the work rather than the fashion.

Among the changes in theater, the reduction in the number of fringe companies has been a crucial factor. In *Stage Right* (1994) John Bull has commented on the problematics of defining "what little remains of an alternative theatre tradition" within which Wandor was active. In spite of the strengths of the Second Wave of women playwrights mentioned in Wandor's influential *Carry On, Understudies,* twenty years later the situation is not greatly improved in terms of opportunities for new writers, particularly women and/or those with more overt political concerns. The economic effects of Thatcherism, the relatively small number of women in powerful positions within theater institutions, and the aging, retirement, or mellowing of the (mostly male) artistic directors who were more radical in the 1970s have all contributed to the narrowing of opportunities and a tendency to support salable commodities such as the late-1990s spate of "New Brutalism" among young writers.

As even a partial list of Wandor's radio and television work indicates, she has been quite productive throughout the 1980s and 1990s. Her television adaptation of William Luce's 1976 stage play about Emily Dickinson, *The Belle of Amherst,* for Thames TV in 1986 won an International Emmy Award in 1987. *The Story of an Hour,* based on a Kate Chopin short story, was made by Thames TV in 1988. Wandor has been nominated for the Sony Radio Award three times and was runner-up in 1984 for her dramatization of H. G. Wells's *Kipps* (1905). She was runner-up for the Pye Radio Award in 1979 for *Dust in the Sugar House,* about writer Antonia White, and nominated for Writer's Guild Awards for radio dramatization in 1994 for *The Jungle Book* and 1995 for *The Piano.* Since the 1990s Wandor has also worked on performances combining text and music with The Siena Ensemble and other musicians, including a 1994 adaptation of John Milton's *Samson Agonistes* (1671).

Michelene Wandor's critical works also continue to feature strongly on the reading lists for undergraduates of theatre studies and performing arts. Critical consensus accepts that her perceptive commentary on plays and her sociologically informed analysis of theater institutions and the period context provide valuable personal insights on the alternative theater movement in Britain. Even if, as Goodman suggests, some of Wandor's plays are "now somewhat dated," Wandor's contribution as both creator and critic is intrinsic to the development of feminist theater practice in Britain.

References:

Elaine Aston, *An Introduction to Feminism & Theatre* (London & New York: Routledge, 1995);

Catherine Belsey, *Critical Practice* (London: Methuen New Accents, 1980);

John Bull, *New British Political Dramatists* (London: Macmillan, 1984);

Bull, *Stage Right* (London: Macmillan, 1994);

Sandy Craig, ed., *Dreams & Deconstructions* (London: Amber Lane Press, 1980);

Lizbeth Goodman, *Contemporary Feminist Theatres: To Each Her Own* (London & New York: Routledge, 1993);

Trevor R. Griffiths and Margaret Llewellyn-Jones, *British & Irish Women Dramatists Since 1958* (Buckingham & Philadelphia: Open University Press, 1993);

Catherine Itzin, *Stages in the Revolution: Political Theatre in Britain Since 1968* (London: Methuen, 1980);

P. Lawley, ed., *Contemporary Literature: Women Dramatists* (London: St. James Press, 1993).

Arnold Wesker
(24 May 1932 -)

Anne Etienne
University College Cork

See also the Wesker entry in *DLB 13: British Dramatists Since World War II*.

PLAY PRODUCTIONS: *Chicken Soup with Barley,* Coventry, Belgrade Theatre, 7 July 1958; London, Royal Court Theatre, 14 July 1958;

Roots, Coventry, Belgrade Theatre, 25 May 1959; London, Royal Court Theatre, 30 June 1959 (transferred 30 July 1959 to Duke of York's Theatre); New York, Mayfair Theatre, 6 March 1961;

The Kitchen, short version, London, Royal Court Theatre, 13 September 1959; full production, Coventry, Belgrade Theatre, 19 June 1961; London, Royal Court Theatre, 27 June 1961; New York, New Theatre Workshop, 9 May 1966; New York, New 81st St. Theatre, 13 June 1966; revised, Madison, University of Wisconsin, Madison, October 1990;

I'm Talking About Jerusalem, Coventry, Belgrade Theatre, 28 March 1960; London, Royal Court Theatre, 27 July 1960;

Chips with Everything, London, Royal Court Theatre, 27 April 1962; New York, Plymouth Theatre, 1 October 1963;

The Nottingham Captain, libretto by Wesker, Wellingborough, Centre 42 Festival, 11 September 1962;

Their Very Own and Golden City, Brussels, Belgium National Theatre, 13 August 1965; London, Royal Court Theatre, 19 May 1966;

The Four Seasons, Coventry, Belgrade Theatre, 24 August 1965; London, Saville Theatre, 21 September 1965; New York, Theatre Four, 14 March 1968; revised, Mold, Theatr Clwyd, 4 November 2002;

The Friends, Stockholm, Stadsteater, 24 January 1970; London, Roundhouse, 19 May 1970;

The Old Ones, London, Royal Court Theatre, 8 August 1972; revised, Munich, Kammerspiele Theatre, February 1973; New York, Theatre at the Lambs Club, 6 December 1974;

Arnold Wesker (photograph by Erich Stering; from the frontispiece of Reade W. Dornan, Arnold Wesker Revisited, *1994; Thomas Cooper Library, University of South Carolina; used by permission of Arnold Wesker)*

The Wedding Feast, based on Fyodor Dostoevsky's "An Unpleasant Predicament," Stockholm, Stadtsteater, 8 May 1974; revised, Leeds, Leeds Playhouse, 20 January 1977; revised again, Ohio, Dennison University, 1995;

The Journalists, professional reading, Highgate, Jackson's Lane Community Centre, 13 July 1975; amateur production, Coventry, Criterion Theatre, 27 March 1977; workshop production, Los Angeles, 1979; professional production, Wilhelmshaven, West Germany, 10 October 1981; London, Questors Theatre, 1996;

The Merchant, based on William Shakespeare's *The Merchant of Venice,* Stockholm, Royal Dramaten Theater, 8 October 1976; Philadelphia, Forrest Theatre, 2 September 1977; Washington, D.C.,

Kennedy Center, 29 September 1977; New York, Plymouth Theatre, 16 November 1977; Birmingham, Birmingham Repertory Theatre, 12 October 1978; revised as *Shylock*, dramatized reading, London, Riverside Studios, 16 October 1989;

Love Letters on Blue Paper, Syracuse, New York, Syracuse Stage, 14 October 1977; London, Cottesloe Theatre (National Theatre), 15 February 1978;

Caritas, London, Cottesloe Theatre (National Theatre), 7 October 1981; opera version, with music by Robert Saxton, Wakefield, Wakefield Opera House, 21 November 1991;

Four Portraits, Tokyo, Mitzukoshi Royal Theatre, 2 July 1982; Edinburgh, Edinburgh Festival, 20 August 1984; London, Man in the Moon Theatre, 20 October 1987;

Annie Wobbler, Birmingham, Birmingham Repertory Theatre Studio, 5 July 1983; London, New End Theatre, 26 July 1983; London, Fortune Theatre, 13 November 1984; New York, Westbeth Theatre Centre, 16 October 1986;

Sullied Hand, Edinburgh, Edinburgh Festival, Theatre at The Netherbow, 10 August 1984;

One More Ride on the Merry Go Round, Leicester, Phoenix Theatre, 25 April 1985;

Yardsale, Edinburgh, Fourth RSC/W. H. Smith Festival, 12 August 1985; performed with *Whatever Happened to Betty Lemon,* London, Hammersmith Lyric Studio, 17 February 1987;

Whatever Happened to Betty Lemon, Paris, Théâtre du Rond-Point, 12 November 1986; performed with *Yardsale,* London, Hammersmith Lyric Studio, 17 February 1987;

When God Wanted a Son, professional reading, Highgate, Jackson's Lane Community Centre, 19 February 1989; full production, London, New End Theatre, 6 February 1997;

Beorhtel's Hill, book by Wesker, music by Ian Stewart, Basildon, Towngate Theatre, 6 June 1989;

The Mistress, Arezzo, Festival of One Act Plays, 18 November 1991; performed with *Break, My Heart,* Cardiff, Sherman Theatre, 4 June 1997;

Three Women Talking [later retitled *Men Die, Women Survive*], Chicago, Northlight Theatre, 15 January 1992;

Letter to a Daughter, Seoul, Sanwoolim Theatre Company, 20 March 1992;

Wild Spring, Tokyo, Bungaku-za Theatre Company, 14 October 1994;

Blood Libel, text by Wesker, music by Derek Barnes, Norwich, Norwich Playhouse, 1 February 1996;

The Confession, reading, London, Lyric Hammersmith Studio, 12 April 1997;

Break, My Heart, performed with *The Mistress,* Cardiff, Sherman Theatre, 4 June 1997; performed with *The Four Seasons,* London, Blue Elephant Theatre, 10 March 2003;

Denial, Bristol, Bristol Old Vic, 16 May 2000;

The Kitchen [musical version], text by Wesker, music by Barnes and Barrington Pheloung, lyrics by Nigel Forde, Tokyo, 16 July 2000;

Groupie, Naples, Festival di Todi, 21 July 2002;

Letter to Myself, Hay-on-Wye, Hay Community Centre, 30 May 2004.

BOOKS: *Roots* (Harmondsworth, U.K.: Penguin, 1959);

I'm Talking About Jerusalem (Harmondsworth, U.K.: Penguin, 1960);

The Wesker Trilogy (London: Cape, 1960; New York: Random House, 1961)–comprises *Chicken Soup with Barley, Roots,* and *I'm Talking About Jerusalem;*

The Modern Playwright, or, O, Mother, Is It Worth It? (Oxford: Gemini, 1960);

Labour & the Arts II, or What, Then, Is to Be Done? (Oxford: Gemini, 1960);

Chicken Soup with Barley (London: Evans, 1961);

The Kitchen (London: Cape, 1961; New York: Random House, 1962);

Chips with Everything (London: Cape, 1962; New York: Random House, 1963);

Their Very Own and Golden City (London: Cape, 1966);

The Four Seasons (London: Cape, 1966);

The Friends (London: Cape, 1970);

Fears of Fragmentation (London: Cape, 1970);

Six Sundays in January (London: Cape, 1971)–comprises *Pools, The Nottingham Captain, Menace, Six Sundays in January,* and *The London Diary for Stockholm;*

The Old Ones (London: Cape, 1973);

Say Goodbye, You May Never See Them Again: Scenes from Two East-End Backgrounds, text by Wesker, paintings by John Allin (London: Cape, 1974);

Love Letters on Blue Paper: Three Stories (London: Cape, 1974; New York: Harper & Row, 1975)–comprises *The Man Who Became Afraid, A Time of Dying,* and *Love Letters on Blue Paper;*

The Journalists (London: Writers and Readers Publishing Cooperative, 1975);

Words as Definitions of Experience (London: Writers and Readers Publishing Cooperative, 1976);

The Plays of Arnold Wesker, 2 volumes (New York: Harper & Row, 1976, 1977)–comprises volume 1, *The Kitchen, Chicken Soup with Barley, Roots, I'm Talking about Jerusalem,* and *Chips with Everything;* and volume 2, *The Four Seasons, Their Very Own and Golden City, Menace, The Friends,* and *The Old Ones;*

Journey into Journalism: A Very Personal Account in Four Parts (London: Writers and Readers Publishing Cooperative, 1977);

Love Letters on Blue Paper [play] (London: TQ Publications with Writers and Readers Publishing Cooperative, 1978);

Fatlips: A Story for Children (London: Writers and Readers Publishing Cooperative, 1978; New York, Harper & Row, 1978);

Said the Old Man to the Young Man: Three Stories (London: Cape, 1978)—comprises *The Man Who Would Never Write Like Balzac, Said the Old Man to the Young Man,* and *The Visit;*

The Journalists: A Triptych (London: Cape, 1979)—comprises *The Journalists,* "A Journal of the Writing of *The Journalists,*" and *Journey into Journalism;*

Chips with Everything, The Friends, The Old Ones, Love Letters on Blue Paper [play] (Harmondsworth, U.K.: Penguin, 1980); revised as *Chips with Everything and Other Plays* (London & New York: Penguin, 1990);

The Journalists, The Wedding Feast, The Merchant (Harmondsworth, U.K.: Penguin, 1980); revised as *Shylock and Other Plays* (London & New York: Penguin, 1990);

Love Letters on Blue Paper and Other Stories (Harmondsworth, U.K. & New York: Penguin, 1980)—comprises *Six Sundays in January, Love Letters on Blue Paper, The Man Who Became Afraid,* and *The Visit;* augmented with *Said the Old Man to the Young Man,* 1990;

Caritas (London: Cape, 1981);

The Kitchen, The Four Seasons, Their Very Own and Golden City (Harmondsworth, U.K. & New York: Penguin, 1981); revised as *The Kitchen and Other Plays* (London: Penguin, 1990);

The Merchant, revised version, edited by Glenda Leeming (London: Methuen, 1983);

Distinctions (London: Cape, 1985);

One-Woman Plays (Harmondsworth, U.K.: Penguin, 1989)—comprises *Yardsale, Whatever Happened to Betty Lemon, Four Portraits, The Mistress,* and *Annie Wobbler;*

Lady Othello and Other Plays (London: Penguin, 1990)—comprises *One More Ride on the Merry Go Round, Caritas, When God Wanted a Son, Lady Othello,* and *Bluey;*

As Much As I Dare: An Autobiography (1932–1959) (London: Century, 1994);

Wild Spring and Other Plays (London: Penguin, 1994)—comprises *Badenheim 1939, Beorhtel's Hill, Three Women Talking, Letter to a Daughter, Blood Libel,* and *Wild Spring;*

The Birth of Shylock and the Death of Zero Mostel: Diary of a Play 1973 to 1980 (London: Quartet, 1997);

Break, My Heart (Cardiff: Drama Association of Wales, 1997);

The King's Daughters: Twelve Erotic Stories (London: Quartet, 1998);

Plays 1: The Wesker Trilogy (London: Methuen, 2001);

Plays 2: One-Woman Plays (London: Methuen, 2001)—comprises *Annie Wobbler, Four Portraits, Yardsale, Whatever Happened to Betty Lemon, The Mistress,* and *Letter to a Daughter.*

PRODUCED SCRIPTS: *Menace,* television, BBC, December 1963;

The Trilogy, television and radio, BBC, 1964;

Love Letters on Blue Paper, television, BBC, 2 March 1975;

The Kitchen, television, BBC, 1976;

Chips with Everything, television, BBC, 1977;

Annie, Anna, Annabella [Annie Wobbler], radio, Suddeutscher Rundfunk (Germany), 3 February 1983;

Caritas, radio, BBC Radio 3, 1983;

Yardsale, radio, BBC Radio 3, 6 October 1984;

Bluey, radio, Cologne Radio, 16 May 1985; BBC Radio 3, 11 December 1985;

Letter to a Daughter, television, Norwegian television, September 1992;

Roots, television, BBC2, 1992;

Break, My Heart, television, HTV, 1997.

OTHER: "A Mini Autobiography in Three Acts and a Prologue," in *Contemporary Authors Autobiography Series,* volume 7 (Detroit: Gale Research, 1988);

Little Old Lady, in *New Plays 1,* edited by Peter Terson (Oxford: Oxford University Press, 1989);

Shoeshine, in *New Plays 3,* edited by Terson (Oxford: Oxford University Press, 1989).

SELECTED PERIODICAL PUBLICATIONS—UNCOLLECTED: "Prole Playwrights," *New Statesman* (28 February 1959);

"Vision! Vision! Mr Woodcock," *New Statesman* (30 July 1960);

"The Strange Affair of the Actors' Revolt," *Sunday Times,* 30 August 1971;

"The Smaller Picture," *Guardian* (15 March 2003), <http://books.guardian.co.uk/review/story/0,,913643,00.html>.

Hailed in the 1960s as a left-wing playwright and champion of "kitchen sink" drama, Arnold Wesker has since been relegated to the place of outsider in British theater. This accepted view of him as a "congenital outsider" (Michael Billington, *Guardian,* 20 May 2000) or "unique outsider" (Ronald Bryden, *The Observer*, 20 May 1966) may derive from contradictory images of him. Though he continues to write new plays, he is best known to the British public for his early achievements in relationship with, in particular, the Royal Court Theatre. Similarly, in spite of the socialist and anti-Establishment views he expressed in such plays as *The Kitchen* (performed in 1959, published in 1961) and *Chips with Everything* (performed and published in 1962), he is now regarded by critics as having shifted to a bourgeois stance. He is also renowned for founding Centre 42, a cultural center aimed at popularizing the arts, mostly through trade-union participation; since the project eventually foundered for lack of financial backing, he retreated from the public and political spotlight. He is additionally an outsider insofar as his plays are rarely premiered in London, though he is an internationally recognized name in English drama and his plays are successfully performed worldwide. An outsider in his own country, then, he defies easy categorization. An Angry Young Man, a working-class author, a naturalist dramatist, and a Jewish writer, he fits none of these labels individually, but his work reflects upon them all. As he wrote in "A Mini Autobiography in Three Acts and a Prologue" (1988), he would prefer to think that "a sense of the free spirit pervades" his work.

His image as a social writer, an Angry Young Man, and a kitchen-sink dramatist was built on his early plays, which explore the everyday lives and struggles of individuals and the social groups to which they belong. Wesker's work is not restricted to the class conflict, but the label may well have led the commercial audience to discard him once the fashion had faded. In another shortcut to understanding his career, he has been compared with George Bernard Shaw, using the stage as a platform for socialism. The parallel with Shaw, however, ignores Wesker's claim (expressed, for example, in his 2003 *Guardian* article "The Smaller Picture") that he uses experience, rather than ideas, as the inspiration for his work.

Wesker was born into a Jewish working-class family in Stepney (in the East End of London) on 24 May 1932. His parents, Joseph Wesker, a Russian garment worker, and Leah (born Perlmutter), of Hungarian Jewish origins, are the models for the Jewish family in his "Wesker Trilogy"—*Chicken Soup with Barley* (performed in 1958, published in 1960), *Roots* (performed and published in 1959), and *I'm Talking about Jerusalem* (performed and published in 1960). In the third of these plays he also dramatizes the experiment of his sister, Della, and her husband, Ralph Saltiel, in Norfolk. (Wesker's other sibling, a brother named Mervyn, had died of meningitis in infancy in 1925.) At the beginning of World War II Wesker was evacuated to various places in Wales and England, and in Barnstaple, Devon, he discovered his passion for the stage when he played King Cophetua in a dramatization of Alfred Tennyson's poem "The Beggar Maid" (1842). He returned to the East End in 1943 to attend Upton House Central School in Hackney. There he learned bookkeeping, typing, and shorthand, and at the age of thirteen he wrote, directed, and acted in his first play for a school concert he had also organized. His formal education ended when he was sixteen.

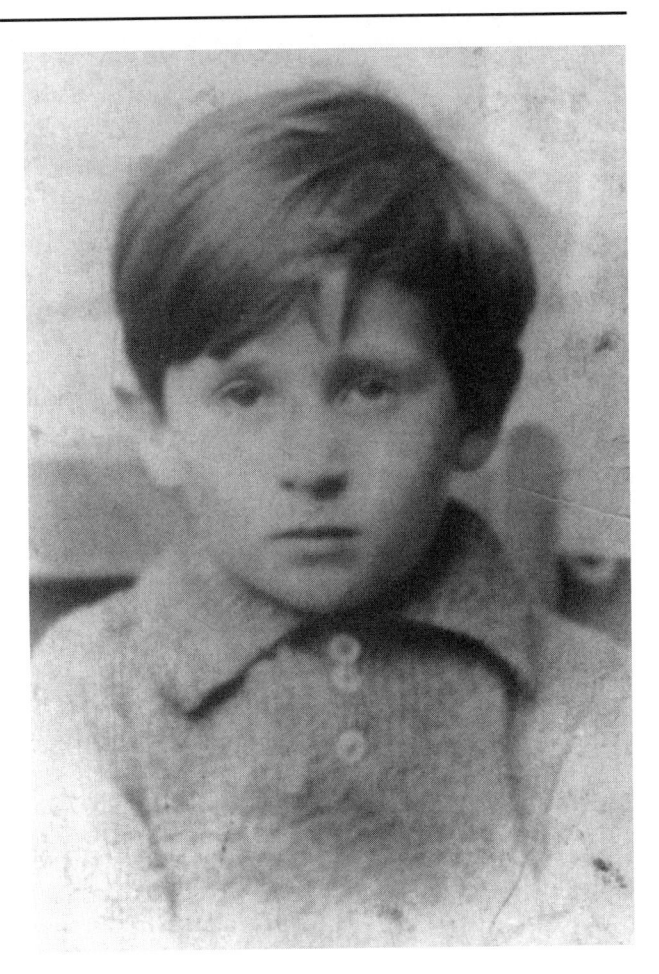

Wesker circa 1937, age five (from As Much As I Dare: An Autobiography [1932–1959], *1994; College of Charleston Library; used by permission of Arnold Wesker)*

Having failed to secure a grant, despite being accepted by the Royal Academy of Dramatic Art (RADA) in 1948, he turned to several jobs such as furniture maker's apprentice, bookshop assistant, and carpenter's and plumber's mate. In 1950 he began his national service in the Royal Air Force, a situation that provided him with the material for *Chips with Everything*. After his discharge in 1952, he took on various jobs in Norfolk and met his future wife, Doreen "Dusty" Bicker, in the Bell Hotel, where they were both working. Returning to London in 1954, he trained as a pastry cook and worked in the Parisian restaurant Le Rallye in 1956. This experience supplied not only the money he needed to enter the London School of Film Technique but also material for his first play, *The Kitchen,* written in 1957.

As Wesker recalls in "A Mini Autobiography in Three Acts and a Prologue" about his studies at the London School of Film Technique in 1956 and 1957, he would have opted for the cinema rather than the stage, but for two reasons: first, "the *Observer* play competition," for which he wrote *The Kitchen,* and second, John Osborne's play *Look Back in Anger* (1956), in which he "just recognized that things *could* be done in the theatre, and immediately went home and wrote *Chicken Soup.*" A portrait of the disintegration of a politically conscious family, paralleling the disintegration of an ideology, *Chicken Soup with Barley* is—as Wesker wrote in "The Smaller Picture"—his "attempt to understand 20 years in the life of my family" and was prompted by quarrels with his mother.

Its chronological scope ranges in three acts from 1936 to 1956. Against the political background, the social group represented by the Kahns and their relatives and friends is portrayed from their original enthusiastic certainties to their final disillusionment with communism. In the first act, the Kahns (Harry, Sarah, and their children, Ada and Ronnie) and their East End Jewish community participate in the 1936 Cable Street demonstration against an anti-Semitic march of Sir Oswald Mosley's British Union of Fascists. By the end of World War II, in the second act, only Sarah and Ronnie are still willing to fight for their political beliefs. Ada and her husband, Dave, who has returned embittered from the Spanish Civil War, have forsaken any hope of reform and retreated to Norfolk. In the final act, Sarah is presented as a lonely character, still clinging to her ideals of welfare socialism in 1955 and 1956. She becomes a political symbol, since her friends abandoned her just as they have abandoned activism. When Ronnie finally returns home, from Paris, where he was working in a kitchen, he attacks her stubborn blindness to political facts, having lost all illusion since the Soviet crushing of the Hungarian uprising of 1956.

Amid this collapse of hope and political faith, Sarah stands firm and preserves her ideals, insisting on the equation between communist values and caring. As evidence, she recalls the eponymous episode of *Chicken Soup with Barley:*

> When Ada had diptheria and I was pregnant I asked Daddy to carry her to the hospital. He wouldn't.... He disappeared. It was Mrs Bernstein who saved her.... It was Mrs Bernstein's soup. Ada still has that taste in her mouth—chicken soup with barley. She says it is a friendly taste—ask her. That saved her.

By giving Sarah the last line, "If you don't care you'll die," Wesker allows her utopian vision of the welfare state to end a play in which every other character has become indifferent to their social and political environment.

In 1957 Wesker met movie director Lindsay Anderson at the London School of Film Technique. Anderson was enthusiastic about *The Kitchen* and *Chicken Soup with Barley* and sent them to George Devine, founder of the English Stage Company and artistic director at the Royal Court Theatre, where *Look Back in Anger* had begun a revival of British drama and led to the coining of the expression Angry Young Men. (Wesker is adamant in refuting the "Angry Young Man" label, however, and claims that none of his contemporaries at the Royal Court Theatre were angry, since they were all making a living out of their writing.) Devine held some doubts about *Chicken Soup with Barley:* the content and twenty-year timespan were both new and difficult. He therefore favored a provincial premiere at the Belgrade Theatre, Coventry, before bringing the play to the Royal Court Theatre. As Wesker recalled in an e-mail to Anne Etienne (13 July 2003), "Around that time they [the Royal Court Theatre] had agreed to celebrate 50 years of repertory theatre by inviting four rep theaters to bring one of their productions for a week's run each. They were not happy with what The Belgrade wanted to bring and so they suggested they consider *Chicken Soup With Barley*. Bryan Bailey, the director of The Belgrade, read it, loved it, and agreed."

Rehearsal time had to be restricted to two weeks, and Anderson, feeling he needed three weeks, left the play in the hands of the young director John Dexter. The play successfully opened at the Belgrade Theatre in Coventry on 7 July 1958 and transferred one week later to the Royal Court Theatre for a second run. In November the play earned Wesker an Arts Council award designed to encourage promising young playwrights. His career was launched. That same year, he married Dusty Bicker, with whom he has three children, two boys and a girl (born in 1959, 1961, and 1962).

Though the Royal Court Theatre commissioned Wesker to write *Roots,* that play also premiered at the Belgrade Theatre before transferring to the Royal Court Theatre. The naturalistic style of *Roots* (for example, the reproduction of the Norfolk dialect and its slow pace of speech) suggests, for Glenda Leeming and Simon Trussler, the conformity of the play to the "mainstream of documentary drama." Yet, the heroine's climactic self-discovery makes it the most dramatic play of the Trilogy. The play features the Bryants, the family of Beatie, who is the girlfriend of Ronnie Kahn from *Chicken Soup with Barley*. In a sharp contrast with the time span of *Chicken Soup with Barley* and *I'm Talking about Jerusalem*, the action in *Roots* takes place within two weeks, in 1959. It centers on the character of Beatie, who is presented as a powerful, buoyant presence. Her constant activity—cleaning, cooking, taking a bath, impersonating and quoting Ronnie in his lectures to her, preparing all the family for the expected arrival of Ronnie—dissociates her from her stagnant family. In act 1, Beatie returns to her rural Norfolk community to announce Ronnie's impending visit. Act 2 bears evidence of her conflicting cultural status when she tries to educate the members of her family as Ronnie has tried to educate her. The climax occurs in the third act: Beatie receives a letter informing her of Ronnie's decision to end their relationship "for ignoring every suggestion I ever made." Attacked by the family she had attempted to change according to Ronnie's precepts, she suddenly voices her own cultural choices. Ending as it does with a cultural and linguistic awakening, the play is "a paradigm for the social problem and the solution that Centre 42 was intended to translate into reality" (Reade W. Dornan, ed., *Arnold Wesker: A Casebook*, 1998).

Beatie represents a conflict between two worlds, the life-denying rural community upbringing and the stimulating environment provided by Ronnie in London. Thus she is divided, as is most vividly manifest in act 2, in her claim to roots. The humor prevalent in Wesker's plays is displayed in this case through the irony of the title. As farm laborers, the Bryants are identified by the traditional aspect of their work. But the routine of their primitive lives numbs them, and they show no interest in the outside world. Culturally and intellectually disconnected, they are without roots. In contrast, Ronnie, the son of immigrants, belongs to a community and has created his own roots. As Ronald Hayman points out, the conflict between the two ways of life arises when Beatie attempts to take the role of educator, and "the cultural life of Beatie's family is measured against the yardstick of what Ronnie has taught Beatie." The list of activities discussed by Beatie opposes Ronnie's cultural background with what he defines as "third-rate": Bizet/pop music, books/comics, high art/entertainment. The didactic dimension of the episode is reminiscent of Wesker's vision for Centre 42: it is not directed solely at Mrs. Bryant but at the public generally.

After Dexter had made a success of *Roots*, Devine gave him an opportunity to direct *The Kitchen* (which Devine initially thought impossible to mount), but only in shortened form as a "Sunday Night Production Without Decor" at the Royal Court Theatre on 13 and 20 September 1959. Devine had conceived these productions as a means to test plays he judged too risky for the English Stage Company to undertake. The series gave an outlet to promising playwrights and offered an alternative to full-scale productions of works about which members of the Council of the Royal Court Theatre might feel uneasy. A full production of *The Kitchen* opened at the Belgrade Theatre, Coventry, on 19 June 1961, before transferring to the Royal Court Theatre on 27 June. Despite Devine's distinct lack of warmth for Wesker's work, he admired the production, and his appreciation was shared by the audience. The success of the play was further crowned by a praising review by the influential drama critic for *The Observer*, Kenneth Tynan.

The Kitchen deals with one working day in the lives of the thirty chefs, waitresses, and kitchen porters of the Tivoli restaurant. The action is concerned with the daily routine of the workers, the rush and the petty quarrels and grumbles. The action is supplemented with a subplot consisting of a love affair between Peter, a German chef, and Monique, a married English waitress. Their affair comes to an end with a dramatic climax when Peter chops the gas pipe in a fit of raging frustration. The play is constructed in two parts representing the two work shifts, separated by a lyrical interlude corresponding to the peaceful after-lunch break, during which some of the staff reveal their dreams. *The Kitchen* illustrates Wesker's creative process of drawing material from personal experience and reshaping it through dramatization. As Leeming and Trussler have pointed out, the working place of the kitchen is a microcosm, "a dramatic metaphor for industrial capitalist society." Wesker's own assessment in the published text emphasizes the microcosmic allegory: "The world might have been a stage for Shakespeare but to me it is a kitchen." When Peter's angry gesture reduces the activity of the kitchen to a standstill and the busy atmosphere to silence, Marango, the restaurant owner, defines the working place as the world: "I don't know what more to give a man. He works, he eats, I give him money. . . . I live in the right world, don't I?" His rhetorical questions are echoed in a final interrogation that remains unanswered as the curtain falls: "What is there more?" For Robert Wilcher, the answer is to be found in the Trilogy, since it "explores human and political complexities of the problems asked in *The Kitchen*."

Leeming and Trussler describe the stylistic technique of this play as "at once realistic and representative." This combination was underlined in its first performances at the Royal Court Theatre, directed by Dexter, in which all the cooking and food preparation were mimed, and the setting, designed by Jocelyn Herbert, verged on minimalism. This particular staging befitted the minimal nature of the plot, since Wesker's

Wesker and Doreen "Dusty" Bicker on their wedding day, 14 November 1958 (from As Much As I Dare: An Autobiography [1932–1959], *1994; College of Charleston Library; used by permission of Arnold Wesker)*

aim, as he stated in *As Much As I Dare: An Autobiography (1932–1959)* (1994), was to re-create "the experiences of working under pressure, illustrating the dehumanising effects of the work process." The kitchen represents any workplace: the characters, of various nationalities, are typified by their jobs in the kitchen, thereby symbolizing the universal worker. Yet, the autobiographical basis of the play also allows for detailed realism, which has prompted its description as "théâtre trouvé," be it in the quick-paced dialogue of the rushed shifts or when the kitchen staff express their individual expectations of a compassionate society, respectful of their longings.

Despite a cast of thirty, and the technical and choreographical difficulties it presents, *The Kitchen* is Wesker's most performed play worldwide. Its lasting appeal is explained by a style that defies fashion, the modernity of its themes, and the various critical responses it has prompted. It has been regarded as "socialist-humanist, passive nihilist, utopian socialist and romantic expressionist" (Dornan, ed., *Arnold Wesker: A Casebook*).

Chicken Soup with Barley and *Roots* received critical acclaim and became a financial success for the Royal Court Theatre when they were revived in 1960 to form a repertoire with the third part of the Trilogy, *I'm Talking About Jerusalem*. The public usually favors *Roots* because it offers an optimistic view with Beatie's liberating self-discovery. *Roots* can be regarded as a thematic as well as structural introduction to *I'm Talking About Jerusalem*. Both plays are set in rural Norfolk, and the absent observer Ronnie reappears in the last play to comment on his sister's experiment to plant roots for a socialist Jerusalem at a time when the Conservatives have won the General Election.

In three acts, the play tells of Ada and Dave Simmonds's attempts to work and live in a community where, unlike in *The Kitchen,* the individual man is not merely a tool within the dehumanizing capitalist machine. Dave and Ada are disillusioned about their young communist hopes and try to "live"—rather than talk about—a traditionally socialist ideal: "not words. At last more than just words."

In act 1, set in 1946, they have left the Kahn family to settle in the middle of the fields where Dave will develop his trade as a furniture maker. According to Sarah, their isolated socialist utopia away from London is bound to fail, since "what's socialism without human beings?" Act 2, one year later, shows that the numbing effect of factory work has left its mark on Dave. As he struggles to build up his workshop and trade, he is confronted with the failed socialist experiment of their old friend Libby Dobson. Further visits from Ada's aunts in the third act emphasize the lonely and doomed nature of their venture. They eventually have to move back to London.

Despite their trust in the reforming ability of the individual, Ada and Dave realize that they must fight industrial competition even in Norfolk, where craftsmanship cannot win over mass production. Yet, they fail because their isolation is psychological as well as geographical and social. They receive no support from their family and friends. Therefore, Dave comes to distrust the socialist vision, because his Jerusalem never soared. His utopia crushed, he realizes that though he may have pursued his craft diligently, his beautiful furniture was only for those who could afford it. Ronnie's final plea that visions "do work! And even if they don't work then for God's sake let's try and behave as though they do—or else nothing will work" is an optimistic statement that pervades Wesker's writing.

The Trilogy established Wesker's reputation as a major dramatist and also created a closely knit relationship with director Dexter and designer Herbert. Hayman applauds the Trilogy as "the first serious and successful political plays to be written in England." Wesker, however, showed early discontent with the political tag; in a letter to the editor, published in the *New Statesman* (28 February 1959), he stated, "I didn't write *Chicken Soup* simply because I wanted to amuse you with 'working-class types' but because I saw my characters within the compass of a personal vision. I have a personal vision, you know, and I will not be tolerated as a passing phase." Hence, his political stance avoids propaganda to stress the emotional commitment of individuals to their beliefs: socialism is identified with caring for the working-class people, whether groups or individuals. In the Trilogy, Wesker concludes that socialist values may work for the individual but fail when applied to the group for lack of caring; as Harry Kahn says in *Chicken Soup with Barley,* "You can't alter people. You can only give them some love and hope they take it."

The plays composing the Wesker Trilogy are the most overtly autobiographical of his work. In an interview included in Hayman's study, Wesker admitted to taking his parents as models for Harry and Sarah Kahn: "They are—in so far as it is possible—total re-creations. So are most of the characters, with the only exception of me." He delved into his early diaries about his father for the character of Harry as well as incorporating remembered sentences uttered by his mother and sister for the roles of Sarah and Ada. The fact that Ronald is an anagram for Arnold also signals Wesker as his own source for the character who links the plays together, a tool "to allow the real heroes to shine," as he wrote in *As Much As I Dare*. Yet, Ronnie is disillusioned at the end of the Trilogy, whereas its author continues in his later plays to translate into theatrical action his belief that words are bridges.

Communication marks a central concern in all of Wesker's plays and is not solely accomplished by words. In most of his plays, either the action is set in a kitchen or food is prepared and offered. Incidentally, the Trilogy, more than *The Kitchen,* is responsible for the phrase "kitchen sink theater."

Wesker's next play, *Chips with Everything,* is a dramatic rewriting of Wesker's correspondence when he was completing his national military service. He has also suggested that the main characters of Pip and Charles may have been inspired by two sides of his personality, a statement that would explain their complementary dynamic action and Wesker's claim that "*Chips* is preoccupied with knowledge versus ignorance, caring versus indifference, tolerance versus bigotry." As in *The Kitchen,* the setting—in this case, an army camp—is a microcosm where hierarchy is prevalent. According to Hayman, the strength of the play lies in the depiction of the ruler/ruled relationship: "Because of their clear-cut division of personnel into officers and men and their rigid hierarchy which subdivides both categories into ranks, the armed services have often been used before as an image of society but *Chips* embodies a more serious, powerful and systematic attack on the class system." Like *The Kitchen* and in contrast with the Trilogy, the class and identity struggle that *Chips with Everything* dramatizes is removed from the friendly setting of the family and shifted to an unfamiliar public context: "You're not at home."

In eighteen scenes, Wesker portrays eight weeks of numbing military drills in a manner he defines as "stylised naturalism." Attention is drawn to the nine conscripts, who are all well-rounded characters, while the officers, appearing more rarely, are stylized as archetypes of authority. Wesker relinquishes the classical three-act division to adopt a Brechtian structure of a series of sketches, snapshot episodes depicting relevant parts of their training: the bayonet drill, the Christmas party where the officers' patronizing attitude is deliberately emphasized, the night expedition to retrieve coke. Action is built on two interactive plots. On the one hand, a friendship develops between two conscripts, Pip and Charles, respectively from upper-class and working-class backgrounds. Pip is fascinated by the habits of the working class, as he recalls his visit to working-class settings where people want chips with everything, just as his knowledge attracts Charles. On the other hand, Pip is selected by the officers to become one of them, despite his initial defiant refusal to follow his father's path. The officers finally reach their goal by ignoring his protests. However, a sour rebellion surges when Smiler, another conscript, is persecuted by the ruling class. In this penultimate scene, the conscripts unite against authority, led in this revolution by Charles, and Pip symbolically assumes the rank of officer by putting on a uniform. Hence the play suggests that revolution can only be effected by the ruled and never by the ruling class.

The play warns, through Pip's example, "how rebellions were accommodated and defused," whether through consent or apathy. His identity as a leader manifests itself to the recruits when he organizes the coke-stealing maneuver. The last confrontation between men and officers is precisely the threatening situation that Pip had tried to initiate throughout the play. However, it is Charles, previously condemned by Pip for his apathy, who takes the lead, defying the officers and uniting the conscripts to defend Smiler. Mutiny is avoided as Pip takes over his officer's role.

Since its first production in April 1962 at the Royal Court Theatre, *Chips with Everything* has been one of Wesker's most popular plays, acclaimed critically and commercially. Though elements of its stylization surprised the reviewers who had Wesker pegged as a social realist, the popular appeal of *Chips with Everything* assured West End transfers. In the *Sunday Times* (29 April 1962) Harold Hobson wrote the most consequential comment on the work, describing it as "the first anti-Establishment play of which the Establishment has cause to be afraid." *Chips with Everything* was subsequently voted best play of 1962 and was Wesker's first work to be produced on Broadway, in 1963. It was revived at the National Theatre in September 1997.

His first five plays firmly established Wesker's voice and talent in the British theater. His artistic achievement was complemented in the 1960s by a grand-scale endeavor to change theater audience, based on the principle "that art is a common heritage, not the habit of a few," as he wrote in a 1960 article titled "Vision! Vision! Mr Woodcock." This vision materialized into Centre 42. At the invitation of the Oxford Student Drama Festival in 1960, Wesker gave a lecture in which he attacked the Labour Party for neglecting the fact that socialism was not "merely an economic organisation of society but a way of living based on the assumption that life is rich, rewarding and that human beings deserve it." The full text was then distributed to every trade-union leader in the country as the pamphlet *The Modern Playwright, or, O, Mother, Is It Worth It?* (1960). His vision was further enunciated in *Labour & the Arts II, or What, Then, Is to Be Done?* (1960), a pamphlet that suggested projects and the active involvement of the trade unions through an inquiry into the state of the arts. As a result, in September 1960, three trade unions placed a resolution before the Trades Union Congress (T.U.C.), calling for recognition of the importance of the arts in community life and for an inquiry into the means by which trade unions could improve cultural activities. This resolution, number 42 on the agenda, was rejected by the General Council but unanimously endorsed by the T.U.C.

This sanction was encouragement enough for Wesker. He launched into action by rallying like-minded artists such as Doris Lessing, John McGrath, and Shelagh Delaney, and persuaded them "to adopt the T.U.C. resolution as a starting point for their plans" (*Fears of Fragmentation*, 1970). Their objective was to found an arts center that would serve as a "cultural hub" for artists to make the best in art available for popular audiences. Wesker, as founder, was elected artistic director of Centre 42. As they had deemed the trade-union movement to be the best medium to reach as many people as possible, they let the unions know that their services could be hired—though the agreement was for the artists invited to ask only the minimum fee or no fee at all. In 1961 they were invited by the Wellingborough Trades Council to help them mount a membership recruiting festival in their town. The following year, in 1962, six festivals went out on tour at the invitation of provincial trade-union councils in Wellingborough, Bristol, Leeds, Leicester, Nottingham, and Birmingham. The festivals, organized with local workers' committees, created a deficit of £38,000 despite their popular success. The financial aspect, as well as the difficulty inherent in working from offices, induced Wesker to refuse the invitations that had been made for 1963 and 1964 festivals. He wanted a home for Centre 42.

Centre 42's efforts concentrated on building a multiart center aimed at popular audiences. By 1963 Wesker had chosen the Roundhouse, an old railway shed in Chalk Farm, North London, to convert into a base. Money was needed to materialize his plans. He met with the Labour prime minister Harold Wilson and the Minister for the Arts Jennie Lee to discuss Centre 42 plans and hopes. Wilson showed his appreciation of the project by suggesting George Hoskins as a fund-raiser. In 1964 Wesker was given the lease of the Roundhouse as a permanent base for Centre 42. Between 1964 and 1966 the models for the conversion were completed, but Centre 42 needed £650,000 to effect the conversion and run it; the fund-raising proved insufficient by 1965. Hoskins therefore suggested a seven-year schedule during which the conversion of the building would start as a performing space for hire by external companies. Wesker had to accept this compromise of a self-supporting commercial enterprise. In addition, Centre 42 set up a Roundhouse Trust. The prime minister acknowledged the new plan in 1967. When Wesker was offered, and turned down, the rank of Commander of the British Empire the same year, he asked Wilson to support Centre 42 instead but received no practical support. Dissatisfied, Wesker saw the conversion of the Roundhouse where Centre 42 had been unable to raise enough money to perform. In December 1970, Wesker resigned from the Roundhouse Trust and the artistic directorship of Centre 42, thereby dissolving it.

Retrospectively, Wesker commented in a 2002 interview with Andrea Matias: "Arts for everyone we never believed this possible in Centre 42. We felt that the audience for the arts would always be small, a minority. What we couldn't know was how small was small, or how big that minority could be." Despite its achievements, Wesker still considers Centre 42 a failure.

During his involvement in Centre 42, Wesker wrote two plays in 1963 and 1964, *The Four Seasons* and *Their Very Own and Golden City*, both performed in 1965 and published in 1966. Though independent, they are companion pieces: both reflect on Wesker's Centre 42 experience and deal respectively with private and public disillusionment. For Leeming and Trussler, "*Our Very Own and Golden City* is *The Four Seasons* turned inside out: the former is the more complete in its panorama of the public and private influences upon its main characters' lives, but it drastically selects and subordinates these private elements, whereas *The Four Seasons* is set physically within its own isolated, intimate, introspective world."

The Four Seasons describes in four parts, from winter to autumn, the rise and fall of a love affair between Adam and Beatrice. Both have had painful relationships and decide to spend a year in a cottage secluded from the rest of the world. In winter, Adam is the sole speaking character, since Beatrice is in a catatonic state. In spring, his caring has willed her into sharing memories. They are in love by summer, when Beatrice asks him to begin a relationship outside the confines of the house. Because he hesitates, their relationship lingers and finally dies in autumn.

This lyrical play is essentially regarded as a symbolic work: the cyclic framework of the four seasons points to the recurrence of the couple's past relationships and the inevitability of their love's ending. The pessimism of the play lies not in the end of their affair but in the fact that their year is but a repetition of their previous failures. Compassion for their imperfections fails to alter the inevitable issue, since their mistakes are unvarying.

Leeming and Trussler point out that "the names Adam and Beatrice, once given, cannot simply slough off their associations of Man as Everyman, originally sinful, and Woman as poetic, mythic love-object." Nevertheless, in the epilogue, Wesker argues against seeing the characters as archetypes of "man" and "woman." In view of the play as a response to Wesker's private pain during the Centre 42 experiment, biographical elements present themselves, the initials of the characters being shared by Wesker and his friend Beba Lavrin, also an acknowledged model for the character of Kate in *Their Very Own and Golden City*.

The stylized structure and language again came as a surprise for critics expecting another naturalistic composition. For its premiere at the Belgrade Theatre on 24 August 1965, the reviews were hostile. While recognizing "the trap of creating a pseudo-poetic dialogue," Wesker vindicated his stylistic choice as a personal artistic evolution. But the exclusion of the outside world and the lack of action were recognized as the main flaw. Hence, "the best moment comes when . . . the man proudly makes an apple strudel to delight his love" (*The Times*, 11 September 1965). The mirror public image presented in *Their Very Own and Golden City*, however, was received just as unfavorably.

The themes of *Their Very Own and Golden City* are compromise and the sad difference between dreams of youth and realities of age. Wesker further explains that this allegorical play is a metaphor for the compromise he experienced during the ten years spent developing Centre 42. Like *The Four Seasons*, it treats a personal experience in a nonnaturalistic mode. Like *Chips with Everything*, it is organized in an episodic series of overlapping or counterpointing scenes. As in *Chicken Soup*

Patsy Byrne, Charles Kay, and Joan Plowright in the 1959 Royal Court Theatre production of Wesker's play Roots, *in which a young woman returns from London and tries to awaken social consciousness in her isolated, rural Norfolk family (from Glenda Leeming,* Wesker the Playwright, *1983; Thomas Cooper Library, University of South Carolina; used by permission of Arnold Wesker)*

with Barley, the action covers decades—in this case some sixty years. The distinctive feature of *Their Very Own and Golden City* is in the technique of flash-forward, which allows for this lengthy time span. The central characters are the children who open the play in the soaring Durham Cathedral: gathered around would-be architect Andy Cobham are his friends Jessie, Paul, and Stoney. Their presence, set in 1926, is recurrent throughout the play. A parallel is drawn between their young vision and enthusiasm for the better world that they would build and the older Andy's attempted enactment of this vision. Once he becomes an architect, Andy joins trade unions to find financial support for the six utopian cities he plans to build. Having opposed the political choices of his mentor Jake Latham, he is assisted in his meandering quest in political and industrial circles by Kate, an impoverished aristocrat who is in love with him. Andy sacrifices his family and friends in the relentless pursuit of his vision and eventually sacrifices his vision itself through nine steps of compromise. In the end, the image of an old and defeated Andy is countered by the ultimate scene, in which the defiant youths leave the cathedral where their utopia was enunciated as a communal vision of hope.

The biographical links to Wesker's Centre 42 experiment are strong. Andy's and Wesker's visions prove unattainable given the political and economic climates. Like Wesker, Andy fails to secure more than the token support of the T.U.C. Andy succeeded in building one city, and Wesker organized two festivals, the second having toured six cities. In an unpublished 13 July 2003 e-mail Wesker acknowledged the modeling of Kate on his Centre 42 assistant Lavrin: "Just as Beba's double-edged sword of mocking criticism both shaped for the better and distorted for the worse the development of Centre Fortytwo, so Kate's advice contributed to the step by step compromises in the building of the cities." Finally, Andy's initial rejection of patchwork solutions derives from Wesker's own fears of fragmentation and belief that it is the artist's purpose to arrange and unify these fragments.

The first British production of *Their Very Own and Golden City* at the Royal Court Theatre in May 1966 failed to be as commercially viable as previous Wesker plays. The critics, though more restrained than toward *The Four Seasons,* censured it. This failure had much to do with William Gaskill's role as director, since he did not understand Wesker's work as well as Dexter did, and he made the wrong decision of using the same actors for the young and older characters of Andy, Jessie, Paul, and Stoney. However, critics generally thought that the play lacked feeling and that Wesker should have avoided using his experience with Centre 42 as the theme of a play he wanted to be an epic.

Wesker's next play, *The Friends* (performed and published in 1970), presents a continuity with *Their Very Own and Golden City* in that the failure of Centre 42 is expressed through the exploration of death, the central event in the play. The debate at the core of the play centers around cultural and political issues that were met by Wesker as administrator of Centre 42. Yet, this return to the naturalistic mode also has parallels with *The Kitchen.* The focus is not on one protagonist but on a group: Esther, who is dying of leukemia; her lover Roland; her brother, Manfred; and their friends and working partners Crispin, Tessa, Simone, and Macey. As in *The Kitchen,* there is also a tight setting for place and action, as the play takes place in Esther's room, around her deathbed, within twenty-four hours. From a thematic perspective, *The Friends* is a reversed image of *The Kitchen:* in the latter, work was everything and left no time for friendship, whereas *The Friends* evokes a long friendship that has developed into a working relationship until work is finally excluded to focus on the initial bonds. As Wesker acknowledged in *As Much As I Dare,* these characters' disillusionment reveals that his own "ambivalence about the working class . . . had grown into a full-frontal confession." His lack of faith in his own social class is given full expression in Manfred's desperate outburst: "The working class! Hate them! It's coming, Macey. Despise them! I can hear myself, it's coming. Hate them! The working class, my class, offend me. Their cowardly acquiescence, their rotten ordinariness—everything about them—hate them! There!"

In the first act, all the friends gather around Esther, and the act closes with her death. It is expository and climactic at the same time. All are childhood friends from a working-class Northern background who have bonded despite the fact that Esther and Manfred are Jewish. Simone, an upper-class Southerner, is the one outsider who nevertheless finds an ally in Macey, the Jewish manager of their clothing shops. Once influential trend-makers, they failed to appeal to the working class with their beautiful designs. They have grown so dissatisfied that they have stopped creating and are carelessly facing the bankruptcy of their six shops. The second act witnesses their psychological and emotional collapse at the death of the unifying person in their group. They all face their own inadequacies and attempt to confront aging and death. Their unity is ultimately saved when Simone reintroduces Esther at the center of their life, by placing her body on her chair: the friends irresistibly gather around it, facing a portrait of Lenin as an image of their working-class and revolutionary past. Despite dying halfway through the play, Esther remains the main character, representing both the true artist and the true revolutionary, still professing the value of life, past and present. Through Simone's mise-en-scène she unifies once more characters who had abandoned their will to communicate.

The first British performance in May 1970 received mixed reviews and failed to meet with commercial success. Wesker directed the production at the Roundhouse, a space badly suited to the intimacy of the action. He met with great difficulties during rehearsals with the actor who was cast as Roland, Victor Henry. As Wesker recalls in *As Much As I Dare,* Henry's violent nature and less than latent anti-Semitism led him to sabotage the production by not learning the lines and eventually feigning an epilectic fit on the night of the premiere. As hurtful personally was the condemnation of the play by McGrath in the radical magazine *Black Dwarf* (12 June 1966): "What [Wesker] must do is not to confuse anybody, including himself into thinking that he is in any way socialist, or that this play relates in any way to any possible form of socialist theatre." Despite initially rejecting McGrath's argument, Wesker concluded in his autobiography than McGrath might have been right concerning his politics. Wesker responded to the scathing critics by denouncing, in various sources, the damaging effects of reviews to his freedom to experiment as an artist; his fight against "lilliputianism" had started.

Nevertheless, Wesker pursued his research into nonnarrative theater with the comedy *The Old Ones* (performed in 1972, published in 1973). In this play the order of the contrasting scenes does not respond to a logical linearity but to "emotional rhythm and thematic progression," as Wilcher notes; the episodic structure of the play reproduces that of *Chips with Everything* and *Their Very Own and Golden City*. The connection between each of the twenty-four scenes is reduced to the fact that the characters are friends or relatives. The old ones of the title are optimistic Manny; his wife, Gerda; his pessimistic brother, Boomy; his sister, Sarah; and her friends Teressa, Millie, and Jack, the only Gentile character. The young ones are their children, Rudi (Sarah's nephew), Martin (Boomy's son), and Rosa (Sarah's daughter), who represents Wesker. The play was directly inspired by Wesker's relatives, and he admitted in *Theatre Quarterly* (1977) that "you can imagine that all the old ones in all the plays are the same people."

The plot focuses on the conflict between optimism and pessimism played through the characters of Manny and Boomy. Their contradictory attitudes are expressed via a ritualistic quarrel in which they best each other with classical quotations proving the essence of life as good or evil. Their quarrel exposes two myths: "The first charts the progressive fragmentation of language and intellect to the level of violent, speechless youths. The other celebrates the continuation of a prelapsarian state of mutual sympathy" (Dornan, ed., *Arnold Wesker: A Casebook*). Hence, debate centers on the struggle against violence and aging as well as the survival of traditions. In this concern for the value of life and inheritance, the play thematically parallels *The Friends*. The survival of the past is portrayed here by a didactic reenactment of the festival of Succoth, the symbol of joy, which forms the framework of the play.

Despite the optimism displayed in *The Old Ones*, its production at the Royal Court Theatre in August 1972 under the direction of Dexter failed to raise the critical acclaim of his earlier plays or to satisfy either author or director. Wesker was all the more disillusioned because *The Old Ones* had been planned to open at the National Theatre, but a quarrel between literary manager Tynan and Dexter resulted in the play being mounted at the Royal Court Theatre. At a time when Wesker was waiting for his reputation to be consolidated, the National Theatre was a symbol that eluded him.

Further and harsher disappointment came with his next play, *The Journalists* (performed and published in 1975). Hayman propounds that "newspaper life can simultaneously be treated naturalistically and used as a microscosm of a country's mental life." In Wesker's metaphor for lilliputianism—epitomized in the main character's repeated question "who does he think he is?"—Wesker was not so much attacking the Establishment as defending himself against the journalistic ego. His assessment of the play in *As Much As I Dare* is that he "could not paint friend entirely white and enemies entirely black" and that "characters questioned literary, artistic, social and political authorities, or at least the cant in vogue whether of left or right."

The play, set in the offices of the *Sunday Paper*, covers six days in six different weeks in order to relate both the growing pressure exerted on the journalists and the sense of a typical working day. The structure is adapted to the snapshot quality of the scenes, as every column is represented with its own obsessions: the women's page, the arts, the sport section, features, foreign desk, business, and the editor's office. Because of the density of the project, there is no in-depth characterization, and the dramatic interest is concentrated in an accurate rendition of the aspects of newspaper life. The main character is Mary Mortimer, the star political reporter, whose objective is to bring down Morgan King, Labour M.P. (an offstage character who has been identified by some critics as Wesker but who Wesker claims was inspired by Labour M. P. Anthony Wedgewood Benn). Mortimer attempts to reveal a supposed link between King and guerilla action. By the end of the play she has gathered enough evidence to print her story, but the editor pretends she is too late for her article to be published. This refusal is because of his discovery that Mary's son is himself involved in King's terrorist gang, a fact unknown to Mary.

Wesker spent two months in the offices of the *Sunday Times* to gather material for his play. He details this experience in *Journey into Journalism: A Very Personal Account in Four Parts* (1977). In November 1971 David Jones, one of the artistic directors of the Royal Shakespeare Company (RSC), let Wesker know the RSC was interested in plays with large casts and would like to read his play on journalism. Trevor Nunn confirmed they would like to produce the play for the 1972–1973 season at the Aldwych Theatre. An opening date was set for 19 October 1972. When Wesker, in collaboration with Jones, had completed the rewrites, most of the actors turned down the roles that they had been offered. The reasons for their decision are detailed in an article by Wesker printed in the *Sunday Times* (30 August 1981). On his return, Jones assessed the seriousness of the situation, the first instance of censorship

Scene from the 1961 Royal Court Theatre production of Wesker's 1959 play The Kitchen, *which depicts a day in the lives of the staff at a large restaurant and was based on Wesker's experiences as a cook in London and Paris in the mid 1950s (photograph by Richard Sadler; from Glenda Leeming,* Wesker the Playwright, *1983; Thomas Cooper Library, University of South Carolina; used by permission of Arnold Wesker)*

exercised by actors: the company was refusing a play that the management had already accepted. Since the actors could not be forced to perform in view of their contract, and it would prove too expensive to import actors, postponing the premiere was ruled out. The RSC production was entirely canceled.

Wesker sued the RSC for damages. In addition to the bad reputation attached to the play after the company's breach of contract, Wesker argued that the RSC production was to be the world premiere of the play; though the rights had already been sold in Belgium, Germany, and Sweden, no prior performance was permitted. The law case was finally settled out of court in November 1980.

Wesker's own delayed and honest view in the 1981 article takes his past career into consideration:

> The actors and others could be right, *The Journalists* could be an awful play. Perhaps yes, but perhaps not. I only know that the directors of the RCT [Royal Court Theatre] did not at first think my trilogy could work, or *The Kitchen*, or *Chips with Everything*. Peggy Ashcroft rescued *Roots*, the late Bryan Bailey of the Belgrade Theatre in Coventry rescued *The Kitchen*, Bob Swash rescued *Chips with Everything*. There is a similar story to tell for all my plays since the majority can't "hear" them until they are performed. When, I ask myself, will *my* experience, expertise, track-record be trusted? . . . My play was about the lilliputian mentality, and the actors had responded in a lilliputian manner—they'd brought down a daring and ambitious play.

The RSC trial unquestionably tarnished Wesker's reputation in London theatrical circles, and his outspokenness toward his critics and toward the increasing importance given to the director over the author (as in an open letter to Nunn on Wesker's website, <http://www.arnold-wesker.com>) has created some sort of resistance. The first performance of *The Journalists* in Great Britain on 13 July 1975 was a rehearsed reading with Sheila Allen and Ian McKellen, organized to raise funds for the Jackson's Lane Community Centre in Highgate. It was performed in an amateur production at the Criterion Theatre in Coventry two years later, with professional productions in West Germany in 1981 and at the amateur, lottery-funded Questors Theatre in London in 1996.

Adapted from Fyodor Dostoevsky's 1861 short story "An Unpleasant Predicament," *The Wedding Feast* (performed in 1974, published in 1980) portrays in a prelude and two acts the bitter disillusionment of Louis Litvanov, a rich shoe manufacturer in a Norfolk town. Having been raised in an immigrant working-class background, Litvanov believes in the equality between employer and employees. He sympathizes with his workers' predicament, allowing them social benefits economically unsound for his factory, and believes that his sympathy is reciprocated by an affectionate loyalty from his employees. The play proceeds from the hypothesis put forward by the outsider character of Hammond: "Supposing you went to their homes. There. Where they live. What then?" Litvanov's utopian view is put to the test when he passes the house of Knocker White, one of his workers, on the day of Knocker's wedding.

There is a sharp contrast between his fantasies of brotherhood and the embarrassment his uninvited presence provokes. The wedding celebration invites a comedic treatment. Nevertheless, the shoe game played at the party illustrates that Litvanov's presence and drunken willingness to enter into the celebration is resented as an intrusion. The game is a blindman's-bluff variant: each member of the circle either throws a shoe to another participant or must strike with it the blindfolded player, who must then try to grab the person wielding the shoe. When Litvanov's turn comes to be in the middle, the game degenerates, and he is finally beaten up by his workers. The game is symbolic of Louis's inaccurate socialist views because he is blind to his workers' actual feelings and because they attack him with their shoes, the tools of his flourishing business. When he awakes from a drunken sleep the following morning, Litvanov accepts his secretary's advice—"Just give them the sweet, sweet illusion that they're equal to any man. Stop pretending it's a reality"—with a fatalistic "Yes, that's the way it has to be."

The first British production took place at the Leeds Playhouse on 20 January 1977, and the play received the best notices since *Chips with Everything*. The critical triumph led to an intended transfer to the Phoenix Theatre in London; but untoward circumstances forbade it, ending the potentiality of a commercial success.

The Merchant (performed in 1976, published in 1980, later retitled *Shylock*), Wesker's counterhandling of the three stories in William Shakespeare's *The Merchant of Venice* (circa 1596–1597), is best read in conjunction with his account of its production in New York, *The Birth of Shylock and the Death of Zero Mostel: Diary of a Play 1973 to 1980* (1997). The book details every rewriting of the play as well as the work involved between Wesker and Dexter in their last collaboration. Wesker developed Shaw's argument that Shakespeare's Shylock was unrealistic in what Christopher Innes describes as "a point by point reversal of its source, justified as accurately reflecting historical reality opposing Shakespeare's racist fantasy." The opposition is also marked in Wesker's play by the friendship between Shylock and Antonio. Wesker gives Shylock a new Jewish perspective (in which the bond of the pound of flesh is presented as a mocking of Venetian law that insultingly insisted upon contracts in dealings with Jews), and the play illustrates the familiar theme of the utopian ideal of an enlightened society. In his monologue Shylock exalts the need of bibliophile knowledge to ameliorate the judicial system and as a means of self-defense against prejudice:

> And where, where I ask you, could that worldly, new education come from to produce that new law, that new government? Tell me. Why, from books! Where else? . . . Amazing! Knowledge, like underground springs, fresh and constantly there, till one day–up! Bubbling! . . . The word! Unsuspected! Written! Printed! Indestructible! Boom! I love it!

Shylock is both the most admired and the most representative example of the Jewish fear of ignorance, that, in *As Much As I Dare,* Wesker describes as "a cesspit breeding inferiority complexes out of which creeps hatred of what is unknown, mob violence against what is different." Wesker's reverence for knowledge is also an expression of his avowed regret at not having had a university education. Shylock initiates a long list of lecturers, professors, and researchers among Wesker's characters. As Hayman points out, Shylock the teacher, educated and warned by books, exposes "the Venetians as comparable to the Nazis in their hostility to learning and literature."

The Merchant, which premiered in Stockholm, was originally to be staged in New York starring Mostel, an event that promised both critical and commercial recognition. Mostel's death a few days after the first Philadelphia preview in September 1977, combined with the retirement of the influential American critic Clive Barnes of *The New York Times,* who had enthused about the play on his WQXR Radio show, ended Wesker's chance for a breakthrough in New York. The reviews for the Birmingham production in October 1978, notably Ned Chaillet's in *The Times,* were favorable, but the play failed to transfer to the West End.

Adapted from its eponymous short story written in 1974, *Love Letters on Blue Paper* was completed in 1976 and staged at the National Theatre, on its Cottesloe stage, in February 1978. This one-act play centers on the relationship between Victor Marsden, a retired trade-union leader (inspired by Robert Copping, the headmaster of the Hearsley Hall school, and Victor Feather, the general secretary of the T.U.C. between 1969 and 1973, both of whom deeply influenced Wesker) who is dying of leukemia, and his wife, Sonia. He refuses to confide in her regarding the seriousness of his condition. He prefers to call upon his protégé Maurice Stapleton, a professor of art, to face his impending death and reassess his fierce will to live. Sonia writes him letters with no beginning, ending, address, or signature. The letters revisit their life together and evolve from fond recollections to declarations of the love that she had failed to express.

Wilcher notes that, compared with the short story, the play shifts the emphasis from the resilience of the capitalist system to the failure of socialism to supply a worthy alternative. The reviews were mixed for Wesker's first play at the National Theatre, most critics considering the oversentimentality of the narrative as best suited to a movie version.

Wesker's next completed play, *One More Ride on the Merry Go Round* (performed in 1985, published in 1990), written in 1978, is one of two plays, along with *Lady Othello* (published in 1990, but unperformed), that Wesker describes as coming from his "blue bawdy period." He explains in his autobiography: "If stimulating people to think and feel, laugh and cry, even to take action in their lives, is a valid function of art, can stimulating one of the most vital and driving of human urges—the sexual urge—be denied?"

In *One More Ride on the Merry Go Round*, Jason, a Cambridge professor of philosophy, and his wife, Nita, are separated. They have both found the passion that they were seeking during their marriage in their respective lovers Monica and Matt. Each act begins with one of the couples having an orgasm. The first act, set in Jason's flat, presents his loss of interest in work and his dilemma about quitting his job. The professorial triumvirate he invites to his fiftieth-birthday party gives him no satisfactory solution to alleviate his doubts. The second act takes place in the home of Nita, who works to raise money for the Third World. The subplot concerns their daughter, Christine, a professional photographer who is dissatisfied with her work, and Jason's illegitimate German son, Eckhard, who is "a brilliant conjurer." Eckhard's function is both "to reflect the quest of both Jason and Nita for the magic they were unable to find in each other" (Dornan, ed., *Arnold Wesker: A Casebook*) and to acknowledge Wesker's Swedish daughter, Elsa. Wesker's interest in rhetorics is reflected in the linguistic reason given for Jason and Nita's divorce: their marriage was spent with each trying to best the other until one could have the last word, a quarreling process reminiscent of Boomy and Manny's ritual in *The Old Ones*. Leeming notes that "like many farces, this one ends with a lot of slamming doors as the characters pop in and out trying to have the last word." The play opened in April 1985 at Leicester's Phoenix Theatre, where it had a three-week run.

Lady Othello was adapted in 1987 from a movie script Wesker wrote in 1980. The script was bought by Goldcrest but was never produced, since the company went bankrupt before filming began. The play is concerned with the exclusive nature of sexual love. In this one-week-long utopia, Stanton, an aging Jewish English professor, dreams of a second youth with Rosie, a voluptuous and clever African American student. Nevertheless, at the end of the play, Stanton realizes that this glorious episode in his life can only remain a dream. The one relationship that allows him to function is the one he shares with his wife and two children.

Having revisited Renaissance Venetian justice for *The Merchant*, Wesker delved into more historical research and completed five historical plays between 1980 and 2002. The main plot of *Caritas* (performed and published in 1981) is set amid the peasants' uprising of 1381 against the tutelage of the Church. It describes the spiritual quest of a young anchoress, Christine, for mystical union with God. Both social and religious narratives explore the pursuit of liberty and happiness, from the perspective of the group and the individual. Both attempts founder. After three years, Christine realizes she was not called to be an anchoress and asks to be released from her desolate cell. As the Church rejects her request, she is driven to insanity. This metaphor for delusion "stages the danger of the worldly and otherworldly visions which distort the view of reality and lead to inhumanity, violence and a crippled life in anticipation of their future implementation" (Dornan, ed., *Arnold Wesker: A Casebook*).

Caritas was Wesker's second play to be staged at the National Theatre, in 1981. Despite the inherent poetry of the text, the production was unsatisfactory, and the play has only been revived in operatic form in 1991.

In his six "one-woman plays," written between 1980 and 1990, Wesker is concerned with the struggles that women must experience to find their identities and to control a place in the social order. Like Beatie's epiphany in *Roots*, their quest for identity is not only expressed through their control of language but also depends upon it. The chief characteristics of all these women is that they are strong, willful, aggressive or defensive, and unencumbered with moral issues. These realistic plays blend a heightened sense of irony with a stylized language and content that endow them with a genuine poetic dimension.

Written for a festival in Japan on the subject of "the mother," the first of these plays, *Four Portraits* (performed in 1982, published in 1989), overcomes the archetypal use of the mother. With the exception of Deborah, a "mother earth" figure, they are unhappy, frustrated, grumpy, or neurotic, whether old or young. All of them, however, are possessed of a sense of humor that encourages them to go on. Each of them is alone on the stage and has offstage interlocutors. Ruth, the unmarried mother, addresses her daughter, the "Divine Brat," who finally obeys and joins her, ending the vignette. Naomi, seventy, is the mother who never was: her only family and reason to survive is her nephew, who regularly phones her. Miriam, on the psychiatrist's couch, describes herself as the failed mother, daughter of an "unworldly mother." The play was first staged in the United Kingdom at the 1984 Edinburgh Festival and was produced in October 1987 at the Man in the Moon Theatre, London.

Annie Wobbler (performed in 1983, published in 1989) presents a portrait of three women who confront themselves with their flaws and learn, or fail, to overcome them. Annie, the tramp and cleaning lady, was inspired by a washing woman employed in the 1930s by Wesker's family, the poor Jewish family Annie describes in the play. Her memories of past jobs illustrate the fact that she does not belong anywhere and is still searching for her identity. She looks in the mirror and sees "this face but I don't know nothin' about it, 'cept it's growing old.... Funny feeling looking at yourself and not knowing what you see. So I don't do it much." When she throws aside her costume, Annie reveals the next character, Anna, a stunning, young, red-haired woman clad in black underwear. Anna is the only character of the three to be portrayed in a gender-conscious way. A bright postgraduate, she prepares for a date and addresses the mirror with her identity dilemma while dressing up: should she play down her intelligence and emphasize her looks for her date, or hide her sexuality to flaunt her knowledge? She solves the dilemma in one defiant line: "I've got brains and black underwear and I'm not ashamed." Discarding one dress, she then turns into the third character, Annabella Wharton, a writer who is being interviewed after the success of her third novel.

In the course of the interview, Annabella adopts three attitudes toward the invisible interviewer, illustrating the states of mind artists go through. She first offers a modest image, exposing her fears of being attacked in the same way Wesker was condemned by some critics. Like Wesker, she writes a collection of clues, is a compulsive scribbler, and keeps a diary. The mode of defense of the second Annabella is aggression. She clearly assesses her power and, certain of her identity, uses the mirror only to check her image, not to doubt it or question it. The last interview, without the interviewer's voice-over, is answered honestly, as she slowly undresses in front of the mirror in a reversal of Anna's action, revealing the fragile image of the doubtful artist and of the aging woman.

The coke-stealing episode from a 1962 Cameri Theatre (Tel-Aviv) production of Wesker's 1962 play Chips with Everything, *in which a rebellious young Royal Air Force conscript is ultimately pushed into accepting a position as an officer (photograph by Mula & Haramaty; from Glenda Leeming,* Wesker the Playwright, *1983; Thomas Cooper Library, University of South Carolina; used by permission of Arnold Wesker)*

Annie Wobbler was written for actress Nichola McAuliffe. It opened in July 1983 at Birmingham's Repertory Theatre and was transferred in the same month to the New End Theatre in Hampstead, London, from where it was revived for transfer to the Fortune Theatre in the West End in 1984.

Yardsale (performed in 1985, published in 1989) explores in eight scenes the phases Stephanie goes through after her husband, Sheldon, has deserted her. Memories and considerations are expressed through the steps to her recovery, which range from depression to vilification of her husband. She attempts to emancipate herself in her new status as a single woman, but she is reminded of her loss wherever she goes. In the last scene, she goes to a yard sale and is faced with discarded objects and her own loneliness, calling for an absent interlocutor. Under the cover of the story of a marital breakdown, *Yardsale* can be read as a metaphor for the relationship between Wesker and his audience.

Whatever Happened to Betty Lemon (performed in 1986, published in 1989) focuses on "Me. Betty Lemon nee Rivkind from Dalston Junction," former athlete, now crippled, former socialist, and now Lady Lemon. Betty is presented in her morning routine on the day that she receives a letter announcing that she is to be honored as Handicapped Woman of the Year. This event prompts the improvisation of speeches and comic vociferations against all forms of crippling. Betty offers clues as to Wesker's political beliefs when she describes her youth as a socialist "because in those days there was no other name for what I believed." She also voices his humanist concerns through her opposition to different forms of handicap. A realistic study of old age and survival, this play is, as Wilcher comments, a "comic triumph over adversity." Written as a companion piece to *Yardsale* for actress Sheila Steafel, it was performed in England at the Lyric Theatre Studio, London, in 1987 by Brenda Bruce, directed by the author.

At the same time as he was writing the one-woman plays, Wesker enlarged the focus of his individual studies with two plays. *When God Wanted a Son* (performed in 1989, published in 1990) and *Men Die, Women Survive* (performed in 1992, published in 1994 under its original title, *Three Women Talking*) both explore the dynamics of couples after their separation.

The first part of *When God Wanted a Son* opens with Connie, an unsuccessful stand-up comedian, performing her self-deprecating act in a cabaret. She returns to the home of her mother, Martha, in an attempt to solve her identity crisis. In the second act, Connie's father, Joshua, a Jewish professor of semantics, also comes to Martha's, uninvited and unwelcome, to request her financial support for his project. Martha is a fiercely anti-Semitic Gentile who cannot bring herself to pronounce the word "Jew" and is equally unable to acknowledge that what finally revolted her in Joshua was his Jewishness. This inability to convey her repulsion, to talk to and about Joshua (he remains "he" or "him"), illustrates the deep-rooted nature of anti-Semitism. It also contrasts with Joshua's semantic hegemony. As a result of both his presence and his semantic mastery, she screams her irrational hatred at the end of both acts. Nevertheless, Joshua is not given an entirely blameless role. Martha attempts a reconciliation by baking him a birthday cake. In a previous scene, the offer of food is equated with the offer of communication: the game consists in guessing the elaborate ingredients and praising Martha's inventiveness. Joshua refuses to participate in the game and ignores Martha's pleas for recognition. Communication is severed on both sides, epitomized in Martha's final cries and Joshua's conclusion that she, as an anti-Semite, "will never have peace." Beneath its dark theme and ending, the play explores the limits of what can or cannot be ridiculed and is extremely funny in its irreverent humor. In full production at the New End Theatre in February 1997, the play received good reviews.

In *Men Die, Women Survive,* Wesker pursues his panegyric of women and states his belief that the twentieth century belongs to them. Minerva was deserted by Montcrieff, a writer, and felt chaos. Mischa, a Hebrew scholar, left Leo and was reborn in the process. Claire, researcher of shadow cabinet minister Vincent, embodies the private pain of the mistress, as Vincent has just abandoned her. The three women meet for dinner in an attempt to console Claire. Each has prepared one course, delineating the three parts of the play. Interspersed between their memories and thoughts about their relationships, one actor plays out short scenes from the celibate life of the three men. The play echoes other works. The story of the battered wife in love with literature in *Break, My Heart* (performed and published in 1997) is related here as a newspaper feature. Mischa's scholarly decree, "Jews and women! Oppressed and hated for knowing too much," recalls Joshua's claim in *When God Wanted a Son.* Her view that "physical deficiencies invite derision" whereas "emotional ones invite pity" revisits Betty Lemon's comic and moving exploration of handicap. Montcrieff's self-denunciation as a writer/vulture that "picks at the dead and the partly living. All my best lines are other people's" is reminiscent of the thieving metaphor in *Yardsale.* The world premiere of the play took place at the Northlight Theater, Chicago, in 1992.

Badenheim 1939 (published in 1994), another of the historical plays, is an adaptation of Aharon Appelfeld's 1979 novel about Jews gathered in the middle-class-turned-bohemian Austrian spa of Badenheim before they are transported to a Polish concentration camp. Every year most of the characters meet around the event of the arts festival. In 1939, they seem unaware, until the end, of the fate that awaits them, as "sanitation inspectors" and barbed wire appear: "Well! If the coaches are so dirty it must mean that we have not far to go." In five parts and thirty-eight scenes, Wesker presents with a delicate humor and poignant emotion an abhorrent part of Western history. The play, written in 1987, has not been performed to date because it needs a venue with the resources of a National Theatre or university theater to accommodate the large cast.

Little Old Lady and *Shoeshine,* both written in 1987 and published in 1989, are two short plays for young people. Each explores a familiar theme. Set in the carriage of an underground train, *Little Old Lady* explores once again the fighting spirit of the old when faced with injustice and blatant violation of their democratic rights. The eponymous lady is the only character who dares to

ACT ONE

Sc. 1.

Venice, 1563. The Ghetto Nuovo.
SHYLOCK'S study. It is strewn
with books and manuscripts.

SHYLOCK, a 'loan-banker', with his
friend, ANTONIO, a merchant, are
leisurely cataloguing.

ANTONIO is by the table, writing, as
SHYLOCK reads out the titles and places
them on his shelves.

They are old friends, and old. ~~Middle-age has passed them. They are~~ in
their ~~early~~ *middle* sixties.

Shylock   (reading out) 'Lesser book of Precepts'. Author, Isaac of Corbeil. England. Thirteenth century. (ANTONIO writes) Hebrew/English Dictionary. Author. R. David Kimhi. England. Thirteenth century. Not too fast for you, Antonio?

Antonio   It's not the most elegant script, but I'm speedy.

Shylock   And I'm ~~too~~ eager. I know it. But here, the last of the manuscripts and then we begin with the printed books. ~~Ah, dear friend, I've~~ Such treasures to show you, you'll be thrilled, ~~astounded, humiliated, and~~ you'll be - I can't wait. But write, one more, and then we'll rest. I promise you. I'll bring out my wines, and fuss and - the last one. I promise, promise.

Antonio   Do I complain, *Ah!* Shylock! Look! I'm waiting.

Shylock   A saint I have for a friend.

Antonio   And what *does the saint* ~~do I~~ have?

Shylock   An over-grown schoolboy. I know it! The worst of the deal. But -

Antonio   I'm waiting, Shylock.

Shylock   Deed. Legal. (Anglo-Jewish. Twelth century. I can't read the name. Probably drawn up by a businessman himself. *(Boring)* ~~But~~ what a mastery ~~of it shows~~ of Talmudic Law. I love them, those old men, their cleverness, their deeds, their wide ranging talents. Feel it! ~~The~~ *it!* Touch ~~the past -~~ ~~Antonio, you look sad. I've overworked you. Abused a~~ *special* ~~friendship. Here. Drink. (offers wine) Drink and It's a special~~ ~~understand me. I've waited ten years to bring my books~~ out ~~from hiding.~~ ~~XXXXXXXX~~ Do you know what that means for a collector? Ten years? ~~August 12, 1553 - the day of the burning of the books.~~ Ha! The scheme of things! 'The Talmud and kindred Hebrew literature?' they said, 'Blasphemy!' 'Burn them!' And there they burned, on the

Corrected typescript page from Wesker's 1989 play Shylock, *a revised version of* The Merchant, *his 1976 reworking of William Shakespeare's* The Merchant of Venice *(by permission of Harry Ransom Humanities Research Center, University of Texas at Austin, and Arnold Wesker)*

defy a thug who has lit a cigarette in this restricted, microcosmic, nonsmoking environment. The climax builds as, distressed by her own boldness and the lack of support from the other commuters, she warns him repeatedly that she will have to stop the train if he refuses to extinguish his cigarette. In *Shoeshine* a young man, having recently completed a degree in philosophy, explores the issues of survival and individual choices. Faced with unemployment, he decides to earn his living by shining people's shoes in the streets. Despite the opinions of his family and friends that this trade is demeaning for someone with a university education, and despite being attacked by thugs, he continues to set up his shoeshine box. Both plays celebrate the resilience of individuals who take action rather than being inanimate elements in their hostile environments.

In sharp contrast with Betty Lemon, Samantha in the next one-woman play, *The Mistress* (published in 1989, performed in 1991), is a desolate figure. A thirty-nine-year-old talented dress designer, she is set in the environment of her workshop and waits, in vain, for a phone call from her married lover. Her dilemma about her relationship with her lover is verbalized in dialogues with her mannequins while she ponders on life priorities and her own social role by selecting her charities. First performed in Italy, this play was staged at Cardiff's Sherman Theatre in June 1997 in a double bill with *Break, My Heart,* a one-act play that explores the cycle of domestic violence in a working-class couple.

Commissioned for the fortieth anniversary in 1989 of Basildon, one of the postwar new towns, *Beorhtel's Hill* (performed in 1989, published in 1994), titled for the Saxon name for Basildon, is a community play designed for 125 performers. As in *Badenheim 1939,* Wesker is concerned with "strangers in their midst," from the viewpoint of the East Enders who first settled in Basildon. The play pleads for tolerance toward recent immigrants, characterized in the Patel family, who are Ugandan refugees. The other issue pervading the play is "the dream versus the reality." The development of the town is described through a diary kept by the character Brenda, who has witnessed the changes in the town from the beginning and tries to adapt to her changing environment. The development is also embodied by the narrator, who is "sour and sweet by turns." The hopeful image that life never ceases is enacted in the recurrent sequence of different generations of children chasing the end of the rainbow.

Although *Yardsale* was staged in France as a fifth vignette to *Four Portraits* (Stephanie embodying the abandoned mother), *Letter to a Daughter* (performed in 1992, published in 1994) is a thematically more suitable coupling, with Melanie as the inadequate mother. The last of the one-woman plays, it shows a singer/songwriter trying to write a letter of advice to her daughter, whom she seldom sees because of her professional schedule. The advice transforms itself into a mea culpa for her shortcomings as a mother. The six parts are each concluded with a song, illustrating the different drafts of her letter/introspection. As Melanie the performer is called onstage, the letter still reads: "My dear daughter, Marike, I have been meaning to write to you for some time. . . ." The play premiered in Seoul, Korea, in 1992 and was staged at the 1998 Edinburgh Festival. In 2003 Wesker completed *Letter to Myself* (performed in 2004), a one-act play in which Melanie's daughter, age thirteen, writes a letter to herself that is to be read on her eighteenth birthday.

Originally written for the radio in 1984, *Bluey* (broadcast in 1985, published in 1990) is a one-act play about suppressed guilt. It concerns the introspective journey of Hilary Hawkins, a judge who comes to question a past he had subconsciously obliterated when a particular court case stirs his confidence and memories. The leitmotiv "Don't forget" is finally associated with an incident in his student days when he forgot to shout a warning before throwing down the lead ("bluey" in slang) from the roof he was working on. As a result, the face of a fellow worker was severely damaged. His lack of courage to meet the man he has scarred echoes another episode of his past, when he avoided seeing a dying girlfriend. His guilty feelings have finally surfaced, but he confides his actions only to his diary that cannot condemn nor judge nor pity.

The stranger as the hostile Other is once more at the center of the plot in *Blood Libel* (published in 1994, performed in 1996). Commissioned by the new Norwich Playhouse and written in 1991, it dramatizes the twelfth-century summary investigation and trial of Jews for the rape and murder of a Christian child in the woods of Norwich. The Jews were accused of killing young William to use his blood for Passover, hence creating the initial "blood libel." Elias, the prior of the church of Norwich, contradicted the evidence presented, and the charge was dropped. After twenty years, the monks of Norwich demand that William's martyrdom be recognized. Pilgrims gather eagerly, awaiting miracles from the blessed and martyred child, thereby enriching the church.

Starting with the story as it was told, the four parts emphasize religious and social prejudice against the Jews. Wesker also presents unsentimentally the conflicts that the trial raised within the clergy about the charge of ritual murder. The attack of the stranger on William is reenacted at regular intervals, identifying the true nature of the crime from a modern perspective and in contrast to the claims of the monks.

Another play concerned with women's voices was *Wild Spring* (performed and published in 1994), written for Bruce; it presents the relationships that Gertie, a

Wesker in his London study in the early 1980s (from Glenda Leeming, Wesker the Playwright, *1983; Thomas Cooper Library, University of South Carolina; used by permission of Arnold Wesker)*

stage actress, develops with two black men within a scope of fifteen years. In 1976, Gertrude Matthews is forty and a revered actress. She befriends Sam, a nineteen-year-old parking attendant who believes he cannot aspire to any other career. She believes that she can be much more than an actress. In 1991, she is a broken figure, abandoned by her theater company. She has fallen in love with Kennedy, the thirty-year-old company manager. He believes he can be an actor, whereas his one gift is enterprise. Through these three portraits, aptly set in the world of the theater, Wesker illustrates the complex tensions of individuals with their own projected or illusory images, using the central theme of acting as a metaphor for self-deceit. The play premiered in Tokyo in 1994 and later had a three-year run in Budapest.

Written in 1997, *Denial* was performed in May 2000 at the Bristol Old Vic, where it received good reviews. It details the process of self-deceit involved in false-memory syndrome and the devastating consequences of false accusations of child abuse on an innocent family. Jenny has been unhappy in her marriage and her career and seeks the help of a therapist when she gives up on both. Valerie Morgan is a social worker who has specialized in battered wives and sexually abused children. She finds an easy solution to Jenny's angst: by the fifth consultation, she observes symptoms that may be displayed by incest victims. She proceeds to distort Jenny's childhood memories, making her believe that she was abused by her father. Interwoven between the therapist's sessions are scenes in which Jenny's father, mother, and sister are trying to understand her accusation and to survive it together. In the final scene–the carefully planned confrontation between Jenny and her parents– her father, Matthew, confesses his "guilt" in a speech that is in essence a celebration of parenthood:

I bit their bums. No let me finish. It gets even worse. We *both* bit their bums. Even worse–we let them bite our bums. Jenny's right–we tampered with her. We used to have bum-biting days. And everyone squealed, and everyone shrieked. Got hiccups from shrieking and squealing, and laughing and fearing.... My worst of worstest confessions. I loved, absolutely loved bathing them–splashing them, squirting them, blowing bubbles for them, and then–rubbing them in with baby oil.... Oh, we tampered with them all right.

The play ends with Jenny's "haunted, confused, uncertain" howl as she turns to Valerie, realizing that her psychological conclusions belong to the land of "could bes." *Denial* identifies the therapist as a manipulator and therapy as a prison that creates dependency.

Groupie (first performed on radio, then onstage in Italy, in 2002) shows Wesker at his best. It is the story of a cantankerous, secluded, neglected painter who is gradually taken out of his shell and out of his flat by Mattie, a cheery sixty-year-old woman, who has read his autobiography and started a correspondence with him because they grew up in the same East End streets. In 2005, the play is entering its third year touring in Italy after an excellent critical response, and its UK premiere is planned for the London Old Vic.

Not yet performed or published, but planned for October 2005 at the Greenwich Theatre in London, Wesker's play "Longitude" (written in 2002) is based on Dava Sobel's 1995 book. In the eighteenth century, Parliament offered £20,000 to whoever would devise a means of finding longitude, therefore saving many lives lost at sea. John Harrison, a carpenter and joiner, constructed a reliable clock; but the conception, trials, and technical improvements of the clock, as well as petty rivalries, meant that he was never awarded the full prize. The play focuses in two acts on the struggle of an uneducated but talented man for recognition by the Establishment. It is reminiscent of *Their Very Own and Golden City* both because of the lengthy time span of the action and in the conflict between the individual and authority. Nevertheless, in "Longitude," the compromise is presented as a forward dynamic toward the completion of the main character's lifework.

It would be a mistake to think of Arnold Wesker's career only in terms of the socially engaged utopia of his plays of the 1950s and 1960s. His friend, the writer Margaret Drabble, has sketched a convincing insight to understanding him and the lukewarm enthusiasm with which his plays have been met in London since the mid 1960s:

> "Those who dismiss me" is a characteristic Wesker phrase. He is sensitive to attack, and admits that one adverse criticism hurts him more than many praises can cheer him. But unlike most people who feel hurt, he conducts long battles in newspapers. . . . If anyone is going to rehabilitate Wesker, it will be Wesker himself, by refusing to sit back in the comfortable slot of Angry Young Dramatist, or to grow into the role of Betrayed Middle Aged Man. (quoted in Dornan, ed., *Arnold Wesker: A Casebook*)

He clearly will not sit back. On the public side, he believes in the importance of criticism in a democracy. On the literary side, with a revival of *The Kitchen* in Paris in April 2003 and production projects in the pipeline, Wesker remains a "compulsive scribbler" and an eclectic artist. He is writing his first novel after successful attempts at short stories and the erotic tales *The King's Daughters* (1998). The latest examples of his dramatic work explore, in a dramatic idiom he has mastered, private and public themes in a dynamic that subtly blends both together.

Interviews:

Catherine Itzin, Glenda Leeming, and Simon Trussler, Interview with Wesker, *Theatre Quarterly*, 7 (1977);

John O'Mahony, "Piques and Troughs: Profile on Arnold Wesker," *Guardian* (25 May 2002) <http://www.guardian.co.uk/saturday_review/story/0,,721464,00.html>;

Andrea Matias, "Turntable 3," *Roundhouse News Sheet* (5 July 2002).

References:

Arnold Wesker, Playwright <http://www.arnoldwesker.com>;

John Russell Brown, *Theatre Language: A Study of Arden, Osborne, Pinter and Wesker* (London: Allen Lane, 1972);

Colin Chambers and Mike Prior, *Playwrights' Progress: Patterns of Postwar British Drama* (Oxford: Amber Lane, 1987);

Reade W. Dornan, *Arnold Wesker Revisited* (New York: Twayne, 1994);

Dornan, ed., *Arnold Wesker: A Casebook* (London & New York: Garland, 1998);

Ronald Hayman, *Arnold Wesker* (London: Heinemann, 1970; third edition, 1979);

Christopher Innes, *Modern British Drama 1890–1990* (Cambridge: Cambridge University Press, 1995);

Catherine Itzin, *Stages in the Revolution: Political Theatre in Britain Since 1968* (London: Eyre Methuen, 1980);

Glenda Leeming, *Wesker the Playwright* (London: Methuen, 1983);

Leeming and Simon Trussler, *The Plays of Arnold Wesker: An Assessment* (London: Gollancz, 1971);

Leeming, ed., *Wesker on File* (London: Methuen, 1985);

Harold U. Ribalow, *Arnold Wesker* (New York: Twayne, 1965);

John Russell Taylor, *Anger and After: A Guide to the New British Drama* (London: Methuen, 1969);

Michelene Wandor, *Look Back in Gender: Sexuality and the Family in Post-War British Drama* (London: Methuen, 1987);

Robert Wilcher, *Understanding Arnold Wesker* (Columbia: University of South Carolina Press, 1991);

Katharine J. Worth, *Revolutions in Modern British Drama* (London: Bell, 1972).

Papers:

Arnold Wesker's papers are in the Harry Ransom Humanities Research Center, University of Texas at Austin <http://www.hrc.utexas.edu/research/fa/wesker.html>.

E. A. Whitehead
(Ted Whitehead)
(3 April 1933 –   )

Tony Dunn
University of Portsmouth

PLAY PRODUCTIONS: *The Foursome,* London, Royal Court Theatre Upstairs, 17 March 1971; London, Fortune Theatre, 4 May 1971; Washington, D.C., 1972; New York, 1973;

Alpha Beta, London, Royal Court Theatre, 26 January 1972; London, Apollo Theatre, May 1972; New York, 1973;

The Sea Anchor, London, Royal Court Theatre Upstairs, 11 July 1974; New York, 1982;

Old Flames, Bristol, Bristol Old Vic Studio, 28 October 1975; London, Arts Theatre, 19 February 1976; New York, Arts Theatre Alliance, 1978;

Mecca, London, Open Space Theatre, 7 July 1977; New York, 1980;

The Man Who Fell in Love with His Wife, London, Lyric Studio Theatre, 27 February 1984; New York, 1988;

The Dance of Death, adapted from August Strindberg's play, Oxford, Playhouse, 31 January 1984 (part one); London, Riverside Theatre, 30 May 1985 (parts one and two).

BOOKS: *The Foursome* (London: Faber & Faber, 1972);
Alpha Beta (London: Faber & Faber, 1972);
The Sea Anchor (London: Faber & Faber, 1975);
Old Flames (London: Faber & Faber, 1976);
Mecca (London: Faber & Faber, 1977);
World's End (London: BBC Publications, 1981);
The Man Who Fell in Love with His Wife (London & Boston: Faber & Faber, 1984);
Plays (London: Oberon, 2001)—comprises *The Foursome, Alpha Beta, The Sea Anchor,* and *The Punishment.*

PRODUCED SCRIPTS: *Under the Age,* television, BBC2, 20 March 1972;
The Punishment, television, BBC2, 14 October 1972;
Alpha Beta, motion picture, Memorial Enterprises, 1973;
The Peddler, television, BBC1, 23 March 1976;
The Proofing Session, television, BBC1, 17 May 1977;

Ted Whitehead, 1977 (photograph by Donald Cooper; from Plays and Players, *February 1978; Thomas Cooper Library, University of South Carolina)*

The Irish Connection, television, ITV, 1979;
Sweet Nothings, television, BBC1, 4 April 1980;
World's End, television, BBC1, 1 October 1981;
The Detective, adapted from Paul Ferris's novel, television, BBC1, 10 May 1985;
The Life and Loves of a She-Devil, adapted from Fay Weldon's novel, television, BBC2, 8 October 1986;
The Old Goat Gone, radio, BBC Radio 3, 1987;
The Free Frenchman, adapted from Piers Paul Read's book, television, ITV, 8 November 1989;
The Cloning of Joanna May, adapted from Weldon's novel, television, ITV, 26 January 1992;
A Question of Guilt, television, ITV, 1993;
Tess of the D'Urbervilles, adapted from Thomas Hardy's novel, television, ITV, 8 March 1998;
The Blonde Bombshell, television, ITV, 26 April 1999;
The Mayor of Casterbridge, adapted from Hardy's novel, television, ITV, 17 August 2003.

Cover for the publication of Whitehead's 1972 play. The premiere starred Rachel Roberts and Albert Finney (pictured) in the story of a disintegrating marriage (photograph by John Haynes; Thomas Cooper Library, University of South Carolina).

OTHER: *The Punishment,* in *Prompt Three,* edited by A. Durband (London: Hutchinson, 1976), pp. 111–127.

E. A. Whitehead's stage plays span the 1970s. They register the pain and confusion attendant upon the erosion of patriarchy as a secure framework to interpret the family, sex, and marriage; however, Whitehead's characters, male and female, do not articulate their crises in these terms. They are neither ideologues nor intellectuals. But they are articulate, and often witty, up to those moments when language breaks down into physical violence: no class, and neither gender, is exempt from this pattern. Whitehead thus attempts to dislocate such deep-seated associations in English culture as the equation of the working class with inarticulate animalism, the middle class with urbane self-control, and woman with the image of ethereal nurturer. The catalyst for the deconstruction of such stereotypes is the final entry of women into civil society. While this observation is now a banal one, the interest of Whitehead's work is that he dramatized this process throughout a period, the 1970s, when it was both uneven and unpredictable. He was struggling to find new ways of expression within old artistic forms. Whitehead summarized his approach to themes and methods in contemporary drama in a revealing interview in *Television Today* (1986), in which he stated he is concerned above all with "the mainstream area" of "relationships between men and women, repression and the frustration felt by women." He adds that he has "little sympathy with those who are concerned with experiment. I'm not interested in experiment for its own sake, but in mastering the traditional uses of drama—of narrative, character development and telling a good story."

Edward Anthony Whitehead (sometimes credited as Ted Whitehead) was born in Liverpool on 3 April 1933. His father, Edward Whitehead, was a compositor on the *Liverpool Post,* and his mother, Catherine Curran Whitehead, was a factory worker in the local plant of the Metal Box Company. He gained a scholarship to the direct-grant grammar school St. Francis Xavier's College, which was then run by the Jesuits. He graduated with a bachelor of arts (honors) degree in English from Christ's College, Cambridge, in 1955 and later obtained a master of arts from the same university. In 1958 he married Kathleen Horton, with whom he has two daughters; the couple divorced in 1976. Between 1959 and 1965 he had a variety of employments, including positions as milkman, salesman, and teacher. He was an advertising copywriter and account executive from 1965 to 1971. Since the success of his first play, *The Foursome* (performed in 1971, published in 1972), he has been a full-time writer for stage, radio, and television, producing both original work and adaptations of classic and contemporary novels. He was resident dramatist at the Royal Court Theatre from 1971 to 1972 and a fellow in creative writing at Bulmershe College, Berkshire, for the 1975–1976 academic year. He won the George Devine Award from the English Stage Company in 1971 and, in the same year, the *Evening Standard* Drama Award, both for *The Foursome.* In 1976 he married script editor Gwenda Bagshaw.

The Foursome is set in the sandhills of Freshfield, a venue for courting couples near Liverpool. Two men in their twenties, Tim and Harry, attempt—sometimes mockingly, sometimes seriously—to seduce two younger girls, Marie and Bella, whom they have picked up in a Liverpool pub the night before. The three acts span a hot summer's day from late morning to early evening. The men enact a series of rapid switches between withdrawal from and approach to the girls. In act 1 they perform a mock striptease in front of the girls, playing the roles of male hunk and coy female. Marie and Bella are a delighted audience. Parodic homosexual "routines" are repeated throughout the play. Yet, the men also make their heterosexual intentions clear: as Harry is lying near Marie after the striptease, she asks him what he is doing; "Looking up your frock," he answers.

The girls appreciate this frank approach, and in act 2 they turn it back on the men. Harry and Tim have called the girls "prick-teasers," so Marie and Bella call them "cunt-teasers." However, the subsequent horseplay with a beach ball turns vicious as the men throw hard to hurt; Harry holds Marie's head down and pours sand on her face; and Tim empties the girls' handbags into the sand and calls their contents "Muck." He then launches into a tirade about when he had the job of painting the ladies' restroom in a club in Slater Street, Liverpool. He was disgusted by the sickening smell of "cunt and . . . scent." He thought of "the birds all collecting up there in front of that bloody great mirror, covering themselves with muck" and "us blokes waiting downstairs for the little angels." He burns one of Bella's stockings with a lighter, and the two men force the girls into the sea to wash off their makeup.

Act 3 seems to effect a reconciliation. The men gather up the girls' makeup, and Marie and Bella placidly apply it as the men watch them in silence. Two moments of idyll seem to counter the previous violence: Marie is delighted with the beauty of the squirrels she has seen in the woods, and Bella recounts when she was crowned Queen of the May. Then Marie announces that her period—"the drips"—has come on, and the girls go to the woods for privacy. Tim and Harry will not stay, even to give them a lift back to town. "Dirty cows!" they say to each other and exit.

For Benedict Nightingale of *The New Statesman* (14 May 1971), this work was "as keen and sharp a new play as I have seen for months," though he thought it somewhat vitiated by an overemphasis in the production on "a mild homosexual crush between the two males." Irving Wardle of *The Times* (19 May 1921) commented on Whitehead's use of a "deliberately impoverished laconic Scouse [native of Liverpool] dialogue," but broadened his analysis to locate the play within "the twisted sexual tradition of the north," where "the boys feel nothing but hostility for their partners; and their lust is only a form of aggression." Kenneth Hurren of *The Spectator* (15 May 1971) thought that Whitehead "communicates a revulsion" for these sex lives "without making satisfactory drama of it."

The sex war continues, but at the level of adult marriage, in Whitehead's next play, *Alpha Beta* (performed and published in 1972). This work is much more ambitious technically. Its three acts cover nine years in the marriage of Mr. and Mrs. Elliott, aged twenty-nine and twenty-six respectively. He is a dock manager, and she is a housewife and mother to their two children, Tony and Sarah, who never appear onstage. The single set is their lounge. Mrs. Elliott is decorating it in white in act 1, the winter of 1962. It is full of sunshine and with a crammed bookcase in act 2, the spring of 1966. It is untidy and poorly decorated in the last act, the summer of 1971. The room is the minitheater for the degeneration and collapse of the Elliotts' marriage. Mr. Elliott is the driving force for its dissolution. He desires freedom, first for himself, then as a social right for all. For him their marriage has already broken down as the play opens. He is on the brink of moving out and taking a mistress. Mrs. Elliott refuses a separation and considers him emotionally arrested. She believes in what she calls "the MORAL law" and will never consent to divorce her husband, despite the fact that by the second act he is openly keeping a mistress and by the third act he has left home. She is determined that, at some stage, Mr. Elliott's "slut," Eileen, will "pay," and that Mr. Elliott's freedom will always be circumscribed.

The third act centers on two long speeches in which each of the Elliotts declares the reasons for the actions they have taken. Mr. Elliott's speech locates his dissatisfaction with his marriage within a larger social context: "in future," he announces, "men and women are going to share free and equal unions that last because they want them to last. Not because they're *forced!*" He finishes with a fervent faith in a future when "Free men . . . will live freely . . . with free women!" Mrs. Elliott's analysis derives from her observation of her husband's character. She thinks he is "a real old Catholic missionary at heart" who is attracted to women who are lonely or shy and then offers to "*complete* them. You offer them *your* vitality, *your* resilience, *your* confidence . . . but instead of saving anybody you're actually enslaving them." His altruism, in her view, leads to total ownership of the woman. The danger for the woman is that, once he has gotten her completely committed to him, he drops her and gallops off to some new crusade. He is, in her view, even more dangerous because he is unconscious of his motives. The two views are equally plausible but, in relation to marriage, incompatible. Mrs. Elliott threatens suicide; Mr. Elliott dares her to do it and exits; and his wife

Cover for the publication of Whitehead's 1974 play about the sexual entanglements among four young people played by Marjorie Yates, Peter Armitage, Alison Steadman, and David Daker (pictured) in the London premiere (Thomas Cooper Library, University of South Carolina)

pours the Nembutal into the sink and is left alone in a near-catatonic state.

Critics were divided as to where Whitehead intended audience sympathies to lie. Wardle in *The Times* (27 January 1972) thought that while the production was "solidly on the man's side" since viewers are "taken inside his head, asked to sympathize with his fantasies," Whitehead's characterization of him is "evasive." Nightingale in *The New Statesman* (4 February 1972) agreed that, as the play proceeds, Mrs. Elliott "begins to look more and more in the wrong," but that her husband emerges as "an impossibly articulate spokesman for Ibsenite honesty and Lawrentian joy." Hurren in *The Spectator* (5 February 1972) doubted the range of register Whitehead had given his characters and commented on the playwright's "curiously elevated notions of working-class speech." He also doubted Whitehead's dramatic skills, calling *Alpha Beta* not a play but "rather a dispute and a deadlock." Nightingale, by contrast, declared, "No British dramatist has portrayed a nastier marriage."

With Whitehead's next play, *The Sea Anchor* (performed in 1974, published in 1975), theme and language converge to make the "freedom" announced by Mr. Elliott and contested by Mrs. Elliott the central issue. On a jetty at Dublin Bay, two men (Andy, in his thirties, and Les, in his twenties) and two women (Sylvia, a teenager, and Jean, in her twenties) wait, over two days, for Jean's lover Nick to arrive after a lone crossing from Liverpool in a ten-foot dinghy. All the characters are engaged in adulterous relationships, but that freedom is circumscribed by marriage and convention. Odysseus-figure Nick, who "does exactly what he wants to do," is their model of a truly free man. But the longer they wait, the more critical they become; the more the sea fog obscures their view, the more clearly they see him. Les, an engineer and former naval man, points out that Nick has no mechanical skills and no backup batteries. All the energy is, in fact, on the jetty. Andy, who boasts of three hundred extramarital relationships but declares "I'd never let it interfere with the family," thinks Nick married too young and that his obsession with freedom was an envious fantasy of the lives he imagined were being led by the next teenage generation, "sexually free in a way we hadn't been." Jean envies Sylvia because she is young and free, but Sylvia wants to have children with Les, who has a wife and family and has become disillusioned with domestic life. Jean herself offered once to leave Nick–to "free him"–but she found she could not live without him, although "every so often I could strangle him." Andy is in constant communication with his wife and Nick's, who are waiting for news of his arrival. The four protagonists break up and realign with mutual accusations of betrayal and commitment. The squabbles continue in the third and last act, with no definite news of Nick. Sylvia seeks a commitment from Les, who says, "I could stand the thought of not sharing a life with you, but I couldn't stand not seeing you tomorrow." Sylvia cries and kisses him, but his ambivalence sums up the uncertain relationships between all the men and women in the play. A launch finally emerges from the mist, towing a dinghy into the harbor. The boat had been found empty, "riding on the sea anchor."

For Wardle in *The Times* (15 July 1974), *The Sea Anchor* is a companion piece to *The Foursome*. Both plays have four characters "bound together by a shared taste for drink and copulation," and the message is "these people are no good at pleasure." But he concluded that *The Sea Anchor* is a far better piece than Whitehead's previous plays because it is "much fairer to women." The play, nonetheless, demonstrates what Wardle called the playwright's great failing: "his taste for a kind of sentimental violence." For Nightingale in *The New Statesman* (19 July 1974), the piece is well written and tense but "depressing," because the protagonists seem "resigned to anomie and sexual misery." He commented that Whitehead is "to sex what Edward Bond is to violence and cruelty, a high priest of misanthropy."

Edward, a cardboard salesman in his late thirties, is the focus of attention in *Old Flames* (performed in 1975, published in 1976). He has been invited to dinner on her houseboat by Sally, a liberated woman in her early twenties. Edward calls her "the first *modern* woman I've known" because she is so free. He sees in her the incarnation of the new Women's Liberation Movement and presents himself as pro-emancipation: "I think the Libbers have a point. I think men abuse women." Edward attributes his failures in relationships with women to his Roman Catholic upbringing, in which women have been represented as either whores or madonnas, and he suspects that his most enduring love is for his mother. Sally allows him to kiss and fondle her but is unimpressed by his new attitudes. When the rest of the guests arrive, the point of the evening becomes clearer. They are three of the women with whom he has failed to establish a satisfactory relationship. Julie, in her mid twenties, was his second wife. He abandoned her when she had a serious illness, and when she recovered, she created a new life for herself working in an art gallery. Diana, his first former wife, arrives. He left her and their children without financial support, and they were evicted from their home. Diana had maintained the family by working as a typist. Edward's "first love" now enters–his mother, Muriel. She accuses him of neglecting his father while the latter was dying from stomach cancer, cutting all ties with his family, and abandoning his wives and children. Edward attempts to defend himself by accusing Diana of being a poor housekeeper and Julie of paranoid jealousy. Muriel, with an echo of Mrs. Elliott's analysis of her husband in *Alpha Beta,* sums him up as being a "dab hand" at "making women suffer." The tone of these exchanges, however, is low-key, as if the women were announcing indisputable facts. Edward congratulates them all on the civilized conduct of their lives and of the evening. He finally asks, "What's for supper?" and Sally replies, "You."

The second act is a discussion between the women of their differing opportunities for happiness, according to their ages and upbringings. Their fathers were silent and repressed, and their men seemed guided only by sexual desires. Marriage emerges as the block on their desires, and masturbation seems preferable to sex with these idiotic men. Unmarried Sally again emerges as the "free woman" of the future. She kisses Diana and Muriel, both of whom resist, but Julie welcomes her advances. Sally has had a much more adventurous sexual history than the other women, including mixed-sex threesomes and a boyfriend who discovered he was gay. Muriel reveals, however, that she too has a history, a short-lived and idyllic relationship with a young communist who talked to her about "art and poetry." The three once-married women take off their wedding rings and put them ceremonially in a bowl. Then, in a parody of the Eucharist, they eat some meat and drink some red liquid, and Sally raises a glass "In memory of Edward."

The Times ran two reviews. The first, by Charles Lewsen (31 October 1975), on the debut of the play at the Bristol Old Vic Studio, praised its construction and called it a "balance of vitriol and compassion." In the

Julie T. Wallace in Whitehead's 1986 television adaptation of Fay Weldon's 1983 novel, The Life and Loves of a She-Devil *(photograph © BBC Photographic Library; from George W. Brandt, ed.,* British Television Drama in the 1980s, *1993; Thomas Cooper Library, University of South Carolina)*

second review, for the London debut, Wardle (20 February 1976) detected "Euripidean ironies" in the denoument of the play and calls the second act "a pent-up hymn of hate to the male animal." He commended the balance between different, opposing readings that the play provides: it can be interpreted as "a sex revolution document" or "an expression of profound masculine self-loathing." For Nightingale in *The New Statesman* (27 February 1976), the play provided "a frank recognition of what most of us have felt in our more disgusted and self-disgusted moments." Hurren concluded in *The Spectator* (28 February 1976) that "It is not that he [Whitehead] hates either men or women; he just deplores the heterosexual urge that leads to the enslavement of men and the betrayal of women."

A twenty-year-old woman is again the catalyst for action in *Mecca* (performed and published in 1977). Sandy is a medical student and the youngest among a tourist party of six English people holidaying in Morocco. She has been taken under the kindly wing of Andrew, a left-leaning doctor in his late forties. His wife, Eunice, some ten years younger, suspects his interest is as much sexual as paternal. A more ambiguous couple is Jill, a copywriter in her late thirties, and her husband, Martin, an army major of the same age. Theirs is really a "white" marriage, since Martin is homosexual and more interested in the Arab boys beyond the tourist compound where the stage action takes place than in any of the women within it. The remaining tourist is Ian, a professional footballer in his mid twenties. His attempt to have sex with Jill on the beach is reported as a failure, as he suffers from premature ejaculation. Sandy, therefore, is the only unattached and sanguine member of the group. She is also the only one of the tourists to try learning the language of the country. The older woman, Jill, envies Sandy her freedom from conventions. "She seems so free and easy and full of life," says Jill in the first scene, and she adds that young women such as Sandy "don't go hurtling into middle age as soon as they get married and have kids, like our lot. . . . We were taught to spend our youth trying to look mature and our maturity trying to look young." For Jill, in fact, Sandy is an entirely new breed of woman, who would actually enjoy sex and men. She is a "kind of twentieth century virgin" in her innocent sensuality. This innocence, however, provokes the central action of the play.

Sandy is keen to explore the town outside the compound walls, alone if necessary, although Andrew and Martin warn her of the dangers. She offers wine to an Arab boy who hangs around the compound and whom Martin has already humiliated by making him jump like a dog for a handful of sweets. Sandy wanders outside the compound dressed only in a towel and is later found raped. In their reactions, some of her fellow tourists reveal different sides to their characters. Jill, the liberal sensualist, denounces all Arabs as animals. Her cynical husband tries to deal with the catastrophe with a tact and understanding that takes into account local sensibilities about unattached women. Andrew's liberal mask slips, and he beats to death, with no clear evidence as to his guilt, the Arab boy with whom Sandy has talked earlier. The women commiserate with Sandy, but she refuses to play the abused woman. "I'm in one piece. I'm alive, I'm not damaged," she says. She acknowledges she was foolish to wander outside unprotected, and she does not consider a rape as the defining experience of her sexual life. Eunice, outraged by Sandy's refusal to play the expected melodramatic role, hits her and silences her. All the tourists are compromised in the end, since they buy their way out of the murder while the Moroccan hotel manager looks on sardonically.

In a review-essay for *The Spectator* (16 July 1977) John Peter discusses *Mecca* and other plays by Whitehead. For him the play "provides us with the exciting spectacle of a writer in progress: of a man whose vision is widening and maturing at the same time." He finds, however, that its weakness lies "not in its structure so much as in its plotting," because Whitehead is a "dramatist of situations with implications and echoes reaching out, like tentacles, into his characters' past or future." For Wardle in *The Times* (8 July 1977) "The exposition is a beautiful piece of craftsmanship. Whitehead knows exactly how far each of the characters will go; and he shows a fine sense for concealment as well as revelation." Nightingale, by contrast, concluded in *The New Statesman* (15 July 1977) that "if *Mecca* were less self-conscious about its moral intentions" it would be "a good play instead of what it finally is, an exceedingly interesting one."

An older woman, Mary Fearon, aged thirty-eight, provokes a crisis of a different kind for her husband, Tom, forty-one, in Whitehead's last full-length play, *The Man Who Fell in Love with His Wife* (performed and published in 1984). The play represents a break in Whitehead's developing and financially lucrative career, from the late 1970s on, as a television writer of single plays, series, and adaptations. The Fearons' child, Susy, is at college and contemplating moving into a flat in the student area of Toxteth, Liverpool, and Mary has gotten her first job, in the civil service. With their familial responsibilities diminished, Tom is impelled to revisit his courting youth with his wife. He plays jazz and Motown records of the late 1950s and early 1960s. He begins to neglect his own job, which is a secure one as a manager of the Liverpool docks. The play pivots around a moment when the women are leaving the domestic space and the man wants them to remain. Tom is extremely jealous of his wife's other life in the office, but his jealousy also refuels his sexual passion for her. He has her wear sexy underwear and pose for Instamatic photographs, but Mary's heart is not in it. She loves Tom, but his ardor is stifling. He even drags her out on a freezing trip down memory lane to a beach near Liverpool that was a favorite courting spot for them twenty years before. He gives up his job to spy on her during the day and pesters her at work. Susy regards her father's behavior with amused contempt. Mary is encouraged to move out, and move on, by her friend at work, Julia, a divorcée in her thirties. She still has dreams of romantic love, which Susy rejects.

Susy sees Mary and Julia as "precursors" of a new definition of love as "a kind of charged friendship," although that does not stop Susy from marrying her boyfriend. But the prerequisite for such friendship, as the structure of the play makes clear, is ownership of personal space. By the end of the play, the family house has been sold; Mary has her own flat with a minimal decor of stripped wooden floor and Indian carpet; and Tom lives in a place "like a cell belonging to a dirty monk." Both have new "places," and each sees the other differently. They are, as Mary observes, "strangers now," but this alienation is one not of hatred but rather a result of new knowledge. Tom has struggled out of the framework of Catholic dogma for interpreting male/female relations and is making a lot of money driving his own cab. Mary has a new partner, Allen, and Tom is mobile and free. Mary speaks the last lines as she comes back into her sitting room after dressing for an evening out with Allen. "How do I look?" she asks Tom. But he has gone while she was dressing. The implication is that she does not need her former husband's gaze to be herself. The Platters' song "Only You" is the last music played. It was one of the triggers for Tom to revive their courtship. Now it signifies that the self, to be true, needs to be alone and set its own standards.

Giles Gordon had a negative reaction to this play in his review for *The Spectator* (10 March 1984). He deduced that Whitehead "despises the marital condition" and had "a horrid feeling he [the playwright] admires the selfish and ludicrous Tom more than he does the balanced and caring Mary." John Barber in *The Daily Telegraph* (28 February 1984), also took issue with Tom's "uncomprehending selfishness (which he calls commitment) [and which] becomes wearisome and monotonous." Michael Billington, by contrast, found Whitehead, in a *Guardian* review (28 February 1984), "scrupulously fair to both sides" and concluded that "Mr. Whitehead captures in plain, direct language the dilemma of countless modern couples caught between the crack-up of a fixed morality and the quest for something new." For Wardle, in his *Times* review (28 February 1984), the best writing "lies in the mercilessly confessional portrait of Tom: an old-style Liverpool Catholic chauvinist, fully convinced that his wife 'belongs' to him, and that any possessive extremity can be justified in the name of love." Sheridan Morley, for *Punch* (7 March 1984), took a similar approach, seeing the playwright as "largely concerned with a specific kind of Liverpool Irish Catholic guilt deeply linked to male chauvinism and impenetrable to outsiders."

With his last stage play, as with his previous ones, Whitehead provoked differing reactions among the critics. The bulk of Whitehead's subsequent work has been for television, where the conventions of realism have been more congenial for a writer who, as he said in the *Television Today* interview, is primarily interested in character and linear narrative. But his interest in depicting male-female relationships that refuse the clichés of victimhood to either party surfaces in certain of his television adaptations. His versions of two novels by Fay Weldon, *The Life and Loves of a She-Devil* (broadcast in 1986) and *The Cloning of Joanna May* (broadcast in 1992), give no simple comfort either to feminists or their opponents. His adaptations of two Thomas Hardy novels, *Tess of the D'Urbervilles* (broadcast in 1998) and *The Mayor of Casterbridge* (broadcast in 2003), signal an ongoing regard for the ambiguities and hypocrisies of marriage. His original television movie on the life of British actress Diana Dors, *The Blonde Bombshell* (broadcast in 1999), portrays her as both winner and loser in the confused postwar race to redefine British female sexuality. The tensions between personal freedom and social codes continue to occupy Whitehead's work.

Interviews:

Sheridan Morley, "Ted Whitehead on the International Fringe," *Times,* 6 July 1977, p. 9;

Albert-Reiner Glaap, "From the Horse's Mouth: Questions from German Students to Living British Dramatists," in *Literatur in der Schule,* no. 5 (Trier: WVG Wissenschaftliche Verlagsgesellschaft mbH, 1978), pp. 1–17;

"Putting the Emphasis on Telling a Good Story," *Television Today,* 23 January 1986, p. 18.

References:

Liz Bird and Jo Eliot, "The Life and Loves of a She-Devil (Fay Weldon–Ted Whitehead)," in *British Television Drama in the 1980s,* edited by George W. Brandt (Cambridge & New York: Cambridge University Press, 1993), pp. 214–233;

John Peter, "Questioning," *Spectator,* 16 July 1977, p. 27.

Christopher Wilkinson
(4 May 1941 -   )

Derek Paget
University of Reading

PLAY PRODUCTIONS: *Their First Evening Alone Together,* Sheffield, Little Theatre, Spring 1969; Sheffield, Sheffield Playhouse, 1971;

Wally, Molly and Polly, Sheffield, Little Theatre, 1969;

Strip Jack Naked, Sheffield, Sheffield Playhouse, 29 April 1970; London, Royal Court Theatre, 1970;

Teasdale's Follies, text by Wilkinson and Frank Hatherley, music by Jeremy Barlow, Sheffield, Sheffield Playhouse, 1971;

Dynamo, London, King's Head Theatre Club, 28 June 1971; Edinburgh, Traverse Theatre, 4 September 1971;

Plays for Rubber Go-Go Girls, Portable Theatre tour, 28 June 1971; London, Hampstead Theatre Club, 9 August 1971; Edinburgh, Edinburgh Festival, August 1971; revised, London, Oval House, 6 September 1972;

I Was Hitler's Maid, Sheffield, Sheffield Playhouse, 29 June 1971; London, King's Head Theatre Club, 3 August 1971;

Sawn Off at the Knees, by Wilkinson and Veronica Thirlaway, Sheffield, Crucible Theatre, May 1978.

PRODUCED SCRIPT: *Their First Evening Alone Together,* radio, BBC Radio 3, 1 December 1971.

Christopher Wilkinson (photograph by Ian Tilton; courtesy of Christopher Wilkinson)

Christopher Wilkinson is a writer who was part of the post-1968 revolution in British theater. His reputation was made through a contribution to the challenging and provocative material produced by small-scale theater groups working at that time in opposition to mainstream theater. This new kind of theater, sometimes called "fringe" or "alternative" theater, had its period of maximum activity and influence in the ten years following the abolition of the Lord Chamberlain's Office in 1968. The touring, community, and constituency-based groups of this period, and the personnel who worked in and for them, reshaped British theater practice in fundamental ways in the late 1960s and early 1970s. A "grass roots" movement, fringe theater is comparable to (but had little actual continuity with) the "theaters of the left" of the period between the two world wars. Both movements represent creative attempts to open up British theater to political ideas and to performance methodologies inimical to the dominant ideologies of British cultural life.

Wilkinson's work, however, has not survived the 1968–1978 period. While several of his contemporaries (such as Howard Brenton, David Hare, and David Edgar) went on to become established mainstream artists working with the most prestigious companies in Britain (the National Theatre, the Royal Shakespeare Company), Wilkinson's works have never been published or produced since that time. These writers, and others, went on to dominate the major theatrical institutions in the 1980s and to work also in television and movies; but Wilkinson's work remains locked into the earlier conjuncture that produced it. He returned to acting, teaching, and local activism and wrote no more plays after 1978.

Yet, this factor makes him an interesting figure culturally; he is, and seems likely to remain, emphatically "of his time." He is not alone, of course; a glance at the "Chronology" section of Catherine Itzin's 1980 *Stages in the Revolution* will show that for every Brenton and Hare there were many writers such as Wilkinson whose works are now forgotten and unpublished. But inscribed in his work are some of the contradictions of a volatile period, and this characteristic makes him in many ways a good example of writers of the era.

Wilkinson was born in Ipswich on 4 May 1941. His father, Oliver Marlow Wilkinson, was an actor, director, and playwright, while his mother worked in a bank, and he has a brother and three sisters. Wilkinson was educated at an upper-class private school (Lancing College) and then went to Bristol University in 1959, earning a B.A. honors degree in drama in 1962. After graduation he worked as an actor at the Hampstead Theatre Club under the direction of James Roose-Evans and then in repertory at the Sheffield Playhouse. He married the painter Veronica Thirlaway in 1962; they divorced in the 1980s. They have one daughter, Alys, born on 18 March 1963.

He joined the Sheffield Playhouse as an actor, but his writing developed to the point where he became resident dramatist at the Playhouse (1970–1971). He also became involved with their Theatre in Education (TIE) program and in the innovative company Vanguard Theatre in its first incarnation at the Playhouse. This company was one of many that attempted to reach out with their performances to audiences not accustomed to going to the theater. He was prominent, too, in small-scale theater festivals in and around Sheffield. From the combination of these interests came Wilkinson's participation, with directors Glen Walford and Frank Hatherley, in the Little Theatre, housed in a former soup kitchen leased by the Sheffield Playhouse. This theater was a venue for avant-garde pieces at night and for TIE work during the day in the late 1960s and early 1970s. It is where Wilkinson's first plays, mostly one-act dark comedies, were produced. *Their First Evening Alone Together* (performed in 1969) features a writer and his partner who achieve a kind of harmony by referring to themselves in the third person as if taking part in a work of fiction. *Wally, Molly and Polly* (performed in 1969) is about a couple guided by questions from a compatibility machine toward a bogus harmony of cliché. Other Little Theatre productions on which Wilkinson worked with Walford and Hatherley were more like one-off events in which the audience was invited to participate; for example, *Doris and Sybilla* (performed in 1969) used illustrations from a Victorian novel in the manner of a tarot pack to dramatize stories made up by the audience, while *Papers* (performed in 1969) explored the treatment of a child murderer as presented in the Sunday tabloids.

In 1970 Wilkinson's play *Strip Jack Naked* had its premiere at Sheffield Playhouse, then received a Sunday night "Production Without Decor" at the Royal Court Theatre. The "Productions Without Decor" series had originally been conceived by artistic director George Devine as a forum for new works that might be too controversial or experimental for a regular full-scale production. As the title indicates, *Strip Jack Naked* already showed Wilkinson's fascination with the sensational, the salacious, and the melodramatic. As Michael Billington wrote in the (London) *Times* (11 May 1970), the play "shows a guilt-ridden young recluse being tried, tortured, humiliated and killed by the sadistic representatives of an unspecified authority." Billington called the play a "surrealistic nightmare."

Wilkinson soon became interested in the kinds of collaborative play-making that typified many artists' attempts during this period to find alternatives to traditional single-author writing. His most successful work was skeletal on the page and relied on actors and directors exploring in rehearsal the potential of the ideas and themes suggested. This exploration was done through the acting games and extended improvisations that became one of the many features of British alternative play-making. In this respect the working methods of alternative theater were different from conventional ways of rehearsing. These methods liberated actors from the tedious "marking and blocking" style used by repertory and West End theaters. It also released them from the repressive aspects of Stanislavskian psychological styles of acting into the libertarian athleticism of Artaudian physical theater. The sparseness of a Wilkinson script marked out its writer's planned retreat from the logocentric.

Three of Wilkinson's plays came to national attention when they were produced in London by two of the most important of the fringe companies: Portable Theatre and Soho Theatre. Productions by these companies received reviews from national newspaper drama critics. The plays in question—*Plays for Rubber Go-Go Girls*, *Dynamo*, and *I Was Hitler's Maid*, all produced in 1971—constitute his main claim for continued critical interest.

Portable and Soho Theatres were instrumental in bringing Wilkinson to a wider public and to metropolitan attention, but their importance to alternative-theater history in general is much greater. Portable Theatre was founded in 1968 and run by Hare, Brenton, and Snoo Wilson, partly as a vehicle for their own writing. The company became a kind of market leader for small-scale touring companies with an interest in new writing with provocative themes. Finding, as many of the younger generation of playwrights did, that the established theater was resistant to new work, they simply produced their own work and found new venues to show it. As their name implies, Portable Theatre's style was minimalist, allowing set and performers to be transported, often in a single van, to venues far and wide. Companies such as Portable Theatre had to be prepared to set up almost anywhere; they performed in conventional spaces that often had no previous connection with theater at all. Their material was part of the politicized 1960s, but the primary motivation of the company was always to access audiences and to get their writers' work produced despite a hostile theatrical environment. Portable Theatre was more like the cabaret troupes of Weimar, Germany, and unlike the "direct action" political-theater groups of the period (7:84, General Will, and Red Ladder, for example).

The other fringe company to produce Wilkinson's work was one that did not habitually tour but also specialized in new writing. The London-based Soho (later the Soho Poly) Theatre Company was founded in 1968 and run by Frederick Proud and Verity Bargate as a "lunchtime theatre club." This company was committed fully to the relatively new concept of lunchtime theater, so its plays were restricted to a one-hour duration. Its first theater was in Soho, next door to the Better Books shop, and the founders' flat was in Archer Street (where planning and even rehearsal for productions often took place). The company lost this space in the early 1970s and eventually found a permanent home in Riding House Street in 1972. Temporarily homeless during 1971, Soho Theatre used the King's Head Theatre Club in Islington for a series of productions that helped to put lunchtime theater on the map as a concept (in London at least). As its name suggests, the King's Head had been an ordinary Victorian neighborhood pub until it was taken over in 1970 by a Canadian couple, Dan and Joan Crawford. They transformed it into one of London's premier new lunchtime and evening venues for small-scale theater.

Lunchtime theater had various important advantages, not the least of which was the opportunity it afforded to actors working in the evenings in the West End (and also to London-based actors out of work) to showcase themselves for agents, producers, and directors. This opportunity was especially important for young actors, even more numerous than young play-

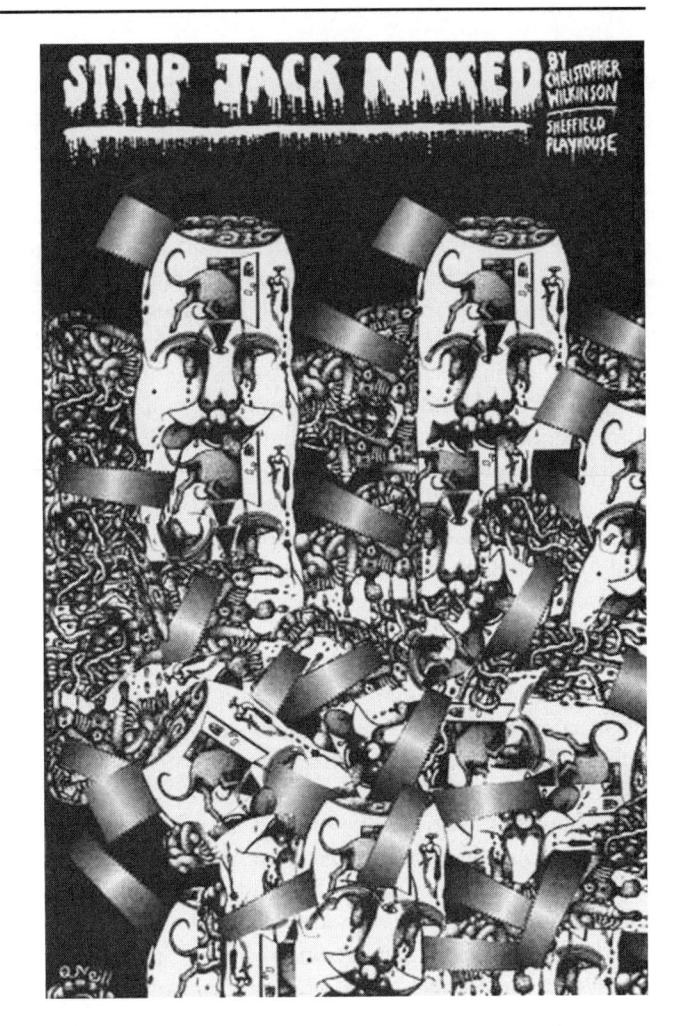

Poster for Wilkinson's 1970 play, in which a young recluse is tortured and killed by figures representing an unnamed authority (courtesy of Christopher Wilkinson)

wrights, but more established performers too began to notice the advantages of showing their range in experimental work. By making themselves into "clubs," these provisional institutions sidestepped Equity rules and enabled the work to be done at little expense (indeed, much of it was done for traveling expenses only). The whole system of companies and venues at the time was underwritten by government grants that were rescinded in the 1980s.

These venues and companies (along with many others such as the Oval House, the Ambiance, the Bush, Hull Truck, Welfare State, and Gay Sweatshop) became a powerful force in postwar British drama in the wake of the abolition in 1968 of the Lord Chamberlain's Office. The censorship exercised by this office had haunted scores of playwrights over the years, preventing them from articulating the full range of their legitimate artistic concerns. Censorship was particularly irksome in the context of the democratic freedoms being sought in the 1960s by a younger postwar generation. For many people, the so-called Student Revolution of 1968 was the culmination of this force for general social change. The strikes, occupations of university administrations, anti–Vietnam War demonstrations, sit-ins, and general protest against outmoded establishments throughout Western Europe and the United States seemed to herald a new democratic age. Left-wing politics and libertarian philosophies animated the thinking of the new generation, which was supported and inspired by the rock-music industry and some of its celebrated practitioners. Such movements throughout the arts were frequently in conflict with an older generation resistant to change.

British theater had a particularly conservative and insular aspect in the immediate postwar period, perennially resistant to much of the practice that had transformed European theater between the wars. This conservatism was shaken up after the first production of *Look Back in Anger* at the Royal Court Theatre in 1956. The style of Joan Littlewood's Theatre Workshop company also began to make an impact at this time. The nonnaturalistic theatrical methodology of Charles Chilton's *Oh, What a Lovely War* (1963), for example, was particularly influential on the fledging fringe because it demonstrated that there were ways of telling and showing onstage beyond the scope of the naturalist/realist theater modes that (then as now) tended to dominate mainstream practice. Fringe theater enjoyed a phenomenal burst of creativity and influence once the restrictive influence of the Lord Chamberlain's Office had been removed. Material formerly subject to censorship suddenly became possible to stage.

The political debates of this period were mirrored in the content of much of the new drama, which actively aligned itself with wider political movements of the Left. The political nature of the young dramatists' work is often highlighted in accounts of this period, and rightly so; but part of the revolution involved new thinking about race, gender, and sexuality. These subjects were also debated in the plays of the new dramatists making their names outside mainstream theater. The important contemporary question of the representation of sex and sexuality is especially important, and problematical, when considering Wilkinson's work.

In hindsight, some of the work of the period exploited new sexual freedoms in particularly questionable ways. For many people the production that most symbolized the post–Lord Chamberlain era was not a political play at all, but the revue *Oh! Calcutta!*, which opened at the Royalty Theatre in 1969. The idea for this series of sexually provocative sketches came from theater critic (and, at the time, National Theatre literary manager) Kenneth Tynan. A pantheon of contemporary writers, including Joe Orton and John Lennon, contributed to *Oh! Calcutta!*, which was hugely successful in commercial (if not in critical) terms. While there was both male and female nudity in *Oh! Calcutta!*, the show was promoted in a way that exploited its female performers. In its vulgarity, it epitomized the double bind evident in many treatments of sex and sexuality in the new, supposedly free and sexually liberated era. For one thing, it showed that the distinction between honest and open theatrical representation of sex and sexuality on the one hand, and pornography on the other, was not necessarily more easily established once the blunt instrument of censorship had been abolished.

Wilkinson's fascination with violent sex was probably one of the features of his work that attracted Portable Theatre to his work. *Plays for Rubber Go-Go Girls*, directed by Malcolm Griffiths, was first produced by Portable Theatre in 1971 and was seen at festivals in York, Leeds, Sheffield, Nottingham, and Cardiff. As well as the tour, the show had a week at the Hampstead Theatre Club. A second Portable company produced a revised version of the piece at the Oval House within a year. By 1981 the feminist writer and critic Michelene Wandor had concluded that another Portable play, the collectively written *Lay By* (1971), "often comes close to being simply titillatory, a reproduction of the very phenomenon (media exploitation of sex and violence) it sought to expose." *I Was Hitler's Maid*, *Plays for Rubber Go-Go Girls*, and *Dynamo* (which played the Traverse Theatre at lunchtime during the 1971 Edinburgh Festival while *Lay By* played the evening slot) all bear out this crucial feminist caveat. These three productions used a high-energy style of presentation based on tabloid newspapers and pornographic cartoons that relied heavily on female nudity as simultaneous attraction and provocation.

The series of vignettes that constitute *Plays for Rubber Go-Go Girls* was largely based on the fantasies of comic magazines (some of which were allegedly produced for U.S. troops in Vietnam). The play mounted an attack on American imperialism via graphic depictions of the kinds of male fantasy that result from a combination of repressed sexuality and a belief in the essential rightness of the American way of life, with its "God on our side" justifications for political dominance. In this two-dimensional comic-book world, the "rubber go-go girls" of the title were endlessly used, killed, and recycled by the male players, springing happily to life again after violent abuse as carbon-copy figures of fantasy in the manner of popular entertainment genres from Captain America to James Bond. The final sketch gave a clue as to the source of this "female as gratifier" model by spoofing the upbringing of the archetypal "All-American girl." The style of a bad American TV sitcom gave this section its satirical cutting edge. The result was, according to taste, either a hilariously subversive entertainment or a needlessly exploitative piece of semipornography. Whichever line was taken, most reviewers admired the energy of the young cast (which included Patricia Hodge). Irving Wardle in the *Times* (10 August 1971) pronounced it "a complete justification of the author's methods."

The same critic "heartily disliked" (*Times*, 1 July 1971) both *Dynamo* and *I Was Hitler's Maid,* as did many of his colleagues. Soho put on *Dynamo* at the King's Head Theatre in 1971, and the play proved so popular with audiences that its run (unusually for the time) was extended. *I Was Hitler's Maid,* directed by Wilkinson himself, was produced there also in 1971 as an evening show. The subtitle of the script for *Dynamo* was "A Second-hand Experience," which neatly articulates Wilkinson's interest in the (at the time) largely unexamined clichés of popular entertainment. *Dynamo* rested upon two ideas yoked together by the violence of theatrical montage: on the one hand, the performances of a classically seedy strip club; on the other, the "performance" of interrogators questioning and torturing a political detainee. The first part of the idea was consistent with Wilkinson's interest in the kinds of popular entertainment often "disavowed," even by their performers and audiences. The second he took from a 1959 book, *Gangrene,* an account of the behavior of French police and security forces during the Algerian War of Independence (1954–1962). The book describes a 1958 case in which a suspect was tortured by being wired up to an electrical dynamo and given ever-increasing shocks as the interrogators tried to compel confession.

Dynamo was structured around four strippers' acts, performed on a set that represented a cross-section of a typical Soho strip club. Opened to the audience's view, therefore, was both changing room and stage. They were thus able to watch each stripper strip twice over: once in preparation for her act (changing from street to performance clothes), and once during her act. The first three strippers performed in conventional strip-show style. For example, in the second–"Bella's Act"–a girl hitched a ride and (to the Rolling Stones' version of the song "Hitchhiker") had her clothes removed by the car driver. In "Celia's Act," what Wilkinson's scenario describes as "Conscious masturbation images" were used with an onstage mirror doubling the image of the stripper.

For "Daphne's Act," the stripper was joined by four men (the manager, emcee, and bouncers of the club, hitherto lounging around in front of the house). These men became the security police of the Algeria story/her male exploiters. The girl/boy (Daphne's cos-

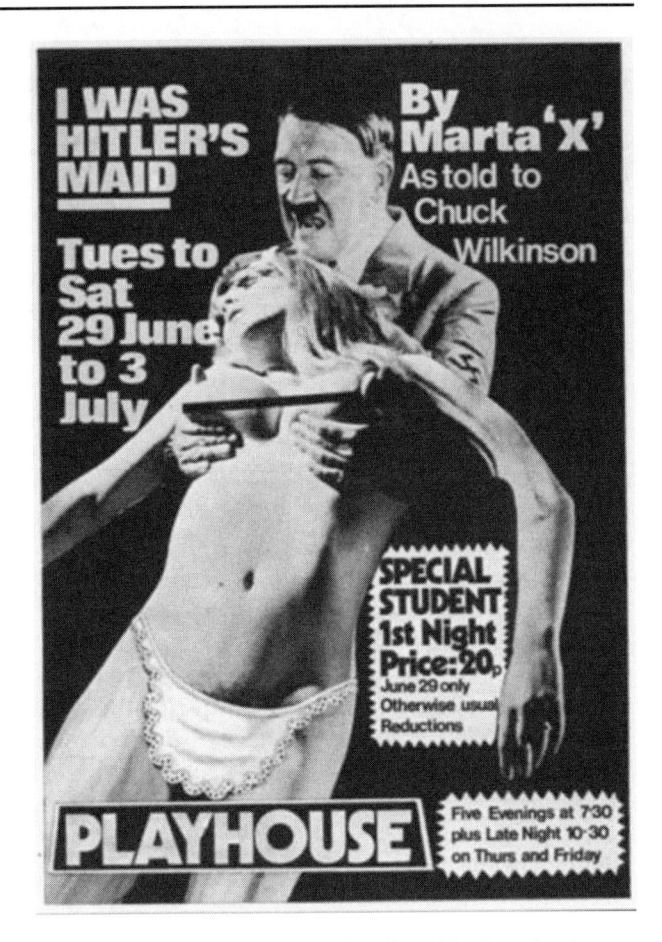

Poster for Wilkinson's 1971 play, directed by the author, in which violence and sexual fantasies from comic books allegedly given to American soldiers in Vietnam are presented in an exaggerated, lurid fashion to shock and provoke audiences (courtesy of Christopher Wilkinson)

tume was deliberately androgynous) was subjected to a five-stage interrogation (described in Wilkinson's scenario as "The Search," "The Inspector's Interrogation," "The Kicking," "The Psychological Warfare Expert," and "Dynamo") after which he/she "confesses" in direct address. The routine was choreographed to contemporary pop music in strip-club style (for example, The Jackson Five's contemporary hit "The Love You Save" accompanied "The Search"). The nonnaturalism both of strip-club "performance" and of the play itself was capped by the completely naturalistic confession in which Daphne admits pathetically to the alienated emptiness of her real life as a stripper. The lengthy speech ends lamely: "And then there's the boys [the bouncers], well, I don't really know them, but they've always been friendly, never bothered me, you know, and they're always good for a laugh . . . and that's it, I think . . . Is that what you wanted? . . . (Laugh)."

The problematical nature of Wilkinson's work is typified by the success of *Dynamo*. It was an inventive idea, creatively realized, and the erotic connection between the sadomasochism of political torture and the voyeurism of strip clubs was vividly evoked. In both cases, questions were posed about the male and his desires. Audiences were made to feel complicit in complex ways, forced to become voyeurs whether they wanted to be or not. As a final link with the exploitative *Oh! Calcutta!*, two of the performers (Jenny Runacre as Amy, the first of the strippers, and Linda Marlowe as Daphne) were appearing in the evenings in that same show.

In *I Was Hitler's Maid,* Wilkinson experimented again with simultaneous stage action. The play was once again based on violent and sexually explicit American comics that Wilkinson alleged were like those issued by the U.S. Army to its serving GIs. Scenes depicting violent rape and murder were performed in a lurid cartoon style intended to provoke and upset audiences. Wardle called the piece "alienated cheesecake" and warned of the dangers of inviting "the very responses it sets out to demolish" (*Times*, 1 July 1971). By this time, the metropolitan critics clearly felt that the ambiguity surrounding Wilkinson's material was more than simply provocative. Harold Hobson in the *Sunday Times* (15 August 1971) remarked that the "degree of political integrity" in *I Was Hitler's Maid* was "difficult to determine." He showed his mounting disdain (and undercut the intention to shock in Wilkinson's production) by observing that the actor Alun Armstrong "vomits very well" in the show.

Following the success of *Dynamo,* the American experimental movie director Steve Dwoskin made a motion picture called *Dyn Amo* in 1972. Shown at both the Cannes and Toulon Film Festivals of that year, the movie acquired a small but lasting reputation for its innovative style. The cast of the Soho Theatre production was used for this movie, but a different product emerged, one with which Wilkinson was not involved. In its two-hour running time, *Dyn Amo* uses only two lines of dialogue from Wilkinson's original play.

In 1972 Wilkinson worked with a Free School project, and then in 1973, with Susan Atkins and his then partner Thirlaway, he formed the Sheffield drop-in center Meatwhistle. For three years they directed and administered this self-styled "theatre/arts/junk workshop" and its associated educational group. Meatwhistle was a variant of the kind of arts labs formed from the late 1960s on, and it was the point of emergence for several early-1980s rock bands (Human League and Heaven 17, for example).

Wilkinson's last play to date, *Sawn Off at the Knees* (written with Thirlaway), was performed at the Crucible Theatre in Sheffield in 1978. The play is set in what appears to be a home furnishings department in a store. Two young couples are acting out a series of marital situations while receiving the director's orders over a loudspeaker and having their pictures taken by photographers. As Eric Short wrote in the *Daily Telegraph* (8 May 1978), *Sawn Off at the Knees* is "all about (and staged amid) shop-window dummies—that is to say, the stunted emotionalism of people living according to the agony columns." Short considered the play "remarkable."

Since then, Christopher Wilkinson has pursued a career as an activist and itinerant actor. In 1988 he married Margaret Dixon, a textile designer. He has appeared onstage in productions ranging from Joe Orton's *Entertaining Mr. Sloane* (1964) at the Derby Playhouse in 1989 to William Shakespeare's *The Taming of the Shrew* with the Royal Shakespeare Company in 2000, and he has worked in movies and on television series, including *Emmerdale* (1996) and *Coronation Street* (1998). In 2002 he formed Yellow Leaf Theatre Company with two other actor-writers, Alan Meadows and Vanessa Rosenthal. While his performance work makes it more likely that he will be recognized as an actor rather than as a playwright, he is nevertheless a noteworthy representative of a particular time and place in British drama.

References:

John Bull, *New British Political Dramatists* (London: Macmillan, 1984);

Sandy Craig, ed., *Dreams and Deconstructions: Alternative Theatre in Britain* (Ambergate, U.K.: Amber Lane Press, 1980);

Andrew Davies, *Other Theatres: The Development of Alternative and Experimental Theatre in Britain* (London: Macmillan, 1987);

John Elsom, *Post-war British Theatre* (London & Boston: Routledge & Kegan Paul, 1979);

Catherine Itzin, *Stages in the Revolution: Political Theatre in Britain since 1968* (London: Eyre Methuen, 1980);

Tom Milne, ed., *The "Time Out" Film Guide* (Harmondsworth, U.K.: Penguin, 1991), p. 190;

Michelene Wandor, *Understudies: Theatre and Sexual Politics* (London: Methuen, 1981).

Ted Willis

(13 January 1918 – 22 December 1992)

Derek Paget
University of Reading

PLAY PRODUCTIONS: *Erna Kremer,* London, Unity Theatre and Unity Outside Show Group, 1941;

Sabotage! London, Unity Theatre, 1 March 1942;

Gabriel Perri, London, Unity Outside Show Group, 1942;

Buster, London, Unity Theatre, 1943; London, Arts Theatre, 13 July 1943;

What Are We Fighting For? Army Bureau of Current Affairs (ABCA) Play Unit, 1944;

Where Do We Go From Here? ABCA Play Unit, 1944;

All Change Here, London, Unity Theatre, 15 June 1944; Bristol, Unity Theatre, 1946;

The Yellow Star, London, Unity Theatre, 6 April 1945;

God Bless the Guv'nor, London, Unity Theatre, 26 December 1945;

The Bells Are Ringing, tour, Unity Mobile, 1945;

All One Battle, London, Coliseum, 1945;

What Happens To Love? London, Unity Theatre, 5 March 1947;

The Magnificent Moodies, London, Embassy Theatre, Swiss Cottage, 1948;

No Trees in the Street, Liverpool, Liverpool Playhouse, 31 May 1948; London, St. James Theatre, 27 July 1948; London, New Cross Empire, 1949;

The Jolly George, tour, Unity Mobile, 1949;

The Lady Purrs, London, Embassy Theatre, Swiss Cottage, 1949;

The Eyes of Youth, adapted from Rosemary Timperley's novel *A Dread of Burning,* Worthing, Connaught Theatre, 1951;

The Blue Lamp, by Willis and Jan Read, Worthing, Connaught Theatre, 22 October 1951; London, Hippodrome, 19 November 1952;

A Kiss for Adèle, adapted by Willis and Talbot Rothwell from Pierre Barillet and Jean Pierre Grédy's *Le Don d'Adèle,* London, Royal Court Theatre, 26 November 1952;

Doctor in the House, adapted from Richard Gordon's novel, Brighton, Theatre Royal, 23 July 1956; London, Victoria Palace, 30 July 1956;

Ted Willis (portrait by June Mendoza; from the dust jacket for The Bells of Autumn: The Third Season of Rosie Carr, *1991; Richland County Public Library)*

Brothers in Law, adapted from Henry Cecil's novel, tour, 1957;

313

Hot Summer Night, Bournemouth, Pavilion Theatre, 29 September 1958; London, New Theatre, 26 November 1958;

When in Rome, adapted from Pietro Garinei and Sandor Giovanni's *Buonanotte, Bettina,* Oxford, New Theatre, 2 December 1959; London, Adelphi Theatre, 26 December 1959;

Mother, adapted from Maksim Gorky's novel, Croydon, Fairfield Halls, 1961;

Doctor at Sea, adapted from Gordon's novel, Bromley, Churchill Theatre, 1961;

Woman in a Dressing Gown, Bromley, Churchill Theatre, 1963; London, 1964;

A Slow Roll of Drums, Bromley, Churchill Theatre, 1964;

A Murder of Crows, Bromley, Churchill Theatre, 1966;

Queenie, Guildford, Yvonne Arnaud Theatre, 18 June 1968; London, Comedy Theatre, July 1968;

Dead on Saturday, Leatherhead, Thorndike Theatre, 1972;

Mr. Polly, adapted from H. G. Wells's novel *The History of Mr. Polly,* Bromley, Churchill Theatre, 4 July 1977;

Stardust, Bromley, Churchill Theatre, 1983;

Tommy Boy, Richmond and provincial tour, 1988;

Intent to Kill, Bromley, Churchill Theatre, 1990.

BOOKS: *Fighting Youth of Russia: The Story of the Young Men and Women of the Soviet Union* (London: Russia Today Society, 1942);

Buster (London: Fore Publications, 1943);

God Bless the Guv'nor (London: New Theatre Publications, 1946);

No Trees in the Street (London: Deane, 1949);

The Blue Lamp: A Novel from the Film-Script (London: Convoy, 1950);

The Lady Purrs: A Farcical Comedy in Three Acts (London: Deane / Boston: Baker, 1950);

George Comes Home: A Play in One Act for Women (London: S. French, 1955);

Doctor in the House: A Comedy in Three Acts, adapted from Richard Gordon's novel (London: Evans Brothers, 1957; New York: S. French, 1957);

Woman in a Dressing Gown (London: Evans Brothers, 1957);

The Devil's Churchyard: A New Dixon of Dock Green Adventure (London: Parrish, 1957);

Seven Gates to Nowhere (London: Parrish, 1958);

Brothers in Law: A Comedy in Three Acts, adapted from Henry Cecil's book (London: S. French, 1959);

Hot Summer Night: A Play in Three Acts (London: S. French, 1959);

Woman in a Dressing Gown, and Other Television Plays (London: Barrie & Rockliff, 1959)—comprises *The Writer and Television, Woman in a Dressing Gown, The Young and the Guilty,* and *Look in Any Window;*

Dixon of Dock Green: My Life by George Dixon, by Willis and Charles Hatton (London: W. Kimber, 1960);

The Eyes of Youth: A Play in Two Acts, adapted from Rosemary Timperley's novel *A Dread of Burning* (London: Evans Brothers, 1960);

Doctor at Sea: A Farcical Comedy in Three Acts, adapted from Gordon's novel (London: Evans Brothers, 1961);

The Little Goldmine: A Play in One Act (London: S. French, 1962);

Whatever Happened to Tom Mix? The Story of One of My Lives (London: Cassell, 1970);

Dead on Saturday (London: Odanti Script Services, 1970);

Death May Surprise Us (London: Macmillan, 1974);

Westminster One (London: Macmillan, 1974; New York: Putnam, 1975);

The Left-Handed Sleeper: A Novel (London: Macmillan, 1975; New York: Putnam, 1976);

Man-eater (London: Macmillan, 1976; New York: Morrow, 1977);

The Churchill Commando (London: Macmillan, 1977; New York: Morrow, 1977);

The Buckingham Palace Connection (London: Macmillan, 1978; New York: Morrow, 1978);

The Lions of Judah (London: Macmillan, 1979; New York: Holt, Rinehart & Winston, 1980);

The Naked Sun (London & New York: Macmillan, 1980);

The Most Beautiful Girl in the World (London: Macmillan, 1982);

Spring at the Winged Horse: The First Season of Rosie Carr (London: Macmillan, 1983; New York: Morrow, 1983);

A Problem for Mother Christmas (London: Gollancz, 1986);

The Green Leaves of Summer: The Second Season of Rosie Carr (London: Macmillan, 1988; New York: St. Martin's Press, 1989);

The Bells of Autumn: The Third Season of Rosie Carr (London: Macmillan, 1991; New York: St. Martin's Press, 1991);

Evening All: Fifty Years Over a Hot Typewriter (London: Macmillan, 1991);

The Plume of Feathers (London: Macmillan, 1993).

PRODUCED SCRIPTS: *Holiday Camp,* motion picture, Gainsborough, 1947;

Mrs. Dale's Diary, radio, BBC, 1948;

Good Time Girl, adapted by Willis, Muriel Box, and Sydney Box from Arthur La Bern's novel *Night Darkens the Streets,* motion picture, Triton/Rank, 1948;

The Huggetts Abroad, by Willis, Gerard Bryant, Keith Campbell, Denis Constanduros, and Mabel Constanduros, motion picture, Gainsborough/Rank, 1949;

The Blue Lamp, by Willis, Jan Read, and T. E. B. Clarke, motion picture, Ealing/Rank, 1950;

The Pattern of Marriage, television, BBC, 11 March – 22 May 1953;

Trouble in Store, by Willis, John Paddy Carstairs, and Maurice Cowan, motion picture, GFD/Two Cities, 1953;

Dixon of Dock Green, television, BBC, 1955–1963;

Woman in a Dressing Gown, television, ITV (Associated Rediffusion), July 1956;

The Young and the Guilty, television, ITV (Associated Rediffusion), November 1956;

It's Great to Be Young! motion picture, AB-Pathé/Marble Arch, 1956;

Woman in a Dressing Gown, motion picture, Godwin-Willis/AB-Pathé, 1957;

Look in Any Window, television, ITV (Associated Rediffusion), January 1958;

No Trees in the Street, motion picture, ABP/Allegro, 1958;

Strictly for the Sparrows, television, 1958;

Hot Summer Night, television, *Armchair Theatre,* ITV (ABC), 1 February 1959;

Scent of Fear, television, *Armchair Theatre,* ITV (ABC), 1959;

Doctor in the House, television, BBC, 5 June 1960;

Days of Vengeance, 6 episodes by Willis and Edward J. Mason, television, BBC, 8 June – 13 July 1960;

Flower of Evil, 6 episodes by Willis and Mason, television, BBC, 11 October – 15 November 1961;

Flame in the Streets, motion picture, Rank/Somerset, 1961;

Outbreak of Murder, 7 episodes by Willis and Mason, television, BBC, 21 July – 1 September 1962;

Big Bertha, radio, BBC, 1962;

Bitter Harvest, adapted by Willis and Patrick Hamilton from Frederic Halbert and Sandra Halbert's novel, motion picture, Rank/Independent Artists, 1963;

Sergeant Cork, created by Willis, television, Associated Television, 1963–1966;

Taxi, television, BBC1, 1963–1964;

The Four Seasons of Rosie Carr, television, BBC1, 4 – 25 July 1964;

The Sullavan Brothers, created by Willis, television, Associated Television, 1964–1965;

The Ballad of Queenie Swann, television, 1966;

Mrs. Thursday, created by Willis, television, Associated Television, 1966–1967;

Virgin of the Secret Service, created by Willis, television, ITV (Associated Television), 1968;

Crime of Passion, television, ITV (Associated Television), 1970–1973;

The Adventures of Black Beauty, television, ITV (London Weekend/Talbot/Fremantle), 1972–1974;

Hunter's Walk, created by Willis, television, Associated Television, 1973–1976;

Barney's Last Battle, television, ITV (Associated Television), 2 May 1976;

Street Party, television, 1977;

And No Birds Sing, radio, BBC, 1979.

Always modest about his talents and abilities as a writer, Ted Willis once observed that nothing he had written would be remembered after his death. This statement seems unnecessarily self-deprecating but may represent his own overvaluing of theater over electronic media. Certainly, his theater work was only ever modestly successful and is unlikely to survive the test of time; his was a minor voice in the great postwar theatrical debates. But his contribution to television drama cannot be overvalued, and his creation of the long-running series *Dixon of Dock Green* (which ran from 1955 to 1976, and for which he wrote until 1963) would alone have guaranteed him posthumous fame. Willis, a working-class writer, became one of the most successful television dramatists of his generation, because of his shrewd and intelligent understanding both of the formal demands of a mass medium and of the mass audience that it serves. This talent was recognized within the industry when a tribute program on Willis's work was screened in 1975 on ITV. In the 1970s, the *Guinness Book of Records* regularly listed him as the "most prolific writer in television history."

Edward Henry (Ted) Willis was born into a working-class family in Tottenham, North London, on 13 January 1918. His father, John Alfred Willis, was a bus driver; his mother, Maria, was a domestic servant. He had one sister, Peggy. After attending West Green Elementary School, Shoreditch, Willis won a scholarship to Downhills Central School, Tottenham. Something of a firebrand in his youth, he was known as the "Boy Orator of Tottenham." He left at fourteen to begin to contribute to the family income, like so many of his generation had to in the period between the wars. He held several jobs after leaving school, including working for London Transport (like his father). He became a socialist at the age of seventeen and was a member of the Labour Party in the 1930s. He joined and became active in a variety of left-wing organizations such as the League of Youth, the British Youth Peace Assembly, and the Spanish Youth Foodship Committee (formed during the Spanish Civil War); Willis went to Spain several times on behalf of this latter group.

He resigned from the Labour Party in 1939 rather than be expelled during one of Labour's periodic

Willis's wife, Audrey Hale, in a 1944 production at the Unity Theatre in London, where they met (from Evening All: Fifty Years Over a Hot Typewriter, *1991; University of Alabama Libraries)*

purges of its left wing. He joined the Communist Party and remained a member throughout the war years. In his 1991 volume of autobiography, *Evening All: Fifty Years Over a Hot Typewriter,* he describes how "going on the tramp" during the 1930s focused his dawning ambition to be a writer. He became involved in the left-wing Unity Theatre in London in 1940, writing first under the pseudonym John Bishop. He met his wife, Audrey Hale, at Unity during World War II, when she was appearing in one of the famous Unity pantomimes, and they married in 1944. The couple had a daughter, Sally Ann, and a son, John Willis, who became a prominent television executive.

Ted Willis's first efforts at writing for the stage were the type of propagandist pieces in which such leftist theater groups as Unity specialized in the prewar period, but his biggest early success was *Buster* (performed and published in 1943), a naturalistic contemporary comedy about a Cockney family (which Unity revived in 1950). The play displayed many of Willis's characteristic strengths and weaknesses as a writer: a good ear for the speech of "ordinary" people (the kind rarely featured in the professional theater of the prewar period); a generous view of the collective nature of working-class society; a keen sense of humor; a tendency toward sentimentality; and a softer politics compared to some other Unity writing of the time. J. B. Priestley, the Communist M.P. Willie Gallacher, and Labour politicians such as Aneurin Bevan all recognized and encouraged Willis. At Unity he also had the benefit of some experienced and capable directors: Eric Capon, for example, directed *Buster*.

During World War II he further developed his skills as a playwright. Having joined the Royal Fusiliers, he was dismissed as a result of political activity, a fact he much regretted by the time he recounted the incident in his first volume of autobiography, *Whatever Happened to Tom Mix? The Story of One of My Lives* (1970). But he persuaded the military authorities that he should be allowed to work first for the Army Kinematic Unit, then for the Army Bureau of Current Affairs (ABCA). In the former, he scripted documentaries used in training (for example, on the firing of the Bren gun); in the latter, he joined the celebrated Play Unit run by Major Michael MacOwan, an actor turned producer who had achieved prominence in the 1930s when he produced a string of prestigious, classic plays in the West End.

At ABCA, MacOwan encouraged his group of left-wing writers to engage with the project of educating soldiers (both about the war effort itself and about the new postwar society for which they were fighting) through entertaining plays with a documentary base. Willis, with his experience at Unity, was well suited for this task and wrote two remarkable documentary dramas, *What Are We Fighting For?* and *Where Do We Go From Here?* (both performed in 1944). These dramas used techniques culled from European and American, as well as native British, traditions of working-class theater. If these traditions were familiar to between-the-wars leftist theater groups (in their common efforts to dramatize problems and issues for subsequent discussion by audiences), they were less so for audiences from outside such circles. One of the theatrical innovations commonly used was the "staged interruption." A cast member placed in the audience would object vociferously from the floor to some provocative point being made onstage. Time after time this unexpected interruption, disrupting the spectacle, would encourage audience participation in active debate. In *Where Do We Go From Here?*

Jack Warner, Arthur Rigby, Moira Mannion, Peter Byrne, and Jeannette Hutchinson in the popular television series Dixon of Dock Green *(1955–1976), which Willis created around a character from his 1950 movie and 1951 stage play* The Blue Lamp *(photograph by the BBC; from Tise Vahimagi, ed.,* British Television: An Illustrated Guide, *1994; Thomas Cooper Library, University of South Carolina)*

the projected postwar settlement proposed in the Beveridge Report of 1942 was laid out and explained to a constituency that had the opportunity to vote in 1945 on the issues being dramatized. Some scholars have claimed that the work of ABCA–and specifically the contribution of plays such as *Where Do We Go From Here?*–was not without influence in paving the way for the Labour Party's landslide electoral victory of 1945.

Willis's plays for Unity during this period were sometimes of a lighter nature, but he took seriously the responsibilities of a leftist perspective in the fight against fascism. *The Yellow Star* (performed in 1945), for example, was about the Holocaust (and was also Willis's first attempt at direction). Closer to home, issues of gender politics featured in *All Change Here* (performed in 1944), a documentary play about the "clippies" (female bus conductors who staffed the London bus service during the war). *God Bless the Guv'nor,* first produced at Unity in December 1945, was a humorous take on the class struggle and was structured like a Victorian melodrama. One of Unity's enduring favorites, the play was revived on three occasions, and Willis signed away his rights to it as a gift to Unity in 1965.

Willis's immediate postwar theater experience involved a brave but doomed attempt to professionalize Unity Theatre, an effort in which he was aided by his friend Oscar Lewenstein (who later became a major force in postwar theater as a producer). Causing immense controversy within a group that had a political as much as a theatrical focus, Willis worked hard to make his vision of a left-wing professional theater a reality. He was the key figure in the Unity of the 1940s, but by common consent (including his own rigorously honest self-assessment) he lacked the resources as a producer, and sufficient talent as a director, to make the bold experiment work. During this period (1945–1948) he was also theater critic for the Communist Party newspaper the *Daily Worker* and editor of various Unity-based periodicals such as *New Theatre*. When Joseph Stalin refused to allow Russian "war brides" to join their British servicemen husbands after the war, Willis left the Communist Party in protest, transferring his political allegiance back to Labour. Willis was also still producing his own work, which included *What Happens to Love?* (performed in 1947), on the subject of divorce, in the style of a "Living Newspaper" (a documentary play that called for specific action to solve a particular social problem).

Colin Chambers has written a detailed account of Willis's considerable role in the history of Unity Theatre. One of the difficulties of documenting the early career of such a writer is his prolific output, but the greater difficulty is the provisional nature of much of the theater work with which he was engaged. Unity was a prototype "fringe" theater, servicing all manner of political causes through one-off plays such as *All One Battle* (performed in 1945, a tribute to Spanish veterans) and mass declamations such as *Gabriel Perri* (performed in 1942, celebrating the life of a French communist martyr of 1941). Two points must be made about such work: first, although it was provisional and has not been as fully documented as mainstream work, it should not be regarded as unimportant; second, in Willis's case it provided a dramaturgical training that stood him in good stead for the rest of his prolific career.

After World War II, Willis began to write for the "new media"—movies, radio, and television—and one must look especially to the latter to judge Willis's significance as a popular writer. The pattern for his theater work was set early and continued throughout his career: he wrote plays, comedies, and even musicals with social themes, and he wrote and adapted farces; productions of his work generally toured, with the hope of finding sufficient success to justify a West End run. Sometimes his plays made it to a West End theater (as with *No Trees in the Street* in 1948), and sometimes they were successfully received by critics (as with *Hot Summer Night,* an early treatment of the "color bar" problem, performed in 1958). But he only found long-running success with what might be regarded as theatrical hackwork (such as his 1956 adaptation of Richard Gordon's *Doctor in the House*).

Willis started to enjoy popular success as a writer for the new media as early as 1947, when he wrote the screenplay for the motion picture *Holiday Camp*. The holiday camp was a significant part of postwar culture, in which working-class families had access for the first time to affordable, efficiently organized, and companionable holidays. For this movie, Willis created a representative working-class family, the Huggetts. Mr. and Mrs. Huggett were played by Jack Warner and Kathleen Harrison, two actors who became central to Willis's postwar success in television. Not only were more Huggett movies made, but the family also became the subject of a radio comedy series, *Meet the Huggetts* (1953–1961). Willis was also a scriptwriter in the early days of the long-running radio soap *Mrs. Dale's Diary* (from 1948), having gained experience in radio as part of the script team on *The Robinsons* (1945–1948). Willis was fired from *Mrs. Dale's Diary* after about a year when he offered a script that jokingly proposed the wiping out of the whole Dale clan in a spectacular charabanc accident.

His first television writing was close to lived experience, as was much of his subsequent work. Willis wrote the dramatized documentary series *The Pattern of Marriage* (1953) for producer Caryl Doncaster (whose work for the BBC can be seen as the continuation, by new means, of the informative entertainment goals of ABCA). *The Pattern of Marriage* was an examination of the legalities surrounding, and the social damage caused by, divorce (which Willis had already explored *What Happens to Love?*). In one sense, Willis's career in television matches his work with Unity: he was involved in the creation of many programs and series, for some of which he contributed scripts. As a working writer who made no great claim to "star" status, he was involved in project after project, especially in the 1950s and 1960s.

The notion of a play or series of plays that gave a documentary account of ordinary people's lives is what led Willis to his most famous television drama creation, a series that began in 1955. *Dixon of Dock Green* was a highly successful police series that followed "an ordinary copper patrolling his beat around Dock Green" (in the words of a title song added later in its long run). The fictional working-class London district of Dock Green was loosely based on Paddington Green and on Whitechapel, the principal locations for Willis's preparatory research. For his protagonist, Willis both literally and metaphorically revived a character from the 1950 movie *The Blue Lamp* (also a 1951 play), which he wrote in collaboration with Ealing Films script editor Jan Read.

The Blue Lamp was set in seedy, bombed-out, postwar London. A kindly policeman, George Dixon (played by Warner), is killed in a shooting, and the movie followed events leading to the arrest of a young spiv played by Dirk Bogarde. The screenplay credit for the movie was given to Ealing's star writer of the period, T. E. B. Clarke, who was brought in by producer Michael Balcon to take over Willis and Read's half-finished project. Nobody, however, is in any doubt that *The Blue Lamp* was fundamentally Willis's creation. He based George Dixon, he subsequently wrote, on an inspector called Mott, who had worked his way up from the beat in the East End and who

Willis and actor Roy Castle at the 1977 premiere of Mr. Polly, *Willis's musical adaptation of H. G. Wells's 1910 novel* The History of Mr. Polly *(from* Evening All: Fifty Years Over a Hot Typewriter, *1991; University of Alabama Libraries)*

saw himself as part policeman, part social worker, and part friend and confidant to the denizens of his "manor," Whitechapel. (Mott, who made a great impression on Willis, also supplied him with the idea and title for the 1965 anthology play series *Knock on Any Door*.)

George Dixon, and the series to which he gave his name, attracted much mockery from the mid 1960s onward. This derision was probably inevitable; Dixon was the creation of a different era, a time before postwar change broke up the working-class solidarity that Willis remembered from his youth and celebrated in his writing. Moreover, by the time Willis left the actual script team in 1963, the altogether harder-edged realism of the BBC's new police series *Z Cars* (from 1962) was providing an onscreen contrast to what was sometimes perceived as a coziness of tone and style and the lack of a social cutting edge in *Dixon of Dock Green*. One stylistic constant in the program was the opening and closing address to the camera by Warner, in character, and this element was particularly mocked by those who thought the show was a sentimental relic rather than documentary reality. Warner always began with a salute and the words "Evening all!," after which he would outline the opening situation of the drama. At the conclusion, he would appear again, with some valedictory observations. The 1960s satire show *That Was The Week That Was* memorably spoofed this element by imagining what the opening address would be like translated into "franglais," for transmission in France. (The model was *Maigret*, with its French accents, another successful 1960s television police series.)

But in this direct address, confidently handled by a limited but excellent character actor, can be seen Willis's Unity origins, and the nonnaturalism of the device was interesting in formal terms. The resolute determination for television drama to be realist in the 1960s looks less impressive, more a matter of developing conventions, in retrospect. Also difficult to counter is the popularity of *Dixon of Dock Green*. It is easy to marshal an elitist argument against the series, which often grossly simplified and even caricatured important social themes. However, taken as a significant piece of cultural material, inscribed with many of the key debates of its time, it is perhaps better regarded as the last gasp of an older generation in new times (which were themselves less than perfect). The implied viewer for these texts was emphatically nostalgic for qualities of ordinary life that, rightly or wrongly, they saw being expunged in the "never had it so good" materialism of the postwar world. Among a generation now in retirement, the series is still revered.

Willis went on to create and sometimes write for other successful television drama series such as *Taxi* (1963–1964), *Sergeant Cork* (1963–1966), *Mrs. Thursday* (1966–1967), and *Hunter's Walk* (1973–1976). Two of these were vehicles for comedy character actors (Sid James in *Taxi*, Harrison in *Mrs. Thursday*), while the others were different takes on the police series. None were as successful as *Dixon of Dock Green*, but Willis continued writing prolifically for television, screen, and stage. In the 1980s he added popular novels to his portfolio, enjoying a run of success with thrillers. In the concluding chapter of his second autobiography, he expresses modest pride in several of his works, including the 1988 drama *Tommy Boy*, set in the period of World War I. But this stage play, like most of his others, did not attract West End backers.

As well as being prolific in his writing, Willis was active throughout his life in the interests of his fellow writers, as befitted a lifelong trade unionist. He was twice president of the Writers' Guild (1958–1968, 1976–1979). He was also a fellow of both the Royal Television Society and the Royal Society for the Arts, and he became a Labour Life Peer in 1963. As Lord Willis of Chislehurst, he served on several House of Lords committees. Although a *Sunday Times* article of 30 May 1976 characterized him as a "rare speaker" in the Upper House, it must be remembered that he was working abroad for much of the last two decades of his life. He spoke out against racism in 1971 education debates, introduced two Public Lending Right bills, supported both the abolition of theater censorship in 1968 and an unsuccessful Blasphemy Bill in 1978, and opposed the homophobic "Clause 28" in 1988. When he died of natural causes on 22 December 1992, he was in the process of working on a sequel to the series that had made his name. The new series, projected but never completed, returned to his greatest success; it was to be about George Dixon's grandson Charles Dixon Crawford and set in London's Docklands, another location of significant end-of-century social change. Several obituaries dubbed Ted Willis "the people's playwright," a suitable epitaph for a writer who always remained interested in the issues of ordinary people.

References:

Ellen Baskin, *Serials on British Television 1950–1994* (Aldershot: Scolar, 1996);

George W. Brandt, ed., *British Television Drama* (Cambridge: Cambridge University Press, 1981);

Colin Chambers, *The Story of Unity Theatre* (London: Lawrence & Wishart, 1989);

Paul Cornell, Martin Day, and Keith Topping, *The Guinness Book of Classic British TV* (Enfield: Guinness Publishing, 1993), pp. 243–247;

Andrew Davies, *Other Theatres: The Development of Alternative and Experimental Theatre in Britain* (London: Macmillan, 1987);

Jeff Evans, *The Guinness Television Encyclopedia* (London: Guinness Publishing, 1995), pp. 157, 264, 353, 470, 514–515;

Oscar Lewenstein, *Kicking Against the Pricks: A Theatre Producer Looks Back* (London: Nick Hern, 1994);

Tise Vahimagi, ed., *British Television: An Illustrated Guide* (Oxford: Oxford University Press, 1994).

Appendix 1

Playwriting for the Seventies: Old Theatres, New Audiences, and the Politics of Revolution

John Arden, Bruce Birchall, Caryl Churchill, Margaretta D'Arcy, David Edgar, Pam Gems, Steve Gooch, Malcolm Griffiths, David Halliwell, Roger Howard, Roy Kift, Michelene Wandor, Arnold Wesker, Snoo Wilson, Olwen Wymark discuss

Playwriting for the Seventies: Old Theatres, New Audiences, and the Politics of Revolution

From *Theatre Quarterly*, 6, no. 24 (Winter 1976–1977)

The 'fifties was the decade of the great discovery of British playwrights. The 'sixties saw the growth of regional theatre, of the 'fringe', and of itinerant companies. Its later years also saw the decline in fortune of some of the major writers of the earlier period, as well as producing a number of dramatists who have stayed out of the mainstream of commercial and subsidized theatre, and preferred to work in the developing area of alternative theatre.

In mid-decade, what prospects do the 'seventies hold for the playwright? It is possible, in retrospect, to chart the ebb and flow of the various 'waves' of theatre between 1956 and 1968. It is less easy to drop a convenient anchor in the midstream of the 'seventies.

Theatre Quarterly *therefore invited fourteen contemporary British playwrights—some well established, some less so—to discuss the role of the writer in the present, confused state of the theatre, to describe the conditions under which they work—what they are, how they have come about, and how they can be altered—and to look at their hopes and fears for the future.*

The discussion is the edited transcript of this meeting, which was held in July 1976 at Oval House, Kennington, under the chairmanship of Malcolm Griffiths, in association with whom TQ *organized the event. For six hours on a Saturday in the middle of the heatwave the playwrights discussed the changes that have taken place in the last ten years—for better, and for worse.*

The debate ranged widely, covering such issues as the 'monopoly' of the major subsidized theatres and their methods of dealing with writers; the growth of alternative theatre, and the opportunities it presents to writers economically, artistically, and (most important) politically; the obligations of the writer to take a moral and political stance in society; the problems of publication in an economic recession; the relation of writers to academics and critics; and the increasing difficulty of getting plays into print—the latter coinciding, however, with TQ's *own plans for our* New Plays *series, launched simultaneously with this issue, and described on page 73.*

Problems of content were, again and again, stressed as opposed to problems of craft. The role of the Arts Council was discussed at length, both in terms of its structure and its stewardship of public money. The writers attempted to define 'political' theatre, and the relation of the theatre and of theatre writers towards Northern Ireland, towards the women's movement, and towards social problems such as housing, child welfare and abortion. They were particularly concerned about the relation between the writer and other theatre workers, and proposed a more productive, collaborative alternative to the role of the director. And they analyzed the difficult issue of a wage structure for writers in their unconventional working situation.

By the end of the day, the writers had reached some clear conclusions on how to improve their working conditions—from some arguably utopian ideas for radically restructuring the production process, to concrete, practical suggestions that could be put into effect in the immediate future—perhaps through the agency of the Theatre Writers Group which, as we go to press, has taken the decision to transform itself into the Theatre Writers Union, and to take immediate, effective action to secure a better deal for writers from the National Theatre.

What became obvious, from the desire of so many writers of such different kinds to come together out of their traditional isolation to discuss their common problems, is that things certainly have changed in the past ten years and that, if the writers have anything to do with it, things will have changed further and faster by the end of the 'seventies. As the growth of the Theatre Writers Group testifies, playwrights are increasingly conscious of themselves as workers with a job to do within society. And, perhaps more significantly, they have a new collective consciousness of themselves as a work force, and of the people for whom their products are produced.

Snoo Wilson was invited but unable to attend, and has provided the first of three 'postscripts' on page 74: the others, by Roger Howard and Bruce Birchall, provide contrasting afterthoughts to the discussion. It should also be noted that David Edgar and Arnold Wesker were unable to be present for the earlier part of the discussion. This was how the chairman, Malcolm Griffiths, opened the day's proceedings.

Griffiths: Perhaps we should start with the changes which have happened within theatre and to the writer for the theatre in the last ten years. For the writer working in theatre there have been major obstacles, but also more freedom and greater access to the machinery of production. Have there not?

Halliwell: Certainly there are more opportunities now than ten years ago, more plays done, however inadequately or otherwise. The greatest change is the development of a grass-roots movement—people doing it themselves, from 'below,' not waiting to be asked from above, or to be given permission. I started as a writer by doing precisely that. When we decided to do *Little Malcolm* in 1965—the actors and the directors and me—we decided we'd have to put it on ourselves, to find the money from somewhere ourselves, hire a theatre, and put it on. Which is what we did. And I remember at that time many people thought we were crackers. Rather like a book writer publishing his own book—you know, the sort of thing you're *not* supposed to do, pay for your own book to be printed: that's what amateurs do, we were told. But this is precisely the way of working that has grown since then. I imagine now that on any given day there must be more people working on the so-called fringe than there are in the so-called legitimate theatre. Though fringe is really now an outdated word for this kind of actvitity.

Gooch: But the greater the resources you're using in the theatre—the larger the sums of money involved—the *less* freedom you have. In other words, it's easy enough to be free and 'doing your own thing' when you're all on social security, or when you're working in a small place with a small number of people. But the more you try and work with bigger resources, the more your hands are tied administratively. And, in the end, politically.

Griffiths: Do you mean you become institutionalized?

Arden: It is difficult to do your own thing on the fringe if it involves the employment of a large number of actors and technical staff. For economic reasons. And if you go to one of the big companies—the National or the Aldwych, or the Royal Court—you find that you *cannot* as a writer anyway do your own thing. What happens is, the director does *his* thing with the material you provide. The more the commercial theatre—the old West End theatre—has declined, the more the best acting and directing talent has tended to go into the big subsidized theatres. In this situation, the director, as an individual, has found himself in a position of power, and the directors in places like the Aldwych and the National are the people who control the policy.

The final decisions, as to whether or not a play should be produced and how it is to be produced and for how long, are made by professional directors. The dirrctor controls the work-force of actors, stage hands, technicians and lighting and sound experts. The author only comes in for each play, and he or she is automatically in a minority. The point is, the writer should *not* be working under the instructions of the director, because the play has been previously written on the author's own initiative. The whole relationship of the writer to these theatres is very external and unsatisfactory, or so I have discovered. If there is any controversy about the interpretation of the play—the method, the style, the performances—then the director—with the actors, and the designer and the musical director under his control, and all in the same little power group—is in a position to make the decisions. This isn't a new problem, obviously: playwrights have been complaining about this for a very long time indeed. But it has been accentuated by the big subsidized theatres because they are the monopoly. The Aldwych and the National and the Royal Court are supposedly in competition, but if you get a bad name in one, it spreads. And they do more or less control the market for work of a certain type.

Monopoly of the Big Three

Halliwell: You mean large-scale work?

Arden: Large-scale work, which needs a lot of money to present and may not necessarily be financially rewarding, is much harder to put on now. I wrote *Serjeant Musgrave's Dance* in 1959, and George Devine put it on at the Court because he thought it was an interesting play, but he lost a lot of money on it. No one is daring to lose the money these days. That particular play would not be put on at any of these theatres now.

D'Arcy: The very existence of this monopoly group—the National, the Aldwych and the Royal Court—also determines what plays are being sold abroad to big theatres. If you get a play on at one of the three big theatres, then a large part of your income will probably thereafter come from productions of that play abroad.

Halliwell: John Arden was talking about the Royal Court risking money in 1959: now the Royal Court doesn't have the money to take that kind of risk.

Wandor: But isn't that partly because of some of the actual changes that have taken place in the last ten years? It is now possible to put on some of that work in other contexts, contexts in which there is little financial reward, but which have political implications. The sort of work that a lot of us are doing is not the sort of work that would *ever* be put on by the three big theatres. And if we *choose* to do that kind of work, we're going to be cut off from subsidized theatre income anyway. Unless we can change the policies and the people who are in control of them. To me the discussion about the three big national companies is fascinating, because I don't think my work even exists for them. I feel very much an outsider, not just in relation to the big monopolies, but also in relation to a lot of what is called fringe and political theatre as well. What has affected me is feminist theatre. Since 1970, alongside the development of agitprop and politically conscious theatre across the whole spectrum of left politics, there has been the growth of interest in feminist theatre. Initially it was an agitprop adjunct to the women's movement. But more recently it has been developing in a much more complex way as a kind of equal rights movement within theatre, with women taking a more active part in areas they haven't previously had access to. There are more women writing: some of them see themselves as consciously feminist, some of them don't necessarily. But activism among women has, I think, begun to affect what is happening in the theatre, though it still has far to go.

Gems: Yes, there is a consciousness of this among men writers, reflected in their work, ranging from contempt, fright, lip-service, through speculation and attempts at political take-over. The cliché is that feminism is deviationist: tell that to women in harems, or to married women trying to keep up in their own professions . . . No political party has a good history towards women . . . Through, as I say, speculation to true open-ended curiosity—that is, real political essence, and fraternal insight into our difficulties. However, although a lot of writers are more conscious of women as people, at a most vital time in their history, women are still, in the main, being written about by men. If you take several years out to have your children, and don't farm them off or neglect them, then you lose out with your work . . . you lose seniority, experience and it's very hard to get back. You come back as an apprentice, but ten, twenty years too old. The insights of mature women, are, by and large, lost to the theatre. I don't think it's any accident that there are still so very few good parts written for women. Look at the prototypes we see on television of women: they are still quite traditional. You get all kinds of new males prototypes—*The Sweeny,* Maurice Colbourne—but women remain winsome and unthreatening. And if you write a play from a feminist angle, the critics—male, most of them of course—you've hardly drawn breath before they're screaming 'unfair,' 'loaded,' and implying that the unfairness of your argument is, of course, because you're a female and can't stick to the point. It's academic, anyway, since most of us are still stuck, and will be until we can insist on a ragbag theatre where our children are welcome. I've never felt the big theatres had much to do with me—I think it's the class thing. You feel intimidated in a way you never do going to a pop show or the cinema.

Arden: Certainly, the individuals who operate the power in these big monopolies are not feminists at all: they are totally controlled by males.

D'Arcy: There is a kind of thinking that says—'Let's not bother with the National Theatre, let's not bother with the Royal Court, we're fringe, we're pure.' There seems to be a complete division. The National people don't look to see what the fringe is doing, the fringe on the whole doesn't look to see what the National is doing. I think *this* actually could be a trap. The National people say it is everyone's theatre, and *our* money is certainly subsidizing it. They've got three theatres, including an experimental theatre, which most fringe workers are actually subsidizing, but not having the use of. This is absolutely appalling.

Arden: There are a lot of dramatists alive and working who want to try things that haven't been done before—for all sorts of reasons, without consideration of commercial return necessarily, but perhaps for an artistic reason, a communication with an audience. If the National Theatre really is *our* theatre, then it ought to be providing the location for this to be done.

D'Arcy: In the early days of the Royal Court when they had their Sunday nights, the actors and playwrights were only paid a small amount of money, but a successful Sunday night meant your play was immediately bought abroad. It was an international shop window. What worries me is that the fringe has not had the status, and it really ought to by now.

Wymark: Surely the same sort of people go to the fringe and see plays there now?

Arden: I don't know whether they do, because the fringe is so large and widespread and there's so much going on. Maybe this *Alternative Theatre Handbook* will help people to know more about what's going on. I don't think people on the continent realize quite what has happened over the past ten years. They are still looking to the big subsidized theatres as the home of living art.

Halliwell: We used to get a lot of people from the continent at lunchtime, who used to see a show listed in *Time Out.* And they must have heard something beforehand to

David Halliwell

Founded and ran Quipu, Britain's first fringe company, from 1966 to 1976. His stage plays include Little Malcolm and His Struggle Against the Eunuchs, K.D. Dufford, A Last Belch for the Great Auk, Janitress Thrilled by Prehensile Penis, A Who's Who of Flapland, *and* Muck from Three Angles. *He has also written widely for television, and directed many plays, the most recent being* The Only Way Out, *by George Thatcher, at the Royal Court Theatre Upstairs (published in the pilot issue of* New Plays). *He is at present resident dramatist at the Royal Court Theatre, writing a new play commissioned by the Court, and running the New Writers Workshops there.*

---

know what was worth going to. A lot of people *do* go to small fringe theatres in London.

D'Arcy: There seems to be a division now between the established theatre, the big subsidized theatres and the fringe. And ironically, the way 'up' for the fringe now is through the West End. It's the West End often that's picked up the exciting things from the fringe.

Churchill: I want to clear up a few points about the Royal Court. I am very critical of it in lots of ways, but there seems to be a bit of confusion here. For instance, when they closed the Theatre Upstairs, they wondered whether continuing Sunday nights would be any substitute. And it was felt it was unsatisfactory to writers just to have one performance. The Theatre Upstairs has opened again, and I would have thought that that was better than Sunday nights. When the Royal Court started, because then there wasn't any fringe, then Sunday nights attracted more attention. That attention is now, naturally, more diffused, because there is so much other fringe, perhaps so much that attention isn't paid to it abroad in the same way any more. I think there is still an element of risk taking at the Royal Court: they do things like Edward Bond's *Fool* and lose on it.

Arden: They used to do fringe plays, but they don't now.

Halliwell: They've only just reopened Upstairs again, and what policy they pursue remains to be seen, but they did use to have a lot of fringe, and a lot of influence on the fringe.

Kift: Ten years ago playwrights seemed to be riding on a wave of complacency, assuming that what happened at the Royal Court in the new wave from 1956 onwards gave them some natural right to enter the kingdom of the British Theatre for ever more. People like yourselves–John Arden and Arnold Wesker. Now we–and you–are in a crisis, the same crisis. That's the reason we're here today.

Arden: There was a period of boom in the theatre in the 'sixties.

Kift: Yes, mirrored in what happened at the Royal Court. There one man, the director, George Devine, decided he was going to put writers in the centre of the theatre where they rightly belonged. When he was there, there were writers in the office; when Gaskill followed him, at least there were scripts in the office; when Lewenstein was there, there were budgets; and now that Nicholas Wright and Robert Kidd are there, it's anybody's guess. Now I do not mean to say that just because the Royal Court has declined and become just an elephantine bureaucratic institution, that that is the reason that playwriting has declined. But there is a parallel there from which we might learn a lesson.

Griffiths: It has been suggested that the increase in subsidy in the last ten years–which has been quite colossal– has led to an entrenched monopoly by the subsidy organization. A lot of community theatre companies, political companies, might disagree, in that they are receiving greatly increased subsidies to do their work. Is it your feeling that the increase in subsidy within the establishment theatre has led to greater restriction?

Churchill: You can get enough money now to get a play done and have it seen around the country, so you don't feel dependent in the same way you would have done when the Arts Council tradition was different.

D'Arcy: Our position personally is now worse. We are earning less money than ever before. We have a smaller market for our plays than ever before.

Griffiths: You have worked on *The Island of the Mighty* with the Royal Shakespeare Company, *Ballygombeen Bequest* with 7:84, and the *Non-Stop Conolly Show* in Dublin–three very different situations. What is the difference between

Roy Kift

began his theatre career as an actor. He turned to writing plays in 1971, and was resident writer with the Freehold Company for two years. In 1974 he won the Thames Television Playwrights Award, and took up a year's residence with the Northcott Theatre, Exeter. His plays have been seen at the Royal Court Upstairs, Hampstead Theatre, Institute of Contemporary Arts, Traverse, and also in Amsterdam, Rotterdam, Zurich, and the La Mama Theatre in New York. He is a member of the Drama Panel of the Arts Council of Great Britain.

dealing with a large subsidized organization, a small subsidized organization and a non-subsidized theatre?

D'Arcy: We are really at the bottom of the ladder; it has not in any way improved either our status or our income.

Churchill: In what sense your status?

D'Arcy: Normally status seems that if you've got a play put on by an illustrious company like 7:84 or at the Aldwych, then commissions come rolling in. But we have just had *The Non-Stop Conolly Show* refused by just about every London management.

Griffiths: And a number of good plays don't get done again after their first productions. There's been no real breakthrough in the production vehicles of the major subsidized organizations. Very few will take up new work and there's been a tremendous retrenchment—towards nostalgia and revivals of safe plays. In the last ten years there has been very little 'freeing' of access to the production business in the major subsidized companies.

Gems: I think it's even worse than that. The Royal Court puts a show together, gets it recognized and a West End manager picks it up. Big shows are tried out in the provinces, subsidized theatre productions transfer to the West End and become 'joint productions,' in such a way that subsidized theatre *itself* is becoming commercial. I think this is fairly ominous.

Arts Council and Alternative Theatre

Wandor: This situation has affected the development of the fringe—and of political theatre. It was quite obvious that the work many people wanted to do couldn't be done in the context of the existing theatrical institutions. So people went off, did their own thing, and put pressure on the Arts Council to provide money for that kind of alternative theatre. And now—partly because playwrights and groups quite rightly have a very strong consciousness of the economic needs for their own survival—they are putting pressure on the Arts Council to subsidize them increasingly, since they obviously can't survive on any commercial basis. This in turn produces the paradoxical situation of having to go for money to people whose policies you don't agree with and are fighting against. There was a sinister little note in *Time Out* this week—I don't know whether anyone noticed it— to say that a number of political theatre groups were being investigated by the Arts Council, including Mayday, Red Ladder and Recreation Ground. The implication seems to be that political pressure is being brought to stop subsidy going to groups that put over a fairly strong and consistent left-wing line. It isn't an announcement of government policy—yet it is a rumour put out to alert people.

Griffiths: Which has got substance.

Kift: It's significant in that respect that probably the only fringe show that the Secretary General of the Arts Council has ever seen was seen here at the Oval—a show by Foco Novo, *The Nine Days and Saltley Gates,* about the General Strike and the 1972 miners' strike. And members of the Arts Council Drama Panel were actually asked for a written report about what we thought of it.

Griffiths: This has happened time and again.

Arden: *The Ballygombeen Bequest* had trouble.

Griffiths: Yes. The Arts Council, for all its liberalism, in fact penalised the 7:84 company, which did that play, for a whole eighteen months afterwards. They are doing the same again with Foco Novo.

> ### Steve Gooch
>
> *Born in 1945, educated in south London and at Cambridge University, where he read French and German. Started 'writing' in 1969, doing workshop shows at Oval House with Brighton Combination. Translation of Brecht's* Man is Man *produced at Royal Court in 1971, and by the RSC in 1975. Translation of Harold Mueller's* Big Wolf *staged at Royal Court in 1972. Will Wat, if Not What Will? about the peasants' uprising of 1381, and translation of Brecht's* The Mother *for Half Moon Theatre, also done in 1972, as were his adaptation of Voltaire's* Candide *for the Victoria, Stoke, and a theatre-in-education play about prisons for the Northcott, Exeter.* Female Transport *and* Dick, *a Christmas show about Dick Turpin for the Half Moon, seen in 1973, and in 1974* The Motor Show, *about union struggles at Fords of Dagenham (with Paul Thompson), and a translation of Fassbinder's* Cock Artist *for the Almost Free.* Strike '26 *written with Frank McDermott for a Popular Theatre tour in 1975. This year he has written* Made in Britain, *with Paul Thompson, about the British motor industry, seen at Oxford Playhouse, and* Our Land, Our Lives, *about the agribusiness, for 7:84 Theatre Company.*

Arden: In fact, there was a question asked about the Foco Novo play by a Tory MP in the *Daily Telegraph* . . .

D'Arcy: And *The Sunday Telegraph* also got us into trouble over *The Ballygombeen Bequest*.

Griffiths: All that we as Drama Panel members can do is to say, 'I believe this tampering is political censorship', and to reject any attempt to cut subsidy to these people on such grounds. Not that that makes any real difference.

Churchill: If our money is coming from people we are opposed to politically, a point is going to come, inevitably, when we are going to be in conflict with them. So, one can't expect subsidy indefinitely.

Griffiths: But the important argument is, in fact, that our money doesn't actually *come* from people we are in political disagreement with, our money is *administered* by people whom we politically disagree with. Our money comes from the mass of the population, comes from taxes from the mass of the population, and from the very companies that are trying to take theatre back to the masses of the population—companies like Foco Novo and Red Ladder, which are being or may be penalized by the Arts Council administration. I think it is important for us to realize this. Because we can make a link with our audiences in a way that the Arts Council never dreamt of, in spite of the reasons for which it was originally set up.

D'Arcy: The new Gulbenkian report on arts patronage suggests that local authorities should distribute the money, which would mean groups like Red Ladder, who are moving out of London, are going to be at the whim of an unsympathetic local council. The idea of local government subsidy may look liberal, but it will mean that groups going out to the masses in the regions—where there isn't a lot of theatrical knowledge—might be penalized.

Restrictions in the Reps

Birchall: In the rep system, there is another form of political censorship. The theatre boards there appoint the directors, and it's the theatre boards and their attitude which decide who the director will be. Of course, they tend to choose the sort of director they think will toe the line. Theatre boards in most of the provinces are composed of well-meaning amateurs and a few people from the local council. In the last few weeks we've had reassessments come in to the Arts Council, and it has been significant that those theatres in real artistic trouble have a large number of local authority people on their boards. The censorship starts there; the director then involves himself in a form of self-censorship in deciding his repertory, because he wants to maintain his relationship with the board. That in turn determines the sort of plays he does, which directly affects our income and our living. By putting on one of our plays, his position might be in jeopardy with the board.

Gooch: There are quite a lot of directors who *are* sympathetic to our work, directors of the same kind of age group. Now what is interesting is that those directors have been, at different times, appointed as artistic directors of repertory companies and have tried to follow progressive policies, tried to do new work—and have come a cropper. Very often because of the policies dictated by local councils or theatre boards. It is interesting that the influence of new directors has changed very little in ten years. Directors thrown up by the work they've done in the fringe have not succeeded naturally to those jobs and those positions that one might have expected them to. I wonder why.

Arden: The objection is not to the directors as such, so much as the people who employ them.

Griffiths: Ninety per cent of the work in the theatre is still *written* plays—old plays or new plays—but still written plays that people go to see. And yet, between you as writer and the audience, there seems to be an incredible barrier, obstacle after obstacle after obstacle after obstacle. Has reaching an audience really got better or worse in the past ten years?

Kift: In rep it's getting worse. We've seen some of the casu-

Roger Howard

Born 1938. Eleven of his plays were published in Slaughter Night *by Calder and Boyars in 1971, and four in* New Short Plays *by Methuen in 1968. Recent productions of his work have included* The Tragedy of Mao in the Lin Piao Period *(played at the ICA under the title* History of the Tenth Struggle*), and* The Great Tide, *at the Mercury Theatre, Colchester. Worked as a teacher at Nankai and Peking Universities in China from 1965 to 1967 and 1972 to 1974, researching a biography of Mao Tse-Tung, published by Allen and Unwin as* Mao Tse-Tung and the Chinese People. *Received an Arts Council playwriting bursary in 1975, and is currently Fellow in Creative Writing at the University of York.*

alties—yourself, Robert Walker, Jane Howell at Exeter, who flogged her heart out trying to adopt some kind of constructive policy towards writers, and Clare Venebles in Lincoln, who decided her last season was going to be one big fling. It turned out to be not *only* artistically successful, but the most financially successful season that they'd ever had—and she was promptly put out on her arse. Philip Hedley also left Lincoln out of despair. In the repertory system there are about sixty theatres, but I think you'd be hard put now to find more than perhaps four actively concerned with putting on new plays. The rest either have no policy or a positively antagonistic policy towards any kind of new writing.

Wymark: Don't provincial theatres now often have a studio, which they didn't ten years ago? Where productions are sometimes more successful than in the big theatres?

Halliwell: That's absolutely true. But the studio theatres reflect what's happening at the Court, for example, where suddenly the nerve was lost and they could push upstairs what had been downstairs, and still retain some kind of conscience. The studio theatres seem to have been built as a sop to the conscience.

Arden: But they've been closing many of them, haven't they?

Kift: The work has gradually been cut down more and more.

Wymark: I am only saying that in the last ten years I've had plays put on in the studio theatres of major reps that I wouldn't have done before.

Gooch: But the question now is whether that is going to continue. It certainly doesn't look like it: it *isn't* developing.

Wandor: But it has produced a fantastic upsurge of new writing. Perhaps everybody else here has been writing for the last ten years, but I certainly haven't. And I know a lot of other people who have been writing for less than ten years, who perhaps wouldn't have started writing seriously if there hadn't been prospects of more diverse outlets. But possibly that is going to decline, too.

Gooch: We seem to be assuming that there is a living to be made from the big companies, but when the National is paying its literary manager £8,000 a year to administer a budget of £5,000 for his writers, there's something wrong! The National was commissioning at £200 a play until last year: now it's gone up to all of £250, perhaps £300! Then there's the RSC, which comes to the Arts Council for extra money to pay royalties for new playwrights they put on at the Other Place, because they can't (that is, don't want to) afford to pay them proper rewards. Seven and a half per cent of peanuts at the Other Place is going to be half a crisp. There is no hope of a living from the major subsidized companies, so we are left with the fringe. And the fringe, thank God, do their damndest to rustle up money to help us write plays. But you cannot write large public plays for the fringe, because the fringe has not got the financial resources to put them on. So there one is, stuck with agitprop plays, with actors doubling like mad, using cloth caps and bowler hats. Or you're forced back to little domestic dramas, which bear no relation to what is going on in England or the world.

Economics of Modern Marketing

Howard: I think it's important to look at what's happened economically in the theatre over the last twenty years. Increasingly, theatres are in competition with television and film and other forms of entertainment that can be sold in a much harder way, and have a 'loud' appeal. When the different forms of entertainment are competing, what tends to happen is that they get isolated more and more from one

Bruce Birchall

lives in Sheffield, having left London because of pressure in the squatting and short-life housing jungle. Helped to lead the long and embittered fight to win Arts Council grants for fringe and community theatre groups. Back on the dole again—and looking forward to his £1.80 rise in November—after the ACGB revenue grant to West London Theatre Workshop was cut off. Convinced that theatre workers are not the only workers who can make theatre; that plays, and all cultural products, to be useful in furthering the class struggle, must arise from it; that until theatre workers have sorted out the correct relationship between party and class all the talk of 'company democracy' and of 'what play shall we do next?' is so much bullshit. 'Put politics in command, and art can then be useful.'

another. And to push a product, a great battery of publicity is needed. To make any kind of impact, a new play has to be 'sold' very heavily. Unless there's a piece of luck—writing the 'right play at the right time'. There's no sort of ongoing sense of an audience anywhere: there's no ongoing sense of a programme of work in the theatres. So every time a new production goes on, it is an individual product that has to be 'sold' individually, which requires huge expenditure and an administrative machine to get the play across to the public. Now, the bigger that machine gets, the bigger the gap between us and our audience. There is less chance of a play which turns up on the doorstep being fed through that machine to the public. The only way you can reverse that situation is by going *to* your audience, with as light an administrative machine and with as few costs as possible. That's the only way of restoring human contact, the only way to avoid being steam-rollered out by these administrative machines.

Griffiths: So increased subsidy is diminishing rather than increasing the accessibility of theatre?

Gooch: Subsidy will decrease the accessibility of theatre so long as theatre is in competition with other forms of entertainment. Because the subsidy is actually going towards making the theatre a better public competitor, as opposed to creating access. The selling machines come between the writer and the audience.

Wandor: Are you suggesting that it would be better to put energy into developing more small theatre networks (which the fringe is, in some cases, consciously doing), where people make plays and take them to people; or setting up small theatre machines? Is that more viable than battering at the doors of the big nationals?

Gooch: We are caught in this dilemma. Certainly in my experience when my work's been done by the relatively poor, relatively small outfits, the quality of communication between the people producing the play and the people consuming the play has been at its best. When I've used the reps, with huge staffs, then the work has somehow had the blood sucked from it. But the contradiction is that even if your work can be done on that smaller scale, you can't make a living from it.

D'Arcy: When you talk about marketing a play, are you talking about the West End? I mean, if a play is done at the National, normally they don't have to have special marketing. A play on at the National automatically gets a kind of stamp, like in the EEC, so its's Grade A, and you automatically get a full house, while the amount of publicity they give to an individual play is very, very small.

Gooch: I was talking more about the reps.

D'Arcy: What kind of people go to the reps?

Kift: A standard, middle-class repertory audience. Middle- aged people, whose kids, I presume, are over twelve or thirteen, so that they don't have to get baby-sitters. Sheffield, for example, only got away from that syndrome when they did *Stirrings in Sheffield,* a local show about the steel industry. It played 103 performances and I don't think there was a person in Sheffield who didn't see that show. We'd get stopped in the street by people! It was a bloody awful show, for what it was saying, but at least it got people into the theatre, presumably because they could recognize it had something to say about themselves.

Educating the Audience

D'Arcy: Didn't Sheffield carry on that policy?

Kift: Well, it wasn't a policy. It was just a lucky shot. Somebody said, 'Let's do a play about the steel workers of Sheffield', and they thought, 'Wow, what a flash of genius'.

Wandor: Aren't shows like that one and theatre in education and alternative theatre having an impact on possible future audiences?

Caryl Churchill

started writing plays at Oxford, where several were seen in student productions. She then had about eight plays produced on BBC Radio. In 1972 her first stage play, Owners, *was staged at the Royal Court Theatre Upstairs, and in 1975* Objections to Sex and Violence *was seen in the main theatre. Moving Clocks Go Slow was done at the Theatre Upstairs in 1975, and this year* Light Shining in Buckinghamshire *was staged by Joint Stock Theatre Company in the same theatre, and on tour. Her new play,* Vinegar Tom, *written for the Monstrous Regiment of Women, is published in the pilot series of* New Plays.

Birchall: If anything, it's putting them off going to 'the' theatre.

Griffiths: Creating a demand that 'grown-up' theatre can't satisfy?

Gooch: Right. I've worked here at the Oval with teenagers on the point of leaving school and found in them a wonderful creativity and inventiveness and originality in what they do in workshops. And then what happens? They leave school and work for the Post Office or the Inland Revenue, and they watch *Monty Python* on telly, and the originality and the standard of creativity and original thinking in their work declines drastically. While kids are in school all kinds of things can be opened up, but the moment they have to earn their living, their lives are much more circumscribed.

Wymark: Why haven't they become the fringe audiences?

Wandor: It's to do with what the fringe does, as much as what the reps do—with the content of what's being produced, which we haven't discussed. There's such a vast range—for example, there are the very experimental, weird, sort of aesthetic fringe groups, a lot of which are not consciously political, but perhaps quite anarchic.

D'Arcy: And there are the ones, in the late 'fifties, which turned against formalism.

Arden: That's us.

D'Arcy: So their audiences would be young?

Wandor: What I'm saying is, that possibly the young people who have been worked with so carefully by theatre-in-education groups would be put off by the political and aesthetic experimentation which goes on a lot in the fringe. There's a gap, perhaps, between the theatre-in-education groups and the 'grown-up' fringe theatre.

Griffiths: I work at Nottingham with students of 19 to 21—and believe it or not, what they are really excited about are things like *Dames at Sea*, slick, camp musicals.

Wymark: I think that is quite a dangerous generalization, I really do.

Griffiths: I am talking about students, in particular.

Wymark: Students *you* have met and worked with perhaps, but the students I've worked with, for example, don't give me that impression at all. I think they would go to see alternative theatre if they knew more about it, or if they didn't feel it was quite so exclusive. They are doing very similar work themselves. I get the feeling that there is some kind of elitist feel about fringe companies that puts students off and makes them feel scruffy and uninitiated. But students I know certainly don't go flocking off to *Dames at Sea*.

Griffiths: I'm still trying to work out why so few students have seen any of the community or alternative theatre companies at work.

Wymark: I think it could well be a lack of publicity. Also—how many companies take productions to universities and polytechnics? They do take them to factories, etc. And most commercial, political theatre is very one-sided, and not an exciting experience unless one hasn't discovered socialism and then suddenly does. A bit like a revival meeting—either it hits you or it doesn't. But in the *Rocky Horror Show*—I went with my kids—they set out to entertain the audience, and everyone was having a great time. It was really an enjoyable experience, for the actors in it and for the audience. Unlike when I went to the ICA to see *The Nine Days and the Saltley Gates*. There were forty people in the audience, and no one spoke to each other. They were all very serious.

Arden: What you get is vibrations from the stage into the audience, saying: 'We're doing something good for you'. It doesn't matter whether it's a political play or an aesthetic play, or an erotic play, you still get those vibrations and it puts people off.

D'Arcy: The critics come along, get their little book out and write down all the symbols.

Olwen Wymark

American born, and the widow of Patrick Wymark, she began writing for the theatre in 1965. Her first plays were produced at the Glasgow Citizens Theatre in 1966, and in a triple bill at the Edinburgh Festival in 1967 which subsequently toured Poland, Yugoslavia, and Brussels. Two volumes of her one-act plays have been published by Calder and Boyars, and all have been staged in London fringe theatres. In 1973–74 she worked as script writer for Common Stock Theatre, and was for two seasons resident dramatist with Unicorn Children's Theatre. First full-length play staged at the Haymarket, Leicester, in 1975. Presently she is writer in residence at Kingston Polytechnic.

Gooch: Theatre becomes a serious cultural event which has nothing to do with life as a whole.

Wandor: But it could. It depends on what the play is and how it's done. In some respects it's quite difficult to do a serious political play or even a serious aesthetic experiment that isn't either catchy and sensational, or terribly earnest.

Entertainment and Instruction

Gooch: I don't believe there must be a necessary division between entertainment and instruction, and I don't think anybody would really want a division. I go back to my previous argument, and suggest that the division comes from competing for audiences. So you make your product as glossy and as attractive as possible, to make it entertaining. When I did *Made in Britain* —about the motor industry—in Oxford, it was interesting that the middle-class strangers to the motor industry who saw the play were completely unmoved by it, bored out of their minds. It was a difficult play for them. But the car workers were engaged by it, interested, and thrilled to see their lives reflected. And also to be in the Oxford Playhouse an unfamiliar building which had always seemed a long way away from where they lived and worked.

D'Arcy: What percentage of the audience were car workers?

Gooch: The houses were overall poor—we probably 'broke' the Oxford Playhouse. But the percentage of car workers was quite high, over the whole period a bit more than half. We played it first of all in the workers' social club and a community centre, and *there* the audience was nearly all from the plant. What was smashing was just the quality of response that you got from the audience of workers.

Howard: I have returned recently from four years in China and I find a lot more activity under the heading of 'alternative' theatre than before I went away. But I wonder what the advantages are of being a writer, and taking a show from place to place where you have to try to attract all sorts of audiences, rather than writing in a specific locality—a geographical or a class locality—and with your group, composing a play as a part of the expression of a group or a class, or a particular geo-grahical area?

Gooch: The socialist groups tour, yes, but they try to do so within a class community. If their dates are organized by trade unionists or a string of contacts in the labour movement, then in fact, they are not having to attract or excite audiences in the way one would if one were taking a straightforward package any old where. Over a period of years, you can build up a trust and a relationship with that audience, so that, although you are not in a specific community, you do have a position in a class community which is identifiable, and which in some senses brings you closer and gives you a more immediate relationship with your audience. What groups do who don't tour to the labour movement someone else should say.

Griffiths: Take the example of Portable Theatre, which was set up in 1968 by writers for writers to tour new plays. You could go to one place and be packed out, and you could go to another place with the same play and it would be empty. You always played to totally different audiences, and the play would be changed according to where you were. It would often be 'dead'. To take a new play on tour turned out to be not a good enough reason in itself for doing it. There was no real ongoing contact with the audiences. Sometimes it worked, sometimes it didn't. That was Portable's dilemma. To start with, it was an aggressive stance: 'Fuck you, let's put on new work, nobody else will. Let's go out and do it.' Then you get the questions, 'Why are we doing it?' 'Who are we doing it for?' 'What is it we are doing?'

Birchall: It's always the same people on the 'socialist' circuits, rather like socialist films playing to the same people.

Griffiths: I think the writers like David Hare and Snoo Wil-

Pam Gems

was born in Hampshire, and went to Manchester University after the war as an ex-service student to read psychology. Has worked as wages clerk, cashier, factory hand, sheet metal worker, cine-gun assistant and projectionist, char, washer-up, usherette, croc handbag renovator, antique dealer, audience researcher, laundry worker, jobbing gardener. Her plays include Betty's Wonderful Christmas, My Warren, After Birthday, Up in Sweden, The Aimiable Courtship of Miz Venus and Wild Bill, Piaf *(unproduced),* The Project, Go West Young Woman, Queen Christina *and* Persephone *(unproduced),* Guinevere, *and* Dead Fish.

son eventually lost interest in writing for Portable, in a situation where they couldn't control the content of their plays. They lost the original impetus of getting their work on, and decided to go back and try out situations where they felt they could communicate their ideas from a director to an audience. Touring became a token way of getting things done.

Howard: In China they have touring companies which are highly professional, to be compared with the National Theatre or other large theatre companies here. But most of the theatre work goes on in the work places, arising from the work experience of a particular group of people—production workers, office workers, or peasants. If they tour, it's only as a result of having done good work in their work place. They would evolve a tour by first playing in their own workshop and then playing to other workshops in the same factory. If the result is good, they play it to the neighborhood around. So a tour evolves in that way. Then they might go to a large town or provincial city, if they are a peasant group, and perhaps get invited to a festival in Peking or one of the larger cities. But a tour builds up from the work places, so that it then reflects the work experience of the group, shared in a cumulative fashion with other workers.

Birchall: Are there writers involved, or is a play totally evolved by the participants?

Howard: There is usually a writer as one member of the working group.

Birchall: But these companies would really be what we would call amateur? Are they workers in a car factory, or whatever, who do the theatre work in their spare time? Or are they people who actually devote long periods of time doing the plays and getting paid for it? Professionals?

Howard: It varies from group to group. Some are completely 'spare time', others are being paid by the work place. As production workers, they get wages, but they do theatre work.

Arden: What you're saying is that in China a factory is regarded as requiring a theatre troupe, just as in this country it would be regarded as requiring a canteen?

Howard: Yes, exactly. It's part of the cultural work of the factory.

Wandor: Is the subject matter always related to the work? Or might they do a play about something completely different?

Howard: It arises almost inevitably from the work, but it reflects national and international subjects or circumstances. Something arises from the particular and becomes general—if it's a good show.

Birchall: Who decides what shows should be done?

Howard: Usually it starts at the factory. Suggestions from workshops or from the floor, governed partly by what people know can be done—what actors there are, who is good at doing what—storytelling or ballet or Peking Opera or skits, songs and dances, whatever. There is a group in each factory responsible for coordinating, for bringing ideas together and putting them into shape in an experimental way.

Arden: Do they just discover that somebody who already works in a factory happens to be able to write or act or sing, or do they take on trained people?

Howard: They have professional advisors from professional theatres—on *technique*. Particularly for the Peking Opera which is very difficult to learn, and some forms of ballet, adopted from the West.

Isolated Writer or Social Being?

Gems: Here, one used not to have a choice of being other than solitary. Writing used to be something you conceived in your own head and then did, and when it was a finished product, you had to try and sell it somewhere. You can still do it that way, but it is also possible to go and work with a group.

Michelene Wandor

took a degree in English at Cambridge University, and is now divorced with two sons—seen with her in this picture. She started writing plays seven years ago, and has had various short plays produced on the fringe, most recently a sequence of five short feminist pieces, To Die Among Friends, *with Paradise Foundry. She is poetry editor and a regular reviewer for* Time Out, *and writes regularly for the feminist monthly* Spare Rib. *She received an Arts Council bursary in 1975–76 to work on full-length plays. She is concerned to bring together feminist and socialist elements without producing either journalistic or simplistic agitprop theatre.*

Wandor: Most groups do have a fairly clear idea of what sort of audiences they are trying to reach. A lot of them have discussions after their plays. And a lot of groups, as a matter of political principle, decide to make the plays themselves, rather than employing someone, a writer from the outside, to produce something for them. There is a desire amongst people now to develop areas of their own creativity, which isn't possible in the conventional theatre. Groups like this have developed a very good relationship with the audiences they go to—like people in the labour movement, or in the case of the Women's Theatre Group, schools. WTG have aimed at girls who are on the verge of leaving school, and they've had to develop a very close relationship with their audiences, simply because the plays won't work if they don't. They get feedback from the people they take the plays to, and criticism and comments which they can then incorporate into their work. That's quite rare in itself and now writers are beginning to be involved in that kind of process, working with groups they've got views in common with. Obviously, writers need to have a shared point of view with a group before they can work together in that kind of way.

Gooch: Ironically, theatre has *always* been a social art. Only now is the idea of the isolated writer seen to be a romantic nineteenth century myth. The point is, however, that we have been isolated not only from our audiences, but from each other, and from directors, from actors, and so on. If you can find a way of working collectively and having artistic control as a group, then you also share a collective experience with your audience. And you can begin to provide a real alternative to the society and culture we live with at the moment. It is very important for writers to force themselves out of their private world, and to confront new situations, to confront people who think differently.

Wymark: I don't see that as a challenge. And I don't see the writer writing by himself as a romantic nineteenth-century idea. There has to be room for the individual creative act. I don't think community theatre and group theatre writing should be a substitute for that. There are two different experiences.

D'Arcy: I would like to raise a point about political groups having political discussions. I would like to know how far groups are aligned to political parties? I find too many so-called political theatre groups–apolitical. I was talking to an actress in one of these companies who said 'We stand united on the Irish situation', but she did not seem to know which faction to be united with. And she said, 'After the show, we have political discussions'. Now what kind of political discussions can that actress have? I think none–unless she and her group are aligned to a political party. Otherwise, they can just say–'Let's have socialism' in a general way. My own isolation is due to the fact that I don't believe that any of these groups are truly political. What they are, is extremely conservative within socialist policies. They make sure they don't offend anyone, on this so-called socialist circuit.

Gooch: What you're really saying is that you disagree with their particular political position, aren't you?

D'Arcy: I don't believe there's any such thing as a political theatre group in this country. There is now just some sort of stereotyped left-wing theatre.

Politics—and Parties

Birchall: You can't say that they're not political just because you disagree with their politics.

D'Arcy: I think that what is wrong in England is that too many have a *generalized* political attitude. Until everyone has an actual political theory, we can't move any further forward. I think that people are being duped by the generalized, 'Oh, well, let's have socialism' of Foco Novo, for example. They never mentioned the role of the Communist Party in 1926. Now how ever can you do a General Strike play with-

John Arden and Margaretta D'Arcy

are married, and live in Ireland. They have written jointly The Business of Good Government, Ars Longa Vita Brevis, The Royal Pardon, The Hero Rises Up, The Island of the Mighty, *and, most recently*, The Non-Stop Connolly Show, *which was in production at the Almost Free at the time of the symposium. This was Margaretta D'Arcy's first working visit to Britain for several years, and she has stressed that she wishes her remarks to be understood as the comments of a visiting playwright.*

out mentioning the Communist Party? I mean, who's kidding who?

Wandor: Plays can be specifically political without being party political. Red Ladder did a play on housing and Women's Theatre Group did a play on contraception and sex education both of which had very limited and confined aims. But the contraception and sex education play, for example, came out very clearly with two or three specific messages: that girls and women should try to talk to each other more, and how that could come about. They tried to tackle the double binds that lots of women teachers are in, being themselves very repressed and being unable to talk about it. They were very specific and very limited in their aim—to try and raise the consciousness of audiences they were with. But I regard that as political theatre.

D'Arcy: That's educational, not political.

Wandor: Isn't it? They questioned what it meant for women to have control over their own bodies, and, by extension, the role of women. You can't do everything in a fifty minute play. You can't raise a revolution in one hour in the theatre! There is an important difference between these groups, and the ones who wave a flag and say, 'If you only get the right kind of moral inspiration, then we'll have socialism next week'.

Arden: There are two sorts of political groups. And the distinctions between them are blurred. There is the group that actually springs from a political party. The WRP, for example, periodically puts on plays, using professional actors and writers to present them. There you have a party which wants a play to present a certain line that the party has already worked out theoretically. Then there is the other sort of group, which unfortunately, presents a very similar image to the audience, but seems in their discussions to be confusing themselves with a political party.

D'Arcy: Most of us—other than the anarchists—agree that the way to overthrow capitalism is by having a party. And it's pointless to talk about the overthrow of capitalism and wanting socialism without in any way telling the audience how.

Arden: Or which way to go.

D'Arcy: What the hell is going on, when a company says, 'Well, we're superior to parties,' or 'There's no party that suits us' . . . ?

Wymark: Haven't we got an obligation to raise people's understanding and comprehension?

D'Arcy: Perhaps, but don't call that *political*, or that it is the work of a *political* group.

Wymark: But if you are trying to raise their political consciousness . . .

D'Arcy: You can say that you are a consciousness-raising group on socialist issues. Let me make it quite clear that when I talk about 'political' writers and groups, I intend this in a narrow sense of groups and individuals within groups, who claim an overt political purpose for their theatre work. I am certainly not talking about individual playwrights who are writing their own individual plays on political themes for the general public theatre. But a *political* group is one that has a definite *political plan*, which, if followed out, as sure as night follows day, will bring about the overthrow of capitalism.

Wandor: You mean there is a distinction between a revolutionary theatre group and a group which sees itself as having a very specific political function?

Arden: Politics are precise.

D'Arcy: Precisely! And you must work in a political party to get what you want. Women controlling their own bodies is not just left-wing: the same is true of housing or old age pensions. These are even occasionally conservative party issues. They are *not politics* but a social way into consciousness. It is like what happened at the end of the nineteenth century when you got do-gooders starting up the Worker's Educational Association, to get the workers reading and washing themselves! That is what the groups are doing now. They are actually stopping the revolutionary potential of this country. Notice that not one of these so-called left-wing companies mentions Ireland. They talk about the 1926 strike, or the Scottish Nationalist Movement, but Ireland is never

Arnold Wesker

achieved prominence in the late 'fifties with The Kitchen *and the plays of the 'Wesker Trilogy'–* Chicken Soup with Barley, Roots, *and* I'm Talking about Jerusalem. Chips with Everything *proved to be his one and only 'commercial' success to date, in 1962, and although* The Four Seasons *followed in 1965,* Their Very Own and Golden City *in 1966, and* The Friends *in 1970, this last play provoked such hostile criticism that Wesker replied at length in his article 'Casual Condemnations' in TQ2 (1971).* The Old Ones *was staged at the Royal Court in 1971,* The Journalists *controversially failed to reach the stage of the Aldwych later that year, and his most recent work,* The Merchant, *will open on Broadway later in 1977.*

mentioned. One show shed great tears for Chile and as the lights went down the guitarist came out, and sang, 'One day the troops will be over here, too, unless you do something about it.' This at the very time British troops are in Northern Ireland! If you are political, the role of British imperialism has got to be analyzed.

Wandor: But you can't make a complete analysis of monopoly capitalism in a single play.

Centrality of Northern Ireland

D'Arcy: When you talk about Chile, you can certainly make a connection with Northern Ireland. But there's no mention of Northern Ireland at all. There is an imperialist war going on there. It's not going on in Chile, it's going on fifty miles from this country. Right now.

Wandor: Do you think that everyone should be making revolutionary plays about Northern Ireland and nothing else?

D'Arcy: I definitely think that you cannot have revolutionary theatre in this country until the issue of Northern Ireland is faced. The British government at the moment is up in the Human Rights Court in Strasbourg for cruelty–what are you all going to do about that? You can't suddenly come along to the British public after you've been putting on your plays about child-rearing and housing and so forth and suddenly say, 'We're terribly sorry, folks, after all these years we are actually found guilty of cruelty.' What about internment, Bloody Sunday, the bombs which are going off, the Prevention of Terrorism Act? Why don't you mention these things in your plays? These are part of society.

Wandor: Because one can't write about everything at the same time.

D'Arcy: That is the reason why there's no revolution in this country. The weakness of 'progressive' politics in this country is reflected in the political theatre of this country– which is always on single issues. That is the way the capitalists stay in power. They let us all waste our energy pursuing single issues in isolation. Because as Marx and Engels said–and these groups always claim to be Marxist–'there can be no revolution in England until Ireland is off its back.' If you were in America at the time of the Vietnam War and you had groups only doing plays on housing, you would say, 'Crazy people, what are you doing? The most important thing is your imperialist war. Why is imperialism not mentioned?'

Wymark: It's not the *only* important thing.

D'Arcy: It is tied up with everything else.

Wandor: I think some people are frightened of fighting imperialism at the moment because the conditions of their particular circumstances make it impossible for them to take part effectively in the direct and immediate struggle against imperialism.

D'Arcy: You are involved in the struggle against imperialism whether you like it or not–because it's going on all the time.

Wandor: But there are different ways of being involved. People need–in order to become politically active in a revolutionary sense–not only a change in their consciousness, but the opportunity to become active. I think that's why it's crucially important to make distinctions between theatre which makes revolutionary statements in a general way and theatre which takes a stand on a single issue for, say, educational reasons.

D'Arcy: But imperialism is not a single issue. That is what disagreement is about.

Wandor: I am not saying it's a single issue, I am saying you can't lump everything into being either revolutionary or not.

D'Arcy: When we talk about the Irish situation, people say 'I'm terribly involved in the things that I'm doing,' and there

David Edgar

was a journalist until 1972, when he took up full-time writing. He has written extensively for fringe theatre, television, and radio, his past work including Excuses, Excuses, *at the Belgrade, Coventry, and the Open Space,* Operation Iskra *for Paradise Foundry, and* Dick Deterred, *seen at the Bush and the ICA. He has also written a number of political documentaries, including five for General Will, and two for repertory theatres—Bristol and Birmingham. His more recent work includes* Saigon Rose *for the Traverse,* Blood Sports, *seen at the Bush, and* Destiny, *staged by the RSC at The Other Place. He is now working on a new show for 7:84.*

is a total censorship of the Irish situation. It is quite ridiculous to say, 'I'm very sorry, we have no time.' The National Theatre says that, the Labour Party says that, the Communist Party says that—everyone says that. What I'm saying is that the so-called socialist theatre in this country is blindfolded in what it's doing. If I could just read out what Hugh Jenkins, former Minister of the Arts, was saying recently: 'The discontents of the post-Imperial British arise in part from their inability to discover a place in the world appropriate to the autumn of a former top nation. Hence the reluctance to shed responsibilities beyond our reduced strength and hence the search for a little grey home in the West of Europe.' (He nearly said 'Ireland'?) 'We are the most inventive and prolific artistic nation in the modern world. I further suggest that this excellence is more important than our old military supremacy, and that if we will undertake an agonizing reappraisal of ourselves, we have it in our power to regain our self-confidence on a different level with great advantage to our economic position. In the arts . . . can be found our success story and one so convincing as to bring encouragement and pride to every other aspect of our national life.' That is what your role is! And you don't have an empire, except for Northern Ireland, which you are ignoring.

Wandor: But wouldn't you agree that there are different tactics. If people said, 'Stop writing plays and get out on the street,' presumably you would argue that you could better use your skills through the work you do to fight imperialism. And I'd argue the same. You're wrong to make what I think is not a very constructive distinction between what you define as political, and therefore revolutionary, and everything else. I don't think the class struggle operates in that kind of way.

D'Arcy: What I'm saying is there is a total censorship in the British media on the Irish situation. Every time someone raises the issue of Ireland, there are excuses—'We can't do this,' and 'We can't do that.' There is an imperialist war going on! The most that anyone has achieved here has been two thousand people on the demonstration against the Terrorist Act. We are now moving forward into a fascist state, while everyone goes on advocating birth controls and abortions. There are more important things to do. We are in the battle between fascism and socialism.

Wandor: Yet fascism seeks, in particular ways, to repress women!

Griffiths: How effective do you think theatre can ever actually be in raising these issues and putting them across publicly?

D'Arcy: In South India, and I'm sure it's the same in China, theatre is used effectively, it has enormous power. And when there are attempts to censor a play, to stop its production, they don't just take the play off, which is what happens here. When David Hare and Howard Brenton, and I think five others, put on the play *England's Ireland* and found it extremely difficult to get bookings, they just dropped the whole Irish thing and went on to something else. If you are in a dangerous field, you are going to be stopped, as we found with our own *Ballygombeen Bequest*. And if you write on Northern Ireland, you will find it extremely difficult to get bookings—from trade unions, or from the Communist Party. Because Ireland is an absolutely red hot issue which is going to split the country.

Griffiths: Are you saying, in fact, that in British theatre there still exists a 'Gentleman's Agreement' on what you're allowed to say?

Arden: Yes.

D'Arcy: There is very little information on Northern Ireland in the British press, so unless people are really politically aware, they will not be able to get the information. The knowledge people have is inadequate. *The Guardian*—the great liberal paper which goes on about birth control, abortion, child care, battered babies and everything else—exercises censorship on the Irish situation. The only paper in which you'll find anything about the Irish situation, actually, is the *Daily Telegraph*—unless you are willing to look at the alternative newspapers, or Irish newspapers.

Griffiths: So you are making two points. You are quite clearly upset about the companies who call themselves political theatre companies. And you are putting forward a platform for action on Ireland for theatre workers, trying to get over what you feel is the critical issue which must be faced . . .

D'Arcy: . . . which has got to be faced before this country is actually swallowed up. People go on about Portugal, Greece, Chile, but why don't they go on about what's happening in their own country? There are bombs going off in this country, people are being killed, there have been hunger strikes, devastation has taken place, 1,700 people have been arrested over the past two years, there's harrassment in ghetto groups in this country. And what are the intellectuals doing about it?

Birchall: I was approached by the Troops Out Movement about a year ago to do a play for a Week of Action that was to be mounted. There were to be rallies and public meetings in six major cities calling for 'British imperialism out of Ireland' and the right of the Irish people to self-determination. The Arts Council turned down the application for a play to tour and perform at six major rallies. The reasons given were that I had another group out on the road doing another play, but pretty clearly, what the Ardens are saying is right. A play on Ireland was too hot to handle for the Arts Council, and it was not given a grant. There must be more instances of such censorship that we're not aware of, too. I think the political identity of the Troops Out Movement as an organization exacerbated the general self-censorship on the subject of Ireland, though. Political organisations get people to meetings and they create ready-made audiences, so by its own liberal logic the Arts Council ought to be pleased that you're getting to a lot of people. That there are a lot of 'bums on seats'. But I think they're basically frightened of the bums getting off their seats and marching about and demonstrating.

D'Arcy: We could have got a grant from the Arts Council for putting on the *Connolly* play but the Arts Council turned down the application because we said we lived in Ireland. Ed Berman put the show into production, putting on fourteen one-hour episodes over a fortnight of lunchtimes—an extremely experimental type of thing, which is what the fringe should be doing. But the Arts Council said no. That is definitely censorship.

Birchall: Or if the Arts Council won't give you money to do a play, say for the Troops Out Movement, then it doesn't happen. Because there's no money for the actors. When you start working within what you are permitted to do economically—because it *is* a job, you may lose your perspective as a political activist, trying to do something about issues which strike you as important.

Precedent of French Commitment

D'Arcy: I'd like to raise another issue, illustrated by the role of the French left-wing writers during the Algerian war. As an intellectual body, writers are supposed to be the guardians of morals and culture and values. We are the only body of workers who need not be intimidated because we are not in a factory. Writers have *got* to be the moral force in this country and this is what they're not doing. The French writers took over the moral force. When Simone de Beauvoir organized the march about abortion and divorce, people listened to her, because all the way through there was a consistency on *every single thing* that happened in French life. When the Maoist newspaper editor was put in jail, French writers stood up on his account and their voice was heard. A left-wing writer's role is to stand against the status quo—conservatism, brutality, injustice. That is our role; it has got to be our role. English writers as a body have *always* avoided that role. You cannot have a lively theatre or a lively intellectual class until writers begin to understand first and foremost that they have this role, as obligation to themselves as writers and to their society.

Wandor: I am not denying the truth in what you say, but the problem is putting it into practice. Capitalists are masters at transforming dissent and undermining it, especially in England.

Birchall: And a writer by taking up the kind of position that Sartre did becomes a kind of celebrated phenomenon—'The famous writer today said . . .' If there are a dozen names who mobilize behind every issue, unconnected to an organization . . . well, it splits you off, doesn't it?

D'Arcy: Those people have always played an intellectual role inside the socialist movement.

Gooch: What we haven't got in England is a tradition of intellectuals who have always been involved in political issues.

D'Arcy: Writers here are isolated because too often they have no guts. The ordinary worker sees them sponging on social security, writing their plays. The writers are perfectly all right, Jack—while the workers slog along to the factories.

Birchall: We should not look at examples of what writers have done and are doing in other countries and immediately assume that we can do the same here, because conditions are very different. We have not had a tradition of political/intellectual life that carries weight in quite the same way. We have had political intellectuals and we have had political playwrights in the past, but the dominant culture has always tended to trivialize them, or to make them reformist if they become successful.

D'Arcy: In the old days of the Committees of One Hundred, some writers did march. They were 'civilly disobedient.' They used to take over Rhodesia House, take a stand against brutality. And *that* was what caused the excitement in the theatre ten years ago which has now faded. Because you writers of the fringe are safe. Because as soon as they are attacked they run off saying 'Let's wait.' Which is the role of the Communist Party in this country, too, reflected in its stepping aside from the real issues. As a writer you have got to be imaginatively in advance of the political parties, because you are much freer.

Gooch: But you say that in one breath, and then you criticize the theatre groups which are not aligning themselves with political parties. That's a contradiction. Where exactly do you stand?

D'Arcy: There are two choices for writers who claim that their work is overtly political. One is that they should join a political party. Then it is the duty of those writers to struggle, struggle, struggle inside that party and against capitalist bureaucracy. If they are not in a political party (perhaps no political party will take them!), then their obligation to their audience is to explain what the role of the political party is—not to ignore it, which is what is happening. Writers these days are much more complacent than ten years ago. What are their plays for, I would like to know?

Wandor: To assume that it is possible for writers to have a revolutionary consciousness which develops in complete isolation from any kind of revolutionary practice is certainly ridiculous: writers can't pluck revolutionary theatre out of the air. You may criticize them because they don't directly confront the question of British imperialism, but writers are reflecting existing society, the existing range of the class struggle—from wishy-washy liberalism to reformism, to ultra-left flag-waving.

Craft and Content

Griffiths: Do you see theatre as a means to an end or the end in itself?

Arden: Perhaps it is a means to an end.

Griffiths: I am sure that not everybody would agree with that. For some people the end is something they are trying to create on their own terms. There is craft involved.

Birchall: But you don't write just for the sheer satisfaction of writing—you do it in order to achieve a purpose.

Arden: A play is a conveyance of an idea, whatever the idea is. Even a light comedy about adultery should convey the idea. Theatre is an art which communicates, and it is a two-way communication. Not the same as making a film, which for example can be shown all over the world and remain exactly the same product wherever it's shown. You never know what the audience think of it. A play varies every night: and the quality of the communication varies between the actors and the audience.

Griffiths: The average person in the audience wants to see the craft of the playwright, his ability to put words together, to create characters, all the conventional literary craft of making a play. Surely this is important.

Arden: Not without content. Plays are meaningless without content.

Birchall: But surely craft is simply the most effective way of presenting content—whatever the content.

Arden: We're taking that as read. . . . I assume that a person who writes plays and gets them put on and continues to write plays and get them on has some idea of what the business involves.

D'Arcy: The more complicated the theme, the more challenge there is to clarify.

Arden: But in an ideal world, the playwright, whoever he or she may be, will find when the play is put on that he will be able to learn from the production—why the craft didn't come up to standard. So the next play is perhaps better and then the one after that and so on . . .

Griffiths: Ten years ago this conversation couldn't have happened in the same way. I think that writers would have put the craft before the content.

On Broad Front Issues

Birchall: One of the significant things that has happened in the last ten years is that a group gets commissioned by a political organization—often a broad front organization—a tenants' organization, a group of militant pensioners, whatever. More often that not, it isn't a political party. If you respond to what the working class is organizing, it tends to be a broad front issue. Another change is that the point of productions becomes *one* point and not many. Ten years ago a writer might write a play in one place, send it to an agent in a second, who would send it to a director in a third, who would send it to a company in a fourth, who would perform it in a fifth. Now by putting all the people in the same place in the play-making process, a product is created which is more relevant and useful to the audience. The problem still remains, however—where do correct ideas come from? From the party or the broad front? They come from struggle, from practice. And particular organizations may or may not correctly interpret that struggle and that practice. Perhaps the point is that the play does not *have* to pose the question of the revolutionary party, because what *the play* achieves is to draw people who are on the edge of struggle into struggle. It is *the struggle* that will then pose, in its development, the need for the party. The play simply draws people into struggle, in the first place.

Arden: When you say a broad front issue, do you mean something like contraception or housing?

Birchall: Yes.

Arden: Then it is the job of the playwright and/or group to surprise the people who have commissioned them. In other words, I think the playwright has fallen down on the job if the play that results from the commission turns out to be only on the same ideas that the broad front group has put forward in pamphlets and dialogue. The theatre should extend itself one step further than is expected or obvious. It is the responsibility of the people working in the theatre to find new insights.

D'Arcy: Which will be taken from the broad struggle. Our duty is to read every newspaper, find out exactly what's happening and not just to sit in the middle of the river—which is what most writers do. It is hard work being a writer.

Working Class Consciousness

Arden: Complacency lies in presenting only what you are expected to present. If, for example, you or I were asked to present a play for trade unionists in Liverpool about a strike going on there, it may very well be that the people who commission the play do not want you to bring up the fact that there are antagonistic communities—of Orangemen and Fenians—in Glasgow. But if you feel that this is relevant to the industrial struggle, then it should be put in the play. But then *you may not be allowed to perform that play*. That is where the struggle of the writer and the theatre group comes in. You must make sure that, with whatever tactics you can, you are not forced into simply being 'Yes Men,' and ignoring areas which you have analyzed as being important as the issue you are writing about.

D'Arcy: If one takes the action for one's play from the class struggle, and then that play is censored, the writer is suddenly personally involved in a very real class struggle.

Gooch: I think the fatal flaw in your statement is the word 'suddenly'. We've always had a very real class struggle.

D'Arcy: Strikes happen very suddenly.

Wandor: They don't always.

D'Arcy: No, not always. Some do: some don't. At least one has to be prepared.

Wymark: Wouldn't you say that one of the sad things about England is that the working people in this country don't comprehend, imaginatively, the Irish situation?

D'Arcy: I absolutely disagree with that. The people who do not understand are the middle classes—and the writers. I can talk to any working class person about Ireland and get an immediate, very strong right or left reaction, but it is not what I met at the National Theatre, for example, which claims 'We don't know what is happening,' or 'We've got more important things to do . . .' The working class has a very strong attitude, which is the reason why the Irish situation is so dangerous.

Wymark: My experience is different. The working class people I have met . . .

D'Arcy: When you say working class, you have to go into what kind of working class, by area, etc.

Wymark: Specifically, I met and talked to a bunch of quite young working class people recently who mostly worked in a clothing factory in E.10. The came out strongly and unanimously conservative on almost every issue and it seemed incredible to me that they were totally without sympathy for their working class counterparts in Ireland. And for the first time ever I felt rather passionately about writing a political play for a purpose to get those people to change their views. From my experience living in this country I have found working class attitudes often very conservative indeed.

Gooch: Conservative on some issues. And it's not always the same issues in the same place.

D'Arcy: And if they are conservative on the Irish issue, it is because of the particular area they live in. If you go to any of the big industrial areas like Liverpool or Glasgow, up in the North, feeling is very strong.

Wandor: David Edgar's play *Destiny,* on the National Front, may be an instance where it might be a useful tactical decison to do a play on a single issue—on fascism and racism, which could lead people to a greater understanding. It might look like a single issue but with wider implications. The theatre may reflect the lack of any kind of all-embracing, pushing-forward, revolutionary party in this country, but I don't think that's to condemn the particular plays that people do.

Arden: Can I suggest that a single issue is all right, provided it does not leave the audience at the end with the sensation that everything will be fine once that single issue has been solved? Most of the single issues are presented in isolation without relation to other issues. The playwrights' function is to show the audience that any single issue is going to involve a whole lot of other things which they must be aware of. Of course, a fifty-minute play cannot explain *in detail* what these things are, nobody is suggesting it should.

D'Arcy: But the writer must be *aware* of all the issues. My great fear is that the writers themselves are politically ignorant, so they become involved in a single issue and think that is the be-all and end-all.

Churchill: You seem to be saying two things. One is that the single issue play has limitations, and the other is that people shouldn't just promote socialism in a generalized way. But for some audiences that in itself would be a big step. If people come to a play completely non-political, and they go out opened up to the feeling that socialism is a good idea, that would be much more than most plays achieve. Are you actually saying that a very specific party line should be given to people?

D'Arcy: If you call yourself a *political* group, yes. If you don't have a specific line, don't call yourself a political group and justify it by saying, 'We have "political" discussions afterwards.'

Arden: There is an analogy with commercial advertising. If you mount an advertising campaign to advertise anything, say a product like soap, people want to know where they can buy the soap and what its price is once they've been told its virtues. I think this is what is missing in political theatre.

Birchall: The role of the writer as you describe it seems identical to the role of members of broad front organizations. That is, to bring out the generalized politics by saying, 'So the James White Abortion Bill is defeated, but that doesn't mean the struggle is over.' I think a revolutionary can win people over to revolutionary politics, by working with them, alongside them, in broad front organizations. Not everyone of course. But some. And you do it by advancing a line on the issue in question and arguing for it, and winning people to it. That can work. What won't work is approaching people head-on as a party organization and demanding they join it immediately, rather than first get involved in the particular struggles that arise from their own situation. People become militants before they become revolutionaries. What revolutionary parties can do, and what writers can do, is to help that process to occur . . .

Griffiths: There are tremendous expectations of the writer to comprehend, and to analyze and to communicate all these issues.

Towards a World View

Arden: It is our job to place the expectations as high as possible. I believe firmly that it is the writer's job to present a consistent vision of the entire world as comprehensively as possible. Now obviously that is an objective no writer, or group of actors, can be expected to fulfill completely, but they must strive towards it. What I have felt very strongly about the English theatre lately—when people ask what one feels about it now as compared with a few years ago—is that writers are inclined to develop for themselves a little corner, and simply operate within and not try to get out of it. This is in the context of this *Alternative Theatre Handbook*, which presents all these little groups, all working on their own, doing their own thing, in different parts of the country. Culturally, we are turning into a nation of mice with their own little nests and their own little holes.

Griffiths: But some of these companies certainly have tried to organize themselves and have started to try to make contact between themselves. And so have the writers.

Arden: Well, we wouldn't be here today if that weren't so. And it is very, very difficult, obviously, for actors, and acting groups, and writers to come together into any sort of cultural landscape which makes sense on its own. We'll certainly not expect this to happen within the next week.

Griffiths: Again, there is the contradiction that nearly all writers are in competition with each other.

Arden: I used to think it was a splendid idea that the community, from its rates and taxes, should support artists. But when I see the vast philosophical gap between the artists and the administrators, with Hugh Jenkins saying, 'We are the most inventive and prolific artistic nation in the modern world and this excellence is more important than our old military supremacy, and we have the power to regain our power on a different level,' I change my mind. He is quite clearly conceiving artists as people who will represent a certain image of Britain! And if that image involves the presentation on stage of a Britain torn by all sorts of internal discontents and struggles, it may have the reverse effect to what Jenkins intends. The writer's job is to tell the truth as he sees it, and the politician's job seems to be to present a certain image of the country which foreigners will respect. The two are in conflict.

Subsidy and Social Meaning

Howard: Before I received an Arts Council playwrights' bursary, I was a wage labourer, writing in my spare time. I am alienated as a writer given the conditions of our society, and I think that is to be expected. But it didn't occur to me what a useful condition alienation can be for a writer. The theatre itself serves only a very small fraction of the population. You can write for a theatre, or you can write for a theatre group working in the community doing community plays, but I don't accept that there is a community, anyway. The community is obliterated in our society beneath exchange value. If you play a production geographically, you are not in any sense serving the community: you are serving a geographical area. To my mind, community productions will be possible only in a society that is organized on a socialist basis. Given that the writer *has* to be alienated in one form or another in this society, I want to ask what is the most useful way to be alienated?

Griffiths: But how can we prepare for a situation where we *will* have a role, where there is a social meaning to our situation?

Howard: It seems to me that as a socialist playwright one's groundwork is in and for the production process. If somehow a writer were situated close to the production point, he could begin to help in the preparation of a socialist economic transformation by a type of cultural action. In other words, writing a play with people who work, writing it specifically for them, using their talents. A writer making his writing, in other words, part of the direct production process. Writers notoriously up until recently have been individualistic and have been forced to be alienated individuals. It is comparable to the alienation of the worker, which is the typical alienation of our society. If one were writing in a working place—as opposed to writing in isolation or in a theatre group outside—I think one could work as a catalyst, introducing a theatre culture into an area which has not been expected to contain a culture. In an office, a factory, a farm, it is not expected that cultural and social activities or any activities apart from productive labour, should take place. In a way, it is surprising that in the normal course of capitalist development, while they have seen the necessity over the last century to provide health facilities which were not expected of them a hundred years ago, there hasn't been a move towards the work place as a social unit. The economy still demands that work places are primarily production units and not cultural or social units as well.

Griffiths: Do you think that if individual playwrights were in 'official' positions in places of work, they could be preparing for that moment of change which will come—when work and the product will be seen as an expression of a person's social identity?

Gooch: The work of a socialist playwright should not only be directed at socialist ends, but should take place in the context of the development towards socialism within the present system.

Griffiths: Is it the real issue then, trying to get subsidies and grants?

Howard: I suppose an Arts Council bursary is intended as a springboard, to allow the writer to consolidate his position and move on to more normal forms of wage labour, by being attached to a theatre company—rather than to move back to being a writer in his spare time. It's the place the writer is that is important, and I am questioning where the writer should be. If a waiter wants to be subsidized then where he writes is a very big question. I think it is worth going into the idea of supporting writers for a year or longer, by offering to write in a work place. Conditions have to be attached, but I would have thought that it could be a useful method of re-injecting the writer back into society, rather than forcing him to remain an observer on the outside.

Writing in a Work Place

Arden: The assumption would be that writers working in a work place would be paid by the trade union—or by the management?

Howard: I would obviously propose that an Arts Council subsidy of this sort should be supplemented by the trade unions with some contribution from the management. But, in general, he should be considered to be on the payroll, that is, be a member of the work force of the factory, office, farm. And he should be there under the auspices of the union, not of the management.

Arden: In a colliery there is a man called a checkweighman whom the trade union employs to make sure that the pitmen are not cheated when the coal is weighed. He is a trade union official whom the management have been forced, over years of struggle, to accept. I can see a situation in which, if management started objecting to what was going on, the order of priorities in the trade union backing the writer would be fairly low. The writer would have had to do something to convince the union that he was worth fighting for, and he may not find that easy. It might take years to get going. It sounds very nice theoretically, but the attitudes of the trade unions at the moment would be a barrier.

Howard: That may be so in quite a lot of cases, but success would depend on the particular union branches and on the playwrights. I also agree that there would be a problem of being ingested into the system.

Arden: It is difficult, because there are permanent antagonistic relationships between managements and unions, which everyone recognizes. Managements en masse would object to such an idea very strongly.

Wandor: There are possibilities in other areas. There are embryonic writing schemes where writers go into schools or colleges or other institutions for one or two terms and get paid as writers in residence, which means that they spend part of their time working in a work place and the other part doing what's called their own work. This has been fairly conservatively applied, but it could be a basis to build on. Maybe the idea could be extended into other areas, like industry of agriculture.

D'Arcy: Who would provide the services, the facilities for rehearsals and so on—the union?

Arden: It's difficult enough for unions to get their ordinary union activities carried out in the works. There are always rows about union meetings being called in factories on the bosses' time....

Kirchall: There would be a danger of being shunted into clubs....

Arden: The social clubs are intended, *if they are paid for by the management,* to keep the workers happy on the job in this country at this time....

Griffiths: Let's face it, it's unlikely anything like this would ever happen.

Arden: It's quite different here from in China, where the factories are not under a capitalist management.

Griffiths: I agree. In our society we aren't at that stage. But we have some access to a certain amount of state money for which we should be responsible. This is money that comes from the workers in the first place, and its benefits should go back to them—surely!

Gooch: When we did *The Motor Show* at Fords we were refused a tour of the plant by the Ford management on the grounds that they were preparing a new model. A secret. So we were smuggled into the plant by the shop stewards and shown around. You know, there are aisles in big factories with cross gangways, and as we were being conducted around by one of the stewards a supervisor appeared at the other end of the aisle. So we would go down one and up another—we had this constant game of hide and seek.

Griffiths: The primary battle is to get us out of the ghetto of 'work for the theatre' or 'work for an academic institution,' which are our two places of permanent employment.

Kift: It boils down to how we win the confidence of the unions and workers—normal working people in a working community. We are more like them than 'artists'. I've no idea how we win the I confidence—whether it means actually working for a while in industry—I don't know how one would start to begin to win that confidence.

D'Arcy: The Arts Council annual report says they want money and involvement from the trade unions. So presumably, it's a matter of putting forward a pilot scheme and approaching the trade unions.

Birchall: There is a TUC Committee on the Arts, due to report at the TUC Conference. I don't know precisely what it's done, but it seems to be meeting general secretaries of entertainment unions—that is, all top-level people with no rank and file involvement. Meanwhile on Tyneside there's a body called Tyneside Trade Unionists for the Socialist Arts, mainly at shop steward and convenor level. Such rank and file labour movement bodies need to be built, which support the arts, and they need to control a TUC committee demographically from the base. This way, access to trade union funds may, possibly, occur, insofar as its part of the *official* labour movement. But to return to the point about working in work places, in Manchester a group were doing a play about health cuts, and they decided they wanted to try and involve some nurses from a hospital. They then decided the way to gain their confidence was actually to work themselves in a hospital for six months and abandon doing theatre work. That's a big decision—to give up play-writing for six months to go into an actual work place, to see the issues. As it turned out, two or three of them decided it was more important to *remain* as workers in the hospitals—to act as shop stewards, and to organize as trade unionists in that place of work. Now is that a failure? Are we disappointed if that is the conclusion that we draw from experience? If a play was intended, and did not result?

Arden: I would think not. It merely removes from the theatre people who discover that their interest is elsewhere. The theatre is carrying enough passengers as it is.

D'Arcy: It would have to be an overall policy. If one wanted to have proper theatre groups within the trade union movement, they would have to be put through the Big Machine, wouldn't they?

Griffiths: That is the problem. It is very similar to the problem of putting plays or ideas through the Big Machines of the big subsidized theatres. Perhaps one could make better contact and have more freedom on a grass roots level than if you were a TUC-approved body.

Problems of Patronage

Birchall: There are obviously contradictions in the establishment ideology. There's the chance of using the Arts Council itself, which freely says it wishes to increase access to the arts for the public throughout Great Britain. There's a certain amount of leverage that can be used in saying that we are doing *that,* and then get increased subsidy for it.

Arden: Pressure *can* be put on theatres through organizations. The Society of Irish Playwrights last year told the Abbey Theatre that if they didn't put on six new plays a year by Irish authors in the next season, they were going to establish a boycott and, if necessary, picket the Abbey. Now the Abbey knew perfectly well that the Society of Irish Playwrights does not consist of all the playwrights in Ireland. On the other hand, it does have a sufficient number of well-known playwrights to worry them. In fact, without it ever coming to a confrontation, the Abbey policy has greatly improved. But there is the contradiction of getting public money to do work which actually questions the whole right of the government to run the country the way it does. I believe as long as the money is there, you might as well take it. There are difficulties too in the way it is used as a weapon to dissuade theatre groups from presenting plays on certain 'sensitive' subjects. And it also leads to an unwillingness to take risks. Everybody discusses what the role of the dramatist is, or what the role of the theatre is, and always the first question that arises is, how do we get subsidy? It is a problem, because once subsidy is created people become dependent upon *officials* to be paid. And although it is public money, it is not the *public* that is paying you the money. It is the administrators. There is a contradiction here to do with subsidies which I am worried about.

D'Arcy: Another contradiction on subsidies is that companies don't get money for long periods, for three years, say. They get subsidy for each play. Therefore, they have to let their actors go, and then get new actors. This creates insecurity and lack of continuity. And there is a kind of harassment, making it necessary to churn out so many performances that, in the end, the actor is not doing creative work. Why don't they give you money for a full five years, and after five years let them come along and have a look at what you've done.

Arden: The problem with all patronage—whether it comes from public money or whether it's the old fashioned kind of patronage where Lord Somebody dishes out money for a poet to celebrate him—is that the money is paid on the understanding that it is going to produce a certain product which is thought to be of value to the patron. So quality invariably depends on particular fashions at any given time. You have to look at each specific subsidy and say, 'What are they doing it for?' and 'Is the artist improving himself, or destroying himself while accepting this?' If the article in *Time Out* about Arts Council enquiries into the political interests of companies is true, the whole subsidy question is going to be drawn much more into the open in a controversial way in the very near future.

Griffiths: You were talking about subsidy to groups rather than subsidy to writers as individuals?

Arden: The same thing applies to both, quite honestly. But it is more obvious in relation to groups because they employ more people and are more publicly accountable. An individual can get money off the Arts Council and then go off and spend it on wine and song somewhere and there is nothing they can do about it. But if it's a group, then the administrators of that group are responsible for the living of half a dozen people or more.

Aims of the Arts Council

Griffiths: What does the Arts Council aim to achieve?

Arden: I don't know. Hugh Jenkins says that it is presenting the prestige of the country in a way that the British Army has been unable to do in recent years! Then there was a Tory report, two or three years ago—by Lord Smarty Boots, what's his name, Eccles—which as good as said that the purpose of the Arts Council subsidy was to keep teenagers from hanging round street corners mugging old ladies. That doesn't seem to me to be what I'm in business for! It may be a possible by-product of my plays, I don't know, but....

Kift: The basic philosophical split between those members of the profession who sit on the Drama Panel and members of the Arts Council itself, appointed by the Minister, is that the Arts Council can only judge contemporary theatre in terms of 'excellence,' platonic

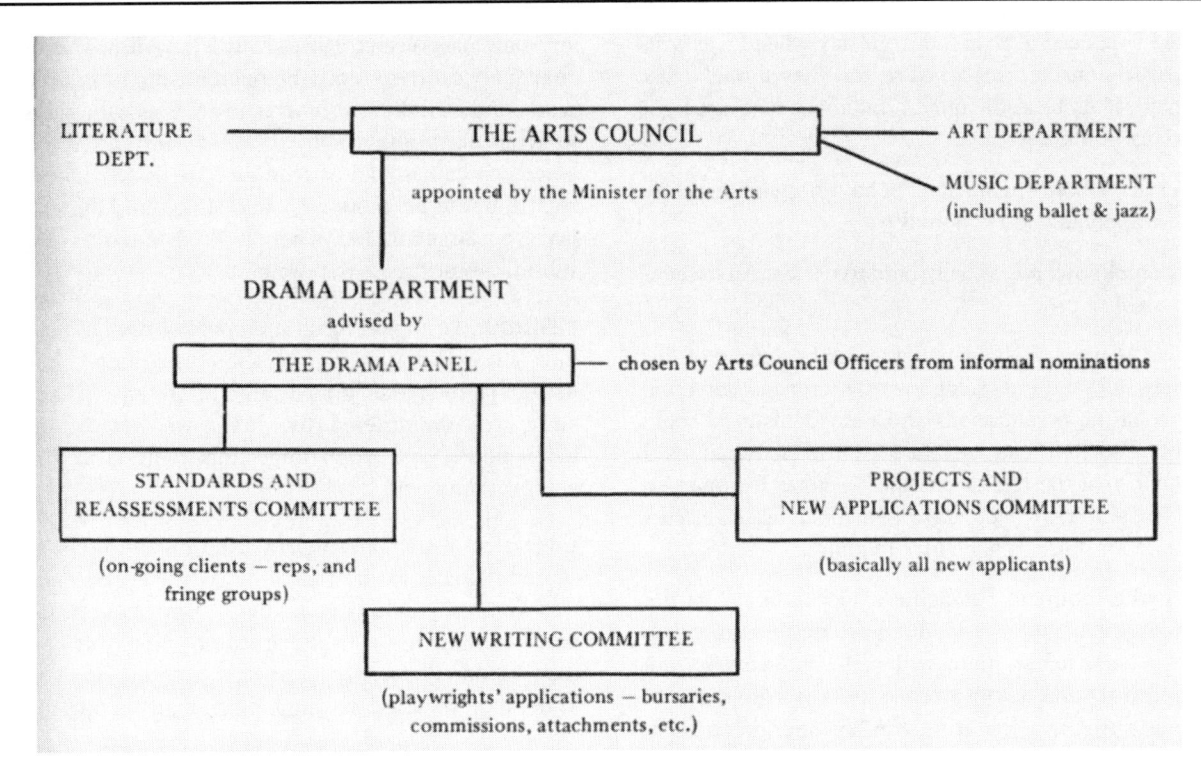

The structure of the Arts Council of Great Britain, with special reference to the Drama Department. All sub-committees are drawn from members of the Drama Panel, but in certain cases members may be co-opted from outside. All recommendations from sub-committees go the Drama Panel for ratification, and finally to the Arts Council itself for approval.

ideas of 'excellence'—whether the work is 'excellent' or not. If orchestras in Chesterfield are playing too many wrong notes, then subsidy is cut off. There is total and utter alienation.

Griffiths: And how does that affect us?

Edgar: I'm much more frightened of members of the Drama Panel than I am by the Arts Council officers and administrators. And I think there is a problem with the left-wing critics. It is good that people like Bernard Levin take over the *Sunday Times,* because then we know where we are. It's the people who praise John McGrath, when he writes scenes with table tops and talking about children's dancing lessons, who seem to me at the moment to destroy radical alternative Marxist theatre by attempting to infiltrate it with bourgeois, individualistic, psychological values. Which means you don't come along to 7:84's *Little Red Hen,* for example, expecting certain messy or dirty working-class humans . . . which could spoil the punch of the production. Instead, you get a kind of political theatre which comes up to standards and criteria set by the critics from national newspapers. The actual human content of that play is highly polished, but amazingly empty. A rough show could have a meaningful content.

Wesker: David Edgar mentions being very upset, worried or frightened by the Drama Panel. Who exactly *are* the Drama Panel?

Edgar: The Drama Panel are the artists who are co-opted on to the Arts Council. They are professional advisors. I am more worried about them than I am about the permanent officers or the grey men in blue suits.

Griffiths: There are professional advisors on the Arts Council panel. The council itself is appointed by the Minister for the Arts. And the Council has its administrative officers to service it, and who service the panels. There has been a head-on confrontation, a very real conflict, between the Drama Panel, with its professional advisors who have been professional theatre workers, and the Council, which obviously looks at the whole of the arts and has to balance off pottery against knitwear, against theatre, against skin-diving, what have you.

Wesker: I knew the structure, I just wondered what each person was thinking when each talked about the Arts Council, what they had in mind?

Kift: Well, there is that group of people appointed by the Minister without reference to anybody whatsoever—that's the Council. The Minister appoints the Council, and then the Council appoints the panels. I think I was appointed because I happened to go in there one day when I was writing an article on the fringe theatre and they thought that 'this chap seems to know quite a bit about it'. And I got phoned up, you know.

Wesker: To whom ought reference have been made before you were appointed, do you think?

Kift: I don't know. It is actually hard to decide. An 'electorate,' if you like.

Griffiths: When I was appointed at the beginning of this year, they did send out voting forms, nominational voting forms to all the organizations and individuals they could think of. And they had back at least 180 nominations. I understand that the highest number of votes for one person was eight. How you have a democratically elected panel is up for discussion. I'd love to know.

Kift: At the moment, I imagine it works like this: the officers together with the Council decide on something called 'a balance,' so they will pick one writer, one administrator, one actor, a few from the conventional repertory system, a few from the big national companies, a few from the fringe, and hope that that will represent a balanced spectrum of overall British theatre opinion.

Wesker: But how much power do you have?

Kift: Well, on the little companies, I should think we have quite a bit. On the RSC, the National Theatre, none whatsoever.

Gooch: There is now an organization which there should have been before, when the left-wing playwrights of the 'fifties and 'sixties were prominent. The Theatre Writers' Group intends to see that people get grants. Because it shouldn't be done on the basis of knowing people's telephone numbers.

Griffiths: Are writers getting a better or worse deal in terms of the whole Arts Council policy now than ten years ago?

Edgar: One thing I find very alarming—I haven't any actual statistics on this apart from experience of two or three theatres in the provinces where I do most of my work—is that there has been a very substantial revolution in the policy of theatre programme construction, whereby the production of new work has become a luxury, an occasional thing you do like a musical. If you don't do a new play for five years, it doesn't really matter. It's difficult for the two members of the Drama Panel here, because one sounds as if one's being personal, and I am sure that these two members of the Drama Panel fought against this. It is alarming to learn that the Birmingham Repertory Theatre has just gone through its longest period without any new plays—since 1921! This is a radical and terrible change. Because reps are the main medium for large-scale work, and I think most of us who are political writers tend to write plays about subjects which are well done with large companies. They tend not to be set in drawing rooms, but to be about wars and strikes and things which involve a large number of people. So that market—regional subsidized theatre—is important.

Griffiths: Time and again members of the Drama Panel have stressed that new work should be done. The problem is that the Arts Council continuously says, 'These theatres are administered by their own boards and are independent,' and don't forget that there is also a local authority involved.

Edgar: So if the Birmingham Rep or any other theatre started doing strip shows and bingo, then presumably the Arts Council would have nothing to say about it? On that basis, they might be justifying subsidy from the Tote, but they wouldn't be justifying subsidy from the Arts Council. What if they started putting football matches on?

Arden: Someone suggested in yesterday's Evening Standard that the Greater London Council subsidize football matches!

Edgar: But if there is an absolutely basic definition that a regional theatre should promote new drama, then the Arts Council could impose sanctions . . .

Wesker: They all say they never look very favourably on theatres which don't have a consistent programme and can't produce new works. . . .

Edgar: If the RSC stopped doing Shakespeare, then the Arts Council might conceivably tap it on the shoulder and say, 'Have you noticed the middle word of your title?'. New work should be as central as that.

Kift: When it actually comes down to hard cash, there is a Finance Department which gets all the figures through before anybody actually decides anything. This year, we were faced with tabled figures to about three million pounds, and they said, please approve these immediately, or the theatres will suffer as a result. True, the Council was faced with not knowing what their allocation would be, until about three days before that. So that was the government's fault. But one's told, well if you hold one up then all the theatres are going to suffer, so one's faced with a shotgun administrative situation.

Griffiths: I think most of the members of the Drama Panel would support any action on behalf of the theatre writers, trying to insist to the Arts Council that they take a stand over this.

Gems: Is there really any point in any of us being on the Drama Panel? Surely the point is that it is more of a danger. Acting as a group of writers, like the Theatre Writers' Group, is a better way of putting on pressure.

Kift: I would say there is a positive point in sitting on those committees. Firstly, you begin to understand more clearly their practical, political way of making decisions over a spectrum of groups. And secondly, if you sit on those committees, you know exactly what is going on, and can within certain limits make information more widely available.

Arden: The real problem is that the authors are co-opted individually onto this panel.

Griffiths: And they are not all writers!

Arden: If on the other hand there was an active theatre writers' union, then the union could elect it's own representatives.

Gooch: There is a very good argument against unions or organizations being represented on any distributive committee in the same way as there is an argument against workers' co-operatives in capitalism.

Edgar: With the exception of the guerrilla fighters that we have in our midst here, the Drama Panel tends to be made up of radical drama critics, people who don't run theatres, people who are fairly high up in the trendy subsidized theatres, left-wing impresarios who have mounted a new attack over the last year or so on theatrical agitprop work.

Griffiths: The Drama Panel does consist mainly of people who are concerned with the management side. We were talking earlier about writers having to work through management structures to get their audience. The Drama Panel reflects that structural control. So when it comes down to it, the cry goes up, 'We haven't enough money,' and the studios get closed down, and new plays don't get put on, and the companies get cut. In what way, then, as writers, do you benefit from the existence of the Arts Council? In what way *should* you benefit? Does it actually do you any good at all? Has your income increased by having guaranteed royalty payments or bursaries?

Birchall: We are still working a productivity deal. And there are unpleasant side effects. With only £600 a play now possible, you still have to write five plays a year to make a wage of £60.00 per week from theatre, which is still less than the national average wage for all male workers. That enables writers to give up their economic base of social security or another job—teaching, whatever—and to try to become full-time writers. If they do, the chance of experiment goes, simply in order to operate because there's never enough money.

Subsidy as Carrot

Gooch: Subsidy operates as a kind of carrot on a stick. It encourages you to do half the job, and it gives you the resources to do half the job. You still have to make commercial products to make up the difference between the subsidy you get and the subsidy you really need.

Griffiths: Is the writer in the same situation as other theatre workers?

Gooch: No, the writer is different. All other theatre workers benefit from the *theatre's* subsidy. The writer is the only person hanging on like grim death hoping that the audience will come in. Even though his reward is related to the whole production—the way it is produced, acted, lit, designed, and finally sold by the publicity machine. If it's kids' plays put on at cut price, then the writer takes a direct cut in wages because his box office gets cut straight away. Part of our fight is to make sure that the writer somehow gets to benefit from the subsidy put into his play by the theatre. How, I don't know. Perhaps the Theatre Writers' Group will say, 'That's what we want,' or demand a strict minimum fee to guarantee the writer's income. All I know is that in Germany and Switzerland they are working out a system whereby the writer can benefit from the amount of subsidy put into his play by the theatre.

Wesker: He gets a percentage on the actual cost of the seat—that is, not just the non-subsidized part of the seat's cost.

Gooch: That's what the Theatre Writers' Group is working towards.

Edgar: I'd like to return to that example of the orchestra in Chesterfield. If it gets a subsidy and it's excellent, and somebody from America or France or Italy comes over and sees it and writes up in his newspaper that it's excellent, then the government can pat itself on the back. And the critics have got to say it's 'excellent'.

Griffiths: The National Theatre, unfortunately, has become our exemplary theatre.

Kift: But what is it that makes it excellent?

Griffiths: The Arts Council gives it a lot of money!

Ideas of 'Excellence'

Wesker: I don't think any of this is true. I think what is meant by excellence is the excellence of the imagination, the excellence of the thought, and the excellence of the execution. And I think that if an audience is confronted with an empty space and six very fine performers performing without any props, that would be recognized as excellent if it were excellently done. I think that the objection is just against tatty productions—which hope they will get by because their hearts are in the right place, when very often one ends up with sloppy thinking and sloppy production. I think that's what is meant by excellence. The Arts Council are quite capable of going to the National Theatre and looking at Ibsen and saying that it's just awful. But if you are talking about the question of excellence, that's what they might mean. Certainly I would mean that.

Kift: But it takes no account of the essential relationship between a theatre performance and a theatre audience, a theatre performance to a certain community of interests. Which is miles away from platonic ideas, which is what Peter Brook called 'rough theatre'.

Arden: Which can either be good or bad. It is hard to define precisely which, until you see a performance and can criticize it specifically.

Griffiths: We have been talking about the National Theatre, and we have talked about a person who earns £8,000 to administer £5,000 for writers. Who are supposed on that to be exemplary?

D'Arcy: But how did he get the job? Was he excellent? That's what we want to find out. Who are the people who lay down the aesthetic values of theatre today? Who are they? Critics? He who does the hiring has to be advised by somebody. Presumably if people get into the National, they are excellent people. Which means that when they were scrubbing away (wherever they were scrubbing) the messenger came along and put down after them, 'Grade A'. And then the Board comes along and says, well *there's* a 'Grade A'! And he gets the job.

Arden: But this is the whole way the English system works. The Church of England for example has been working like this for years. Bishops are supposed to be appointed by the Queen. In fact, they are appointed by the Prime Minister who is advised by other Bishops who to appoint. And so they tend on the whole—unless you've got an odd, eccentric Prime Minister—to appoint a series of people who fall within the standards already laid down by previous holders of the job. When it's applied to the arts, there is a very grave problem, because ideas of excellence have become conservative, traditional ideas. So we are going to end up with a conservative theatre. There is an argument for a conservative tradition in the arts, but it's not the only tradition. There is also the old fashioned experiment which may begin in a tatty well-meaning way, as Arnold Wesker says, but which may end, with experience and with practice, criticizing itself and improving itself.

Wandor: I think it's fairly complicated, because some of the things which effect people's thinking about the theatre don't come from the history of the theatre itself. They come from the history of literature teaching. There is a notion of a classical tradition of literature, the 'great' Cambridge tradition, which is completely untheatrical. There is still the idea that Britain will once again lead the world if it can get back on the right kind of pedestal, and this does affect what people think about the theatre: it affects the way in which the National and the RSC plan their classical programmes. They look for something they would like to think of as a modern classic—which inevitably means, things which are out of date, or very set.

Howard: As long as writers think they are involved in a literary pursuit, they are really on their own. And that is what is meant by excellent plays.

D'Arcy: And this standard is set for all the English speaking areas in the world, like India or ex-colonial Africa.

Wandor: That's where imperialism is a basic part of the culture. There has been a lot of argument in the Poetry Society recently, and most of the news reporters, when they reported it in the national press, were slightly cynical. But one of the things all the journalists agreed about was that the English did poetry best, whatever it was. This came out unconsciously. But they were very sure, and the assumption just tripped off the typewriter with no trouble at all. This kind of cultural superiority is behind a hell of a lot of thinking, not just in the theatre.

Arden: It is very obvious in Ireland, because there is no Irish theatre tradition. There is a tradition of Irish *playwrights,* but the theatre in Ireland was originally set up in the late seventeenth and early eighteenth centuries for the entertainment of the English garrisons. They took all their standards from what was prevalent in England. This situation has never really changed. Even when they formed the Abbey Theatre at the beginning of the century they did it partly on the model of the English repertory movement, and it was Miss Homiman of Manchester who helped them. Nobody has actually found an Irish aesthetic in the *presentation* of plays, although Irish plays are clearly quite different from English plays. The subject matter is different, the use of language is different and so on. This is a problem that each year seems to become more difficult.

D'Arcy: And Ireland has a hell of a lot of Irish actors who begin to act in this 'excellent' style and tradition and become enmeshed in an English way of thinking and acting. And there are no Irish directors.

Arden: Irish directors in Ireland try to imitate what the English directors do here, with the result that you get a lot of stories about how the playwrights' work does not come up to the 'standards of excellence'. Those are the words used. The head of the Abbey was talking on the radio last year about the policy of the Abbey, and he said that they have 'standards' at the Abbey and they cannot put on plays which don't meet those 'standards'. He never said what the standards were. They never seem able to explain to the dramatists why the standards even had to be. I am quite certain that their standards of excellence derived from the British theatre.

Griffiths: So the standards of excellence are determined not by the writers whose plays are being judged, but by the management structure.

D'Arcy: Which is dominated by double-standards and by the English critics.

Finding an 'Alternative' Approach

Griffiths: Do the same notions of 'excellence,' either positively or negatively, apply to alternative fringe?

Gooch: I think people in all forms of theatre are trying to do theatre which moves people and revitalizes their thinking. But nearly everyone working on the fringe suffers from the legacy of the conventional theatre, in the sense that you don't find a completely thought-out theory of alternative theatre, one which is consistent and cohesive and which an entire company can work within. So you have not got a definitive theoretical alternative to conventional theatre. The problem is that because we are all working not only for the fringe, but in the theatre as a whole, we are also subject to pressures, both commercial and artistic, which compromise our focus and concentration on alternative work from the beginning. If you reach a sticky point in rehearsal, you may try to think in an alternative vein, but find the easy answer is the conventional one. You may solve the immediate problem, but you don't push through to something really new. I think that's the most common problem.

Kift: The basic difference in writing for the two areas is that in the conventional theatre the overriding consideration in presenting a play is that it should conform to certain laws about consistency of character and nicely-rounded scenes, well-drawn situations, good psychological conflict. And finally that it doesn't offend too many people with 'bad language'. On the fringe, on the other hand, you *start* by talking about what you are going to say, and then you are going to say it within the medium of theatre.

Edgar: I think areas are getting blurred for the writers. There is a commercial fringe which I think everybody accepts—post-*Kennedy's Children*—a fringe geared to West End transfer. In that sense, that *Teeth 'n' Smiles* is coming off might be rather good news for the fringe. Because it is good for the fringe that that particular bubble should be burst. Forgetting that sector, however, and thinking in terms of the touring groups and the community groups and the provincial situation, and actors and directors who work there, one still gets quite a wide division. The number of actors who will leave Red Ladder, for example, to go into the National Theatre is very few. As for directors . . . yes, well, there may be some. But there is a peculiar contradiction for the writers, that they are unable to eat because the fringe pays so badly, and have to (or indeed sometimes quite legitimately want to) work in a number of different environments, I think that the division between North West Spanner and the National Theatre now is much wider than between the Open Space and the Royal Court. So the situation has changed since six years ago.

Birchall: The reason why there has been a migration by writers towards the more established institutions and established managements is the inadequacy of fringe companies as production vehicles to put the work on, given their small grants. You have the problem with a play in the established theatre that its meaning is suppressed by *their* production vehicle, and unless you play the game and go along with that you'll not get a play on: you'll not be chosen in the first place. The other problem is that on the fringe the size of the cast is limited because the grants are too low! And if we are trying to deal with serious issues, we tend to want large casts. You've got a problem if your play needs twenty or more people to perform it. So it's either the National Theatre, or the Royal Shakespeare Company which must put it on—or not! Sometimes to write what you wish to write, you have exceeded the production capability of a fringe company.

Griffiths: So the contradiction is that the big theatres have the production capability we require to deal with serious topics, but we can't get the meaning to the right audience through established theatres.

Formalism on the Fringe

Wandor: There is a kind of tyranny of formalistic experiment in a lot of fringe companies. Perhaps because the spaces are small and the companies are small, there is this tendency to try and put things on which are just theatrical sensations. They tend to show off how many exciting things they can put on in a small space. It's different from what was being done five or six years ago, when some of the sensational stuff was quite aggressive. *The Connolly Show* reminded me of earlier productions where the audience was put in the middle and actors attacked them from all sides. Now there's a nice interaction between the people doing the plays and the people coming to see them.

Griffiths: How do you avoid sensationalism in your own writing?

Wandor: I feel pushed towards it actually–to write something which is going to be snappy and have two scenes on every page and extraordinary things happening.

Arden: You automatically feel blocked from even starting to think in terms of a relaxed, cool presentation of a theme? You feel that if you are writing a play for fringe theatre, you have got to pep it up whether the subject matter demands it or not?

Wandor: There is some pressure in that direction, yes, because there is a very strong reaction against the post-war naturalism of the commercial West End theatre. And there is a hostility from some people to the kind of stereotyped realism that appears in a lot of agitprop work. So there has been an attempt to find something between the two, which has its own kind of theatrical 'shockingness'. I would quite like to do something that combines all these things–I'll use the word 'political,' if you don't mind–but I mean something that is very clear in what it is saying, so that people can't go away, perhaps like they did from Edward Bond's *Stone,* saying, 'Well, of course it's about this' and then again, 'It's about that'.

Birchall: I think there is a problem within fringe companies to do with the effects of British drama school training. A lot of actors who work on the fringe are still tainted by very bourgeois ideas about theatre style. And if for the first time a democratic company of actors are getting a chance to influence the content and style of the play, there might be quite a serious conflict between the way the writer sees the material, and what the actors believe they find satisfying to act in the conventions they are used to from their training.

D'Arcy: But, on the other hand, you find actors in some alternative companies who haven't had the training which relates to practical experience. They have worked with groups who have not pushed them and they are a dead weight.

Wesker: I am waiting for someone to say that the Ardens are applying pointless standards of excellence, or make me understand what their objection to 'excellence' was.

Arden: What I understand the Arts Council to mean by excellence bears no relation to five or six flesh and blood people playing in a sweaty room to thirty or forty people on hard seats. Basically, an imperfect, temporal atmosphere is being judged according to some eternal concept of platonic values, which bears no relationship to the process of communication by one group to another. I am not in any way putting down the standards of an art, or an artist trying to create an artifact. I would merely say that in creating a play, one is working in a very, very difficult area of art. There are certain standards, and obviously certain questions you have to ask yourself while you are writing the play. And *after* you have written it. Otherwise there is no way in which you are going to look at your own piece of work and say, 'Well, that's bad because. . .'. Obviously, you are going to use standards of selectivity, and 'excellence'. What I'm saying about the Arts Council is that it tends to think that a piece of theatre exists as a piece of literature *per se,* without reference to any other form of communication.

D'Arcy: You know, I think that they actually treat theatre as if it was an aesthetic object, as if it was like a piece of pottery.

Economics of Playwriting

Griffiths: Can we move on to the more practical problem of how writers should be paid?

Gooch: The only proper way to begin to tap that problem is to see things in terms of a minimum weekly wage. If you are in a semi-subsidized situation, you're going to come across all kinds of anomalies—where people are half wage labourer and half selling commercial wares. So it's virtually impossible to think out one scheme which is consistent and logical and which answers the needs of writers. You are almost bound to have a mixture. The important principle is to make sure that a writer working full time in the business for theatre managements or groups should earn a better wage.

Arden: The difficulty is the definition of being 'in work'. This can be impossible to determine and regulate in any normal way. You might be asked to supply a play or plays to a particular theatre group who assess a rate of pay which you receive while you are doing that. But, on the other hand, you might have the bright idea that doesn't appear to fit any particular theatre group operating at that moment. But you may hope that in two years time, say, there will be some market for it. The writer is the only person who can say whether he is in work or not.

Wymark: Sometimes there are weeks of not getting anywhere with your work, and then suddenly it might all come clear in your mind. The whole way of subsequently assessing your time is affected. If you're working in a group, it's easier to calculate.

Gooch: That's why I was saying you are bound to get mixed situations. One way you can try to cope with it, is to earn a bit over the top on certain projects. I, in effect, buy myself time to write—my private work, if you like, in the hope that I am going to sell that later, and that that is going to pay for the time it took later.

Edgar: We all know that the actual writing of a play in physical terms, varies. But this applies to a lot of other theatre workers. How long does it take a designer to think of an idea? How long does Guy Wolfenden, who is employed permanently by the RSC, take to write a fanfare? Twenty seconds? Three weeks? Who decides that?

Wesker: I am sure they view it as a legitimate means of giving a wage to a composer who is going to be able to compose his serious music in the meantime.

Griffiths: That doesn't happen to writers in the theatre. Why is that?

Arden: It does happen to some extent.

D'Arcy: With writers in residence.

Writers under Contract

Gooch: I think the principle of contract-writing schemes where you are employed to do a job is reasonable. There seems to be no more reason in the world why a theatre shouldn't employ you from time to time, through the Arts Council, to do the job of writing something which is never necessarily going to get done. Or if you are a new writer, just to encourage you. It seems to me that the Arts Council can and should dole out sabbaticals quite easily. It does so to many people, anyway, who earn far more than we do. But the concept of paying a writer to produce a piece of work, so he becomes an employee, seems to me a very good one.

Halliwell: There is one difference between the composer and the writer. A writer can never fully be an employee, in that his play originates a theatre production. The script is the first thing—so either the script is done, in which case the whole process is set in motion, or the script isn't. The composer comes into the process when the play is already in production.

Arden: There was an educational programme on television, a documentary on how particular medieval medical papers were organized in the fourteenth century. There was a city that wanted a medical play to celebrate the fact that they had come, more or less unscathed, through the Black Death. And they put it out to tender. There were two particular people who applied. One was a clergyman who was good on theology, and the other was a professional poet. But his charges were too high and they went for the clergyman. He took far too long to write the script and they had to go to the other fellow who was charging them more. It was put out to tender, and that was the result.

D'Arcy: Say you get a contract from a theatre which says, 'We want six plays', one on the homeless, one on abortion or whatever, and so on. And they send a tender out to writers, who can then apply. I am very well suited to exploring problems about homeless women, say, and send in a play with three or four characters. In that kind of situation the whole business of talking about excellence becomes completely irrational.

Gems: Who is going to judge the excellence of the tenders?

Wandor: I think there may be something in trying to push the artists-in-residence idea. Because if writers are attached to particular theatres, not all of which have nasty managements, it might be possible for writers to be freed of the burden of the free-lance status, which is very insecure. You wouldn't have to feel that awful piece-work pressure. And it might make for better relations between writers and theatre companies, where ideas can be generated from other people. You needn't necessarily have an authoritarian mandate where the writers are simply told what to do. The writers-in-residence idea might solve the living wage problem *and* the working relationship between writers and theatres.

D'Arcy: What about writers who have got families? I've been offered these residencies and it's just impossible.

Wandor: I agree.

Arden: I had to give up a university job, a writing residency at a university, because my family is in Ireland and it just was not possible under the circumstances for us all to transplant, or for me to separate from them. Residencies are not easy except for young people without any ties.

Wandor: It depends on how much money is offered. I couldn't afford to work with any group on any kind of commission they could offer, because I need to earn far more than anybody could offer me. So I am pushed back into sitting staring at my typewriter.

Gooch: I think that the resident writer thing is very complicated. I have been through it twice. Once was at a theatre where I had worked quite happily before, where they did a play of mine, and it did very well, and has done well in other places subsequently. So I suppose that in the long term it was a good relationship. The second place was a very unlikely place for me to be. And what happened there was that I suddenly had a year's 'bought' time, and the freedom to write something more private. I was not directly commissioned, so I had this tendency just to *splurge*. All the frustrations that we normally have were gone, and I was able to say, 'Right the time's paid for, I can write what I like, although of course it's to be a brief from this theatre.' What happened in that situation was that the theatre didn't like the play and that by the time it was due to go on the theatre had just lost £15,000 on new plays, and could not contemplate another large-scale work. I think that unless you've got, in advance, a very good, close, working relationship with a director, or the director of a theatre, writing in residence can be a way of buying time and writing. But there's no guarantee that the work will get on, or that cross fertilization of ideas will take place.

Wesker: Don't writers find that sometimes a play takes years to write and sometimes two weeks?

Edgar: Obviously, things go wrong. There are millions of performances that could have done better with another three weeks or years of time. To assume that writers are somehow distinct from other workers in the entertainment industry, that they are surrounded by mystique, is dangerous. It merely justifies them in not meeting deadlines. Actors have to meet a deadline—they have to be there on the first night.

How Long to Write a Play?

Arden: There is a crucial difference between the author's work and the actor's—which is that the actor starts with a script, the author has to start with nothing. He has to think of an idea and that can take a hell of a time.

D'Arcy: But if the idea is 'given'?

Arden: Oh, if the idea is given, then that's quite a different thing. I am not talking about doing a play on a specific subject or in a specific style.

Edgar: There *are* obviously differences and these should be reflected. The Theatre Writers' Group is assuming that it takes six months to produce two hours worth of material.

Wesker: I think that's reasonable.

Edgar: I think it is absolutely reasonable. But I think there are elitist and mystifying concepts about writers, which writers exploit. It allows one to be moody and difficult in rehearsals.

D'Arcy: When you have to produce a play in two weeks, it's amazing that one can actually do it. It's true that if the pressure is on, it can make you productive.

Wesker: It's absolutely the reverse for me. I am paralyzed under pressure.

Wandor: It varies according to whether you are getting feedback from a group or a director while you are working. If you sit on your own and have to be your own critic, assessing it as you go along, it is more difficult.

Arden: I always take longer to write things that I'm not doing for anybody specifically. But when I have been commissioned by a theatre to provide a play, I work better.

Edgar: Let me make it clear. I think two weeks is absurd. All I am saying is that a professional writer knows and can calculate to an extent how long something is going to take. To base the way that writers are paid on the assumption that it is impossible to calculate the amount of time which is needed to produce a play is clearly no use.

Wesker: But that assumes that there are elements in the process which are constant—like you remain twenty-five years old all your life, set yourself the same challenges. And my experience is that growing older makes it more difficult to write, that you expect more complicated things from yourself, set yourself greater challenges. And this increases the amount of time. These are elements which must be taken into consideration when talking about what is expected, how much time is expected for a writer to produce anything. And what about things like research?

Edgar: So you are saying it is impossible to consider any kind of writer's wage on a realistic level?

Wesker: Absolutely. "If I had the power of prophecy to look around this table and say, 'I know that at the end of his lifetime or her lifetime, *that* person is going to produce the seven plays that Chekhov produced," I would say, 'Give that one £1,000, £3,000, £5,000, £10,000 a year for the next year and let us have those plays.' One hasn't got that power, of course, but it's a way of expressing what I think about it, the creative process and what it merits. And I don't think that's creating any mystique. It's just acknowledging what it seems to me centuries and centuries of the creative process has proven–there can be no rules, deadlines, or dogmas.

Gooch: I think that's true, but it's also true that it's very difficult to earn enough money when one is caught between a wage-earning situation and a fee situation. The price of the tickets that we get our royalty income from is not real. And we haven't got any criteria on which to base our weekly work. So we have got to have something. I think David Edgar's idea of the jobbing, gun-toting, have-typewriter-will-travel writer is quite good in certain situations. There are certain jobs you can do on that basis. But I think there has got to be room for writers who need to get away from theatre people. I have to get away from them. Frequently.

Arden: You can't possibly predict or budget for the Chekhovs. What we've got to do is to produce writers who are capable of providing enough plays to keep a regular flow of entertained audiences in and out of the theatre.

Griffiths: But how many new plays is it possible for writers actually to get produced–even though they may have written bloody good scripts?

Rift: Sitting on the Arts Council's New Writing Committee, we were given a list of new plays which had been written–whether by people who had been given a royalty or commissioned–and I don't think a single one was in the process of production. Certainly that list was one of the richest seams of writing I'd ever seen–but it was totally ignored in terms of production.

The Case of Arnold Wesker

Griffiths: I would recount the classic case of Arnold Wesker–somebody who has got three or four plays on the books and a considerable reputation, for whom there would seem to be no outlet in the British theatre, no one willing to produce them. Is that right?

Wesker: The situation has slightly changed. At Leeds they have decided to do one of the plays and Dexter is going to direct another–the last one, *The Merchant*, but in New York first. There is still no production for *The Journalists*, though.

Griffiths: What do you do in that situation?

Wesker: I get very furious. But each play actually had a different history. *The Journalists* was contracted to the wrong company, the RSC, and the actors refused to perform it. I have a photostat of a letter signed by two of the actors on behalf of the company saying they did not want to do The Journalists. And what the letter says is, 'We are much more excited'– and I am sure they were right–'by the John Arden play'. The letter says this. I don't think one should draw conclusions about the rights of the actors from this–I think that *The Journalists* happened at one moment in the history of the company and John and Margaretta's *Island of the Mighty* happened at another moment, and the circumstances had changed. My play seems to have arrived at a moment when the actors were feeling the high point of their strength, and were actually able to exercise it. And then within months they lost that power. It may be that the management found that they were tyrannized by the actors at the moment of my play, and they weren't going to have any more of it, so they put their foot down when the Ardens' play came along. I'm suing the RSC, so we'll know more when it comes into court.

Griffiths: There is a whole British theatre structure outside the RSC and there are people who are beginning to pick up your work on the reputation that you have. What factors do you think influence this?

Wesker: I have often tried to give answers to this. I think it's a mixture of a number of things. I think that generations of writers come in waves, and I think that new directors want to discover their own writers. So they will, and this is fine. This should be encouraged. New directors come along bringing with them new writers. I think that's one of the reasons. I also think that my plays require a lot of money. *The Journalists* has 33 characters and *The Wedding Feast* has 16, with four different settings.

Arden: I am sure that is part of the problem. Because you were writing *The Journalists* at the same time as we were working on *The Island of the Mighty*, and both plays were probably conceived when things were fairly good economically in the theatre. Then there was a sudden slump, wasn't there, around the beginning of the seventies?

Wesker: I don't think that either of our plays were to do with that slump. I really think–look, my reputation is very strained in this country. My plays have only ever lasted a few weeks–any of the plays with the exception of *Chips with Everything*, which had a commercial run, mainly because the audience thought it was a comedy. *Roots* flopped in the West End: it failed after two or three weeks. All the plays have only had a few weeks' run at the Royal Court. You see, I've never exactly been a popular English writer. It's just that my plays came at a time when everyone was taking notice of the British theatre. I don't know of any other way to account for it. I think also that I took on the critics, which doesn't help. Critics took notice of that and when the time came, Harold Hobson put the boot in. I don't think writers should take it, though–what they get from critics—and not scream. I feel very much between two camps now. I had a moment of feeling that I was in among the establishment—but there are two kinds of establishment now, there's the fringe-establishment and the establishment-establishment, and I find myself falling between the two. There's as much boulevardism on the left, you know, as there is on the right. But the reputation of all of us, I think John, is so strong abroad that we can go on, despite what is happening to us in England . . .

Arden: No, *our* plays have never really gone abroad, because of the translation problem . . .

Wesker: But the early plays . . .

Arden: We were never successful abroad with them, either. You are running in Warsaw and Japan, but our early plays have never been successful—at the most two or three-week runs in Berlin. The translations have been mostly terrible, or so I am told.

Griffiths: A point which comes up which is interesting to me is that of finding a director who believes in your work and who will push it through . . .

Wesker: This is nearly always what happens here and also abroad. It always depends on one man who feels that your play is worthwhile.

Dictatorship of the Directors?

Griffiths: Is that right? Is it a fact that a director decides whether you're good? Isn't this rather strange?

Wesker: Yes, and I think that there should be the beginnings of a movement for a real writers' theatre, by which I mean a theatre in which writers direct their own works and really become all-round craftsmen in the theatre. And in order to avoid this problem of who chooses whose work, there should be some sort of spontaneous coming together of about three or four writers who have proven themselves, to form a group which produces at least their own plays if not other writers' as well.

D'Arcy: Who does the plays after the first production? This is another difficulty. If you direct your own play, then no other directors would want to take your play on.

Wesker: That doesn't matter. You direct it and it goes on in the same way as if it had been directed by a director. And one way round many of the problems we've been discussing is that the writer and the director should be the same person. I am not saying that all writers are directors and that all directors should be writers, or that all actors should direct, but I do think that these three things—acting, writing, directing—could all be part of one job. They have been separated over the last fifty years or so, and we should now combine all three again. I don't mean that everyone can do everything equally well, but we should all have a go at it. And some people may be equally good at two of the jobs.

Griffiths: There are special relationships between the script and the writer, and the performers and the writer and possibly the designer—with people who are strongly opposite. The director fights on behalf of the writer.

Howard: At the same time you get a dangerous situation when the writer is director, if the edges of the roles aren't quite clear.

Arden: We've been talking about the writer's relationship with the theatre in terms of wage structure. But I think that if writers are going to be involved with a theatre, it should be the business of the playwright—part of his professional expertise—to know how to direct actors. The word 'playwright' means a person who *makes* plays. It doesn't necessarily mean that they just *write* them: making them includes moving the actors on stage and making the actors perform. The essential relationship to look for—and we haven't got to it yet, and I know there are plenty of writers who have never had the opportunity to get it and can't do it, and don't think they can, and so on—is not one in which the writer feeds his idea to the director who then feeds it on to the actor, but the direct relationship between the writer and the *actors*. There would, in fact, be a third party to this relationship who would be the stage manager, whose role would be of a somewhat higher status than that of the stage manager at the moment. The actual work commonly done by the director should be apportioned out between the writer and the stage manager.

D'Arcy: The stage manager would be the objective person.

Griffiths: Designers are often at the other end of the management structure from the writers, but their visual contribution is vitally important . . .

Wesker: I found that my experience of directing *Their Very Own and Golden City* in Denmark was very much affected by Hayden Griffen, who designed a really interesting set and gave me a way of doing the play.

Arden: Again, there should be a closer relationship between the writer and the designer. Frequently the writer hardly ever meets the designer. The director chooses the designer, and introduces him to the writer—you perhaps sit around with a cup of coffee for a couple of hours and the designer goes away and is never seen again by the writer. The designer may show the models and drawings and so on to the director, but unless there is an obvious problem, the designer doesn't see the writer.

New Production Relationships?

Griffiths: We're talking about creating a quite new interaction between the most important people—the writer, performer, designer. What we're asking is to eliminate the old management structure.

Arden: The management structure is not only the middle man, but an alienating and alienated hierarchy. In theatres like the RSC or the National, the director, the designer, the musical director are a group of specialists who operate from theatre offices. The actors belong to the Green Room and the dressing rooms, and the author comes in at the front door, sits in the stalls, and has no connection whatever with a great deal of what's going on in his play.

Wandor: I am not absolutely sure that the abolition of the director is the best answer. One of the problems is that writers are in competition with each other. In most companies it's the director who is ultimately responsible—and I think the kind of antagonism and the keeping apart of the writer and the actors and all the other people who work in the production company has been very damaging to writers. Directors may have you along if there are some things which aren't clear, but as soon as they've decided they've had as much as they need, they say, 'Okay, we don't need you around any more'. It may be as much a question of transforming relations between a writer and a director as getting rid of the director. There may be a different kind of function for a director figure, though I am not necessarily sure what it would be. There may be no necessity to abolish the director as a figure, but rather to transform the role and function.

D'Arcy: When writers have written very personal plays, one then needs a director's relationship with an actor to draw out the psychological relationships, like in a love affair. But if you're talking about public plays, which actors can understand anyway, where no groping around inside the actor's guts is required, then the stage manager should be sufficient.

Gooch: A good director will have good insights into a work. So much is added to the fabric of a play, just by having another sympathetic imagination at work on the job. And if there is a good relationship, between the writer and the director, a good relationship with the actors is made easier. And you will have the full benefit of the imagination of the actors—the skills and talents they bring to the play.

D'Arcy: The actors are the most important element.

Gooch: Their talent should never be underestimated in any way.

D'Arcy: They really have the sole responsibility for the play. But you will find that the director's contract stipulates overall control—which is what we found at the RSC. Writers should have at least equal rights with the director.

Arden: At the present moment, in the present administrative structures, you have theatres with one or more directors permanently on the staff. And most of the plays produced by that theatre are directed by those directors. The writer enters with his play, the theatre management accepts the play, and signs on one of them to be the director.

D'Arcy: This system relates to concepts of 'excellence'. We all think we're not very good as playwrights until somebody comes along and says, 'You really are a playwright!' We feel we cannot push ourselves or praise ourselves. First somebody has got to come and judge it and put the grade on it.

Griffiths: That's a hangover from the nineteenth century actor-manager tradition.

Arden: It isn't quite. The old actor-manager was an autocrat and he was very often abominable to authors. But at least he was an actor choosing work that he himself could appear in. Now we have a new profession which didn't exist in the nineteenth century—people who neither act, write, play a trumpet or paint the scenery, and yet are supposed to be able to tell what is a good play. This is the director. The menial is called the stage manager.

Equal Status for Playwrights

Wesker: The trouble with all discussion like this is that they become 'either/or'. There's been too much good work by directors throughout the world to deny the validity of the function of the director. We've also seen productions that have made our hair stand on end. And those of us who have directed have felt that we've learned something, that we've got closer to the work and enjoyed it. Directing is the continuation of the act of writing: you're really getting your last draft when you're directing it. This is how I feel. Obviously, not every writer is temperamentally suited to doing this, or, if he is, would want to. But there are some, and there are some who could be brought into existence, being made aware of talents and appetites they didn't think they could or should have.

D'Arcy: If the contracts were changed so writers had equal status, we would have no objection at all to directors.

Wymark: Do you have some kind of artibrator in case of a head-on clash?

D'Arcy: Well, it's normally the management.

Wymark: You would have to have a legal contract between writer and director?

D'Arcy: If the production were a disaster, then the management would be the one to intervene. Also, if you had a clash between the writer and an actor.

Wymark: It would have to be understood that the management might come in on the side of the writer.

Gooch: I think there would be a danger in calling it co-directing—which is often difficult even amongst directors.

D'Arcy: I believe the American Guild of Playwrights has come up with the idea of having writers on the contract described as co-directors, because the directors want royalties for every stage direction or something.

Arden: It would depend on the personal relationships, whether it would work.

D'Arcy: He doesn't have to be called co-director! He could be called anything so long as he was equal.

Gooch: It is quite important to have somebody else other than the director who anyway has to handle the administrative tasks. A director should have the authority and responsibility of working in the front line with the actors. It is sometimes very difficult to get the necessary distance from what you're doing to be sufficiently critical. A co-directorship can work very well, in the sense that the writer, another director, a back-row, more critical one, who can communicate with the actors directly, but never in a way that blocks the main channel towards the director as such.

Arden: At the moment the typical contractual system is biased against the writer.

D'Arcy: That's because the director is an integral part of the management.

Griffiths: The director is, in fact, also the employer. Or is the employing agency. He selects the play, the cast, the design.

Arden: And this word 'director' has to cover both the artistic and administrative functions. Maybe in retaliation playwrights would have to cease to call themselves playwrights—we would have to call ourselves controllers of scripts, something like that.

Griffiths: So in terms of relationships between writers and other theatre workers, it is this ambiguous role of the director which has to be questioned critically.

Edgar: There are a lot of actors who find this person—the writer—whom they meet about three times, who sits at the back, very strange. They're all dead scared and they don't like him. If he's famous, they're intimidated; if he's not, they think he's incompetent, that he doesn't really know anything about it.

D'Arcy: They feel a greater responsibility when the writer is there. If there is a director, the actors feel very little responsibility. It's the director who tells them everything to do.

Arden: I've never actually asked an actor what the writer's psychological effect is. If rehearsal is in progress and an actor is standing on stage giving a speech or whatever, he may suddenly see the author at the back of the auditorium lean over and whisper in the director's ear. Then the director says, 'Just a moment, luv,' and then there's all this sort of conflab and the director says, 'Yes, well, now I think it would be better if you did so and so'. The actor doesn't know what was being said, and sometimes what has been said is in praise of the actor, but as often as not, it's something that would have upset him. He knows this, and a lot of actors actually hate writers because of this.

Kift: I think the value of a writer attached to a theatre is that he can actually see the day to day mechanics of what happens.

Drawing Some Conclusions

Griffiths: We've covered, since this morning, an enormous range of situations, problems, possibilities facing writers. But are there any practical things which could and should be done? In the short term, not the long term?

Arden: Equality with directors on the contract. If it could only be achieved.

Gooch: And a minimum living wage for writers: the Arts Council should positively discriminate in favour of writers and hold back revenue which should only be released to those theatres which put on new plays. Writers cannot practically withdraw their labour, so the major public patron should act to defend these people. There should be provisions for writers, comparable to provisions for buildings, for example. Provisions for playwrights (which was £112,000 this year!) is matched in its poverty only by lack of provisions for novelists, poets and other creative, living artists.

D'Arcy: We could do what the Society of Irish Playwrights does—insist that out of all the money given to the theatre, so much should be given out to new plays. And it should be worked out on a statistical basis so the bigger theatres like the National Theatre should have to put on so many more new plays.

Gooch: And the Arts Council should also start to institute immediately some form of rewarding writers other than just mere box office percentages. Whether by demanding a percentage of a subsidy or demanding a certain minimum for a writer and his work.

Strength through Organization

Birchall: I think it's also up to us to develop the Theatre Writers' Group as a body really organized nationally and regionally. If all the writers in Yorkshire, say, are organized, they could effect the programme of the Playhouse and Sheffield Crucible. Much as the Irish Society of Playwrights did with the Abbey Theatre.

Howard: I don't think the Arts Council *will* act, so it is up to the Theatre Writers' Group to make them act. I would think the Theatre Writers' Group from its embryonic state is now going to grow to a much stronger position. It must try to embrace all the theatre writers in this country, and put pressure on both the Arts Council and the theatres directly, on behalf of its members.

Wymark: So TWG could say, 'We won't give you any new plays until the policy everywhere is more new plays and more money for new plays.

Birchall: I think it's also very important to forge links with organizations in the labour movement. At the South Yorkshire Federation of Trades Councils, there's talk of setting up a permanent Entertainments Sub-committee, a body to promote plays and organize commissions from working class organizations, not only in the work place, but also in tenants associations and so on.

D'Arcy: And questionnaires could be used in schools and universities to find out how many people are going to plays and what they want.

Griffiths: There is the idea of royalty payments.

Birchall: Wonderful. Every time a theatre does Shakespeare, he could get paid royalties, which, because he's dead, he can't actually receive, so they would go into a fund for new writers. Shakespeare is doing a living writer out of a job! For every Shakespeare play that's put on, there's one of us who's not getting a chance. Blacklegged by Shakespeare! The scab!

Griffiths: Are you saying Shakespeare should not be put on, full stop?

Arden: I think there could be less Shakespeare.

D'Arcy: Couldn't a levy be put on academics as well—who write about us for their theses? It's your time that is spent helping them.

Wesker: It costs me about £100 a year just in postage.

D'Arcy: So if they wish to write about you, they should have to pay for it.

Wesker: No, I don't think so. I think it's one of the social responsibilities of being a writer.

Arden: I was in an Australian university last year. There was a man there writing something about Pinter, and when I went into his office one day, all over the wall he had cuttings pinned up about Pinter's plays, cuttings from magazines, a great wall chart. And there was a whole new exhibit about the scandal about what's her name—Lady Fraser. I thought—well really!

D'Arcy: And there was the absurd situation when John was in New York teaching playwrights how to write plays, a lecturer was upstairs giving lectures on him, who never even asked him upstairs. It was like he was dead. Once you get on to the academic shelf, that really is the end of you. No one wants to know.

Problems of Publication

Gooch: Our plays don't get published. And publication is terribly important.

Arden: Publication is a serious problem now. I have been writing plays since 1958, which have all been published because the original plays were at the Royal Court, and either Penguin or Methuen were automatically publishing all the Royal Court plays in those days. As somebody has said, there was an air of complacency. Yes, one did get complacent in expecting, for example, that if your play was on, and you had been published several times by the same publishing house, they would inevitably publish you again. But now the *Non-Stop Connolly Show* has been refused publication by Methuen: we had a talk with the man from Methuen two days ago, who said quite definitely that they could not publish it. They are running out of money, and it's a long play. The relationship between the number of pages assessed against the number of people who buy plays, apparently makes it difficult to get the whole play published. And if it's not published, then nobody will do it.

Griffiths: So it is very hard to get scripts published now. What do you think can be done about that?

Wandor: I think we are going to be forced to publish our own things. Dinah Brooke and I have done just that as no publisher was, or would probably ever be, interested in publishing our plays.

D'Arcy: But then there's the problem of distribution.

Wandor: But there are alternative distribution networks, though it means doing a bit of work oneself. Theatre writers share the same problems as other socialist writers. Dinah Brooke and I published seven of our own plays, at first a thousand copies. I distributed them together with Feminist Books from a feminist distributor in Leeds. We sold out the first thousand very quickly and we printed another five hundred–which made us feel fantastic. And some of my plays have been done in five or six places all over the country as a consequence–which would never have been done had I not published them. And it didn't cost us all that much to do it. Certainly, companies like Methuen have cut back. They can't afford to take risks–as they put it.

Gooch: I think publication is good because it's another source of income. But I find it quite encouraging that publication has ceased to be the criterion of success it used to be. Obviously, it still has meaning in some academic quarters, but anybody who really knows the theatre is not going to say *Ballygombeen Bequest* isn't an important part of the development of John Arden and Margaretta D'Arcy just because they can't actually pick it up and read it.

Arden: But if your play is not published, it will never be done. The important thing about books is that the people who buy them are often the people who wish to produce the plays.

Edgar: Methuen producing glossy scripts may be very nice, but it is not all that relevant to what is going on in the theatre. If you took published plays as a criterion of what is going on in the theatre, then you would have a very strange and jaundiced view of English theatre. And I think in a perverse kind of way, that's rather good. Because it has made people realize that theatre is a medium of performance primarily, not of literature. On the other hand, there clearly is a problem in getting second productions. But that seems to be a problem that Methuen or Calder and Boyars don't solve anyway. It's a problem that could be solved simply by duplicating, an inexpensive and efficient way of producing scripts for people to buy and read and produce.

Do-It-Yourself Scripts

Wandor: What's interesting is that there's always been that possibility for people on the fringe, yet it hasn't been done very much. I think there's some kind of blockage in theatre people's thinking–that the theatre is ephemeral and not worth recording.

Gooch: I'd like to see a system where one had subscribers which could include, for example, all the reps, and all the small theatre companies, as well as individuals, for either a play a month, or a quarter. Some system whereby institutions and universities and theatres could all subscribe. With some form of state subsidy and through writers' organizations, you could run a very simple system of script distribution which would solve this problem of second performances.

Wymark: The Northern Playwrights' Society has arranged with Newcastle Library for every play submitted to be duplicated. They keep one copy of every play and lend the other one. That is a possibility which could be pursued. But going to libraries for plays? Certainly, you can't go on sending out manuscripts endlessly–they get lost, they cost money.

Birchall: Could there not be a theatre quarterly which published abstracts of a play–even ones that are currently being written?

Edgar: It's perfectly simple when a theatre wants to do Pinter's *Old Times,* for example. It expects to go out and buy a copy of *Old Times* in a bookshop. They read it and decide whether they want to do it. They may possibly buy some more to give to the actors. But for us it seems to be a perpetual problem. It now costs a quid a script to do it yourself, not counting labour time, to produce thirty copies. This is a problem which solidarity could help to solve–if everybody refused to send scripts to theatres which asked for them without some rental or fixed fee system. Then you wouldn't get this scandalous situation where theatres hang on to your property and refuse to send it back. I've often thought of sending coppers around to theatres to demand back what is effectively a piece of stolen property! It's all part and parcel of the raw deal that writers usually get. When a theatre asks to see your play, you send away your eighteenth copy and you've got only one left, and then what? You've got to produce more, spend more money you don't earn and haven't got. When I was at Exeter, I'd see this huge pile of scripts. Nobody had any responsibility to sift through them. They were just gradually mouldering away, until someone would come along and say, 'What about the play I sent you–ten years ago?' There must be a lot of people around thinking, 'Oh, this could be my big break', or 'They're obviously reading my play seriously'–when in fact the scripts are rotting away and never get read. There is no mechanism in many theatres, apart from the Royal Court, maybe, for reading and responding to plays.

Wandor: They are very slow even at the Court.

D'Arcy: Wasn't it eight months before somebody read one of Osborne's recent plays? Which then they didn't do. Not that he should be treated any better than anyone else, but it's symbolic of how writers are regarded and treated.

Appendix 2:

Michael Billington Reviews the Past in British Theatre and Celebrates the New Breed

Michael Billington Reviews the Past in British Theatre and Celebrates the New Breed

From *The Guardian* (London), 6 July 2002

British theatre is facing a period of momentous change. London's commercial sector is still reeling from the impact of September 11: despite the recent influx of star names, West End business is down by a reputed 15%.

Meanwhile, in the subsidised sector, there is upheaval. The beleaguered Royal Shakespeare Company (RSC) is urgently hunting for a new director, following Adrian Noble's resignation, and faces a huge deficit this year. At the National, Nicholas Hytner is gearing up to take over from Sir Trevor Nunn, and already has plans to radically redefine the Olivier stage and introduce a cheap ticket policy.

With new directors also due at the Almeida, the Donmar Warehouse, the West Yorkshire Playhouse, Chichester and Hampstead, our national theatre is poised for its biggest shakeup in decades.

Yet change is also opportunity. The West End now has to seize on the tourist defection to discover a new, and preferably younger, native audience. And the RSC, after the collective nervous breakdown of the past year, has to go back to its roots and recreate itself as a permanent company.

If there are grounds for hope, it is that British theatre has always shown itself capable of self-renewal, and has a 50-year tradition on which to draw, based on a pragmatic mix of subsidy and commerce, a vibrant regional theatre and a firm belief in the centrality of the dramatist.

But if British theatre has largely prospered over the past half century, there is another key reason: tensions within society itself. In 1962, the former U.S. secretary of state Dean Acheson famously said that Britain "has lost an empire but not yet found a role."

You could add that our whole postwar history is one of unresolved national conflicts. We have spent years trying to reconcile our superpower pretensions with our economic under-performance, our love of tradition with our commitment to modernity, our attachment to America with our tentative affiliation to Europe.

One could add a whole list of issues—class, race and monarchy—on which the nation remains deeply divided. The very things about Britain that make many people tear their hair out are, paradoxically, the same things that have helped produce great drama.

Each decade takes on a distinct character. The 1950s is acknowledged as the era when theatre shook off its postwar sloth, when realism asserted itself over fantasy and prose over poetry; and the opening night of John Osborne's *Look Back In Anger* at the Royal Court on May 8, 1956, has acquired a mythical resonance. I'd be the last to deny either the enduring power or instant appeal of the play: as a swottish sixth-former at the time, I recall giving a solemn lecture on the phenomenon of the Angry Young Man.

But while Osborne's play opened the door to new writers and put the Royal Court at the centre of the theatrical map, it wasn't quite the lone grenade it now appears. Even before Osborne's arrival, there were signs, both in theatre and in culture at large, that the old certainties were being eroded.

In 1953, a radical genius called Joan Littlewood took over the derelict Theatre Royal in Stratford East, London, to offer fast, fluid, beautifully choreographed versions of the classics. The following year saw the publication of *Lucky Jim* and *Lord Of The Flies,* two novels that subverted ideas of academic deference and innate goodness; 1955 witnessed the British debuts of Brecht, Ionesco and Beckett: the premiere of *Waiting For Godot,* in Tom Stoppard's words, "redefined the minima of theatrical validity." For the provincial young, of course, the really big event was a movie called *Rock Around The Clock,* which prompted Dionysiac dancing in the aisles.

If the ground started to shift in the 1950s, the 1960s was a truly miraculous decade. Now trashed by the right as an era when pop stars and hairdressers became famous, it was, in fact, a period of irreversible social change: capital punishment was abolished, abortion legalised and homosexuality decriminalised. It was also the most exciting decade for British theatre since the 1590s; one that not only produced great plays, but also established a basic framework from which we have lived ever since.

In Stratford-upon-Avon, Peter Hall, who had seen the benefits of permanent institutions during national service in Germany, created the Royal Shakespeare Company. In London, in 1963, Laurence Olivier established a National Theatre company at the Old Vic. And around the country, a thousand flowers bloomed: in Chichester, Nottingham, Bolton, Stoke-on-Trent and Edinburgh, new theatres opened their doors.

British theatre also shed much of its insularity. In 1964, Peter Daubeny set up an annual world theatre season at the Aldwych, London, that led to fascinating cross-fertilisation. In the same year, Peter Brook, with Charles Marowitz, ran a Theatre of Cruelty season at Lamda (London Academy of Music and Dramatic Art), which not only introduced us to Artaud, but also legitimised experiment.

But it was the quality of the writing that really distinguished the 1960s, a point recently proved by a rash of revivals—Pinter's *The Homecoming*, Peter Nichols's *A Day In The Death Of Joe Egg*, Osborne's *Luther*, David Rudkin's *Afore Night Come* and David Storey's *In Celebration*. The Royal Court's 1965 production of Edward Bond's *Saved*, in which a baby is stoned to death in its pram, prompted a prosecution by the Lord Chamberlain, which led, three years later, to the abolition of his ludicrous powers as a theatrical censor.

But the Royal Court had no monopoly on talent in the 1960s. Stoppard, Ayckbourn and Orton appeared on rival stages. Littlewood produced the phenomenal *Oh What A Lovely War!*, which changed attitudes to the military-political establishment that had sanctioned the carnage of 1914–18. Towards the end of the decade, young writers such as David Hare and Howard Brenton started to appear in mobile touring companies or pocket-sized fringe theatres.

The 1960s changed British theatre forever. The reasons were partly pragmatic. Harold Wilson appointed as minister for the arts Jennie Lee, who brought a missionary fervour to her job and secured vital increases in Arts Council funding. The theatrical renaissance was also sparked by social tensions: plays such as *Saved* and *Loot* attacked the creation of an educationally deprived underclass and police corruption.

But the decade's key legacy, aside from two national companies and a host of regional theatres, was the idea that theatre was an oppositional force—something that questioned both government policies and society's underlying values.

Much of the best writing of the 1970s, assisted by the growth of fringe theatre, was powered by a belief that theatre had a directly political function. This produced many transient agitprop plays, but it also yielded a wealth of first rate writing: Trevor Griffiths's *The Party* and *Comedians,* David Hare's *Knuckle* and *Plenty,* David Edgar's *Destiny* and John McGrath's *The Cheviot, the Stag, and the Black, Black Oil.*

By the end of the 1970s, however, there was a feeling that the party was over. Dramatists increasingly drifted to television. Visits from foreign companies became occasional treats. Audacious experiment declined.

The election of Margaret Thatcher in 1979 had as radical an impact on theatre as it did on other aspects of British life. There was still good work, not least under Peter Hall at the newly built National Theatre, and at enterprising venues such as the Glasgow Citizens, Manchester's Royal Exchange and Scarborough's Stephen Joseph Theatre. But, having promised no "candle-end economies" in the arts, the Thatcher government gave us just that.

It seems to me no accident that the Thatcherite 1980s were characterised by the rise and rise of the musical: a form that, with a few exceptions, appeals to our desire for escape and that actively celebrates capitalism. This was the decade of *Cats, The Phantom Of The Opera* and *Les Miserables;* and, if anyone objects that the last-named stimulates revolutionary fervour, I'd say that it actually makes poverty picturesque.

What was depressing, however, was the way the national companies felt that they, too, had to jump on the musical bandwagon: the National gave us *Jean Seberg* and the RSC *Carrie,* which the sudden onset of a kidney stone thankfully prevented me from seeing.

Of course, no decade is a writeoff. Women's theatre groups and black and Asian companies made steady advances in the 1980s. And there were some outstanding individual events: *The Mysteries, Les Liaisons Dangereuses,* Caryl Churchill's *Serious Money,* Hare and Brenton's *Pravda,* Judi Dench's *Cleopatra,* Antony Sher's *Richard III.*

But by the start of the 1990s, there was a sense of a theatre running on empty—of national institutions in need of renewal, of mounting regional deficits, of a theatre defined by its capacity to create musical spectacles. Victorian values had triumphantly been reasserted.

The scrape-and-save attitude to funding persisted for much of the 1990s, but there was at least a renewal of confidence. Much of the credit belongs to specific individuals. Max Stafford-Clark heroically kept the Royal Court alive during difficult years. Taking over in 1994, Stephen Daldry built on that inheritance by pummelling us with new writers, notably Sarah Kane and Mark Ravenhill, and also Jez Butterworth, Joe Penhall, Martin McDonagh, Nick Grosso, Rebecca Prichard and Ayub Khan-Din. It was like the mid-1950s all over again.

Add to that a Scottish renaissance, with writers such as David Harrower and David Greig, and the platform given by the Bush Theatre to writers Conor McPherson, Billy Roche, David Eldridge and Charlotte Jones, and it was as if the energy repressed during the Thatcher years had suddenly been unleashed.

One growth industry during the 1990s was that of bilious media attacks on theatre as outdated and irrelevant. But the facts suggested otherwise. Hare's state-of-the-nation trilogy at the National, wisely promoted by Richard Eyre, was hardly the product of a dead medium. The Almeida, under Jonathan Kent and Ian McDiarmid, made Islington a centre of enlightened internationalism. Sam Mendes did fine work at the Donmar. And two touring companies, Cheek By Jowl and Theatre de Complicite, became a byword for adventure on the international circuit. You only had to travel to realise that British theatre, however despised at home, was highly prized abroad.

This doesn't mean that all in the garden is lovely. We need to rejuvenate the theatre audience. We also have to reflect Britain's multicultural diversity. Increasingly, we seem to live in an "event culture" that obscures the value of grassroots work: a Rattigan or Priestley revival at a regional rep may not sound sexy, but it can be as important to the health of the national theatre as county cricket is to Test match achievement.

But, even if Utopia is still some way off, there are grounds for rational optimism. The £25m injected into the English system by the Arts Council will stave off potential disaster, and fresh talent is emerging in the industry, much of it celebrated in these pages.

Above all, new plays are still being written; and that, for all the quality of our acting, direction and design, is the supremely important fact. You cannot live by classics and musicals alone; and any theatre that can produce plays as good as Michael Wynne's *The People Are Friendly,* Richard Cameron's *The Glee Club* or Peter Gill's *The York Realist* is clearly not dead and buried. It is as if the narrative that began in the 1950s—and that was tragically interrupted in the 1980s—has at last been fruitfully resumed.

Books for Further Reading

Acheson, James, ed. *British and Irish Drama Since 1960*. London: Macmillan, 1993.

Adams, David. *Stage Welsh*. Llandysul: Gomer, 1996.

Allsop, Kenneth. *The Angry Decade: A Survey of the Cultural Revolt of the Nineteen-Fifties*. London: Peter Owen, 1958.

Anderson, Michael. *Anger and Detachment: A Study of Arden, Osborne and Pinter*. London: Pitman, 1976.

Ansorge, Peter. *Disrupting the Spectacle: Five Years of Experimental and Fringe Theatre in Britain*. London: Pitman, 1975.

Arden, John. *To Present the Pretence: Essays on the Theatre and its Public*. London: Eyre Methuen, 1977.

Armstrong, William, ed. *Experimental Drama*. London: G. Bell, 1963.

Barnes, Philip. *A Companion to Post-War British Theatre*. London: Croom Helm, 1986.

Bell, Sam Hanna. *The Theatre in Ulster: A Survey of the Dramatic Movement in Ulster from 1902 to the Present Day*. Dublin: Gill & Macmillan, 1972.

Bigsby, C. W. E., ed. *Contemporary English Drama,* Stratford-upon-Avon Studies, no. 19. London: Edward Arnold, 1981.

Billington, Michael. *One Night Stands: A Critic's View of Modern British Theatre*. London: Nick Hern, 1993.

Black, Kitty. *Upper Circle*. London: Methuen, 1984.

Bock, Hedwig, and Albert Wertheim, eds. *Essays on Contemporary British Drama*. Munich: Max Hueber Verlag, 1981.

Brandt, George. *British Television Drama*. Cambridge: Cambridge University Press, 1981.

Brown, Ivor. *Theatre 1954–1955*. London: Max Reinhardt, 1955.

Brown. *Theatre 1955–1956*. London: Max Reinhardt, 1956.

Brown, John Russell, ed. *Modern British Dramatists*. Englewood Cliffs, N.J.: Prentice-Hall, 1984.

Browne, Terry. *Playwrights' Theatre: The English Stage Company at the Royal Court Theatre*. London: Pitman, 1975.

Bull, John. *New British Political Dramatists*. London: Macmillan, 1984.

Bull. *Stage Right: Crisis and Recovery in British Contemporary Mainstream Theatre*. Houndmills, U.K.: Macmillan, 1994.

Calder, Angus. *The People's War*. London: Cape, 1969.

Books for Further Reading

Cameron, Alasdair, ed. *Scot-Free: New Scottish Plays*. London: Nick Hern, 1990.

Cave, Richard. *New British Drama in Performance on the London Stage: 1970–1985*. Gerrards Cross, U.K.: Colin Smythe, 1987.

Chambers, Colin. *Other Spaces: New Theatre and the RSC*. London: Eyre Methuen, 1980.

Chambers. *Peggy: The Life of Margaret Ramsay*. London: Nick Hern, 1997.

Chambers and Mike Prior. *Playwrights' Progress: Patterns of Post-War British Drama*. Oxford: Amber Lane, 1987.

Cohn, Ruby. *Retreats from Realism in Recent English Drama*. Cambridge: Cambridge University Press, 1991.

Coveney, Michael. *The Citz: Twenty One Years of the Glasgow Citizens Theatre*. London: Nick Hern, 1990.

Cowell, Raymond. *Twelve Modern Dramatists*. Oxford: Pergamon Press, 1967.

Craig, Sandy. *Dreams and Deconstructions: Alternative Theatre in Britain*. London: Amber Lane, 1980.

Daubeny, Peter. *My World of Theatre*. London: Cape, 1971.

Davies, Andrew. *Other Theatres: The Development of Alternative and Experimental Theatre in Britain*. Basingstoke: Macmillan, 1987.

Doty, Gresdna, and Billy Harbin, eds. *Inside the Royal Court Theatre 1956–81*. Baton Rouge: Louisiana State University Press, 1990.

Duff, Charles. *The Lost Summer: The Heyday of the West End Theatre*. London: Nick Hern, 1995.

Edgar, David. *The Second Time as Farce: Reflections on the Drama of Mean Times*. London: Lawrence & Wishart, 1988.

Edwardes, Pamela, ed. *Frontline Intelligence I: New Plays for the Nineties*. London: Methuen, 1993.

Edwardes, ed. *Frontline Intelligence II: New Plays for the Nineties*. London: Methuen, 1994.

Elsom, John. *Post-War British Theatre*. London: Routledge & Kegan Paul, 1976.

Elsom, ed. *Post-War British Theatre Criticism*. London: Routledge & Kegan Paul, 1981.

Esslin, Martin. *Brief Chronicles: Essays on Modern Theatre*. London: Temple Smith, 1970.

Esslin. *The Theatre of the Absurd*. London: Penguin, 1965.

Etherton, Michael. *Contemporary Irish Dramatists*. London: Macmillan Education, 1989.

Fay, Gerard. *The Abbey Theatre*. London: Hollis & Carter, 1958.

Findlater, Richard. *Banned!: A Review of Theatrical Censorship in Britain*. London: MacGibbon & Kee, 1967.

Findlater. *The Unholy Trade*. London: Gollancz, 1952.

Findlater, ed. *At the Royal Court: Twenty Five Years of the English Stage Company*. Derbyshire: Amber Lane Press, 1981.

Findlay, Bill, ed. *A History of Scottish Theatre*. Edinburgh: Polygon, 1996.

Fitz-Simon, Christopher. *The Irish Theatre.* London: Thames & Hudson, 1983.

Genet, Jacqueline, and Richard Cave, eds. *Perspectives on Irish Drama and Theatre.* Gerards Cross: Colin Smythe, 1990.

Goodman, Lizbeth. *Contemporary Feminist Theatres: To Each Her Own.* London: Routledge, 1993.

Goorney, Howard. *The Theatre Workshop Story.* London: Eyre Methuen, 1981.

Griffiths, Trevor, and Margaret Llewellyn-Jones, eds. *British and Irish Women Dramatists Since 1958: A Critical Handbook.* Buckingham: Open University Press, 1993.

Harrington, John, ed. *Modern Irish Drama.* New York: Norton, 1991.

Hart, Lynda, ed. *Making a Spectacle: Feminist Essays on Contemporary Women's Theatre.* Ann Arbor: University of Michigan Press, 1989.

Harwood, Kate, ed. *First Run: New Plays by New Writers.* London: Nick Hern, 1989.

Hayman, Ronald. *British Theatre Since 1955.* Oxford: Oxford University Press, 1979.

Hayman. *The Set Up: An Anatomy of the English Theatre Today.* London: Methuen, 1969.

Haynes, Jim. *Thanks for Coming!* London: Faber & Faber, 1984.

Herbert, A. P. *No Fine on Fun: The Comical History of the Entertainments Duty.* London: Methuen, 1957.

Hinchcliffe, A. P. *British Theatre 1950–1970.* Oxford: Blackwell, 1974.

Hobson, Harold. *Theatre in Britain: A Personal View.* Oxford: Phaidon, 1984.

Huggett, Richard. *Binkie Beaumont: Eminence Grise of the West End Theatre 1933–1973.* London: Hodder & Stoughton, 1989.

Hunt, Albert. *Hopes for Great Happenings.* London: Eyre Methuen, 1976.

Hunt, Hugh, Kenneth Richards, and John Russell Taylor. *The Revels History of Drama in English.* London: Eyre Methuen, 1978.

Innes, Christopher. *Avant Garde Theatre 1892–1992.* London: Routledge, 1993.

Innes. *Modern British Drama 1890–1990.* Cambridge: Cambridge University Press, 1991.

Itzin, Catherine. *Stages in the Revolution: Political Theatre in Britain since 1968.* London: Eyre Methuen, 1980.

Jackson, Anthony, and George Rowell. *The Repertory Movement: A History of Regional Theatre in Britain.* Cambridge: Cambridge University Press, 1984.

Johnston, John. *The Lord Chamberlain's Blue Pencil.* London: Hodder & Stoughton, 1990.

Jones, Dedwydd. *Black Book on the Welsh Theatre.* Lausanne: Iolo, 1980.

Joseph, Stephen. *Theatre in the Round.* London: Barrie & Rockliff, 1967.

Kerensky, Oleg. *The New British Drama: Fourteen Playwrights since Osborne and Pinter.* London: Hamilton, 1977.

Books for Further Reading

Kershaw, Baz. *The Politics of Performance: Radical Theatre as Cultural Intervention*. London: Routledge, 1992.

Keyssar, Helene. *Feminist Theatre: An Introduction to Plays of Contemporary British and American Women*. London: Macmillan, 1984.

Kitchin, Laurence. *Mid-Century Drama*. London: Faber & Faber, 1960.

Lacey, Stephen. *British Realist Theatre: The New Wave in Context 1956–65*. London: Routledge, 1995.

Lambert, J. W. *Drama in Britain 1964–1973*. Harlow, U.K.: British Council, 1974.

Lewis, Justin. *Art, Culture and Enterprise: The Politics of Art and the Cultural Industries*. London: Routledge, 1990.

Lewis, Peter. *The Fifties: Portrait of an Age*. London: Cupid, 1988.

Littlewood, Joan. *Joan's Book: Joan Littlewood's Peculiar History As She Tells It*. London: Methuen, 1994.

Lloyd-Evans, Barbara, and Gareth Lloyd-Evans, eds. *Plays in Review 1956–1980: British Drama and the Critics*. London: Batsford, 1985.

Mander, Raymond, and Joe Mitchenson. *The Theatres of London*. London: New English Library, 1975.

Marowitz, Charles. *Confessions of a Counterfeit Critic: A London Theatre Notebook, 1958–1971*. London: Eyre Methuen, 1973.

Marowitz, Tom Milne, and Owen Hale. *The Encore Reader: A Chronicle of the New Drama*. London: Methuen, 1965.

McFadyen, Edward. *The British Theatre, 1956–1977: A Personal View*. London: National Book League, 1977.

McGrath, John. *The Bone Won't Break: On Theatre and Hope in Hard Times*. London: Methuen, 1990.

McGrath. *A Good Night Out: Popular Theatre: Audience, Class and Form*. London: Eyre Methuen, 1981.

McMillan, Joyce. *The Traverse Theatre Story, 1963–1988*. London: Methuen, 1988.

Mikhail, Edward H. *Contemporary British Drama, 1959–1976: An Annotated Critical Bibliography*. London: Macmillan, 1976.

Moore-Gilbert, Bart, and John Seed, eds. *Cultural Revolution: The Challenge of the Arts in the 1960s*. London: Routledge, 1992.

Murray, Christopher. *Twentieth-Century Irish Drama: Mirror up to Nation*. Manchester: Manchester University Press, 1997.

Noble, Peter. *British Theatre*. London: British Yearbooks, 1946.

Ó hAodha, Micheál. *Theatre in Ireland*. Oxford: Blackwell, 1974.

Osborne, John. *A Better Class of Person: An Autobiography 1929–1956*. Harmondsworth, U.K.: Penguin, 1982.

Peacock, Keith. *Radical Stages: Alternative History in Modern British Drama*. New York: Greenwood Press, 1991.

Pick, John. *The Theatre Industry*. London: Comedia, 1985.

Pick. *The West End: Mismanagement and Snobbery*. Eastbourne, U.K.: Offord, 1983.

Price, Cecil. *The Professional Theatre in Wales*. Swansea: University of Swansea, 1984.

Rabey, David Ian. *British and Irish Political Drama in the Twentieth Century: Implicating the Audience*. London: Macmillan, 1986.

Rebellato, Dan. *1956 And All That: The Making of Modern British Drama*. London: Routledge, 1999.

Richtarik, Marilynn. *Acting Between the Lines: The Field Day Company and Irish Cultural Politics, 1980–1984*. Oxford: Clarendon Press, 1994.

Roberts, Philip. *The Royal Court Theatre 1965–1972*. London: Routledge & Kegan Paul, 1986.

Roche, Anthony. *Contemporary Irish Drama: From Beckett to McGuiness*. Dublin: Gill & McMillan, 1994.

Sanderson, Michael. *From Irving to Olivier: A Social History of the Acting Profession in England 1880–1983*. London: Athlone, 1984.

Shank, Theodore, ed. *Contemporary British Theatre*. London: Macmillan, 1994.

Shellard, Dominic. *British Theatre since the War*. London: Yale University Press, 1999.

Shellard. *Harold Hobson: Witness and Judge. The Theatre Criticism of Harold Hobson*. Keele: Keele University Press, 1995.

Shellard, ed. *British Theatre in the 1950s*. Sheffield: Sheffield Academic Press, 2000.

Simpson, Alan. *Beckett and Behan, and a Theatre in Dublin*. London: Routledge & Kegan Paul, 1962.

Stevenson, Randall, and Gavin Wallace. *Scottish Theatre Since the Seventies*. Edinburgh: Edinburgh University Press, 1996.

Taylor, Anna-Marie, ed. *Staging Wales: Welsh Theatre 1979–1997*. Cardiff: University of Wales, 1997.

Taylor, John Russell. *Anger and After: A Guide to the New British Drama*. London: Methuen, 1962.

Taylor. *The Rise and Fall of the Well-Made Play*. London: Methuen, 1967.

Taylor. *The Second Wave: British Drama of the Sixties*. London: Eyre Methuen, 1978.

Trewin, John Courtenay. *Drama 1945–1950*. London: Longmans, Green, 1951.

Trussler, Simon, ed. *New Theatre Voices of the Seventies: Sixteen Interviews from* Theatre Quarterly, *1970–1980*. London: Eyre Methuen, 1981.

Tushingham, David, ed. *Critical Mass*. London: Methuen, 1996.

Tushingham, ed. *Food for the Soul: A New Generation of British Theatremakers*. London: Methuen, 1994.

Tushingham, ed. *Not What I Am: The Experience of Performing*. London: Methuen, 1995.

Tynan, Kathleen. *Curtains: Selections from the Drama, Criticism and Related Writings*. London: Longmans, 1961.

Tynan. *The Life of Kenneth Tynan*. London: Methuen, 1988.

Tynan. *Tynan Right & Left: Plays, Films, People, Places, and Events*. London: Longmans, 1967.

Books for Further Reading

Tynan. *A View of the English Stage, 1944–1963*. London: Davis-Poynter, 1975.

Wager, Walter, ed. *The Playwrights Speak*. London: Longman, 1969.

White, Michael. *Empty Seats*. London: Hamilton, 1984.

Worth, Katherine. *Revolutions in English Drama*. London: Bell, 1972.

Wu, Duncan. *Six Contemporary Dramatists: Bennett, Potter, Gray, Brenton, Hare, Ayckbourn*. Basingstoke: Macmillan, 1995.

Zeifman, Hersch, and Cynthia Zimmerman, eds. *Contemporary British Drama 1970–90: Essays from "Modern Drama."* Basingstoke: Macmillan, 1993.

Contributors

Peter Billingham . . . . *Bath Spa University College*
Ian Brown . . . . *Perthshire, Scotland*
Roy Connolly . . . . *Edge Hill College*
Francesca Coppa . . . . *Muhlenberg College*
Tony Dunn . . . . *University of Portsmouth*
Anne Etienne . . . . *University College Cork*
Ben Francombe . . . . *University College Chichester*
David Grant . . . . *Queen's University, Belfast*
Frances Gray . . . . *University of Sheffield*
Ksenija Horvat . . . . *Queen Margaret University College, Edinburgh*
Lucy Kay . . . . *Liverpool Hope University College*
Ronald Knowles . . . . *University of Reading*
Susanne Kries . . . . *Universität Potsdam*
Margaret Llewellyn-Jones . . . . *London Metropolitan University*
Catherine MacGregor . . . . *New York, New York*
Kara McKechnie . . . . *University of Leeds*
Derek Paget . . . . *University of Reading*
Jeremy Ridgman . . . . *Roehampton University*
Nic Ros . . . . *University of Wales Bangor*
Aleks Sierz . . . . *London*
Andy W. Smith . . . . *University of Wales, Newport*
Ioan Williams . . . . *University of Wales Aberystwyth*

Cumulative Index

Dictionary of Literary Biography, Volumes 1-310
Dictionary of Literary Biography Yearbook, 1980-2002
Dictionary of Literary Biography Documentary Series, Volumes 1-19
Concise Dictionary of American Literary Biography, Volumes 1-7
Concise Dictionary of British Literary Biography, Volumes 1-8
Concise Dictionary of World Literary Biography, Volumes 1-4

Cumulative Index

DLB before number: *Dictionary of Literary Biography,* Volumes 1-310
Y before number: *Dictionary of Literary Biography Yearbook,* 1980-2002
DS before number: *Dictionary of Literary Biography Documentary Series,* Volumes 1-19
CDALB before number: *Concise Dictionary of American Literary Biography,* Volumes 1-7
CDBLB before number: *Concise Dictionary of British Literary Biography,* Volumes 1-8
CDWLB before number: *Concise Dictionary of World Literary Biography,* Volumes 1-4

A

Aakjær, Jeppe 1866-1930 . . . . DLB-214
Aarestrup, Emil 1800-1856 . . . . DLB-300
Abbey, Edward 1927-1989 . . . . DLB-256, 275
Abbey, Edwin Austin 1852-1911 . . . . DLB-188
Abbey, Maj. J. R. 1894-1969 . . . . DLB-201
Abbey Press DLB-49
The Abbey Theatre and Irish Drama,
 1900-1945 . . . . DLB-10
Abbot, Willis J. 1863-1934 . . . . DLB-29
Abbott, Edwin A. 1838-1926 . . . . DLB-178
Abbott, Jacob 1803-1879 . . . . DLB-1, 42, 243
Abbott, Lee K. 1947- DLB-130
Abbott, Lyman 1835-1922 . . . . DLB-79
Abbott, Robert S. 1868-1940 . . . . DLB-29, 91
Abe Kōbō 1924-1993 . . . . DLB-182
Abelaira, Augusto 1926- DLB-287
Abelard, Peter circa 1079-1142? DLB-115, 208
Abelard-Schuman DLB-46
Abell, Arunah S. 1806-1888 . . . . DLB-43
Abell, Kjeld 1901-1961 . . . . DLB-214
Abercrombie, Lascelles 1881-1938 . . . . DLB-19
 The Friends of the Dymock
  Poets Y-00
Aberdeen University Press Limited DLB-106
Abish, Walter 1931- DLB-130, 227
Ablesimov, Aleksandr Onisimovich
 1742-1783 . . . . DLB-150
Abraham à Sancta Clara 1644-1709 . . . . . . DLB-168
Abrahams, Peter
 1919- DLB-117, 225; CDWLB-3
Abramov, Fedor Aleksandrovich
 1920-1983 . . . . DLB-302
Abrams, M. H. 1912- DLB-67
Abramson, Jesse 1904-1979 . . . . DLB-241
Abrogans circa 790-800 . . . . DLB-148
Abschatz, Hans Aßmann von
 1646-1699 . . . . DLB-168
Abse, Dannie 1923- DLB-27, 245
Abutsu-ni 1221-1283 . . . . DLB-203
Academy Chicago Publishers DLB-46

Accius circa 170 B.C.-circa 80 B.C. DLB-211
Accrocca, Elio Filippo 1923-1996 . . . . DLB-128
Ace Books DLB-46
Achebe, Chinua 1930- DLB-117; CDWLB-3
Achtenberg, Herbert 1938- DLB-124
Ackerman, Diane 1948- DLB-120
Ackroyd, Peter 1949- DLB-155, 231
Acorn, Milton 1923-1986 . . . . DLB-53
Acosta, Oscar Zeta 1935?-1974? DLB-82
Acosta Torres, José 1925- DLB-209
Actors Theatre of Louisville DLB-7
Adair, Gilbert 1944- DLB-194
Adair, James 1709?-1783? DLB-30
Aðalsteinn Kristmundsson (see Steinn Steinarr)
Adam, Graeme Mercer 1839-1912 . . . . DLB-99
Adam, Robert Borthwick, II
 1863-1940 . . . . DLB-187
Adame, Leonard 1947- DLB-82
Adameșteanu, Gabriel 1942- DLB-232
Adamic, Louis 1898-1951 . . . . DLB-9
Adams, Abigail 1744-1818 . . . . DLB-183, 200
Adams, Alice 1926-1999 . . . . DLB-234; Y-86
Adams, Bertha Leith (Mrs. Leith Adams,
 Mrs. R. S. de Courcy Laffan)
 1837?-1912 . . . . DLB-240
Adams, Brooks 1848-1927 . . . . DLB-47
Adams, Charles Francis, Jr. 1835-1915 . . . . DLB-47
Adams, Douglas 1952-2001 . . . . DLB-261; Y-83
Adams, Franklin P. 1881-1960 . . . . DLB-29
Adams, Hannah 1755-1832 . . . . DLB-200
Adams, Henry 1838-1918 . . . . . . DLB-12, 47, 189
Adams, Herbert Baxter 1850-1901 . . . . DLB-47
Adams, James Truslow
 1878-1949 . . . . DLB-17; DS-17
Adams, John 1735-1826 . . . . DLB-31, 183
Adams, John Quincy 1767-1848 . . . . DLB-37
Adams, Léonie 1899-1988 . . . . DLB-48
Adams, Levi 1802-1832 . . . . DLB-99
Adams, Richard 1920- DLB-261
Adams, Samuel 1722-1803 . . . . DLB-31, 43
Adams, Sarah Fuller Flower
 1805-1848 . . . . DLB-199

Adams, Thomas 1582/1583-1652 . . . . DLB-151
Adams, William Taylor 1822-1897 . . . . DLB-42
J. S. and C. Adams [publishing house] DLB-49
Adamson, Harold 1906-1980 . . . . DLB-265
Adamson, Sir John 1867-1950 . . . . DLB-98
Adamson, Robert 1943- DLB-289
Adcock, Arthur St. John 1864-1930 . . . . . . DLB-135
Adcock, Betty 1938- DLB-105
 "Certain Gifts" DLB-105
 Tribute to James Dickey Y-97
Adcock, Fleur 1934- DLB-40
Addams, Jane 1860-1935 . . . . DLB-303
Addison, Joseph
 1672-1719 . . . . DLB-101; CDBLB-2
Ade, George 1866-1944 . . . . DLB-11, 25
Adeler, Max (see Clark, Charles Heber)
Adlard, Mark 1932- DLB-261
Adler, Richard 1921- DLB-265
Adonias Filho
 (Adonias Aguiar Filho)
 1915-1990 . . . . DLB-145, 307
Adorno, Theodor W. 1903-1969 . . . . DLB-242
Adoum, Jorge Enrique 1926- DLB-283
Advance Publishing Company DLB-49
Ady, Endre 1877-1919 . . . . . . DLB-215; CDWLB-4
AE 1867-1935 . . . . DLB-19; CDBLB-5
Ælfric circa 955-circa 1010 . . . . DLB-146
Aeschines circa 390 B.C.-circa 320 B.C. DLB-176
Aeschylus 525-524 B.C.-456-455 B.C.
 . . . . DLB-176; CDWLB-1
Aesthetic Papers DLB-1
Aesthetics
 Eighteenth-Century Aesthetic
  Theories DLB-31
African Literature
 Letter from Khartoum Y-90
African American
 Afro-American Literary Critics:
  An Introduction DLB-33
 The Black Aesthetic: Background DS-8
 The Black Arts Movement,
  by Larry Neal DLB-38

375

Black Theaters and Theater Organizations
 in America, 1961-1982:
 A Research List DLB-38

Black Theatre: A Forum [excerpts] ... DLB-38

Callaloo [journal]..................... Y-87

Community and Commentators:
 Black Theatre and Its Critics..... DLB-38

The Emergence of Black
 Women Writers.............. DS-8

The Hatch-Billops Collection........ DLB-76

A Look at the Contemporary Black
 Theatre Movement DLB-38

The Moorland-Spingarn Research
 Center...................... DLB-76

"The Negro as a Writer," by
 G. M. McClellan DLB-50

"Negro Poets and Their Poetry," by
 Wallace Thurman DLB-50

Olaudah Equiano and Unfinished Journeys:
 The Slave-Narrative Tradition and
 Twentieth-Century Continuities, by
 Paul Edwards and Pauline T.
 Wangman DLB-117

PHYLON (Fourth Quarter, 1950),
 The Negro in Literature:
 The Current Scene DLB-76

The Schomburg Center for Research
 in Black Culture DLB-76

Three Documents [poets], by John
 Edward Bruce DLB-50

After Dinner Opera Company Y-92
Agassiz, Elizabeth Cary 1822-1907...... DLB-189
Agassiz, Louis 1807-1873 .... DLB-1, 235
Agee, James
 1909-1955 .... DLB-2, 26, 152; CDALB-1

The Agee Legacy: A Conference at
 the University of Tennessee
 at Knoxville Y-89

Aguilera Malta, Demetrio 1909-1981 .... DLB-145
Aguirre, Isidora 1919- DLB-305
Agustini, Delmira 1886-1914 .... DLB-290
Ahlin, Lars 1915-1997................ DLB-257
Ai 1947- DLB-120
Aichinger, Ilse 1921- DLB-85, 299
Aickman, Robert 1914-1981............ DLB-261
Aidoo, Ama Ata 1942- DLB-117; CDWLB-3
Aiken, Conrad
 1889-1973 .... DLB-9, 45, 102; CDALB-5
Aiken, Joan 1924- DLB-161
Aikin, Lucy 1781-1864 .... DLB-144, 163
Ainsworth, William Harrison
 1805-1882 .... DLB-21
Aistis, Jonas 1904-1973 ..... DLB-220; CDWLB-4
Aitken, George A. 1860-1917 .... DLB-149
Robert Aitken [publishing house] DLB-49
Aitmatov, Chingiz 1928- DLB-302
Akenside, Mark 1721-1770 .... DLB-109
Akhamatova, Anna Andreevna
 1889-1966 .... DLB-295
Akins, Zoë 1886-1958................ DLB-26
Aksakov, Ivan Sergeevich 1823-1826 .....DLB-277

Aksakov, Sergei Timofeevich
 1791-1859..................... DLB-198
Aksyonov, Vassily 1932- DLB-302
Akunin, Boris (Grigorii Shalvovich
 Chkhartishvili) 1956- DLB-285
Akutagawa Ryūnosuke 1892-1927 .... DLB-180
Alabaster, William 1568-1640 .... DLB-132
Alain de Lille circa 1116-1202/1203 ..... DLB-208
Alain-Fournier 1886-1914 .... DLB-65
Alanus de Insulis (see Alain de Lille)
Alarcón, Francisco X. 1954- DLB-122
Alarcón, Justo S. 1930- DLB-209
Alba, Nanina 1915-1968................ DLB-41
Albee, Edward 1928- ... DLB-7, 266; CDALB-1
Albert, Octavia 1853-ca. 1889 .... DLB-221
Albert the Great circa 1200-1280 .... DLB-115
Alberti, Rafael 1902-1999............. DLB-108
Albertinus, Aegidius circa 1560-1620 .... DLB-164
Alcaeus born circa 620 B.C. DLB-176
Alcoforado, Mariana, the Portuguese Nun
 1640-1723..................... DLB-287
Alcott, Amos Bronson
 1799-1888............... DLB-1, 223; DS-5
Alcott, Louisa May 1832-1888
 ... DLB-1, 42, 79, 223, 239; DS-14; CDALB-3
Alcott, William Andrus 1798-1859.... DLB-1, 243
Alcuin circa 732-804................. DLB-148
Alden, Henry Mills 1836-1919 .... DLB-79
Alden, Isabella 1841-1930 .... DLB-42
John B. Alden [publishing house] DLB-49
Alden, Beardsley, and Company DLB-49
Aldington, Richard
 1892-1962 ....DLB-20, 36, 100, 149
Aldis, Dorothy 1896-1966 .... DLB-22
Aldis, H. G. 1863-1919................ DLB-184
Aldiss, Brian W. 1925- DLB-14, 261, 271
Aldrich, Thomas Bailey
 1836-1907..........DLB-42, 71, 74, 79
Alegría, Ciro 1909-1967 .... DLB-113
Alegría, Claribel 1924- DLB-145, 283
Aleixandre, Vicente 1898-1984......... DLB-108
Aleksandravičius, Jonas (see Aistis, Jonas)
Aleksandrov, Aleksandr Andreevich
 (see Durova, Nadezhda Andreevna)
Alekseeva, Marina Anatol'evna
 (see Marinina, Aleksandra)
Alencar, José de 1829-1877 .... DLB-307
Aleramo, Sibilla (Rena Pierangeli Faccio)
 1876-1960.................. DLB-114, 264
Aleshkovsky, Petr Markovich 1957- ... DLB-285
Alexander, Cecil Frances 1818-1895..... DLB-199
Alexander, Charles 1868-1923 .... DLB-91
Charles Wesley Alexander
 [publishing house] DLB-49
Alexander, James 1691-1756........... DLB-24
Alexander, Lloyd 1924- DLB-52
Alexander, Sir William, Earl of Stirling
 1577?-1640 .... DLB-121

Alexie, Sherman 1966- DLB-175, 206, 278
Alexis, Willibald 1798-1871 .... DLB-133
Alfred, King 849-899 .... DLB-146
Alger, Horatio, Jr. 1832-1899........... DLB-42
Algonquin Books of Chapel Hill DLB-46
Algren, Nelson
 1909-1981 .... DLB-9; Y-81, 82; CDALB-1

Nelson Algren: An International
 Symposium Y-00

Aljamiado Literature.................. DLB-286
Allan, Andrew 1907-1974 .... DLB-88
Allan, Ted 1916-1995................. DLB-68
Allbeury, Ted 1917- DLB-87
Alldritt, Keith 1935- DLB-14
Allen, Dick 1939- DLB-282
Allen, Ethan 1738-1789 .... DLB-31
Allen, Frederick Lewis 1890-1954 ....DLB-137
Allen, Gay Wilson 1903-1995 .....DLB-103; Y-95
Allen, George 1808-1876 .... DLB-59
Allen, Grant 1848-1899 ....DLB-70, 92, 178
Allen, Henry W. 1912-1991 .... Y-85
Allen, Hervey 1889-1949 .... DLB-9, 45
Allen, James 1739-1808................ DLB-31
Allen, James Lane 1849-1925 .... DLB-71
Allen, Jay Presson 1922- DLB-26
John Allen and Company DLB-49
Allen, Paula Gunn 1939- DLB-175
Allen, Samuel W. 1917- DLB-41
Allen, Woody 1935- DLB-44
George Allen [publishing house]......... DLB-106
George Allen and Unwin Limited DLB-112
Allende, Isabel 1942- DLB-145; CDWLB-3
Alline, Henry 1748-1784 .... DLB-99
Allingham, Margery 1904-1966 .... DLB-77

The Margery Allingham Society Y-98

Allingham, William 1824-1889.......... DLB-35
W. L. Allison [publishing house] DLB-49
The *Alliterative Morte Arthure and the Stanzaic
 Morte Arthur* circa 1350-1400 ... DLB-146
Allott, Kenneth 1912-1973 .... DLB-20
Allston, Washington 1779-1843 ...... DLB-1, 235
Almeida, Manuel Antônio de
 1831-1861 .... DLB-307
John Almon [publishing house] DLB-154
Alonzo, Dámaso 1898-1990 .... DLB-108
Alsop, George 1636-post 1673 .... DLB-24
Alsop, Richard 1761-1815.............. DLB-37
Henry Altemus and Company.......... DLB-49
Altenberg, Peter 1885-1919 .... DLB-81
Althusser, Louis 1918-1990 .... DLB-242
Altolaguirre, Manuel 1905-1959........ DLB-108
Aluko, T. M. 1918- DLB-117
Alurista 1947- DLB-82
Alvarez, A. 1929- DLB-14, 40
Alvarez, Julia 1950- DLB-282

376

Alvaro, Corrado 1895-1956............DLB-264	Amis, Martin 1949- DLB-14, 194	Anhalt, Edward 1914-2000 ....DLB-26
Alver, Betti 1906-1989......DLB-220; CDWLB-4	Ammianus Marcellinus circa A.D. 330-A.D. 395 ....DLB-211	Anissimov, Myriam 1943- DLB-299
Amadi, Elechi 1934- DLB-117	Ammons, A. R. 1926-2001 ....DLB-5, 165	Anker, Nini Roll 1873-1942..............DLB-297
Amado, Jorge 1912-2001 ....DLB-113	Amory, Thomas 1691?-1788............DLB-39	Annenkov, Pavel Vasil'evich 1813?-1887 ....DLB-277
Amalrik, Andrei 1938-1980 ....DLB-302	Anania, Michael 1939- DLB-193	Annensky, Innokentii Fedorovich 1855-1909 ....DLB-295
Ambler, Eric 1909-1998.................DLB-77	Anaya, Rudolfo A. 1937- DLB-82, 206, 278	Henry F. Anners [publishing house] DLB-49
The Library of America................DLB-46	*Ancrene Riwle* circa 1200-1225............DLB-146	*Annolied* between 1077 and 1081.........DLB-148
The Library of America: An Assessment After Two Decades Y-02	Andersch, Alfred 1914-1980 ....DLB-69	Anscombe, G. E. M. 1919-2001.........DLB-262
America: or, A Poem on the Settlement of the British Colonies, by Timothy Dwight DLB-37	Andersen, Benny 1929- DLB-214	Anselm of Canterbury 1033-1109 ....DLB-115
	Andersen, Hans Christian 1805-1875 ....DLB-300	Anstey, F. 1856-1934 ....DLB-141, 178
	Anderson, Alexander 1775-1870 ....DLB-188	Anthologizing New Formalism DLB-282
American Bible Society Department of Library, Archives, and Institutional Research Y-97	Anderson, David 1929- DLB-241	Anthony, Michael 1932- DLB-125
	Anderson, Frederick Irving 1877-1947 ....DLB-202	Anthony, Piers 1934- DLB-8
American Conservatory Theatre DLB-7	Anderson, Margaret 1886-1973 ....DLB-4, 91	Anthony, Susanna 1726-1791............DLB-200
	Anderson, Maxwell 1888-1959 .... DLB-7, 228	Antin, David 1932- DLB-169
American Culture American Proletarian Culture: The Twenties and Thirties........ DS-11	Anderson, Patrick 1915-1979............DLB-68	Antin, Mary 1881-1949 .... DLB-221; Y-84
	Anderson, Paul Y. 1893-1938 ....DLB-29	Anton Ulrich, Duke of Brunswick-Lüneburg 1633-1714 ....DLB-168
Studies in American Jewish Literature Y-02	Anderson, Poul 1926-2001 ....DLB-8	
The American Library in Paris Y-93	Tribute to Isaac Asimov Y-92	Antschel, Paul (see Celan, Paul)
American Literature The Literary Scene and Situation and . . . (Who Besides Oprah) Really Runs American Literature? Y-99	Anderson, Robert 1750-1830 ....DLB-142	Antunes, António Lobo 1942- DLB-287
	Anderson, Robert 1917- DLB-7	Anyidoho, Kofi 1947- DLB-157
	Anderson, Sherwood 1876-1941 .....DLB-4, 9, 86; DS-1; CDALB-4	Anzaldúa, Gloria 1942- DLB-122
		Anzengruber, Ludwig 1839-1889 ....DLB-129
Who Owns American Literature, by Henry Taylor Y-94	Andrade, Jorge (Aluísio Jorge Andrade Franco) 1922-1984 ....DLB-307	Apess, William 1798-1839 .... DLB-175, 243
		Apodaca, Rudy S. 1939- DLB-82
Who Runs American Literature? Y-94	Andrade, Mario de 1893-1945..........DLB-307	Apollinaire, Guillaume 1880-1918.......DLB-258
American News Company..............DLB-49	Andrade, Oswald de (José Oswald de Sousa Andrade) 1890-1954 ....DLB-307	Apollonius Rhodius third century B.C. ... DLB-176
A Century of Poetry, a Lifetime of Collecting: J. M. Edelstein's Collection of Twentieth-Century American Poetry............ Y-02		Apple, Max 1941- DLB-130
	Andreae, Johann Valentin 1586-1654 ....DLB-164	Appelfeld, Aharon 1932- DLB-299
	Andreas Capellanus flourished circa 1185...............DLB-208	D. Appleton and Company DLB-49
The American Poets' Corner: The First Three Years (1983-1986)............. Y-86		Appleton-Century-Crofts.................DLB-46
	Andreas-Salomé, Lou 1861-1937 ....DLB-66	Applewhite, James 1935- DLB-105
American Publishing Company.........DLB-49	Andreev, Leonid Nikolaevich 1871-1919 ....DLB-295	Tribute to James Dickey..............Y-97
American Spectator [Editorial] Rationale From the Initial Issue of the American Spectator (November 1932)...............DLB-137		Apple-wood Books..................DLB-46
	Andres, Stefan 1906-1970 ....DLB-69	April, Jean-Pierre 1948- DLB-251
	Andresen, Sophia de Mello Breyner 1919- DLB-287	Apukhtin, Aleksei Nikolaevich 1840-1893 ....DLB-277
American Stationers' Company.........DLB-49	Andreu, Blanca 1959- DLB-134	Apuleius circa A.D. 125-post A.D. 164 .... DLB-211; CDWLB-1
The American Studies Association of Norway......................... Y-00	Andrewes, Lancelot 1555-1626 ..... DLB-151, 172	
	Andrews, Charles M. 1863-1943.........DLB-17	Aquin, Hubert 1929-1977 ....DLB-53
American Sunday-School Union DLB-49	Andrews, Miles Peter ?-1814 ....DLB-89	Aquinas, Thomas 1224/1225-1274 ......DLB-115
American Temperance Union DLB-49	Andrews, Stephen Pearl 1812-1886.......DLB-250	Aragon, Louis 1897-1982.......... DLB-72, 258
American Tract Society DLB-49	Andrian, Leopold von 1875-1951 ....DLB-81	Aragon, Vernacular Translations in the Crowns of Castile and 1352-1515....DLB-286
The American Trust for the British Library .. Y-96	Andrić, Ivo 1892-1975 ...... DLB-147; CDWLB-4	
American Writers' Congress 25-27 April 1935 ....DLB-303	Andrieux, Louis (see Aragon, Louis)	Aralica, Ivan 1930- DLB-181
	Andrus, Silas, and Son.................DLB-49	Aratus of Soli circa 315 B.C.-circa 239 B.C. DLB-176
American Writers Congress The American Writers Congress (9-12 October 1981) Y-81	Andrzejewski, Jerzy 1909-1983 ....DLB-215	
	Angell, James Burrill 1829-1916 ....DLB-64	Arbasino, Alberto 1930- DLB-196
The American Writers Congress: A Report on Continuing Business Y-81	Angell, Roger 1920- DLB-171, 185	Arbor House Publishing Company.......DLB-46
	Angelou, Maya 1928- DLB-38; CDALB-7	Arbuthnot, John 1667-1735 ....DLB-101
Ames, Fisher 1758-1808................DLB-37	Tribute to Julian Mayfield............. Y-84	Arcadia House...................DLB-46
Ames, Mary Clemmer 1831-1884 ....DLB-23	Anger, Jane flourished 1589............DLB-136	Arce, Julio G. (see Ulica, Jorge)
Ames, William 1576-1633 ....DLB-281	Angers, Félicité (see Conan, Laure)	Archer, William 1856-1924 ....DLB-10
Amiel, Henri-Frédéric 1821-1881........DLB-217	*The Anglo-Saxon Chronicle* circa 890-1154...................DLB-146	Archilochhus mid seventh century B.C.E. DLB-176
Amini, Johari M. 1935- DLB-41		
Amis, Kingsley 1922-1995 ..... DLB-15, 27, 100, 139, Y-96; CDBLB-7	Angus and Robertson (UK) Limited DLB-112	

Cumulative Index

The Archpoet circa 1130?-? DLB-148
Archpriest Avvakum (Petrovich)
  1620?-1682. . . . . DLB-150
Arden, John 1930- DLB-13, 245
Arden of Faversham DLB-62
Ardis Publishers Y-89
Ardizzone, Edward 1900-1979 . . . . . . DLB-160
Arellano, Juan Estevan 1947- DLB-122
The Arena Publishing Company DLB-49
Arena Stage. DLB-7
Arenas, Reinaldo 1943-1990. . . . . DLB-145
Arendt, Hannah 1906-1975 . . . . DLB-242
Arensberg, Ann 1937- Y-82
Arghezi, Tudor 1880-1967. . . . DLB-220; CDWLB-4
Arguedas, José María 1911-1969 . . . . DLB-113
Argüelles, Hugo 1932-2003 . . . . DLB-305
Argueta, Manlio 1936- DLB-145
Arias, Ron 1941- DLB-82
Arishima Takeo 1878-1923. . . . . DLB-180
Aristophanes circa 446 B.C.-circa 386 B.C.
  . . . . DLB-176; CDWLB-1
Aristotle 384 B.C.-322 B.C.
  . . . . DLB-176; CDWLB-1
Ariyoshi Sawako 1931-1984. . . . . DLB-182
Arland, Marcel 1899-1986 . . . . DLB-72
Arlen, Michael 1895-1956 . . . . . . DLB-36, 77, 162
Arlt, Roberto 1900-1942. . . . . DLB-305
Armah, Ayi Kwei 1939- . . . DLB-117; CDWLB-3
Armantrout, Rae 1947- DLB-193
Der arme Hartmann ?-after 1150 . . . . . . DLB-148
Armed Services Editions. DLB-46
Armitage, G. E. (Robert Edric) 1956- . . DLB-267
Armstrong, Martin Donisthorpe
  1882-1974. DLB-197
Armstrong, Richard 1903- DLB-160
Armstrong, Terence Ian Fytton (see Gawsworth, John)
Arnauld, Antoine 1612-1694. . . . . DLB-268
Arndt, Ernst Moritz 1769-1860. . . . . DLB-90
Arnim, Achim von 1781-1831. . . . . DLB-90
Arnim, Bettina von 1785-1859 . . . . DLB-90
Arnim, Elizabeth von (Countess Mary Annette
  Beauchamp Russell) 1866-1941 . . . . DLB-197
Arno Press DLB-46
Arnold, Edwin 1832-1904 . . . . DLB-35
Arnold, Edwin L. 1857-1935. . . . . DLB-178
Arnold, Matthew
  1822-1888 . . . . DLB-32, 57; CDBLB-4
  Preface to *Poems* (1853). DLB-32
Arnold, Thomas 1795-1842 . . . . DLB-55
Edward Arnold [publishing house]. DLB-112
Arnott, Peter 1962- DLB-233
Arnow, Harriette Simpson 1908-1986 . . . . DLB-6
Arp, Bill (see Smith, Charles Henry)
Arpino, Giovanni 1927-1987. . . . . DLB-177
Arrebo, Anders 1587-1637 . . . . DLB-300
Arreola, Juan José 1918-2001 . . . . DLB-113

Arrian circa 89-circa 155. . . . . DLB-176
J. W. Arrowsmith [publishing house] DLB-106
Arrufat, Antón 1935- DLB-305
Art
  John Dos Passos: Artist Y-99
  The First Post-Impressionist
    Exhibition. DS-5
  The Omega Workshops DS-10
  The Second Post-Impressionist
    Exhibition .DS-5
Artaud, Antonin 1896-1948 . . . . DLB-258
Artel, Jorge 1909-1994 . . . . DLB-283
Arthur, Timothy Shay
  1809-1885 . . . . . . .DLB-3, 42, 79, 250; DS-13
Artmann, H. C. 1921-2000. . . . . DLB-85
Artsybashev, Mikhail Petrovich
  1878-1927. DLB-295
Arvin, Newton 1900-1963 . . . . DLB-103
Asch, Nathan 1902-1964 . . . . DLB-4, 28
  Nathan Asch Remembers Ford Madox
    Ford, Sam Roth, and Hart Crane Y-02
Ascham, Roger 1515/1516-1568. . . . . DLB-236
Aseev, Nikolai Nikolaevich
  1889-1963 . . . . DLB-295
Ash, John 1948- DLB-40
Ashbery, John 1927- DLB-5, 165; Y-81
Ashbridge, Elizabeth 1713-1755 . . . . DLB-200
Ashburnham, Bertram Lord
  1797-1878 . . . . DLB-184
Ashendene Press. DLB-112
Asher, Sandy 1942- Y-83
Ashton, Winifred (see Dane, Clemence)
Asimov, Isaac 1920-1992 . . . . .DLB-8; Y-92
  Tribute to John Ciardi Y-86
Askew, Anne circa 1521-1546 . . . . DLB-136
Aspazija 1865-1943. . . . . . . DLB-220; CDWLB-4
Asselin, Olivar 1874-1937 . . . . DLB-92
The Association of American Publishers Y-99
The Association for Documentary Editing. . . . Y-00
The Association for the Study of
  Literature and Environment (ASLE) Y-99
Astell, Mary 1666-1731. . . . . DLB-252
Astley, Thea 1925- DLB-289
Astley, William (see Warung, Price)
Asturias, Miguel Ángel
  1899-1974. . . . . . . .DLB-113, 290; CDWLB-3
Atava, S. (see Terpigorev, Sergei Nikolaevich)
Atheneum Publishers DLB-46
Atherton, Gertrude 1857-1948 . . . . .DLB-9, 78, 186
Athlone Press DLB-112
Atkins, Josiah circa 1755-1781 . . . . DLB-31
Atkins, Russell 1926- DLB-41
Atkinson, Kate 1951- DLB-267
Atkinson, Louisa 1834-1872 . . . . DLB-230
The Atlantic Monthly Press DLB-46
Attaway, William 1911-1986 . . . . DLB-76
Atwood, Margaret 1939- DLB-53, 251

Aubert, Alvin 1930- DLB-41
Aubert de Gaspé, Phillipe-Ignace-François
  1814-1841. . . . . DLB-99
Aubert de Gaspé, Phillipe-Joseph
  1786-1871. . . . . DLB-99
Aubin, Napoléon 1812-1890. . . . . DLB-99
Aubin, Penelope
  1685-circa 1731 . . . . DLB-39
  Preface to *The Life of Charlotta
    du Pont* (1723). DLB-39
Aubrey-Fletcher, Henry Lancelot (see Wade, Henry)
Auchincloss, Louis 1917- DLB-2, 244; Y-80
Auden, W. H.
  1907-1973 . . . . DLB-10, 20; CDBLB-6
Audio Art in America: A Personal Memoir . . . Y-85
Audubon, John James 1785-1851 . . . . . . DLB-248
Audubon, John Woodhouse
  1812-1862 . . . . DLB-183
Auerbach, Berthold 1812-1882. . . . . DLB-133
Auernheimer, Raoul 1876-1948 . . . . DLB-81
Augier, Emile 1820-1889 . . . . DLB-192
Augustine 354-430 . . . . DLB-115
Aulnoy, Marie-Catherine Le Jumel
  de Barneville, comtesse d'
  1650/1651-1705. . . . . .DLB-268
Aulus Gellius
  circa A.D. 125-circa A.D. 180?. DLB-211
Austen, Jane 1775-1817 . . . . . . DLB-116; CDBLB-3
Auster, Paul 1947- DLB-227
Austin, Alfred 1835-1913 . . . . DLB-35
Austin, J. L. 1911-1960. . . . . DLB-262
Austin, Jane Goodwin 1831-1894. . . . . . . DLB-202
Austin, John 1790-1859. . . . . DLB-262
Austin, Mary Hunter
  1868-1934 . . . . DLB-9, 78, 206, 221, 275
Austin, William 1778-1841 . . . . DLB-74
Australie (Emily Manning)
  1845-1890 . . . . DLB-230
Authors and Newspapers Association DLB-46
Authors' Publishing Company DLB-49
Avallone, Michael 1924-1999 . . . . . .DLB-306; Y-99
  Tribute to John D. MacDonald Y-86
  Tribute to Kenneth Millar Y-83
  Tribute to Raymond Chandler Y-88
Avalon Books DLB-46
Avancini, Nicolaus 1611-1686 . . . . DLB-164
Avendaño, Fausto 1941- DLB-82
Averroës 1126-1198 . . . . DLB-115
Avery, Gillian 1926- DLB-161
Avicenna 980-1037 . . . . DLB-115
Ávila Jiménez, Antonio 1898-1965 . . . . . . DLB-283
Avison, Margaret 1918-1987. . . . . DLB-53
Avon Books DLB-46
Avyžius, Jonas 1922-1999. . . . . DLB-220
Awdry, Wilbert Vere 1911-1997 . . . . DLB-160
Awoonor, Kofi 1935- DLB-117
Ayckbourn, Alan 1939- DLB-13, 245
Ayer, A. J. 1910-1989 . . . . DLB-262

Aymé, Marcel 1902-1967 . . . . DLB-72

Aytoun, Sir Robert 1570-1638 . . . . DLB-121

Aytoun, William Edmondstoune
  1813-1865 . . . . DLB-32, 159

Azevedo, Aluísio 1857-1913 . . . . DLB-307

Azevedo, Manuel Antônio Álvares de
  1831-1852 . . . . DLB-307

B

B.V. (see Thomson, James)

Babbitt, Irving 1865-1933 . . . . DLB-63

Babbitt, Natalie 1932- DLB-52

John Babcock [publishing house] DLB-49

Babel, Isaak Emmanuilovich
  1894-1940 . . . . DLB-272

Babits, Mihály 1883-1941 . . . DLB-215; CDWLB-4

Babrius circa 150-200 . . . . DLB-176

Babson, Marian 1929- DLB-276

Baca, Jimmy Santiago 1952- DLB-122

Bacchelli, Riccardo 1891-1985 . . . . DLB-264

Bache, Benjamin Franklin 1769-1798 . . . . . DLB-43

Bachelard, Gaston 1884-1962 . . . . DLB-296

Bacheller, Irving 1859-1950 . . . . DLB-202

Bachmann, Ingeborg 1926-1973 . . . . DLB-85

Bačinskaitė-Bučienė, Salomėja (see Nėris, Salomėja)

Bacon, Delia 1811-1859 . . . . DLB-1, 243

Bacon, Francis
  1561-1626 . . . . . DLB-151, 236, 252; CDBLB-1

Bacon, Sir Nicholas circa 1510-1579 . . . . . DLB-132

Bacon, Roger circa 1214/1220-1292 . . . . . DLB-115

Bacon, Thomas circa 1700-1768 . . . . DLB-31

Bacovia, George
  1881-1957 . . . . DLB-220; CDWLB-4

Richard G. Badger and Company DLB-49

Bagaduce Music Lending Library Y-00

Bage, Robert 1728-1801 . . . . DLB-39

Bagehot, Walter 1826-1877 . . . . DLB-55

Baggesen, Jens 1764-1826 . . . . DLB-300

Bagley, Desmond 1923-1983 . . . . DLB-87

Bagley, Sarah G. 1806-1848? DLB-239

Bagnold, Enid 1889-1981 . . . DLB-13, 160, 191, 245

Bagryana, Elisaveta
  1893-1991 . . . . DLB-147; CDWLB-4

Bahr, Hermann 1863-1934 . . . . DLB-81, 118

Bailey, Abigail Abbot
  1746-1815 . . . . DLB-200

Bailey, Alfred Goldsworthy 1905- DLB-68

Bailey, H. C. 1878-1961 . . . . DLB-77

Bailey, Jacob 1731-1808 . . . . DLB-99

Bailey, Paul 1937- DLB-14, 271

Bailey, Philip James 1816-1902 . . . . DLB-32

Francis Bailey [publishing house] DLB-49

Baillargeon, Pierre 1916-1967 . . . . DLB-88

Baillie, Hugh 1890-1966 . . . . DLB-29

Baillie, Joanna 1762-1851 . . . . DLB-93

Bailyn, Bernard 1922- DLB-17

Bain, Alexander
  English Composition and Rhetoric (1866)
  [excerpt] DLB-57

Bainbridge, Beryl 1933- DLB-14, 231

Baird, Irene 1901-1981 . . . . DLB-68

Baker, Augustine 1575-1641 . . . . DLB-151

Baker, Carlos 1909-1987 . . . . DLB-103

Baker, David 1954- DLB-120

Baker, George Pierce 1866-1935 . . . . DLB-266

Baker, Herschel C. 1914-1990 . . . . DLB-111

Baker, Houston A., Jr. 1943- DLB-67

Baker, Howard
  Tribute to Caroline Gordon Y-81
  Tribute to Katherine Anne Porter Y-80

Baker, Nicholson 1957- DLB-227; Y-00
  Review of Nicholson Baker's *Double Fold:
    Libraries and the Assault on Paper* Y-00

Baker, Samuel White 1821-1893 . . . . DLB-166

Baker, Thomas 1656-1740 . . . . DLB-213

Walter H. Baker Company
  ("Baker's Plays") DLB-49

The Baker and Taylor Company DLB-49

Bakhtin, Mikhail Mikhailovich
  1895-1975 . . . . DLB-242

Bakunin, Mikhail Aleksandrovich
  1814-1876 . . . . DLB-277

Balaban, John 1943- DLB-120

Bald, Wambly 1902- DLB-4

Balde, Jacob 1604-1668 . . . . DLB-164

Balderston, John 1889-1954 . . . . DLB-26

Baldwin, James 1924-1987
  . . . . . DLB-2, 7, 33, 249, 278; Y-87; CDALB-1

Baldwin, Joseph Glover
  1815-1864 . . . . DLB-3, 11, 248

Baldwin, Louisa (Mrs. Alfred Baldwin)
  1845-1925 . . . . DLB-240

Baldwin, William circa 1515-1563 . . . . DLB-132

Richard and Anne Baldwin
  [publishing house] DLB-170

Bale, John 1495-1563 . . . . DLB-132

Balestrini, Nanni 1935- DLB-128, 196

Balfour, Sir Andrew 1630-1694 . . . . DLB-213

Balfour, Arthur James 1848-1930 . . . . DLB-190

Balfour, Sir James 1600-1657 . . . . DLB-213

Ballantine Books DLB-46

Ballantyne, R. M. 1825-1894 . . . . DLB-163

Ballard, J. G. 1930- DLB-14, 207, 261

Ballard, Martha Moore 1735-1812 . . . . . . DLB-200

Ballerini, Luigi 1940- DLB-128

Ballou, Maturin Murray (Lieutenant Murray)
  1820-1895 . . . . DLB-79, 189

Robert O. Ballou [publishing house] DLB-46

Bal'mont, Konstantin Dmitrievich
  1867-1942 . . . . DLB-295

Balzac, Guez de 1597?-1654 . . . . DLB-268

Balzac, Honoré de 1799-1855 . . . . DLB-119

Bambara, Toni Cade
  1939-1995 . . . . DLB-38, 218; CDALB-7

Bamford, Samuel 1788-1872 . . . . DLB-190

A. L. Bancroft and Company DLB-49

Bancroft, George 1800-1891 . . . DLB-1, 30, 59, 243

Bancroft, Hubert Howe 1832-1918 . . . DLB-47, 140

Bandeira, Manuel 1886-1968 . . . . DLB-307

Bandelier, Adolph F. 1840-1914 . . . . DLB-186

Bang, Herman 1857-1912 . . . . DLB-300

Bangs, John Kendrick 1862-1922 . . . . . DLB-11, 79

Banim, John 1798-1842 . . . . DLB-116, 158, 159

Banim, Michael 1796-1874 . . . . DLB-158, 159

Banks, Iain (M.) 1954- DLB-194, 261

Banks, John circa 1653-1706 . . . . DLB-80

Banks, Russell 1940- DLB-130, 278

Bannerman, Helen 1862-1946 . . . . DLB-141

Bantam Books DLB-46

Banti, Anna 1895-1985 . . . . DLB-177

Banville, John 1945- DLB-14, 271

Banville, Théodore de 1823-1891 . . . . DLB-217

Baraka, Amiri
  1934- DLB-5, 7, 16, 38; DS-8; CDALB-1

Barańczak, Stanisław 1946- DLB-232

Baranskaia, Natal'ia Vladimirovna
  1908- DLB-302

Baratynsky, Evgenii Abramovich
  1800-1844 . . . . DLB-205

Barba-Jacob, Porfirio 1883-1942 . . . . DLB-283

Barbauld, Anna Laetitia
  1743-1825 . . . . DLB-107, 109, 142, 158

Barbeau, Marius 1883-1969 . . . . DLB-92

Barber, John Warner 1798-1885 . . . . DLB-30

Bàrberi Squarotti, Giorgio 1929- DLB-128

Barbey d'Aurevilly, Jules-Amédée
  1808-1889 . . . . DLB-119

Barbier, Auguste 1805-1882 . . . . DLB-217

Barbilian, Dan (see Barbu, Ion)

Barbour, John circa 1316-1395 . . . . DLB-146

Barbour, Ralph Henry 1870-1944 . . . . DLB-22

Barbu, Ion 1895-1961 . . . . . . DLB-220; CDWLB-4

Barbusse, Henri 1873-1935 . . . . DLB-65

Barclay, Alexander circa 1475-1552 . . . . . . DLB-132

E. E. Barclay and Company DLB-49

C. W. Bardeen [publishing house] DLB-49

Barham, Richard Harris 1788-1845 . . . . . . DLB-159

Barich, Bill 1943- DLB-185

Baring, Maurice 1874-1945 . . . . DLB-34

Baring-Gould, Sabine 1834-1924 . . . . DLB-156, 190

Barker, A. L. 1918- DLB-14, 139

Barker, Clive 1952- DLB-261

Barker, Dudley (see Black, Lionel)

Barker, George 1913-1991 . . . . DLB-20

Barker, Harley Granville 1877-1946 . . . . . . DLB-10

Barker, Howard 1946- DLB-13, 233

Barker, James Nelson 1784-1858 . . . . DLB-37

Barker, Jane 1652-1727 . . . . DLB-39, 131

Barker, Lady Mary Anne 1831-1911 . . . . . DLB-166

Barker, Pat 1943- DLB-271

Barker, William circa 1520-after 1576 . . . . DLB-132

Arthur Barker Limited DLB-112
Barkov, Ivan Semenovich 1732-1768 . . . . DLB-150
Barks, Coleman 1937- DLB-5
Barlach, Ernst 1870-1938 . . . . DLB-56, 118
Barlow, Joel 1754-1812 . . . . DLB-37
   The Prospect of Peace (1778) DLB-37
Barnard, John 1681-1770 . . . . DLB-24
Barnard, Marjorie (M. Barnard Eldershaw)
   1897-1987 . . . . DLB-260
Barnard, Robert 1936- DLB-276
Barne, Kitty (Mary Catherine Barne)
   1883-1957 . . . . DLB-160
Barnes, Barnabe 1571-1609 . . . . DLB-132
Barnes, Djuna 1892-1982 . . . . DLB-4, 9, 45; DS-15
Barnes, Jim 1933- DLB-175
Barnes, Julian 1946- DLB-194; Y-93
   Notes for a Checklist of Publications Y-01
Barnes, Margaret Ayer 1886-1967 . . . . DLB-9
Barnes, Peter 1931- DLB-13, 233
Barnes, William 1801-1886 . . . . DLB-32
A. S. Barnes and Company DLB-49
Barnes and Noble Books DLB-46
Barnet, Miguel 1940- DLB-145
Barney, Natalie 1876-1972 . . . . DLB-4; DS-15
Barnfield, Richard 1574-1627 . . . . DLB-172
Richard W. Baron [publishing house] DLB-46
Barr, Amelia Edith Huddleston
   1831-1919 . . . . DLB-202, 221
Barr, Robert 1850-1912 . . . . DLB-70, 92
Barral, Carlos 1928-1989 . . . . DLB-134
Barrax, Gerald William 1933- DLB-41, 120
Barrès, Maurice 1862-1923 . . . . DLB-123
Barreno, Maria Isabel (see The Three Marias:
   A Landmark Case in Portuguese
   Literary History)
Barrett, Eaton Stannard 1786-1820 . . . . . . DLB-116
Barrie, J. M.
   1860-1937 . . . . . DLB-10, 141, 156; CDBLB-5
Barrie and Jenkins DLB-112
Barrio, Raymond 1921- DLB-82
Barrios, Gregg 1945- DLB-122
Barry, Philip 1896-1949 . . . . DLB-7, 228
Barry, Robertine (see Françoise)
Barry, Sebastian 1955- DLB-245
Barse and Hopkins DLB-46
Barstow, Stan 1928- DLB-14, 139, 207
   Tribute to John Braine Y-86
Barth, John 1930- DLB-2, 227
Barthelme, Donald
   1931-1989 . . . . DLB-2, 234; Y-80, 89
Barthelme, Frederick 1943- DLB-244; Y-85
Barthes, Roland 1915-1980 . . . . DLB-296
Bartholomew, Frank 1898-1985 . . . . DLB-127
Bartlett, John 1820-1905 . . . . DLB-1, 235
Bartol, Cyrus Augustus 1813-1900 . . . . DLB-1, 235
Barton, Bernard 1784-1849 . . . . DLB-96

Barton, John ca. 1610-1675 . . . . DLB-236
Barton, Thomas Pennant 1803-1869 . . . . DLB-140
Bartram, John 1699-1777 . . . . DLB-31
Bartram, William 1739-1823 . . . . DLB-37
Barykova, Anna Pavlovna 1839-1893 . . . . DLB-277
Basic Books DLB-46
Basille, Theodore (see Becon, Thomas)
Bass, Rick 1958- DLB-212, 275
Bass, T. J. 1932- Y-81
Bassani, Giorgio 1916-2000 . . . . DLB-128, 177, 299
Basse, William circa 1583-1653 . . . . DLB-121
Bassett, John Spencer 1867-1928 . . . . DLB-17
Bassler, Thomas Joseph (see Bass, T. J.)
Bate, Walter Jackson 1918-1999 . . . . . DLB-67, 103
Bateman, Stephen circa 1510-1584 . . . . . . DLB-136
Christopher Bateman
   [publishing house] DLB-170
Bates, H. E. 1905-1974 . . . . DLB-162, 191
Bates, Katharine Lee 1859-1929 . . . . DLB-71
Batiushkov, Konstantin Nikolaevich
   1787-1855 . . . . DLB-205
B. T. Batsford [publishing house] DLB-106
Battiscombe, Georgina 1905- DLB-155
The Battle of Maldon circa 1000 . . . . DLB-146
Baudelaire, Charles 1821-1867 . . . . DLB-217
Baudrillard, Jean 1929- DLB-296
Bauer, Bruno 1809-1882 . . . . DLB-133
Bauer, Wolfgang 1941- DLB-124
Baum, L. Frank 1856-1919 . . . . DLB-22
Baum, Vicki 1888-1960 . . . . DLB-85
Baumbach, Jonathan 1933- Y-80
Bausch, Richard 1945- DLB-130
   Tribute to James Dickey Y-97
   Tribute to Peter Taylor Y-94
Bausch, Robert 1945- DLB-218
Bawden, Nina 1925- DLB-14, 161, 207
Bax, Clifford 1886-1962 . . . . DLB-10, 100
Baxter, Charles 1947- DLB-130
Bayer, Eleanor (see Perry, Eleanor)
Bayer, Konrad 1932-1964 . . . . DLB-85
Bayle, Pierre 1647-1706 . . . . DLB-268
Bayley, Barrington J. 1937- DLB-261
Baynes, Pauline 1922- DLB-160
Baynton, Barbara 1857-1929 . . . . DLB-230
Bazin, Hervé (Jean Pierre Marie Hervé-Bazin)
   1911-1996 . . . . DLB-83
The BBC Four Samuel Johnson Prize
   for Non-fiction Y-02
Beach, Sylvia
   1887-1962 . . . . DLB-4; DS-15
Beacon Press DLB-49
Beadle and Adams DLB-49
Beagle, Peter S. 1939- Y-80
Beal, M. F. 1937- Y-81
Beale, Howard K. 1899-1959 . . . . DLB-17

Beard, Charles A. 1874-1948 . . . . DLB-17
Beat Generation (Beats)
   As I See It, by Carolyn Cassady DLB-16
   A Beat Chronology: The First Twenty-five
     Years, 1944-1969 . . . . DLB-16
   The Commercialization of the Image
     of Revolt, by Kenneth Rexroth . . . DLB-16
   Four Essays on the Beat Generation . . DLB-16
   in New York City DLB-237
   in the West DLB-237
   Outlaw Days DLB-16
   Periodicals of DLB-16
Beattie, Ann 1947- DLB-218, 278; Y-82
Beattie, James 1735-1803 . . . . DLB-109
Beatty, Chester 1875-1968 . . . . DLB-201
Beauchemin, Nérée 1850-1931 . . . . DLB-92
Beauchemin, Yves 1941- DLB-60
Beaugrand, Honoré 1848-1906 . . . . DLB-99
Beaulieu, Victor-Lévy 1945- DLB-53
Beaumont, Francis circa 1584-1616
   and Fletcher, John
   1579-1625 . . . . DLB-58; CDBLB-1
Beaumont, Sir John 1583?-1627 . . . . DLB-121
Beaumont, Joseph 1616-1699 . . . . DLB-126
Beauvoir, Simone de 1908-1986 . . . . . DLB-72; Y-86
   Personal Tribute to Simone de Beauvoir . . . Y-86
Beaver, Bruce 1928- DLB-289
Becher, Ulrich 1910-1990 . . . . DLB-69
Becker, Carl 1873-1945 . . . . DLB-17
Becker, Jurek 1937-1997 . . . . DLB-75, 299
Becker, Jurgen 1932- DLB-75
Beckett, Samuel 1906-1989
   . . . . DLB-13, 15, 233; Y-90; CDBLB-7
Beckford, William 1760-1844 . . . . . . DLB-39, 213
Beckham, Barry 1944- DLB-33
Bećković, Matija 1939- DLB-181
Becon, Thomas circa 1512-1567 . . . . DLB-136
Becque, Henry 1837-1899 . . . . DLB-192
Beddoes, Thomas 1760-1808 . . . . DLB-158
Beddoes, Thomas Lovell 1803-1849 . . . . . DLB-96
Bede circa 673-735 . . . . DLB-146
Bedford-Jones, H. 1887-1949 . . . . DLB-251
Bedregal, Yolanda 1913-1999 . . . . DLB-283
Beebe, William 1877-1962 . . . . DLB-275
Beecher, Catharine Esther
   1800-1878 . . . . DLB-1, 243
Beecher, Henry Ward
   1813-1887 . . . . DLB-3, 43, 250
Beer, George L. 1872-1920 . . . . DLB-47
Beer, Johann 1655-1700 . . . . DLB-168
Beer, Patricia 1919-1999 . . . . DLB-40
Beerbohm, Max 1872-1956 . . . . DLB-34, 100
Beer-Hofmann, Richard 1866-1945 . . . . . . DLB-81
Beers, Henry A. 1847-1926 . . . . DLB-71
S. O. Beeton [publishing house] DLB-106
Begley, Louis 1933- DLB-299
Bégon, Elisabeth 1696-1755 . . . . DLB-99

Behan, Brendan 1923-1964 ....DLB-13, 233; CDBLB-7

Behn, Aphra 1640?-1689.......DLB-39, 80, 131

Behn, Harry 1898-1973 ....DLB-61

Behrman, S. N. 1893-1973 ....DLB-7, 44

Beklemishev, Iurii Solomonvich (see Krymov, Iurii Solomonovich)

Belaney, Archibald Stansfeld (see Grey Owl)

Belasco, David 1853-1931 ....DLB-7

Clarke Belford and Company DLB-49

Belgian Luxembourg American Studies Association Y-01

Belinsky, Vissarion Grigor'evich 1811-1848 ....DLB-198

Belitt, Ben 1911- DLB-5

Belknap, Jeremy 1744-1798 ....DLB-30, 37

Bell, Adrian 1901-1980 ....DLB-191

Bell, Clive 1881-1964...................DS-10

Bell, Daniel 1919- DLB-246

Bell, Gertrude Margaret Lowthian 1868-1926 ....DLB-174

Bell, James Madison 1826-1902........DLB-50

Bell, Madison Smartt 1957- DLB-218, 278

Tribute to Andrew Nelson Lytle........ Y-95

Tribute to Peter Taylor................ Y-94

Bell, Marvin 1937- DLB-5

Bell, Millicent 1919- DLB-111

Bell, Quentin 1910-1996 ....DLB-155

Bell, Vanessa 1879-1961..................DS-10

George Bell and Sons...................DLB-106

Robert Bell [publishing house]..........DLB-49

Bellamy, Edward 1850-1898 ....DLB-12

Bellamy, Joseph 1719-1790.............DLB-31

John Bellamy [publishing house] DLB-170

La Belle Assemblée 1806-1837 ....DLB-110

Bellezza, Dario 1944-1996 ....DLB-128

Belli, Carlos Germán 1927- DLB-290

Belli, Gioconda 1948- DLB-290

Belloc, Hilaire 1870-1953 .... DLB-19, 100, 141, 174

Belloc, Madame (see Parkes, Bessie Rayner)

Bellonci, Maria 1902-1986 ....DLB-196

Bellow, Saul 1915- DLB-2, 28, 299; Y-82; DS-3; CDALB-1

Tribute to Isaac Bashevis Singer Y-91

Belmont Productions DLB-46

Belov, Vasilii Ivanovich 1932- DLB-302

Bels, Alberts 1938- DLB-232

Belševica, Vizma 1931- DLB-232; CDWLB-4

Bely, Andrei 1880-1934 ....DLB-295

Bemelmans, Ludwig 1898-1962..........DLB-22

Bemis, Samuel Flagg 1891-1973..........DLB-17

William Bemrose [publishing house] DLB-106

Ben no Naishi 1228?-1271? DLB-203

Benchley, Robert 1889-1945 ....DLB-11

Bencúr, Matej (see Kukučín, Martin)

Benedetti, Mario 1920- DLB-113

Benedict, Pinckney 1964- DLB-244

Benedict, Ruth 1887-1948 ....DLB-246

Benedictus, David 1938- DLB-14

Benedikt Gröndal 1826-1907 ....DLB-293

Benedikt, Michael 1935- DLB-5

Benediktov, Vladimir Grigor'evich 1807-1873.....................DLB-205

Benét, Stephen Vincent 1898-1943 .... DLB-4, 48, 102, 249

Stephen Vincent Benét Centenary Y-97

Benét, William Rose 1886-1950 ....DLB-45

Benford, Gregory 1941- Y-82

Benítez, Sandra 1941- DLB-292

Benjamin, Park 1809-1864..... DLB-3, 59, 73, 250

Benjamin, Peter (see Cunningham, Peter)

Benjamin, S. G. W. 1837-1914..........DLB-189

Benjamin, Walter 1892-1940...........DLB-242

Benlowes, Edward 1602-1676 ....DLB-126

Benn, Gottfried 1886-1956 ....DLB-56

Benn Brothers Limited................DLB-106

Bennett, Alan 1934- DLB-310

Bennett, Arnold 1867-1931 ....DLB-10, 34, 98, 135; CDBLB-5

The Arnold Bennett Society Y-98

Bennett, Charles 1899-1995............DLB-44

Bennett, Emerson 1822-1905...........DLB-202

Bennett, Gwendolyn 1902-1981 ....DLB-51

Bennett, Hal 1930- DLB-33

Bennett, James Gordon 1795-1872.......DLB-43

Bennett, James Gordon, Jr. 1841-1918.....DLB-23

Bennett, John 1865-1956 ....DLB-42

Bennett, Louise 1919- DLB-117; CDWLB-3

Benni, Stefano 1947- DLB-196

Benoit, Jacques 1941- DLB-60

Benson, A. C. 1862-1925...............DLB-98

Benson, E. F. 1867-1940............DLB-135, 153

The E. F. Benson Society Y-98

The Tilling Society Y-98

Benson, Jackson J. 1930- DLB-111

Benson, Robert Hugh 1871-1914 ....DLB-153

Benson, Stella 1892-1933 ....DLB-36, 162

Bent, James Theodore 1852-1897 ....DLB-174

Bent, Mabel Virginia Anna ?-? DLB-174

Bentham, Jeremy 1748-1832 ... DLB-107, 158, 252

Bentley, E. C. 1875-1956 ....DLB-70

Bentley, Phyllis 1894-1977.............DLB-191

Bentley, Richard 1662-1742 ....DLB-252

Richard Bentley [publishing house]......DLB-106

Benton, Robert 1932-   and Newman, David 1937- DLB-44

Benziger Brothers.....................DLB-49

Beowulf circa 900-1000 or 790-825 ....DLB-146; CDBLB-1

Berent, Wacław 1873-1940 ....DLB-215

Beresford, Anne 1929- DLB-40

Beresford, John Davys 1873-1947 .... DLB-162, 178, 197

"Experiment in the Novel" (1929) [excerpt] DLB-36

Beresford-Howe, Constance 1922- DLB-88

R. G. Berford Company DLB-49

Berg, Elizabeth 1948- DLB-292

Berg, Stephen 1934- DLB-5

Bergengruen, Werner 1892-1964 ....DLB-56

Berger, John 1926- DLB-14, 207

Berger, Meyer 1898-1959 ....DLB-29

Berger, Thomas 1924- DLB-2; Y-80

A Statement by Thomas Berger Y-80

Bergman, Hjalmar 1883-1931 ....DLB-259

Bergman, Ingmar 1918- DLB-257

Berkeley, Anthony 1893-1971 ....DLB-77

Berkeley, George 1685-1753 .... DLB-31, 101, 252

The Berkley Publishing Corporation......DLB-46

Berkman, Alexander 1870-1936........DLB-303

Berlin, Irving 1888-1989 ....DLB-265

Berlin, Lucia 1936- DLB-130

Berman, Marshall 1940- DLB-246

Berman, Sabina 1955- DLB-305

Bernal, Vicente J. 1888-1915 ....DLB-82

Bernanos, Georges 1888-1948 ....DLB-72

Bernard, Catherine 1663?-1712 ....DLB-268

Bernard, Harry 1898-1979...............DLB-92

Bernard, John 1756-1828 ....DLB-37

Bernard of Chartres circa 1060-1124?....DLB-115

Bernard of Clairvaux 1090-1153........DLB-208

Bernard, Richard 1568-1641/1642.......DLB-281

Bernard Silvestris flourished circa 1130-1160 ....DLB-208

Bernari, Carlo 1909-1992 ....DLB-177

Bernhard, Thomas 1931-1989 .... DLB-85, 124; CDWLB-2

Berniéres, Louis de 1954- DLB-271

Bernstein, Charles 1950- DLB-169

Berriault, Gina 1926-1999 ....DLB-130

Berrigan, Daniel 1921- DLB-5

Berrigan, Ted 1934-1983.............DLB-5, 169

Berry, Wendell 1934- DLB-5, 6, 234, 275

Berryman, John 1914-1972 ....DLB-48; CDALB-1

Bersianik, Louky 1930- DLB-60

Thomas Berthelet [publishing house] DLB-170

Berto, Giuseppe 1914-1978 ....DLB-177

Bertocci, Peter Anthony 1910-1989......DLB-279

Bertolucci, Attilio 1911-2000 ....DLB-128

Berton, Pierre 1920- DLB-68

Bertrand, Louis "Aloysius" 1807-1841....DLB-217

Besant, Sir Walter 1836-1901 ......DLB-135, 190

Bessa-Luís, Agustina 1922- DLB-287

Bessette, Gerard 1920- DLB-53

Bessie, Alvah 1904-1985 ....DLB-26

Bester, Alfred 1913-1987 ....DLB-8

Besterman, Theodore 1904-1976 . . . . DLB-201

Beston, Henry (Henry Beston Sheahan)
    1888-1968 . . . . DLB-275

Best-Seller Lists
    An Assessment Y-84

    What's Really Wrong With
        Bestseller Lists Y-84

Bestuzhev, Aleksandr Aleksandrovich
    (Marlinsky) 1797-1837 . . . . DLB-198

Bestuzhev, Nikolai Aleksandrovich
    1791-1855 . . . . DLB-198

Betham-Edwards, Matilda Barbara
    (see Edwards, Matilda Barbara Betham-)

Betjeman, John
    1906-1984 . . . . DLB-20; Y-84; CDBLB-7

Betocchi, Carlo 1899-1986 . . . . DLB-128

Bettarini, Mariella 1942- DLB-128

Betts, Doris 1932- DLB-218; Y-82

Beveridge, Albert J. 1862-1927 . . . . DLB-17

Beverley, Robert circa 1673-1722 . . . . DLB-24, 30

Bevilacqua, Alberto 1934- DLB-196

Bevington, Louisa Sarah 1845-1895 . . . . . DLB-199

Beyle, Marie-Henri (see Stendhal)

Białoszewski, Miron 1922-1983 . . . . DLB-232

Bianco, Margery Williams 1881-1944 . . . DLB-160

Bibaud, Adèle 1854-1941 . . . . DLB-92

Bibaud, Michel 1782-1857 . . . . DLB-99

Bibliography
    Bibliographical and Textual Scholarship
        Since World War II Y-89

    Center for Bibliographical Studies and
        Research at the University of
        California, Riverside Y-91

    The Great Bibliographers Series Y-93

    Primary Bibliography: A Retrospective . . Y-95

Bichsel, Peter 1935- DLB-75

Bickerstaff, Isaac John 1733-circa 1808 . . . . DLB-89

Drexel Biddle [publishing house] DLB-49

Bidermann, Jacob
    1577 or 1578-1639 . . . . DLB-164

Bidwell, Walter Hilliard 1798-1881 . . . . . . DLB-79

Biehl, Charlotta Dorothea 1731-1788 . . . . DLB-300

Bienek, Horst 1930-1990 . . . . DLB-75

Bierbaum, Otto Julius 1865-1910 . . . . DLB-66

Bierce, Ambrose 1842-1914?
    . . . . . . DLB-11, 12, 23, 71, 74, 186; CDALB-3

Bigelow, William F. 1879-1966 . . . . DLB-91

Biggers, Earl Derr 1884-1933 . . . . DLB-306

Biggle, Lloyd, Jr. 1923- DLB-8

Bigiaretti, Libero 1905-1993 . . . . DLB-177

Bigland, Eileen 1898-1970 . . . . DLB-195

Biglow, Hosea (see Lowell, James Russell)

Bigongiari, Piero 1914-1997 . . . . DLB-128

Bilac, Olavo 1865-1918 . . . . DLB-307

Bilenchi, Romano 1909-1989 . . . . DLB-264

Billinger, Richard 1890-1965 . . . . DLB-124

Billings, Hammatt 1818-1874 . . . . DLB-188

Billings, John Shaw 1898-1975 . . . . DLB-137

Billings, Josh (see Shaw, Henry Wheeler)

Binding, Rudolf G. 1867-1938 . . . . DLB-66

Bingay, Malcolm 1884-1953 . . . . DLB-241

Bingham, Caleb 1757-1817 . . . . DLB-42

Bingham, George Barry 1906-1988 . . . . . DLB-127

Bingham, Sallie 1937- DLB-234

William Bingley [publishing house] DLB-154

Binyon, Laurence 1869-1943 . . . . DLB-19

Biographia Brittanica DLB-142

Biography
    Biographical Documents Y-84, 85

    A Celebration of Literary Biography Y-98

    Conference on Modern Biography Y-85

    The Cult of Biography
        Excerpts from the Second Folio Debate:
        "Biographies are generally a disease of
        English Literature" Y-86

    New Approaches to Biography: Challenges
        from Critical Theory, USC Conference
        on Literary Studies, 1990 . . . . Y-90

    "The New Biography," by Virginia Woolf,
        New York Herald Tribune,
        30 October 1927 . . . . DLB-149

    "The Practice of Biography," in *The English
        Sense of Humour and Other Essays*, by
        Harold Nicolson DLB-149

    "Principles of Biography," in *Elizabethan
        and Other Essays*, by Sidney Lee . . DLB-149

    Remarks at the Opening of "The Biographical
        Part of Literature" Exhibition, by
        William R. Cagle Y-98

    Survey of Literary Biographies Y-00

    A Transit of Poets and Others: American
        Biography in 1982 . . . . Y-82

    The Year in Literary
        Biography Y-83–01

Biography, The Practice of:
    An Interview with B. L. Reid Y-83

    An Interview with David Herbert Donald . . Y-87

    An Interview with Humphrey Carpenter . . . Y-84

    An Interview with Joan Mellen Y-94

    An Interview with John Caldwell Guilds . . . Y-92

    An Interview with William Manchester . . . Y-85

John Bioren [publishing house] DLB-49

Bioy Casares, Adolfo 1914-1999 . . . . DLB-113

Bird, Isabella Lucy 1831-1904 . . . . DLB-166

Bird, Robert Montgomery 1806-1854 . . . DLB-202

Bird, William 1888-1963 . . . . DLB-4; DS-15

    The Cost of the *Cantos*: William Bird
        to Ezra Pound Y-01

Birken, Sigmund von 1626-1681 . . . . DLB-164

Birney, Earle 1904-1995 . . . . DLB-88

Birrell, Augustine 1850-1933 . . . . DLB-98

Bisher, Furman 1918- DLB-171

Bishop, Elizabeth
    1911-1979 . . . . DLB-5, 169; CDALB-6

    The Elizabeth Bishop Society Y-01

Bishop, John Peale 1892-1944 . . . . . DLB-4, 9, 45

Bismarck, Otto von 1815-1898 . . . . DLB-129

Bisset, Robert 1759-1805 . . . . DLB-142

Bissett, Bill 1939- DLB-53

Bitov, Andrei Georgievich 1937- DLB-302

Bitzius, Albert (see Gotthelf, Jeremias)

Bjørnboe, Jens 1920-1976 . . . . DLB-297

Bjørnvig, Thorkild 1918- DLB-214

Black, David (D. M.) 1941- DLB-40

Black, Gavin (Oswald Morris Wynd)
    1913-1998 . . . . DLB-276

Black, Lionel (Dudley Barker)
    1910-1980 . . . . DLB-276

Black, Winifred 1863-1936 . . . . DLB-25

Walter J. Black [publishing house] DLB-46

Blackamore, Arthur 1679-? DLB-24, 39

Blackburn, Alexander L. 1929- Y-85

Blackburn, John 1923-1993 . . . . DLB-261

Blackburn, Paul 1926-1971 . . . . DLB-16; Y-81

Blackburn, Thomas 1916-1977 . . . . DLB-27

Blacker, Terence 1948- DLB-271

Blackmore, R. D. 1825-1900 . . . . DLB-18

Blackmore, Sir Richard 1654-1729 . . . . . . DLB-131

Blackmur, R. P. 1904-1965 . . . . DLB-63

Blackwell, Alice Stone 1857-1950 . . . . DLB-303

Basil Blackwell, Publisher DLB-106

Blackwood, Algernon Henry
    1869-1951 . . . . DLB-153, 156, 178

Blackwood, Caroline 1931-1996 . . . . DLB-14, 207

William Blackwood and Sons, Ltd. DLB-154

Blackwood's Edinburgh Magazine
    1817-1980 . . . . DLB-110

Blades, William 1824-1890 . . . . DLB-184

Blaga, Lucian 1895-1961 . . . . DLB-220

Blagden, Isabella 1817?-1873 . . . . DLB-199

Blair, Eric Arthur (see Orwell, George)

Blair, Francis Preston 1791-1876 . . . . DLB-43

Blair, Hugh
    Lectures on Rhetoric and Belles Lettres (1783),
        [excerpts] DLB-31

Blair, James circa 1655-1743 . . . . DLB-24

Blair, John Durburrow 1759-1823 . . . . DLB-37

Blais, Marie-Claire 1939- DLB-53

Blaise, Clark 1940- DLB-53

Blake, George 1893-1961 . . . . DLB-191

Blake, Lillie Devereux 1833-1913 . . . . DLB-202, 221

Blake, Nicholas (C. Day Lewis)
    1904-1972 . . . . DLB-77

Blake, William
    1757-1827 . . . . DLB-93, 154, 163; CDBLB-3

The Blakiston Company DLB-49

Blanchard, Stephen 1950- DLB-267

Blanchot, Maurice 1907-2003 . . . . DLB-72, 296

Blanckenburg, Christian Friedrich von
    1744-1796 . . . . DLB-94

Blandiana, Ana 1942- DLB-232; CDWLB-4

Blanshard, Brand 1892-1987 . . . . DLB-279

Blaser, Robin 1925- DLB-165

Blaumanis, Rudolfs 1863-1908 . . . . DLB-220

Bleasdale, Alan 1946- DLB-245

Bledsoe, Albert Taylor 1809-1877 .... DLB-3, 79, 248

Bleecker, Ann Eliza 1752-1783 .... DLB-200

Blelock and Company DLB-49

Blennerhassett, Margaret Agnew 1773-1842 .... DLB-99

Geoffrey Bles [publishing house] DLB-112

Blessington, Marguerite, Countess of 1789-1849 .... DLB-166

Blew, Mary Clearman 1939- DLB-256

Blicher, Steen Steensen 1782-1848 ...... DLB-300

The Blickling Homilies circa 971 .... DLB-146

Blind, Mathilde 1841-1896 .... DLB-199

Blish, James 1921-1975 .... DLB-8

E. Bliss and E. White [publishing house] DLB-49

Bliven, Bruce 1889-1977 .... DLB-137

Blixen, Karen 1885-1962 .... DLB-214

Bloch, Ernst 1885-1977 .... DLB-296

Bloch, Robert 1917-1994 .... DLB-44

    Tribute to John D. MacDonald Y-86

Block, Lawrence 1938- DLB-226

Block, Rudolph (see Lessing, Bruno)

Blok, Aleksandr Aleksandrovich 1880-1921 .... DLB-295

Blondal, Patricia 1926-1959 .... DLB-88

Bloom, Harold 1930- DLB-67

Bloomer, Amelia 1818-1894 .... DLB-79

Bloomfield, Robert 1766-1823 .... DLB-93

Bloomsbury Group DS-10

    The *Dreannought* Hoax DS-10

Bloor, Ella Reeve 1862-1951 .... DLB-303

Blotner, Joseph 1923- DLB-111

Blount, Thomas 1618?-1679 .... DLB-236

Bloy, Léon 1846-1917 .... DLB-123

Blume, Judy 1938- DLB-52

    Tribute to Theodor Seuss Geisel Y-91

Blunck, Hans Friedrich 1888-1961 ..... DLB-66

Blunden, Edmund 1896-1974 ... DLB-20, 100, 155

Blundeville, Thomas 1522?-1606 ...... DLB-236

Blunt, Lady Anne Isabella Noel 1837-1917 .... DLB-174

Blunt, Wilfrid Scawen 1840-1922 ... DLB-19, 174

Bly, Nellie (see Cochrane, Elizabeth)

Bly, Robert 1926- DLB-5

Blyton, Enid 1897-1968 .... DLB-160

Boaden, James 1762-1839 .... DLB-89

Boal, Augusto 1931- DLB-307

Boas, Frederick S. 1862-1957 .... DLB-149

The Bobbs-Merrill Company DLB-46, 291

    The Bobbs-Merrill Archive at the Lilly Library, Indiana University Y-90

Boborykin, Petr Dmitrievich 1836-1921 .... DLB-238

Bobrov, Semen Sergeevich 1763?-1810 .... DLB-150

Bobrowski, Johannes 1917-1965 .... DLB-75

Bocage, Manuel Maria Barbosa du 1765-1805 .... DLB-287

Bodenheim, Maxwell 1892-1954 .... DLB-9, 45

Bodenstedt, Friedrich von 1819-1892 ... DLB-129

Bodini, Vittorio 1914-1970 .... DLB-128

Bodkin, M. McDonnell 1850-1933 ..... DLB-70

Bodley, Sir Thomas 1545-1613 ...... DLB-213

Bodley Head DLB-112

Bodmer, Johann Jakob 1698-1783 ..... DLB-97

Bodmershof, Imma von 1895-1982 .... DLB-85

Bodsworth, Fred 1918- DLB-68

Böðvar Guðmundsson 1939- DLB-293

Boehm, Sydney 1908- DLB-44

Boer, Charles 1939- DLB-5

Boethius circa 480-circa 524 .... DLB-115

Boethius of Dacia circa 1240-? DLB-115

Bogan, Louise 1897-1970 .... DLB-45, 169

Bogarde, Dirk 1921-1999 .... DLB-14

Bogdanov, Aleksandr Aleksandrovich 1873-1928 .... DLB-295

Bogdanovich, Ippolit Fedorovich circa 1743-1803 .... DLB-150

David Bogue [publishing house] DLB-106

Bohjalian, Chris 1960- DLB-292

Böhme, Jakob 1575-1624 .... DLB-164

H. G. Bohn [publishing house] DLB-106

Bohse, August 1661-1742 .... DLB-168

Boie, Heinrich Christian 1744-1806 .... DLB-94

Boileau-Despréaux, Nicolas 1636-1711 ... DLB-268

Bojunga, Lygia 1932- DLB-307

Bok, Edward W. 1863-1930 ...... DLB-91; DS-16

Boland, Eavan 1944- DLB-40

Boldrewood, Rolf (Thomas Alexander Browne) 1826?-1915 .... DLB-230

Bolingbroke, Henry St. John, Viscount 1678-1751 .... DLB-101

Böll, Heinrich 1917-1985 .... DLB-69; Y-85; CDWLB-2

Bolling, Robert 1738-1775 .... DLB-31

Bolotov, Andrei Timofeevich 1738-1833 .... DLB-150

Bolt, Carol 1941- DLB-60

Bolt, Robert 1924-1995 .... DLB-13, 233

Bolton, Herbert E. 1870-1953 .... DLB-17

Bonaventura DLB-90

Bonaventure circa 1217-1274 .... DLB-115

Bonaviri, Giuseppe 1924- DLB-177

Bond, Edward 1934- DLB-13, 310

Bond, Michael 1926- DLB-161

Bondarev, Iurii Vasil'evich 1924- DLB-302

Albert and Charles Boni [publishing house] DLB-46

Boni and Liveright DLB-46

Bonnefoy, Yves 1923- DLB-258

Bonner, Marita 1899-1971 .... DLB-228

Bonner, Paul Hyde 1893-1968 .... DS-17

Bonner, Sherwood (see McDowell, Katharine Sherwood Bonner)

Robert Bonner's Sons DLB-49

Bonnin, Gertrude Simmons (see Zitkala-Ša)

Bonsanti, Alessandro 1904-1984 ...... DLB-177

Bontempelli, Massimo 1878-1960 ..... DLB-264

Bontemps, Arna 1902-1973 .... DLB-48, 51

The Book Buyer (1867-1880, 1884-1918, 1935-1938) DS-13

The Book League of America DLB-46

Book Reviewing
    The American Book Review: A Sketch .. Y-92
    Book Reviewing and the Literary Scene Y-96, 97
    Book Reviewing in America Y-87–94
    Book Reviewing in America and the Literary Scene Y-95
    Book Reviewing in Texas Y-94
    Book Reviews in Glossy Magazines Y-95
    Do They or Don't They? Writers Reading Book Reviews Y-01
    The Most Powerful Book Review in America [*New York Times Book Review*] Y-82
    Some Surprises and Universal Truths ... Y-92
    The Year in Book Reviewing and the Literary Situation Y-98

Book Supply Company DLB-49

The Book Trade History Group Y-93

The Booker Prize Y-96–98
    Address by Anthony Thwaite, Chairman of the Booker Prize Judges Comments from Former Booker Prize Winners Y-86

Boorde, Andrew circa 1490-1549 ...... DLB-136

Boorstin, Daniel J. 1914- DLB-17
    Tribute to Archibald MacLeish Y-82
    Tribute to Charles Scribner Jr. Y-95

Booth, Franklin 1874-1948 .... DLB-188

Booth, Mary L. 1831-1889 .... DLB-79

Booth, Philip 1925- Y-82

Booth, Wayne C. 1921- DLB-67

Booth, William 1829-1912 .... DLB-190

Bor, Josef 1906-1979 .... DLB-299

Borchardt, Rudolf 1877-1945 .... DLB-66

Borchert, Wolfgang 1921-1947 ..... DLB-69, 124

Bording, Anders 1619-1677 .... DLB-300

Borel, Pétrus 1809-1859 .... DLB-119

Borgen, Johan 1902-1979 .... DLB-297

Borges, Jorge Luis 1899-1986 ... DLB-113, 283; Y-86; CDWLB-3
    The Poetry of Jorge Luis Borges Y-86
    A Personal Tribute Y-86

Borgese, Giuseppe Antonio 1882-1952 ... DLB-264

Börne, Ludwig 1786-1837 .... DLB-90

Bornstein, Miriam 1950- DLB-209

Borowski, Tadeusz 1922-1951 .... DLB-215; CDWLB-4

Borrow, George 1803-1881 ...... DLB-21, 55, 166

Bosanquet, Bernard 1848-1923........ DLB-262

Bosch, Juan 1909-2001 .... DLB-145

Bosco, Henri 1888-1976 .... DLB-72

Bosco, Monique 1927- DLB-53

Bosman, Herman Charles 1905-1951.... DLB-225

Bossuet, Jacques-Bénigne 1627-1704...... DLB-268

Bostic, Joe 1908-1988 .... DLB-241

Boston, Lucy M. 1892-1990 .... DLB-161

Boston Quarterly Review DLB-1

Boston University
   Editorial Institute at Boston University ... Y-00
   Special Collections at Boston University .. Y-99

Boswell, James
   1740-1795 .... DLB-104, 142; CDBLB-2

Boswell, Robert 1953- DLB-234

Bosworth, David...................... Y-82
   Excerpt from "Excerpts from a Report of the Commission," in *The Death of Descartes* Y-82

Bote, Hermann circa 1460-circa 1520 ... DLB-179

Botev, Khristo 1847-1876 .... DLB-147

Botkin, Vasilii Petrovich 1811-1869...... DLB-277

Botta, Anne C. Lynch 1815-1891...... DLB-3, 250

Botto, Ján (see Krasko, Ivan)

Bottome, Phyllis 1882-1963 .... DLB-197

Bottomley, Gordon 1874-1948 .... DLB-10

Bottoms, David 1949- DLB-120; Y-83
   Tribute to James Dickey Y-97

Bottrall, Ronald 1906- DLB-20

Bouchardy, Joseph 1810-1870 .... DLB-192

Boucher, Anthony 1911-1968.......... DLB-8

Boucher, Jonathan 1738-1804.......... DLB-31

Boucher de Boucherville, Georges
   1814-1894................... DLB-99

Boudreau, Daniel (see Coste, Donat)

Bouhours, Dominique 1628-1702........ DLB-268

Bourassa, Napoléon 1827-1916........ DLB-99

Bourget, Paul 1852-1935 .... DLB-123

Bourinot, John George 1837-1902...... DLB-99

Bourjaily, Vance 1922- DLB-2, 143

Bourne, Edward Gaylord 1860-1908..... DLB-47

Bourne, Randolph 1886-1918.......... DLB-63

Bousoño, Carlos 1923- DLB-108

Bousquet, Joë 1897-1950.............. DLB-72

Bova, Ben 1932- Y-81

Bovard, Oliver K. 1872-1945 .... DLB-25

Bove, Emmanuel 1898-1945............ DLB-72

Bowen, Elizabeth
   1899-1973......... DLB-15, 162; CDBLB-7

Bowen, Francis 1811-1890 ...... DLB-1, 59, 235

Bowen, John 1924- DLB-13

Bowen, Marjorie 1886-1952.......... DLB-153

Bowen-Merrill Company DLB-49

Bowering, George 1935- DLB-53

Bowers, Bathsheba 1671-1718.......... DLB-200

Bowers, Claude G. 1878-1958 .... DLB-17

Bowers, Edgar 1924-2000.............. DLB-5

Bowers, Fredson Thayer
   1905-1991 .... DLB-140; Y-91
   The Editorial Style of Fredson Bowers ... Y-91
   Fredson Bowers and Studies in Bibliography Y-91
   Fredson Bowers and the Cambridge Beaumont and Fletcher Y-91
   Fredson Bowers as Critic of Renaissance Dramatic Literature............. Y-91
   Fredson Bowers as Music Critic....... Y-91
   Fredson Bowers, Master Teacher Y-91
   An Interview [on Nabokov].......... Y-80
   Working with Fredson Bowers Y-91

Bowles, Paul 1910-1999 ..... DLB-5, 6, 218; Y-99

Bowles, Samuel, III 1826-1878 .... DLB-43

Bowles, William Lisle 1762-1850 ...... DLB-93

Bowman, Louise Morey 1882-1944..... DLB-68

Bowne, Borden Parker 1847-1919......DLB-270

Boyd, James 1888-1944 .... DLB-9; DS-16

Boyd, John 1912-2002 .... DLB-310

Boyd, John 1919- DLB-8

Boyd, Martin 1893-1972.............. DLB-260

Boyd, Thomas 1898-1935 .... DLB-9; DS-16

Boyd, William 1952- DLB-231

Boye, Karin 1900-1941................ DLB-259

Boyesen, Hjalmar Hjorth
   1848-1895 .... DLB-12, 71; DS-13

Boylan, Clare 1948- DLB-267

Boyle, Kay 1902-1992 DLB-4, 9, 48, 86; DS-15;
   .... Y-93

Boyle, Roger, Earl of Orrery 1621-1679... DLB-80

Boyle, T. Coraghessan
   1948- DLB-218, 278; Y-86

Božić, Mirko 1919- DLB-181

Brackenbury, Alison 1953- DLB-40

Brackenridge, Hugh Henry
   1748-1816...................DLB-11, 37
   The Rising Glory of America........ DLB-37

Brackett, Charles 1892-1969.......... DLB-26

Brackett, Leigh 1915-1978 .... DLB-8, 26

John Bradburn [publishing house] DLB-49

Bradbury, Malcolm 1932-2000.......DLB-14, 207

Bradbury, Ray 1920- DLB-2, 8; CDALB-6

Bradbury and Evans................. DLB-106

Braddon, Mary Elizabeth
   1835-1915 .... DLB-18, 70, 156

Bradford, Andrew 1686-1742 ...... DLB-43, 73

Bradford, Gamaliel 1863-1932 .... DLB-17

Bradford, John 1749-1830.............. DLB-43

Bradford, Roark 1896-1948 .... DLB-86

Bradford, William 1590-1657 ...... DLB-24, 30

Bradford, William, III 1719-1791 .... DLB-43, 73

Bradlaugh, Charles 1833-1891........ DLB-57

Bradley, David 1950- DLB-33

Bradley, F. H. 1846-1924 .... DLB-262

Bradley, Katherine Harris (see Field, Michael)

Bradley, Marion Zimmer 1930-1999 ...... DLB-8

Bradley, William Aspenwall 1878-1939 .... DLB-4

Ira Bradley and Company DLB-49

J. W. Bradley and Company DLB-49

Bradshaw, Henry 1831-1886 .... DLB-184

Bradstreet, Anne
   1612 or 1613-1672 .... DLB-24; CDALB-2

Bradūnas, Kazys 1917- DLB-220

Bradwardine, Thomas circa 1295-1349 .. DLB-115

Brady, Frank 1924-1986.............. DLB-111

Frederic A. Brady [publishing house] DLB-49

Braga, Rubem 1913-1990.............. DLB-307

Bragg, Melvyn 1939- DLB-14, 271

Brahe, Tycho 1546-1601 .... DLB-300

Charles H. Brainard [publishing house] ... DLB-49

Braine, John
   1922-1986 .... DLB-15; Y-86; CDBLB-7

Braithwait, Richard 1588-1673........ DLB-151

Braithwaite, William Stanley
   1878-1962................. DLB-50, 54

Bräker, Ulrich 1735-1798 .... DLB-94

Bramah, Ernest 1868-1942............ DLB-70

Branagan, Thomas 1774-1843 .... DLB-37

Brancati, Vitaliano 1907-1954......... DLB-264

Branch, William Blackwell 1927- DLB-76

Brand, Christianna 1907-1988 ....DLB-276

Brand, Max (see Faust, Frederick Schiller)

Brandão, Raul 1867-1930 .... DLB-287

Branden Press.................... DLB-46

Brandes, Georg 1842-1927 .... DLB-300

Branner, H.C. 1903-1966 .... DLB-214

Brant, Sebastian 1457-1521..............DLB-179

Brassey, Lady Annie (Allnutt)
   1839-1887 .... DLB-166

Brathwaite, Edward Kamau
   1930- DLB-125; CDWLB-3

Brault, Jacques 1933- DLB-53

Braun, Matt 1932- DLB-212

Braun, Volker 1939- DLB-75, 124

Brautigan, Richard
   1935-1984 ....DLB-2, 5, 206; Y-80, 84

Braxton, Joanne M. 1950- DLB-41

Bray, Anne Eliza 1790-1883 .... DLB-116

Bray, Thomas 1656-1730 .... DLB-24

Brazdžionis, Bernardas 1907- DLB-220

George Braziller [publishing house] DLB-46

The Bread Loaf Writers' Conference 1983 ... Y-84

Breasted, James Henry 1865-1935 ...... DLB-47

Brecht, Bertolt
   1898-1956 ....DLB-56, 124; CDWLB-2

Bredel, Willi 1901-1964 .... DLB-56

Bregendahl, Marie 1867-1940........ DLB-214

Breitinger, Johann Jakob 1701-1776 ...... DLB-97

Brekke, Paal 1923-1993 .... DLB-297

Bremser, Bonnie 1939- DLB-16

Bremser, Ray 1934-1998 .... DLB-16

Brennan, Christopher 1870-1932........DLB-230
Brentano, Bernard von 1901-1964........DLB-56
Brentano, Clemens 1778-1842...........DLB-90
Brentano, Franz 1838-1917............DLB-296
Brentano's..........................DLB-49
Brenton, Howard 1942-................DLB-13
Breslin, Jimmy 1929-1996............DLB-185
Breton, André 1896-1966........DLB-65, 258
Breton, Nicholas circa 1555-circa 1626...DLB-136
The Breton Lays
    1300-early fifteenth century........DLB-146
Brett, Simon 1945-..................DLB-276
Brewer, Gil 1922-1983...............DLB-306
Brewer, Luther A. 1858-1933.........DLB-187
Brewer, Warren and Putnam...........DLB-46
Brewster, Elizabeth 1922-............DLB-60
Breytenbach, Breyten 1939-..........DLB-225
Bridge, Ann (Lady Mary Dolling Sanders
    O'Malley) 1889-1974..............DLB-191
Bridge, Horatio 1806-1893...........DLB-183
Bridgers, Sue Ellen 1942-............DLB-52
Bridges, Robert
    1844-1930............DLB-19, 98; CDBLB-5
The Bridgewater Library.............DLB-213
Bridie, James 1888-1951..............DLB-10
Brieux, Eugene 1858-1932............DLB-192
Brigadere, Anna
    1861-1933............DLB-220; CDWLB-4
Briggs, Charles Frederick
    1804-1877........................DLB-3, 250
Brighouse, Harold 1882-1958..........DLB-10
Bright, Mary Chavelita Dunne
    (see Egerton, George)
Brightman, Edgar Sheffield 1884-1953...DLB-270
B. J. Brimmer Company................DLB-46
Brines, Francisco 1932-..............DLB-134
Brink, André 1935-..................DLB-225
Brinley, George, Jr. 1817-1875.......DLB-140
Brinnin, John Malcolm 1916-1998......DLB-48
Brisbane, Albert 1809-1890........DLB-3, 250
Brisbane, Arthur 1864-1936...........DLB-25
British Academy......................DLB-112
The British Critic 1793-1843.......DLB-110
British Library
    The American Trust for the
        British Library.................Y-96
    The British Library and the Regular
        Readers' Group..................Y-91
    Building the New British Library
        at St Pancras...................Y-94
British Literary Prizes..........DLB-207; Y-98
British Literature
    The "Angry Young Men"............DLB-15
    Author-Printers, 1476-1599.......DLB-167
    The Comic Tradition Continued....DLB-15
    Documents on Sixteenth-Century
        Literature..................DLB-167, 172
    Eikon Basilike 1649..............DLB-151

Letter from London....................Y-96
A Mirror for Magistrates...........DLB-167
"Modern English Prose" (1876),
    by George Saintsbury..............DLB-57
Sex, Class, Politics, and Religion [in the
    British Novel, 1930-1959].........DLB-15
Victorians on Rhetoric and Prose
    Style............................DLB-57
The Year in British Fiction.........Y-99–01
"You've Never Had It So Good," Gusted
    by "Winds of Change": British
    Fiction in the 1950s, 1960s,
    and After.........................DLB-14
British Literature, Old and Middle English
Anglo-Norman Literature in the
    Development of Middle English
    Literature.......................DLB-146
The *Alliterative Morte Arthure* and the
    Stanzaic Morte Arthur
    circa 1350-1400..................DLB-146
Ancrene Riwle circa 1200-1225......DLB-146
The Anglo-Saxon Chronicle circa
    890-1154........................DLB-146
The Battle of Maldon circa 1000....DLB-146
Beowulf circa 900-1000 or
    790-825...............DLB-146; CDBLB-1
The Blickling Homilies circa 971....DLB-146
The Breton Lays
    1300-early fifteenth century.....DLB-146
The Castle of Perseverance
    circa 1400-1425..................DLB-146
The Celtic Background to Medieval
    English Literature...............DLB-146
The Chester Plays circa 1505-1532;
    revisions until 1575.............DLB-146
Cursor Mundi circa 1300............DLB-146
The English Language: 410
    to 1500..........................DLB-146
The Germanic Epic and Old English
    Heroic Poetry: *Widsith, Waldere*,
    and *The Fight at Finnsburg*.....DLB-146
Judith circa 930...................DLB-146
The Matter of England 1240-1400.....DLB-146
The Matter of Rome early twelfth to
    late fifteenth centuries.........DLB-146
Middle English Literature:
    An Introduction..................DLB-146
The Middle English Lyric............DLB-146
Morality Plays: *Mankind* circa 1450-1500
    and *Everyman* circa 1500........DLB-146
N-Town Plays circa 1468 to early
    sixteenth century................DLB-146
Old English Literature:
    An Introduction..................DLB-146
Old English Riddles
    eighth to tenth centuries........DLB-146
The Owl and the Nightingale
    circa 1189-1199..................DLB-146
The Paston Letters 1422-1509.......DLB-146
The Seafarer circa 970.............DLB-146
The *South English Legendary* circa
    thirteenth to fifteenth centuries....DLB-146
*The British Review and London Critical
    Journal* 1811-1825...............DLB-110

Brito, Aristeo 1942-.................DLB-122
Brittain, Vera 1893-1970.............DLB-191
Briusov, Valerii Iakovlevich
    1873-1924........................DLB-295
Brizeux, Auguste 1803-1858...........DLB-217
Broadway Publishing Company..........DLB-46
Broch, Hermann
    1886-1951..........DLB-85, 124; CDWLB-2
Brochu, André 1942-..................DLB-53
Brock, Edwin 1927-1997................DLB-40
Brockes, Barthold Heinrich 1680-1747...DLB-168
Brod, Max 1884-1968..................DLB-81
Brodber, Erna 1940-.................DLB-157
Brodhead, John R. 1814-1873..........DLB-30
Brodkey, Harold 1930-1996...........DLB-130
Brodsky, Joseph (Iosif Aleksandrovich
    Brodsky) 1940-1996........DLB-285; Y-87
    Nobel Lecture 1987................Y-87
Brodsky, Michael 1948-..............DLB-244
Broeg, Bob 1918-....................DLB-171
Brøgger, Suzanne 1944-..............DLB-214
Brome, Richard circa 1590-1652.......DLB-58
Brome, Vincent 1910-................DLB-155
Bromfield, Louis 1896-1956.......DLB-4, 9, 86
Bromige, David 1933-................DLB-193
Broner, E. M. 1930-.................DLB-28
    Tribute to Bernard Malamud........Y-86
Bronk, William 1918-1999............DLB-165
Bronnen, Arnolt 1895-1959...........DLB-124
Brontë, Anne 1820-1849.........DLB-21, 199
Brontë, Charlotte
    1816-1855........DLB-21, 159, 199; CDBLB-4
Brontë, Emily
    1818-1848........DLB-21, 32, 199; CDBLB-4
The Brontë Society....................Y-98
Brook, Stephen 1947-................DLB-204
Brook Farm 1841-1847..........DLB-1; 223; DS-5
Brooke, Frances 1724-1789.........DLB-39, 99
Brooke, Henry 1703?-1783.............DLB-39
Brooke, L. Leslie 1862-1940.........DLB-141
Brooke, Margaret, Ranee of Sarawak
    1849-1936........................DLB-174
Brooke, Rupert
    1887-1915...........DLB-19, 216; CDBLB-6
    The Friends of the Dymock Poets...Y-00
Brooker, Bertram 1888-1955...........DLB-88
Brooke-Rose, Christine 1923-.....DLB-14, 231
Brookner, Anita 1928-.........DLB-194; Y-87
Brooks, Charles Timothy 1813-1883...DLB-1, 243
Brooks, Cleanth 1906-1994........DLB-63; Y-94
    Tribute to Katherine Anne Porter...Y-80
    Tribute to Walker Percy...........Y-90
Brooks, Gwendolyn
    1917-2000.........DLB-5, 76, 165; CDALB-1
    Tribute to Julian Mayfield........Y-84
Brooks, Jeremy 1926-................DLB-14
Brooks, Mel 1926-..................DLB-26

Brooks, Noah 1830-1903 . . . . DLB-42; DS-13

Brooks, Richard 1912-1992 . . . . DLB-44

Brooks, Van Wyck 1886-1963 . . . DLB-45, 63, 103

Brophy, Brigid 1929-1995 . . . . DLB-14, 70, 271

Brophy, John 1899-1965. . . . . DLB-191

Brorson, Hans Adolph 1694-1764 . . . . . . DLB-300

Brossard, Chandler 1922-1993 . . . . DLB-16

Brossard, Nicole 1943- DLB-53

Broster, Dorothy Kathleen 1877-1950 . . . . DLB-160

Brother Antoninus (see Everson, William)

Brotherton, Lord 1856-1930 . . . . DLB-184

Brougham, John 1810-1880 . . . . DLB-11

Brougham and Vaux, Henry Peter Brougham, Baron 1778-1868 . . . DLB-110, 158

Broughton, James 1913-1999 . . . . DLB-5

Broughton, Rhoda 1840-1920 . . . . DLB-18

Broun, Heywood 1888-1939 . . . . DLB-29, 171

Browder, Earl 1891-1973 . . . . DLB-303

Brown, Alice 1856-1948 . . . . DLB-78

Brown, Bob 1886-1959 . . . . DLB-4, 45; DS-15

Brown, Cecil 1943- DLB-33

Brown, Charles Brockden 1771-1810 . . . . DLB-37, 59, 73; CDALB-2

Brown, Christy 1932-1981 . . . . DLB-14

Brown, Dee 1908-2002 . . . . Y-80

Brown, Frank London 1927-1962 . . . . DLB-76

Brown, Fredric 1906-1972 . . . . DLB-8

Brown, George Mackay 1921-1996 . . . . DLB-14, 27, 139, 271

Brown, Harry 1917-1986 . . . . DLB-26

Brown, Ian 1945- DLB-310

Brown, Larry 1951- DLB-234, 292

Brown, Lew 1893-1958 . . . . DLB-265

Brown, Marcia 1918- DLB-61

Brown, Margaret Wise 1910-1952 . . . . DLB-22

Brown, Morna Doris (see Ferrars, Elizabeth)

Brown, Oliver Madox 1855-1874 . . . . DLB-21

Brown, Sterling 1901-1989 . . . . . . DLB-48, 51, 63

Brown, T. E. 1830-1897 . . . . DLB-35

Brown, Thomas Alexander (see Boldrewood, Rolf)

Brown, Warren 1894-1978 . . . . DLB-241

Brown, William Hill 1765-1793 . . . . DLB-37

Brown, William Wells 1815-1884 . . . . DLB-3, 50, 183, 248

Brown University The Festival of Vanguard Narrative Y-93

Browne, Charles Farrar 1834-1867 . . . . DLB-11

Browne, Frances 1816-1879 . . . . DLB-199

Browne, Francis Fisher 1843-1913 . . . . DLB-79

Browne, Howard 1908-1999 . . . . DLB-226

Browne, J. Ross 1821-1875 . . . . DLB-202

Browne, Michael Dennis 1940- DLB-40

Browne, Sir Thomas 1605-1682 . . . . DLB-151

Browne, William, of Tavistock 1590-1645 . . . . DLB-121

Browne, Wynyard 1911-1964 . . . . . . DLB-13, 233

Browne and Nolan DLB-106

Brownell, W. C. 1851-1928 . . . . DLB-71

Browning, Elizabeth Barrett 1806-1861 . . . . DLB-32, 199; CDBLB-4

Browning, Robert 1812-1889 . . . . DLB-32, 163; CDBLB-4

Essay on Chatterton DLB-32

Introductory Essay: *Letters of Percy Bysshe Shelley* (1852) DLB-32

"The Novel in [Robert Browning's] 'The Ring and the Book'" (1912), by Henry James DLB-32

Brownjohn, Allan 1931- DLB-40

Tribute to John Betjeman Y-84

Brownson, Orestes Augustus 1803-1876 . . . . DLB-1, 59, 73, 243; DS-5

Bruccoli, Matthew J. 1931- DLB-103

Joseph [Heller] and George [V. Higgins] . . . Y-99

Response [to Busch on Fitzgerald] Y-96

Tribute to Albert Erskine Y-93

Tribute to Charles E. Feinberg Y-88

Working with Fredson Bowers Y-91

Bruce, Charles 1906-1971 . . . . DLB-68

Bruce, John Edward 1856-1924

Three Documents [African American poets] DLB-50

Bruce, Leo 1903-1979 . . . . DLB-77

Bruce, Mary Grant 1878-1958 . . . . DLB-230

Bruce, Philip Alexander 1856-1933 . . . . . . DLB-47

Bruce-Novoa, Juan 1944- DLB-82

Bruckman, Clyde 1894-1955 . . . . DLB-26

Bruckner, Ferdinand 1891-1958 . . . . DLB-118

Brundage, John Herbert (see Herbert, John)

Brunner, John 1934-1995 . . . . DLB-261

Tribute to Theodore Sturgeon Y-85

Brutus, Dennis 1924- DLB-117, 225; CDWLB-3

Bryan, C. D. B. 1936- DLB-185

Bryan, William Jennings 1860-1925 . . . . . DLB-303

Bryant, Arthur 1899-1985 . . . . DLB-149

Bryant, William Cullen 1794-1878 . . . . DLB-3, 43, 59, 189, 250; CDALB-2

Bryce, James 1838-1922 . . . . DLB-166, 190

Bryce Echenique, Alfredo 1939- DLB-145; CDWLB-3

Bryden, Bill 1942- DLB-233

Brydges, Sir Samuel Egerton 1762-1837 . . . . DLB-107, 142

Bryskett, Lodowick 1546?-1612 . . . . DLB-167

Buchan, John 1875-1940 . . . . DLB-34, 70, 156

Buchanan, George 1506-1582 . . . . DLB-132

Buchanan, Robert 1841-1901 . . . . DLB-18, 35

"The Fleshly School of Poetry and Other Phenomena of the Day" (1872) DLB-35

"The Fleshly School of Poetry: Mr. D. G. Rossetti" (1871), by Thomas Maitland DLB-35

Buchler, Justus 1914-1991 . . . . DLB-279

Buchman, Sidney 1902-1975 . . . . DLB-26

Buchner, Augustus 1591-1661 . . . . DLB-164

Büchner, Georg 1813-1837 . . . . DLB-133; CDWLB-2

Bucholtz, Andreas Heinrich 1607-1671 . . . . DLB-168

Buck, Pearl S. 1892-1973 . . DLB-9, 102; CDALB-7

Bucke, Charles 1781-1846 . . . . DLB-110

Bucke, Richard Maurice 1837-1902 . . . . . . DLB-99

Buckingham, Edwin 1810-1833 . . . . DLB-73

Buckingham, Joseph Tinker 1779-1861 . . . DLB-73

Buckler, Ernest 1908-1984 . . . . DLB-68

Buckley, Vincent 1925-1988 . . . . DLB-289

Buckley, William F., Jr. 1925- DLB-137; Y-80

Publisher's Statement From the Initial Issue of *National Review* (19 November 1955) DLB-137

Buckminster, Joseph Stevens 1784-1812 . . . . DLB-37

Buckner, Robert 1906- DLB-26

Budd, Thomas ?-1698 . . . . DLB-24

Budrys, A. J. 1931- DLB-8

Buechner, Frederick 1926- Y-80

Buell, John 1927- DLB-53

Buenaventura, Enrique 1925-2003 . . . . . . DLB-305

Bufalino, Gesualdo 1920-1996 . . . . DLB-196

Job Buffum [publishing house] DLB-49

Bugnet, Georges 1879-1981 . . . . DLB-92

Buies, Arthur 1840-1901 . . . . DLB-99

Bukiet, Melvin Jules 1953- DLB-299

Bukowski, Charles 1920-1994 . . . . DLB-5, 130, 169

Bulatović, Miodrag 1930-1991 . . . . DLB-181; CDWLB-4

Bulgakov, Mikhail Afanas'evich 1891-1940 . . . . DLB-272

Bulgarin, Faddei Venediktovich 1789-1859 . . . . DLB-198

Bulger, Bozeman 1877-1932 . . . . DLB-171

Bull, Olaf 1883-1933 . . . . DLB-297

Bullein, William between 1520 and 1530-1576 . . . . DLB-167

Bullins, Ed 1935- DLB-7, 38, 249

Bulwer, John 1606-1656 . . . . DLB-236

Bulwer-Lytton, Edward (also Edward Bulwer) 1803-1873 . . . . DLB-21

"On Art in Fiction" (1838) DLB-21

Bumpus, Jerry 1937- Y-81

Bunce and Brother DLB-49

Bunner, H. C. 1855-1896 . . . . DLB-78, 79

Bunting, Basil 1900-1985 . . . . DLB-20

Buntline, Ned (Edward Zane Carroll Judson) 1821-1886 . . . . DLB-186

Bunyan, John 1628-1688 . . . . . DLB-39; CDBLB-2

The Author's Apology for His Book DLB-39

Burch, Robert 1925- DLB-52

Burciaga, José Antonio 1940- DLB-82

Burdekin, Katharine (Murray Constantine) 1896-1963 . . . . DLB-255

Bürger, Gottfried August 1747-1794.......DLB-94

Burgess, Anthony (John Anthony Burgess Wilson) 1917-1993 ......DLB-14, 194, 261; CDBLB-8

   The Anthony Burgess Archive at the Harry Ransom Humanities Research Center................Y-98

   Anthony Burgess's *99 Novels*: An Opinion Poll.................Y-84

Burgess, Gelett 1866-1951................DLB-11

Burgess, John W. 1844-1931..............DLB-47

Burgess, Thornton W. 1874-1965..........DLB-22

Burgess, Stringer and Company...........DLB-49

Burgos, Julia de 1914-1953..............DLB-290

Burick, Si 1909-1986...................DLB-171

Burk, John Daly circa 1772-1808.........DLB-37

Burk, Ronnie 1955-.....................DLB-209

Burke, Edmund 1729?-1797........DLB-104, 252

Burke, James Lee 1936-.................DLB-226

Burke, Johnny 1908-1964................DLB-265

Burke, Kenneth 1897-1993..........DLB-45, 63

Burke, Thomas 1886-1945................DLB-197

Burley, Dan 1907-1962..................DLB-241

Burley, W. J. 1914-....................DLB-276

Burlingame, Edward Livermore 1848-1922................DLB-79

Burman, Carina 1960-...................DLB-257

Burnet, Gilbert 1643-1715...............DLB-101

Burnett, Frances Hodgson 1849-1924..........DLB-42, 141; DS-13, 14

Burnett, W. R. 1899-1982...........DLB-9, 226

Burnett, Whit 1899-1973................DLB-137

Burney, Fanny 1752-1840.................DLB-39

   Dedication, *The Wanderer* (1814)......DLB-39

   Preface to *Evelina* (1778).............DLB-39

Burns, Alan 1929-.................DLB-14, 194

Burns, Joanne 1945-....................DLB-289

Burns, John Horne 1916-1953..............Y-85

Burns, Robert 1759-1796......DLB-109; CDBLB-3

Burns and Oates........................DLB-106

Burnshaw, Stanley 1906-.........DLB-48; Y-97

   James Dickey and Stanley Burnshaw Correspondence.................Y-02

   Review of Stanley Burnshaw: The Collected Poems and Selected Prose..........................Y-02

   Tribute to Robert Penn Warren........Y-89

Burr, C. Chauncey 1815?-1883............DLB-79

Burr, Esther Edwards 1732-1758.........DLB-200

Burroughs, Edgar Rice 1875-1950..........DLB-8

   The Burroughs Bibliophiles.............Y-98

Burroughs, John 1837-1921..........DLB-64, 275

Burroughs, Margaret T. G. 1917-........DLB-41

Burroughs, William S., Jr. 1947-1981.....DLB-16

Burroughs, William Seward 1914-1997
..........DLB-2, 8, 16, 152, 237; Y-81, 97

Burroway, Janet 1936-...................DLB-6

Burt, Maxwell Struthers 1882-1954................DLB-86; DS-16

A. L. Burt and Company.................DLB-49

Burton, Hester 1913-...................DLB-161

Burton, Isabel Arundell 1831-1896......DLB-166

Burton, Miles (see Rhode, John)

Burton, Richard Francis 1821-1890..............DLB-55, 166, 184

Burton, Robert 1577-1640...............DLB-151

Burton, Virginia Lee 1909-1968..........DLB-22

Burton, William Evans 1804-1860........DLB-73

Burwell, Adam Hood 1790-1849..........DLB-99

Bury, Lady Charlotte 1775-1861........DLB-116

Busch, Frederick 1941-..............DLB-6, 218

   Excerpts from Frederick Busch's USC Remarks [on F. Scott Fitzgerald].....Y-96

   Tribute to James Laughlin..............Y-97

   Tribute to Raymond Carver............Y-88

Busch, Niven 1903-1991.................DLB-44

Bushnell, Horace 1802-1876..............DS-13

Business & Literature
   The Claims of Business and Literature: An Undergraduate Essay by Maxwell Perkins..................Y-01

Bussières, Arthur de 1877-1913...........DLB-92

Butler, Charles circa 1560-1647.........DLB-236

Butler, Guy 1918-......................DLB-225

Butler, Joseph 1692-1752................DLB-252

Butler, Josephine Elizabeth 1828-1906................DLB-190

Butler, Juan 1942-1981..................DLB-53

Butler, Judith 1956-...................DLB-246

Butler, Octavia E. 1947-................DLB-33

Butler, Pierce 1884-1953...............DLB-187

Butler, Robert Olen 1945-..............DLB-173

Butler, Samuel 1613-1680.........DLB-101, 126

Butler, Samuel 1835-1902.......DLB-18, 57, 174; CDBLB-5

Butler, William Francis 1838-1910......DLB-166

E. H. Butler and Company..............DLB-49

Butor, Michel 1926-....................DLB-83

Nathaniel Butter [publishing house].....DLB-170

Butterworth, Hezekiah 1839-1905........DLB-42

Buttitta, Ignazio 1899-1997............DLB-114

Butts, Mary 1890-1937..................DLB-240

Buzo, Alex 1944-......................DLB-289

Buzzati, Dino 1906-1972................DLB-177

Byars, Betsy 1928-.....................DLB-52

Byatt, A. S. 1936-................DLB-14, 194

Byles, Mather 1707-1788................DLB-24

Henry Bynneman [publishing house].....DLB-170

Bynner, Witter 1881-1968................DLB-54

Byrd, William circa 1543-1623..........DLB-172

Byrd, William, II 1674-1744........DLB-24, 140

Byrne, John Keyes (see Leonard, Hugh)

Byron, George Gordon, Lord 1788-1824.........DLB-96, 110; CDBLB-3

   The Byron Society of America..........Y-00

Byron, Robert 1905-1941...............DLB-195

C

Caballero Bonald, José Manuel 1926-.........................DLB-108

Cabañero, Eladio 1930-.................DLB-134

Cabell, James Branch 1879-1958......DLB-9, 78

Cabeza de Baca, Manuel 1853-1915.....DLB-122

Cabeza de Baca Gilbert, Fabiola 1898-.........................DLB-122

Cable, George Washington 1844-1925...............DLB-12, 74; DS-13

Cable, Mildred 1878-1952...............DLB-195

Cabral, Manuel del 1907-1999..........DLB-283

Cabral de Melo Neto, João 1920-1999........................DLB-307

Cabrera, Lydia 1900-1991...............DLB-145

Cabrera Infante, Guillermo 1929-..............DLB-113; CDWLB-3

Cabrujas, José Ignacio 1937-1995.......DLB-305

Cadell [publishing house]..............DLB-154

Cady, Edwin H. 1917-...................DLB-103

Caedmon flourished 658-680.............DLB-146

Caedmon School circa 660-899..........DLB-146

Caesar, Irving 1895-1996...............DLB-265

Cafés, Brasseries, and Bistros..........DS-15

Cage, John 1912-1992..................DLB-193

Cahan, Abraham 1860-1951.......DLB-9, 25, 28

Cahn, Sammy 1913-1993................DLB-265

Cain, George 1943-.....................DLB-33

Cain, James M. 1892-1977..............DLB-226

Cain, Paul (Peter Ruric, George Sims) 1902-1966......................DLB-306

Caird, Edward 1835-1908...............DLB-262

Caird, Mona 1854-1932.................DLB-197

Čaks, Aleksandrs 1901-1950...............DLB-220; CDWLB-4

Caldecott, Randolph 1846-1886.........DLB-163

John Calder Limited [Publishing house]................DLB-112

Calderón de la Barca, Fanny 1804-1882....................DLB-183

Caldwell, Ben 1937-....................DLB-38

Caldwell, Erskine 1903-1987.........DLB-9, 86

H. M. Caldwell Company................DLB-49

Caldwell, Taylor 1900-1985..............DS-17

Calhoun, John C. 1782-1850........DLB-3, 248

Călinescu, George 1899-1965...........DLB-220

Calisher, Hortense 1911-.............DLB-2, 218

Calkins, Mary Whiton 1863-1930.......DLB-270

Callaghan, Mary Rose 1944-............DLB-207

Callaghan, Morley 1903-1990......DLB-68; DS-15

Callahan, S. Alice 1868-1894........DLB-175, 221

Callaloo [journal]........................Y-87

Callimachus circa 305 B.C.-240 B.C......DLB-176

Calmer, Edgar 1907-.....................DLB-4

Calverley, C. S. 1831-1884..............DLB-35

Cumulative Index

Calvert, George Henry
 1803-1889 .... DLB-1, 64, 248
Calverton, V. F. (George Goetz)
 1900-1940. .... DLB-303
Calvino, Italo 1923-1985 .... DLB-196
Cambridge, Ada 1844-1926 .... DLB-230
Cambridge Press. DLB-49
Cambridge Songs (Carmina Cantabrigensia)
 circa 1050. .... DLB-148
Cambridge University
 Cambridge and the Apostles DS-5
Cambridge University Press. DLB-170
Camden, William 1551-1623 .... DLB-172
Camden House: An Interview with
 James Hardin Y-92
Cameron, Eleanor 1912-2000 .... DLB-52
Cameron, George Frederick
 1854-1885 .... DLB-99
Cameron, Lucy Lyttelton 1781-1858 ... DLB-163
Cameron, Peter 1959- DLB-234
Cameron, William Bleasdell 1862-1951 ... DLB-99
Camm, John 1718-1778 .... DLB-31
Camões, Luís de 1524-1580 .... DLB-287
Camon, Ferdinando 1935- DLB-196
Camp, Walter 1859-1925 .... DLB-241
Campana, Dino 1885-1932 .... DLB-114
Campbell, Bebe Moore 1950- DLB-227
Campbell, David 1915-1979 .... DLB-260
Campbell, Gabrielle Margaret Vere
 (see Shearing, Joseph, and Bowen, Marjorie)
Campbell, James Dykes 1838-1895 ..... DLB-144
Campbell, James Edwin 1867-1896. ...... DLB-50
Campbell, John 1653-1728 .... DLB-43
Campbell, John W., Jr. 1910-1971 .... DLB-8
Campbell, Ramsey 1946- DLB-261
Campbell, Robert 1927-2000 .... DLB-306
Campbell, Roy 1901-1957 .... DLB-20, 225
Campbell, Thomas 1777-1844. ...... DLB-93, 144
Campbell, William Edward (see March, William)
Campbell, William Wilfred 1858-1918. ... DLB-92
Campion, Edmund 1539-1581 .... DLB-167
Campion, Thomas
 1567-1620. .... DLB-58, 172; CDBLB-1
Campo, Rafael 1964- DLB-282
Campton, David 1924- DLB-245
Camus, Albert 1913-1960 .... DLB-72
Camus, Jean-Pierre 1584-1652 .... DLB-268
The Canadian Publishers' Records Database .. Y-96
Canby, Henry Seidel 1878-1961 .... DLB-91
Cancioneros DLB-286
Candelaria, Cordelia 1943- DLB-82
Candelaria, Nash 1928- DLB-82
Canetti, Elias
 1905-1994 ...... DLB-85, 124; CDWLB-2
Canham, Erwin Dain 1904-1982 .... DLB-127
Canitz, Friedrich Rudolph Ludwig von
 1654-1699 .... DLB-168

Cankar, Ivan 1876-1918 ..... DLB-147; CDWLB-4
Cannan, Gilbert 1884-1955 .... DLB-10, 197
Cannan, Joanna 1896-1961 .... DLB-191
Cannell, Kathleen 1891-1974 .... DLB-4
Cannell, Skipwith 1887-1957 .... DLB-45
Canning, George 1770-1827 .... DLB-158
Cannon, Jimmy 1910-1973 .... DLB-171
Cano, Daniel 1947- DLB-209
 Old Dogs / New Tricks? New
 Technologies, the Canon, and the
 Structure of the Profession Y-02
Cantú, Norma Elia 1947- DLB-209
Cantwell, Robert 1908-1978 .... DLB-9
Jonathan Cape and Harrison Smith
 [publishing house] DLB-46
Jonathan Cape Limited. DLB-112
Čapek, Karel 1890-1938 .... DLB-215; CDWLB-4
Capen, Joseph 1658-1725 .... DLB-24
Capes, Bernard 1854-1918 .... DLB-156
Capote, Truman 1924-1984
 .... DLB-2, 185, 227; Y-80, 84; CDALB-1
Capps, Benjamin 1922- DLB-256
Caproni, Giorgio 1912-1990 .... DLB-128
Caragiale, Mateiu Ioan 1885-1936 ..... DLB-220
Carballido, Emilio 1925- DLB-305
Cardarelli, Vincenzo 1887-1959 .... DLB-114
Cardenal, Ernesto 1925- DLB-290
Cárdenas, Reyes 1948- DLB-122
Cardinal, Marie 1929-2001. .... DLB-83
Cardoza y Aragón, Luis 1901-1992 ..... DLB-290
Carew, Jan 1920- DLB-157
Carew, Thomas 1594 or 1595-1640 .... DLB-126
Carey, Henry circa 1687-1689-1743 ...... DLB-84
Carey, Mathew 1760-1839 .... DLB-37, 73
M. Carey and Company DLB-49
Carey, Peter 1943- DLB-289
Carey and Hart DLB-49
Carlell, Lodowick 1602-1675 .... DLB-58
Carleton, William 1794-1869 .... DLB-159
G. W. Carleton [publishing house]. DLB-49
Carlile, Richard 1790-1843 .... DLB-110, 158
Carlson, Ron 1947- DLB-244
Carlyle, Jane Welsh 1801-1866 .... DLB-55
Carlyle, Thomas
 1795-1881 .... DLB-55, 144; CDBLB-3
 "The Hero as Man of Letters:
 Johnson, Rousseau, Burns"
 (1841) [excerpt] DLB-57
 The Hero as Poet. Dante; Shakspeare
 (1841) DLB-32
Carman, Bliss 1861-1929 .... DLB-92
Carmina Burana circa 1230 .... DLB-138
Carnap, Rudolf 1891-1970 .... DLB-270
Carnero, Guillermo 1947- DLB-108
Carossa, Hans 1878-1956 .... DLB-66
Carpenter, Humphrey
 1946- DLB-155; Y-84, 99

Carpenter, Stephen Cullen ?-1820? DLB-73
Carpentier, Alejo
 1904-1980 .... DLB-113; CDWLB-3
Carr, Emily (1871-1945) DLB-68
Carr, John Dickson 1906-1977 .... DLB-306
Carr, Marina 1964- DLB-245
Carr, Virginia Spencer 1929- DLB-111; Y-00
Carrera Andrade, Jorge 1903-1978. ..... DLB-283
Carrier, Roch 1937- DLB-53
Carrillo, Adolfo 1855-1926. .... DLB-122
Carroll, Gladys Hasty 1904- DLB-9
Carroll, John 1735-1815 .... DLB-37
Carroll, John 1809-1884 .... DLB-99
Carroll, Lewis
 1832-1898 .... DLB-18, 163, 178; CDBLB-4
 The Lewis Carroll Centenary Y-98
 The Lewis Carroll Society
 of North America Y-00
Carroll, Paul 1927- DLB-16
Carroll, Paul Vincent 1900-1968 .... DLB-10
Carroll and Graf Publishers DLB-46
Carruth, Hayden 1921- DLB-5, 165
 Tribute to James Dickey Y-97
 Tribute to Raymond Carver Y-88
Carryl, Charles E. 1841-1920. .... DLB-42
Carson, Anne 1950- DLB-193
Carson, Rachel 1907-1964 .... DLB-275
Carswell, Catherine 1879-1946. .... DLB-36
Cartagena, Alfonso de ca. 1384-1456 .... DLB-286
Cartagena, Teresa de 1425?-? DLB-286
Cărtărescu, Mirea 1956- DLB-232
Carter, Angela 1940-1992 ...... DLB-14, 207, 261
Carter, Elizabeth 1717-1806 .... DLB-109
Carter, Henry (see Leslie, Frank)
Carter, Hodding, Jr. 1907-1972 .... DLB-127
Carter, Jared 1939- DLB-282
Carter, John 1905-1975 .... DLB-201
Carter, Landon 1710-1778 .... DLB-31
Carter, Lin 1930-1988 .... Y-81
Carter, Martin 1927-1997 .... DLB-117; CDWLB-3
Carter, Robert, and Brothers DLB-49
Carter and Hendee DLB-49
Cartwright, Jim 1958- DLB-245
Cartwright, John 1740-1824 .... DLB-158
Cartwright, William circa 1611-1643 .... DLB-126
Caruthers, William Alexander
 1802-1846 .... DLB-3, 248
Carver, Jonathan 1710-1780 .... DLB-31
Carver, Raymond 1938-1988 ... DLB-130; Y-83, 88
 First Strauss "Livings" Awarded to Cynthia
 Ozick and Raymond Carver
 An Interview with Raymond Carver ... Y-83
Carvic, Heron 1917?-1980 .... DLB-276
Cary, Alice 1820-1871 .... DLB-202
Cary, Joyce 1888-1957 ... DLB-15, 100; CDBLB-6
Cary, Patrick 1623?-1657 .... DLB-131

388

Casal, Julián del 1863-1893 . . . . DLB-283	Cela, Camilo José 1916-2002. . . . . Y-89	Chandler, Otis 1927- DLB-127
Case, John 1540-1600 . . . . DLB-281	Nobel Lecture 1989. . . . . Y-89	Chandler, Raymond 1888-1959 . . . . DLB-226, 253; DS-6; CDALB-5
Casey, Gavin 1907-1964 . . . . DLB-260	Celan, Paul 1920-1970 . . . . DLB-69; CDWLB-2	Raymond Chandler Centenary. Y-88
Casey, Juanita 1925- DLB-14	Celati, Gianni 1937- DLB-196	Channing, Edward 1856-1931. . . . . DLB-17
Casey, Michael 1947- DLB-5	Celaya, Gabriel 1911-1991 . . . . DLB-108	Channing, Edward Tyrrell 1790-1856 . . . . DLB-1, 59, 235
Cassady, Carolyn 1923- DLB-16	Céline, Louis-Ferdinand 1894-1961. . . . . . . DLB-72	
"As I See It". DLB-16	Celtis, Conrad 1459-1508 . . . . DLB-179	Channing, William Ellery 1780-1842 . . . . DLB-1, 59, 235
Cassady, Neal 1926-1968 . . . . DLB-16, 237	Cendrars, Blaise 1887-1961 . . . . DLB-258	Channing, William Ellery, II 1817-1901 . . . . DLB-1, 223
Cassell and Company DLB-106	The Steinbeck Centennial Y-02	
Cassell Publishing Company DLB-49	Censorship The Island Trees Case: A Symposium on School Library Censorship. Y-82	Channing, William Henry 1810-1884 . . . . DLB-1, 59, 243
Cassill, R. V. 1919- DLB-6, 218; Y-02		Chapelain, Jean 1595-1674 . . . . DLB-268
Tribute to James Dickey Y-97	Center for Bibliographical Studies and Research at the University of California, Riverside Y-91	Chaplin, Charlie 1889-1977 . . . . DLB-44
Cassity, Turner 1929- DLB-105; Y-02		Chapman, George 1559 or 1560-1634 . . . . DLB-62, 121
Cassius Dio circa 155/164-post 229 . . . . . . DLB-176	Center for Book Research Y-84	
Cassola, Carlo 1917-1987. . . . . DLB-177	The Center for the Book in the Library of Congress Y-93	Chapman, Olive Murray 1892-1977 . . . . . DLB-195
Castellano, Olivia 1944- DLB-122		Chapman, R. W. 1881-1960 . . . . DLB-201
Castellanos, Rosario 1925-1974 . . . . DLB-113, 290; CDWLB-3	A New Voice: The Center for the Book's First Five Years Y-83	Chapman, William 1850-1917 . . . . DLB-99
	Centlivre, Susanna 1669?-1723 . . . . DLB-84	John Chapman [publishing house]. DLB-106
Castelo Branco, Camilo 1825-1890 . . . . . . DLB-287	The Centre for Writing, Publishing and Printing History at the University of Reading. Y-00	Chapman and Hall [publishing house] . . . DLB-106
Castile, Protest Poetry in DLB-286		Chappell, Fred 1936- DLB-6, 105
Castile and Aragon, Vernacular Translations in Crowns of 1352-1515 . . . . DLB-286		"A Detail in a Poem". DLB-105
	The Century Company. DLB-49	Tribute to Peter Taylor. Y-94
Castillo, Ana 1953- DLB-122, 227	A Century of Poetry, a Lifetime of Collecting: J. M. Edelstein's Collection of Twentieth-Century American Poetry Y-02	Chappell, William 1582-1649 . . . . DLB-236
Castillo, Rafael C. 1950- DLB-209		Char, René 1907-1988 . . . . DLB-258
The Castle of Perserverance circa 1400-1425. . . . . DLB-146	Cernuda, Luis 1902-1963 . . . . DLB-134	Charbonneau, Jean 1875-1960. . . . . DLB-92
	Cerruto, Oscar 1912-1981 . . . . DLB-283	Charbonneau, Robert 1911-1967 . . . . DLB-68
Castlemon, Harry (see Fosdick, Charles Austin)	Cervantes, Lorna Dee 1954- DLB-82	Charles, Gerda 1914- DLB-14
Castro, Consuelo de 1946- DLB-307	de Céspedes, Alba 1911-1997 . . . . DLB-264	William Charles [publishing house]. DLB-49
Castro Alves, Antônio de 1847-1871 . . . . . DLB-307	Ch., T. (see Marchenko, Anastasiia Iakovlevna)	Charles d'Orléans 1394-1465 . . . . DLB-208
Čašule, Kole 1921- DLB-181	Chaadaev, Petr Iakovlevich 1794-1856 . . . . DLB-198	Charley (see Mann, Charles)
Caswall, Edward 1814-1878. . . . . DLB-32		Charskaia, Lidiia 1875-1937. . . . . DLB-295
Catacalos, Rosemary 1944- DLB-122	Chabon, Michael 1963- DLB-278	Charteris, Leslie 1907-1993 . . . . DLB-77
Cather, Willa 1873-1947 . . . . DLB-9, 54, 78, 256; DS-1; CDALB-3	Chacel, Rosa 1898-1994 . . . . DLB-134	Chartier, Alain circa 1385-1430. . . . . DLB-208
	Chacón, Eusebio 1869-1948 . . . . DLB-82	Charyn, Jerome 1937- Y-83
The Willa Cather Pioneer Memorial and Education Foundation Y-00	Chacón, Felipe Maximiliano 1873-?. DLB-82	Chase, Borden 1900-1971 . . . . DLB-26
	Chadwick, Henry 1824-1908. . . . . DLB-241	Chase, Edna Woolman 1877-1957 . . . . DLB-91
Catherine II (Ekaterina Alekseevna), "The Great," Empress of Russia 1729-1796 . . . DLB-150	Chadwyck-Healey's Full-Text Literary Databases: Editing Commercial Databases of Primary Literary Texts Y-95	Chase, James Hadley (René Raymond) 1906-1985 . . . . DLB-276
Catherwood, Mary Hartwell 1847-1902 . . . DLB-78		
Catledge, Turner 1901-1983 . . . . DLB-127		Chase, Mary Coyle 1907-1981 . . . . DLB-228
Catlin, George 1796-1872. . . . . . . DLB-186, 189	Challans, Eileen Mary (see Renault, Mary)	Chase-Riboud, Barbara 1936- DLB-33
Cato the Elder 234 B.C.-149 B.C. DLB-211	Chalmers, George 1742-1825. . . . . DLB-30	Chateaubriand, François-René de 1768-1848 . . . . DLB-119
Cattafi, Bartolo 1922-1979 . . . . DLB-128	Chaloner, Sir Thomas 1520-1565 . . . . DLB-167	
Catton, Bruce 1899-1978 . . . . DLB-17	Chamberlain, Samuel S. 1851-1916. . . . . . . DLB-25	Chatterton, Thomas 1752-1770 . . . . DLB-109
Catullus circa 84 B.C.-54 B.C. DLB-211; CDWLB-1	Chamberland, Paul 1939- DLB-60	Essay on Chatterton (1842), by Robert Browning DLB-32
	Chamberlin, William Henry 1897-1969. . . . DLB-29	
Causley, Charles 1917- DLB-27	Chambers, Charles Haddon 1860-1921 . . . DLB-10	Chatto and Windus. DLB-106
Caute, David 1936- DLB-14, 231	Chambers, María Cristina (see Mena, María Cristina)	Chatwin, Bruce 1940-1989 . . . . DLB-194, 204
Cavendish, Duchess of Newcastle, Margaret Lucas 1623?-1673 . . . . DLB-131, 252, 281	Chambers, Robert W. 1865-1933 . . . . DLB-202	Chaucer, Geoffrey 1340?-1400 . . . . DLB-146; CDBLB-1
	W. and R. Chambers [publishing house] DLB-106	
Cawein, Madison 1865-1914. . . . . DLB-54		New Chaucer Society Y-00
William Caxton [publishing house] DLB-170	Chambers, Whittaker 1901-1961 . . . . DLB-303	Chaudhuri, Amit 1962- DLB-267
The Caxton Printers, Limited DLB-46	Chamisso, Adelbert von 1781-1838. . . . . . . DLB-90	Chauncy, Charles 1705-1787 . . . . DLB-24
Caylor, O. P. 1849-1897 . . . . DLB-241	Champfleury 1821-1889 . . . . DLB-119	Chauveau, Pierre-Joseph-Olivier 1820-1890 . . . . DLB-99
Cayrol, Jean 1911- DLB-83	Chandler, Harry 1864-1944 . . . . DLB-29	
Cecil, Lord David 1902-1986 . . . . DLB-155	Chandler, Norman 1899-1973 . . . . DLB-127	Chávez, Denise 1948- DLB-122

Cumulative Index

DLB 310

Chávez, Fray Angélico 1910-1996 . . . . DLB-82
Chayefsky, Paddy 1923-1981 . . . . . DLB-7, 44; Y-81
Cheesman, Evelyn 1881-1969 . . . . DLB-195
Cheever, Ezekiel 1615-1708 . . . . DLB-24
Cheever, George Barrell 1807-1890 . . . . . . DLB-59
Cheever, John 1912-1982
. . . . .DLB-2, 102, 227; Y-80, 82; CDALB-1
Cheever, Susan 1943- Y-82
Cheke, Sir John 1514-1557 . . . . DLB-132
Chekhov, Anton Pavlovich 1860-1904. . . .DLB-277
Chelsea House DLB-46
Chênedollé, Charles de 1769-1833 . . . . . . DLB-217
Cheney, Brainard
    Tribute to Caroline Gordon Y-81
Cheney, Ednah Dow 1824-1904 . . . . . DLB-1, 223
Cheney, Harriet Vaughan 1796-1889. . . . . DLB-99
Chénier, Marie-Joseph 1764-1811. . . . . . . DLB-192
Chernyshevsky, Nikolai Gavrilovich
    1828-1889 . . . . DLB-238
Cherry, Kelly 1940. Y-83
Cherryh, C. J. 1942- Y-80
Chesebro', Caroline 1825-1873 . . . . DLB-202
Chesney, Sir George Tomkyns
    1830-1895 . . . . DLB-190
Chesnut, Mary Boykin 1823-1886 . . . . . . DLB-239
Chesnutt, Charles Waddell
    1858-1932 . . . . .DLB-12, 50, 78
Chesson, Mrs. Nora (see Hopper, Nora)
Chester, Alfred 1928-1971 . . . . DLB-130
Chester, George Randolph 1869-1924 . . . DLB-78
The Chester Plays circa 1505-1532;
    revisions until 1575 . . . . DLB-146
Chesterfield, Philip Dormer Stanhope,
    Fourth Earl of 1694-1773 . . . . DLB-104
Chesterton, G. K. 1874-1936
    . . .DLB-10, 19, 34, 70, 98, 149, 178; CDBLB-6
    "The Ethics of Elfland" (1908). DLB-178
Chettle, Henry
    circa 1560-circa 1607 . . . . DLB-136
Cheuse, Alan 1940- DLB-244
Chew, Ada Nield 1870-1945. . . . . DLB-135
Cheyney, Edward P. 1861-1947 . . . . DLB-47
Chiara, Piero 1913-1986. . . . . .DLB-177
Chicanos
    Chicano History. DLB-82
    Chicano Language. DLB-82
    Chicano Literature: A Bibliography . . .DLB-209
    A Contemporary Flourescence of Chicano
        Literature. Y-84
    Literatura Chicanesca: The View From
        Without. DLB-82
Child, Francis James 1825-1896 . . . DLB-1, 64, 235
Child, Lydia Maria 1802-1880 . . . . DLB-1, 74, 243
Child, Philip 1898-1978 . . . . DLB-68
Childers, Erskine 1870-1922 . . . . DLB-70
Children's Literature
    Afterword: Propaganda, Namby-Pamby,
        and Some Books of Distinction . . . DLB-52
    Children's Book Awards and Prizes. . . DLB-61

Children's Book Illustration in the
    Twentieth Century DLB-61
Children's Illustrators, 1800-1880 . . . DLB-163
The Harry Potter Phenomenon. Y-99
    Pony Stories, Omnibus
        Essay on DLB-160
The Reality of One Woman's Dream:
    The de Grummond Children's
    Literature Collection Y-99
School Stories, 1914-1960 . . . . DLB-160
The Year in Children's
    Books. Y-92–96, 98–01
The Year in Children's Literature Y-97
Childress, Alice 1916-1994 . . . . .DLB-7, 38, 249
Childress, Mark 1957- DLB-292
Childs, George W. 1829-1894 . . . . DLB-23
Chilton Book Company DLB-46
Chin, Frank 1940- DLB-206
Chinweizu 1943- DLB-157
Chitham, Edward 1932- DLB-155
Chittenden, Hiram Martin 1858-1917 . . . . DLB-47
Chivers, Thomas Holley 1809-1858 . . DLB-3, 248
Chkhartishvili, Grigorii Shalvovich
    (see Akunin, Boris)
Chocano, José Santos 1875-1934 . . . . DLB-290
Cholmondeley, Mary 1859-1925 . . . . DLB-197
Chomsky, Noam 1928- DLB-246
Chopin, Kate 1850-1904. . . DLB-12, 78; CDALB-3
Chopin, René 1885-1953 . . . . DLB-92
Choquette, Adrienne 1915-1973 . . . . DLB-68
Choquette, Robert 1905-1991 . . . . DLB-68
Choyce, Lesley 1951- DLB-251
Chrétien de Troyes
    circa 1140-circa 1190 . . . . DLB-208
Christensen, Inger 1935- DLB-214
Christensen, Lars Saabye 1953- DLB-297
The Christian Examiner DLB-1
The Christian Publishing Company DLB-49
Christie, Agatha
    1890-1976. . . . . . . .DLB-13, 77, 245; CDBLB-6
Christine de Pizan
    circa 1365-circa 1431 . . . . DLB-208
Christopher, John (Sam Youd) 1922- . . DLB-255
Christus und die Samariterin circa 950. . . . . . DLB-148
Christy, Howard Chandler 1873-1952 . . . DLB-188
Chukovskaia, Lidiia 1907-1996 . . . . DLB-302
Chulkov, Mikhail Dmitrievich
    1743?-1792 . . . . DLB-150
Church, Benjamin 1734-1778 . . . . DLB-31
Church, Francis Pharcellus 1839-1906 . . . . DLB-79
Church, Peggy Pond 1903-1986. . . . . DLB-212
Church, Richard 1893-1972 . . . . DLB-191
Church, William Conant 1836-1917 . . . . . DLB-79
Churchill, Caryl 1938- DLB-13, 310
Churchill, Charles 1731-1764 . . . . DLB-109
Churchill, Winston 1871-1947 . . . . DLB-202
Churchill, Sir Winston
    1874-1965. . . . . . . DLB-100; DS-16; CDBLB-5

Churchyard, Thomas 1520?-1604 . . . . . . DLB-132
E. Churton and Company DLB-106
Chute, Marchette 1909-1994 . . . . DLB-103
Ciardi, John 1916-1986 . . . . .DLB-5; Y-86
Cibber, Colley 1671-1757 . . . . DLB-84
Cicero 106 B.C.-43 B.C. DLB-211, CDWLB-1
Cima, Annalisa 1941- DLB-128
Čingo, Živko 1935-1987. . . . . DLB-181
Cioran, E. M. 1911-1995 . . . . DLB-220
Čipkus, Alfonsas (see Nyka-Niliūnas, Alfonsas)
Cirese, Eugenio 1884-1955. . . . . DLB-114
Cīrulis, Jānis (see Bels, Alberts)
Cisneros, Antonio 1942- DLB-290
Cisneros, Sandra 1954- DLB-122, 152
City Lights Books. DLB-46
Civil War (1861–1865)
    Battles and Leaders of the Civil War. . . DLB-47
    Official Records of the Rebellion DLB-47
    Recording the Civil War DLB-47
Cixous, Hélène 1937- DLB-83, 242
Clampitt, Amy 1920-1994 . . . . DLB-105
    Tribute to Alfred A. Knopf Y-84
Clancy, Tom 1947- DLB-227
Clapper, Raymond 1892-1944 . . . . DLB-29
Clare, John 1793-1864 . . . . DLB-55, 96
Clarendon, Edward Hyde, Earl of
    1609-1674 . . . . DLB-101
Clark, Alfred Alexander Gordon
    (see Hare, Cyril)
Clark, Ann Nolan 1896- DLB-52
Clark, C. E. Frazer, Jr. 1925-2001 . . DLB-187; Y-01
    C. E. Frazer Clark Jr. and
        Hawthorne Bibliography. DLB-269
    The Publications of C. E. Frazer
        Clark Jr.. . . . . DLB-269
Clark, Catherine Anthony 1892-1977 . . . . DLB-68
Clark, Charles Heber 1841-1915 . . . . DLB-11
Clark, Davis Wasgatt 1812-1871 . . . . DLB-79
Clark, Douglas 1919-1993 . . . . .DLB-276
Clark, Eleanor 1913- DLB-6
Clark, J. P. 1935- DLB-117; CDWLB-3
Clark, Lewis Gaylord
    1808-1873 . . . . .DLB-3, 64, 73, 250
Clark, Mary Higgins 1929- DLB-306
Clark, Walter Van Tilburg
    1909-1971 . . . . DLB-9, 206
Clark, William 1770-1838 . . . . DLB-183, 186
Clark, William Andrews, Jr.
    1877-1934 .DLB-187
C. M. Clark Publishing Company DLB-46
Clarke, Sir Arthur C. 1917- DLB-261
    Tribute to Theodore Sturgeon. Y-85
Clarke, Austin 1896-1974 . . . . DLB-10, 20
Clarke, Austin C. 1934- DLB-53, 125
Clarke, Gillian 1937- DLB-40
Clarke, James Freeman
    1810-1888 . . . . DLB-1, 59, 235; DS-5

Clarke, John circa 1596-1658..........DLB-281
Clarke, Lindsay 1939- DLB-231
Clarke, Marcus 1846-1881............DLB-230
Clarke, Pauline 1921- DLB-161
Clarke, Rebecca Sophia 1833-1906.......DLB-42
Clarke, Samuel 1675-1729............DLB-252
Robert Clarke and Company DLB-49
Clarkson, Thomas 1760-1846..........DLB-158
Claudel, Paul 1868-1955..........DLB-192, 258
Claudius, Matthias 1740-1815..........DLB-97
Clausen, Andy 1943- DLB-16
Claussen, Sophus 1865-1931..........DLB-300
Clawson, John L. 1865-1933..........DLB-187
Claxton, Remsen and Haffelfinger DLB-49
Clay, Cassius Marcellus 1810-1903.......DLB-43
Clayton, Richard (see Haggard, William)
Cleage, Pearl 1948- DLB-228
Cleary, Beverly 1916- DLB-52
Cleary, Kate McPhelim 1863-1905 .....DLB-221
Cleaver, Vera 1919-1992 and
  Cleaver, Bill 1920-1981............DLB-52
Cleeve, Brian 1921- DLB-276
Cleland, John 1710-1789.............DLB-39
Clemens, Samuel Langhorne (Mark Twain)
  1835-1910 ....DLB-11, 12, 23, 64, 74,
                         186, 189; CDALB-3
  Comments From Authors and Scholars on
    their First Reading of *Huck Finn*.....Y-85
  Huck at 100: How Old Is
    Huckleberry Finn? Y-85
  Mark Twain on Perpetual Copyright Y-92
  A New Edition of *Huck Finn* Y-85
Clement, Hal 1922- DLB-8
Clemo, Jack 1916- DLB-27
Clephane, Elizabeth Cecilia 1830-1869...DLB-199
Cleveland, John 1613-1658 ....DLB-126
Cliff, Michelle 1946- DLB-157; CDWLB-3
Clifford, Lady Anne 1590-1676.........DLB-151
Clifford, James L. 1901-1978 ....DLB-103
Clifford, Lucy 1853?-1929.....DLB-135, 141, 197
Clift, Charmian 1923-1969 ....DLB-260
Clifton, Lucille 1936- DLB-5, 41
Clines, Francis X. 1938- DLB-185
Clive, Caroline (V) 1801-1873..........DLB-199
Edward J. Clode [publishing house].......DLB-46
Clough, Arthur Hugh 1819-1861 ....DLB-32
Cloutier, Cécile 1930- DLB-60
Clouts, Sidney 1926-1982 ....DLB-225
Clutton-Brock, Arthur 1868-1924 ....DLB-98
Coates, Robert M.
  1897-1973............DLB-4, 9, 102; DS-15
Coatsworth, Elizabeth 1893-1986 ....DLB-22
Cobb, Charles E., Jr. 1943- DLB-41
Cobb, Frank I. 1869-1923 ....DLB-25
Cobb, Irvin S. 1876-1944......DLB-11, 25, 86
Cobbe, Frances Power 1822-1904.......DLB-190

Cobbett, William 1763-1835 .... DLB-43, 107, 158
Cobbledick, Gordon 1898-1969 .... DLB-171
Cochran, Thomas C. 1902- DLB-17
Cochrane, Elizabeth 1867-1922 ......DLB-25, 189
Cockerell, Sir Sydney 1867-1962 ....DLB-201
Cockerill, John A. 1845-1896...........DLB-23
Cocteau, Jean 1889-1963...........DLB-65, 258
Coderre, Emile (see Jean Narrache)
Cody, Liza 1944- DLB-276
Coe, Jonathan 1961- DLB-231
Coetzee, J. M. 1940- DLB-225
Coffee, Lenore J. 1900?-1984............DLB-44
Coffin, Robert P. Tristram 1892-1955....DLB-45
Coghill, Mrs. Harry (see Walker, Anna Louisa)
Cogswell, Fred 1917- DLB-60
Cogswell, Mason Fitch 1761-1830........DLB-37
Cohan, George M. 1878-1942.......... DLB-249
Cohen, Arthur A. 1928-1986...........DLB-28
Cohen, Leonard 1934- DLB-53
Cohen, Matt 1942- DLB-53
Cohen, Morris Raphael 1880-1947 ..... DLB-270
Colasanti, Marina 1937- DLB-307
Colbeck, Norman 1903-1987...........DLB-201
Colden, Cadwallader
  1688-1776 .... DLB-24, 30, 270
Colden, Jane 1724-1766 .... DLB-200
Cole, Barry 1936- DLB-14
Cole, George Watson 1850-1939 ....DLB-140
Colegate, Isabel 1931- DLB-14, 231
Coleman, Emily Holmes 1899-1974 ....DLB-4
Coleman, Wanda 1946- DLB-130
Coleridge, Hartley 1796-1849 ....DLB-96
Coleridge, Mary 1861-1907.........DLB-19, 98
Coleridge, Samuel Taylor
  1772-1834 .... DLB-93, 107; CDBLB-3
Coleridge, Sara 1802-1852............DLB-199
Colet, John 1467-1519 .... DLB-132
Colette 1873-1954 .... DLB-65
Colette, Sidonie Gabrielle (see Colette)
Colinas, Antonio 1946- DLB-134
Coll, Joseph Clement 1881-1921........DLB-188
A Century of Poetry, a Lifetime of Collecting:
  J. M. Edelstein's Collection of
  Twentieth-Century American Poetry Y-02
Collier, John 1901-1980............ DLB-77, 255
Collier, John Payne 1789-1883.........DLB-184
Collier, Mary 1690-1762 ....DLB-95
Collier, Robert J. 1876-1918...........DLB-91
P. F. Collier [publishing house] DLB-49
Collin and Small DLB-49
Collingwood, R. G. 1889-1943 .... DLB-262
Collingwood, W. G. 1854-1932.........DLB-149
Collins, An floruit circa 1653..........DLB-131
Collins, Anthony 1676-1729 ....DLB-252
Collins, Merle 1950- DLB-157

Collins, Michael 1964- DLB-267
Collins, Michael (see Lynds, Dennis)
Collins, Mortimer 1827-1876.........DLB-21, 35
Collins, Tom (see Furphy, Joseph)
Collins, Wilkie
  1824-1889........DLB-18, 70, 159; CDBLB-4
  "The Unknown Public" (1858)
    [excerpt] DLB-57
  The Wilkie Collins Society Y-98
Collins, William 1721-1759 ....DLB-109
Isaac Collins [publishing house]..........DLB-49
William Collins, Sons and Company DLB-154
Collis, Maurice 1889-1973.............DLB-195
Collyer, Mary 1716?-1763?............DLB-39
Colman, Benjamin 1673-1747 ....DLB-24
Colman, George, the Elder 1732-1794.....DLB-89
Colman, George, the Younger
  1762-1836 .... DLB-89
S. Colman [publishing house] DLB-49
Colombo, John Robert 1936- DLB-53
Colonial Literature DLB-307
Colquhoun, Patrick 1745-1820 ....DLB-158
Colter, Cyrus 1910-2002 ....DLB-33
Colum, Padraic 1881-1972............DLB-19
The Columbia History of the American Novel
  A Symposium on...................Y-92
Columella fl. first century A.D...........DLB-211
Colvin, Sir Sidney 1845-1927 ....DLB-149
Colwin, Laurie 1944-1992........ DLB-218; Y-80
Comden, Betty 1915- and
  Green, Adolph 1918- DLB-44, 265
Comi, Girolamo 1890-1968............DLB-114
Comisso, Giovanni 1895-1969 ....DLB-264
Commager, Henry Steele 1902-1998......DLB-17
Commynes, Philippe de
  circa 1447-1511 ....DLB-208
Compton, D. G. 1930- DLB-261
Compton-Burnett, Ivy 1884?-1969........DLB-36
Conan, Laure (Félicité Angers)
  1845-1924 .... DLB-99
Concord, Massachusetts
  Concord History and Life...........DLB-223
  Concord: Literary History
    of a Town....................DLB-223
  The Old Manse, by Hawthorne DLB-223
  The Thoreauvian Pilgrimage: The
    Structure of an American Cult ... DLB-223
Concrete Poetry...................DLB-307
Conde, Carmen 1901-1996 ....DLB-108
Congreve, William
  1670-1729 ....DLB-39, 84; CDBLB-2
  Preface to *Incognita* (1692) DLB-39
W. B. Conkey Company...............DLB-49
Conn, Stewart 1936- DLB-233
Connell, Evan S., Jr. 1924- DLB-2; Y-81
Connelly, Marc 1890-1980 .... DLB-7; Y-80
Connolly, Cyril 1903-1974 ....DLB-98
Connolly, James B. 1868-1957...........DLB-78

Cumulative Index   DLB 310

Connor, Ralph (Charles William Gordon) 1860-1937 .... DLB-92

Connor, Tony 1930- DLB-40

Conquest, Robert 1917- DLB-27

Conrad, Joseph 1857-1924 .... DLB-10, 34, 98, 156; CDBLB-5

John Conrad and Company DLB-49

Conroy, Jack 1899-1990 .... Y-81

    A Tribute [to Nelson Algren] Y-81

Conroy, Pat 1945- DLB-6

Considine, Bob 1906-1975 .... DLB-241

Consolo, Vincenzo 1933- DLB-196

Constable, Henry 1562-1613 .... DLB-136

Archibald Constable and Company DLB-154

Constable and Company Limited DLB-112

Constant, Benjamin 1767-1830 .... DLB-119

Constant de Rebecque, Henri-Benjamin de (see Constant, Benjamin)

Constantine, David 1944- DLB-40

Constantine, Murray (see Burdekin, Katharine)

Constantin-Weyer, Maurice 1881-1964 ... DLB-92

Contempo (magazine)
    Contempo Caravan: Kites in a Windstorm Y-85

The Continental Publishing Company DLB-49

A Conversation between William Riggan and Janette Turner Hospital Y-02

Conversations with Editors Y-95

Conway, Anne 1631-1679 .... DLB-252

Conway, Moncure Daniel 1832-1907 .... DLB-1, 223

Cook, Ebenezer circa 1667-circa 1732 .... DLB-24

Cook, Edward Tyas 1857-1919 .... DLB-149

Cook, Eliza 1818-1889 .... DLB-199

Cook, George Cram 1873-1924 .... DLB-266

Cook, Michael 1933-1994 .... DLB-53

David C. Cook Publishing Company DLB-49

Cooke, George Willis 1848-1923 .... DLB-71

Cooke, John Esten 1830-1886 .... DLB-3, 248

Cooke, Philip Pendleton 1816-1850 .... DLB-3, 59, 248

Cooke, Rose Terry 1827-1892 .... DLB-12, 74

Increase Cooke and Company DLB-49

Cook-Lynn, Elizabeth 1930- DLB-175

Coolbrith, Ina 1841-1928 .... DLB-54, 186

Cooley, Peter 1940- DLB-105

    "Into the Mirror" DLB-105

Coolidge, Clark 1939- DLB-193

Coolidge, Susan (see Woolsey, Sarah Chauncy)

George Coolidge [publishing house] DLB-49

Cooper, Anna Julia 1858-1964 .... DLB-221

Cooper, Edith Emma 1862-1913 .... DLB-240

Cooper, Giles 1918-1966 .... DLB-13

Cooper, J. California 19??- DLB-212

Cooper, James Fenimore 1789-1851 .... DLB-3, 183, 250; CDALB-2

The Bicentennial of James Fenimore Cooper: An International Celebration Y-89

The James Fenimore Cooper Society Y-01

Cooper, Kent 1880-1965 .... DLB-29

Cooper, Susan 1935- DLB-161, 261

Cooper, Susan Fenimore 1813-1894 ..... DLB-239

William Cooper [publishing house] DLB-170

J. Coote [publishing house] DLB-154

Coover, Robert 1932- DLB-2, 227; Y-81

    Tribute to Donald Barthelme Y-89

    Tribute to Theodor Seuss Geisel Y-91

Copeland and Day DLB-49

Ćopić, Branko 1915-1984 .... DLB-181

Copland, Robert 1470?-1548 .... DLB-136

Coppard, A. E. 1878-1957 .... DLB-162

Coppée, François 1842-1908 .... DLB-217

Coppel, Alfred 1921- Y-83

    Tribute to Jessamyn West Y-84

Coppola, Francis Ford 1939- DLB-44

Copway, George (Kah-ge-ga-gah-bowh) 1818-1869 .... DLB-175, 183

Copyright
    The Development of the Author's Copyright in Britain DLB-154

    The Digital Millennium Copyright Act: Expanding Copyright Protection in Cyberspace and Beyond Y-98

    Editorial: The Extension of Copyright ... Y-02

    Mark Twain on Perpetual Copyright Y-92

    Public Domain and the Violation of Texts Y-97

    The Question of American Copyright in the Nineteenth Century
    Preface, by George Haven Putnam
    The Evolution of Copyright, by Brander Matthews
    Summary of Copyright Legislation in the United States, by R. R. Bowker
    Analysis of the Provisions of the Copyright Law of 1891, by George Haven Putnam
    The Contest for International Copyright, by George Haven Putnam
    Cheap Books and Good Books, by Brander Matthews DLB-49

    Writers and Their Copyright Holders: the WATCH Project Y-94

Corazzini, Sergio 1886-1907 .... DLB-114

Corbett, Richard 1582-1635 .... DLB-121

Corbière, Tristan 1845-1875 .... DLB-217

Corcoran, Barbara 1911- DLB-52

Cordelli, Franco 1943- DLB-196

Corelli, Marie 1855-1924 .... DLB-34, 156

Corle, Edwin 1906-1956 .... Y-85

Corman, Cid 1924- DLB-5, 193

Cormier, Robert 1925-2000 ... DLB-52; CDALB-6

    Tribute to Theodor Seuss Geisel Y-91

Corn, Alfred 1943- DLB-120, 282; Y-80

Corneille, Pierre 1606-1684 .... DLB-268

Cornford, Frances 1886-1960 .... DLB-240

Cornish, Sam 1935- DLB-41

Cornish, William circa 1465-circa 1524 .... DLB-132

Cornwall, Barry (see Procter, Bryan Waller)

Cornwallis, Sir William, the Younger circa 1579-1614 .... DLB-151

Cornwell, David John Moore (see le Carré, John)

Cornwell, Patricia 1956- DLB-306

Coronel Urtecho, José 1906-1994 ...... DLB-290

Corpi, Lucha 1945- DLB-82

Corrington, John William 1932-1988 .... DLB-6, 244

Corriveau, Monique 1927-1976 .... DLB-251

Corrothers, James D. 1869-1917 .... DLB-50

Corso, Gregory 1930-2001 .... DLB-5, 16, 237

Cortázar, Julio 1914-1984 .... DLB-113; CDWLB-3

Cortéz, Carlos 1923- DLB-209

Cortez, Jayne 1936- DLB-41

Corvinus, Gottlieb Siegmund 1677-1746 .... DLB-168

Corvo, Baron (see Rolfe, Frederick William)

Cory, Annie Sophie (see Cross, Victoria)

Cory, Desmond (Shaun Lloyd McCarthy) 1928- DLB-276

Cory, William Johnson 1823-1892 ...... DLB-35

Coryate, Thomas 1577?-1617 .... DLB-151, 172

Ćosić, Dobrica 1921- DLB-181; CDWLB-4

Cosin, John 1595-1672 .... DLB-151, 213

Cosmopolitan Book Corporation DLB-46

Cossa, Roberto 1934- DLB-305

Costa, Maria Velho da (see The Three Marias: A Landmark Case in Portuguese Literary History)

Costain, Thomas B. 1885-1965 .... DLB-9

Coste, Donat (Daniel Boudreau) 1912-1957 .... DLB-88

Costello, Louisa Stuart 1799-1870 ...... DLB-166

Cota-Cárdenas, Margarita 1941- DLB-122

Côté, Denis 1954- DLB-251

Cotten, Bruce 1873-1954 .... DLB-187

Cotter, Joseph Seamon, Jr. 1895-1919 .... DLB-50

Cotter, Joseph Seamon, Sr. 1861-1949 .... DLB-50

Joseph Cottle [publishing house] DLB-154

Cotton, Charles 1630-1687 .... DLB-131

Cotton, John 1584-1652 .... DLB-24

Cotton, Sir Robert Bruce 1571-1631 ..... DLB-213

Coulter, John 1888-1980 .... DLB-68

Cournos, John 1881-1966 .... DLB-54

Courteline, Georges 1858-1929 .... DLB-192

Cousins, Margaret 1905-1996 .... DLB-137

Cousins, Norman 1915-1990 .... DLB-137

Couvreur, Jessie (see Tasma)

Coventry, Francis 1725-1754 .... DLB-39

    Dedication, *The History of Pompey the Little* (1751) DLB-39

Coverdale, Miles 1487 or 1488-1569 .... DLB-167

N. Coverly [publishing house] DLB-49

Covici-Friede DLB-46

Cowan, Peter 1914-2002 . . . . .DLB-260

Coward, Noel
  1899-1973 . . . . DLB-10, 245; CDBLB-6

Coward, McCann and Geoghegan DLB-46

Cowles, Gardner 1861-1946 . . . . .DLB-29

Cowles, Gardner "Mike", Jr.
  1903-1985 . . . . DLB-127, 137

Cowley, Abraham 1618-1667 . . . . .DLB-131, 151

Cowley, Hannah 1743-1809 . . . . .DLB-89

Cowley, Malcolm
  1898-1989 . . . . DLB-4, 48; DS-15; Y-81, 89

Cowper, Richard (John Middleton Murry Jr.)
  1926-2002 .DLB-261

Cowper, William 1731-1800 . . . . . . .DLB-104, 109

Cox, A. B. (see Berkeley, Anthony)

Cox, James McMahon 1903-1974 . . . . . . .DLB-127

Cox, James Middleton 1870-1957 . . . . . . .DLB-127

Cox, Leonard circa 1495-circa 1550 . . . . .DLB-281

Cox, Palmer 1840-1924 . . . . .DLB-42

Coxe, Louis 1918-1993 . . . . .DLB-5

Coxe, Tench 1755-1824 . . . . .DLB-37

Cozzens, Frederick S. 1818-1869 . . . . .DLB-202

Cozzens, James Gould 1903-1978 . . . .
  . . . . .DLB-9, 294; Y-84; DS-2; CDALB-1

  Cozzens's *Michael Scarlett* Y-97

  Ernest Hemingway's Reaction to
    James Gould Cozzens Y-98

  James Gould Cozzens—A View
    from Afar Y-97

  James Gould Cozzens: How to
    Read Him Y-97

  James Gould Cozzens Symposium and
    Exhibition at the University of
    South Carolina, Columbia Y-00

  Mens Rea (or Something) Y-97

  Novels for Grown-Ups Y-97

Crabbe, George 1754-1832 . . . . .DLB-93

Crace, Jim 1946- DLB-231

Crackanthorpe, Hubert 1870-1896 . . . . . .DLB-135

Craddock, Charles Egbert (see Murfree, Mary N.)

Cradock, Thomas 1718-1770 . . . . .DLB-31

Craig, Daniel H. 1811-1895 . . . . .DLB-43

Craik, Dinah Maria 1826-1887 . . . . . .DLB-35, 163

Cramer, Richard Ben 1950- DLB-185

Cranch, Christopher Pearse
  1813-1892 . . . . .DLB-1, 42, 243; DS-5

Crane, Hart 1899-1932 . . . . .DLB-4, 48; CDALB-4

  Nathan Asch Remembers Ford Madox
    Ford, Sam Roth, and Hart Crane Y-02

Crane, R. S. 1886-1967 . . . . .DLB-63

Crane, Stephen
  1871-1900 . . . . .DLB-12, 54, 78; CDALB-3

  Stephen Crane: A Revaluation, Virginia
    Tech Conference, 1989 . . . . .Y-89

  The Stephen Crane Society Y-98, 01

Crane, Walter 1845-1915 . . . . .DLB-163

Cranmer, Thomas 1489-1556 . . . . . . .DLB-132, 213

Crapsey, Adelaide 1878-1914 . . . . .DLB-54

Crashaw, Richard 1612/1613-1649 . . . . . .DLB-126

Craven, Avery 1885-1980 . . . . .DLB-17

Crawford, Charles 1752-circa 1815 . . . . . . .DLB-31

Crawford, F. Marion 1854-1909 . . . . .DLB-71

Crawford, Isabel Valancy 1850-1887 . . . . . .DLB-92

Crawley, Alan 1887-1975 . . . . .DLB-68

Crayon, Geoffrey (see Irving, Washington)

Crayon, Porte (see Strother, David Hunter)

Creamer, Robert W. 1922- DLB-171

Creasey, John 1908-1973 . . . . .DLB-77

Creative Age Press DLB-46

Creative Nonfiction .Y-02

William Creech [publishing house] DLB-154

Thomas Creede [publishing house] DLB-170

Creel, George 1876-1953 . . . . .DLB-25

Creeley, Robert 1926-
  . . . . DLB-5, 16, 169; DS-17

Creelman, James
  1859-1915 . . . . .DLB-23

Cregan, David 1931- DLB-13

Creighton, Donald 1902-1979 . . . . .DLB-88

Crémazie, Octave 1827-1879 . . . . .DLB-99

Crémer, Victoriano 1909?- DLB-108

Crescas, Hasdai circa 1340-1412? DLB-115

Crespo, Angel 1926-1995 . . . . .DLB-134

Cresset Press DLB-112

Cresswell, Helen 1934- DLB-161

Crèvecoeur, Michel Guillaume Jean de
  1735-1813 . . . . .DLB-37

Crewe, Candida 1964- DLB-207

Crews, Harry 1935- DLB-6, 143, 185

Crichton, Michael (John Lange, Jeffrey Hudson,
  Michael Douglas) 1942- DLB-292; Y-81

Crispin, Edmund (Robert Bruce Montgomery)
  1921-1978 . . . . .DLB-87

Cristofer, Michael 1946- DLB-7

Criticism
  Afro-American Literary Critics:
    An Introduction DLB-33

  The Consolidation of Opinion: Critical
    Responses to the Modernists DLB-36

  "Criticism in Relation to Novels"
    (1863), by G. H. Lewes DLB-21

  The Limits of Pluralism DLB-67

  Modern Critical Terms, Schools, and
    Movements DLB-67

  "Panic Among the Philistines":
    A Postscript, An Interview
    with Bryan Griffin Y-81

  The Recovery of Literature: Criticism
    in the 1990s: A Symposium Y-91

  The Stealthy School of Criticism (1871),
    by Dante Gabriel Rossetti DLB-35

Crnjanski, Miloš
  1893-1977 . . . . .DLB-147; CDWLB-4

Crocker, Hannah Mather 1752-1829 . . . . .DLB-200

Crockett, David (Davy)
  1786-1836 . . . . DLB-3, 11, 183, 248

Croft-Cooke, Rupert (see Bruce, Leo)

Crofts, Freeman Wills 1879-1957 . . . . .DLB-77

Croker, John Wilson 1780-1857 . . . . .DLB-110

Croly, George 1780-1860 . . . . .DLB-159

Croly, Herbert 1869-1930 . . . . .DLB-91

Croly, Jane Cunningham 1829-1901 . . . . . .DLB-23

Crompton, Richmal 1890-1969 . . . . .DLB-160

Cronin, A. J. 1896-1981 . . . . .DLB-191

Cros, Charles 1842-1888 . . . . .DLB-217

Crosby, Caresse 1892-1970 and
  Crosby, Harry 1898-1929 and . .DLB-4; DS-15

Crosby, Harry 1898-1929 . . . . .DLB-48

Crosland, Camilla Toulmin (Mrs. Newton
  Crosland) 1812-1895 . . . . .DLB-240

Cross, Amanda (Carolyn G. Heilbrun)
  1926-2003 .DLB-306

Cross, Gillian 1945- DLB-161

Cross, Victoria 1868-1952 . . . . .DLB-135, 197

Crossley-Holland, Kevin 1941- DLB-40, 161

Crothers, Rachel 1870-1958 . . . . .DLB-7, 266

Thomas Y. Crowell Company DLB-49

Crowley, John 1942- Y-82

Crowley, Mart 1935- DLB-7, 266

Crown Publishers DLB-46

Crowne, John 1641-1712 . . . . .DLB-80

Crowninshield, Edward Augustus
  1817-1859 .DLB-140

Crowninshield, Frank 1872-1947 . . . . .DLB-91

Croy, Homer 1883-1965 . . . . .DLB-4

Crumley, James 1939- DLB-226; Y-84

Cruse, Mary Anne 1825?-1910 . . . . .DLB-239

Cruz, Migdalia 1958- DLB-249

Cruz, Sor Juana Inés de la 1651-1695 . . . .DLB-305

Cruz, Victor Hernández 1949- DLB-41

Cruz e Sousa, João 1861-1898 . . . . .DLB-307

Csokor, Franz Theodor 1885-1969 . . . . . . .DLB-81

Csoóri, Sándor 1930- DLB-232; CDWLB-4

Cuadra, Pablo Antonio 1912-2002 . . . . . .DLB-290

Cuala Press DLB-112

Cudworth, Ralph 1617-1688 . . . . .DLB-252

Cugoano, Quobna Ottabah 1797-?. Y-02

Cullen, Countee
  1903-1946 . . . . .DLB-4, 48, 51; CDALB-4

Culler, Jonathan D. 1944- DLB-67, 246

Cullinan, Elizabeth 1933- DLB-234

Culverwel, Nathaniel 1619?-1651? DLB-252

Cumberland, Richard 1732-1811 . . . . .DLB-89

Cummings, Constance Gordon
  1837-1924 .DLB-174

Cummings, E. E.
  1894-1962 . . . . .DLB-4, 48; CDALB-5

  The E. E. Cummings Society Y-01

Cummings, Ray 1887-1957 . . . . .DLB-8

Cummings and Hilliard DLB-49

Cummins, Maria Susanna 1827-1866 . . . . .DLB-42

Cumpián, Carlos 1953- DLB-209

Cunard, Nancy 1896-1965 . . . . .DLB-240

Joseph Cundall [publishing house] DLB-106

Cumulative Index

Cuney, Waring 1906-1976 .... DLB-51
Cuney-Hare, Maude 1874-1936 .... DLB-52
Cunha, Euclides da 1866-1909 .... DLB-307
Cunningham, Allan
   1784-1842 .... DLB-116, 144
Cunningham, J. V. 1911-1985 .... DLB-5
Cunningham, Michael 1952- DLB-292
Cunningham, Peter (Peter Lauder, Peter
   Benjamin) 1947- DLB-267
Peter F. Cunningham
   [publishing house] DLB-49
Cunqueiro, Alvaro 1911-1981 .... DLB-134
Cuomo, George 1929- Y-80
Cupples, Upham and Company DLB-49
Cupples and Leon DLB-46
Cuppy, Will 1884-1949 .... DLB-11
Curiel, Barbara Brinson 1956- DLB-209
Edmund Curll [publishing house] DLB-154
Currie, James 1756-1805 .... DLB-142
Currie, Mary Montgomerie Lamb Singleton,
   Lady Currie (see Fane, Violet)
Cursor Mundi circa 1300 .... DLB-146
Curti, Merle E. 1897-1996 .... DLB-17
Curtis, Anthony 1926- DLB-155
Curtis, Cyrus H. K. 1850-1933 .... DLB-91
Curtis, George William
   1824-1892 .... DLB-1, 43, 223
Curzon, Robert 1810-1873 .... DLB-166
Curzon, Sarah Anne 1833-1898 .... DLB-99
Cusack, Dymphna 1902-1981 .... DLB-260
Cushing, Eliza Lanesford
   1794-1886 .... DLB-99
Cushing, Harvey 1869-1939 .... DLB-187
Custance, Olive (Lady Alfred Douglas)
   1874-1944 .... DLB-240
Cynewulf circa 770-840 .... DLB-146
Cyrano de Bergerac, Savinien de
   1619-1655 .... DLB-268
Czepko, Daniel 1605-1660 .... DLB-164
Czerniawski, Adam 1934- DLB-232

D

Dabit, Eugène 1898-1936 .... DLB-65
Daborne, Robert circa 1580-1628 ..... DLB-58
Dąbrowska, Maria
   1889-1965 .... DLB-215; CDWLB-4
Dacey, Philip 1939- DLB-105
   "Eyes Across Centuries:
   Contemporary Poetry and 'That
   Vision Thing,'" DLB-105
Dach, Simon 1605-1659 .... DLB-164
Dagerman, Stig 1923-1954 .... DLB-259
Daggett, Rollin M. 1831-1901 .... DLB-79
D'Aguiar, Fred 1960- DLB-157
Dahl, Roald 1916-1990 .... DLB-139, 255
   Tribute to Alfred A. Knopf Y-84
Dahlberg, Edward 1900-1977 .... DLB-48
Dahn, Felix 1834-1912 .... DLB-129

The Daily Worker DLB-303
Dal', Vladimir Ivanovich (Kazak Vladimir
   Lugansky) 1801-1872 .... DLB-198
Dale, Peter 1938- DLB-40
Daley, Arthur 1904-1974 .... DLB-171
Dall, Caroline Healey 1822-1912 .... DLB-1, 235
Dallas, E. S. 1828-1879 .... DLB-55
   The Gay Science [excerpt](1866) DLB-21
The Dallas Theater Center DLB-7
D'Alton, Louis 1900-1951 .... DLB-10
Dalton, Roque 1935-1975 .... DLB-283
Daly, Carroll John 1889-1958 .... DLB-226
Daly, T. A. 1871-1948 .... DLB-11
Damon, S. Foster 1893-1971 .... DLB-45
William S. Damrell [publishing house] .. DLB-49
Dana, Charles A. 1819-1897 ..... DLB-3, 23, 250
Dana, Richard Henry, Jr.
   1815-1882 .... DLB-1, 183, 235
Dandridge, Ray Garfield DLB-51
Dane, Clemence 1887-1965 .... DLB-10, 197
Danforth, John 1660-1730 .... DLB-24
Danforth, Samuel, I 1626-1674 ...... DLB-24
Danforth, Samuel, II 1666-1727 ..... DLB-24
Daniel, John M. 1825-1865 .... DLB-43
Daniel, Samuel 1562 or 1563-1619 .... DLB-62
Daniel Press DLB-106
Daniel', Iulii 1925-1988 .... DLB-302
Daniells, Roy 1902-1979 .... DLB-68
Daniels, Jim 1956- DLB-120
Daniels, Jonathan 1902-1981 .... DLB-127
Daniels, Josephus 1862-1948 .... DLB-29
Daniels, Sarah 1957- DLB-245
Danilevsky, Grigorii Petrovich
   1829-1890 .... DLB-238
Dannay, Frederic 1905-1982 .... DLB-137
Danner, Margaret Esse 1915- DLB-41
John Danter [publishing house] DLB-170
Dantin, Louis (Eugene Seers)
   1865-1945 .... DLB-92
Danto, Arthur C. 1924- DLB-279
Danzig, Allison 1898-1987 .... DLB-171
D'Arcy, Ella circa 1857-1937 .... DLB-135
Darío, Rubén 1867-1916 .... DLB-290
Dark, Eleanor 1901-1985 .... DLB-260
Darke, Nick 1948- DLB-233
Darley, Felix Octavious Carr
   1822-1888 .... DLB-188
Darley, George 1795-1846 .... DLB-96
Darmesteter, Madame James
   (see Robinson, A. Mary F.)
Darrow, Clarence 1857-1938 .... DLB-303
Darwin, Charles 1809-1882 ...... DLB-57, 166
Darwin, Erasmus 1731-1802 .... DLB-93
Daryush, Elizabeth 1887-1977 .... DLB-20
Dashkova, Ekaterina Romanovna
   (née Vorontsova) 1743-1810 .... DLB-150

Dashwood, Edmée Elizabeth Monica de la Pasture
   (see Delafield, E. M.)
Daudet, Alphonse 1840-1897 .... DLB-123
d'Aulaire, Edgar Parin 1898- and
   d'Aulaire, Ingri 1904- DLB-22
Davenant, Sir William 1606-1668 ... DLB-58, 126
Davenport, Guy 1927- DLB-130
   Tribute to John Gardner Y-82
Davenport, Marcia 1903-1996 .... DS-17
Davenport, Robert ?-? DLB-58
Daves, Delmer 1904-1977 .... DLB-26
Davey, Frank 1940- DLB-53
Davidson, Avram 1923-1993 .... DLB-8
Davidson, Donald 1893-1968 .... DLB-45
Davidson, Donald 1917- DLB-279
Davidson, John 1857-1909 .... DLB-19
Davidson, Lionel 1922- DLB-14, 276
Davidson, Robyn 1950- DLB-204
Davidson, Sara 1943- DLB-185
Davið Stefánsson frá Fagraskógi
   1895-1964 .... DLB-293
Davie, Donald 1922- DLB-27
Davie, Elspeth 1919-1995 .... DLB-139
Davies, Sir John 1569-1626 .... DLB-172
Davies, John, of Hereford 1565?-1618 .. DLB-121
Davies, Rhys 1901-1978 .... DLB-139, 191
Davies, Robertson 1913-1995 .... DLB-68
Davies, Samuel 1723-1761 .... DLB-31
Davies, Thomas 1712?-1785 ..... DLB-142, 154
Davies, W. H. 1871-1940 .... DLB-19, 174
Peter Davies Limited DLB-112
Davin, Nicholas Flood 1840?-1901 .... DLB-99
Daviot, Gordon 1896?-1952 .... DLB-10
   (see also Tey, Josephine)
Davis, Arthur Hoey (see Rudd, Steele)
Davis, Benjamin J. 1903-1964 .... DLB-303
Davis, Charles A. (Major J. Downing)
   1795-1867 .... DLB-11
Davis, Clyde Brion 1894-1962 .... DLB-9
Davis, Dick 1945- DLB-40, 282
Davis, Frank Marshall 1905-1987 ..... DLB-51
Davis, H. L. 1894-1960 .... DLB-9, 206
Davis, John 1774-1854 .... DLB-37
Davis, Lydia 1947- DLB-130
Davis, Margaret Thomson 1926- DLB-14
Davis, Ossie 1917- DLB-7, 38, 249
Davis, Owen 1874-1956 .... DLB-249
Davis, Paxton 1925-1994 .... Y-89
Davis, Rebecca Harding
   1831-1910 .... DLB-74, 239
Davis, Richard Harding 1864-1916
   .... DLB-12, 23, 78, 79, 189; DS-13
Davis, Samuel Cole 1764-1809 .... DLB-37
Davis, Samuel Post 1850-1918 .... DLB-202
Davison, Frank Dalby 1893-1970 .... DLB-260
Davison, Peter 1928- DLB-5

Davydov, Denis Vasil'evich 1784-1839 .... DLB-205
Davys, Mary 1674-1732 .... DLB-39
    Preface to *The Works of Mrs. Davys* (1725) DLB-39
DAW Books DLB-46
Dawe, Bruce 1930- DLB-289
Dawson, Ernest 1882-1947 .... DLB-140; Y-02
Dawson, Fielding 1930- DLB-130
Dawson, Sarah Morgan 1842-1909 ...... DLB-239
Dawson, William 1704-1752 .... DLB-31
Day, Angel flourished 1583-1599 ... DLB-167, 236
Day, Benjamin Henry 1810-1889 .... DLB-43
Day, Clarence 1874-1935 .... DLB-11
Day, Dorothy 1897-1980 .... DLB-29
Day, Frank Parker 1881-1950 .... DLB-92
Day, John circa 1574-circa 1640 .... DLB-62
Day, Thomas 1748-1789 .... DLB-39
John Day [publishing house] DLB-170
The John Day Company DLB-46
Mahlon Day [publishing house] DLB-49
Day Lewis, C. (see Blake, Nicholas)
Dazai Osamu 1909-1948 .... DLB-182
Deacon, William Arthur 1890-1977 ...... DLB-68
Deal, Borden 1922-1985 .... DLB-6
de Angeli, Marguerite 1889-1987 .... DLB-22
De Angelis, Milo 1951- DLB-128
Debord, Guy 1931-1994 .... DLB-296
De Bow, J. D. B. 1820-1867 ...... DLB-3, 79, 248
Debs, Eugene V. 1855-1926 .... DLB-303
de Bruyn, Günter 1926- DLB-75
de Camp, L. Sprague 1907-2000 .... DLB-8
De Carlo, Andrea 1952- DLB-196
De Casas, Celso A. 1944- DLB-209
Dechert, Robert 1895-1975 .... DLB-187
Dedications, Inscriptions, and Annotations Y-01–02
Dee, John 1527-1608 or 1609 .... DLB-136, 213
Deeping, George Warwick 1877-1950 .... DLB-153
Defoe, Daniel 1660-1731 .... DLB-39, 95, 101; CDBLB-2
    Preface to *Colonel Jack* (1722) DLB-39
    Preface to *The Farther Adventures of Robinson Crusoe* (1719) DLB-39
    Preface to *Moll Flanders* (1722) DLB-39
    Preface to *Robinson Crusoe* (1719) DLB-39
    Preface to *Roxana* (1724) DLB-39
de Fontaine, Felix Gregory 1834-1896 .... DLB-43
De Forest, John William 1826-1906 .... DLB-12, 189
DeFrees, Madeline 1919- DLB-105
    "The Poet's Kaleidoscope: The Element of Surprise in the Making of the Poem" DLB-105
DeGolyer, Everette Lee 1886-1956 ...... DLB-187
de Graff, Robert 1895-1981 .... Y-81
de Graft, Joe 1924-1978 .... DLB-117

De Heinrico circa 980? DLB-148
Deighton, Len 1929- DLB-87; CDBLB-8
DeJong, Meindert 1906-1991 .... DLB-52
Dekker, Thomas circa 1572-1632 ...... DLB-62, 172; CDBLB-1
Delacorte, George T., Jr. 1894-1991 ...... DLB-91
Delafield, E. M. 1890-1943 .... DLB-34
Delahaye, Guy (Guillaume Lahaise) 1888-1969 .... DLB-92
de la Mare, Walter 1873-1956 .... DLB-19, 153, 162, 255; CDBLB-6
Deland, Margaret 1857-1945 .... DLB-78
Delaney, Shelagh 1939- DLB-13; CDBLB-8
Delano, Amasa 1763-1823 .... DLB-183
Delany, Martin Robinson 1812-1885 ..... DLB-50
Delany, Samuel R. 1942- DLB-8, 33
de la Roche, Mazo 1879-1961 .... DLB-68
Delavigne, Jean François Casimir 1793-1843 .... DLB-192
Delbanco, Nicholas 1942- DLB-6, 234
Delblanc, Sven 1931-1992 .... DLB-257
Del Castillo, Ramón 1949- DLB-209
Deledda, Grazia 1871-1936 .... DLB-264
De León, Nephtal 1945- DLB-82
Deleuze, Gilles 1925-1995 .... DLB-296
Delfini, Antonio 1907-1963 .... DLB-264
Delgado, Abelardo Barrientos 1931- DLB-82
Del Giudice, Daniele 1949- DLB-196
De Libero, Libero 1906-1981 .... DLB-114
DeLillo, Don 1936- DLB-6, 173
de Lint, Charles 1951- DLB-251
de Lisser H. G. 1878-1944 .... DLB-117
Dell, Floyd 1887-1969 .... DLB-9
Dell Publishing Company DLB-46
delle Grazie, Marie Eugene 1864-1931 .... DLB-81
Deloney, Thomas died 1600 .... DLB-167
Deloria, Ella C. 1889-1971 .... DLB-175
Deloria, Vine, Jr. 1933- DLB-175
del Rey, Lester 1915-1993 .... DLB-8
Del Vecchio, John M. 1947- DS-9
Del'vig, Anton Antonovich 1798-1831 .... DLB-205
de Man, Paul 1919-1983 .... DLB-67
DeMarinis, Rick 1934- DLB-218
Demby, William 1922- DLB-33
De Mille, James 1833-1880 .... DLB-99, 251
de Mille, William 1878-1955 .... DLB-266
Deming, Philander 1829-1915 .... DLB-74
Deml, Jakub 1878-1961 .... DLB-215
Demorest, William Jennings 1822-1895 ... DLB-79
De Morgan, William 1839-1917 .... DLB-153
Demosthenes 384 B.C.-322 B.C. DLB-176
Henry Denham [publishing house] DLB-170
Denham, Sir John 1615-1669 .... DLB-58, 126
Denison, Merrill 1893-1975 .... DLB-92
T. S. Denison and Company DLB-49

Dennery, Adolphe Philippe 1811-1899 ... DLB-192
Dennie, Joseph 1768-1812 ..... DLB-37, 43, 59, 73
Dennis, C. J. 1876-1938 .... DLB-260
Dennis, John 1658-1734 .... DLB-101
Dennis, Nigel 1912-1989 .... DLB-13, 15, 233
Denslow, W. W. 1856-1915 .... DLB-188
Dent, J. M., and Sons DLB-112
Dent, Lester 1904-1959 .... DLB-306
Dent, Tom 1932-1998 .... DLB-38
Denton, Daniel circa 1626-1703 .... DLB-24
DePaola, Tomie 1934- DLB-61
De Quille, Dan 1829-1898 .... DLB-186
De Quincey, Thomas 1785-1859 .... DLB-110, 144; CDBLB-3
    "Rhetoric" (1828; revised, 1859) [excerpt] DLB-57
    "Style" (1840; revised, 1859) [excerpt] DLB-57
Derby, George Horatio 1823-1861 .... DLB-11
J. C. Derby and Company DLB-49
Derby and Miller DLB-49
De Ricci, Seymour 1881-1942 .... DLB-201
Derleth, August 1909-1971 .... DLB-9; DS-17
Derrida, Jacques 1930- DLB-242
The Derrydale Press DLB-46
Derzhavin, Gavriil Romanovich 1743-1816 .... DLB-150
Desai, Anita 1937- DLB-271
Desaulniers, Gonzalve 1863-1934 .... DLB-92
Desbordes-Valmore, Marceline 1786-1859 .... DLB-217
Descartes, René 1596-1650 .... DLB-268
Deschamps, Emile 1791-1871 .... DLB-217
Deschamps, Eustache 1340?-1404 ...... DLB-208
Desbiens, Jean-Paul 1927- DLB-53
des Forêts, Louis-Rene 1918-2001 .... DLB-83
Desiato, Luca 1941- DLB-196
Desjardins, Marie-Catherine (see Villedieu, Madame de)
Desnica, Vladan 1905-1967 .... DLB-181
Desnos, Robert 1900-1945 .... DLB-258
DesRochers, Alfred 1901-1978 .... DLB-68
Desrosiers, Léo-Paul 1896-1967 .... DLB-68
Dessaulles, Louis-Antoine 1819-1895 .... DLB-99
Dessì, Giuseppe 1909-1977 .... DLB-177
Destouches, Louis-Ferdinand (see Céline, Louis-Ferdinand)
DeSylva, Buddy 1895-1950 .... DLB-265
De Tabley, Lord 1835-1895 .... DLB-35
Deutsch, Babette 1895-1982 .... DLB-45
Deutsch, Niklaus Manuel (see Manuel, Niklaus)
André Deutsch Limited DLB-112
Devanny, Jean 1894-1962 .... DLB-260
Deveaux, Alexis 1948- DLB-38
De Vere, Aubrey 1814-1902 .... DLB-35
Devereux, second Earl of Essex, Robert 1565-1601 .... DLB-136

Cumulative Index

The Devin-Adair Company DLB-46
De Vinne, Theodore Low
   1828-1914. . . . . DLB-187
Devlin, Anne 1951- DLB-245
DeVoto, Bernard 1897-1955. . . . . DLB-9, 256
De Vries, Peter 1910-1993 . . . . DLB-6; Y-82
   Tribute to Albert Erskine. Y-93
Dewart, Edward Hartley 1828-1903. . . . . . DLB-99
Dewdney, Christopher 1951- DLB-60
Dewdney, Selwyn 1909-1979 . . . . DLB-68
Dewey, John 1859-1952 . . . . DLB-246, 270
Dewey, Orville 1794-1882 . . . . DLB-243
Dewey, Thomas B. 1915-1981 . . . . DLB-226
DeWitt, Robert M., Publisher DLB-49
DeWolfe, Fiske and Company DLB-49
Dexter, Colin 1930- DLB-87
de Young, M. H. 1849-1925. . . . . DLB-25
Dhlomo, H. I. E. 1903-1956. . . . . DLB-157, 225
Dhuoda circa 803-after 843 . . . . DLB-148
The Dial 1840-1844. . . . . DLB-223
The Dial Press DLB-46
Diamond, I. A. L. 1920-1988 . . . . DLB-26
Dias Gomes, Alfredo 1922-1999. . . . . . . DLB-307
Dibble, L. Grace 1902-1998 . . . . DLB-204
Dibdin, Thomas Frognall
   1776-1847 . . . . DLB-184
Di Cicco, Pier Giorgio 1949- DLB-60
Dick, Philip K. 1928-1982 . . . . DLB-8
Dick and Fitzgerald. DLB-49
Dickens, Charles 1812-1870
   . . . . DLB-21, 55, 70, 159,
   166; DS-5; CDBLB-4
Dickey, Eric Jerome 1961- DLB-292
Dickey, James 1923-1997 . . . . DLB-5, 193;
   Y-82, 93, 96, 97; DS-7, 19; CDALB-6
   James Dickey and Stanley Burnshaw
     Correspondence Y-02
   James Dickey at Seventy–A Tribute Y-93
   James Dickey, American Poet Y-96
   The James Dickey Society Y-99
   The Life of James Dickey: A Lecture to
     the Friends of the Emory Libraries,
     by Henry Hart. Y-98
   Tribute to Archibald MacLeish Y-82
   Tribute to Malcolm Cowley Y-89
   Tribute to Truman Capote Y-84
   Tributes [to Dickey]. Y-97
Dickey, William
   1928-1994 . . . . DLB-5
Dickinson, Emily
   1830-1886 . . . . DLB-1, 243; CDALB-3
Dickinson, John 1732-1808. . . . . DLB-31
Dickinson, Jonathan 1688-1747. . . . . DLB-24
Dickinson, Patric 1914- DLB-27
Dickinson, Peter 1927- DLB-87, 161, 276
John Dicks [publishing house] DLB-106
Dickson, Gordon R.
   1923-2001 . . . . DLB-8

Dictionary of Literary Biography
   Annual Awards for *Dictionary of
   Literary Biography* Editors and
   Contributors Y-98–02
*Dictionary of Literary Biography
   Yearbook* Awards. Y-92–93, 97–02
The Dictionary of National Biography DLB-144
Didion, Joan 1934-
   . . . . DLB-2, 173, 185; Y-81, 86; CDALB-6
Di Donato, Pietro 1911- DLB-9
Die Fürstliche Bibliothek Corvey Y-96
Diego, Gerardo 1896-1987 . . . . DLB-134
Dietz, Howard 1896-1983 . . . . DLB-265
Digby, Everard 1550?-1605 . . . . DLB-281
Digges, Thomas circa 1546-1595 . . . . DLB-136
The Digital Millennium Copyright Act:
   Expanding Copyright Protection in
   Cyberspace and Beyond Y-98
Diktonius, Elmer 1896-1961. . . . . DLB-259
Dillard, Annie 1945- DLB-275, 278; Y-80
Dillard, R. H. W. 1937- DLB-5, 244
Charles T. Dillingham Company. DLB-49
G. W. Dillingham Company DLB-49
Edward and Charles Dilly
   [publishing house] DLB-154
Dilthey, Wilhelm 1833-1911 . . . . DLB-129
Dimitrova, Blaga 1922- . . . DLB-181; CDWLB-4
Dimov, Dimitr 1909-1966 . . . . DLB-181
Dimsdale, Thomas J. 1831?-1866. . . . . . . DLB-186
Dinescu, Mircea 1950- DLB-232
Dinesen, Isak (see Blixen, Karen)
Dingelstedt, Franz von 1814-1881 . . . . . . DLB-133
Dinis, Júlio (Joaquim Guilherme
   Gomes Coelho) 1839-1871. . . . . DLB-287
Dintenfass, Mark 1941- Y-84
Diogenes, Jr. (see Brougham, John)
Diogenes Laertius circa 200 . . . . DLB-176
DiPrima, Diane 1934- DLB-5, 16
Disch, Thomas M. 1940- DLB-8, 282
Diski, Jenny 1947- DLB-271
Disney, Walt 1901-1966. . . . . DLB-22
Disraeli, Benjamin 1804-1881. . . . . DLB-21, 55
D'Israeli, Isaac 1766-1848 . . . . DLB-107
DLB Award for Distinguished
   Literary Criticism. Y-02
Ditlevsen, Tove 1917-1976 . . . . DLB-214
Ditzen, Rudolf (see Fallada, Hans)
Dix, Dorothea Lynde 1802-1887 . . . . . DLB-1, 235
Dix, Dorothy (see Gilmer, Elizabeth Meriwether)
Dix, Edwards and Company DLB-49
Dix, Gertrude circa 1874-? DLB-197
Dixie, Florence Douglas 1857-1905 . . . . . DLB-174
Dixon, Ella Hepworth
   1855 or 1857-1932 . . . . DLB-197
Dixon, Paige (see Corcoran, Barbara)
Dixon, Richard Watson 1833-1900 . . . . . . DLB-19
Dixon, Stephen 1936- DLB-130

DLB Award for Distinguished
   Literary Criticism. Y-02
Dmitriev, Andrei Viktorovich 1956- . . DLB-285
Dmitriev, Ivan Ivanovich 1760-1837. . . . . DLB-150
Dobell, Bertram 1842-1914 . . . . DLB-184
Dobell, Sydney 1824-1874 . . . . DLB-32
Dobie, J. Frank 1888-1964 . . . . DLB-212
Dobles Yzaguirre, Julieta 1943- DLB-283
Döblin, Alfred 1878-1957 . . . . DLB-66; CDWLB-2
Dobroliubov, Nikolai Aleksandrovich
   1836-1861 . . . . DLB-277
Dobson, Austin 1840-1921. . . . . DLB-35, 144
Dobson, Rosemary 1920- DLB-260
Doctorow, E. L.
   1931- DLB-2, 28, 173; Y-80; CDALB-6
Dodd, Susan M. 1946- DLB-244
Dodd, William E. 1869-1940 . . . . DLB-17
Anne Dodd [publishing house]. DLB-154
Dodd, Mead and Company DLB-49
Doderer, Heimito von 1896-1966 . . . . . . DLB-85
B. W. Dodge and Company. DLB-46
Dodge, Mary Abigail 1833-1896 . . . . . . DLB-221
Dodge, Mary Mapes
   1831?-1905. . . . . DLB-42, 79; DS-13
Dodge Publishing Company DLB-49
Dodgson, Charles Lutwidge (see Carroll, Lewis)
Dodsley, Robert 1703-1764. . . . . DLB-95
R. Dodsley [publishing house] DLB-154
Dodson, Owen 1914-1983 . . . . DLB-76
Dodwell, Christina 1951- DLB-204
Doestlcks, Q. K. Philander, P. B.
   (see Thomson, Mortimer)
Doheny, Carrie Estelle 1875-1958 . . . . . . DLB-140
Doherty, John 1798?-1854 . . . . DLB-190
Doig, Ivan 1939- DLB-206
Doinaş, Ştefan Augustin 1922- DLB-232
Domínguez, Sylvia Maida 1935- DLB-122
Donaghy, Michael 1954- DLB-282
Patrick Donahoe [publishing house] DLB-49
Donald, David H. 1920- DLB-17; Y-87
Donaldson, Scott 1928- DLB-111
Doni, Rodolfo 1919- DLB-177
Donleavy, J. P. 1926- DLB-6, 173
Donnadieu, Marguerite (see Duras, Marguerite)
Donne, John
   1572-1631. . . . . DLB-121, 151; CDBLB-1
Donnelly, Ignatius 1831-1901. . . . . DLB-12
R. R. Donnelley and Sons Company DLB-49
Donoghue, Emma 1969- DLB-267
Donohue and Henneberry DLB-49
Donoso, José 1924-1996 . . . . . DLB-113; CDWLB-3
M. Doolady [publishing house] DLB-49
Dooley, Ebon (see Ebon)
Doolittle, Hilda 1886-1961 . . . . . DLB-4, 45; DS-15
Doplicher, Fabio 1938- DLB-128
Dor, Milo 1923- DLB-85

George H. Doran Company DLB-46

Dorgelès, Roland 1886-1973 ....DLB-65

Dorn, Edward 1929-1999 ....DLB-5

Dorr, Rheta Childe 1866-1948 ....DLB-25

Dorris, Michael 1945-1997.............DLB-175

Dorset and Middlesex, Charles Sackville,
　Lord Buckhurst, Earl of 1643-1706....DLB-131

Dorsey, Candas Jane 1952- DLB-251

Dorst, Tankred 1925- DLB-75, 124

Dos Passos, John 1896-1970
　..............DLB-4, 9; DS-1, 15; CDALB-5

　John Dos Passos: A Centennial
　　Commemoration Y-96

　John Dos Passos: Artist................Y-99

　John Dos Passos Newsletter Y-00

　U.S.A. (Documentary).............DLB-274

Dostoevsky, Fyodor 1821-1881.........DLB-238

Doubleday and Company DLB-49

Doubrovsky, Serge 1928- DLB-299

Dougall, Lily 1858-1923 ....DLB-92

Doughty, Charles M.
　1843-1926................ DLB-19, 57, 174

Douglas, Lady Alfred (see Custance, Olive)

Douglas, Ellen (Josephine Ayres Haxton)
　1921-...........................DLB-292

Douglas, Gavin 1476-1522.............DLB-132

Douglas, Keith 1920-1944 ....DLB-27

Douglas, Norman 1868-1952........DLB-34, 195

Douglass, Frederick 1817-1895
　.........DLB-1, 43, 50, 79, 243; CDALB-2

　Frederick Douglass Creative Arts Center Y-01

Douglass, William circa 1691-1752 ....DLB-24

Dourado, Autran 1926- DLB-145, 307

Dove, Arthur G. 1880-1946............DLB-188

Dove, Rita 1952- DLB-120; CDALB-7

Dover Publications....................DLB-46

Doves Press DLB-112

Dovlatov, Sergei Donatovich
　1941-1990 ....DLB-285

Dowden, Edward 1843-1913........DLB-35, 149

Dowell, Coleman 1925-1985 ....DLB-130

Dowland, John 1563-1626...............DLB-172

Downes, Gwladys 1915- DLB-88

Downing, J., Major (see Davis, Charles A.)

Downing, Major Jack (see Smith, Seba)

Dowriche, Anne
　before 1560-after 1613...............DLB-172

Dowson, Ernest 1867-1900 .... DLB-19, 135

William Doxey [publishing house]........DLB-49

Doyle, Sir Arthur Conan
　1859-1930 ... DLB-18, 70, 156, 178; CDBLB-5

　The Priory Scholars of New York........Y-99

Doyle, Kirby 1932- DLB-16

Doyle, Roddy 1958- DLB-194

Drabble, Margaret
　1939- DLB-14, 155, 231; CDBLB-8

　Tribute to Graham Greene Y-91

Drach, Albert 1902-1995 ....DLB-85

Drachmann, Holger 1846-1908.........DLB-300

Dragojević, Danijel 1934- DLB-181

Dragún, Osvaldo 1929-1999 ....DLB-305

Drake, Samuel Gardner 1798-1875 ......DLB-187

Drama (*See* Theater)

The Dramatic Publishing Company DLB-49

Dramatists Play Service DLB-46

Drant, Thomas
　early 1540s?-1578 ....DLB-167

Draper, John W. 1811-1882 ....DLB-30

Draper, Lyman C. 1815-1891 ....DLB-30

Drayton, Michael 1563-1631............DLB-121

Dreiser, Theodore 1871-1945
　....... DLB-9, 12, 102, 137; DS-1; CDALB-3

　The International Theodore Dreiser
　　Society Y-01

　Notes from the Underground
　　of *Sister Carrie* Y-01

Dresser, Davis 1904-1977 ....DLB-226

Drew, Elizabeth A.
　"A Note on Technique" [excerpt]
　(1926) DLB-36

Drewitz, Ingeborg 1923-1986 ....DLB-75

Drieu La Rochelle, Pierre 1893-1945......DLB-72

Drinker, Elizabeth 1735-1807...........DLB-200

Drinkwater, John 1882-1937 ..... DLB-10, 19, 149

　The Friends of the Dymock Poets........Y-00

Droste-Hülshoff, Annette von
　1797-1848............DLB-133; CDWLB-2

The Drue Heinz Literature Prize
　Excerpt from "Excerpts from a Report
　of the Commission," in David
　Bosworth's *The Death of Descartes*
　An Interview with David Bosworth Y-82

Drummond, William, of Hawthornden
　1585-1649 ....DLB-121, 213

Drummond, William Henry 1854-1907 ...DLB-92

Drummond de Andrade, Carlos
　1902-1987 ....DLB-307

Druzhinin, Aleksandr Vasil'evich
　1824-1864 ....DLB-238

Dryden, Charles 1860?-1931...........DLB-171

Dryden, John
　1631-1700 ......DLB-80, 101, 131; CDBLB-2

Držić, Marin
　circa 1508-1567 .... DLB-147; CDWLB-4

Duane, William 1760-1835 ....DLB-43

Dubé, Marcel 1930- DLB-53

Dubé, Rodolphe (see Hertel, François)

Dubie, Norman 1945- DLB-120

Dubin, Al 1891-1945 ....DLB-265

Dubois, Silvia 1788 or 1789?-1889........DLB-239

Du Bois, W. E. B.
　1868-1963 .... DLB-47, 50, 91, 246; CDALB-3

Du Bois, William Pène 1916-1993 ....DLB-61

Dubrovina, Ekaterina Oskarovna
　1846-1913 ....DLB-238

Dubus, Andre 1936-1999.............DLB-130

　Tribute to Michael M. Rea Y-97

Dubus, Andre, III 1959- DLB-292

Ducange, Victor 1783-1833 ....DLB-192

Du Chaillu, Paul Belloni 1831?-1903 ....DLB-189

Ducharme, Réjean 1941- DLB-60

Dučić, Jovan 1871-1943..... DLB-147; CDWLB-4

Duck, Stephen 1705?-1756..............DLB-95

Gerald Duckworth and Company
　Limited DLB-112

Duclaux, Madame Mary (see Robinson, A. Mary F.)

Dudek, Louis 1918-2001 ....DLB-88

Dudintsev, Vladimir Dmitrievich
　1918-1998 ....DLB-302

Dudley-Smith, Trevor (see Hall, Adam)

Duell, Sloan and Pearce...............DLB-46

Duerer, Albrecht 1471-1528............DLB-179

Duff Gordon, Lucie 1821-1869 ....DLB-166

Dufferin, Helen Lady, Countess of Gifford
　1807-1867 ....DLB-199

Duffield and Green DLB-46

Duffy, Maureen 1933- DLB-14, 310

Dufief, Nicholas Gouin 1776-1834.......DLB-187

Dufresne, John 1948- DLB-292

Dugan, Alan 1923- DLB-5

Dugard, William 1606-1662 .....DLB-170, 281

William Dugard [publishing house]......DLB-170

Dugas, Marcel 1883-1947 ....DLB-92

William Dugdale [publishing house] DLB-106

Duhamel, Georges 1884-1966 ....DLB-65

Dujardin, Edouard 1861-1949..........DLB-123

Dukes, Ashley 1885-1959 ....DLB-10

Dumas, Alexandre *fils* 1824-1895 ....DLB-192

Dumas, Alexandre *père* 1802-1870 .....DLB-119, 192

Dumas, Henry 1934-1968 ....DLB-41

du Maurier, Daphne 1907-1989........DLB-191

Du Maurier, George 1834-1896 .... DLB-153, 178

Dummett, Michael 1925- DLB-262

Dunbar, Paul Laurence
　1872-1906 ....DLB-50, 54, 78; CDALB-3

　Introduction to *Lyrics of Lowly Life* (1896),
　　by William Dean Howells DLB-50

Dunbar, William
　circa 1460-circa 1522..........DLB-132, 146

Duncan, Dave 1933- DLB-251

Duncan, David James 1952- DLB-256

Duncan, Norman 1871-1916 ....DLB-92

Duncan, Quince 1940- DLB-145

Duncan, Robert 1919-1988 .... DLB-5, 16, 193

Duncan, Ronald 1914-1982.............DLB-13

Duncan, Sara Jeannette 1861-1922 ....DLB-92

Dunigan, Edward, and Brother..........DLB-49

Dunlap, John 1747-1812...............DLB-43

Dunlap, William 1766-1839 .... DLB-30, 37, 59

Dunlop, William "Tiger" 1792-1848 ......DLB-99

Dunmore, Helen 1952- DLB-267

Dunn, Douglas 1942- DLB-40

Dunn, Harvey Thomas 1884-1952 ......DLB-188

Cumulative Index

Dunn, Stephen 1939- DLB-105
    "The Good, The Not So Good" DLB-105
Dunne, Dominick 1925- DLB-306
Dunne, Finley Peter 1867-1936 ...... DLB-11, 23
Dunne, John Gregory 1932- Y-80
Dunne, Philip 1908-1992 .... DLB-26
Dunning, Ralph Cheever 1878-1930 ...... DLB-4
Dunning, William A. 1857-1922 .... DLB-17
Duns Scotus, John circa 1266-1308 ..... DLB-115
Dunsany, Lord (Edward John Moreton
    Drax Plunkett, Baron Dunsany)
    1878-1957 .... DLB-10, 77, 153, 156, 255
Dunton, W. Herbert 1878-1936 .... DLB-188
John Dunton [publishing house] DLB-170
Dupin, Amantine-Aurore-Lucile (see Sand, George)
Dupuy, Eliza Ann 1814-1880 .... DLB-248
Durack, Mary 1913-1994 .... DLB-260
Durand, Lucile (see Bersianik, Louky)
Duranti, Francesca 1935- DLB-196
Duranty, Walter 1884-1957 .... DLB-29
Duras, Marguerite (Marguerite Donnadieu)
    1914-1996 .... DLB-83
Durfey, Thomas 1653-1723 .... DLB-80
Durova, Nadezhda Andreevna
    (Aleksandr Andreevich Aleksandrov)
    1783-1866 .... DLB-198
Durrell, Lawrence 1912-1990
    .... DLB-15, 27, 204; Y-90; CDBLB-7
William Durrell [publishing house] DLB-49
Dürrenmatt, Friedrich
    1921-1990 .... DLB-69, 124; CDWLB-2
Duston, Hannah 1657-1737 .... DLB-200
Dutt, Toru 1856-1877 .... DLB-240
E. P. Dutton and Company DLB-49
Duun, Olav 1876-1939 .... DLB-297
Duvoisin, Roger 1904-1980 .... DLB-61
Duyckinck, Evert Augustus
    1816-1878 .... DLB-3, 64, 250
Duyckinck, George L.
    1823-1863 .... DLB-3, 250
Duyckinck and Company DLB-49
Dwight, John Sullivan 1813-1893 ..... DLB-1, 235
Dwight, Timothy 1752-1817 .... DLB-37
    America: or, A Poem on the Settlement
    of the British Colonies, by
    Timothy Dwight DLB-37
Dybek, Stuart 1942- DLB-130
    Tribute to Michael M. Rea Y-97
Dyer, Charles 1928- DLB-13
Dyer, Sir Edward 1543-1607 .... DLB-136
Dyer, George 1755-1841 .... DLB-93
Dyer, John 1699-1757 .... DLB-95
Dyk, Viktor 1877-1931 .... DLB-215
Dylan, Bob 1941- DLB-16

E

Eager, Edward 1911-1964 .... DLB-22
Eagleton, Terry 1943- DLB-242

Eames, Wilberforce
    1855-1937 .... DLB-140
Earle, Alice Morse
    1853-1911 .... DLB-221
Earle, John 1600 or 1601-1665 .... DLB-151
James H. Earle and Company DLB-49
East Europe
    Independence and Destruction,
    1918-1941 .... DLB-220
    Social Theory and Ethnography:
    Languageand Ethnicity in
    Western versus Eastern Man ... DLB-220
Eastlake, William 1917-1997 .... DLB-6, 206
Eastman, Carol ?- DLB-44
Eastman, Charles A. (Ohiyesa)
    1858-1939 .... DLB-175
Eastman, Max 1883-1969 .... DLB-91
Eaton, Daniel Isaac 1753-1814 .... DLB-158
Eaton, Edith Maude 1865-1914 .... DLB-221
Eaton, Winnifred 1875-1954 .... DLB-221
Eberhart, Richard 1904- DLB-48; CDALB-1
    Tribute to Robert Penn Warren Y-89
Ebner, Jeannie 1918- DLB-85
Ebner-Eschenbach, Marie von
    1830-1916 .... DLB-81
Ebon 1942- DLB-41
E-Books' Second Act in Libraries Y-02
Ecbasis Captivi circa 1045 .... DLB-148
Ecco Press DLB-46
Eckhart, Meister circa 1260-circa 1328 ... DLB-115
The Eclectic Review 1805-1868 .... DLB-110
Eco, Umberto 1932- DLB-196, 242
Eddison, E. R. 1882-1945 .... DLB-255
Edel, Leon 1907-1997 .... DLB-103
Edelfeldt, Inger 1956- DLB-257
A Century of Poetry, a Lifetime of Collecting:
    J. M. Edelstein's Collection of Twentieth-
    Century American Poetry Y-02
Edes, Benjamin 1732-1803 .... DLB-43
Edgar, David 1948- DLB-13, 233
    Viewpoint: Politics and
    Performance DLB-13
Edgerton, Clyde 1944- DLB-278
Edgeworth, Maria
    1768-1849 .... DLB-116, 159, 163
The Edinburgh Review 1802-1929 .... DLB-110
Edinburgh University Press DLB-112
Editing
    Conversations with Editors Y-95
    Editorial Statements DLB-137
    The Editorial Style of Fredson Bowers ... Y-91
    Editorial: The Extension of Copyright ... Y-02
    We See the Editor at Work Y-97
    Whose *Ulysses?* The Function of Editing .. Y-97
The Editor Publishing Company DLB-49
Editorial Institute at Boston University Y-00
Edmonds, Helen Woods Ferguson
    (see Kavan, Anna)

Edmonds, Randolph 1900-1983 .... DLB-51
Edmonds, Walter D. 1903-1998 .... DLB-9
Edric, Robert (see Armitage, G. E.)
Edschmid, Kasimir 1890-1966 .... DLB-56
Edson, Margaret 1961- DLB-266
Edson, Russell 1935- DLB-244
Edwards, Amelia Anne Blandford
    1831-1892 .... DLB-174
Edwards, Dic 1953- DLB-245
Edwards, Edward 1812-1886 .... DLB-184
Edwards, Jonathan 1703-1758 .... DLB-24, 270
Edwards, Jonathan, Jr. 1745-1801 .... DLB-37
Edwards, Junius 1929- DLB-33
Edwards, Matilda Barbara Betham
    1836-1919 .... DLB-174
Edwards, Richard 1524-1566 .... DLB-62
Edwards, Sarah Pierpont 1710-1758 ..... DLB-200
James Edwards [publishing house] DLB-154
Effinger, George Alec 1947- DLB-8
Egerton, George 1859-1945 .... DLB-135
Eggleston, Edward 1837-1902 .... DLB-12
Eggleston, Wilfred 1901-1986 .... DLB-92
Eglītis, Anšlavs 1906-1993 .... DLB-220
Eguren, José María 1874-1942 .... DLB-290
Ehrenreich, Barbara 1941- DLB-246
Ehrenstein, Albert 1886-1950 .... DLB-81
Ehrhart, W. D. 1948- DS-9
Ehrlich, Gretel 1946- DLB-212, 275
Eich, Günter 1907-1972 .... DLB-69, 124
Eichendorff, Joseph Freiherr von
    1788-1857 .... DLB-90
Eifukumon'in 1271-1342 .... DLB-203
Eigner, Larry 1926-1996 .... DLB-5, 193
Eikon Basilike 1649 .... DLB-151
Eilhart von Oberge
    circa 1140-circa 1195 .... DLB-148
Einar Benediktsson 1864-1940 .... DLB-293
Einar Kárason 1955- DLB-293
Einar Már Guðmundsson 1954- DLB-293
Einhard circa 770-840 .... DLB-148
Eiseley, Loren 1907-1977 .... DLB-275, DS-17
Eisenberg, Deborah 1945- DLB-244
Eisenreich, Herbert 1925-1986 .... DLB-85
Eisner, Kurt 1867-1919 .... DLB-66
Ekelöf, Gunnar 1907-1968 .... DLB-259
Eklund, Gordon 1945- Y-83
Ekman, Kerstin 1933- DLB-257
Ekwensi, Cyprian 1921- DLB-117; CDWLB-3
Elaw, Zilpha circa 1790-? DLB-239
George Eld [publishing house] DLB-170
Elder, Lonne, III 1931- DLB-7, 38, 44
Paul Elder and Company DLB-49
Eldershaw, Flora (M. Barnard Eldershaw)
    1897-1956 .... DLB-260
Eldershaw, M. Barnard (see Barnard, Marjorie and
    Eldershaw, Flora)

The Electronic Text Center and the Electronic Archive of Early American Fiction at the University of Virginia Library Y-98

Eliade, Mircea 1907-1986 . . . . DLB-220; CDWLB-4

Elie, Robert 1915-1973 . . . . DLB-88

Elin Pelin 1877-1949 . . . . DLB-147; CDWLB-4

Eliot, George 1819-1880 . . . . DLB-21, 35, 55; CDBLB-4

    The George Eliot Fellowship Y-99

Eliot, John 1604-1690 . . . . DLB-24

Eliot, T. S. 1888-1965
. . . . DLB-7, 10, 45, 63, 245; CDALB-5

    T. S. Eliot Centennial: The Return of the Old Possum Y-88

    The T. S. Eliot Society: Celebration and Scholarship, 1980-1999 . . . . Y-99

Eliot's Court Press DLB-170

Elizabeth I 1533-1603 . . . . DLB-136

Elizabeth von Nassau-Saarbrücken after 1393-1456 . . . . DLB-179

Elizondo, Salvador 1932- DLB-145

Elizondo, Sergio 1930- DLB-82

Elkin, Stanley 1930-1995 . . . . DLB-2, 28, 218, 278; Y-80

Elles, Dora Amy (see Wentworth, Patricia)

Ellet, Elizabeth F. 1818?-1877 . . . . DLB-30

Elliot, Ebenezer 1781-1849 . . . . DLB-96, 190

Elliot, Frances Minto (Dickinson) 1820-1898 . . . . DLB-166

Elliott, Charlotte 1789-1871 . . . . DLB-199

Elliott, George 1923- DLB-68

Elliott, George P. 1918-1980 . . . . DLB-244

Elliott, Janice 1931-1995 . . . . DLB-14

Elliott, Sarah Barnwell 1848-1928 . . . . . . DLB-221

Elliott, Sumner Locke 1917-1991 . . . . . . DLB-289

Elliott, Thomes and Talbot DLB-49

Elliott, William, III 1788-1863 . . . . . . DLB-3, 248

Ellin, Stanley 1916-1986 . . . . DLB-306

Ellis, Alice Thomas (Anna Margaret Haycraft) 1932- DLB-194

Ellis, Bret Easton 1964- DLB-292

Ellis, Edward S. 1840-1916 . . . . DLB-42

Ellis, George E.
    "The New Controversy Concerning Miracles DS-5

Ellis, Havelock 1859-1939 . . . . DLB-190

Frederick Staridge Ellis [publishing house] DLB-106

The George H. Ellis Company DLB-49

Ellison, Harlan 1934- DLB-8

    Tribute to Isaac Asimov Y-92

Ellison, Ralph 1914-1994 . . . DLB-2, 76, 227; Y-94; CDALB-1

Ellmann, Richard 1918-1987 . . . . . . DLB-103; Y-87

Ellroy, James 1948- DLB-226; Y-91

    Tribute to John D. MacDonald Y-86

    Tribute to Raymond Chandler Y-88

Eluard, Paul 1895-1952 . . . . DLB-258

Elyot, Thomas 1490?-1546 . . . . DLB-136

Emanuel, James Andrew 1921- DLB-41

Emecheta, Buchi 1944- DLB-117; CDWLB-3

Emerson, Ralph Waldo 1803-1882 . . . . . . DLB-1, 59, 73, 183, 223, 270; DS-5; CDALB-2

    Ralph Waldo Emerson in 1982 . . . . Y-82

    The Ralph Waldo Emerson Society Y-99

Emerson, William 1769-1811 . . . . DLB-37

Emerson, William R. 1923-1997 . . . . Y-97

Emin, Fedor Aleksandrovich circa 1735-1770 . . . . DLB-150

Emmanuel, Pierre 1916-1984 . . . . DLB-258

Empedocles fifth century B.C. DLB-176

Empson, William 1906-1984 . . . . DLB-20

Enchi Fumiko 1905-1986 . . . . DLB-182

Ende, Michael 1929-1995 . . . . DLB-75

Endō Shūsaku 1923-1996 . . . . DLB-182

Engel, Marian 1933-1985 . . . . DLB-53

Engel'gardt, Sof'ia Vladimirovna 1828-1894 . . . . DLB-277

Engels, Friedrich 1820-1895 . . . . DLB-129

Engle, Paul 1908- DLB-48

    Tribute to Robert Penn Warren Y-89

English, Thomas Dunn 1819-1902 . . . . . . DLB-202

Ennius 239 B.C.-169 B.C. DLB-211

Enquist, Per Olov 1934- DLB-257

Enright, Anne 1962- DLB-267

Enright, D. J. 1920- DLB-27

Enright, Elizabeth 1909-1968 . . . . DLB-22

Epictetus circa 55-circa 125-130 . . . . DLB-176

Epicurus 342/341 B.C.-271/270 B.C. DLB-176

Epps, Bernard 1936- DLB-53

Epshtein, Mikhail Naumovich 1950- . . . DLB-285

Epstein, Julius 1909-2000 and Epstein, Philip 1909-1952 . . . . DLB-26

Epstein, Leslie 1938- DLB-299

Editors, Conversations with Y-95

Equiano, Olaudah circa 1745-1797 . . . . . . DLB-37, 50; CDWLB-3

    Olaudah Equiano and Unfinished Journeys: The Slave-Narrative Tradition and Twentieth-Century Continuities DLB-117

Eragny Press DLB-112

Erasmus, Desiderius 1467-1536 . . . . DLB-136

Erba, Luciano 1922- DLB-128

Erdman, Nikolai Robertovich 1900-1970 . . . . DLB-272

Erdrich, Louise 1954- DLB-152, 175, 206; CDALB-7

Erenburg, Il'ia Grigor'evich 1891-1967 . . . DLB-272

Erichsen-Brown, Gwethalyn Graham (see Graham, Gwethalyn)

Eriugena, John Scottus circa 810-877 . . . . DLB-115

Ernst, Paul 1866-1933 . . . . DLB-66, 118

Erofeev, Venedikt Vasil'evich 1938-1990 . . . . DLB-285

Erofeev, Viktor Vladimirovich 1947- . . . DLB-285

Ershov, Petr Pavlovich 1815-1869 . . . . DLB-205

Erskine, Albert 1911-1993 . . . . Y-93

    At Home with Albert Erskine Y-00

Erskine, John 1879-1951 . . . . DLB-9, 102

Erskine, Mrs. Steuart ?-1948 . . . . DLB-195

Ertel', Aleksandr Ivanovich 1855-1908 . . . . DLB-238

Ervine, St. John Greer 1883-1971 . . . . DLB-10

Eschenburg, Johann Joachim 1743-1820 . . . . DLB-97

Escofet, Cristina 1945- DLB-305

Escoto, Julio 1944- DLB-145

Esdaile, Arundell 1880-1956 . . . . DLB-201

Esenin, Sergei Aleksandrovich 1895-1925 . . . . DLB-295

Eshleman, Clayton 1935- DLB-5

Espaillat, Rhina P. 1932- DLB-282

Espanca, Florbela 1894-1930 . . . . DLB-287

Espriu, Salvador 1913-1985 . . . . DLB-134

Ess Ess Publishing Company DLB-49

Essex House Press DLB-112

Esson, Louis 1878-1943 . . . . DLB-260

Essop, Ahmed 1931- DLB-225

Esterházy, Péter 1950- DLB-232; CDWLB-4

Estes, Eleanor 1906-1988 . . . . DLB-22

Estes and Lauriat DLB-49

Estleman, Loren D. 1952- DLB-226

Eszterhas, Joe 1944- DLB-185

Etherege, George 1636-circa 1692 . . . . DLB-80

Ethridge, Mark, Sr. 1896-1981 . . . . DLB-127

Ets, Marie Hall 1893-1984 . . . . DLB-22

Etter, David 1928- DLB-105

Ettner, Johann Christoph 1654-1724 . . . . DLB-168

Eudora Welty Remembered in Two Exhibits Y-02

Eugene Gant's Projected Works Y-01

Eupolemius flourished circa 1095 . . . . . . DLB-148

Euripides circa 484 B.C.-407/406 B.C.
. . . . DLB-176; CDWLB-1

Evans, Augusta Jane 1835-1909 . . . . DLB-239

Evans, Caradoc 1878-1945 . . . . DLB-162

Evans, Charles 1850-1935 . . . . DLB-187

Evans, Donald 1884-1921 . . . . DLB-54

Evans, George Henry 1805-1856 . . . . DLB-43

Evans, Hubert 1892-1986 . . . . DLB-92

Evans, Mari 1923- DLB-41

Evans, Mary Ann (see Eliot, George)

Evans, Nathaniel 1742-1767 . . . . DLB-31

Evans, Sebastian 1830-1909 . . . . DLB-35

Evans, Ray 1915- DLB-265

M. Evans and Company DLB-46

Evaristi, Marcella 1953- DLB-233

Everett, Alexander Hill 1790-1847 . . . . . . DLB-59

Everett, Edward 1794-1865 . . . . . . DLB-1, 59, 235

Everson, R. G. 1903- DLB-88

Cumulative Index

Everson, William 1912-1994 ..... DLB-5, 16, 212
Ewald, Johannes 1743-1781 .... DLB-300
Ewart, Gavin 1916-1995 .... DLB-40
Ewing, Juliana Horatia
    1841-1885 .... DLB-21, 163
The Examiner 1808-1881 .... DLB-110
Exley, Frederick 1929-1992 .... DLB-143; Y-81
Editorial: The Extension of Copyright Y-02
von Eyb, Albrecht 1420-1475 .... DLB-179
Eyre and Spottiswoode DLB-106
Ezera, Regīna 1930- DLB-232
Ezzo ?-after 1065 .... DLB-148

F

Faber, Frederick William 1814-1863 ...... DLB-32
Faber and Faber Limited DLB-112
Faccio, Rena (see Aleramo, Sibilla)
Facsimiles
    The Uses of Facsimile: A Symposium Y-90
Fadeev, Aleksandr Aleksandrovich
    1901-1956 .... DLB-272
Fagundo, Ana María 1938- DLB-134
Fainzil'berg, Il'ia Arnol'dovich
    (see Il'f, Il'ia and Petrov, Evgenii)
Fair, Ronald L. 1932- DLB-33
Fairfax, Beatrice (see Manning, Marie)
Fairlie, Gerard 1899-1983 .... DLB-77
Faldbakken, Knut 1941- DLB-297
Falkberget, Johan (Johan Petter Lillebakken)
    1879-1967 .... DLB-297
Fallada, Hans 1893-1947 .... DLB-56
Fancher, Betsy 1928- Y-83
Fane, Violet 1843-1905 .... DLB-35
Fanfrolico Press DLB-112
Fanning, Katherine 1927- DLB-127
Fanon, Frantz 1925-1961 .... DLB-296
Fanshawe, Sir Richard 1608-1666 ...... DLB-126
Fantasy Press Publishers DLB-46
Fante, John 1909-1983 .... DLB-130; Y-83
Al-Farabi circa 870-950 .... DLB-115
Farabough, Laura 1949- DLB-228
Farah, Nuruddin 1945- DLB-125; CDWLB-3
Farber, Norma 1909-1984 .... DLB-61
Fargue, Léon-Paul 1876-1947 .... DLB-258
Farigoule, Louis (see Romains, Jules)
Farjeon, Eleanor 1881-1965 .... DLB-160
Farley, Harriet 1812-1907 .... DLB-239
Farley, Walter 1920-1989 .... DLB-22
Farmborough, Florence 1887-1978 ..... DLB-204
Farmer, Penelope 1939- DLB-161
Farmer, Philip José 1918- DLB-8
Farnaby, Thomas 1575?-1647 .... DLB-236
Farningham, Marianne (see Hearn, Mary Anne)
Farquhar, George circa 1677-1707 ...... DLB-84
Farquharson, Martha (see Finley, Martha)
Farrar, Frederic William 1831-1903 .... DLB-163

Farrar, Straus and Giroux DLB-46
Farrar and Rinehart DLB-46
Farrell, J. G. 1935-1979 .... DLB-14, 271
Farrell, James T. 1904-1979 ... DLB-4, 9, 86; DS-2
Fast, Howard 1914- DLB-9
Faulkner, William 1897-1962
    ....DLB-9, 11, 44, 102; DS-2; Y-86; CDALB-5
    Faulkner and Yoknapatawpha
      Conference, Oxford, Mississippi Y-97
    Faulkner Centennial Addresses Y-97
    "Faulkner 100–Celebrating the Work,"
      University of South Carolina,
      Columbia Y-97
    Impressions of William Faulkner Y-97
    William Faulkner and the People-to-People
      Program Y-86
    William Faulkner Centenary
      Celebrations Y-97
    The William Faulkner Society Y-99
George Faulkner [publishing house] DLB-154
Faulks, Sebastian 1953- DLB-207
Fauset, Jessie Redmon 1882-1961 .... DLB-51
Faust, Frederick Schiller (Max Brand)
    1892-1944 .... DLB-256
Faust, Irvin
    1924- DLB-2, 28, 218, 278; Y-80, 00
    I Wake Up Screaming [Response to
      Ken Auletta] Y-97
    Tribute to Bernard Malamud Y-86
    Tribute to Isaac Bashevis Singer Y-91
    Tribute to Meyer Levin Y-81
Fawcett, Edgar 1847-1904 .... DLB-202
Fawcett, Millicent Garrett 1847-1929 .... DLB-190
Fawcett Books DLB-46
Fay, Theodore Sedgwick 1807-1898 ..... DLB-202
Fearing, Kenneth 1902-1961 .... DLB-9
Federal Writers' Project DLB-46
Federman, Raymond 1928- Y-80
Fedin, Konstantin Aleksandrovich
    1892-1977 .... DLB-272
Fedorov, Innokentii Vasil'evich
    (see Omulevsky, Innokentii Vasil'evich)
Feiffer, Jules 1929- DLB-7, 44
Feinberg, Charles E. 1899-1988 ....DLB-187; Y-88
Feind, Barthold 1678-1721 .... DLB-168
Feinstein, Elaine 1930- DLB-14, 40
Feirstein, Frederick 1940- DLB-282
Feiss, Paul Louis 1875-1952 .... DLB-187
Feldman, Irving 1928- DLB-169
Felipe, Carlos 1911-1975 .... DLB-305
Felipe, Léon 1884-1968 .... DLB-108
Fell, Frederick, Publishers DLB-46
Fellowship of Southern Writers Y-98
Felltham, Owen 1602?-1668 .... DLB-126, 151
Felman, Shoshana 1942- DLB-246
Fels, Ludwig 1946- DLB-75
Felton, Cornelius Conway
    1807-1862 .... DLB-1, 235

Mothe-Fénelon, François de Salignac de la
    1651-1715 .... DLB-268
Fenn, Harry 1837-1911 .... DLB-188
Fennario, David 1947- DLB-60
Fenner, Dudley 1558?-1587? DLB-236
Fenno, Jenny 1765?-1803 .... DLB-200
Fenno, John 1751-1798 .... DLB-43
R. F. Fenno and Company DLB-49
Fenoglio, Beppe 1922-1963 .... DLB-177
Fenton, Geoffrey 1539?-1608 .... DLB-136
Fenton, James 1949- DLB-40
    The Hemingway/Fenton
      Correspondence Y-02
Ferber, Edna 1885-1968 ...... DLB-9, 28, 86, 266
Ferdinand, Vallery, III (see Salaam, Kalamu ya)
Ferguson, Sir Samuel 1810-1886 .... DLB-32
Ferguson, William Scott 1875-1954 ...... DLB-47
Fergusson, Robert 1750-1774 .... DLB-109
Ferland, Albert 1872-1943 .... DLB-92
Ferlinghetti, Lawrence
    1919- DLB-5, 16; CDALB-1
    Tribute to Kenneth Rexroth Y-82
Fermor, Patrick Leigh 1915- DLB-204
Fern, Fanny (see Parton, Sara Payson Willis)
Ferrars, Elizabeth (Morna Doris Brown)
    1907-1995 .... DLB-87
Ferré, Rosario 1942- DLB-145
Ferreira, Vergílio 1916-1996 .... DLB-287
E. Ferret and Company DLB-49
Ferrier, Susan 1782-1854 .... DLB-116
Ferril, Thomas Hornsby 1896-1988 ..... DLB-206
Ferrini, Vincent 1913- DLB-48
Ferron, Jacques 1921-1985 .... DLB-60
Ferron, Madeleine 1922- DLB-53
Ferrucci, Franco 1936- DLB-196
Fet, Afanasii Afanas'evich
    1820?-1892 .... DLB-277
Fetridge and Company DLB-49
Feuchtersleben, Ernst Freiherr von
    1806-1849 .... DLB-133
Feuchtwanger, Lion 1884-1958 .... DLB-66
Feuerbach, Ludwig 1804-1872 .... DLB-133
Feuillet, Octave 1821-1890 .... DLB-192
Feydeau, Georges 1862-1921 .... DLB-192
Fibiger, Mathilde 1830-1872 .... DLB-300
Fichte, Johann Gottlieb 1762-1814 ...... DLB-90
Ficke, Arthur Davison 1883-1945 .... DLB-54
Fiction
    American Fiction and the 1930s DLB-9
    Fiction Best-Sellers, 1910-1945 .... DLB-9
    Postmodern Holocaust Fiction DLB-299
    The Year in Fiction Y-84, 86, 89, 94–99
    The Year in Fiction: A Biased View Y-83
    The Year in U.S. Fiction Y-00, 01
    The Year's Work in Fiction: A Survey ... Y-82
Fiedler, Leslie A. 1917- DLB-28, 67

Tribute to Bernard Malamud Y-86
Tribute to James Dickey Y-97
Field, Barron 1789-1846 . . . . DLB-230
Field, Edward 1924- DLB-105
Field, Eugene 1850-1895 . . DLB-23, 42, 140; DS-13
Field, John 1545?-1588 . . . . DLB-167
Field, Joseph M. 1810-1856 . . . . DLB-248
Field, Marshall, III 1893-1956 . . . . DLB-127
Field, Marshall, IV 1916-1965 . . . . DLB-127
Field, Marshall, V 1941- DLB-127
Field, Michael (Katherine Harris Bradley)
  1846-1914 . . . . DLB-240
"The Poetry File" DLB-105
Field, Nathan 1587-1619 or 1620 . . . . DLB-58
Field, Rachel 1894-1942 . . . . DLB-9, 22
Fielding, Helen 1958- DLB-231
Fielding, Henry
  1707-1754 . . . . DLB-39, 84, 101; CDBLB-2
  "Defense of *Amelia*" (1752) DLB-39
  The History of the Adventures of Joseph Andrews
    [excerpt] (1742) DLB-39
  Letter to [Samuel] Richardson on *Clarissa*
    (1748) DLB-39
  Preface to *Joseph Andrews* (1742) DLB-39
  Preface to Sarah Fielding's *Familiar
    Letters* (1747) [excerpt] DLB-39
  Preface to Sarah Fielding's *The
    Adventures of David Simple* (1744) . . . DLB-39
  Review of *Clarissa* (1748) DLB-39
  Tom Jones (1749) [excerpt] DLB-39
Fielding, Sarah 1710-1768 . . . . DLB-39
  Preface to *The Cry* (1754) DLB-39
Fields, Annie Adams 1834-1915 . . . . DLB-221
Fields, Dorothy 1905-1974 . . . . DLB-265
Fields, James T. 1817-1881 . . . . DLB-1, 235
Fields, Julia 1938- DLB-41
Fields, Osgood and Company DLB-49
Fields, W. C. 1880-1946 . . . . DLB-44
Fierstein, Harvey 1954- DLB-266
Figes, Eva 1932- DLB-14, 271
Figuera, Angela 1902-1984 . . . . DLB-108
Filmer, Sir Robert 1586-1653 . . . . DLB-151
Filson, John circa 1753-1788 . . . . DLB-37
Finch, Anne, Countess of Winchilsea
  1661-1720 . . . . DLB-95
Finch, Annie 1956- DLB-282
Finch, Robert 1900- DLB-88
Findley, Timothy 1930-2002 . . . . DLB-53
Finlay, Ian Hamilton 1925- DLB-40
Finley, Martha 1828-1909 . . . . DLB-42
Finn, Elizabeth Anne (McCaul)
  1825-1921 . . . . DLB-166
Finnegan, Seamus 1949- DLB-245
Finney, Jack 1911-1995 . . . . DLB-8
Finney, Walter Braden (see Finney, Jack)
Firbank, Ronald 1886-1926 . . . . DLB-36
Firmin, Giles 1615-1697 . . . . DLB-24

First Edition Library/Collectors'
  Reprints, Inc. Y-91
Fischart, Johann
  1546 or 1547-1590 or 1591 . . . . DLB-179
Fischer, Karoline Auguste Fernandine
  1764-1842 . . . . DLB-94
Fischer, Tibor 1959- DLB-231
Fish, Stanley 1938- DLB-67
Fishacre, Richard 1205-1248 . . . . DLB-115
Fisher, Clay (see Allen, Henry W.)
Fisher, Dorothy Canfield 1879-1958 . . . DLB-9, 102
Fisher, Leonard Everett 1924- DLB-61
Fisher, Roy 1930- DLB-40
Fisher, Rudolph 1897-1934 . . . . DLB-51, 102
Fisher, Steve 1913-1980 . . . . DLB-226
Fisher, Sydney George 1856-1927 . . . . DLB-47
Fisher, Vardis 1895-1968 . . . . DLB-9, 206
Fiske, John 1608-1677 . . . . DLB-24
Fiske, John 1842-1901 . . . . DLB-47, 64
Fitch, Thomas circa 1700-1774 . . . . DLB-31
Fitch, William Clyde 1865-1909 . . . . DLB-7
FitzGerald, Edward 1809-1883 . . . . DLB-32
Fitzgerald, F. Scott 1896-1940
  . . . . DLB-4, 9, 86; Y-81, 92;
    DS-1, 15, 16; CDALB-4
  F. Scott Fitzgerald: A Descriptive
    Bibliography, Supplement (2001) Y-01
  F. Scott Fitzgerald Centenary
    Celebrations Y-96
  F. Scott Fitzgerald Inducted into the
    American Poets' Corner at St. John
    the Divine; Ezra Pound Banned Y-99
  "F. Scott Fitzgerald: St. Paul's Native Son
    and Distinguished American Writer":
    University of Minnesota Conference,
    29-31 October 1982 . . . . Y-82
  First International F. Scott Fitzgerald
    Conference Y-92
  The Great Gatsby (Documentary) DLB-219
  Tender Is the Night (Documentary) DLB-273
Fitzgerald, Penelope 1916- DLB-14, 194
Fitzgerald, Robert 1910-1985 . . . . Y-80
FitzGerald, Robert D. 1902-1987 . . . . DLB-260
Fitzgerald, Thomas 1819-1891 . . . . DLB-23
Fitzgerald, Zelda Sayre 1900-1948 . . . . Y-84
Fitzhugh, Louise 1928-1974 . . . . DLB-52
Fitzhugh, William circa 1651-1701 . . . . DLB-24
Flagg, James Montgomery 1877-1960 . . . . . DLB-188
Flanagan, Thomas 1923-2002 . . . . Y-80
Flanner, Hildegarde 1899-1987 . . . . DLB-48
Flanner, Janet 1892-1978 . . . . DLB-4; DS-15
Flannery, Peter 1951- DLB-233
Flaubert, Gustave 1821-1880 . . . . DLB-119, 301
Flavin, Martin 1883-1967 . . . . DLB-9
Fleck, Konrad (flourished circa 1220) DLB-138
Flecker, James Elroy 1884-1915 . . . . DLB-10, 19
Fleeson, Doris 1901-1970 . . . . DLB-29
Fleißer, Marieluise 1901-1974 . . . . DLB-56, 124

Fleischer, Nat 1887-1972 . . . . DLB-241
Fleming, Abraham 1552?-1607 . . . . DLB-236
Fleming, Ian 1908-1964 . . . DLB-87, 201; CDBLB-7
Fleming, Joan 1908-1980 . . . . DLB-276
Fleming, May Agnes 1840-1880 . . . . DLB-99
Fleming, Paul 1609-1640 . . . . DLB-164
Fleming, Peter 1907-1971 . . . . DLB-195
Fletcher, Giles, the Elder 1546-1611 . . . . . DLB-136
Fletcher, Giles, the Younger
  1585 or 1586-1623 . . . . DLB-121
Fletcher, J. S. 1863-1935 . . . . DLB-70
Fletcher, John 1579-1625 . . . . DLB-58
Fletcher, John Gould 1886-1950 . . . . DLB-4, 45
Fletcher, Phineas 1582-1650 . . . . DLB-121
Flieg, Helmut (see Heym, Stefan)
Flint, F. S. 1885-1960 . . . . DLB-19
Flint, Timothy 1780-1840 . . . . DLB-73, 186
Fløgstad, Kjartan 1944- DLB-297
Florensky, Pavel Aleksandrovich
  1882-1937 . . . . DLB-295
Flores, Juan de fl. 1470-1500 . . . . DLB-286
Flores-Williams, Jason 1969- DLB-209
Florio, John 1553?-1625 . . . . DLB-172
Fludd, Robert 1574-1637 . . . . DLB-281
Flynn, Elizabeth Gurley 1890-1964 . . . . . . DLB-303
Fo, Dario 1926- Y-97
  Nobel Lecture 1997: Contra Jogulatores
    Obloquentes Y-97
Foden, Giles 1967- DLB-267
Fofanov, Konstantin Mikhailovich
  1862-1911 . . . . DLB-277
Foix, J. V. 1893-1987 . . . . DLB-134
Foley, Martha 1897-1977 . . . . DLB-137
Folger, Henry Clay 1857-1930 . . . . DLB-140
Folio Society DLB-112
Follain, Jean 1903-1971 . . . . DLB-258
Follen, Charles 1796-1840 . . . . DLB-235
Follen, Eliza Lee (Cabot) 1787-1860 . . . . DLB-1, 235
Follett, Ken 1949- DLB-87; Y-81
Follett Publishing Company DLB-46
John West Folsom [publishing house] DLB-49
Folz, Hans
  between 1435 and 1440-1513 . . . . DLB-179
Fonseca, Manuel da 1911-1993 . . . . DLB-287
Fonseca, Rubem 1925- DLB-307
Fontane, Theodor
  1819-1898 . . . . DLB-129; CDWLB-2
Fontenelle, Bernard Le Bovier de
  1657-1757 . . . . DLB-268
Fontes, Montserrat 1940- DLB-209
Fonvisin, Denis Ivanovich
  1744 or 1745-1792 . . . . DLB-150
Foote, Horton 1916- DLB-26, 266
Foote, Mary Hallock
  1847-1938 . . . . DLB-186, 188, 202, 221
Foote, Samuel 1721-1777 . . . . DLB-89
Foote, Shelby 1916- DLB-2, 17

Forbes, Calvin 1945- ... DLB-41	Foster, Hannah Webster 1758-1840 ... DLB-37, 200	Frattini, Alberto 1922- ... DLB-128
Forbes, Ester 1891-1967 ... DLB-22	Foster, John 1648-1681 ... DLB-24	Frau Ava ?-1127 ... DLB-148
Forbes, Rosita 1893?-1967 ... DLB-195	Foster, Michael 1904-1956 ... DLB-9	Fraunce, Abraham 1558?-1592 or 1593 .. DLB-236
Forbes and Company ... DLB-49	Foster, Myles Birket 1825-1899 ... DLB-184	Frayn, Michael 1933- ... DLB-13, 14, 194, 245
Force, Peter 1790-1868 ... DLB-30	Foster, William Z. 1881-1961 ... DLB-303	Frazier, Charles 1950- ... DLB-292
Forché, Carolyn 1950- ... DLB-5, 193	Foucault, Michel 1926-1984 ... DLB-242	Fréchette, Louis-Honoré 1839-1908 ... DLB-99
Ford, Charles Henri 1913-2002 ... DLB-4, 48	Robert and Andrew Foulis [publishing house] ... DLB-154	Frederic, Harold 1856-1898 ... DLB-12, 23; DS-13
Ford, Corey 1902-1969 ... DLB-11	Fouqué, Caroline de la Motte 1774-1831 ... DLB-90	Freed, Arthur 1894-1973 ... DLB-265
Ford, Ford Madox 1873-1939 ... DLB-34, 98, 162; CDBLB-6	Fouqué, Friedrich de la Motte 1777-1843 ... DLB-90	Freeling, Nicolas 1927- ... DLB-87
Nathan Asch Remembers Ford Madox Ford, Sam Roth, and Hart Crane ... Y-02	Four Seas Company ... DLB-46	Tribute to Georges Simenon ... Y-89
J. B. Ford and Company ... DLB-49	Four Winds Press ... DLB-46	Freeman, Douglas Southall 1886-1953 ... DLB-17; DS-17
Ford, Jesse Hill 1928-1996 ... DLB-6	Fournier, Henri Alban (see Alain-Fournier)	Freeman, Joseph 1897-1965 ... DLB-303
Ford, John 1586-? ... DLB-58; CDBLB-1	Fowler, Christopher 1953- ... DLB-267	Freeman, Judith 1946- ... DLB-256
Ford, R. A. D. 1915- ... DLB-88	Fowler, Connie May 1958- ... DLB-292	Freeman, Legh Richmond 1842-1915 ... DLB-23
Ford, Richard 1944- ... DLB-227	Fowler and Wells Company ... DLB-49	Freeman, Mary E. Wilkins 1852-1930 ... DLB-12, 78, 221
Ford, Worthington C. 1858-1941 ... DLB-47	Fowles, John 1926- ... DLB-14, 139, 207; CDBLB-8	Freeman, R. Austin 1862-1943 ... DLB-70
Fords, Howard, and Hulbert ... DLB-49	Fox, John 1939- ... DLB-245	Freidank circa 1170-circa 1233 ... DLB-138
Foreman, Carl 1914-1984 ... DLB-26	Fox, John, Jr. 1862 or 1863-1919 ... DLB-9; DS-13	Freiligrath, Ferdinand 1810-1876 ... DLB-133
Forester, C. S. 1899-1966 ... DLB-191	Fox, Paula 1923- ... DLB-52	Fremlin, Celia 1914- ... DLB-276
The C. S. Forester Society ... Y-00	Fox, Richard Kyle 1846-1922 ... DLB-79	Frémont, Jessie Benton 1834-1902 ... DLB-183
Forester, Frank (see Herbert, Henry William)	Fox, William Price 1926- ... DLB-2; Y-81	Frémont, John Charles 1813-1890 ... DLB-183, 186
Anthologizing New Formalism ... DLB-282	Remembering Joe Heller ... Y-99	French, Alice 1850-1934 ... DLB-74; DS-13
The Little Magazines of the New Formalism ... DLB-282	Richard K. Fox [publishing house] ... DLB-49	French, David 1939- ... DLB-53
The New Narrative Poetry ... DLB-282	Foxe, John 1517-1587 ... DLB-132	French, Evangeline 1869-1960 ... DLB-195
Presses of the New Formalism and the New Narrative ... DLB-282	Fraenkel, Michael 1896-1957 ... DLB-4	French, Francesca 1871-1960 ... DLB-195
The Prosody of the New Formalism ... DLB-282	France, Anatole 1844-1924 ... DLB-123	James French [publishing house] ... DLB-49
Younger Women Poets of the New Formalism ... DLB-282	France, Richard 1938- ... DLB-7	Samuel French [publishing house] ... DLB-49
Forman, Harry Buxton 1842-1917 ... DLB-184	Francis, Convers 1795-1863 ... DLB-1, 235	Samuel French, Limited ... DLB-106
Fornés, María Irene 1930- ... DLB-7	Francis, Dick 1920- ... DLB-87; CDBLB-8	French Literature
Forrest, Leon 1937-1997 ... DLB-33	Francis, Sir Frank 1901-1988 ... DLB-201	Epic and Beast Epic ... DLB-208
Forsh, Ol'ga Dmitrievna 1873-1961 ... DLB-272	Francis, Jeffrey, Lord 1773-1850 ... DLB-107	French Arthurian Literature ... DLB-208
Forster, E. M. 1879-1970 ... DLB-34, 98, 162, 178, 195; DS-10; CDBLB-6	C. S. Francis [publishing house] ... DLB-49	Lyric Poetry ... DLB-268
"Fantasy," from Aspects of the Novel (1927) ... DLB-178	Franck, Sebastian 1499-1542 ... DLB-179	Other Poets ... DLB-217
Forster, Georg 1754-1794 ... DLB-94	Francke, Kuno 1855-1930 ... DLB-71	Poetry in Nineteenth-Century France: Cultural Background and Critical Commentary ... DLB-217
Forster, John 1812-1876 ... DLB-144	Françoise (Robertine Barry) 1863-1910 ... DLB-92	Roman de la Rose: Guillaume de Lorris 1200 to 1205-circa 1230, Jean de Meun 1235/1240-circa 1305 ... DLB-208
Forster, Margaret 1938- ... DLB-155, 271	François, Louise von 1817-1893 ... DLB-129	Saints' Lives ... DLB-208
Forsyth, Frederick 1938- ... DLB-87	Frank, Bruno 1887-1945 ... DLB-118	Troubadours, Trobaíritz, and Trouvères ... DLB-208
Forsyth, William "Literary Style" (1857) [excerpt] ... DLB-57	Frank, Leonhard 1882-1961 ... DLB-56, 118	French Theater Medieval French Drama ... DLB-208
Forten, Charlotte L. 1837-1914 ... DLB-50, 239	Frank, Melvin 1913-1988 ... DLB-26	Parisian Theater, Fall 1984: Toward a New Baroque ... Y-85
Pages from Her Diary ... DLB-50	Frank, Waldo 1889-1967 ... DLB-9, 63	Freneau, Philip 1752-1832 ... DLB-37, 43
Fortini, Franco 1917-1994 ... DLB-128	Franken, Rose 1895?-1988 ... DLB-228, Y-84	The Rising Glory of America ... DLB-37
Fortune, Mary ca. 1833-ca. 1910 ... DLB-230	Franklin, Benjamin 1706-1790 ... DLB-24, 43, 73, 183; CDALB-2	Freni, Melo 1934- ... DLB-128
Fortune, T. Thomas 1856-1928 ... DLB-23	Franklin, James 1697-1735 ... DLB-43	Freshfield, Douglas W. 1845-1934 ... DLB-174
Fosdick, Charles Austin 1842-1915 ... DLB-42	Franklin, John 1786-1847 ... DLB-99	Freud, Sigmund 1856-1939 ... DLB-296
Fosse, Jon 1959- ... DLB-297	Franklin, Miles 1879-1954 ... DLB-230	Freytag, Gustav 1816-1895 ... DLB-129
Foster, David 1944- ... DLB-289	Franklin Library ... DLB-46	Frída Á. Sigurðardóttir 1940- ... DLB-293
Foster, Genevieve 1893-1979 ... DLB-61	Frantz, Ralph Jules 1902-1979 ... DLB-4	Fridegård, Jan 1897-1968 ... DLB-259
	Franzos, Karl Emil 1848-1904 ... DLB-129	Fried, Erich 1921-1988 ... DLB-85
	Fraser, Antonia 1932- ... DLB-276	
	Fraser, G. S. 1915-1980 ... DLB-27	
	Fraser, Kathleen 1935- ... DLB-169	

Friedan, Betty 1921- DLB-246
Friedman, Bruce Jay 1930- DLB-2, 28, 244
Friedman, Carl 1952- DLB-299
Friedman, Kinky 1944- DLB-292
Friedrich von Hausen circa 1171-1190....DLB-138
Friel, Brian 1929- DLB-13
Friend, Krebs 1895?-1967? DLB-4
Fries, Fritz Rudolf 1935- DLB-75
Frisch, Max
  1911-1991 ....DLB-69, 124; CDWLB-2
Frischlin, Nicodemus 1547-1590 ....DLB-179
Frischmuth, Barbara 1941- DLB-85
Fritz, Jean 1915- DLB-52
Froissart, Jean circa 1337-circa 1404......DLB-208
Fromm, Erich 1900-1980...............DLB-296
Fromentin, Eugene 1820-1876 ....DLB-123
Frontinus circa A.D. 35-A.D. 103/104 ....DLB-211
Frost, A. B. 1851-1928.........DLB-188; DS-13
Frost, Robert
  1874-1963 ....DLB-54; DS-7; CDALB-4
  The Friends of the Dymock Poets........Y-00
Frostenson, Katarina 1953- DLB-257
Frothingham, Octavius Brooks
  1822-1895 ....DLB-1, 243
Froude, James Anthony
  1818-1894 ....DLB-18, 57, 144
Fruitlands 1843-1844..........DLB-1, 223; DS-5
Fry, Christopher 1907- DLB-13
  Tribute to John Betjeman Y-84
Fry, Roger 1866-1934 ....DS-10
Fry, Stephen 1957- DLB-207
Frye, Northrop 1912-1991 ......DLB-67, 68, 246
Fuchs, Daniel 1909-1993 .....DLB-9, 26, 28; Y-93
  Tribute to Isaac Bashevis Singer Y-91
Fuentes, Carlos 1928- DLB-113; CDWLB-3
Fuertes, Gloria 1918-1998 ....DLB-108
Fugard, Athol 1932- DLB-225
The Fugitives and the Agrarians:
  The First Exhibition Y-85
Fujiwara no Shunzei 1114-1204 ....DLB-203
Fujiwara no Tameaki 1230s?-1290s?.....DLB-203
Fujiwara no Tameie 1198-1275 ....DLB-203
Fujiwara no Teika 1162-1241 ....DLB-203
Fuks, Ladislav 1923-1994 ....DLB-299
Fulbecke, William 1560-1603?..........DLB-172
Fuller, Charles 1939- DLB-38, 266
Fuller, Henry Blake 1857-1929...........DLB-12
Fuller, John 1937- DLB-40
Fuller, Margaret (see Fuller, Sarah)
Fuller, Roy 1912-1991 ....DLB-15, 20
  Tribute to Christopher Isherwood Y-86
Fuller, Samuel 1912-1997 ....DLB-26
Fuller, Sarah 1810-1850 ....DLB-1, 59, 73,
                    183, 223, 239; DS-5; CDALB-2
Fuller, Thomas 1608-1661................DLB-151
Fullerton, Hugh 1873-1945 ....DLB-171

Fullwood, William flourished 1568......DLB-236
Fulton, Alice 1952- DLB-193
Fulton, Len 1934- Y-86
Fulton, Robin 1937- DLB-40
Furbank, P. N. 1920- DLB-155
Furetière, Antoine 1619-1688...........DLB-268
Furman, Laura 1945- Y-86
Furmanov, Dmitrii Andreevich
  1891-1926 ....DLB-272
Furness, Horace Howard 1833-1912......DLB-64
Furness, William Henry
  1802-1896 ....DLB-1, 235
Furnivall, Frederick James 1825-1910 ....DLB-184
Furphy, Joseph (Tom Collins)
  1843-1912 ....DLB-230
Furthman, Jules 1888-1966 ....DLB-26
  Shakespeare and Montaigne: A
    Symposium by Jules Furthman......Y-02
Furui Yoshikichi 1937- DLB-182
Fushimi, Emperor 1265-1317...........DLB-203
Futabatei Shimei (Hasegawa Tatsunosuke)
  1864-1909 ....DLB-180
Fyleman, Rose 1877-1957..............DLB-160

G

Gaarder, Jostein 1952- DLB-297
Gadallah, Leslie 1939- DLB-251
Gadamer, Hans-Georg 1900-2002.......DLB-296
Gadda, Carlo Emilio 1893-1973 ....DLB-177
Gaddis, William 1922-1998 ....DLB-2, 278
  William Gaddis: A Tribute............Y-99
Gág, Wanda 1893-1946................DLB-22
Gagarin, Ivan Sergeevich 1814-1882 .....DLB-198
Gagnon, Madeleine 1938- DLB-60
Gaiman, Neil 1960- DLB-261
Gaine, Hugh 1726-1807.................DLB-43
  Hugh Gaine [publishing house] DLB-49
Gaines, Ernest J.
  1933- DLB-2, 33, 152; Y-80; CDALB-6
Gaiser, Gerd 1908-1976.................DLB-69
Gaitskill, Mary 1954- DLB-244
Galarza, Ernesto 1905-1984.............DLB-122
Galaxy Science Fiction Novels..........DLB-46
Galbraith, Robert (or Caubraith)
  circa 1483-1544...................DLB-281
Gale, Zona 1874-1938 ....DLB-9, 228, 78
Galen of Pergamon 129-after 210 ....DLB-176
Gales, Winifred Marshall 1761-1839.....DLB-200
Medieval Galician-Portuguese Poetry DLB-287
Gall, Louise von 1815-1855..............DLB-133
Gallagher, Tess 1943- DLB-120, 212, 244
Gallagher, Wes 1911- DLB-127
Gallagher, William Davis 1808-1894......DLB-73
Gallant, Mavis 1922- DLB-53
Gallegos, María Magdalena 1935- DLB-209
Gallico, Paul 1897-1976 ....DLB-9, 171

Gallop, Jane 1952- DLB-246
Galloway, Grace Growden 1727-1782....DLB-200
Gallup, Donald 1913-2000.............DLB-187
Galsworthy, John 1867-1933
  .....DLB-10, 34, 98, 162; DS-16; CDBLB-5
Galt, John 1779-1839 ....DLB-99, 116, 159
Galton, Sir Francis 1822-1911 ....DLB-166
Galvin, Brendan 1938- DLB-5
Gambaro, Griselda 1928- DLB-305
Gambit..............................DLB-46
Gamboa, Reymundo 1948- DLB-122
Gammer Gurton's Needle DLB-62
Gan, Elena Andreevna (Zeneida R-va)
  1814-1842 ....DLB-198
Gandlevsky, Sergei Markovich 1952- ..DLB-285
Gannett, Frank E. 1876-1957..........DLB-29
Gao Xingjian 1940- Y-00
  Nobel Lecture 2000: "The Case for
    Literature" Y-00
Gaos, Vicente 1919-1980...............DLB-134
García, Andrew 1854?-1943 ....DLB-209
García, Cristina 1958- DLB-292
García, Lionel G. 1935- DLB-82
García, Richard 1941- DLB-209
García, Santiago 1928- DLB-305
García Márquez, Gabriel
  1928- DLB-113; Y-82; CDWLB-3
  The Magical World of Macondo Y-82
  Nobel Lecture 1982: The Solitude of
    Latin America....................Y-82
  A Tribute to Gabriel García Márquez....Y-82
García Marruz, Fina 1923- DLB-283
García-Camarillo, Cecilio 1943- DLB-209
Gardam, Jane 1928- DLB-14, 161, 231
Gardell, Jonas 1963- DLB-257
Garden, Alexander circa 1685-1756.......DLB-31
Gardiner, John Rolfe 1936- DLB-244
Gardiner, Margaret Power Farmer
  (see Blessington, Marguerite, Countess of)
Gardner, John
  1933-1982 ....DLB-2; Y-82; CDALB-7
Garfield, Leon 1921-1996 ....DLB-161
Garis, Howard R. 1873-1962............DLB-22
Garland, Hamlin 1860-1940 ..DLB-12, 71, 78, 186
  The Hamlin Garland Society Y-01
Garneau, François-Xavier 1809-1866 ....DLB-99
Garneau, Hector de Saint-Denys
  1912-1943 ....DLB-88
Garneau, Michel 1939- DLB-53
Garner, Alan 1934- DLB-161, 261
Garner, Hugh 1913-1979.................DLB-68
Garnett, David 1892-1981...............DLB-34
Garnett, Eve 1900-1991 ....DLB-160
Garnett, Richard 1835-1906 ....DLB-184
Garrard, Lewis H. 1829-1887 ....DLB-186
Garraty, John A. 1920- DLB-17

403

Cumulative Index

Garrett, Almeida (João Baptista da Silva Leitão de Almeida Garrett) 1799-1854 . . . . DLB-287

Garrett, George 1929- DLB-2, 5, 130, 152; Y-83

    Literary Prizes Y-00

    My Summer Reading Orgy: Reading for Fun and Games: One Reader's Report on the Summer of 2001 . . . . . . Y-01

    A Summing Up at Century's End Y-99

    Tribute to James Dickey Y-97

    Tribute to Michael M. Rea Y-97

    Tribute to Paxton Davis Y-94

    Tribute to Peter Taylor Y-94

    Tribute to William Goyen Y-83

    A Writer Talking: A Collage Y-00

Garrett, John Work 1872-1942 . . . . DLB-187

Garrick, David 1717-1779 . . . . DLB-84, 213

Garrison, William Lloyd 1805-1879 . . . . DLB-1, 43, 235; CDALB-2

Garro, Elena 1920-1998 . . . . DLB-145

Garshin, Vsevolod Mikhailovich 1855-1888 . . . . DLB-277

Garth, Samuel 1661-1719 . . . . DLB-95

Garve, Andrew 1908-2001 . . . . DLB-87

Gary, Romain 1914-1980 . . . . DLB-83, 299

Gascoigne, George 1539?-1577 . . . . DLB-136

Gascoyne, David 1916-2001 . . . . DLB-20

Gash, Jonathan (John Grant) 1933- . . . DLB-276

Gaskell, Elizabeth Cleghorn 1810-1865 . . . . . . DLB-21, 144, 159; CDBLB-4

    The Gaskell Society Y-98

Gaskell, Jane 1941- DLB-261

Gaspey, Thomas 1788-1871 . . . . DLB-116

Gass, William H. 1924- DLB-2, 227

Gates, Doris 1901-1987 . . . . DLB-22

Gates, Henry Louis, Jr. 1950- DLB-67

Gates, Lewis E. 1860-1924 . . . . DLB-71

Gatto, Alfonso 1909-1976 . . . . DLB-114

Gault, William Campbell 1910-1995 . . . . DLB-226

    Tribute to Kenneth Millar Y-83

Gaunt, Mary 1861-1942 . . . . DLB-174, 230

Gautier, Théophile 1811-1872 . . . . DLB-119

Gautreaux, Tim 1947- DLB-292

Gauvreau, Claude 1925-1971 . . . . DLB-88

The Gawain-Poet flourished circa 1350-1400 . . . . DLB-146

Gawsworth, John (Terence Ian Fytton Armstrong) 1912-1970 . . . . DLB-255

Gay, Ebenezer 1696-1787 . . . . DLB-24

Gay, John 1685-1732 . . . . DLB-84, 95

Gayarré, Charles E. A. 1805-1895 . . . . DLB-30

Charles Gaylord [publishing house] DLB-49

Gaylord, Edward King 1873-1974 . . . . . . DLB-127

Gaylord, Edward Lewis 1919- DLB-127

Gébler, Carlo 1954- DLB-271

Geda, Sigitas 1943- DLB-232

Geddes, Gary 1940- DLB-60

Geddes, Virgil 1897- DLB-4

Gedeon (Georgii Andreevich Krinovsky) circa 1730-1763 . . . . DLB-150

Gee, Maggie 1948- DLB-207

Gee, Shirley 1932- DLB-245

Geibel, Emanuel 1815-1884 . . . . DLB-129

Geiogamah, Hanay 1945- DLB-175

Geis, Bernard, Associates DLB-46

Geisel, Theodor Seuss 1904-1991 . . . . DLB-61; Y-91

Gelb, Arthur 1924- DLB-103

Gelb, Barbara 1926- DLB-103

Gelber, Jack 1932- DLB-7, 228

Gélinas, Gratien 1909-1999 . . . . DLB-88

Gellert, Christian Füerchtegott 1715-1769 . . . . DLB-97

Gellhorn, Martha 1908-1998 . . . . Y-82, 98

Gems, Pam 1925- DLB-13

Genet, Jean 1910-1986 . . . . DLB-72; Y-86

Genette, Gérard 1930- DLB-242

Genevoix, Maurice 1890-1980 . . . . DLB-65

Genis, Aleksandr Aleksandrovich 1953- DLB-285

Genovese, Eugene D. 1930- DLB-17

Gent, Peter 1942- Y-82

Geoffrey of Monmouth circa 1100-1155 . . . . DLB-146

George, Elizabeth 1949- DLB-306

George, Henry 1839-1897 . . . . DLB-23

George, Jean Craighead 1919- DLB-52

George, W. L. 1882-1926 . . . . DLB-197

George III, King of Great Britain and Ireland 1738-1820 . . . . DLB-213

Georgslied 896? DLB-148

Gerber, Merrill Joan 1938- DLB-218

Gerhardie, William 1895-1977 . . . . DLB-36

Gerhardt, Paul 1607-1676 . . . . DLB-164

Gérin, Winifred 1901-1981 . . . . DLB-155

Gérin-Lajoie, Antoine 1824-1882 . . . . DLB-99

German Literature
    A Call to Letters and an Invitation to the Electric Chair DLB-75

    The Conversion of an Unpolitical Man DLB-66

    The German Radio Play DLB-124

    The German Transformation from the Baroque to the Enlightenment DLB-97

    Germanophilism DLB-66

    A Letter from a New Germany Y-90

    The Making of a People DLB-66

    The Novel of Impressionism DLB-66

    Pattern and Paradigm: History as Design DLB-75

    Premisses DLB-66

    The 'Twenties and Berlin DLB-66

    Wolfram von Eschenbach's Parzival: Prologue and Book 3 . . . . DLB-138

    Writers and Politics: 1871-1918 . . . . . . DLB-66

German Literature, Middle Ages
    Abrogans circa 790-800 . . . . DLB-148

    Annolied between 1077 and 1081 . . . . . DLB-148

    The Arthurian Tradition and Its European Context DLB-138

    Cambridge Songs (Carmina Cantabrigensia) circa 1050 . . . . DLB-148

    Christus und die Samariterin circa 950 . . DLB-148

    De Heinrico circa 980? DLB-148

    Ecbasis Captivi circa 1045 . . . . DLB-148

    Georgslied 896? DLB-148

    German Literature and Culture from Charlemagne to the Early Courtly Period DLB-148; CDWLB-2

    The Germanic Epic and Old English Heroic Poetry: Widsith, Waldere, and The Fight at Finnsburg DLB-146

    Graf Rudolf between circa 1170 and circa 1185 . . . . DLB-148

    Heliand circa 850 . . . . DLB-148

    Das Hildesbrandslied circa 820 . . . . DLB-148; CDWLB-2

    Kaiserchronik circa 1147 . . . . DLB-148

    The Legends of the Saints and a Medieval Christian Worldview DLB-148

    Ludus de Antichristo circa 1160 . . . . . . DLB-148

    Ludwigslied 881 or 882 . . . . DLB-148

    Muspilli circa 790-circa 850 . . . . DLB-148

    Old German Genesis and Old German Exodus circa 1050-circa 1130 . . . . DLB-148

    Old High German Charms and Blessings DLB-148; CDWLB-2

    The Old High German Isidor circa 790-800 . . . . DLB-148

    Petruslied circa 854? DLB-148

    Physiologus circa 1070-circa 1150 . . . . . DLB-148

    Ruodlieb circa 1050-1075 . . . . DLB-148

    "Spielmannsepen" (circa 1152 circa 1500) DLB-148

    The Strasbourg Oaths 842 . . . . DLB-148

    Tatian circa 830 . . . . DLB-148

    Waltharius circa 825 . . . . DLB-148

    Wessobrunner Gebet circa 787-815 . . . . DLB-148

German Theater
    German Drama 800-1280 . . . . DLB-138

    German Drama from Naturalism to Fascism: 1889-1933 . . . . DLB-118

Gernsback, Hugo 1884-1967 . . . . DLB-8, 137

Gerould, Katharine Fullerton 1879-1944 . . . . DLB-78

Samuel Gerrish [publishing house] DLB-49

Gerrold, David 1944- DLB-8

Gersão, Teolinda 1940- DLB-287

Gershon, Karen 1923-1993 . . . . DLB-299

Gershwin, Ira 1896-1983 . . . . DLB-265

    The Ira Gershwin Centenary Y-96

Gerson, Jean 1363-1429 . . . . DLB-208

Gersonides 1288-1344 . . . . DLB-115

Gerstäcker, Friedrich 1816-1872 . . . . DLB-129

Gertsen, Aleksandr Ivanovich (see Herzen, Alexander)

Gerstenberg, Heinrich Wilhelm von 1737-1823........DLB-97

Gervinus, Georg Gottfried 1805-1871........DLB-133

Gery, John 1953-........DLB-282

Geßner, Solomon 1730-1788........DLB-97

Geston, Mark S. 1946-........DLB-8

Al-Ghazali 1058-1111........DLB-115

Gibbings, Robert 1889-1958........DLB-195

Gibbon, Edward 1737-1794........DLB-104

Gibbon, John Murray 1875-1952........DLB-92

Gibbon, Lewis Grassic (see Mitchell, James Leslie)

Gibbons, Floyd 1887-1939........DLB-25

Gibbons, Kaye 1960-........DLB-292

Gibbons, Reginald 1947-........DLB-120

Gibbons, William ?-?........DLB-73

Gibson, Charles Dana 1867-1944........DLB-188; DS-13

Gibson, Graeme 1934-........DLB-53

Gibson, Margaret 1944-........DLB-120

Gibson, Margaret Dunlop 1843-1920........DLB-174

Gibson, Wilfrid 1878-1962........DLB-19

The Friends of the Dymock Poets........Y-00

Gibson, William 1914-........DLB-7

Gibson, William 1948-........DLB-251

Gide, André 1869-1951........DLB-65

Giguère, Diane 1937-........DLB-53

Giguère, Roland 1929-........DLB-60

Gil de Biedma, Jaime 1929-1990........DLB-108

Gil-Albert, Juan 1906-1994........DLB-134

Gilbert, Anthony 1899-1973........DLB-77

Gilbert, Elizabeth 1969-........DLB-292

Gilbert, Sir Humphrey 1537-1583........DLB-136

Gilbert, Michael 1912-........DLB-87

Gilbert, Sandra M. 1936-........DLB-120, 246

Gilchrist, Alexander 1828-1861........DLB-144

Gilchrist, Ellen 1935-........DLB-130

Gilder, Jeannette L. 1849-1916........DLB-79

Gilder, Richard Watson 1844-1909........DLB-64, 79

Gildersleeve, Basil 1831-1924........DLB-71

Giles, Henry 1809-1882........DLB-64

Giles of Rome circa 1243-1316........DLB-115

Gilfillan, George 1813-1878........DLB-144

Gill, Eric 1882-1940........DLB-98

Gill, Sarah Prince 1728-1771........DLB-200

William F. Gill Company........DLB-49

Gillespie, A. Lincoln, Jr. 1895-1950........DLB-4

Gillespie, Haven 1883-1975........DLB-265

Gilliam, Florence ?-?........DLB-4

Gilliatt, Penelope 1932-1993........DLB-14

Gillott, Jacky 1939-1980........DLB-14

Gilman, Caroline H. 1794-1888........DLB-3, 73

Gilman, Charlotte Perkins 1860-1935........DLB-221

The Charlotte Perkins Gilman Society........Y-99

W. and J. Gilman [publishing house]........DLB-49

Gilmer, Elizabeth Meriwether 1861-1951........DLB-29

Gilmer, Francis Walker 1790-1826........DLB-37

Gilmore, Mary 1865-1962........DLB-260

Gilroy, Frank D. 1925-........DLB-7

Gimferrer, Pere (Pedro) 1945-........DLB-134

Gingrich, Arnold 1903-1976........DLB-137

Prospectus From the Initial Issue of Esquire (Autumn 1933)........DLB-137

"With the Editorial Ken," Prospectus From the Initial Issue of Ken (7 April 1938)........DLB-137

Ginsberg, Allen 1926-1997........DLB-5, 16, 169, 237; CDALB-1

Ginzburg, Evgeniia 1904-1977........DLB-302

Ginzburg, Lidiia Iakovlevna 1902-1990........DLB-302

Ginzburg, Natalia 1916-1991........DLB-177

Ginzkey, Franz Karl 1871-1963........DLB-81

Gioia, Dana 1950-........DLB-120, 282

Giono, Jean 1895-1970........DLB-72

Giotti, Virgilio 1885-1957........DLB-114

Giovanni, Nikki 1943-........DLB-5, 41; CDALB-7

Giovannitti, Arturo 1884-1959........DLB-303

Gipson, Lawrence Henry 1880-1971........DLB-17

Girard, Rodolphe 1879-1956........DLB-92

Giraudoux, Jean 1882-1944........DLB-65

Girondo, Oliverio 1891-1967........DLB-283

Gissing, George 1857-1903........DLB-18, 135, 184

The Place of Realism in Fiction (1895)........DLB-18

Giudici, Giovanni 1924-........DLB-128

Giuliani, Alfredo 1924-........DLB-128

Gjellerup, Karl 1857-1919........DLB-300

Glackens, William J. 1870-1938........DLB-188

Gladilin, Anatolii Tikhonovich 1935-........DLB-302

Gladkov, Fedor Vasil'evich 1883-1958........DLB-272

Gladstone, William Ewart 1809-1898........DLB-57, 184

Glaeser, Ernst 1902-1963........DLB-69

Glancy, Diane 1941-........DLB-175

Glanvill, Joseph 1636-1680........DLB-252

Glanville, Brian 1931-........DLB-15, 139

Glapthorne, Henry 1610-1643?........DLB-58

Glasgow, Ellen 1873-1945........DLB-9, 12

The Ellen Glasgow Society........Y-01

Glasier, Katharine Bruce 1867-1950........DLB-190

Glaspell, Susan 1876-1948........DLB-7, 9, 78, 228

Glass, Montague 1877-1934........DLB-11

Glassco, John 1909-1981........DLB-68

Glauser, Friedrich 1896-1938........DLB-56

F. Gleason's Publishing Hall........DLB-49

Gleim, Johann Wilhelm Ludwig 1719-1803........DLB-97

Glendinning, Robin 1938-........DLB-310

Glendinning, Victoria 1937-........DLB-155

Glidden, Frederick Dilley (Luke Short) 1908-1975........DLB-256

Glinka, Fedor Nikolaevich 1786-1880........DLB-205

Glover, Keith 1966-........DLB-249

Glover, Richard 1712-1785........DLB-95

Glover, Sue 1943-........DLB-310

Glück, Louise 1943-........DLB-5

Glyn, Elinor 1864-1943........DLB-153

Gnedich, Nikolai Ivanovich 1784-1833........DLB-205

Gobineau, Joseph-Arthur de 1816-1882........DLB-123

Godber, John 1956-........DLB-233

Godbout, Jacques 1933-........DLB-53

Goddard, Morrill 1865-1937........DLB-25

Goddard, William 1740-1817........DLB-43

Godden, Rumer 1907-1998........DLB-161

Godey, Louis A. 1804-1878........DLB-73

Godey and McMichael........DLB-49

Godfrey, Dave 1938-........DLB-60

Godfrey, Thomas 1736-1763........DLB-31

Godine, David R., Publisher........DLB-46

Godkin, E. L. 1831-1902........DLB-79

Godolphin, Sidney 1610-1643........DLB-126

Godwin, Gail 1937-........DLB-6, 234

M. J. Godwin and Company........DLB-154

Godwin, Mary Jane Clairmont 1766-1841........DLB-163

Godwin, Parke 1816-1904........DLB-3, 64, 250

Godwin, William 1756-1836........DLB-39, 104, 142, 158, 163, 262; CDBLB-3

Preface to St. Leon (1799)........DLB-39

Goering, Reinhard 1887-1936........DLB-118

Goes, Albrecht 1908-........DLB-69

Goethe, Johann Wolfgang von 1749-1832........DLB-94; CDWLB-2

Goetz, Curt 1888-1960........DLB-124

Goffe, Thomas circa 1592-1629........DLB-58

Goffstein, M. B. 1940-........DLB-61

Gogarty, Oliver St. John 1878-1957........DLB-15, 19

Gogol, Nikolai Vasil'evich 1809-1852........DLB-198

Goines, Donald 1937-1974........DLB-33

Gold, Herbert 1924-........DLB-2; Y-81

Tribute to William Saroyan........Y-81

Gold, Michael 1893-1967........DLB-9, 28

Goldbarth, Albert 1948-........DLB-120

Goldberg, Dick 1947-........DLB-7

Golden Cockerel Press........DLB-112

Golding, Arthur 1536-1606........DLB-136

Golding, Louis 1895-1958........DLB-195

Golding, William 1911-1993........DLB-15, 100, 255; Y-83; CDBLB-7

Nobel Lecture 1993........Y-83

The Stature of William Golding........Y-83

Goldman, Emma 1869-1940........DLB-221

Cumulative Index

Goldman, William 1931- DLB-44
Goldring, Douglas 1887-1960 .... DLB-197
Goldschmidt, Meir Aron 1819-1887 .... DLB-300
Goldsmith, Oliver 1730?-1774
 .... DLB-39, 89, 104, 109, 142; CDBLB-2
Goldsmith, Oliver 1794-1861 .... DLB-99
Goldsmith Publishing Company DLB-46
Goldstein, Richard 1944- DLB-185
Gollancz, Sir Israel 1864-1930 .... DLB-201
Victor Gollancz Limited DLB-112
Gomberville, Marin Le Roy, sieur de
 1600?-1674 .... DLB-268
Gombrowicz, Witold
 1904-1969 .... DLB-215; CDWLB-4
Gómez-Quiñones, Juan 1942- DLB-122
Laurence James Gomme
 [publishing house] DLB-46
Gompers, Samuel 1850-1924 .... DLB-303
Gonçalves Dias, Antônio 1823-1864 .... DLB-307
Goncharov, Ivan Aleksandrovich
 1812-1891 .... DLB-238
Goncourt, Edmond de 1822-1896 ..... DLB-123
Goncourt, Jules de 1830-1870 .... DLB-123
Gonzales, Rodolfo "Corky" 1928- DLB-122
Gonzales-Berry, Erlinda 1942- DLB-209
 "Chicano Language" DLB-82
González, Angel 1925- DLB-108
Gonzalez, Genaro 1949- DLB-122
González, Otto-Raúl 1921- DLB-290
Gonzalez, Ray 1952- DLB-122
González de Mireles, Jovita
 1899-1983 .... DLB-122
González Martínez, Enrique 1871-1952 .. DLB-290
González-T., César A. 1931- DLB-82
Goodis, David 1917-1967 .... DLB-226
Goodison, Lorna 1947- DLB-157
Goodman, Allegra 1967- DLB-244
Goodman, Nelson 1906-1998 .... DLB-279
Goodman, Paul 1911-1972 .... DLB-130, 246
The Goodman Theatre DLB-7
Goodrich, Frances 1891-1984 and
 Hackett, Albert 1900-1995 .... DLB-26
Goodrich, Samuel Griswold
 1793-1860 .... DLB-1, 42, 73, 243
S. G. Goodrich [publishing house] DLB-49
C. E. Goodspeed and Company DLB-49
Goodwin, Stephen 1943- Y-82
Googe, Barnabe 1540-1594 .... DLB-132
Gookin, Daniel 1612-1687 .... DLB-24
Goran, Lester 1928- DLB-244
Gordimer, Nadine 1923- DLB-225; Y-91
 Nobel Lecture 1991 .... Y-91
Gordon, Adam Lindsay 1833-1870 ..... DLB-230
Gordon, Caroline
 1895-1981 ...... DLB-4, 9, 102; DS-17; Y-81
Gordon, Charles F. (see OyamO)
Gordon, Charles William (see Connor, Ralph)

Gordon, Giles 1940- DLB-14, 139, 207
Gordon, Helen Cameron, Lady Russell
 1867-1949 .... DLB-195
Gordon, Lyndall 1941- DLB-155
Gordon, Mack 1904-1959 .... DLB-265
Gordon, Mary 1949- DLB-6; Y-81
Gordone, Charles 1925-1995 .... DLB-7
Gore, Catherine 1800-1861 .... DLB-116
Gore-Booth, Eva 1870-1926 .... DLB-240
Gores, Joe 1931- DLB-226; Y-02
 Tribute to Kenneth Millar Y-83
 Tribute to Raymond Chandler Y-88
Gorey, Edward 1925-2000 .... DLB-61
Gorgias of Leontini
 circa 485 B.C.-376 B.C. DLB-176
Gor'ky, Maksim 1868-1936 .... DLB-295
Gorodetsky, Sergei Mitrofanovich
 1884-1967 .... DLB-295
Gorostiza, José 1901-1979 .... DLB-290
Görres, Joseph 1776-1848 .... DLB-90
Gosse, Edmund 1849-1928 ..... DLB-57, 144, 184
Gosson, Stephen 1554-1624 .... DLB-172
 The Schoole of Abuse (1579) DLB-172
Gotanda, Philip Kan 1951- DLB-266
Gotlieb, Phyllis 1926- DLB-88, 251
Go-Toba 1180-1239 .... DLB-203
Gottfried von Straßburg
 died before 1230 ...... DLB-138; CDWLB-2
Gotthelf, Jeremias 1797-1854 .... DLB-133
Gottschalk circa 804/808-869 .... DLB-148
Gottsched, Johann Christoph
 1700-1766 .... DLB-97
Götz, Johann Nikolaus 1721-1781 ..... DLB-97
Goudge, Elizabeth 1900-1984 .... DLB-191
Gough, John B. 1817-1886 .... DLB-243
Gould, Wallace 1882-1940 .... DLB-54
Govoni, Corrado 1884-1965 .... DLB-114
Govrin, Michal 1950- DLB-299
Gower, John circa 1330-1408 .... DLB-146
Goyen, William 1915-1983 ..... DLB-2, 218; Y-83
Goytisolo, José Agustín 1928- DLB-134
Gozzano, Guido 1883-1916 .... DLB-114
Grabbe, Christian Dietrich 1801-1836 ... DLB-133
Gracq, Julien (Louis Poirier) 1910- DLB-83
Grady, Henry W. 1850-1889 .... DLB-23
Graf, Oskar Maria 1894-1967 .... DLB-56
Graf Rudolf between circa 1170 and
 circa 1185 .... DLB-148
Graff, Gerald 1937- DLB-246
Richard Grafton [publishing house] DLB-170
Grafton, Sue 1940- DLB-226
Graham, Frank 1893-1965 .... DLB-241
Graham, George Rex 1813-1894 ...... DLB-73
Graham, Gwethalyn (Gwethalyn Graham
 Erichsen-Brown) 1913-1965 .... DLB-88
Graham, Jorie 1951- DLB-120

Graham, Katharine 1917-2001 .... DLB-127
Graham, Lorenz 1902-1989 .... DLB-76
Graham, Philip 1915-1963 .... DLB-127
Graham, R. B. Cunninghame
 1852-1936 .... DLB-98, 135, 174
Graham, Shirley 1896-1977 .... DLB-76
Graham, Stephen 1884-1975 .... DLB-195
Graham, W. S. 1918-1986 .... DLB-20
William H. Graham [publishing house] ... DLB-49
Graham, Winston 1910- DLB-77
Grahame, Kenneth 1859-1932 ... DLB-34, 141, 178
Grainger, Martin Allerdale 1874-1941 .... DLB-92
Gramatky, Hardie 1907-1979 .... DLB-22
Gramcko, Ida 1924-1994 .... DLB-290
Gramsci, Antonio 1891-1937 .... DLB-296
Grand, Sarah 1854-1943 .... DLB-135, 197
Grandbois, Alain 1900-1975 .... DLB-92
Grandson, Oton de circa 1345-1397 .... DLB-208
Grange, John circa 1556-? DLB-136
Granger, Thomas 1578-1627 .... DLB-281
Granich, Irwin (see Gold, Michael)
Granin, Daniil 1918- DLB-302
Granovsky, Timofei Nikolaevich
 1813-1855 .... DLB-198
Grant, Anne MacVicar 1755-1838 ..... DLB-200
Grant, Duncan 1885-1978 .... DS-10
Grant, George 1918-1988 .... DLB-88
Grant, George Monro 1835-1902 ...... DLB-99
Grant, Harry J. 1881-1963 .... DLB-29
Grant, James Edward 1905-1966 ..... DLB-26
Grant, John (see Gash, Jonathan)
War of the Words (and Pictures): The Creation
 of a Graphic Novel Y-02
Grass, Günter 1927- ... DLB-75, 124; CDWLB-2
 Nobel Lecture 1999:
 "To Be Continued . . ." Y-99
 Tribute to Helen Wolff Y-94
Grasty, Charles H. 1863-1924 .... DLB-25
Grau, Shirley Ann 1929- DLB-2, 218
Graves, John 1920- Y-83
Graves, Richard 1715-1804 .... DLB-39
Graves, Robert 1895-1985
 ....DLB-20, 100, 191; DS-18; Y-85; CDBLB-6
 The St. John's College
 Robert Graves Trust Y-96
Gray, Alasdair 1934- DLB-194, 261
Gray, Asa 1810-1888 .... DLB-1, 235
Gray, David 1838-1861 .... DLB-32
Gray, Simon 1936- DLB-13
Gray, Thomas 1716-1771 ..... DLB-109; CDBLB-2
Grayson, Richard 1951- DLB-234
Grayson, William J. 1788-1863 .... DLB-3, 64, 248
The Great Bibliographers Series Y-93
The Great Gatsby (Documentary) DLB-219
"The Greatness of Southern Literature":
 League of the South Institute for the

Study of Southern Culture and History Y-02

Grech, Nikolai Ivanovich 1787-1867 ..... DLB-198

Greeley, Horace 1811-1872 ... DLB-3, 43, 189, 250

Green, Adolph 1915-2002 .... DLB-44, 265

Green, Anna Katharine 1846-1935 .... DLB-202, 221

Green, Duff 1791-1875 .... DLB-43

Green, Elizabeth Shippen 1871-1954 ..... DLB-188

Green, Gerald 1922- DLB-28

Green, Henry 1905-1973 .... DLB-15

Green, Jonas 1712-1767 .... DLB-31

Green, Joseph 1706-1780 .... DLB-31

Green, Julien 1900-1998 .... DLB-4, 72

Green, Paul 1894-1981 ..... DLB-7, 9, 249; Y-81

Green, T. H. 1836-1882 .... DLB-190, 262

Green, Terence M. 1947- DLB-251

T. and S. Green [publishing house] DLB-49

Green Tiger Press DLB-46

Timothy Green [publishing house] DLB-49

Greenaway, Kate 1846-1901 .... DLB-141

Greenberg: Publisher DLB-46

Greene, Asa 1789-1838 .... DLB-11

Greene, Belle da Costa 1883-1950 .... DLB-187

Greene, Graham 1904-1991
.... DLB-13, 15, 77, 100, 162, 201, 204; Y-85, 91; CDBLB-7

Tribute to Christopher Isherwood Y-86

Greene, Robert 1558-1592 .... DLB-62, 167

Greene, Robert Bernard (Bob), Jr. 1947- DLB-185

Benjamin H Greene [publishing house] DLB-49

Greenfield, George 1917-2000 .... Y-91, 00

Derek Robinson's Review of George Greenfield's *Rich Dust* Y-02

Greenhow, Robert 1800-1854 .... DLB-30

Greenlee, William B. 1872-1953 .... DLB-187

Greenough, Horatio 1805-1852 .... DLB-1, 235

Greenwell, Dora 1821-1882 .... DLB-35, 199

Greenwillow Books DLB-46

Greenwood, Grace (see Lippincott, Sara Jane Clarke)

Greenwood, Walter 1903-1974 ..... DLB-10, 191

Greer, Ben 1948- DLB-6

Greflinger, Georg 1620?-1677 .... DLB-164

Greg, W. R. 1809-1881 .... DLB-55

Greg, W. W. 1875-1959 .... DLB-201

Gregg, Josiah 1806-1850 .... DLB-183, 186

Gregg Press DLB-46

Gregory, Horace 1898-1982 .... DLB-48

Gregory, Isabella Augusta Persse, Lady 1852-1932 .... DLB-10

Gregory of Rimini circa 1300-1358 ...... DLB-115

Gregynog Press DLB-112

Greiff, León de 1895-1976 .... DLB-283

Greiffenberg, Catharina Regina von 1633-1694 .... DLB-168

Greig, Noël 1944- DLB-245

Grekova, Irina (Elena Sergeevna Venttsel') 1907- DLB-302

Grenfell, Wilfred Thomason 1865-1940 .... DLB-92

Gress, Elsa 1919-1988 .... DLB-214

Greve, Felix Paul (see Grove, Frederick Philip)

Greville, Fulke, First Lord Brooke 1554-1628 .... DLB-62, 172

Grey, Sir George, K.C.B. 1812-1898 ..... DLB-184

Grey, Lady Jane 1537-1554 .... DLB-132

Grey, Zane 1872-1939 .... DLB-9, 212

Zane Grey's West Society Y-00

Grey Owl (Archibald Stansfeld Belaney) 1888-1938 .... DLB-92; DS-17

Grey Walls Press DLB-112

Griboedov, Aleksandr Sergeevich 1795?-1829 .... DLB-205

Grice, Paul 1913-1988 .... DLB-279

Grier, Eldon 1917- DLB-88

Grieve, C. M. (see MacDiarmid, Hugh)

Griffin, Bartholomew flourished 1596 .... DLB-172

Griffin, Bryan
 "Panic Among the Philistines": A Postscript, An Interview with Bryan Griffin Y-81

Griffin, Gerald 1803-1840 .... DLB-159

The Griffin Poetry Prize Y-00

Griffith, Elizabeth 1727?-1793 .... DLB-39, 89
 Preface to *The Delicate Distress* (1769) ... DLB-39

Griffith, George 1857-1906 .... DLB-178

Ralph Griffiths [publishing house] DLB-154

Griffiths, Trevor 1935- DLB-13, 245

S. C. Griggs and Company DLB-49

Griggs, Sutton Elbert 1872-1930 .... DLB-50

Grignon, Claude-Henri 1894-1976 .... DLB-68

Grigor'ev, Apollon Aleksandrovich 1822-1864 .... DLB-277

Grigorovich, Dmitrii Vasil'evich 1822-1899 .... DLB-238

Grigson, Geoffrey 1905-1985 .... DLB-27

Grillparzer, Franz 1791-1872 .... DLB-133; CDWLB-2

Grimald, Nicholas circa 1519-circa 1562 .... DLB-136

Grimké, Angelina Weld 1880-1958 .... DLB-50, 54

Grimké, Sarah Moore 1792-1873 .... DLB-239

Grimm, Hans 1875-1959 .... DLB-66

Grimm, Jacob 1785-1863 .... DLB-90

Grimm, Wilhelm 1786-1859 .... DLB-90; CDWLB-2

Grimmelshausen, Johann Jacob Christoffel von 1621 or 1622-1676 ...... DLB-168; CDWLB-2

Grimshaw, Beatrice Ethel 1871-1953 .... DLB-174

Grímur Thomsen 1820-1896 .... DLB-293

Grin, Aleksandr Stepanovich 1880-1932 .... DLB-272

Grindal, Edmund 1519 or 1520-1583 .... DLB-132

Gripe, Maria (Kristina) 1923- DLB-257

Griswold, Rufus Wilmot 1815-1857 .... DLB-3, 59, 250

Gronlund, Laurence 1846-1899 .... DLB-303

Grosart, Alexander Balloch 1827-1899 ... DLB-184

Grosholz, Emily 1950- DLB-282

Gross, Milt 1895-1953 .... DLB-11

Grosset and Dunlap DLB-49

Grosseteste, Robert circa 1160-1253 ..... DLB-115

Grossman, Allen 1932- DLB-193

Grossman, David 1954- DLB-299

Grossman, Vasilii Semenovich 1905-1964 .... DLB-272

Grossman Publishers DLB-46

Grosvenor, Gilbert H. 1875-1966 .... DLB-91

Groth, Klaus 1819-1899 .... DLB-129

Groulx, Lionel 1878-1967 .... DLB-68

Grove, Frederick Philip (Felix Paul Greve) 1879-1948 .... DLB-92

Grove Press DLB-46

Groys, Boris Efimovich 1947- DLB-285

Grubb, Davis 1919-1980 .... DLB-6

Gruelle, Johnny 1880-1938 .... DLB-22

von Grumbach, Argula 1492-after 1563? DLB-179

Grundtvig, N. F. S. 1783-1872 .... DLB-300

Grymeston, Elizabeth before 1563-before 1604 .... DLB-136

Grynberg, Henryk 1936- DLB-299

Gryphius, Andreas 1616-1664 .... DLB-164; CDWLB-2

Gryphius, Christian 1649-1706 .... DLB-168

Guare, John 1938- DLB-7, 249

Guarnieri, Gianfrancesco 1934- DLB-307

Guberman, Igor Mironovich 1936- DLB-285

Guðbergur Bergsson 1932- DLB-293

Guðmundur Böðvarsson 1904-1974 ..... DLB-293

Guðmundur Gíslason Hagalín 1898-1985 .... DLB-293

Guðmundur Magnússon (see Jón Trausti)

Guerra, Tonino 1920- DLB-128

Guest, Barbara 1920- DLB-5, 193

Guèvremont, Germaine 1893-1968 .... DLB-68

Guglielminetti, Amalia 1881-1941 ...... DLB-264

Guidacci, Margherita 1921-1992 .... DLB-128

Guillén, Jorge 1893-1984 .... DLB-108

Guillén, Nicolás 1902-1989 .... DLB-283

Guilloux, Louis 1899-1980 .... DLB-72

Guilpin, Everard circa 1572-after 1608? DLB-136

Guiney, Louise Imogen 1861-1920 .... DLB-54

Guiterman, Arthur 1871-1943 .... DLB-11

Gumilev, Nikolai Stepanovich 1886-1921 .... DLB-295

Günderrode, Caroline von 1780-1806 .... DLB-90

Gundulić, Ivan 1589-1638 ... DLB-147; CDWLB-4

Gunesekera, Romesh 1954- DLB-267

Gunn, Bill 1934-1989 .... DLB-38
Gunn, James E. 1923- DLB-8
Gunn, Neil M. 1891-1973 .... DLB-15
Gunn, Thom 1929- DLB-27; CDBLB-8
Gunnar Gunnarsson 1889-1975 .... DLB-293
Gunnars, Kristjana 1948- DLB-60
Günther, Johann Christian 1695-1723 ... DLB-168
Gurik, Robert 1932- DLB-60
Gurney, A. R. 1930- DLB-266
Gurney, Ivor 1890-1937 .... Y-02
    The Ivor Gurney Society Y-98
Guro, Elena Genrikhovna 1877-1913 .... DLB-295
Gustafson, Ralph 1909-1995 .... DLB-88
Gustafsson, Lars 1936- DLB-257
Gütersloh, Albert Paris 1887-1973 .... DLB-81
Guterson, David 1956- DLB-292
Guthrie, A. B., Jr. 1901-1991 .... DLB-6, 212
Guthrie, Ramon 1896-1973 .... DLB-4
Guthrie, Thomas Anstey (see Anstey, FC)
Guthrie, Woody 1912-1967 .... DLB-303
The Guthrie Theater DLB-7
Gutiérrez Nájera, Manuel 1859-1895 .... DLB-290
Guttormur J. Guttormsson 1878-1966 ... DLB-293
Gutzkow, Karl 1811-1878 .... DLB-133
Guy, Ray 1939- DLB-60
Guy, Rosa 1925- DLB-33
Guyot, Arnold 1807-1884 .... DS-13
Gwynn, R. S. 1948- DLB-282
Gwynne, Erskine 1898-1948 .... DLB-4
Gyles, John 1680-1755 .... DLB-99
Gyllembourg, Thomasine 1773-1856 .... DLB-300
Gyllensten, Lars 1921- DLB-257
Gyrðir Elíasson 1961- DLB-293
Gysin, Brion 1916-1986 .... DLB-16

H

H.D. (see Doolittle, Hilda)
Habermas, Jürgen 1929- DLB-242
Habington, William 1605-1654 .... DLB-126
Hacker, Marilyn 1942- DLB-120, 282
Hackett, Albert 1900-1995 .... DLB-26
Hacks, Peter 1928- DLB-124
Hadas, Rachel 1948- DLB-120, 282
Hadden, Briton 1898-1929 .... DLB-91
Hagedorn, Friedrich von 1708-1754 ..... DLB-168
Hagelstange, Rudolf 1912-1984 .... DLB-69
Hagerup, Inger 1905-1985 .... DLB-297
Haggard, H. Rider
  1856-1925 .... DLB-70, 156, 174, 178
Haggard, William (Richard Clayton)
  1907-1993 .... DLB-276; Y-93
Hagy, Alyson 1960- DLB-244
Hahn-Hahn, Ida Gräfin von 1805-1880 .. DLB-133
Haig-Brown, Roderick 1908-1976 .... DLB-88
Haight, Gordon S. 1901-1985 .... DLB-103

Hailey, Arthur 1920- DLB-88; Y-82
Haines, John 1924- DLB-5, 212
Hake, Edward flourished 1566-1604 .... DLB-136
Hake, Thomas Gordon 1809-1895 .... DLB-32
Hakluyt, Richard 1552?-1616 .... DLB-136
Halas, František 1901-1949 .... DLB-215
Halbe, Max 1865-1944 .... DLB-118
Halberstam, David 1934- DLB-241
Haldane, Charlotte 1894-1969 .... DLB-191
Haldane, J. B. S. 1892-1964 .... DLB-160
Haldeman, Joe 1943- DLB-8
Haldeman-Julius Company DLB-46
Hale, E. J., and Son DLB-49
Hale, Edward Everett
  1822-1909 .... DLB-1, 42, 74, 235
Hale, Janet Campbell 1946- DLB-175
Hale, Kathleen 1898-2000 .... DLB-160
Hale, Leo Thomas (see Ebon)
Hale, Lucretia Peabody 1820-1900 ...... DLB-42
Hale, Nancy
  1908-1988 .... DLB-86; DS-17; Y-80, 88
Hale, Sarah Josepha (Buell)
  1788-1879 .... DLB-1, 42, 73, 243
Hale, Susan 1833-1910 .... DLB-221
Hales, John 1584-1656 .... DLB-151
Halévy, Ludovic 1834-1908 .... DLB-192
Haley, Alex 1921-1992 .... DLB-38; CDALB-7
Haliburton, Thomas Chandler
  1796-1865 .... DLB-11, 99
Hall, Adam (Trevor Dudley-Smith)
  1920-1995 .... DLB-276
Hall, Anna Maria 1800-1881 .... DLB-159
Hall, Donald 1928- DLB-5
Hall, Edward 1497-1547 .... DLB-132
Hall, Halsey 1898-1977 .... DLB-241
Hall, James 1793-1868 .... DLB-73, 74
Hall, Joseph 1574-1656 .... DLB-121, 151
Hall, Radclyffe 1880-1943 .... DLB-191
Hall, Rodney 1935- DLB-289
Hall, Sarah Ewing 1761-1830 .... DLB-200
Hall, Stuart 1932- DLB-242
Samuel Hall [publishing house] DLB-49
Hallam, Arthur Henry 1811-1833 .... DLB-32
  On Some of the Characteristics of
  Modern Poetry and On the
  Lyrical Poems of Alfred
  Tennyson (1831) DLB-32
Halldór Laxness (Halldór Guðjónsson)
  1902-1998 .... DLB-293
Halleck, Fitz-Greene 1790-1867 ...... DLB-3, 250
Haller, Albrecht von 1708-1777 .... DLB-168
Halliday, Brett (see Dresser, Davis)
Halliwell-Phillipps, James Orchard
  1820-1889 .... DLB-184
Hallmann, Johann Christian
  1640-1704 or 1716? DLB-168
Hallmark Editions DLB-46
Halper, Albert 1904-1984 .... DLB-9

Halperin, John William 1941- DLB-111
Halstead, Murat 1829-1908 .... DLB-23
Hamann, Johann Georg 1730-1788 ...... DLB-97
Hamburger, Michael 1924- DLB-27
Hamilton, Alexander 1712-1756 .... DLB-31
Hamilton, Alexander 1755?-1804 .... DLB-37
Hamilton, Cicely 1872-1952 .... DLB-10, 197
Hamilton, Edmond 1904-1977 .... DLB-8
Hamilton, Elizabeth 1758-1816 ...... DLB-116, 158
Hamilton, Gail (see Corcoran, Barbara)
Hamilton, Gail (see Dodge, Mary Abigail)
Hamish Hamilton Limited DLB-112
Hamilton, Hugo 1953- DLB-267
Hamilton, Ian 1938-2001 .... DLB-40, 155
Hamilton, Janet 1795-1873 .... DLB-199
Hamilton, Mary Agnes 1884-1962 ...... DLB-197
Hamilton, Patrick 1904-1962 .... DLB-10, 191
Hamilton, Virginia 1936-2002 ... DLB-33, 52; Y-01
Hamilton, Sir William 1788-1856 ...... DLB-262
Hamilton-Paterson, James 1941- DLB-267
Hammerstein, Oscar, 2nd 1895-1960 .... DLB-265
Hammett, Dashiell
  1894-1961 .... DLB-226; DS-6; CDALB-5
  An Appeal in *TAC* Y-91
  The Glass Key and Other Dashiell
    Hammett Mysteries Y-96
  Knopf to Hammett: The Editoral
    Correspondence Y-00
  The Maltese Falcon (Documentary) DLB-280
Hammon, Jupiter 1711-died between
  1790 and 1806 .... DLB-31, 50
Hammond, John ?-1663 .... DLB-24
Hamner, Earl 1923- DLB-6
Hampson, John 1901-1955 .... DLB-191
Hampton, Christopher 1946- DLB-13
Hamsun, Knut 1859-1952 .... DLB-297
Handel-Mazzetti, Enrica von 1871-1955 ... DLB-81
Handke, Peter 1942- DLB-85, 124
Handlin, Oscar 1915- DLB-17
Hankin, St. John 1869-1909 .... DLB-10
Hanley, Clifford 1922- DLB-14
Hanley, James 1901-1985 .... DLB-191
Hannah, Barry 1942- DLB-6, 234
Hannay, James 1827-1873 .... DLB-21
Hannes Hafstein 1861-1922 .... DLB-293
Hano, Arnold 1922- DLB-241
Hanrahan, Barbara 1939-1991 .... DLB-289
Hansberry, Lorraine
  1930-1965 .... DLB-7, 38; CDALB-1
Hansen, Martin A. 1909-1955 .... DLB-214
Hansen, Thorkild 1927-1989 .... DLB-214
Hanson, Elizabeth 1684-1737 .... DLB-200
Hapgood, Norman 1868-1937 .... DLB-91
Happel, Eberhard Werner 1647-1690 ... DLB-168
Harbach, Otto 1873-1963 .... DLB-265
The Harbinger 1845-1849 .... DLB-1, 223

Harburg, E. Y. "Yip" 1896-1981 . . . . .DLB-265
Harcourt Brace Jovanovich DLB-46
Hardenberg, Friedrich von (see Novalis)
Harding, Walter 1917- DLB-111
Hardwick, Elizabeth 1916- DLB-6
Hardy, Alexandre 1572?-1632. . . . . .DLB-268
Hardy, Frank 1917-1994 . . . . .DLB-260
Hardy, Thomas
   1840-1928 . . . . . . .DLB-18, 19, 135; CDBLB-5
   "Candour in English Fiction" (1890) . . .DLB-18
Hare, Cyril 1900-1958. . . . . .DLB-77
Hare, David 1947- DLB-13, 310
Hare, R. M. 1919-2002 . . . . .DLB-262
Hargrove, Marion 1919- DLB-11
Häring, Georg Wilhelm Heinrich
   (see Alexis, Willibald)
Harington, Donald 1935- DLB-152
Harington, Sir John 1560-1612 . . . . .DLB-136
Harjo, Joy 1951- DLB-120, 175
Harkness, Margaret (John Law)
   1854-1923 . . . . .DLB-197
Harley, Edward, second Earl of Oxford
   1689-1741 . . . . .DLB-213
Harley, Robert, first Earl of Oxford
   1661-1724 . . . . .DLB-213
Harlow, Robert 1923- DLB-60
Harman, Thomas flourished 1566-1573 . . .DLB-136
Harness, Charles L. 1915- DLB-8
Harnett, Cynthia 1893-1981 . . . . .DLB-161
Harnick, Sheldon 1924- DLB-265
   Tribute to Ira Gershwin Y-96
   Tribute to Lorenz Hart Y-95
Harper, Edith Alice Mary (see Wickham, Anna)
Harper, Fletcher 1806-1877 . . . . .DLB-79
Harper, Frances Ellen Watkins
   1825-1911 . . . . .DLB-50, 221
Harper, Michael S. 1938- DLB-41
Harper and Brothers DLB-49
Harpur, Charles 1813-1868. . . . . .DLB-230
Harraden, Beatrice 1864-1943 . . . . .DLB-153
George G. Harrap and Company
   Limited DLB-112
Harriot, Thomas 1560-1621 . . . . .DLB-136
Harris, Alexander 1805-1874. . . . . .DLB-230
Harris, Benjamin ?-circa 1720 . . . . . . .DLB-42, 43
Harris, Christie 1907-2002. . . . . .DLB-88
Harris, Errol E. 1908- DLB-279
Harris, Frank 1856-1931 . . . . .DLB-156, 197
Harris, George Washington
   1814-1869 . . . . .DLB-3, 11, 248
Harris, Joanne 1964- DLB-271
Harris, Joel Chandler
   1848-1908 . . . . .DLB-11, 23, 42, 78, 91
   The Joel Chandler Harris Association. . . .Y-99
Harris, Mark 1922- DLB-2; Y-80
   Tribute to Frederick A. Pottle Y-87
Harris, William Torrey 1835-1909 . . . . . . .DLB-270

Harris, Wilson 1921- DLB-117; CDWLB-3
Harrison, Mrs. Burton
   (see Harrison, Constance Cary)
Harrison, Charles Yale 1898-1954. . . . . . . .DLB-68
Harrison, Constance Cary 1843-1920. . . .DLB-221
Harrison, Frederic 1831-1923 . . . . . . .DLB-57, 190
   "On Style in English Prose" (1898). . . .DLB-57
Harrison, Harry 1925- DLB-8
James P. Harrison Company DLB-49
Harrison, Jim 1937- Y-82
Harrison, M. John 1945- DLB-261
Harrison, Mary St. Leger Kingsley
   (see Malet, Lucas)
Harrison, Paul Carter 1936- DLB-38
Harrison, Susan Frances 1859-1935. . . . . . .DLB-99
Harrison, Tony 1937- DLB-40, 245
Harrison, William 1535-1593 . . . . .DLB-136
Harrison, William 1933- DLB-234
Harrisse, Henry 1829-1910 . . . . .DLB-47
The Harry Ransom Humanities Research Center
   at the University of Texas at Austin Y-00
Harryman, Carla 1952- DLB-193
Harsdörffer, Georg Philipp 1607-1658. . . .DLB-164
Harsent, David 1942- DLB-40
Hart, Albert Bushnell 1854-1943 . . . . .DLB-17
Hart, Anne 1768-1834 . . . . .DLB-200
Hart, Elizabeth 1771-1833 . . . . .DLB-200
Hart, Julia Catherine 1796-1867. . . . . .DLB-99
Hart, Lorenz 1895-1943. . . . . .DLB-265
   Larry Hart: Still an Influence Y-95
   Lorenz Hart: An American Lyricist Y-95
   The Lorenz Hart Centenary Y-95
Hart, Moss 1904-1961 . . . . .DLB-7, 266
Hart, Oliver 1723-1795 . . . . .DLB-31
Rupert Hart-Davis Limited DLB-112
Harte, Bret 1836-1902
   . . . . .DLB-12, 64, 74, 79, 186; CDALB-3
Harte, Edward Holmead 1922- DLB-127
Harte, Houston Harriman 1927- DLB-127
Hartlaub, Felix 1913-1945 . . . . .DLB-56
Hartlebon, Otto Erich 1864-1905 . . . . . . .DLB-118
Hartley, David 1705-1757 . . . . .DLB-252
Hartley, L. P. 1895-1972 . . . . .DLB-15, 139
Hartley, Marsden 1877-1943 . . . . .DLB-54
Hartling, Peter 1933- DLB-75
Hartman, Geoffrey H. 1929- DLB-67
Hartmann, Sadakichi 1867-1944 . . . . .DLB-54
Hartmann von Aue
   circa 1160-circa 1205. . . .DLB-138; CDWLB-2
Hartshorne, Charles 1897-2000 . . . . .DLB-270
Haruf, Kent 1943- DLB-292
Harvey, Gabriel 1550?-1631 . . . DLB-167, 213, 281
Harvey, Jack (see Rankin, Ian)
Harvey, Jean-Charles 1891-1967. . . . . .DLB-88
Harvill Press Limited. DLB-112
Harwood, Gwen 1920-1995. . . . . .DLB-289

Harwood, Lee 1939- DLB-40
Harwood, Ronald 1934- DLB-13
Hašek, Jaroslav 1883-1923 . .DLB-215; CDWLB-4
Haskins, Charles Homer 1870-1937 . . . . . .DLB-47
Haslam, Gerald 1937- DLB-212
Hass, Robert 1941- DLB-105, 206
Hasselstrom, Linda M. 1943- DLB-256
Hastings, Michael 1938- DLB-233
Hatar, Győző 1914- DLB-215
The Hatch-Billops Collection DLB-76
Hathaway, William 1944- DLB-120
Hatherly, Ana 1929- DLB-287
Hauch, Carsten 1790-1872. . . . . .DLB-300
Hauff, Wilhelm 1802-1827 . . . . .DLB-90
Hauge, Olav H. 1908-1994 . . . . .DLB-297
Haugen, Paal-Helge 1945- DLB-297
Haugwitz, August Adolph von
   1647-1706. .DLB-168
Hauptmann, Carl 1858-1921 . . . . . .DLB-66, 118
Hauptmann, Gerhart
   1862-1946 . . . . .DLB-66, 118; CDWLB-2
Hauser, Marianne 1910- Y-83
Havel, Václav 1936- DLB-232; CDWLB-4
Haven, Alice B. Neal 1827-1863 . . . . .DLB-250
Havergal, Frances Ridley 1836-1879 . . . . .DLB-199
Hawes, Stephen 1475?-before 1529 . . . . .DLB-132
Hawker, Robert Stephen 1803-1875 . . . . .DLB-32
Hawkes, John
   1925-1998 . . . . .DLB-2, 7, 227; Y-80, Y-98
   John Hawkes: A Tribute. Y-98
   Tribute to Donald Barthelme Y-89
Hawkesworth, John 1720-1773 . . . . .DLB-142
Hawkins, Sir Anthony Hope (see Hope, Anthony)
Hawkins, Sir John 1719-1789 . . . . . . .DLB-104, 142
Hawkins, Walter Everette 1883-? DLB-50
Hawthorne, Nathaniel 1804-1864
   . . .DLB-1, 74, 183, 223, 269; DS-5; CDALB-2
   The Nathaniel Hawthorne Society Y-00
   The Old Manse. DLB-223
Hawthorne, Sophia Peabody
   1809-1871 . . . . .DLB-183, 239
Hay, John 1835-1905. . . . . .DLB-12, 47, 189
Hay, John 1915- DLB-275
Hayashi Fumiko 1903-1951. . . . . .DLB-180
Haycox, Ernest 1899-1950 . . . . .DLB-206
Haycraft, Anna Margaret (see Ellis, Alice Thomas)
Hayden, Robert
   1913-1980 . . . . .DLB-5, 76; CDALB-1
Haydon, Benjamin Robert 1786-1846 . . .DLB-110
Hayes, John Michael 1919- DLB-26
Hayley, William 1745-1820. . . . . . . .DLB-93, 142
Haym, Rudolf 1821-1901 . . . . .DLB-129
Hayman, Robert 1575-1629. . . . . .DLB-99
Hayman, Ronald 1932- DLB-155
Hayne, Paul Hamilton
   1830-1886 . . . . .DLB-3, 64, 79, 248

Cumulative Index

Hays, Mary 1760-1843 .... DLB-142, 158

Hayward, John 1905-1965 .... DLB-201

Haywood, Eliza 1693?-1756 .... DLB-39

    Dedication of *Lasselia* [excerpt] (1723) DLB-39

    Preface to *The Disguis'd Prince* [excerpt] (1723) DLB-39

    The Tea-Table [excerpt] DLB-39

Haywood, William D. 1869-1928 ...... DLB-303

Willis P. Hazard [publishing house] DLB-49

Hazlitt, William 1778-1830 .... DLB-110, 158

Hazzard, Shirley 1931- DLB-289; Y-82

Head, Bessie 1937-1986 .... DLB-117, 225; CDWLB-3

Headley, Joel T. 1813-1897 .. DLB-30, 183; DS-13

Heaney, Seamus 1939- .. DLB-40; Y-95; CDBLB-8

    Nobel Lecture 1994: Crediting Poetry Y-95

Heard, Nathan C. 1936- DLB-33

Hearn, Lafcadio 1850-1904 .....DLB-12, 78, 189

Hearn, Mary Anne (Marianne Farningham, Eva Hope) 1834-1909 .... DLB-240

Hearne, John 1926- DLB-117

Hearne, Samuel 1745-1792 .... DLB-99

Hearne, Thomas 1678?-1735 .... DLB-213

Hearst, William Randolph 1863-1951 .... DLB-25

Hearst, William Randolph, Jr. 1908-1993 .... DLB-127

Heartman, Charles Frederick 1883-1953 .... DLB-187

Heath, Catherine 1924- DLB-14

Heath, James Ewell 1792-1862 .... DLB-248

Heath, Roy A. K. 1926- DLB-117

Heath-Stubbs, John 1918- DLB-27

Heavysege, Charles 1816-1876 .... DLB-99

Hebbel, Friedrich 1813-1863 .... DLB-129; CDWLB-2

Hebel, Johann Peter 1760-1826 .... DLB-90

Heber, Richard 1774-1833 .... DLB-184

Hébert, Anne 1916-2000 .... DLB-68

Hébert, Jacques 1923- DLB-53

Hecht, Anthony 1923- DLB-5, 169

Hecht, Ben 1894-1964 ....DLB-7, 9, 25, 26, 28, 86

Hecker, Isaac Thomas 1819-1888 .... DLB-1, 243

Hedge, Frederic Henry 1805-1890 .... DLB-1, 59, 243; DS-5

Hefner, Hugh M. 1926- DLB-137

Hegel, Georg Wilhelm Friedrich 1770-1831 .... DLB-90

Heiberg, Johan Ludvig 1791-1860 ...... DLB-300

Heiberg, Johanne Luise 1812-1890 ...... DLB-300

Heide, Robert 1939- DLB-249

Heidegger, Martin 1889-1976 .... DLB-296

Heidish, Marcy 1947- Y-82

Heißenbüttel, Helmut 1921-1996 .... DLB-75

Heike monogatari DLB-203

Hein, Christoph 1944- ... DLB-124; CDWLB-2

Hein, Piet 1905-1996 .... DLB-214

Heine, Heinrich 1797-1856 ... DLB-90; CDWLB-2

Heinemann, Larry 1944- DS-9

William Heinemann Limited DLB-112

Heinesen, William 1900-1991 .... DLB-214

Heinlein, Robert A. 1907-1988 .... DLB-8

Heinrich, Willi 1920- DLB-75

Heinrich Julius of Brunswick 1564-1613 .... DLB-164

Heinrich von dem Türlîn flourished circa 1230 .... DLB-138

Heinrich von Melk flourished after 1160 .... DLB-148

Heinrich von Veldeke circa 1145-circa 1190 .... DLB-138

Heinse, Wilhelm 1746-1803 .... DLB-94

Heinz, W. C. 1915- DLB-171

Heiskell, John 1872-1972 .... DLB-127

Hejinian, Lyn 1941- DLB-165

Helder, Herberto 1930- DLB-287

Heliand circa 850 .... DLB-148

Heller, Joseph 1923-1999 ......DLB-2, 28, 227; Y-80, 99, 02

    Excerpts from Joseph Heller's USC Address, "The Literature of Despair" Y-96

    Remembering Joe Heller, by William Price Fox Y-99

    A Tribute to Joseph Heller Y-99

Heller, Michael 1937- DLB-165

Hellman, Lillian 1906-1984 ..... DLB-7, 228; Y-84

Hellwig, Johann 1609-1674 .... DLB-164

Helprin, Mark 1947- Y-85; CDALB-7

Helwig, David 1938- DLB-60

Hemans, Felicia 1793-1835 .... DLB-96

Hemenway, Abby Maria 1828-1890 .... DLB-243

Hemingway, Ernest 1899-1961 .... DLB-4, 9, 102, 210; Y-81, 87, 99; DS-1, 15, 16; CDALB-4

    A Centennial Celebration Y-99

    Come to Papa Y-99

    The Ernest Hemingway Collection at the John F. Kennedy Library Y-99

    Ernest Hemingway Declines to Introduce *War and Peace* Y-01

    Ernest Hemingway's Reaction to James Gould Cozzens Y-98

    Ernest Hemingway's Toronto Journalism Revisited: With Three Previously Unrecorded Stories Y-92

    Falsifying Hemingway Y-96

    A Farewell to Arms (Documentary) DLB-308

    Hemingway Centenary Celebration at the JFK Library Y-99

    The Hemingway/Fenton Correspondence Y-02

    Hemingway in the JFK Y-99

    The Hemingway Letters Project Finds an Editor Y-02

    Hemingway Salesmen's Dummies Y-00

    Hemingway: Twenty-Five Years Later ... Y-85

    A Literary Archaeologist Digs On: A Brief Interview with Michael Reynolds Y-99

    Not Immediately Discernible . . . but Eventually Quite Clear: The *First Light* and *Final Years* of Hemingway's Centenary Y-99

    Packaging Papa: *The Garden of Eden* Y-86

    Second International Hemingway Colloquium: Cuba Y-98

Hémon, Louis 1880-1913 .... DLB-92

Hempel, Amy 1951- DLB-218

Hempel, Carl G. 1905-1997 ....DLB-279

Hemphill, Paul 1936- Y-87

Hénault, Gilles 1920-1996 .... DLB-88

Henchman, Daniel 1689-1761 .... DLB-24

Henderson, Alice Corbin 1881-1949 ..... DLB-54

Henderson, Archibald 1877-1963 .... DLB-103

Henderson, David 1942- DLB-41

Henderson, George Wylie 1904-1965 ... DLB-51

Henderson, Zenna 1917-1983 .... DLB-8

Henighan, Tom 1934- DLB-251

Henisch, Peter 1943- DLB-85

Henley, Beth 1952- Y-86

Henley, William Ernest 1849-1903 ...... DLB-19

Henniker, Florence 1855-1923 .... DLB-135

Henning, Rachel 1826-1914 .... DLB-230

Henningsen, Agnes 1868-1962 .... DLB-214

Henry, Alexander 1739-1824 .... DLB-99

Henry, Buck 1930- DLB-26

Henry, Marguerite 1902-1997 .... DLB-22

Henry, O. (see Porter, William Sydney)

Henry, Robert Selph 1889-1970 ....DLB-17

Henry, Will (see Allen, Henry W.)

Henry VIII of England 1491-1547 ...... DLB-132

Henry of Ghent circa 1217-1229 - 1293 .... DLB-115

Henryson, Robert 1420s or 1430s-circa 1505 .... DLB-146

Henschke, Alfred (see Klabund)

Hensher, Philip 1965- DLB-267

Hensley, Sophie Almon 1866-1946 ...... DLB-99

Henson, Lance 1944- DLB-175

Henty, G. A. 1832-1902 .... DLB-18, 141

    The Henty Society Y-98

Hentz, Caroline Lee 1800-1856 ...... DLB-3, 248

Heraclitus flourished circa 500 B.C. DLB-176

Herbert, Agnes circa 1880-1960 ....DLB-174

Herbert, Alan Patrick 1890-1971 .....DLB-10, 191

Herbert, Edward, Lord, of Cherbury 1582-1648 ....DLB-121, 151, 252

Herbert, Frank 1920-1986 ..... DLB-8; CDALB-7

Herbert, George 1593-1633 .. DLB-126; CDBLB-1

Herbert, Henry William 1807-1858 .... DLB-3, 73

Herbert, John 1926- DLB-53

Herbert, Mary Sidney, Countess of Pembroke (see Sidney, Mary)

Herbert, Xavier 1901-1984 . . . . DLB-260
Herbert, Zbigniew
   1924-1998 . . . . DLB-232; CDWLB-4
Herbst, Josephine 1892-1969 . . . . DLB-9
Herburger, Gunter 1932- DLB-75, 124
Herculano, Alexandre 1810-1877 . . . . DLB-287
Hercules, Frank E. M. 1917-1996 . . . . DLB-33
Herder, Johann Gottfried 1744-1803 . . . . . . DLB-97
B. Herder Book Company DLB-49
Heredia, José-María de 1842-1905 . . . . DLB-217
Herford, Charles Harold 1853-1931 . . . . . DLB-149
Hergesheimer, Joseph 1880-1954 . . . . . . DLB-9, 102
Heritage Press DLB-46
Hermann the Lame 1013-1054 . . . . DLB-148
Hermes, Johann Timotheu 1738-1821 . . . . . DLB-97
Hermlin, Stephan 1915-1997 . . . . DLB-69
Hernández, Alfonso C. 1938- DLB-122
Hernández, Inés 1947- DLB-122
Hernández, Miguel 1910-1942 . . . . DLB-134
Hernton, Calvin C. 1932- DLB-38
Herodotus circa 484 B.C.-circa 420 B.C.
    . . . . DLB-176; CDWLB-1
Heron, Robert 1764-1807 . . . . DLB-142
Herr, Michael 1940- DLB-185
Herrera, Darío 1870-1914 . . . . DLB-290
Herrera, Juan Felipe 1948- DLB-122
E. R. Herrick and Company DLB-49
Herrick, Robert 1591-1674 . . . . DLB-126
Herrick, Robert 1868-1938 . . . . DLB-9, 12, 78
Herrick, William 1915- Y-83
Herrmann, John 1900-1959 . . . . DLB-4
Hersey, John
   1914-1993 . . . DLB-6, 185, 278, 299; CDALB-7
Hertel, François 1905-1985 . . . . DLB-68
Hervé-Bazin, Jean Pierre Marie (see Bazin, Hervé)
Hervey, John, Lord 1696-1743 . . . . DLB-101
Herwig, Georg 1817-1875 . . . . DLB-133
Herzen, Alexander (Aleksandr Ivanovich
   Gersten) 1812-1870 . . . . DLB-277
Herzog, Emile Salomon Wilhelm
   (see Maurois, André)
Hesiod eighth century B.C. DLB-176
Hesse, Hermann
   1877-1962 . . . . DLB-66; CDWLB-2
Hessus, Eobanus 1488-1540 . . . . DLB-179
Heureka! (see Kertész, Imre and Nobel Prize
   in Literature: 2002) Y-02
Hewat, Alexander circa 1743-circa 1824 . . . DLB-30
Hewett, Dorothy 1923-2002 . . . . DLB-289
Hewitt, John 1907-1987 . . . . DLB-27
Hewlett, Maurice 1861-1923 . . . . DLB-34, 156
Heyen, William 1940- DLB-5
Heyer, Georgette 1902-1974 . . . . DLB-77, 191
Heym, Stefan 1913-2001 . . . . DLB-69
Heyse, Paul 1830-1914 . . . . DLB-129
Heytesbury, William
   circa 1310-1372 or 1373 . . . . DLB-115

Heyward, Dorothy 1890-1961 . . . . DLB-7, 249
Heyward, DuBose 1885-1940 . . . DLB-7, 9, 45, 249
Heywood, John 1497?-1580? DLB-136
Heywood, Thomas 1573 or 1574-1641 . . . . DLB-62
Hiaasen, Carl 1953- DLB-292
Hibberd, Jack 1940- DLB-289
Hibbs, Ben 1901-1975 . . . . DLB-137
   "The Saturday Evening Post reaffirms
   a policy," Ben Hibb's Statement
   in *The Saturday Evening Post*
   (16 May 1942) DLB-137
Hichens, Robert S. 1864-1950 . . . . DLB-153
Hickey, Emily 1845-1924 . . . . DLB-199
Hickman, William Albert 1877-1957 . . . . . . DLB-92
Hicks, Granville 1901-1982 . . . . DLB-246
Hidalgo, José Luis 1919-1947 . . . . DLB-108
Hiebert, Paul 1892-1987 . . . . DLB-68
Hieng, Andrej 1925- DLB-181
Hierro, José 1922-2002 . . . . DLB-108
Higgins, Aidan 1927- DLB-14
Higgins, Colin 1941-1988 . . . . DLB-26
Higgins, George V.
   1939-1999 . . . . DLB-2; Y-81, 98–99
   Afterword [in response to Cozzen's
   Mens Rea (or Something)] Y-97
   At End of Day: The Last George V.
   Higgins Novel Y-99
   The Books of George V. Higgins:
   A Checklist of Editions
   and Printings Y-00
   George V. Higgins in Class Y-02
   Tribute to Alfred A. Knopf Y-84
   Tributes to George V. Higgins Y-99
   "What You Lose on the Swings You Make
   Up on the Merry-Go-Round" . . . Y-99
Higginson, Thomas Wentworth
   1823-1911 . . . . DLB-1, 64, 243
Highsmith, Patricia 1921-1995 . . . . DLB-306
Highwater, Jamake 1942?- DLB-52; Y-85
Hijuelos, Oscar 1951- DLB-145
Hildegard von Bingen 1098-1179 . . . . DLB-148
Das Hildesbrandslied
   circa 820 . . . . DLB-148; CDWLB-2
Hildesheimer, Wolfgang 1916-1991 . . DLB-69, 124
Hildreth, Richard 1807-1865 . . . DLB-1, 30, 59, 235
Hill, Aaron 1685-1750 . . . . DLB-84
Hill, Geoffrey 1932- DLB-40; CDBLB-8
George M. Hill Company DLB-49
Hill, "Sir" John 1714?-1775 . . . . DLB-39
Lawrence Hill and Company,
   Publishers DLB-46
Hill, Joe 1879-1915 . . . . DLB-303
Hill, Leslie 1880-1960 . . . . DLB-51
Hill, Reginald 1936- DLB-276
Hill, Susan 1942- DLB-14, 139
Hill, Walter 1942- DLB-44
Hill and Wang DLB-46
Hillberry, Conrad 1928- DLB-120

Hillerman, Tony 1925- DLB-206, 306
Hilliard, Gray and Company DLB-49
Hills, Lee 1906-2000 . . . . DLB-127
Hillyer, Robert 1895-1961 . . . . DLB-54
Hilsenrath, Edgar 1926- DLB-299
Hilton, James 1900-1954 . . . . DLB-34, 77
Hilton, Walter died 1396 . . . . DLB-146
Hilton and Company DLB-49
Himes, Chester 1909-1984 . . . DLB-2, 76, 143, 226
Joseph Hindmarsh [publishing house] DLB-170
Hine, Daryl 1936- DLB-60
Hingley, Ronald 1920- DLB-155
Hinojosa-Smith, Rolando 1929- DLB-82
Hinton, S. E. 1948- CDALB-7
Hippel, Theodor Gottlieb von
   1741-1796 . . . . DLB-97
Hippius, Zinaida Nikolaevna
   1869-1945 . . . . DLB-295
Hippocrates of Cos flourished circa
   425 B.C. DLB-176; CDWLB-1
Hirabayashi Taiko 1905-1972 . . . . DLB-180
Hirsch, E. D., Jr. 1928- DLB-67
Hirsch, Edward 1950- DLB-120
"Historical Novel," The Holocaust DLB-299
Hoagland, Edward 1932- DLB-6
Hoagland, Everett H., III 1942- DLB-41
Hoban, Russell 1925- DLB-52; Y-90
Hobbes, Thomas 1588-1679 . . . DLB-151, 252, 281
Hobby, Oveta 1905-1995 . . . . DLB-127
Hobby, William 1878-1964 . . . . DLB-127
Hobsbaum, Philip 1932- DLB-40
Hobsbawn, Eric (Francis Newton)
   1917- DLB-296
Hobson, Laura Z. 1900- DLB-28
Hobson, Sarah 1947- DLB-204
Hoby, Thomas 1530-1566 . . . . DLB-132
Hoccleve, Thomas
   circa 1368-circa 1437 . . . . DLB-146
Hoch, Edward D. 1930- DLB-306
Hochhuth, Rolf 1931- DLB-124
Hochman, Sandra 1936- DLB-5
Hocken, Thomas Morland 1836-1910 . . . . DLB-184
Hocking, William Ernest 1873-1966 . . . . . DLB-270
Hodder and Stoughton, Limited DLB-106
Hodgins, Jack 1938- DLB-60
Hodgman, Helen 1945- DLB-14
Hodgskin, Thomas 1787-1869 . . . . DLB-158
Hodgson, Ralph 1871-1962 . . . . DLB-19
Hodgson, William Hope
   1877-1918 . . . . DLB-70, 153, 156, 178
Hoe, Robert, III 1839-1909 . . . . DLB-187
Hoeg, Peter 1957- DLB-214
Hoel, Sigurd 1890-1960 . . . . DLB-297
Hoem, Edvard 1949- DLB-297
Hoffenstein, Samuel 1890-1947 . . . . DLB-11
Hoffman, Alice 1952- DLB-292

Hoffman, Charles Fenno 1806-1884... DLB-3, 250	Holmes, Richard 1945- DLB-155	Hopkinson, Nalo 1960- DLB-251
Hoffman, Daniel 1923- DLB-5	Holmes, Thomas James 1874-1959...... DLB-187	Hopper, Nora (Mrs. Nora Chesson) 1871-1906................. DLB-240
Tribute to Robert Graves............ Y-85	The Holocaust "Historical Novel"...... DLB-299	Hoppin, Augustus 1828-1896......... DLB-188
Hoffmann, E. T. A. 1776-1822............ DLB-90; CDWLB-2	Holocaust Fiction, Postmodern......... DLB-299	Hora, Josef 1891-1945 ...... DLB-215; CDWLB-4
Hoffman, Frank B. 1888-1958 .... DLB-188	Holocaust Novel, The "Second-Generation" DLB-299	Horace 65 B.C.-8 B.C........ DLB-211; CDWLB-1
Hoffman, William 1925- DLB-234	Holroyd, Michael 1935- DLB-155; Y-99	Horgan, Paul 1903-1995...... DLB-102, 212; Y-85
Tribute to Paxton Davis Y-94	Holst, Hermann E. von 1841-1904 ...... DLB-47	Tribute to Alfred A. Knopf Y-84
Hoffmanswaldau, Christian Hoffman von 1616-1679.................. DLB-168	Holt, John 1721-1784 .... DLB-43	Horizon Press..................... DLB-46
Hofmann, Michael 1957- DLB-40	Henry Holt and Company DLB-49, 284	Horkheimer, Max 1895-1973.......... DLB-296
Hofmannsthal, Hugo von 1874-1929..........DLB-81, 118; CDWLB-2	Holt, Rinehart and Winston........... DLB-46	Hornby, C. H. St. John 1867-1946...... DLB-201
Hofmo, Gunvor 1921-1995 .... DLB-297	Holtby, Winifred 1898-1935 .... DLB-191	Hornby, Nick 1957- DLB-207
Hofstadter, Richard 1916-1970.......DLB-17, 246	Holthusen, Hans Egon 1913-1997 ...... DLB-69	Horne, Frank 1899-1974........... DLB-51
Hogan, Desmond 1950- DLB-14	Hölty, Ludwig Christoph Heinrich 1748-1776................... DLB-94	Horne, Richard Henry (Hengist) 1802 or 1803-1884 .... DLB-32
Hogan, Linda 1947- DLB-175	Holub, Miroslav 1923-1998 .... DLB-232; CDWLB-4	Horne, Thomas 1608-1654 .... DLB-281
Hogan and Thompson DLB-49	Holz, Arno 1863-1929 .... DLB-118	Horney, Karen 1885-1952 .... DLB-246
Hogarth Press................ DLB-112; DS-10	Home, Henry, Lord Kames (see Kames, Henry Home, Lord)	Hornung, E. W. 1866-1921 .... DLB-70
Hogg, James 1770-1835....... DLB-93, 116, 159	Home, John 1722-1808................. DLB-84	Horovitz, Israel 1939- DLB-7
Hohberg, Wolfgang Helmhard Freiherr von 1612-1688................... DLB-168	Home, William Douglas 1912- DLB-13	Horta, Maria Teresa (see The Three Marias: A Landmark Case in Portuguese Literary History)
von Hohenheim, Philippus Aureolus Theophrastus Bombastus (see Paracelsus)	Home Publishing Company DLB-49	Horton, George Moses 1797?-1883?...... DLB-50
Hohl, Ludwig 1904-1980 .... DLB-56	Homer circa eighth-seventh centuries B.C. DLB-176; CDWLB-1	George Moses Horton Society.......... Y-99
Højholt, Per 1928- DLB-214	Homer, Winslow 1836-1910 .... DLB-188	Horváth, Ödön von 1901-1938 ..... DLB-85, 124
Holan, Vladimir 1905-1980 .... DLB-215	Homes, Geoffrey (see Mainwaring, Daniel)	Horwood, Harold 1923- DLB-60
Holberg, Ludvig 1684-1754 .... DLB-300	Honan, Park 1928- DLB-111	E. and E. Hosford [publishing house]..... DLB-49
Holbrook, David 1923- DLB-14, 40	Hone, William 1780-1842..........DLB-110, 158	Hoskens, Jane Fenn 1693-1770? DLB-200
Holcroft, Thomas 1745-1809 .... DLB-39, 89, 158	Hongo, Garrett Kaoru 1951- DLB-120	Hoskyns, John circa 1566-1638 .... DLB-121, 281
Preface to *Alwyn* (1780)............ DLB-39	Honig, Edwin 1919- DLB-5	Hosokawa Yūsai 1535-1610 .... DLB-203
Holden, Jonathan 1941- DLB-105	Hood, Hugh 1928-2000 .... DLB-53	Hospers, John 1918- DLB-279
"Contemporary Verse Story-telling" .. DLB-105	Hood, Mary 1946- DLB-234	Hostovský, Egon 1908-1973 .... DLB-215
Holden, Molly 1927-1981.............. DLB-40	Hood, Thomas 1799-1845 .... DLB-96	Hotchkiss and Company DLB-49
Hölderlin, Friedrich 1770-1843............. DLB-90; CDWLB-2	Hook, Sidney 1902-1989 ....DLB-279	Hough, Emerson 1857-1923 .... DLB-9, 212
Holdstock, Robert 1948- DLB-261	Hook, Theodore 1788-1841 .... DLB-116	Houghton, Stanley 1881-1913 .... DLB-10
Holiday House DLB-46	Hooker, Jeremy 1941- DLB-40	Houghton Mifflin Company DLB-49
Holinshed, Raphael died 1580 .... DLB-167	Hooker, Richard 1554-1600 .... DLB-132	*Hours at Home* DS-13
Holland, J. G. 1819-1881 ....DS-13	Hooker, Thomas 1586-1647 .... DLB-24	Household, Geoffrey 1900-1988 .... DLB-87
Holland, Norman N. 1927- DLB-67	hooks, bell 1952- DLB-246	Housman, A. E. 1859-1936 ... DLB-19; CDBLB-5
Hollander, John 1929- DLB-5	Hooper, Johnson Jones 1815-1862 .... DLB-3, 11, 248	Housman, Laurence 1865-1959 .... DLB-10
Holley, Marietta 1836-1926 .... DLB-11	Hope, A. D. 1907-2000............. DLB-289	Houston, Pam 1962- DLB-244
Hollinghurst, Alan 1954- DLB-207	Hope, Anthony 1863-1933........ DLB-153, 156	Houwald, Ernst von 1778-1845 .... DLB-90
Hollingsworth, Margaret 1940- DLB-60	Hope, Christopher 1944- DLB-225	Hovey, Richard 1864-1900 .... DLB-54
Hollo, Anselm 1934- DLB-40	Hope, Eva (see Hearn, Mary Anne)	Howard, Donald R. 1927-1987........ DLB-111
Holloway, Emory 1885-1977 .... DLB-103	Hope, Laurence (Adela Florence Cory Nicolson) 1865-1904......... DLB-240	Howard, Maureen 1930- Y-83
Holloway, John 1920- DLB-27	Hopkins, Ellice 1836-1904 .... DLB-190	Howard, Richard 1929- DLB-5
Holloway House Publishing Company ... DLB-46	Hopkins, Gerard Manley 1844-1889 .... DLB-35, 57; CDBLB-5	Howard, Roy W. 1883-1964 .... DLB-29
Holme, Constance 1880-1955 .... DLB-34	Hopkins, John ?-1570 .... DLB-132	Howard, Sidney 1891-1939 ....DLB-7, 26, 249
Holmes, Abraham S. 1821?-1908........ DLB-99	Hopkins, John H., and Son............ DLB-46	Howard, Thomas, second Earl of Arundel 1585-1646 .... DLB-213
Holmes, John Clellon 1926-1988 .... DLB-16, 237	Hopkins, Lemuel 1750-1801 .... DLB-37	Howe, E. W. 1853-1937............ DLB-12, 25
"Four Essays on the Beat Generation"................. DLB-16	Hopkins, Pauline Elizabeth 1859-1930.... DLB-50	Howe, Henry 1816-1893 .... DLB-30
Holmes, Mary Jane 1825-1907 ..... DLB-202, 221	Hopkins, Samuel 1721-1803 .... DLB-31	Howe, Irving 1920-1993............ DLB-67
Holmes, Oliver Wendell 1809-1894 ...... DLB-1, 189, 235; CDALB-2	Hopkinson, Francis 1737-1791 .... DLB-31	Howe, Joseph 1804-1873 .... DLB-99
		Howe, Julia Ward 1819-1910.... DLB-1, 189, 235
		Howe, Percival Presland 1886-1944..... DLB-149

Howe, Susan 1937- DLB-120
Howell, Clark, Sr. 1863-1936 ....DLB-25
Howell, Evan P. 1839-1905.............DLB-23
Howell, James 1594?-1666.............DLB-151
Howell, Soskin and Company DLB-46
Howell, Warren Richardson
  1912-1984 ....DLB-140
Howells, William Dean 1837-1920
  .... DLB-12, 64, 74, 79, 189; CDALB-3
  Introduction to Paul Laurence
    Dunbar's *Lyrics of Lowly Life*
    (1896) DLB-50
  The William Dean Howells Society Y-01
Howitt, Mary 1799-1888 ....DLB-110, 199
Howitt, William 1792-1879 ....DLB-110
Hoyem, Andrew 1935- DLB-5
Hoyers, Anna Ovena 1584-1655........DLB-164
Hoyle, Fred 1915-2001 ....DLB-261
Hoyos, Angela de 1940- DLB-82
Henry Hoyt [publishing house].........DLB-49
Hoyt, Palmer 1897-1979..............DLB-127
Hrabal, Bohumil 1914-1997..........DLB-232
Hrabanus Maurus 776?-856..........DLB-148
Hronský, Josef Cíger 1896-1960 ......DLB-215
Hrotsvit of Gandersheim
  circa 935-circa 1000................DLB-148
Hubbard, Elbert 1856-1915...........DLB-91
Hubbard, Kin 1868-1930..............DLB-11
Hubbard, William circa 1621-1704 ......DLB-24
Huber, Therese 1764-1829............DLB-90
Huch, Friedrich 1873-1913.............DLB-66
Huch, Ricarda 1864-1947 ....DLB-66
Huddle, David 1942- DLB-130
Hudgins, Andrew 1951- DLB-120, 282
Hudson, Henry Norman 1814-1886 ......DLB-64
Hudson, Stephen 1868?-1944 ....DLB-197
Hudson, W. H. 1841-1922 ..... DLB-98, 153, 174
Hudson and Goodwin.................DLB-49
Huebsch, B. W., oral history............Y-99
B. W. Huebsch [publishing house].......DLB-46
Hueffer, Oliver Madox 1876-1931......DLB-197
Huet, Pierre Daniel
  Preface to *The History of Romances*
  (1715) DLB-39
Hugh of St. Victor circa 1096-1141 ......DLB-208
Hughes, David 1930- DLB-14
Hughes, Dusty 1947- DLB-233
Hughes, Hatcher 1881-1945 ....DLB-249
Hughes, John 1677-1720...............DLB-84
Hughes, Langston 1902-1967 ....DLB-4, 7, 48,
      51, 86, 228; ; DS-15; CDALB-5
Hughes, Richard 1900-1976..........DLB-15, 161
Hughes, Ted 1930-1998 ....DLB-40, 161
Hughes, Thomas 1822-1896 ....DLB-18, 163
Hugo, Richard 1923-1982 ....DLB-5, 206
Hugo, Victor 1802-1885 ..... DLB-119, 192, 217
Hugo Awards and Nebula Awards DLB-8

Huidobro, Vicente 1893-1948.........DLB-283
Hull, Richard 1896-1973 ....DLB-77
Hulda (Unnur Benediktsdóttir Bjarklind)
  1881-1946 ....DLB-293
Hulme, T. E. 1883-1917 ....DLB-19
Hulton, Anne ?-1779? DLB-200
Humboldt, Alexander von 1769-1859 .....DLB-90
Humboldt, Wilhelm von 1767-1835......DLB-90
Hume, David 1711-1776...........DLB-104, 252
Hume, Fergus 1859-1932...............DLB-70
Hume, Sophia 1702-1774 ....DLB-200
Hume-Rothery, Mary Catherine
  1824-1885 ....DLB-240
Humishuma
  (see Mourning Dove)
Hummer, T. R. 1950- DLB-120
Humor
  American Humor: A Historical
    Survey DLB-11
  American Humor Studies Association.....Y-99
  The Comic Tradition Continued
    [in the British Novel] DLB-15
  Humorous Book Illustration DLB-11
  International Society for Humor Studies.. Y-99
  Newspaper Syndication of American
    Humor DLB-11
  Selected Humorous Magazines
    (1820-1950).....................DLB-11
Bruce Humphries [publishing house] DLB-46
Humphrey, Duke of Gloucester
  1391-1447 ....DLB-213
Humphrey, William
  1924-1997 .... DLB-6, 212, 234, 278
Humphreys, David 1752-1818...........DLB-37
Humphreys, Emyr 1919- DLB-15
Humphreys, Josephine 1945- DLB-292
Huncke, Herbert 1915-1996 ....DLB-16
Huneker, James Gibbons 1857-1921 ......DLB-71
Hunold, Christian Friedrich
  1681-1721 ....DLB-168
Hunt, Irene 1907- DLB-52
Hunt, Leigh 1784-1859 ....DLB-96, 110, 144
Hunt, Violet 1862-1942............. DLB-162, 197
Hunt, William Gibbes 1791-1833 ....DLB-73
Hunter, Evan (Ed McBain)
  1926- DLB-306; Y-82
  Tribute to John D. MacDonald........Y-86
Hunter, Jim 1939- DLB-14
Hunter, Kristin 1931- DLB-33
  Tribute to Julian Mayfield............Y-84
Hunter, Mollie 1922- DLB-161
Hunter, N. C. 1908-1971 ....DLB-10
Hunter-Duvar, John 1821-1899 ....DLB-99
Huntington, Henry E. 1850-1927 ....DLB-140
  The Henry E. Huntington Library Y-92
Huntington, Susan Mansfield
  1791-1823 ....DLB-200
Hurd and Houghton..................DLB-49

Hurst, Fannie 1889-1968 ....DLB-86
Hurst and Blackett....................DLB-106
Hurst and Company DLB-49
Hurston, Zora Neale
  1901?-1960 ....DLB-51, 86; CDALB-7
Husserl, Edmund 1859-1938...........DLB-296
Husson, Jules-François-Félix (see Champfleury)
Huston, John 1906-1987 ....DLB-26
Hutcheson, Francis 1694-1746 ......DLB-31, 252
Hutchinson, Ron 1947- DLB-245
Hutchinson, R. C. 1907-1975 ....DLB-191
Hutchinson, Thomas 1711-1780 ......DLB-30, 31
Hutchinson and Company
  (Publishers) Limited DLB-112
Huth, Angela 1938- DLB-271
Hutton, Richard Holt
  1826-1897 ....DLB-57
von Hutten, Ulrich 1488-1523..........DLB-179
Huxley, Aldous 1894-1963
  ...... DLB-36, 100, 162, 195, 255; CDBLB-6
Huxley, Elspeth Josceline
  1907-1997 ....DLB-77, 204
Huxley, T. H. 1825-1895 ....DLB-57
Huyghue, Douglas Smith 1816-1891......DLB-99
Huysmans, Joris-Karl 1848-1907 ....DLB-123
Hwang, David Henry
  1957- DLB-212, 228
Hyde, Donald 1909-1966 ....DLB-187
Hyde, Mary 1912- DLB-187
Hyman, Trina Schart 1939- DLB-61

I

Iavorsky, Stefan 1658-1722 ....DLB-150
Iazykov, Nikolai Mikhailovich
  1803-1846 ....DLB-205
Ibáñez, Armando P. 1949- DLB-209
Ibáñez, Sara de 1909-1971 ....DLB-290
Ibarbourou, Juana de 1892-1979 ....DLB-290
Ibn Bajja circa 1077-1138 ....DLB-115
Ibn Gabirol, Solomon
  circa 1021-circa 1058................DLB-115
Ibuse Masuji 1898-1993...............DLB-180
Ichijō Kanera
  (see Ichijō Kaneyoshi)
Ichijō Kaneyoshi (Ichijō Kanera)
  1402-1481 ....DLB-203
Iffland, August Wilhelm
  1759-1814 ....DLB-94
Iggulden, John 1917- DLB-289
Ignatieff, Michael 1947- DLB-267
Ignatow, David 1914-1997..............DLB-5
Ike, Chukwuemeka 1931- DLB-157
Ikkyū Sōjun 1394-1481 ....DLB-203
Iles, Francis
  (see Berkeley, Anthony)
Il'f, Il'ia (Il'ia Arnol'dovich Fainzil'berg)
  1897-1937 ....DLB-272
Illich, Ivan 1926-2002 ....DLB-242

Illustration
- Children's Book Illustration in the Twentieth Century DLB-61
- Children's Illustrators, 1800-1880 . . . DLB-163
- Early American Book Illustration DLB-49
- The Iconography of Science-Fiction Art DLB-8
- The Illustration of Early German Literary Manuscripts, circa 1150-circa 1300 . . . . DLB-148
- Minor Illustrators, 1880-1914 . . . . . . DLB-141

Illyés, Gyula 1902-1983 . . . . DLB-215; CDWLB-4
Imbs, Bravig 1904-1946 . . . . DLB-4; DS-15
Imbuga, Francis D. 1947- DLB-157
Immermann, Karl 1796-1840 . . . . DLB-133
Inchbald, Elizabeth 1753-1821 . . . . . . DLB-39, 89
Indiana University Press Y-02
Ingamells, Rex 1913-1955 . . . . DLB-260
Inge, William 1913-1973 . . . DLB-7, 249; CDALB-1
Ingelow, Jean 1820-1897 . . . . DLB-35, 163
Ingemann, B. S. 1789-1862 . . . . DLB-300
Ingersoll, Ralph 1900-1985 . . . . DLB-127
The Ingersoll Prizes Y-84
Ingoldsby, Thomas (see Barham, Richard Harris)
Ingraham, Joseph Holt 1809-1860 . . . . DLB-3, 248
Inman, John 1805-1850 . . . . DLB-73
Innerhofer, Franz 1944- DLB-85
Innes, Michael (J. I. M. Stewart) 1906-1994 . . . . DLB-276
Innis, Harold Adams 1894-1952 . . . . DLB-88
Innis, Mary Quayle 1899-1972 . . . . DLB-88
Inō Sōgi 1421-1502 . . . . DLB-203
Inoue Yasushi 1907-1991 . . . . DLB-182
"The Greatness of Southern Literature": League of the South Institute for the Study of Southern Culture and History Y-02
International Publishers Company DLB-46
Internet (publishing and commerce)
- Author Websites Y-97
- The Book Trade and the Internet Y-00
- E-Books Turn the Corner Y-98
- The E-Researcher: Possibilities and Pitfalls Y-00
- Interviews on E-publishing Y-00
- John Updike on the Internet Y-97
- LitCheck Website Y-01
- Virtual Books and Enemies of Books Y-00

Interviews
- Adoff, Arnold Y-01
- Aldridge, John W. Y-91
- Anastas, Benjamin Y-98
- Baker, Nicholson Y-00
- Bank, Melissa Y-98
- Bass, T. J. Y-80
- Bernstein, Harriet Y-82
- Betts, Doris Y-82
- Bosworth, David Y-82

Bottoms, David Y-83
Bowers, Fredson Y-80
Burnshaw, Stanley Y-97
Carpenter, Humphrey Y-84, 99
Carr, Virginia Spencer Y-00
Carver, Raymond Y-83
Cherry, Kelly Y-83
Conroy, Jack Y-81
Coppel, Alfred Y-83
Cowley, Malcolm Y-81
Davis, Paxton Y-89
Devito, Carlo Y-94
De Vries, Peter Y-82
Dickey, James Y-82
Donald, David Herbert Y-87
Editors, Conversations with Y-95
Ellroy, James Y-91
Fancher, Betsy Y-83
Faust, Irvin Y-00
Fulton, Len Y-86
Furst, Alan Y-01
Garrett, George Y-83
Gelfman, Jane Y-93
Goldwater, Walter Y-93
Gores, Joe Y-02
Greenfield, George Y-91
Griffin, Bryan Y-81
Groom, Winston Y-01
Guilds, John Caldwell Y-92
Hamilton, Virginia Y-01
Hardin, James Y-92
Harris, Mark Y-80
Harrison, Jim Y-82
Hazzard, Shirley Y-82
Herrick, William Y-01
Higgins, George V. Y-98
Hoban, Russell Y-90
Holroyd, Michael Y-99
Horowitz, Glen Y-90
Iggulden, John Y-01
Jakes, John Y-83
Jenkinson, Edward B. Y-82
Jenks, Tom Y-86
Kaplan, Justin Y-86
King, Florence Y-85
Klopfer, Donald S. Y-97
Krug, Judith Y-82
Lamm, Donald Y-95
Laughlin, James Y-96
Lawrence, Starling Y-95
Lindsay, Jack Y-84
Mailer, Norman Y-97
Manchester, William Y-85
Max, D. T. Y-94

McCormack, Thomas Y-98
McNamara, Katherine Y-97
Mellen, Joan Y-94
Menaker, Daniel Y-97
Mooneyham, Lamarr Y-82
Murray, Les Y-01
Nosworth, David Y-82
O'Connor, Patrick Y-84, 99
Ozick, Cynthia Y-83
Penner, Jonathan Y-83
Pennington, Lee Y-82
Penzler, Otto Y-96
Plimpton, George Y-99
Potok, Chaim Y-84
Powell, Padgett Y-01
Prescott, Peter S. Y-86
Rabe, David Y-91
Rechy, John Y-82
Reid, B. L. Y-83
Reynolds, Michael Y-95, 99
Robinson, Derek Y-02
Rollyson, Carl Y-97
Rosset, Barney Y-02
Schlafly, Phyllis Y-82
Schroeder, Patricia Y-99
Schulberg, Budd Y-81, 01
Scribner, Charles, III Y-94
Sipper, Ralph Y-94
Smith, Cork Y-95
Staley, Thomas F. Y-00
Styron, William Y-80
Talese, Nan Y-94
Thornton, John Y-94
Toth, Susan Allen Y-86
Tyler, Anne Y-82
Vaughan, Samuel Y-97
Von Ogtrop, Kristin Y-92
Wallenstein, Barry Y-92
Weintraub, Stanley Y-82
Williams, J. Chamberlain Y-84

Into the Past: William Jovanovich's Reflections in Publishing Y-02
Ireland, David 1927- DLB-289
The National Library of Ireland's New James Joyce Manuscripts Y-02
Irigaray, Luce 1930- DLB-296
Irving, John 1942- DLB-6, 278; Y-82
Irving, Washington 1783-1859 . . . . DLB-3, 11, 30, 59, 73, 74, 183, 186, 250; CDALB-2
Irwin, Grace 1907- DLB-68
Irwin, Will 1873-1948 . . . . DLB-25
Isaksson, Ulla 1916-2000 . . . . DLB-257
Iser, Wolfgang 1926- DLB-242
Isherwood, Christopher 1904-1986 . . . . DLB-15, 195; Y-86

The Christopher Isherwood Archive,
  The Huntington Library............ Y-99
Ishiguro, Kazuo 1954- DLB-194
Ishikawa Jun 1899-1987............... DLB-182
Iskander, Fazil' Abdulevich 1929- DLB-302
The Island Trees Case: A Symposium on
  School Library Censorship
  An Interview with Judith Krug
  An Interview with Phyllis Schlafly
  An Interview with Edward B. Jenkinson
  An Interview with Lamarr Mooneyham
  An Interview with Harriet Bernstein..... Y-82
Islas, Arturo
  1938-1991...................... DLB-122
Issit, Debbie 1966- DLB-233
Ivanišević, Drago 1907-1981........... DLB-181
Ivanov, Viacheslav Ivanovich
  1866-1949...................... DLB-295
Ivanov, Vsevolod Viacheslavovich
  1895-1963...................... DLB-272
Ivaska, Astrīde 1926- DLB-232
M. J. Ivers and Company............... DLB-49
Iwaniuk, Wacław 1915- DLB-215
Iwano Hōmei 1873-1920 .... DLB-180
Iwaszkiewicz, Jarosław 1894-1980 ...... DLB-215
Iyayi, Festus 1947- DLB-157
Izumi Kyōka 1873-1939................ DLB-180

J

Jackmon, Marvin E. (see Marvin X)
Jacks, L. P. 1860-1955................ DLB-135
Jackson, Angela 1951- DLB-41
Jackson, Charles 1903-1968........... DLB-234
Jackson, Helen Hunt
  1830-1885 .... DLB-42, 47, 186, 189
Jackson, Holbrook 1874-1948 .... DLB-98
Jackson, Laura Riding 1901-1991 ...... DLB-48
Jackson, Shirley
  1916-1965.......... DLB-6, 234; CDALB-1
Jacob, Max 1876-1944................. DLB-258
Jacob, Naomi 1884?-1964 .... DLB-191
Jacob, Piers Anthony Dillingham
  (see Anthony, Piers)
Jacob, Violet 1863-1946............... DLB-240
Jacobi, Friedrich Heinrich 1743-1819..... DLB-94
Jacobi, Johann Georg 1740-1841 .... DLB-97
George W. Jacobs and Company DLB-49
Jacobs, Harriet 1813-1897 .... DLB-239
Jacobs, Joseph 1854-1916.............. DLB-141
Jacobs, W. W. 1863-1943 .... DLB-135
  The W. W. Jacobs Appreciation Society.. Y-98
Jacobsen, J. P. 1847-1885............. DLB-300
Jacobsen, Jørgen-Frantz 1900-1938 ..... DLB-214
Jacobsen, Josephine 1908- DLB-244
Jacobsen, Rolf 1907-1994.............. DLB-297
Jacobson, Dan 1929- DLB-14, 207, 225
Jacobson, Howard 1942- DLB-207
Jacques de Vitry circa 1160/1170-1240 ... DLB-208

Jæger, Frank 1926-1977............... DLB-214
William Jaggard [publishing house]...... DLB-170
Jahier, Piero 1884-1966............ DLB-114, 264
Jahnn, Hans Henny 1894-1959 ...... DLB-56, 124
Jaimes, Freyre, Ricardo 1866?-1933 ..... DLB-283
Jakes, John 1932- DLB-278; Y-83
  Tribute to John Gardner............. Y-82
  Tribute to John D. MacDonald......... Y-86
Jakobína Johnson (Jakobína Sigurbjarnardóttir)
  1883-1977...................... DLB-293
Jakobson, Roman 1896-1982........... DLB-242
James, Alice 1848-1892 .... DLB-221
James, C. L. R. 1901-1989............. DLB-125
James, George P. R. 1801-1860 .... DLB-116
James, Henry 1843-1916
  ..... DLB-12, 71, 74, 189; DS-13; CDALB-3
  "The Future of the Novel" (1899)..... DLB-18
  "The Novel in [Robert Browning's]
  'The Ring and the Book'"
  (1912) DLB-32
James, John circa 1633-1729........... DLB-24
James, M. R. 1862-1936............ DLB-156, 201
James, Naomi 1949- DLB-204
James, P. D. (Phyllis Dorothy James White)
  1920- DLB-87, 276; DS-17; CDBLB-8
  Tribute to Charles Scribner Jr. Y-95
James, Thomas 1572?-1629 .... DLB-213
U. P. James [publishing house] DLB-49
James, Will 1892-1942................. DS-16
James, William 1842-1910............ DLB-270
James VI of Scotland, I of England
  1566-1625 .... DLB-151, 172
  Ane Schort Treatise Conteining Some Revlis
  and Cautelis to Be Obseruit and
  Eschewit in Scottis Poesi (1584)..... DLB-172
Jameson, Anna 1794-1860 .... DLB-99, 166
Jameson, Fredric 1934- DLB-67
Jameson, J. Franklin 1859-1937 .... DLB-17
Jameson, Storm 1891-1986 .... DLB-36
Jančar, Drago 1948- DLB-181
Janés, Clara 1940- DLB-134
Janevski, Slavko 1920- DLB-181; CDWLB-4
Janowitz, Tama 1957- DLB-292
Jansson, Tove 1914-2001............... DLB-257
Janvier, Thomas 1849-1913............. DLB-202
Japan
  "The Development of Meiji Japan"... DLB-180
  "Encounter with the West"......... DLB-180
Japanese Literature
  Letter from Japan Y-94, 98
  Medieval Travel Diaries DLB-203
  Surveys: 1987-1995 .... DLB-182
Jaramillo, Cleofas M. 1878-1956 .... DLB-122
Jaramillo Levi, Enrique 1944- DLB-290
Jarman, Mark 1952- DLB-120, 282
Jarrell, Randall
  1914-1965 .... DLB-48, 52; CDALB-1
Jarrold and Sons DLB-106

Jarry, Alfred 1873-1907 .... DLB-192, 258
Jarves, James Jackson 1818-1888........ DLB-189
Jasmin, Claude 1930- DLB-60
Jaunsudrabiņš, Jānis 1877-1962 .... DLB-220
Jay, John 1745-1829................... DLB-31
Jean de Garlande (see John of Garland)
Jefferies, Richard 1848-1887 .... DLB-98, 141
  The Richard Jefferies Society Y-98
Jeffers, Lance 1919-1985 .... DLB-41
Jeffers, Robinson
  1887-1962 .... DLB-45, 212; CDALB-4
Jefferson, Thomas
  1743-1826 .... DLB-31, 183; CDALB-2
Jégé 1866-1940....................... DLB-215
Jelinek, Elfriede 1946- DLB-85
Jellicoe, Ann 1927- DLB-13, 233
Jemison, Mary circa 1742-1833 .... DLB-239
Jenkins, Dan 1929- DLB-241
Jenkins, Elizabeth 1905- DLB-155
Jenkins, Robin 1912- DLB-14, 271
Jenkins, William Fitzgerald (see Leinster, Murray)
Herbert Jenkins Limited DLB-112
Jennings, Elizabeth 1926- DLB-27
Jens, Walter 1923- DLB-69
Jensen, Axel 1932-2003 .... DLB-297
Jensen, Johannes V. 1873-1950 .... DLB-214
Jensen, Merrill 1905-1980 .... DLB-17
Jensen, Thit 1876-1957................ DLB-214
Jephson, Robert 1736-1803 .... DLB-89
Jerome, Jerome K. 1859-1927 .... DLB-10, 34, 135
  The Jerome K. Jerome Society Y-98
Jerome, Judson 1927-1991 .... DLB-105
  "Reflections: After a Tornado" DLB-105
Jerrold, Douglas 1803-1857 .... DLB-158, 159
Jersild, Per Christian 1935- DLB-257
Jesse, F. Tennyson 1888-1958 .... DLB-77
Jewel, John 1522-1571 .... DLB-236
John P. Jewett and Company............ DLB-49
Jewett, Sarah Orne 1849-1909 .... DLB-12, 74, 221
The Jewish Publication Society DLB-49
Studies in American Jewish Literature....... Y-02
Jewitt, John Rodgers 1783-1821......... DLB-99
Jewsbury, Geraldine 1812-1880.......... DLB-21
Jewsbury, Maria Jane 1800-1833 .... DLB-199
Jhabvala, Ruth Prawer 1927- DLB-139, 194
Jiménez, Juan Ramón 1881-1958 .... DLB-134
Jin, Ha 1956- DLB-244, 292
Joans, Ted 1928- DLB-16, 41
Jōha 1525-1602 .... DLB-203
Jóhann Sigurjónsson 1880-1919......... DLB-293
Jóhannes úr Kötlum 1899-1972 .... DLB-293
Johannis de Garlandia (see John of Garland)
John, Errol 1924-1988................ DLB-233
John, Eugenie (see Marlitt, E.)

John of Dumbleton circa 1310-circa 1349 . . . . DLB-115	Johnston, David Claypole 1798?-1865 . . . DLB-188	Johsson, Tor 1916-1951 . . . . DLB-297
John of Garland (Jean de Garlande, Johannis de Garlandia) circa 1195-circa 1272 . . . . DLB-208	Johnston, Denis 1901-1984. . . . . DLB-10	Jordan, June 1936- DLB-38
	Johnston, Ellen 1835-1873 . . . . DLB-199	Jorgensen, Johannes 1866-1956 . . . . DLB-300
	Johnston, George 1912-1970 . . . . DLB-260	Joseph, Jenny 1932- DLB-40
The John Reed Clubs DLB-303	Johnston, George 1913- DLB-88	Joseph and George Y-99
Johns, Captain W. E. 1893-1968 . . . . DLB-160	Johnston, Sir Harry 1858-1927 . . . . .DLB-174	Michael Joseph Limited DLB-112
Johnson, Mrs. A. E. ca. 1858-1922 . . . . . . DLB-221	Johnston, Jennifer 1930- DLB-14	Josephson, Matthew 1899-1978 . . . . DLB-4
Johnson, Amelia (see Johnson, Mrs. A. E.)	Johnston, Mary 1870-1936 . . . . DLB-9	Josephus, Flavius 37-100 . . . . .DLB-176
Johnson, B. S. 1933-1973 . . . . DLB-14, 40	Johnston, Richard Malcolm 1822-1898 . . . DLB-74	Josephy, Alvin M., Jr. Tribute to Alfred A. Knopf Y-84
Johnson, Charles 1679-1748 . . . . DLB-84	Johnstone, Charles 1719?-1800? DLB-39	
Johnson, Charles 1948- DLB-33, 278	Johst, Hanns 1890-1978 . . . . DLB-124	Josiah Allen's Wife (see Holley, Marietta)
Johnson, Charles S. 1893-1956 . . . . . . DLB-51, 91	Jökull Jakobsson 1933-1978 . . . . DLB-293	Josipovici, Gabriel 1940- DLB-14
Johnson, Colin (Mudrooroo) 1938- . . . DLB-289	Jolas, Eugene 1894-1952 . . . . DLB-4, 45	Josselyn, John ?-1675 . . . . DLB-24
Johnson, Denis 1949- DLB-120	Jón Stefán Sveinsson or Svensson (see Nonni)	Joudry, Patricia 1921-2000 . . . . DLB-88
Johnson, Diane 1934- Y-80	Jón Trausti (Guðmundur Magnússon) 1873-1918 . . . . DLB-293	Jouve, Pierre Jean 1887-1976 . . . . DLB-258
Johnson, Dorothy M. 1905–1984 . . . . DLB-206		Jovanovich, William 1920-2001 . . . . Y-01
Johnson, E. Pauline (Tekahionwake) 1861-1913 . . . . .DLB-175	Jón úr Vör (Jón Jónsson) 1917-2000 . . . . DLB-293	Into the Past: William Jovanovich's Reflections on Publishing Y-02
	Jónas Hallgrímsson 1807-1845 . . . . DLB-293	
Johnson, Edgar 1901-1995 . . . . DLB-103	Jones, Alice C. 1853-1933 . . . . DLB-92	[Response to Ken Auletta] Y-97
Johnson, Edward 1598-1672 . . . . DLB-24	Jones, Charles C., Jr. 1831-1893 . . . . DLB-30	The Temper of the West: William Jovanovich Y-02
Johnson, Eyvind 1900-1976 . . . . DLB-259	Jones, D. G. 1929- DLB-53	
Johnson, Fenton 1888-1958 . . . . DLB-45, 50	Jones, David 1895-1974 . . . . DLB-20, 100; CDBLB-7	Tribute to Charles Scribner Jr. Y-95
Johnson, Georgia Douglas 1877?-1966 . . . . DLB-51, 249		Jovine, Francesco 1902-1950 . . . . DLB-264
	Jones, Diana Wynne 1934- DLB-161	Jovine, Giuseppe 1922- DLB-128
Johnson, Gerald W. 1890-1980 . . . . DLB-29	Jones, Ebenezer 1820-1860 . . . . DLB-32	Joyaux, Philippe (see Sollers, Philippe)
Johnson, Greg 1953- DLB-234	Jones, Ernest 1819-1868 . . . . DLB-32	Joyce, Adrien (see Eastman, Carol)
Johnson, Helene 1907-1995 . . . . DLB-51	Jones, Gayl 1949- DLB-33, 278	Joyce, James 1882-1941 . . . . .DLB-10, 19, 36, 162, 247; CDBLB-6
Jacob Johnson and Company DLB-49	Jones, George 1800-1870 . . . . DLB-183	
Johnson, James Weldon 1871-1938 . . . . DLB-51; CDALB-4	Jones, Glyn 1905-1995 . . . . DLB-15	Danis Rose and the Rendering of Ulysses . . . Y-97
	Jones, Gwyn 1907- DLB-15, 139	James Joyce Centenary: Dublin, 1982 . . . . Y-82
Johnson, John H. 1918- DLB-137	Jones, Henry Arthur 1851-1929 . . . . DLB-10	James Joyce Conference Y-85
"Backstage," Statement From the Initial Issue of Ebony (November 1945) DLB-137	Jones, Hugh circa 1692-1760 . . . . DLB-24	A Joyce (Con)Text: Danis Rose and the Remaking of Ulysses Y-97
	Jones, James 1921-1977 . . . . . . .DLB-2, 143; DS-17	
	James Jones Papers in the Handy Writers' Colony Collection at the University of Illinois at Springfield Y-98	The National Library of Ireland's New James Joyce Manuscripts Y-02
Johnson, Joseph [publishing house] DLB-154		
Johnson, Linton Kwesi 1952- DLB-157		The New Ulysses Y-84
Johnson, Lionel 1867-1902 . . . . DLB-19		Public Domain and the Violation of Texts Y-97
Johnson, Nunnally 1897-1977 . . . . DLB-26	The James Jones Society Y-92	
Johnson, Owen 1878-1952 . . . . Y-87	Jones, Jenkin Lloyd 1911- DLB-127	The Quinn Draft of James Joyce's Circe Manuscript Y-00
Johnson, Pamela Hansford 1912-1981 . . . . DLB-15	Jones, John Beauchamp 1810-1866 . . . . . . DLB-202	
Johnson, Pauline 1861-1913 . . . . DLB-92	Jones, Joseph, Major (see Thompson, William Tappan)	Stephen Joyce's Letter to the Editor of The Irish Times Y-97
Johnson, Ronald 1935-1998 . . . . DLB-169		
Johnson, Samuel 1696-1772 . . . DLB-24; CDBLB-2	Jones, LeRoi (see Baraka, Amiri)	Ulysses, Reader's Edition: First Reactions . . Y-97
Johnson, Samuel 1709-1784 . . . . DLB-39, 95, 104, 142, 213	Jones, Lewis 1897-1939 . . . . DLB-15	We See the Editor at Work Y-97
	Jones, Madison 1925- DLB-152	Whose Ulysses? The Function of Editing . . Y-97
Rambler, no. 4 (1750) [excerpt] DLB-39	Jones, Marie 1951- DLB-233	Jozsef, Attila 1905-1937 . . . . DLB-215; CDWLB-4
The BBC Four Samuel Johnson Prize for Non-fiction Y-02	Jones, Preston 1936-1979 . . . . DLB-7	Juarroz, Roberto 1925-1995 . . . . DLB-283
	Jones, Rodney 1950- DLB-120	Orange Judd Publishing Company DLB-49
Johnson, Samuel 1822-1882 . . . . DLB-1, 243	Jones, Thom 1945- DLB-244	Judd, Sylvester 1813-1853 . . . . DLB-1, 243
Johnson, Susanna 1730-1810 . . . . DLB-200	Jones, Sir William 1746-1794 . . . . DLB-109	Judith circa 930 . . . . DLB-146
Johnson, Terry 1955- DLB-233	Jones, William Alfred 1817-1900 . . . . DLB-59	Juel-Hansen, Erna 1845-1922 . . . . DLB-300
Johnson, Uwe 1934-1984 . . . . . DLB-75; CDWLB-2	Jones's Publishing House DLB-49	Julian of Norwich 1342-circa 1420 . . . . . DLB-1146
Benjamin Johnson [publishing house] DLB-49	Jong, Erica 1942- DLB-2, 5, 28, 152	Julius Caesar 100 B.C.-44 B.C. DLB-211; CDWLB-1
Benjamin, Jacob, and Robert Johnson [publishing house] DLB-49	Jonke, Gert F. 1946- DLB-85	
	Jonson, Ben 1572?-1637 . . . . DLB-62, 121; CDBLB-1	June, Jennie (see Croly, Jane Cunningham)
Johnston, Annie Fellows 1863-1931 . . . . . . DLB-42		Jung, Carl Gustav 1875-1961 . . . . DLB-296
Johnston, Basil H. 1929- DLB-60		Jung, Franz 1888-1963 . . . . DLB-118

Jünger, Ernst 1895- DLB-56; CDWLB-2
Der jüngere Titurel circa 1275 ....DLB-138
Jung-Stilling, Johann Heinrich
   1740-1817.......................DLB-94
Junqueiro, Abílio Manuel Guerra
   1850-1923......................DLB-287
Justice, Donald 1925- Y-83
Juvenal circa A.D. 60-circa A.D. 130
   ....DLB-211; CDWLB-1
The Juvenile Library
   (see M. J. Godwin and Company)

K

Kacew, Romain (see Gary, Romain)
Kafka, Franz 1883-1924......DLB-81; CDWLB-2
Kahn, Gus 1886-1941 ....DLB-265
Kahn, Roger 1927- DLB-171
Kaikō Takeshi 1939-1989 ....DLB-182
Káinn (Kristján Níels Jónsson/Kristjan
   Niels Julius) 1860-1936..........DLB-293
Kaiser, Georg 1878-1945 ....DLB-124; CDWLB-2
Kaiserchronik circa 1147 ....DLB-148
Kaleb, Vjekoslav 1905- DLB-181
Kalechofsky, Roberta 1931- DLB-28
Kaler, James Otis 1848-1912 ....DLB-12, 42
Kalmar, Bert 1884-1947................DLB-265
Kamensky, Vasilii Vasil'evich
   1884-1961......................DLB-295
Kames, Henry Home, Lord
   1696-1782..................DLB-31, 104
Kamo no Chōmei (Kamo no Nagaakira)
   1153 or 1155-1216 ....DLB-203
Kamo no Nagaakira (see Kamo no Chōmei)
Kampmann, Christian 1939-1988 ....DLB-214
Kandel, Lenore 1932- DLB-16
Kane, Sarah 1971-1999 ....DLB-310
Kanin, Garson 1912-1999 ....DLB-7
   A Tribute (to Marc Connelly)..........Y-80
Kaniuk, Yoram 1930- DLB-299
Kant, Hermann 1926- DLB-75
Kant, Immanuel 1724-1804 ....DLB-94
Kantemir, Antiokh Dmitrievich
   1708-1744......................DLB-150
Kantor, MacKinlay 1904-1977.........DLB-9, 102
Kanze Kōjirō Nobumitsu 1435-1516.....DLB-203
Kanze Motokiyo (see Zeimi)
Kaplan, Fred 1937- DLB-111
Kaplan, Johanna 1942- DLB-28
Kaplan, Justin 1925- DLB-111; Y-86
Kaplinski, Jaan 1941- DLB-232
Kapnist, Vasilii Vasilevich 1758?-1823 ...DLB-150
Karadžić,Vuk Stefanović
   1787-1864............DLB-147; CDWLB-4
Karamzin, Nikolai Mikhailovich
   1766-1826......................DLB-150
Karinthy, Frigyes 1887-1938 ....DLB-215
Karmel, Ilona 1925-2000 ....DLB-299
Karsch, Anna Louisa 1722-1791.........DLB-97

Kasack, Hermann 1896-1966...........DLB-69
Kasai Zenzō 1887-1927................DLB-180
Kaschnitz, Marie Luise 1901-1974........DLB-69
Kassák, Lajos 1887-1967...............DLB-215
Kaštelan, Jure 1919-1990..............DLB-147
Kästner, Erich 1899-1974...............DLB-56
Kataev, Evgenii Petrovich
   (see Il'f, Il'ia and Petrov, Evgenii)
Kataev, Valentin Petrovich 1897-1986....DLB-272
Katenin, Pavel Aleksandrovich
   1792-1853......................DLB-205
Kattan, Naim 1928- DLB-53
Katz, Steve 1935- Y-83
Ka-Tzetnik 135633 (Yehiel Dinur)
   1909-2001......................DLB-299
Kauffman, Janet 1945- DLB-218; Y-86
Kauffmann, Samuel 1898-1971.........DLB-127
Kaufman, Bob 1925-1986............DLB-16, 41
Kaufman, George S. 1889-1961...........DLB-7
Kaufmann, Walter 1921-1980 ....DLB-279
Kavan, Anna (Helen Woods Ferguson
   Edmonds) 1901-1968 ....DLB-255
Kavanagh, P. J. 1931- DLB-40
Kavanagh, Patrick 1904-1967 ....DLB-15, 20
Kaverin, Veniamin Aleksandrovich
   (Veniamin Aleksandrovich Zil'ber)
   1902-1989......................DLB-272
Kawabata Yasunari 1899-1972.........DLB-180
Kay, Guy Gavriel 1954- DLB-251
Kaye-Smith, Sheila 1887-1956 ....DLB-36
Kazakov, Iurii Pavlovich 1927-1982......DLB-302
Kazin, Alfred 1915-1998 ....DLB-67
Keane, John B. 1928- DLB-13
Keary, Annie 1825-1879...............DLB-163
Keary, Eliza 1827-1918................DLB-240
Keating, H. R. F. 1926- DLB-87
Keatley, Charlotte 1960- DLB-245
Keats, Ezra Jack 1916-1983 ....DLB-61
Keats, John 1795-1821 ....DLB-96, 110; CDBLB-3
Keble, John 1792-1866...........DLB-32, 55
Keckley, Elizabeth 1818?-1907..........DLB-239
Keeble, John 1944- Y-83
Keeffe, Barrie 1945- DLB-13, 245
Keeley, James 1867-1934 ....DLB-25
W. B. Keen, Cooke and Company DLB-49
The Mystery of Carolyn Keene............Y-02
Kefala, Antigone 1935- DLB-289
Keillor, Garrison 1942- Y-87
Keith, Marian (Mary Esther MacGregor)
   1874?-1961......................DLB-92
Keller, Gary D. 1943- DLB-82
Keller, Gottfried
   1819-1890............DLB-129; CDWLB-2
Keller, Helen 1880-1968 ....DLB-303
Kelley, Edith Summers 1884-1956........DLB-9
Kelley, Emma Dunham ?-? DLB-221
Kelley, Florence 1859-1932 ....DLB-303

Kelley, William Melvin 1937- DLB-33
Kellogg, Ansel Nash 1832-1886.........DLB-23
Kellogg, Steven 1941- DLB-61
Kelly, George E. 1887-1974 ....DLB-7, 249
Kelly, Hugh 1739-1777................DLB-89
Kelly, Piet and Company DLB-49
Kelly, Robert 1935- DLB-5, 130, 165
Kelman, James 1946- DLB-194
Kelmscott Press DLB-112
Kelton, Elmer 1926- DLB-256
Kemble, E. W. 1861-1933..............DLB-188
Kemble, Fanny 1809-1893..............DLB-32
Kemelman, Harry 1908-1996..........DLB-28
Kempe, Margery circa 1373-1438......DLB-146
Kempinski, Tom 1938- DLB-310
Kempner, Friederike 1836-1904........DLB-129
Kempowski, Walter 1929- DLB-75
Kenan, Randall 1963- DLB-292
Claude Kendall [publishing company].....DLB-46
Kendall, Henry 1839-1882............DLB-230
Kendall, May 1861-1943..............DLB-240
Kendell, George 1809-1867............DLB-43
Keneally, Thomas 1935- DLB-289, 299
Kenedy, P. J., and Sons DLB-49
Kenkō circa 1283-circa 1352 ....DLB-203
Kenna, Peter 1930-1987...............DLB-289
Kennan, George 1845-1924............DLB-189
Kennedy, A. L. 1965- DLB-271
Kennedy, Adrienne 1931- DLB-38
Kennedy, John Pendleton 1795-1870...DLB-3, 248
Kennedy, Leo 1907-2000 ....DLB-88
Kennedy, Margaret 1896-1967 ....DLB-36
Kennedy, Patrick 1801-1873 ....DLB-159
Kennedy, Richard S. 1920- DLB-111; Y-02
Kennedy, William 1928- DLB-143; Y-85
Kennedy, X. J. 1929- DLB-5
   Tribute to John Ciardi Y-86
Kennelly, Brendan 1936- DLB-40
Kenner, Hugh 1923- DLB-67
   Tribute to Cleanth Brooks Y-80
Mitchell Kennerley [publishing house] DLB-46
Kenny, Maurice 1929- DLB-175
Kent, Frank R. 1877-1958 ....DLB-29
Kenyon, Jane 1947-1995 ....DLB-120
Kenzheev, Bakhyt Shkurullaevich
   1950-.........................DLB-285
Keough, Hugh Edmund 1864-1912......DLB-171
Keppler and Schwartzmann DLB-49
Ker, John, third Duke of Roxburghe
   1740-1804......................DLB-213
Ker, N. R. 1908-1982 ....DLB-201
Kerlan, Irvin 1912-1963................DLB-187
Kermode, Frank 1919- DLB-242
Kern, Jerome 1885-1945 ....DLB-187
Kernaghan, Eileen 1939- DLB-251

Cumulative Index

Kerner, Justinus 1786-1862 . . . . DLB-90
Kerouac, Jack
1922-1969 . . DLB-2, 16, 237; DS-3; CDALB-1
   Auction of Jack Kerouac's
      On the Road Scroll Y-01
   The Jack Kerouac Revival Y-95
   "Re-meeting of Old Friends":
      The Jack Kerouac Conference Y-82
   Statement of Correction to "The Jack
      Kerouac Revival" Y-96
Kerouac, Jan 1952-1996 . . . . DLB-16
Charles H. Kerr and Company DLB-49
Kerr, Orpheus C. (see Newell, Robert Henry)
Kersh, Gerald 1911-1968 . . . . DLB-255
Kertész, Imre DLB-299; Y-02
Kesey, Ken
1935-2001 . . . . . . DLB-2, 16, 206; CDALB-6
Kessel, Joseph 1898-1979 . . . . DLB-72
Kessel, Martin 1901-1990 . . . . DLB-56
Kesten, Hermann 1900-1996 . . . . DLB-56
Keun, Irmgard 1905-1982 . . . . DLB-69
Key, Ellen 1849-1926 . . . . DLB-259
Key and Biddle DLB-49
Keynes, Sir Geoffrey 1887-1982 . . . . DLB-201
Keynes, John Maynard 1883-1946 . . . . DS-10
Keyserling, Eduard von 1855-1918 . . . . . . DLB-66
Khan, Ismith 1925-2002 . . . . DLB-125
Kharitonov, Evgenii Vladimirovich
1941-1981 . . . . DLB-285
Kharitonov, Mark Sergeevich 1937- . . . DLB-285
Khaytov, Nikolay 1919- DLB-181
Khemnitser, Ivan Ivanovich
1745-1784 . . . . DLB-150
Kheraskov, Mikhail Matveevich
1733-1807 . . . . DLB-150
Khlebnikov, Velimir 1885-1922 . . . . DLB-295
Khomiakov, Aleksei Stepanovich
1804-1860 . . . . DLB-205
Khristov, Boris 1945- DLB-181
Khvoshchinskaia, Nadezhda Dmitrievna
1824-1889 . . . . DLB-238
Khvostov, Dmitrii Ivanovich
1757-1835 . . . . DLB-150
Kibirov, Timur Iur'evich (Timur
Iur'evich Zapoev) 1955- DLB-285
Kidd, Adam 1802?-1831 . . . . DLB-99
William Kidd [publishing house] DLB-106
Kidde, Harald 1878-1918 . . . . DLB-300
Kidder, Tracy 1945- DLB-185
Kiely, Benedict 1919- DLB-15
Kieran, John 1892-1981 . . . . DLB-171
Kierkegaard, Søren 1813-1855 . . . . DLB-300
Kies, Marietta 1853-1899 . . . . DLB-270
Kiggins and Kellogg DLB-49
Kiley, Jed 1889-1962 . . . . DLB-4
Kilgore, Bernard 1908-1967 . . . . DLB-127
Kilian, Crawford 1941- DLB-251
Killens, John Oliver 1916-1987 . . . . DLB-33

   Tribute to Julian Mayfield Y-84
Killigrew, Anne 1660-1685 . . . . DLB-131
Killigrew, Thomas 1612-1683 . . . . DLB-58
Kilmer, Joyce 1886-1918 . . . . DLB-45
Kilroy, Thomas 1934- DLB-233
Kilwardby, Robert circa 1215-1279 . . . . . DLB-115
Kilworth, Garry 1941- DLB-261
Kim, Anatolii Andreevich 1939- DLB-285
Kimball, Richard Burleigh 1816-1892 . . . DLB-202
Kincaid, Jamaica 1949-
   . . . . DLB-157, 227; CDALB-7; CDWLB-3
Kinck, Hans Ernst 1865-1926 . . . . DLB-297
King, Charles 1844-1933 . . . . DLB-186
King, Clarence 1842-1901 . . . . DLB-12
King, Florence 1936- Y-85
King, Francis 1923- DLB-15, 139
King, Grace 1852-1932 . . . . DLB-12, 78
King, Harriet Hamilton 1840-1920 . . . . . . DLB-199
King, Henry 1592-1669 . . . . DLB-126
Solomon King [publishing house] DLB-49
King, Stephen 1947- DLB-143; Y-80
King, Susan Petigru 1824-1875 . . . . DLB-239
King, Thomas 1943- DLB-175
King, Woodie, Jr. 1937- DLB-38
Kinglake, Alexander William
1809-1891 . . . . DLB-55, 166
Kingo, Thomas 1634-1703 . . . . DLB-300
Kingsbury, Donald 1929- DLB-251
Kingsley, Charles
1819-1875 . . . . DLB-21, 32, 163, 178, 190
Kingsley, Henry 1830-1876 . . . . DLB-21, 230
Kingsley, Mary Henrietta 1862-1900 . . . . . DLB-174
Kingsley, Sidney 1906-1995 . . . . DLB-7
Kingsmill, Hugh 1889-1949 . . . . DLB-149
Kingsolver, Barbara
1955- DLB-206; CDALB-7
Kingston, Maxine Hong
1940- DLB-173, 212; Y-80; CDALB-7
Kingston, William Henry Giles
1814-1880 . . . . DLB-163
Kinnan, Mary Lewis 1763-1848 . . . . DLB-200
Kinnell, Galway 1927- DLB-5; Y-87
Kinsella, Thomas 1928- DLB-27
Kipling, Rudyard 1865-1936
   . . . . DLB-19, 34, 141, 156; CDBLB-5
Kipphardt, Heinar 1922-1982 . . . . DLB-124
Kirby, William 1817-1906 . . . . DLB-99
Kircher, Athanasius 1602-1680 . . . . DLB-164
Kireevsky, Ivan Vasil'evich 1806-1856 . . . DLB-198
Kireevsky, Petr Vasil'evich 1808-1856 . . . DLB-205
Kirk, Hans 1898-1962 . . . . DLB-214
Kirk, John Foster 1824-1904 . . . . DLB-79
Kirkconnell, Watson 1895-1977 . . . . DLB-68
Kirkland, Caroline M.
1801-1864 . . . . DLB-3, 73, 74, 250; DS-13
Kirkland, Joseph 1830-1893 . . . . DLB-12
Francis Kirkman [publishing house] DLB-170

Kirkpatrick, Clayton 1915- DLB-127
Kirkup, James 1918- DLB-27
Kirouac, Conrad (see Marie-Victorin, Frère)
Kirsch, Sarah 1935- DLB-75
Kirst, Hans Hellmut 1914-1989 . . . . DLB-69
Kiš, Danilo 1935-1989 . . . . DLB-181; CDWLB-4
Kita Morio 1927- DLB-182
Kitcat, Mabel Greenhow 1859-1922 . . . . . DLB-135
Kitchin, C. H. B. 1895-1967 . . . . DLB-77
Kittredge, William 1932- DLB-212, 244
Kiukhel'beker, Vil'gel'm Karlovich
1797-1846 . . . . DLB-205
Kizer, Carolyn 1925- DLB-5, 169
Kjaerstad, Jan 1953- DLB-297
Klabund 1890-1928 . . . . DLB-66
Klaj, Johann 1616-1656 . . . . DLB-164
Klappert, Peter 1942- DLB-5
Klass, Philip (see Tenn, William)
Klein, A. M. 1909-1972 . . . . DLB-68
Kleist, Ewald von 1715-1759 . . . . DLB-97
Kleist, Heinrich von
1777-1811 . . . . DLB-90; CDWLB-2
Klíma, Ivan 1931- DLB-232; CDWLB-4
Klimentev, Andrei Platonovic
   (see Platonov, Andrei Platonovich)
Klinger, Friedrich Maximilian
1752-1831 . . . . DLB-94
Kliuev, Nikolai Alekseevich 1884-1937 . . DLB-295
Kliushnikov, Viktor Petrovich
1841-1892 . . . . DLB-238
Klopfer, Donald S.
   Impressions of William Faulkner Y-97
   Oral History Interview with Donald
      S. Klopfer Y-97
   Tribute to Alfred A. Knopf Y-84
Klopstock, Friedrich Gottlieb
1724-1803 . . . . DLB-97
Klopstock, Meta 1728-1758 . . . . DLB-97
Kluge, Alexander 1932- DLB-75
Kluge, P. F. 1942- Y-02
Knapp, Joseph Palmer 1864-1951 . . . . DLB-91
Knapp, Samuel Lorenzo 1783-1838 . . . . . . DLB-59
J. J. and P. Knapton [publishing house] . . DLB-154
Kniazhnin, Iakov Borisovich
1740-1791 . . . . DLB-150
Knickerbocker, Diedrich (see Irving, Washington)
Knigge, Adolph Franz Friedrich Ludwig,
   Freiherr von 1752-1796 . . . . DLB-94
Charles Knight and Company DLB-106
Knight, Damon 1922-2002 . . . . DLB-8
Knight, Etheridge 1931-1992 . . . . DLB-41
Knight, John S. 1894-1981 . . . . DLB-29
Knight, Sarah Kemble 1666-1727 . . . . DLB-24, 200
Knight-Bruce, G. W. H. 1852-1896 . . . . . . DLB-174
Knister, Raymond 1899-1932 . . . . DLB-68
Knoblock, Edward 1874-1945 . . . . DLB-10
Knopf, Alfred A. 1892-1984 . . . . Y-84

Knopf to Hammett: The Editoral Correspondence Y-00
Alfred A. Knopf [publishing house] DLB-46
Knorr von Rosenroth, Christian 1636-1689 .... DLB-168
Knowles, John 1926- DLB-6; CDALB-6
Knox, Frank 1874-1944 .... DLB-29
Knox, John circa 1514-1572 .... DLB-132
Knox, John Armoy 1850-1906 .... DLB-23
Knox, Lucy 1845-1884 .... DLB-240
Knox, Ronald Arbuthnott 1888-1957 ..... DLB-77
Knox, Thomas Wallace 1835-1896 ...... DLB-189
Knudsen, Jakob 1858-1917 .... DLB-300
Kobayashi Takiji 1903-1933 .... DLB-180
Kober, Arthur 1900-1975 .... DLB-11
Kobiakova, Aleksandra Petrovna 1823-1892 .... DLB-238
Kocbek, Edvard 1904-1981 ... DLB-147; CDWLB-4
Koch, C. J. 1932- DLB-289
Koch, Howard 1902-1995 .... DLB-26
Koch, Kenneth 1925-2002 .... DLB-5
Kōda Rohan 1867-1947 .... DLB-180
Koehler, Ted 1894-1973 .... DLB-265
Koenigsberg, Moses 1879-1945 .... DLB-25
Koeppen, Wolfgang 1906-1996 .... DLB-69
Koertge, Ronald 1940- DLB-105
Koestler, Arthur 1905-1983 ...... Y-83; CDBLB-7
Kohn, John S. Van E. 1906-1976 .... DLB-187
Kokhanovskaia (see Sokhanskaia, Nadezhda Stepanova)
Kokoschka, Oskar 1886-1980 .... DLB-124
Kolb, Annette 1870-1967 .... DLB-66
Kolbenheyer, Erwin Guido 1878-1962 .... DLB-66, 124
Kolleritsch, Alfred 1931- DLB-85
Kolodny, Annette 1941- DLB-67
Kol'tsov, Aleksei Vasil'evich 1809-1842 .... DLB-205
Komarov, Matvei circa 1730-1812 .... DLB-150
Komroff, Manuel 1890-1974 .... DLB-4
Komunyakaa, Yusef 1947- DLB-120
Kondoleon, Harry 1955-1994 .... DLB-266
Koneski, Blaže 1921-1993 ... DLB-181; CDWLB-4
Konigsburg, E. L. 1930- DLB-52
Konparu Zenchiku 1405-1468? DLB-203
Konrád, György 1933- DLB-232; CDWLB-4
Konrad von Würzburg circa 1230-1287 .... DLB-138
Konstantinov, Aleko 1863-1897 .... DLB-147
Konwicki, Tadeusz 1926- DLB-232
Koontz, Dean 1945- DLB-292
Kooser, Ted 1939- DLB-105
Kopit, Arthur 1937- DLB-7
Kops, Bernard 1926?- DLB-13
Kornbluth, C. M. 1923-1958 .... DLB-8
Körner, Theodor 1791-1813 .... DLB-90

Kornfeld, Paul 1889-1942 .... DLB-118
Korolenko, Vladimir Galaktionovich 1853-1921 .... DLB-277
Kosinski, Jerzy 1933-1991 ...... DLB-2, 299; Y-82
Kosmač, Ciril 1910-1980 .... DLB-181
Kosovel, Srečko 1904-1926 .... DLB-147
Kostrov, Ermil Ivanovich 1755-1796 ..... DLB-150
Kotzebue, August von 1761-1819 .... DLB-94
Kotzwinkle, William 1938- DLB-173
Kovačić, Ante 1854-1889 .... DLB-147
Kovalevskaia, Sof'ia Vasil'evna 1850-1891 .... DLB-277
Kovič, Kajetan 1931- DLB-181
Kozlov, Ivan Ivanovich 1779-1840 .... DLB-205
Kracauer, Siegfried 1889-1966 .... DLB-296
Kraf, Elaine 1946- Y-81
Kramer, Jane 1938- DLB-185
Kramer, Larry 1935- DLB-249
Kramer, Mark 1944- DLB-185
Kranjčević, Silvije Strahimir 1865-1908 ... DLB-147
Krasko, Ivan 1876-1958 .... DLB-215
Krasna, Norman 1909-1984 .... DLB-26
Kraus, Hans Peter 1907-1988 .... DLB-187
Kraus, Karl 1874-1936 .... DLB-118
Krause, Herbert 1905-1976 .... DLB-256
Krauss, Ruth 1911-1993 .... DLB-52
Kreisel, Henry 1922-1991 .... DLB-88
Krestovsky V. (see Khvoshchinskaia, Nadezhda Dmitrievna)
Krestovsky, Vsevolod Vladimirovich 1839-1895 .... DLB-238
Kreuder, Ernst 1903-1972 .... DLB-69
Krėvė-Mickevičius, Vincas 1882-1954 .... DLB-220
Kreymborg, Alfred 1883-1966 .... DLB-4, 54
Krieger, Murray 1923- DLB-67
Krim, Seymour 1922-1989 .... DLB-16
Kripke, Saul 1940- DLB-279
Kristensen, Tom 1893-1974 .... DLB-214
Kristeva, Julia 1941- DLB-242
Kristján Níels Jónsson/Kristjan Niels Julius (see Káinn)
Kritzer, Hyman W. 1918-2002 .... Y-02
Krivulin, Viktor Borisovich 1944-2001 ... DLB-285
Krleža, Miroslav 1893-1981 .... DLB-147; CDWLB-4
Krock, Arthur 1886-1974 .... DLB-29
Kroetsch, Robert 1927- DLB-53
Kropotkin, Petr Alekseevich 1842-1921 .. DLB-277
Kross, Jaan 1920- DLB-232
Kruchenykh, Aleksei Eliseevich 1886-1968 .... DLB-295
Krúdy, Gyula 1878-1933 .... DLB-215
Krutch, Joseph Wood 1893-1970 .... DLB-63, 206, 275
Krylov, Ivan Andreevich 1769-1844 .... DLB-150

Krymov, Iurii Solomonovich (Iurii Solomonovich Beklemishev) 1908-1941 .... DLB-272
Kubin, Alfred 1877-1959 .... DLB-81
Kubrick, Stanley 1928-1999 .... DLB-26
Kudrun circa 1230-1240 .... DLB-138
Kuffstein, Hans Ludwig von 1582-1656 .. DLB-164
Kuhlmann, Quirinus 1651-1689 .... DLB-168
Kuhn, Thomas S. 1922-1996 .... DLB-279
Kuhnau, Johann 1660-1722 .... DLB-168
Kukol'nik, Nestor Vasil'evich 1809-1868 .... DLB-205
Kukučín, Martin 1860-1928 .... DLB-215; CDWLB-4
Kumin, Maxine 1925- DLB-5
Kuncewicz, Maria 1895-1989 .... DLB-215
Kundera, Milan 1929- DLB-232; CDWLB-4
Kunene, Mazisi 1930- DLB-117
Kunikida Doppo 1869-1908 .... DLB-180
Kunitz, Stanley 1905- DLB-48
Kunjufu, Johari M. (see Amini, Johari M.)
Kunnert, Gunter 1929- DLB-75
Kunze, Reiner 1933- DLB-75
Kupferberg, Tuli 1923- DLB-16
Kuprin, Aleksandr Ivanovich 1870-1938 .... DLB-295
Kuraev, Mikhail Nikolaevich 1939- DLB-285
Kurahashi Yumiko 1935- DLB-182
Kureishi, Hanif 1954- DLB-194, 245
Kürnberger, Ferdinand 1821-1879 ...... DLB-129
Kurz, Isolde 1853-1944 .... DLB-66
Kusenberg, Kurt 1904-1983 .... DLB-69
Kushchevsky, Ivan Afanas'evich 1847-1876 .... DLB-238
Kushner, Tony 1956- DLB-228
Kuttner, Henry 1915-1958 .... DLB-8
Kuzmin, Mikhail Alekseevich 1872-1936 .... DLB-295
Kuznetsov, Anatoli 1929-1979 .... DLB-299, 302
Kyd, Thomas 1558-1594 .... DLB-62
Kyffin, Maurice circa 1560?-1598 .... DLB-136
Kyger, Joanne 1934- DLB-16
Kyne, Peter B. 1880-1957 .... DLB-78
Kyōgoku Tamekane 1254-1332 .... DLB-203
Kyrklund, Willy 1921- DLB-257

L

L. E. L. (see Landon, Letitia Elizabeth)
Laberge, Albert 1871-1960 .... DLB-68
Laberge, Marie 1950- DLB-60
Labiche, Eugène 1815-1888 .... DLB-192
Labrunie, Gerard (see Nerval, Gerard de)
La Bruyère, Jean de 1645-1696 .... DLB-268
La Calprenède 1609?-1663 .... DLB-268
Lacan, Jacques 1901-1981 .... DLB-296
La Capria, Raffaele 1922- DLB-196

Lacombe, Patrice
(see Trullier-Lacombe, Joseph Patrice)

Lacretelle, Jacques de 1888-1985 . . . . DLB-65

Lacy, Ed 1911-1968 . . . . DLB-226

Lacy, Sam 1903- DLB-171

Ladd, Joseph Brown 1764-1786 . . . . DLB-37

La Farge, Oliver 1901-1963 . . . . DLB-9

Lafayette, Marie-Madeleine, comtesse de
1634-1693 . . . . DLB-268

Laffan, Mrs. R. S. de Courcy
(see Adams, Bertha Leith)

Lafferty, R. A. 1914-2002 . . . . DLB-8

La Flesche, Francis 1857-1932 . . . . .DLB-175

La Fontaine, Jean de 1621-1695 . . . . DLB-268

Laforge, Jules 1860-1887 . . . . DLB-217

Lagerkvist, Pär 1891-1974 . . . . DLB-259

Lagerlöf, Selma
1858-1940 . . . . DLB-259

Lagorio, Gina 1922- DLB-196

La Guma, Alex
1925-1985 . . . . DLB-117, 225; CDWLB-3

Lahaise, Guillaume (see Delahaye, Guy)

Lahontan, Louis-Armand de Lom d'Arce,
Baron de 1666-1715? DLB-99

Laing, Kojo 1946- DLB-157

Laird, Carobeth 1895-1983 . . . . Y-82

Laird and Lee DLB-49

Lake, Paul 1951- DLB-282

Lalić, Ivan V. 1931-1996 . . . . DLB-181

Lalić, Mihailo 1914-1992 . . . . DLB-181

Lalonde, Michèle 1937- DLB-60

Lamantia, Philip 1927- DLB-16

Lamartine, Alphonse de
1790-1869 . . . . DLB-217

Lamb, Lady Caroline
1785-1828 . . . . DLB-116

Lamb, Charles
1775-1834 . . . . . . .DLB-93, 107, 163; CDBLB-3

Lamb, Mary 1764-1874 . . . . DLB-163

Lambert, Angela 1940- DLB-271

Lambert, Betty 1933-1983 . . . . DLB-60

Lamm, Donald
Goodbye, Gutenberg? A Lecture at
the New York Public Library,
18 April 1995 . . . . Y-95

Lamming, George
1927- DLB-125; CDWLB-3

La Mothe Le Vayer, François de
1588-1672 . . . . DLB-268

L'Amour, Louis 1908-1988 . . . . . . DLB-206; Y-80

Lampman, Archibald 1861-1899 . . . . DLB-92

Lamson, Wolffe and Company DLB-49

Lancer Books DLB-46

Lanchester, John 1962- DLB-267

Lander, Peter (see Cunningham, Peter)

Landesman, Jay 1919- and
Landesman, Fran 1927- DLB-16

Landolfi, Tommaso 1908-1979 . . . . .DLB-177

Landon, Letitia Elizabeth 1802-1838 . . . . . DLB-96

Landor, Walter Savage 1775-1864 . . . .DLB-93, 107

Landry, Napoléon-P. 1884-1956 . . . . DLB-92

Landvik, Lorna 1954- DLB-292

Lane, Charles 1800-1870 . . . . . . DLB-1, 223; DS-5

Lane, F. C. 1885-1984 . . . . DLB-241

Lane, Laurence W. 1890-1967 . . . . DLB-91

Lane, M. Travis 1934- DLB-60

Lane, Patrick 1939- DLB-53

Lane, Pinkie Gordon 1923- DLB-41

John Lane Company DLB-49

Laney, Al 1896-1988 . . . . .DLB-4, 171

Lang, Andrew 1844-1912 . . . . . . DLB-98, 141, 184

Langer, Susanne K. 1895-1985 . . . . .DLB-270

Langevin, André 1927- DLB-60

Langford, David 1953- DLB-261

Langgässer, Elisabeth 1899-1950 . . . . DLB-69

Langhorne, John 1735-1779 . . . . DLB-109

Langland, William circa 1330-circa 1400 . DLB-146

Langton, Anna 1804-1893 . . . . DLB-99

Lanham, Edwin 1904-1979 . . . . DLB-4

Lanier, Sidney 1842-1881 . . . . DLB-64; DS-13

Lanyer, Aemilia 1569-1645 . . . . DLB-121

Lapointe, Gatien 1931-1983 . . . . DLB-88

Lapointe, Paul-Marie 1929- DLB-88

Larcom, Lucy 1824-1893 . . . . DLB-221, 243

Lardner, John 1912-1960 . . . . .DLB-171

Lardner, Ring 1885-1933
. . . . . . .DLB-11, 25, 86, 171; DS-16; CDALB-4

Lardner 100: Ring Lardner
Centennial Symposium Y-85

Lardner, Ring, Jr. 1915-2000 . . . . . .DLB-26, Y-00

Larkin, Philip 1922-1985 . . . . . DLB-27; CDBLB-8

The Philip Larkin Society Y-99

La Roche, Sophie von 1730-1807 . . . . DLB-94

La Rochefoucauld, François duc de
1613-1680 . . . . DLB-268

La Rocque, Gilbert 1943-1984 . . . . DLB-60

Laroque de Roquebrune, Robert
(see Roquebrune, Robert de)

Larrick, Nancy 1910- DLB-61

Lars, Claudia 1899-1974 . . . . DLB-283

Larsen, Nella 1893-1964 . . . . DLB-51

Larsen, Thøger 1875-1928 . . . . DLB-300

Larson, Clinton F. 1919-1994 . . . . DLB-256

La Sale, Antoine de
circa 1386-1460/1467 . . . . DLB-208

Lasch, Christopher 1932-1994 . . . . DLB-246

Lasker-Schüler, Else 1869-1945 . . . . . DLB-66, 124

Lasnier, Rina 1915-1997 . . . . DLB-88

Lassalle, Ferdinand 1825-1864 . . . . DLB-129

Late-Medieval Castilian Theater DLB-286

Latham, Robert 1912-1995 . . . . DLB-201

Lathan, Emma (Mary Jane Latsis [1927-1997] and
Martha Henissart [1929-   ]) DLB-306

Lathrop, Dorothy P. 1891-1980 . . . . DLB-22

Lathrop, George Parsons 1851-1898 . . . . . DLB-71

Lathrop, John, Jr. 1772-1820 . . . . DLB-37

Latimer, Hugh 1492?-1555 . . . . DLB-136

Latimore, Jewel Christine McLawler
(see Amini, Johari M.)

Latin Literature, The Uniqueness of DLB-211

La Tour du Pin, Patrice de 1911-1975 . . . DLB-258

Latymer, William 1498-1583 . . . . DLB-132

Laube, Heinrich 1806-1884 . . . . DLB-133

Laud, William 1573-1645 . . . . DLB-213

Laughlin, James 1914-1997 . . . . . .DLB-48; Y-96, 97

A Tribute [to Henry Miller] Y-80

Tribute to Albert Erskine Y-93

Tribute to Kenneth Rexroth Y-82

Tribute to Malcolm Cowley Y-89

Laumer, Keith 1925-1993 . . . . DLB-8

Lauremberg, Johann 1590-1658 . . . . DLB-164

Laurence, Margaret 1926-1987 . . . . DLB-53

Laurentius von Schnüffis 1633-1702 . . . . DLB-168

Laurents, Arthur 1918- DLB-26

Laurie, Annie (see Black, Winifred)

Laut, Agnes Christiana 1871-1936 . . . . . . DLB-92

Lauterbach, Ann 1942- DLB-193

Lautréamont, Isidore Lucien Ducasse,
Comte de 1846-1870 . . . . .DLB-217

Lavater, Johann Kaspar 1741-1801 . . . . . . DLB-97

Lavin, Mary 1912-1996 . . . . DLB-15

Law, John (see Harkness, Margaret)

Lawes, Henry 1596-1662 . . . . DLB-126

Lawler, Ray 1921- DLB-289

Lawless, Anthony (see MacDonald, Philip)

Lawless, Emily (The Hon. Emily Lawless)
1845-1913 . . . . DLB-240

Lawrence, D. H. 1885-1930
. . . . . .DLB-10, 19, 36, 98, 162, 195; CDBLB-6

The D. H. Lawrence Society of
North America Y-00

Lawrence, David 1888-1973 . . . . DLB-29

Lawrence, Jerome 1915- DLB-228

Lawrence, Seymour 1926-1994 . . . . Y-94

Tribute to Richard Yates Y-92

Lawrence, T. E. 1888-1935 . . . . DLB-195

The T. E. Lawrence Society Y-98

Lawson, George 1598-1678 . . . . DLB-213

Lawson, Henry 1867-1922 . . . . DLB-230

Lawson, John ?-1711 . . . . DLB-24

Lawson, John Howard 1894-1977 . . . . . DLB-228

Lawson, Louisa Albury 1848-1920 . . . . . . DLB-230

Lawson, Robert 1892-1957 . . . . DLB-22

Lawson, Victor F. 1850-1925 . . . . DLB-25

Layard, Austen Henry 1817-1894 . . . . . . DLB-166

Layton, Irving 1912- DLB-88

LaZamon flourished circa 1200 . . . . DLB-146

Lazarević, Laza K. 1851-1890 . . . . .DLB-147

Lazarus, George 1904-1997 . . . . DLB-201

Lazhechnikov, Ivan Ivanovich
1792-1869 . . . . DLB-198

Lea, Henry Charles 1825-1909 . . . . .DLB-47	Legaré, Hugh Swinton 1797-1843. . . . . .DLB-3, 59, 73, 248	Lermontov, Mikhail Iur'evich 1814-1841 . . . . .DLB-205
Lea, Sydney 1942- DLB-120, 282	Legaré, James Mathewes 1823-1859 . . . .DLB-3, 248	Lerner, Alan Jay 1918-1986. . . . . .DLB-265
Lea, Tom 1907-2001 . . . . .DLB-6	Léger, Antoine-J. 1880-1950 . . . . .DLB-88	Lerner, Max 1902-1992. . . . . .DLB-29
Leacock, John 1729-1802. . . . . .DLB-31	Leggett, William 1801-1839. . . . . .DLB-250	Lernet-Holenia, Alexander 1897-1976 . . . . .DLB-85
Leacock, Stephen 1869-1944 . . . . .DLB-92	Le Guin, Ursula K.	Le Rossignol, James 1866-1969 . . . . .DLB-92
Lead, Jane Ward 1623-1704. . . . . .DLB-131	1929- DLB-8, 52, 256, 275; CDALB-6	Lescarbot, Marc circa 1570-1642 . . . . .DLB-99
Leadenhall Press DLB-106	Lehman, Ernest 1920- DLB-44	LeSeur, William Dawson 1840-1917 . . . . . .DLB-92
"The Greatness of Southern Literature": League of the South Institute for the Study of Southern Culture and History Y-02	Lehmann, John 1907-1989 . . . . DLB-27, 100	LeSieg, Theo. (see Geisel, Theodor Seuss)
	John Lehmann Limited DLB-112	Leskov, Nikolai Semenovich 1831-1895 . . . . .DLB-238
	Lehmann, Rosamond 1901-1990. . . . . .DLB-15	
Leakey, Caroline Woolmer 1827-1881 . . . .DLB-230	Lehmann, Wilhelm 1882-1968 . . . . .DLB-56	Leslie, Doris before 1902-1982 . . . . .DLB-191
Leapor, Mary 1722-1746 . . . . .DLB-109	Leiber, Fritz 1910-1992 . . . . .DLB-8	Leslie, Eliza 1787-1858 . . . . .DLB-202
Lear, Edward 1812-1888 . . . . . . .DLB-32, 163, 166	Leibniz, Gottfried Wilhelm 1646-1716. . . .DLB-168	Leslie, Frank (Henry Carter) 1821-1880 .DLB-43, 79
Leary, Timothy 1920-1996 . . . . .DLB-16	Leicester University Press DLB-112	
W. A. Leary and Company. DLB-49	Leigh, Carolyn 1926-1983 . . . . .DLB-265	Frank Leslie [publishing house] DLB-49
Léautaud, Paul 1872-1956 . . . . .DLB-65	Leigh, W. R. 1866-1955 . . . . .DLB-188	Leśmian, Bolesław 1878-1937 . . . . .DLB-215
Leavis, F. R. 1895-1978 . . . . .DLB-242	Leinster, Murray 1896-1975 . . . . .DLB-8	Lesperance, John 1835?-1891 . . . . .DLB-99
Leavitt, David 1961- DLB-130	Leiser, Bill 1898-1965 . . . . .DLB-241	Lessing, Bruno 1870-1940 . . . . .DLB-28
Leavitt and Allen DLB-49	Leisewitz, Johann Anton 1752-1806. . . . . . .DLB-94	Lessing, Doris 1919- DLB-15, 139; Y-85; CDBLB-8
Le Blond, Mrs. Aubrey 1861-1934 . . . . . .DLB-174	Leitch, Maurice 1933- DLB-14	
le Carré, John (David John Moore Cornwell) 1931- DLB-87; CDBLB-8	Leithauser, Brad 1943- DLB-120, 282	Lessing, Gotthold Ephraim 1729-1781 . . . . DLB-97; CDWLB-2
	Leland, Charles G. 1824-1903. . . . . .DLB-11	
Tribute to Graham Greene Y-91	Leland, John 1503?-1552 . . . . .DLB-136	The Lessing Society Y-00
Tribute to George Greenfield Y-00	Lemay, Pamphile 1837-1918 . . . . .DLB-99	Le Sueur, Meridel 1900-1996 . . . . .DLB-303
Lécavelé, Roland (see Dorgeles, Roland)	Lemelin, Roger 1919-1992. . . . . .DLB-88	Lettau, Reinhard 1929-1996 . . . . .DLB-75
Lechlitner, Ruth 1901- DLB-48	Lemercier, Louis-Jean-Népomucène 1771-1840 . . . . .DLB-192	The Hemingway Letters Project Finds an Editor Y-02
Leclerc, Félix 1914-1988 . . . . .DLB-60		
Le Clézio, J. M. G. 1940- DLB-83	Le Moine, James MacPherson 1825-1912 . .DLB-99	Lever, Charles 1806-1872 . . . . .DLB-21
Leder, Rudolf (see Hermlin, Stephan)	Lemon, Mark 1809-1870 . . . . .DLB-163	Lever, Ralph ca. 1527-1585 . . . . .DLB-236
Lederer, Charles 1910-1976. . . . . .DLB-26	Le Moyne, Jean 1913-1996 . . . . .DLB-88	Leverson, Ada 1862-1933 . . . . .DLB-153
Ledwidge, Francis 1887-1917 . . . . .DLB-20	Lemperly, Paul 1858-1939. . . . . .DLB-187	Levertov, Denise 1923-1997 . . . . .DLB-5, 165; CDALB-7
Lee, Dennis 1939- DLB-53	Leñero, Vicente 1933- DLB-305	
Lee, Don L. (see Madhubuti, Haki R.)	L'Engle, Madeleine 1918- DLB-52	Levi, Peter 1931-2000 . . . . .DLB-40
Lee, George W. 1894-1976 . . . . .DLB-51	Lennart, Isobel 1915-1971 . . . . .DLB-44	Levi, Primo 1919-1987. . . . . DLB-177, 299
Lee, Harper 1926- DLB-6; CDALB-1	Lennox, Charlotte 1729 or 1730-1804 . . . . .DLB-39	Levien, Sonya 1888-1960 . . . . .DLB-44
Lee, Harriet 1757-1851 and Lee, Sophia 1750-1824. . . . . .DLB-39	Lenox, James 1800-1880 . . . . .DLB-140	Levin, Meyer 1905-1981 . . . . DLB-9, 28; Y-81
	Lenski, Lois 1893-1974 . . . . .DLB-22	Levin, Phillis 1954- DLB-282
Lee, Laurie 1914-1997 . . . . .DLB-27	Lentricchia, Frank 1940- DLB-246	Lévinas, Emmanuel 1906-1995 . . . . .DLB-296
Lee, Leslie 1935- DLB-266	Lenz, Hermann 1913-1998 . . . . .DLB-69	Levine, Norman 1923- DLB-88
Lee, Li-Young 1957- DLB-165	Lenz, J. M. R. 1751-1792 . . . . .DLB-94	Levine, Philip 1928- DLB-5
Lee, Manfred B. 1905-1971 . . . . .DLB-137	Lenz, Siegfried 1926- DLB-75	Levis, Larry 1946- DLB-120
Lee, Nathaniel circa 1645-1692 . . . . .DLB-80	Leonard, Elmore 1925- DLB-173, 226	Lévi-Strauss, Claude 1908- DLB-242
Lee, Robert E. 1918-1994 . . . . .DLB-228	Leonard, Hugh 1926- DLB-13	Levitov, Aleksandr Ivanovich 1835?-1877 . . . . .DLB-277
Lee, Sir Sidney 1859-1926 . . . . .DLB-149, 184	Leonard, William Ellery 1876-1944 . . . . . .DLB-54	
"Principles of Biography," in Elizabethan and Other Essays DLB-149	Leonov, Leonid Maksimovich 1899-1994 . . . . .DLB-272	Levy, Amy 1861-1889. . . . . .DLB-156, 240
		Levy, Benn Wolfe 1900-1973 . . . . . .DLB-13; Y-81
Lee, Tanith 1947- DLB-261	Leonowens, Anna 1834-1914 . . . . . . .DLB-99, 166	Levy, Deborah 1959- DLB-310
Lee, Vernon 1856-1935 . . . . .DLB-57, 153, 156, 174, 178	Leont'ev, Konstantin Nikolaevich 1831-1891 . . . . .DLB-277	Lewald, Fanny 1811-1889 . . . . .DLB-129
		Lewes, George Henry 1817-1878 . . . . .DLB-55, 144
Lee and Shepard DLB-49	Leopold, Aldo 1887-1948. . . . . .DLB-275	"Criticism in Relation to Novels" (1863) DLB-21
Le Fanu, Joseph Sheridan 1814-1873 . . . . DLB-21, 70, 159, 178	LePan, Douglas 1914-1998 . . . . .DLB-88	
	Lepik, Kalju 1920-1999 . . . . .DLB-232	The Principles of Success in Literature (1865) [excerpt]. DLB-57
Leffland, Ella 1931- Y-84	Leprohon, Rosanna Eleanor 1829-1879. . . .DLB-99	
le Fort, Gertrud von 1876-1971 . . . . .DLB-66	Le Queux, William 1864-1927 . . . . .DLB-70	Lewis, Agnes Smith 1843-1926 . . . . .DLB-174
Le Gallienne, Richard 1866-1947. . . . . .DLB-4		Lewis, Alfred H. 1857-1914 . . . . .DLB-25, 186
		Lewis, Alun 1915-1944 . . . . .DLB-20, 162

Lewis, C. Day (see Day Lewis, C.)	Lima, Jorge de 1893-1953............DLB-307	National Book Critics Circle Awards Y-00–01
Lewis, C. I. 1883-1964 ....DLB-270	Lima Barreto, Afonso Henriques de 1881-1922 .... DLB-307	The National Jewish Book Awards Y-85
Lewis, C. S. 1898-1963 .... DLB-15, 100, 160, 255; CDBLB-7	Limited Editions Club DLB-46	Nobel Prize Y-80–02
The New York C. S. Lewis Society Y-99	Limón, Graciela 1938- DLB-209	Winning an Edgar.................. Y-98
Lewis, Charles B. 1842-1924 .... DLB-11	Lincoln and Edmands................ DLB-49	*The Literary Chronicle and Weekly Review 1819-1828* DLB-110
Lewis, David 1941-2001................DLB-279	Lind, Jakov 1927- DLB-299	Literary Periodicals:
Lewis, Henry Clay 1825-1850 .... DLB-3, 248	Linda Vilhjálmsdóttir 1958- DLB-293	*Callaloo* Y-87
Lewis, Janet 1899-1999.................. Y-87	Lindesay, Ethel Forence (see Richardson, Henry Handel)	Expatriates in Paris DS-15
Tribute to Katherine Anne Porter Y-80	Lindgren, Astrid 1907-2002 .... DLB-257	New Literary Periodicals: A Report for 1987 .... Y-87
Lewis, Matthew Gregory 1775-1818................DLB-39, 158, 178	Lindgren, Torgny 1938- DLB-257	A Report for 1988 .... Y-88
Lewis, Meriwether 1774-1809...... DLB-183, 186	Lindsay, Alexander William, Twenty-fifth Earl of Crawford 1812-1880 ... DLB-184	A Report for 1989 .... Y-89
Lewis, Norman 1908- DLB-204	Lindsay, Sir David circa 1485-1555 ..... DLB-132	A Report for 1990 .... Y-90
Lewis, R. W. B. 1917- DLB-111	Lindsay, David 1878-1945 .... DLB-255	A Report for 1991 .... Y-91
Lewis, Richard circa 1700-1734......... DLB-24	Lindsay, Jack 1900-1990................ Y-84	A Report for 1992 .... Y-92
Lewis, Saunders 1893-1985 .... DLB-310	Lindsay, Lady (Caroline Blanche Elizabeth Fitzroy Lindsay) 1844-1912 .... DLB-199	A Report for 1993 .... Y-93
Lewis, Sinclair 1885-1951 ..... DLB-9, 102; DS-1; CDALB-4	Lindsay, Norman 1879-1969 .... DLB-260	Literary Research Archives
Sinclair Lewis Centennial Conference Y-85	Lindsay, Vachel 1879-1931............. DLB-54; CDALB-3	The Anthony Burgess Archive at the Harry Ransom Humanities Research Center Y-98
The Sinclair Lewis Society............. Y-99	Linebarger, Paul Myron Anthony (see Smith, Cordwainer)	Archives of Charles Scribner's Sons..... DS-17
Lewis, Wilmarth Sheldon 1895-1979 .... DLB-140	Link, Arthur S. 1920-1998 .... DLB-17	Berg Collection of English and American Literature of the New York Public Library Y-83
Lewis, Wyndham 1882-1957 .... DLB-15	Linn, Ed 1922-2000 .... DLB-241	The Bobbs-Merrill Archive at the Lilly Library, Indiana University Y-90
Time and Western Man [excerpt] (1927) DLB-36	Linn, John Blair 1777-1804 .... DLB-37	Die Fürstliche Bibliothek Corvey........ Y-96
Lewisohn, Ludwig 1882-1955 .. DLB-4, 9, 28, 102	Lins, Osman 1924-1978 ....DLB-145, 307	Guide to the Archives of Publishers, Journals, and Literary Agents in North American Libraries........... Y-93
Leyendecker, J. C. 1874-1951........... DLB-188	Linton, Eliza Lynn 1822-1898 .... DLB-18	The Henry E. Huntington Library Y-92
Leyner, Mark 1956- DLB-292	Linton, William James 1812-1897....... DLB-32	The Humanities Research Center, University of Texas............... Y-82
Lezama Lima, José 1910-1976...... DLB-113, 283	Barnaby Bernard Lintot [publishing house] DLB-170	The John Carter Brown Library Y-85
L'Heureux, John 1934- DLB-244	Lion Books....................... DLB-46	Kent State Special Collections Y-86
Libbey, Laura Jean 1862-1924 .... DLB-221	Lionni, Leo 1910-1999 .... DLB-61	The Lilly Library Y-84
Libedinsky, Iurii Nikolaevich 1898-1959 .... DLB-272	Lippard, George 1822-1854 .... DLB-202	The Modern Literary Manuscripts Collection in the Special Collections of the Washington University Libraries Y-87
The Liberator DLB-303	Lippincott, Sara Jane Clarke 1823-1904 .... DLB-43	
Library History Group................ Y-01	J. B. Lippincott Company............. DLB-49	A Publisher's Archives: G. P. Putnam Y-92
E-Books' Second Act in Libraries Y-02	Lippmann, Walter 1889-1974........ DLB-29	Special Collections at Boston University Y-99
The Library of America DLB-46	Lipton, Lawrence 1898-1975 .... DLB-16	The University of Virginia Libraries Y-91
The Library of America: An Assessment After Two Decades Y-02	Lisboa, Irene 1892-1958.............. DLB-287	The William Charvat American Fiction Collection at the Ohio State University Libraries Y-92
Licensing Act of 1737 .... DLB-84	Liscow, Christian Ludwig 1701-1760 ..... DLB-97	
Leonard Lichfield I [publishing house] DLB-170	Lish, Gordon 1934- DLB-130	Literary Societies Y-98–02
Lichtenberg, Georg Christoph 1742-1799 .... DLB-94	Tribute to Donald Barthelme.......... Y-89	The Margery Allingham Society Y-98
The Liddle Collection................. Y-97	Tribute to James Dickey Y-97	The American Studies Association of Norway..................... Y-00
Lidman, Sara 1923- DLB-257	Lisle, Charles-Marie-René Leconte de 1818-1894 .... DLB-217	The Arnold Bennett Society.......... Y-98
Lieb, Fred 1888-1980 ....DLB-171	Lispector, Clarice 1925?-1977 ....DLB-113, 307; CDWLB-3	The Association for the Study of Literature and Environment (ASLE) Y-99
Liebling, A. J. 1904-1963 ....DLB-4, 171	LitCheck Website...................... Y-01	
Lieutenant Murray (see Ballou, Maturin Murray)	Literary Awards and Honors Y-81–02	Belgian Luxembourg American Studies Association Y-01
Lighthall, William Douw 1857-1954...... DLB-92	Booker Prize.............. Y-86, 96–98	
Lihn, Enrique 1929-1988 .... DLB-283	The Drue Heinz Literature Prize Y-82	The E. F. Benson Society............. Y-98
Lilar, Françoise (see Mallet-Joris, Françoise)	The Elmer Holmes Bobst Awards in Arts and Letters................. Y-87	The Elizabeth Bishop Society........... Y-01
Lili'uokalani, Queen 1838-1917 .... DLB-221		
Lillo, George 1691-1739 .... DLB-84	The Griffin Poetry Prize Y-00	
Lilly, J. K., Jr. 1893-1966 .... DLB-140	Literary Prizes [British] DLB-15, 207	
Lilly, Wait and Company............. DLB-49		
Lily, William circa 1468-1522 .... DLB-132		

The [Edgar Rice] Burroughs Bibliophiles	Y-98	
The Byron Society of America	Y-00	
The Lewis Carroll Society of North America	Y-00	
The Willa Cather Pioneer Memorial and Education Foundation	Y-00	
New Chaucer Society	Y-00	
The Wilkie Collins Society	Y-98	
The James Fenimore Cooper Society	Y-01	
The Stephen Crane Society	Y-98, 01	
The E. E. Cummings Society	Y-01	
The James Dickey Society	Y-99	
John Dos Passos Newsletter	Y-00	
The Priory Scholars [Sir Arthur Conan Doyle] of New York	Y-99	
The International Theodore Dreiser Society	Y-01	
The Friends of the Dymock Poets	Y-00	
The George Eliot Fellowship	Y-99	
The T. S. Eliot Society: Celebration and Scholarship, 1980-1999	Y-99	
The Ralph Waldo Emerson Society	Y-99	
The William Faulkner Society	Y-99	
The C. S. Forester Society	Y-00	
The Hamlin Garland Society	Y-01	
The [Elizabeth] Gaskell Society	Y-98	
The Charlotte Perkins Gilman Society	Y-99	
The Ellen Glasgow Society	Y-01	
Zane Grey's West Society	Y-00	
The Ivor Gurney Society	Y-98	
The Joel Chandler Harris Association	Y-99	
The Nathaniel Hawthorne Society	Y-00	
The [George Alfred] Henty Society	Y-98	
George Moses Horton Society	Y-99	
The William Dean Howells Society	Y-01	
WW2 HMSO Paperbacks Society	Y-98	
American Humor Studies Association	Y-99	
International Society for Humor Studies	Y-99	
The W. W. Jacobs Appreciation Society	Y-98	
The Richard Jefferies Society	Y-98	
The Jerome K. Jerome Society	Y-98	
The D. H. Lawrence Society of North America	Y-00	
The T. E. Lawrence Society	Y-98	
The [Gotthold] Lessing Society	Y-00	
The New York C. S. Lewis Society	Y-99	
The Sinclair Lewis Society	Y-99	
The Jack London Research Center	Y-00	
The Jack London Society	Y-99	
The Cormac McCarthy Society	Y-99	
The Melville Society	Y-01	
The Arthur Miller Society	Y-01	
The Milton Society of America	Y-00	
International Marianne Moore Society	Y-98	
International Nabokov Society	Y-99	

The Vladimir Nabokov Society	Y-01	
The Flannery O'Connor Society	Y-99	
The Wilfred Owen Association	Y-98	
Penguin Collectors' Society	Y-98	
The [E. A.] Poe Studies Association	Y-99	
The Katherine Anne Porter Society	Y-01	
The Beatrix Potter Society	Y-98	
The Ezra Pound Society	Y-01	
The Powys Society	Y-98	
Proust Society of America	Y-00	
The Dorothy L. Sayers Society	Y-98	
The Bernard Shaw Society	Y-99	
The Society for the Study of Southern Literature	Y-00	
The Wallace Stevens Society	Y-99	
The Harriet Beecher Stowe Center	Y-00	
The R. S. Surtees Society	Y-98	
The Thoreau Society	Y-99	
The Tilling [E. F. Benson] Society	Y-98	
The Trollope Societies	Y-00	
H. G. Wells Society	Y-98	
The Western Literature Association	Y-99	
The William Carlos Williams Society	Y-99	
The Henry Williamson Society	Y-98	
The [Nero] Wolfe Pack	Y-99	
The Thomas Wolfe Society	Y-99	
Worldwide Wodehouse Societies	Y-98	
The W. B. Yeats Society of N.Y.	Y-99	
The Charlotte M. Yonge Fellowship	Y-98	
Literary Theory The Year in Literary Theory	Y-92–Y-93	
Literature at Nurse, or Circulating Morals (1885), by George Moore	DLB-18	
Litt, Toby 1968-	DLB-267	
Littell, Eliakim 1797-1870	DLB-79	
Littell, Robert S. 1831-1896	DLB-79	
Little, Brown and Company	DLB-49	
Little Magazines and Newspapers	DS-15	
Selected English-Language Little Magazines and Newspapers [France, 1920-1939]	DLB-4	
The Little Magazines of the New Formalism	DLB-282	
The Little Review 1914-1929	DS-15	
Littlewood, Joan 1914-2002	DLB-13	
Lively, Penelope 1933-	DLB-14, 161, 207	
Liverpool University Press	DLB-112	
The Lives of the Poets (1753)	DLB-142	
Livesay, Dorothy 1909-1996	DLB-68	
Livesay, Florence Randal 1874-1953	DLB-92	
Livings, Henry 1929-1998	DLB-13	
Livingston, Anne Howe 1763-1841	DLB-37, 200	
Livingston, Jay 1915-2001	DLB-265	
Livingston, Myra Cohn 1926-1996	DLB-61	
Livingston, William 1723-1790	DLB-31	
Livingstone, David 1813-1873	DLB-166	

Livingstone, Douglas 1932-1996	DLB-225	
Livshits, Benedikt Konstantinovich 1886-1938 or 1939	DLB-295	
Livy 59 B.C.-A.D. 17	DLB-211; CDWLB-1	
Liyong, Taban lo (see Taban lo Liyong)		
Lizárraga, Sylvia S. 1925-	DLB-82	
Llewellyn, Richard 1906-1983	DLB-15	
Lloréns Torres, Luis 1876-1944	DLB-290	
Edward Lloyd [publishing house]	DLB-106	
Lobato, José Bento Monteiro 1882-1948	DLB-307	
Lobel, Arnold 1933-	DLB-61	
Lochhead, Liz 1947-	DLB-310	
Lochridge, Betsy Hopkins (see Fancher, Betsy)		
Locke, Alain 1886-1954	DLB-51	
Locke, David Ross 1833-1888	DLB-11, 23	
Locke, John 1632-1704	DLB-31, 101, 213, 252	
Locke, Richard Adams 1800-1871	DLB-43	
Locker-Lampson, Frederick 1821-1895	DLB-35, 184	
Lockhart, John Gibson 1794-1854	DLB-110, 116, 144	
Lockridge, Francis 1896-1963	DLB-306	
Lockridge, Richard 1898-1982	DLB-306	
Lockridge, Ross, Jr. 1914-1948	DLB-143; Y-80	
Locrine and Selimus	DLB-62	
Lodge, David 1935-	DLB-14, 194	
Lodge, George Cabot 1873-1909	DLB-54	
Lodge, Henry Cabot 1850-1924	DLB-47	
Lodge, Thomas 1558-1625	DLB-172	
Defence of Poetry (1579) [excerpt]	DLB-172	
Loeb, Harold 1891-1974	DLB-4; DS-15	
Loeb, William 1905-1981	DLB-127	
Loesser, Frank 1910-1969	DLB-265	
Lofting, Hugh 1886-1947	DLB-160	
Logan, Deborah Norris 1761-1839	DLB-200	
Logan, James 1674-1751	DLB-24, 140	
Logan, John 1923-1987	DLB-5	
Logan, Martha Daniell 1704?-1779	DLB-200	
Logan, William 1950-	DLB-120	
Logau, Friedrich von 1605-1655	DLB-164	
Logue, Christopher 1926-	DLB-27	
Lohenstein, Daniel Casper von 1635-1683	DLB-168	
Lo-Johansson, Ivar 1901-1990	DLB-259	
Lokert, George (or Lockhart) circa 1485-1547	DLB-281	
Lomonosov, Mikhail Vasil'evich 1711-1765	DLB-150	
London, Jack 1876-1916	DLB-8, 12, 78, 212; CDALB-3	
The Jack London Research Center	Y-00	
The Jack London Society	Y-99	
The London Magazine 1820-1829	DLB-110	
Long, David 1948-	DLB-244	
Long, H., and Brother	DLB-49	
Long, Haniel 1888-1956	DLB-45	

Cumulative Index

Long, Ray 1878-1935 .... DLB-137
Longfellow, Henry Wadsworth
    1807-1882 .... DLB-1, 59, 235; CDALB-2
Longfellow, Samuel 1819-1892 .... DLB-1
Longford, Elizabeth 1906-2002 .... DLB-155
    Tribute to Alfred A. Knopf Y-84
Longinus circa first century DLB-176
Longley, Michael 1939- DLB-40
T. Longman [publishing house] DLB-154
Longmans, Green and Company DLB-49
Longmore, George 1793?-1867 .... DLB-99
Longstreet, Augustus Baldwin
    1790-1870 .... DLB-3, 11, 74, 248
D. Longworth [publishing house] DLB-49
Lønn, Øystein 1936- DLB-297
Lonsdale, Frederick 1881-1954 .... DLB-10
Loos, Anita 1893-1981 .... DLB-11, 26, 228; Y-81
Lopate, Phillip 1943- Y-80
Lopes, Fernão 1380/1390?-1460? DLB-287
Lopez, Barry 1945- DLB-256, 275
López, Diana (see Isabella, Ríos)
López, Josefina 1969- DLB-209
López de Mendoza, Íñigo
    (see Santillana, Marqués de)
López Velarde, Ramón 1888-1921 ...... DLB-290
Loranger, Jean-Aubert 1896-1942 .... DLB-92
Lorca, Federico García 1898-1936 ..... DLB-108
Lord, John Keast 1818-1872 .... DLB-99
Lorde, Audre 1934-1992 .... DLB-41
Lorimer, George Horace 1867-1937 ..... DLB-91
A. K. Loring [publishing house] DLB-49
Loring and Mussey DLB-46
Lorris, Guillaume de (see Roman de la Rose)
Lossing, Benson J. 1813-1891 .... DLB-30
Lothar, Ernst 1890-1974 .... DLB-81
D. Lothrop and Company DLB-49
Lothrop, Harriet M. 1844-1924 .... DLB-42
Loti, Pierre 1850-1923 .... DLB-123
Lotichius Secundus, Petrus 1528-1560 .... DLB-179
Lott, Emmeline ?-? DLB-166
Louisiana State University Press Y-97
Lounsbury, Thomas R. 1838-1915 .... DLB-71
Louÿs, Pierre 1870-1925 .... DLB-123
Løveid, Cecile 1951- DLB-297
Lovejoy, Arthur O. 1873-1962 .... DLB-270
Lovelace, Earl 1935- DLB-125; CDWLB-3
Lovelace, Richard 1618-1657 .... DLB-131
John W. Lovell Company DLB-49
Lovell, Coryell and Company DLB-49
Lover, Samuel 1797-1868 .... DLB-159, 190
Lovesey, Peter 1936- DLB-87
    Tribute to Georges Simenon Y-89
Lovinescu, Eugen
    1881-1943 .... DLB-220; CDWLB-4
Lovingood, Sut
    (see Harris, George Washington)

Low, Samuel 1765-? DLB-37
Lowell, Amy 1874-1925 .... DLB-54, 140
Lowell, James Russell 1819-1891
    ...... DLB-1, 11, 64, 79, 189, 235; CDALB-2
Lowell, Robert
    1917-1977 .... DLB-5, 169; CDALB-7
Lowenfels, Walter 1897-1976 .... DLB-4
Lowndes, Marie Belloc 1868-1947 ...... DLB-70
Lowndes, William Thomas 1798-1843 ... DLB-184
Humphrey Lownes [publishing house] ... DLB-170
Lowry, Lois 1937- DLB-52
Lowry, Malcolm 1909-1957 ... DLB-15; CDBLB-7
Lowther, Pat 1935-1975 .... DLB-53
Loy, Mina 1882-1966 .... DLB-4, 54
Loynaz, Dulce María 1902-1997 .... DLB-283
Lozeau, Albert 1878-1924 .... DLB-92
Lubbock, Percy 1879-1965 .... DLB-149
Lucan A.D. 39-A.D. 65 .... DLB-211
Lucas, E. V. 1868-1938 .... DLB-98, 149, 153
Fielding Lucas Jr. [publishing house] DLB-49
Luce, Clare Booth 1903-1987 .... DLB-228
Luce, Henry R. 1898-1967 .... DLB-91
John W. Luce and Company DLB-46
Lucena, Juan de ca. 1430-1501 .... DLB-286
Lucian circa 120-180 .... DLB-176
Lucie-Smith, Edward 1933- DLB-40
Lucilius circa 180 B.C.-102/101 B.C. DLB-211
Lucini, Gian Pietro 1867-1914 .... DLB-114
Luco Cruchaga, Germán 1894-1936 .... DLB-305
Lucretius circa 94 B.C.-circa 49 B.C.
    .... DLB-211; CDWLB-1
Luder, Peter circa 1415-1472 .... DLB-179
Ludlam, Charles 1943-1987 .... DLB-266
Ludlum, Robert 1927-2001 .... Y-82
Ludus de Antichristo circa 1160 .... DLB-148
Ludvigson, Susan 1942- DLB-120
Ludwig, Jack 1922- DLB-60
Ludwig, Otto 1813-1865 .... DLB-129
Ludwigslied 881 or 882 .... DLB-148
Luera, Yolanda 1953- DLB-122
Luft, Lya 1938- DLB-145
Lugansky, Kazak Vladimir
    (see Dal', Vladimir Ivanovich)
Lugn, Kristina 1948- DLB-257
Lugones, Leopoldo 1874-1938 .... DLB-283
Luhan, Mabel Dodge 1879-1962 .... DLB-303
Lukács, Georg (see Lukács, György)
Lukács, György
    1885-1971 .... DLB-215, 242; CDWLB-4
Luke, Peter 1919- DLB-13
Lummis, Charles F. 1859-1928 .... DLB-186
Lundkvist, Artur 1906-1991 .... DLB-259
Lunts, Lev Natanovich 1901-1924 ...... DLB-272
F. M. Lupton Company DLB-49
Lupus of Ferrières circa 805-circa 862 ... DLB-148
Lurie, Alison 1926- DLB-2

Lussu, Emilio 1890-1975 .... DLB-264
Lustig, Arnošt 1926- DLB-232, 299
Luther, Martin
    1483-1546 .... DLB-179; CDWLB-2
Luzi, Mario 1914- DLB-128
L'vov, Nikolai Aleksandrovich
    1751-1803 .... DLB-150
Lyall, Gavin 1932- DLB-87
Lydgate, John circa 1370-1450 .... DLB-146
Lyly, John circa 1554-1606 .... DLB-62, 167
Lynch, Martin 1950- DLB-310
Lynch, Patricia 1898-1972 .... DLB-160
Lynch, Richard flourished 1596-1601 ... DLB-172
Lynd, Robert 1879-1949 .... DLB-98
Lynds, Dennis (Michael Collins)
    1924- DLB-306
    Tribute to John D. MacDonald Y-86
    Tribute to Kenneth Millar Y-83
    Why I Write Mysteries: Night and Day .. Y-85
Lyon, Matthew 1749-1822 .... DLB-43
Lyotard, Jean-François 1924-1998 ..... DLB-242
Lyricists
    Additional Lyricists: 1920-1960 ..... DLB-265
Lysias circa 459 B.C.-circa 380 B.C. DLB-176
Lytle, Andrew 1902-1995 .... DLB-6; Y-95
    Tribute to Caroline Gordon Y-81
    Tribute to Katherine Anne Porter Y-80
Lytton, Edward
    (see Bulwer-Lytton, Edward)
Lytton, Edward Robert Bulwer
    1831-1891 .... DLB-32

M

Maass, Joachim 1901-1972 .... DLB-69
Mabie, Hamilton Wright 1845-1916 ..... DLB-71
Mac A'Ghobhainn, Iain (see Smith, Iain Crichton)
MacArthur, Charles 1895-1956 ..... DLB-7, 25, 44
Macaulay, Catherine 1731-1791 .... DLB-104
Macaulay, David 1945- DLB-61
Macaulay, Rose 1881-1958 .... DLB-36
Macaulay, Thomas Babington
    1800-1859 .... DLB-32, 55; CDBLB-4
Macaulay Company DLB-46
MacBeth, George 1932-1992 .... DLB-40
Macbeth, Madge 1880-1965 .... DLB-92
MacCaig, Norman 1910-1996 .... DLB-27
MacDiarmid, Hugh
    1892-1978 .... DLB-20; CDBLB-7
MacDonald, Cynthia 1928- DLB-105
MacDonald, George 1824-1905 .... DLB-18, 163, 178
MacDonald, John D.
    1916-1986 .... DLB-8, 306; Y-86
MacDonald, Philip 1899?-1980 .... DLB-77
Macdonald, Ross (see Millar, Kenneth)
Macdonald, Sharman 1951- DLB-245
MacDonald, Wilson 1880-1967 .... DLB-92
Macdonald and Company (Publishers) .. DLB-112

MacEwen, Gwendolyn 1941-1987....DLB-53, 251

Macfadden, Bernarr 1868-1955.......DLB-25, 91

MacGregor, John 1825-1892............DLB-166

MacGregor, Mary Esther (see Keith, Marian)

Macherey, Pierre 1938- DLB-296

Machado, Antonio 1875-1939............DLB-108

Machado, Manuel 1874-1947............DLB-108

Machado de Assis, Joaquim Maria
    1839-1908..................DLB-307

Machar, Agnes Maule 1837-1927.........DLB-92

Machaut, Guillaume de
    circa 1300-1377..................DLB-208

Machen, Arthur Llewelyn Jones
    1863-1947..............DLB-36, 156, 178

MacIlmaine, Roland fl. 1574............DLB-281

MacInnes, Colin 1914-1976.............DLB-14

MacInnes, Helen 1907-1985.............DLB-87

Mac Intyre, Tom 1931-...............DLB-245

Mačiulis, Jonas (see Maironis, Jonas)

Mack, Maynard 1909- DLB-111

Mackall, Leonard L. 1879-1937.........DLB-140

MacKay, Isabel Ecclestone 1875-1928.....DLB-92

MacKaye, Percy 1875-1956..............DLB-54

Macken, Walter 1915-1967..............DLB-13

Mackenzie, Alexander 1763-1820........DLB-99

Mackenzie, Alexander Slidell
    1803-1848.....................DLB-183

Mackenzie, Compton 1883-1972.....DLB-34, 100

Mackenzie, Henry 1745-1831............DLB-39

    The Lounger, no. 20 (1785)............DLB-39

Mackenzie, Kenneth (Seaforth Mackenzie)
    1913-1955.....................DLB-260

Mackenzie, William 1758-1828..........DLB-187

Mackey, Nathaniel 1947- DLB-169

Mackey, Shena 1944- DLB-231

Mackey, William Wellington 1937- DLB-38

Mackintosh, Elizabeth (see Tey, Josephine)

Mackintosh, Sir James 1765-1832.......DLB-158

Macklin, Charles 1699-1797............DLB-89

Maclaren, Ian (see Watson, John)

MacLaverty, Bernard 1942- DLB-267

MacLean, Alistair 1922-1987...........DLB-276

MacLean, Katherine Anne 1925- DLB-8

Maclean, Norman 1902-1990...........DLB-206

MacLeish, Archibald 1892-1982
    ......DLB-4, 7, 45; Y-82; DS-15; CDALB-7

MacLennan, Hugh 1907-1990............DLB-68

MacLeod, Alistair 1936- DLB-60

Macleod, Fiona (see Sharp, William)

Macleod, Norman 1906-1985............DLB-4

Mac Low, Jackson 1922- DLB-193

Macmillan and Company..............DLB-106

The Macmillan Company..............DLB-49

Macmillan's English Men of Letters,
    First Series (1878-1892)............DLB-144

MacNamara, Brinsley 1890-1963........DLB-10

MacNeice, Louis 1907-1963..........DLB-10, 20

Macphail, Andrew 1864-1938............DLB-92

Macpherson, James 1736-1796..........DLB-109

Macpherson, Jay 1931- DLB-53

Macpherson, Jeanie 1884-1946..........DLB-44

Macrae Smith Company................DLB-46

MacRaye, Lucy Betty (see Webling, Lucy)

John Macrone [publishing house]........DLB-106

MacShane, Frank 1927-1999............DLB-111

Macy-Masius..........................DLB-46

Madden, David 1933- DLB-6

Madden, Sir Frederic 1801-1873........DLB-184

Maddow, Ben 1909-1992...............DLB-44

Maddux, Rachel 1912-1983.......DLB-234; Y-93

Madgett, Naomi Long 1923- DLB-76

Madhubuti, Haki R. 1942- DLB-5, 41; DS-8

Madison, James 1751-1836............DLB-37

Madsen, Svend Åge 1939- DLB-214

Madrigal, Alfonso Fernández de (El Tostado)
    ca. 1405-1455.................DLB-286

Maeterlinck, Maurice 1862-1949........DLB-192

Mafūz, Najīb 1911- Y-88

    Nobel Lecture 1988..................Y-88

The Little Magazines of the
    New Formalism................DLB-282

Magee, David 1905-1977..............DLB-187

Maginn, William 1794-1842.......DLB-110, 159

Magoffin, Susan Shelby 1827-1855......DLB-239

Mahan, Alfred Thayer 1840-1914........DLB-47

Maheux-Forcier, Louise 1929- DLB-60

Mahin, John Lee 1902-1984............DLB-44

Mahon, Derek 1941- DLB-40

Maiakovsky, Vladimir Vladimirovich
    1893-1930....................DLB-295

Maikov, Apollon Nikolaevich
    1821-1897....................DLB-277

Maikov, Vasilii Ivanovich 1728-1778.....DLB-150

Mailer, Norman 1923-
    ......DLB-2, 16, 28, 185, 278; Y-80, 83, 97;
    DS-3; CDALB-6

    Tribute to Isaac Bashevis Singer........Y-91

    Tribute to Meyer Levin..............Y-81

Maillart, Ella 1903-1997...............DLB-195

Maillet, Adrienne 1885-1963............DLB-68

Maillet, Antonine 1929- DLB-60

Maillu, David G. 1939- DLB-157

Maimonides, Moses 1138-1204.........DLB-115

Main Selections of the Book-of-the-Month
    Club, 1926-1945..................DLB-9

Mainwaring, Daniel 1902-1977.........DLB-44

Mair, Charles 1838-1927..............DLB-99

Mair, John circa 1467-1550............DLB-281

Maironis, Jonas 1862-1932..DLB-220; CDWLB-4

Mais, Roger 1905-1955.......DLB-125; CDWLB-3

Maitland, Sara 1950- DLB-271

Major, Andre 1942- DLB-60

Major, Charles 1856-1913.............DLB-202

Major, Clarence 1936- DLB-33

Major, Kevin 1949-...................DLB-60

Major Books........................DLB-46

Makanin, Vladimir Semenovich
    1937- DLB-285

Makarenko, Anton Semenovich
    1888-1939....................DLB-272

Makemie, Francis circa 1658-1708.......DLB-24

The Making of Americans Contract..........Y-98

Maksimov, Vladimir Emel'ianovich
    1930-1995....................DLB-302

Maksimović, Desanka
    1898-1993............DLB-147; CDWLB-4

Malamud, Bernard 1914-1986
    ......DLB-2, 28, 152; Y-80, 86; CDALB-1

    Bernard Malamud Archive at the
    Harry Ransom Humanities
    Research Center..................Y-00

Mălăncioiu, Ileana 1940- DLB-232

Malaparte, Curzio
    (Kurt Erich Suckert) 1898-1957....DLB-264

Malerba, Luigi 1927- DLB-196

Malet, Lucas 1852-1931...............DLB-153

Mallarmé, Stéphane 1842-1898........DLB-217

Malleson, Lucy Beatrice (see Gilbert, Anthony)

Mallet-Joris, Françoise (Françoise Lilar)
    1930- DLB-83

Mallock, W. H. 1849-1923.........DLB-18, 57

    "Every Man His Own Poet; or,
    The Inspired Singer's Recipe
    Book" (1877).................DLB-35

    "Le Style c'est l'homme" (1892)......DLB-57

    Memoirs of Life and Literature (1920),
    [excerpt]...................DLB-57

Malone, Dumas 1892-1986.............DLB-17

Malone, Edmond 1741-1812............DLB-142

Malory, Sir Thomas
    circa 1400-1410 - 1471....DLB-146; CDBLB-1

Malouf, David 1934- DLB-289

Malpede, Karen 1945- DLB-249

Malraux, André 1901-1976.............DLB-72

Malthus, Thomas Robert
    1766-1834................DLB-107, 158

Maltz, Albert 1908-1985..............DLB-102

Malzberg, Barry N. 1939- DLB-8

Mamet, David 1947- DLB-7

Mamin, Dmitrii Narkisovich
    1852-1912....................DLB-238

Manaka, Matsemela 1956- DLB-157

Manchester University Press...........DLB-112

Mandel, Eli 1922-1992................DLB-53

Mandel'shtam, Nadezhda Iakovlevna
    1899-1980....................DLB-302

Mandel'shtam, Osip Emil'evich
    1891-1938....................DLB-295

Mandeville, Bernard 1670-1733........DLB-101

Mandeville, Sir John
    mid fourteenth century...........DLB-146

Cumulative Index

Mandiargues, André Pieyre de
1909-1991 . . . . DLB-83

Manea, Norman 1936- DLB-232

Manfred, Frederick 1912-1994 . . . . DLB-6, 212, 227

Manfredi, Gianfranco 1948- DLB-196

Mangan, Sherry 1904-1961 . . . . DLB-4

Manganelli, Giorgio 1922-1990 . . . . DLB-196

Manilius fl. first century A.D. DLB-211

Mankiewicz, Herman 1897-1953 . . . . DLB-26

Mankiewicz, Joseph L. 1909-1993 . . . . DLB-44

Mankowitz, Wolf 1924-1998 . . . . DLB-15

Manley, Delarivière 1672?-1724 . . . . . DLB-39, 80

Preface to *The Secret History, of Queen
Zarah, and the Zarazians* (1705) DLB-39

Mann, Abby 1927- DLB-44

Mann, Charles 1929-1998 . . . . Y-98

Mann, Emily 1952- DLB-266

Mann, Heinrich 1871-1950 . . . . DLB-66, 118

Mann, Horace 1796-1859 . . . . DLB-1, 235

Mann, Klaus 1906-1949 . . . . DLB-56

Mann, Mary Peabody 1806-1887 . . . . DLB-239

Mann, Thomas 1875-1955 . . . DLB-66; CDWLB-2

Mann, William D'Alton 1839-1920 . . . . . DLB-137

Mannin, Ethel 1900-1984 . . . . DLB-191, 195

Manning, Emily (see Australie)

Manning, Frederic 1882-1935 . . . . DLB-260

Manning, Laurence 1899-1972 . . . . DLB-251

Manning, Marie 1873?-1945 . . . . DLB-29

Manning and Loring DLB-49

Mannyng, Robert flourished
1303-1338 . . . . DLB-146

Mano, D. Keith 1942- DLB-6

Manor Books DLB-46

Manrique, Gómez 1412?-1490 . . . . DLB-286

Manrique, Jorge ca. 1440-1479 . . . . DLB-286

Mansfield, Katherine 1888-1923 . . . . DLB-162

Mantel, Hilary 1952- DLB-271

Manuel, Niklaus circa 1484-1530 . . . . DLB-179

Manzini, Gianna 1896-1974 . . . . DLB-177

Mapanje, Jack 1944- DLB-157

Maraini, Dacia 1936- DLB-196

Maramzin, Vladimir Rafailovich
1934- DLB-302

March, William (William Edward Campbell)
1893-1954 . . . . DLB-9, 86

Marchand, Leslie A. 1900-1999 . . . . DLB-103

Marchant, Bessie 1862-1941 . . . . DLB-160

Marchant, Tony 1959- DLB-245

Marchenko, Anastasiia Iakovlevna
1830-1880 . . . . DLB-238

Marchessault, Jovette 1938- DLB-60

Marcinkevičius, Justinas 1930- DLB-232

Marcos, Plínio (Plínio Marcos de Barros)
1935-1999 . . . . DLB-307

Marcus, Frank 1928- DLB-13

Marcuse, Herbert 1898-1979 . . . . DLB-242

Marden, Orison Swett 1850-1924 . . . . DLB-137

Marechera, Dambudzo 1952-1987 . . . . . . DLB-157

Marek, Richard, Books DLB-46

Mares, E. A. 1938- DLB-122

Margulies, Donald 1954- DLB-228

Mariani, Paul 1940- DLB-111

Marie de France flourished 1160-1178 . . . DLB-208

Marie-Victorin, Frère (Conrad Kirouac)
1885-1944 . . . . DLB-92

Marin, Biagio 1891-1985 . . . . DLB-128

Marinetti, Filippo Tommaso
1876-1944 . . . . DLB-114, 264

Marinina, Aleksandra (Marina Anatol'evna
Alekseeva) 1957- DLB-285

Marinković, Ranko
1913- DLB-147; CDWLB-4

Marion, Frances 1886-1973 . . . . DLB-44

Marius, Richard C. 1933-1999 . . . . Y-85

Markevich, Boleslav Mikhailovich
1822-1884 . . . . DLB-238

Markfield, Wallace 1926-2002 . . . . DLB-2, 28

Markham, Edwin 1852-1940 . . . . DLB-54, 186

Markle, Fletcher 1921-1991 . . . . DLB-68; Y-91

Marlatt, Daphne 1942- DLB-60

Marlitt, E. 1825-1887 . . . . DLB-129

Marlowe, Christopher
1564-1593 . . . . DLB-62; CDBLB-1

Marlyn, John 1912- DLB-88

Marmion, Shakerley 1603-1639 . . . . DLB-58

Der Marner before 1230-circa 1287 . . . . . DLB-138

Marnham, Patrick 1943- DLB-204

The *Marprelate Tracts* 1588-1589 . . . . DLB-132

Marquand, John P. 1893-1960 . . . . DLB-9, 102

Marques, Helena 1935- DLB-287

Marqués, René 1919-1979 . . . . DLB-113, 305

Marquis, Don 1878-1937 . . . . DLB-11, 25

Marriott, Anne 1913-1997 . . . . DLB-68

Marryat, Frederick 1792-1848 . . . . . . DLB-21, 163

Marsh, Capen, Lyon and Webb DLB-49

Marsh, George Perkins
1801-1882 . . . . DLB-1, 64, 243

Marsh, James 1794-1842 . . . . DLB-1, 59

Marsh, Narcissus 1638-1713 . . . . DLB-213

Marsh, Ngaio 1899-1982 . . . . DLB-77

Marshall, Alan 1902-1984 . . . . DLB-260

Marshall, Edison 1894-1967 . . . . DLB-102

Marshall, Edward 1932- DLB-16

Marshall, Emma 1828-1899 . . . . DLB-163

Marshall, James 1942-1992 . . . . DLB-61

Marshall, Joyce 1913- DLB-88

Marshall, Paule 1929- DLB-33, 157, 227

Marshall, Tom 1938-1993 . . . . DLB-60

Marsilius of Padua
circa 1275-circa 1342 . . . . DLB-115

Mars-Jones, Adam 1954- DLB-207

Marson, Una 1905-1965 . . . . DLB-157

Marston, John 1576-1634 . . . . DLB-58, 172

Marston, Philip Bourke 1850-1887 . . . . . . DLB-35

Martens, Kurt 1870-1945 . . . . DLB-66

Martí, José 1853-1895 . . . . DLB-290

Martial circa A.D. 40-circa A.D. 103
. . . . DLB-211; CDWLB-1

William S. Martien [publishing house] DLB-49

Martin, Abe (see Hubbard, Kin)

Martin, Catherine ca. 1847-1937 . . . . DLB-230

Martin, Charles 1942- DLB-120, 282

Martin, Claire 1914- DLB-60

Martin, David 1915-1997 . . . . DLB-260

Martin, Jay 1935- DLB-111

Martin, Johann (see Laurentius von Schnüffis)

Martin, Thomas 1696-1771 . . . . DLB-213

Martin, Violet Florence (see Ross, Martin)

Martin du Gard, Roger 1881-1958 . . . . . . DLB-65

Martineau, Harriet
1802-1876 . . . . . DLB-21, 55, 159, 163, 166, 190

Martínez, Demetria 1960- DLB-209

Martínez de Toledo, Alfonso
1398?-1468 . . . . DLB-286

Martínez, Eliud 1935- DLB-122

Martínez, Max 1943- DLB-82

Martínez, Rubén 1962- DLB-209

Martinson, Harry 1904-1978 . . . . DLB-259

Martinson, Moa 1890-1964 . . . . DLB-259

Martone, Michael 1955- DLB-218

Martyn, Edward 1859-1923 . . . . DLB-10

Marvell, Andrew
1621-1678 . . . . DLB-131; CDBLB-2

Marvin X 1944- DLB-38

Marx, Karl 1818-1883 . . . . DLB-129

Marzials, Theo 1850-1920 . . . . DLB-35

Masefield, John 1878-1967
. . . . DLB-10, 19, 153, 160; CDBLB-5

Masham, Damaris Cudworth, Lady
1659-1708 . . . . DLB-252

Masino, Paola 1908-1989 . . . . DLB-264

Mason, A. E. W. 1865-1948 . . . . DLB-70

Mason, Bobbie Ann
1940- DLB-173; Y-87; CDALB-7

Mason, F. van Wyck (Geoffrey Coffin, Frank W.
Mason, Ward Weaver) 1901-1978 . . . DLB-306

Mason, William 1725-1797 . . . . DLB-142

Mason Brothers DLB-49

The Massachusetts Quarterly Review
1847-1850 . . . . DLB-1

The Masses DLB-303

Massey, Gerald 1828-1907 . . . . DLB-32

Massey, Linton R. 1900-1974 . . . . DLB-187

Massie, Allan 1938- DLB-271

Massinger, Philip 1583-1640 . . . . DLB-58

Masson, David 1822-1907 . . . . DLB-144

Masters, Edgar Lee
1868-1950 . . . . DLB-54; CDALB-3

Masters, Hilary 1928- DLB-244

Mastronardi, Lucio 1930-1979 . . . . DLB-177

Matevski, Mateja 1929- ...DLB-181; CDWLB-4	Mayes, Wendell 1919-1992............DLB-26	McCullagh, Joseph B. 1842-1896........DLB-23
Mather, Cotton 1663-1728.......DLB-24, 30, 140; CDALB-2	Mayfield, Julian 1928-1984........DLB-33; Y-84	McCullers, Carson 1917-1967.....DLB-2, 7, 173, 228; CDALB-1
Mather, Increase 1639-1723.............DLB-24	Mayhew, Henry 1812-1887....DLB-18, 55, 190	McCulloch, Thomas 1776-1843..........DLB-99
Mather, Richard 1596-1669............DLB-24	Mayhew, Jonathan 1720-1766...........DLB-31	McDermott, Alice 1953-............DLB-292
Matheson, Annie 1853-1924...........DLB-240	Mayne, Ethel Colburn 1865-1941.......DLB-197	McDonald, Forrest 1927-.............DLB-17
Matheson, Richard 1926-..........DLB-8, 44	Mayne, Jasper 1604-1672..............DLB-126	McDonald, Walter 1934-........DLB-105, DS-9
Matheus, John F. 1887-..............DLB-51	Mayne, Seymour 1944-..............DLB-60	"Getting Started: Accepting the Regions You Own–or Which Own You"..............DLB-105
Mathews, Cornelius 1817?-1889...DLB-3, 64, 250	Mayor, Flora Macdonald 1872-1932.....DLB-36	
Elkin Mathews [publishing house]......DLB-112	Mayröcker, Friederike 1924-..........DLB-85	Tribute to James Dickey..............Y-97
Mathews, John Joseph 1894-1979.......DLB-175	Mazrui, Ali A. 1933-................DLB-125	McDougall, Colin 1917-1984...........DLB-68
Mathias, Roland 1915-................DLB-27	Mažuranić, Ivan 1814-1890............DLB-147	McDowell, Katharine Sherwood Bonner 1849-1883................DLB-202, 239
Mathis, June 1892-1927..............DLB-44	Mazursky, Paul 1930-................DLB-44	
Mathis, Sharon Bell 1937-............DLB-33	McAlmon, Robert 1896-1956...DLB-4, 45; DS-15	Obolensky McDowell [publishing house]................DLB-46
Matković, Marijan 1915-1985..........DLB-181	"A Night at Bricktop's"..............Y-01	
Matoš, Antun Gustav 1873-1914........DLB-147	McArthur, Peter 1866-1924............DLB-92	McEwan, Ian 1948-............DLB-14, 194
Matos Paoli, Francisco 1915-2000.......DLB-290	McAuley, James 1917-1976............DLB-260	McFadden, David 1940-..............DLB-60
Matsumoto Seichō 1909-1992..........DLB-182	Robert M. McBride and Company.......DLB-46	McFall, Frances Elizabeth Clarke (see Grand, Sarah)
The Matter of England 1240-1400......DLB-146	McCabe, Patrick 1955-...............DLB-194	
The Matter of Rome early twelfth to late fifteenth century.................DLB-146	McCafferty, Owen 1961-..............DLB-310	McFarland, Ron 1942-...............DLB-256
	McCaffrey, Anne 1926-..............DLB-8	McFarlane, Leslie 1902-1977..........DLB-88
Matthew of Vendôme circa 1130-circa 1200..............DLB-208	McCann, Colum 1965-...............DLB-267	McFee, William 1881-1966...........DLB-153
	McCarthy, Cormac 1933-....DLB-6, 143, 256	McGahern, John 1934-..........DLB-14, 231
Matthews, Brander 1852-1929..DLB-71, 78; DS-13	The Cormac McCarthy Society.........Y-99	McGee, Thomas D'Arcy 1825-1868......DLB-99
Matthews, Jack 1925-.................DLB-6	McCarthy, Mary 1912-1989........DLB-2; Y-81	McGeehan, W. O. 1879-1933......DLB-25, 171
Matthews, Victoria Earle 1861-1907.....DLB-221	McCarthy, Shaun Lloyd (see Cory, Desmond)	McGill, Ralph 1898-1969.............DLB-29
Matthews, William 1942-1997............DLB-5	McCay, Winsor 1871-1934............DLB-22	McGinley, Phyllis 1905-1978........DLB-11, 48
Matthías Jochumsson 1835-1920........DLB-293	McClane, Albert Jules 1922-1991......DLB-171	McGinniss, Joe 1942-................DLB-185
Matthías Johannessen 1930-...........DLB-293	McClatchy, C. K. 1858-1936...........DLB-25	McGirt, James E. 1874-1930..........DLB-50
Matthiessen, F. O. 1902-1950..........DLB-63	McClellan, George Marion 1860-1934....DLB-50	McGlashan and Gill................DLB-106
Matthiessen, Peter 1927-......DLB-6, 173, 275	"The Negro as a Writer"............DLB-50	McGough, Roger 1937-..............DLB-40
Maturin, Charles Robert 1780-1824.....DLB-178	McCloskey, Robert 1914-.............DLB-22	McGrath, John 1935-................DLB-233
Maugham, W. Somerset 1874-1965 ....DLB-10, 36, 77, 100, 162, 195; CDBLB-6	McCloy, Helen 1904-1992............DLB-306	McGrath, Patrick 1950-..............DLB-231
	McClung, Nellie Letitia 1873-1951......DLB-92	McGraw-Hill......................DLB-46
Maupassant, Guy de 1850-1893........DLB-123	McClure, James 1939-...............DLB-276	McGuane, Thomas 1939-....DLB-2, 212; Y-80
Maupin, Armistead 1944-............DLB-278	McClure, Joanna 1930-..............DLB-16	Tribute to Seymour Lawrence..........Y-94
Mauriac, Claude 1914-1996...........DLB-83	McClure, Michael 1932-..............DLB-16	McGuckian, Medbh 1950-............DLB-40
Mauriac, François 1885-1970..........DLB-65	McClure, Phillips and Company........DLB-46	McGuffey, William Holmes 1800-1873....DLB-42
Maurice, Frederick Denison 1805-1872....DLB-55	McClure, S. S. 1857-1949.............DLB-91	McGuinness, Frank 1953-............DLB-245
Maurois, André 1885-1967............DLB-65	A. C. McClurg and Company.........DLB-49	McHenry, James 1785-1845...........DLB-202
Maury, James 1718-1769..............DLB-31	McCluskey, John A., Jr. 1944-.........DLB-33	McIlvanney, William 1936-......DLB-14, 207
Mavor, Elizabeth 1927-..............DLB-14	McCollum, Michael A. 1946-..........Y-87	McIlwraith, Jean Newton 1859-1938......DLB-92
Mavor, Osborne Henry (see Bridie, James)	McConnell, William C. 1917-..........DLB-88	McInerney, Jay 1955-................DLB-292
Maxwell, Gavin 1914-1969...........DLB-204	McCord, David 1897-1997............DLB-61	McInerny, Ralph 1929-..............DLB-306
Maxwell, William 1908-2000............DLB-218, 278; Y-80	McCord, Louisa S. 1810-1879.........DLB-248	McIntosh, Maria Jane 1803-1878....DLB-239, 248
	McCorkle, Jill 1958-............DLB-234; Y-87	McIntyre, James 1827-1906...........DLB-99
Tribute to Nancy Hale................Y-88	McCorkle, Samuel Eusebius 1746-1811....DLB-37	McIntyre, O. O. 1884-1938............DLB-25
H. Maxwell [publishing house].........DLB-49	McCormick, Anne O'Hare 1880-1954....DLB-29	McKay, Claude 1889-1948....DLB-4, 45, 51, 117
John Maxwell [publishing house]......DLB-106	McCormick, Kenneth Dale 1906-1997......Y-97	The David McKay Company..........DLB-49
May, Elaine 1932-..................DLB-44	McCormick, Robert R. 1880-1955......DLB-29	McKean, William V. 1820-1903.........DLB-23
May, Karl 1842-1912................DLB-129	McCourt, Edward 1907-1972..........DLB-88	McKenna, Stephen 1888-1967..........DLB-197
May, Thomas 1595/1596-1650..........DLB-58	McCoy, Horace 1897-1955.............DLB-9	The McKenzie Trust....................Y-96
Mayer, Bernadette 1945-.............DLB-165	McCrae, Hugh 1876-1958............DLB-260	McKerrow, R. B. 1872-1940..........DLB-201
Mayer, Mercer 1943-................DLB-61	McCrae, John 1872-1918.............DLB-92	McKinley, Robin 1952-..............DLB-52
Mayer, O. B. 1818-1891..........DLB-3, 248	McCrumb, Sharyn 1948-............DLB-306	McKnight, Reginald 1956-...........DLB-234
Mayes, Herbert R. 1900-1987.........DLB-137		

427

McLachlan, Alexander 1818-1896 . . . . DLB-99
McLaren, Floris Clark 1904-1978 . . . . DLB-68
McLaverty, Michael 1907- DLB-15
McLean, Duncan 1964- DLB-267
McLean, John R. 1848-1916 . . . . DLB-23
McLean, William L. 1852-1931 . . . . DLB-25
McLennan, William 1856-1904 . . . . DLB-92
McLoughlin Brothers DLB-49
McLuhan, Marshall 1911-1980 . . . . DLB-88
McMaster, John Bach 1852-1932 . . . . DLB-47
McMillan, Terri 1951- DLB-292
McMurtry, Larry 1936-
 . . . . DLB-2, 143, 256; Y-80, 87; CDALB-6
McNally, Terrence 1939- DLB-7, 249
McNeil, Florence 1937- DLB-60
McNeile, Herman Cyril 1888-1937 . . . . . . DLB-77
McNickle, D'Arcy 1904-1977 . . . . . . DLB-175, 212
McPhee, John 1931- DLB-185, 275
McPherson, James Alan 1943- DLB-38, 244
McPherson, Sandra 1943- Y-86
McTaggart, J. M. E. 1866-1925 . . . . DLB-262
McWhirter, George 1939- DLB-60
McWilliam, Candia 1955- DLB-267
McWilliams, Carey 1905-1980 . . . . DLB-137
 "*The Nation's* Future," Carey
  McWilliams's Editorial Policy
  in *Nation* DLB-137
Mda, Zakes 1948- DLB-225
Mead, George Herbert 1863-1931 . . . . DLB-270
Mead, L. T. 1844-1914 . . . . DLB-141
Mead, Matthew 1924- DLB-40
Mead, Taylor ?- DLB-16
Meany, Tom 1903-1964 . . . . DLB-171
Mechthild von Magdeburg
 circa 1207-circa 1282 . . . . DLB-138
Medieval Galician-Portuguese Poetry DLB-287
Medill, Joseph 1823-1899 . . . . DLB-43
Medoff, Mark 1940- DLB-7
Meek, Alexander Beaufort
 1814-1865 . . . . DLB-3, 248
Meeke, Mary ?-1816? DLB-116
Mei, Lev Aleksandrovich 1822-1862 . . . . . DLB-277
Meinke, Peter 1932- DLB-5
Meireles, Cecília 1901-1964 . . . . DLB-307
Mejia Vallejo, Manuel 1923- DLB-113
Melanchthon, Philipp 1497-1560 . . . . DLB-179
Melançon, Robert 1947- DLB-60
Mell, Max 1882-1971 . . . . DLB-81, 124
Mellow, James R. 1926-1997 . . . . DLB-111
Mel'nikov, Pavel Ivanovich 1818-1883 . . . DLB-238
Meltzer, David 1937- DLB-16
Meltzer, Milton 1915- DLB-61
Melville, Elizabeth, Lady Culross
 circa 1585-1640 . . . . DLB-172
Melville, Herman
 1819-1891 . . . . DLB-3, 74, 250; CDALB-2

The Melville Society Y-01
Melville, James
 (Roy Peter Martin) 1931- DLB-276
Mena, Juan de 1411-1456 . . . . DLB-286
Mena, María Cristina 1893-1965 . . . DLB-209, 221
Menander 342-341 B.C.-circa 292-291 B.C.
 . . . . DLB-176; CDWLB-1
Menantes (see Hunold, Christian Friedrich)
Mencke, Johann Burckhard 1674-1732 . . . DLB-168
Mencken, H. L. 1880-1956
 . . . . DLB-11, 29, 63, 137, 222; CDALB-4
 "Berlin, February, 1917" Y-00
 From the Initial Issue of *American Mercury*
  (January 1924) DLB-137
 Mencken and Nietzsche: An
  Unpublished Excerpt from H. L.
  Mencken's *My Life as Author and
  Editor* Y-93
Mendelssohn, Moses 1729-1786 . . . . DLB-97
Mendes, Catulle 1841-1909 . . . . DLB-217
Méndez M., Miguel 1930- DLB-82
The Mercantile Library of New York Y-96
Mercer, Cecil William (see Yates, Dornford)
Mercer, David 1928-1980 . . . . DLB-13, 310
Mercer, John 1704-1768 . . . . DLB-31
Mercer, Johnny 1909-1976 . . . . DLB-265
Meredith, George
 1828-1909 . . . . DLB-18, 35, 57, 159; CDBLB-4
Meredith, Louisa Anne 1812-1895 . . DLB-166, 230
Meredith, Owen
 (see Lytton, Edward Robert Bulwer)
Meredith, William 1919- DLB-5
Meres, Francis
 Palladis Tamia, Wits Treasurie (1598)
 [excerpt] DLB-172
Merezhkovsky, Dmitrii Sergeevich
 1865-1941 . . . . DLB-295
Mergerle, Johann Ulrich
 (see Abraham ä Sancta Clara)
Mérimée, Prosper 1803-1870 . . . . . . DLB-119, 192
Merivale, John Herman 1779-1844 . . . . . . DLB-96
Meriwether, Louise 1923- DLB-33
Merleau-Ponty, Maurice 1908-1961 . . . . . DLB-296
Merlin Press DLB-112
Merriam, Eve 1916-1992 . . . . DLB-61
The Merriam Company DLB-49
Merril, Judith 1923-1997 . . . . DLB-251
 Tribute to Theodore Sturgeon Y-85
Merrill, James 1926-1995 . . . . . . DLB-5, 165; Y-85
Merrill and Baker DLB-49
The Mershon Company DLB-49
Merton, Thomas 1915-1968 . . . . DLB-48; Y-81
Merwin, W. S. 1927- DLB-5, 169
Julian Messner [publishing house] DLB-46
Mészöly, Miklós 1921- DLB-232
J. Metcalf [publishing house] DLB-49
Metcalf, John 1938- DLB-60
The Methodist Book Concern DLB-49

Methuen and Company DLB-112
Meun, Jean de (see *Roman de la Rose*)
Mew, Charlotte 1869-1928 . . . . DLB-19, 135
Mewshaw, Michael 1943- Y-80
 Tribute to Albert Erskine Y-93
Meyer, Conrad Ferdinand 1825-1898 . . . DLB-129
Meyer, E. Y. 1946- DLB-75
Meyer, Eugene 1875-1959 . . . . DLB-29
Meyer, Michael 1921-2000 . . . . DLB-155
Meyers, Jeffrey 1939- DLB-111
Meynell, Alice 1847-1922 . . . . DLB-19, 98
Meynell, Viola 1885-1956 . . . . DLB-153
Meyrink, Gustav 1868-1932 . . . . DLB-81
Mézières, Philipe de circa 1327-1405 . . . . DLB-208
Michael, Ib 1945- DLB-214
Michael, Livi 1960- DLB-267
Michaëlis, Karen 1872-1950 . . . . DLB-214
Michaels, Anne 1958- DLB-299
Michaels, Leonard 1933- DLB-130
Michaux, Henri 1899-1984 . . . . DLB-258
Micheaux, Oscar 1884-1951 . . . . DLB-50
Michel of Northgate, Dan
 circa 1265-circa 1340 . . . . DLB-146
Micheline, Jack 1929-1998 . . . . DLB-16
Michener, James A. 1907?-1997 . . . . DLB-6
Micklejohn, George circa 1717-1818 . . . . . DLB-31
Middle Hill Press DLB-106
Middleton, Christopher 1926- DLB-40
Middleton, Richard 1882-1911 . . . . DLB-156
Middleton, Stanley 1919- DLB-14
Middleton, Thomas 1580-1627 . . . . DLB-58
Miegel, Agnes 1879-1964 . . . . DLB-56
Miežalitis, Eduardas 1919-1997 . . . . DLB-220
Miguéis, José Rodrigues 1901-1980 . . . . . DLB-287
Mihailović, Dragoslav 1930- DLB-181
Mihalić, Slavko 1928- DLB-181
Mikhailov, A.
 (see Sheller, Aleksandr Konstantinovich)
Mikhailov, Mikhail Larionovich
 1829-1865 . . . . DLB-238
Mikhailovsky, Nikolai Konstantinovich
 1842-1904 . . . . DLB-277
Miles, Josephine 1911-1985 . . . . DLB-48
Miles, Susan (Ursula Wyllie Roberts)
 1888-1975 . . . . DLB-240
Miliković, Branko 1934-1961 . . . . DLB-181
Milius, John 1944- DLB-44
Mill, James 1773-1836 . . . . DLB-107, 158, 262
Mill, John Stuart
 1806-1873 . . . . . . DLB-55, 190, 262; CDBLB-4
 Thoughts on Poetry and Its Varieties
  (1833) DLB-32
Andrew Millar [publishing house] DLB-154
Millar, Kenneth
 1915-1983 . . . . DLB-2, 226; Y-83; DS-6
Millay, Edna St. Vincent
 1892-1950 . . . . DLB-45, 249; CDALB-4

Millen, Sarah Gertrude 1888-1968 ......DLB-225
Miller, Andrew 1960- DLB-267
Miller, Arthur 1915-2005...DLB-7, 266; CDALB-1
   The Arthur Miller Society............Y-01
Miller, Caroline 1903-1992 ....DLB-9
Miller, Eugene Ethelbert 1950- DLB-41
   Tribute to Julian Mayfield............Y-84
Miller, Heather Ross 1939- DLB-120
Miller, Henry
   1891-1980........DLB-4, 9; Y-80; CDALB-5
Miller, Hugh 1802-1856 ....DLB-190
Miller, J. Hillis 1928- DLB-67
Miller, Jason 1939- DLB-7
Miller, Joaquin 1839-1913 ....DLB-186
Miller, May 1899-1995 ....DLB-41
Miller, Paul 1906-1991................DLB-127
Miller, Perry 1905-1963.............DLB-17, 63
Miller, Sue 1943- DLB-143
Miller, Vassar 1924-1998...............DLB-105
Miller, Walter M., Jr. 1923-1996.........DLB-8
Miller, Webb 1892-1940 ....DLB-29
James Miller [publishing house].........DLB-49
Millett, Kate 1934- DLB-246
Millhauser, Steven 1943- DLB-2
Millican, Arthenia J. Bates 1920- DLB-38
Milligan, Alice 1866-1953 ....DLB-240
Mills, Magnus 1954- DLB-267
Mills and Boon DLB-112
Milman, Henry Hart 1796-1868 ....DLB-96
Milne, A. A. 1882-1956 .....DLB-10, 77, 100, 160
Milner, Ron 1938- DLB-38
William Milner [publishing house] DLB-106
Milnes, Richard Monckton (Lord Houghton)
   1809-1885...................DLB-32, 184
Milton, John
   1608-1674.....DLB-131, 151, 281; CDBLB-2
   The Milton Society of America.........Y-00
Miłosz, Czesław 1911- DLB-215; CDWLB-4
Minakami Tsutomu 1919- DLB-182
Minamoto no Sanetomo 1192-1219......DLB-203
Minco, Marga 1920- DLB-299
The Minerva Press DLB-154
Minnesang circa 1150-1280 ....DLB-138
   The Music of *Minnesang* DLB-138
Minns, Susan 1839-1938 ....DLB-140
Minton, Balch and Company DLB-46
Mirbeau, Octave 1848-1917.......DLB-123, 192
Mirk, John died after 1414?............DLB-146
Miró, Ricardo 1883-1940................DLB-290
Miron, Gaston 1928-1996...............DLB-60
A Mirror for Magistrates DLB-167
Mishima Yukio 1925-1970.............DLB-182
Mistral, Gabriela 1889-1957............DLB-283
Mitchel, Jonathan 1624-1668...........DLB-24
Mitchell, Adrian 1932- DLB-40

Mitchell, Donald Grant
   1822-1908...............DLB-1, 243; DS-13
Mitchell, Gladys 1901-1983.............DLB-77
Mitchell, James Leslie 1901-1935........DLB-15
Mitchell, John (see Slater, Patrick)
Mitchell, John Ames 1845-1918..........DLB-79
Mitchell, Joseph 1908-1996 ....DLB-185; Y-96
Mitchell, Julian 1935- DLB-14
Mitchell, Ken 1940- DLB-60
Mitchell, Langdon 1862-1935 ....DLB-7
Mitchell, Loften 1919- DLB-38
Mitchell, Margaret 1900-1949 ...DLB-9; CDALB-7
Mitchell, S. Weir 1829-1914 ....DLB-202
Mitchell, W. J. T. 1942- DLB-246
Mitchell, W. O. 1914-1998 ....DLB-88
Mitchison, Naomi Margaret (Haldane)
   1897-1999 ....DLB-160, 191, 255
Mitford, Mary Russell 1787-1855....DLB-110, 116
Mitford, Nancy 1904-1973..............DLB-191
Mittelholzer, Edgar
   1909-1965 ....DLB-117; CDWLB-3
Mitterer, Erika 1906- DLB-85
Mitterer, Felix 1948- DLB-124
Mitternacht, Johann Sebastian
   1613-1679 ....DLB-168
Miyamoto Yuriko 1899-1951 ....DLB-180
Mizener, Arthur 1907-1988 ....DLB-103
Mo, Timothy 1950- DLB-194
Moberg, Vilhelm 1898-1973 ....DLB-259
Modern Age Books DLB-46
Modern Language Association of America
   The Modern Language Association of
   America Celebrates Its Centennial ..Y-84
The Modern Library.................DLB-46
Modiano, Patrick 1945- DLB-83, 299
Moffat, Yard and Company DLB-46
Moffet, Thomas 1553-1604 ....DLB-136
Mofolo, Thomas 1876-1948 ....DLB-225
Mohr, Nicholasa 1938- DLB-145
Moix, Ana María 1947- DLB-134
Molesworth, Louisa 1839-1921 ....DLB-135
Molière (Jean-Baptiste Poquelin)
   1622-1673 ....DLB-268
Møller, Poul Martin 1794-1838 ....DLB-300
Möllhausen, Balduin 1825-1905 ....DLB-129
Molnár, Ferenc 1878-1952 ...DLB-215; CDWLB-4
Molnár, Miklós (see Mészöly, Miklós)
Momaday, N. Scott
   1934- DLB-143, 175, 256; CDALB-7
Monkhouse, Allan 1858-1936 ....DLB-10
Monro, Harold 1879-1932.............DLB-19
Monroe, Harriet 1860-1936.........DLB-54, 91
Monsarrat, Nicholas 1910-1979 ....DLB-15
Montagu, Lady Mary Wortley
   1689-1762 ....DLB-95, 101
Montague, C. E. 1867-1928 ....DLB-197
Montague, John 1929- DLB-40

Montale, Eugenio 1896-1981..........DLB-114
Montalvo, Garci Rodríguez de
   ca. 1450?-before 1505 ....DLB-286
Montalvo, José 1946-1994...........DLB-209
Monterroso, Augusto 1921-2003........DLB-145
Montesquiou, Robert de 1855-1921.....DLB-217
Montgomerie, Alexander
   circa 1550?-1598.................DLB-167
Montgomery, James 1771-1854......DLB-93, 158
Montgomery, John 1919- DLB-16
Montgomery, Lucy Maud
   1874-1942 ....DLB-92; DS-14
Montgomery, Marion 1925- DLB-6
Montgomery, Robert Bruce (see Crispin, Edmund)
Montherlant, Henry de 1896-1972.......DLB-72
The Monthly Review 1749-1844 ....DLB-110
Monti, Ricardo 1944- DLB-305
Montigny, Louvigny de 1876-1955......DLB-92
Montoya, José 1932- DLB-122
Moodie, John Wedderburn Dunbar
   1797-1869 ....DLB-99
Moodie, Susanna 1803-1885 ....DLB-99
Moody, Joshua circa 1633-1697..........DLB-24
Moody, William Vaughn 1869-1910....DLB-7, 54
Moorcock, Michael 1939- DLB-14, 231, 261
Moore, Alan 1953- DLB-261
Moore, Brian 1921-1999 ....DLB-251
Moore, Catherine L. 1911-1987..........DLB-8
Moore, Clement Clarke 1779-1863 ......DLB-42
Moore, Dora Mavor 1888-1979..........DLB-92
Moore, G. E. 1873-1958 ....DLB-262
Moore, George 1852-1933....DLB-10, 18, 57, 135
   Literature at Nurse, or Circulating Morals
   (1885) DLB-18
Moore, Lorrie 1957- DLB-234
Moore, Marianne
   1887-1972 ....DLB-45; DS-7; CDALB-5
   International Marianne Moore Society ...Y-98
Moore, Mavor 1919- DLB-88
Moore, Richard 1927- DLB-105
   "The No Self, the Little Self, and
   the Poets" DLB-105
Moore, T. Sturge 1870-1944 ....DLB-19
Moore, Thomas 1779-1852 ....DLB-96, 144
Moore, Ward 1903-1978 ....DLB-8
Moore, Wilstach, Keys and Company DLB-49
Moorehead, Alan 1901-1983............DLB-204
Moorhouse, Frank 1938- DLB-289
Moorhouse, Geoffrey 1931- DLB-204
The Moorland-Spingarn Research
   Center DLB-76
Moorman, Mary C. 1905-1994 ....DLB-155
Mora, Pat 1942- DLB-209
Moraes, Vinicius de 1913-1980 ....DLB-307
Moraga, Cherríe 1952- DLB-82, 249
Morales, Alejandro 1944- DLB-82
Morales, Mario Roberto 1947- DLB-145

Morales, Rafael 1919- DLB-108

Morality Plays: *Mankind* circa 1450-1500 and *Everyman* circa 1500 .... DLB-146

Morand, Paul (1888-1976) DLB-65

Morante, Elsa 1912-1985 .... DLB-177

Morata, Olympia Fulvia 1526-1555 .... DLB-179

Moravia, Alberto 1907-1990 .... DLB-177

Mordaunt, Elinor 1872-1942 .... DLB-174

Mordovtsev, Daniil Lukich 1830-1905 .... DLB-238

More, Hannah 1745-1833 .... DLB-107, 109, 116, 158

More, Henry 1614-1687 .... DLB-126, 252

More, Sir Thomas 1477/1478-1535 .... DLB-136, 281

Morejón, Nancy 1944- DLB-283

Morency, Pierre 1942- DLB-60

Moreno, Dorinda 1939- DLB-122

Moretti, Marino 1885-1979 .... DLB-114, 264

Morgan, Berry 1919- DLB-6

Morgan, Charles 1894-1958 .... DLB-34, 100

Morgan, Edmund S. 1916- DLB-17

Morgan, Edwin 1920- DLB-27

Morgan, John Pierpont 1837-1913 .... DLB-140

Morgan, John Pierpont, Jr. 1867-1943 .... DLB-140

Morgan, Robert 1944- DLB-120, 292

Morgan, Sydney Owenson, Lady 1776?-1859 .... DLB-116, 158

Morgner, Irmtraud 1933-1990 .... DLB-75

Morhof, Daniel Georg 1639-1691 .... DLB-164

Mori Ōgai 1862-1922 .... DLB-180

Móricz, Zsigmond 1879-1942 .... DLB-215

Morier, James Justinian 1782 or 1783?-1849 .... DLB-116

Mörike, Eduard 1804-1875 .... DLB-133

Morin, Paul 1889-1963 .... DLB-92

Morison, Richard 1514?-1556 .... DLB-136

Morison, Samuel Eliot 1887-1976 .... DLB-17

Morison, Stanley 1889-1967 .... DLB-201

Moritz, Karl Philipp 1756-1793 .... DLB-94

Moriz von Craûn circa 1220-1230 .... DLB-138

Morley, Christopher 1890-1957 .... DLB-9

Morley, John 1838-1923 .... DLB-57, 144, 190

Moro, César 1903-1956 .... DLB-290

Morris, George Pope 1802-1864 .... DLB-73

Morris, James Humphrey (see Morris, Jan)

Morris, Jan 1926- DLB-204

Morris, Lewis 1833-1907 .... DLB-35

Morris, Margaret 1737-1816 .... DLB-200

Morris, Mary McGarry 1943- DLB-292

Morris, Richard B. 1904-1989 .... DLB-17

Morris, William 1834-1896 .... DLB-18, 35, 57, 156, 178, 184; CDBLB-4

Morris, Willie 1934-1999 .... Y-80

    Tribute to Irwin Shaw Y-84

    Tribute to James Dickey Y-97

Morris, Wright 1910-1998 .... DLB-2, 206, 218; Y-81

Morrison, Arthur 1863-1945 .... DLB-70, 135, 197

Morrison, Charles Clayton 1874-1966 .... DLB-91

Morrison, John 1904-1998 .... DLB-260

Morrison, Toni 1931- DLB-6, 33, 143; Y-81, 93; CDALB-6

    Nobel Lecture 1993 .... Y-93

Morrissy, Mary 1957- DLB-267

William Morrow and Company DLB-46

Morse, James Herbert 1841-1923 .... DLB-71

Morse, Jedidiah 1761-1826 .... DLB-37

Morse, John T., Jr. 1840-1937 .... DLB-47

Morselli, Guido 1912-1973 .... DLB-177

Morte Arthure, the *Alliterative* and the *Stanzaic* circa 1350-1400 .... DLB-146

Mortimer, Favell Lee 1802-1878 .... DLB-163

Mortimer, John 1923- DLB-13, 245, 271; CDBLB-8

Morton, Carlos 1942- DLB-122

Morton, H. V. 1892-1979 .... DLB-195

John P. Morton and Company DLB-49

Morton, Nathaniel 1613-1685 .... DLB-24

Morton, Sarah Wentworth 1759-1846 .... DLB-37

Morton, Thomas circa 1579-circa 1647 .... DLB-24

Moscherosch, Johann Michael 1601-1669 .... DLB-164

Humphrey Moseley [publishing house] DLB-170

Möser, Justus 1720-1794 .... DLB-97

Mosley, Nicholas 1923- DLB-14, 207

Mosley, Walter 1952- DLB-306

Moss, Arthur 1889-1969 .... DLB-4

Moss, Howard 1922-1987 .... DLB-5

Moss, Thylias 1954- DLB-120

Motion, Andrew 1952- DLB-40

Motley, John Lothrop 1814-1877 .... DLB-1, 30, 59, 235

Motley, Willard 1909-1965 .... DLB-76, 143

Mott, Lucretia 1793-1880 .... DLB-239

Benjamin Motte Jr. [publishing house] DLB-154

Motteux, Peter Anthony 1663-1718 .... DLB-80

Mottram, R. H. 1883-1971 .... DLB-36

Mount, Ferdinand 1939- DLB-231

Mouré, Erin 1955- DLB-60

Mourning Dove (Humishuma) between 1882 and 1888?-1936 .... DLB-175, 221

Movies

    Fiction into Film, 1928-1975: A List of Movies Based on the Works of Authors in British Novelists, 1930-1959 .... DLB-15

    Movies from Books, 1920-1974 .... DLB-9

Mowat, Farley 1921- DLB-68

A. R. Mowbray and Company, Limited DLB-106

Mowrer, Edgar Ansel 1892-1977 .... DLB-29

Mowrer, Paul Scott 1887-1971 .... DLB-29

Edward Moxon [publishing house] DLB-106

Joseph Moxon [publishing house] DLB-170

Moyes, Patricia 1923-2000 .... DLB-276

Mphahlele, Es'kia (Ezekiel) 1919- DLB-125, 225; CDWLB-3

Mrożek, Sławomir 1930- DLB-232; CDWLB-4

Mtshali, Oswald Mbuyiseni 1940- DLB-125, 225

Mucedorus DLB-62

Mudford, William 1782-1848 .... DLB-159

Mudrooroo (see Johnson, Colin)

Mueller, Lisel 1924- DLB-105

Muhajir, El (see Marvin X)

Muhajir, Nazzam Al Fitnah (see Marvin X)

Mühlbach, Luise 1814-1873 .... DLB-133

Muir, Edwin 1887-1959 .... DLB-20, 100, 191

Muir, Helen 1937- DLB-14

Muir, John 1838-1914 .... DLB-186, 275

Muir, Percy 1894-1979 .... DLB-201

Mujū Ichien 1226-1312 .... DLB-203

Mukherjee, Bharati 1940- DLB-60, 218

Mulcaster, Richard 1531 or 1532-1611 .... DLB-167

Muldoon, Paul 1951- DLB-40

Mulisch, Harry 1927- DLB-299

Müller, Friedrich (see Müller, Maler)

Müller, Heiner 1929-1995 .... DLB-124

Müller, Maler 1749-1825 .... DLB-94

Muller, Marcia 1944- DLB-226

Müller, Wilhelm 1794-1827 .... DLB-90

Mumford, Lewis 1895-1990 .... DLB-63

Munby, A. N. L. 1913-1974 .... DLB-201

Munby, Arthur Joseph 1828-1910 .... DLB-35

Munday, Anthony 1560-1633 .... DLB-62, 172

Mundt, Clara (see Mühlbach, Luise)

Mundt, Theodore 1808-1861 .... DLB-133

Munford, Robert circa 1737-1783 .... DLB-31

Mungoshi, Charles 1947- DLB-157

Munk, Kaj 1898-1944 .... DLB-214

Munonye, John 1929- DLB-117

Munro, Alice 1931- DLB-53

George Munro [publishing house] DLB-49

Munro, H. H. 1870-1916 .... DLB-34, 162; CDBLB-5

Munro, Neil 1864-1930 .... DLB-156

Norman L. Munro [publishing house] DLB-49

Munroe, Kirk 1850-1930 .... DLB-42

Munroe and Francis DLB-49

James Munroe and Company DLB-49

Joel Munsell [publishing house] DLB-49

Munsey, Frank A. 1854-1925 .... DLB-25, 91

Frank A. Munsey and Company DLB-49

Murakami Haruki 1949- DLB-182

Murav'ev, Mikhail Nikitich 1757-1807 .... DLB-150

Murdoch, Iris 1919-1999 .... DLB-14, 194, 233; CDBLB-8

DLB 310 — Cumulative Index

Murdock, James
  From *Sketches of Modern Philosophy* DS-5
Murdoch, Rupert 1931- DLB-127
Murfree, Mary N. 1850-1922 . . . . DLB-12, 74
Murger, Henry 1822-1861 . . . . DLB-119
Murger, Louis-Henri (see Murger, Henry)
Murnane, Gerald 1939- DLB-289
Murner, Thomas 1475-1537 . . . . DLB-179
Muro, Amado 1915-1971 . . . . DLB-82
Murphy, Arthur 1727-1805 . . . . DLB-89, 142
Murphy, Beatrice M. 1908-1992 . . . . DLB-76
Murphy, Dervla 1931- DLB-204
Murphy, Emily 1868-1933 . . . . DLB-99
Murphy, Jack 1923-1980 . . . . DLB-241
John Murphy and Company DLB-49
Murphy, John H., III 1916- DLB-127
Murphy, Richard 1927-1993 . . . . DLB-40
Murphy, Tom 1935- DLB-310
Murray, Albert L. 1916- DLB-38
Murray, Gilbert 1866-1957 . . . . DLB-10
Murray, Jim 1919-1998 . . . . DLB-241
John Murray [publishing house] DLB-154
Murray, Judith Sargent 1751-1820 . . . . DLB-37, 200
Murray, Les 1938- DLB-289
Murray, Pauli 1910-1985 . . . . DLB-41
Murry, John Middleton 1889-1957 . . . . . . DLB-149
  "The Break-Up of the Novel"
    (1922) DLB-36
Murry, John Middleton, Jr. (see Cowper, Richard)
Musäus, Johann Karl August 1735-1787 . . . . DLB-97
Muschg, Adolf 1934- DLB-75
Musil, Robert
  1880-1942 . . . . DLB-81, 124; CDWLB-2
Muspilli circa 790-circa 850 . . . . DLB-148
Musset, Alfred de 1810-1857 . . . . DLB-192, 217
Benjamin B. Mussey
  and Company DLB-49
Muste, A. J. 1885-1967 . . . . DLB-303
Mutafchieva, Vera 1929- DLB-181
Mutis, Alvaro 1923- DLB-283
Mwangi, Meja 1948- DLB-125
Myers, Frederic W. H.
  1843-1901 . . . . DLB-190
Myers, Gustavus 1872-1942 . . . . DLB-47
Myers, L. H. 1881-1944 . . . . DLB-15
Myers, Walter Dean 1937- DLB-33
Myerson, Julie 1960- DLB-267
Mykle, Agnar 1915-1994 . . . . DLB-297
Mykolaitis-Putinas,
  Vincas 1893-1967 . . . . DLB-220
Myles, Eileen 1949- DLB-193
Myrdal, Jan 1927- DLB-257
Mystery
  1985: The Year of the Mystery:
    A Symposium Y-85
  Comments from Other Writers Y-85
  The Second Annual New York Festival
    of Mystery Y-00
  Why I Read Mysteries Y-85
  Why I Write Mysteries: Night and Day,
    by Michael Collins Y-85

N

Na Prous Boneta circa 1296-1328 . . . . DLB-208
Nabl, Franz 1883-1974 . . . . DLB-81
Nabakov, Véra 1902-1991 . . . . Y-91
Nabokov, Vladimir 1899-1977 . . DLB-2, 244, 278;
                        Y-80, 91; DS-3; CDALB-1
  International Nabokov Society Y-99
  An Interview [On Nabokov], by
    Fredson Bowers Y-80
  Nabokov Festival at Cornell Y-83
  The Vladimir Nabokov Archive in the
    Berg Collection of the New York
    Public Library: An Overview Y-91
  The Vladimir Nabokov Society Y-01
Nádaši, Ladislav (see Jégé)
Naden, Constance 1858-1889 . . . . DLB-199
Nadezhdin, Nikolai Ivanovich
  1804-1856 . . . . DLB-198
Nadson, Semen Iakovlevich 1862-1887 . . . DLB-277
Naevius circa 265 B.C.-201 B.C. DLB-211
Nafis and Cornish DLB-49
Nagai Kafū 1879-1959 . . . . DLB-180
Nagel, Ernest 1901-1985 . . . . DLB-279
Nagibin, Iurii Markovich 1920-1994 . . . . . DLB-302
Nagrodskaia, Evdokiia Apollonovna
  1866-1930 . . . . DLB-295
Naipaul, Shiva 1945-1985 . . . . DLB-157; Y-85
Naipaul, V. S. 1932- DLB-125, 204, 207;
                    Y-85, Y-01; CDBLB-8; CDWLB-3
  Nobel Lecture 2001: "Two Worlds" Y-01
Nakagami Kenji 1946-1992 . . . . DLB-182
Nakano-in Masatada no Musume (see Nijō, Lady)
Nałkowska, Zofia 1884-1954 . . . . DLB-215
Namora, Fernando 1919-1989 . . . . DLB-287
Joseph Nancrede [publishing house] DLB-49
Naranjo, Carmen 1930- DLB-145
Narbikova, Valeriia Spartakovna
  1958- DLB-285
Narezhny, Vasilii Trofimovich
  1780-1825 . . . . DLB-198
Narrache, Jean (Emile Coderre)
  1893-1970 . . . . DLB-92
Nasby, Petroleum Vesuvius (see Locke, David Ross)
Eveleigh Nash [publishing house] DLB-112
Nash, Ogden 1902-1971 . . . . DLB-11
Nashe, Thomas 1567-1601? DLB-167
Nason, Jerry 1910-1986 . . . . DLB-241
Nasr, Seyyed Hossein 1933- DLB-279
Nast, Condé 1873-1942 . . . . DLB-91
Nast, Thomas 1840-1902 . . . . DLB-188
Nastasijević, Momčilo 1894-1938 . . . . DLB-147
Nathan, George Jean 1882-1958 . . . . DLB-137
Nathan, Robert 1894-1985 . . . . DLB-9
Nation, Carry A. 1846-1911 . . . . DLB-303
National Book Critics Circle Awards Y-00–01
The National Jewish Book Awards Y-85
Natsume Sōseki 1867-1916 . . . . DLB-180
Naughton, Bill 1910-1992 . . . . DLB-13
Nava, Michael 1954- DLB-306
Navarro, Joe 1953- DLB-209
Naylor, Gloria 1950- DLB-173
Nazor, Vladimir 1876-1949 . . . . DLB-147
Ndebele, Njabulo 1948- DLB-157, 225
Neagoe, Peter 1881-1960 . . . . DLB-4
Neal, John 1793-1876 . . . . DLB-1, 59, 243
Neal, Joseph C. 1807-1847 . . . . DLB-11
Neal, Larry 1937-1981 . . . . DLB-38
The Neale Publishing Company DLB-49
Nearing, Scott 1883-1983 . . . . DLB-303
Nebel, Frederick 1903-1967 . . . . DLB-226
Nebrija, Antonio de 1442 or 1444-1522 . . DLB-286
Nedreaas, Torborg 1906-1987 . . . . DLB-297
F. Tennyson Neely [publishing house] DLB-49
Negoițescu, Ion 1921-1993 . . . . DLB-220
Negri, Ada 1870-1945 . . . . DLB-114
Neihardt, John G. 1881-1973 . . . . DLB-9, 54, 256
Neidhart von Reuental
  circa 1185-circa 1240 . . . . DLB-138
Neilson, John Shaw 1872-1942 . . . . DLB-230
Nekrasov, Nikolai Alekseevich
  1821-1877 . . . . DLB-277
Nekrasov, Viktor Platonovich
  1911-1987 . . . . DLB-302
Neledinsky-Meletsky, Iurii Aleksandrovich
  1752-1828 . . . . DLB-150
Nelligan, Emile 1879-1941 . . . . DLB-92
Nelson, Alice Moore Dunbar 1875-1935 . . . DLB-50
Nelson, Antonya 1961- DLB-244
Nelson, Kent 1943- DLB-234
Nelson, Richard K. 1941- DLB-275
Nelson, Thomas, and Sons [U.K.] DLB-106
Nelson, Thomas, and Sons [U.S.] DLB-49
Nelson, William 1908-1978 . . . . DLB-103
Nelson, William Rockhill 1841-1915 . . . . . . DLB-23
Nemerov, Howard 1920-1991 . . . . . DLB-5, 6; Y-83
Németh, László 1901-1975 . . . . DLB-215
Nepos circa 100 B.C.-post 27 B.C. DLB-211
Nėris, Salomėja 1904-1945 . . . . . DLB-220; CDWLB-4
Neruda, Pablo 1904-1973 . . . . DLB-283
Nerval, Gérard de 1808-1855 . . . . DLB-217
Nervo, Amado 1870-1919 . . . . DLB-290
Nesbit, E. 1858-1924 . . . . DLB-141, 153, 178
Ness, Evaline 1911-1986 . . . . DLB-61
Nestroy, Johann 1801-1862 . . . . DLB-133
Nettleship, R. L. 1846-1892 . . . . DLB-262
Neugeboren, Jay 1938- DLB-28
Neukirch, Benjamin 1655-1729 . . . . DLB-168

Neumann, Alfred 1895-1952 .... DLB-56
Neumann, Ferenc (see Molnár, Ferenc)
Neumark, Georg 1621-1681 .... DLB-164
Neumeister, Erdmann 1671-1756 ...... DLB-168
Nevins, Allan 1890-1971 .... DLB-17; DS-17
Nevinson, Henry Woodd 1856-1941 .... DLB-135
The New American Library DLB-46
New Directions Publishing Corporation ... DLB-46
The New Monthly Magazine 1814-1884 .... DLB-110
New York Times Book Review Y-82
John Newbery [publishing house] DLB-154
Newbolt, Henry 1862-1938 .... DLB-19
Newbound, Bernard Slade (see Slade, Bernard)
Newby, Eric 1919- DLB-204
Newby, P. H. 1918- DLB-15
Thomas Cautley Newby
 [publishing house] DLB-106
Newcomb, Charles King 1820-1894 ... DLB-1, 223
Newell, Peter 1862-1924 .... DLB-42
Newell, Robert Henry 1836-1901 .... DLB-11
Newhouse, Samuel I. 1895-1979 .... DLB-127
Newman, Cecil Earl 1903-1976 .... DLB-127
Newman, David 1937- DLB-44
Newman, Frances 1883-1928 .... Y-80
Newman, Francis William 1805-1897 .... DLB-190
Newman, G. F. 1946- DLB-310
Newman, John Henry
 1801-1890 .... DLB-18, 32, 55
Mark Newman [publishing house] DLB-49
Newmarch, Rosa Harriet 1857-1940 ..... DLB-240
George Newnes Limited DLB-112
Newsome, Effie Lee 1885-1979 .... DLB-76
Newton, A. Edward 1864-1940 .... DLB-140
Newton, Sir Isaac 1642-1727 .... DLB-252
Nexø, Martin Andersen 1869-1954 ..... DLB-214
Nezval, Vítěslav
 1900-1958 .... DLB-215; CDWLB-4
Ngugi wa Thiong'o
 1938- DLB-125; CDWLB-3
Niatum, Duane 1938- DLB-175
The *Nibelungenlied* and the *Klage*
 circa 1200 .... DLB-138
Nichol, B. P. 1944-1988 .... DLB-53
Nicholas of Cusa 1401-1464 .... DLB-115
Nichols, Ann 1891?-1966 .... DLB-249
Nichols, Beverly 1898-1983 .... DLB-191
Nichols, Dudley 1895-1960 .... DLB-26
Nichols, Grace 1950- DLB-157
Nichols, John 1940- Y-82
Nichols, Mary Sargeant (Neal) Gove
 1810-1884 .... DLB-1, 243
Nichols, Peter 1927- DLB-13, 245
Nichols, Roy F. 1896-1973 .... DLB-17
Nichols, Ruth 1948- DLB-60
Nicholson, Edward Williams Byron
 1849-1912 .... DLB-184

Nicholson, Geoff 1953- DLB-271
Nicholson, Norman 1914- DLB-27
Nicholson, William 1872-1949 .... DLB-141
Ní Chuilleanáin, Eiléan 1942- DLB-40
Nicol, Eric 1919- DLB-68
Nicolai, Friedrich 1733-1811 .... DLB-97
Nicolas de Clamanges circa 1363-1437 ... DLB-208
Nicolay, John G. 1832-1901 and
 Hay, John 1838-1905 .... DLB-47
Nicole, Pierre 1625-1695 .... DLB-268
Nicolson, Adela Florence Cory (see Hope, Laurence)
Nicolson, Harold 1886-1968 .... DLB-100, 149
 "The Practice of Biography," in
 *The English Sense of Humour and
 Other Essays* DLB-149
Nicolson, Nigel 1917- DLB-155
Niebuhr, Reinhold 1892-1971 .... DLB-17; DS-17
Niedecker, Lorine 1903-1970 .... DLB-48
Nieman, Lucius W. 1857-1935 .... DLB-25
Nietzsche, Friedrich
 1844-1900 .... DLB-129; CDWLB-2
 Mencken and Nietzsche: An Unpublished
 Excerpt from H. L. Mencken's *My Life
 as Author and Editor* Y-93
Nievo, Stanislao 1928- DLB-196
Niggli, Josefina 1910-1983 .... Y-80
Nightingale, Florence 1820-1910 ...... DLB-166
Nijō, Lady (Nakano-in Masatada no Musume)
 1258-after 1306 .... DLB-203
Nijō Yoshimoto 1320-1388 .... DLB-203
Nikitin, Ivan Savvich 1824-1861 ...... DLB-277
Nikitin, Nikolai Nikolaevich 1895-1963 ... DLB-272
Nikolev, Nikolai Petrovich 1758-1815 ... DLB-150
Niles, Hezekiah 1777-1839 .... DLB-43
Nims, John Frederick 1913-1999 .... DLB-5
 Tribute to Nancy Hale Y-88
Nin, Anaïs 1903-1977 .... DLB-2, 4, 152
Nína Björk Árnadóttir 1941-2000 ...... DLB-293
Niño, Raúl 1961- DLB-209
Nissenson, Hugh 1933- DLB-28
Niven, Frederick John 1878-1944 ...... DLB-92
Niven, Larry 1938- DLB-8
Nixon, Howard M. 1909-1983 .... DLB-201
Nizan, Paul 1905-1940 .... DLB-72
Njegoš, Petar II Petrović
 1813-1851 .... DLB-147; CDWLB-4
Nkosi, Lewis 1936- DLB-157, 225
Noah, Mordecai M. 1785-1851 .... DLB-250
Noailles, Anna de 1876-1933 .... DLB-258
Nobel Peace Prize
 The Nobel Prize and Literary Politics Y-88
 Elie Wiesel Y-86
Nobel Prize in Literature
 Joseph Brodsky Y-87
 Camilo José Cela Y-89
 Dario Fo Y-97
 Gabriel García Márquez Y-82

 William Golding Y-83
 Nadine Gordimer Y-91
 Günter Grass Y-99
 Seamus Heaney Y-95
 Imre Kertész Y-02
 Najīb Mahfūz Y-88
 Toni Morrison Y-93
 V. S. Naipaul Y-01
 Kenzaburō Ōe Y-94
 Octavio Paz Y-90
 José Saramago Y-98
 Jaroslav Seifert Y-84
 Claude Simon Y-85
 Wole Soyinka Y-86
 Wisława Szymborska Y-96
 Derek Walcott Y-92
 Gao Xingjian Y-00
Nobre, António 1867-1900 .... DLB-287
Nodier, Charles 1780-1844 .... DLB-119
Noël, Marie (Marie Mélanie Rouget)
 1883-1967 .... DLB-258
Noel, Roden 1834-1894 .... DLB-35
Nogami Yaeko 1885-1985 .... DLB-180
Nogo, Rajko Petrov 1945- DLB-181
Nolan, William F. 1928- DLB-8
 Tribute to Raymond Chandler Y-88
Noland, C. F. M. 1810?-1858 .... DLB-11
Noma Hiroshi 1915-1991 .... DLB-182
Nonesuch Press DLB-112
Creative Nonfiction Y-02
Nonni (Jón Stefán Sveinsson or Svensson)
 1857-1944 .... DLB-293
Noon, Jeff 1957- DLB-267
Noonan, Robert Phillipe (see Tressell, Robert)
Noonday Press DLB-46
Noone, John 1936- DLB-14
Nora, Eugenio de 1923- DLB-134
Nordan, Lewis 1939- DLB-234
Nordbrandt, Henrik 1945- DLB-214
Nordhoff, Charles 1887-1947 .... DLB-9
Norén, Lars 1944- DLB-257
Norfolk, Lawrence 1963- DLB-267
Norman, Charles 1904-1996 .... DLB-111
Norman, Marsha 1947- DLB-266; Y-84
Norris, Charles G. 1881-1945 .... DLB-9
Norris, Frank
 1870-1902 .... DLB-12, 71, 186; CDALB-3
Norris, Helen 1916- DLB-292
Norris, John 1657-1712 .... DLB-252
Norris, Leslie 1921- DLB-27, 256
Norse, Harold 1916- DLB-16
Norte, Marisela 1955- DLB-209
North, Marianne 1830-1890 .... DLB-174
North Point Press DLB-46
Nortje, Arthur 1942-1970 .... DLB-125, 225

Norton, Alice Mary (see Norton, Andre)

Norton, Andre 1912- DLB-8, 52

Norton, Andrews 1786-1853 .... DLB-1, 235; DS-5

Norton, Caroline 1808-1877.... DLB-21, 159, 199

Norton, Charles Eliot
1827-1908 .... DLB-1, 64, 235

Norton, John 1606-1663 ....DLB-24

Norton, Mary 1903-1992...............DLB-160

Norton, Thomas 1532-1584 ....DLB-62

W. W. Norton and Company DLB-46

Norwood, Robert 1874-1932 ....DLB-92

Nosaka Akiyuki 1930- DLB-182

Nossack, Hans Erich 1901-1977.........DLB-69

Notker Balbulus circa 840-912..........DLB-148

Notker III of Saint Gall
circa 950-1022..................DLB-148

Notker von Zweifalten ?-1095 ....DLB-148

Nourse, Alan E. 1928- DLB-8

Novak, Slobodan 1924- DLB-181

Novak, Vjenceslav 1859-1905 ....DLB-147

Novakovich, Josip 1956- DLB-244

Novalis 1772-1801 .... DLB-90; CDWLB-2

Novaro, Mario 1868-1944 ....DLB-114

Novás Calvo, Lino 1903-1983 ....DLB-145

Novelists
Library Journal Statements and
Questionnaires from First Novelists ... Y-87

Novels
The Columbia History of the American Novel
A Symposium on Y-92

The Great Modern Library Scam Y-98

Novels for Grown-Ups Y-97

The Proletarian Novel................DLB-9

Novel, The "Second-Generation" Holocaust
............................DLB-299

The Year in the Novel...... Y-87–88, Y-90–93

Novels, British
"The Break-Up of the Novel" (1922),
by John Middleton Murry DLB-36

The Consolidation of Opinion: Critical
Responses to the Modernists DLB-36

"Criticism in Relation to Novels"
(1863), by G. H. Lewes DLB-21

"Experiment in the Novel" (1929)
[excerpt], by John D. Beresford ...DLB-36

"The Future of the Novel" (1899), by
Henry James DLB-18

The Gay Science (1866), by E. S. Dallas
[excerpt] DLB-21

A Haughty and Proud Generation
(1922), by Ford Madox Hueffer ...DLB-36

Literary Effects of World War II DLB-15

"Modern Novelists –Great and Small"
(1855), by Margaret Oliphant.....DLB-21

The Modernists (1932),
by Joseph Warren Beach DLB-36

A Note on Technique (1926), by
Elizabeth A. Drew [excerpts] DLB-36

Novel-Reading: *The Works of Charles
Dickens; The Works of W. Makepeace*

Thackeray (1879),
by Anthony Trollope DLB-21

Novels with a Purpose (1864), by
Justin M'Carthy DLB-21

"On Art in Fiction" (1838),
by Edward Bulwer DLB-21

The Present State of the English Novel
(1892), by George Saintsbury.....DLB-18

Representative Men and Women:
A Historical Perspective on
the British Novel, 1930-1960 .....DLB-15

"The Revolt" (1937), by Mary Colum
[excerpts]....................DLB-36

"Sensation Novels" (1863), by
H. L. Manse DLB-21

Sex, Class, Politics, and Religion [in
the British Novel, 1930-1959].....DLB-15

Time and Western Man (1927),
by Wyndham Lewis [excerpts] DLB-36

Noventa, Giacomo 1898-1960..........DLB-114

Novikov, Nikolai Ivanovich
1744-1818 ....DLB-150

Novomeský, Laco 1904-1976..........DLB-215

Nowlan, Alden 1933-1983..............DLB-53

Noyes, Alfred 1880-1958...............DLB-20

Noyes, Crosby S. 1825-1908 ....DLB-23

Noyes, Nicholas 1647-1717..............DLB-24

Noyes, Theodore W. 1858-1946.........DLB-29

Nozick, Robert 1938-2002 ....DLB-279

N-Town Plays circa 1468 to early
sixteenth century DLB-146

Nugent, Frank 1908-1965 ....DLB-44

Nušić, Branislav 1864-1938 .. DLB-147; CDWLB-4

David Nutt [publishing house]........DLB-106

Nwapa, Flora 1931-1993 .... DLB-125; CDWLB-3

Nye, Edgar Wilson (Bill)
1850-1896.................DLB-11, 23, 186

Nye, Naomi Shihab 1952- DLB-120

Nye, Robert 1939- DLB-14, 271

Nyka-Niliūnas, Alfonsas 1919- DLB-220

O

Oakes, Urian circa 1631-1681 ....DLB-24

Oakes Smith, Elizabeth
1806-1893 ....DLB-1, 239, 243

Oakley, Violet 1874-1961 ....DLB-188

Oates, Joyce Carol 1938-
.............DLB-2, 5, 130; Y-81; CDALB-6

Tribute to Michael M. Rea Y-97

Ōba Minako 1930- DLB-182

Ober, Frederick Albion 1849-1913 ......DLB-189

Ober, William 1920-1993 .... Y-93

Oberholtzer, Ellis Paxson 1868-1936......DLB-47

The Obituary as Literary Form............ Y-02

Obradović, Dositej 1740?-1811 ....DLB-147

O'Brien, Charlotte Grace 1845-1909.....DLB-240

O'Brien, Edna 1932- ...DLB-14, 231; CDBLB-8

O'Brien, Fitz-James 1828-1862 ....DLB-74

O'Brien, Flann (see O'Nolan, Brian)

O'Brien, Kate 1897-1974 ....DLB-15

O'Brien, Tim
1946- DLB-152; Y-80; DS-9; CDALB-7

O'Casey, Sean 1880-1964 .....DLB-10; CDBLB-6

Occom, Samson 1723-1792 ....DLB-175

Occomy, Marita Bonner 1899-1971.......DLB-51

Ochs, Adolph S. 1858-1935.............DLB-25

Ochs-Oakes, George Washington
1861-1931 ....DLB-137

O'Connor, Flannery 1925-1964
........DLB-2, 152; Y-80; DS-12; CDALB-1

The Flannery O'Connor Society........ Y-99

O'Connor, Frank 1903-1966...........DLB-162

O'Connor, Joseph 1963- DLB-267

Octopus Publishing Group DLB-112

Oda Sakunosuke 1913-1947 ....DLB-182

Odell, Jonathan 1737-1818 ....DLB-31, 99

O'Dell, Scott 1903-1989.................DLB-52

Odets, Clifford 1906-1963 .... DLB-7, 26

Odhams Press Limited DLB-112

Odio, Eunice 1922-1974................DLB-283

Odoevsky, Aleksandr Ivanovich
1802-1839 ....DLB-205

Odoevsky, Vladimir Fedorovich
1804 or 1803-1869 ....DLB-198

O'Donnell, Peter 1920- DLB-87

O'Donovan, Michael (see O'Connor, Frank)

O'Dowd, Bernard 1866-1953 ....DLB-230

Ōe, Kenzaburō 1935- DLB-182; Y-94

Nobel Lecture 1994: Japan, the
Ambiguous, and Myself Y-94

Oehlenschläger, Adam 1779-1850 ....DLB-300

O'Faolain, Julia 1932- DLB-14, 231

O'Faolain, Sean 1900-1991 ....DLB-15, 162

Off-Loop Theatres.....................DLB-7

Offord, Carl Ruthven 1910- DLB-76

O'Flaherty, Liam 1896-1984 ... DLB-36, 162; Y-84

Ogarev, Nikolai Platonovich 1813-1877 .. DLB-277

J. S. Ogilvie and Company DLB-49

Ogilvy, Eliza 1822-1912................DLB-199

Ogot, Grace 1930- DLB-125

O'Grady, Desmond 1935- DLB-40

Ogunyemi, Wale 1939- DLB-157

O'Hagan, Howard 1902-1982...........DLB-68

O'Hara, Frank 1926-1966 ....DLB-5, 16, 193

O'Hara, John
1905-1970 ....DLB-9, 86; DS-2; CDALB-5

John O'Hara's Pottsville Journalism Y-88

O'Hare, Kate Richards 1876-1948.......DLB-303

O'Hegarty, P. S. 1879-1955 ....DLB-201

Ohio State University
The William Charvat American Fiction
Collection at the Ohio State
University Libraries Y-92

Okara, Gabriel 1921- DLB-125; CDWLB-3

O'Keeffe, John 1747-1833................DLB-89

Nicholas Okes [publishing house] DLB-170

Okigbo, Christopher 1930-1967........... DLB-125; CDWLB-3
Okot p'Bitek 1931-1982 .... DLB-125; CDWLB-3
Okpewho, Isidore 1941- DLB-157
Okri, Ben 1959- DLB-157, 231
Ólafur Jóhann Sigurðsson 1918-1988.... DLB-293
Old Dogs / New Tricks? New Technologies, the Canon, and the Structure of the Profession..................... Y-02
Old Franklin Publishing House DLB-49
Old German Genesis and *Old German Exodus* circa 1050-circa 1130 .... DLB-148
The *Old High German Isidor* circa 790-800 .... DLB-148
Older, Fremont 1856-1935............. DLB-25
Oldham, John 1653-1683............. DLB-131
Oldman, C. B. 1894-1969............. DLB-201
Olds, Sharon 1942- DLB-120
Olearius, Adam 1599-1671............. DLB-164
O'Leary, Ellen 1831-1889............. DLB-240
O'Leary, Juan E. 1879-1969 .... DLB-290
Olesha, Iurii Karlovich 1899-1960 ..... DLB-272
Oliphant, Laurence 1829?-1888 ..... DLB-18, 166
Oliphant, Margaret 1828-1897 .. DLB-18, 159, 190
"Modern Novelists–Great and Small" (1855) DLB-21
Oliveira, Carlos de 1921-1981 .... DLB-287
Oliver, Chad 1928-1993............... DLB-8
Oliver, Mary 1935- DLB-5, 193
Ollier, Claude 1922- DLB-83
Olsen, Tillie 1912/1913- DLB-28, 206; Y-80; CDALB-7
Olson, Charles 1910-1970........ DLB-5, 16, 193
Olson, Elder 1909- DLB-48, 63
Olson, Sigurd F. 1899-1982 ....DLB-275
The Omega Workshops.................DS-10
Omotoso, Kole 1943- DLB-125
Omulevsky, Innokentii Vasil'evich 1836 [or 1837]-1883................ DLB-238
Ondaatje, Michael 1943- DLB-60
O'Neill, Eugene 1888-1953..... DLB-7; CDALB-5
Eugene O'Neill Memorial Theater Center DLB-7
Eugene O'Neill's Letters: A Review...... Y-88
Onetti, Juan Carlos 1909-1994 .... DLB-113; CDWLB-3
Onions, George Oliver 1872-1961 ...... DLB-153
Onofri, Arturo 1885-1928 .... DLB-114
O'Nolan, Brian 1911-1966 .... DLB-231
Oodgeroo of the Tribe Noonuccal (Kath Walker) 1920-1993 .... DLB-289
Opie, Amelia 1769-1853 .... DLB-116, 159
Opitz, Martin 1597-1639............... DLB-164
Oppen, George 1908-1984 .... DLB-5, 165
Oppenheim, E. Phillips 1866-1946....... DLB-70
Oppenheim, James 1882-1932 .... DLB-28
Oppenheimer, Joel 1930-1988 .... DLB-5, 193
Optic, Oliver (see Adams, William Taylor)

Orczy, Emma, Baroness 1865-1947 ...... DLB-70
Oregon Shakespeare Festival Y-00
Origo, Iris 1902-1988................. DLB-155
O'Riordan, Kate 1960- DLB-267
Orlovitz, Gil 1918-1973 .... DLB-2, 5
Orlovsky, Peter 1933- DLB-16
Ormond, John 1923- DLB-27
Ornitz, Samuel 1890-1957 .... DLB-28, 44
O'Rourke, P. J. 1947- DLB-185
Orozco, Olga 1920-1999............. DLB-283
Orten, Jiří 1919-1941 .... DLB-215
Ortese, Anna Maria 1914- DLB-177
Ortiz, Simon J. 1941- DLB-120, 175, 256
Ortnit and *Wolfdietrich* circa 1225-1250.... DLB-138
Orton, Joe 1933-1967 .... DLB-13, 310; CDBLB-8
Orwell, George (Eric Arthur Blair) 1903-1950 .. DLB-15, 98, 195, 255; CDBLB-7
The Orwell Year Y-84
(Re-)Publishing Orwell............ Y-86
Ory, Carlos Edmundo de 1923- DLB-134
Osbey, Brenda Marie 1957- DLB-120
Osbon, B. S. 1827-1912............... DLB-43
Osborn, Sarah 1714-1796 .... DLB-200
Osborne, John 1929-1994..... DLB-13; CDBLB-7
Osgood, Frances Sargent 1811-1850..... DLB-250
Osgood, Herbert L. 1855-1918......... DLB-47
James R. Osgood and Company DLB-49
Osgood, McIlvaine and Company..... DLB-112
O'Shaughnessy, Arthur 1844-1881....... DLB-35
Patrick O'Shea [publishing house] DLB-49
Osipov, Nikolai Petrovich 1751-1799 .... DLB-150
Oskison, John Milton 1879-1947 ....DLB-175
Osler, Sir William 1849-1919.......... DLB-184
Osofisan, Femi 1946- DLB-125; CDWLB-3
Ostenso, Martha 1900-1963 .... DLB-92
Ostrauskas, Kostas 1926- DLB-232
Ostriker, Alicia 1937- DLB-120
Ostrovsky, Aleksandr Nikolaevich 1823-1886 ....DLB-277
Ostrovsky, Nikolai Alekseevich 1904-1936 ....DLB-272
Osundare, Niyi 1947- DLB-157; CDWLB-3
Oswald, Eleazer 1755-1795 .... DLB-43
Oswald von Wolkenstein 1376 or 1377-1445 ....DLB-179
Otero, Blas de 1916-1979 .... DLB-134
Otero, Miguel Antonio 1859-1944 .... DLB-82
Otero, Nina 1881-1965................ DLB-209
Otero Silva, Miguel 1908-1985........ DLB-145
Otfried von Weißenburg circa 800-circa 875? DLB-148
Otis, Broaders and Company........... DLB-49
Otis, James (see Kaler, James Otis)
Otis, James, Jr. 1725-1783 .... DLB-31
Ottaway, James 1911-2000............. DLB-127
Ottendorfer, Oswald 1826-1900......... DLB-23

Ottieri, Ottiero 1924- DLB-177
Otto-Peters, Louise 1819-1895 .... DLB-129
Otway, Thomas 1652-1685 .... DLB-80
Ouellette, Fernand 1930- DLB-60
Ouida 1839-1908 .... DLB-18, 156
Outing Publishing Company DLB-46
Overbury, Sir Thomas circa 1581-1613 .... DLB-151
The Overlook Press DLB-46
Ovid 43 B.C.-A.D. 17........DLB-211; CDWLB-1
Owen, Guy 1925- DLB-5
Owen, John 1564-1622............... DLB-121
John Owen [publishing house] DLB-49
Peter Owen Limited DLB-112
Owen, Robert 1771-1858 ....DLB-107, 158
Owen, Wilfred 1893-1918 .... DLB-20; DS-18; CDBLB-6
A Centenary Celebration............ Y-93
The Wilfred Owen Association Y-98
The *Owl and the Nightingale* circa 1189-1199 .... DLB-146
Owsley, Frank L. 1890-1956 ....DLB-17
Oxford, Seventeenth Earl of, Edward de Vere 1550-1604................DLB-172
OyamO (Charles F. Gordon) 1943- DLB-266
Ozerov, Vladislav Aleksandrovich 1769-1816...................... DLB-150
Ozick, Cynthia 1928- ...DLB-28, 152, 299; Y-82
First Strauss "Livings" Awarded to Cynthia Ozick and Raymond Carver An Interview with Cynthia Ozick.... Y-83
Tribute to Michael M. Rea Y-97

P

Pace, Richard 1482?-1536 .... DLB-167
Pacey, Desmond 1917-1975 .... DLB-88
Pacheco, José Emilio 1939- DLB-290
Pack, Robert 1929- DLB-5
Padell Publishing Company DLB-46
Padgett, Ron 1942- DLB-5
Padilla, Ernesto Chávez 1944- DLB-122
L. C. Page and Company.............. DLB-49
Page, Louise 1955- DLB-233
Page, P. K. 1916- DLB-68
Page, Thomas Nelson 1853-1922 ....DLB-12, 78; DS-13
Page, Walter Hines 1855-1918........DLB-71, 91
Paget, Francis Edward 1806-1882 ...... DLB-163
Paget, Violet (see Lee, Vernon)
Pagliarani, Elio 1927- DLB-128
Pain, Barry 1864-1928 ....DLB-135, 197
Pain, Philip ?-circa 1666................ DLB-24
Paine, Robert Treat, Jr. 1773-1811 ...... DLB-37
Paine, Thomas 1737-1809 .... DLB-31, 43, 73, 158; CDALB-2
Painter, George D. 1914- DLB-155

Painter, William 1540?-1594 . . . . DLB-136
Palazzeschi, Aldo 1885-1974 . . . . DLB-114, 264
Palei, Marina Anatol'evna 1955- DLB-285
Palencia, Alfonso de 1424-1492 . . . . DLB-286
Palés Matos, Luis 1898-1959 . . . . DLB-290
Paley, Grace 1922- DLB-28, 218
Paley, William 1743-1805 . . . . DLB-252
Palfrey, John Gorham
  1796-1881 . . . . DLB-1, 30, 235
Palgrave, Francis Turner 1824-1897 . . . . . . DLB-35
Palmer, Joe H. 1904-1952 . . . . DLB-171
Palmer, Michael 1943- DLB-169
Palmer, Nettie 1885-1964 . . . . DLB-260
Palmer, Vance 1885-1959 . . . . DLB-260
Paltock, Robert 1697-1767 . . . . DLB-39
Paludan, Jacob 1896-1975 . . . . DLB-214
Paludin-Müller, Frederik 1809-1876 . . . . . DLB-300
Pan Books Limited DLB-112
Panaev, Ivan Ivanovich 1812-1862 . . . . . . DLB-198
Panaeva, Avdot'ia Iakovlevna
  1820-1893 . . . . DLB-238
Panama, Norman 1914- and
  Frank, Melvin 1913-1988 . . . . DLB-26
Pancake, Breece D'J 1952-1979 . . . . DLB-130
Panduro, Leif 1923-1977 . . . . DLB-214
Panero, Leopoldo 1909-1962 . . . . DLB-108
Pangborn, Edgar 1909-1976 . . . . DLB-8
Panizzi, Sir Anthony 1797-1879 . . . . DLB-184
Panneton, Philippe (see Ringuet)
Panova, Vera Fedorovna 1905-1973 . . . . . DLB-302
Panshin, Alexei 1940- DLB-8
Pansy (see Alden, Isabella)
Pantheon Books DLB-46
Papadat-Bengescu, Hortensia
  1876-1955 . . . . DLB-220
Papantonio, Michael 1907-1976 . . . . DLB-187
Paperback Library DLB-46
Paperback Science Fiction DLB-8
Papini, Giovanni 1881-1956 . . . . DLB-264
Paquet, Alfons 1881-1944 . . . . DLB-66
Paracelsus 1493-1541 . . . . DLB-179
Paradis, Suzanne 1936- DLB-53
Páral, Vladimír, 1932- DLB-232
Pardoe, Julia 1804-1862 . . . . DLB-166
Paredes, Américo 1915-1999 . . . . DLB-209
Pareja Diezcanseco, Alfredo 1908-1993 . . . DLB-145
Parents' Magazine Press DLB-46
Paretsky, Sara 1947- DLB-306
Parfit, Derek 1942- DLB-262
Parise, Goffredo 1929-1986 . . . . DLB-177
Parish, Mitchell 1900-1993 . . . . DLB-265
Parizeau, Alice 1930-1990 . . . . DLB-60
Park, Ruth 1923?- DLB-260
Parke, John 1754-1789 . . . . DLB-31
Parker, Dan 1893-1967 . . . . DLB-241

Parker, Dorothy 1893-1967 . . . . DLB-11, 45, 86
Parker, Gilbert 1860-1932 . . . . DLB-99
Parker, James 1714-1770 . . . . DLB-43
Parker, John [publishing house] DLB-106
Parker, Matthew 1504-1575 . . . . DLB-213
Parker, Robert B. 1932- DLB-306
Parker, Stewart 1941-1988 . . . . DLB-245
Parker, Theodore 1810-1860 . . . . DLB-1, 235; DS-5
Parker, William Riley 1906-1968 . . . . DLB-103
J. H. Parker [publishing house] DLB-106
Parkes, Bessie Rayner (Madame Belloc)
  1829-1925 . . . . DLB-240
Parkman, Francis
  1823-1893 . . . . DLB-1, 30, 183, 186, 235
Parks, Gordon 1912- DLB-33
Parks, Tim 1954- DLB-231
Parks, William 1698-1750 . . . . DLB-43
William Parks [publishing house] DLB-49
Parley, Peter (see Goodrich, Samuel Griswold)
Parmenides late sixth-fifth century B.C. . . . DLB-176
Parnell, Thomas 1679-1718 . . . . DLB-95
Parnicki, Teodor 1908-1988 . . . . DLB-215
Parnok, Sofiia Iakovlevna (Parnokh)
  1885-1933 . . . . DLB-295
Parr, Catherine 1513?-1548 . . . . DLB-136
Parra, Nicanor 1914- DLB-283
Parrington, Vernon L. 1871-1929 . . . . . . DLB-17, 63
Parrish, Maxfield 1870-1966 . . . . DLB-188
Parronchi, Alessandro 1914- DLB-128
Parshchikov, Aleksei Maksimovich
  (Raiderman) 1954- DLB-285
Partisan Review DLB-303
Parton, James 1822-1891 . . . . DLB-30
Parton, Sara Payson Willis
  1811-1872 . . . . DLB-43, 74, 239
S. W. Partridge and Company DLB-106
Parun, Vesna 1922- DLB-181; CDWLB-4
Pascal, Blaise 1623-1662 . . . . DLB-268
Pasinetti, Pier Maria 1913- DLB-177
  Tribute to Albert Erskine Y-93
Pasolini, Pier Paolo 1922-1975 . . . . . . DLB-128, 177
Pastan, Linda 1932- DLB-5
Pasternak, Boris
  1890-1960 . . . . DLB-302
Paston, George (Emily Morse Symonds)
  1860-1936 . . . . DLB-149, 197
The Paston Letters 1422-1509 . . . . DLB-146
Pastorius, Francis Daniel
  1651-circa 1720 . . . . DLB-24
Patchen, Kenneth 1911-1972 . . . . DLB-16, 48
Pater, Walter 1839-1894 . . DLB-57, 156; CDBLB-4
  Aesthetic Poetry (1873) DLB-35
  "Style" (1888) [excerpt] DLB-57
Paterson, A. B. "Banjo" 1864-1941 . . . . . . DLB-230
Paterson, Katherine 1932- DLB-52
Patmore, Coventry 1823-1896 . . . . DLB-35, 98
Paton, Alan 1903-1988 . . . . DLB-225; DS-17

Paton, Joseph Noel 1821-1901 . . . . DLB-35
Paton Walsh, Jill 1937- DLB-161
Patrick, Edwin Hill ("Ted") 1901-1964 . . . DLB-137
Patrick, John 1906-1995 . . . . DLB-7
Pattee, Fred Lewis 1863-1950 . . . . DLB-71
Patterson, Alicia 1906-1963 . . . . DLB-127
Patterson, Eleanor Medill 1881-1948 . . . . . DLB-29
Patterson, Eugene 1923- DLB-127
Patterson, Joseph Medill 1879-1946 . . . . . . DLB-29
Pattillo, Henry 1726-1801 . . . . DLB-37
Paul, Elliot 1891-1958 . . . . DLB-4; DS-15
Paul, Jean (see Richter, Johann Paul Friedrich)
Paul, Kegan, Trench, Trubner and
  Company Limited DLB-106
Peter Paul Book Company DLB-49
Stanley Paul and Company Limited DLB-112
Paulding, James Kirke
  1778-1860 . . . . DLB-3, 59, 74, 250
Paulin, Tom 1949- DLB-40
Pauper, Peter, Press DLB-46
Paustovsky, Konstantin Georgievich
  1892-1968 . . . . DLB-272
Pavese, Cesare 1908-1950 . . . . DLB-128, 177
Pavić, Milorad 1929- DLB-181; CDWLB-4
Pavlov, Konstantin 1933- DLB-181
Pavlov, Nikolai Filippovich 1803-1864 . . . . DLB-198
Pavlova, Karolina Karlovna 1807-1893 . . . . DLB-205
Pavlović, Miodrag
  1928- DLB-181; CDWLB-4
Pavlovsky, Eduardo 1933- DLB-305
Paxton, John 1911-1985 . . . . DLB-44
Payn, James 1830-1898 . . . . DLB-18
Payne, John 1842-1916 . . . . DLB-35
Payne, John Howard 1791-1852 . . . . DLB-37
Payson and Clarke DLB-46
Paz, Octavio 1914-1998 . . . . DLB-290; Y-90, 98
  Nobel Lecture 1990 . . . . Y-90
Pazzi, Roberto 1946- DLB-196
Pea, Enrico 1881-1958 . . . . DLB-264
Peabody, Elizabeth Palmer
  1804-1894 . . . . DLB-1, 223
  Preface to *Record of a School:
    Exemplifying the General Principles
    of Spiritual Culture* DS-5
Elizabeth Palmer Peabody
  [publishing house] DLB-49
Peabody, Josephine Preston 1874-1922 . . . DLB-249
Peabody, Oliver William Bourn
  1799-1848 . . . . DLB-59
Peace, Roger 1899-1968 . . . . DLB-127
Peacham, Henry 1578-1644? DLB-151
Peacham, Henry, the Elder
  1547-1634 . . . . DLB-172, 236
Peachtree Publishers, Limited DLB-46
Peacock, Molly 1947- DLB-120
Peacock, Thomas Love 1785-1866 . . . DLB-96, 116
Pead, Deuel ?-1727 . . . . DLB-24

Cumulative Index

Peake, Mervyn 1911-1968 ..... DLB-15, 160, 255
Peale, Rembrandt 1778-1860 .... DLB-183
Pear Tree Press..................... DLB-112
Pearce, Philippa 1920- DLB-161
H. B. Pearson [publishing house] DLB-49
Pearson, Hesketh 1887-1964........... DLB-149
Peattie, Donald Culross 1898-1964 ..... DLB-275
Pechersky, Andrei (see Mel'nikov, Pavel Ivanovich)
Peck, George W. 1840-1916......... DLB-23, 42
H. C. Peck and Theo. Bliss
   [publishing house] DLB-49
Peck, Harry Thurston 1856-1914..... DLB-71, 91
Peden, William 1913-1999 .... DLB-234
   Tribute to William Goyen Y-83
Peele, George 1556-1596 .... DLB-62, 167
Pegler, Westbrook 1894-1969 ....DLB-171
Péguy, Charles 1873-1914 .... DLB-258
Peirce, Charles Sanders 1839-1914.......DLB-270
Pekić, Borislav 1930-1992... DLB-181; CDWLB-4
Pelecanos, George P. 1957- DLB-306
Pelevin, Viktor Olegovich 1962- DLB-285
Pellegrini and Cudahy DLB-46
Pelletier, Aimé (see Vac, Bertrand)
Pelletier, Francine 1959- DLB-251
Pellicer, Carlos 1897?-1977 .... DLB-290
Pemberton, Sir Max 1863-1950 .... DLB-70
de la Peña, Terri 1947- DLB-209
Penfield, Edward 1866-1925.......... DLB-188
Penguin Books [U.K.]............... DLB-112
   Fifty Penguin Years Y-85
   Penguin Collectors' Society Y-98
Penguin Books [U.S.] DLB-46
Penn, William 1644-1718 .... DLB-24
Penn Publishing Company............ DLB-49
Penna, Sandro 1906-1977 .... DLB-114
Pennell, Joseph 1857-1926............ DLB-188
Penner, Jonathan 1940- Y-83
Pennington, Lee 1939- Y-82
Penton, Brian 1904-1951 .... DLB-260
Pepper, Stephen C. 1891-1972 ....DLB-270
Pepys, Samuel
   1633-1703......... DLB-101, 213; CDBLB-2
Percy, Thomas 1729-1811 .... DLB-104
Percy, Walker 1916-1990........DLB-2; Y-80, 90
   Tribute to Caroline Gordon Y-81
Percy, William 1575-1648.............DLB-172
Perec, Georges 1936-1982 .... DLB-83, 299
Perelman, Bob 1947- DLB-193
Perelman, S. J. 1904-1979 .... DLB-11, 44
Pérez de Guzmán, Fernán
   ca. 1377-ca. 1460................ DLB-286
Perez, Raymundo "Tigre"
   1946- DLB-122
Peri Rossi, Cristina 1941- DLB-145, 290
Perkins, Eugene 1932- DLB-41

Perkins, Maxwell
   The Claims of Business and Literature:
   An Undergraduate Essay Y-01
Perkins, William 1558-1602........... DLB-281
Perkoff, Stuart Z. 1930-1974............ DLB-16
Perley, Moses Henry 1804-1862 .... DLB-99
Permabooks DLB-46
Perovsky, Aleksei Alekseevich
   (Antonii Pogorel'sky) 1787-1836 ... DLB-198
Perrault, Charles 1628-1703...........DLB-268
Perri, Henry 1561-1617 .... DLB-236
Perrin, Alice 1867-1934.............. DLB-156
Perry, Anne 1938- DLB-276
Perry, Bliss 1860-1954 .... DLB-71
Perry, Eleanor 1915-1981 .... DLB-44
Perry, Henry (see Perri, Henry)
Perry, Matthew 1794-1858 .... DLB-183
Perry, Sampson 1747-1823 .... DLB-158
Perse, Saint-John 1887-1975 .... DLB-258
Persius A.D. 34-A.D. 62............ DLB-211
Perutz, Leo 1882-1957 .... DLB-81
Pesetsky, Bette 1932- DLB-130
Pessanha, Camilo 1867-1926 .... DLB-287
Pessoa, Fernando 1888-1935 .... DLB-287
Pestalozzi, Johann Heinrich 1746-1827 .... DLB-94
Peter, Laurence J. 1919-1990 .... DLB-53
Peter of Spain circa 1205-1277 .... DLB-115
Peterkin, Julia 1880-1961 .... DLB-9
Peters, Ellis (Edith Pargeter)
   1913-1995 ....DLB-276
Peters, Lenrie 1932- DLB-117
Peters, Robert 1924- DLB-105
   "Foreword to *Ludwig of Baviria*" DLB-105
Petersham, Maud 1889-1971 and
   Petersham, Miska 1888-1960......... DLB-22
Peterson, Charles Jacobs 1819-1887 ...... DLB-79
Peterson, Len 1917- DLB-88
Peterson, Levi S. 1933- DLB-206
Peterson, Louis 1922-1998 .... DLB-76
Peterson, T. B., and Brothers DLB-49
Petitclair, Pierre 1813-1860............ DLB-99
Petrescu, Camil 1894-1957 .... DLB-220
Petronius circa A.D. 20-A.D. 66
   .... DLB-211; CDWLB-1
Petrov, Aleksandar 1938- DLB-181
Petrov, Evgenii (Evgenii Petrovich Kataev)
   1903-1942 ....DLB-272
Petrov, Gavriil 1730-1801............ DLB-150
Petrov, Valeri 1920- DLB-181
Petrov, Vasilii Petrovich 1736-1799 ..... DLB-150
Petrović, Rastko
   1898-1949 ....DLB-147; CDWLB-4
Petrushevskaia, Liudmila Stefanovna
   1938- DLB-285
Petruslied circa 854?................... DLB-148
Petry, Ann 1908-1997................. DLB-76
Pettie, George circa 1548-1589 .... DLB-136

Pétur Gunnarsson 1947- DLB-293
Peyton, K. M. 1929- DLB-161
Pfaffe Konrad flourished circa 1172 ..... DLB-148
Pfaffe Lamprecht flourished circa 1150 .. DLB-148
Pfeiffer, Emily 1827-1890 .... DLB-199
Pforzheimer, Carl H. 1879-1957........ DLB-140
Phaedrus circa 18 B.C.-circa A.D. 50 ..... DLB-211
Phaer, Thomas 1510?-1560 .... DLB-167
Phaidon Press Limited DLB-112
Pharr, Robert Deane 1916-1992......... DLB-33
Phelps, Elizabeth Stuart 1815-1852..... DLB-202
Phelps, Elizabeth Stuart 1844-1911....DLB-74, 221
Philander von der Linde
   (see Mencke, Johann Burckhard)
Philby, H. St. John B. 1885-1960 .... DLB-195
Philip, Marlene Nourbese 1947- DLB-157
Philippe, Charles-Louis 1874-1909....... DLB-65
Philips, John 1676-1708................. DLB-95
Philips, Katherine 1632-1664 .... DLB-131
Phillipps, Sir Thomas 1792-1872........ DLB-184
Phillips, Caryl 1958- DLB-157
Phillips, David Graham
   1867-1911.............. DLB-9, 12, 303
Phillips, Jayne Anne 1952- DLB-292; Y-80
   Tribute to Seymour Lawrence.......... Y-94
Phillips, Robert 1938- DLB-105
   "Finding, Losing, Reclaiming: A Note
   on My Poems" DLB-105
   Tribute to William Goyen Y-83
Phillips, Stephen 1864-1915 .... DLB-10
Phillips, Ulrich B. 1877-1934.............DLB-17
Phillips, Wendell 1811-1884.......... DLB-235
Phillips, Willard 1784-1873 .... DLB-59
Phillips, William 1907-2002 ....DLB-137
Phillips, Sampson and Company DLB-49
Phillpotts, Adelaide Eden (Adelaide Ross)
   1896-1993 .... DLB-191
Phillpotts, Eden 1862-1960...DLB-10, 70, 135, 153
Philo circa 20-15 B.C.-circa A.D. 50.......DLB-176
Philosophical Library DLB-46
Philosophy
   Eighteenth-Century Philosophical
   Background.................. DLB-31
   Philosophic Thought in Boston DLB-235
   Translators of the Twelfth Century:
   Literary Issues Raised and
   Impact Created DLB-115
Elihu Phinney [publishing house]........ DLB-49
Phoenix, John (see Derby, George Horatio)
PHYLON (Fourth Quarter, 1950),
   The Negro in Literature:
   The Current Scene.............. DLB-76
Physiologus circa 1070-circa 1150 .... DLB-148
Piccolo, Lucio 1903-1969 .... DLB-114
Pickard, Tom 1946- DLB-40
William Pickering [publishing house].... DLB-106
Pickthall, Marjorie 1883-1922 .... DLB-92

Picoult, Jodi 1966- DLB-292	Platen, August von 1796-1835 ....DLB-90	Contempo Caravan: Kites in a Windstorm..................... Y-85
Pictorial Printing Company............DLB-49	Plantinga, Alvin 1932- DLB-279	"Contemporary Verse Story-telling," by Jonathan Holden...........DLB-105
Piel, Gerard 1915- DLB-137	Plath, Sylvia 1932-1963........DLB-5, 6, 152; CDALB-1	"A Detail in a Poem," by Fred Chappell....................DLB-105
"An Announcement to Our Readers," Gerard Piel's Statement in *Scientific American* (April 1948)...........DLB-137	Plato circa 428 B.C.-348-347 B.C. DLB-176; CDWLB-1	"The English Renaissance of Art" (1908), by Oscar Wilde DLB-35
Pielmeier, John 1949- DLB-266	Plato, Ann 1824?-?...................DLB-239	"Every Man His Own Poet; or, The Inspired Singer's Recipe Book" (1877), by H. W. Mallock.................DLB-35
Piercy, Marge 1936- DLB-120, 227	Platon 1737-1812......................DLB-150	
Pierro, Albino 1916-1995..............DLB-128	Platonov, Andrei Platonovich (Andrei Platonovich Klimentev) 1899-1951 . . .DLB-272	
Pignotti, Lamberto 1926- DLB-128	Platt, Charles 1945- DLB-261	
Pike, Albert 1809-1891 ....DLB-74	Platt and Munk Company...............DLB-46	"Eyes Across Centuries: Contemporary Poetry and 'That Vision Thing,'" by Philip Dacey DLB-105
Pike, Zebulon Montgomery 1779-1813 . . .DLB-183	Plautus circa 254 B.C.-184 B.C. DLB-211; CDWLB-1	
Pillat, Ion 1891-1945 ....DLB-220	Playboy Press........................DLB-46	A Field Guide to Recent Schools of American Poetry Y-86
Pil'niak, Boris Andreevich (Boris Andreevich Vogau) 1894-1938.................DLB-272	John Playford [publishing house]........DLB-170	"Finding, Losing, Reclaiming: A Note on My Poems, by Robert Phillips"...........DLB-105
Pilon, Jean-Guy 1930- DLB-60	Der Pleier flourished circa 1250.........DLB-138	
Pinar, Florencia fl. ca. late fifteenth century DLB-286	Pleijel, Agneta 1940- DLB-257	"The Fleshly School of Poetry and Other Phenomena of the Day" (1872) . . .DLB-35
Pinckney, Eliza Lucas 1722-1793 ....DLB-200	Plenzdorf, Ulrich 1934- DLB-75	
Pinckney, Josephine 1895-1957 ....DLB-6	Pleshcheev, Aleksei Nikolaevich 1825?-1893 .... DLB-277	"The Fleshly School of Poetry: Mr. D. G. Rossetti" (1871) DLB-35
Pindar circa 518 B.C.-circa 438 B.C. DLB-176; CDWLB-1	Plessen, Elizabeth 1944- DLB-75	The G. Ross Roy Scottish Poetry Collection at the University of South Carolina . . Y-89
Pindar, Peter (see Wolcot, John)	Pletnev, Petr Aleksandrovich 1792-1865 ....DLB-205	"Getting Started: Accepting the Regions You Own–or Which Own You," by Walter McDonald...........DLB-105
Pineda, Cecile 1942- DLB-209	Pliekšāne, Elza Rozenberga (see Aspazija)	
Pinero, Arthur Wing 1855-1934 ....DLB-10	Pliekšāns, Jānis (see Rainis, Jānis)	
Piñero, Miguel 1946-1988 ....DLB-266	Plievier, Theodor 1892-1955............DLB-69	"The Good, The Not So Good," by Stephen Dunn................DLB-105
Pinget, Robert 1919-1997...............DLB-83	Plimpton, George 1927-2003 . . DLB-185, 241; Y-99	The Griffin Poetry Prize Y-00
Pinkney, Edward Coote 1802-1828......DLB-248	Pliny the Elder A.D. 23/24-A.D. 79 ....DLB-211	The Hero as Poet. Dante; Shakspeare (1841), by Thomas Carlyle DLB-32
Pinnacle Books.......................DLB-46	Pliny the Younger circa A.D. 61-A.D. 112 ....DLB-211	
Piñon, Nélida 1935- DLB-145, 307	Plomer, William 1903-1973 .... DLB-20, 162, 191, 225	"Images and 'Images,'" by Charles Simic.......................DLB-105
Pinsky, Robert 1940- Y-82		
Reappointed Poet Laureate............ Y-98	Plotinus 204-270.......... DLB-176; CDWLB-1	"Into the Mirror," by Peter Cooley...DLB-105
Pinter, Harold 1930- ...DLB-13, 310; CDBLB-8	Plowright, Teresa 1952- DLB-251	"Knots into Webs: Some Autobiographical Sources," by Dabney Stuart DLB-105
Writing for the Theatre.............DLB-13	Plume, Thomas 1630-1704 ....DLB-213	
Pinto, Fernão Mendes 1509/1511?-1583 . .DLB-287	Plumly, Stanley 1939- DLB-5, 193	"L'Envoi" (1882), by Oscar Wilde DLB-35
Piontek, Heinz 1925- DLB-75	Plumpp, Sterling D. 1940- DLB-41	"Living in Ruin," by Gerald Stern . . . DLB-105
Piozzi, Hester Lynch [Thrale] 1741-1821 ....DLB-104, 142	Plunkett, James 1920- DLB-14	Looking for the Golden Mountain: Poetry Reviewing................ Y-89
Piper, H. Beam 1904-1964...............DLB-8	Plutarch circa 46-circa 120....... DLB-176; CDWLB-1	Lyric Poetry (French)..............DLB-268
Piper, Watty DLB-22		Medieval Galician-Portuguese Poetry.....................DLB-287
Pirandello, Luigi 1867-1936 ....DLB-264	Plymell, Charles 1935- DLB-16	
Pirckheimer, Caritas 1467-1532.........DLB-179	Pocket Books........................DLB-46	"The No Self, the Little Self, and the Poets," by Richard Moore DLB-105
Pirckheimer, Willibald 1470-1530 ....DLB-179	Podestá, José J. 1858-1937..............DLB-305	
Pires, José Cardoso 1925-1998 ....DLB-287	Poe, Edgar Allan 1809-1849 ....DLB-3, 59, 73, 74, 248; CDALB-2	On Some of the Characteristics of Modern Poetry and On the Lyrical Poems of Alfred Tennyson (1831).........DLB-32
Pisar, Samuel 1929- Y-83		
Pisarev, Dmitrii Ivanovich 1840-1868 ....DLB-277	The Poe Studies Association........... Y-99	The Pitt Poetry Series: Poetry Publishing Today....................... Y-85
Pisemsky, Aleksei Feofilaktovich 1821-1881 ....DLB-238	Poe, James 1921-1980 ....DLB-44	
Pitkin, Timothy 1766-1847 ....DLB-30	The Poet Laureate of the United States...... Y-86	"The Poetry File," by Edward Field......................DLB-105
Pitter, Ruth 1897- DLB-20	Statements from Former Consultants in Poetry...................... Y-86	Poetry in Nineteenth-Century France: Cultural Background and Critical Commentary DLB-217
Pix, Mary 1666-1709 ....DLB-80	Poetry Aesthetic Poetry (1873) DLB-35	
Pixerécourt, René Charles Guilbert de 1773-1844 ....DLB-192		The Poetry of Jorge Luis Borges......... Y-86
Pizarnik, Alejandra 1936-1972 ....DLB-283	A Century of Poetry, a Lifetime of Collecting: J. M. Edelstein's Collection of Twentieth- Century American Poetry Y-02	"The Poet's Kaleidoscope: The Element of Surprise in the Making of the Poem" by Madeline DeFrees DLB-105
Plá, Josefina 1909-1999 ....DLB-290		
Plaatje, Sol T. 1876-1932 ....DLB-125, 225		The Pre-Raphaelite Controversy DLB-35
Plante, David 1940- Y-83	"Certain Gifts," by Betty Adcock DLB-105	
	Concrete Poetry DLB-307	Protest Poetry in Castile DLB-286

437

Cumulative Index

"Reflections: After a Tornado,"
 by Judson Jerome DLB-105
Statements from Former Consultants
 in Poetry Y-86
Statements on the Art of Poetry DLB-54
The Study of Poetry (1880), by
 Matthew Arnold DLB-35
A Survey of Poetry Anthologies,
 1879-1960 . . . . DLB-54
Thoughts on Poetry and Its Varieties
 (1833), by John Stuart Mill DLB-32
Under the Microscope (1872), by
 A. C. Swinburne DLB-35
The Unterberg Poetry Center of the
 92nd Street Y. Y-98
Victorian Poetry: Five Critical
 Views. DLBV-35
Year in Poetry Y-83–92, 94–01
Year's Work in American Poetry Y-82
Poets
 The Lives of the Poets (1753) DLB-142
 Minor Poets of the Earlier
  Seventeenth Century DLB-121
 Other British Poets Who Fell
  in the Great War DLB-216
 Other Poets [French] DLB-217
 Second-Generation Minor Poets of
  the Seventeenth Century DLB-126
 Third-Generation Minor Poets of
  the Seventeenth Century DLB-131
Pogodin, Mikhail Petrovich 1800-1875 . . . DLB-198
Pogorel'sky, Antonii
 (see Perovsky, Aleksei Alekseevich)
Pohl, Frederik 1919- DLB-8
 Tribute to Isaac Asimov Y-92
 Tribute to Theodore Sturgeon Y-85
Poirier, Louis (see Gracq, Julien)
Poláček, Karel 1892-1945 . . . DLB-215; CDWLB-4
Polanyi, Michael 1891-1976 . . . . DLB-100
Pole, Reginald 1500-1558 . . . . DLB-132
Polevoi, Nikolai Alekseevich 1796-1846 . . DLB-198
Polezhaev, Aleksandr Ivanovich
 1804-1838 . . . . DLB-205
Poliakoff, Stephen 1952- DLB-13
Polidori, John William 1795-1821. . . . . . . DLB-116
Polite, Carlene Hatcher 1932- DLB-33
Pollard, Alfred W. 1859-1944 . . . . DLB-201
Pollard, Edward A. 1832-1872 . . . . DLB-30
Pollard, Graham 1903-1976 . . . . DLB-201
Pollard, Percival 1869-1911 . . . . DLB-71
Pollard and Moss DLB-49
Pollock, Sharon 1936- DLB-60
Polonsky, Abraham 1910-1999 . . . . DLB-26
Polonsky, Iakov Petrovich 1819-1898 . . . . DLB-277
Polotsky, Simeon 1629-1680 . . . . DLB-150
Polybius circa 200 B.C.-118 B.C. DLB-176
Pomialovsky, Nikolai Gerasimovich
 1835-1863 . . . . DLB-238
Pomilio, Mario 1921-1990 . . . . DLB-177

Pompéia, Raul (Raul d'Avila Pompéia)
 1863-1895 . . . . DLB-307
Ponce, Mary Helen 1938- DLB-122
Ponce-Montoya, Juanita 1949- DLB-122
Ponet, John 1516?-1556 . . . . DLB-132
Ponge, Francis 1899-1988 . . . . DLB-258; Y-02
Poniatowska, Elena
 1933- DLB-113; CDWLB-3
Ponsard, François 1814-1867 . . . . DLB-192
William Ponsonby [publishing house] DLB-170
Pontiggia, Giuseppe 1934- DLB-196
Pontoppidan, Henrik 1857-1943 . . . . DLB-300
Pony Stories, Omnibus Essay on DLB-160
Poole, Ernest 1880-1950 . . . . DLB-9
Poole, Sophia 1804-1891 . . . . DLB-166
Poore, Benjamin Perley 1820-1887 . . . . . . DLB-23
Popa, Vasko 1922-1991 . . . . DLB-181; CDWLB-4
Pope, Abbie Hanscom 1858-1894 . . . . . . DLB-140
Pope, Alexander
 1688-1744 . . . . . . DLB-95, 101, 213; CDBLB-2
Popov, Aleksandr Serafimovich
 (see Serafimovich, Aleksandr Serafimovich)
Popov, Evgenii Anatol'evich 1946- DLB-285
Popov, Mikhail Ivanovich
 1742-circa 1790 . . . . DLB-150
Popović, Aleksandar 1929-1996 . . . . DLB-181
Popper, Karl 1902-1994 . . . . DLB-262
Popular Culture Association/
 American Culture Association Y-99
Popular Library DLB-46
Poquelin, Jean-Baptiste (see Molière)
Porete, Marguerite ?-1310 . . . . DLB-208
Porlock, Martin (see MacDonald, Philip)
Porpoise Press DLB-112
Porta, Antonio 1935-1989 . . . . DLB-128
Porter, Anna Maria 1780-1832 . . . . . DLB-116, 159
Porter, Cole 1891-1964 . . . . DLB-265
Porter, David 1780-1843 . . . . DLB-183
Porter, Eleanor H. 1868-1920 . . . . DLB-9
Porter, Gene Stratton (see Stratton-Porter, Gene)
Porter, Hal 1911-1984 . . . . DLB-260
Porter, Henry ?-? DLB-62
Porter, Jane 1776-1850 . . . . DLB-116, 159
Porter, Katherine Anne 1890-1980
 . . . . DLB-4, 9, 102; Y-80; DS-12; CDALB-7
 The Katherine Anne Porter Society Y-01
Porter, Peter 1929- DLB-40, 289
Porter, William Sydney (O. Henry)
 1862-1910 . . . . DLB-12, 78, 79; CDALB-3
Porter, William T. 1809-1858 . . . . DLB-3, 43, 250
Porter and Coates DLB-49
Portillo Trambley, Estela 1927-1998 . . . . . DLB-209
Portis, Charles 1933- DLB-6
Medieval Galician-Portuguese Poetry DLB-287
Posey, Alexander 1873-1908 . . . . DLB-175
Postans, Marianne circa 1810-1865 . . . . . DLB-166
Postgate, Raymond 1896-1971 . . . . DLB-276

Postl, Carl (see Sealsfield, Carl)
Postmodern Holocaust Fiction DLB-299
Poston, Ted 1906-1974 . . . . DLB-51
Potekhin, Aleksei Antipovich
 1829-1908 . . . . DLB-238
Potok, Chaim 1929-2002 . . . . DLB-28, 152
 A Conversation with Chaim Potok Y-84
 Tribute to Bernard Malamud Y-86
Potter, Beatrix 1866-1943 . . . . DLB-141
 The Beatrix Potter Society Y-98
Potter, David M. 1910-1971 . . . . DLB-17
Potter, Dennis 1935-1994 . . . . DLB-233
John E. Potter and Company DLB-49
Pottle, Frederick A. 1897-1987 . . . . DLB-103; Y-87
Poulin, Jacques 1937- DLB-60
Pound, Ezra 1885-1972
 . . . . DLB-4, 45, 63; DS-15; CDALB-4
 The Cost of the *Cantos:* William Bird
  to Ezra Pound Y-01
 The Ezra Pound Society Y-01
Poverman, C. E. 1944- DLB-234
Povey, Meic 1950- DLB-310
Povich, Shirley 1905-1998 . . . . DLB-171
Powell, Anthony 1905-2000 . . . DLB-15; CDBLB-7
 The Anthony Powell Society: Powell and
  the First Biennial Conference Y-01
Powell, Dawn 1897-1965
 Dawn Powell, Where Have You Been
  All Our Lives? Y-97
Powell, John Wesley 1834-1902 . . . . DLB-186
Powell, Padgett 1952- DLB-234
Powers, J. F. 1917-1999 . . . . DLB-130
Powers, Jimmy 1903-1995 . . . . DLB-241
Pownall, David 1938- DLB-14
Powys, John Cowper 1872-1963 . . . . DLB-15, 255
Powys, Llewelyn 1884-1939 . . . . DLB-98
Powys, T. F. 1875-1953 . . . . DLB-36, 162
 The Powys Society Y-98
Poynter, Nelson 1903-1978 . . . . DLB-127
Prado, Adélia 1935- DLB-307
Prado, Pedro 1886-1952 . . . . DLB-283
Prados, Emilio 1899-1962 . . . . DLB-134
Praed, Mrs. Caroline (see Praed, Rosa)
Praed, Rosa (Mrs. Caroline Praed)
 1851-1935 . . . . DLB-230
Praed, Winthrop Mackworth 1802-1839 . . DLB-96
Praeger Publishers DLB-46
Praetorius, Johannes 1630-1680 . . . . DLB-168
Pratolini, Vasco 1913-1991 . . . . DLB-177
Pratt, E. J. 1882-1964 . . . . DLB-92
Pratt, Samuel Jackson 1749-1814 . . . . DLB-39
Preciado Martin, Patricia 1939- DLB-209
Préfontaine, Yves 1937- DLB-53
Prelutsky, Jack 1940- DLB-61
Prentice, George D. 1802-1870 . . . . DLB-43
Prentice-Hall DLB-46

Prescott, Orville 1906-1996 . . . . Y-96
Prescott, William Hickling
   1796-1859 . . . . DLB-1, 30, 59, 235
Prešeren, Francè
   1800-1849 . . . . DLB-147; CDWLB-4
Presses (See also Publishing)
   Small Presses in Great Britain and
      Ireland, 1960-1985 . . . . DLB-40
   Small Presses I: Jargon Society Y-84
   Small Presses II: The Spirit That Moves
      Us Press Y-85
   Small Presses III: Pushcart Press Y-87
Preston, Margaret Junkin
   1820-1897 . . . . DLB-239, 248
Preston, May Wilson 1873-1949 . . . . DLB-188
Preston, Thomas 1537-1598 . . . . DLB-62
Prévert, Jacques 1900-1977 . . . . DLB-258
Price, Anthony 1928- DLB-276
Price, Reynolds 1933- DLB-2, 218, 278
Price, Richard 1723-1791 . . . . DLB-158
Price, Richard 1949- Y-81
Prichard, Katharine Susannah
   1883-1969 . . . . DLB-260
Prideaux, John 1578-1650 . . . . DLB-236
Priest, Christopher 1943- DLB-14, 207, 261
Priestley, J. B. 1894-1984
    . . . DLB-10, 34, 77, 100, 139; Y-84; CDBLB-6
Priestley, Joseph 1733-1804 . . . . DLB-252
Prigov, Dmitrii Aleksandrovich 1940- . . DLB-285
Prime, Benjamin Young 1733-1791 . . . . . . DLB-31
Primrose, Diana floruit circa 1630 . . . . DLB-126
Prince, F. T. 1912- DLB-20
Prince, Nancy Gardner 1799-? DLB-239
Prince, Thomas 1687-1758 . . . . DLB-24, 140
Pringle, Thomas 1789-1834 . . . . DLB-225
Printz, Wolfgang Casper 1641-1717 . . . . . . DLB-168
Prior, Matthew 1664-1721 . . . . DLB-95
Prisco, Michele 1920- DLB-177
Prishvin, Mikhail Mikhailovich
   1873-1954 . . . . DLB-272
Pritchard, William H. 1932- DLB-111
Pritchett, V. S. 1900-1997 . . . . DLB-15, 139
Probyn, May 1856 or 1857-1909 . . . . DLB-199
Procter, Adelaide Anne 1825-1864 . . . DLB-32, 199
Procter, Bryan Waller 1787-1874 . . . . DLB-96, 144
Proctor, Robert 1868-1903 . . . . DLB-184
Prokopovich, Feofan 1681?-1736 . . . . DLB-150
Prokosch, Frederic 1906-1989 . . . . DLB-48
Pronzini, Bill 1943- DLB-226
Propertius circa 50 B.C.-post 16 B.C.
   . . . . DLB-211; CDWLB-1
Propper, Dan 1937- DLB-16
Prose, Francine 1947- DLB-234
Protagoras circa 490 B.C.-420 B.C. DLB-176
Protest Poetry in Castile
   ca. 1445-ca. 1506 . . . . DLB-286
Proud, Robert 1728-1813 . . . . DLB-30
Proust, Marcel 1871-1922 . . . . DLB-65

Marcel Proust at 129 and the Proust
   Society of America Y-00
Marcel Proust's *Remembrance of Things Past*:
   The Rediscovered Galley Proofs Y-00
Prutkov, Koz'ma Petrovich 1803-1863 . . . DLB-277
Prynne, J. H. 1936- DLB-40
Przybyszewski, Stanislaw 1868-1927 . . . . . . DLB-66
Pseudo-Dionysius the Areopagite floruit
   circa 500 . . . . DLB-115
Public Lending Right in America
   PLR and the Meaning of Literary
      Property Y-83
   Statement by Sen. Charles
      McC. Mathias, Jr. PLR Y-83
   Statements on PLR by American Writers . . Y-83
Public Lending Right in the United Kingdom
   The First Year in the United Kingdom . . . Y-83
Publishers [listed by individual names]
   Publishers, Conversations with:
      An Interview with Charles Scribner III . . Y-94
      An Interview with Donald Lamm Y-95
      An Interview with James Laughlin Y-96
      An Interview with Patrick O'Connor Y-84
Publishing
   The Art and Mystery of Publishing:
      Interviews Y-97
   Book Publishing Accounting: Some Basic
      Concepts Y-98
   1873 Publishers' Catalogues DLB-49
   The Literary Scene 2002: Publishing, Book
      Reviewing, and Literary Journalism . . Y-02
   Main Trends in Twentieth-Century
      Book Clubs DLB-46
   Overview of U.S. Book Publishing,
      1910-1945 . . . . DLB-9
   The Pitt Poetry Series: Poetry Publishing
      Today Y-85
   Publishing Fiction at LSU Press Y-87
   The Publishing Industry in 1998:
      Sturm-und-drang.com Y-98
   The Publishing Industry in 1999 . . . . Y-99
   Publishers and Agents: The Columbia
      Connection Y-87
   Responses to Ken Auletta Y-97
   Southern Writers Between the Wars . . . DLB-9
   The State of Publishing Y-97
   Trends in Twentieth-Century
      Mass Market Publishing DLB-46
   The Year in Book Publishing Y-86
Pückler-Muskau, Hermann von
   1785-1871 . . . . DLB-133
Pufendorf, Samuel von 1632-1694 . . . . DLB-168
Pugh, Edwin William 1874-1930 . . . . DLB-135
Pugin, A. Welby 1812-1852 . . . . DLB-55
Puig, Manuel 1932-1990 . . . . DLB-113; CDWLB-3
Pulgar, Hernando del (Fernando del Pulgar)
   ca. 1436-ca. 1492 . . . . DLB-286
Pulitzer, Joseph 1847-1911 . . . . DLB-23
Pulitzer, Joseph, Jr. 1885-1955 . . . . DLB-29
Pulitzer Prizes for the Novel, 1917-1945 . . . . DLB-9
Pulliam, Eugene 1889-1975 . . . . DLB-127

Purcell, Deirdre 1945- DLB-267
Purchas, Samuel 1577?-1626 . . . . DLB-151
Purdy, Al 1918-2000 . . . . DLB-88
Purdy, James 1923- DLB-2, 218
Purdy, Ken W. 1913-1972 . . . . DLB-137
Pusey, Edward Bouverie 1800-1882 . . . . . . DLB-55
Pushkin, Aleksandr Sergeevich
   1799-1837 . . . . DLB-205
Pushkin, Vasilii L'vovich
   1766-1830 . . . . DLB-205
Putnam, George Palmer
   1814-1872 . . . . DLB-3, 79, 250, 254
G. P. Putnam [publishing house] DLB-254
G. P. Putnam's Sons [U.K.] DLB-106
G. P. Putnam's Sons [U.S.] DLB-49
   A Publisher's Archives: G. P. Putnam . . . Y-92
Putnam, Hilary 1926- DLB-279
Putnam, Samuel 1892-1950 . . . . DLB-4; DS-15
Puttenham, George 1529?-1590 . . . . DLB-281
Puzo, Mario 1920-1999 . . . . DLB-6
Pyle, Ernie 1900-1945 . . . . DLB-29
Pyle, Howard
   1853-1911 . . . . DLB-42, 188; DS-13
Pyle, Robert Michael 1947- DLB-275
Pym, Barbara 1913-1980 . . . . . . DLB-14, 207; Y-87
Pynchon, Thomas 1937- DLB-2, 173
Pyramid Books DLB-46
Pyrnelle, Louise-Clarke 1850-1907 . . . . DLB-42
Pythagoras circa 570 B.C.-? DLB-176

Q

Quad, M. (see Lewis, Charles B.)
Quaritch, Bernard 1819-1899 . . . . DLB-184
Quarles, Francis 1592-1644 . . . . DLB-126
The Quarterly Review 1809-1967 . . . . DLB-110
Quasimodo, Salvatore 1901-1968 . . . . DLB-114
Queen, Ellery (see Dannay, Frederic, and
   Manfred B. Lee)
Queen, Frank 1822-1882 . . . . DLB-241
The Queen City Publishing House DLB-49
Queirós, Eça de 1845-1900 . . . . DLB-287
Queneau, Raymond 1903-1976 . . . . . DLB-72, 258
Quennell, Peter 1905-1993 . . . . DLB-155, 195
Quental, Antero de 1842-1891 . . . . DLB-287
Quesada, José Luis 1948- DLB-290
Quesnel, Joseph 1746-1809 . . . . DLB-99
Quiller-Couch, Sir Arthur Thomas
   1863-1944 . . . . DLB-135, 153, 190
Quin, Ann 1936-1973 . . . . DLB-14, 231
Quinault, Philippe 1635-1688 . . . . DLB-268
Quincy, Samuel, of Georgia ?-? DLB-31
Quincy, Samuel, of Massachusetts
   1734-1789 . . . . DLB-31
Quindlen, Anna 1952- DLB-292
Quine, W. V. 1908-2000 . . . . DLB-279
Quinn, Anthony 1915-2001 . . . . DLB-122

Cumulative Index

Quinn, John 1870-1924.................DLB-187
Quiñónez, Naomi 1951-............DLB-209
Quintana, Leroy V. 1944-............DLB-82
Quintana, Miguel de 1671-1748
    A Forerunner of Chicano
        Literature...................DLB-122
Quintilian
    circa A.D. 40-circa A.D. 96.........DLB-211
Quintus Curtius Rufus
    fl. A.D. 35...................DLB-211
Harlin Quist Books...................DLB-46
Quoirez, Françoise (see Sagan, Françoise)

R

Raabe, Wilhelm 1831-1910............DLB-129
Raban, Jonathan 1942-..............DLB-204
Rabe, David 1940-.........DLB-7, 228; Y-91
Raboni, Giovanni 1932-.............DLB-128
Rachilde 1860-1953..............DLB-123, 192
Racin, Kočo 1908-1943..............DLB-147
Racine, Jean 1639-1699..............DLB-268
Rackham, Arthur 1867-1939..........DLB-141
Raczymow, Henri 1948-..............DLB-299
Radauskas, Henrikas
    1910-1970............DLB-220; CDWLB-4
Radcliffe, Ann 1764-1823..........DLB-39, 178
Raddall, Thomas 1903-1994...........DLB-68
Radford, Dollie 1858-1920...........DLB-240
Radichkov, Yordan 1929-............DLB-181
Radiguet, Raymond 1903-1923.........DLB-65
Radishchev, Aleksandr Nikolaevich
    1749-1802..................DLB-150
Radnóti, Miklós
    1909-1944..........DLB-215; CDWLB-4
Radrigán, Juan 1937-...............DLB-305
Radványi, Netty Reiling (see Seghers, Anna)
Rahv, Philip 1908-1973.............DLB-137
Raich, Semen Egorovich 1792-1855.....DLB-205
Raičković, Stevan 1928-............DLB-181
Raiderman (see Parshchikov, Aleksei Maksimovich)
Raimund, Ferdinand Jakob 1790-1836....DLB-90
Raine, Craig 1944-.................DLB-40
Raine, Kathleen 1908-..............DLB-20
Rainis, Jānis 1865-1929.....DLB-220; CDWLB-4
Rainolde, Richard
    circa 1530-1606.........DLB-136, 236
Rainolds, John 1549-1607............DLB-281
Rakić, Milan 1876-1938.....DLB-147; CDWLB-4
Rakosi, Carl 1903-.................DLB-193
Ralegh, Sir Walter
    1554?-1618..........DLB-172; CDBLB-1
Raleigh, Walter
    Style (1897) [excerpt]..............DLB-57
Ralin, Radoy 1923-.................DLB-181
Ralph, Julian 1853-1903.............DLB-23
Ramat, Silvio 1939-.................DLB-128
Ramée, Marie Louise de la (see Ouida)

Ramírez, Sergío 1942-..............DLB-145
Ramke, Bin 1947-...................DLB-120
Ramler, Karl Wilhelm 1725-1798......DLB-97
Ramon Ribeyro, Julio 1929-1994......DLB-145
Ramos, Graciliano 1892-1953.........DLB-307
Ramos, Manuel 1948-................DLB-209
Ramos Sucre, José Antonio 1890-1930...DLB-290
Ramous, Mario 1924-................DLB-128
Rampersad, Arnold 1941-............DLB-111
Ramsay, Allan 1684 or 1685-1758.....DLB-95
Ramsay, David 1749-1815.............DLB-30
Ramsay, Martha Laurens 1759-1811....DLB-200
Ramsey, Frank P. 1903-1930..........DLB-262
Ranch, Hieronimus Justesen
    1539-1607...................DLB-300
Ranck, Katherine Quintana 1942-.....DLB-122
Rand, Avery and Company.............DLB-49
Rand, Ayn 1905-1982....DLB-227, 279; CDALB-7
Rand McNally and Company............DLB-49
Randall, David Anton 1905-1975......DLB-140
Randall, Dudley 1914-...............DLB-41
Randall, Henry S. 1811-1876..........DLB-30
Randall, James G. 1881-1953..........DLB-17
    The Randall Jarrell Symposium: A Small
        Collection of Randall Jarrells........Y-86
    Excerpts From Papers Delivered at the
        Randall Jarrel Symposium..........Y-86
Randall, John Herman, Jr. 1899-1980...DLB-279
Randolph, A. Philip 1889-1979........DLB-91
Anson D. F. Randolph
    [publishing house]...............DLB-49
Randolph, Thomas 1605-1635......DLB-58, 126
Random House........................DLB-46
Rankin, Ian (Jack Harvey) 1960-.....DLB-267
Henry Ranlet [publishing house].......DLB-49
Ransom, Harry 1908-1976.............DLB-187
Ransom, John Crowe
    1888-1974.........DLB-45, 63; CDALB-7
Ransome, Arthur 1884-1967...........DLB-160
Raphael, Frederic 1931-.............DLB-14
Raphaelson, Samson 1896-1983........DLB-44
Rare Book Dealers
    Bertram Rota and His Bookshop.......Y-91
    An Interview with Glenn Horowitz.....Y-90
    An Interview with Otto Penzler.......Y-96
    An Interview with Ralph Sipper........Y-94
    New York City Bookshops in the
        1930s and 1940s: The Recollections
        of Walter Goldwater.............Y-93
Rare Books
    Research in the American Antiquarian
        Book Trade....................Y-97
    Two Hundred Years of Rare Books and
        Literary Collections at the
        University of South Carolina.......Y-00
Rascón Banda, Víctor Hugo 1948-.....DLB-305
Rashi circa 1040-1105................DLB-208
Raskin, Ellen 1928-1984..............DLB-52

Rasputin, Valentin Grigor'evich
    1937-......................DLB-302
Rastell, John 1475?-1536..........DLB-136, 170
Rattigan, Terence
    1911-1977.............DLB-13; CDBLB-7
Raven, Simon 1927-2001..............DLB-271
Ravenhill, Mark 1966-...............DLB-310
Ravnkilde, Adda 1862-1883...........DLB-300
Rawicz, Piotr 1919-1982.............DLB-299
Rawlings, Marjorie Kinnan 1896-1953
    ....DLB-9, 22, 102; DS-17; CDALB-7
Rawlinson, Richard 1690-1755........DLB-213
Rawlinson, Thomas 1681-1725.........DLB-213
Rawls, John 1921-2002...............DLB-279
Raworth, Tom 1938-..................DLB-40
Ray, David 1932-....................DLB-5
Ray, Gordon Norton 1915-1986....DLB-103, 140
Ray, Henrietta Cordelia 1849-1916....DLB-50
Raymond, Ernest 1888-1974...........DLB-191
Raymond, Henry J. 1820-1869......DLB-43, 79
Raymond, René (see Chase, James Hadley)
Razaf, Andy 1895-1973...............DLB-265
Rea, Michael 1927-1996...............Y-97
    Michael M. Rea and the Rea Award for
        the Short Story................Y-97
Reach, Angus 1821-1856..............DLB-70
Read, Herbert 1893-1968...........DLB-20, 149
Read, Martha Meredith..............DLB-200
Read, Opie 1852-1939................DLB-23
Read, Piers Paul 1941-..............DLB-14
Reade, Charles 1814-1884............DLB-21
Reader's Digest Condensed Books......DLB-46
Readers Ulysses Symposium............Y-97
Reading, Peter 1946-................DLB-40
Reading Series in New York City.......Y-96
Reaney, James 1926-.................DLB-68
Rebhun, Paul 1500?-1546.............DLB-179
Rèbora, Clemente 1885-1957..........DLB-114
Rebreanu, Liviu 1885-1944...........DLB-220
Rechy, John 1931-..........DLB-122, 278; Y-82
Redding, J. Saunders 1906-1988.....DLB-63, 76
J. S. Redfield [publishing house].......DLB-49
Redgrove, Peter 1932-...............DLB-40
Redmon, Anne 1943-...................Y-86
Redmond, Eugene B. 1937-............DLB-41
Redol, Alves 1911-1969..............DLB-287
James Redpath [publishing house]......DLB-49
Reed, Henry 1808-1854...............DLB-59
Reed, Henry 1914-1986...............DLB-27
Reed, Ishmael
    1938-........DLB-2, 5, 33, 169, 227; DS-8
Reed, Rex 1938-.....................DLB-185
Reed, Sampson 1800-1880...........DLB-1, 235
Reed, Talbot Baines 1852-1893........DLB-141
Reedy, William Marion 1862-1920.....DLB-91
Reese, Lizette Woodworth 1856-1935....DLB-54

Reese, Thomas 1742-1796 . . . . DLB-37
Reeve, Clara 1729-1807 . . . . DLB-39
 Preface to *The Old English Baron*
  (1778) DLB-39
 The Progress of Romance (1785)
  [excerpt] DLB-39
Reeves, James 1909-1978 . . . . DLB-161
Reeves, John 1926- DLB-88
Reeves-Stevens, Garfield 1953- DLB-251
Régio, José (José Maria dos Reis Pereira)
 1901-1969 . . . . DLB-287
Henry Regnery Company DLB-46
Rêgo, José Lins do 1901-1957 . . . . DLB-307
Rehberg, Hans 1901-1963 . . . . DLB-124
Rehfisch, Hans José 1891-1960 . . . . DLB-124
Reich, Ebbe Kløvedal 1940- DLB-214
Reid, Alastair 1926- DLB-27
Reid, B. L. 1918-1990 . . . . DLB-111
Reid, Christopher 1949- DLB-40
Reid, Forrest 1875-1947 . . . . DLB-153
Reid, Helen Rogers 1882-1970 . . . . DLB-29
Reid, James ?-? DLB-31
Reid, Mayne 1818-1883 . . . . DLB-21, 163
Reid, Thomas 1710-1796 . . . . DLB-31, 252
Reid, V. S. (Vic) 1913-1987 . . . . DLB-125
Reid, Whitelaw 1837-1912 . . . . DLB-23
Reilly and Lee Publishing Company DLB-46
Reimann, Brigitte 1933-1973 . . . . DLB-75
Reinmar der Alte circa 1165-circa 1205 . . . DLB-138
Reinmar von Zweter
 circa 1200-circa 1250 . . . . DLB-138
Reisch, Walter 1903-1983 . . . . DLB-44
Reizei Family DLB-203
Religion
 A Crisis of Culture: The Changing
  Role of Religion in the
  New Republic DLB-37
Remarque, Erich Maria
 1898-1970 . . . . DLB-56; CDWLB-2
Remington, Frederic
 1861-1909 . . . . DLB-12, 186, 188
Remizov, Aleksei Mikhailovich
 1877-1957 . . . . DLB-295
Renaud, Jacques 1943- DLB-60
Renault, Mary 1905-1983 . . . . Y-83
Rendell, Ruth (Barbara Vine)
 1930- DLB-87, 276
Rensselaer, Maria van Cortlandt van
 1645-1689 . . . . DLB-200
Repplier, Agnes 1855-1950 . . . . DLB-221
Reshetnikov, Fedor Mikhailovich
 1841-1871 . . . . DLB-238
Rettenbacher, Simon 1634-1706 . . . . DLB-168
Retz, Jean-François-Paul de Gondi,
 cardinal de 1613-1679 . . . . DLB-268
Reuchlin, Johannes 1455-1522 . . . . DLB-179
Reuter, Christian 1665-after 1712 . . . . . . DLB-168
Fleming H. Revell Company DLB-49
Reverdy, Pierre 1889-1960 . . . . DLB-258

Reuter, Fritz 1810-1874 . . . . DLB-129
Reuter, Gabriele 1859-1941 . . . . DLB-66
Reventlow, Franziska Gräfin zu
 1871-1918 . . . . DLB-66
Review of Reviews Office DLB-112
Rexroth, Kenneth 1905-1982
 . . . . . . DLB-16, 48, 165, 212; Y-82; CDALB-1
 The Commercialization of the Image
  of Revolt DLB-16
Rey, H. A. 1898-1977 . . . . DLB-22
Reyes, Carlos José 1941- DLB-305
Reynal and Hitchcock DLB-46
Reynolds, G. W. M. 1814-1879 . . . . DLB-21
Reynolds, John Hamilton
 1794-1852 . . . . DLB-96
Reynolds, Sir Joshua 1723-1792 . . . . DLB-104
Reynolds, Mack 1917-1983 . . . . DLB-8
Reznikoff, Charles 1894-1976 . . . . DLB-28, 45
Rhetoric
 Continental European Rhetoricians,
  1400-1600, and Their Influence
  in Reaissance England DLB-236
 A Finding Guide to Key Works on
  Microfilm DLB-236
 Glossary of Terms and Definitions of
  Rhetoic and Logic DLB-236
Rhett, Robert Barnwell 1800-1876 . . . . . . DLB-43
Rhode, John 1884-1964 . . . . DLB-77
Rhodes, Eugene Manlove 1869-1934 . . . . DLB-256
Rhodes, James Ford 1848-1927 . . . . DLB-47
Rhodes, Richard 1937- DLB-185
Rhys, Jean 1890-1979
 . . . . DLB-36, 117, 162; CDBLB-7; CDWLB-3
Ribeiro, Bernadim
 fl. ca. 1475/1482-1526/1544 . . . . . . DLB-287
Ricardo, David 1772-1823 . . . . DLB-107, 158
Ricardou, Jean 1932- DLB-83
Rice, Anne (A. N. Roquelare, Anne Rampling)
 1941- DLB-292
Rice, Christopher 1978- DLB-292
Rice, Elmer 1892-1967 . . . . DLB-4, 7
Rice, Grantland 1880-1954 . . . . DLB-29, 171
Rich, Adrienne 1929- DLB-5, 67; CDALB-7
Richard, Mark 1955- DLB-234
Richard de Fournival
 1201-1259 or 1260 . . . . DLB-208
Richards, David Adams 1950- DLB-53
Richards, George circa 1760-1814 . . . . . . DLB-37
Richards, I. A. 1893-1979 . . . . DLB-27
Richards, Laura E. 1850-1943 . . . . DLB-42
Richards, William Carey 1818-1892 . . . . . DLB-73
Grant Richards [publishing house] DLB-112
Richardson, Charles F. 1851-1913 . . . . . . DLB-71
Richardson, Dorothy M. 1873-1957 . . . . . DLB-36
 The Novels of Dorothy Richardson
  (1918), by May Sinclair DLB-36
Richardson, Henry Handel
 (Ethel Florence Lindsay Robertson)
 1870-1946 . . . . DLB-197, 230

Richardson, Jack 1935- DLB-7
Richardson, John 1796-1852 . . . . DLB-99
Richardson, Samuel
 1689-1761 . . . . DLB-39, 154; CDBLB-2
 Introductory Letters from the Second
  Edition of *Pamela* (1741) DLB-39
 Postscript to [the Third Edition of]
  Clarissa (1751) DLB-39
 Preface to the First Edition of
  Pamela (1740) DLB-39
 Preface to the Third Edition of
  Clarissa (1751) [excerpt] DLB-39
 Preface to Volume 1 of *Clarissa*
  (1747) DLB-39
 Preface to Volume 3 of *Clarissa*
  (1748) DLB-39
Richardson, Willis 1889-1977 . . . . DLB-51
Riche, Barnabe 1542-1617 . . . . DLB-136
Richepin, Jean 1849-1926 . . . . DLB-192
Richler, Mordecai 1931-2001 . . . . DLB-53
Richter, Conrad 1890-1968 . . . . DLB-9, 212
Richter, Hans Werner 1908-1993 . . . . DLB-69
Richter, Johann Paul Friedrich
 1763-1825 . . . . DLB-94; CDWLB-2
Joseph Rickerby [publishing house] DLB-106
Rickword, Edgell 1898-1982 . . . . DLB-20
Riddell, Charlotte 1832-1906 . . . . DLB-156
Riddell, John (see Ford, Corey)
Ridge, John Rollin 1827-1867 . . . . DLB-175
Ridge, Lola 1873-1941 . . . . DLB-54
Ridge, William Pett 1859-1930 . . . . DLB-135
Riding, Laura (see Jackson, Laura Riding)
Ridler, Anne 1912- DLB-27
Ridruego, Dionisio 1912-1975 . . . . DLB-108
Riel, Louis 1844-1885 . . . . DLB-99
Riemer, Johannes 1648-1714 . . . . DLB-168
Rifbjerg, Klaus 1931- DLB-214
Riffaterre, Michael 1924- DLB-67
A Conversation between William Riggan
 and Janette Turner Hospital Y-02
Riggs, Lynn 1899-1954 . . . . DLB-175
Riis, Jacob 1849-1914 . . . . DLB-23
John C. Riker [publishing house] DLB-49
Riley, James 1777-1840 . . . . DLB-183
Riley, John 1938-1978 . . . . DLB-40
Rilke, Rainer Maria
 1875-1926 . . . . DLB-81; CDWLB-2
Rimanelli, Giose 1926- DLB-177
Rimbaud, Jean-Nicolas-Arthur
 1854-1891 . . . . DLB-217
Rinehart and Company DLB-46
Ringuet 1895-1960 . . . . DLB-68
Ringwood, Gwen Pharis 1910-1984 . . . . . DLB-88
Rinser, Luise 1911- DLB-69
Ríos, Alberto 1952- DLB-122
Ríos, Isabella 1948- DLB-82
Ripley, Arthur 1895-1961 . . . . DLB-44
Ripley, George 1802-1880 . . . . . DLB-1, 64, 73, 235

The Rising Glory of America:
Three Poems DLB-37

The Rising Glory of America: Written in 1771
(1786), by Hugh Henry Brackenridge
and Philip Freneau DLB-37

Riskin, Robert 1897-1955 .... DLB-26

Risse, Heinz 1898- DLB-69

Rist, Johann 1607-1667 .... DLB-164

Ristikivi, Karl 1912-1977............ DLB-220

Ritchie, Anna Mowatt 1819-1870 ..... DLB-3, 250

Ritchie, Anne Thackeray 1837-1919...... DLB-18

Ritchie, Thomas 1778-1854 .... DLB-43

The Ritz Paris Hemingway Award......... Y-85

    Mario Varga Llosa's Acceptance Speech . . Y-85

Rivard, Adjutor 1868-1945............ DLB-92

Rive, Richard 1931-1989 .... DLB-125, 225

Rivera, José 1955- DLB-249

Rivera, Marina 1942- DLB-122

Rivera, Tomás 1935-1984 .... DLB-82

Rivers, Conrad Kent 1933-1968........ DLB-41

Riverside Press DLB-49

Rivington, James circa 1724-1802........ DLB-43

Charles Rivington [publishing house].... DLB-154

Rivkin, Allen 1903-1990................ DLB-26

Roa Bastos, Augusto 1917- DLB-113

Robbe-Grillet, Alain 1922- DLB-83

Robbins, Tom 1936- Y-80

Roberts, Charles G. D. 1860-1943 ..... DLB-92

Roberts, Dorothy 1906-1993 .... DLB-88

Roberts, Elizabeth Madox
1881-1941 .... DLB-9, 54, 102

Roberts, John (see Swynnerton, Thomas)

Roberts, Keith 1935-2000............ DLB-261

Roberts, Kenneth 1885-1957 .... DLB-9

Roberts, Michèle 1949- DLB-231

Roberts, Theodore Goodridge
1877-1953 .... DLB-92

Roberts, Ursula Wyllie (see Miles, Susan)

Roberts, William 1767-1849 .... DLB-142

James Roberts [publishing house]....... DLB-154

Roberts Brothers..................... DLB-49

A. M. Robertson and Company......... DLB-49

Robertson, Ethel Florence Lindesay
(see Richardson, Henry Handel)

Robertson, William 1721-1793 .... DLB-104

Robin, Leo 1895-1984 .... DLB-265

Robins, Elizabeth 1862-1952 .... DLB-197

Robinson, A. Mary F. (Madame James
Darmesteter, Madame Mary
Duclaux) 1857-1944 .... DLB-240

Robinson, Casey 1903-1979 .... DLB-44

Robinson, Derek.................... Y-02

Robinson, Edwin Arlington
1869-1935 .... DLB-54; CDALB-3

    Review by Derek Robinson of George
    Greenfield's *Rich Dust*............. Y-02

Robinson, Henry Crabb 1775-1867 ..... DLB-107

Robinson, James Harvey 1863-1936 ..... DLB-47

Robinson, Lennox 1886-1958 .... DLB-10

Robinson, Mabel Louise 1874-1962...... DLB-22

Robinson, Marilynne 1943- DLB-206

Robinson, Mary 1758-1800 .... DLB-158

Robinson, Richard circa 1545-1607 ..... DLB-167

Robinson, Therese 1797-1870 .... DLB-59, 133

Robison, Mary 1949- DLB-130

Roblès, Emmanuel 1914-1995 .... DLB-83

Roccatagliata Ceccardi, Ceccardo
1871-1919.................... DLB-114

Rocha, Adolfo Correira da (see Torga, Miguel)

Roche, Billy 1949- DLB-233

Rochester, John Wilmot, Earl of
1647-1680..................... DLB-131

Rochon, Esther 1948- DLB-251

Rock, Howard 1911-1976............ DLB-127

Rockwell, Norman Perceval 1894-1978 .. DLB-188

Rodgers, Carolyn M. 1945- DLB-41

Rodgers, W. R. 1909-1969 .... DLB-20

Rodney, Lester 1911- DLB-241

Rodrigues, Nelson 1912-1980......... DLB-307

Rodríguez, Claudio 1934-1999 .... DLB-134

Rodríguez, Joe D. 1943- DLB-209

Rodríguez, Luis J. 1954- DLB-209

Rodriguez, Richard 1944- DLB-82, 256

Rodríguez Julia, Edgardo 1946- DLB-145

Roe, E. P. 1838-1888 .... DLB-202

Roethke, Theodore
1908-1963 .... DLB-5, 206; CDALB-1

Rogers, Jane 1952- DLB-194

Rogers, Pattiann 1940- DLB-105

Rogers, Samuel 1763-1855 .... DLB-93

Rogers, Will 1879-1935 .... DLB-11

Rohmer, Sax 1883-1959 .... DLB-70

Roiphe, Anne 1935- Y-80

Rojas, Arnold R. 1896-1988 .... DLB-82

Rojas, Fernando de ca. 1475-1541 ...... DLB-286

Rolfe, Edwin (Solomon Fishman)
1909-1954 .... DLB-303

Rolfe, Frederick William
1860-1913 .... DLB-34, 156

Rolland, Romain 1866-1944........... DLB-65

Rolle, Richard circa 1290-1300 - 1340 ... DLB-146

Rölvaag, O. E. 1876-1931 .... DLB-9, 212

Romains, Jules 1885-1972 .... DLB-65

A. Roman and Company DLB-49

Roman de la Rose: Guillaume de Lorris
1200/1205-circa 1230, Jean de
Meun 1235-1240-circa 1305........ DLB-208

Romano, Lalla 1906-2001 ....DLB-177

Romano, Octavio 1923- DLB-122

Rome, Harold 1908-1993............ DLB-265

Romero, Leo 1950- DLB-122

Romero, Lin 1947- DLB-122

Romero, Orlando 1945- DLB-82

Rook, Clarence 1863-1915............ DLB-135

Roosevelt, Theodore
1858-1919 .... DLB-47, 186, 275

Root, Waverley 1903-1982 .... DLB-4

Root, William Pitt 1941- DLB-120

Roquebrune, Robert de 1889-1978..... DLB-68

Rorty, Richard 1931- DLB-246, 279

Rosa, João Guimarães 1908-1967 ...DLB-113, 307

Rosales, Luis 1910-1992............ DLB-134

Roscoe, William 1753-1831 .... DLB-163

Rose, Reginald 1920-2002 .... DLB-26

Rose, Wendy 1948- DLB-175

Rosegger, Peter 1843-1918........... DLB-129

Rosei, Peter 1946- DLB-85

Rosen, Norma 1925- DLB-28

Rosenbach, A. S. W. 1876-1952 ...... DLB-140

Rosenbaum, Ron 1946- DLB-185

Rosenbaum, Thane 1960- DLB-299

Rosenberg, Isaac 1890-1918........ DLB-20, 216

Rosenfeld, Isaac 1918-1956 .... DLB-28

Rosenthal, Harold 1914-1999.......... DLB-241

    Jimmy, Red, and Others: Harold
    Rosenthal Remembers the Stars of
    the Press Box.................. Y-01

Rosenthal, M. L. 1917-1996 .... DLB-5

Rosenwald, Lessing J. 1891-1979 ....DLB-187

Ross, Alexander 1591-1654 .... DLB-151

Ross, Harold 1892-1951.............DLB-137

Ross, Jerry 1926-1955 .... DLB-265

Ross, Leonard Q. (see Rosten, Leo)

Ross, Lillian 1927- DLB-185

Ross, Martin 1862-1915 .... DLB-135

Ross, Sinclair 1908-1996............. DLB-88

Ross, W. W. E. 1894-1966 .... DLB-88

Rosselli, Amelia 1930-1996 .... DLB-128

Rossen, Robert 1908-1966 .... DLB-26

Rosset, Barney Y-02

Rossetti, Christina 1830-1894... DLB-35, 163, 240

Rossetti, Dante Gabriel
1828-1882 .... DLB-35; CDBLB-4

    The Stealthy School of
    Criticism (1871)............... DLB-35

Rossner, Judith 1935- DLB-6

Rostand, Edmond 1868-1918.......... DLB-192

Rosten, Leo 1908-1997 .... DLB-11

Rostenberg, Leona 1908- DLB-140

Rostopchina, Evdokiia Petrovna
1811-1858 .... DLB-205

Rostovsky, Dimitrii 1651-1709 .... DLB-150

Rota, Bertram 1903-1966 .... DLB-201

    Bertram Rota and His Bookshop....... Y-91

Roth, Gerhard 1942- DLB-85, 124

Roth, Henry 1906?-1995 .... DLB-28

Roth, Joseph 1894-1939 .... DLB-85

Roth, Philip
1933- DLB-2, 28, 173; Y-82; CDALB-6

Rothenberg, Jerome 1931- DLB-5, 193
Rothschild Family DLB-184
Rotimi, Ola 1938- DLB-125
Rotrou, Jean 1609-1650 ....DLB-268
Routhier, Adolphe-Basile 1839-1920 .....DLB-99
Routier, Simone 1901-1987 ....DLB-88
George Routledge and Sons...........DLB-106
Roversi, Roberto 1923- DLB-128
Rowe, Elizabeth Singer 1674-1737 .....DLB-39, 95
Rowe, Nicholas 1674-1718.............DLB-84
Rowlands, Ian 1964- DLB-310
Rowlands, Samuel circa 1570-1630 .....DLB-121
Rowlandson, Mary
   circa 1637-circa 1711 ....DLB-24, 200
Rowley, William circa 1585-1626 ....DLB-58
Rowling, J. K.
   The Harry Potter Phenomenon Y-99
Rowse, A. L. 1903-1997................DLB-155
Rowson, Susanna Haswell
   circa 1762-1824 .... DLB-37, 200
Roy, Camille 1870-1943................DLB-92
The G. Ross Roy Scottish Poetry Collection
   at the University of South Carolina Y-89
Roy, Gabrielle 1909-1983 ....DLB-68
Roy, Jules 1907-2000 ....DLB-83
The Royal Court Theatre and the English
   Stage Company.................DLB-13
The Royal Court Theatre and the New
   Drama......................DLB-10
The Royal Shakespeare Company
   at the Swan Y-88
Royall, Anne Newport 1769-1854 ....DLB-43, 248
Royce, Josiah 1855-1916 ....DLB-270
The Roycroft Printing Shop DLB-49
Royde-Smith, Naomi 1875-1964 ....DLB-191
Royster, Vermont 1914-1996 ....DLB-127
Richard Royston [publishing house] DLB-170
Rozanov, Vasilii Vasil'evich
   1856-1919 ....DLB-295
Różewicz, Tadeusz 1921- DLB-232
Ruark, Gibbons 1941- DLB-120
Ruban, Vasilii Grigorevich 1742-1795 ...DLB-150
Rubens, Bernice 1928- DLB-14, 207
Rubião, Murilo 1916-1991.............DLB-307
Rubina, Dina Il'inichna 1953- DLB-285
Rubinshtein, Lev Semenovich 1947- DLB-285
Rudd and Carleton DLB-49
Rudd, Steele (Arthur Hoey Davis).....DLB-230
Rudkin, David 1936- DLB-13
Rudnick, Paul 1957- DLB-266
Rudnicki, Adolf 1909-1990 ....DLB-299
Rudolf von Ems circa 1200-circa 1254 ...DLB-138
Ruffin, Josephine St. Pierre 1842-1924 ....DLB-79
Ruganda, John 1941- DLB-157
Ruggles, Henry Joseph 1813-1906 ......DLB-64
Ruiz de Burton, María Amparo
   1832-1895 ....DLB-209, 221

Rukeyser, Muriel 1913-1980............DLB-48
Rule, Jane 1931- DLB-60
Rulfo, Juan 1918-1986......DLB-113; CDWLB-3
Rumaker, Michael 1932- DLB-16
Rumens, Carol 1944- DLB-40
Rummo, Paul-Eerik 1942- DLB-232
Runyon, Damon
   1880-1946................ DLB-11, 86, 171
Ruodlieb circa 1050-1075...............DLB-148
Rush, Benjamin 1746-1813 ....DLB-37
Rush, Rebecca 1779-?..................DLB-200
Rushdie, Salman 1947- DLB-194
Rusk, Ralph L. 1888-1962..............DLB-103
Ruskin, John
   1819-1900 ......DLB-55, 163, 190; CDBLB-4
Russ, Joanna 1937- DLB-8
Russell, Benjamin 1761-1845...........DLB-43
Russell, Bertrand 1872-1970........DLB-100, 262
Russell, Charles Edward 1860-1941 ......DLB-25
Russell, Charles M. 1864-1926 ....DLB-188
Russell, Eric Frank 1905-1978 ....DLB-255
Russell, Fred 1906-2003...............DLB-241
Russell, George William (see AE)
Russell, Countess Mary Annette Beauchamp
   (see Arnim, Elizabeth von)
Russell, Willy 1947- DLB-233
B. B. Russell and Company.............DLB-49
R. H. Russell and Son DLB-49
Rutebeuf flourished 1249-1277 ....DLB-208
Rutherford, Mark 1831-1913............DLB-18
Ruxton, George Frederick
   1821-1848 ....DLB-186
R-va, Zeneida (see Gan, Elena Andreevna)
Ryan, James 1952- DLB-267
Ryan, Michael 1946- Y-82
Ryan, Oscar 1904- DLB-68
Rybakov, Anatolii Naumovich
   1911-1994 ....DLB-302
Ryder, Jack 1871-1936.................DLB-241
Ryga, George 1932-1987 ....DLB-60
Rylands, Enriqueta Augustina Tennant
   1843-1908 ....DLB-184
Rylands, John 1801-1888...............DLB-184
Ryle, Gilbert 1900-1976 ....DLB-262
Ryleev, Kondratii Fedorovich
   1795-1826 ....DLB-205
Rymer, Thomas 1643?-1713 ....DLB-101
Ryskind, Morrie 1895-1985.............DLB-26
Rzhevsky, Aleksei Andreevich
   1737-1804....................DLB-150

S

The Saalfield Publishing Company.......DLB-46
Saba, Umberto 1883-1957 ....DLB-114
Sábato, Ernesto 1911- DLB-145; CDWLB-3
Saberhagen, Fred 1930- DLB-8
Sabin, Joseph 1821-1881 ....DLB-187

Sabino, Fernando (Fernando Tavares Sabino)
   1923- DLB-307
Sacer, Gottfried Wilhelm 1635-1699.....DLB-168
Sachs, Hans 1494-1576 ..... DLB-179; CDWLB-2
Sá-Carneiro, Mário de 1890-1916.......DLB-287
Sack, John 1930- DLB-185
Sackler, Howard 1929-1982 ....DLB-7
Sackville, Lady Margaret 1881-1963.....DLB-240
Sackville, Thomas 1536-1608 and
   Norton, Thomas 1532-1584 ....DLB-62
Sackville, Thomas 1536-1608 ....DLB-132
Sackville-West, Edward 1901-1965 ......DLB-191
Sackville-West, Vita 1892-1962 ......DLB-34, 195
Sá de Miranda, Francisco de
   1481-1588? DLB-287
Sadlier, Mary Anne 1820-1903 ....DLB-99
D. and J. Sadlier and Company.........DLB-49
Sadoff, Ira 1945- DLB-120
Sadoveanu, Mihail 1880-1961 ....DLB-220
Sadur, Nina Nikolaevna 1950- DLB-285
Sáenz, Benjamin Alire 1954- DLB-209
Saenz, Jaime 1921-1986...........DLB-145, 283
Saffin, John circa 1626-1710............DLB-24
Sagan, Françoise 1935- DLB-83
Sage, Robert 1899-1962.................DLB-4
Sagel, Jim 1947- DLB-82
Sagendorph, Robb Hansell 1900-1970....DLB-137
Sahagún, Carlos 1938- DLB-108
Sahkomaapii, Piitai (see Highwater, Jamake)
Sahl, Hans 1902-1993 ....DLB-69
Said, Edward W. 1935- DLB-67
Saigyō 1118-1190 ....DLB-203
Saiko, George 1892-1962...............DLB-85
Sainte-Beuve, Charles-Augustin
   1804-1869 ....DLB-217
Saint-Exupéry, Antoine de 1900-1944 .....DLB-72
St. John, J. Allen 1872-1957 ....DLB-188
St John, Madeleine 1942- DLB-267
St. Johns, Adela Rogers 1894-1988 ......DLB-29
St. Omer, Garth 1931- DLB-117
Saint Pierre, Michel de 1916-1987 ....DLB-83
St. Dominic's Press DLB-112
The St. John's College Robert Graves Trust.. Y-96
St. Martin's Press....................DLB-46
St. Nicholas 1873-1881.................. DS-13
Saintsbury, George 1845-1933....... DLB-57, 149
   "Modern English Prose" (1876) DLB-57
   The Present State of the English
      Novel (1892), ...DLB-18
Saiokuken Sōchō 1448-1532 ....DLB-203
Saki (see Munro, H. H.)
Salaam, Kalamu ya 1947- DLB-38
Šalamun, Tomaž 1941- ...DLB-181; CDWLB-4
Salas, Floyd 1931- DLB-82
Sálaz-Marquez, Rubén 1935- DLB-122
Salcedo, Hugo 1964- DLB-305

Cumulative Index

Salemson, Harold J. 1910-1988..........DLB-4
Salesbury, William 1520?-1584?........DLB-281
Salinas, Luis Omar 1937-............DLB-82
Salinas, Pedro 1891-1951.............DLB-134
Salinger, J. D. 1919-..........DLB-2, 102, 173; CDALB-1
Salkey, Andrew 1928-............DLB-125
Sallust circa 86 B.C.-35 B.C.
..................DLB-211; CDWLB-1
Salt, Waldo 1914-1987...............DLB-44
Salter, James 1925-................DLB-130
Salter, Mary Jo 1954-..............DLB-120
Saltus, Edgar 1855-1921.............DLB-202
Saltykov, Mikhail Evgrafovich 1826-1889...................DLB-238
Salustri, Carlo Alberto (see Trilussa)
Salverson, Laura Goodman 1890-1970....DLB-92
Samain, Albert 1858-1900...........DLB-217
Sampson, Richard Henry (see Hull, Richard)
Samuels, Ernest 1903-1996...........DLB-111
Sanborn, Franklin Benjamin 1831-1917..............DLB-1, 223
Sánchez, Luis Rafael 1936-......DLB-145, 305
Sánchez, Philomeno "Phil" 1917-.....DLB-122
Sánchez, Ricardo 1941-1995..........DLB-82
Sánchez, Saúl 1943-...............DLB-209
Sanchez, Sonia 1934-..........DLB-41; DS-8
Sánchez de Arévalo, Rodrigo 1404-1470...................DLB-286
Sánchez, Florencio 1875-1910..........DLB-305
Sand, George 1804-1876..........DLB-119, 192
Sandburg, Carl 1878-1967...........DLB-17, 54; CDALB-3
Sandel, Cora (Sara Fabricius) 1880-1974....................DLB-297
Sandemose, Aksel 1899-1965..........DLB-297
Sanders, Edward 1939-..........DLB-16, 244
Sanderson, Robert 1587-1663.........DLB-281
Sandoz, Mari 1896-1966.........DLB-9, 212
Sandwell, B. K. 1876-1954............DLB-92
Sandy, Stephen 1934-..............DLB-165
Sandys, George 1578-1644........DLB-24, 121
Sangster, Charles 1822-1893..........DLB-99
Sanguineti, Edoardo 1930-...........DLB-128
Sanjōnishi Sanetaka 1455-1537........DLB-203
San Pedro, Diego de fl. ca. 1492.......DLB-286
Sansay, Leonora ?-after 1823.........DLB-200
Sansom, William 1912-1976...........DLB-139
Sant'Anna, Affonso Romano de 1937-......................DLB-307
Santayana, George 1863-1952......DLB-54, 71, 246, 270; DS-13
Santiago, Danny 1911-1988..........DLB-122
Santillana, Marqués de (Íñigo López de Mendoza) 1398-1458...................DLB-286
Santmyer, Helen Hooven 1895-1986.......Y-84
Sanvitale, Francesca 1928-..........DLB-196

Sapidus, Joannes 1490-1561.........DLB-179
Sapir, Edward 1884-1939.............DLB-92
Sapper (see McNeile, Herman Cyril)
Sappho circa 620 B.C.-circa 550 B.C.
..................DLB-176; CDWLB-1
Saramago, José 1922-.........DLB-287; Y-98
 Nobel Lecture 1998: How Characters Became the Masters and the Author Their Apprentice..................Y-98
Sarban (John W. Wall) 1910-1989......DLB-255
Sardou, Victorien 1831-1908..........DLB-192
Sarduy, Severo 1937-1993............DLB-113
Sargent, Pamela 1948-................DLB-8
Saro-Wiwa, Ken 1941-..............DLB-157
Saroyan, Aram
 Rites of Passage [on William Saroyan]....Y-83
Saroyan, William 1908-1981.....DLB-7, 9, 86; Y-81; CDALB-7
Sarraute, Nathalie 1900-1999..........DLB-83
Sarrazin, Albertine 1937-1967..........DLB-83
Sarris, Greg 1952-................DLB-175
Sarton, May 1912-1995..........DLB-48; Y-81
Sartre, Jean-Paul 1905-1980........DLB-72, 296
Sassoon, Siegfried 1886-1967..........DLB-20, 191; DS-18
 A Centenary Essay..................Y-86
 Tributes from Vivien F. Clarke and Michael Thorpe..................Y-86
Sata Ineko 1904-.................DLB-180
Saturday Review Press.................DLB-46
Saunders, James 1925-..............DLB-13
Saunders, John Monk 1897-1940.......DLB-26
Saunders, Margaret Marshall 1861-1947......................DLB-92
Saunders and Otley.................DLB-106
Saussure, Ferdinand de 1857-1913......DLB-242
Savage, James 1784-1873.............DLB-30
Savage, Marmion W. 1803?-1872........DLB-21
Savage, Richard 1697?-1743...........DLB-95
Savard, Félix-Antoine 1896-1982........DLB-68
Savery, Henry 1791-1842.............DLB-230
Saville, (Leonard) Malcolm 1901-1982...DLB-160
Savinio, Alberto 1891-1952...........DLB-264
Sawyer, Robert J. 1960-............DLB-251
Sawyer, Ruth 1880-1970..............DLB-22
Sayers, Dorothy L. 1893-1957.....DLB-10, 36, 77, 100; CDBLB-6
 The Dorothy L. Sayers Society.........Y-98
Sayle, Charles Edward 1864-1924......DLB-184
Sayles, John Thomas 1950-..........DLB-44
Sbarbaro, Camillo 1888-1967..........DLB-114
Scalapino, Leslie 1947-.............DLB-193
Scannell, Vernon 1922-..............DLB-27
Scarry, Richard 1919-1994............DLB-61
Schack, Hans Egede 1820-1859.........DLB-300
Schaefer, Jack 1907-1991.............DLB-212
Schaeffer, Albrecht 1885-1950..........DLB-66

Schaeffer, Susan Fromberg 1941-...DLB-28, 299
Schaff, Philip 1819-1893................DS-13
Schaper, Edzard 1908-1984...........DLB-69
Scharf, J. Thomas 1843-1898..........DLB-47
Schede, Paul Melissus 1539-1602........DLB-179
Scheffel, Joseph Viktor von 1826-1886...DLB-129
Scheffler, Johann 1624-1677..........DLB-164
Schelling, Friedrich Wilhelm Joseph von 1775-1854....................DLB-90
Scherer, Wilhelm 1841-1886..........DLB-129
Scherfig, Hans 1905-1979............DLB-214
Schickele, René 1883-1940...........DLB-66
Schiff, Dorothy 1903-1989............DLB-127
Schiller, Friedrich 1759-1805.............DLB-94; CDWLB-2
Schirmer, David 1623-1687...........DLB-164
Schlaf, Johannes 1862-1941..........DLB-118
Schlegel, August Wilhelm 1767-1845.....DLB-94
Schlegel, Dorothea 1763-1839.........DLB-90
Schlegel, Friedrich 1772-1829.........DLB-90
Schleiermacher, Friedrich 1768-1834.....DLB-90
Schlesinger, Arthur M., Jr. 1917-......DLB-17
Schlumberger, Jean 1877-1968..........DLB-65
Schmid, Eduard Hermann Wilhelm (see Edschmid, Kasimir)
Schmidt, Arno 1914-1979.............DLB-69
Schmidt, Johann Kaspar (see Stirner, Max)
Schmidt, Michael 1947-..............DLB-40
Schmidtbonn, Wilhelm August 1876-1952.....................DLB-118
Schmitz, Aron Hector (see Svevo, Italo)
Schmitz, James H. 1911-1981............DLB-8
Schnabel, Johann Gottfried 1692-1760...DLB-168
Schnackenberg, Gjertrud 1953-......DLB-120
Schnitzler, Arthur 1862-1931.........DLB-81, 118; CDWLB-2
Schnurre, Wolfdietrich 1920-1989.......DLB-69
Schocken Books.....................DLB-46
Scholartis Press....................DLB-112
Scholderer, Victor 1880-1971..........DLB-201
The Schomburg Center for Research in Black Culture..................DLB-76
Schönbeck, Virgilio (see Giotti, Virgilio)
Schönherr, Karl 1867-1943...........DLB-118
Schoolcraft, Jane Johnston 1800-1841.....DLB-175
School Stories, 1914-1960.............DLB-160
Schopenhauer, Arthur 1788-1860........DLB-90
Schopenhauer, Johanna 1766-1838......DLB-90
Schorer, Mark 1908-1977.............DLB-103
Schottelius, Justus Georg 1612-1676.....DLB-164
Schouler, James 1839-1920............DLB-47
Schoultz, Solveig von 1907-1996........DLB-259
Schrader, Paul 1946-................DLB-44
Schreiner, Olive 1855-1920..........DLB-18, 156, 190, 225
Schroeder, Andreas 1946-............DLB-53

Schubart, Christian Friedrich Daniel 1739-1791 .... DLB-97
Schubert, Gotthilf Heinrich 1780-1860 .... DLB-90
Schücking, Levin 1814-1883 .... DLB-133
Schulberg, Budd 1914- DLB-6, 26, 28; Y-81
  Excerpts from USC Presentation [on F. Scott Fitzgerald] Y-96
F. J. Schulte and Company............. DLB-49
Schulz, Bruno 1892-1942.... DLB-215; CDWLB-4
Schulze, Hans (see Praetorius, Johannes)
Schupp, Johann Balthasar 1610-1661..... DLB-164
Schurz, Carl 1829-1906 .... DLB-23
Schuyler, George S. 1895-1977 ...... DLB-29, 51
Schuyler, James 1923-1991 .... DLB-5, 169
Schwartz, Delmore 1913-1966 .... DLB-28, 48
Schwartz, Jonathan 1938- Y-82
Schwartz, Lynne Sharon 1939- DLB-218
Schwarz, Sibylle 1621-1638 .... DLB-164
Schwarz-Bart, Andre 1928- DLB-299
Schwerner, Armand 1927-1999 .... DLB-165
Schwob, Marcel 1867-1905 .... DLB-123
Sciascia, Leonardo 1921-1989 .... DLB-177
Science Fiction and Fantasy
  Documents in British Fantasy and Science Fiction DLB-178
  Hugo Awards and Nebula Awards DLB-8
  The Iconography of Science-Fiction Art DLB-8
  The New Wave................ DLB-8
  Paperback Science Fiction DLB-8
  Science Fantasy DLB-8
  Science-Fiction Fandom and Conventions DLB-8
  Science-Fiction Fanzines: The Time Binders DLB-8
  Science-Fiction Films DLB-8
  Science Fiction Writers of America and the Nebula Award DLB-8
  Selected Science-Fiction Magazines and Anthologies................. DLB-8
  A World Chronology of Important Science Fiction Works (1818-1979) DLB-8
  The Year in Science Fiction and Fantasy. Y-00, 01
Scot, Reginald circa 1538-1599 .... DLB-136
Scotellaro, Rocco 1923-1953 .... DLB-128
Scott, Alicia Anne (Lady John Scott) 1810-1900 .... DLB-240
Scott, Catharine Amy Dawson 1865-1934 .... DLB-240
Scott, Dennis 1939-1991 .... DLB-125
Scott, Dixon 1881-1915 .... DLB-98
Scott, Duncan Campbell 1862-1947....... DLB-92
Scott, Evelyn 1893-1963 .... DLB-9, 48
Scott, F. R. 1899-1985 .... DLB-88
Scott, Frederick George 1861-1944 ...... DLB-92
Scott, Geoffrey 1884-1929 .... DLB-149
Scott, Harvey W. 1838-1910 .... DLB-23

Scott, Lady Jane (see Scott, Alicia Anne)
Scott, Paul 1920-1978............. DLB-14, 207
Scott, Sarah 1723-1795 .... DLB-39
Scott, Tom 1918- DLB-27
Scott, Sir Walter 1771-1832 ..... DLB-93, 107, 116, 144, 159; CDBLB-3
Scott, William Bell 1811-1890 .... DLB-32
Walter Scott Publishing Company Limited DLB-112
William R. Scott [publishing house]......DLB-46
Scott-Heron, Gil 1949- DLB-41
Scribe, Eugene 1791-1861 .... DLB-192
Scribner, Arthur Hawley 1859-1932 .... DS-13, 16
Scribner, Charles 1854-1930 .... DS-13, 16
Scribner, Charles, Jr. 1921-1995 .... Y-95
  Reminiscences.................... DS-17
Charles Scribner's Sons DLB-49; DS-13, 16, 17
  Archives of Charles Scribner's Sons DS-17
Scribner's Magazine.................. DS-13
Scribner's Monthly................... DS-13
Scripps, E. W. 1854-1926 .... DLB-25
Scudder, Horace Elisha 1838-1902 .... DLB-42, 71
Scudder, Vida Dutton 1861-1954 .... DLB-71
Scudéry, Madeleine de 1607-1701 .... DLB-268
Scupham, Peter 1933- DLB-40
Seabrook, William 1886-1945 .... DLB-4
Seabury, Samuel 1729-1796 .... DLB-31
Seacole, Mary Jane Grant 1805-1881..... DLB-166
The Seafarer circa 970 .... DLB-146
Sealsfield, Charles (Carl Postl) 1793-1864 .... DLB-133, 186
Searle, John R. 1932- DLB-279
Sears, Edward I. 1819?-1876 .... DLB-79
Sears Publishing Company DLB-46
Seaton, George 1911-1979 .... DLB-44
Seaton, William Winston 1785-1866...... DLB-43
Martin Secker [publishing house]........DLB-112
Martin Secker, and Warburg Limited DLB-112
The "Second Generation" Holocaust Novel.................... DLB-299
Sedgwick, Arthur George 1844-1915...... DLB-64
Sedgwick, Catharine Maria 1789-1867 .... DLB-1, 74, 183, 239, 243
Sedgwick, Ellery 1872-1960............ DLB-91
Sedgwick, Eve Kosofsky 1950- DLB-246
Sedley, Sir Charles 1639-1701 .... DLB-131
Seeberg, Peter 1925-1999 .... DLB-214
Seeger, Alan 1888-1916 .... DLB-45
Seers, Eugene (see Dantin, Louis)
Segal, Erich 1937- Y-86
Segal, Lore 1928- DLB-299
Šegedin, Petar 1909- DLB-181
Seghers, Anna 1900-1983 .... DLB-69; CDWLB-2
Seid, Ruth (see Sinclair, Jo)
Seidel, Frederick Lewis 1936- Y-84
Seidel, Ina 1885-1974................. DLB-56

Seifert, Jaroslav 1901-1986 .... DLB-215; Y-84; CDWLB-4
  Jaroslav Seifert Through the Eyes of the English-Speaking Reader Y-84
  Three Poems by Jaroslav Seifert........ Y-84
Seifullina, Lidiia Nikolaevna 1889-1954 .. DLB-272
Seigenthaler, John 1927- DLB-127
Seizin Press DLB-112
Séjour, Victor 1817-1874 ....DLB-50
Séjour Marcou et Ferrand, Juan Victor (see Séjour, Victor)
Sekowski, Jósef-Julian, Baron Brambeus (see Senkovsky, Osip Ivanovich)
Selby, Bettina 1934- DLB-204
Selby, Hubert, Jr. 1928- DLB-2, 227
Selden, George 1929-1989............. DLB-52
Selden, John 1584-1654 .... DLB-213
Selenić, Slobodan 1933-1995 .... DLB-181
Self, Edwin F. 1920- DLB-137
Self, Will 1961- DLB-207
Seligman, Edwin R. A. 1861-1939 .... DLB-47
Selimović, Meša 1910-1982 .... DLB-181; CDWLB-4
Sellars, Wilfrid 1912-1989 .... DLB-279
Sellings, Arthur (Arthur Gordon Ley) 1911-1968 .... DLB-261
Selous, Frederick Courteney 1851-1917 .. DLB-174
Seltzer, Chester E. (see Muro, Amado)
Thomas Seltzer [publishing house] DLB-46
Selvon, Sam 1923-1994 ..... DLB-125; CDWLB-3
Semel, Nava 1954- DLB-299
Semmes, Raphael 1809-1877 .... DLB-189
Senancour, Etienne de 1770-1846 .... DLB-119
Sena, Jorge de 1919-1978............. DLB-287
Sendak, Maurice 1928- DLB-61
Seneca the Elder circa 54 B.C.-circa A.D. 40 .... DLB-211
Seneca the Younger circa 1 B.C.-A.D. 65 ...... DLB-211; CDWLB-1
Senécal, Eva 1905- DLB-92
Sengstacke, John 1912-1997 .... DLB-127
Senior, Olive 1941- DLB-157
Senkovsky, Osip Ivanovich (Józef-Julian Sekowski, Baron Brambeus) 1800-1858................... DLB-198
Šenoa, August 1838-1881 ... DLB-147; CDWLB-4
Sepamla, Sipho 1932- DLB-157, 225
Serafimovich, Aleksandr Serafimovich (Aleksandr Serafimovich Popov) 1863-1949 .... DLB-272
Serao, Matilde 1856-1927 .... DLB-264
Seredy, Kate 1899-1975 .... DLB-22
Sereni, Vittorio 1913-1983............ DLB-128
William Seres [publishing house] DLB-170
Sergeev-Tsensky, Sergei Nikolaevich (Sergei Nikolaevich Sergeev) 1875-1958 .... DLB-272
Serling, Rod 1924-1975 ....DLB-26
Sernine, Daniel 1955- DLB-251

Serote, Mongane Wally 1944- . . . DLB-125, 225	Shapir, Ol'ga Andreevna 1850-1916. . . . . DLB-295	Shepard, Sam 1943- DLB-7, 212
Serraillier, Ian 1912-1994 . . . . DLB-161	Shapiro, Karl 1913-2000. . . . . DLB-48	Shepard, Thomas I, 1604 or 1605-1649. . . DLB-24
Serrano, Nina 1934- DLB-122	Sharon Publications DLB-46	Shepard, Thomas, II, 1635-1677 . . . . DLB-24
Service, Robert 1874-1958 . . . . DLB-92	Sharov, Vladimir Aleksandrovich 1952- DLB-285	Shepherd, Luke flourished 1547-1554 . . . DLB-136
Sessler, Charles 1854-1935 . . . . DLB-187	Sharp, Margery 1905-1991 . . . . DLB-161	Sherburne, Edward 1616-1702 . . . . DLB-131
Seth, Vikram 1952- DLB-120, 271	Sharp, William 1855-1905 . . . . DLB-156	Sheridan, Frances 1724-1766. . . . . DLB-39, 84
Seton, Elizabeth Ann 1774-1821 . . . . DLB-200	Sharpe, Tom 1928- DLB-14, 231	Sheridan, Richard Brinsley 1751-1816. . . . . DLB-89; CDBLB-2
Seton, Ernest Thompson 1860-1942 . . . . DLB-92; DS-13	Shaw, Albert 1857-1947 . . . . DLB-91	Sherman, Francis 1871-1926. . . . . DLB-92
Seton, John circa 1509-1567 . . . . DLB-281	Shaw, George Bernard 1856-1950 . . . . . . .DLB-10, 57, 190, CDBLB-6	Sherman, Martin 1938- DLB-228
Setouchi Harumi 1922- DLB-182	The Bernard Shaw Society. Y-99	Sherriff, R. C. 1896-1975 . . . . . .DLB-10, 191, 233
Settle, Mary Lee 1918- DLB-6	"Stage Censorship: The Rejected Statement" (1911) [excerpts]. DLB-10	Sherrod, Blackie 1919- DLB-241
Seume, Johann Gottfried 1763-1810 . . . . . DLB-94	Shaw, Henry Wheeler 1818-1885 . . . . DLB-11	Sherry, Norman 1935- DLB-155
Seuse, Heinrich 1295?-1366 . . . . .DLB-179	Shaw, Irwin 1913-1984 . . . . . DLB-6, 102; Y-84; CDALB-1	Tribute to Graham Greene Y-91
Seuss, Dr. (see Geisel, Theodor Seuss)	Shaw, Joseph T. 1874-1952. . . . . DLB-137	Sherry, Richard 1506-1551 or 1555 . . . . . DLB-236
Severianin, Igor' 1887-1941. . . . . DLB-295	"As I Was Saying," Joseph T. Shaw's Editorial Rationale in Black Mask (January 1927) DLB-137	Sherwood, Mary Martha 1775-1851 . . . . . DLB-163
Severin, Timothy 1940- DLB-204		Sherwood, Robert E. 1896-1955 . . .DLB-7, 26, 249
Sévigné, Marie de Rabutin Chantal, Madame de 1626-1696 . . . . DLB-268	Shaw, Mary 1854-1929. . . . . DLB-228	Shevyrev, Stepan Petrovich 1806-1864 . . . . DLB-205
Sewall, Joseph 1688-1769 . . . . DLB-24	Shaw, Robert 1927-1978 . . . . DLB-13, 14	Shiel, M. P. 1865-1947 . . . . DLB-153
Sewall, Richard B. 1908- DLB-111	Shaw, Robert B. 1947- DLB-120	Shiels, George 1886-1949 . . . . DLB-10
Sewall, Samuel 1652-1730. . . . . DLB-24	Shawn, Wallace 1943- DLB-266	Shiga Naoya 1883-1971 . . . . DLB-180
Sewell, Anna 1820-1878 . . . . DLB-163	Shawn, William 1907-1992 . . . . DLB-137	Shiina Rinzō 1911-1973 . . . . DLB-182
Sexton, Anne 1928-1974 . . . DLB-5, 169; CDALB-1	Frank Shay [publishing house] DLB-46	Shikishi Naishinnō 1153?-1201 . . . . DLB-203
Seymour-Smith, Martin 1928-1998. . . . . . DLB-155	Shchedrin, N. (see Saltykov, Mikhail Evgrafovich)	Shillaber, Benjamin Penhallow 1814-1890 . . . . DLB-1, 11, 235
Sgorlon, Carlo 1930- DLB-196	Shcherbakova, Galina Nikolaevna 1932- DLB-285	
Shaara, Michael 1929-1988. . . . . Y-83		Shimao Toshio 1917-1986 . . . . DLB-182
Shabel'skaia, Aleksandra Stanislavovna 1845-1921 . . . . DLB-238	Shcherbina, Nikolai Fedorovich 1821-1869 . . . . .DLB-277	Shimazaki Tōson 1872-1943. . . . . DLB-180
Shadwell, Thomas 1641?-1692. . . . . DLB-80	Shea, John Gilmary 1824-1892. . . . . DLB-30	Shimose, Pedro 1940- DLB-283
Shaffer, Anthony 1926- DLB-13	Sheaffer, Louis 1912-1993 . . . . DLB-103	Shine, Ted 1931- DLB-38
Shaffer, Peter 1926- DLB-13, 233; CDBLB-8	Sheahan, Henry Beston (see Beston, Henry)	Shinkei 1406-1475. . . . . DLB-203
Shaftesbury, Anthony Ashley Cooper, Third Earl of 1671-1713 . . . . DLB-101	Shearing, Joseph 1886-1952 . . . . DLB-70	Ship, Reuben 1915-1975 . . . . DLB-88
	Shebbeare, John 1709-1788 . . . . DLB-39	Shirer, William L. 1904-1993 . . . . DLB-4
Shaginian, Marietta Sergeevna 1888-1982 . . . . DLB-272	Sheckley, Robert 1928- DLB-8	Shirinsky-Shikhmatov, Sergii Aleksandrovich 1783-1837. . . . . DLB-150
Shairp, Mordaunt 1887-1939 . . . . DLB-10	Shedd, William G. T. 1820-1894 . . . . DLB-64	
Shakespeare, Nicholas 1957- DLB-231	Sheed, Wilfrid 1930- DLB-6	Shirley, James 1596-1666 . . . . DLB-58
Shakespeare, William 1564-1616. . . . . . DLB-62, 172, 263; CDBLB-1	Sheed and Ward [U.S.]. DLB-46	Shishkov, Aleksandr Semenovich 1753-1841. . . . . DLB-150
The New Variorum Shakespeare Y-85	Sheed and Ward Limited [U.K.] DLB-112	Shockley, Ann Allen 1927- DLB-33
Shakespeare and Montaigne: A Symposium by Jules Furthman Y-02	Sheldon, Alice B. (see Tiptree, James, Jr.)	Sholokhov, Mikhail Aleksandrovich 1905-1984 . . . . .DLB-272
	Sheldon, Edward 1886-1946. . . . . DLB-7	
$6,166,000 for a Book! Observations on The Shakespeare First Folio: The History of the Book Y-01	Sheldon and Company. DLB-49	Shōno Junzō 1921- DLB-182
	Sheller, Aleksandr Konstantinovich 1838-1900 . . . . DLB-238	Shore, Arabella 1820?-1901 . . . . DLB-199
Taylor-Made Shakespeare? Or Is "Shall I Die?" the Long-Lost Text of Bottom's Dream? Y-85		Shore, Louisa 1824-1895 . . . . DLB-199
	Shelley, Mary Wollstonecraft 1797-1851 . . . . .DLB-110, 116, 159, 178; CDBLB-3	Short, Luke (see Glidden, Frederick Dilley)
The Shakespeare Globe Trust Y-93		Peter Short [publishing house] DLB-170
Shakespeare Head Press DLB-112	Preface to Frankenstein; or, The Modern Prometheus (1818) DLB-178	Shorter, Dora Sigerson 1866-1918 . . . . . . DLB-240
Shakhova, Elisaveta Nikitichna 1822-1899 .DLB-277		Shorthouse, Joseph Henry 1834-1903 . . . . DLB-18
	Shelley, Percy Bysshe 1792-1822 . . . . . DLB-96, 110, 158; CDBLB-3	Short Stories Michael M. Rea and the Rea Award for the Short Story. Y-97
Shakhovskoi, Aleksandr Aleksandrovich 1777-1846 . . . . DLB-150	Shelnutt, Eve 1941- DLB-130	
Shalamov, Varlam Tikhonovich 1907-1982 . . . . DLB-302	Shenshin (see Fet, Afanasii Afanas'evich)	The Year in Short Stories. Y-87
	Shenstone, William 1714-1763 . . . . DLB-95	The Year in the Short Story Y-88, 90–93
Shange, Ntozake 1948- DLB-38, 249	Shepard, Clark and Brown. DLB-49	Shōtetsu 1381-1459. . . . . DLB-203
Shapcott, Thomas W. 1935- DLB-289	Shepard, Ernest Howard 1879-1976 . . . . . DLB-160	Showalter, Elaine 1941- DLB-67
		Shreve, Anita 1946- DLB-292

446

Shukshin, Vasilii Makarovich
  1929-1974 .... DLB-302
Shulevitz, Uri 1935- DLB-61
Shulman, Max 1919-1988 .... DLB-11
Shute, Henry A. 1856-1943 .... DLB-9
Shute, Nevil (Nevil Shute Norway)
  1899-1960 .... DLB-255
Shuttle, Penelope 1947- DLB-14, 40
Shvarts, Evgenii L'vovich 1896-1958 ..... DLB-272
Sibbes, Richard 1577-1635 .... DLB-151
Sibiriak, D. (see Mamin, Dmitrii Narkisovich)
Siddal, Elizabeth Eleanor 1829-1862 ..... DLB-199
Sidgwick, Ethel 1877-1970 .... DLB-197
Sidgwick, Henry 1838-1900 .... DLB-262
Sidgwick and Jackson Limited DLB-112
Sidney, Margaret (see Lothrop, Harriet M.)
Sidney, Mary 1561-1621 .... DLB-167
Sidney, Sir Philip
  1554-1586 .... DLB-167; CDBLB-1
  An Apologie for Poetrie (the Olney edition,
  1595, of *Defence of Poesie*) DLB-167
Sidney's Press DLB-49
Sierra, Rubén 1946- DLB-122
Sierra Club Books DLB-49
Siger of Brabant circa 1240-circa 1284... DLB-115
Sigourney, Lydia Huntley
  1791-1865 ...... DLB-1, 42, 73, 183, 239, 243
Silkin, Jon 1930-1997 .... DLB-27
Silko, Leslie Marmon
  1948- DLB-143, 175, 256, 275
Silliman, Benjamin 1779-1864 .... DLB-183
Silliman, Ron 1946- DLB-169
Silliphant, Stirling 1918-1996 .... DLB-26
Sillitoe, Alan 1928- DLB-14, 139; CDBLB-8
  Tribute to J. B. Priestly Y-84
Silman, Roberta 1934- DLB-28
Silone, Ignazio (Secondino Tranquilli)
  1900-1978 .... DLB-264
Silva, Beverly 1930- DLB-122
Silva, Clara 1905-1976 .... DLB-290
Silva, José Asunció 1865-1896 .... DLB-283
Silverberg, Robert 1935- DLB-8
Silverman, Kaja 1947- DLB-246
Silverman, Kenneth 1936- DLB-111
Simak, Clifford D. 1904-1988 .... DLB-8
Simcoe, Elizabeth 1762-1850 .... DLB-99
Simcox, Edith Jemima 1844-1901 ...... DLB-190
Simcox, George Augustus 1841-1905 .... DLB-35
Sime, Jessie Georgina 1868-1958 ...... DLB-92
Simenon, Georges 1903-1989 ..... DLB-72; Y-89
Simic, Charles 1938- DLB-105
  "Images and 'Images'" DLB-105
Simionescu, Mircea Horia 1928- DLB-232
Simmel, Georg 1858-1918 .... DLB-296
Simmel, Johannes Mario 1924- DLB-69
Valentine Simmes [publishing house] ... DLB-170

Simmons, Ernest J. 1903-1972 .... DLB-103
Simmons, Herbert Alfred 1930- DLB-33
Simmons, James 1933- DLB-40
Simms, William Gilmore
  1806-1870 .... DLB-3, 30, 59, 73, 248
Simms and M'Intyre DLB-106
Simon, Claude 1913- DLB-83; Y-85
  Nobel Lecture Y-85
Simon, Neil 1927- DLB-7, 266
Simon and Schuster DLB-46
Simonov, Konstantin Mikhailovich
  1915-1979 .... DLB-302
Simons, Katherine Drayton Mayrant
  1890-1969 .... Y-83
Simović, Ljubomir 1935- DLB-181
Simpkin and Marshall
  [publishing house] DLB-154
Simpson, Helen 1897-1940 .... DLB-77
Simpson, Louis 1923- DLB-5
Simpson, N. F. 1919- DLB-13
Sims, George 1923- DLB-87; Y-99
Sims, George Robert 1847-1922 ... DLB-35, 70, 135
Sinán, Rogelio 1902-1994 .... DLB-145, 290
Sinclair, Andrew 1935- DLB-14
Sinclair, Bertrand William 1881-1972 .... DLB-92
Sinclair, Catherine 1800-1864 .... DLB-163
Sinclair, Jo 1913-1995 .... DLB-28
Sinclair, Lister 1921- DLB-88
Sinclair, May 1863-1946 .... DLB-36, 135
  The Novels of Dorothy Richardson
  (1918) DLB-36
Sinclair, Upton 1878-1968 ...... DLB-9; CDALB-5
Upton Sinclair [publishing house] DLB-46
Singer, Isaac Bashevis 1904-1991
  .... DLB-6, 28, 52, 278; Y-91; CDALB-1
Singer, Mark 1950- DLB-185
Singmaster, Elsie 1879-1958 .... DLB-9
Siniavsky, Andrei (Abram Tertz)
  1925-1997 .... DLB-302
Sinisgalli, Leonardo 1908-1981 .... DLB-114
Siodmak, Curt 1902-2000 .... DLB-44
Sîrbu, Ion D. 1919-1989 .... DLB-232
Siringo, Charles A. 1855-1928 .... DLB-186
Sissman, L. E. 1928-1976 .... DLB-5
Sisson, C. H. 1914- DLB-27
Sitwell, Edith 1887-1964 ...... DLB-20; CDBLB-7
Sitwell, Osbert 1892-1969 .... DLB-100, 195
Skácel, Jan 1922-1989 .... DLB-232
Skalbe, Kārlis 1879-1945 .... DLB-220
Skármeta, Antonio
  1940- DLB-145; CDWLB-3
Skavronsky, A. (see Danilevsky, Grigorii Petrovich)
Skeat, Walter W. 1835-1912 .... DLB-184
William Skeffington [publishing house] ... DLB-106
Skelton, John 1463-1529 .... DLB-136
Skelton, Robin 1925-1997 .... DLB-27, 53
Škéma, Antanas 1910-1961 .... DLB-220

Skinner, Constance Lindsay
  1877-1939 .... DLB-92
Skinner, John Stuart 1788-1851 .... DLB-73
Skipsey, Joseph 1832-1903 .... DLB-35
Skou-Hansen, Tage 1925- DLB-214
Skrzynecki, Peter 1945- DLB-289
Škvorecký, Josef 1924- DLB-232; CDWLB-4
Slade, Bernard 1930- DLB-53
Slamnig, Ivan 1930- DLB-181
Slančeková, Božena (see Timrava)
Slataper, Scipio 1888-1915 .... DLB-264
Slater, Patrick 1880-1951 .... DLB-68
Slaveykov, Pencho 1866-1912 .... DLB-147
Slaviček, Milivoj 1929- DLB-181
Slavitt, David 1935- DLB-5, 6
Sleigh, Burrows Willcocks Arthur
  1821-1869 .... DLB-99
Sleptsov, Vasilii Alekseevich 1836-1878... DLB-277
Slesinger, Tess 1905-1945 .... DLB-102
Slessor, Kenneth 1901-1971 .... DLB-260
Slick, Sam (see Haliburton, Thomas Chandler)
Sloan, John 1871-1951 .... DLB-188
Sloane, William, Associates DLB-46
Slonimsky, Mikhail Leonidovich
  1897-1972 .... DLB-272
Sluchevsky, Konstantin Konstantinovich
  1837-1904 .... DLB-277
Small, Maynard and Company DLB-49
Smart, Christopher 1722-1771 .... DLB-109
Smart, David A. 1892-1957 .... DLB-137
Smart, Elizabeth 1913-1986 .... DLB-88
Smart, J. J. C. 1920- DLB-262
Smedley, Menella Bute 1820?-1877 ..... DLB-199
William Smellie [publishing house] DLB-154
Smiles, Samuel 1812-1904 .... DLB-55
Smiley, Jane 1949- DLB-227, 234
Smith, A. J. M. 1902-1980 .... DLB-88
Smith, Adam 1723-1790 .... DLB-104, 252
Smith, Adam (George Jerome Waldo
  Goodman) 1930- DLB-185
Smith, Alexander 1829-1867 .... DLB-32, 55
  "On the Writing of Essays" (1862).... DLB-57
Smith, Amanda 1837-1915 .... DLB-221
Smith, Betty 1896-1972 .... Y-82
Smith, Carol Sturm 1938- Y-81
Smith, Charles Henry 1826-1903 .... DLB-11
Smith, Charlotte 1749-1806 .... DLB-39, 109
Smith, Chet 1899-1973 .... DLB-171
Smith, Cordwainer 1913-1966 .... DLB-8
Smith, Dave 1942- DLB-5
  Tribute to James Dickey Y-97
  Tribute to John Gardner Y-82
Smith, Dodie 1896- DLB-10
Smith, Doris Buchanan 1934- DLB-52
Smith, E. E. 1890-1965 .... DLB-8
Smith, Elihu Hubbard 1771-1798 .... DLB-37

Cumulative Index

Smith, Elizabeth Oakes (Prince)
(see Oakes Smith, Elizabeth)

Smith, Eunice 1757-1823 .... DLB-200

Smith, F. Hopkinson 1838-1915 .... DS-13

Smith, George D. 1870-1920 .... DLB-140

Smith, George O. 1911-1981 .... DLB-8

Smith, Goldwin 1823-1910 .... DLB-99

Smith, H. Allen 1907-1976 .... DLB-11, 29

Smith, Harry B. 1860-1936 .... DLB-187

Smith, Hazel Brannon 1914-1994 .... DLB-127

Smith, Henry circa 1560-circa 1591 ..... DLB-136

Smith, Horatio (Horace)
1779-1849 .... DLB-96, 116

Smith, Iain Crichton 1928-1998 ..... DLB-40, 139

Smith, J. Allen 1860-1924 .... DLB-47

Smith, James 1775-1839 .... DLB-96

Smith, Jessie Willcox 1863-1935 .... DLB-188

Smith, John 1580-1631 .... DLB-24, 30

Smith, John 1618-1652 .... DLB-252

Smith, Josiah 1704-1781 .... DLB-24

Smith, Ken 1938- DLB-40

Smith, Lee 1944- DLB-143; Y-83

Smith, Logan Pearsall 1865-1946 .... DLB-98

Smith, Margaret Bayard 1778-1844 ..... DLB-248

Smith, Mark 1935- Y-82

Smith, Michael 1698-circa 1771 .... DLB-31

Smith, Pauline 1882-1959 .... DLB-225

Smith, Red 1905-1982 .... DLB-29, 171

Smith, Roswell 1829-1892 .... DLB-79

Smith, Samuel Harrison 1772-1845 .... DLB-43

Smith, Samuel Stanhope 1751-1819 .... DLB-37

Smith, Sarah (see Stretton, Hesba)

Smith, Sarah Pogson 1774-1870 .... DLB-200

Smith, Seba 1792-1868 .... DLB-1, 11, 243

Smith, Stevie 1902-1971 .... DLB-20

Smith, Sydney 1771-1845 .... DLB-107

Smith, Sydney Goodsir 1915-1975 .... DLB-27

Smith, Sir Thomas 1513-1577 .... DLB-132

Smith, W. Gordon 1928-1996 .... DLB-310

Smith, Wendell 1914-1972 .... DLB-171

Smith, William flourished 1595-1597 .... DLB-136

Smith, William 1727-1803 .... DLB-31

A General Idea of the College of Mirania
(1753) [excerpts] DLB-31

Smith, William 1728-1793 .... DLB-30

Smith, William Gardner 1927-1974 ...... DLB-76

Smith, William Henry 1808-1872 .... DLB-159

Smith, William Jay 1918- DLB-5

Smith, Elder and Company DLB-154

Harrison Smith and Robert Haas
[publishing house] DLB-46

J. Stilman Smith and Company DLB-49

W. B. Smith and Company DLB-49

W. H. Smith and Son DLB-106

Leonard Smithers [publishing house] DLB-112

Smollett, Tobias
1721-1771 .... DLB-39, 104; CDBLB-2

Dedication to *Ferdinand Count Fathom*
(1753) DLB-39

Preface to *Ferdinand Count Fathom*
(1753) DLB-39

Preface to *Roderick Random* (1748) DLB-39

Smythe, Francis Sydney 1900-1949 ..... DLB-195

Snelling, William Joseph 1804-1848 ..... DLB-202

Snellings, Rolland (see Touré, Askia Muhammad)

Snodgrass, W. D. 1926- DLB-5

Snorri Hjartarson 1906-1986 .... DLB-293

Snow, C. P.
1905-1980 .... DLB-15, 77; DS-17; CDBLB-7

Snyder, Gary
1930- DLB-5, 16, 165, 212, 237, 275

Sobiloff, Hy 1912-1970 .... DLB-48

The Society for Textual Scholarship and
TEXT Y-87

The Society for the History of Authorship,
Reading and Publishing Y-92

Söderberg, Hjalmar 1869-1941 .... DLB-259

Södergran, Edith 1892-1923 .... DLB-259

Soffici, Ardengo 1879-1964 .... DLB-114, 264

Sofola, 'Zulu 1938- DLB-157

Sokhanskaia, Nadezhda Stepanovna
(Kokhanovskaia) 1823?-1884 .... DLB-277

Sokolov, Sasha (Aleksandr Vsevolodovich
Sokolov) 1943- DLB-285

Solano, Solita 1888-1975 .... DLB-4

Soldati, Mario 1906-1999 .... DLB-177

Soledad (see Zamudio, Adela)

Šoljan, Antun 1932-1993 .... DLB-181

Sollers, Philippe (Philippe Joyaux)
1936- DLB-83

Sollogub, Vladimir Aleksandrovich
1813-1882 .... DLB-198

Sollors, Werner 1943- DBL-246

Solmi, Sergio 1899-1981 .... DLB-114

Sologub, Fedor 1863-1927 .... DLB-295

Solomon, Carl 1928- DLB-16

Solórzano, Carlos 1922- DLB-305

Soloukhin, Vladimir Alekseevich
1924-1997 .... DLB-302

Solov'ev, Sergei Mikhailovich
1885-1942 .... DLB-295

Solov'ev, Vladimir Sergeevich
1853-1900 .... DLB-295

Solstad, Dag 1941- DLB-297

Solway, David 1941- DLB-53

Solzhenitsyn, Aleksandr
1918- DLB-302
Solzhenitsyn and America Y-85

Some Basic Notes on Three Modern Genres:
Interview, Blurb, and Obituary Y-02

Somerville, Edith Œnone 1858-1949 .... DLB-135

Somov, Orest Mikhailovich 1793-1833 ... DLB-198

Sønderby, Knud 1909-1966 .... DLB-214

Song, Cathy 1955- DLB-169

Sonnevi, Göran 1939- DLB-257

Sono Ayako 1931- DLB-182

Sontag, Susan 1933-2004 .... DLB-2, 67

Sophocles 497/496 B.C.-406/405 B.C.
.... DLB-176; CDWLB-1

Šopov, Aco 1923-1982 .... DLB-181

Sorel, Charles ca.1600-1674 .... DLB-268

Sørensen, Villy 1929- DLB-214

Sorensen, Virginia 1912-1991 .... DLB-206

Sorge, Reinhard Johannes 1892-1916 ... DLB-118

Sorokin, Vladimir Georgievich
1955- DLB-285

Sorrentino, Gilbert 1929- DLB-5, 173; Y-80

Sosa, Roberto 1930- DLB-290

Sotheby, James 1682-1742 .... DLB-213

Sotheby, John 1740-1807 .... DLB-213

Sotheby, Samuel 1771-1842 .... DLB-213

Sotheby, Samuel Leigh 1805-1861 ...... DLB-213

Sotheby, William 1757-1833 .... DLB-93, 213

Soto, Gary 1952- DLB-82

Soueif, Ahdaf 1950- DLB-267

Souster, Raymond 1921- DLB-88

The *South English Legendary* circa
thirteenth-fifteenth centuries DLB-146

Southerland, Ellease 1943- DLB-33

Southern, Terry 1924-1995 .... DLB-2

Southern Illinois University Press Y-95

Southern Literature
Fellowship of Southern Writers Y-98

The Fugitives and the Agrarians:
The First Exhibition Y-85

"The Greatness of Southern Literature":
League of the South Institute for the
Study of Southern Culture and
History Y-02

The Society for the Study of
Southern Literature Y-00

Southern Writers Between the Wars ... DLB-9

Southerne, Thomas 1659-1746 .... DLB-80

Southey, Caroline Anne Bowles
1786-1854 .... DLB-116

Southey, Robert 1774-1843 ...... DLB-93, 107, 142

Southwell, Robert 1561?-1595 .... DLB-167

Southworth, E. D. E. N. 1819-1899 .... DLB-239

Sowande, Bode 1948- DLB-157

Tace Sowle [publishing house] DLB-170

Soyfer, Jura 1912-1939 .... DLB-124

Soyinka, Wole
1934- DLB-125; Y-86, Y-87; CDWLB-3
Nobel Lecture 1986: This Past Must
Address Its Present Y-86

Spacks, Barry 1931- DLB-105

Spalding, Frances 1950- DLB-155

Spanish Travel Writers of the
Late Middle Ages DLB-286

Spark, Muriel 1918- DLB-15, 139; CDBLB-7

Michael Sparke [publishing house] DLB-170

Sparks, Jared 1789-1866 ...... DLB-1, 30, 235

Sparshott, Francis 1926- DLB-60

Späth, Gerold 1939- DLB-75	Tribute to Isaac Asimov Y-92	Steadman, Mark 1930- DLB-6
Spatola, Adriano 1941-1988...........DLB-128	Spires, Elizabeth 1952- DLB-120	Stearns, Harold E. 1891-1943 ......DLB-4; DS-15
Spaziani, Maria Luisa 1924- DLB-128	Spitteler, Carl 1845-1924.............DLB-129	Stebnitsky, M. (see Leskov, Nikolai Semenovich)
Specimens of Foreign Standard Literature 1838-1842......................DLB-1	Spivak, Lawrence E. 1900- DLB-137	Stedman, Edmund Clarence 1833-1908 ...DLB-64
The Spectator 1828- DLB-110	Spofford, Harriet Prescott 1835-1921................DLB-74, 221	Steegmuller, Francis 1906-1994.........DLB-111
Spedding, James 1808-1881...........DLB-144	Sports	Steel, Flora Annie 1847-1929.......DLB-153, 156
Spee von Langenfeld, Friedrich 1591-1635....................DLB-164	Jimmy, Red, and Others: Harold Rosenthal Remembers the Stars of the Press Box Y-01	Steele, Max 1922- Y-80
Speght, Rachel 1597-after 1630 ....DLB-126		Steele, Richard 1672-1729 ....DLB-84, 101; CDBLB-2
Speke, John Hanning 1827-1864 ....DLB-166	The Literature of Boxing in England through Arthur Conan Doyle....... Y-01	Steele, Timothy 1948- DLB-120
Spellman, A. B. 1935- DLB-41	Notable Twentieth-Century Books about Sports DLB-241	Steele, Wilbur Daniel 1886-1970 ....DLB-86
Spence, Catherine Helen 1825-1910 .....DLB-230	Sprigge, Timothy L. S. 1932- DLB-262	Wallace Markfield's "Steeplechase"......... Y-02
Spence, Thomas 1750-1814............DLB-158	Spring, Howard 1889-1965 ....DLB-191	Steere, Richard circa 1643-1721.........DLB-24
Spencer, Anne 1882-1975...........DLB-51, 54	Squibob (see Derby, George Horatio)	Stefán frá Hvítadal (Stefán Sigurðsson) 1887-1933....................DLB-293
Spencer, Charles, third Earl of Sunderland 1674-1722....................DLB-213	Squier, E. G. 1821-1888..............DLB-189	Stefán Guðmundsson (see Stephan G. Stephansson)
Spencer, Elizabeth 1921- DLB-6, 218	Stableford, Brian 1948- DLB-261	Stefán Hörður Grímsson 1919 or 1920-2002 ....DLB-293
Spencer, George John, Second Earl Spencer 1758-1834....................DLB-184	Stacpoole, H. de Vere 1863-1951 ....DLB-153	Steffens, Lincoln 1866-1936...........DLB-303
	Staël, Germaine de 1766-1817 ......DLB-119, 192	Stefanovski, Goran 1952- DLB-181
Spencer, Herbert 1820-1903 ....DLB-57, 262	Staël-Holstein, Anne-Louise Germaine de (see Staël, Germaine de)	Stegner, Wallace 1909-1993..........DLB-9, 206, 275; Y-93
"The Philosophy of Style" (1852).....DLB-57	Staffeldt, Schack 1769-1826 ....DLB-300	Stehr, Hermann 1864-1940 ....DLB-66
Spencer, Scott 1945- Y-86	Stafford, Jean 1915-1979 ....DLB-2, 173	Steig, William 1907- DLB-61
Spender, J. A. 1862-1942 ....DLB-98	Stafford, William 1914-1993 ....DLB-5, 206	Stein, Gertrude 1874-1946 ....DLB-4, 54, 86, 228; DS-15; CDALB-4
Spender, Stephen 1909-1995 .. DLB-20; CDBLB-7	Stallings, Laurence 1894-1968 ....DLB-7, 44	
Spener, Philipp Jakob 1635-1705 ....DLB-164	Stallworthy, Jon 1935- DLB-40	Stein, Leo 1872-1947 ....DLB-4
Spenser, Edmund circa 1552-1599........DLB-167; CDBLB-1	Stampp, Kenneth M. 1912- DLB-17	Stein and Day Publishers..............DLB-46
Envoy from *The Shepheardes Calender*....DLB-167	Stănescu, Nichita 1933-1983 ....DLB-232	Steinbeck, John 1902-1968 ....DLB-7, 9, 212, 275, 309; DS-2; CDALB-5
"The Generall Argument of the Whole Booke," from *The Shepheardes Calender* DLB-167	Stanev, Emiliyan 1907-1979 ....DLB-181	John Steinbeck Research Center, San Jose State University Y-85
	Stanford, Ann 1916- DLB-5	
	Stanihurst, Richard 1547-1618.........DLB-281	The Steinbeck Centennial............. Y-02
"A Letter of the Authors Expounding His Whole Intention in the Course of this Worke: Which for that It Giueth Great Light to the Reader, for the Better Vnderstanding Is Hereunto Annexed," from *The Faerie Qveene* (1590) DLB-167	Stanitsky, N. (see Panaeva, Avdot'ia Iakovlevna)	Steinem, Gloria 1934- DLB-246
	Stankevich, Nikolai Vladimirovich 1813-1840....................DLB-198	Steiner, George 1929- DLB-67, 299
		Steinhoewel, Heinrich 1411/1412-1479 ...DLB-179
	Stanković, Borisav ("Bora") 1876-1927 ....DLB-147; CDWLB-4	Steinn Steinarr (Aðalsteinn Kristmundsson) 1908-1958....................DLB-293
"To His Booke," from *The Shepheardes Calender* (1579) ...DLB-167	Stanley, Henry M. 1841-1904 ....DLB-189; DS-13	Steinunn Sigurðardóttir 1950- DLB-293
"To the Most Excellent and Learned Both Orator and Poete, Mayster Gabriell Haruey, His Verie Special and Singular Good Frend E. K. Commendeth the Good Lyking of This His Labour, and the Patronage of the New Poete," from *The Shepheardes Calender* DLB-167	Stanley, Thomas 1625-1678...........DLB-131	Steloff, Ida Frances 1887-1989 ....DLB-187
	Stannard, Martin 1947- DLB-155	Stendhal 1783-1842 ....DLB-119
	William Stansby [publishing house]......DLB-170	Stephan G. Stephansson (Stefán Guðmundsson) 1853-1927....................DLB-293
	Stanton, Elizabeth Cady 1815-1902......DLB-79	
	Stanton, Frank L. 1857-1927 ....DLB-25	Stephen, Leslie 1832-1904 ......DLB-57, 144, 190
	Stanton, Maura 1946- DLB-120	Stephen Family (Bloomsbury Group) DS-10
	Stapledon, Olaf 1886-1950..........DLB-15, 255	Stephens, A. G. 1865-1933 ....DLB-230
Sperr, Martin 1944- DLB-124	Star Spangled Banner Office DLB-49	Stephens, Alexander H. 1812-1883 ....DLB-47
Spewack, Bella Cowen 1899-1990.......DLB-266	Stark, Freya 1893-1993 ....DLB-195	Stephens, Alice Barber 1858-1932.......DLB-188
Spewack, Samuel 1899-1971 ....DLB-266	Starkey, Thomas circa 1499-1538 ....DLB-132	Stephens, Ann 1810-1886 ....DLB-3, 73, 250
Spicer, Jack 1925-1965............DLB-5, 16, 193	Starkie, Walter 1894-1976 ....DLB-195	Stephens, Charles Asbury 1844?-1931 ....DLB-42
Spiegelman, Art 1948- DLB-299	Starkweather, David 1935- DLB-7	Stephens, James 1882?-1950 ... DLB-19, 153, 162
Spielberg, Peter 1929- Y-81	Starrett, Vincent 1886-1974 ....DLB-187	Stephens, John Lloyd 1805-1852....DLB-183, 250
Spielhagen, Friedrich 1829-1911 ....DLB-129	Stationers' Company of London, The....DLB-170	Stephens, Michael 1946- DLB-234
"*Spielmannsepen*" (circa 1152-circa 1500) ...DLB-148	Statius circa A.D. 45-A.D. 96..........DLB-211	Stephensen, P. R. 1901-1965 ....DLB-260
Spier, Peter 1927- DLB-61	Stead, Christina 1902-1983 ....DLB-260	Sterling, George 1869-1926 ....DLB-54
Spillane, Mickey 1918- DLB-226	Stead, Robert J. C. 1880-1959 ....DLB-92	Sterling, James 1701-1763.............DLB-24
Spink, J. G. Taylor 1888-1962 ....DLB-241		Sterling, John 1806-1844 ....DLB-116
Spinrad, Norman 1940- DLB-8		

Stern, Gerald 1925- DLB-105
   "Living in Ruin"................... DLB-105
Stern, Gladys B. 1890-1973............ DLB-197
Stern, Madeleine B. 1912- DLB-111, 140
Stern, Richard 1928- DLB-218; Y-87
Stern, Stewart 1922- DLB-26
Sterne, Laurence 1713-1768 ... DLB-39; CDBLB-2
Sternheim, Carl 1878-1942 .... DLB-56, 118
Sternhold, Thomas ?-1549 .... DLB-132
Steuart, David 1747-1824 .... DLB-213
Stevens, Henry 1819-1886 .... DLB-140
Stevens, Wallace 1879-1955 ... DLB-54; CDALB-5
   The Wallace Stevens Society Y-99
Stevenson, Anne 1933- DLB-40
Stevenson, D. E. 1892-1973 .... DLB-191
Stevenson, Lionel 1902-1973 .... DLB-155
Stevenson, Robert Louis
   1850-1894 ....DLB-18, 57, 141, 156, 174;
                                 DS-13; CDBLB-5
   "On Style in Literature:
     Its Technical Elements" (1885) ... DLB-57
Stewart, Donald Ogden
   1894-1980 .... DLB-4, 11, 26; DS-15
Stewart, Douglas 1913-1985........... DLB-260
Stewart, Dugald 1753-1828............. DLB-31
Stewart, George, Jr. 1848-1906 .... DLB-99
Stewart, George R. 1895-1980 .... DLB-8
Stewart, Harold 1916-1995 .... DLB-260
Stewart, J. I. M. (see Innes, Michael)
Stewart, Maria W. 1803?-1879 .... DLB-239
Stewart, Randall 1896-1964 .... DLB-103
Stewart, Sean 1965- DLB-251
Stewart and Kidd Company............. DLB-46
Sthen, Hans Christensen 1544-1610..... DLB-300
Stickney, Trumbull 1874-1904 .... DLB-54
Stieler, Caspar 1632-1707 .... DLB-164
Stifter, Adalbert
   1805-1868 .... DLB-133; CDWLB-2
Stiles, Ezra 1727-1795 .... DLB-31
Still, James 1906-2001............. DLB-9; Y-01
Stirling, S. M. 1953- DLB-251
Stirner, Max 1806-1856 .... DLB-129
Stith, William 1707-1755 .... DLB-31
Stivens, Dal 1911-1997 .... DLB-260
Elliot Stock [publishing house] DLB-106
Stockton, Annis Boudinot 1736-1801 .... DLB-200
Stockton, Frank R.
   1834-1902 .... DLB-42, 74; DS-13
Stockton, J. Roy 1892-1972............ DLB-241
Ashbel Stoddard [publishing house] DLB-49
Stoddard, Charles Warren 1843-1909 ... DLB-186
Stoddard, Elizabeth 1823-1902 .... DLB-202
Stoddard, Richard Henry
   1825-1903 .... DLB-3, 64, 250; DS-13
Stoddard, Solomon 1643-1729 .... DLB-24
Stoker, Bram
   1847-1912 ......DLB-36, 70, 178; CDBLB-5

On Writing *Dracula,* from the
   Introduction to *Dracula* (1897) DLB-178
Dracula (Documentary)............ DLB-304
Frederick A. Stokes Company DLB-49
Stokes, Thomas L. 1898-1958 .... DLB-29
Stokesbury, Leon 1945- DLB-120
Stolberg, Christian Graf zu 1748-1821 .... DLB-94
Stolberg, Friedrich Leopold Graf zu
   1750-1819........................ DLB-94
Stone, Lucy 1818-1893............. DLB-79, 239
Stone, Melville 1848-1929 .... DLB-25
Stone, Robert 1937- DLB-152
Stone, Ruth 1915- DLB-105
Stone, Samuel 1602-1663 .... DLB-24
Stone, William Leete 1792-1844........ DLB-202
Herbert S. Stone and Company DLB-49
Stone and Kimball DLB-49
Stoppard, Tom
   1937- DLB-13, 233; Y-85; CDBLB-8
   Playwrights and Professors DLB-13
Storey, Anthony 1928- DLB-14
Storey, David 1933- DLB-13, 14, 207, 245
Storm, Theodor
   1817-1888............ DLB-129; CDWLB-2
Storni, Alfonsina 1892-1938 .... DLB-283
Story, Thomas circa 1670-1742......... DLB-31
Story, William Wetmore 1819-1895... DLB-1, 235
Storytelling: A Contemporary Renaissance ... Y-84
Stoughton, William 1631-1701 .... DLB-24
Stout, Rex 1886-1975 .... DLB-306
Stow, John 1525-1605................. DLB-132
Stow, Randolph 1935- DLB-260
Stowe, Harriet Beecher 1811-1896..... DLB-1,12,
          42, 74, 189, 239, 243; CDALB-3
   The Harriet Beecher Stowe Center Y-00
Stowe, Leland 1899-1994 .... DLB-29
Stoyanov, Dimitr Ivanov (see Elin Pelin)
Strabo 64/63 B.C.-circa A.D. 25 ....DLB-176
Strachey, Lytton 1880-1932 ..... DLB-149; DS-10
   Preface to *Eminent Victorians*......... DLB-149
William Strahan [publishing house] DLB-154
Strahan and Company DLB-106
Strand, Mark 1934- DLB-5
The Strasbourg Oaths 842 .... DLB-148
Stratemeyer, Edward 1862-1930 .... DLB-42
Strati, Saverio 1924- DLB-177
Stratton and Barnard DLB-49
Stratton-Porter, Gene
   1863-1924 .... DLB-221; DS-14
Straub, Peter 1943- Y-84
Strauß, Botho 1944- DLB-124
Strauß, David Friedrich 1808-1874...... DLB-133
The Strawberry Hill Press DLB-154
Strawson, P. F. 1919- DLB-262
Streatfeild, Noel 1895-1986 .... DLB-160
Street, Cecil John Charles (see Rhode, John)

Street, G. S. 1867-1936 .... DLB-135
Street and Smith DLB-49
Streeter, Edward 1891-1976 .... DLB-11
Streeter, Thomas Winthrop 1883-1965 .. DLB-140
Stretton, Hesba 1832-1911......... DLB-163, 190
Stribling, T. S. 1881-1965................ DLB-9
Der Stricker circa 1190-circa 1250 ...... DLB-138
Strickland, Samuel 1804-1867.......... DLB-99
Strindberg, August 1849-1912 .... DLB-259
Stringer, Arthur 1874-1950............ DLB-92
Stringer and Townsend DLB-49
Strittmatter, Erwin 1912-1994 .... DLB-69
Strniša, Gregor 1930-1987 .... DLB-181
Strode, William 1630-1645............ DLB-126
Strong, L. A. G. 1896-1958 .... DLB-191
Strother, David Hunter (Porte Crayon)
   1816-1888 .... DLB-3, 248
Strouse, Jean 1945- DLB-111
Strugatsky, Arkadii Natanovich
   1925- DLB-302
Strugatsky, Boris Natanovich 1933- ... DLB-302
Stuart, Dabney 1937- DLB-105
   "Knots into Webs: Some
     Autobiographical Sources" DLB-105
Stuart, Jesse 1906-1984......DLB-9, 48, 102; Y-84
Lyle Stuart [publishing house] DLB-46
Stuart, Ruth McEnery 1849?-1917...... DLB-202
Stub, Ambrosius 1705-1758 .... DLB-300
Stubbs, Harry Clement (see Clement, Hal)
Stubenberg, Johann Wilhelm von
   1619-1663 .... DLB-164
Stuckenberg, Viggo 1763-1905 .... DLB-300
Studebaker, William V. 1947- DLB-256
Studies in American Jewish Literature Y-02
Studio............................ DLB-112
Stump, Al 1916-1995 .... DLB-241
Sturgeon, Theodore
   1918-1985 ....DLB-8; Y-85
Sturges, Preston 1898-1959 .... DLB-26
Styron, William
   1925- DLB-2, 143, 299; Y-80; CDALB-6
   Tribute to James Dickey Y-97
Suárez, Clementina 1902-1991......... DLB-290
Suárez, Mario 1925- DLB-82
Suassuna, Ariano 1927- DLB-307
Such, Peter 1939- DLB-60
Suckling, Sir John 1609-1641? DLB-58, 126
Suckow, Ruth 1892-1960 .... DLB-9, 102
Sudermann, Hermann 1857-1928....... DLB-118
Sue, Eugène 1804-1857............... DLB-119
Sue, Marie-Joseph (see Sue, Eugène)
Suetonius circa A.D. 69-post A.D. 122 .... DLB-211
Suggs, Simon (see Hooper, Johnson Jones)
Sui Sin Far (see Eaton, Edith Maude)
Suits, Gustav 1883-1956.... DLB-220; CDWLB-4
Sukenick, Ronald 1932- DLB-173; Y-81

An Author's Response... Y-82	Sylvester, Josuah 1562 or 1563-1618.....DLB-121	Tapahonso, Luci 1953- DLB-175
Sukhovo-Kobylin, Aleksandr Vasil'evich 1817-1903 ....DLB-277	Symonds, Emily Morse (see Paston, George)	The Mark Taper Forum DLB-7
Suknaski, Andrew 1942- DLB-53	Symonds, John Addington 1840-1893 .... DLB-57, 144	Taradash, Daniel 1913- DLB-44
Sullivan, Alan 1868-1947 ....DLB-92	"Personal Style" (1890)............DLB-57	Tarasov-Rodionov, Aleksandr Ignat'evich 1885-1938 ....DLB-272
Sullivan, C. Gardner 1886-1965 ....DLB-26	Symons, A. J. A. 1900-1941...........DLB-149	Tarbell, Ida M. 1857-1944.............DLB-47
Sullivan, Frank 1892-1976 ....DLB-11	Symons, Arthur 1865-1945 ...... DLB-19, 57, 149	Tardivel, Jules-Paul 1851-1905 ....DLB-99
Sulte, Benjamin 1841-1923 ....DLB-99	Symons, Julian 1912-1994 ..... DLB-87, 155; Y-92	Targan, Barry 1932-...............DLB-130
Sulzberger, Arthur Hays 1891-1968 .....DLB-127	Julian Symons at Eighty Y-92	Tribute to John Gardner.............. Y-82
Sulzberger, Arthur Ochs 1926- DLB-127	Symons, Scott 1933- DLB-53	Tarkington, Booth 1869-1946........DLB-9, 102
Sulzer, Johann Georg 1720-1779.........DLB-97	Synge, John Millington 1871-1909 ....DLB-10, 19; CDBLB-5	Tashlin, Frank 1913-1972 ....DLB-44
Sumarokov, Aleksandr Petrovich 1717-1777 ....DLB-150	Synge Summer School: J. M. Synge and the Irish Theater, Rathdrum, County Wiclow, Ireland............ Y-93	Tasma (Jessie Couvreur) 1848-1897.....DLB-230
Summers, Hollis 1916- DLB-6		Tate, Allen 1899-1979 ...... DLB-4, 45, 63; DS-17
Sumner, Charles 1811-1874............DLB-235	Syrett, Netta 1865-1943 .... DLB-135, 197	Tate, James 1943- DLB-5, 169
Sumner, William Graham 1840-1910 ....DLB-270	Szabó, Lőrinc 1900-1957 ....DLB-215	Tate, Nahum circa 1652-1715 ....DLB-80
Henry A. Sumner [publishing house].................DLB-49	Szabó, Magda 1917- DLB-215	Tatian circa 830 ....DLB-148
Sundman, Per Olof 1922-1992 ....DLB-257	Szymborska, Wisława 1923- DLB-232, Y-96; CDWLB-4	Taufer, Veno 1933- DLB-181
Supervielle, Jules 1884-1960 ....DLB-258		Tauler, Johannes circa 1300-1361 ....DLB-179
Surtees, Robert Smith 1803-1864.........DLB-21	Nobel Lecture 1996: The Poet and the World Y-96	Tavares, Salette 1922-1994 ....DLB-287
The R. S. Surtees Society Y-98		Tavčar, Ivan 1851-1923.............DLB-147
Sutcliffe, Matthew 1550?-1629.........DLB-281	**T**	Taverner, Richard ca. 1505-1575........DLB-236
Sutcliffe, William 1971- DLB-271		Taylor, Ann 1782-1866 ....DLB-163
Sutherland, Efua Theodora 1924-1996 ...DLB-117	Taban lo Liyong 1939?- DLB-125	Taylor, Bayard 1825-1878....... DLB-3, 189, 250
Sutherland, John 1919-1956............DLB-68	Tablada, José Juan 1871-1945 ....DLB-290	Taylor, Bert Leston 1866-1921 ....DLB-25
Sutro, Alfred 1863-1933...............DLB-10	Tabori, George 1914- DLB-245	Taylor, Charles H. 1846-1921 ....DLB-25
Svava Jakobsdóttir 1930- DLB-293	Tabucchi, Antonio 1943- DLB-196	Taylor, Edward circa 1642-1729 ....DLB-24
Svendsen, Hanne Marie 1933- DLB-214	Taché, Joseph-Charles 1820-1894 ....DLB-99	Taylor, Elizabeth 1912-1975 ....DLB-139
Svevo, Italo (Ettore Schmitz) 1861-1928 ....DLB-264	Tachihara Masaaki 1926-1980..........DLB-182	Taylor, Sir Henry 1800-1886 ....DLB-32
	Tacitus circa A.D. 55-circa A.D. 117 .... DLB-211; CDWLB-1	Taylor, Henry 1942- DLB-5
Swados, Harvey 1920-1972 ....DLB-2		Who Owns American Literature Y-94
Swain, Charles 1801-1874 ....DLB-32	Tadijanović, Dragutin 1905- DLB-181	Taylor, Jane 1783-1824 ....DLB-163
Swallow Press DLB-46	Tafdrup, Pia 1952- DLB-214	Taylor, Jeremy circa 1613-1667..........DLB-151
Swan Sonnenschein Limited DLB-106	Tafolla, Carmen 1951- DLB-82	Taylor, John 1577 or 1578 - 1653 ....DLB-121
Swanberg, W. A. 1907-1992............DLB-103	Taggard, Genevieve 1894-1948..........DLB-45	Taylor, Mildred D. 1943- DLB-52
Swedish Literature The Literature of the Modern Breakthrough DLB-259	Taggart, John 1942- DLB-193	Taylor, Peter 1917-1994... DLB-218, 278; Y-81, 94
	Tagger, Theodor (see Bruckner, Ferdinand)	Taylor, Susie King 1848-1912 ....DLB-221
	Taiheiki late fourteenth century.........DLB-203	Taylor, William Howland 1901-1966 ....DLB-241
Swenson, May 1919-1989 ....DLB-5	Tait, J. Selwin, and Sons DLB-49	William Taylor and Company DLB-49
Swerling, Jo 1897- DLB-44	Tait's Edinburgh Magazine 1832-1861......DLB-110	Teale, Edwin Way 1899-1980...........DLB-275
Swift, Graham 1949- DLB-194	The Takarazaka Revue Company.......... Y-91	Teasdale, Sara 1884-1933 ....DLB-45
Swift, Jonathan 1667-1745........DLB-39, 95, 101; CDBLB-2	Talander (see Bohse, August)	Teillier, Jorge 1935-1996 ....DLB-283
	Talese, Gay 1932- DLB-185	Telles, Lygia Fagundes 1924- DLB-113, 307
Swinburne, A. C. 1837-1909 ....DLB-35, 57; CDBLB-4	Tribute to Irwin Shaw................ Y-84	The Temper of the West: William Jovanovich ... Y-02
Under the Microscope (1872) DLB-35	Talev, Dimitr 1898-1966 ....DLB-181	Temple, Sir William 1555?-1627........DLB-281
Swineshead, Richard floruit circa 1350 ...DLB-115	Taliaferro, H. E. 1811-1875 ....DLB-202	Temple, Sir William 1628-1699.........DLB-101
Swinnerton, Frank 1884-1982 ....DLB-34	Tallent, Elizabeth 1954- DLB-130	Temple, William F. 1914-1989 ....DLB-255
Swisshelm, Jane Grey 1815-1884.........DLB-43	TallMountain, Mary 1918-1994 ....DLB-193	Temrizov, A. (see Marchenko, Anastasia Iakovlevna)
Swope, Herbert Bayard 1882-1958 ....DLB-25	Talvj 1797-1870 ....DLB-59, 133	Tench, Watkin ca. 1758-1833 ....DLB-230
Swords, James ?-1844 ....DLB-73	Tamási, Áron 1897-1966 ....DLB-215	Tender Is the Night (Documentary).......DLB-273
Swords, Thomas 1763-1843.............DLB-73	Tammsaare, A. H. 1878-1940 ....DLB-220; CDWLB-4	Tendriakov, Vladimir Fedorovich 1923-1984.....................DLB-302
T. and J. Swords and Company DLB-49	Tan, Amy 1952- DLB-173; CDALB-7	Tenn, William 1919- DLB-8
Swynnerton, Thomas (John Roberts) circa 1500-1554..................DLB-281	Tandori, Dezső 1938- DLB-232	Tennant, Emma 1937- DLB-14
	Tanner, Thomas 1673/1674-1735 ....DLB-213	Tenney, Tabitha Gilman 1762-1837 .. DLB-37, 200
Sykes, Ella C. ?-1939 ....DLB-174	Tanizaki Jun'ichirō 1886-1965 ....DLB-180	Tennyson, Alfred 1809-1892...DLB-32; CDBLB-4

On Some of the Characteristics of Modern Poetry and On the Lyrical Poems of Alfred Tennyson (1831) DLB-32

Tennyson, Frederick 1807-1898 .... DLB-32

Tenorio, Arthur 1924- DLB-209

Tepl, Johannes von circa 1350-1414/1415 .... DLB-179

Tepliakov, Viktor Grigor'evich 1804-1842 .... DLB-205

Terence circa 184 B.C.-159 B.C. or after DLB-211; CDWLB-1

Terhune, Albert Payson 1872-1942 .... DLB-9

Terhune, Mary Virginia 1830-1922 .... DS-13

Terpigorev, Sergei Nikolaevich (S. Atava) 1841-1895 .... DLB-277

Terry, Megan 1932- DLB-7, 249

Terson, Peter 1932- DLB-13

Tesich, Steve 1943-1996 .... Y-83

Tessa, Delio 1886-1939 .... DLB-114

Testori, Giovanni 1923-1993 .... DLB-128, 177

Texas
   The Year in Texas Literature Y-98

Tey, Josephine 1896?-1952 .... DLB-77

Thacher, James 1754-1844 .... DLB-37

Thacher, John Boyd 1847-1909 .... DLB-187

Thackeray, William Makepeace 1811-1863 ... DLB-21, 55, 159, 163; CDBLB-4

Thames and Hudson Limited DLB-112

Thanet, Octave (see French, Alice)

Thaxter, Celia Laighton 1835-1894 .... DLB-239

Thayer, Caroline Matilda Warren 1785-1844 .... DLB-200

Thayer, Douglas H. 1929- DLB-256

Theater
   Black Theatre: A Forum [excerpts] ... DLB-38
   Community and Commentators: Black Theatre and Its Critics DLB-38
   German Drama from Naturalism to Fascism: 1889-1933 .... DLB-118
   A Look at the Contemporary Black Theatre Movement DLB-38
   The Lord Chamberlain's Office and Stage Censorship in England DLB-10
   New Forces at Work in the American Theatre: 1915-1925 .... DLB-7
   Off Broadway and Off-Off Broadway .. DLB-7
   Oregon Shakespeare Festival Y-00
   Plays, Playwrights, and Playgoers DLB-84
   Playwrights on the Theater DLB-80
   Playwrights and Professors DLB-13
   Producing Dear Bunny, Dear Volodya: The Friendship and the Feud Y-97
   Viewpoint: Politics and Performance, by David Edgar DLB-13
   Writing for the Theatre, by Harold Pinter DLB-13
   The Year in Drama Y-82–85, 87-98
   The Year in U.S. Drama Y-00

Theater, English and Irish
   Anti-Theatrical Tracts DLB-263
   The Chester Plays circa 1505-1532; revisions until 1575 .... DLB-146
   Dangerous Years: London Theater, 1939-1945 .... DLB-10
   A Defense of Actors DLB-263
   The Development of Lighting in the Staging of Drama, 1900-1945 .... DLB-10
   Education DLB-263
   The End of English Stage Censorship, 1945-1968 .... DLB-13
   Epigrams and Satires DLB-263
   Eyewitnesses and Historians DLB-263
   Fringe and Alternative Theater in Great Britain DLB-13
   The Great War and the Theater, 1914-1918 [Great Britain] DLB-10
   Licensing Act of 1737 .... DLB-84
   Morality Plays: Mankind circa 1450-1500 and Everyman circa 1500 .... DLB-146
   The New Variorum Shakespeare Y-85
   N-Town Plays circa 1468 to early sixteenth century DLB-146
   Politics and the Theater DLB-263
   Practical Matters DLB-263
   Prologues, Epilogues, Epistles to Readers, and Excerpts from Plays DLB-263
   The Publication of English Renaissance Plays DLB-62
   Regulations for the Theater DLB-263
   Sources for the Study of Tudor and Stuart Drama DLB-62
   Stage Censorship: "The Rejected Statement" (1911), by Bernard Shaw [excerpts] DLB-10
   Synge Summer School: J. M. Synge and the Irish Theater, Rathdrum, County Wiclow, Ireland Y-93
   The Theater in Shakespeare's Time .. DLB-62
   The Theatre Guild DLB-7
   The Townely Plays fifteenth and sixteenth centuries DLB-146
   The Year in British Drama Y-99–01
   The Year in Drama: London Y-90
   The Year in London Theatre Y-92
   A Yorkshire Tragedy DLB-58

Theaters
   The Abbey Theatre and Irish Drama, 1900-1945 .... DLB-10
   Actors Theatre of Louisville DLB-7
   American Conservatory Theatre DLB-7
   Arena Stage DLB-7
   Black Theaters and Theater Organizations in America, 1961-1982: A Research List DLB-38
   The Dallas Theater Center DLB-7
   Eugene O'Neill Memorial Theater Center DLB-7
   The Goodman Theatre DLB-7
   The Guthrie Theater DLB-7

The Mark Taper Forum DLB-7

The National Theatre and the Royal Shakespeare Company: The National Companies DLB-13

Off-Loop Theatres DLB-7

The Royal Court Theatre and the English Stage Company DLB-13

The Royal Court Theatre and the New Drama DLB-10

The Takarazaka Revue Company Y-91

Thegan and the Astronomer flourished circa 850 .... DLB-148

Thelwall, John 1764-1834 .... DLB-93, 158

Theocritus circa 300 B.C.-260 B.C. DLB-176

Theodorescu, Ion N. (see Arghezi, Tudor)

Theodulf circa 760-circa 821 .... DLB-148

Theophrastus circa 371 B.C.-287 B.C. DLB-176

Thériault, Yves 1915-1983 .... DLB-88

Thério, Adrien 1925- DLB-53

Theroux, Paul 1941- DLB-2, 218; CDALB-7

Thesiger, Wilfred 1910- DLB-204

They All Came to Paris DS-15

Thibaudeau, Colleen 1925- DLB-88

Thiele, Colin 1920- DLB-289

Thielen, Benedict 1903-1965 .... DLB-102

Thiong'o Ngugi wa (see Ngugi wa Thiong'o)

This Quarter 1925-1927, 1929-1932 .... DS-15

Thoma, Ludwig 1867-1921 .... DLB-66

Thoma, Richard 1902- DLB-4

Thomas, Audrey 1935- DLB-60

Thomas, D. M. 1935- DLB-40, 207, 299; Y-82; CDBLB-8
   The Plagiarism Controversy Y-82

Thomas, Dylan 1914-1953 ...... DLB-13, 20, 139; CDBLB-7
   The Dylan Thomas Celebration Y-99

Thomas, Ed 1961- DLB-310

Thomas, Edward 1878-1917 .... DLB-19, 98, 156, 216
   The Friends of the Dymock Poets Y-00

Thomas, Frederick William 1806-1866 .. DLB-202

Thomas, Gwyn 1913-1981 .... DLB-15, 245

Thomas, Isaiah 1750-1831 .... DLB-43, 73, 187

Thomas, Johann 1624-1679 .... DLB-168

Thomas, John 1900-1932 .... DLB-4

Thomas, Joyce Carol 1938- DLB-33

Thomas, Lewis 1913-1993 .... DLB-275

Thomas, Lorenzo 1944- DLB-41

Thomas, Norman 1884-1968 .... DLB-303

Thomas, R. S. 1915-2000 ..... DLB-27; CDBLB-8

Isaiah Thomas [publishing house] DLB-49

Thomasîn von Zerclære circa 1186-circa 1259 .... DLB-138

Thomason, George 1602?-1666 .... DLB-213

Thomasius, Christian 1655-1728 .... DLB-168

Thompson, Daniel Pierce 1795-1868 .... DLB-202

Thompson, David 1770-1857 .... DLB-99

Thompson, Dorothy 1893-1961 . . . . .DLB-29

Thompson, E. P. 1924-1993 . . . . .DLB-242

Thompson, Flora 1876-1947 . . . . .DLB-240

Thompson, Francis
1859-1907 . . . . DLB-19; CDBLB-5

Thompson, George Selden (see Selden, George)

Thompson, Henry Yates 1838-1928 . . . . .DLB-184

Thompson, Hunter S. 1939-2005 . . . . . . .DLB-185

Thompson, Jim 1906-1977. . . . . .DLB-226

Thompson, John 1938-1976. . . . . .DLB-60

Thompson, John R. 1823-1873 . . . . DLB-3, 73, 248

Thompson, Lawrance 1906-1973. . . . . . . .DLB-103

Thompson, Maurice 1844-1901. . . . . . . DLB-71, 74

Thompson, Ruth Plumly 1891-1976 . . . . . .DLB-22

Thompson, Thomas Phillips 1843-1933 . . .DLB-99

Thompson, William 1775-1833 . . . . .DLB-158

Thompson, William Tappan
1812-1882 . . . . .DLB-3, 11, 248

Thomson, Cockburn
"Modern Style" (1857) [excerpt] DLB-57

Thomson, Edward William 1849-1924 . . . .DLB-92

Thomson, James 1700-1748 . . . . .DLB-95

Thomson, James 1834-1882 . . . . .DLB-35

Thomson, Joseph 1858-1895 . . . . .DLB-174

Thomson, Mortimer 1831-1875. . . . . .DLB-11

Thomson, Rupert 1955- DLB-267

Thon, Melanie Rae 1957- DLB-244

Thor Vilhjálmsson 1925- DLB-293

Þórarinn Eldjárn 1949- DLB-293

Þórbergur Þórðarson 1888-1974 . . . . .DLB-293

Thoreau, Henry David 1817-1862 . . . DLB-1, 183,
    223, 270, 298; DS-5; CDALB-2

The Thoreau Society Y-99

The Thoreauvian Pilgrimage: The
    Structure of an American Cult . . .DLB-223

Thorne, William 1568?-1630. . . . . .DLB-281

Thornton, John F.
    [Repsonse to Ken Auletta] Y-97

Thorpe, Adam 1956- DLB-231

Thorpe, Thomas Bangs
1815-1878 . . . . .DLB-3, 11, 248

Thorup, Kirsten 1942- DLB-214

Thotl, Birgitte 1610-1662. . . . . .DLB-300

Thrale, Hester Lynch
(see Piozzi, Hester Lynch [Thrale])

The Three Marias: A Landmark Case in
    Portuguese Literary History
    (Maria Isabel Barreno, 1939- ;
    Maria Teresa Horta, 1937- ;
    Maria Velho da Costa, 1938-) DLB-287

Thubron, Colin 1939- DLB-204, 231

Thucydides
    circa 455 B.C.-circa 395 B.C. DLB-176

Thulstrup, Thure de 1848-1930 . . . . .DLB-188

Thümmel, Moritz August von
1738-1817 .DLB-97

Thurber, James
1894-1961 . . . . .DLB-4, 11, 22, 102; CDALB-5

Thurman, Wallace 1902-1934. . . . . .DLB-51

"Negro Poets and Their Poetry". DLB-50

Thwaite, Anthony 1930- DLB-40

    The Booker Prize, Address Y-86

Thwaites, Reuben Gold 1853-1913 . . . . . .DLB-47

Tibullus circa 54 B.C.-circa 19 B.C. DLB-211

Ticknor, George 1791-1871 . . . .DLB-1, 59, 140, 235

Ticknor and Fields. DLB-49

Ticknor and Fields (revived) DLB-46

Tieck, Ludwig 1773-1853. . . . . DLB-90; CDWLB-2

Tietjens, Eunice 1884-1944 . . . . .DLB-54

Tikkanen, Märta 1935- DLB-257

Tilghman, Christopher circa 1948. . . . . . .DLB-244

Tilney, Edmund circa 1536-1610. . . . . . . .DLB-136

Charles Tilt [publishing house] DLB-106

J. E. Tilton and Company DLB-49

Time-Life Books DLB-46

Times Books .DLB-46

Timothy, Peter circa 1725-1782 . . . . .DLB-43

Timrava 1867-1951 . . . . .DLB-215

Timrod, Henry 1828-1867. . . . . .DLB-3, 248

Tindal, Henrietta 1818?-1879 . . . . .DLB-199

Tinker, Chauncey Brewster 1876-1963 . . . .DLB-140

Tinsley Brothers DLB-106

Tiptree, James, Jr. 1915-1987 . . . . .DLB-8

Tišma, Aleksandar 1924- DLB-181

Titus, Edward William
1870-1952 . . . . .DLB-4; DS-15

Tiutchev, Fedor Ivanovich 1803-1873 . . . .DLB-205

Tlali, Miriam 1933- DLB-157, 225

Todd, Barbara Euphan 1890-1976. . . . . . .DLB-160

Todorov, Tzvetan 1939- DLB-242

Tofte, Robert
    1561 or 1562-1619 or 1620. . . . . . . .DLB-172

Tóibín, Colm 1955- DLB-271

Toklas, Alice B. 1877-1967 . . . . . . .DLB-4; DS-15

Tokuda Shūsei 1872-1943 . . . . .DLB-180

Toland, John 1670-1722 . . . . .DLB-252

Tolkien, J. R. R.
1892-1973 . . . . . .DLB-15, 160, 255; CDBLB-6

Toller, Ernst 1893-1939 . . . . .DLB-124

Tollet, Elizabeth 1694-1754 . . . . .DLB-95

Tolson, Melvin B. 1898-1966 . . . . . . .DLB-48, 76

Tolstaya, Tatyana 1951- DLB-285

Tolstoy, Aleksei Konstantinovich
1817-1875. . . . . .DLB-238

Tolstoy, Aleksei Nikolaevich 1883-1945 . .DLB-272

Tolstoy, Leo 1828-1910 . . . . .DLB-238

Tomalin, Claire 1933- DLB-155

Tómas Guðmundsson 1901-1983 . . . . . . .DLB-293

Tomasi di Lampedusa, Giuseppe
1896-1957 . . . . .DLB-177

Tomlinson, Charles 1927- DLB-40

Tomlinson, H. M. 1873-1958 . . . DLB-36, 100, 195

Abel Tompkins [publishing house] DLB-49

Tompson, Benjamin 1642-1714 . . . . .DLB-24

Tomson, Graham R.
    (see Watson, Rosamund Marriott)

Ton'a 1289-1372 . . . . .DLB-203

Tondelli, Pier Vittorio 1955-1991 . . . . . . .DLB-196

Tonks, Rosemary 1932- DLB-14, 207

Tonna, Charlotte Elizabeth 1790-1846 . . .DLB-163

Jacob Tonson the Elder
    [publishing house] DLB-170

Toole, John Kennedy 1937-1969 . . . . Y-81

Toomer, Jean
    1894-1967 . . . . .DLB-45, 51; CDALB-4

Topsoe, Vilhelm 1840-1881 . . . . .DLB-300

Tor Books DLB-46

Torberg, Friedrich 1908-1979 . . . . .DLB-85

Torga, Miguel (Adolfo Correira da Rocha)
1907-1995 . . . . .DLB-287

Torrence, Ridgely 1874-1950. . . . . . . .DLB-54, 249

Torres-Metzger, Joseph V. 1933- DLB-122

El Tostado (see Madrigal, Alfonso Fernández de)

Toth, Susan Allen 1940- Y-86

Richard Tottell [publishing house]. DLB-170

    "The Printer to the Reader,"
    (1557) .DLB-167

Tough-Guy Literature DLB-9

Touré, Askia Muhammad 1938- DLB-41

Tourgée, Albion W. 1838-1905 . . . . .DLB-79

Tournemir, Elizaveta Sailhas de (see Tur, Evgeniia)

Tourneur, Cyril circa 1580-1626 . . . . .DLB-58

Tournier, Michel 1924- DLB-83

Frank Tousey [publishing house]. DLB-49

Tower Publications DLB-46

Towne, Benjamin circa 1740-1793 . . . . . . .DLB-43

Towne, Robert 1936- DLB-44

The Townely Plays fifteenth and sixteenth
    centuries .DLB-146

Townsend, Sue 1946- DLB-271

Townshend, Aurelian
    by 1583-circa 1651 . . . . .DLB-121

Toy, Barbara 1908-2001 . . . . .DLB-204

Tozzi, Federigo 1883-1920 . . . . .DLB-264

Tracy, Honor 1913-1989 . . . . .DLB-15

Traherne, Thomas 1637?-1674 . . . . .DLB-131

Traill, Catharine Parr 1802-1899 . . . . .DLB-99

Train, Arthur 1875-1945 . . . . .DLB-86; DS-16

Tranquilli, Secondino (see Silone, Ignazio)

The Transatlantic Publishing Company . . .DLB-49

The Transatlantic Review 1924-1925 . . . . DS-15

The Transcendental Club
1836-1840 . . . . .DLB-1; DLB-223

Transcendentalism. DLB-1; DLB-223; DS-5

    "A Response from America," by
    John A. Heraud DS-5

    Publications and Social Movements DLB-1

    The Rise of Transcendentalism,
    1815-1860 . . . . DS-5

    Transcendentalists, American DS-5

"What Is Transcendentalism? By a
    Thinking Man," by James
    Kinnard Jr. DS-5
transition 1927-1938 ....DS-15
Translations (Vernacular) in the Crowns of
    Castile and Aragon 1352-1515......DLB-286
Tranströmer, Tomas 1931- DLB-257
Tranter, John 1943- DLB-289
Travel Writing
    American Travel Writing, 1776-1864
        (checklist)..................DLB-183
    British Travel Writing, 1940-1997
        (checklist)..................DLB-204
    Travel Writers of the Late
        Middle Ages DLB-286
    (1876-1909) DLB-174
    (1837-1875) DLB-166
    (1910-1939) DLB-195
Traven, B. 1882?/1890?-1969?.......DLB-9, 56
Travers, Ben 1886-1980 ....DLB-10, 233
Travers, P. L. (Pamela Lyndon)
    1899-1996 ....DLB-160
Trediakovsky, Vasilii Kirillovich
    1703-1769 ....DLB-150
Treece, Henry 1911-1966...........DLB-160
Treitel, Jonathan 1959- DLB-267
Trejo, Ernesto 1950-1991............DLB-122
Trelawny, Edward John
    1792-1881................DLB-110, 116, 144
Tremain, Rose 1943- DLB-14, 271
Tremblay, Michel 1942- DLB-60
Trent, William P. 1862-1939 ....DLB-47, 71
Trescot, William Henry 1822-1898 ....DLB-30
Tressell, Robert (Robert Phillipe Noonan)
    1870-1911 ....DLB-197
Trevelyan, Sir George Otto
    1838-1928 ....DLB-144
Trevisa, John circa 1342-circa 1402 .....DLB-146
Trevisan, Dalton 1925- DLB-307
Trevor, William 1928- DLB-14, 139
Triana, José 1931- DLB-305
Trierer Floyris circa 1170-1180 ....DLB-138
Trifonov, Iurii Valentinovich
    1925-1981 ....DLB-302
Trillin, Calvin 1935- DLB-185
Trilling, Lionel 1905-1975 ....DLB-28, 63
Trilussa 1871-1950 ....DLB-114
Trimmer, Sarah 1741-1810 ....DLB-158
Triolet, Elsa 1896-1970................DLB-72
Tripp, John 1927- DLB-40
Trocchi, Alexander 1925-1984.........DLB-15
Troisi, Dante 1920-1989..............DLB-196
Trollope, Anthony
    1815-1882........DLB-21, 57, 159; CDBLB-4
    Novel-Reading: *The Works of Charles
        Dickens; The Works of W. Makepeace
        Thackeray* (1879) DLB-21
    The Trollope Societies................Y-00
Trollope, Frances 1779-1863........DLB-21, 166

Trollope, Joanna 1943- DLB-207
Troop, Elizabeth 1931- DLB-14
Tropicália.........................DLB-307
Trotter, Catharine 1679-1749.......DLB-84, 252
Trotti, Lamar 1898-1952 ....DLB-44
Trottier, Pierre 1925- DLB-60
Trotzig, Birgitta 1929- DLB-257
Troupe, Quincy Thomas, Jr. 1943- DLB-41
John F. Trow and Company DLB-49
Trowbridge, John Townsend 1827-1916 .DLB-202
Trudel, Jean-Louis 1967- DLB-251
Truillier-Lacombe, Joseph-Patrice
    1807-1863.......................DLB-99
Trumbo, Dalton 1905-1976 ....DLB-26
Trumbull, Benjamin 1735-1820 ....DLB-30
Trumbull, John 1750-1831 ....DLB-31
Trumbull, John 1756-1843 ....DLB-183
Truth, Sojourner 1797?-1883 ....DLB-239
Tscherning, Andreas 1611-1659......DLB-164
Tsubouchi Shōyō 1859-1935 ....DLB-180
Tsvetaeva, Marina Ivanovna 1892-1941..DLB-295
Tuchman, Barbara W.
    Tribute to Alfred A. Knopf Y-84
Tucholsky, Kurt 1890-1935 ....DLB-56
Tucker, Charlotte Maria
    1821-1893 ....DLB-163, 190
Tucker, George 1775-1861........DLB-3, 30, 248
Tucker, James 1808?-1866? DLB-230
Tucker, Nathaniel Beverley
    1784-1851......................DLB-3, 248
Tucker, St. George 1752-1827 ....DLB-37
Tuckerman, Frederick Goddard
    1821-1873......................DLB-243
Tuckerman, Henry Theodore 1813-1871...DLB-64
Tumas, Juozas (see Vaizgantas)
Tunis, John R. 1889-1975.........DLB-22, 171
Tunstall, Cuthbert 1474-1559..........DLB-132
Tunström, Göran 1937-2000 ....DLB-257
Tuohy, Frank 1925- DLB-14, 139
Tupper, Martin F. 1810-1889 ....DLB-32
Tur, Evgeniia 1815-1892 ....DLB-238
Turbyfill, Mark 1896-1991............DLB-45
Turco, Lewis 1934- Y-84
    Tribute to John Ciardi................Y-86
Turgenev, Aleksandr Ivanovich
    1784-1845 ....DLB-198
Turgenev, Ivan Sergeevich 1818-1883 ...DLB-238
Turnbull, Alexander H. 1868-1918 .....DLB-184
Turnbull, Andrew 1921-1970..........DLB-103
Turnbull, Gael 1928- DLB-40
Turner, Arlin 1909-1980 ....DLB-103
Turner, Charles (Tennyson)
    1808-1879........................DLB-32
Turner, Ethel 1872-1958..............DLB-230
Turner, Frederick 1943- DLB-40
Turner, Frederick Jackson
    1861-1932 ....DLB-17, 186

A Conversation between William Riggan
    and Janette Turner Hospital Y-02
Turner, Joseph Addison 1826-1868 .....DLB-79
Turpin, Waters Edward 1910-1968......DLB-51
Turrini, Peter 1944- DLB-124
Tutuola, Amos
    1920-1997 ....DLB-125; CDWLB-3
Twain, Mark (see Clemens, Samuel Langhorne)
Tweedie, Ethel Brilliana
    circa 1860-1940 ....DLB-174
A Century of Poetry, a Lifetime of
    Collecting: J. M. Edelstein's
    Collection of Twentieth-
    Century American Poetry YB-02
Twombly, Wells 1935-1977 ....DLB-241
Twysden, Sir Roger 1597-1672.........DLB-213
Tyler, Anne
    1941- DLB-6, 143; Y-82; CDALB-7
Tyler, Mary Palmer 1775-1866........DLB-200
Tyler, Moses Coit 1835-1900.........DLB-47, 64
Tyler, Royall 1757-1826 ....DLB-37
Tylor, Edward Burnett 1832-1917 ......DLB-57
Tynan, Katharine 1861-1931 ......DLB-153, 240
Tyndale, William circa 1494-1536......DLB-132
Tyree, Omar 1969- DLB-292

U

Uchida, Yoshika 1921-1992..........CDALB-7
Udall, Nicholas 1504-1556............DLB-62
Ugrêsić, Dubravka 1949- DLB-181
Uhland, Ludwig 1787-1862............DLB-90
Uhse, Bodo 1904-1963................DLB-69
Ujević, Augustin "Tin"
    1891-1955 ....DLB-147
Ulenhart, Niclas flourished circa 1600 ...DLB-164
Ulfeldt, Leonora Christina 1621-1698 ...DLB-300
Ulibarrí, Sabine R. 1919- DLB-82
Ulica, Jorge 1870-1926 ....DLB-82
Ulitskaya, Liudmila Evgen'evna
    1943- DLB-285
Ulivi, Ferruccio 1912- DLB-196
Ulizio, B. George 1889-1969 ....DLB-140
Ulrich von Liechtenstein
    circa 1200-circa 1275 ....DLB-138
Ulrich von Zatzikhoven
    before 1194-after 1214.............DLB-138
Unaipon, David 1872-1967............DLB-230
Unamuno, Miguel de 1864-1936 ......DLB-108
Under, Marie 1883-1980 ...DLB-220; CDWLB-4
Underhill, Evelyn 1875-1941 ....DLB-240
Undset, Sigrid 1882-1949 ....DLB-297
Ungaretti, Giuseppe 1888-1970 ......DLB-114
Unger, Friederike Helene 1741-1813 ....DLB-94
United States Book Company DLB-49
Universal Publishing and Distributing
    Corporation.....................DLB-46
University of Colorado
    Special Collections at the University of
    Colorado at Boulder Y-98

Indiana University Press Y-02
The University of Iowa
    Writers' Workshop Golden Jubilee....... Y-86
University of Missouri Press Y-01
University of South Carolina
    The G. Ross Roy Scottish
    Poetry Collection Y-89
    Two Hundred Years of Rare Books and
        Literary Collections at the
        University of South Carolina Y-00
The University of South Carolina Press Y-94
University of Virginia
    The Book Arts Press at the University
        of Virginia...................... Y-96
    The Electronic Text Center and the
        Electronic Archive of Early American
        Fiction at the University of Virginia
        Library Y-98
    University of Virginia Libraries Y-91
University of Wales Press DLB-112
University Press of Florida Y-00
University Press of Kansas Y-98
University Press of Mississippi Y-99
Unnur Benediktsdóttir Bjarklind (see Hulda)
Uno Chiyo 1897-1996 ....DLB-180
Unruh, Fritz von 1885-1970........DLB-56, 118
Unsworth, Barry 1930- DLB-194
Unt, Mati 1944- DLB-232
The Unterberg Poetry Center of the
    92nd Street Y...................... Y-98
Untermeyer, Louis 1885-1977 ....DLB-303
T. Fisher Unwin [publishing house]......DLB-106
Upchurch, Boyd B. (see Boyd, John)
Updike, John 1932- ... DLB-2, 5, 143, 218, 227;
    Y-80, 82; DS-3; CDALB-6
    John Updike on the Internet Y-97
    Tribute to Alfred A. Knopf........... Y-84
    Tribute to John Ciardi Y-86
Upīts, Andrejs 1877-1970 ....DLB-220
Uppdal, Kristofer 1878-1961 ....DLB-297
Upton, Bertha 1849-1912 ....DLB-141
Upton, Charles 1948- DLB-16
Upton, Florence K. 1873-1922..........DLB-141
Upward, Allen 1863-1926...............DLB-36
Urban, Milo 1904-1982................DLB-215
Ureña de Henríquez, Salomé
    1850-1897 ....DLB-283
Urfé, Honoré d' 1567-1625 ....DLB-268
Urista, Alberto Baltazar (see Alurista)
Urquhart, Fred 1912-1995..............DLB-139
Urrea, Luis Alberto 1955- DLB-209
Urzidil, Johannes 1896-1970 ....DLB-85
Usigli, Rodolfo 1905-1979 ....DLB-305
Usk, Thomas died 1388 ....DLB-146
Uslar Pietri, Arturo 1906-2001 ....DLB-113
Uspensky, Gleb Ivanovich 1843-1902....DLB-277
Ussher, James 1581-1656...............DLB-213
Ustinov, Peter 1921- DLB-13

Uttley, Alison 1884-1976 ....DLB-160
Uz, Johann Peter 1720-1796............DLB-97

V

Vadianus, Joachim 1484-1551 ....DLB-179
Vac, Bertrand (Aimé Pelletier) 1914- DLB-88
Vācietis, Ojārs 1933-1983 ....DLB-232
Vaculík, Ludvík 1926- DLB-232
Vaičiulaitis, Antanas 1906-1992 ....DLB-220
Vaičiūnaite, Judita 1937- DLB-232
Vail, Laurence 1891-1968 ....DLB-4
Vail, Petr L'vovich 1949- DLB-285
Vailland, Roger 1907-1965.............DLB-83
Vaižgantas 1869-1933 ....DLB-220
Vajda, Ernest 1887-1954 ....DLB-44
Valdés, Gina 1943- DLB-122
Valdez, Luis Miguel 1940- DLB-122
Valduga, Patrizia 1953- DLB-128
Vale Press DLB-112
Valente, José Angel 1929-2000 ....DLB-108
Valenzuela, Luisa 1938- ... DLB-113; CDWLB-3
Valera, Diego de 1412-1488 ....DLB-286
Valeri, Diego 1887-1976...............DLB-128
Valerius Flaccus fl. circa A.D. 92 ....DLB-211
Valerius Maximus fl. circa A.D. 31........DLB-211
Valéry, Paul 1871-1945 ....DLB-258
Valesio, Paolo 1939- DLB-196
Valgardson, W. D. 1939- DLB-60
Valle, Luz 1899-1971 ....DLB-290
Valle, Víctor Manuel 1950- DLB-122
Valle-Inclán, Ramón del 1866-1936......DLB-134
Vallejo, Armando 1949- DLB-122
Vallejo, César Abraham 1892-1938......DLB-290
Vallès, Jules 1832-1885 ....DLB-123
Vallette, Marguerite Eymery (see Rachilde)
Valverde, José María 1926-1996 ....DLB-108
Vampilov, Aleksandr Valentinovich (A. Sanin)
    1937-1972.......................DLB-302
Van Allsburg, Chris 1949- DLB-61
Van Anda, Carr 1864-1945.............DLB-25
Vanbrugh, Sir John 1664-1726..........DLB-80
Vance, Jack 1916?- DLB-8
Vančura, Vladislav
    1891-1942 ....DLB-215; CDWLB-4
van der Post, Laurens 1906-1996 ......DLB-204
Van Dine, S. S. (see Wright, Williard Huntington)
Van Doren, Mark 1894-1972............DLB-45
van Druten, John 1901-1957 ....DLB-10
Van Duyn, Mona 1921- DLB-5
    Tribute to James Dickey Y-97
Van Dyke, Henry 1852-1933 .....DLB-71; DS-13
Van Dyke, Henry 1928- DLB-33
Van Dyke, John C. 1856-1932 ....DLB-186
Vane, Sutton 1888-1963 ....DLB-10
Van Gieson, Judith 1941- DLB-306

Vanguard Press.......................DLB-46
van Gulik, Robert Hans 1910-1967........ DS-17
van Itallie, Jean-Claude 1936- DLB-7
Van Loan, Charles E. 1876-1919........DLB-171
Vann, Robert L. 1879-1940.............DLB-29
Van Rensselaer, Mariana Griswold
    1851-1934 ....DLB-47
Van Rensselaer, Mrs. Schuyler
    (see Van Rensselaer, Mariana Griswold)
Van Vechten, Carl 1880-1964.......DLB-4, 9, 51
van Vogt, A. E. 1912-2000 ....DLB-8, 251
Varela, Blanca 1926- DLB-290
Vargas Llosa, Mario
    1936- DLB-145; CDWLB-3
    Acceptance Speech for the Ritz Paris
        Hemingway Award............... Y-85
Varley, John 1947- Y-81
Varnhagen von Ense, Karl August
    1785-1858 ....DLB-90
Varnhagen von Ense, Rahel
    1771-1833 ....DLB-90
Varro 116 B.C.-27 B.C. DLB-211
Vasilenko, Svetlana Vladimirovna
    1956- DLB-285
Vasiliu, George (see Bacovia, George)
Vásquez, Richard 1928- DLB-209
Vásquez Montalbán, Manuel 1939- DLB-134
Vassa, Gustavus (see Equiano, Olaudah)
Vassalli, Sebastiano 1941- DLB-128, 196
Vaugelas, Claude Favre de 1585-1650 ....DLB-268
Vaughan, Henry 1621-1695 ....DLB-131
Vaughan, Thomas 1621-1666...........DLB-131
Vaughn, Robert 1592?-1667 ....DLB-213
Vaux, Thomas, Lord 1509-1556 ....DLB-132
Vazov, Ivan 1850-1921 ......DLB-147; CDWLB-4
Véa, Alfredo, Jr. 1950- DLB-209
Veblen, Thorstein 1857-1929...........DLB-246
Vedel, Anders Sørensen 1542-1616......DLB-300
Vega, Janine Pommy 1942- DLB-16
Veiller, Anthony 1903-1965 ....DLB-44
Velásquez-Trevino, Gloria 1949- DLB-122
Veley, Margaret 1843-1887 ....DLB-199
Velleius Paterculus
    circa 20 B.C.-circa A.D. 30 ....DLB-211
Veloz Maggiolo, Marcio 1936- DLB-145
Vel'tman, Aleksandr Fomich
    1800-1870 ....DLB-198
Venegas, Daniel ?-? DLB-82
Venevitinov, Dmitrii Vladimirovich
    1805-1827 ....DLB-205
Verbitskaia, Anastasiia Alekseevna
    1861-1928 ....DLB-295
Verde, Cesário 1855-1886...............DLB-287
Vergil, Polydore circa 1470-1555........DLB-132
Veríssimo, Erico 1905-1975 ......DLB-145, 307
Verlaine, Paul 1844-1896 ....DLB-217
Vernacular Translations in the Crowns of
    Castile and Aragon 1352-1515 ......DLB-286

Cumulative Index

Verne, Jules 1828-1905 .... DLB-123
Verplanck, Gulian C. 1786-1870 .... DLB-59
Very, Jones 1813-1880 .... DLB-1, 243; DS-5
Vesaas, Halldis Moren 1907-1995 ...... DLB-297
Vesaas, Tarjei 1897-1970 .... DLB-297
Vian, Boris 1920-1959 .... DLB-72
Viazemsky, Petr Andreevich
  1792-1878 .... DLB-205
Vicars, Thomas 1591-1638 .... DLB-236
Vicente, Gil 1465-1536/1540? DLB-287
Vickers, Roy 1888?-1965 .... DLB-77
Vickery, Sukey 1779-1821 .... DLB-200
Victoria 1819-1901 .... DLB-55
Victoria Press DLB-106
Vidal, Gore 1925- DLB-6, 152; CDALB-7
Vidal, Mary Theresa 1815-1873 .... DLB-230
Vidmer, Richards 1898-1978 .... DLB-241
Viebig, Clara 1860-1952 .... DLB-66
Vieira, António, S. J. (Antonio Vieyra)
  1608-1697 .... DLB-307
Viereck, George Sylvester 1884-1962 ..... DLB-54
Viereck, Peter 1916- DLB-5
Vietnam War (ended 1975)
  Resources for the Study of Vietnam War
    Literature DLB-9
Viets, Roger 1738-1811 .... DLB-99
Vigil-Piñon, Evangelina 1949- DLB-122
Vigneault, Gilles 1928- DLB-60
Vigny, Alfred de 1797-1863 ..... DLB-119, 192, 217
Vigolo, Giorgio 1894-1983 .... DLB-114
Vik, Bjørg 1935- DLB-297
The Viking Press DLB-46
Vilde, Eduard 1865-1933 .... DLB-220
Vilinskaia, Mariia Aleksandrovna
  (see Vovchok, Marko)
Villanueva, Alma Luz 1944- DLB-122
Villanueva, Tino 1941- DLB-82
Villard, Henry 1835-1900 .... DLB-23
Villard, Oswald Garrison 1872-1949 .. DLB-25, 91
Villarreal, Edit 1944- DLB-209
Villarreal, José Antonio 1924- DLB-82
Villaseñor, Victor 1940- DLB-209
Villedieu, Madame de (Marie-Catherine
  Desjardins) 1640?-1683 .... DLB-268
Villegas de Magnón, Leonor
  1876-1955 .... DLB-122
Villehardouin, Geoffroi de
  circa 1150-1215 .... DLB-208
Villemaire, Yolande 1949- DLB-60
Villena, Enrique de
  ca. 1382/84-1432 .... DLB-286
Villena, Luis Antonio de 1951- DLB-134
Villiers, George, Second Duke
  of Buckingham 1628-1687 .... DLB-80
Villiers de l'Isle-Adam, Jean-Marie
  Mathias Philippe-Auguste,
  Comte de 1838-1889 .... DLB-123, 192
Villon, François 1431-circa 1463? DLB-208

Vine Press DLB-112
Viorst, Judith ?- DLB-52
Vipont, Elfrida (Elfrida Vipont Foulds,
  Charles Vipont) 1902-1992 .... DLB-160
Viramontes, Helena María 1954- DLB-122
Virgil 70 B.C.-19 B.C. DLB-211; CDWLB-1
Vischer, Friedrich Theodor
  1807-1887 .... DLB-133
Vitier, Cintio 1921- DLB-283
Vitruvius circa 85 B.C.-circa 15 B.C. DLB-211
Vitry, Philippe de 1291-1361 .... DLB-208
Vittorini, Elio 1908-1966 .... DLB-264
Vivanco, Luis Felipe 1907-1975 .... DLB-108
Vivian, E. Charles (Charles Henry Cannell,
  Charles Henry Vivian, Jack Mann,
  Barry Lynd) 1882-1947 .... DLB-255
Viviani, Cesare 1947- DLB-128
Vivien, Renée 1877-1909 .... DLB-217
Vizenor, Gerald 1934- DLB-175, 227
Vizetelly and Company DLB-106
Vladimov, Georgii
  1931-2003 .... DLB-302
Voaden, Herman 1903-1991 .... DLB-88
Voß, Johann Heinrich 1751-1826 .... DLB-90
Vogau, Boris Andreevich
  (see Pil'niak, Boris Andreevich)
Voigt, Ellen Bryant 1943- DLB-120
Voinovich, Vladimir Nikolaevich
  1932- DLB-302
Vojnović, Ivo 1857-1929 ..... DLB-147; CDWLB-4
Vold, Jan Erik 1939- DLB-297
Volkoff, Vladimir 1932- DLB-83
P. F. Volland Company DLB-46
Vollbehr, Otto H. F.
  1872?-1945 or 1946 .... DLB-187
Vologdin (see Zasodimsky, Pavel Vladimirovich)
Voloshin, Maksimilian Aleksandrovich
  1877-1932 .... DLB-295
Volponi, Paolo 1924-1994 .... DLB-177
Vonarburg, Élisabeth 1947- DLB-251
von der Grün, Max 1926- DLB-75
Vonnegut, Kurt 1922- DLB-2, 8, 152;
                              Y-80; DS-3; CDALB-6
  Tribute to Isaac Asimov Y-92
  Tribute to Richard Brautigan Y-84
Voranc, Prežihov 1893-1950 .... DLB-147
Voronsky, Aleksandr Konstantinovich
  1884-1937 .... DLB-272
Vorse, Mary Heaton 1874-1966 .... DLB-303
Vovchok, Marko 1833-1907 .... DLB-238
Voynich, E. L. 1864-1960 .... DLB-197
Vroman, Mary Elizabeth
  circa 1924-1967 .... DLB-33

W

Wace, Robert ("Maistre")
  circa 1100-circa 1175 .... DLB-146
Wackenroder, Wilhelm Heinrich
  1773-1798 .... DLB-90

Wackernagel, Wilhelm 1806-1869 ...... DLB-133
Waddell, Helen 1889-1965 .... DLB-240
Waddington, Miriam 1917- DLB-68
Wade, Henry 1887-1969 .... DLB-77
Wagenknecht, Edward 1900- DLB-103
Wägner, Elin 1882-1949 .... DLB-259
Wagner, Heinrich Leopold 1747-1779 .... DLB-94
Wagner, Henry R. 1862-1957 .... DLB-140
Wagner, Richard 1813-1883 .... DLB-129
Wagoner, David 1926- DLB-5, 256
Wah, Fred 1939- DLB-60
Waiblinger, Wilhelm 1804-1830 .... DLB-90
Wain, John
  1925-1994 ...DLB-15, 27, 139, 155; CDBLB-8
  Tribute to J. B. Priestly Y-84
Wainwright, Jeffrey 1944- DLB-40
Waite, Peirce and Company DLB-49
Wakeman, Stephen H. 1859-1924 ...... DLB-187
Wakoski, Diane 1937- DLB-5
Walahfrid Strabo circa 808-849 .... DLB-148
Henry Z. Walck [publishing house] DLB-46
Walcott, Derek
  1930- DLB-117; Y-81, 92; CDWLB-3
  Nobel Lecture 1992: The Antilles:
    Fragments of Epic Memory Y-92
Robert Waldegrave [publishing house] ...DLB-170
Waldis, Burkhard circa 1490-1556? ... DLB-178
Waldman, Anne 1945- DLB-16
Waldrop, Rosmarie 1935- DLB-169
Walker, Alice 1900-1982 .... DLB-201
Walker, Alice
  1944- DLB-6, 33, 143; CDALB-6
Walker, Annie Louisa (Mrs. Harry Coghill)
  circa 1836-1907 .... DLB-240
Walker, George F. 1947- DLB-60
Walker, John Brisben 1847-1931 .... DLB-79
Walker, Joseph A. 1935- DLB-38
Walker, Kath (see Oodgeroo of the Tribe Noonuccal)
Walker, Margaret 1915-1998 .... DLB-76, 152
Walker, Obadiah 1616-1699 .... DLB-281
Walker, Ted 1934- DLB-40
Walker, Evans and Cogswell Company DLB-49
Wall, John F. (see Sarban)
Wallace, Alfred Russel 1823-1913 ...... DLB-190
Wallace, Dewitt 1889-1981 .... DLB-137
Wallace, Edgar 1875-1932 .... DLB-70
Wallace, Lew 1827-1905 .... DLB-202
Wallace, Lila Acheson 1889-1984 ...... DLB-137
"A Word of Thanks," From the Initial
  Issue of Reader's Digest
  (February 1922) DLB-137
Wallace, Naomi 1960- DLB-249
Wallace Markfield's "Steeplechase" Y-02
Wallace-Crabbe, Chris 1934- DLB-289
Wallant, Edward Lewis
  1926-1962 .... DLB-2, 28, 143, 299
Waller, Edmund 1606-1687 .... DLB-126

Walpole, Horace 1717-1797 . . . . . DLB-39, 104, 213
   Preface to the First Edition of
      The Castle of Otranto (1764) DLB-39, 178
   Preface to the Second Edition of
      The Castle of Otranto (1765) DLB-39, 178
Walpole, Hugh 1884-1941. . . . . DLB-34
Walrond, Eric 1898-1966 . . . . DLB-51
Walser, Martin 1927- DLB-75, 124
Walser, Robert 1878-1956 . . . . DLB-66
Walsh, Ernest 1895-1926. . . . . .DLB-4, 45
Walsh, Robert 1784-1859 . . . . .DLB-59
Walters, Henry 1848-1931 . . . . DLB-140
Waltharius circa 825 . . . . .DLB-148
Walther von der Vogelweide
    circa 1170-circa 1230 . . . . .DLB-138
Walton, Izaak
    1593-1683 . . . . DLB-151, 213; CDBLB-1
Wambaugh, Joseph 1937- DLB-6; Y-83
Wand, Alfred Rudolph 1828-1891 . . . . . . DLB-188
Wandor, Michelene 1940- DLB-310
Waniek, Marilyn Nelson 1946- DLB-120
Wanley, Humphrey 1672-1726 . . . . DLB-213
War of the Words (and Pictures):
    The Creation of a Graphic Novel Y-02
Warburton, William 1698-1779 . . . . .DLB-104
Ward, Aileen 1919- DLB-111
Ward, Artemus (see Browne, Charles Farrar)
Ward, Arthur Henry Sarsfield (see Rohmer, Sax)
Ward, Douglas Turner 1930- DLB-7, 38
Ward, Mrs. Humphry 1851-1920 . . . . DLB-18
Ward, James 1843-1925. . . . . .DLB-262
Ward, Lynd 1905-1985 . . . . .DLB-22
Ward, Lock and Company DLB-106
Ward, Nathaniel circa 1578-1652 . . . . DLB-24
Ward, Theodore 1902-1983 . . . . DLB-76
Wardle, Ralph 1909-1988 . . . . DLB-103
Ware, Henry, Jr. 1794-1843 . . . . .DLB-235
Ware, William 1797-1852 . . . . .DLB-1, 235
Warfield, Catherine Ann 1816-1877 . . . . . .DLB-248
Waring, Anna Letitia 1823-1910 . . . . DLB-240
Frederick Warne and Company [U.K.] DLB-106
Frederick Warne and Company [U.S.] DLB-49
Warner, Anne 1869-1913 . . . . .DLB-202
Warner, Charles Dudley 1829-1900 . . . . . . DLB-64
Warner, Marina 1946- DLB-194
Warner, Rex 1905-1986 . . . . .DLB-15
Warner, Susan 1819-1885 . . . . DLB-3, 42, 239, 250
Warner, Sylvia Townsend
    1893-1978 . . . . .DLB-34, 139
Warner, William 1558-1609 . . . . DLB-172
Warner Books DLB-46
Warr, Bertram 1917-1943 . . . . DLB-88
Warren, John Byrne Leicester
    (see De Tabley, Lord)
Warren, Lella 1899-1982. . . . . Y-83
Warren, Mercy Otis 1728-1814 . . . . . . DLB-31, 200

Warren, Robert Penn 1905-1989 . . . . . DLB-2, 48,
                          152; Y-80, 89; CDALB-6
   Tribute to Katherine Anne Porter Y-80
Warren, Samuel 1807-1877 . . . . DLB-190
Die Wartburgkrieg circa 1230-circa 1280 . . . DLB-138
Warton, Joseph 1722-1800. . . . . DLB-104, 109
Warton, Thomas 1728-1790 . . . . . . .DLB-104, 109
Warung, Price (William Astley)
    1855-1911 . . . . .DLB-230
Washington, George 1732-1799 . . . . DLB-31
Washington, Ned 1901-1976 . . . . .DLB-265
Wassermann, Jakob 1873-1934 . . . . .DLB-66
Wasserstein, Wendy 1950- DLB-228
Wassmo, Herbjorg 1942- DLB-297
Wasson, David Atwood 1823-1887 . . . . DLB-1, 223
Watanna, Onoto (see Eaton, Winnifred)
Waten, Judah 1911?-1985 . . . . DLB-289
Waterhouse, Keith 1929- DLB-13, 15
Waterman, Andrew 1940- DLB-40
Waters, Frank 1902-1995 . . . . . . DLB-212; Y-86
Waters, Michael 1949- DLB-120
Watkins, Tobias 1780-1855 . . . . DLB-73
Watkins, Vernon 1906-1967 . . . . DLB-20
Watmough, David 1926- DLB-53
Watson, Colin 1920-1983 . . . . DLB-276
Watson, Ian 1943- DLB-261
Watson, James Wreford (see Wreford, James)
Watson, John 1850-1907 . . . . DLB-156
Watson, Rosamund Marriott
    (Graham R. Tomson) 1860-1911 . . . . DLB-240
Watson, Sheila 1909-1998 . . . . DLB-60
Watson, Thomas 1545?-1592 . . . . .DLB-132
Watson, Wilfred 1911- DLB-60
W. J. Watt and Company DLB-46
Watten, Barrett 1948- DLB-193
Watterson, Henry 1840-1921 . . . . .DLB-25
Watts, Alan 1915-1973 . . . . DLB-16
Watts, Isaac 1674-1748 . . . . DLB-95
Franklin Watts [publishing house] DLB-46
Waugh, Alec 1898-1981 . . . . .DLB-191
Waugh, Auberon 1939-2000 . . . DLB-14, 194; Y-00
Waugh, Evelyn 1903-1966 . . . . DLB-15, 162, 195;
                                     CDBLB-6
Way and Williams DLB-49
Wayman, Tom 1945- DLB-53
Weatherly, Tom 1942- DLB-41
Weaver, Gordon 1937- DLB-130
Weaver, Robert 1921- DLB-88
Webb, Beatrice 1858-1943 . . . . .DLB-190
Webb, Francis 1925-1973 . . . . DLB-260
Webb, Frank J. ?-? DLB-50
Webb, James Watson 1802-1884. . . . . DLB-43
Webb, Mary 1881-1927 . . . . DLB-34
Webb, Phyllis 1927- DLB-53
Webb, Sidney 1859-1947 . . . . DLB-190

Webb, Walter Prescott 1888-1963 . . . . DLB-17
Webbe, William ?-1591 . . . . DLB-132
Webber, Charles Wilkins 1819-1856? DLB-202
Weber, Max 1864-1920 . . . . DLB-296
Webling, Lucy (Lucy Betty MacRaye)
    1877-1952 . . . . DLB-240
Webling, Peggy (Arthur Weston)
    1871-1949 . . . . .DLB-240
Webster, Augusta 1837-1894 . . . . DLB-35, 240
Webster, John
    1579 or 1580-1634? DLB-58; CDBLB-1
   The Melbourne Manuscript Y-86
Webster, Noah
    1758-1843 . . . . DLB-1, 37, 42, 43, 73, 243
Webster, Paul Francis 1907-1984 . . . . .DLB-265
Charles L. Webster and Company DLB-49
Weckherlin, Georg Rodolf 1584-1653 . . . .DLB-164
Wedekind, Frank
    1864-1918 . . . . DLB-118; CDWLB-2
Weeks, Edward Augustus, Jr.
    1898-1989 . . . . .DLB-137
Weeks, Stephen B. 1865-1918 . . . . DLB-187
Weems, Mason Locke 1759-1825 . . DLB-30, 37, 42
Weerth, Georg 1822-1856 . . . . DLB-129
Weidenfeld and Nicolson DLB-112
Weidman, Jerome 1913-1998 . . . . DLB-28
Weigl, Bruce 1949- DLB-120
Weil, Jiří 1900-1959 . . . . DLB-299
Weinbaum, Stanley Grauman
    1902-1935 . . . . DLB-8
Weiner, Andrew 1949- DLB-251
Weintraub, Stanley 1929- DLB-111; Y82
Weise, Christian 1642-1708 . . . . DLB-168
Weisenborn, Gunther 1902-1969 . . . . DLB-69, 124
Weiss, John 1818-1879 . . . . DLB-1, 243
Weiss, Paul 1901-2002 . . . . .DLB-279
Weiss, Peter 1916-1982 . . . . DLB-69, 124
Weiss, Theodore 1916- DLB-5
Weiß, Ernst 1882-1940 . . . . DLB-81
Weiße, Christian Felix 1726-1804 . . . . .DLB-97
Weitling, Wilhelm 1808-1871 . . . . .DLB-129
Welch, James 1940- DLB-175, 256
Welch, Lew 1926-1971? DLB-16
Weldon, Fay 1931- DLB-14, 194; CDBLB-8
Wellek, René 1903-1995 . . . . DLB-63
Wells, Carolyn 1862-1942 . . . . .DLB-11
Wells, Charles Jeremiah
    circa 1800-1879 . . . . DLB-32
Wells, Gabriel 1862-1946 . . . . .DLB-140
Wells, H. G. 1866-1946
      . . . . DLB-34, 70, 156, 178; CDBLB-6
   H. G. Wells Society Y-98
   Preface to *The Scientific Romances of*
      H. G. Wells (1933) DLB-178
Wells, Helena 1758?-1824 . . . . DLB-200
Wells, Rebecca 1952- DLB-292
Wells, Robert 1947- DLB-40
Wells-Barnett, Ida B. 1862-1931 . . . . . DLB-23, 221

Cumulative Index

Welsh, Irvine 1958- DLB-271	Wetzel, Friedrich Gottlob 1779-1819 ..... DLB-90	Whitehead, Alfred North 1861-1947 ....DLB-100, 262
Welty, Eudora 1909-2001 ......DLB-2, 102, 143; Y-87, 01; DS-12; CDALB-1	Weyman, Stanley J. 1855-1928 .... DLB-141, 156	Whitehead, E. A. (Ted Whitehead) 1933- DLB-310
Eudora Welty: Eye of the Storyteller.....Y-87	Wezel, Johann Karl 1747-1819 .... DLB-94	Whitehead, James 1936- Y-81
Eudora Welty Newsletter.................Y-99	Whalen, Philip 1923-2002 .... DLB-16	Whitehead, William 1715-1785..... DLB-84, 109
Eudora Welty's Funeral...............Y-01	Whalley, George 1915-1983............ DLB-88	Whitfield, James Monroe 1822-1871 ..... DLB-50
Eudora Welty's Ninetieth Birthday Y-99	Wharton, Edith 1862-1937.........DLB-4, 9, 12, 78, 189; DS-13; CDALB-3	Whitfield, Raoul 1898-1945 .... DLB-226
Eudora Welty Remembered in Two Exhibits...................Y-02	Wharton, William 1920s?- Y-80	Whitgift, John circa 1533-1604........ DLB-132
Wendell, Barrett 1855-1921 .... DLB-71	Whately, Mary Louisa 1824-1889 ..... DLB-166	Whiting, John 1917-1963 .... DLB-13
Wentworth, Patricia 1878-1961 .... DLB-77	Whately, Richard 1787-1863........... DLB-190	Whiting, Samuel 1597-1679 .... DLB-24
Wentworth, William Charles 1790-1872.................... DLB-230	Elements of Rhetoric (1828; revised, 1846) [excerpt]......... DLB-57	Whitlock, Brand 1869-1934............ DLB-12
Werder, Diederich von dem 1584-1657 .. DLB-164	Wheatley, Dennis 1897-1977 ....DLB-77, 255	Whitman, Albery Allson 1851-1901.... DLB-50
Werfel, Franz 1890-1945 .... DLB-81, 124	Wheatley, Phillis circa 1754-1784....... DLB-31, 50; CDALB-2	Whitman, Alden 1913-1990 .... Y-91
Werner, Zacharias 1768-1823........... DLB-94	Wheeler, Anna Doyle 1785-1848?..... DLB-158	Whitman, Sarah Helen (Power) 1803-1878............... DLB-1, 243
The Werner Company................ DLB-49	Wheeler, Charles Stearns 1816-1843 .. DLB-1, 223	Whitman, Walt 1819-1892 ... DLB-3, 64, 224, 250; CDALB-2
Wersba, Barbara 1932- DLB-52	Wheeler, Monroe 1900-1988 .... DLB-4	Albert Whitman and Company DLB-46
Wescott, Glenway 1901-1987........... DLB-4, 9, 102; DS-15	Wheelock, John Hall 1886-1978......... DLB-45	Whitman Publishing Company DLB-46
Wesker, Arnold 1932- .. DLB-13, 310; CDBLB-8	From John Hall Wheelock's Oral Memoir...................Y-01	Whitney, Geoffrey 1548 or 1552?-1601............... DLB-136
Wesley, Charles 1707-1788 .... DLB-95	Wheelwright, J. B. 1897-1940 .... DLB-45	Whitney, Isabella flourished 1566-1573 .. DLB-136
Wesley, John 1703-1791 .... DLB-104	Wheelwright, John circa 1592-1679 ..... DLB-24	Whitney, John Hay 1904-1982.........DLB-127
Wesley, Mary 1912-2002 .... DLB-231	Whetstone, George 1550-1587 .... DLB-136	Whittemore, Reed 1919-1995 .... DLB-5
Wesley, Richard 1945- DLB-38	Whetstone, Colonel Pete (see Noland, C. F. M.)	Whittier, John Greenleaf 1807-1892........... DLB-1, 243; CDALB-2
Wessel, Johan Herman 1742-1785 ..... DLB-300	Whewell, William 1794-1866 .... DLB-262	Whittlesey House................ DLB-46
A. Wessels and Company DLB-46	Whichcote, Benjamin 1609?-1683 ..... DLB-252	Wickham, Anna (Edith Alice Mary Harper) 1884-1947 .... DLB-240
Wessobrunner Gebet circa 787-815 .... DLB-148	Whicher, Stephen E. 1915-1961........ DLB-111	Wickram, Georg circa 1505-circa 1561 ...DLB-179
West, Anthony 1914-1988 .... DLB-15	Whipple, Edwin Percy 1819-1886 ..... DLB-1, 64	Wicomb, Zoë 1948- DLB-225
Tribute to Liam O'Flaherty Y-84	Whitaker, Alexander 1585-1617......... DLB-24	Wideman, John Edgar 1941- DLB-33, 143
West, Cheryl L. 1957- DLB-266	Whitaker, Daniel K. 1801-1881 .... DLB-73	Widener, Harry Elkins 1885-1912...... DLB-140
West, Cornel 1953- DLB-246	Whitcher, Frances Miriam 1812-1852 .... DLB-11, 202	Wiebe, Rudy 1934- DLB-60
West, Dorothy 1907-1998............. DLB-76	White, Andrew 1579-1656 .... DLB-24	Wiechert, Ernst 1887-1950 .... DLB-56
West, Jessamyn 1902-1984 ..... DLB-6; Y-84	White, Andrew Dickson 1832-1918...... DLB-47	Wied, Gustav 1858-1914 .... DLB-300
West, Mae 1892-1980.................. DLB-44	White, E. B. 1899-1985 ... DLB-11, 22; CDALB-7	Wied, Martina 1882-1957............. DLB-85
West, Michael Lee 1953- DLB-292	White, Edgar B. 1947- DLB-38	Wiehe, Evelyn May Clowes (see Mordaunt, Elinor)
West, Michelle Sagara 1963- DLB-251	White, Edmund 1940- DLB-227	Wieland, Christoph Martin 1733-1813.... DLB-97
West, Morris 1916-1999 .... DLB-289	White, Ethel Lina 1887-1944 .... DLB-77	Wienbarg, Ludolf 1802-1872 .... DLB-133
West, Nathanael 1903-1940 .... DLB-4, 9, 28; CDALB-5	White, Hayden V. 1928- DLB-246	Wieners, John 1934- DLB-16
West, Paul 1930- DLB-14	White, Henry Kirke 1785-1806 .... DLB-96	Wier, Ester 1910- DLB-52
West, Rebecca 1892-1983......... DLB-36; Y-83	White, Horace 1834-1916 .... DLB-23	Wiesel, Elie 1928- DLB-83, 299; Y-86, 87; CDALB-7
West, Richard 1941- DLB-185	White, James 1928-1999.............. DLB-261	Nobel Lecture 1986: Hope, Despair and Memory Y-86
West and Johnson DLB-49	White, Patrick 1912-1990............. DLB-260	Wiggin, Kate Douglas 1856-1923........ DLB-42
Westcott, Edward Noyes 1846-1898 .... DLB-202	White, Phyllis Dorothy James (see James, P. D.)	Wigglesworth, Michael 1631-1705 ...... DLB-24
The Western Literature Association........ Y-99	White, Richard Grant 1821-1885........ DLB-64	Wilberforce, William 1759-1833....... DLB-158
The Western Messenger 1835-1841 ....DLB-1; DLB-223	White, T. H. 1906-1964.......... DLB-160, 255	Wilbrandt, Adolf 1837-1911........... DLB-129
Western Publishing Company DLB-46	White, Walter 1893-1955.............. DLB-51	Wilbur, Richard 1921- .. DLB-5, 169; CDALB-7
Western Writers of America Y-99	Wilcox, James 1949- DLB-292	Tribute to Robert Penn Warren Y-89
The Westminster Review 1824-1914 .... DLB-110	William White and Company DLB-49	Wilcox, James 1949- DLB-292
Weston, Arthur (see Webling, Peggy)	White, William Allen 1868-1944 ...... DLB-9, 25	Wild, Peter 1940- DLB-5
Weston, Elizabeth Jane circa 1582-1612 .. DLB-172	White, William Anthony Parker (see Boucher, Anthony)	Wilde, Lady Jane Francesca Elgee 1821?-1896.................... DLB-199
Wetherald, Agnes Ethelwyn 1857-1940 ... DLB-99	White, William Hale (see Rutherford, Mark)	
Wetherell, Elizabeth (see Warner, Susan)	Whitchurch, Victor L. 1868-1933....... DLB-70	
Wetherell, W. D. 1948- DLB-234		

Wilde, Oscar 1854-1900
  . DLB-10, 19, 34, 57, 141, 156, 190; CDBLB-5
  "The Critic as Artist" (1891).........DLB-57
  "The Decay of Lying" (1889)........DLB-18
  "The English Renaissance of Art" (1908)..................DLB-35
  "L'Envoi" (1882)..................DLB-35
  Oscar Wilde Conference at Hofstra University.................... Y-00
Wilde, Richard Henry 1789-1847 ......DLB-3, 59
W. A. Wilde Company DLB-49
Wilder, Billy 1906- DLB-26
Wilder, Laura Ingalls 1867-1957 .....DLB-22, 256
Wilder, Thornton 1897-1975........DLB-4, 7, 9, 228; CDALB-7
  Thornton Wilder Centenary at Yale..... Y-97
Wildgans, Anton 1881-1932 ....DLB-118
Wiley, Bell Irvin 1906-1980..............DLB-17
John Wiley and Sons DLB-49
Wilhelm, Kate 1928- DLB-8
Wilkes, Charles 1798-1877..............DLB-183
Wilkes, George 1817-1885 ....DLB-79
Wilkins, John 1614-1672 ....DLB-236
Wilkinson, Anne 1910-1961 ....DLB-88
Wilkinson, Christopher 1941- DLB-310
Wilkinson, Eliza Yonge 1757-circa 1813 ....DLB-200
Wilkinson, Sylvia 1940- Y-86
Wilkinson, William Cleaver 1833-1920 ...DLB-71
Willard, Barbara 1909-1994 ....DLB-161
Willard, Emma 1787-1870...........DLB-239
Willard, Frances E. 1839-1898..........DLB-221
Willard, Nancy 1936- DLB-5, 52
Willard, Samuel 1640-1707 ....DLB-24
L. Willard [publishing house] DLB-49
Willeford, Charles 1919-1988 ....DLB-226
William of Auvergne 1190-1249 ....DLB-115
William of Conches circa 1090-circa 1154................DLB-115
William of Ockham circa 1285-1347 .....DLB-115
William of Sherwood 1200/1205-1266/1271 ....DLB-115
The William Charvat American Fiction Collection at the Ohio State University Libraries Y-92
Williams, Ben Ames 1889-1953.........DLB-102
Williams, C. K. 1936- DLB-5
Williams, Chancellor 1905-1992 ....DLB-76
Williams, Charles 1886-1945... DLB-100, 153, 255
Williams, Denis 1923-1998 ....DLB-117
Williams, Emlyn 1905-1987............DLB-10, 77
Williams, Garth 1912-1996 ....DLB-22
Williams, George Washington 1849-1891 ....DLB-47
Williams, Heathcote 1941- DLB-13
Williams, Helen Maria 1761-1827 ....DLB-158
Williams, Hugo 1942- DLB-40
Williams, Isaac 1802-1865 ....DLB-32

Williams, Joan 1928- DLB-6
Williams, Joe 1889-1972 ....DLB-241
Williams, John A. 1925- DLB-2, 33
Williams, John E. 1922-1994............DLB-6
Williams, Jonathan 1929- DLB-5
Williams, Miller 1930- DLB-105
Williams, Nigel 1948- DLB-231
Williams, Raymond 1921-1988 ....DLB-14, 231, 242
Williams, Roger circa 1603-1683........DLB-24
Williams, Rowland 1817-1870 ....DLB-184
Williams, Samm-Art 1946- DLB-38
Williams, Sherley Anne 1944-1999 ....DLB-41
Williams, T. Harry 1909-1979...........DLB-17
Williams, Tennessee 1911-1983 ..... DLB-7; Y-83; DS-4; CDALB-1
Williams, Terry Tempest 1955- ... DLB-206, 275
Williams, Ursula Moray 1911- DLB-160
Williams, Valentine 1883-1946 ....DLB-77
Williams, William Appleman 1921- DLB-17
Williams, William Carlos 1883-1963......DLB-4, 16, 54, 86; CDALB-4
  The William Carlos Williams Society.... Y-99
Williams, Wirt 1921- DLB-6
A. Williams and Company DLB-49
Williams Brothers DLB-49
Wililiamson, David 1942- DLB-289
Williamson, Henry 1895-1977..........DLB-191
  The Henry Williamson Society........ Y-98
Williamson, Jack 1908- DLB-8
Willingham, Calder Baynard, Jr. 1922-1995 ....DLB-2, 44
Williram of Ebersberg circa 1020-1085 ...DLB-148
Willis, John circa 1572-1625 ....DLB-281
Willis, Nathaniel Parker 1806-1867 ....DLB-3, 59, 73, 74, 183, 250; DS-13
Willis, Ted 1918-1992.................DLB-310
Willkomm, Ernst 1810-1886 ....DLB-133
Wills, Garry 1934- DLB-246
  Tribute to Kenneth Dale McCormick.... Y-97
Willson, Meredith 1902-1984 ....DLB-265
Willumsen, Dorrit 1940- DLB-214
Wilmer, Clive 1945- DLB-40
Wilson, A. N. 1950- DLB-14, 155, 194
Wilson, Angus 1913-1991 ...... DLB-15, 139, 155
Wilson, Arthur 1595-1652................DLB-58
Wilson, August 1945- DLB-228
Wilson, Augusta Jane Evans 1835-1909 ...DLB-42
Wilson, Colin 1931- DLB-14, 194
  Tribute to J. B. Priestly Y-84
Wilson, Edmund 1895-1972 ....DLB-63
Wilson, Ethel 1888-1980 ....DLB-68
Wilson, F. P. 1889-1963................DLB-201
Wilson, Harriet E. 1827/1828?-1863?.........DLB-50, 239, 243
Wilson, Harry Leon 1867-1939..........DLB-9

Wilson, John 1588-1667 ....DLB-24
Wilson, John 1785-1854...............DLB-110
Wilson, John Anthony Burgess (see Burgess, Anthony)
Wilson, John Dover 1881-1969.........DLB-201
Wilson, Lanford 1937- DLB-7
Wilson, Margaret 1882-1973 ....DLB-9
Wilson, Michael 1914-1978 ....DLB-44
Wilson, Mona 1872-1954 ....DLB-149
Wilson, Robert Charles 1953- DLB-251
Wilson, Robert McLiam 1964- DLB-267
Wilson, Robley 1930- DLB-218
Wilson, Romer 1891-1930..............DLB-191
Wilson, Thomas 1524-1581 ....DLB-132, 236
Wilson, Woodrow 1856-1924...........DLB-47
Effingham Wilson [publishing house] DLB-154
Wimpfeling, Jakob 1450-1528 ....DLB-179
Wimsatt, William K., Jr. 1907-1975 .....DLB-63
Winchell, Walter 1897-1972.............DLB-29
J. Winchester [publishing house] DLB-49
Winckelmann, Johann Joachim 1717-1768 ....DLB-97
Winckler, Paul 1630-1686............DLB-164
Wind, Herbert Warren 1916- DLB-171
John Windet [publishing house] DLB-170
Windham, Donald 1920- DLB-6
Wing, Donald Goddard 1904-1972 .....DLB-187
Wing, John M. 1844-1917 ....DLB-187
Allan Wingate [publishing house] DLB-112
Winnemucca, Sarah 1844-1921 ....DLB-175
Winnifrith, Tom 1938- DLB-155
Winsloe, Christa 1888-1944 ....DLB-124
Winslow, Anna Green 1759-1780 ....DLB-200
Winsor, Justin 1831-1897 ....DLB-47
John C. Winston Company.............DLB-49
Winters, Yvor 1900-1968 ....DLB-48
Winterson, Jeanette 1959- DLB-207, 261
Winther, Christian 1796-1876 ....DLB-300
Winthrop, John 1588-1649 ....DLB-24, 30
Winthrop, John, Jr. 1606-1676..........DLB-24
Winthrop, Margaret Tyndal 1591-1647 ..DLB-200
Winthrop, Theodore 1828-1861 ....DLB-202
Wirt, William 1772-1834...............DLB-37
Wise, John 1652-1725 ....DLB-24
Wise, Thomas James 1859-1937 ....DLB-184
Wiseman, Adele 1928-1992.............DLB-88
Wishart and Company DLB-112
Wisner, George 1812-1849 ....DLB-43
Wister, Owen 1860-1938.........DLB-9, 78, 186
Wister, Sarah 1761-1804 ....DLB-200
Wither, George 1588-1667 ....DLB-121
Witherspoon, John 1723-1794 ....DLB-31
  The Works of the Rev. John Witherspoon (1800-1801) [excerpts] DLB-31
Withrow, William Henry 1839-1908 .....DLB-99

459

Witkacy (see Witkiewicz, Stanisław Ignacy)

Witkiewicz, Stanisław Ignacy
1885-1939 .... DLB-215; CDWLB-4

Wittenwiler, Heinrich before 1387-
circa 1414?................... DLB-179

Wittgenstein, Ludwig 1889-1951 .... DLB-262

Wittig, Monique 1935- DLB-83

Wodehouse, P. G.
1881-1975.......... DLB-34, 162; CDBLB-6

    Worldwide Wodehouse Societies Y-98

Wohmann, Gabriele 1932- DLB-75

Woiwode, Larry 1941- DLB-6

    Tribute to John Gardner Y-82

Wolcot, John 1738-1819 .... DLB-109

Wolcott, Roger 1679-1767 .... DLB-24

Wolf, Christa 1929- DLB-75; CDWLB-2

Wolf, Friedrich 1888-1953 .... DLB-124

Wolfe, Gene 1931- DLB-8

Wolfe, Thomas 1900-1938...................
DLB-9, 102, 229; Y-85; DS-2, DS-16; CDALB-5

    "All the Faults of Youth and Inexperience":
    A Reader's Report on
    Thomas Wolfe's *O Lost* Y-01

    Emendations for *Look Homeward, Angel*.... Y-00

    Eugene Gant's Projected Works Y-01

    Fire at the Old Kentucky Home
    [Thomas Wolfe Memorial] Y-98

    Thomas Wolfe Centennial
    Celebration in Asheville Y-00

    The Thomas Wolfe Collection at
    the University of North Carolina
    at Chapel Hill Y-97

    The Thomas Wolfe Society......... Y-97, 99

Wolfe, Tom 1931- DLB-152, 185

John Wolfe [publishing house] DLB-170

Reyner (Reginald) Wolfe
[publishing house] DLB-170

Wolfenstein, Martha 1869-1906........ DLB-221

Wolff, David (see Maddow, Ben)

Wolff, Egon 1926- DLB-305

Wolff, Helen 1906-1994................. Y-94

Wolff, Tobias 1945- DLB-130

    Tribute to Michael M. Rea Y-97

    Tribute to Raymond Carver Y-88

Wolfram von Eschenbach
circa 1170-after 1220 ... DLB-138; CDWLB-2

    Wolfram von Eschenbach's *Parzival*:
    Prologue and Book 3.......... DLB-138

Wolker, Jiří 1900-1924.............. DLB-215

Wollstonecraft, Mary 1759-1797
.... DLB-39, 104, 158, 252; CDBLB-3

Women
    Women's Work, Women's Sphere:
    Selected Comments from Women
    Writers DLB-200

Wondratschek, Wolf 1943- DLB-75

Wong, Elizabeth 1958- DLB-266

Wood, Anthony à 1632-1695.......... DLB-213

Wood, Benjamin 1820-1900 .... DLB-23

Wood, Charles 1932-1980 .... DLB-13

The Charles Wood Affair:
    A Playwright Revived Y-83

Wood, Mrs. Henry 1814-1887......... DLB-18

Wood, Joanna E. 1867-1927............ DLB-92

Wood, Sally Sayward Barrell Keating
1759-1855...................... DLB-200

Wood, William ?-?................. DLB-24

Samuel Wood [publishing house]........ DLB-49

Woodberry, George Edward
1855-1930 ....DLB-71, 103

Woodbridge, Benjamin 1622-1684....... DLB-24

Woodbridge, Frederick J. E. 1867-1940 ...DLB-270

Woodcock, George 1912-1995 .... DLB-88

Woodhull, Victoria C. 1838-1927 .... DLB-79

Woodmason, Charles circa 1720-?....... DLB-31

Woodress, James Leslie, Jr. 1916- DLB-111

Woods, Margaret L. 1855-1945........ DLB-240

Woodson, Carter G. 1875-1950 .... DLB-17

Woodward, C. Vann 1908-1999 .... DLB-17

Woodward, Stanley 1895-1965 ....DLB-171

Woodworth, Samuel 1785-1842 .... DLB-250

Wooler, Thomas 1785 or 1786-1853 .... DLB-158

Woolf, David (see Maddow, Ben)

Woolf, Douglas 1922-1992 .... DLB-244

Woolf, Leonard 1880-1969 ......DLB-100; DS-10

Woolf, Virginia 1882-1941
.... DLB-36, 100, 162; DS-10; CDBLB-6

    "The New Biography," *New York Herald
    Tribune*, 30 October 1927....... DLB-149

Woollcott, Alexander 1887-1943 .... DLB-29

Woolman, John 1720-1772 .... DLB-31

Woolner, Thomas 1825-1892 .... DLB-35

Woolrich, Cornell 1903-1968......... DLB-226

Woolsey, Sarah Chauncy 1835-1905..... DLB-42

Woolson, Constance Fenimore
1840-1894 ....DLB-12, 74, 189, 221

Worcester, Joseph Emerson
1784-1865................... DLB-1, 235

Wynkyn de Worde [publishing house] ...DLB-170

Wordsworth, Christopher 1807-1885.... DLB-166

Wordsworth, Dorothy 1771-1855.......DLB-107

Wordsworth, Elizabeth
1840-1932 .... DLB-98

Wordsworth, William
1770-1850.......... DLB-93, 107; CDBLB-3

Workman, Fanny Bullock
1859-1925 .... DLB-189

World Literatue Today: A Journal for the
New Millennium Y-01

World Publishing Company DLB-46

World War I (1914-1918) DS-18

    The Great War Exhibit and Symposium
    at the University of South Carolina .. Y-97

    The Liddle Collection and First World
    War Research Y-97

    Other British Poets Who Fell
    in the Great War............. DLB-216

    The Seventy-Fifth Anniversary of
    the Armistice: The Wilfred Owen
    Centenary and the Great War Exhibit
    at the University of Virginia Y-93

World War II (1939-1945)
    Literary Effects of World War II..... DLB-15

    World War II Writers Symposium
    at the University of South Carolina,
    12-14 April 1995................ Y-95

    WW2 HMSO Paperbacks Society....... Y-98

R. Worthington and Company DLB-49

Wotton, Sir Henry 1568-1639 .... DLB-121

Wouk, Herman 1915- Y-82; CDALB-7

    Tribute to James Dickey Y-97

Wreford, James 1915- DLB-88

Wren, Sir Christopher 1632-1723 .... DLB-213

Wren, Percival Christopher 1885-1941 .. DLB-153

Wrenn, John Henry 1841-1911 .... DLB-140

Wright, C. D. 1949- DLB-120

Wright, Charles 1935- DLB-165; Y-82

Wright, Charles Stevenson 1932- DLB-33

Wright, Chauncey 1830-1875..........DLB-270

Wright, Frances 1795-1852........... DLB-73

Wright, Harold Bell 1872-1944 .... DLB-9

Wright, James 1927-1980
.... DLB-5, 169; CDALB-7

Wright, Jay 1935- DLB-41

Wright, Judith 1915-2000............ DLB-260

Wright, Louis B. 1899-1984...........DLB-17

Wright, Richard
1908-1960 .... DLB-76, 102; DS-2; CDALB-5

Wright, Richard B. 1937- DLB-53

Wright, S. Fowler 1874-1965 .... DLB-255

Wright, Sarah Elizabeth 1928- DLB-33

Wright, T. H. "Style" (1877) [excerpt] DLB-57

Wright, Willard Huntington (S. S. Van Dine)
1887-1939................. DLB-306; DS-16

Wrightson, Patricia 1921- DLB-289

Wrigley, Robert 1951- DLB-256

Writers' Forum Y-85

Writing
    A Writing Life Y-02

    On Learning to Write Y-88

    The Profession of Authorship:
    Scribblers for Bread.............. Y-89

    A Writer Talking: A Collage......... Y-00

Wroth, Lawrence C. 1884-1970.........DLB-187

Wroth, Lady Mary 1587-1653 .... DLB-121

Wurlitzer, Rudolph 1937- DLB-173

Wyatt, Sir Thomas circa 1503-1542..... DLB-132

Wycherley, William
1641-1715................ DLB-80; CDBLB-2

Wyclif, John circa 1335-1384 .... DLB-146

Wyeth, N. C. 1882-1945 .... DLB-188; DS-16

Wyle, Niklas von circa 1415-1479 ....DLB-179

Wylie, Elinor 1885-1928 .... DLB-9, 45

Wylie, Philip 1902-1971 .... DLB-9

Wyllie, John Cook 1908-1968 .... DLB-140

Wyman, Lillie Buffum Chace
1847-1929..................... DLB-202

Wymark, Olwen 1934- DLB-233

Wynd, Oswald Morris (see Black, Gavin)

Wyndham, John (John Wyndham Parkes
Lucas Beynon Harris) 1903-1969 ... DLB-255

Wynne-Tyson, Esmé 1898-1972 . . . . DLB-191

X

Xenophon circa 430 B.C.-circa 356 B.C. DLB-176

Y

Yasuoka Shōtarō 1920- DLB-182
Yates, Dornford 1885-1960 . . . . DLB-77, 153
Yates, J. Michael 1938- DLB-60
Yates, Richard 1926-1992 . . . DLB-2, 234; Y-81, 92
Yau, John 1950- DLB-234
Yavorov, Peyo 1878-1914 . . . . DLB-147
Yearsley, Ann 1753-1806 . . . . DLB-109
Yeats, William Butler
    1865-1939 . . . . DLB-10, 19, 98, 156; CDBLB-5
    The W. B. Yeats Society of N.Y. Y-99
Yellen, Jack 1892-1991 . . . . DLB-265
Yep, Laurence 1948- DLB-52
Yerby, Frank 1916-1991 . . . . DLB-76
Yezierska, Anzia 1880-1970 . . . . DLB-28, 221
Yolen, Jane 1939- DLB-52
Yonge, Charlotte Mary 1823-1901 . . . DLB-18, 163
    The Charlotte M. Yonge Fellowship Y-98
The York Cycle circa 1376-circa 1569 . . . . DLB-146
A Yorkshire Tragedy DLB-58
Thomas Yoseloff [publishing house] DLB-46
Youd, Sam (see Christopher, John)
Young, A. S. "Doc" 1919-1996 . . . . DLB-241
Young, Al 1939- DLB-33
Young, Arthur 1741-1820 . . . . DLB-158
Young, Dick 1917 or 1918-1987 . . . . DLB-171
Young, Edward 1683-1765 . . . . DLB-95
Young, Frank A. "Fay" 1884-1957 . . . . . . DLB-241
Young, Francis Brett 1884-1954 . . . . DLB-191
Young, Gavin 1928- DLB-204
Young, Stark 1881-1963 . . . . . DLB-9, 102; DS-16
Young, Waldeman 1880-1938 . . . . DLB-26
William Young [publishing house] DLB-49
Young Bear, Ray A. 1950- DLB-175

Yourcenar, Marguerite 1903-1987 . . . DLB-72; Y-88
Yovkov, Yordan 1880-1937 . . . DLB-147; CDWLB-4

Z

Zachariä, Friedrich Wilhelm 1726-1777 . . . . DLB-97
Zagajewski, Adam 1945- DLB-232
Zagoskin, Mikhail Nikolaevich
    1789-1852 . . . . DLB-198
Zajc, Dane 1929- DLB-181
Zālīte, Māra 1952- DLB-232
Zalygin, Sergei Pavlovich
    1913-2000 . . . . DLB-302
Zamiatin, Evgenii Ivanovich 1884-1937 . . . DLB-272
Zamora, Bernice 1938- DLB-82
Zamudio, Adela (Soledad) 1854-1928 . . . . DLB-283
Zand, Herbert 1923-1970 . . . . DLB-85
Zangwill, Israel 1864-1926 . . . . . . DLB-10, 135, 197
Zanzotto, Andrea 1921- DLB-128
Zapata Olivella, Manuel 1920- DLB-113
Zapoev, Timur Iur'evich
    (see Kibirov, Timur Iur'evich)
Zasodimsky, Pavel Vladimirovich
    1843-1912 . . . . DLB-238
Zebra Books DLB-46
Zebrowski, George 1945- DLB-8
Zech, Paul 1881-1946 . . . . DLB-56
Zeidner, Lisa 1955- DLB-120
Zeidonis, Imants 1933- DLB-232
Zeimi (Kanze Motokiyo) 1363-1443 . . . . . DLB-203
Zelazny, Roger 1937-1995 . . . . DLB-8
Zenger, John Peter 1697-1746 . . . . DLB-24, 43
Zepheria DLB-172
Zesen, Philipp von 1619-1689 . . . . DLB-164
Zhadovskaia, Iuliia Valerianovna
    1824-1883 . . . . DLB-277
Zhukova, Mar'ia Semenovna
    1805-1855 . . . . DLB-277
Zhukovsky, Vasilii Andreevich
    1783-1852 . . . . DLB-205
Zhvanetsky, Mikhail Mikhailovich
    1934- DLB-285
G. B. Zieber and Company DLB-49

Ziedonis, Imants 1933- CDWLB-4
Zieroth, Dale 1946- DLB-60
Zigler und Kliphausen, Heinrich
    Anshelm von 1663-1697 . . . . DLB-168
Zil'ber, Veniamin Aleksandrovich
    (see Kaverin, Veniamin Aleksandrovich)
Zimmer, Paul 1934- DLB-5
Zinberg, Len (see Lacy, Ed)
Zincgref, Julius Wilhelm 1591-1635 . . . . . DLB-164
Zindel, Paul 1936- DLB-7, 52; CDALB-7
Zinnes, Harriet 1919- DLB-193
Zinov'ev, Aleksandr Aleksandrovich
    1922- DLB-302
Zinov'eva-Annibal, Lidiia Dmitrievna
    1865 or 1866-1907 . . . . DLB-295
Zinzendorf, Nikolaus Ludwig von
    1700-1760 . . . . DLB-168
Zitkala-Ša 1876-1938 . . . . DLB-175
Zīverts, Mārtiņš 1903-1990 . . . . DLB-220
Zlatovratsky, Nikolai Nikolaevich
    1845-1911 . . . . DLB-238
Zola, Emile 1840-1902 . . . . DLB-123
Zolla, Elémire 1926- DLB-196
Zolotow, Charlotte 1915- DLB-52
Zoshchenko, Mikhail Mikhailovich
    1895-1958 . . . . DLB-272
Zschokke, Heinrich 1771-1848 . . . . DLB-94
Zubly, John Joachim 1724-1781 . . . . DLB-31
Zu-Bolton, Ahmos, II 1936- DLB-41
Zuckmayer, Carl 1896-1977 . . . . DLB-56, 124
Zukofsky, Louis 1904-1978 . . . . DLB-5, 165
Zupan, Vitomil 1914-1987 . . . . DLB-181
Župančič, Oton 1878-1949 . . . DLB-147; CDWLB-4
zur Mühlen, Hermynia 1883-1951 . . . . . . DLB-56
Zweig, Arnold 1887-1968 . . . . DLB-66
Zweig, Stefan 1881-1942 . . . . DLB-81, 118
Zwinger, Ann 1925- DLB-275
Zwingli, Huldrych 1484-1531 . . . . DLB-179

Ø

Øverland, Arnulf 1889-1968 . . . . DLB-297

ISBN 0-7876-8128-8

90000

PR
736
.B683

2005